P9-DFS-633

CENTRAL PROCESS	PRIME ADAPTIVE EGO QUALITY	CORE PATHOLOGY	APPLIED TOPIC
			Abortion
Mutuality with the caregiver	Hope	Withdrawal	The role of the parents
Imitation	Will	Compulsion	Childcare
Identification	Purpose	Inhibition	School readiness
Education	Competence	Inertia	Violence in the lives of children
Peer pressure	Fidelity to others	Dissociation	Adolescent alcohol and drug use
Role experimentation	Fidelity to values	Repudiation	Dropping out of college
Mutuality among peers	Love	Exclusivity	Divorce
Person-environment interaction and creativity	Care	Rejectivity	Discrimination in the workplace
Introspection	Wisdom	Disdain	Retirement
Social support	Confidence	Diffidence	Meeting the needs of the frail elderly

ELEVENTH EDITION

Development Through Life

A Psychosocial Approach

Barbara M. Newman
University of Rhode Island

and

Philip R. Newman
University of Rhode Island

WADSWORTH
CENGAGE Learning™

Australia • Brazil • Japan • Korea • Mexico • Singapore • Spain • United Kingdom • United States

WADSWORTH
CENGAGE Learning

Development Through Life: A Psychosocial Approach
Barbara M. Newman and Philip R Newman

Publisher/Executive Editor: Linda Schreiber-Ganster

Acquisitions Editor: Jaime Perkins

Developmental Editor: Rebecca Dashiell

Assistant Editor: Kelly Miller

Editorial Assistant: Jessica Alderman

Media Editor: Mary Noel

Marketing Manager: Jessica Egbert

Marketing Assistant: Janay Pryor

Marketing Communications Manager: Laura Localio

Content Project Manager: Charlene M. Carpentier

Design Director: Rob Hugel

Art Director: Vernon Boes

Print Buyer: Mary Beth Hennebury

Rights Acquisitions Specialist: Dean Dauphinais

Production Service: Cadmus

Text Designer: Lisa Buckley Design

Photo Researcher: Bill Smith Group

Text Researcher: Karyn Morrison

Copy Editor: Steve Burr/Danielle Lake

Cover Designer: Lisa Henry

Cover Image: © 2010 Estate of Pablo Picasso/Artists Rights Society
(ARS), New York © Superstock © 2010 Estate of Pablo Picasso/
Artists Rights Society (ARS), New York

Compositor: Cadmus

© 2012, 2009 Wadsworth, Cengage Learning

ALL RIGHTS RESERVED. No part of this work covered by the copyright herein
may be reproduced, transmitted, stored, or used in any form or by any means
graphic, electronic, or mechanical, including but not limited to photocopying,
recording, scanning, digitizing, taping, Web distribution, information networks,
or information storage a nd retrieval systems, except as permitted under
Section 107 or 108 of the 1976 United States Copyright Act, without the prior
written permission of the publisher.

For product information and technology assistance, contact us at
Cengage Learning Customer & Sales Support, 1-800-354-9706.
For permission to use material from this text or product,
submit all requests online at **www.cengage.com/permissions.**
Further permissions questions can be e-mailed to
permissionrequest@cengage.com.

Library of Congress Control Number: 2010941421

Student Edition:
ISBN-13: 978-1-111-34466-5
ISBN-10: 1-111-34466-3

Loose-leaf Edition:
ISBN-13: 978-1-111-34468-9
ISBN-10: 1-111-34468-X

Wadsworth
20 Davis Drive
Belmont, CA 94002-3098
USA

Cengage Learning is a leading provider of customized learning solutions with
office locations around the globe, including Singapore, the United Kingdom,
Australia, Mexico, Brazil, and Japan. Locate your local office at **www.cengage
.com/global.**

Cengage Learning products are represented in Canada by Nelson Education, Ltd.

To learn more about Wadsworth, visit **www.cengage.com/wadsworth**
Purchase any of our products at your local college store or at our preferred
online store **www.CengageBrain.com.**

Printed in the United States of America
3 4 5 6 7 14 13 12

Brief Contents

Contents

CHAPTER 5

Infancy (First 24 Months)   136

CHAPTER 6

Toddlerhood (Ages 2 and 3)   194

CHAPTER 7

Early School Age (4 to 6 Years)   238

CHAPTER 8

Middle Childhood (6 to 11 Years)   288

CHAPTER 9

Early Adolescence (12 to 18 Years) 334

CHAPTER 10

Later Adolescence (18 to 24 Years) 386

CHAPTER 11

Early Adulthood (24 to 34 Years) 428

CHAPTER 12

Middle Adulthood (34 to 60 Years)   482

CHAPTER 13

Later Adulthood (60 to 75 Years)   526

CHAPTER 14

Elderhood (75 Until Death)   562

CHAPTER 15

Understanding Death, Dying, and Bereavement 600

APPENDIX

The Research Process A-1

Preface

The first edition of *Development Through Life* was published in 1975. Since that time, the science of human development and changes in longevity have converged to create a remarkable revision of our understanding of the life course including new insights about the prenatal period and infancy, new ideas about the transition from adolescence to adulthood, and new views about aging.

Today, the years of infancy and childhood comprise a smaller percentage of the life span than was the case in 1975. At the same time, researchers have looked in much greater detail at the prenatal stage as a dynamic period when learning begins, the environment impacts the developmental trajectory, and conditions of pregnancy influence fetal growth. Research on infant development, particularly development in the first days and weeks of life, has flourished and resulted in a greater appreciation for the cognitive and sensory capacities of the newborn. The expanding field of evolutionary psychology has shed new light on the adaptive capacities of infants and the features of the parent-infant relationship that contribute to survival and long-term growth.

The application of developmental systems theory has provided many new insights into the way change occurs. We view development as a product of the interaction of many levels at once, each potentially altering the other. For example, at the macro level, the resources of parents, their workplace, and their extended family relationships may all contribute to prenatal health, and infant well-being. At the micro level, changes in muscle strength, coordination, and balance contribute to new motor capacities that result in crawling or walking. Many behaviors that were once viewed as a product of genetically guided maturation are now understood as requiring a component of self-directed problem solving.

In 1975, we offered a revision of Erikson's theory by introducing two stages of adolescence, early adolescence with the psychosocial crisis of group identity versus alienation, and later adolescence, with the psychosocial crisis of personal identity versus role confusion. Today, scholars are describing an ever more gradual transition out of adolescence into adulthood, such that the period we call later adolescence is lasting well into the decade of the twenties. Research on brain development, educational and occupational attainment, and relationships with family all point to the idea that the life commitments that used to be formed in the decade of the twenties are being forestalled for many young people into their late twenties and thirties.

The slowed emergence into adulthood is due in part to the expanding life expectancy. If people can expect to live to 85 or 90, what is the urgency of settling down in family, work, or community commitments? Other explanations include the lengthening period of education and training necessary to take one's place in a postindustrial labor market, and the invention of effective birth control, resulting in changing patterns of marriage and childbearing.

Life expectancy in the United States has changed over the past 35 years, so that today those who are already age 65 can expect to live another 19 years. Those in the period of later life, which we call elderhood, are the fastest-growing segment of the U.S. population. As the baby boomers age, they will contribute to an even greater proportion of the population in elderhood. And these elders are enjoying a period of life that is more active, less constrained by financial limitations, and more continuously informed about healthy lifestyle practices than ever before.

In the current edition of *Development Through Life*, we have included reference to the conditions of life in other industrialized countries. In that regard, we have been troubled to note many ways in which life in the United States, as exciting and promising as it is, does not compare favorably. As you read, you will note that infant mortality, student performance in math and science, teen pregnancies, school dropouts, children and adolescents who are victims of violent crime, children in poverty, children who experience multiple parental transitions, adults who are homeless, and longevity are all less favorable in the United States than in many other countries. These comparisons lead us to urge students and scholars in human development to address the challenges of how to continue to promote optimal development through the life span.

The Stage Approach

The text provides a thorough chronological introduction to the study of human development from conception through elderhood. We examine physical, intellectual, social, and emotional growth in each of the 11 stages, emphasizing that development results from the interdependence of these areas at every stage. This strategy gives full attention to important developmental themes that recur in different stages of life. For each life stage, the process of development is linked to internal conflicts, changing self-awareness, and a dynamic social environment. As a result, students gain a sense of a multidimensional person, striving toward new levels of competence and mastery, embedded in multiple contexts.

Advantages of the Psychosocial Framework

Psychosocial theory provides an organizing conceptual framework that highlights the continuous interaction and integration of individual competencies with the demands and resources of culture. Development is viewed as a product of genetic, maturational, societal, and self-directed factors. The psychosocial framework helps students think about how people make meaning of their experiences, and how efforts at meaning making change over the life span. Applying this integrated perspective to an analysis of human development has several advantages:

- Although the subject matter is potentially overwhelming, the psychosocial framework helps to identify and emphasize themes and directions of growth across the life span.
- The psychosocial framework helps readers assess the influence of experiences during earlier life stages on later development.
- The psychosocial framework clarifies how one's past, present, and expectations of the future are systematically connected to the lives of people who are older and younger. This perspective highlights issues of intergenerational transmission and the reciprocal influences of the generations.
- The psychosocial framework offers a hopeful outlook on the total life course. Positive psychological capacities, such as hope, purpose, love, and caring, promote growth and help to clarify how a personal worldview develops. The promise of continuous growth in later adulthood and elderhood validates the struggles of childhood, adolescence, and adulthood.
- The psychosocial perspective locates development within a framework of significant relationships. This helps students appreciate the idea that a sense of self and a sense of others emerge and mature together, fostering the simultaneous and complementary processes of autonomy and connection.

The Life-Span Perspective

When we wrote the first edition of *Development Through Life*, we had just completed graduate study, had two young children, and were in the midst of early adulthood. Now, at the publication of the 11th edition, we are looking forward to the birth of our third grandchild; our three adult children are living in cities across the country and are thriving in their careers, and we are experiencing the new challenges of later adulthood.

The psychosocial life-span perspective has been a valuable orienting framework for our scholarly work as well as our personal lives. It has provided insights into the birth and parenting of our three children; the deaths of our parents; the successes, disappointments, and transitions of our work lives; and the conflicts and delights of our relationship as husband and wife. The themes of this book have allowed us to anticipate and cope with the challenges of adult life, and to remain hopeful in the face of crises. We hope that the ideas presented in this text will provide these same benefits to you.

In addition to enhancing self-understanding, the life-span perspective is a means of comprehending the conflicts, opportunities, and achievements of central importance to people living through different stages than one's own. In this respect, it challenges our egocentrism. The life-span perspective assumes an interconnection among people at every period of life. This knowledge helps guide interactions with others so that they are optimally sensitive, supportive, and facilitative for growth at each life stage.

Effects of Cultural and Historical Contexts

Studying development over the course of life requires sensitivity to the ways societies change over time. The developing person exists in a changing cultural and historical context. Events since the 10th edition of *Development Through Life* was published include the election of our first African American president; continuing wars in Iraq and Afghanistan and the large number of injuries and deaths associated with these wars; the devastation and relocation of thousands associated with the earthquake in Haiti and floods in Pakistan; the mortgage crisis in the United States and the associated worldwide financial recession; a massive oil drilling catastrophe in the Gulf of Mexico with related economic, cultural, and environmental impacts; the loss of millions of jobs in the United States and the highest unemployment rate in 20 years; the formation of new political parties clamoring for less government; and the continued spread of the AIDS epidemic in Africa and China. There is growing international awareness of global warming, which is associated with renewed efforts to make lifestyle changes at the personal, community, and corporate levels. These are just a few examples of the contexts in which development takes place that may dramatically alter people's lived experiences. Nothing could be more fascinating than trying to understand patterns of continuity and change over the life course within the context of a changing environment.

Effects of Poverty, Discrimination, and Other Forms of Societal Oppression

The number of children in the United States who lived in families with incomes below the poverty level in 2009 was 15.5 million, or 20.7% of all children. Numerous examples of the ways that poverty, discrimination, and various forms of societal oppression affect individual development are interwoven throughout the text. The expanding literature aids the further analysis of poverty by pointing out how its impact cascades from increased risks during the prenatal period through disruptions in physical, cognitive, and emotional development in childhood, in adolescence, and into adult life. At the same time, increased research on resilience illustrates the remarkable capacities for growth and adaptation at every period of life.

Organization

The following summarizes the basic organization of the text.

Introducing the Field: Chapters 1 to 3

Chapter 1 describes the orientation and assumptions of the text and introduces the life-span perspective. Chapter 2 introduces the role of theory in human development and outlines significant ideas about change and growth from seven theoretical perspectives. The presentation of each theory emphasizes its basic features, its implications for the study of human development, and its links to the psychosocial framework. Chapter 3 introduces basic concepts of psychosocial theory, including an analysis of its strengths and weaknesses. As in the 10th edition, the chapter on the research process was shortened and moved to the appendix, based on user feedback.

The Latest on Fetal Development and Genetics: Chapter 4

In Chapter 4, fetal development is presented, highlighting the bidirectional influences of the fetus and the pregnant woman within her social and cultural environments. Continuing discoveries in the field of behavioral genetics have been included in this revision. The chapter traces changes in physical and sensory development across three trimesters. We have emphasized research on the risks to fetal development associated with a pregnant woman's exposure to a wide range of substances, especially nicotine, alcohol, caffeine, other drugs, and environmental toxins. Poverty is discussed as a context that increases risks for suboptimal development. This chapter includes a detailed description of cultural differences in the way pregnancy and childbirth are conceptualized, providing a first model for considering the psychosocial process as it will unfold in subsequent chapters.

Growth and Development from Infancy to Elderhood: Chapters 5 to 14

Chapters 5 through 14 trace basic patterns of normal growth and development in infancy, toddlerhood, early school age, middle childhood, early adolescence, later adolescence, early adulthood, middle adulthood, later adulthood, and elderhood. In these chapters we consider how individuals organize and interpret their experience, noting changes in their behavior, attitudes, worldview, and the coping strategies that they use in the face of changing environmental demands.

Each chapter begins with an examination of four or five of the critical developmental tasks of the stage. These tasks reflect global aspects of development, including physical maturation, sensory and motor competence, cognitive maturation, emotional development, social relationships, and self-understanding. We consider the psychosocial crisis of each stage in some detail. We also show how successfully resolving a crisis helps individuals develop a prime adaptive ego quality and how unsuccessful resolution leads to core pathology. Although most people grow developmentally—albeit with pain and struggle—others do not. People who acquire prime adaptive ego qualities are more likely to lead active, flexible, agentic lives, and be resilient in the face of stressors. People who acquire core pathologies are more likely to lead withdrawn, guarded lives; they are more vulnerable to stressors resulting in greater risk of mental and physical health problems.

Applied Topics at the End of Each Chapter

We conclude each chapter by applying research and theory to a topic of societal importance. These applied topics provide an opportunity for students to link the research and theory about normative developmental processes to the analysis of pressing social concerns. The flyleaf on the front cover of the book contains an overview of the basic tasks, crises, and applied topics for each stage of life.

Understanding Death, Dying, and Bereavement: Chapter 15

The book closes with a chapter that addresses end-of-life issues within a psychosocial framework. As with the developmental stage chapters, the topic illustrates the interaction of the biological, psychological, and societal systems as they contribute to the experiences of dying, grieving, and bereavement. The chapter includes definitions of death, the process of dying, death-related rituals, grief, and bereavement, including a focus on the role of culture in shaping ideas about death and expressions of grief. We conclude the chapter with a discussion of the opportunities for psychosocial growth that are a result of bereavement and the considerations of one's own mortality.

New to This Edition

The 11th edition has retained the basic structure and positive developmental emphasis of previous editions. We continue to strive to make the text clear, readable, and thought provoking, while still capturing the complexities and novel concepts that make the study of human development so fascinating. Many new sections bring greater clarity, elaboration, and a fresh way of thinking about a topic. The text has been completely updated. New research findings and recent census data have been integrated into the narrative. The following list highlights examples of the new material in each chapter.

Chapter 1: "The Development Through Life Perspective"

- The case of Patrick Jonathan Carmichael is systematically linked to the discussion of biological, psychological, and societal systems.
- A new emphasis on meaning making.
- Discussion of technology and its influences on the societal system.
- New data on life expectancy at birth for four groups from 1970 to 2004.
- Discussion of the discrepancy in longevity between African American and Anglo populations in the United States.
- International data on life expectancy at birth for 220 countries.

Chapter 2: "Major Theories for Understanding Human Development"

- Revised explanation of the role of theory in the study of human development.
- Introduction to the concept of resilience.
- Distinction between theory, research, and fact.
- New discussion of evolutionary theory and William James' theory of consciousness.
- New discussion of ego psychology in psychosexual theory.
- New box focusing on cognitive behavioral therapy.
- In theories of learning, we have expanded the discussions of social learning and cognitive behaviorism.
- In cultural theory, new research on the role of culture in shaping the neural pathways.
- In social role theory, a new case example of social identity in a Pakistani American adolescent.
- In systems theory, we present new research about the importance of having links to multiple systems as a buffer against depression.
- New research about how workplace conditions contribute to role strain in the parent role.

Chapter 3: "Psychosocial Theory"

- Analyzes the case of Erik Erikson throughout the chapter using the basic concepts of psychosocial theory.

- Expands the discussion of resilience as an aspect of coping.
- New evidence from longitudinal research supporting the sequence of psychosocial stages.

Chapter 4: "The Period of Pregnancy and Prenatal Development"

- New section about epigenetics including imprinting and epigenetic marks.
- Discussion of plasticity as it relates to the interaction of genes and the environment.
- Explanation about how some genotypes flourish in certain environments but not in others.
- New data about assisted reproductive technology cycles and success.
- New discussion of adoption as an alternative to childbearing.
- Research on fetal memory.
- New data about the increasing incidence of cesarean delivery.
- Expanded discussion of stress, especially workplace stress, and its impact on pregnancy and fetal development.
- New research on how men think about their responsibility for their partner's pregnancy.
- New studies linking poverty, ethnicity, and smoking to the risk of preterm delivery.
- Findings from a Task Force of the American Psychological Association on the relationship of abortion to mental health.

Chapter 5: "Infancy"

- Addition of communication as a developmental task, including language perception, communication with gestures, grammar recognition, and first words.
- Expanded discussion of neural development, including transient exuberance—the rapid increase in the number of neurons, dendrites, and synapses during the first 2 years of life.
- New section on information processing, including attention, processing speed, memory, and representational skills.
- Possible benefits of insecure attachment under conditions of danger or threat.
- Increased discussion of the sense of mistrust among abused infants and infants' sensitivity to increased hostility in the household.
- Increased discussion of the role of nutrition and safety concerns related to food as part of the role of parents.
- Three features of parenting quality that relate to optimal development: sensitivity, cognitive stimulation, and warmth.
- Quotation about how infants play with their fathers.

Chapter 6: "Toddlerhood"

- Discussion of the fact that toddlers are not getting enough moderate to vigorous physical activity to support optimal physical development.

- Impact of the television on language development in toddlerhood.
- A new explanation for theory of mind and a new example of theory of mind research.
- Section on the qualities of early attachment and experiences of shame.
- New studies about the long-lasting consequences of exposure to poverty in young children.
- New studies about the relationship of early, high-quality child care and academic performance in sixth grade.
- New studies about the effects of low-quality child care.
- Costs as well as benefits of bilingualism.
- Introduces the idea of relational aggression.

Chapter 7: "Early School Age"

- Use of gender labels is linked to gender stereotyped play.
- Clarification of concepts of gender permanence and gender constancy.
- Expanded discussion of gender nonconformity and gender dysphoria (the desire to be the opposite sex).
- The principle of care and caring is added to the discussion of moral development.
- New discussion of the relationship between playing violent video games and moral development.
- Discussion about the fact that unstructured, child-initiated play time is dwindling.
- New section on media play.
- New data about family risk factors and reading scores from kindergarten through third grade.

Chapter 8: "Middle Childhood"

- International agreement to stop the use of children as soldiers in armed conflict.
- Expanded definition of social competence.
- New discussion of the role of sibling relationships as they influence social development.
- New discussion of ways to help children who are socially anxious to increase their sense of closeness to friends.
- Section on the use of the Internet to supplement face-to-face friendship.
- New research about bullying.
- Results of policy report indicating that current mathematics instruction is of poor quality.
- Discussion about the impact of early deprivation on higher level skill mastery.
- Expanded discussion of reading as a complex skill.
- Introduced feelings of pride and the attributions that lead to feelings of pride in the discussion of self-evaluation.
- New discussion of cooperation and the evolutionary basis for cooperative behavior.
- Results from the American Psychological Association's report on stress in America, which highlights aspects of their lives that children worry about.
- New information about the number of children who are victims of corporal punishment in their school.

Chapter 9: "Early Adolescence"

- New discussion of early adolescence as a time of positive strides toward maturity.
- New research about how peers influence a girl's body dissatisfaction.
- New research about the secular trend.
- New data suggesting that there is a delay in the onset of sexual experience.
- Risk factors for becoming a teen mother.
- New data about the likelihood of pregnant teens having an abortion.
- New data about characteristics of teen fathers.
- More extensive discussion of brain development.
- New examples of the ways that high school experiences may foster formal operational reasoning.
- New discussion of the interaction of cognition and emotion and the way the brain processes emotions.
- Research showing that depression plays a role in engaging in stressful interpersonal relationships, which then increases depression.
- The role of common home language for forming peer groups.
- Examples of how Chinese early adolescents view parents' efforts to control their behavior.
- New research on the development of ethnic identity.
- Added discussion of how hostile and aggressive parenting can lead to increased feelings of alienation for early adolescent children.
- Narrative about feelings of alienation by a Bosnian immigrant.
- New discussion of four contexts for predicting alcohol misuse: parents, peers, school, and neighborhood.

Chapter 10: "Later Adolescence"

- New introduction explaining our rationale for calling the stage later adolescence rather than emerging adulthood.
- New data showing the percentages of men and women at three ages who have completed the five markers of adult status.
- New research about later adolescents' living arrangements and their relationships with their parents.
- New research on financial self-sufficiency.
- New box on human development and diversity explaining third gender.
- New studies focusing on the sexual and reproductive health of later adolescents.
- Discussion of the contribution of community service in fostering moral development.
- Added a discussion of the concept of career decision-making self-efficacy.
- New discussion of role experimentation as a cycling of commitment formation and commitment reevaluation.
- Added a first-person account of a student who dropped out of college.

Chapter 11: "Early Adulthood"

- New discussion of how the transition into adulthood has changed.
- Expanded discussion of cohabitation.
- Expanded discussion of relationships between partners of the same sex.
- Discussion of speed dating and online dating as new ways of finding a partner.
- Expanded discussion of the positivity bias and the similarity bias as ways of strengthening partners' commitment to one another.
- New discussion of the communal norm and the exchange norm as explanations for how relationships are sustained in the early years of marriage.
- Expanded discussion of decisions about childbearing, including unintended pregnancies and characteristics of the firstborn that influence the decision to have another child.
- New section about problems during pregnancy and maternal depression.
- New section on adoption as an alternative to childbearing.
- In section on work, there is a new section on retraining in the context of massive firings and economic recession.
- New discussion of workers who experience hostility from their supervisors.
- New discussion of national comparison and the poverty rate and the limited resources dedicated to workers in the United States.
- Added discussion of online social networking.
- Added section on the benefits of sleep.
- New international data about bike riding and walking as contributors to fitness.
- Expanded discussion about the adaptive value of love.

Chapter 12: "Middle Adulthood"

- Data from the Organization for Economic Cooperation and Development that provides an international comparison of the working conditions of adults.
- Introduces the concept of adaptive leadership.
- Expands the discussion of interpersonal skills that are needed for effective career management with special emphasis on working in teams.
- Updates the discussion about the use of estrogen therapy for menopausal women.
- Comparison of how fathers and mothers interact with their children when they come home from work.
- Expands the definition of filial obligation including a discussion about its measurement.
- Expands the presentation about building and preserving a positive parent-child relationship as parents age.
- New research on the relationship of generativity to well-being for people who are parents and people who are childless.
- Introduces the case of Bernie Madoff as an example of stagnation.
- New discussions of sex discrimination, age discrimination, race discrimination, and sexual harassment.

Chapter 13: "Later Adulthood"

- New analysis of life goals, including goal domains, goal orientation, and goal-related actions.
- Discussion of openness to experience and sense of humor as aspects of personality that are associated with well-being.
- New research on changes in cognitive abilities across the life span.
- New first-person narrative from grandparents discussing raising their grandchildren.
- Expands the discussion of death anxiety among older adults.
- New data about the increasing involvement of older adults in the labor force and delaying retirement.
- New case study: Anna Quinlin explains her decision to retire as a writer for *Newsweek*.
- New box, "Applying Theory and Research to Life" on patterns of adaptation to widowhood.

Chapter 14: "Elderhood"

- Explanation of the term elderhood as a final stage of the life span.
- Identifies seven components of fitness to assess for the elderly.
- New data about the percentage of the elderly who engage in physical activity.
- New discussion of insomnia in elderhood.
- New discussions of osteoarthritis and osteoporosis.
- New data about the percentage of people in three age groups who need help in the activities of daily living.
- Discussion about online resources that allow elders to pool their experiences and support each other.
- In the discussion of the psychosocial crisis of immortality versus extinction, adds the notion of transcendent future time.
- Updates the symptoms and causes of dementia.

Chapter 15: "Understanding Death, Dying and Bereavement"

- First-person account of a woman describing what she thinks are the benefits of registering her advanced directive.
- Results of a British study describing 12 principles of a good death.
- New first-person account of a woman who changed from being an intensive care nurse to working in hospice.
- Expands the discussion of Oregon Death With Dignity Act.
- Updated information on the moral acceptability of physician-assisted suicide.
- New data from a Gallop poll about Americans' beliefs about heaven.

Features That Support Learning

Several features are included in the 11th edition that we expect will contribute to the learning process.

Basic Chapter Pedagogy

Each chapter begins with an outline and a list of objectives. These can be used to guide the reader to the main topics and help summarize basic ideas of the chapter. The chapter objectives are repeated at the point in the text where the material addressing each objective is presented, and again in the chapter summary to help students connect the material in the chapter to the major themes. Glossary terms are presented in boldface to help introduce new concepts. Each chapter ends with a chapter summary, which highlights main ideas in an integrative fashion, and a set of questions. With these questions, we hope to encourage students to synthesize information across chapters, to link topics in the text to their own experiences, and to think about how they might relate ideas from the chapters to applied settings. A list of key terms and page numbers is included to draw attention to important ideas presented in the chapter.

Boxed Features

Two types of boxed features are included to extend discussion on topics of special interest:

Applying Theory and Research to Life illustrates how new research and theory can be applied to concerns of daily social life.

Human Development and Diversity presents a wide range of human differences that shape the nature of development at various stages of life.

Each box concludes with a group of critical thinking questions to encourage students to make connections with the topics in the text.

Case Studies

- *Case Studies* and accompanying questions encourage students to apply concepts from the chapter to real-life experiences. The cases can be a focus for self-study or used in groups to foster discussion regarding the application of the main ideas in the chapter.

Acknowledgments

The works of Erik Erikson and Robert Havighurst have guided and inspired our own intellectual development. The combined contributions of these scholars have shaped the basic direction of psychosocial theory and have guided an enormous amount of research in human development. They directed us to look at the process of growth and change across the life span. They recognized the intimate interweaving of the individual's life story with a sociohistorical context, emphasizing societal pressures that call for new levels of functioning at each life stage. In their writing, they com-

municated an underlying optimism about each person's resilience, adaptability, and immense capacity for growth that finds new expression in the work of positive psychology. At the same time, they wrote with a moral passion about our responsibility as teachers, therapists, parents, scholars, and citizens to create a caring society. We celebrate these ideas and continue their expression in the 11th edition of *Development Through Life*.

We want to express our thanks to our many students, colleagues, and friends who shared their experiences and expertise. Through the years, our mentors, Bill McKeachie and Jim Kelly, have been unfailing sources of support and fresh ideas. Theirs are the voices of wisdom we count on, reminding us of the values of good scholarship and a generous heart. Our former students, Brenda Lohman and Laura Landry Meyer, were excellent collaborators on our life-span development case book. For this edition, we want to thank Clarissa Uttley who revised the Student Study Guide and prepared the Instructor's resource materials. Phil was Clarissa's academic advisor when she was an undergraduate student. He encouraged her to go on for her master's degree in human development, and then her Ph.D. in psychology. She is now a faculty member at Plymouth State University in Plymouth, New Hampshire. It has been a delight to work with her and watch her flourish. With each new edition, we turn to our children and their families to offer new observations, try out ideas, and talk over controversies. At each stage, they bring new talents and perspectives that enrich our efforts.

The 11th edition was produced under the guidance of our editor, Jaime Perkins, the managing development editor, Jeremy Judson, and a team of developmental editors including Dan Moneypenny, Kirk Bomont, Shannon LeMay Finn, and Rebecca Dashiell. Their advice, encouragement, support, and vision have been instrumental in bringing this edition to fruition. We are very lucky to have had the benefit of their creative energy. In addition, we would like to express our appreciation to the other professionals at Wadsworth who have helped make this book possible: Charlene Carpentier, Content Project Manager; Vernon Boes, Art Director; Kelly Miller, Assistant Editor; Mary Noel, Media Editor; Jessica Egbert, Marketing Manager; Laura Localio, Marketing Communications Manager; and Janay Pryor, Marketing Coordinator.

Finally, we acknowledge the thoughtful, constructive comments and suggestions of the following reviewers: Diane D. Ashe, Valencia Community College; Verneda P. Hamm Baugh, Kean University; Shannon Bert, University of Oklahoma; Bridget Danielle Byrd, University of North Carolina–Wilmington; Kay Fernandes, Trident Technical College; Jerry Green, Tarrant County College; Pamela B. Hill, San Antonio College; Leslee K. Pollina, Southeast Missouri State University; Marylou Robins, San Jacinto College; Jaylene Krieg Schaefer, University of Cincinnati; Debra L. Stout, California State University–Fullerton; and Shannon Welch, University of Idaho.

Supplements: Print, Video, and Electronic

Development Through Life: A Psychosocial Approach, 11th edition, is accompanied by a wide array of supplementary resources prepared for both the instructor and student.

For the Instructor

Instructor's Manual with Test Bank
ISBN-10: 1111349010 | ISBN-13: 9781111349011

The Instructor's Manual (written by Clarissa Uttley of Plymouth State University) contains resources designed to streamline and maximize the effectiveness of your course preparation. The content includes lecture suggestions, discussion topics, teaching notes, class projects, and video suggestions. The Test Bank offers over 2,000 questions, including multiple-choice, true/false, matching, and essay questions. The multiple-choice questions include page references, difficulty, and question-type, along with the correct answer. Test Bank questions are keyed to chapter objectives.

PowerLecture with ExamView®
ISBN-10: 1111349037 | ISBN-13: 9781111349035

This one-stop lecture and class preparation tool contains ready-to-use Microsoft PowerPoint slides (written by Clarissa Uttley of Plymouth State University) and allows you to assemble, edit, publish, and present custom lectures for your course. PowerLecture lets you bring together text-specific lecture outlines and art from Newman and Newman's text, along with videos or your own materials—culminating in a powerful, personalized, media-enhanced presentation. The CD-ROM also includes the ExamView® assessment and tutorial system, which guides you step by step through the process of creating tests.

For the Student

Study Guide
ISBN-10: 1111349045 | ISBN-13: 9781111349042

For each chapter, this student resource (written by Barbara M. Newman, Philip R. Newman, and Clarissa Uttley of Plymouth State University) includes the chapter outline, the learning objectives, a pre-test of 20 true-or-false questions, matching and focusing questions, a 20-item multiple-choice post-test, and a "Suggestions for Further Observation and Study" section that includes key terms that can be further researched.

Life-Span Development: A Case Book
ISBN-10: 053459767X | ISBN-13 9780534597672

Written by Barbara M. Newman (University of Rhode Island), Philip R. Newman (University of Rhode Island), Laura Landry-Meyer (Bowling Green State University), and Brenda J. Lohman (Iowa State University), *LIFE-SPAN DEVELOPMENT: A CASE BOOK* uses lively, contemporary case studies to illustrate development transitions and challenges in every stage of life. The authors have chosen these cases for their ability to fascinate, engage, and stimulate. Together with thought-provoking questions for analysis, the case studies create a learning experience that helps readers use multiple perspectives to analyze and interpret life events.

WebTutor™ on BlackBoard or WebCT

Jumpstart your course with customizable, rich, text-specific content within your Course Management System. Whether you want to Web-enable your class or put an entire course online, WebTutor™ delivers. WebTutor™ offers a wide array of resources including quizzing, videos, and more. Visit webtutor.cengage.com to learn more.

Psychology CourseMate

To access additional course materials, including CourseMate, please visit **www.cengagebrain.com**. At the CengageBrain.com home page, search for the ISBN of your title (from the back cover of your book) using the search box at the top of the page. This will take you to the product page where these resources can be found. Psychology CourseMate includes an integrated eBook, interactive teaching and learning tools including quizzes, flashcards, videos, and more, and EngagementTracker, a first-of-its-kind tool that monitors student engagement in the course.

Brief Author Biographies

Philip R. Newman (Ph.D., University of Michigan) is involved in research on the transition to high school and on group identity and alienation. His current projects include a book about how high schools can meet the psychosocial needs of adolescents, and the development of a protocol for counselors to assess psychosocial maturity and problems in living based on the framework presented in *Development Through Life*. He has taught courses in introductory psychology, adolescence, social psychology, developmental psychology, counseling, and family, school, and community contexts for development. He served as the director for research and evaluation of the Young Scholars Program at the Ohio State University and as the director of the Human Behavior Curriculum Project for the American Psychological Association. He is a fellow of the American Psychological Association, the Society for the Psychological Study of Social Issues (SPSSI), and the American Orthopsychiatric Association. For fun, Phil enjoys photography, reading mysteries, attending concerts and Broadway plays, and watching baseball. He homeschooled his three children through elementary and middle school.

Barbara M. Newman (Ph.D., University of Michigan) is a professor in the department of Human Development and Family Studies at the University of Rhode Island. She has also been on the faculty at Russell Sage College and the Ohio State University, where she served as department chair in Human Development and Family Science and as associate provost for faculty recruitment and development. She teaches courses in life-span development, adolescence, human development and family theories, and the research process. Also an active researcher, Dr. Newman's interests focus on social and emotional development in adolescence, parent-child relationships in early adolescence, and factors that promote success in the transition to high school and college. Her current research is an analysis of the sense of belonging among college freshmen. She is a member of the teaching committee of the Society for Research in Child Development. For fun, Barbara enjoys reading, practicing the piano, making up projects with her grandchildren, taking walks along Narragansett Bay and Block Island Sound, and spending time with her family.

Together, the Newmans have worked on programs to bring low-income minority youths to college and have studied the processes involved in their academic success. They are co-authors of 13 books, including a recent book on theories of human development, and numerous articles in the field of human development. They met by the Mason Hall elevator at the University of Michigan, fell in love at first sight, and have been married for 44 years.

This edition of *Development Through Life*
is dedicated to our grandchildren.

© 2011 Estate of Pablo Picasso/Artists Rights Society (ARS), New York/Picasso, Pablo (1881–1973)/Private Collection/Photo © Sotheby's

Through play, children extend their ideas about what is possible in the present and in the future. A child with a hobbyhorse can be a cowhand, a police officer, a palace guard, or a wizard riding a dragon. In the study of human development, we strive to understand how individuals make meaning of their experiences and shape the direction of their lives from the playful inventions of childhood to the creative and inspiring wisdoms of elderhood.

The Development Through Life Perspective

Chapter Objectives

1. To introduce the basic assumptions that guide the orientation of the text.

2. To introduce the psychosocial approach to the study of development, including the interrelationship among the biological, psychological, and societal systems.

3. To note historical changes in life expectancy and examine the implications of these changes for the study of development over the life span.

PATRICK JONATHAN CARMICHAEL was born the son of a free man who had earned his way out of slavery in North Carolina before moving to Alabama and the Rump plantation. Carmichael attended Snowhill Institute, which was modeled after Booker T. Washington's Tuskegee Institute. It was here that the dream for his own school began. After graduating from high school, he taught for five years, then founded Purdue Hill Industrial High.

"The state put up just seventy-five dollars a year for expenses," Carmichael says. "Students paid tuition of twenty-five cents a year and paid in chickens or cans of syrup if they didn't have the money. You couldn't get a dime out of a state to build a Negro school back then. I'd write letters to people all over the country who I thought had a little charity about them to help us. I'd be the last man to put his light out because I'd be writing letters."

"He got twenty-five dollars a month," Carmichael's son adds. "He fed us kids by farming, getting up before dawn to work the fields, raise chickens and cattle and pigs. He had a big garden. All his earnings went back into the school. At night he'd write those letters to wealthy people in Boston or New York, trying to get a little money for the school. He was persistent. A little at a time. People in the area built the school. It started out as a one-room school with one teacher and eleven students and grew to a twelve-room school with two hundred and fifty students and ten teachers."

When this interview was conducted, Patrick Jonathan Carmichael was living with his son and daughter-in-law.

He was 101 years old but had been with them for only the past few years. After retiring from his career in education in 1958, he lived alone on his farm until he broke his hip after going out to feed his cattle; he was 97 at the time.

"I didn't get along with my father when I was younger," says his son. "He was such a hard-working, disciplined man. Now it's different. It's like we're getting another chance. I have to take care of him, do things for him like shave him. He needs me and we're developing more of a buddy relationship." (Heynen, 1990, p. 9. Patrick Jonathan Carmichael, born 1886, interviewed in 1987.)

Think for a moment about Patrick Jonathan Carmichael: his hopes, determination, sacrifices, family, accomplishments, and disappointments; the new challenges he must have faced as he retired from education, lived alone, and formed new, interdependent relationships with his son and daughter-in-law. Think of living 100 years—so many changes and so much to learn; so many losses and so many victories. What do we know of development through life? How can we conceptualize the dynamic development of individuals within the contexts of their societies, the period of history in which they grew up and entered adulthood, their families, their values and goals, and the obstacles they faced? How can we study patterns of change and growth in populations and still preserve an understanding of the intriguing uniqueness of individual lives? These are some of the challenging questions facing the discipline of human development. ∎

The study of human development is puzzling. Our goal is to gain a more accurate understanding of how individuals make sense of their experiences, adapt to their environments, cope with challenges, and continue to develop from one period of life to the next. This process is as individual as each person's life story and is influenced by such factors as gender, ethnicity, cultural identity, health, socioeconomic status, education, sexual orientation, physical

Growth occurs at every stage of life. Within a large family, we have opportunities to observe family resemblances and individual differences; patterns of **continuity** from year to year as well as evidence of maturation and change.

© Ariel Skelley/Corbis

abilities and disabilities, and historical and social contexts. Even though each person's life is unique, common patterns of experience and meaning allow us to know and care for one another and contribute to one another's well-being. The life-span approach to human development strives to identify and account for patterns of transition and transformation from one period of life to another while recognizing both intergroup differences and individual variations within groups (Smith & Baltes, 1999).

This chapter provides a brief introduction to three topics that are central to the study of the **life span**. First, we outline five assumptions about human development that guide the orientation of the text. Second, we introduce the concept of a **psychosocial approach** to development. Third, we review data about **life expectancy** to start you thinking in a concrete way about the course of your life and the decisions you make that may directly influence your life story.

Assumptions of the Text

Objective 1. To introduce the basic assumptions that guide the orientation of the text.

Our perspective on development through life makes the following five assumptions that are critical to the orientation of this book:

1. *Growth occurs at every period of life, from conception through very old age.* At each period, new capacities emerge, new roles are undertaken, new challenges must be faced, and, as a result, a new orientation toward self and society unfolds. The concept of life-span development implies **plasticity**, a capacity for adaptive reorganization at the neurological, psychological, and behavioral levels.

2. *Individual lives show both continuity and developmental change over time.* An awareness of the processes that contribute to both continuity and change is central to an understanding of human development. *Continuity* refers to stability in characteristics from one period of life to another. It also refers to a sense of sameness over time built on a history of memories, identity, and reflected self. **Developmental change** refers to patterns of growth and reorganization. Change may be attributed to biological maturation, systematic socialization, self-directed striving, and to the interaction of these forces.

3. *We need to understand the whole person, because we function in an integrated manner.* To achieve such an understanding, we need to study the major developments in physical, social, emotional, and cognitive capacities and their interrelationships. We also need to study actions, the many forms of observable behavior. Each system serves as a stimulus for the others, with the overall purpose of enhancing the person's adaptive capacities.

4. *Behavior must be interpreted in the context of relevant settings and personal relationships.* Human beings are highly skilled in adapting to their environments. The meaning of a given behavior pattern or behavior change must be interpreted in light of the significant physical and social environments in which it occurs.

5. *People contribute actively to their development.* These contributions take many forms, including the expression of tastes and preferences, choices and goals, and one's willingness to embrace or resist cultural and societal

expectations. One of the most critical ways in which a person contributes to his or her development is through the creation of significant social relationships, which then form a context for social support and socialization. Some societies offer more opportunities for choice and promote a person's ability to mold the direction of development, whereas others have fewer resources, are more restrictive, or place less value on individuality (Veenhoven, 2000).

A Psychosocial Approach: The Interaction of the Biological, Psychological, and Societal Systems

Objective 2. To introduce the psychosocial approach to the study of development, including the interrelationship among the biological, psychological, and societal systems.

Erik Erikson (1963, p. 37) wrote that human life as the individual experiences it is produced by the interaction and modification of three major systems: the biological system, the psychological system, and the societal system. Each system can be examined for patterns of continuity and change over the life course. Each system can be modified by self-guided choices. The integration of the biological, psychological, and societal systems leads to a complex, **biopsychosocial** dynamic portrait of human thought and behavior.

In many developmental analyses of behavior, you may come across the terms "nature" and "nurture." These terms are often used as shorthand for thinking about the roles of genetics and environments in guiding development. Typically, nature refers to genetic predispositions or potentials and inborn or innate qualities that guide the unfolding of capacities and traits. Nurture refers to the patterns of socialization and care that the person receives. The science of development is often been presented as the study of the ways nature and nurture interact to produce a certain outcome, for example intelligence, assertiveness, or hopefulness.

In *Development Through Life* we take a somewhat different approach by expanding the analysis to three interrelated systems: the biological, the societal, and the psychological systems. Rather than thinking of the developing person as passively shaped by forces of nature and nurture, we think of the person as actively engaged in the developmental process through the application of the psychological system. The psychological system is the **meaning-making** system that seeks out information, integrates information from many sources, and evaluates experiences as positive or negative, encouraging or threatening. Over time, and drawing upon genetically based resources as well as environmental

facilitation, the person becomes increasingly able to make plans, set goals, make choices and decisions, and interpret inner feelings and thoughts (Ryan & Deci, 2000). The stories of individual lives are a product of this interpretive capacity of the psychological system as much as they are a result of the unfolding of genetically guided capacities and environmental or societal resources and constraints. Depending on their experiences and predispositions, some people are more proactive in shaping the course of their development while others are more passive. The psychosocial approach is an attempt to sketch out the ways that a person's worldview and sense of self in society change as a product of the interaction of these three dynamic systems over the course of life.

The Biological System

The **biological system** includes all those processes necessary for the physical functioning of the organism and for mental activity (see Figure 1.1). The brain and spinal cord (the central nervous system) and the peripheral nervous system are components of the biological system through which all sensory information is received, processed, and transmitted to guide behavior. Biological processes develop and change as a consequence of genetically guided maturation; environmental stimulation and resources, including social interactions,

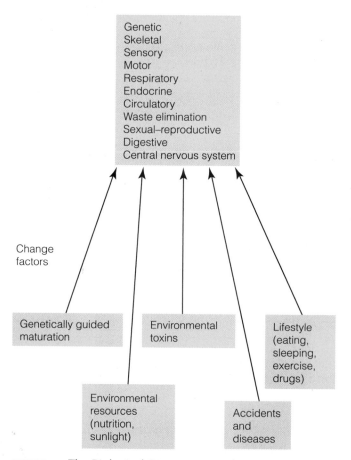

FIGURE 1.1 The Biological System

cognitive challenges, and nutrition; exposure to environmental toxins; encounters with accidents and diseases; and lifestyle patterns of behavior.

Cultures differ in their support of physical growth and health, depending on the availability of adequate nutritional resources, approaches to the treatment of illness, exposure to environmental toxins and hazardous conditions, and the availability of information about healthy lifestyle choices.

Some components of the biological system influence the maturation of other components of the biological system. For example, when the infant's limbs achieve a certain length and muscle strength, the baby is able to reach out from a sitting position to begin crawling—a new form of locomotion. This results in new opportunities for exploration of the environment which in turn results in new neural networks and changes in the organization of the brain. The biological system is itself a multilevel, dynamic system in which maturation at one level can have profound, and sometimes unexpected, consequences for maturation at another level.

In the case of Patrick Jonathan Carmichael, two examples of the influences of the biological system on his life experiences are his **longevity** and his physical strength. He lived a long time in good health. His uncommon hardiness, brought about by a combination of genes, a life of rigorous exercise, and a healthy lifestyle, contributed to his ability to endure the physical demands of his life and to achieve many of his career goals, while still supporting his family. The experience of breaking his hip at an advanced age is an example of how changes in the biological system can modify the social and psychological systems. Looking at Figure 1.1, can you think of other aspects of the biological system that may have been important in shaping Patrick Jonathan Carmichael's life story?

The Psychological System

The **psychological system** includes those mental processes central to a person's ability to make meaning of experiences and take action (see Figure 1.2). Emotion, memory, perception, motivation, thinking and reasoning, language, symbolic abilities, and one's orientation to the future are examples of psychological processes. When these processes are integrated, they provide the resources for processing information, solving problems, and navigating reality. In the case of Patrick Jonathan Carmichael, the influence of the psychological system can be appreciated when one considers his motivation, his persistence, his academic abilities, his independence, his ingenuity, his goals, and his sense of self-discipline.

Like the biological processes, psychological processes develop and change over one's life span. Change is guided in part by genetic information. The capacity for intellectual functioning and the direction of cognitive maturation are genetically guided. A number of genetically transmitted diseases result in intellectual impairment and a reduced capacity for learning. Change also results from the accumulation

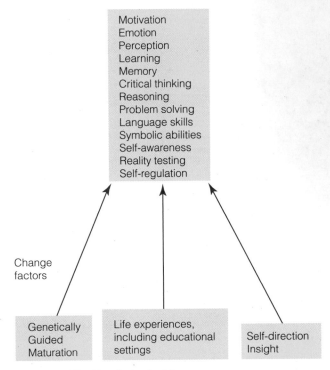

FIGURE 1.2 The Psychological System

of experiences and from encounters with various educational settings which impact brain development and result in new cognitive structures and new approaches to problem solving. Psychological processes can be enhanced by numerous life experiences including the quality of parenting one receives, interactions with friends, opportunities for play of all types, travel, reading, exposure to music, art, poetry, and the dramatic arts, and schooling. Finally, change can be self-directed. A person can decide to pursue a new interest, learn another language, or adopt a new set of ideas. People can strive to achieve new levels of **self-insight**, to be more aware of their thoughts and feelings, and less defensive. There is evidence to suggest that self-insight is a vital component of positive mental health (Wilson, 2009).

The Societal System

The **societal system** includes social roles; social support; **culture**, including rituals, myths, and social expectations; media; leadership styles; communication patterns; family organization; ethnic and subcultural influences; political ideologies and forms of government; religions; patterns of economic prosperity or **poverty**; conditions of war or peace; and exposure to racism, sexism, and other forms of discrimination, intolerance, or intergroup hostility. The societal system encompasses those processes that foster or disrupt a person's sense of social integration and social identity (see Figure 1.3). Through laws and public policies, political and economic structures, and educational opportunities, societies influence the psychosocial development of individuals and alter the life course for future generations (de St. Aubin, McAdams,

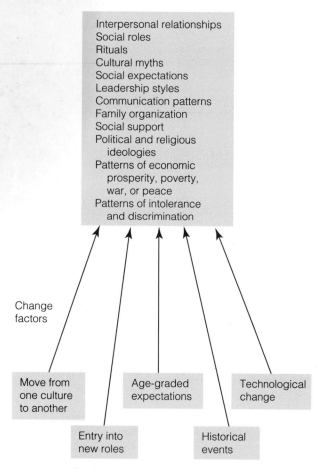

FIGURE 1.3 The Societal System

& Kim, 2004). Societal processes may change over one's life span. The process of modernization may bring exposure to new levels of education, new technologies, encounters with more diverse groups of people, and new forms of work. These changes are likely to result in more individualistic values, new priorities about which skills are valued, and changing patterns of family life (Greenfield, 2009).

Technological innovations can modify the societal system. For example, television, cell phones, personal computers, and the Internet have modified a person's access to information, patterns of informal interaction, and the ease with which individuals and groups can collaborate. Websites such as Facebook, MySpace, or LinkedIn create virtual social networks where people can establish and preserve connections, even when they are physically far apart, recreating the sense of neighborhood and facilitating interactions among people with common interests. These technologies have altered children's roles, providing them with resources that can allow them to function at new levels of autonomy and competence. In many families, children teach their parents and grandparents how to make use of the new technologies, elevating their role within the family. The widespread distribution of cell phones reduces barriers to communication, a change that has an impact on patterns of communication among parents

and children, loved ones, friends, and colleagues. Cell phones make it possible to communicate in a variety of modes including text messages, voice mail, shared images, and email as well as traditional telephone talk. We can hypothesize that cell phones may contribute to sustaining intimate relationships and preserving bonds of closeness in a time when people are extremely busy trying to manage multiple roles.

Historical events can also influence the societal system, altering social roles, access to resources, economic conditions, and one's sense of personal safety or security. For example, although we do not yet have a systematic analysis of the societal impacts of the events of September 11, 2001, or the sudden economic collapse of 2008, we can hypothesize that these events will have an enduring influence on people's sense of safety, economic security, and confidence in key social institutions. In response to these crises, the government has instituted new levels of surveillance, new restrictions, and new laws which become integrated into the "way of life." Some researchers speculate that recent experiences of economic instability may result in revised aspirations about accumulating material wealth, leading to the adoption of a more modest standard of living, and a greater desire to be part of a meaningful and caring social community (Novotney, 2009).

In this text, the role of culture is emphasized as it contributes to the pattern, pace, and direction of development. Societies differ in their **worldviews**, including the emphasis placed on collectivism or individualism, ideas about the major sources of stress and ways to alleviate stress, and beliefs about which groups are viewed as more powerful or more important than others. Societies differ in their emphasis on and belief in science, spirituality, and fatalism. They differ in their **age-graded expectations**, such as when a person is considered to be a child, an adult, or an elder, and how people in these age roles should be treated. They differ in their definitions of morality, beauty, bravery, wealth, and other ideals that may define individual and group aspirations. As you read the text, you will encounter boxes entitled Human Development and Diversity. These boxes provide examples of how norms of development might be viewed differently in different cultures or ethnic groups. We hope these examples will help sensitize you to the role of culture in defining what may be viewed as appropriate, optimal, or normal behavior.

The societal system is illustrated in the case of Patrick Jonathan Carmichael by the importance of Carmichael's educational experiences at the Snowhill Institute, the discriminatory practices that resulted in no state funding for Negro education, the involvement of other families in the community in encouraging education for their children, the philanthropic donations from benefactors outside the community, and the changing nature of Carmichael's relationship with his son.

The Psychosocial Impact of Poverty

In thinking about the impact of societal factors on development, we want to highlight the context of poverty as a major obstacle to optimal development. (See the Applying Theory and Research to Life box.) Racism, sexism, ageism, homophobia, and discrimination against individuals with physical, intellectual, and emotional disabilities are other examples. However, under conditions of poverty, individuals have fewer options and less opportunity to escape or avoid these other societal deterrents. Poverty has powerful and potentially pervasive effects on the biological and psychological systems across the life span.

In 2008, an estimated 14 million U.S. children lived in families with incomes at or below the poverty level, and another 16 million lived in families at up to twice the poverty level. More than half of these children lived in families where a parent worked full time (National Center for Children in Poverty, 2009). These figures do not take into account the full impact of the recent recession, because many families that were marginally above the poverty level are now unemployed or underemployed, and still others have lost their homes to foreclosures.

African-American, Hispanic, and Native-American families are overrepresented among those living in poverty, and their experiences of poverty are likely to be long lasting. For individuals in these ethnic groups, the stresses associated with the chronic conditions of poverty are linked with earlier exposure to health risks and higher exposure to environmental hazards.

In and of itself, poverty does not place inevitable limits on development. There are many instances, both famous and less well known, of children who grew up in poverty and achieved eminence (Harrington & Boardman, 2000). We need only think of the case of Patrick Jonathan Carmichael to recognize that many children flourish under conditions of meager family resources. In fact, some people choose to live very modest material lives in order to achieve other important goals. However, it is well documented that poverty increases the risks that individuals face, including risks associated with malnutrition, poor quality health care, living in poor quality and overcrowded housing, living in a hazardous or dangerous neighborhood, and attending ineffective schools. Poverty is linked with reduced access to the basic resources associated with health and survival (Yoo, Slack, & Holl, 2009; Crosnoe & Huston, 2007). Exposure to these risk factors early and continuously throughout childhood is associated with higher incidences of health problems, greater challenges in achieving the developmental tasks of each life stage, disruptions in family and work trajectories, and reduced life expectancy (Hayward, Crimmins, Miles, & Yang, 2000; Knitzer, 2007).

Because of the complex and pervasive impact of poverty on development, we introduce it as a fundamental societal theme. Issues related to the impact of poverty on patterns of development and family life will be addressed in more detail in subsequent chapters.

Overview of the Psychosocial Approach

The **psychosocial approach** seeks to understand development as a product of interactions among biological, psychological, and societal processes. Changes in one of the three systems (biological, psychological, or societal) generally bring about changes in the others. As an example, consider the emerging field of **social cognitive neuroscience**. This field explores the neurological processes associated with the ways we perceive social information and reason about others. The field draws on an evolutionary perspective that suggests that human beings are social animals whose survival depended on being able to communicate with others and to establish and preserve social bonds. As a result, neural mechanisms have developed that are uniquely organized to detect social messages of exclusion and trustworthiness. In the ancient past, those humans who were able to make accurate, rapid judgments about whether someone or some situation was safe or dangerous, trustworthy or threatening, had a survival advantage (Chen, 2009). This social cognitive advantage, firmly embedded in the brain's neural networks, has been passed along from one generation to the next, contributing to the way modern humans detect and assess their social environment.

The capacities for representing self and others, for perspective taking and empathy, and for engaging in effective social communication develop over time as the social information-processing areas of the brain are stimulated in diverse and culturally guided forms of social interaction (Wood, 2003). The biological system recognizes and processes social stimulation. The societal system creates the contexts for social interactions and introduces complex patterns of values and priorities for social behavior. Further, the psychological system internalizes these values and assigns unique meaning to social events. So, for example, researchers find that in a task that requires recognition of one's own face and the face of a familiar other, Westerners who tend to emphasize self-related events recognize their own face more quickly, and East Asians, who tend to emphasize social connections among people, recognize the familiar other more quickly (Sui, Liu, & Han, 2009).

Throughout life, personal relationships occupy our attention. Some of these relationships are more important than others, but their quality and diversity provide a basis for the study of one's psychosocial development. As we progress through the stages of life, most of us develop an increasing capacity to initiate new relationships and to innovate in our thoughts and actions so as to direct the course of our lives.

At each period of life, people spend much of their time mastering a unique group of psychological tasks that provide essential learning for social adaptation within their society. Each life stage brings a normative crisis, which is viewed as a tension between one's competencies and the new demands of society. People strive to reduce this tension by using a variety of familiar coping strategies and by learning new ones. A positive resolution of each crisis provides new social abilities and a new understanding of the self and others that enhance a person's capacity to adapt successfully in succeeding stages. A negative resolution of each crisis typically results in defensiveness, rigidity, or withdrawal, which decreases a person's ability for successful social adaptation in succeeding stages.

Poverty

Conditions Leading to Poverty

Since the 1960s, five factors have contributed to an increase in the number of families living in poverty: (1) the decline in well-paying, blue-collar jobs; (2) large increases in single-mother households due to births to unmarried women and to divorce; (3) the erosion of the economic safety net for poor families, including the decline in cash transfers and benefits to families in the welfare program, Transitional Assistance to Needy Families; (4) the decline in the purchasing power of the minimum wage; and (5) the economic recession of 2008 which resulted in dramatic increases in unemployment, homelessness, and loss of retirement savings (Hernandez, 1993; Pavetti, 2000). Adjusted for inflation, the purchasing power of the minimum wage in 2009 ($7.25 per hour) was 17% less than it was in 1968 (Economic Policy Institute, 2009).

The way the current poverty level is estimated has been criticized as flawed for two major reasons: First, the poverty level was established in the 1960s based on an estimate of how much an average family spends on food. At that time, families spent about 1/3 of their income on food, so the poverty level was set at three times the cost of a typical "shopping basket" of consumables. Today, food is only 1/7th of an average family's expenses. Costs for rent, transportation, child care, and health/medical expenses have increased much faster than the costs of food. Second, the poverty level is a national standard that does not take into account regional variations in the cost of living. For example, one estimate of basic needs found that the average cost of basic housing and utilities for a family of four would cost $15,816 per year in New York City, and $10,224

Poverty is a powerful characteristic of the societal system. Children growing up in poverty are exposed to stressors and hazards that can severely restrict development.

in Houston, TX (National Center for Children in Poverty, 2009). Neither the federal guidelines about the poverty level nor a Basic Budget approach to estimating the poverty level includes any category for savings or emergency funds.

Poverty is transitory for some families—such as when a wage earner becomes unemployed and then finds new work—but persistent over the life course for others. For unmarried women who become mothers in adolescence, poverty is often a result of interrupted education, the inability to work full time (usually because of time needed to care for their children), and the low-paying jobs that are available to those with limited educational attainment. Furthermore, many of these young mothers are growing up in families that are already living in poverty. Eighty-five percent of children whose parents do not have a high-school diploma live in low-income families (National Center for Children in Poverty, 2009).

Divorce places many women and their children into poverty. In many instances, the family was already encountering financial strain, which is known to be one of the primary factors associated with divorce. However, following divorce, an estimated 27% of divorced women and their children fall below the poverty line (Chase-Lansdale, 1993). The level of poverty experienced by newly divorced women is aggravated by the failure of many fathers to pay child support (Smock & Manning, 1997). Poverty for these families is sometimes transitory, because many divorced women remarry or are able to find adequate employment after a year or two. However, in one study, 48% of respondents reported lower income even five years after the divorce (Thabes, 1997). With increases in women's education and career prospects, opportunities for women to emerge from poverty after divorce are likely to improve.

© Nathan Benn/CORBIS

Negative Consequences of Poverty

Persistent poverty and exposure to poverty during infancy and early childhood are associated with greater vulnerability and more negative consequences to health, cognitive development and school achievement, and mental health.

Health. Exposure to poverty during the prenatal period is associated with increased risks for having premature babies and babies that are small for gestational age (Nepomnyaschy, 2009). According to the National Center for Children in Poverty (2009), two consequences of poverty have a significant impact on health. First, children in low-income families are likely to experience food insecurity; second, they are likely to lack health insurance. Children in low-income families are more likely to be in fair or poor health and lack access to quality health care. Children in low-income families often lack treatment for existing physical health problems, such as asthma, or go untreated for infections that then become more serious and can result in long-term chronic conditions. For a family in poverty, a visit to a doctor that costs $75 is a significant and possibly prohibitive expense.

Education. Higher family income is consistently associated with higher academic achievement (Gershoff, 2003; Lee & Burkham, 2002). Children in low-income families begin kindergarten with a substantial disadvantage with regard to specific academic skills such as counting, recognizing letters of the alphabet, and reading. By the time they are in the third grade, children in low-income families have an average vocabulary of 4,000 words compared to a vocabulary of 12,000 words for children from middle income families (Klein & Knitzer, 2007). Research on seasonal fluctuations in learning shows that children from low-income families and low-resource communities have substantially fewer learning opportunities over the summer. Each fall they begin school behind their middle-income peers year after year. In addition, the inequity in school resources and educational opportunities across communities is well documented. As a result, by the time children from low-income families reach the ninth grade, they have significantly lower test scores, are less likely to be placed in college-preparatory tracks, and are more likely to drop out of high school than their higher socioeconomic (SES) peers (Alexander, Entwisle, & Olson, 2007). When children from poor families attend schools where there are students from a greater diversity of economic backgrounds, the poor students tend to be viewed as less competent by the teachers and the wealthier students. This may create an added burden on their academic self-concept and result in lower academic performance (Crosnoe, 2009).

Mental Health. Recent neuroscience research has clarified the significance of the quality of early life experiences. Earliest experiences shape the establishment of neural networks, including the way the brain processes information and manages emotions. A key ingredient of early brain development is the quality of caregiving relationships, especially the ability of caregivers to be appropriately nurturing, responsive, and stimulating.

Children from low-income families are more likely to be exposed prenatally to factors such as maternal malnutrition, cigarette smoke, alcohol, and environmental toxins that disrupt neural development. Infants and young children are more likely to be exposed to parental depression, other diagnosable mental disorders, and parental adversities including domestic violence and substance abuse that disrupt or destabilize caregiving. In addition, threats to safety are of special concern to children living in low-income neighborhoods where exposure to uncontrollable violence on the streets and near the school is associated with symptoms of post-traumatic stress (Caughy, Nettles, O'Campo, & Lohrfink, 2006).

These risk factors have been associated with a number of short- and long-term consequences for children including depression, acting-out behaviors, difficulty concentrating, and school problems. Living in poverty is associated with higher rates of learning problems and diagnosable disorders in older children (Knitzer & Cooper, 2006). These often lead to juvenile justice involvement and higher school drop-out rates. Two-thirds of youth with mental health problems have been found to drop out of high school (Wagner, 2005).

Critical Thinking Questions

1. What are some examples of ways that social and economic policies can increase or decrease the number of families in poverty?

2. What is meant by the phrase "the cycle of poverty"? How might the experiences of growing up in poverty influence one's adjustment as an adolescent? as an adult?

3. What do you think would be the most important, immediate steps that a society could take to reduce the negative consequences of poverty?

4. If you had to choose between giving money directly to families in poverty by increasing the minimum wage or investing in higher quality schools, health care insurance, and housing, which would you do? Why?

Left: Image copyright Eoliverong 2010. Used under license from Shutterstock.com   Top Right: © 2010/Thinkstock Jupiterimages Corporation
Bottom Right: ©2010 Ariel Skelley/Jupiterimages Corporation

The desire to experience a loving relationship remains strong throughout life. However, the self one brings to a loving relationship changes at each stage. How might experiences of love change from adolescence to early adulthood to later adulthood?

CASE STUDY

ROSE

The interaction of the biological, the psychological, and the societal systems.

Rose is a 60-year-old woman who has been having serious attacks of dizziness and shortness of breath as Thanksgiving approaches. Rose is usually active and energetic. In the past, she looked forward to entertaining her family, which used to include three married daughters, one married son, their spouses, and their children. However, her son has recently been divorced. Feelings between him and his ex-wife are bitter. Any attempts on Rose's part to communicate with her former daughter-in-law or granddaughter are met with outbursts of hostility from her son. Although Rose is very fond of her daughter-in-law and granddaughter, she knows that she cannot invite them to the family gathering without stirring up intense conflict with her son. Rose's daughters suggest having the dinner at one of their homes in order to prevent further conflict. They hope this solution will take some of the pressure off their mother and ease the attacks. Rose agrees, but her attacks continue.

ANALYSIS

How are the biological, psychological, and societal systems involved in Rose's situation? We might hypothesize that her physical symptoms, dizziness and shortness of breath, are due to an inability to resolve a difficult family conflict. Psychological and societal demands may elicit responses from the biological system, as they commonly do in people under stress. The biological system often alerts a person to the severity of a threat or crisis through the development of physical symptoms. Rose might visit her family doctor in order to evaluate whether her symptoms are a result of high blood pressure or early signs of heart disease. There may be medication that can help reduce these symptoms, allowing Rose to feel less anxious and more confident about her role in the family.

Rose's psychological system is involved in interpreting her son's behavior, which she views as forcing her to choose between him and her daughter-in-law and granddaughter. She might also use psychological processes to try to arrive at a solution to the conflict. So far, Rose has not identified any satisfactory solution. Although she can avoid the conflict most of the time, the impending Thanksgiving dinner is forcing her to confront it directly.

The psychological system includes Rose's self-concept as well as her emotional state. Through memory, Rose retains a sense of her family at earlier periods, when they enjoyed greater closeness. Having to face a Thanksgiving dinner at which she will feel angry at her son or guilty about excluding her daughter-in-law and granddaughter places her in a fundamental conflict. The Thanksgiving meal is also a symbolic event, representing Rose's idea of family unity, which she cannot achieve.

The societal system influences the situation at several levels. First, there are the societal expectations regarding the mother role: Mother is nurturing, loving, and protecting. But Rose cannot be nurturing without sending messages of rejection either to her son or to her daughter-in-law and granddaughter. Second, social norms for relating to various family members after a divorce are unclear. How should Rose behave toward her son's former spouse? How should she relate to her grandchild if her son is no longer the child's custodial parent? Rose is confused about what to do. Third, the Thanksgiving celebration has social, religious, and cultural significance. This family ritual was performed in Rose's home when she was a child, and she has carried it through in her own home as an adult. Now, however, she is being forced to pass the responsibility for this gathering to her daughter before she is ready to do so and, as a result, Rose is likely to feel a special sense of loss. She will also lose the sense of family unity that she has tried to preserve.

CRITICAL THINKING QUESTIONS

1. How does this case illustrate the interconnections among the biological, psychological, and societal systems?
2. Given what you know about the assumptions of psychosocial theory, how might Rose's stage of development influence her perceptions of this situation and her approach to coping with this conflict?
3. How might you pose a research question based on the information raised in this case study? (For example, how likely is it that parents experience health problems following their child's divorce?)
4. How might Rose's social support system, especially her daughters, be involved in helping her cope with this conflict?
5. How might the current conflict impact future psychosocial development for Rose? Consider the assumptions of the text as you try to answer this question.

Meaning Making

The meaning we make of our experiences changes over the course of life. Think about the concept of love as an example. In infancy, love is almost entirely physical. It is the pervasive sense of comfort and security that we feel in the presence of our caregivers. By adolescence, the idea of love includes loyalty, emotional closeness, and sexuality. In adulthood, the concept of love may expand to include a new emphasis on companionship and open communication. The need to be loved and to give love remains important throughout life, but the self we bring to a loving relationship, the context within which the relationship is established, and the signs we look for as evidence of love change with age.

Meaning is created out of efforts to interpret and integrate the experiences of the biological, psychological, and societal systems. A primary focus of this meaning making is the search for **identity**. Humans struggle to define themselves—to achieve a sense of identity—through a sense of connectedness with certain other people and groups and through feelings of distinctiveness from others. We establish categories that define to whom we are connected, about whom we care, and which of our own qualities we admire. We also establish categories that define those to whom we are not connected, those about whom we do not care, and those qualities of our own that we reject or deny. These categories provide us with an orientation toward certain kinds of people and away from others, toward certain life choices and away from others. The psychosocial perspective brings to light the dynamic interplay of the roles of the self and the others, the I and the We, as they contribute to the emergence of identity over the life course.

The Life Span

Objective 3. To note historical changes in life expectancy and examine the implications of these changes for the study of development over the life span.

The study of human development requires an analysis of the life span and a view of the periods of life that are embedded within it. Unlike other primates, humans have a relatively long period of childhood during which we depend on adults to feed and protect us. Without some form of adult care, infants and young children younger than age six or seven cannot survive. Human evolution has resulted in a life span characterized by a prolonged period of dependency, a gradual transition to reproductive maturity, and significant length (Gibbons, 2008). In modern times, with expanded longevity, childhood takes up a relatively smaller percentage of one's life; the period of active, productive adulthood expands; and the period when people are considered very old or elderly is pushed ahead to increasingly advanced ages. Over the past 100 years, adolescence has changed from a relatively brief period of five or six years from puberty until a young person was ready to engage in the work and family roles of adulthood, to a period of ten to fifteen years, as puberty begins earlier and entry into adult roles is increasingly delayed. Thus, the lifespan itself is a fluid concept that is influenced by the biological, psychological, and societal systems.

TABLE 1.1 Average Remaining Lifetime at Various Ages, 1900–2005

AGE	2005	1989	1978	1968	1954	1939–1941	1929–1931	1900–1902
At birth	77.8	75.3	73.3	70.2	69.6	63.6	59.3	49.2
65 years	18.7	17.2	16.3	14.6	14.4	12.8	12.3	11.9
75 years	12.0	10.9	10.4	9.1	9.0	7.6	7.3	7.1
80 years	9.2	8.3	8.1	6.8	6.9	5.7	5.4	5.3

Source: U.S. Census Bureau, 1984, 1992, 1997, 2000, 2003, 2009.

Life Expectancy

How long does one expect to live? At what age is one considered to be adult? old? ancient? If the life expectancy at birth is 50, then a person who is 65 might be considered quite elderly. However, if the life expectancy at birth is 77, then a person who is 65 might be considered to be in the prime of life.

Life expectancy is a projection of the number of years one can expect to live. Think back to the case of Patrick Jonathan Carmichael, who was living alone and working on his farm until the age of 97. According to population statistics, the life expectancy for someone born in 1900 was 49.2. Among Carmichael's cohort of African-American men, the life expectancy was 32.5. If you consider African-American men who reached the age of 65 in the 1950s, the additional life expectancy was 13.5 years. Patrick Jonathan Carmichael lived to be much older than the norm for his group. The task of mapping one's future depends on how long one expects to live. Naturally, for specific individuals, we can make only rough predictions. We know that some lives may be cut short by a disaster, an accident, or an illness. On the other hand, some people are exceptionally long lived.

Table 1.1 presents data on the average life expectancy of people in the United States during eight time periods. Look at the top row of the table, labeled "at birth." The average life expectancy of people born at the beginning of the 20th century was about 49 years. Over the course of the 20th century, we observed increasingly longer life expectancies. In the year 2005, people had a life expectancy at birth 28.6 years longer than they had in 1900; a 58% increase in average life expectancy in one century!

You may be wondering how we can know about the life expectancy of people who were born in the year 2005. Not many years have passed to record deaths and life expectancy estimates for this group. The National Center for Health Statistics calculates life expectancy tables based on the number of deaths at each age for a particular year, information from the U.S. Census Bureau about the number of people who are alive at each age, and information from the Medicare program about the likelihood of dying among those aged 85 years and older (Arias, 2007). So whereas the life expectancy information about people born in 1900 is based on the actual rates of death experienced by that group over time, the life expectancy projections for people born in 2005 are based on a summary of the death rates in the year 2005 for people at each age.

The next few lines in Table 1.1 show that people who reach an advanced age (65, 75, or 80 years) in each of the time periods have a longer life expectancy than the people who were born in those time periods. For example, a person born in 1900 could expect to live until age 49; but a person who was already 65 in 1900 could expect to live an additional 12 years to age 77. These data suggest that hazards during the early and middle years of life shorten the average life expectancy at birth. Infant mortality was a major factor in limiting life expectancy at the turn of the 20th century. Furthermore, many women died in childbirth, and respiratory diseases and heart disease were serious threats to life during the middle adult years. If one survived these common killers, one's chance for a long later life increased.

Today, more and more adults are anticipating an extended period of what we refer to as "elderhood"—age 75 and beyond. Over the past 100 years, the U.S. population has changed from one shaped like a pyramid with a large number of children and adolescents, and relatively fewer adults at each advanced age, to a population that looks more like a rectangle, with a relatively smaller percentage of children and adolescents, and a relatively larger percentage of adults including a growing percentage of those in advanced old age. These changes have major implications for a wide range of social policies regarding education, employment, retirement, health care, and social security benefits.

Figure 1.4 provides a visual comparison of life expectancy at birth for four race–sex groups from 1970 to 2004. Over time, life expectancy has increased for all four groups. However, the figure illustrates a consistent gap in life expectancy for males and females as well as for African Americans and Anglos. Since 1979, the gap in life expectancy between males and females has decreased from 7.8 years to 5.2 years; the gap between African Americans and Anglos has also decreased to 5.2 years. At birth, Anglo females have the longest life expectancy (80.8 years), and African-American males have the shortest (69.5 years) (Arias, 2007).

Men die at younger ages than women in countries around the world. There are biological, societal, and behavioral explanations for women's longevity advantage, but this discrepancy is not fully understood and is still being investigated. Although more male than female infants are born, more males die at each age than females. Some researchers

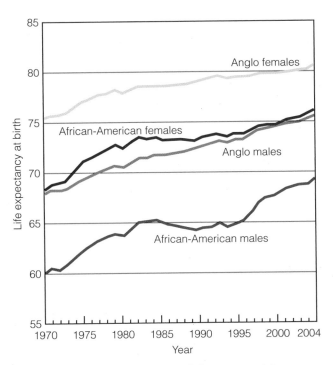

FIGURE 1.4 Life Expectancy at Birth by Race and Sex: 1970—2004

suggest that estrogen has a protective effect that helps reduce women's risk of heart disease during the childbearing years. Others suggest that because men are physically larger on average than women, their cells must reproduce more often and are at greater risk of exhausting their regenerative potential. Although women suffered higher mortality rates during childbirth at the beginning of the 20th century, the risks associated with childbirth have been substantially reduced. In contrast, men continue to be exposed to more risks associated with physical labor, military service, accidents, and injuries than women. One of the most commonly cited explanations for men's greater risk of heart disease and lung cancer is their more widespread exposure to cigarette smoking. Some researchers suggest that the change in cigarette smoking, both the increase in the number of women who smoke and the reduction in the number of men who smoke, contributes to the narrowing of the longevity advantage of women (Shrestha, 2006).

The discrepancy in longevity between the African-American and Anglo populations in the United States can be seen in higher rates of death among the African-American population from a wide range of causes including cardiovascular diseases, infections, lung disease, diabetes, and traumatic injuries associated with motor vehicle accidents, homicide, and other accidents. These health disparities can be attributed to the confounding of factors, many of which are associated with lifelong exposure to poverty and inadequate access to health care resources. Starting in infancy, more African-American babies are born with low birth weight, making them more vulnerable to infant mortality. Poverty

is associated with prenatal and infant malnutrition. African-American men are more likely to work in hazardous conditions where they may be exposed to toxins, injury, and, at the same time, where employers do not provide health insurance benefits.

One factor that has been found to be associated with improved health is marriage. Healthy adults are more likely to find partners and marry. At the same time, married couples are more likely to be embedded in an effective social network, to engage in healthy behaviors, and to live longer. Whereas 91% of Anglo women born in 1950 have married, only 75% of African-American women of this cohort have married (Bramlett & Mosher, 2002). Projections suggest that this percentage could decline further in the years ahead as a result of the disproportionate number of African-American men who die in early and middle adulthood, are incarcerated, or are unemployed (Winkelby & Cubbin, 2004). Across all economic groups, exposure to racial discrimination is itself a lifelong source of stress which can have deleterious psychological and physiological consequences (Shrestha, 2006; Arias, 2007).

Projections of Life Expectancy

Table 1.2 shows projections of life expectancy for the years 2015 and 2020 for men and women separately by race. The life expectancy of both men and women is projected to increase.

One question that has been raised is whether the increase in life expectancy can continue in the years ahead. Some researchers have suggested that the primary diseases that resulted in mortality of infants and adults have already been brought under control. They project that increases in life expectancy will be more modest over the coming 50 years, leading to an estimated life expectancy at birth of around 80 to 83 years in the United States.

The reasoning behind this view is that as the life expectancy increases, it takes greater declines in the death rate at every age to increase the life expectancy further. From this perspective, researchers argue that it is unlikely that there will be major improvements in the death rate of those under age 50 that would significantly add to their life expectancy. The conditions associated with death among older age groups are intimately linked to basic biological conditions of aging that, at present, are poorly understood. Many experts

TABLE 1.2 Projections for Life Expectancy at Birth for the Years 2015 and 2020 by Sex and Race

	2015		2020	
RACE	**MALE**	**FEMALE**	**MALE**	**FEMALE**
Anglo	77.1	81.8	77.7	82.4
African American	71.4	78.2	72.6	79.2

Source: U.S. Census Bureau, 2009, Table 100.

suggest that the best we can hope for is a healthier rather than a longer period of later life (Hayflick, 2000; Olshansky, Carnes, & Desesquelles, 2001).

On the other hand, a recent government report finds that the United States is 48th among 227 countries and territories in life expectancy at birth. The life expectancy in developed countries including Canada, Greece, Australia, Switzerland, Japan, and Singapore is already greater than the life expectancy projected for people in the United States in the year 2015. It is difficult to imagine that over the next 25 years the United States would not be able to make progress in advancing average longevity to at least catch up with the life expectancy that is already being experienced in other countries around the world (Shrestha, 2006).

A second question is whether there is an absolute limit to the human life span. Currently, the oldest woman whose date of birth could be authenticated was Jeanne Calment of France, who died at age 122 years, 164 days, and, for a man, Christian Mortensen (a Danish immigrant to the United States), who died at age 115 years, 252 days. Some scientists, many of whom are investigating the genetic bases of aging and longevity, are optimistic about substantial increases in longevity. Experiments with genetic engineering in flies, worms, and mice have been able to increase longevity in these species by 50%. Other research has found that imposing near-starvation dietary restrictions results in significant increases in longevity in mice. These studies may not have immediate relevance for humans, but they suggest paths for further investigation (Couzin, 2003; Kirkwood, 2001). Some futurists argue that there is no necessary limit to human longevity. They suggest that with each generation comes the possibility of new discoveries and new adaptations that will extend longevity (De Magalhaes, 2003).

Factors That Contribute to Longevity

Looking back over the past 50 years, improvements in longevity have been attributed to major reductions in the death rates from diseases of the heart and cerebrovascular diseases (commonly referred to as stroke). These improvements have been brought about by medical advances in diagnosis, emergency treatment, new medicines, and new patterns of care; changes in individual behavior patterns, especially smoking cessation and management of high blood pressure; and changes in social policies that provide greater access to medical resources, especially the introduction of Medicare and Medicaid.

As we look to the future, there may be continued improvement in the death rates from these diseases, but we also expect new medical advances in the prevention and treatment of diseases such as cancer and diabetes, which have not shown much change in the death rate since the 1950s. Given the extent of investment in medical research and the heightened awareness of the health risks associated with obesity, we may expect important gains in prevention and treatment in the next 50 years (Shrestha, 2006).

At present, we are the only developed country in the world that does not have national health coverage, resulting in a significant proportion of the population that does not have health insurance. Presumably, longevity in the United States would improve once a universal health insurance program is established (Cohen, 2004).

When you try to estimate your own life expectancy, you must consider projections for people in your country, region, and state, and in your age, educational, racial, and sex groups. Furthermore, research with identical twins finds that some components of longevity are genetically guided. People with long-lived ancestors are likely to be long lived themselves. Moreover, individual lifestyle factors have a great impact on longevity.

Of the many factors that have been studied, education has been consistently linked to health and longevity. Across many societies with many different models of educational opportunity, increases in years of schooling predict added years of life. The benefit of more years of education for longevity has been observed among African Americans and Anglos, men and women. These benefits are explained in part by the relationship of education and wealth. People with more schooling have higher paying jobs. In addition, people with better paying jobs may have greater control over their time and less exposure to dangerous work conditions. Finally, more schooling is associated with better decision-making skills that may influence health care, risk taking, and better self-monitoring of one's health status (Cutler & Lieras-Muney, 2006; Lieras-Muney, 2005).

In addition to education, a variety of demographic, health, and lifestyle factors are associated with longevity and a high level of functioning in later life. These factors include the following: family income; being married; the absence of hypertension, arthritis, or back pain; being a nonsmoker; having normal weight; and consuming a moderate amount of alcohol. A growing body of research emphasizes the potential benefits of a well-balanced diet combined with the strategic

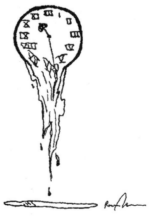

Age is relative, as is time. As the life span increases, the way we calculate our sense of maturity and aging changes. How old do you feel you are? In what way does your sense of being old depend on the situation?

use of vitamin and mineral supplements to slow the cellular damage associated with aging (Carper, 1995; Harman, Holliday, & Meydani, 1998; Rusting, 1992). Other research highlights the value of daily activity—even 20 to 30 minutes of exercise and movement—for promoting health and longevity (Brown et al., 2003). Social integration has been identified as a factor that influences health and longevity across the lifespan, from childhood through very old age (Uchino, Cacciopo, & Kiekolt-Glaser, 1996; Berkman, Glass, Brissette, & Seeman, 2000; Kolata, 2007).

Personal Assumptions about One's Life Expectancy

Many of our most important life decisions are made with either an implicit or explicit assumption about how long we expect to live. Our perception of our life expectancy has an impact on our behavior, self-concept, attitudes, and outlook on the future. For example, Colleen expects to live to be about 80 years old. She reasons that there is no rush about getting married because, even if she waits until she is 40, she will still have 40 years of married life, and that is a long time to get along with one partner. In contrast, Tyler expects to live to be about 25. Several of his older brothers' friends died of gunshot wounds, others died from drug overdoses, and some died in prison. He believes that he may as well take all the risks and have all the fun he can in life, because his time is short. He hopes to have lots of babies by many women so that some part of him will live on. Marie is celebrating her 90th birthday. She had expected to live to about age 75. Most of her friends and all her older siblings are dead. She is puzzled by the idea of having lived so long and sometimes wonders about the purpose of her long life.

As we look to the future, advances in medical technology and treatment coupled with improved support services for older adults can lead to higher standards of living and new levels of functioning in later life. On the other hand, inequities in the distribution of health care services and other societal supports may result in a growing disparity in the quality of later life for various segments of the population.

Chapter Summary

Objective 1. To introduce the basic assumptions that guide the orientation of the text.

This book presents the story of human development across the life span. The analysis is based on five assumptions: (1) Growth occurs at every period of life, from conception through very old age. (2) Individual lives show continuity and change as they progress through time. (3) We need to understand the whole person, because we function in an integrated manner. (4) Every person's behavior must be analyzed in the context of relevant settings and personal relationships. (5) People contribute actively to their development.

Objective 2. To introduce the psychosocial approach to the study of development, including the inter-relationship among the biological, psychological, and societal systems.

Psychosocial theory, which provides the organizing framework for the book, emphasizes interaction among the biological, psychological, and societal systems. As a result of maturation and change in each of these systems, individuals' beliefs about themselves and their relationships are modified. Although each life story is unique, we can identify important common patterns, allowing us to anticipate the future and to understand one another.

Objective 3. To note historical changes in life expectancy and examine the implications of these changes for the study of development over the life span.

Demographic information about the life span stimulates thought about one's own life expectancy. In the United States, the average life expectancy increased by more than 50% during the 20th century. This dramatic change affects how each of us views our own future. We need to study human development in a constantly changing context. We can never be satisfied that the information from earlier periods will hold true for future generations.

Key Terms

age-graded expectations, 8
biological system, 6
biopsychosocial, 6
continuity, 5
culture, 7
developmental change, 5
identity, 13

life expectancy, 5
life span, 5
longevity, 7
meaning-making, 6
plasticity, 5
poverty, 7

psychological system, 7
psychosocial approach, 5
self-insight, 7
social cognitive neuroscience, 9
societal system, 7
worldview, 8

Further Reflection

1. How might people's own decisions and goals influence the course of their development?
2. What are some examples in your own experience of how the biological, psychological, and societal systems interact?
3. What are your own direct experiences with poverty? How might poverty influence the biological, psychological, and societal systems and, thereby, influence the direction of development?
4. What are the critical settings in which development takes place? How do these settings change with age?
5. How does your culture influence your view of the life span? For example, what messages from your family, community, or ethnic group influence your sense of the distinctions between childhood, adolescence, adulthood, and elderhood?
6. What are your current thoughts about your life expectancy? What are you doing now to increase your chances of living a long, healthy life?
7. How would you account for the fact that more education is associated with greater longevity in many countries around the world?
8. What are some implications for social policy of the increased size of the adult and aging populations in comparison to the size of the population of young children and adolescents?

Psychology CourseMate

To access additional course materials, including CourseMate, please visit www.cengagebrain.com. At the Cengagebrain.com home page, search for the ISBN of your title (from the back cover of your book) using the search box at the top of the page. This will take you to the product page where these resources can be found.

Casebook

For additional case material related to this chapter, see the case of "Mabel," in *Life Span Development: A Case Book,* by Barbara and Philip Newman, Laura Landry-Meyer, and Brenda J. Lohman, page 215. This case of a 93-year-old woman who is adapting to the physical changes of aging provides an opportunity to examine the interaction of the biological, psychological, and societal systems as they influence development in later life. It also introduces some of the challenges of coping successfully with extreme longevity.

© 2011 Estate of Pablo Picasso/Artists Rights Society (ARS), New York/Standing Nude, c.1909–1910 (oil on canvas)/Private Collection/Photo © Christie's Images/The Bridgeman Art Library International

Cubism is like theoretical painting. It moves beyond the surface to reveal the elements of which the subject is composed. Theories provide ways of understanding behavior by introducing structures and processes that are not immediately observable.

CHAPTER 2

Major Theories for Understanding Human Development

Chapter Objectives

1. To define the concept of theory and explain how theories contribute to the study of development.

2. To review the basic concepts of seven major theories and their implications for the study of human development:

   2a. Evolutionary theory

   2b. Psychosexual theory

   2c. Cognitive developmental theories

   2d. Theories of learning

   2e. Cultural theory

   2f. Social role theory

   2g. Systems theory

IMAGINE THAT YOU are taking a road trip across the country. To plan your route and find your way, you will need a map of the United States that indicates the major highways and the location of urban centers and scenic areas. However, you will probably want to get more detailed maps of the states you will visit. Once you arrive at a city, or a state or national park, you will need tourist maps showing the historic sites, shopping areas, hotels, and walking trails so that you can enjoy each spot to its fullest.

With respect to this book, psychosocial theory is like the map of the United States: It provides a broad, conceptual umbrella for the study of human development. We provided an overview of the psychosocial approach in Chapter 1. More detail about that theory will be presented in Chapter 3. However, we need other theories to explain behavior at different levels of analysis. The theories presented in this chapter are like the maps of states, cities, and special scenic areas. They guide research and thinking in specific areas of human development. This chapter does not provide comprehensive coverage of all theories of human development, but a group of theories selected for their significant impact in guiding research and intervention. Many theories presented here continue to be evaluated and challenged as new and competing ideas about human behavior emerge.

First, we consider the role of theory in the study of human development, including a definition of theory and an analysis of what a theory of development is likely to explain. Then we present basic concepts of seven major theories of human development. The *theory of evolution* provides a broad picture of species change over long time periods. Evolutionary theory places the study of individual development in the context of the history of the species. It links humans with other animal species and suggests ways of thinking about key periods of the life span that are critical for species survival. A forerunner of psychosocial theory, *psychosexual theory* explains the relationship of mental activity to changing needs, wishes, and drives, with a particular focus on the role of sexual and aggressive needs. *Cognitive theory* describes the maturation of capacities for logical thought. *Learning theories*, *cultural theory*, *social role theory*, and *developmental systems theory* each introduce mechanisms that explain how environments guide the content and direction of growth.

In each section, a brief explanation of the theory and a few major constructs are presented, along with an analysis of the theory's contributions to the study of development and links to the psychosocial approach. In subsequent chapters, additional ideas from many of the theories will be presented as they relate to specific topics. ■

What Is a Theory?

Objective 1. To define the concept of theory and explain how theories contribute to the study of development.

A **theory** is a logical system of concepts that helps explain observations and contributes to the development of a body of knowledge. We all have our informal, intuitive theories about social life. For example, the adage "The acorn doesn't fall far from the tree" is an informal theory, which predicts that children are going to grow up to behave a lot like their parents. However, the idea of a scientific theory is quite different from an informal set of beliefs. In order for a set of ideas to reach the level of a formal scientific theory, it has to be supported by extensive evidence, including systematic experimentation and observation (Zimmerman, 2009).

A formal scientific theory is a set of interconnected statements, including assumptions, definitions, and hypotheses, which explain and interpret observations. The function of this set of interconnected statements is to describe unobservable structures, mechanisms, or processes and to relate them to one another and to observable events.

Major theories reorganize the way we think about and understand the world. Einstein's theory of relativity showed us that matter and energy are two forms of the same thing rather than totally distinct. Freud's theory of psychosexual development showed us that emotional conflicts can be expressed unconsciously through physical symptoms. Once a scientific theory is introduced, it leads the way for testing and elaboration through additional research.

A formal theory should meet certain requirements. It should be *logical* and *internally consistent*, with no contradictory statements. The hypothetical constructs should be translatable into *testable* hypotheses that can be explored through systematic research. The theory should be *parsimonious*, which means that the theory should be simple, relying on as few assumptions, constructs, and propositions as possible while still accurately accounting for the observations. Parsimony is relative. For example, Freud hypothesized that there were five stages of development; Erikson hypothesized that there were eight stages of development. Using the principle of parsimony, one might conclude that Freud's theory is a better one. However, Erikson's theory provides a more differentiated view of adulthood and aging, and, as a result, his theory offers more insight into the process of development over the life span. On the other hand, a theory that suggests 30 or 40 stages of life might be viewed as overly complex and less parsimonious than one that provides a smaller number of integrated periods. Finally, a theory should integrate previous research, and it should deal with a relatively large area of science (Miller, 2009). Most current developmental theories do not meet all of these requirements of formal, scientific theories. However, they offer a language of constructs and hypotheses that guides systematic inquiry and can compare observations in order to build a body of knowledge.

In order to understand a theory, we must answer three questions:

1. **Which phenomena is the theory trying to explain**?
   A theory of intellectual development may include hypotheses about the evolution of the brain, the growth of logical thinking, or the capacity to use symbolism. Such a theory is less likely to explain fears, motives, or friendship. Understanding the focus of the theory helps to identify its **range of applicability**. Although principles from one theory may have relevance to another area of knowledge, a theory is evaluated in terms of the behavior it was originally intended to explain.

2. **What assumptions does the theory make**?
   Assumptions are the guiding premises underlying the logic of a theory. In order to evaluate a theory, you must first understand what its assumptions are. Charles Darwin assumed that lower life forms "progress" to higher forms in the process of evolution. Freud assumed that all behavior is motivated and that the unconscious is a "storehouse" of motives and wishes. The assumptions of any theory may or may not be correct. Assumptions may be influenced by the following:

   - The cultural context that dominates the theorist's period of history
   - The sample of observations from which the theorist has drawn inferences
   - The current knowledge base of the field
   - The intellectual capacities of the theorist

3. **What does the theory predict**?
   Theories add new levels of understanding by suggesting causal relationships, unifying diverse observations, and identifying the importance of events that may have gone unnoticed. Theories of human development offer explanations regarding the origins and functions of human behavior, predictions about changes that can be expected in behavior from one period of life to the next, and hypotheses about the mechanisms or processes that account for change.

   There are many different types of theories, each with its own **range of applicability**. For example, there are personality theories, theories of learning, theories of decision making, theories of conflict resolution, theories of group dynamics, theories of leadership, theories of counseling, theories of social work practice, and theories of family formation. Just within the field of human development, there are many theories including those that account for language development, theories that focus on emotional bonds between parents and their children, and theories that address processes of change from one generation to the next.

A theory of development usually helps to explain how people change and grow over time, as well as how to account for continuity (Thomas, 1999). We expect a theory of human development to provide explanations about six questions:

1. **What is the *direction* of change over the life span**?
   We assume that there is a direction to development, that it is not random. Development is not the same as changing one's hairstyle or deciding one day to play tennis and the next to play soccer. Theories of development offer some big ideas about maturity and shed light on important ways in which thought, self-understanding, the capacity for social relationships, and the capacity for adaptation become increasingly complex and integrated through the course of life. Some theories suggest that change takes place in a sequence of stages or qualitatively distinct periods of life. Other theories suggest processes that account for gradual change or highlight

significant events that result in transitions at various points in life.

2. **What are the *mechanisms* that account for growth from conception through old age? Do these mechanisms vary across the life span?**

Theories of development identify the processes or experiences that bring about systematic change. In this chapter and throughout the text, we will present and explain a variety of mechanisms theorists offer for how growth and development occur. Some theories emphasize a biologically based, genetically guided plan for development. Others emphasize the role of the environment in shaping behavior and providing roles or settings that support new levels of functioning. Still other theories emphasize the ongoing interaction of biological and environmental factors, characterizing development as a process of adaptive self-organization.

3. **How relevant are *early experiences* for later development?**

Theories of development offer different ideas about the significance of early experiences for the psychological and behavioral organization of later periods of life. Some theories suggest that incidents from infancy and childhood play a powerful role in guiding the direction of development well into adulthood. Other theories emphasize the influence of contemporary events in guiding development by viewing the person as continuously adapting to new demands and new opportunities.

One important question that emerges in the study of development is the degree to which individuals can be characterized as **resilient** in the face of early stresses or deprivation. Current work in cognitive neuroscience suggests that there is a high degree of plasticity in the human brain. In cases of injury, one area of the brain can reorganize to take over functions of another area. Plasticity is observed across the life span, well into later life. The human brain has evolved to have a great degree of flexibility, being able to adapt to a wide range of family, cultural, language, and environmental conditions. At the same time, there is a growing literature about the risks of early exposure to harsh parenting and the long-term consequences of these early negative experiences. This research suggests that events that unfold early in life may set a person on a trajectory that intensifies certain ways of thinking and feeling and narrows the options for recovery.

4. **How do physical, cognitive, emotional, and social functions interact?**

Most theories of human development focus on a specific domain such as cognition, learning, social relationships, or the expression and management of emotions. However, they also consider the interplay of other domains. For example, according to social learning theory, feelings of tension or anxiety in the learning situation can influence a person's confidence about whether a new skill can be mastered. According to cognitive theory, emotions can contribute to the person's attention and motivation to persist in seeking the solution to a problem.

5. **How do the *environmental* and *social contexts* affect individual development?**

Individuals develop in context. Theories of human development provide ways of conceptualizing context and of highlighting which aspects of context are especially important in shaping the directions of growth. Should we focus on mother as context? Father? Both parents? Siblings? Friends? Spouse? School? Work? The physical environment of home or neighborhood? How do social constructions, including social class, race, ethnicity, and religion, become integrated into a person's life story? How and in what ways do they matter?

Research on the interaction of environment and genetic predisposition has illustrated the complexity of these questions. For example, some genes are highly responsive to environmental influences. A serotonin transporter gene, 5-HTTLPR, has a short and long allele. Earlier studies had linked the gene to vulnerability to depression. Recent studies have shown that individuals who have two short alleles are more vulnerable to depression as young adults if they grew up in a cold, emotionally distant, or harsh family environment. Individuals with this same genetic makeup are less likely than others to experience depression if they grew up in a warm, nurturing, and supportive environment (Taylor et al., 2006). This kind of research illustrates the need for theories of development to consider the interactions of biological factors and environmental conditions that may be relevant at particular periods of life.

6. **What factors are likely to place the person *at risk* at specific periods of the life span?**

Although humans have an enormous capacity for adaptation, some combination of conditions is likely to impede optimal growth. Each theory of human development provides constructs that help us understand the nature of risks as well as predictions about conditions that increase risks. Some theories also offer differentiated views of risk across the life span or at different critical life transitions. We look to theories of human development to help us understand how development might be disrupted.

In the field of human development, **theory** is differentiated from **research** and from **facts**. The research process, which is described in some detail in the appendix, may be guided by theory. However, the research process is a separate approach to building a knowledge base. For example, Piaget's cognitive developmental theory introduced the idea that through direct interaction with the physical world, infants gradually construct a scheme for the permanent object. Piaget believed that infants gradually, through the first 18 months of life, gain an understanding that objects do not cease to exist even when they are out of sight. A growing body of research was stimulated by this theory, which addresses questions of what infants appear to know or expect about objects, and at what point in development this knowledge can be observed. The research relies on direct observations and experimental manipulations in order to describe what infants understand about objects. The results of this research have led to a more differentiated view of what infants know about objects depending on the nature of the task, the kind of response the baby is required to make, and the setting where the baby is being studied. Thus, research often uncovers a more detailed analysis than is presented in the original theoretical formulation.

Facts are distinct from the theories that might try to explain or account for them. For example, in Chapter 1, we pointed out that life expectancy at birth in the United States has increased over 50% from 1900 to the present. This fact is indisputable. There may be several theories about the factors that account for changes in longevity, each of which might influence the direction of research about longevity. However, these theories do not change the facts.

The Theory of Evolution

Objective 2a. To review the basic concepts of the theory of evolution and its implications for the study of human development.

The theory of evolution explains how diverse and increasingly more complex life forms come to exist. Evolutionary theory assumes that the natural laws that apply to plant and animal life also apply to humans. The **law of natural selection** explains how, over generations, species gradually change to respond to changing environmental conditions (Darwin, 1859/1979). Natural selection operates at the level of genes that are passed, via an organism's reproductive process, from one generation to the next. Reproductive success, sometimes called **fitness**, varies among members of a species (Archer, 1991).

Every species produces more offspring than can survive to reproduce, because of limitations of the food supply and natural dangers. Darwin observed that there was quite a bit of variability among members of the same species in any given location. Some individuals were better suited than others to their immediate environment and, thus, were more likely to survive, mate, and produce offspring. These offspring were also more likely to have characteristics appropriate for that location. Over time, those members of the species that had the selective advantage would be more likely to survive and reproduce,

thus passing their genetic characteristics on to future generations. This process is called **adaptation**. If the environment changed (e.g., in climate), only certain variations of organisms would survive, and again some species would evolve. Failure to adapt would lead to species **extinction**. Thus, in the context of changing environmental conditions, the variability within a species ensures the species' continuation or its development into new forms. Darwin viewed evolutionary change as taking place slowly and incrementally as individual organisms adapt and populations with similar adaptive characteristics come to dominate an environment or **ecological niche**.

Darwin described two aspects of evolution (Mayr, 1991). One is the gradual change within a species over time from earlier to later forms. For example, even though they are the same species, chimpanzees alive today are not identical to the chimpanzees that lived thousands of years ago. They have had to adapt to changing environmental conditions, including alterations in food sources, landscapes, and threats. The second form of evolution is the breaking away from an earlier evolutionary lineage and the establishment of a new branch in the phylogenetic tree. This is the process of **speciation** that contributes to biological diversity. For example, some combination of events led to the separation of the hominids from homo erectus to homo sapiens about 250,000 years ago (Enard et al., 2002). For an exciting presentation on human evolution, go to the website of the American Museum of Natural History in New York City and go to the section on the Hall of Human Origins. Click on the History of Human Evolution.

The concept of **inclusive fitness** was later added to the theory of natural selection (Hamilton, 1964). This idea suggests that fitness is not only determined by an individual's success in passing genes along to the next generation through reproduction. A characteristic can be selected if the genes are passed along to the next generation by promoting the survival and reproductive success of others who carry those genes. In human groups, behaviors that support one's family members or that make it possible for one's kin to be more attractive in the mating process would be considered examples of inclusive fitness. This concept highlights the adaptive advantage of supportive kin networks that selectively direct their resources toward members of their family, kinship network, tribe, or ethnic group.

Advances in the field of genetics coupled with advances in neuroscience have begun to shed new light on the evolutionary process (Begley, 2007). By analyzing the human genome, one can better compare humans to primates and other mammals, leading to a clearer understanding of the likely points at which the brains of various species diverged. For example, in an analysis of the Y chromosome in a variety of populations, Peter Underhill and colleagues (Underhill et al., 2000) have estimated that all humans alive today are descendants of a small group of about 4,000 men and women who left Africa less than 100,000 years ago and settled throughout the rest of the world. These humans carried the FOXP2 gene

From an evolutionary perspective, the attachment behavioral system is central to the offspring's survival. Adults have strategies for monitoring and protecting their young, and infants have capacities for alerting their caregivers when they are frightened or upset. What behaviors in human infant-mother pairs help them stay connected in times of distress?

that supports advanced language capacity and other symbolic and representational arts.

Ethology. Two subspecialties that have emerged from evolutionary theory are *ethology* and *evolutionary psychology.* **Ethology** is the study of the functional significance of expressive behavior in its social context from an evolutionary perspective (LaFreniere, 2000). This means that ethologists focus on describing the unique adaptive behaviors of specific species, such as mating, caregiving, play, or strategies for obtaining resources. They are especially interested in behaviors that appear to be spontaneous and that provide some type of adaptive advantage. An example is the infant's smile. Smiles occur early in the postnatal period. They function as a powerful signal that evokes a caregiving response. Over time, the infant's smile takes on a more complex meaning within the social context. Yet it begins as an unlearned behavior that has important survival value. Through comparisons among species, the study of the conditions that evoke and maintain adaptive behaviors helps to clarify the role of behavior in the long-term survival of the species (Charlesworth, 1992).

Evolutionary Psychology. **Evolutionary psychology** is the study of the evolutionary origins of mental structures, emotions, and social behavior. Whereas ethology focuses

on analyzing adaptive behavior patterns across species, evolutionary psychology draws on principles of evolution to understand the human mind. "The mind is a set of information processing machines that were designed by natural selection to solve adaptive problems faced by our hunter-gatherer ancestors" (Cosmides & Tooby, 1997). This focus takes us to a time when humans lived in small, nomadic groups, traveling from place to place to find sources of food and trying to protect themselves from the dangers of predatory animals, weather, illness, and other humans. This way of life existed for more than 2 million years, during which time various human species (along with their human minds) emerged. From this perspective, the mind is highly adapted to solve the problems faced by these human ancestors, but it may not be well adapted to solve the new problems that have emerged in our recent industrial and postindustrial way of life.

From an evolutionary perspective, any behavior can be assessed by asking a few basic questions: What behavior is necessary to achieve a goal? How much energy is needed to achieve the goal? When should the organism stop the activity? What should the organism do next? These questions suggest that the organism has to recognize the nature of a problem and bring to bear the best "tool" needed to solve the problem (Neese, 2001). There are start-up costs to beginning any new behavior, so the most adaptive responses will contribute to long-term fitness. Once a behavior has been started, the organism has to assess how hard and how long to persist at the task. There is risk in putting too much energy into one problem and ignoring other important tasks.

The work of David Buss on mating strategies provides an example of the approach that evolutionary psychology takes to understanding human behavior. According to evolutionary theory, one of the key components of fitness is the mating process.

> Successful mating requires solutions of a number of difficult adaptive problems. These include selecting a fertile mate, out-competing same-sex rivals in attracting a mate, fending off mate poachers (those who try to lure one's mate away), preventing the mate from leaving, and engaging in all of the necessarily sexual and social behaviors required for successful conception to take place. (Buss, 2006, p. 239)

Based on this analysis, Buss argued that the mate preferences of one sex will influence the basis upon which members of the opposite sex will compete to attract a mate. These two factors co-evolve. In other words, the qualities that are viewed as desirable by one sex influence the ways that the opposite sex competes. As a result, in subsequent generations the qualities that are most highly desired by one sex will be more likely to be present in the opposite sex. In cross-national research, Buss found that women in many different cultures valued men who were likely to be successful breadwinners and who exhibited such qualities as ambition, industriousness, and high social status. These qualities are hypothesized to support the woman's concern that her long-term partner will invest in her and her offspring. In contrast, men consistently valued physical appearance more than women did, especially physical features that convey health and a likelihood of reproductive success. Thus men view women as desirable partners who are youthful, have clear smooth skin, shiny hair, full lips, and a nicely rounded symmetrical body—features that convey the promise of fertility (Buss, 2006). Thus, according to the theory, in an effort to compete for the affections of women men would emphasize their high status, industriousness, and financial success. In order to compete for men, women would emphasize their physical attractiveness.

Implications for Human Development

Darwin's theory of evolution by means of natural selection provided the foundational theoretical framework for much of American psychology through its influences on William James, G. Stanley Hall, John Dewey, and their students. An underlying premise of natural selection is that new or emerging capacities are retained as a result of their adaptive value. This perspective was elaborated by William James in defense of consciousness itself. James argued that consciousness evolved and has been preserved among humans because it contributes positively to the chances of survival. By being able to set a goal, plan a course of action, assess progress toward that goal, and modify actions as needed, consciousness and its corollary, free will, increase the ability of human beings to adapt effectively to whatever environments or environmental changes they encounter (James, 1890; Dewey, 1896; Green, 2009).

With its focus on reproductive success, evolutionary theory highlights three phases of the life span: (1) healthy growth and development leading up to the reproductive period; (2) success in mating and the conception of offspring; and (3) the ability to parent offspring so they can survive, reach reproductive age, and bear offspring of their own (Charlesworth, 1992).

Humans are most vulnerable during infancy and childhood. Children require nurture and care in order to survive to reproductive age. Biological capacities and the environments in which they can be expressed operate together to produce behavior. A genetic plan, shaped through hundreds of generations, guides infants' predispositions, capacities, and sensitivities. Evolutionary theory points out that infants come into the world with a range of innate capacities and potentials. They are able to establish social contact, organize information, and recognize and communicate their needs.

The genetic potential of human infants is much greater than the behaviors actually exhibited in any particular cultural context. Infants have to be able to respond to the specific language environment, diet, parenting behaviors, and other physical and social contexts in which they are born. Particular environments are likely to take advantage of

certain genetic predispositions and not others. Infants must adapt to a variety of environmental conditions including differences in the quality of parenting, adequacy of resources, and competition for resources with other siblings. Childhood experiences shape the future of the human species by providing the context for the establishment of attachments, meaningful social competence, and problem-solving capacities. These in turn have a bearing on an individual's behavior in adulthood—particularly the ability to form intimate relationships and to parent one's offspring. In adolescence and adulthood, the evolutionary focus shifts to emerging reproductive capacities—the ability to find a mate, to reproduce, and to rear one's young so that they can reach their own reproductive age. With advanced age, the forces of selection weaken. Because early humans died at a relatively young age due to predators, diseases, and environmental hazards, the selective advantage of characteristics that might be noticeable in later life was not preserved. As a result, the genome does not guide the direction of development to preserve high levels of functioning in later life as it so clearly does in infancy, childhood, and the transition through puberty to reproductive adulthood (Baltes, 1997). More rests on culture, lifestyle, and social resources to support successful aging.

The evolutionary perspective draws attention to the interconnection between an individual's life history and the long-range history of the species. Principles of natural selection operate slowly over generations. However, the reproductive success of individuals over the course of their own life span determines whether their genetic material continues to be represented in the larger population. The evolutionary perspective directs attention to the importance of variability for a species' survival. Although theories of development typically focus on general patterns of continuity and change across individuals, evolutionary theory prompts one to attend to the importance of individual differences in the study of development. These differences help explain how the human species adapts successfully across a wide variety of environmental conditions.

Links to the Psychosocial Approach

The psychosocial approach translates the idea of species adaptation to the individual level. Individuals encounter a necessary developmental struggle between their own traits and capacities and the requirements and demands of the environment. Each generation within a society faces similar challenges to cycle critical resources to the young, to form enduring social bonds that will result in a reproductive environment, to nurture competence and a capacity for caring in the new generation of adults, and to inspire younger generations with hope and anticipation about the prospects of growing old. Within cultural groups, rites and rituals serve to protect and preserve resources, direct the rearing of children, and assist individuals through key transitions. Groups that adapt successfully are those that effectively cycle resources,

TABLE 2.1 Basic Concepts of Evolutionary Theory

Natural selection
Fitness
Inclusive fitness
Adaptation
Extinction
Ecological niche
Speciation
Ethology
Evolutionary psychology

help new members, and pass along information that will help individuals cope with future challenges. For a list of the key concepts of evolutionary theory, see Table 2.1.

Psychosexual Theory

Objective 2b. To review the basic concepts of psychosexual theory and their implications for the study of human development.

Evolutionary theory calls attention to the importance of the reproductive functions as they contribute to fitness and long-term species adaptation. In contrast, psychosexual theory focuses on the impact of sexual and aggressive drives on the individual's psychological functioning. It distinguishes between the impact of drives on mental activity and their effect on reproductive functions. The theory assumes that very young children have strong sexual and aggressive drives that find unique modes of expression through successive developmental stages. Throughout childhood, adolescence, and adult life, sexual and aggressive drives operate to direct aspects of one's fantasies, self-concept, problem-solving strategies, and social interactions.

A unique feature of psychosexual theory is the importance placed on childhood experiences for shaping adult thoughts and behavior. The theory focuses on both normative and pathological patterns of growth and development that result from the socialization pressures that act on biologically based drives. The theory highlights the relevance of certain primary social relationships, especially the mother-child and father-child dyads, for their role in determining the expression and gratification of needs and the internalization of moral standards. Many contributions of psychosexual theory continue to influence the study of development and approaches to therapeutic interventions.

Seven ideas from psychosexual theory are reviewed in the chapter: (1) motivation and behavior, (2) domains of consciousness, (3) the structure of personality, (4) stages of development, (5) defense mechanisms, (6) object

relations theory, and (7) ego psychology. All are contemporary elaborations of psychosexual theory.

Motivation and Behavior

Freud assumed that all behavior (except that resulting from fatigue) is motivated. He thought that all behavior has meaning; it does not occur randomly or without purpose. Many of the concepts of psychosexual theory attempt to describe the processes by which sexual and aggressive drives motivate behavior. A related assumption of psychosexual theory is that there is an area of the mind called the **unconscious** that is a storehouse of powerful, primitive motives of which the person is unaware. Unconscious as well as conscious motives may motivate behavior simultaneously. Thus, behaviors that may appear to be somewhat unusual or extremely intense are described as **multiply determined**—that is, a single behavior expresses many motives, some of which the person can recognize and control and others that are guided by unconscious thought.

Freud's analysis of normal development as well as his explanations for specific forms of mental illness are derived from his understanding of the ways that sexual and aggressive drives press for expression and are inhibited or given various outlets in thoughts, dreams, behaviors, and symptoms. The term *drive* is sometimes referred to as psychic energy, tension, instincts, or *libido*. **Drives** can be thought of as sexual and aggressive forces that have a biological or somatic origin—they are a result of some metabolic function, but are also intimately linked to psychological processes. Freud envisioned a model in which the energy behind the drives builds up as it seeks satisfaction. The psychic energy that is embodied in these drives can be expressed in a variety of ways, but the energy itself will not be destroyed. Drives have a power or force. A person can experience a drive along a continuum from mild to strong. Drives have an aim—a desire to be satisfied that may be handled immediately, delayed, or possibly redirected so that it is only partly satisfied. When possible, drives are satisfied immediately to reduce tension and achieve a state of equilibrium. Drives have an object—a person or thing that allows the drive to achieve its aim. The object of the drive is closely linked to the specific environment in which the child functions. Thus, in order to understand how drives are satisfied one must have a concrete understanding of the social and physical resources that are available to a child at a specific developmental period (Ritvo & Solnit, 1995). Over time, a person becomes able to delay the satisfaction of the drives and finds increasingly flexible and socially appropriate ways to achieve satisfaction.

Domains of Consciousness

One of the most enduring contributions of psychosexual theory is the analysis of the topography of mental activity (see Figure 2.1). Freud thought the human mind was like an iceberg. **Conscious processes** are the tip that protrudes out of the water; they make up only a small part of the mind. Our conscious thoughts are fleeting. We can have only a few of them at any one time. As soon as energy is diverted from a thought or image, it disappears from consciousness.

© Bjanka Kadic/Alamy

Freud's patients visited him in his office in Vienna, surrounded by cultural artifacts that were sources of stimulation to his own thinking. Central to the office was the famous couch. Freud invented the technique of free association as a way to gain insight into the unconscious.

The **preconscious** is analogous to the part of the iceberg near the waterline. Material in the preconscious can be made conscious if attention is directed to it. Preconscious thoughts are readily accessible to consciousness through focused attention. You may not be thinking about your hometown or favorite desserts right now, but if someone were to ask you about either of them you could readily recall and discuss them.

The **unconscious**, like the rest of the iceberg, is hidden from view. It is a vast network of content and processes that are actively barred from consciousness. Freud hypothesized that the content of the unconscious, including wishes, fears, impulses, and repressed memories, plays a major role in guiding behavior even though we cannot explain the connections consciously. Freud included in his use of the term *unconscious* unintentional behaviors, such as slips of the tongue or mistakes, the source or cause of which the person is unaware (Bargh & Morsella, 2008). Behaviors that are unusual or extremely intense may not make sense if they are explained only in terms of conscious motives. However, through certain techniques used in psychotherapy, the link between unconscious wishes and fears and overt behaviors often can be established.

Here is an example of the complexity of the process. A patient of Freud's who had recently been married sometimes forgot his wife's name. Freud hypothesized that consciously the man felt he loved his wife and thought they were happy together. Freud thought that forgetting the wife's name provided a clue to the content of the man's unconscious. In his unconscious, the man had strong, negative feelings about his wife, feelings that were so unacceptable that they could not be allowed expression. By forgetting his wife's name, Freud reasoned that the young man could express some level of hostility toward her and, at the same time, punish himself for his unconscious anger toward her.

Three Structures of Personality

Freud (1933/1964) described three components of personality: the id, the ego, and the superego. In his writings about these structures, Freud suggested a developmental progression in which id exists alone at birth, ego emerges during infancy, and the superego takes shape in early childhood. In adulthood, the three structures must find an effective pattern of interaction in order to support adaptation.

Id. The **id** is the source of instincts and impulses. It is the primary source of psychic energy, and it exists from birth. Freud believed that newborn infants' mental processes were comprised completely of id impulses, and that the ego and superego emerged later, drawing their energy from the id.

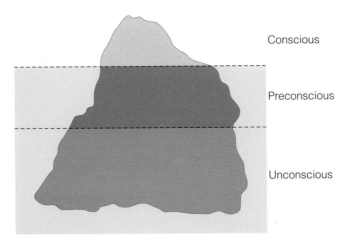

Conscious

Preconscious

Unconscious

FIGURE 2.1 Topography of Mental Activity: Domains of Consciousness

© 2011 Estate of Pablo Picasso/Artists Rights Society (ARS), New York

In each of us, the id is the source of instincts and impulses. At age 22, Picasso drew this devilish caricature of himself, suggesting his impulsive, primate nature.

The id expresses its demands according to the **pleasure principle**: People are motivated to seek pleasure and avoid pain. The pleasure principle does not take into account the feelings of others, society's norms, or agreements between people. Its rule is to achieve the immediate satisfaction of impulses and discharge of energy. When you lie to a friend to protect your image, or when you cut ahead of people in line so you won't have to wait, you are operating according to the pleasure principle.

The logic of the id is also the logic of dreams. This kind of thinking is called **primary process thought**. It is characterized by a lack of concern for the constraints of reality. In primary process thought, there are no negatives. Everything is yes. There is no time. Nothing happens in the past or in the future. Everything is now. Symbolism becomes flexible. One object may symbolize many things, and many different objects may mean the same thing. Many male faces can all represent the father. The image of a house may be a symbol for one's mother, a lover, or the female genitalia as well as for a house.

Ego. Ego is a term that has two related meanings. One is the idea of ego as a person's self, including one's physical self, self-concept, self-esteem, and mental representations of the self in relation to others. This sense of ego emerges as psychic energy is directed toward the self—a process that is sometimes called primary narcissism. The idea is that the sense of self is born out of self-love, an enthusiasm and excitement for one's body, one's experiences, and one's emerging sense of agency. The second idea of ego refers to all mental functions that have to

do with the person's relation to the environment. It includes a multitude of cognitive processes such as perception, learning, memory, judgment, self-awareness, and language skills that allow a person to take in information, process it, assess its implications, and select a course of action. Freud thought the ego begins to develop in the first six or eight months of life and is well established by the age of 2 or 3. Other scholars view the ego processes as present from birth (Moore, 1995). Of course, much change and growth occur over time as the ego responds to demands from the environment and finds strategies that support effective functioning. The ego also responds to the demands of the id and the superego and helps the person satisfy needs, live up to ideals and standards, and establish a healthy emotional balance.

The ego operates according to the **reality principle**. Under this principle, the ego protects the person by waiting to gratify id impulses until a socially acceptable form of expression or gratification can be found. In the ego, primary process thought becomes subordinated to a more reality-oriented process, called **secondary process thought**. This process begins to dominate as the ego matures.

Secondary process thought is the kind of logical, sequential thinking that we usually mean when we discuss thinking. It allows people to plan and act in order to engage the world and to achieve gratification in personally and socially acceptable ways. It enables people to delay gratification. It helps people assess plans by examining whether they will really work. This last process is called **reality testing**.

Superego. The **superego** includes both a punishing and a rewarding function. The conscience, which includes ideas about which behaviors and thoughts are improper, unacceptable, and wrong, carries out the punishing function. The ego ideal, which includes ideas about what behaviors and thoughts are admirable, acceptable, and worthy of praise, carries out the rewarding function. Freud's work led him to conclude that the superego does not begin to develop until the age of 5 or 6 and probably is not firmly established until several years later. Other theorists have suggested that the roots of the superego emerge in infancy as the child becomes differentiated from the caregiver and aware of the possibility of disrupting the close bond with this loving object (Klein, 1948). Because it is formed during early childhood, the superego tends to be harsh and unrealistic in its demands. It is often just as illogical and unrelenting in its search for proper behavior as the id is in its search for pleasure. When a child thinks about behaving in a morally unacceptable way, the superego sends a warning by producing feelings of anxiety and guilt.

The superego is developed through a process called **identification**. Motivated by love, fear, and admiration, children actively imitate their parents' characteristics and internalize their values. Through identification, parents' values become the ideals and aspirations of their children. In this way, the moral standards of a society are transmitted from one generation to the next.

The Relationship of Id, Ego, and Superego. Ego processes work toward satisfying id impulses through thoughts and actions without generating strong feelings of guilt in the superego. In one sense, the ego processes serve both the id and the superego, striving to provide gratification, but in morally and socially acceptable ways. In another sense, ego is the executive of personality. The strength of the ego determines the person's effectiveness in meeting needs, handling the demands of the superego, and dealing with the demands of reality. If the ego is strong and can establish a good balance among id, superego, and environmental demands, the person is satisfied and free from immobilizing guilt and feelings of worthlessness.

When id and superego are stronger than ego, the person may be tossed and turned psychologically by strong desires for pleasure and strong constraints against attaining those desires. When environmental demands are strong and the ego is weak, for example when an adolescent is confronted by strong pressures for peer conformity and the threat of peer rejection, a person may also be overwhelmed. According to psychosexual theory, it is the breakdown of the ego that leads to mental disorder.

Stages of Development

Freud assumed that the most significant developments in personality take place during five life stages from infancy through adolescence with the primary emphasis given to the first five or six years of life. After that time, according to Freud, the essential pattern for expressing and controlling impulses has been established. Later life serves only to uncover new modes of gratification and new sources of frustration.

The stages Freud described reflect his emphasis on sexuality as a driving force. Freud used the term **sexuality** quite broadly, referring to the full range of physical pleasure, from sucking to sexual intercourse. He also attached a positive, life-force symbolism to the concept of sexuality, suggesting that sexual impulses provide a thrust toward growth and renewal. At each stage, a particular body zone is of heightened sexual importance. The shift in focus from one body zone to the next is due largely to the biologically based unfolding of physical maturation. The five stages Freud identified are the oral, anal, phallic, latent, and genital stages.

During the **oral stage**, in the first year of life, the mouth is the site of sexual and aggressive gratification. Babies use their mouths to explore the environment, to express tension, and to experience pleasure. Freud characterized infants as passive and dependent. They take things in, absorbing experience just as they swallow milk. As infants learn to delay gratification, the ego becomes more clearly differentiated and they become aware of the distinction between the self and others. With this awareness comes the realization that all wishes cannot be satisfied.

In the **anal stage**, during the second year of life, the anus is the most sexualized body part. With the development of the sphincter muscles, a child learns to expel or withhold feces at will. The conflict at this stage focuses on the subordination of the child's will to the demands of the culture (via parents) for appropriate toilet habits.

The **phallic stage** begins during the third year of life and may last until the child is 6. It is a period of heightened genital sensitivity in the absence of the hormonal changes that accompany puberty. Freud described the behavior of children at this stage as bisexual. They direct sexualized activity toward both sexes and engage in self-stimulation. This is the stage during which the Oedipal or Electra complex is observed.

The **Oedipal complex** in boys and the **Electra complex** in girls result from ambivalence surrounding heightened sexuality. According to psychosexual theory, the child has a strong, sexualized attraction to the parent of the opposite sex, and the same-sex parent becomes a fantasized rival. The child may desire to have the exclusive attention of one parent and may fantasize that the other parent will leave, or perhaps die. At the same time, the child fears that amorous overtures toward the desired parent may result in hostility or retribution from the parent of the same sex. The child also worries that this beloved, same-sex parent will withdraw love. Parental threats intended to prevent the child from masturbating, and fantasies of the possibility of castration or bodily mutilation, may add to the child's fears that sexualized fantasies are going to result in punishment or withdrawal of love.

An important component of the Oedipal or Electra complex dynamic is the view of the young child as engaged in complex, conflicting wishes that involve the mother-father-child triad. Many competing impulses come into play: the conflict between wanting to satisfy sexual drives and the awareness that self-stimulation is not socially acceptable; the conflict between wanting to remain a child who is loved and cared for by both parents and the desire to assume a more mature role in the eyes of the opposite-sex parent; the anger and rivalry experienced toward the same-sex parent and the desire to preserve that parent's love and admiration; and the pressures to embrace one's own gender identity and the envy one feels toward the opposite sex. In a successful resolution of the Oedipal or Electra conflict, the superego emerges as a strong structure that aids the ego in controlling unacceptable impulses. Through a process of identification with one's parents' moral and ethical values, the child achieves a new level of autonomy, and at the same time receives the admiration and approval of both parents who see the child as moving in the direction of maturity and self-control. Most of the intense and painful conflicts of this period are repressed, and the ego emerges with a new degree of self-esteem and confidence about the child's place in the family structure (Tyson & Tyson, 1995).

Once the Oedipal or Electra conflict is resolved, the child enters a period of **latency**. During this stage, which lasts from about 7 years until puberty, no new significant conflicts or impulses arise. The primary personality development during this period is the maturation of the ego.

A final stage of development begins with the onset of puberty: the **genital stage**. During this period, the person finds ways of satisfying sexual impulses in mature, dyadic relationships. Adolescence brings about a reawakening of Oedipal or Electra conflicts and a reworking of earlier childhood identifications. Freud explained the tension of adolescence as the result of the sexual threat that the mature adolescent poses to the family unit. In an effort to avoid this threat, adolescents may withdraw from their families or temporarily devalue their parents. With the selection of a permanent sex partner, the threat of intimacy between young people and their parents diminishes. At the end of adolescence, a more autonomous relationship with one's parents becomes possible.

Freud believed that the psychological conflicts that arise during adolescence and adulthood result from a failure to satisfy or express specific childhood wishes. At any of the childhood stages, sexualized impulses may have been so frustrated or overindulged that the person continues to seek their gratification at later stages of life. Freud used the term **fixation** to refer to continued use of pleasure-seeking or anxiety-reducing behaviors appropriate to an earlier stage of development. Because no person can possibly satisfy all wishes at every life stage, normal development depends on the ability to channel the energy from those impulses into activities that either symbolize the impulses or express them in a socially acceptable form. This process is called **sublimation**. During adolescence and early adulthood, patterns of impulse expression, fixation, and sublimation crystallize into a life orientation. From this point on, the content of the id, the regulating functions of the superego, and the executive functions of the ego rework the struggles of childhood through repeated episodes of engagement, conflict, and impulse gratification or frustration.

Defense Mechanisms

Much of the ego's work involves mediating the conflicts between the id's demands for gratification and the superego's demands for good behavior. This work is conducted outside the person's awareness. When unconscious conflicts threaten to break through into consciousness, the person experiences anxiety. If the ego functions effectively, it pushes these conflicts into the unconscious, thereby protecting the person from unpleasant emotions. The ego satisfies desires in acceptable ways by directing behavior and social interaction.

Strong, unresolvable conflicts may leave a person in a state of constant anxiety and symptoms may emerge. A person who feels a desire that is thought to be very "bad," such as an unconscious wish to harm a parent or to be sexually intimate with a sibling, may experience anxiety without recognizing its source. The unexpressed drive continues to seek gratification. The unpleasant emotional state may preoccupy the person and make it difficult to handle the normal demands of day-to-day life. **Defense mechanisms** protect the person from anxiety so that effective functioning can be preserved. They distort, substitute, or completely block out the source of the conflict. They are usually initiated unconsciously. Often the defense mechanism used depends on a person's age and the intensity of the perceived threat. Younger children tend to use denial and repression (pushing

thoughts from awareness). A more diverse set of defenses, requiring greater cognitive complexity, becomes available in the course of development. In situations of greatest threat, denial is often the initial defense used, regardless of age.

According to Freud, the basic defense mechanism is **repression**, a process whereby unacceptable impulses are pushed into the unconscious. It is as if a wall were constructed between the unconscious and the conscious mind so that anxiety-provoking thoughts and feelings cannot enter consciousness. With unacceptable thoughts and impulses far from awareness, the person is protected from uncomfortable feelings of anxiety and may devote the remaining psychic energy to interchange with the interpersonal and physical environments. This defensive strategy has two major costs. First, it takes energy to continue to protect the conscious mind from these thoughts, thereby reducing the amount of mental energy available to cope with other daily demands. Second, if too many thoughts and feelings are relegated to repression, the person loses the use of the emotional system as a means of monitoring and evaluating reality.

The following are defense mechanisms:

Repression: Unacceptable wishes are barred from conscious thought.

Projection: Unacceptable wishes are attributed to someone else.

Reaction formation: Unacceptable feelings are expressed by the opposite feelings.

Regression: One avoids confronting conflicts and stresses by reverting to behaviors that were effective and comforting at an earlier life stage.

Displacement: Unacceptable impulses are expressed toward a substitute target.

Rationalization: Unacceptable feelings and actions are justified by logical or pseudo-logical explanations.

Isolation: Feelings are separated from thoughts.

Denial: Parts of external reality are denied.

Sublimation: Unacceptable wishes are channeled to socially acceptable behaviors.

All people resort to defense mechanisms at various times in their lives. These mechanisms not only reduce anxiety but may lead to positive social outcomes. Physicians who use isolation may be able to function effectively because they are able to apply their knowledge without being hindered by their feelings. Children who rationalize defeat may be able to protect their self-esteem by viewing themselves favorably. The child who projects angry feelings onto someone else may find that this technique stimulates a competitive orientation that enhances performance.

Regression is an especially important defense when considered from a developmental perspective. Many theorists suggest that development is a "spiraling" process in which forward movement and increased integration of complex functions may alternate with temporary backsliding or return to a more comfortable, less demanding position. In psychosexual theory, regression may occur when a person (child or adult) reverts to an earlier form of drive satisfaction, immature forms of relationships with others, lower moral standards, or more simplistic ways of thinking and solving problems. Anna Freud (1965) and Peter Blos (1967) both wrote about the idea that regression can serve ego development if it is not met with extreme disapproval. Sometimes it is necessary to return to an earlier mode of functioning in order to resolve conflicts that were inadequately resolved at that time, or to engage in a kind of playful childishness in order to achieve a new level of mastery. Most obviously, in the creative process, a certain amount of regressive fantasy can unlock possible associations that make sense according to primary process thinking but are censored in secondary process thinking (Tyson & Tyson, 1995).

Object Relations Theory

Object relations theory is a modern adaptation of psychoanalytic theory that places less emphasis on the drives of aggression and sexuality as motivational forces and more emphasis on human relationships as the primary motivational force in life (Kernberg, 2005). Freud originally used the term *object* to mean a person or thing that allows the drive to achieve its aim. Drives are of two types: libidinal and aggressive. Accordingly, objects became a key component of Freud's drive/structural model of the human psyche. In contrast to Freud's views, however, many theorists have moved toward a relational/structural model of the psyche in which an object is the target of relational needs in human development. Although there are many different object relations theorists, most agree that humans have an innate drive to form and maintain relationships, and that this is the fundamental human need that forms a context against which other drives, such as libidinal and aggressive, gain meaning.

The **object relations paradigm** emerged and has been consolidated within psychoanalytic thought over the past 70 years (Borden, 2000). Theorists such as W. R. D. Fairbairn, Melanie Klein, Harry Stack Sullivan, Donald Winnicut, and Heinz Kohut are forerunners in this perspective. They stress that humans have basic needs for connection, contact, and meaningful interpersonal relationships throughout life. According to this view, infants have a very limited sense of self. The self is formed in relationship with the primary objects, especially the mother. Margaret Mahler (Mahler & Furer, 1968; Mahler, Pine, & Bergman, 1975) described the self as taking shape in three stages over the first two years of life. At first, the infant simply enjoys the isolated events of the caregiving relationship. In this context, drives are satisfied and a sense of frustration is followed by a sense of satisfaction when needs are met. In the second phase, infants enjoy engaging in more rhythmic interactions with the mother, initiating interactions that are not necessarily focused around meeting basic needs. In the final stage, a process of separation and individuation occurs that continues throughout infancy and into adolescence and adult life.

In this phase, a tension arises between wanting to explore the environment beyond the mother, and wanting to be reassured of the mother's continuous presence. During this time, there is an assumption that infants have a hard time integrating the positive and negative interactions they have with their mother, leading to splitting between the good and the bad mother.

By about 24 months, the child is able to integrate the frustrating, angry, and loving memories of interactions with mother into a stable representation of self and other. The child achieves a greater tolerance for strains in the relationship with the mother, knowing that the basic bond is pleasurable and positive. Over time, the representation of the integrated, loving, caring mother is internalized through identification, so that the child can use this representation for self-comfort. At the same time, the internalization of the loving mother contributes positively to the child's sense of self-esteem. "I am someone who is safe, loved, and valued." The child experiences the stability of not only giving and receiving love in the interpersonal domain, but integrates a sense of being loveable into a component of the constant self. The process is viewed as ongoing because this representation may be altered through subsequent life events, and the internalized representation of the mother is never a complete substitute for the real mother's love (Tyson & Tyson, 1995).

The path toward maturity requires that the person achieve a sense of vitality, stability, and inner cohesiveness that is formulated through interpersonal transactions. In the relational perspective, psychopathology or dysfunction arises when a person internalizes rigid, rejecting, or neglectful relational experiences and then uses these internalizations to anticipate or respond to real-life social encounters. Because the internalized relational pattern is familiar and well learned, the person is reluctant to give it up even if it leads to feelings of isolation, anxiety, or self-loathing (Messer & Warren, 1995).

Ego Psychology

In his structural theory, Freud introduced the concept of ego and its executive functions in managing the expression of impulses, negotiating between the id and the superego, striving to attain goals embedded in the ego ideal, and assessing reality. Anna Freud took these ideas further in *The Ego and the Mechanisms of Defense* (1936/1946), outlining new ego capacities that emerge from infancy through adolescence. She highlighted the various threats that the id poses to the ego at each stage of development, and provided a classification of the defense mechanisms the ego uses to protect itself from unruly and unacceptable impulses.

Anna Freud gave special attention to the period of adolescence as a time of increased sexual and aggressive energy that is linked to the biological changes of puberty. At this time, children are likely to be overwhelmed by libidinal energy and the ego is more or less fighting for its life. Anger and aggression become more intense, sometimes to the point of getting out of hand. Appetites become enormous. Oral and anal interests come to the surface again expressed as pleasure in dirt and disorder, exhibitionistic tendencies, brutality, cruelty to animals, and enjoyment of various forms of vulgarity. In her clinical cases, Anna Freud observed that previously successful defense mechanisms threatened to fall to pieces as intense sexual impulses emerged. During this period, the ego may employ very rigid defenses in order to deny the instinctual drives. Adolescents may vacillate in their behavior from loving to mean, compliant to rebellious, or self-centered to altruistic, as the ego tries to assert itself in the midst of conflicting and newly energized libidinal forces.

Peter Blos expanded the concept of ego and the mechanisms of defense by identifying the coping mechanisms that emerge in adolescence as young people find ways of adapting psychologically to the physical transitions of puberty. By the end of adolescence, those ego conflicts present at the beginning of puberty are transformed into more manageable aspects of identity construction and expression. Blos noted five major accomplishments of ego development for young people who navigate adolescence successfully:

1. Judgment, interests, intellect, and other ego functions emerge that are specific to the individual and very stable.
2. The conflict-free area of the ego expands, allowing adolescents to find satisfaction in new relationships and experiences.
3. An irreversible sexual identity is formed.
4. The egocentrism of the child is replaced by a balance between thoughts about oneself and thoughts about others.
5. A wall separating one's public and private selves is established.

In *Ego Psychology and the Problem of Adaptation* (1939), Heinz Hartmann suggested that not all aspects of the ego's functioning arise out of conflict between id and superego. He introduced the concept of the conflict-free sphere of the ego, including basic adaptive functions such as perception, recognition of objects, problem solving, motor development, and language. Hartmann thought that the concepts of ego, id, and superego were more accurately viewed as three interrelated components of mental functioning that could expand or contract under the influence of one another. He offered a developmental picture of the ego beginning with early differentiation and distinction between id and ego, a process of growing clarity between self and the external reality, a shift from early self-love to investment in others, and to the eventual achievement of adaptive, reality-based thinking.

Building on Hartmann's work, Edith Jacobson (1964) described how the self is shaped through identification with others and achieves new levels of autonomy in adolescence through the incorporation of moral codes and ethical values. According to Jacobson, the superego is not always a threat to the ego. It can become a stimulus for new levels of ego development when anxiety or guilt signals a need for a new standard of moral behavior.

In their extension of the concept of ego, Rubin and Gertrude Blanck (1986) moved from a view of many ego functions to a more executive, integrated analysis of ego. Ego psychology has become a study of the development and differentiation of the ego as integrative, adaptive, and goal directed. Jane Loevinger (1976) offered a nine-stage theory of ego development, with adolescence characterized as a time of conformity to the group, and self-conscious awareness of the reactions of others. In her theory the ego is at once an intricate composite of multiple capacities, including planning, assessing, defending, coping, and mediating, and the integration of these with other aspects of self-concept, self-esteem, moral judgment, and personal identity, which gives the person substance, individuality, and location in the social world.

Implications for Human Development

Psychosexual theory emphasizes the importance of the tension between interpersonal demands and intrapsychic demands in shaping personality. The ego develops skills for dealing with the realities of the interpersonal world. It also develops skills for satisfying personal needs and for imposing personal standards and aspirations about the way these needs are satisfied. The expectations of others—particularly parents—are internalized and given personal meaning in the formation of the superego. By developing this idea, Freud was able to show how a child translates the demands of the interpersonal world into a personal way of functioning. At the same time, new demands and experiences continue to play a role in the development of personality. Freud focused on the effects of sexual impulses on personal and interpersonal life throughout adulthood.

One of the major early contributions of psychosexual theory was the identification of the influence of childhood experiences on adult behavior. Freud argued that the basic dynamics of personality are established by the age of 6 or 7. Psychosexual theory was unique in its focus on stages of development, family interactions, and unresolved family conflicts as explanations for ongoing adult behavior. The emphasis Freud gave to the importance of parenting practices and their implications for psychosexual development has provided one of the few theoretical frameworks for examining parent-child relationships. Many of the early empirical studies in developmental psychology focused on issues that derived from Freud's theory, such as childrearing and discipline practices, moral development, and childhood aggression.

The psychosexual approach recognizes the importance of motives, emotions, and fantasies that guide behavior. Within this framework, human behavior springs at least as much from emotional needs as from reason. The psychosexual theory suggests that unconscious motives and wishes explain behaviors that otherwise might not make sense. Many domains of mental activity—including fantasies, dreams, primary process thoughts and symbols, and defense mechanisms—influence how individuals make meaning from their experiences. Through the construct of the unconscious, Freud provided a means for explaining thoughts and behaviors that appear irrational, self-destructive, or contradictory. The idea that development involves efforts to find acceptable outlets for strong, often socially unacceptable impulses still guides therapeutic interventions with children, adolescents, and adults.

Another critical contribution is Freud's recognition of the role of sexual impulses during childhood. Freud believed that a sexual relationship with a loving partner is important for healthy adult functioning. Sexual impulses have a direct outlet in behavior during adult life. However, Freud argued that children also have needs for sexual stimulation and satisfaction, but have no acceptable means to satisfy those needs. Today, we are more aware of a child's need for hugging, snuggling, and physical warmth with loving caregivers, but most adults still find it difficult to acknowledge that young children have sexual impulses. Childhood wishes and needs, bottled up in the unconscious, guide behavior indirectly through symbolic expression, dreams, or, in some cases, the symptoms of mental disorders. We need only look at a daily newspaper to recognize that the acceptance and expression of sexual impulses continue to be points of conflict in modern society. Controversies over sexual dysfunction, sexual abuse, rape by strangers and acquaintances, sexual harassment in the workplace, sexually transmitted diseases, contraception, abortion, infidelity, and homophobia reveal the difficulties that Americans have in dealing with the expression of sexual impulses.

Links to the Psychosocial Approach

Both psychosexual theory and psychosocial theory are stage theories that address basic, qualitative changes in self-understanding and social orientation. Erikson, having been trained in psychoanalysis under Anna Freud and mentored by Sigmund Freud and other members of the Analytic Institute, readily acknowledged his intellectual ties to Freud's psychosexual theory. Psychosexual theory deals with conflicts that the child experiences in satisfying basic needs and impulses, especially sexual and aggressive impulses, within socially acceptable boundaries. The psychosocial approach expands this view by considering the broad range of social demands and social expectations that confront children at each point in development as well as the wide variety of competencies and social resources that children have for meeting those demands.

Both the psychosocial approach and psychosexual theory describe characteristics and functions of the ego system. However, the psychosocial approach goes beyond childhood and adolescence, suggesting the direction for ego development in early, middle, and later adulthood. The psychosocial approach gives a greater role to the individual in guiding and shaping the direction of development through the use of coping strategies that redefine conflicts and identify new resources.

TABLE 2.2 Basic Concepts of Psychosexual Theory

Drives
Preconscious
Unconscious
Id
Ego
Superego
Primary process thought
Pleasure principle
Reality principle
Secondary process thought
Stages of development: oral, anal, phallic, latency, genital
Identification
Oedipal conflict
Electra conflict
Defense mechanisms
Object relations theory

Psychosexual theory suggests that basic issues of personal development are in place by adolescence. The results of this development are then played out for the remainder of adult life in a person's defensive style, fixations, typical sexual behavior and sexual fantasies, and the strategies for sublimating sexual and aggressive impulses. In contrast, the psychosocial approach assumes that development goes on throughout life. The skills resulting from accomplishing new developmental tasks are learned, and new social abilities are achieved. The radius of significant relationships expands, bringing new expectations and new sources of social support. As new conflicts arise, they stimulate new growth, and new ego qualities emerge as a result of successfully coping with each new challenge. For a list of the key concepts of psychosexual theory, see Table 2.2.

Cognitive Developmental Theories

Objective 2c. To review the basic concepts of cognitive developmental theories and their implications for the study of human development.

Cognition is the process of organizing and making meaning of experience. In psychosexual theory, this function was assigned to the ego. Interpreting a statement, solving a problem, synthesizing information, critically analyzing a complex task—all of these are cognitive activities. Cognitive developmental theory focuses specifically on how knowing emerges and is transformed into logical, systematic capacities for reasoning and problem solving. Perhaps the most widely known and influential of the modern cognitive theorists is Jean Piaget. His concepts provide the initial focus of this section. Recent interest in the social framework within which cognition develops has been stimulated by the work of L. S. Vygotsky. Several of his important contributions, introduced toward the end of this section, complement and expand the developmental perspective on how cognition emerges and changes over the life course.

Basic Concepts in Piaget's Theory

According to Piaget, every organism strives to achieve equilibrium. **Equilibrium** is a balance of organized structures, whether motor, sensory, or cognitive. When structures are in equilibrium, they provide effective ways of interacting with the environment. Whenever changes in the organism or in the environment require a revision of the basic structures, they are thrown into **disequilibrium** (Piaget, 1978/1985). Piaget focused on how equilibrium is achieved with the environment through the formation of schemes (the structure or organization of action in thought) and operations (the mental manipulation of schemes and concepts) that form systematic, logical structures for comprehending and analyzing experience, and on how equilibrium is achieved within the schemes and operations themselves.

Equilibrium is achieved through **adaptation**—a process of gradually modifying existing schemes and operations in order to take into account changes or discrepancies between what is known and what is being experienced (see Figure 2.2). Adaptation is a two-part process in which the continuity of existing schemes and the possibility of altering schemes

interact. One part of adaptation is **assimilation**—the tendency to interpret new experiences in terms of an existing scheme. Assimilation contributes to the continuity of knowing. The second part of adaptation is **accommodation**—the tendency to modify familiar schemes in order to account for new dimensions of the object or event that are revealed through experience. Assimilation is a conservative process that operates to preserve existing structures by incorporating new information and confirming that what is already known is useful in making sense of new experiences. Accommodation is a progressive process that operates to alter existing structures in light of new information, thereby creating the basis for future assimilation (van Geert, 1998).

Piaget hypothesized that cognitive development occurs in four stages, each of which is characterized by a unique capacity for organizing and interpreting information. At each new stage, competencies of the earlier stages are not lost but are integrated into a qualitatively new approach to thinking and knowing. The essential features of these stages are introduced here. They will be discussed in greater detail in subsequent chapters. In general, Piaget's theory describes the path in the development of cognition from direct action on objects in infancy to mental actions (operations) and the relationships among mental operations in adolescence.

The first stage, **sensorimotor intelligence**, begins at birth and lasts until approximately 18 months of age. This stage is characterized by the formation of increasingly complex sensory and motor schemes that allow infants to organize and exercise some control over their environment.

The second stage, **preoperational thought**, begins when the child learns a language and ends at about age 5 or 6.

FIGURE 2.2 Adaptation = Assimilation + Accommodation

Experimentation with a string is an example of sensorimotor exploration. This infant is discovering the properties of the string through tactile, visual, and motor strategies. What are some examples of sensorimotor exploration that you continue to use as an adult?

During this stage, children develop the tools for representing schemes symbolically through language, imitation, imagery, symbolic play, and symbolic drawing. Their knowledge is still very much tied to their own perceptions.

The third stage, **concrete operational thought**, begins about age 6 or 7 and ends in early adolescence, around age 11 or 12. During this stage, children begin to appreciate the logical necessity of certain causal relationships. They can manipulate categories, classification systems, and hierarchies in groups. They are more successful at solving problems that are clearly tied to physical reality than at generating hypotheses about purely philosophical or abstract concepts.

The final stage of cognitive development, **formal operational thought**, begins in adolescence and persists through adulthood. This level of thinking permits a person to conceptualize about many simultaneously interacting variables. It allows for the creation of a system of laws or rules that can be used for problem solving. Formal operational thought reflects the quality of intelligence on which science and philosophy are built.

At the start of each new stage, the child experiences a type of **egocentrism** or limitation in point of view. With experience, children gain new objectivity about their perspective and are able to step back from the situation and see it more flexibly.

Implications for Human Development

Piaget's theory has had an enormous influence on our understanding of cognition and the way we think about the reasoning capacities of infants and young children. Six implications of the theory for the study of child development are discussed here. First, the theory suggests that cognition has its base in the biological capacities of the human infant—that knowledge is derived from action. For example, infants learn about the features of objects by grasping and sucking on them. Knowledge is constructed rather than passively absorbed. Children as well as adults select, explore, and experiment with objects and later with ideas. They create their knowledge through this active engagement.

As the knower changes, so does what is known. For example, an infant may know a ball through its touch, how it feels in the hand or mouth, through its appearance, and through its response to the infant's actions. A toddler may become aware of the functions of a ball by kicking, throwing, rolling, and bouncing it. At later ages, children understand more about the physical properties of a ball and can link it to other shapes and categories of objects. With each more advanced level of motor, symbolic, and interpersonal capacity, the knower creates a new meaning of objects, people, and the interactions among them. Because of natural interest and through exposure to a wide range of materials, stimuli, and experiences, infants and young children "teach themselves" a great deal of what they know. This perspective has been integrated into instructional strategies in which children are encouraged to construct meaning through direct experience. Through free exploration, which typically requires the coordination of perspectives and the manipulation of interconnected elements, an understanding of the integration of coordinated factors is naturally acquired (Kamii et al., 2001; Kamii, Rummelsburg, & Kari, 2005).

Second, discrepancies between existing schemes and contemporary experiences promote cognitive development. Encounters with all types of novelty—especially experiences that are moderately distinct rather than widely different from what is already known—are important for advancing new ideas and new ways of organizing thought. Extending this idea, encounters with differences in opinion through discussion and reading are just as important in adolescence and adulthood as encounters with different types of sensory materials in infancy and toddlerhood.

Third, infants have the capacity for thinking and problem solving. Although infants do not make use of symbolic strategies, they are able to establish certain logical connections between means and ends that guide their problem-solving efforts.

Fourth, infants, toddlers, and school-age children think in different ways, and the ways they think are different from the ways adults think. This does not mean that their thinking is unorganized or illogical, but the same principles of logic that typically govern adult thought do not govern the thinking of young children.

Fifth, beginning with the period of concrete operations, children can approach problems using many of the principles that are fundamental to scientific reasoning. They can also begin to reason about their reasoning—introducing the importance of **metacognition**, or the many strategies used to guide the way we organize and prepare ourselves to think more clearly and effectively.

Sixth, thinking about the social world is regulated by many of the same principles as thinking about objects in the physical world. As we learn about the principles that govern objects and physical relationships, we are also learning about ourselves and others.

Vygotsky's Concepts of Cognitive Development

Piaget's focus on cognitive development emphasized a process in which children investigate, explore, discover, and rediscover meaning in their world. Although Piaget acknowledged the significance of social factors, especially parents and peers, in the cognitive process, his theory focused on what he believed to be universal processes and stages in the maturation of cognition from infancy through adolescence. In contrast, Vygotsky, often referred to as an interactionist, argued that development can be understood only within a social-historical framework. At the heart of his work is a focus on thinking, especially in childhood, which he links to the development of language and speech.

> The development of the child's thinking depends on his mastery of the social means of thinking, that is, on mastery of speech…. This thesis stems from our *comparison* of the development of inner speech and verbal thinking in man with the development of speech and intellect as it occurs in the animal world and the earliest stages of childhood. This comparison demonstrates that the former does not represent a simple continuation of the latter. The very type of development changes. It changes from a biological form of development to a socio-historical form of development. (Vygotsky, 1987, p. 120)

Vygotsky, like many other theorists and philosophers of his time, was trying to account for the development of higher mental processes from their simpler forms. He saw development as following a continuous path from other animals to humans, and also a discontinuous path. This was captured in his view of *natural* or **lower mental processes**, which could be observed in animal behavior and in the problem-solving behaviors of infants and very young children, and **higher mental processes**, which arise as children encounter and master the cultural tools of their society. He viewed human beings across cultures as both similar to the extent that they shared basic physical characteristics and natural psychological processes, and substantially different depending upon the cultural symbol systems to which they are exposed, and how those systems shape thinking and behavior.

Higher mental processes, particularly language and meaning, emerge from the child's ongoing interactions within social, historical, and cultural contexts, as well as from the child's biological maturation. The child and the culture are intricately interwoven through the process of social interaction. New levels of understanding begin at an interpersonal level as two individuals, initially an infant and an adult, coordinate their interactions. Eventually interpersonal collaboration becomes internalized to make up the child's internal mental framework. Through continuous interaction with others, especially adults and older children, a child revises and advances levels of understanding. Over time, it is the mastery of these **cultural tools** or symbol systems that permits individuals to alter their environments and guide, regulate, and redefine themselves.

Four key concepts in Vygotsky's theory are introduced here: (1) culture as a mediator of cognitive structuring, (2) movement from the intermental to the intramental, (3) inner speech, and (4) the zone of proximal development.

Culture as a Mediator of Cognitive Structuring

Vygotsky argued that cognitive development can be understood only in the context of **culture**. Of the many elements of culture that shape cognition, one that was of special interest to Vygotsky was the idea of tools and signs as human inventions that shape thought. Technical tools such as plows, cars, weapons, and signs—sometimes referred to as *psychological tools*—like symbolic systems, counting systems, and strategies for remembering, modify the person's relationship to the environment. Through the use of tools, humans change the way they organize and think about the world. Vygotsky viewed tools as a means through which the human mind is shaped and modified over the course of history.

Movement from Intermental to Intramental

Perhaps contrary to common sense, Vygotsky argued that high-level mental functions begin in external activity that is gradually reconstructed and internalized. He gave the example of *pointing*. Vygotsky claimed that initially, an infant will reach toward an object that is out of reach, stretching the hand in the direction of the object and making grasping motions with the fingers. This is a movement directed to the object. As soon as the caregiver recognizes that the child wants the object and is able to satisfy the child's request, the child begins to modify the reaching and grasping motion into a socially meaningful gesture—pointing. The caregiver's understanding of the gesture and the **intermental** coordination between caregiver and infant result in an **intramental** process for the infant—an understanding of the special relationship between the desired goal, the caregiver as mediator, and pointing as a meaningful sign.

Inner Speech

Vygotsky (1978) argued that speech plays a central role in self-regulation, self-directed goal attainment, and practical problem solving. He described the problem-solving behaviors of toddlers as involving both speech and action. Toddlers use what was described by Piaget (1952) as **egocentric speech** to accompany their behavior. They talk out loud, but do not seem to be concerned about whether anyone can hear them or understand them. He described the talk as egocentric because it did not seem to have any social intention. Piaget suggested that the development of communication began with inner thinking of a very private, nonsocialized nature. In toddlerhood, he viewed egocentric speech as evidence of the relative absence of social life and the great extent of nonsocialized thoughts that the child is unable to express.

Vygotsky (1987) proposed a completely different developmental pathway to account for egocentric speech and its function. He represented the scheme as: social speech—egocentric speech—inner speech. Vygotsky viewed speech as beginning in the social interactions between children and adults or other children. The first and foremost function of speech is social. Egocentric speech is a transformation of this social speech inward. The child uses speech that was initially acquired through interactions with others to guide personal behaviors. It does not have a social intention; rather, it is a tool that helps to guide problem solving. Vygotsky viewed egocentric speech and actions as part of the same problem-solving function. The more difficult the problem, the more speech is necessary for the child to find a solution. "Children solve practical tasks with the help of their speech, as well as their eyes and hands" (Vygotsky, 1978a, p. 26). Eventually, the egocentric speech of an audible nature dwindles (but does not disappear entirely) and becomes **inner speech.**

The Zone of Proximal Development

Taking the idea of internalization further, Vygotsky offered the concept of the zone of proximal development to explain how learning and development converge. The zone of proximal development is "the distance between the actual developmental level as determined by independent problem solving and the level of potential development as determined through problem solving under adult guidance or in collaboration with more capable peers" (Vygotsky, 1978b, p. 86).

We have all experienced situations in which we were able to solve a task only with the assistance and advice of someone else. The typical efforts of parents to help a child put together a jigsaw puzzle by suggesting strategies, like selecting all the straight-edged pieces first to make the border, or sorting the many pieces into those with a similar color, are examples of how learning takes place within the zone. Vygotsky suggested that the level of competence a person can reach when taking advantage of the guidance of others reflects the functions that are in the process of maturation, as contrasted to those that have already matured. Learning within the zone of proximal development sets into motion the reorganization and internalization of existing developmental competencies, which then become synthesized at a new, higher intramental level.

Implications for Human Development

Vygotsky's theory suggests that the boundaries between the individual and the environment are much less clear than one might infer from most other theories of human development. In fact, Vygotsky directs attention to the guiding role of social interaction and culture in shaping and orienting cognition, thus bringing the study of cognitive development

Vygotsky's theory emphasizes the social context of cognitive development. Children often learn by interacting with older siblings who can answer their questions and show them how to solve problems.

© Robert Brenner/Photo Edit

into much greater harmony with the concepts of psychosocial theory than are seen in Piaget's theory.

Several specific implications of Vygotsky's work can be inferred (Davydov, 1995). First, the mental structures and functioning of people raised in a specific culture will be different from those of people raised in other cultures. In comparison to Piaget, who viewed the emergence of logical thought as largely a universal process, Vygotsky considered the nature of reasoning and problem solving as culturally created. Because of the way in which intermental experiences and networks structure intramental events, one's family and others who influence and control the child's early learning and problem-solving experiences will have a strong influence on the structure of one's thinking.

Second, Vygotsky highlighted the role of language as a cultural tool that links each new generation of children with the history and cultural meaning of their ancestors. Language, especially the spoken word, is a bridge between the interpersonal environment and the child's private thoughts.

Third, the concept of a zone of proximal development links development and learning. It assumes a critical role for adults in the child's environment who can identify where a child is with regard to any particular skill area and can then introduce questions, suggestions, tasks, and strategies to help move them to a new level of competence. Vygotsky believed in the interconnection of the learning and teaching processes, arguing that children could never discover all that is known in a culture's knowledge base just through exploration and experimentation. They need the guidance of more skillful peers and adults.

Finally, an implication of Vygotsky's work is that individuals can promote their own cognitive development by seeking interactions with others who can help draw them to higher levels of functioning within their zone of proximal development.

Links to the Psychosocial Approach

Piaget's cognitive developmental theory and the psychosocial approach focus on development as a product of discrepancies, referred to as *disequilibrium* in cognitive developmental theory and as *psychosocial crises* in psychosocial theory. Piaget's theory, like the psychosocial approach, proposes a set of stages of development, with each stage growing from and integrating the achievements of earlier stages. Piaget's theory did not offer any hypotheses about the qualitative changes that might follow the period of formal operational reasoning, whereas the psychosocial approach makes clear predictions about the direction of ego development in early, middle, and later adulthood.

Piaget focused on the cognitive domain—especially on the process of knowledge acquisition and logical reasoning. The meaning a person makes of a situation depends largely on the stage of mental development attained. Feelings, social relationships, and self-understanding are viewed as cognitive schemes that are constructed with the same logic that the person applies to the understanding of objects. In the psychosocial approach, cognitive development is referred to as ego development—an understanding of how the self emerges and shapes a personal identity with goals, values, beliefs, and strategies for achieving goals within the constraints of the society. Ego development involves planning, making decisions, coping with challenges, and facing the future with a sense of purpose.

Vygotsky's theory provides an important link from Piaget's emphasis on the maturation of logical reasoning to the emphasis of the psychosocial approach on the maturation of self in society by emphasizing the interpersonal nature of cognition. The idea of a zone of proximal development relates closely to the idea of an expanding network of social relationships, capturing the unique interpersonal and cultural context of all aspects of knowing, whether it is knowing about the logic of the physical world or about the logic of relationships. Vygotsky's theory shares with the psychosocial approach a strong emphasis on the role of culture in guiding social and cognitive development. The two theories view development as an ongoing interaction of the person and the cultural context. One might think of Vygotsky's notion of movement from the intermental to the intramental as a forerunner of the psychosocial concept of identity—a gradual internalization and integration of the roles and social expectations of others into a meaningful sense of one's role in society. For a list of the key concepts of cognitive developmental theory, see Table 2.3.

TABLE 2.3 Basic Concepts of Cognitive Developmental Theory

PIAGET'S THEORY

Equilibrium

Adaptation

Assimilation

Accommodation

Sensorimotor intelligence

Preoperational thought

Concrete operational thought

Formal operational thought

Metacognition

VYGOTSKY'S THEORY

Culture

Tools

Language

Intermental processes

Intramental processes

Speech

Inner speech

Egocentric speech

Zone of proximal development

Theories of Learning

Objective 2d. To review the basic concepts of learning theories and their implications for the study of human development.

Human abilities are diverse, flexible, and can be coordinated or integrated to achieve many different goals. An understanding of the processes of learning and teaching requires concepts that are not linked to specific goals, but can be applied broadly across many problem areas (Premack, 2010). For example, observational learning is a common mode through which humans can learn a vast array of behaviors, such as eating with a fork, swinging a bat, speaking in a polite tone of voice, or sharing toys with friends. Learning theorists have proposed mechanisms to account for the relatively permanent changes in behavior that occur as a result of experience. Underlying human beings' extensive capacity to adapt to changes in their environments is their flexible ability to learn. Two theories of learning that have made significant contributions to the study of human development are social learning, and cognitive behaviorism.

Social Learning Theory

The concept of **social learning** evolved from the awareness that much learning takes place as a result of **observation** and **imitation** of other people's behavior (Bandura & Walters, 1963). Changes in behavior can occur without being linked to a specific pattern of positive or negative reinforcement. They can also occur without numerous opportunities for trial-and-error practice. A person can watch someone perform a task or say a new expression and imitate that behavior accurately on the first try. The person being observed is called the **model**; the process of imitating a model is called **modeling.**

Early research in social learning theory was devoted to identifying conditions that determine whether a child will imitate a model (Bandura, 1971, 1977, 1986). Children have been found to imitate aggressive, altruistic, helping, and stingy models. They are most likely to imitate models who appear to be powerful and prestigious, in other words, models who control resources or who are themselves rewarded. Bandura and Walters (1963) suggested that children not only observe the behaviors carried out by a model, but they also watch what happens to the model. When the model's behavior is rewarded, the behavior is more likely to be imitated; when the model's behavior is punished, the behavior is more likely to be avoided. This process is called **vicarious reinforcement**. When naughty behaviors go unpunished, they too are likely to be imitated. Through observational learning, a child can learn a behavior and also acquire the motivation to perform that behavior or to resist performing that behavior depending on what is learned about the consequences linked to that behavior. Thus, observational learning can hold the key to self-regulation and to the internalization of standards for resisting certain behaviors as well as for enacting behaviors (Grusec, 1992).

Social learning theory emphasizes the role of observation and imitation as means of learning new behaviors. Can you think of a new response that you recently learned through imitation?

Bandura (1977) pointed out the distinction between learning and performance. A learner might understand features of a task or demands in a situation that are not evident in the learner's behavior. Social learning theory assumes that a great deal of learning goes on through observation, but that much of it is not observed in behavior unless the reinforcement conditions are conducive.

Recent directions in social learning theory have taken an increasingly cognitive orientation, sometimes referred to as social cognitive theory (Bandura, 1989, 1991, 2001). Through observational learning, the child becomes acquainted with the general concepts of the situation as well as with the specific behaviors. Direct reinforcement or non-reinforcement provides one type of information about how to behave in a certain situation. Moreover, people watch others, learn about the consequences of their actions, and remember what others have told or shown them and what they have read or learned about the situation. Over time, one forms a symbolic representation for the situation, the required behaviors, and the expected outcomes. A worker may learn that with one type of supervisor, it is appropriate to ask lots of questions and offer suggestions for ways of solving problems, whereas with another supervisor, it is better to remain quiet and try not to be noticed. The rules for behavior in each setting are abstracted from what has been observed in watching others, what happened following one's own behavior in the past, and what one understands about the demands in the immediate situation. Through social learning, individuals develop an understanding of the social consequences of behavior, leading to new patterns of behavioral expression and self-regulation. The culmination of this learning process is what Bandura (2001) referred to as efficacy, including planning intentional actions, guiding and directing one's own behaviors toward a goal, and reflecting on one's actions to assess their quality, impact, and purpose.

Implications for Human Development

The principles of social learning theory are assumed to operate in the same way throughout life. The concept of social learning highlights the relevance of models' behavior in guiding the behavior of others. These models may be parents, older siblings, peers, entertainment stars, or sports heroes. Because new models may be encountered at any life stage, new learning through the process of observational learning is always possible. Exposure to a certain array of models and a certain pattern of rewards or punishments results in the encouragement to imitate some behaviors and to inhibit the performance of others. The similarity in behavior among people of the same age reflects their exposure to a common history of models, rewards, and punishments. Recognition of the potential impact one has as a model for others—especially in the role of parent, teacher, clinician, counselor, or supervisor—ought to impart a certain level of self-conscious monitoring about the behaviors one exhibits and the strategies one employs in the presence of those who are likely to perceive one as a model for new learning.

Cognitive Behaviorism

Cognitive behaviorists study the many internal mental activities that influence behavior. Edward Tolman (1932/1967, 1948) introduced the notion of a **cognitive map**—an internal mental representation of the learning environment. According to Tolman, individuals who perform a specific task in a certain environment attend primarily to that task, but they also form a representation of the rest of the setting. The cognitive map includes expectations about the reward system in operation, the existing spatial relationships, and the behaviors accorded the highest priority. An individual's performance in a situation represents only part of the learning that has occurred. The fact that people respond to changes in the environment indicates that a complex mental map actually develops in this situation.

According to Walter Mischel (1973, 1979; Mischel & Shoda, 1995), six types of cognitive and affective factors mediate a person's behavior in a situation and account for continuity in how people respond across situations: encodings;

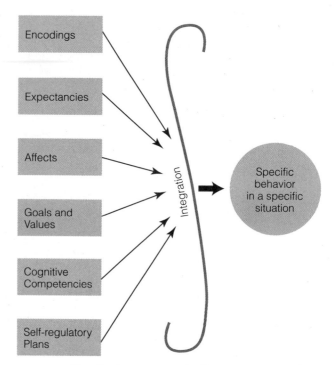

FIGURE 2.3 The Six Cognitive and Affective Dimensions That Influence Behavior

expectancies and beliefs; affects (feelings and emotional responses); goals and values; competencies; and self-regulatory plans (see Figure 2.3). **Encodings** refer to constructs the person has about the self, the situation, and others in the situation. **Expectancies** refer to cognitive assessments about one's ability to perform, ideas about the consequences of one's behavior, and the meaning of events in one's environment.

Affects are the feelings and emotional reactions or physiological responses that are associated with a situation. Feelings of anger, fear, arousal, excitement, or jealousy might interact with expectancies and encodings to guide behavior. **Goals** and **values** are related to the relative importance one places on the outcomes of situations. One person may value high levels of task performance, whereas another may value success in social situations. One's behavior in a situation is influenced by how one values its possible outcomes. **Cognitive competencies** consist of knowledge, skills, and abilities.

Self-regulatory plans are strategies for achieving one's goals, including techniques for managing internal emotional states, creating a plan, and putting the plan into action. In comparison to the notion of classical or operant conditioning, self-regulation focuses on how one leaves the realm of stimulus control in order to gain control over behavior. Self-regulation is especially important in situations where temptations, frustrations, or self-doubt threaten to pull one away from important goals (Mischel & Ayduk, 2002). As people become increasingly aware of the effects of stimuli on their behavior, they can learn to overcome, channel, or eliminate those influences that tempt them to abandon their goals. The box on Cognitive Behavioral Therapy illustrates how the principles of cognitive behaviorism have been incorporated

APPLYING THEORY AND RESEARCH TO LIFE

Cognitive Behavioral Therapy

BUILDING ON THE TRADITIONS of cognitive developmental theory, cognitive behaviorism, and attribution theory, cognitive behavioral therapy is a general term that applies to a variety of therapies that share certain similarities. The central idea is that stimuli or situations produce thoughts that create certain affects (emotions). The affects are produced by the thoughts we have about the stimulus, not by the stimulus itself (Leahy, 2006). Since people differ in the way they categorize and evaluate a stimulus, the same situation might create feelings of discouragement and depression in some people, and feelings of determination in others. For example, one person might react to a bad grade on a test as evidence that she is not smart enough to do well; another person might react to the same grade as evidence that he needs to study harder.

Aaron Beck (1976/1979), the founder of cognitive therapy, began his work in the treatment of depression. He found that patients suffering from depression spoke consistently of themes of loss, incompetence, and failure. They viewed themselves as failures; they perceived their efforts to alter their situation as useless, and their expectancies of the future as bleak. Beck began to focus his therapeutic effort on guiding patients to examine their emotional reactions and automatic assumptions.

The goal of cognitive behavioral therapy is to teach clients ways of unlearning unwanted, negative encodings by examining their thoughts in light of new information or alternative interpretations, and then replacing those thoughts with new, more adaptive encodings (NACBT.org, 2007). The therapy takes an inductive approach, encouraging clients to consider their thoughts as hypotheses that can be questioned or tested and then changed in order to be more appropriately adapted to reality. The therapist focuses on teaching the client rational, self-counseling skills that can be practiced through weekly homework, and applied to daily situations outside of the therapy session. The therapy also teaches clients to examine their problems with a degree of calm detachment. If a person is upset about a problem, then the person actually has two problems, the troubling situation and the distress associated with their reaction to it. Finding ways to reduce the distress allows the person to examine the problem using higher-order cognitive skills rather than affect-driven stress reduction responses.

Cognitive behavioral therapy has been shown to be effective in the treatment of depression, panic disorder, bulimia (an eating disorder), and post-traumatic stress disorder (Baker, McFall, & Shoham, 2009). A number of clinical studies have shown that cognitive behavioral therapy is more long-lasting as a treatment for these disorders than treatment using medication. In other words, once the treatment has ended, patients who have had cognitive behavioral therapy are substantially less likely to relapse than those who were treated with medication. The implication is that for these conditions, a therapeutic process can result in a relatively permanent change in thought, affect, and specific behaviors designed to help the client achieve goals.

Critical Thinking Questions

1. What are the links between the six elements of cognitive behaviorism (Figure 2.3) and cognitive behavioral therapy?

2. Based on what you know about psychosexual theory, what might be some similarities and differences in the therapeutic approaches of psychosexual and cognitive behavioral therapy?

3. What are some ways in which cognitive behavioral therapy builds on Piaget's cognitive developmental theory? How might the therapy be viewed in terms of Vygotsky's idea of the zone of proximal development?

4. What are some limitations to cognitive behavioral therapy? What are some features of the client or the problem that would not lend themselves well to cognitive behavioral therapy?

into a therapeutic approach to help clients alter unwanted or distressing thoughts, affect, and behavior.

Implications for Human Development

Cognitive behaviorism suggests that the learner acquires an outlook on the learning situation that influences subsequent learning and performance. This outlook influences the learner's feeling of familiarity with the task, motivation to undertake the task, optimism about performing the task successfully, and strategies for approaching the task. In addition to everything a parent, teacher, or supervisor might do to structure a learning environment, one must always take into account the outlook that the learner brings to the task. Differences in expectancies, self-control strategies, values, emotional reactions, and goals all influence the way individuals approach a learning situation and the behaviors they are likely to exhibit in the situation.

Cognitive behaviorism suggests that in order to understand why people behave as they do in a specific situation, one needs to understand the meaning that is constructed of the situation, including the integration of expectations, goals, and values and their links to cognitive and behavioral competences and self-regulatory plans. Although information or skills can be learned, they will not be expressed in behavior unless expectations about the self and the environment justify their enactment.

TABLE 2.4 Basic Concepts of Social Learning Theory and Cognitive Behaviorism

SOCIAL LEARNING	COGNITIVE BEHAVIORISM
Observation	Cognitive map
Imitation	Encodings
Model	Expectancies
Modeling	Affects
Vicarious reinforcement	Goals
Social cognition	Values
Self-efficacy	Cognitive competencies
	Self-regulatory plans

Links to the Psychosocial Approach

The learning theories and the psychosocial approach operate at different levels of abstraction. The psychosocial approach assumes that growth and change continue throughout the life span; however, it does not account for the exact processes by which new behaviors, new coping strategies, or new ego strengths are acquired. The learning theories provide explanations for the ways in which the patterns of daily events shape the direction of adaptation and growth. They offer insight into the processes through which society's rules, norms, and customs become internalized and translated into habits, preferences, and expectations, which become generalized across common situations. The learning theories emphasize the significance of the immediate environment in directing the course of growth and also help to explain why habits or patterns of behavior may be difficult to change, even when they appear to be dysfunctional. The key terms introduced by social learning theory and cognitive behaviorism are listed in Table 2.4.

Cultural Theory

Objective 2e. To review the basic concepts of cultural theory and its implications for the study of human development.

The concept of **culture**, although defined in a variety of ways by anthropologists, political scientists, sociologists, and psychologists, refers here to the learned systems of meanings and patterns of behaviors that are shared by a group of people and transmitted from one generation to the next. **Physical culture** encompasses the objects, technologies, structures, tools, and other artifacts of a culture. **Social culture** consists of norms, roles, beliefs, values, rites, and customs (Herkovits, 1948; Triandis et al., 1980; Rohner, 1984; Betancourt & Lopez, 1993; Triandis, 1994).

Culture has been described as a **worldview**—a way of making meaning of the relationships, situations, and objects encountered in daily life. Basic ideas, such as whether people are considered to be in control of nature or a part of nature, who is included in the definition of family, what characteristics are considered signs of mental health or mental illness, which acts are construed as hostile or nurturing, which aspects of the environment are considered dangerous or safe—all these and many other mental constructions are shaped by culture (Kagitcibasi, 1990). Culture guides development, not only through encounters with certain objects, roles, and settings, but also through the meanings linked to actions.

Weisner and Lowe (2004) clarify this process using the term **cultural pathways**. According to this view, adults in each culture have values and goals for themselves and for their children that shape and organize the socialization process and activities of daily life. "Activities are made up of values and goals; resources needed to make the activity happen; people in relationships; the tasks the activity is there to accomplish; emotions and feelings of those engaged in the activity; and a script defining the appropriate, normative way we expect to do that activity" (Weisner & Lowe, 2004, p. 6).

The idea that engaging in the specific routines and activities of daily life shaped developmental pathways was captured early in the field of cultural anthropology through the work of Ruth Benedict. She introduced the principle of **cultural determinism** (Benedict, 1934/1950), which suggests that the individual's psychological experiences are shaped by the expectations, resources, and challenges posed by one's specific cultural group. Similar to the learning theories, cultural determinism suggests that individuals' behaviors are shaped through enculturation, in which culture carriers such as parents, teachers, religious leaders, and elders, teach, model, reward, punish, and use other symbolic strategies to transmit critical practices and values. Two theoretical constructs that allow one to compare cultures are presented here: continuity and discontinuity, and individualism and collectivism.

Continuity and Discontinuity

The extent to which development is viewed as distinct stages of life depends on the degree to which socialization within a culture is characterized by continuity or discontinuity. **Continuity** is found when a child is given information and responsibilities that apply directly to that child's future adult behavior. For example, Margaret Mead (1928/1950) observed that in Samoan society, girls of 6 or 7 years of age commonly took care of their younger siblings. As they grew older, their involvement in the caregiving role increased; however, the behaviors that were expected of them were not substantially changed. When there is continuity, development is a gradual, fluid transformation, in which adult competencies are built directly on childhood accomplishments. **Discontinuity** is found when a child is either barred from activities that are open only to adults or is forced to "unlearn" information or

Kwanzaa was created to strengthen the cultural identity of the African American ethnic group. Family members participate in rituals that highlight a common ancestry and shared cultural values.

behaviors that are accepted in children but considered inappropriate for adults. The change from expectations of virginity before marriage to expectations of sexual responsiveness after marriage is an example of discontinuity. Cultures that have discrete, age-graded expectations for people at different periods of life produce a pattern of development in which age groups have distinct characteristics and appear to function at different skill levels. These societies are likely to be marked by public ceremonies, graduations, and other **rites of passage** from one stage to the next.

Individualism and Collectivism

The dimensions of *individualism* and *collectivism* provide another lens for comparing cultures (Triandis, 1990, 1995, 1998). **Individualism** refers to a worldview in which social behavior is guided largely by personal goals, ambitions, and pleasures, which may or may not coincide with the interests of the group. Independence and personal achievement are valued. When conflicts arise between group and personal goals, it is considered acceptable and perhaps expected that personal goals will come first. **Collectivism** refers to a worldview in which social behavior is guided largely by goals that are shared by a collective, such as a family, tribe, work group, or political or religious association. Interdependence and group solidarity are valued. The in-group creates norms, goals, and beliefs that are enculturated and endorsed by its members. When conflicts arise between group goals and personal goals, a person is expected to act in the best interest of the group.

There is growing evidence to suggest that people from different cultures process social information somewhat differently, influenced in part by the collectivist or individualistic orientation of the culture. For example, both native Chinese and Western adults process information about characteristics of the self in the same area of the prefrontal cortex. However, Chinese adults also process information about characteristics of their mothers in this same area of the brain, an area that in Western adults is involved only in thinking about the self. The implication is that for Chinese adults, a strong cultural tie between self and others is supported by a neural pathway for thinking about self and significant others (Ambady & Bharucha, 2009; Zhu, Zhang, Fan, & Han, 2007).

Cultures have been differentiated as relatively more collectivist or individualist. Across cultures, people have to achieve some of the same basic developmental tasks. But the degree to which the culture is collectivistic or individualistic will influence what the people in a culture think is the ideal state and what is necessary to achieve that state. All cultures have some expectations for the formation of social relationships and social bonds, but the pathways that are emphasized as high quality or most desirable are different. In an individualistic developmental pathway, social obligations are constructed through agreements among the individual participants in the relationship. Opportunities to decide whom you want to have relationships with and how to behave within those relationships are maximized. As a result, there is considerable variability in the nature and quality of interpersonal relationships. In the collectivistic or interdependent developmental pathway, social obligations and responsibilities are more important, and more clearly defined. There is greater consistency in the scripts for specific relationships,

© Tom Wilson/Getty Images

and greater agreement about the importance of preserving those relationships, even when those obligations require personal sacrifice (Greenfield, Keller, Fuligni, & Maynard, 2003). For example, arranged marriages are more common in collectivistic cultures, whereas marriages based on romantic love and personal choice are more common in individualistic cultures.

Typically, societies marked by greater complexity, affluence, social mobility, and cultural diversity tend to be more individualistic in their worldview (Greenfield, 2009). Factors including greater exposure to education, increased access to technology, and increased globalization tend to move cultures away from the collectivistic and toward the individualistic pathways. People within cultures can also be described as adhering to more individualist or collectivist values. Thus, not everyone in a collectivist culture equally endorses the collectivist worldview. Subgroups within a society may differ in how much their values reflect the dominant individualist or collectivist orientation of the larger society. The Human Development and Diversity box provides a discussion of the implications of individualism and collectivism for parenting.

Implications for Human Development

Culture interacts with biological development in determining whether development is perceived as stage-like and how each period of life is experienced. This concept is illustrated by the ways in which different cultures mark an adolescent girl's first menstruation (Mead, 1949/1955). In some societies, people fear menstruation and treat the girl as if she were dangerous to others. In other societies, she is viewed as having powerful magic that will affect her own future and that of the tribe so she is treated with new reverence. In still others, the perceived shamefulness of sex requires that the menstruation be kept as secret as possible. The culture thus determines how a biological change is marked by others and how it is experienced by the person.

Societies vary in the extent to which they expect people to make significant life decisions during each life period and in the range of choices they make available. The United States is a highly individualistic culture. American adolescents are expected to make decisions regarding sex, work, politics, religion, marriage, and education. In each of these areas, the alternatives are complex and varied. As a result, adolescence is prolonged, and the risk of leaving this period without having found a solution to these problems is great. People who emigrate to the United States from more collectivistic cultures or who are members of more collectivistic **subcultures** may experience even more stress during this period as their values for family and group allegiances and their scripts for behavior come into conflict with the individualistic orientation of the larger cultural context. In cultures that offer fewer choices and provide a clearer path from childhood to adulthood, adolescence may be brief and relatively free of psychological stress.

The study of development must be approached with an appreciation for the cultural context. Cultural expectations about the timing for entry into and completion of certain life tasks, such as schooling, work, marriage, childbearing, and political and religious leadership, influence the tempo and tone of one's life history. Cultures also vary in the personal qualities they admire and those they consider inappropriate or shameful. A society's standards of beauty, leadership, and talent determine how easily an individual can achieve status within it.

Cultures not only differ from one another, but some societies are more culturally diverse than others. The process of **globalization** includes "the rapid spread of materials and products, ideas, images, capital flows, and people across spaces and borders (national or otherwise) that formerly were far more difficult if not impossible to connect" (Weisner & Lowe, 2004, p. 6). With increased global travel, migration, global communication systems, and opportunities to study or work in other cultures, most contemporary societies are becoming more culturally diverse than in the past. This means that there may be tensions between dominant and minority cultures as well as conflicts among ethnic groups. Some of the benefits of increased access to goods and technologies that are a by-product of globalization may be counterbalanced by the disintegration of social ties and the loss of meaningful group identity.

Links to the Psychosocial Approach

The psychosocial approach is based on the assumption that culture contributes fundamentally to individual development. Basic cultural values regarding generosity, self-control, independence, or cooperation can be interpreted from infant caregiving practices. Just as evolutionary theory asserts that adaptation is a product of the interaction between the organism and the physical environment, psychosocial theory assumes that individual development is a product of continuous interaction between the developing person and the demands and resources of the cultural environment.

The concept of developmental pathways suggests that all cultures have to address certain developmental tasks, such as the establishment of interpersonal relationships, but the way these pathways are structured, the activities that are included along the path, and the ideals or goals that adults strive to achieve differ across cultures. According to the psychosocial approach, all cultures must be able to adapt to changes in economic, environmental, and intercultural conditions in order to survive. Individual development is interwoven with the ability of the society to adapt and continue. For a list of the key concepts of cultural theory, see Table 2.6.

HUMAN DEVELOPMENT AND DIVERSITY

Implications of Individualism and Collectivism for Parenting Practices

THE CONSTRUCTS OF individualism and collectivism refer to two different value systems that characterize a culture. Individualism encourages and celebrates individual accomplishments and self-expression; collectivism encourages and celebrates interdependence and the strength of the community. Every society requires some blend or balance between these two perspectives. In order to survive, a group must be able to support both the *I* and the *We*, the individual person and the group. However, as one interacts with people from different cultural backgrounds, it is helpful to be aware of the dominant orientation toward either individualism or collectivism in order to achieve greater insight into the person's likely motivations, goals, and sense of moral obligation. Table 2.5 summarizes the features of these two orientations (Trumbull, Rothstein-Fisch, & Greenfield, 2000).

These contrasting values have implications for the behaviors that parents value and the way they interact with their children. Individualist cultures encourage more independent play. They foster a child's autonomy and self-expression by allowing greater physical distance between the child and the caregiver, asking for the child's opinions, and allowing children to have a voice in decision making. Children are praised for doing things on their own and moving toward self-reliance. In both subtle and specific ways, children in individualist cultures are encouraged to compete with each other and to feel pride in their individual achievements.

Children in collectivist cultures are kept closer to their parents or caregivers during infancy. They are more likely to be nurtured through longer periods of breastfeeding,

TABLE 2.5 A Comparison of Individualism and Collectivism

INDIVIDUALISM	COLLECTIVISM
Fosters independence	Fosters interdependence
Values individual achievement	Values group success
Promotes self-expression	Promotes adherence to norms
Values individual thinking	Values group consensus
Associated with egalitarian relationships	Associated with hierarchical roles and respect for elders
Associated with private property and individual ownership	Associated with shared property and group ownership

to be carried or held closely during infancy, and to be socialized through gentle encouragement and indulgences well into childhood. Families in collectivist cultures usually include extended kinship groups that all play an active role in a child's comfort, socialization, and care. Children are taught to be respectful of their elders and to show deference for adults' opinions and decisions. A strong value for sharing and cooperation leads to encouragement for children to share their belongings and to learn from one another. Children are praised for behaviors that evidence responsibility for others, a sense of duty, and commitment to the family (Greenfield & Suzuki, 1998).

Critical Thinking Questions

1. Joan and Dave get married and have a child. Joan comes from a cultural background that has a collectivist orientation. Dave comes from a cultural background that has an individualist orientation. They are discussing how to discipline their young child.
   a. What kinds of strategies might Joan elect to use?
   b. What kinds of strategies might Dave elect to use?
   c. Under what circumstances might they find themselves in conflict over their approach to childrearing?
   d. What kinds of childrearing approaches might they devise that would be acceptable to both of them?
2. Some researchers take issue with the idea that cultures can be characterized as collectivist or individualist. What are the limitations of these concepts? Are they overly simplistic? Do they reflect real differences in people's attitudes and beliefs? Do they help explain differences in the behaviors of people from various cultural backgrounds? What kinds of evidence would you want to have in order to be confident about using these constructs?
3. Aside from the ideas of individualism and collectivism, what other ideas do you find useful in characterizing cultural orientations that are transmitted from one generation to the next?

TABLE 2.6 Basic Concepts from Cultural Theory

Culture	Continuity
Physical culture	Discontinuity
Social culture	Rites of passage
Worldview	Collectivism
Cultural pathways	Individualism
Cultural determinism	Globalization
Enculturation	

Social Role Theory

Objective 2f. To review the basic concepts of social role theory and its implications for the study of human development.

Another approach to thinking about the effect of the environment on development has been suggested by social psychologists such as Orville Brim (1966) and sociologists such as Talcott Parsons (Parsons & Bales, 1955). They traced the process of socialization and personality development through the person's participation in increasingly diverse and complex social roles. A **social role** is any set of behaviors that has a socially agreed-upon function and an accepted code of norms (Brown, 1965; Biddle & Thomas, 1966; Biddle, 1979). The term *role* was taken from the context of the theater. In a play, actors' behaviors are distinct and predictable because each actor has a part to play and follows a script. You will recall this metaphor from Shakespeare's analysis in *As You Like It*, "All the world's a stage, / and all the men and women merely players. / They have their exits and their entrances, / and one man in his time plays many parts" (Act 2, scene 7).

Role theory applies this same framework to social life (Biddle, 1986). The three elements of concern to role theory are the patterned characteristics of social behavior (**role enactment**), the parts or identities a person assumes (**social roles**), and the scripts or shared expectations for behavior that are linked to each part (**role expectations**). Social roles serve as a bridge between the individual and the society. Every society has a range of roles, and individuals learn about the expectations associated with them. As people enter new roles, they modify their behavior to conform to these role expectations. Each role is usually linked to one or more related or **reciprocal roles**. The student and the teacher, the parent and the child, and the salesperson and the customer are reciprocal roles. Each role is partly defined by the other roles that support it. The function of the role is determined by its relation to the surrounding role groups to which it is allied.

Four dimensions are used to analyze the impact of social roles on development: the *number* of roles a person occupies; the *intensity* of role involvement, or how deeply the person identifies with the role; the amount of *time* the role demands; and the extent to which the expectations associated with each role are either highly *structured* or *flexible* and open to improvisation. These features help account for experiences of role strain and role overload as various periods of life when the demands and intensity of multiple roles converge (see the box on Role Strain and Parenthood).

Implications for Human Development

All cultures offer new roles that await individuals as they move from one stage of life to another. Some of these roles may be directly associated with age, such as the role of a high school student. Other roles may be accessible only to those of a certain age who demonstrate other relevant skills, traits, or personal preferences. In many elementary schools, for example, the fifth-grade students become eligible to serve in the role of crossing guard to help the younger children get across the streets near the school. Families, organizations, and the larger community have implicit theories of development that determine what role positions open up for individuals in each age group. Some of the most important life roles persist across several stages, including child, parent, and sibling. The expectations for role performance remain the same in some respects, but change in others. We can begin to see how social roles provide consistency to life experiences and how they prompt new learning.

Involvement in personal relationships and social groups contributes to the formation of one's **social identity**—that aspect of the self-concept that is based on membership in a group or groups and on the importance and emotional salience of that membership (Tajfel, 1981). Some of these role relationships are personal—based on family, friendship, or intimate relationships. Others are political, religious, or ethnic. Some aspects of one's social identity may be associated with a stigmatized group, such as being homeless, unemployed, or on welfare (Deaux, Reid, Mizrahi, & Ethier, 1995). In modern societies, people are members of many groups and form complex social identities, in which many roles and their varying meanings and values are balanced and synthesized. Understanding a person's social identity helps account for which groups a person may view as ingroups and outgroups, why a person might discriminate against certain outgroups, or how a person's views of fairness and justice may be shaped (Simon & Klandermans, 2001).

The idea that one's social identity is crafted from experiences in a variety of roles is illustrated in the following narrative of Azhar, an 18-year-old male.

> Basically I feel that there are three main facets of what I feel are priorities in my life. What shape my decisions. One being my Pakistani heritage. My father and mother are from Pakistan, and growing up I was really ingrained in Pakistani culture, meaning that I was always exposed to the music, the culture, the tradition, the poetry of Iqbal, the whole family

APPLYING THEORY AND RESEARCH TO LIFE

Role Strain and Parenthood

A RECURRING THEME in the literature on parenthood is the experience of role strain. **Role strain** is defined as a sense of difficulty in meeting perceived role expectations or balancing competing role demands (Biddle, 1986). Each of the following dimensions of social roles may contribute to parental role strain: role intensity, time required, the structure or flexibility of the role, and the number and characteristics of other roles. Because the parent role has great intensity, the sense of involvement in all the behaviors associated with the role intensifies, and so does anxiety about failure to meet the expectations of the role. First-time parents especially may have little confidence in their ability to fulfill their roles, and the level of worry associated with the role rises accordingly.

The parent role takes a lot of time. Most first-time parents underestimate how much time infants and toddlers require. When new parents, especially mothers, reflect on the time they spend in a variety of social roles, they point to the parent role as more time consuming than any other role, now or in the past.

Role strain linked with parenting is related to the structure of the role. Some adults have very clear ideas about how they should enact their parent role, but many are unsure. Partners are likely to differ in their views on childrearing techniques. These differences require time to resolve. Because of the hardships or distress they recall from their own child-hoods, many adults do not want to raise their children the way they were raised themselves. They have to learn a new script for this role.

When parenting is added to other adult roles, especially those of worker and spouse, the demands of the new parental role may seem overwhelming. Most parents are also enacting a worker role. Workplace conditions that allow demands of the work role to spill over into family life can be a cause of work-family conflict and role strain. With corporate downsizing, many workers find that they have much more to do, more functions to fill, and increased pressure to do work after hours or at home. The need to make a long commute to work, expectations to bring work home, and expectations to be available for telephone or online interactions from home are all examples of work demands that can increase parental role strain (Voydanoff, 2005).

There are at least five ways to minimize role strain associated with the parent role (Cowan & Cowan, 1988; Newman, 2000; Allen, 2001; Bornstein, 2002):

1. Parents need to focus on a small number of expectations for their parenting role and focus on finding pleasure in meeting those expectations rather than worrying about the many expectations that are not being met.
2. The ability to delegate role responsibilities can reduce role strain. Parents who can hire others to help with some of the parenting responsibilities or who can turn to family members or friends for help will experience less role strain than those who are solely responsible for the parenting role. Couples who can flexibly alter and share household responsibilities in response to the demands of parenting will experience more satisfaction and less strain.
3. The ability to integrate several aspects of the role in one activity can reduce role strain. Some parents become quite inventive about ways to maintain contact with their infant while carrying out household chores

and other work and also preserving time with each other.
4. Role strain is reduced when partners reach consensus about their parent roles. New parents who have resolved their differences regarding childrearing philosophy, child care activities, and the division of household responsibilities experience less role strain and a higher level of marital satisfaction than those who continue to have opposing views on these issues.
5. Either find a work environment that has supportive attitudes and policies regarding work-family coordination, or take steps to change the existing work culture to be more flexible and positive toward workers who must meet concurrent family roles and responsibilities (Allen, 2001).

Critical Thinking Questions

1. How could you tell if parents are experiencing role strain? What kinds of behaviors would you be likely to observe? What types of emotional states might you observe?
2. How might parental role strain influence one's relationships with other family members? How might it influence one's performance as a worker?
3. What factors might make it difficult for partners to reach consensus about childrearing in order to reduce role strain?
4. How might characteristics of the child or children in the family contribute to parental role strain? What are some of these characteristics?
5. What are some demands of the work role that might produce work-family conflict and parental role strain? What are some characteristics of the workplace that might reduce parental role strain?

---

style of being Pakistani.… Then there comes the American aspect of my identity. I love pop culture, I love watching Steven Colbert and Jon Stewart on *The Daily Show*, I love rock music. I love being part of America in general. It gives you so much freedom to express your ideas in whatever ways you want. And then comes Islam, which ties into everything. And it sort of gives me a direction in which I look

to. From the start, as far as I can remember, I was always ingrained in an Islamic household. My parents always emphasized that you should be a good Muslim. We should have strong moral values…following the *sunnah* of the Prophet. And along with that came a lot of education. I was really involved in going to a lot of educational seminars. I was part of some Muslim youth organizations. (Sirin & Fine, p. 122)

The social role of healer can be found in most cultures. Although the costumes and techniques may differ, healers typically have access to knowledge not shared by most of the people in the society. What are some of the role expectations associated with healers in our society?

This narrative illustrates how youth forge a social identity from their early and ongoing family socialization, contemporary interests and preferences, and community expectations and resources.

Links to the Psychosocial Approach

Role relationships provide a central mechanism through which the socialization process takes place. In the psychosocial approach, one might think of the radius of significant relationships as an interconnected web of reciprocal roles and role relationships through which the expectations and demands of society make themselves known. The idea of reciprocity in roles is closely linked to the concept of interdependence of people at different psychosocial stages. The capacity of adults to cope with the challenges of their life stages and to achieve new ego strengths is intricately linked to the ability of children and youth to flourish and grow.

TABLE 2.7 Basic Concepts from Social Role Theory

Social role
Role enactment
Role expectations
Reciprocal roles
Social identity
Role strain

Social role theory helps clarify why this is so important, because children and adults occupy many reciprocal roles.

In the following chapters, we describe a number of life roles especially related to family, school, and work. As the number of roles increases, individuals must learn some of the skills of role playing, role differentiation, and role integration. The developmental crisis of individual identity versus identity confusion emphasizes the challenge of being able to integrate several diverse roles in order to preserve a sense of personal continuity. With each new role, one's self-definition changes and one's potential for influencing the world increases. For a list of the key concepts of social role theory, see Table 2.7.

Systems Theory

Objective 2g. To review the basic concepts of systems theory and its implications for the study of human development.

Systems theories attempt to describe and account for the characteristics of systems and the relationships among the component parts found within the system (Sameroff, 1982). Systems theories take the position that the whole is more than the sum of its parts. Any **system**—whether it is a cell, an organ, an individual, a family, or a corporation—is composed of interdependent elements that share some common goals, interrelated functions, boundaries, and an identity. The system cannot be wholly understood by identifying each of its component parts. The processes and relationships of those parts make for a larger, coherent entity. The language system, for example, is more than the capacity to make vocal utterances, use grammar, and acquire vocabulary. It is the coordination of these elements in a useful way in a context of shared meaning. Similarly, a family system is more than the sum of the characteristics and competencies of the individual family members.

A system cannot violate the laws that govern the functioning of its parts, but at the same time it cannot be explained solely by those laws. Biological functioning cannot violate the laws of physics and chemistry, but the laws of physics

The neighborhood is a microsystem. Children adapt their play to the physical characteristics of their neighborhoods. How might adaptive regulation differ for children who grow up in these two communities?

and chemistry cannot fully explain biological functioning. Similarly, children's capacities for cognitive growth cannot violate the laws of biological functioning, but biological growth does not fully explain the quality of thought.

Individuals, families, communities, schools, and societies are all examples of open systems. Ludwig von Bertalanffy (1950, 1968) defined **open systems** as structures that maintain their organization even though their parts constantly change. Just as the water in a river is constantly changing but the river itself retains its boundaries and course, so the molecules of human cells are constantly changing while the various biological systems retain their coordinated functions.

Systems change in the direction of adjusting to or incorporating more and more of the environment into themselves, in order to prevent disorganization as a result of environmental fluctuations (Sameroff, 1982). **Adaptation**—whether the concept is articulated by Darwin, Piaget, or Bandura—seems to be a fundamental process. Ervin Laszlo (1972) described this property of an open system as **adaptive self-regulation**. A system uses **feedback** mechanisms to identify and respond to environmental changes. The more information about the environment the system is capable of detecting, the more complex these feedback mechanisms must be. When the oxygen level of the environment is reduced, for example, you tend to grow sleepy. While you sleep, your breathing slows, and you use less oxygen. Some of these adjustments are managed unconsciously by the organization of biological systems. Others are managed more deliberately by efforts to minimize the effects of environmental changes. Most systems have a capacity for storing or saving resources so that temporary shortages do not disrupt their operations.

When open systems are confronted by new or changing environmental conditions, they have the capacity for **adaptive self-organization**. The system retains its essential identity by creating new substructures, revising the relationships among components, or creating new, higher levels of organization that coordinate existing substructures.

From the systems perspective, the components and the whole are always in tension. What one understands and observes depends on where one stands in this complex set of interrelationships. All living entities are both parts and wholes. A person is a part of a family, a classroom or work group, a friendship group, and a society. A person is also a whole—a coordinated, complex system composed of physical, cognitive, emotional, social, and self subsystems. Part of the story of human development is told in an analysis of the adaptive regulation and organization of those subsystems. Simultaneously, the story is told in the way larger systems fluctuate and impinge on individuals, forcing adaptive regulation and reorganization as a means of achieving stability at higher levels of system organization.

In an effort to elaborate and clarify the interlocking system of systems in which human behavior takes place, Urie Bronfenbrenner (1979, 1995, 1999) offered the following topography of the environmental structure (see Figure 2.4).

A **microsystem** is a pattern of activities, roles, and interpersonal relations experienced by the developing person in a given setting with particular physical and material characteristics.

A **mesosystem** comprises the interrelations among two or more settings in which the developing person actively participates (e.g., for a child, the relations among home, school, and neighborhood peer group; for an adult, among family, work, and social life).

An **exosystem** refers to one or more settings that do not involve the developing person as an active participant, but in which events occur that affect—or are affected by—what happens in the setting containing the developing person.

The **macrosystem** refers to consistencies in the form and content of lower-order systems (micro-, meso-, and exo-) that exist, or could exist, at the level of the subculture or the culture as a whole, along with any belief systems or ideologies underlying such consistencies (Bronfenbrenner, 1979, pp. 22, 25, 26).

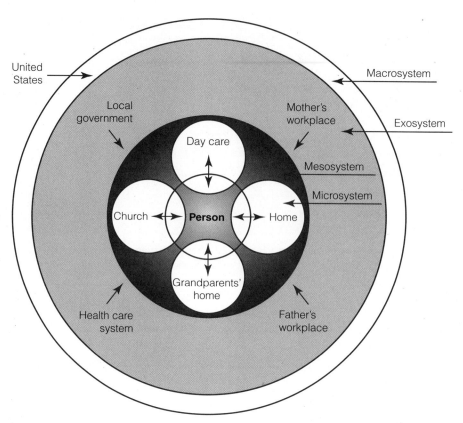

Specific examples of microsystems and systems in the exosystem are given, but many other systems could be shown. Arrows in the mesosystem show a two-way, or bidirectional influence; arrows in the exosystem are unidirectional, because the developing person does not participate in those settings. The person, the microsystems, and the relationship among systems change over time.

FIGURE 2.4 A Topography of the Relationship Among Systems
Source: Adapted from Bronfenbrenner, 1979.

The **chronosystem** refers to time (Bronfenbrenner, 1995). Both the individual and the systems in which that person is embedded change over time. What is more, the relationships among the systems change over time. Some of these changes are patterned, developmental transformations, such as the change in a child's capacity for coordinated movement and voluntary, goal-directed action. Other changes are societal, such as a community decision to restructure a school system from an elementary (Grades K–6), junior high (Grades 7–9), and high school (Grades 10–12) system to an elementary (Grades K–5), middle school (Grades 6–8), and high school (Grades 9–12) system. Finally, some changes reflect the decline or improvement of resources in a setting, as when a neighborhood becomes transformed through urban development.

Bronfenbrenner argued that development is influenced directly by the interactions that take place within a single microsystem, such as the family, and by the similarities and differences in patterns of interaction that occur across the various systems in which the person functions (the mesosystem). Events in adjoining systems, such as decisions in the workplace that affect the parents' work schedule or decisions in city government that affect resources for the local schools, also have an impact on development even though the child does not participate directly in these settings. Furthermore, the roles, norms, and resources within settings as well as the interrelationships among systems have a unique pattern of organization and reflect an underlying set of beliefs and values that differ from one culture or ethnic group to the next. These cultural characteristics are transmitted to the developing person.

Implications for Human Development

Systems theory has been applied to the study of the life span through **developmental systems theory** (Lerner, Dowling, & Roth, 2003). This perspective emphasizes the ongoing interaction and integration across many levels of the human organism from the genetic to the behavioral level, within the nested contexts of the person, family, community, and culture, to consider both continuity and change over individual and historical time. **Plasticity,** the capacity for change, is at the heart of this approach. The **person in the setting** is the focus of analysis. The challenge to developmental systems theory is to understand the reciprocal regulation of the person and the environment over time. How is the person shaped and defined by the contexts in which the person functions? How does the person influence these contexts to foster more optimal environments for growth (Bronfenbrenner, 2004)? In the framework of systems theory, the boundary between the person and the environment is fuzzy; as an open system, a person is continuously influenced by information and resources from the environment and, at the same time, creates or modifies the environment to preserve system functioning.

Systems theory has also been applied to the analysis of family functioning. Family systems theories focus on how families establish and maintain stable patterns of functioning. Families are viewed as emotional units identifiable by certain boundaries and rules (Broderick, 1993). The **boundaries** of the family determine who is considered to be a family member and who is an outsider. They influence the way information, support, and validation of the family unit are sought and the way new members are admitted into the family. Some families have very strict **rules** that maintain a narrow boundary around the family. Few sources of information or contact are admitted. Other families extend the sense of belonging to a wide range of people who bring ideas and resources to the family system.

Family systems are maintained by patterns of communication (Vogl-Bauer, 2003). Positive and negative **feedback loops** operate to stabilize, diminish, or increase certain types of interactions. For example, a feedback loop is positive when a child offers a suggestion and a parent recognizes and compliments the child on that suggestion. As a result, the child is encouraged to continue to offer suggestions, and the parent comes to view the child as someone who has valuable suggestions to offer. A feedback loop is negative if a parent ignores the child's suggestions or scolds the child for making them. The child is less likely to make further suggestions, and the parents' view of the child as someone who has no valuable ideas to offer is confirmed. Many positive and negative feedback loops operate in families to sustain the qualities of the system, such as the power hierarchy, level of conflict, and balance between autonomy and dependence among the members.

One of the most commonly noted characteristics of family systems is the **interdependence** of the family members. Changes in one family member are accompanied by changes in the others. Imagine for a moment that family members are standing in a circle and holding a rope. Each person is trying to exert enough tension on the rope to keep it tight and preserve the circular shape. The amount of tension each person must exert depends on what every other person is doing. Now imagine that one member of the family lets go of the rope and steps away. In order to retain the shape and tension of the rope, everyone else has to adjust his or her grip. Letting go of the rope is an analogy for many kinds of changes that can occur in a family—a parent becomes ill, a child goes off to college, or a parent takes on a demanding job outside of the home. The system adjusts by redefining relationships, modifying patterns of communication, and adjusting its boundaries. The members and their interdependencies change. Similar adjustments must be made if a member is added to the family system or when the system undergoes some other major transition.

The family systems perspective offers a distinct approach to clinical problems. A person who has been identified as dysfunctional is treated not as a lone individual but as part of a family system. From a systems theory perspective, the assumption is that the person's problems are a product of the interactions among family members. The only way to bring about changes in that person's functioning is to alter the functioning of the *other* members of the system as well. If the person is underfunctioning—that is, acting irresponsibly, not communicating, not performing at a level of capability, withdrawing, or acting impulsively—one assumes that others in the family are overfunctioning—that is, assuming many of the person's roles and responsibilities in order to take up the slack. The dysfunctional behavior is maintained because it is a component of an emotional unit. In other words, the dysfunction belongs neither to the person nor to the other family members but to the particular interdependence among the family members that operates to preserve the viability of the family system as a whole (Bowen, 1978).

Family systems are also interdependent with adjacent systems. Thus, the understanding of families requires an analysis of the resources and demands of other social systems that impinge on families and of the opportunities that families have for influencing adjoining systems. A woman who is experiencing an extremely demanding, stressful, and sexist work environment, for example, may be constantly tired, tense, and irritable in her behavior toward her family members. She may bring home the resentments from work in the way she treats and expects to be treated by the men and women in her family. If the job is important to her and her family, no one may be willing to acknowledge the disruptive impact that the work setting is having on family life. Family violence, the effects of unemployment on families, participation of mothers in the labor force, child care, and the role of parents in their children's schooling are all being examined from a systems perspective.

Links to the Psychosocial Approach

The psychosocial approach is quite compatible with the basic assumption of systems theory—that an understanding of development requires an analysis of the person embedded in a number of interrelated systems. Systems theory predicts that systems change through adaptive self-regulation and adaptive self-organization. The direction of this change is not necessarily patterned, except that it is expected to move in the direction of creating new, higher levels of organization to coordinate newly developed substructures. The nature of change is a product of efforts to retain a sense of system identity and boundaries in the face of multiple demands and shifts in environments. According to psychosocial theory, however, change is patterned. At each new stage of life, a person is propelled into increasingly complex social systems and encounters new stimulation for growth through participation in a greater variety of social relationships. As they mature, individuals develop new coping skills and devise strategies for new levels of participation in the social system. Eventually, they create innovative approaches for modifying the social system itself.

TABLE 2.8 Basic Concepts of Systems Theory

System
Open system
Adaptation
Adaptive self-regulation
Adaptive self-organization
Feedback
Microsystem
Mesosystem
Exosystem
Macrosystem
Chronosystem
Boundaries
Rules
Interdependence

Building on the assumption that development is a product of ongoing interactions between the person and society, the psychosocial approach suggests that both the diversity of microsystems in which one is embedded and the quality of one's connections to those microsystems will influence the direction of development. Feelings of belonging, attachment and connection to particular microsystems are associated with lower levels of anxiety, depression, and antisocial behavior. For example, in a study of middle-school-age adolescents, those who had a positive connection to home, school, and neighborhood had better grades in school than those who had low connection to these contexts. Having a positive connection to at least one of these microsystems served as a protective factor, providing a basis for self-esteem and a buffer against depression (Witherspoon, Schotland, Way, & Hughes, 2009). The specific configuration of microsystems and one's role or place in those systems contribute to the positive or negative direction of development over the life span.

For a summary of the key concepts of systems theory, see Table 2.8.

CASE STUDY

JACK MANASKY AND HIS DAUGHTER MARILYN

Jack Manasky has been widowed for six years. He still writes letters to his beloved wife Anna, keeping her up to date on the events of his life. In the following letter, Jack writes of a small episode, but a lot is revealed about Jack's life, his sense of self, and his relationship with his adult daughter.

Dear Anna,

I am writing this from a coffee shop. My seat is by the window. Why, you are thinking, am I sitting in a coffee shop when I have a perfectly good house to sit in? Okay, I will tell you.

Marilyn, our dear daughter, may she have a long and wonderful life, this dear child of ours who is no longer a child, decided last month to cure me. Cure me of what, I do not know. I did not ask. One day she came in. A day no different from any other. I was sitting in the living room watching the television news.

Marilyn went into the kitchen to empty her grocery bags. "Dad," she said. "I bought you new coffee. It's decaffeinated." "What does this mean, decaffeinated?" I asked. This I said from my chair, why should I walk into the kitchen? "Unleaded, Dad. You shouldn't be drinking regular coffee. It's a diuretic."

By this time she was standing in the doorway of the kitchen, folding her paper bag. "It means it takes too much water out of you. You're too old for that."

New? Decaffeinated. Diuretic. Too much water. Let her do what she wants. What did I care?

I forgot about it. The next day, I got up, I fed the birds, read the newspaper, and drank my coffee. No big deal. But that afternoon, a headache. And what a headache, loud, pounding, I could not think. This was not so new to me. Headaches. They come, they go. But this one, it was different. The next day, it was still with me. And the next day also. Like a black cloud, it filled my head with thunder, everywhere I went.

When Marilyn came on the third day, I remembered. "Marilyn," I said, "this decaffeinated coffee, however you call it, it is killing me."

"Ha, ha," she laughed. "It's not killing you, Dad. It's good for you."

"It's murdering me. Go, buy me some coffee. Or tomorrow you will be pouring this decaffeinated coffee on my grave."

"Dad," she said. "You have a headache? You'll get over it. It's not the decaf that's giving it to you. It's from no caffeine. It'll stop soon." She laughed again, and then she was gone. This is what she does. Comes into my house, checks things off her list, and then disappears.

I sat down. "Okay." I said to the floor. "I will buy my own coffee."

Source: From "Starboys" by Elissa Goldberg in *Families in Later Life: Connections and Transitions*, by Alexis J. Walker et al., pp. 250–251. Copyright 2001 Pine Forge Press. Reprinted by permission.

CRITICAL THINKING AND CASE ANALYSIS

Consider what each of the theories discussed in this chapter might have to offer in helping to understand this interaction between an aging, widowed father and his adult daughter.

EVOLUTIONARY THEORY

1. How can evolutionary theory account for Marilyn's motivation to care for her aging father? What aspect of fitness is enhanced when children use their resources to support their parents' longevity and well-being?
2. How would you describe the interactions among the biological, psychological, and societal systems in this case?

PSYCHOSEXUAL THEORY

3. How can psychosexual theory account for Marilyn's motivation to care for her aging father?

4. How can psychosexual theory account for Jack's coping strategy of writing letters to his deceased wife?

5. If Jack watches television news as part of his daily routine, why doesn't he know about decaffeinated coffee? What defense mechanisms might he be using to block out information about the negative effects of coffee on health?

COGNITIVE DEVELOPMENTAL THEORY

6. How would you characterize Marilyn's level of cognitive reasoning as she tries to modify her father's coffee-drinking behavior?

7. How would you characterize Jack's level of cognitive reasoning about the relationship of his headaches to the new coffee?

LEARNING THEORIES

8. How might cognitive behaviorism explain the establishment of a pattern or routine of behavior such as the one Jack describes—feed the birds, read the newspaper, drink a cup of coffee?

9. What is Jack learning about his daughter from her behaviors? "This is what she does. Comes into my house, checks things off her list, and then disappears."

10. What principles of learning theory could help Marilyn be more effective in altering her father's behavior?

CULTURAL THEORY

11. What can you detect from this case about the cultural norms for the relationship of an adult daughter and an aging father?

12. Can you describe a cultural context in which Jack and Marilyn might have a very different type of relationship and a different style of interaction?

13. How is the U.S. cultural value of independence and individualism expressed in the case?

SOCIAL ROLE THEORY

14. How is Marilyn defining her role as an adult child of a widowed father?

15. How is Jack defining his role as Marilyn's father?

16. What role does Anna, Jack's deceased wife, play in Jack's life?

SYSTEMS THEORY

17. How would you evaluate the feedback mechanisms between Jack and Marilyn and their impact on each other's behavior?

18. How might macrosystem values and resources regarding health and nutrition be influencing Marilyn's behavior toward her father?

19. At the end of the case, Jack says, "Okay, I will buy my own coffee." Which concepts presented in this chapter best explain a person's decision to change his behavior in order to achieve a new goal?

Chapter Summary

Objective 1. To define the concept of theory and explain how theories contribute to the study of human development.

A theory is a logical system of concepts that helps explain observations and points to underlying processes or relationships that are not readily observable. In order to understand a theory, one must consider which phenomena the theory is trying to explain, the assumptions that underlie the theory, and the theory's predictions about causal relationships or systematic associations. A theory of human development typically addresses several of the following questions: What is the direction of change over the life span? What are the mechanisms that account for continuity and change? What is the relevance of early experiences for later development? How do physical, cognitive, emotional, and social functions interact? How do the physical and social environments impact development? What factors typically place the person at risk for problems in development at various periods of life?

The seven theoretical perspectives reviewed in this chapter each take a distinct approach to explaining continuity and change across the life span. Table 2.9 provides an overview of the primary emphasis and aspects of development highlighted in each of the theories.

Objective 2a. To review the basic concepts of the theory of evolution and its implications for the study of human development.

Evolutionary theory provides a framework for understanding individual development within the broad perspective of the biological evolution of the human species. Although a life span of 85 or 90 years may seem long, it is but a flicker in the millions of years of biological adaptation. Evolutionary theory highlights the genetically governed aspects of growth and development. The environment provides the specific conditions that require adaptation. However, adaptive change can occur only if it is supported by the genetically based characteristics of the organism. The basic mechanism that accounts for species change over many generations is natural selection.

Ethology, the study of evolutionarily significant behaviors, provides a systematic approach to analyzing reproductive practices, caregiving behaviors, strategies for obtaining resources, and other behaviors that contribute to individual and species survival. Evolutionary psychology focuses on understanding the human mind in terms of the problems of survival it has been shaped to solve.

Objective 2b. To review the basic concepts of psychosexual theory and its implications for the study of human development.

According to psychosexual theory, development follows a biologically determined path in which patterns of social

TABLE 2.9 Overview of Seven Theories of Development

THEORY	EMPHASIS	SPECIFIC ASPECTS OF HUMAN DEVELOPMENT
Evolutionary theory	The emergence and modification of species as a result of natural selection	Fitness and inclusive fitness; the adaptive value of species' characteristics
Psychosexual theory	The origins and development of mental life	Personality development, emotions, motivation, impulse control, morality
Cognitive developmental theories	The origins and development of cognition	The development of reasoning and logical thought from infancy through adolescence; the role of culture and the teaching/learning process
Learning theories	The formation of relatively permanent changes in behavior as a result of experience	Learned behaviors, observational learning, the distinction between learning and performance, affects, expectancies, values, goals and plans
Cultural theory	Learned systems of meanings and patterns of behavior shared by groups and transmitted from one generation to the next	The nature and direction of culturally guided developmental pathways; diversity in worldview
Social role theory	Socially constructed roles and role relationships that bridge the individual and society	The development of the self in social life; role gain, role loss, and the enactment of multiple roles
Systems theory	Processes that account for continuity and change in complex systems	The interdependence of elements within and between systems; emergence of new properties and behaviors as a result of self-regulation and self-organization; bidirectional nature of influence across system boundaries

relationships change as a result of emerging sexual impulses and the sexualization of body zones. Culture plays a major role in establishing the taboos and acceptable patterns of sexual gratification that lead to conflicts, fixations, and strategies for sublimation. The content of the unconscious—including sexual impulses, wishes, and fears—guides behavior and gives it meaning. Psychosexual theory emphasizes the years of infancy and childhood as those in which basic personality patterns are established. It also identifies the family, especially the parent-child relationship, as the primary context within which conflicts related to the socialization of sexual impulses are resolved. In contemporary psychoanalytic theory, interpersonal needs and the relational context of ego development are highlighted in contrast to the drive-based perspective of traditional psychosexual theory.

Objective 2c. To review the basic concepts of cognitive developmental theories and their implications for the study of human development.

Cognitive developmental theories focus on the etiology of rational thought and the capacity for scientific reasoning. Piaget's cognitive theory, like psychosexual theory, views development as the product of a biologically guided plan for growth and change. The elements that make cognitive growth possible are all present in the genetic information that governs the growth of the brain and nervous system. However, the process of intellectual growth requires interaction with a diverse and responsive environment. Cognitive development is fostered by the recognition of discrepancies between existing schemes and new experiences. Through the reciprocal processes of assimilation and accommodation, schemes are modified and integrated to form the basis for organizing and explaining experience. The child is viewed as actively constructing knowledge through sensory, motor, and representational exploration.

Vygotsky's contribution to cognitive theory places the development of higher mental processes in a dynamic social context. Although thinking and reasoning are dependent on biologically based capacities, the way in which mental activity is organized reflects unique characteristics of the social context, especially as culture is transmitted through language, tools, and social relationships.

Objective 2d. To review the basic concepts of learning theories and their implications for the study of human development.

Learning theories focus on the mechanisms that permit individuals to respond to their diverse environments and the changes in thought and behavior that accompany changes in the environment. Behavior can be shaped and modified by systematic changes in environmental conditions. According to learning theorists, human beings have an especially flexible behavioral system. No assumptions are made about universal stages of growth. As conditions in the environment change, response patterns also change. Similarity among individuals at a particular period of life is explained by the fact that they are exposed to similar environmental conditions, patterns of reinforcement, and models. Consistent contingencies between behaviors and their consequences result in the formation of cognitive expectations as well as behaviors.

Objective 2e. To review the basic concepts of cultural theory and its implications for the study of human development.

Cultural theory, like the learning theories, emphasizes the role of the environment in directing the course of development. However, within the cultural theory framework, the focus is on the patterns of meaning that are given to biological maturation as well as the activities and routines that shape developmental pathways. Cultural theory recognizes certain constants in developmental tasks, but the ideal direction and socialization processes for guiding development differ widely across cultural groups. What one defines as the normal or natural pattern and tempo of change in competence, roles, and status depends largely on the way a society recognizes and treats individuals of different ages, sexes, and degrees of kinship.

Objective 2f. To review the basic concepts of social role theory and its implications for the study of human development.

Social role theory suggests that learning is organized around key social functions called roles. As people enact roles, they integrate their behavior into meaningful units. Meaning is provided by the definition of the role and by the expectations of those in reciprocal roles. Development is a product of entry into an increasing number of complex roles over the life span. As children acquire and lose roles, they change their self-definitions and their relationships with social groups. Most societies define roles that are linked with gender, age, marital status, and kinship. These roles provide patterning to the life course. However, the patterns are understood to be products of the structures and functions of the society rather than of genetic information.

Objective 2g. To review the basic concepts of systems theory and its implications for the study of human development.

Systems theory emphasizes the multidimensional sources of influence on individuals and the simultaneous influence of individuals on the systems of which they are a part. Each person is at once a component of one or more larger systems, and a system unto the self. One must approach the study of development from many angles, identifying the critical resources, the flow of resources, and the transformation of resources that underlie an adaptive process of reorganization and growth. This perspective has been applied to an analysis of families and family change as well as to individual development over the life span.

Key Terms

accommodation, 36
adaptation, 36
adaptive self-organization, 51
adaptive self-regulation, 51
affects, 42
anal stage, 31
applied behavioral analysis, 57
assimilation, 36
boundaries, 53
chronosystem, 52
cognition, 35
cognitive competencies, 42
cognitive map, 42
collectivism, 45
concrete operational thought, 37
conscious processes, 29
continuity, 44
cultural determinism, 44
cultural pathways, 44
cultural tools, 38
culture, 38
defense mechanism, 32

developmental systems theory, 52
discontinuity, 44
disequilibrium, 36
drives, 28
ecological niche, 25
ego, 30
egocentric speech, 39
egocentrism, 37
electra complex, 31
equilibrium, 36
ethology, 25
evolutionary psychology, 26
exosystem, 51
expectancies, 42
extinction, 25
feedback, 51
feedback loops, 53
fitness, 25
fixation, 57
formal operational thought, 37
genital stage, 31
goals, 42

higher mental processes, 38
id, 29
identification, 30
imitation, 41
inclusive fitness, 25
individualism, 45
inner speech, 39
interdependence, 53
intermental, 38
intramental, 38
latency, 31
law of natural selection, 25
lower mental processes, 38
macrosystem, 51
mesosystem, 51
metacognition, 38
microsystem, 51
model, 41
modeling, 41
multiply determined, 28
object relations paradigm, 33
object relations theory, 33

Further Reflection

1. Imagine that you had to explain development to a new parent. What mechanisms or processes do the seven theories offer to explain how children grow up and change from infancy into adulthood?

2. Which of the theories is most like your own beliefs about development? Which is least like your own beliefs? Why?

3. In what ways do the theories overlap? Give some examples of ways that two or more of the theories use different words or terms to explain basically the same thing.

4. In what ways do each of the theories offer something unique to the understanding of development? Give some examples of ways in which one or two of the theories contribute something that does not seem to be included in the others.

5. Psychosocial theory assumes that development is a product of the interactions among the biological, psychological, and societal systems. Try to identify the role of these three systems in each of the theories discussed in this chapter.

6. What are the implications of each theory for the educational environment for young children, adolescents, college students, or adult learners? If you were in charge of creating a learning environment, which theory or combination of theories would you draw on to guide your planning and your interaction with students?

Psychology CourseMate

To access additional course materials, including CourseMate, please visit www.cengagebrain.com. At the Cengagebrain .com home page, search for the ISBN of your title (from the back cover of your book) using the search box at the top of the page. This will take you to the product page where these resources can be found.

Casebook

For additional case material related to this chapter, see the case of "A School Debate," in *Life Span Development: A Case Book*, by Barbara and Philip Newman, Laura Landry-Meyer, and Brenda J. Lohman, on page 13. This case focuses on the opinions of teachers and the school principal at a middle school about how to increase school attendance and reduce student tardiness. The varying suggestions reflect the application of different theories of human development to the solution of an important real-world problem. The case provides practice in linking theoretical ideas about causes of behavior to potential strategies for intervention.

© 2011 Estate of Pablo Picasso/Artists Rights Society (ARS), New York/Cameraphoto Arte, Venice/Art Resource, NY

Psychosocial theory focuses on the ongoing interaction of the person and the social environment. Development is a balancing act between positive forces toward growth and negative forces for self-protection and withdrawal. Accompanied by the right music, each life holds the promise for creative energy and meaningful social connection.

Psychosocial Theory

CHAPTER 3

Chapter Objectives

1. To explain the rationale for using psychosocial theory as an organizing framework for the study of human development.

2. To define the six basic concepts of psychosocial theory: stages of development, developmental

tasks, psychosocial crisis, central process for resolving the crisis, radius of significant relationships, and coping.

3. To evaluate psychosocial theory, pointing out its strengths and weaknesses.

IN THIS CHAPTER we introduce the basic concepts of psychosocial theory that provide the integrating framework for our psychosocial approach to the study of human development. Psychosocial theory presents human development as a product of the ongoing interaction between an individual's (*psycho*) biological and psychological needs and abilities on the one hand and societal (*social*) expectations and demands on the other hand. The theory accounts for patterns of individual development that emerge from a biopsychosocial process.

The Rationale for Emphasizing Psychosocial Theory

Objective 1. To explain the rationale for using psychosocial theory as an organizing framework for the study of human development.

We have selected **psychosocial theory** as an organizing framework for the text because of its range and scope. Having read Chapter 2, you probably realize that psychosocial theory is not the only or most widely accepted theory for studying human development. However, it combines three features that make it especially useful as we strive to link the broad field of human development to applications in health, human services, education, and social welfare (Green, 2008):

1. Psychosocial theory addresses growth across the life span, identifying and differentiating central issues from infancy through old age. It also suggests that experiences of adolescence or adulthood can lead to a review and reinterpretation of earlier periods.
2. Psychosocial theory assumes that individuals have the capacity to contribute to their own psychological development at each stage of life. People have the ability to integrate, organize, and conceptualize their experiences in order to protect themselves, cope with challenges, and direct the course of their lives. Therefore, the direction of development is shaped by self-regulation as well as by the ongoing interaction of biological and societal influences.
3. Psychosocial theory takes into consideration the active contribution of **culture** to individual growth. At each life stage, cultural goals, aspirations, and social expectations and requirements make demands that evoke individual

reactions. These reactions influence which of a person's capabilities will be developed further. This vital link between the individual and the culture is a key mechanism of development. Each society has its own view of the qualities that reflect maturity. These qualities are infused into the lives of individuals and help determine the direction of growth within the society.

The person who identified and developed psychosocial theory was Erik H. Erikson. He initially was trained as a psychoanalyst. His theory was influenced by the work of many others, including Sigmund and Anna Freud, Peter Blos, Robert White, Jean Piaget, and Robert Havighurst, whose ideas you will encounter throughout this book. His wife, Joan, was an important intellectual collaborator as well. Erik and Joan worked together to formulate the first presentation of psychosocial theory and its eight stages of development in 1950 (J. M. Erikson, 1988). The case study, which was written by Erikson, gives us a brief look into his early life and leads us to speculate about how his life experiences may have guided the direction of his theoretical work. Just like other great thinkers of his time, being an outsider seems to have had some advantages for Erikson, allowing him to approach the study of human development from a unique and creative point of view (Dunbar, 2000).

CASE STUDY

ERIK H. ERIKSON: A BIOGRAPHICAL CASE STUDY OF PSYCHOSOCIAL DEVELOPMENT

Erik Erikson (1902–1994) illustrates the psychosocial perspective by describing the personal, family, and societal factors that contributed to his own identity crisis.

There is first of all the question of origin, which often looms large in individuals who are driven to be original. I grew up in Karlsruhe in southern Germany as the son of a pediatrician, Dr. Theodor Homburger, and his wife Karla, née Abrahamsen, a native of Copenhagen, Denmark. All through my earlier childhood, they kept secret from me the fact that my mother had been married previously; and that I was the son of a Dane who had abandoned her before my birth. They apparently thought that such secretiveness was not only workable (because children then were not held to know what they had not been told) but also advisable, so that I would feel thoroughly at home in their home. As children will do, I played in with this and more or less forgot the period before the age of three, when mother and I had lived alone. Then her friends had been artists working in the folk style of Hans Thoma of the Black Forest. They, I believe, provided my first male imprinting before I had to come to terms with that intruder, the bearded doctor, with his healing love and mysterious instruments. Later, I enjoyed going back and forth between the painters' studios and our house, the first floor of which, in the afternoons, was filled with tense and trusting mothers and children. My sense of being "different" took refuge (as it is apt to do even in children without such acute life problems) in fantasies of how I, the son of much better parents, had been altogether a foundling. In the meantime, however, my adoptive father was anything but the proverbial stepfather. He had

given me his last name (which I have retained as a middle name) and expected me to become a doctor like himself.

Identity problems sharpen with that turn in puberty when images of future roles become inescapable. My stepfather was the only professional man (and a highly respected one) in an intensely Jewish small bourgeois family, while I (coming from a racially mixed Scandinavian background) was blond and blue-eyed, and grew flagrantly tall. Before long, then, I was referred to as "goy" in my stepfather's temple; while to my schoolmates I was a "Jew." Although during World War I, I tried desperately to be a good German chauvinist, I became a "Dane" when Denmark remained neutral.

At the time, like other youths with artistic or literary aspirations, I became intensely alienated from everything my bourgeois family stood for. At that point, I set out to be different. After graduation from the type of high school called a humanistic Gymnasium, . . . I went to art school, but always again took to wandering. . . . And in those days every self-respecting stranger in his own (northern) culture drifted sooner or later to Italy, where endless time was spent soaking up the southern sun and the ubiquitous sights with their grand blend of artifact and nature. I was a "Bohemian" then.

Source: Erikson, 1975.

CRITICAL THINKING QUESTIONS

As you think about this autobiographical case, consider the following questions:

1. Why did Erikson feel like a "stranger in his own culture"?
2. What are the biological, psychological, and societal factors that contributed to Erikson's identity crisis?
3. What factors from childhood appear to be influencing his experiences as an adolescent?
4. Who are the significant figures in Erikson's life, the radius of significant others, who influenced his sense of how he should behave and who he should strive to become?
5. What factors might have contributed to Erikson's ability to cope with the challenges of this period of his life, eventually finding a direction and meaning to which he could commit his talent and energy?
6. Based on Erikson's account of his childhood and adolescence, how might his life experiences and cultural context have influenced the nature and focus of his psychosocial theory?

Erik H. Erikson and Joan Erikson, the parents of psychosocial theory.

Basic Concepts of Psychosocial Theory

Objective 2. To define the six basic concepts of psychosocial theory: stages of development, developmental tasks, psychosocial crisis, central process for resolving the crisis, radius of significant relationships, and coping.

Psychosocial theory, as we use it in this book, offers an organizational framework for considering individual

© 2010 Jupiterimages Corporation

Dressed in her ball gown and wearing the traditional tiara, Lucinda dances with her father at her Quinceanara. This cultural celebration of the 15th birthday marks Lucinda's transition into young womanhood.

development within the larger perspective of psychosocial evolution. **Psychosocial evolution**, a construct proposed by Julian Huxley (1941, 1942), refers to the range of human abilities that allows us to gather knowledge from our ancestors and transmit it to our descendants. Childrearing practices, education, and modes of communication are examples of mechanisms that transmit information and ways of thinking from one generation to the next. At the same time, people devise new information, new ways of thinking, and new ways of teaching their discoveries to others. In this way, psychosocial evolution has proceeded at a rapid pace, bringing with it changes in technology and ideology that have allowed us to create and modify our physical and social environments. The transmission of values and knowledge across generations requires the maturation of individuals who are capable of creating knowledge, symbolizing it, adapting it, and transferring it to others. At the same time, societies change, posing new challenges for adaptation. People change and grow, enhancing their potential for carrying their own and succeeding generations forward.

Psychosocial theory accounts for systematic change over the life span through six basic concepts: (1) stages of development, (2) developmental tasks, (3) psychosocial crises, (4) a central process for resolving the crisis at each stage, (5) a radiating network of significant relationships, and (6) coping—the new behavior people generate to meet new challenges. These concepts will be defined in the following sections. However, each concept includes stage-specific content that will be elaborated on in subsequent chapters.

Stages of Development

A **developmental stage** is a period of life that is characterized by a specific underlying organization. At every stage, some characteristics differentiate that stage from the preceding and succeeding stages. Stage theories propose a specific direction for development. At each stage, the accomplishments from the previous stages provide resources for mastering the new challenges. In the process of development, it is not uncommon to observe patterns of plateaus, where the level of competence remains steady while the person integrates new abilities, followed by a spurt of rapid reorganization as the person attains a new, more complex level of functioning (Dawson, Commons, Wilson, & Fischer, 2005). Each stage is unique and leads to the acquisition of new skills related to new capabilities (Davison, King, Kitchener, & Parker, 1980; Fischer & Silvern, 1985; Miller, 2002).

Within the framework of psychosocial theory, the concept of stages of development refers to a pattern of changes in the self-concept based on new cognitive capacities, new learning, and the acquisition of new relationship skills. At each stage, the biological, psychological, and societal systems converge around a set of defining challenges that require a new view of the self in society, and a new way of relating to others (Whitbourne, Sneed, & Sayer, 2009). You can verify the stage concept through reflection on your own past. You can probably recall earlier periods when you were very preoccupied by efforts first to gain your parents' approval, then to win acceptance by your peers, and later to understand yourself. Each of these concerns may have appeared all-encompassing at the time, but eventually each gave way to a new preoccupation. At each stage, you were confronted with a unique set of problems that required the integration of your personal needs and skills with the social demands of your culture. The end product was a new way of thinking about the self, and a new approach for engaging in interactions with others.

Erikson (1963) proposed eight stages of psychosocial development. His formulation of these stages can be traced in part to the stages of psychosexual development proposed by Freud and in part to Erikson's own observations and rich mode of thinking. Figure 3.1 shows the chart that Erikson produced in *Childhood and Society* to describe the stages of psychosocial development. The shaded boxes identify the main psychosocial conflicts of each stage. If the conflicts of the stage are handled well, a new sense of mastery or competence emerges. In Erikson's original model, you will note that the periods of life are given names, such as oral–sensory or puberty and adolescence, but no ages. This approach reflects Erikson's emphasis on an individual timetable for development, guided by both biological maturation and cultural expectations, rather than a strict chronological time frame for development.

Erikson (1963) proposed that the stages of development follow the **epigenetic principle**—a biological plan for growth that allows each function to emerge systematically until the fully functioning organism has developed. An assumption of this and other stage theories is that the stages form a sequence. Although one can anticipate challenges that will occur at a later stage, one passes through the stages in an orderly pattern of growth. In the logic of psychosocial theory, the entire life span is required for all the functions of psychosocial development to appear and become integrated. There is no going back to an earlier stage,

because experience makes retreat impossible. In contrast to other stage theories, however, Erikson suggested that one can review and reinterpret previous stages in the light of new insight or new experiences.

Furthermore, the themes of earlier stages may reemerge at any point. Through reflection and insight, a person can find new meaning or a new resolution to an earlier conflict. Joan Erikson reflects on the fluidity and hopefulness in this perspective:

> This sequential growth . . . is now known to be more influenced by the social milieu than was in previous years considered possible. . . . Where a strength is not adequately developed according to the given sequence for its scheduled period of critical resolution, the supports of the environment may bring it into appropriate balance at a later period. Hope remains constant throughout life that more sturdy resolutions of the basic confrontation may be realized. (J. M. Erikson, 1988, pp. 74–75)

		1	2	3	4	5	6	7	8
1.	Oral–sensory	Basic trust vs. Mistrust							
2.	Muscular–anal		Autonomy vs. Shame, doubt						
3.	Locomotor–genital			Initiative vs. Guilt					
4.	Latency				Industry vs. Inferiority				
5.	Puberty and adolescence					Identity vs. Role confusion			
6.	Young adulthood						Intimacy vs. Isolation		
7.	Adulthood							Genera-tivity vs. Stagnation	
8.	Maturity								Ego integrity vs. Despair

FIGURE 3.1 Erikson's Model of the Psychosocial Stages of Development
Source: Erikson, 1963.

The epigenetic principle assumes that it takes the entire life span, from the prenatal period through elderhood for all facets of human capacity to emerge. In later adulthood and elderhood grandparents transmit the wisdom of their generation to their grandchildren by teaching them stories, songs, customs, and beliefs.

© Lawrence Migdale/Photo Researchers

The concept of life stages permits us to consider the various aspects of development, such as physical growth, social relationships, and cognitive capacities, at a given period of life and to speculate about their interrelation. It also encourages a focus on the experiences that are unique to each life period—experiences that deserve to be understood both in their own right and for their contribution to subsequent development. When programs and services are designed to address critical needs in such areas as education, health care, housing, and social welfare, the developmental stage approach allows the designers to focus on the needs and resources of the particular population to be served.

Despite the usefulness of a stage approach, one must avoid thinking of stages as pigeonholes. Being in a given stage does not mean that a person cannot function at other levels. It is not unusual for people to anticipate later challenges before they become dominant. Many children of toddler and preschool age, for example, play house, envisioning having a husband or a wife and children. You might say that, in this play, they are anticipating the issues of intimacy and generativity that lie ahead. The experience of having a child—whether this occurs at age 18, 25, or 35—is likely to raise issues of generativity, even if the theory suggests that this theme is not in its peak ascendancy until middle adulthood (McAdams & de St. Aubin, 1998). Whereas some elements of each psychosocial theme can be observed at all ages, the intensity with which they are expressed at certain times marks their importance in the definition of a developmental stage. Erikson, Erikson, and Kivnick (1986) put it this way:

The epigenetic chart also rightly suggests that the individual is never struggling only with the tension that is focal at the time. Rather, at every successive developmental stage, the individual is also increasingly engaged in the anticipation of tensions that have yet to become focal and in re-experiencing those tensions that were inadequately integrated when they were focal; similarly engaged are those whose age-appropriate integration was then, but is no longer, adequate. (p. 39)

As one leaves a stage, the achievements of that period are neither lost nor irrelevant to later stages. Important ego strengths emerge from the successful resolution of conflicts at every stage. Some of these strengths may be challenged or reorganized as events take place later in life that call into question the essential beliefs established in an earlier period. For example, the psychosocial conflict during early school age is initiative versus guilt. Its positive outcome, a sense of initiative, is a joy in innovation and experimentation and a willingness to take risks in order to learn more about the world. Once achieved, the sense of initiative provides a positive platform for the formation of social relationships and for further creative intellectual inquiry and discovery. However, experiences in a highly authoritarian school environment or in a very judgmental, shaming personal relationship may cause one to inhibit this sense of initiative or to mask it with a facade of indifference.

The concept of the psychosocial stages of development is very good as far as it goes, but Erikson's road map seems incomplete. Three criticisms of this layout of the life span have been raised. First, although the boxes in the figure look very even and comparable, each stage is actually of very different length. Second, the figure suggests discrete shifts from one stage to the next, when in fact the themes of these stages overlap (McAdams & de St. Aubin, 1992). Transitions from stage to stage are not instantaneous. Movement from one stage to the next is the result of changes in several major systems, which takes place gradually. Third, if the idea of psychosocial evolution has validity—and we believe it does—new stages can be expected to develop as a culture evolves.

In this text, we have identified 11 stages of psychosocial development, each with the following approximate age range: (1) *prenatal*, from conception to birth; (2) *infancy*, from birth to 2 years; (3) *toddlerhood*, 2 and 3 years; (4) *early school age*, 4 to 6 years; (5) *middle childhood*, 6 to 12 years; (6) *early adolescence*, 12 to 18 years; (7) *later adolescence*, 18 to 24 years; (8) *early adulthood*, 24 to 34 years; (9) *middle adulthood*, 34 to 60 years; (10) *later adulthood*, 60 to 75 years; and (11) *elderhood,* 75 until death.

By discussing a prenatal stage, two stages of adolescent development rather than one, and elderhood, we are adding three stages to those proposed by Erikson. This revision is a product of our analysis of the research literature, observations through research and practice, discussions with colleagues, and suggestions from other stage theorists.

The addition of these three new stages provides a good demonstration of the process of theory construction. Theories of human development emerge and change within a cultural and historical context. The differentiation of adolescence into two stages, for example, is a product of changes in the timing of onset of puberty in modern society, the expanding need for education and training before entry into the world of work, related changes in the structure of the educational system, and the variety of available life choices in work, marriage, parenting, and ideology.

Figure 3.2 shows the 11 stages of psychosocial development as presented in this textbook. The age range given for each stage is only an approximation. Each person has a uniquely personal timetable for growth. Differences associated with poverty, health, cultural group (e.g., differing rates of longevity), and exposure to environmental risks also lead to different timetables. The lengths of the stages vary, from the 9 months of the prenatal period to the roughly 26 years of middle adulthood.

Developmental Tasks

Robert J. Havighurst first introduced the concept of **developmental tasks**. He believed that human development is a process in which people attempt to learn the tasks required of them by the society to which they are adapting. These tasks change with age, because each society has **age-graded expectations** for behavior. "Living in a modern society is a long series of tasks to learn" (Havighurst, 1972, p. 2). In Havighurst's view, the person who learns well receives satisfaction and reward; the person who does not suffers unhappiness and social disapproval.

Although Havighurst's view of development emphasized the guiding role of society in determining which skills need to be acquired at a certain age, he did not totally ignore the role of physical maturation. Havighurst believed that there are **sensitive periods** for learning developmental tasks—that is, times when the person is most ready to acquire a new ability. Havighurst called these periods **teachable moments**. Most people learn developmental tasks at the time and in the sequence appropriate in their society. If a particular task is not learned during the sensitive period, it may be much more difficult to learn later on.

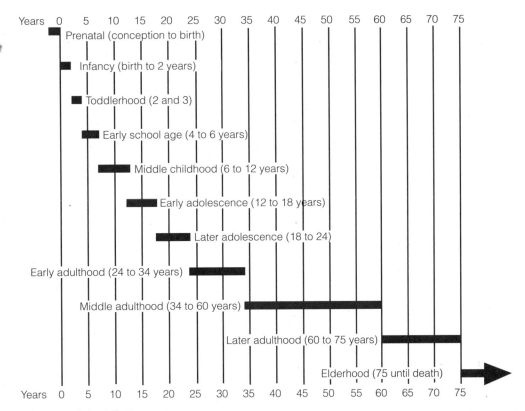

FIGURE 3.2 The 11 Stages of the Life Span

Toddlerhood is a sensitive period for language development, when parent-child conversations are especially critical.

At each stage of life, one faces new developmental tasks that contribute to increased mastery over one's environment. These tasks reflect areas of accomplishment in physical, cognitive, social, and emotional development, as well as development of the self-concept. The specific tasks we identify differ from those outlined in Havighurst's writings. Our choice of tasks is based on broad areas of accomplishment that have been identified by researchers as critical to psychological and social growth at each stage of life in a modern, technological culture. We recognize that the demands for growth may differ according to the orientation and complexity of a particular society. For example, in comparing gender role norms in Iran and the United States, Thomas (1999) pointed out that the legal minimum age for women to marry in Iran is 9 years and that at any age, Iranian women must have permission from their father or grandfather to marry. We have identified early adulthood—roughly ages 24 through 34—as the time when most people in the United States are focusing on exploring intimate relationships and making decisions about marriage. In the United States, women are free to marry without parental or family consent after age 18. Thus, the developmental task associated with establishing a commitment to an intimate partner would be present in both cultures, but the ages at which this task is usually addressed and the context for forming such a commitment differ from one society to the next.

The basic premise associated with the concept of developmental tasks, regardless of their specific content, is that a relatively small number of major psychosocial challenges dominate a person's problem-solving efforts and learning during a given stage of life. As these tasks are mastered, new competencies enhance the person's ability to engage in more complex social relationships and advanced problem solving. Effective mastery of the developmental tasks of a specific stage of life provides building blocks for mastery of the tasks of future stages (Masten, Obradović, & Burt, 2006). We assume that successful cultures will stimulate behavior that helps its members learn what they need to know for both their own survival and that of the group.

In the case presented earlier in the chapter, Erikson provides an example of how the culture supports a person's work on the developmental tasks of a particular life stage. As he was entering later adolescence following graduation from Gymnasium, Erikson took advantage of a culturally accepted period of exploration by traveling to Italy. During this period, he was able to work on several of the developmental tasks of later adolescence, especially gaining greater autonomy from his family, experimenting with possible career paths, and clarifying his values and beliefs by becoming a "Bohemian."

Keep in mind that the person is maturing in a few important domains at once during each period of life. Tasks involving physical, emotional, intellectual, and social growth, as well as growth in one's self-concept, all contribute to one's resources for dealing with the challenges of life. Table 3.1 shows the developmental tasks we have identified as areas of learning for most people in modern society and the stages during which each set of tasks is of primary learning value. There are 42 developmental tasks on the list. Whereas the infant is learning orientations and skills related to the first five, a person at the early adulthood stage has already acquired skills related to 27 tasks from the previous stages. New learning may continue in these areas as well as in the four new developmental tasks faced by the young adult. This helps one appreciate that by the time people reach early adulthood, they have a considerable repertoire of competencies that can be used to cope with the challenges of life. By the stage of elderhood a person has all the areas of previous learning to draw from while working on three new tasks.

Psychosocial Crisis

A **psychosocial crisis** refers to a state of tension that results from the discrepancies between the person's competences at the beginning of a stage, and the society's expectations for behavior at that period of life (Erikson, 1963). For example, in toddlerhood, the second stage of development from roughly ages 2 to 4, the psychosocial crisis is autonomy versus shame and doubt. At the beginning of this stage, the toddler may have established a strong, positive, and trusting relationship with the caregiver. Now the child is expected to function more independently, to take care of some basic needs by oneself, and to exercise new levels of self-control.

TABLE 3.1 Developmental Tasks Associated with the Life Stages

LIFE STAGES*	DEVELOPMENTAL TASKS
Infancy (birth to 2 years)	Maturation of sensory/perceptual, and motor functions
	Sensorimotor intelligence: Processing, organizing and using information
	Communication
	Attachment
	Emotional development
Toddlerhood (2 and 3)	Elaboration of locomotion
	Language development
	Fantasy play
	Self-control
Early school age (4 to 6)	Gender identification
	Early moral development
	Self-theory
	Peer play
Middle childhood (6 to 12)	Friendship
	Concrete operations
	Skill learning
	Self-evaluation
	Team play
Early adolescence (12 to 18)	Physical maturation
	Formal operations
	Emotional development
	Membership in the peer group
	Romantic and sexual relationships
Later adolescence (18 to 24)	Autonomy from parents
	Gender identity
	Internalized morality
	Career choice
Early adulthood (24 to 34)	Exploring intimate relationships
	Childbearing
	Work
	Lifestyle
Middle adulthood (34 to 60)	Managing a career
	Nurturing an intimate relationship
	Expanding caring relationships
	Managing the household
Later adulthood (60 to 75)	Accepting one's life
	Redirecting energy toward new roles and activities
	Promoting intellectual vigor
	Developing a point of view about death
Elderhood (75 until death)	Coping with physical changes of aging
	Developing a psychohistorical perspective
	Traveling through uncharted terrain

*We do not consider the concept of developmental tasks appropriate to the prenatal stage.

These may be experienced as new demands that the child may first encounter with some distress, overreaching by asserting too much autonomy, or being shamed for acting overly dependent. At each stage, the sense of crisis arises because one must make psychological efforts to adjust to the demands of the social environment. The word *crisis* in this context refers to a normal set of stresses and strains rather than to an extraordinary set of events.

Societal demands vary from stage to stage. People experience these demands as mild but persistent expectations for behavior. They may be demands for greater self-control, further development of skills, or a stronger commitment to goals. Before the end of each stage of development, the individual tries to achieve a resolution, adjust to society's demands, and at the same time translate those demands into personal terms. This process produces a state of tension that the individual must reduce in order to proceed to the next stage.

Mastery of the developmental tasks is influenced by the resolution of the psychosocial crisis of the previous stage. This resolution leads to the development of new social capabilities. These capabilities orient the person toward new experiences, a new aptitude for relationships, and new feelings of personal worth as the challenges of the next stage's developmental tasks begin. In turn, the skills learned during a particular stage as a result of work on its developmental tasks provide the tools for the resolution of the psychosocial crisis of that stage. Task accomplishment and crisis resolution interact to produce individual life stories.

Psychosocial Crises of the Life Stages

Table 3.2 lists the psychosocial crisis of each stage of development from infancy through elderhood. This scheme, derived from Erikson's model shown in Figure 3.1, depicts the crises as polarities—for example, trust versus mistrust, and autonomy versus shame and doubt. These contrasting conditions suggest the underlying dimensions along which each psychosocial crisis is resolved. According to psychosocial theory, most people experience both ends of the continuum. The inevitable discrepancy between one's level of development at the beginning of a stage and society's push for a new level of functioning by the end of it creates at least a mild degree of the negative dimension. For example, even within a loving, caring family environment that promotes trust, an infant will experience some moments of frustration or disappointment that result in mistrust.

The outcome of the crisis at each stage is an integration of the two opposing forces. For each person, the relative frequency and significance of positive and negative experiences will contribute to a resolution of the crisis. The likelihood of a completely positive or a completely negative resolution is small. Most individuals resolve the crises in a generally positive direction, supported by a combination of positive experiences and natural maturational tendencies. At each successive stage, however, the likelihood of a negative resolution mounts as the developmental tasks become more complex and the chances of encountering societal barriers to development increase.

To understand the process of growth at each life stage, we have to consider the negative as well as the positive pole of each crisis. The dynamic tension between the positive and negative forces reflects the struggles a person encounters to restrain unbridled impulses, to overcome fears and doubts, and to look past one's own needs to consider the needs of others. The negative poles offer insight into basic areas of human vulnerability. In every psychosocial crisis, experiences at both the positive and negative poles contribute to the total range of a person's adaptive capacities. Although a steady diet of mistrust is undesirable, for example, it is important that a trusting person be able to evaluate situations and people for their trustworthiness. This ability is based in part on experiences of mistrust, which help a person recognize cues about safety or danger in any encounter.

Why conceptualize life in terms of crises? Does this idea adequately portray the experience of the individual, or does it overemphasize conflict and abnormality? The term *crisis* implies that tension and conflict are necessary to the developmental process; crisis and its resolution are viewed as normative, biologically based components of life experience at every stage.

The term *psychosocial* draws attention to the fact that the psychosocial crises are, in part, the result of cultural pressures and expectations. Individuals will experience tension because of the culture's need to socialize and integrate its members. The concept acknowledges the dynamic conflicts between individuality and group membership at each period of life.

In Erikson's case, he attributes the psychosocial crisis around his personal identity to a convergence of biological, psychological, and societal factors. He is physically different from his Jewish family members; he is identified as a religious outsider by his friends; and he is an object of traditional, middle-class family values and expectations that he rejects. As he emerges into later adolescence, he finds his transitional identity as an artist, an identity that he explores for several years before discovering his potential as a teacher, therapist, and theorist.

The exact nature of the psychosocial crisis is not the same at each stage. For example, few cultural limits are placed on infants. The outcome of the psychosocial crisis of infancy depends greatly on the skill of the caregiver. At early school age, the culture stands in fairly direct opposition to

---

TABLE 3.2   The Psychosocial Crises

LIFE STAGE*	PSYCHOSOCIAL CRISIS
Infancy (birth to 2 years)	Trust versus mistrust
Toddlerhood (2 and 3)	Autonomy versus shame and doubt
Early school age (4 to 6)	Initiative versus guilt
Middle childhood (6 to 12)	Industry versus inferiority
Early adolescence (12 to 18)	Group identity versus alienation
Later adolescence (18 to 24)	Individual identity versus identity confusion
Early adulthood (24 to 34)	Intimacy versus isolation
Middle adulthood (34 to 60)	Generativity versus stagnation
Later adulthood (60 to 75)	Integrity versus despair
Elderhood (75 until death)	Immortality versus extinction

*We do not consider the concept of psychosocial crisis appropriate to the prenatal stage.

the child's initiative in some matters by discouraging curiosity or questioning about certain topics, but offers abundant encouragement to initiative in others. In young adulthood, the dominant cultural push is toward the establishment of intimate relationships, yet an individual may be unable to attain intimacy because of the lack of time to cultivate these relationships, competing pressures from the workplace, cultural norms against certain expressions of intimacy, or restrictions against certain types of unions.

As reflected in the epigenetic principle, the succession of crises occurs in a predictable sequence over the life course. Although Erikson did not specify the exact ages for each crisis, the theory hypothesizes an age-related progression, in which each crisis has its time of special ascendancy. The combination of biological, psychological, and societal forces that operate to bring about change has a degree of regularity within society that places each psychosocial crisis at a particular period of life. The research described in the Applying Theory and Research to Life box illustrates one approach for exploring the empirical basis of this concept.

In addition to the predictable psychosocial crises, any number of unforeseen stresses may arise.

Parents' divorce, the death of a sibling, victimization by violence, the loss of a job, and widowhood are examples of unforeseen life crises. The need to cope with them may overwhelm a person, particularly if several crises occur at the same time. The picture of predictable developmental stress that is emphasized in psychosocial theory must be expanded to include the possibility of unanticipated crises. Although these chance events may foster growth and new competencies, they may also result in defensiveness, regression, or dread. The impact of an unpredictable crisis will depend in part on whether the person is in a state of psychosocial crisis

© 2011 Estate of Pablo Picasso/Artists Rights Society (ARS), New York/© Peter Will/SuperStock

Pablo Picasso's son is shown in deep concentration as he sketches at his desk. Through imitation, a child takes ownership of actions and skills that are observed when among adults. It is little wonder that Paulo, surrounded by his father's ongoing artistic activity, would be drawn to imitate it.

© Reuters/CORBIS

The attack on the World Trade Center on September 11, 2001, brought unforeseen crises to thousands. At different developmental stages, people adapt in unique ways to crisis and loss. The impact of this crisis on the subsequent psychosocial development for the generations who experienced it is yet to be understood.

at the time. For example, the unexpected death of a sibling might be exceptionally disruptive for someone who is also in a period of questioning related to personal identity, where matters of family loyalties and commitments to values and beliefs are unresolved.

The combination of predictable crises, unpredictable crises, and unique historical pressures may lead to the resurfacing of prior crises that require reorganization. For example, during early adulthood, when issues of intimacy versus isolation are salient, it is common to find a reworking of industry versus inferiority as well (Whitbourne, Zuschlag, Elliot, & Waterman, 1992). Young adults encounter the very concrete challenges of establishing themselves in the labor market and achieving self-sufficiency. The outcome of this reworking of an earlier crisis will depend in part on historical factors, such as the economic and materialistic orientation of the society as a specific age group enters early adulthood. It will also depend on additional individual factors—especially on whether the adult is able to forge a meaningful occupational role that is consistent with personal and community values (Whitbourne, Sneed, & Sayer, 2009). Thus, the psychosocial crises are not resolved and put to rest once and for all. Each crisis is played and replayed both during ongoing developmental changes and when life events challenge a balance that was achieved earlier.

The Central Process for Resolving the Psychosocial Crisis

Every psychosocial crisis reflects some discrepancy between the person's developmental competencies at the beginning of the stage and new societal pressures for more effective, integrated functioning. How is the discrepancy resolved? What experiences or processes permit the person to interpret the expectations and demands of society and internalize them in order to support change? We have identified a **central process** through which each psychosocial crisis is resolved. The central process suggests a way that the person takes in or makes sense of cultural expectations and undergoes adaptive modifications of the self. The term *process* suggests a means by which the person recognizes new social pressures and expectations, gives these expectations personal meaning, and gradually changes.

The process, unfolding over time, results in a new relationship between self and society. For example, in toddlerhood, the psychosocial crisis raises the question of how children increase their sense of autonomy without risking too many experiences that provoke a sense of shame and doubt. We suggest that *imitation* is the central process for psychosocial growth during toddlerhood (ages 2 and 3). Children expand their range of skills by imitating adults, siblings, television models, playmates, and even animals. Movement toward a sense of autonomy in toddlerhood is facilitated by the child's readiness to imitate, by the variety of models available for observation, and by the variety of behaviors the child has the

TABLE 3.3 The Central Process for Resolving Each Psychosocial Crisis

LIFE STAGE*	CENTRAL PROCESS
Infancy (birth to 2 years)	Mutuality with caregiver
Toddlerhood (2 and 3)	Imitation
Early school age (4 to 6)	Identification
Middle childhood (6 to 12)	Education
Early adolescence (12 to 18)	Peer pressure
Later adolescence (18 to 24)	Role experimentation
Early adulthood (24 to 34)	Mutuality among peers
Middle adulthood (34 to 60)	Person–environment fit and creativity
Later adulthood (60 to 75)	Introspection
Elderhood (75 until death)	Social support

*We do not consider the concept of central process appropriate to the prenatal stage.

opportunity to observe. Through persistent imitative activity, children expand their self-initiated behavior and control over their actions. Repetitive experiences of this kind allow children to believe that they can do more things on their own, advancing their sense of personal autonomy.

The central process for coping with the challenges of each life stage provides both personal and societal mechanisms for taking in new information and reorganizing existing information. It also suggests the means that are most likely to lead to a revision of the psychological system so that the crisis of that particular stage may be resolved. Each central process results in an intensive reworking of the psychological system, including a reorganization of boundaries, values, and images of oneself and others. Table 3.3 shows the central processes that lead to the acquisition of new skills, and the resolution of the psychosocial crisis at each life stage.

Radius of Significant Relationships

Age-related demands on individuals are communicated through **the radius of significant relationships** (Erikson, 1982, p. 31; see Figure 3.4). Initially, a person focuses on a small number of relationships. During childhood, adolescence, and early adulthood, the number of relationships expands, and the quality of these relationships takes on greater variety in depth and intensity. In later adulthood, the person often returns to a small number of extremely important relationships that provide opportunities for great depth and intimacy.

In Erikson's case study, he recalls a network of artists who may have influenced him at a very early age while he was living with his mother. Then, the radius of significant relationships shifted to include his father, Dr. Homburger, who was a trusted and respected professional. As he moved into later adolescence, he found a group of like-minded young people with artistic and literary

Using Autobiographical Memories to Explore Psychosocial Stages of Life

PSYCHOSOCIAL THEORY PREDICTS that the self-concept and worldview are reorganized at each stage of life to highlight new goals and a new relationship of self and society. To explore this idea further, Martin Conway and Alison Holmes (2004) asked adults between the ages of 62 and 89 to recall memories for each decade of their lives from the first 10 years through the decade of the 60s. The participants were asked about the decades in a random order and were given 5 minutes per decade to write down up to 3 memories from that time of life. Each memory was dated to the nearest year and month within the decade. The memories were then coded for the degree to which they reflected themes inherent in the psychosocial crises.

Fifty participants produced 552 memories. Figure 3.3 shows the distribution of memories coded for each psychosocial stage by decade. The two decades from ages 10 to 19 and 20 to 29 produced the largest number of memories. As predicted, memories tied to early psychosocial crises (wanting to be or being nurtured, helped, and taught; having fun and playing; encounters with parents, family members, and teachers) were most frequently recalled in association with the first decade of life. Memories associated with identity and identity

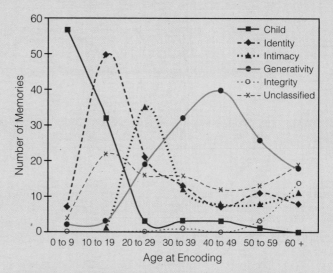

FIGURE 3.3 Lifespan Memory Distribution Curves for Memories Classified by Psychosocial Stage over Seven Decades of Life

Source: Conway, M.A. & Holmes, A. (2004). Psychosocial stages and the accessibility of autobiographical memories across the life cycle. *Journal of Personality, 72,* 461–480. Reprinted by permission.

confusion were most frequent in the second decade of life. Memories related to intimacy were of greatest frequency in the third decade. In contrast to childhood memories that decline noticeably from the first decade of life, memories associated with generativity increased gradually from the 20s to the 40s and continued to be prominent in the decades of the 50s and the 60s. Relatively few memories were coded as reflecting the themes of integrity and despair, but those memories were tied primarily to the decade of the 60s. These findings use biographical memory recall to support the view that the self is reorganized around different goals and preoccupations at various stages of life that reflect the demands and satisfactions associated with the psychosocial crises of those stages.

Critical Thinking Questions

1. What story do the data in Figure 3.3 tell?
2. Given the more detailed conceptualization of psychosocial theory presented in this chapter, and summarized in Figure 3.5, what additional constructs would you want to measure in order to determine the salience of specific psychosocial crises at various periods of life?
3. What other approaches to measurement might you use aside from memory recall to study the question of patterns of psychosocial development?
4. What are the strengths and limitations of using autobiographical memory to study psychosocial development over the stages of life?

ambitions, who supported his feelings of alienation from his traditional family, and offered a milieu of acceptance and care. Subsequently he became immersed in a circle of professional analysts who educated and trained him and offered him a new professional identity.

At each stage of life, the network of significant relationships determines the demands that will be made, how the

person will be taken care of, and the meaning that could be derived from the relationships. The relationship network varies individually, but each person has a network of significant relationships and an increasing readiness to enter into a more complex social life (Vanzetti & Duck, 1996). The quality of these relationships and the norms for interaction are influenced by the nature of the specific social context.

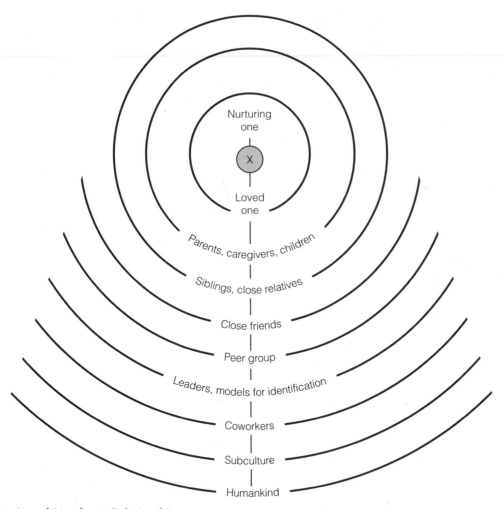

FIGURE 3.4 The Radius of Significant Relationships

Contexts of Development

One way of thinking about the impact of the societal system is to consider individuals as embedded in a kaleidoscope of changing, interconnected systems. Children are members of families. Parents and other relatives are members of other important work and community groups that can influence families. As they get older, children may become members of other institutions, such as child care programs, schools, religious groups, community clubs, or athletic teams. Communities are nested in cities, counties, states, and nations. An understanding of development requires insight into each level of social organization as well as across the culture as a whole. These organizations influence what is expected of its members, the roles they play, the activities they engage in, the resources available to meet these expectations, and the risks they may encounter.

The **contexts of development** embody social, economic, and historical factors. Events such as war, political revolution, famine, or economic collapse may temporarily alter the prevailing childrearing values, opportunities for education or employment, and the availability of resources. Furthermore, these events may increase exposure to violence and separation of family members or provide exposure to other unpredictable stressors that may disrupt the course of development. Family, culture, and ethnic group are three of the major contexts through which the radius of significant relationships is organized.

Families. All over the world, children are raised by small groups or families. Family is the universal primary social context of childhood. The family continues to be a meaningful context throughout life, especially as we think of the relationship of adults with their aging parents, the formation of new families in adulthood, and the lifelong connections among siblings. Historically, the term **family** has referred to a group of people, usually related by blood, marriage, or adoption. In contemporary U.S. society, however, people who view themselves as members of a family may have no legal relationship or shared ancestral bond. The psychosocial meaning of family continues to be defined as individuals who share a common destiny and who experience a sense of emotional intimacy. People in a family care about one another and take care of one another (Price, Price, & McKenry, 2010).

© Philip Newman

As a newborn, Max is the center of a radius of significant relationships, including his mother, grandmother, aunt, and uncles. For all these adults, Max has entered their radius of significant relationships.

Culture. Culture refers to the socially standardized ways of thinking, feeling, and acting that are shared by members of a society. Culture includes the concepts, habits, skills, arts, technology, religion, and government of a people. It encompasses the tools and symbol systems that give structure and meaning to experience. In relation to human development, cultures have implicit theories about the stages of life, the expectations for behavior as one matures, and the nature of one's obligations to the older and younger members of the cultural group. A culture exerts influence directly through families as well as through other social organizations such as churches and schools. As is true for other nations, the United States' culture has a strong, unifying impact on its citizens. Within the United States, there are also noticeable regional cultural patterns marked by unique vocabulary and dialect, mannerisms, and styles of social interaction. Throughout this book, we will note the great differences in what life—including family life—is like in different cultures and note how the integration of person and culture produces distinctive personal experiences for individuals in various cultures.

Ethnic Groups. In addition to the common threads of culture that affect everyone who grows up or lives for a long time in the United States, there are also persistent subcultural forces that shape the daily lives of children and adults. The United States is a complex society made up of people from a vast array of cultures throughout the world. We call these groups ethnic subcultures or **ethnic groups**. People who belong to ethnic groups share socially standardized ways of thinking, feeling, and acting with other members of their group. Holidays such as St. Patrick's Day, Oktoberfest, or Kwanzaa are examples of public occasions that celebrate

the ethnic heritage of particular groups. Current research has focused on the development of ethnic identity, particularly the ways in which one's ethnic heritage and cultural values are integrated into one's personal identity. Ethnic values may include views about family cohesiveness, the importance of certain religious practices, the role and meaning of education, attitudes toward elders, or efforts to preserve a language and customs. The influence of one's ethnic heritage is likely to change from one generation to another. Recent studies examine the role of ethnic values and beliefs for first-generation immigrants as compared to second- and third-generation offspring. Increasing attention is being given to the lifestyles, identity development, parenting practices, and family values of ethnic groups, and we will give special attention to studies that highlight ethnic group comparisons where possible.

Coping Behavior

Coping refers to people's conscious, adaptive efforts to manage stressful events or situations, and their efforts to manage the emotions associated with these stressors (Somerfield & McCrae, 2000). Coping is a process that begins with an **appraisal** of the situation. This includes answers to the following questions: What is the nature of this stressor? How much of a threat is it? How much time do I have to deal with this challenge? How much control do I have over the situation? Following the appraisal, one must enlist cognitive, affective, and behavioral strategies to manage the stress. Lazarus and Folkman (1984) distinguished between coping efforts that are targeted at changing something about the source of stress (*problem-focused coping*) and strategies that are targeted at managing or controlling one's emotions in the face of the stressor (*emotion-focused coping*). Often, these strategies are used together. Claire, who has taken a week of vacation, has returned to work to find a basket full of mail, 20 voice messages, and 80 email messages. She still has her usual daily workload. She decides to take a short lunch and stay an hour late in order to catch up. At the same time, she tries to remain calm and think about the wonderfully relaxing time she had on her vacation so that she does not become depressed by this huge amount of work.

In order to understand how a person copes with a stressful situation, one must consider: (1) the nature of the stressor, (2) how it is perceived by the person, and (3) the range of resources that are available to address the situation (McCubbin & Patterson, 1982; Lazarus, 2000). The coping process depends on the specific stressful situation. One does not cope the same way if the house is on fire or if the baby has a high fever. In the situation of bereavement, for example, there are no actions the grieving person can take to bring the lost loved one back to life. The major coping task for the survivors is to find a way to reconcile themselves to the situation and to carry on with their own lives (Wortman & Boerner, 2007).

The approach to coping also depends on the values, beliefs, and goals of the person or family involved and on how these values, beliefs, and goals lead to a particular interpretation of the stressor event. For example, in one family, the announcement that an oldest child decides to enlist in the military may be greeted with great joy and pride; in another family, that same announcement may be greeted with dismay and disappointment. Both families will worry about the child's safety and will experience the stress of the child's absence. However, the family's beliefs and goals will determine the meaning given to a child's decision to join the military.

Finally, individuals and families differ in the resources that are available to cope with a difficult situation. Resources include such things as social support, information, professional advice, financial resources, and a sense of humor. Fewer resources, or the lack of the appropriate resources, may impede the coping process. In a study exploring how people cope with financial stress, problem-focused coping was found to be more effective in reducing distress than emotion-focused coping (Caplan & Schooler, 2007). Among those participating in this study, those with lower SES resources were found to use more emotion-focused coping strategies and, as a result, had higher levels of psychosocial distress. Lower SES participants had lower self-confidence and a greater degree of fatalism, a belief that events in life are largely out of one's control. These two factors, low self-confidence and high fatalism, were strongly related to the limited use of problem-focused coping. Thus, the study illustrated that the path from low SES to distress over financial strain is brought about largely through perceived lack of control, which interferes with the mobilization of problem-focused coping.

Coping behavior is an important concept in psychosocial theory because it explains how unique and inventive behaviors occur. An important aspect of coping is the ability to redefine or *reappraise* the situation in a positive way. This suggests

creating or reemphasizing the meaning, values, and opportunities embedded in the stressful situation (Folkman & Moskowitz, 2000). For example, as Robert cared for his partner who had AIDS, he took special pleasure in routine, daily events like planning an enjoyable meal that they shared together. In the face of feelings of helplessness about the uncontrollable changes in his partner's condition, Robert also took steps to set attainable goals, like creating a video library of favorite movies that he and his partner could enjoy together. Thus, even while Robert was experiencing many negative emotions, he also found positive experiences in the context of the stress.

Some people are better able to cope with the challenges that they are faced with than others. The term **resilience** is often used to characterize individuals who exhibit positive outcomes in the face of serious threats to development. They may have experienced prolonged, severe poverty; they may have a parent with a serious mental illness; or they may have been exposed to ongoing abuse or violence. Faced with these or other difficulties, resilient individuals show low levels of psychological symptoms, and function effectively in the basic developmental tasks expected for their stage of life (Masten, Obradović, & Burt, 2006). Over time, they create lives that integrate their own personal strengths with the resources and opportunities of their community, meeting the community's expectations for maturity. Although the story of resilience is highly individual, reflecting unique patterns of life challenges and coping strategies, the notion of resilience underscores a widely shared capacity to recover from adversity. There appear to be a small number of factors that support resilience including: "connections to competent and caring adults in the family and community; cognitive and self-regulation skills; positive views of self; and motivation to be effective in the environment" (Masten, 2001, p. 13).

An individual's characteristic style of coping is a dynamic set of actions that changes in response to changing conditions. In research about how individuals cope with chronic pain, for example, participants were asked to make daily entries in a diary and were also prompted several times a day to respond to a set of questions about their appraisal of the situation, their mood, and their behaviors (Tennen, Affleck, Armeli, & Carney, 2000). Participants were most likely to use problem-focused strategies to cope with pain, or to use problem-focused and emotion-focused coping at the same time. However, as time went on, if the pain did not subside with the use of problem-focused strategies, they were likely to turn to emotion-focused solutions. In other words, the coping process was sensitive to the results of various strategies. If a person finds that active efforts to reduce pain are not working, then subsequent coping may shift to seeking spiritual or emotional support or trying to redefine the situation to make it more bearable.

As a result of experiencing mastery and competence through coping, one builds a more positive expectation about being able to face new challenges. The positive consequences of coping help to sustain individuals during prolonged stressors. One can see how, over time, effective coping contributes to development. In the face of threat, coping behavior may

EAN-PHILIPPE KSIAZEK/AFP/Getty Images

After the devastating destruction of the earthquake in Haiti, hundreds of thousands were left homeless. The catastrophic nature of the crisis strains most people's coping capacities. Evens sits bewildered as peacekeeping forces march through the street where he used to live.

allow an individual to act effectively, rather than merely to maintain equilibrium or become disorganized.

According to psychosocial theory, at each stage of life, consistent efforts to face and cope with the psychosocial crisis of the period result in the formation of basic adaptive capacities, referred to as the **prime adaptive ego qualities**. When coping is unsuccessful and the challenges of the period are not adequately mastered, individuals are likely to form maladaptive orientations, referred to as **core pathologies**.

Prime Adaptive Ego Qualities

Erikson (1978) postulated **prime adaptive ego qualities** that develop from the positive resolution of the psychosocial crisis of a given stage and provide resources for coping with the next. He described these qualities as *mental states* that shape the interpretation of life experiences. A sense of competence, for example, permits a person to feel free to exercise wit to solve problems without being weighed down by a sense of inferiority.

The prime adaptive ego qualities and their definitions are listed in Table 3.4. These ego qualities contribute to the person's dominant worldview, which is continuously reformulated to accommodate new ego qualities (Markstrom, Sabino, Turner, & Berman, 1997). The importance of many of the prime adaptive ego qualities, including hope, purpose, competence, love, and wisdom, has been verified by research (Lopez & Snyder, 2003). For example, a new measure, *The Psychosocial Inventory of Ego Strengths*, has been developed to assess the relationship of the prime adaptive ego strengths to psychosocial well-being. As anticipated, higher scores on the psychosocial inventory were correlated with identity achievement, self-esteem, locus of control, empathic concern, and perspective taking (Markstrom & Marshall, 2007).

TABLE 3.4 Prime Adaptive Ego Qualities

LIFE STAGE	EGO QUALITY	DEFINITION
Infancy (birth to 2 years)	Hope	An enduring belief that one can attain one's deep and essential wishes
Toddlerhood (2 and 3)	Will	A determination to exercise free choice and self-control
Early school age (4 to 6)	Purpose	The courage to imagine and pursue valued goals
Middle childhood (6 to 12)	Competence	The free exercise of skill and intelligence in the completion of tasks
Early adolescence (12 to 18)	Fidelity to others	The ability to freely pledge and sustain loyalty to others
Later adolescence (18 to 24)	Fidelity to values	The ability to freely pledge and sustain loyalty to values and ideology
Early adulthood (24 to 34)	Love	A capacity for mutuality that transcends childhood dependency
Middle adulthood (34 to 60)	Care	A commitment to concern about what has been generated
Later adulthood (60 to 75)	Wisdom	A detached yet active concern with life itself in the face of death
Elderhood (75 until death)	Confidence	A conscious trust in oneself and assurance about the meaningfulness of life

Focusing specifically on the ego quality of *hope,* Erikson and his colleagues found that people in later life who were hopeful about their own future and that of their children were more intellectually vigorous and psychologically resilient than those who were less hopeful (Erikson et al., 1986). People with a hopeful attitude have a better chance of maintaining their spirits and strength in the face of crisis than people who are pessimistic. For both young and older adults, the ego strength of hope has been found to be a significant predictor of life satisfaction (Isaacowitz, Vaillant, & Seligman, 2003).

Core Pathologies

Although most people develop the prime adaptive ego qualities, a potential core pathology or destructive force may also emerge as a result of ineffective, negatively balanced crisis resolution at each stage (Erikson, 1982; see Table 3.5). The core pathologies also serve as guiding orientations for behavior. These pathologies move people away from others, tend to prevent further exploration of interpersonal relations, and obstruct the resolution of subsequent psychosocial crises. The energy that would normally be directed toward mastering the developmental tasks of a stage is directed instead toward resisting or avoiding change. The core pathologies are not simply passive limitations or barriers to growth. They are energized worldviews leading to strategies that protect people from further unwanted association with the social system and its persistent, tension-producing demands.

Evaluation of Psychosocial Theory

Objective 3. To evaluate psychosocial theory, pointing out its strengths and weaknesses.

Although we believe that psychosocial theory provides a useful theoretical framework for organizing the vast array of observations in the field of human development, we recognize that it has weaknesses as well as strengths. As a student of development, you must begin to form your own independent judgment of its usefulness and be alert to how the theory may influence your thinking. The strengths and weaknesses of psychosocial theory that are discussed in the following sections are listed in Table 3.6.

Strengths

Psychosocial theory highlights the social nature of human development. Human beings depend for their survival on their capacity to form social bonds and to recognize and respond to social messages. Although the field of psychology has traditionally focused on the thoughts and behaviors of individuals, a growing body of research emphasizes the social nature of mental functioning. Thus, the basic view of development offered by psychosocial theory as a product of interactions between the individual and the social environment is gaining increasing support.

Psychosocial theory provides a broad, integrative context within which to study life-span development (Kiston, 1994; Hopkins, 1995). The theory links the process of child development to stages of adult life, individual development to the nature of culture and society, and the personal and historical past to the personal and societal future. Although many scholars agree that such a broad perspective is necessary, few other theories attempt to address the interplay between individual development and society (Miller, 2002).

Psychosocial theory provides a framework for tracing the process through which self-concept, self-esteem, and self-other boundaries become integrated into a positive, adaptive, socially engaged person (Hamachek, 1985, 1994). Emphasizing the normal, hopeful, and creative aspects of

TABLE 3.5 Core Pathologies

LIFE STAGE	CORE PATHOLOGY	DEFINITION
Infancy (birth to 2 years)	Withdrawal	Social and emotional detachment
Toddlerhood (2 and 3)	Compulsion	Repetitive behaviors motivated by impulse or by restrictions against the expression of impulse
Early school age (4 to 6)	Inhibition	A psychological restraint that prevents freedom of thought, expression, and activity
Middle childhood (6 to 12)	Inertia	A paralysis of action and thought that prevents productive work
Early adolescence (12 to 18)	Dissociation	An inability to connect with others
Later adolescence (18 to 24)	Repudiation	Rejection of roles and values that are viewed as alien to oneself
Early adulthood (24 to 34)	Exclusivity	An elitist shutting out of others
Middle adulthood (34 to 60)	Rejectivity	Unwillingness to include certain others or groups of others in one's generative concern
Later adulthood (60 to 75)	Disdain	A feeling of scorn for the weakness and frailty of oneself and others
Elderhood (75 until death)	Diffidence	An inability to act because of overwhelming self-doubt

Source: Based on Erikson, 1982.

TABLE 3.6 Strengths and Weaknesses of Psychosocial Theory

STRENGTHS	WEAKNESSES
The theory provides a broad, integrative framework within which to study the life span.	Explanations for the mechanisms of crisis resolution and process of moving from one stage to the next need to be developed more fully.
The theory provides insight into the directions of healthy development across the life span.	The idea of a specific number of stages of life and their link to a genetic plan for development is disputed.
Many of the basic ideas of the theory have been operationalized using traditional and novel approaches to assessment.	The theory and much of its supporting research have been dominated by a male, Eurocentric perspective that gives too much emphasis to individuality and not enough attention to connection and social relatedness.
The concept of psychosocial crises, including the positive and negative poles of the crisis, offers a model for considering individual differences within a framework of normal development.	
The concept of the psychosocial crisis identifies predictable tensions between socialization and maturation.	The specific ways that culture encourages or inhibits development at each stage of life are not clearly elaborated.
Longitudinal studies support the general direction of development hypothesized by the theory.	

coping and adaptation, the theory has taken the study of development beyond the deterministic position of psychosexual theory or the mechanistic view of behaviorism, providing an essential conceptual framework for the emergence of positive psychology.

At one time, some argued that a weakness of psychosocial theory was that its basic concepts were presented in language that is abstract and difficult to examine empirically (Crain, 2000; Miller, 2002). However, over the past 20 years, such terms as *hope, inhibition, autonomy, personal identity, intimacy, generativity,* and *integrity*—to name a few—have been operationalized (Christiansen & Palkovitz, 1998; McAdams & de St. Aubin, 1998; Bohlin, Bengtsgard, & Andersson, 2000; Kroger, 2000; Marcia, 2002; Snyder, 2002; Lopez & Snyder, 2003). Concepts central to the theory—such as trust, autonomy, identity achievement, coping, well-being, social support, and intergenerational interdependence—have become thoroughly integrated into contemporary human development scholarship. Researchers have developed instruments to trace the emergence of psychosocial crises and their resolution in samples varying in age from adolescence to later adulthood (Constantinople, 1969; Waterman & Whitbourne, 1981; Darling-Fisher & Leidy, 1988; Hawley, 1988; Domino & Affonso, 1990; Whitbourne et al., 1992; Whitbourne et al., 2009).

Unlike some other theories, psychosocial theory identifies tensions that may disrupt development at each life stage, providing a useful framework for considering individual differences in development. The positive and negative poles of each psychosocial crisis offer a way of thinking about differences in self-concept development at each stage of life as well as a model for considering cumulative differences across the life span. This matrix of crises and stages also provides a useful tool for approaching psychotherapy and counseling.

The concept of normative psychosocial crises is a creative contribution that identifies predictable tensions between socialization and maturation throughout life. Societies, with their structures, laws, roles, rituals, and sanctions, are organized to guide individual growth toward a particular ideal of mature adulthood. However, every society faces problems when it attempts to balance the needs of the individual with the needs of the group. All individuals face some strains as they attempt to experience their individuality while maintaining the support of their groups and attempting to fit into their society. Psychosocial theory offers concepts for exploring these natural tensions.

Longitudinal research using psychosocial theory as a framework for studying patterns of personality change and self-concept development has found support for many of its basic concepts. Changes in psychological outlook that reflect the major themes of the theory—such as industry, identity, intimacy, and generativity—appear to emerge and become consolidated over time (Whitbourne et al., 2009). There is also evidence of a preview of themes prior to their period of maximum ascendancy (Peterson & Steward, 1993) and evidence for the notion of revisitation through which adults are stimulated to rework and reorganize the resolutions of earlier issues (Shibley, 2000).

Weaknesses

One weakness of psychosocial theory is that the explanations of the mechanisms for resolving crises and moving from one stage to the next are not well developed (Miller, 2009). The theory does not offer a universal mechanism for crisis resolution, nor a detailed picture of the kinds of experiences that are necessary at each stage if one is to cope successfully with the crisis of that stage. We have addressed this weakness by including the concepts of developmental tasks and a central process for each stage. The developmental tasks suggest some of the major achievements that permit a person to meet the social expectations of each stage. The central process identifies the primary mechanism through which the person encounters societal expectations and integrates them into a revised sense of self. Using these two constructs, one can begin to clarify the process of movement from one stage to the next.

The specific number of stages and their link to a biologically based plan for development has been criticized. The stages of life unfold in a cultural context. For example, in some societies, the transition from childhood to adulthood is swift, leaving little time or expectation for identity exploration. In many traditional societies, parents choose one's marital partner, there are few occupational choices, and one is guided toward one's vocation from an early age. Thus, although there is always a biological period of pubescence that marks the transition from childhood to adulthood, there may be little justification for two stages of adolescence when the identity formation process is societally constrained (Thomas, 1999). In contrast, in our highly technological society, adolescence appears to be extended for some, especially as the age at first marriage is delayed and the complexity of preparing for and entering the labor market increases. As a reflection of this extension of modern adolescence, we have treated the period from puberty through about age 24 as two stages rather than one, each with its own psychosocial crisis and developmental tasks.

Along this same line of criticism, some scholars have taken a more differentiated view of the stages of adulthood and later life. In later life, health status, life circumstances, and culture interact to produce increasing variation in life stories. Distinctions are made between people of the same chronological age who are referred to as the "young-old" and the "old-old" depending upon their health status and their capacity to manage tasks of daily life (Deeg, Kardaun, & Fozard, 1996; Poon & Harrington, 2006).

In other research, distinctions are made on the basis of chronological age. For example, Leonard Poon has written extensively about the differences between centenarians (people who are 100 or more), octogenarians (people in their 80s), and sexagenarians (people in their 60s) (Martin, Poon, Kim, & Johnson, 1996). Each cohort of older adults has been exposed to different historical crises, educational, health, and occupational opportunities, and shifting societal values. Therefore, it is likely that the normative patterns used to describe development in adulthood and later life will become dated and need reexamination as each younger cohort enters later adulthood and elderhood (Siegler, Poon, Madden, & Welsh, 1996).

We have addressed this concern in part by extending the traditional psychosocial stage approach to adulthood from three stages to four, adding a period called elderhood. In the chapters on adulthood, we also address differences in lifestyle and life course that are attributable to historical and cultural trends. Nevertheless, the increasing life expectancy, accompanied by a longer period of healthy later life and the elaboration of lifestyles, makes it difficult to chart a normative life course from early adulthood into late life.

In this book, you will also read about the important developmental issues of the prenatal period—a stage that

Erikson's theory does not consider, but that clearly plays a central role in setting the stage for a lifetime of vulnerabilities and competencies. These revisions demonstrate the natural evolution of a theoretical framework as it continues to encounter new observations.

Finally, psychosocial theory and related research have been criticized as being dominated by a male, Eurocentric, individualistic perspective that emphasizes the ability to originate plans and take action, called **agency**, over the commitment to and consideration for the well-being of others, called **communion** (Abele & Wojciszke, 2007). Critics have argued that the themes of autonomy, initiative, industry, and personal identity, which reflect individuality, have been equated with psychological maturity. They suggest that relatively little attention has been given to the development of interpersonal connection and social relatedness. These latter themes have been identified as central for an understanding of the psychosocial maturity of girls and young women. They also emerge in the study of collectively oriented ethnic groups—cultures in which maturity is equated with one's ability to support and sustain the success of the family or the extended family group rather than with one's own achievement of status, wealth, or recognition (Boykin, 1994; Josselson, 2003).

Within the framework of psychosocial theory, the theme of connection is addressed directly through the first psychosocial crisis of trust versus mistrust in infancy, but then the thread is lost until early adolescence and early and middle adulthood, when group identity, intimacy, and generativity direct the focus back to the critical links that individuals build with others. The concept of the radius of significant relationships serves to maintain the perspective of the person interwoven in a tapestry of relationships, focusing especially on family and friends in childhood; the family, peer group, love relationships, and close friends in early and later adolescence; and on intimate partners, family, friends, and coworkers in adult life. A basic premise of psychosocial theory is that the self-concept is taking shape in constant interaction with the community (Schlein, 1987, 2007).

To extend the theme of connection, this book elaborates on developing capabilities for social interaction and differences in socialization practices and outcomes for men and women in our society. A variety of social abilities, including empathy, prosocial behavior, interaction skills, and components of social cognition, are traced as they emerge in the context of family relationships, friendship, peer groups, and work. This book considers ethnic groups as well as broader social influences on development and the importance of a collective orientation toward responsibility in caring for children and creating a sense of community.

A Recap of Psychosocial Theory

Figure 3.5 shows development as a building process that incorporates the six constructs of psychosocial theory. The structure grows larger as the radius of significant relationships

While most later adolescents in the U.S. are establishing their identity in the context of college or university, some are forming their identity in the military. How might military training contribute to psychosocial maturity and movement from later adolescence to early adulthood?

expands and as the achievements of earlier stages are integrated into the behavior of the next stage of development.

How can you tell when stage change has occurred? The resolution of the psychosocial crisis of a previous stage provides the ego strengths and skill acquisition needed to face the challenges and expectations of the next stage. The order in which work on each developmental task begins and the rate of skill development or task achievement differ from person to person. These differences may be due to a host of factors such as genetic differences in physical growth and sexual maturation, temperament, quality of parenting, access to resources, and exposure to stressors. Once a person is fully engaged in all the tasks of a new period of life, a new stage of life has begun. The person's energy, motivation, and concerns about self and others are directed toward new goals, and the expectations others have for the person's level of functioning shift. Just as we no longer applaud the 4-year-old for the ability to crawl, we no longer applaud the 30-year-old for

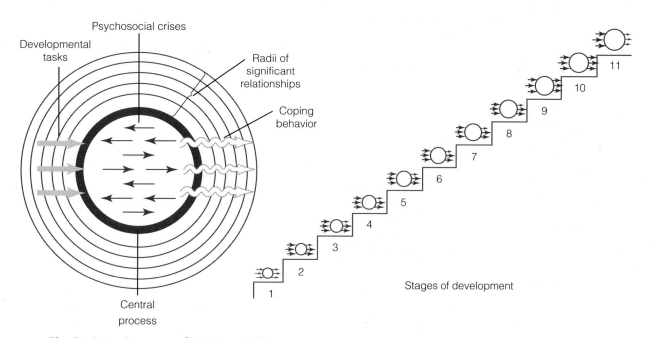

FIGURE 3.5 The Six Basic Concepts of Psychosocial Theory

the ability to hold a steady job. Evidence of a stage change can be marked by new preoccupations and plans, new worries, and a new approach to building and maintaining relationships. A wonderful aspect of human development is the continuing redirection of energy to new ambitions, building upon the satisfactions of prior achievements.

At the beginning of this chapter, we introduced three questions one must ask in order to understand a theory. Let us now answer these questions with respect to psychosocial theory:

Which phenomena is the theory trying to explain? Psychosocial theory attempts to explain human development across the life span—especially patterned changes in self-concept development, which are reflected in self-understanding, identity formation, social relationships, and worldview.

What assumptions does the theory make? Human development is a product of three interacting factors: biological maturation, the interaction between individuals and social groups, and the contributions that individuals make to their own psychological growth.

The theory makes the following five assumptions:

1. Growth occurs at every period of life, from conception through elderhood.
2. Individual lives show continuity and change as they progress through time.
3. In order to understand behavior, one must consider the integration of cognitive, physical, social, and emotional competences, since these domains influence one another.
4. Every person's behavior must be analyzed in the context of relevant settings and personal relationships.
5. People contribute actively to their own development.

What does the theory predict?

1. There are 11 stages of development, which emerge in an ordered sequence. Issues of later stages can be previewed at an earlier time, but each issue has its period of ascendance. It takes the entire life span, from the prenatal period through elderhood, for all aspects of the person's potential to be realized.
2. Developmental tasks are dictated by the interaction of the biological, psychological, and societal systems during each stage.
3. A normal crisis arises at each stage of development, and a central process operates to resolve this crisis. The resolution

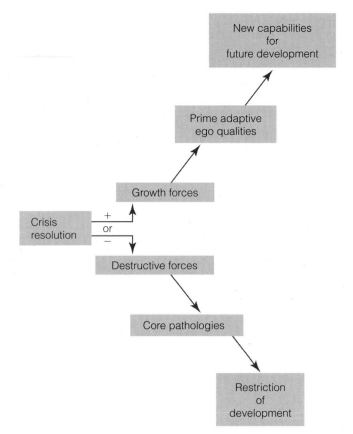

FIGURE 3.6 The Mechanism for Positive and Negative Psychosocial Development

of the crisis at each stage determines one's coping resources, with a positive resolution contributing to ego strengths and a negative resolution contributing to core pathologies.

4. Each person is part of an expanding network of significant relationships that convey society's expectations and demands. These relationships also provide encouragement in the face of challenges.
5. Development will be optimal if a person can create new behaviors and relationships as a result of skill acquisition and successful crisis resolution during each stage of growth. Lack of development and core pathologies result from tendencies that restrict behavior (especially social behavior) in general and new behavior in particular. The mechanisms for positive and negative development are diagrammed in Figure 3.6.

Chapter Summary

Objective 1. To explain the rationale for using psychosocial theory as an organizing framework for the study of human development.

Psychosocial theory offers a life-span view in which development is a product of the interactions between individuals and their social environments. The needs and goals of both the

individual and society must be considered in conceptualizing human development. Predictability is found in the sequence of psychosocial stages, the central process involved in the resolution of the psychosocial crisis at each stage, and the radius of significant relationships. Individuality is expressed in the achievement of the developmental tasks, the balance of the positive and negative poles of each psychosocial crisis and the resulting worldview, and in the style and resources for coping that a person brings to each new life challenge.

Connectivity is achieved in the way the person learns to relate in a radius of significant others who make demands, convey social expectations, and offer social rewards. Over time, the person becomes engaged in increasingly complex social groups and institutions. A person's worldview at a particular age is a product of past identifications and the resolution of previous psychosocial crises, contemporary pressures and opportunities, and hopes for the future. In our society, there is great diversity in the outcomes of this psychosocial process and in the transmission of social expectations from one generation of adults to the next generation of children.

Objective 2. To define the six basic concepts of psychosocial theory.

Psychosocial theory accounts for systematic change over the life span through six basic concepts: (1) stages of development, (2) developmental tasks, (3) psychosocial crises, (4) a central process for resolving the crisis at each stage, (5) a radiating network of significant relationships, and (6) coping—the new behavior people generate to meet new challenges.

The basic concepts of psychosocial theory provide the framework for analyzing development across 11 life stages from the prenatal period through elderhood. Development is viewed as a building process that incorporates the six constructs of psychosocial theory. The structure grows larger as the radius of significant relationships expands, and coping strategies become more varied and complex as the developmental tasks of each stage are mastered and become available to face the challenges and psychosocial crisis of the next stage of life.

Objective 3. To evaluate psychosocial theory, pointing out its strengths and weaknesses.

Psychosocial theory provides a broad, integrative context within which to study life-span development. The strengths and weaknesses of the theory are summarized in Table 3.6. The theory provides insights into the direction of development over the life span, highlighting human strengths and vulnerabilities, and predictable shifts in worldview and self-understanding at each stage. The theory offers a framework for considering the ongoing interaction of individuals and their societies, pointing to the interconnections of people at various stages of life. The theory has been criticized for its lack of clarity about the mechanisms that explain change from one stage to the next. The psychosocial crises have been criticized as overemphasizing values of individuality as compared to values of connection and interdependence.

As You Read on ...

Each chapter of this text, from Chapter 4 through 14, is devoted to one life stage. Chapter 15 covers topics related to death and bereavement across the life span. With the exception of Chapter 4, on pregnancy and prenatal development, each life-stage chapter starts with a discussion of the developmental tasks of that life stage. By tracing developments in physical growth, emotional growth, intellectual skills, social relationships, and self-understanding, you can recognize the interrelationships among all of these dimensions during each period of life.

In the second section of each chapter, the psychosocial crisis of that life stage is described, accounting for the tension by examining the individual's needs and personal resources in light of the dominant societal expectations. In addition to defining the crisis, we conceptualize the central process by which it is resolved. The resolution of the crisis at each stage is tied to new ego strengths and new core pathologies.

At the end of each chapter, we draw on the material we have discussed to analyze a topic that is of persistent concern to our society. These topics are controversial, and they may generate sentiment as they deepen understanding. We intend these sections to stimulate the application of developmental principles to real-world concerns.

Take a moment to study the table on the front leaf of the book. You can use this table as a guide to the major themes of the text. It may help you to see the connections among the topics in a chapter or to trace threads of continuity over several periods of life. You may also use this table in constructing a life map for yourself, which will reveal the levels of tension and the major psychosocial factors that are currently affecting your self-concept and your relationships with others.

Key Terms

age-graded expectations, 67
agency, 80
appraisal, 75
central process, 72
communion, 80
contexts of development, 74
coping, 75
core pathologies, 77

culture, 62
developmental stage, 64
developmental task, 67
epigenetic principle, 65
ethnic groups, 75
family, 74
prime adaptive ego qualities, 77
psychosocial crisis, 68

psychosocial evolution, 64
psychosocial theory, 62
radius of significant relationships, 72
research, 67
resilience, 76
sensitive periods, 67
teachable moment, 67

Further Reflection

Based on your understanding of psychosocial theory, consider the following questions:

1. What are the essential features of a scientific theory? How well does psychosocial theory meet the criteria for a scientific theory?
2. What is the focus or range of applicability of psychosocial theory? What is this theory about?
3. What role does psychosocial theory give to biological maturation and experience in guiding development? How do these factors interact?
4. How do the concepts of psychosocial theory help explain how a person moves from one stage of life to the next?
5. What is coping? How does it fit into the process of development over the life course? Can you describe an example of your own coping behavior as you faced a new or demanding situation in the past few months?
6. How might people at different psychosocial stages differ in the ways they are affected by a similar stressor such as unemployment or death of a parent?

Psychology CourseMate

To access additional course materials, including CourseMate, please visit www.cengagebrain.com. At the CengageBrain.com home page, search for the ISBN of your title (from the back cover of your book) using the search box at the top of the page. This will take you to the product page where these resources can be found.

Casebook

For additional case material related to this chapter, see the case of "Ayesha and the Dinosaurs" in *Life Span Development: A Case Book*, by Barbara and Philip Newman, Laura Landry Meyer, and Brenda J. Lohman, page 100. This case of an engaging 10-year-old illustrates ways in which the psychosocial strengths of trust, autonomy, initiative, and industry come together to support effective problem solving. The case provides an opportunity to discuss the usefulness of the central concepts of psychosocial theory for guiding understanding about positive development.

© 2011 Estate of Pablo Picasso/Artists Rights Society (ARS), New York/Photo © SuperStock

The period of pregnancy involves intricate interactions between the developing fetus and the pregnant woman. The pattern of fetal development is guided by genetic factors, but the pregnant woman's health, social support, and emotional well-being can have substantial impact on fetal growth.

The Period of Pregnancy and Prenatal Development

Chapter Objectives

1. To describe the biochemical basis of genetic information and the process through which it is transmitted from one generation to the next.

2. To identify the contributions of genetic factors to individuality through their role in controlling the rate of development, their contributions to individual traits, and the genetic sources of abnormalities.

3. To trace fetal development through three trimesters of pregnancy, including an understanding of critical periods when normal fetal development can be disrupted.

4. To describe the birth process and factors that contribute to infant mortality.

5. To analyze the reciprocity between the pregnant woman and the developing fetus, focusing on ways in which pregnancy affects a childbearing woman and expectant father and on basic influences on fetal growth, such as maternal age, drug use, nutrition, and environmental toxins.

6. To examine the impact of culture on pregnancy and childbirth.

7. To analyze abortion from a psychosocial perspective, including the legal context, its social and emotional impact on women, and men's views.

WHEN DOES AN individual's life story begin? At birth? At conception? At the births of his parents? At the births of her grandparents? We are each linked back in time, through a lifeline comprising our ancestry, culture, and genetic makeup. This chapter begins the story of development at the molecular level of genes and chromosomes, moves to the physical maturation of the fetus during the prenatal period, and then expands the view of early development by considering the psychosocial, interpersonal, and cultural contexts of the period of pregnancy.

Genetic factors guide the tempo of growth and the emergence of individual characteristics. As the human fetus grows, sensory and motor competencies emerge. The psychosocial environment provides both resources for and challenges to healthy development. Cultural attitudes toward pregnancy and childbirth, poverty and the associated stressors, support from the child's father and other significant family members, maternal nutrition, and exposure to toxins or drugs are among the factors that affect fetal growth.

Genetics and Development

Objective 1. To describe the biochemical basis of genetic information and the process through which it is transmitted from one generation to the next.

Variability, which is so essential for human survival, is guaranteed, in part, by the complexity of the human *genome* (all the genetic material in the chromosomes of a human being) and the mechanisms for genetic inheritance. In this section, we briefly review the biology of genetics and the laws that govern the transmission of genetic information from one generation to the next. As parents, teachers, and human service professionals, we are encouraged to value and respond to human diversity. The growing knowledge about human genetics provides a foundation for appreciating the biological basis of this diversity. An excellent source of information and links about the results, ethics, and future directions of the human genome project can be found on the Human Genome Project website sponsored by the U.S. Department of Energy.

Genes and Chromosomes as Sources of Genetic Information

Genetic information links each new person to the human species in general and also to a specific genetic ancestry. When we discuss inherited characteristics, we are really referring to two different kinds of heredity. The first includes all the genetic information that comes to us as members of the human species. Most inherited genetic information is shared by *all* human beings, such as patterns of motor behavior (e.g., walking upright), brain size, and body structure, including the proportional size of the head, torso, and limbs. Two of the most relevant of these species-related characteristics are the readiness to learn and the inclination to participate in social interaction.

The second kind of heredity consists of characteristics that have been transmitted through a specific *ancestry*. Hair color, skin color, blood group, and height result from the genetic information passed on from one generation to the next. Given all the shared information that is carried in the genome, these individual differences amount to only 0.1% of all DNA (McGuffin, Riley, & Plomin, 2001). Thus, all the ways in which individuals differ genetically from one another is accounted for by a very small percentage of the information carried in the **genes**.

Chromosomes, the long, thin strands of genetic material located in the cell nucleus, are formed from chains of DNA molecules (see Figure 4.1). Most single genes are composed of a piece of DNA that codes for the production of one protein and occupies a specific place on a chromosome. The recent estimate based on **genome** mapping places the number of functional genes between 20,000 and 25,000, or about 2% of the entire genome (U.S. Department of Energy Office of Science, 2004).

The important work of the genes is to produce proteins, which then guide cellular formation and functioning. Proteins, which are large, complex molecules comprised of amino acids, perform most life functions and make up the majority of cellular structures. The constellation of all proteins in a cell is called its **proteome**. Unlike the relatively unchanging genome, the dynamic proteome changes from minute to minute in response to tens of thousands of intra- and extracellular environmental signals. A protein's chemistry and behavior are specified by the gene sequence and by the number and identities of other proteins made in the same cell at the same time and with which it associates and reacts. Therefore, at the cellular level, genetic and environmental information are continuously interacting to influence the functions of the cells (U.S. Department of Energy, 2003).

In each chromosome pair, one chromosome comes from the father and one from the mother. The chromosome pairs differ in size. In 22 pairs of chromosomes, both members are similar in shape and size. They also contain the same kinds of genes. The 23rd pair of chromosomes is a different story: Female humans have two X chromosomes, and male humans have one X and one Y chromosome. The X and Y notation is used because these chromosomes differ in shape and size (the X chromosome is longer than the Y chromosome). There are very few similarities in the genes present on the X and Y chromosomes.

One common misconception is that there is one gene for each specific trait such as sociability, **intelligence**, or criminality. Single genes do not determine most human behaviors (McGuffin, Riley, & Plomin, 2001). Only certain rare disorders such as Huntington's disease have a simple mode of transmission in which a specific mutation confers the certainty of developing the disorder. Most types of behavior have no such clear-cut pattern and depend on interplay between environmental factors and multiple genes (p. 1232).

The Laws of Heredity

The laws that govern the process by which genetic information is transmitted from parent to offspring were discovered by Gregor Mendel (1866), a monk who studied the inherited characteristics of plants, particularly garden peas. His laws were formulated long before the discovery of the biochemical substances that compose genes and chromosomes.

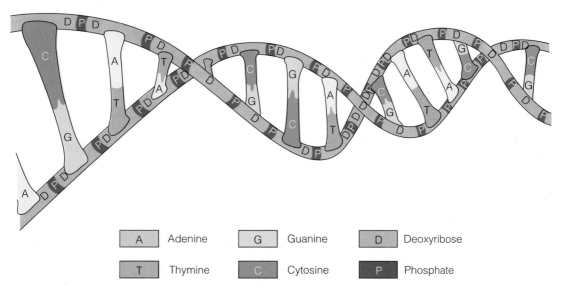

| A | Adenine | G | Guanine | D | Deoxyribose |
| T | Thymine | C | Cytosine | P | Phosphate |

FIGURE 4.1 Diagram of a Small Part of a DNA Molecule. The biochemical basis of genetic information is the DNA (deoxyribonucleic acid) molecule, which has the shape of a double helix (i.e., it looks somewhat like a twisted rope ladder). The sides of this ladder comprise alternating units of sugar (deoxyribose) and phosphate, and its rungs are made up of pairs of nitrogen bases (so named because they contain the element nitrogen as well as hydrogen and carbon). The four nitrogen bases involved are adenine (A), guanine (G), cytosine (C), and thymine (T). They are often referred to by their initial letters, and A, G, C, and T are called the genetic alphabet.

Alleles

In the 22 pairs of identical chromosomes, each gene has at least two possible states or conditions, one on each chromosome in the pair. These alternative states are called **alleles**. Whatever the allelic state of the gene from one parent, the other parent's allele for that gene may be either the same or different. If both alleles are the same, the gene is said to be **homozygous**. If the alleles are different, the gene is **heterozygous**.

Genotype and Phenotype

The genetic information about a trait is called the **genotype** (e.g., the genetic information that encodes skin color). The observed characteristic (e.g., one's actual skin color) is called the **phenotype**. The expression, "There is more here than meets the eye," suggests the difference between genotype and phenotype. Genotype can influence phenotype in three different ways. First, the differences in the allelic states of several genes sometimes result in a **cumulative relation**, in which more than one pair of alleles influences the trait. An example of this kind of relation is the genetic contribution to height. A person whose alleles of different genes are mostly for tallness will be tall; a person who receives many alleles of different genes for shortness will be short. Most people receive a mix of alleles for both tallness and shortness and are of average height.

Second, the differences between alleles may result in **codominance**, in which both genes are expressed in the new cell. An example of codominance is the AB blood type, which results from the joining of an A blood type allele from one parent and a B blood type allele from the other parent. This blood type is not a mixture of A and B, nor is A subordinate to B or B to A; instead, a distinct blood type, AB, is formed.

Third, differences in the allele states of a gene may result in a **dominance** relation. Dominance means that if one allele is present, its characteristic is predominantly observed whether the other allele of the pair is the same or not. The allele that dominates is called the *dominant* allele. The other allele that is present, but whose characteristic is masked by the dominant allele, is called the *recessive* allele. Eye color is the result of a dominance relation. The allele for brown eyes (B) is dominant over the allele for blue eyes (b). The probability that the recessive trait of blue eyes will emerge in the offspring of two heterozygous parents is illustrated in Figure 4.2. The possible combinations of the gene related to brown or blue eye color are BB, Bb, bB, and bb. Only one combination, bb, which will occur on the average in only 25% of the offspring, results in a child with blue eyes. The other three genotypes result in one phenotype—brown eyes.

Adding to the complexity of the laws of heredity are the processes of **epigenetics**, activities at the biochemical level that alter gene expression but do not alter the genome itself. Two of these processes are imprinting and **epigenetic marks**. **Imprinting** is a condition in which genes from either the mother or the father are silenced. At present, 156 imprinted genes have been identified (Luedi et al., 2007). Under conditions of imprinting, the genes from both parents are present on the DNA strands and are copied by the RNA but only the genes from one parent

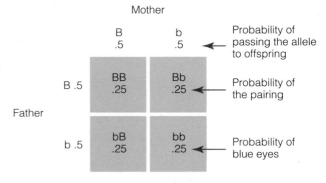

Note: Whenever B allele is present, eyes will be brown.

FIGURE 4.2 Probability of Heterozygous Brown-Eyed Parents Producing Blue-Eyed Offspring

Family resemblance is influenced by the transmission of genes that guide the production of melanin which can be detected in similarity of hair color, eye color, and skin tones.

Image copyright Monkey Business Images 2010. Used under license from Shutterstock.

are used in making proteins. As a result, even though there are two different alleles in the genotype, only the mother's or the father's allele is expressed in the phenotype. There is an assumed adaptive advantage to having some genetic information silenced selectively depending on its origin from the paternal or maternal genetic source, but the mechanisms that might explain or account for this advantage are not yet clear. Many developmental disorders and diseases are linked to imprinted genes, either as a result of the expression of a mutation or recessive condition that is not balanced by the silenced allele, or as a result of some environmental condition that removes the imprinting and thereby increases the impact of the gene. Future study of imprinted genes is expected to contribute significantly to our understanding of the genetic and epigenetic basis of disease (Jirtle & Weidman, 2007).

Epigenetic marks are chemicals that sit on top of the genes and instruct them to switch on or off (Figure 4.3). These marks can be influenced by environmental factors such as overabundant eating, smoking cigarettes at an early age, or having access to particular vitamins during the prenatal period. When the epigenetic marks are altered, the impact is seen in subsequent generations. For example, researchers studied the long-term impact of famine and feast in a small Swedish community. They found that the children and grandchildren of those children who had experienced periods of near starvation followed by a year of overeating had substantially shorter lives than the offspring of those who experienced only the famine, but no overeating. In contrast to the slow process of genetic modification through natural selection, epigenetic studies show how exposure to critical environmental factors at key periods of life can predispose one's children and grandchildren to genetically based vulnerabilities. These environmental influences are distinct from the prenatal exposure of the fetus to malnutrition or toxins, discussed later in this chapter, which may result in developmental delay or disruption. Epigenetic studies link developmentally time-sensitive exposure to environmental conditions to the gene expression in one or more generations of offspring (Pembrey, Bygren et al., 2006; Pembrey, 2008).

Sex-Linked Characteristics

Certain genetic characteristics are said to be **sex linked** because the gene for the specific characteristic is found on the sex chromosomes (X and Y). The female ova carry only X chromosomes. Half of the male sperm carry Y chromosomes, and half carry X chromosomes. Male children can be produced only when a sperm carrying a Y chromosome fertilizes an egg, and the result is an XY combination in the 23rd chromosome pair. All sperm carrying X chromosomes will produce female children.

Sex-linked traits are more likely to be observed in male offspring, even though they may be present in the genotype of female offspring. You will understand this more readily if you visualize the XY chromosome pair. When a trait is carried on the Y chromosome, it will be inherited and transmitted only by male offspring, because only male offspring have the Y chromosome. Interestingly, the Y chromosome is quite

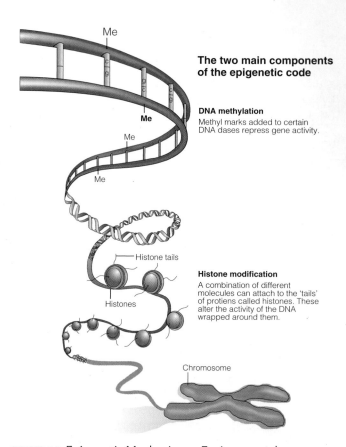

The two main components of the epigenetic code

DNA methylation
Methyl marks added to certain DNA bases repress gene activity.

Me
Me
Me
Me

Histone tails

Histone modification
A combination of different molecules can attach to the 'tails' of proteins called histones. These alter the activity of the DNA wrapped around them.

Histones

Chromosome

FIGURE 4.3 Epigenetic Mechanisms. Environmental conditions such as a rich diet following a period of starvation can alter gene expression. These changes can turn genes on or off and may affect what gets passed down to succeeding generations.

Source: From "Epigenetics: Unfinished Symphony" by J. Qiu, 2006, *Nature, 441*, no. 7090, 143–145. Used by permission of Nature Publishing Group.

small, and few exclusively Y-linked traits have been identified. One of the few key genes that has been located on the Y chromosome is SRY, which is responsible for setting into motion the differentiation of the testes during embryonic development. Once the testes are formed, they begin to produce hormones that account for further differentiation of the male reproductive system.

Sex-linked traits that are carried on the X chromosome are more likely to be observed in male offspring than in female offspring, because male children do not have a second X chromosome to offset the effects of an X-linked trait. Hemophilia A, the most common type of hemophilia, is an example of such a sex-linked trait. Individuals with hemophilia lack a specific blood protein that causes their blood to clot after receiving a wound (ADAM, 2004). The allele for hemophilia is a recessive trait carried on the X chromosome; however, it is most likely to affect men (see Figure 4.4). Half (50%) of the male offspring of female carriers have the disease, and 50% of their female offspring are carriers. All female children of a man with hemophilia are carriers of the trait. This disease affects approximately 1 in 5,000 men.

Other genes are expressed exclusively in one sex but are not found on the sex chromosomes per se. For example, the

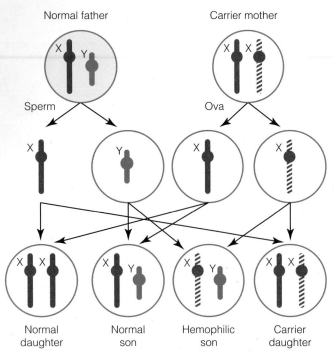

FIGURE 4.4 Sex-Linked Inheritance of Hemophilia. The allele for hemophilia is carried on the X chromosome. If the allele is either heterozygous or homozygous for the dominant trait (normal blood clotting), a female child will have normal blood-clotting capabilities. Only if she is homozygous for the recessive trait (a very rare occurrence) will she be hemophilic. A male child, on the other hand, has only one allele for the clotting gene, which he inherits from his mother. If that allele is dominant, his blood will clot normally, but if it is recessive, he will be hemophilic.

Source: From "The Molecular Genetics of Hemophilia" by R. M. Lawn and G. A. Vehar, 1986, *Scientific American*, 254, p. 50. Copyright © 1986. All rights reserved. Reprinted by permission of Alan Iselin.

genes for male beard development and female breast development are not located on the sex chromosomes. However, these characteristics will emerge only in the presence of the appropriate hormonal environment, which is directed by the sex chromosomes.

Genetic Sources of Individual Differences

Objective 2. To identify the contributions of genetic factors to individuality through their role in controlling the rate of development, their contributions to individual traits, and the genetic sources of abnormalities.

The study of genetics reveals that individual variability is due to the combination of the many variations in environment and experience that confront a growing person and the variability built into the biological mechanisms of heredity. Each adult couple has the potential for producing a great variety of genetically distinct children. Three areas

in which genetic determinants contribute to individual variability are *rate of development, individual traits,* and *abnormal development.*

Genetic Determinants of the Rate of Development

Genes regulate the rate and sequence of maturation. The concept of an epigenetic plan for growth and development is based on the assumption that a genetically guided system promotes or restricts the growth of cells over the life span. Genetic factors have been found to play a role in behavioral development, including the onset of various levels of reasoning, language, and social orientation.

Evidence for the role of genetics in guiding the rate and sequence of development has been provided by studies of identical twins (who have the same genotype). The rates at which identical twins develop are highly correlated, even when those twins are reared apart. A number of characteristics—including the timing of the acquisition of motor skills, personality development, changes in intellectual capacity among aged twins, and the timing of physical maturation—show a strong genetic influence (Bouchard & Pederson, 1999).

Genes can be viewed as internal regulators that set the pace for maturation. They signal the onset of significant developmental changes throughout life, such as growth spurts, the eruption of teeth, puberty, and menopause. They also appear to set the limits of the life span. A small number of genes influence how many times the cells of a specific organism can divide and replicate. Research on three different animal species—fruit flies, worms, and mice—has shown that when the most long-lived of a species are bred, the offspring live longer than average (Barinaga, 1991).

Differences in the rate of development contribute to our understanding of psychosocial growth. Differences in age at crawling or walking, for example, bring children into contact with new aspects of their environments and provide them with changing capacities at different chronological ages. Thus, the genetic processes that regulate readiness for certain kinds of growth and vulnerabilities to particular kinds of stress contribute to systematic differences among individuals. For example, adult expectations for the accomplishment of such specific tasks as toilet training, getting dressed without help, and learning to write interact with the child's developmental level. Disappointment may be conveyed to children who are not able to perform these tasks until later in the developmental spectrum, and pride and approval may be conveyed to developmentally accelerated children.

Genetic Determinants of Individual Traits

Genes contain specific information about a wide range of human characteristics, from eye color and height to the ability to taste a particular substance called phenylthiocarbamide (which to tasters is bitter, but to nontasters has no taste at all). Some characteristics are controlled by a single gene. However, most significant characteristics, such as height, weight, blood group, skin color, and intelligence, are guided by the combined action of several genes. When multiple genes are involved in the regulation of a trait, the possibilities for individual differences in that trait increase. Because many characteristics are regulated by multiple genes, the variety of human phenotypes is enormous.

Genetic factors also play a substantial role in individual differences in personality (Loehlin, 1992; Plomin, 1990, 1994; Loehlin, 1992; Borkenau, Riemann, Angleitner, & Spinath, 2001). Traits such as *sociability* (a tendency to be outgoing), *inhibition* (a tendency to be cautious and socially shy or withdrawn), and *neuroticism* (a tendency to be anxious and emotionally sensitive) are pervasive dimensions of personality that appear to have strong genetic components. Research on the biological basis of sexual orientation suggests that genes may influence the development of the part of the brain that guides sexual behavior (LeVay, 1991). Identical twins are more likely to have the same sexual orientation than are fraternal twins or adoptive siblings (Bailey & Pillard, 1991, 1994). Even in rather specific areas of personality, such as political attitudes, aesthetic preferences, and sense of humor, identical twins show greater similarity than fraternal twins, even when the identical twins are reared apart from each other.

Extending the analysis of the impact of genetics on individual differences, Sandra Scarr (1992) suggested at least three ways in which genetic factors influence the environment of individuals. First, most children are raised by their parents in environments created by their parents. Thus, children receive both their genes and their home environment from a common genetic source—their parents. As an example, a parent who is temperamentally sociable is more likely than a withdrawn or timid parent to have lots of people at the house, to enjoy the companionship of others, and therefore to expose the children to more companionable adults.

Second, people draw out responses from others that are related to their own personality characteristics. Thus, broad, genetically based aspects of one's individuality will affect the kinds of social responses one receives from others, including one's parents.

Third, as people mature and become increasingly assertive in selecting certain experiences and rejecting others, their own temperaments, talents, intelligence, and level of sociability will guide the kinds of environments they select, strengthening certain genetic predispositions while dampening others.

Genetic Determinants of Abnormal Development

In addition to characteristics such as physical appearance, temperament, talent, and intellectual capacity, a wide variety of abnormalities, or *anomalies*, have a genetic cause. The most dramatic anomalies result in a spontaneous abortion of the fetus early in the pregnancy. Approximately 15% to 20% of recognized pregnancies end in first-term spontaneous abortion (Geyman, Oliver, & Sullivan, 1999). The majority of these early-term spontaneous abortions are due to chromosomal abnormalities in the fertilized zygotes (the developing organism formed from the father's sperm and the mother's egg).

Of those infants who survive the neonatal period, an estimated 3% to 5% of newborns have one or more major recognizable anomalies (Cunningham et al., 2001). The incidence of anomalies increases to 6% to 7% as some disorders are diagnosed later in childhood. Some birth defects are linked to a specific chromosome or to a single gene. Other birth defects are linked solely to environmental factors, such as drugs, medications, and fetal and maternal infections. Most malformations, however, result from the interaction of genetic vulnerabilities and environmental hazards, or are of unknown origin (Moore & Persaud, 2003).

Examples of genetic and **chromosomal disorders** are listed in Table 4.1. The disorders are presented in two broad categories: those associated with specific genes and those associated with chromosomal abnormalities. Within those categories, some disorders are found on 1 of the 22 pairs of autosomal chromosomes (chromosomes other than the sex chromosomes), and others are on one of the sex chromosomes. There are more than 1,100 genes for which at least one disease-related mutation or alternate allele has been identified using the map-based approach to gene discovery. However, many diseases are thought to involve multiple genes in some form of interaction. Moreover, many diseases that have an identified genetic basis—such as hypertension, schizophrenia, or coronary artery disease—are expressed in certain environments, including the prenatal environment, and not in others (Peltonen & McKusick, 2001; Fox, Hane, & Pine, 2007).

Certain genetic diseases are linked directly to our ancestry; therefore, their incidence is higher in certain populations than in others (National Institutes of Health, 2007). For example, the incidence of Tay-Sachs disease is especially frequent in Jews who settled in Eastern Europe. One in every 27 Jews in the United States carries the gene. Thalassemia, a disease involving faulty production of hemoglobin (which carries oxygen in the blood), is found most often in people of Mediterranean, Middle Eastern, and Southeast Asian origins. The variety of genetic abnormalities serves to broaden the range of individual variability. Many of these irregularities pose a challenge both to the adaptive capacities of the affected person and to the caregiving capacities of the adults involved.

Genetic Technology and Psychosocial Evolution

Psychosocial evolution has typically been differentiated from biological evolution in that change is accomplished by social mechanisms rather than incorporated in the genetic structure. As a result of scientific knowledge, however, we are entering an era when it is possible to intervene to influence the genotype. One such intervention is **genetic counseling**. Individuals and couples with a family history of a genetic disease—or who for some other reason

TABLE 4.1 Examples of Genetic and Chromosomal Disorders

GENETIC DISORDERS

Autosomal dominant gene

Huntington's chorea: Rapid, jerky, involuntary movements; deterioration of muscle coordination and mental functioning. Symptoms usually do not appear until age 35–50. Caused by genetic defect on chromosome 4.

Marfan's syndrome: Elongated fingers; deformed chest and spine; abnormal heart. Tendons, ligaments, and joint capsules are weak.

Autosomal recessive gene

Albinism: Hair, skin, and eyes lack the pigment melanin. Often accompanied by visual problems and a susceptibility to skin cancer.

Cystic fibrosis: Certain glands do not function properly. The glands in the lining of the bronchial tubes produce excessive amounts of thick mucus, which leads to chronic lung infections. Failure of the pancreas to produce enzymes necessary for the breakdown of fats and their absorption from the intestines leads to malnutrition. Sweat glands are also affected. Often fatal by age 30. Caused by missing base pairs on chromosome 7.

Sickle-cell anemia: Malformation of red blood cells reduces the amount of oxygen they can carry. Results in fatigue, headaches, shortness of breath on exertion, pallor, jaundice, pain, and damage to kidneys, lungs, intestine, and brain.

Tay-Sachs disease: Absence of a certain enzyme results in the buildup of harmful chemicals in the brain. Results in death before age 3.

X-linked recessive gene

Color blindness: Defect of light-sensitive pigment in one or more classes of cone cells in the retina of the eye or an abnormality in or reduced number of cone cells themselves. The two common types are reduced discrimination of light wavelengths within the middle (green) and long (red) parts of the visible spectrum.

Hemophilia: Absence of a blood protein (factor VIII) reduces effectiveness of blood clotting. Severity of disorder varies. Bleeding episodes likely to begin in toddlerhood.

CHROMOSOMAL DISORDERS

Autosomal abnormality

Down syndrome: Additional 21st chromosome; also called trisomy 21. The excess chromosome results in physical and intellectual abnormalities, including IQ in the range of 30–80; distinctive facial features, heart defects, intestinal problems, hearing defects; susceptibility to repeated ear infections. Tendency to develop narrowing of the arteries in adulthood, with attendant increase in risk of heart disease.

Sex-chromosome abnormalities

Turner's syndrome: Usually caused by a lack of one X chromosome in a girl; sometimes one of two X chromosomes is defective; occasionally some base pairs are missing on an X chromosome. These abnormalities result in defective sexual development and infertility, short stature, absence or retarded development of secondary sex characteristics, absence of menstruation, narrowing of the aorta, and a degree of mental retardation.

Klinefelter's syndrome: One or more extra X chromosomes in a boy. This abnormality results in defective sexual development, including enlarged breasts and small testes, infertility, and often mental retardation.

worry about the possibility of transmitting a genetic disease to their children—can have a blood test to identify genes that may result in the inherited disorder. The locations of the genes that account for such abnormalities as Tay-Sachs disease, sickle-cell anemia, Duchenne muscular dystrophy, and cystic fibrosis have been identified. Couples who have reason to believe that they may carry genes for one of these diseases can be advised about the probability of having children who may be afflicted (Medline Plus, 2010). If significant numbers of the carriers of genetic diseases decided not to reproduce, the incidence of these diseases in the population would decline over time. Thus, a psychosocial intervention would modify the gene pool.

Ethical Considerations

Gene transfer; the patenting of new life forms created through genetic engineering; genetic fingerprinting, which is used to help identify criminal suspects; and, most recently, cloning from an adult mammal are some of the topics that are raising new ethical concerns. There is a general consensus that the use of gene therapy to treat serious diseases such as cystic fibrosis or cancer is ethical. There is less agreement about the use of intervention to alter the genetic code at the level of the zygote or to attempt to introduce genes intended to enhance aspects of normal development in humans. Even the advances in identifying genetic markers for specific diseases can lead to ethical dilemmas. There are no federal laws in the United States relating to genetic discrimination in individual insurance coverage or to genetic discrimination in the workplace. Concerns have been raised that insurers will use genetic information to deny or cancel policies based on genetic tests or that employers could use information from genetic tests to screen employee applicants. Individuals are turning down the opportunity to be tested for possible genetic diseases for fear that they will be denied health insurance, life insurance, or employment (U.S. Department of Energy, 2007).

The possibility of reproducing genetically identical clones from human tissue has stirred the conscience of the religious, political, and medical communities. Is it ethical to clone human genes so that great scholars, scientists, and artists can walk the Earth again? Should cloning become an approved technology for coping with infertility? The debate about cloning has extended to include human stem cell research. Through a procedure called **nuclear transplantation**, the nucleus of an egg cell, which contains its DNA, is removed and replaced with the DNA from an adult cell. If this egg, with its new DNA, undergoes cell division and survives for several days, it produces embryonic stem cells. These cells have the potential to develop into any type of organ in the body. Thus, they can be injected in a person with a debilitating disease to replace dead or infected tissues. Because the DNA comes from the person's own healthy cells, there is less risk that the body will reject these stem cells (NIH, 2009). This same procedure, nuclear transplantation, can be used for reproductive cloning. Once the

donor DNA is injected into an egg cell and the cell begins to divide, it can be implanted into a uterus. If the implant survives, it would develop into a fetus with the same DNA as the donor. Although there is strong public opposition to the cloning of humans, the procedure has been used to clone other mammals, and there is growing support for stem cell research.

Gene X Environment Interactions and Behavior

Accomplishments in mapping the human genome still leave us with critical questions about how genes and the environment interact to influence behavior. Genes cannot be expressed without an appropriate environment, including the biological environment at the cellular level and the physical and social environments at the larger systems level. For example, a human being needs to breathe oxygen. If an infant is deprived of oxygen in the prenatal period or during the birth process, a genetic potential for intelligence will not be observed in behavior. What is more, as illustrated in the discussion of epigenetic marks, individuals and their environments are in a state of dynamic interaction and change, each modifying the other.

Genetics and Intelligence

One area that has received considerable attention is the relative contributions of genetic and environmental factors to intelligence. To what extent is a person's intelligence set by hereditary factors? To what extent is it a product of experience? Intelligent behavior requires the successful integration of both. It relies on the structure of the central nervous system and the sense receptors, which are products of genetically guided information. However, the healthy functioning of these systems requires adequate nutrition, rest, and freedom from disease—conditions that vary with the environment. Intelligent behavior builds on experiences with diverse stimuli, social interactions, and schooling—all elements of the physical and social environment.

The influence of genetic factors on intelligence may be observed in two ways. First, specific genetic irregularities can cause degrees of mental retardation. Two examples are Down syndrome and Turner's syndrome (see Table 4.1 for descriptions). These and many other genetic diseases play an indisputable role in restricting intellectual potential.

A second approach to understanding the influence of genetics on intelligence is through the study of family relationships. Family members may be related closely or distantly. The closer the biological relationship, the more similar the genetic makeup. If intelligence is influenced by genetics, close relatives should be more similar in intelligence than distant relatives. Figure 4.5 shows the degree of similarity found in more than 100 studies of intelligence in siblings at four different degrees of relationship. Similarity

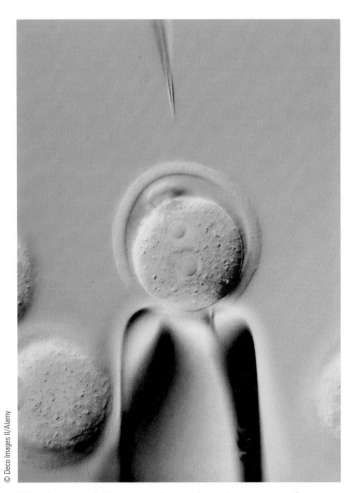

© Deco Images II/Alamy

This photograph illustrates cloning through a process of microinjection of embryonic stem cells into a human ovum.

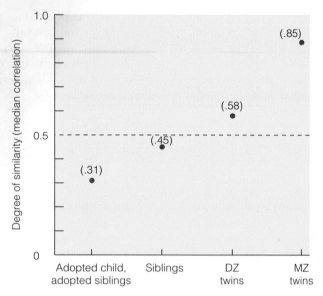

FIGURE 4.5 Similarity in Intelligence Among Siblings at Four Levels of Relationship

Source: From "Familial Studies of Intelligence: A Review," by T. J. Bouchard and M. McGue, 1981, *Science*, 212, 1055–1059. Copyright © 1981 AAAS. Reprinted by permission.

in intelligence increases with the degree of genetic relatedness. The correlation between pairs of monozygotic (identical) twins is .85, providing striking evidence of the contribution of genetics to intelligence. Fraternal, dizygotic (DZ) twins who share the same prenatal, home, and childrearing environments show much less similarity than do MZ twins and not much more than non-twin siblings. An overview of studies that have attempted to evaluate the contribution of genetic factors to cognitive ability suggests that genetics accounts for 50% of the variance, shared environmental factors for 33% of the variance, unshared environmental factors for 17% of the variance, and measurement error for 10% of the variance in intelligence (Gottesman, 1997). One might expect that genetic factors would play a smaller role in measured intelligence with age. However, the data suggest the opposite. Heritability of intelligence increases with age (Plomin & Spinath, 2004). For example, in studies of adopted children, the correlation of IQ between children and their adoptive parents drops to almost zero by the time the children are young adults (Bouchard & Pederson, 1999).

The fact that intelligence is strongly influenced by genetic factors does not imply that environments have no impact; nor that intelligence is fixed and unchangeable. We are just beginning to learn about the role of genes in the structure and functions of the brain and the ways that various genes are related to cognitive capacities. As we will discuss later in the chapter, both the prenatal and postnatal environments have potential impact on the developing nervous system. Access to adequate nutrition, exposure to toxins, and birth trauma can all alter the phenotype with

regard to intelligence. Moreover, tested IQ is only one way of conceptualizing intelligence, a concept that is widely debated in the social sciences. The question of how to think about and study the relationship of genetics and intelligence is moving into new and exciting areas of investigation (Plomin, 2004).

The Norm of Reaction

One way to conceptualize the influence of genetics on behavior is to view the phenotype or observed behavior as a **norm of reaction**—that is, a pattern of possible phenotypes that are likely to be observed under different environmental conditions. This way of thinking about development highlights the importance of the concept of plasticity. **Plasticity** can be conceptualized as the degree of flexibility or variation that can be expressed at the level of an organ, a capacity, or a broad, developmental trajectory. Consider the example of handedness. If you are left handed, and you break your left hand, you can learn to feed yourself with your right hand. It's not as smooth, but it's possible. So handedness, which is genetically influenced, is also plastic. And some people are more readily able to switch from one hand to the other than others; we call them ambidextrous. Some characteristics of personality, intelligence, and emotional response are more plastic than others; that is, they are more sensitive to environmental stimulation or the conditions of childrearing than others. And some children are more malleable than others. Whereas some children are very highly attuned to the social messages and childrearing practices of their parents, others are more resistant to parenting strategies and seem to grow up in tune with their own inner plan (Belsky & Pluess, 2009). Plasticity suggests that specific characteristics can be modified under various environmental conditions, and that some individuals are more responsive to the impact of the environment (for better or worse) than others.

Figure 4.6 shows the hypothetical reaction ranges of three children with respect to intelligence. Child A has greater genetic potential for intelligence than Child B, who has greater potential than Child C. When all three children are in nonstimulating environments, their IQs develop at the lower end of their potential range and the differences among the three phenotypes are reduced. When all three children are in stimulating environments, their IQs develop toward the upper end of their potential range and the differences among the three phenotypes are accentuated. Each child's intellectual ability can be expressed as a range of probable levels that are likely given the child's genetic potential and the quality of the childrearing environment. The more plastic a characteristic, such as intelligence, the more the phenotype will reflect environmental variation. The more channeled or constrained the characteristic, such as the shape of one's eyes or the length of one's fingers, the less environmental factors will influence the expression of the genotype in the phenotype.

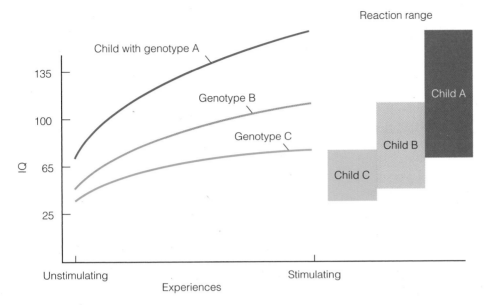

Reaction range

Child with genotype A

Genotype B

Genotype C

Child A

Child B

Child C

IQ

135

100

65

25

Unstimulating

Stimulating

Experiences

FIGURE 4.6 Hypothetical Reaction Range of Intelligence for Three Genotypes

Source: Adapted from "Genetic Aspects of Intelligent Behavior," by I. Gottesman, in N. Ellis (Ed.), *Handbook of Mental Deficiency*, p. 255. Copyright © 1963 McGraw-Hill. Reprinted by permission.

Some genotypes flourish under certain conditions but not others. For example, consider the genotype for behavioral inhibition (Fox, Hane, & Pine, 2007). Behaviorally inhibited children are likely to stop their activity and seek proximity to their caregiver when faced with novel stimuli. Whereas some children have a genotype for intense inhibition, others have a genotype for low levels of inhibition. They are more active, outgoing, and exploratory, and less disrupted or distressed by novelty. In cultures where children are expected to learn through observation and imitation, and where close physical contact between caregivers and mothers is the norm, one might expect the behaviorally inhibited children to be viewed as more normal and to thrive. The outgoing, exploratory, uninhibited children may be perceived as difficult,

disruptive, and may experience more efforts on the part of caregivers to control or constrain their behavior. These children with a genotype that predisposes them to be outgoing and active might experience high levels of distress and self-doubt in this type of environment. In other cultures, where the norm is toward early independence, and encouragement for exploratory behavior, the inhibited infants will require especially sensitive and supportive caregiving in order to thrive. Some parents may add to their inhibited infant's distress by rejecting these infants, conveying impatience with their infant's sensitivity and perceived clinginess, as well as avoidant behavior.

The concept of the norm of reaction can be seen clearly in the outlook for children with Down syndrome (Cody &

© John Henley/CORBIS

Even though children with Down syndrome have mild to moderate disabilities, they also have many talents and abilities. They benefit enormously from early intervention services, including physical, speech, and developmental therapies. Children with Down syndrome enjoy and benefit from social interactions with their typically developing peers.

Kamphaus, 1999; Laws, Byrne, & Buckley, 2000). This condition, which occurs in 1 of every 700 live births, is the most common genetic cause of mental retardation in the United States. In the early part of the 20th century, children born with Down syndrome had a life expectancy of 9 years. Today, the life expectancy of a child with Down syndrome is 30 years, and 25% of individuals with Down syndrome live to age 50. Medical care, early and constant educational intervention, physical therapy, and a nurturing home environment have significant positive results for children with Down syndrome. Participation in a mainstreamed classroom environment has been shown to have significant benefits for these children's vocabulary, grammar, and certain memory skills. Under optimal conditions, individuals with Down syndrome are able to achieve a moderate degree of independence and to participate actively in the life of their schools, communities, and families. Although Down syndrome constrains the probable phenotype, there is a norm of reaction that results from a child's exposure to various degrees of environmental support. Thus, the norm of reaction depends on the specific dynamic interaction of a given genotype in a particular environment.

Normal Fetal Development

Objective 3. To trace fetal development through three trimesters of pregnancy, including an understanding of critical periods when normal fetal development can be disrupted.

Genetic information guides the production of proteins, the formation of body structures, and their interrelated functions. The following description takes us from the cellular level of fertilization to the elaboration of physical and sensory capacities over the three trimesters of pregnancy.

Fertilization

One normal ejaculation contains several hundred million sperm. This large number is necessary to ensure **fertilization**, because most sperm die on the way through the vagina and the uterus. Each microscopic sperm is composed of a pointed head and a tail. The head contains the genetic material necessary for reproduction. The tail moves like a whip as the sperm swims through the cervix and uterus and into the fallopian tubes. Swimming at the rate of 1 inch every 8 minutes, sperm may reach the egg in as little as 30 minutes, but the journey usually takes about 6 hours; sperm can stay alive in the uterus for up to 5 days.

In contrast to a man, who produces billions of sperm in a lifetime, a woman ordinarily releases just one ovum, or egg, each month, midway through the menstrual cycle. In a lifetime of approximately 40 fertile years, during which she can be expected to have two children, the average woman releases approximately 450 eggs. Each woman is born with her complete supply of eggs.

Like the sperm, the ovum is a single cell that contains genetic material. In comparison with body cells, the ovum is quite large (0.12 millimeters), about the size of the period at the end of this sentence. When the ovum is mature, it is encased in a sac of fluid and floats to the surface of the ovary. The sac ruptures and releases the ovum into one of the two fallopian tubes. Millions of feathery, hair-like structures in the fallopian tube sweep around the ovum and gently move it toward the uterus.

Only one sperm can enter the egg. As the first sperm passes through the egg's cell membrane, a rapid change in the membrane's chemistry effectively locks out other sperm. If the ovum is not fertilized within the first 24 hours of its maturity, it begins to disintegrate and is shed along with the lining of the uterus in the next menstrual period.

Once inside the egg cell, the sperm loses its tail, and the head becomes a normal cell nucleus. The egg cell also goes

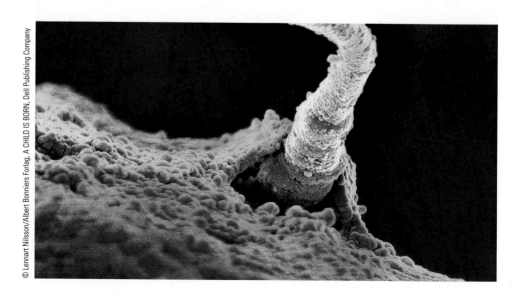

When the sperm breaks through the lining of the egg, a biochemical reaction takes place that prevents other sperm from entering the cell.

© Lennart Nilsson/Albert Bonniers Forlag, A CHILD IS BORN, Dell Publishing Company

through a final change in preparation for fertilization. The **gametes** (egg and sperm cells) contain only one of each chromosome, rather than the full set of 23 pairs. When the cell nuclei of the sperm and the ovum meet in the egg cytoplasm, their separate chromosomal material is integrated into a single set of 23 pairs of chromosomes. At this moment, all the information necessary to activate growth is contained in a single cell.

Twins

The cell produced when the sperm has fertilized the egg is referred to as a **zygote.** The zygote travels down the fallopian tube and divides as it travels toward the uterus without growing larger. After about a week, this mass of cells implants in the uterus. Occasionally, this growing mass of cells divides in two and separates, forming two individuals with the same chromosomal composition. These individuals are referred to as **monozygotic** (MZ) twins, because they come from a single zygote. They are always of the same sex, and are strikingly similar in physical appearance, a characteristic leading to the alternative term **identical twins**.

Fraternal twins occur as a result of multiple ovulations in the same cycle. Each egg develops separately in the ovary, is shed and fertilized individually, and develops separately in the uterus. The result is **dizygotic** (DZ) twins—that is, two-egg twins. Actually, these twins are littermates and may be of different sexes. Genetically, they bear no more resemblance to one another than other children of the same parents. However, they share the same prenatal environment and a more common parenting environment than do most siblings who are born one or more years apart. Approximately 33 in 1,000 live births are multiple births, most of them twins. The ratio of multiple births is notably higher among mothers over age 30, possibly because older mothers are more likely to be using some type of fertility therapy (Martin et al., 2003).

Infertility and Alternative Means of Reproduction

Infertility, or the inability to conceive, can result from problems in the reproductive system of the man, the woman, or both. The risk of infertility increases with age and is associated with exposure to toxins, including cigarette smoke, pesticides, chemical solvents, and fumes from anesthesia (Sinclair & Pressinger, 2001). Research on the emotional impact of infertility suggests that it is a major source of stress. The discovery of infertility may force a couple to reassess the meaning and purpose of their marriage. It may raise doubts in the couple about their self-worth; it often disrupts their satisfaction with their sexual relationship; and it often isolates them because of the difficulty of discussing this personal family problem with others (Haynes & Miller, 2003).

> I have been trying to conceive for 2 years. Each month, at ovulation, I am so sure this will be "the month." And then, like clockwork, my period comes and I spend at least a day feeling depressed. Sex has even become a chore for both me and my partner. This whole infertility roller coaster is definitely hurting our relationship and sex life. Well-meaning friends tell me it will happen when the time is right, but I don't know how to help our relationship in the meantime. (Peterson, 2001)

When couples perceive similar levels of distress about their infertility and are able to communicate with each other about it, they report higher levels of marital satisfaction (Peterson, Newton, & Rosen, 2003). However, it is not uncommon for husbands and wives to have different reactions to infertility and different levels of distress about it, which results in more strained marital relationships. The stressors associated with infertility may go on over a long period. Some couples undergo fertility treatments for years

Identical twins have the same genotype; fraternal twins are no more alike genetically than other siblings. However, both kinds of twins share the same prenatal environment.

© Syracuse Newspapers/Lisa Kratz/The Image Works

Reproductive Technologies

MUCH OF THE DATA about reproductive technology focuses on strategies for artificially fertilizing ova and transferring them to the uterus for the prenatal period. Many websites are available for advice, exchange of information, and encouragement to individuals who are using or thinking about using these new technologies. The following sections describe reproductive technologies in use today.

ARTIFICIAL INSEMINATION

This is an old form of reproductive technology that is commonly used in animal husbandry and more recently has been applied to human fertilization. Sperm that have been donated and frozen are injected into a woman at the time of her ovulation. The most successful approach is to inject the sperm directly into the uterus (IUI, intrauterine insemination), thus bypassing the potentially destructive cervical environment.

Typically, the male partner is the source of the sperm; however, this is not necessary. Some sperm banks keep the donors' characteristics on file, which enables the woman to select the sperm of a donor whose features she desires in her offspring. Other banks blend sperm, so that the recipient cannot trace the donor's identity. In one recent case, a woman froze her husband's sperm and was able to conceive his child using **artificial insemination** after his death. Success rate: 5% to 30% per cycle using IUI (www.IVF-infertility.com, 2007).

FERTILITY DRUGS

Ovulation induction is the artificial stimulation of the ovaries to produce eggs using **fertility drugs**. There is about a 90% chance that the ovaries can be made to work with the right drug(s) so long as the woman does not have a raised baseline FSH level that may indicate ovarian failure (www.ivf-infertility.com, 2007). The administration of fertility drugs usually results in the release of multiple eggs at a cycle, increasing the chances that one egg will be fertilized. In about 20% of cases, multiple births result. Most other

assisted reproductive technologies begin with this step (i.e., using some form of medication to stimulate the ovaries to produce eggs). If this is successful, decisions must be made about how many eggs to fertilize and how many embryos to transfer to the uterus.

IN VITRO FERTILIZATION (FERTILIZATION IN AN ARTIFICIAL ENVIRONMENT)

Eggs are removed from the ovary and placed in a petri dish inside an incubator. A few drops of sperm are then added to the dish. If the eggs are fertilized and the cells begin to divide, they are implanted in the uterus for subsequent development. Typically, two or three embryos are transferred at once in hopes that at least one will implant and mature. Success rate: 32.9% (U.S. Department of Health and Human Services, Centers for Disease Control and Prevention, 2006).

INTRACYTOPLASMIC SPERM INJECTION

A modification of in vitro fertilization in which a sperm is injected directly into the egg. This procedure is used when there is a very low sperm

---

before conceiving or giving up on their hopes for a biologically related child (Savitz-Smith, 2003). Over time, the impact of infertility can become increasingly stressful, leading to high levels of depression as various alternatives are tried and fail (Domar et al., 2000).

In addition to the emotional costs of treatment, there are substantial financial costs amounting to tens of thousands of dollars, most of which is not covered by insurance. Moreover, many procedures are unsuccessful. During 1 year of unprotected sexual relations, 90% of healthy couples achieve pregnancy. Data from 430 U.S. clinics reporting to the National Center for Chronic Disease Prevention and Health Promotion in 2007 provide a picture of the likelihood that a reproductive cycle results in a live birth. The cycle begins with the fertilization of one or more ova using one of the techniques described in the box on reproductive technologies. The 142,435 ART cycles performed at these reporting clinics resulted in 43,412 live births (deliveries of one or more living infants) and 57,565 infants. This is an overall success rate of 30% of live births per ART cycles (U.S. Department

of Health and Human Services, Centers for Disease Control and Prevention, 2009). For more information about infertility and reproductive technologies, you may want to visit the website of the International Council on Infertility Information Dissemination at www.inciid.org

On an encouraging note, studies have reported the positive quality of parenting and positive developmental outcomes for children conceived through **artificial insemination**, **surrogacy**, and **in vitro fertilization** (Golombok, Cook, Bish, & Murray, 1995; Golombok, MacCallum, & Goodman, 2001; Golombok, Murray, Jadva, MacCallum, & Lycett, 2004). Families with children conceived through alternative reproductive technologies have been compared with families with naturally conceived and adopted children. In general, parents of children conceived through both types of assisted reproduction showed more warmth and involvement with their children, higher levels of interaction, and lower levels of stress than the parents of children who were conceived naturally. Parents of adopted children typically scored in between the levels of the other two groups. In a comparison of

count or nonmotile sperm. Embryos produced by in vitro fertilization can be frozen for future use if the initial pregnancy does not reach full term. Success rate: 30.9% (U.S. Department of Health and Human Services, Centers for Disease Control and Prevention, 2006).

GAMETE INTRAFALLOPIAN TRANSFER (GIFT)

Eggs and sperm are transferred into a woman's fallopian tubes. Fertilization takes place as it normally would, within the woman's reproductive system. These eggs and sperm may come from the couple or from other donors. Thus, the fetus may be genetically related to the man or the woman in the couple or to neither. Success rate: 23.3% (U.S. Department of Health and Human Services, Centers for Disease Control and Prevention, 2006).

IN VIVO FERTILIZATION (FERTILIZATION IN A LIVING BODY)

Partners involve another woman in the conception. The second woman, who has demonstrated her fertility, is artificially inseminated with the man's sperm. Once an embryo has formed, it is transferred to the first woman's uterus, which becomes the gestational environment. The child is therefore genetically related to the man but not to the woman.

SURROGATE MOTHER

There are two types of surrogacy, traditional and gestational. In the traditional surrogacy, sperm from an infertile woman's husband are injected into the **surrogate mother** during the time of her monthly ovulation. This is repeated each month until the surrogate becomes pregnant. The surrogate mother bears the child and returns it to the couple at birth. In gestational surrogacy, the couple produces the embryo through IVF and the resulting embryo is implanted in the surrogate. Surrogacy is an expensive and legally complicated procedure. Not all states allow surrogacy, and each state has its own regulations regarding its execution. The Center for Disease Control and Prevention estimated that there were 550 births through surrogacy in 2002 (http://BabyCenter.com, 2006).

Critical Thinking Questions

1. Of the ARTs described, which ones appear to have the best chance of resulting in a live birth?
2. What are the costs associated with these various ARTs? You will have to go to other sources beyond this book to find out about this.
3. What are the risks associated with each method? Again, you will have to draw on additional resources and use your critical thinking skills to address this question.
4. What are the different reasons that people may have for wanting to explore ARTs? What medical or personal circumstances might lead to a preference for one method over another?
5. If you were advising someone who was thinking about using ART, how would you approach the topic? What factors would you want the person to be aware of? What would you point out related to health risks, costs, and success rates?
6. Why might someone prefer using one of these technologies over adopting a child?

parenting experiences for couples who conceived through a successful ART procedure and couples who conceived spontaneously, mothering experiences during the child's first year of life were more positive for the ART mothers. Difficulties with the birth, challenges associated with low-birth-weight babies, and difficulties soothing the babies were perceived as less stressful for the ART mothers than for mothers who conceived through spontaneous fertility (Repokari et al., 2006). In general, the research to date suggests a positive developmental trajectory for mother-infant relationships for infants conceived through in vitro fertilization.

Ethical Considerations. Assisted reproductive technologies (ARTs) have raised many legal and ethical questions. One of these questions focuses on equitable access to these new technologies (Beckman & Harvey, 2005). A variety of social, medical, financial, and legal practices have resulted in limited access to ART for certain groups of women including lesbians, poor women, and women whose ability to rear children is questioned, especially women with certain disabilities and older women (Peterson, 2005). As a result of fertility intervention, a 63-year-old postmenopausal woman gave birth. She was reported to be the oldest birth mother on record (Kalb, 1997). Ethical considerations have been raised about the use of medical technology to keep the birth window open at this advanced age. Concerns focus on the medical complications associated with pregnancy in older women and on whether older men and women can sustain effective parenting as their children move into adolescence while they enter later adulthood.

Another area of ethical concern involves what people consider to be the acceptable use of reproductive technologies. For example, there is a debate about whether couples should be allowed to use reproductive technologies to select the sex of their child or to select for or against certain genetic conditions such as deafness or Down syndrome that are not life threatening (Hollingsworth, 2005; Johnston, 2005). A third ethical concern involves the lack of information for consumers in order to make a reasoned decision about whether to elect to use reproductive technologies. Information about risks, costs, legal considerations, and effectiveness is often not available or not accurate (Wingert, Harvey, Duncan, & Berry, 2005).

Questions are raised about the limits that should be placed on the production and use of embryos in vitro. Should we permit scientists to produce embryos from frozen sperm and egg cells for purposes other than implantation? Thousands of frozen embryos are held in various medical and laboratory facilities in the United States. Research on embryos is important for further understanding of the expression of genetic diseases, for understanding the factors associated with miscarriages, and for improving reproductive technologies. Various countries as well as states within the United States differ in their laws governing the use, preservation, and ownership of embryos produced through ART. Ethical and legal questions are being raised about the rights of parents to determine the fate of these embryos, the embryos' rights to protection and inheritance, and the responsibility of institutes and laboratories to ensure the proper use of the embryos (Krones et al., 2006).

Finally, issues regarding claims to parenthood are called into question. The husband of a woman who is planning to be artificially inseminated must consent to the procedure and agree to assume legal guardianship of the offspring. But are there parental rights associated with being sperm and egg donors? Over the years, a range of new policies and procedures have been instituted to help clarify and limit the rights of all those involved in ART births.

Some adults choose **adoption** as an alternative to child-bearing as a way of having children. Adoption is an alternative to biological reproduction for those who believe that there are already enough children who need families, and for those who have tried alternative reproductive technologies to no avail. Most agencies that provide adoption services suggest that couples who have undergone treatment for infertility need to cope with the grief and disappointment of unsuccessful outcomes before engaging in the adoption process. Once the alternative of adoption is being considered, new decisions must be faced including: international versus domestic adoption; age of child; racial preferences; and adoption from a private service or a public agency. The adoption process typically includes a 3- to 6-month home study in which a social worker gathers information about the adoptive parents. This process allows the adoptive parents to consider the decision to adopt from many angles, and also allows the agency to reach an informed assessment of whether the prospective parents will be able to provide a caring, supportive family for the adoptive child (Pertman, 2000; Arcus & Chambers, 2008).

Development in the First Trimester

The period of pregnancy—typically 40 weeks after the last menstrual period, or 38 weeks from ovulation—is often conceptualized in three 3-month periods called *trimesters*. Perhaps because development is so rapid and dramatic during the first trimester, it is divided further into the **germinal period**, the **embryonic period**, and the **fetal period**. Each trimester brings changes in the status of the developing fetus and its supporting systems. These changes are summarized briefly in Table 4.2 (Moore & Persaud, 2003). The pregnant woman also experiences changes during the trimesters. In the first trimester, many women are not certain that they are pregnant. By the last trimester, though, the woman is usually certain, and so is everyone else!

The Germinal Period

After fertilization, the egg begins to divide. At this time, the cell material is referred to as a **zygote** until implantation.

TABLE 4.2 Major Developments in Fetal Growth during the Three Trimesters

FIRST TRIMESTER	SECOND TRIMESTER	THIRD TRIMESTER
Fertilization	Sucking and swallowing	Nervous system matures
Growth of the amniotic sac	Preference for sweet taste	Coordination of sucking and swallowing
Growth of the placenta	Skin ridges on fingers and toes	Mechanisms for regulating body temperature
Emergence of body parts	Hair on scalp, eyebrows, back, arms, legs	More efficient digestion and excretion
Differentiation of sex organs	Sensitivity to touch, taste, light	Degeneration of the placenta toward the end of the ninth month
Initial formation of central nervous system	Sucks thumb	
Movement	6-month average size: 10 inches, 2 pounds	9-month average size: 20 inches, 7 to 7½ pounds
Grasp reflex		
Babinski reflex		
Heartbeat		
3-month average size: 3 inches, about ²/₅ ounce		

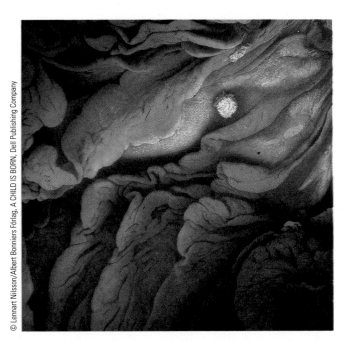

© Lennart Nilsson/Albert Bonniers Förlag, A CHILD IS BORN, Dell Publishing Company

The fertilized egg begins to divide as it travels along the fallopian tube toward the uterus.

The first series of cell divisions does not increase the mass of the cells, nor do the cells take on specialized functions; rather, the cell material is redistributed among several parts. When implantation is successful, by the sixth day after fertilization, the egg makes contact with the lining of the uterus and begins to attach itself there. At this point, the cells are referred to as an **embryo**. Sometimes, the egg does not reach the uterus but attaches itself to the fallopian tube or even to some area of the intestine. The embryo may grow in these locations until the organ ruptures.

The Embryonic Period

The 3 weeks following implantation are devoted primarily to elaboration of the supportive elements that will house the embryo. An **amniotic sac** surrounds the embryo and fills with a clear, watery fluid. This fluid acts as a cushion that buffers the embryo and permits it to move about and change position. Once the embryo is firmly implanted in the uterus, special cells in the placenta produce a hormone that maintains the uterine lining. This hormone is excreted through the kidneys, so a urine sample can be evaluated to determine its presence. Home pregnancy tests are based on the detection of this hormone in a small drop of urine and are accurate 1 or 2 days after implantation. A large number of pregnancies are spontaneously aborted in these early weeks, usually as a result of some major abnormalities of the embryo (Winston & Handyside, 1993).

The **placenta** is an organ that is newly formed with each pregnancy and is expelled at birth. Nutrients necessary for the embryo's growth pass through the placenta, as does the embryo's waste, which then passes into the mother's blood. Thus, the placenta is an exchange station at which adult material is synthesized for the embryo's use and foreign materials harmful to the embryo's development can be screened out. However, this screening is imperfect. Even though the mother's blood and the embryo's blood are separated by independent systems, the placenta permits the two systems to come close enough that oxygen and nutrients from the mother's blood can enter the fetal system and waste products from the fetal system can be removed. In the process, certain substances in the mother's system may affect the fetal system.

Agents that can produce malformations in the fetus while the tissues and organs are forming are referred to as **teratogens**. Teratogens have a wide variety of forms, such as viruses; medicines, alcohol, and other drugs that a pregnant woman takes; and **environmental toxins**. During the first trimester—especially weeks 3 through 9—the embryo is particularly sensitive to the disruptive influences of teratogens (see Figure 4.7).

In the third and fourth weeks, the embryo's cells differentiate rapidly, taking on the specialized structures that will permit them to carry out their unique functions in the body. Similar cells are grouped into tissues that gradually emerge as body organs. The first essential changes include the establishment of the body form as an elongated cylinder and the formation of the precursors of the brain and the heart. The neural tube, which is the structural basis of the central nervous system, begins to take shape at the end of the third week after conception. Cells in the neural tube are produced at the miraculous rate of 250,000 a minute over the first 5 weeks, as the tube is differentiated into five bulges that are the forerunners of the major subdivisions of the brain.

The central nervous system begins to develop early in the prenatal period and continues to develop throughout childhood and adolescence. Most of the neurons that will make up the cerebral cortex are produced by the end of the second trimester. By birth, the infant's brain contains roughly 100 billion neurons, ready to be linked and organized into networks as the infant responds to environmental stimulation and patterned experience (Aoki & Siekevitz, 1988; Nash, 1997). By the end of the fourth week, the head, the upper trunk, and the lower trunk are visible, as are the limb buds and the forerunners of the forebrain, midbrain, hindbrain, eyes, and ears. The embryo has increased 50 times in length and 40,000 times in weight since the moment of fertilization.

By the end of the second month, the embryo looks quite human. It weighs about 2.25 grams and is about 28 millimeters (1 inch) long. Almost all the internal organs are formed, as are the external features of the face, limbs, fingers, and toes. At 8 weeks, the embryo will respond to mild stimulation. The embryonic period ends about 10 weeks after the last menstrual period—most of the essential structures are formed by this time. The term **fetus** is used from this point until birth.

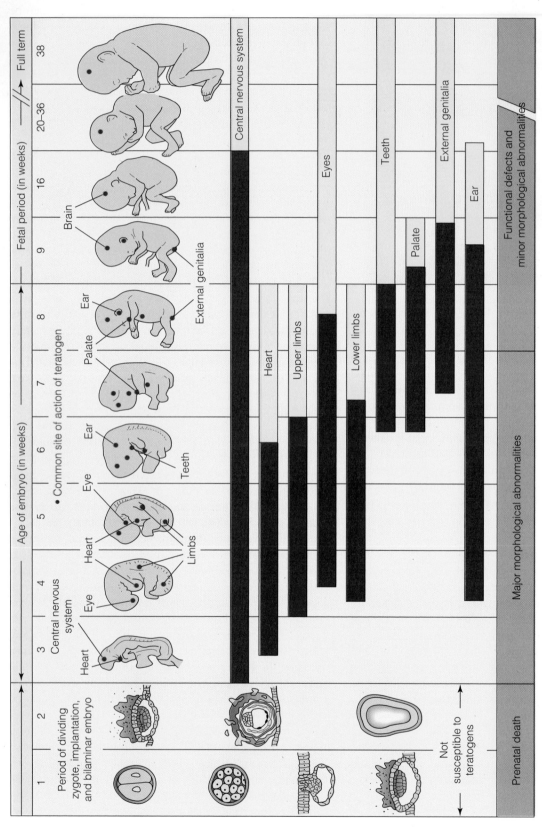

FIGURE 4.7 Critical Periods in Prenatal Development. During the first 2 weeks of development, the embryo is usually not susceptible to teratogens. During these pre-differentiation stages, a substance either damages all or most of the cells of the embryo, resulting in its death, or damages only a few cells, allowing the embryo to recover without developing defects. Dark bars denote highly sensitive periods for particular organs or organ systems; light bars indicate stages that are less sensitive to teratogens. Severe mental retardation may result from the exposure of the embryo or fetus to teratogenic agents, such as high levels of radiation, from the 8th to the 16th week.

Source: From *Before we were born: Essentials of embryology and birth defects*, 6th ed., by K. L. Moore and T.V. N Persaud, p. 130. Copyright © 2003 by W. B. Saunders. Reprinted by permission of Elsevier.

Late in pregnancy, the fetal brain begins to produce hormones that increase the production of estrogen in the placenta. This, in turn, leads to a shift from mild to strong uterine contractions, which result in dilation of the cervix, rupture of the amniotic sac, and delivery (Nathanielsz, 1996). The approximate time from conception to birth is 38 weeks. However, there is a great deal of variability in the duration of pregnancies and in the size of full-term infants, even infants born to the same mother.

The Birth Process

Objective 4. To describe the birth process and factors that contribute to infant mortality.

Birth is initiated by involuntary contractions of the uterine muscles, commonly referred to as **labor**. The length of time from the beginning of labor to the birth of the infant is highly variable. The average time is 14 hours for women undergoing their first labor (*primiparae*) and 8 hours for women undergoing later labors (*multiparae*).

The uterine contractions serve two central functions: *effacement* and *dilation*. **Effacement**, or thinning, is the shortening of the cervical canal. **Dilation** is the gradual enlargement of the cervix from an opening only millimeters wide to one of about 10 centimeters—large enough for the baby to pass through. Effacement and dilation occur without deliberate effort by the mother. Once the cervix is fully enlarged, the mother can assist in the birth by exerting pressure on the abdominal walls of the uterus. The baby, too, helps in the birth process by squirming, turning its head, and pushing against the birth canal.

Stages of Labor

The medical profession describes three stages of labor. The first stage begins with the onset of uterine contractions and ends with the full dilation of the cervix; this is the longest stage. The second stage involves the expulsion of the fetus. It begins at full dilation and ends with the delivery of the baby. The third stage begins with delivery and ends with the expulsion of the placenta. This stage usually lasts 5 to 10 minutes.

These three stages of labor do not precisely parallel the personal experience of childbirth. For example, although the expulsion of the placenta is considered a unique stage of labor in the medical model, it is rarely mentioned in women's accounts of their birth experiences. On the other hand, many of the signs of impending labor that occur in the last weeks of pregnancy are often included in women's accounts of labor.

In terms of the psychological adaptation to the birth process, labor can be viewed as having five phases: (1) early signs that labor is approaching; (2) strong, regular uterine contractions, signaling that labor has begun and generally accompanied by a move from the home to the hospital or birthing center; (3) the transition phase, during which contractions are strong, rest times between contractions are short, and women experience the greatest difficulty or discomfort; (4) the birth process, which allows the mother's active participation in the delivery and is generally accompanied by a move from the labor area to the more sterile delivery room; and (5) the postpartum period, which involves the initial interactions with the newborn, physiological changes that mark a return to the prepregnant state, and the return home. The significant events of these phases are summarized in Table 4.3.

Cesarean Delivery

Sometimes a normal, spontaneous vaginal delivery would be dangerous to the mother or the newborn (Cunningham et al., 2001). One alternative is to remove the baby surgically through an incision in the uterine wall. The procedure, called a **cesarean section**, may have gotten its name from an 8th century BC Roman law, *lex cesarea*, which required that in the case of the death of a pregnant woman, a postmortem operative delivery would be performed, so that the mother and child could be buried separately (Sehdev, 2005). Until as late as the 17th century, infants might be saved through the cesarean section but the operation was usually fatal to mothers.

The incidence of cesarean deliveries in the United States increased from 5.5% of births in 1970 to 32% in 2007 (Menacker & Hamilton, 2010). Cesarean deliveries may be planned or unplanned. The procedure may be used if labor is severely prolonged and the fetus appears to be at risk due to lack of oxygen. It may also be used when the infant is in the breech position (feet or buttocks first rather than head first) or if the mother's pelvis is too small for the infant's head to pass through. Physicians often recommend a repeat cesarean if the woman has delivered by cesarean section before. The rate of cesarean deliveries is higher for mothers age 30 and older than for younger mothers.

The cesarean delivery makes childbirth a surgical procedure, requiring anesthetics, intravenous feeding of the mother, and a prolonged recovery period. Although the procedure undoubtedly saves many infants and mothers who would not survive vaginal childbirth, there is some concern that it is being misused for the convenience of health professionals or busy mothers who want to be able to schedule deliveries and thus avoid waiting for the unpredictable onset of labor. In a national goal statement, *Healthy People 2020*, the U.S. Public Health Service calls for a reduction of the national cesarean rate for both first-time deliveries and for births following a cesarean with an overall rate of 15% (National Center for Health Statistics, 2009)—a goal implying that a substantial number of the current cesarean procedures are not required.

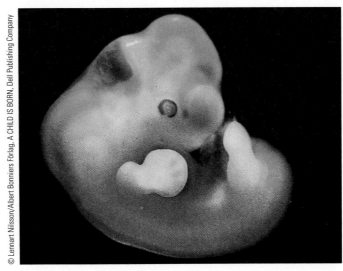

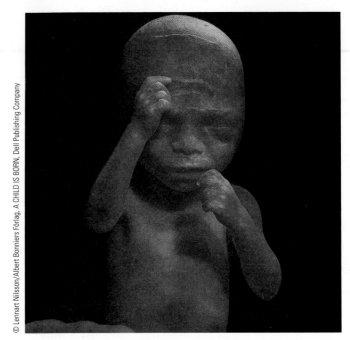

© Lennart Nilsson/Albert Bonniers Förlag, A CHILD IS BORN, Dell Publishing Company

At 23 weeks, the fetus is about 12 inches (30 cm) long, still small enough to have room to swim about in the expanding uterus. As any pregnant woman will tell you, the fetus is active at this stage, kicking, grasping, waving its arms, and turning over.

movement become increasingly coordinated. These patterns suggest a critical integration of the somatic and cardiac processes within the central nervous system. At some point between 28 and 32 weeks, these patterns of increase stop, and are replaced by a leveling off or slight decrease. This pattern is interpreted to mean that a certain critical level of neurological maturation is in place by 32 weeks. Evidence to support this idea is found in the cognitive competence of preterm infants who are born at about 32 weeks (DiPietro et al., 2004).

Additional evidence of cognitive maturation is provided by studies of fetal memory. By the age of 30 weeks gestational age, the fetus appears to recognize and remember the sensation of a vibroacoustic stimulus that is applied to the mother's abdomen. Fetal movement in the second following the stimulus is taken as evidence of a response. The absence of fetal movement on four trials following several consecutive positive responses is taken as evidence of habituation or familiarity with the stimulus. By 38 weeks of gestational age, the fetus recognizes these vibroacoustic stimuli even 4 weeks after the last testing session (Dirix, Nijhuis, Jongsma, & Hornstra, 2009).

Studies of 36- to 39-week-old fetuses have found that they are sensitive to changes in low-pitched musical notes, to pulsing as compared to continuous sounds, and to changes in speech sounds (Groome et al., 2000; Lecanuet, Graniere-Deferre, Jacquet, & DeCasper, 2000; Byers-Heinlein, Burns, & Werker, 2010). In one study, pregnant women recited a children's rhyme aloud every day from the 33rd through the 37th week of fetal development. Monitoring of the fetal heart

rate provided evidence that the fetuses recognized a ta recording of the familiar rhyme in comparison to unfan iar rhymes. All this evidence supports the notion that a fe experiences its mother's speech sounds during the third mester and becomes familiar with the sound of her voice the features of her spoken language (DeCasper et al., 199

The advantages that a full-term fetus has over a prer ture, 28-week-old fetus include: (1) the ability to begin maintain regular breathing; (2) a stronger sucking respor (3) well-coordinated swallowing movements; (4) stror peristalsis and, therefore, more efficient digestion and w excretion; and (5) a more fully balanced control of b temperature.

The full-term fetus has been able to take advant of minerals in the mother's diet for the formation of tc enamel. As the placenta begins to degenerate in the month of pregnancy, antibodies against various diseases have been formed in the mother's blood pass into the bloodstream. They provide the fetus with immunity to n diseases during the first few months of life.

The uterus cannot serve indefinitely as the home o fetus. Several factors lead to the eventual termination o fetal-uterine relationship. First, as the placenta degener antibodies that form in both the mother's and the fe blood would destroy the blood of the other. Second, bec the placenta does not grow much larger than 2 pounds fetus, as it reaches its maximum size, cannot obtain en nutrients to sustain life. Third, the fetal head cannot much larger than the pelvic opening without endange the brain in the birth process. Even though soft conne membranes permit the skull plates to overlap, head size factor that limits fetal growth.

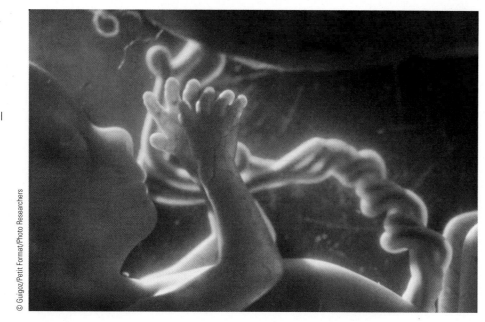

© Guigoz/Petit Format/Photo Researchers

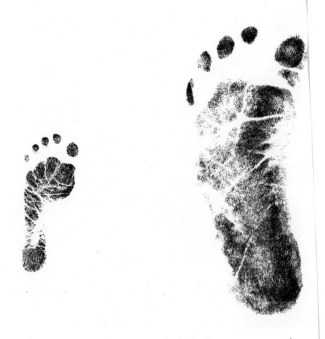

© Brendan Smialowski/AFP/Getty Images

© David Young-Wolff/Photo Edit

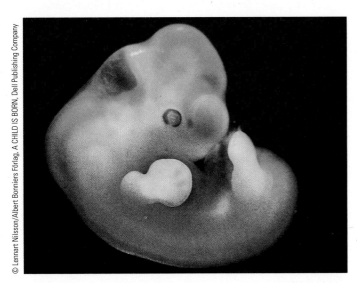

At 5½ weeks, cell differentiation has resulted in an embryo that is about 0.4 inch (1 cm) long. Emerging shapes of the head, arm, and fingers are visible. Many women are not even sure about their pregnancy at this point in fetal development.

At 8 weeks, the fingers are clearly differentiated and the hand is distinct from the forearm. Reflexes sometimes guide the hand toward the face. The fetus is encased in the amniotic sac.

The Fetal Period

In the third month, the fetus grows to 3 inches, and its weight increases to 14 grams. The head is about one third of the total body length. During this month, the fetus assumes the *fetal position*, arms curled up toward the face and knees bent in to the stomach. The eyelids are fused.

A dramatic change takes place in the sex organs during this period. All embryos go through a bisexual stage, during which no sex-linked characteristics can be discerned. Both female and male embryos have a surface mass that becomes the testes in male fetuses and eventually deteriorates in female fetuses, when new sex cells grow to form the ovaries. Both male and female embryos have two sets of sex ducts. In male fetuses, the sperm ducts develop and the female ducts dissolve. In female fetuses, the fallopian tubes, the uterus, and the vagina develop, and the other ducts degenerate. Finally, both male and female embryos have a conical area that is the outlet for the bladder duct. When the male testes develop, this area forms into the penis and scrotum. In female fetuses, it remains to form the clitoris, which is surrounded by the genital swellings of the labia majora.

Differentiation of the male and female genitalia is guided by genetic information. In the presence of the maleness gene, SRY, the undifferentiated embryonic tissue is transformed into the testes. The testes then produce hormones that facilitate the further elaboration of male genitalia and internal reproductive structures. Genes carried on the X chromosome are thought to guide the formation of the ovaries (Crooks & Bauer, 2005).

The genetic factors that produce the differentiation of the fetus as male or female appear to influence more than the formation of the reproductive organs and the production of hormones. Research on the organization and structure of the brain suggests that during fetal and early postnatal development, sex hormones direct male and female brains along slightly different paths. Three areas of the brain—the hypothalamus, amygdala, and hippocampus—have been studied as potential sites for sex differences in structure that may relate to some of the functional areas in which men's and women's problem-solving and cognitive skills differ (Kimura, 1992).

Although males and females are very similar in most psychological variables, and in particular have similar distributions in measured intelligence, studies by numerous researchers have shown that sex differences in hormonal levels influence differences in specific problem-solving areas and intellectual strengths. Some of the areas in which males and females have been shown to differ include: verbal ability, visual-spatial ability, and mathematical ability. We are still not sure what the route is from the developing fetal brain structure to cognitive functioning in childhood and beyond, but it is increasingly clear that anatomical variations in regions of the brain and their interconnections are tied to sex-linked variations in certain specialized problem-solving capacities (Kimura, 2002).

The 3-month-old fetus moves spontaneously and has both a grasp reflex and a Babinski reflex, in which the toes extend and fan out in response to a mild stroke on the sole of the foot. When an amplified stethoscope, called a Doppler, is placed on the mother's abdomen, the fetal heartbeat can be heard through the uterine wall by the expectant parents as well as the physician and nurse. For expectant parents, listening to the fetal heartbeat is one of the first experiences that transforms the fetus from something abstract and remote to a concrete, vital reality.

Development in the Second Trimester

During the second trimester, the average fetus grows to 10 inches and increases in weight to almost 2 pounds. The fetus continues to grow at the rate of about an inch every 10 days from the fifth month until the end of the pregnancy. During this trimester, the uterus itself begins to stretch and grow. It rises into the mother's abdominal cavity and expands until, by the end of the ninth month, it is pushing against the ribs and diaphragm. The reality of a growing life becomes more evident to the pregnant woman during this trimester as she observes the changes in her body and experiences the early fetal movements, called **quickening**. These movements first feel like light bubbles or twitches; later, they can be identified as the foot, elbow, or fist of the restless resident.

During the fourth month, the fetus begins to suck and swallow. Whenever the fetus opens its mouth, amniotic fluid enters and cycles through the system. This fluid provides some nutrients in addition to those absorbed through the placenta. The 4-month-old fetus shows some preference for a sweet taste: If sugar is introduced into the amniotic fluid, it will swallow the fluid at a faster rate.

In the fifth month, the skin begins to thicken, and a cheesy coating of dead cells and oil, the *vernix caseosa*, covers the skin. The individuality of the fetus is marked by the pattern of skin ridges on the fingers and toes. Hair covers the scalp, eyebrows, back, arms, and legs.

The sensory receptors of the fetus are well established by the end of the sixth month. The fetus is sensitive to touch and may react to it with a muscle movement. It will also stick out its tongue in response to a bitter taste. Throughout the sixth month, the nostrils are plugged by skin cells. When these cells dissolve, the nose fills with amniotic fluid; thus, the sense of smell is probably not functional until birth.

The external ear canal is filled with fluid, and the fetus does not tend to respond to sound until the eighth or ninth month; however, the semicircular canals of the inner ear are sensitive to stimulation. The nerve fibers that connect the retina to the brain are developed by 6 months, and infants born prematurely at this time respond to light.

At 25 weeks, the fetus functions well within its uterine environment. It swallows, digests, excretes, moves about, sucks its thumb, rests, and grows. However, the nervous system, which begins to develop at 3 weeks, is still not mature enough to coordinate the many systems that must function simultaneously to ensure survival. Whereas the 22-week-old fetus has almost no chance to survive outside the uterus, the outlook for a 24-week-old fetus is anywhere from 50% to 90%, depending on the quality of the intensive care and the birth conditions. By 30 weeks, survival outside the uterus is almost certain.

Development in the Third Trimester

In the last trimester, the average fetus grows from 10 to 20 inches and increases in weight from 2 to 7 or 7½ pounds. These increases in body size and weight are paralleled by a maturation of the central nervous system. From 20 to 28 weeks of gestational age, fetal heart rate declines and variability and accelerations in heart rate increase. In the third trimester, there are longer periods of quiet between fetal movements. By combining recordings from ultrasound and monitoring of fetal heart rate, patterns of fetal behavioral states have been documented. They include periods of quiet, similar to non-REM sleep in newborns; periods of frequent movement with sleep-like heartbeat, similar to REM sleep; periods of quiet wakefulness; and periods of active wakefulness (Nijhuis, 2003). Moreover, fetal heart rate and fetal

At 16 weeks, the fetus is about 6.4 inches (16 cm) long and is clearly recognizable as a human child. The fetus has assumed what is known as the "fetal position"—arms curled up near the head and legs bent in toward the stomach—a position that remains part of the human behavioral repertoire throughout life.

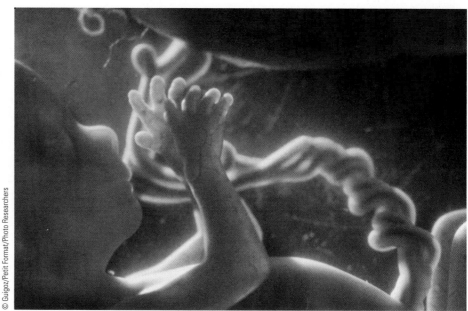

© Guigoz/Petit Format/Photo Researchers

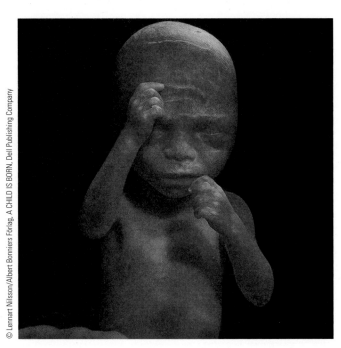

© Lennart Nilsson/Albert Bonniers Förlag, A CHILD IS BORN, Dell Publishing Company

At 23 weeks, the fetus is about 12 inches (30 cm) long, still small enough to have room to swim about in the expanding uterus. As any pregnant woman will tell you, the fetus is active at this stage, kicking, grasping, waving its arms, and turning over.

movement become increasingly coordinated. These patterns suggest a critical integration of the somatic and cardiac processes within the central nervous system. At some point between 28 and 32 weeks, these patterns of increase stop, and are replaced by a leveling off or slight decrease. This pattern is interpreted to mean that a certain critical level of neurological maturation is in place by 32 weeks. Evidence to support this idea is found in the cognitive competence of preterm infants who are born at about 32 weeks (DiPietro et al., 2004).

Additional evidence of cognitive maturation is provided by studies of fetal memory. By the age of 30 weeks gestational age, the fetus appears to recognize and remember the sensation of a vibroacoustic stimulus that is applied to the mother's abdomen. Fetal movement in the second following the stimulus is taken as evidence of a response. The absence of fetal movement on four trials following several consecutive positive responses is taken as evidence of habituation or familiarity with the stimulus. By 38 weeks of gestational age, the fetus recognizes these vibroacoustic stimuli even 4 weeks after the last testing session (Dirix, Nijhuis, Jongsma, & Hornstra, 2009).

Studies of 36- to 39-week-old fetuses have found that they are sensitive to changes in low-pitched musical notes, to pulsing as compared to continuous sounds, and to changes in speech sounds (Groome et al., 2000; Lecanuet, Graniere-Deferre, Jacquet, & DeCasper, 2000; Byers-Heinlein, Burns, & Werker, 2010). In one study, pregnant women recited a children's rhyme aloud every day from the 33rd through the 37th week of fetal development. Monitoring of the fetal heart

rate provided evidence that the fetuses recognized a tape recording of the familiar rhyme in comparison to unfamiliar rhymes. All this evidence supports the notion that a fetus experiences its mother's speech sounds during the third trimester and becomes familiar with the sound of her voice and the features of her spoken language (DeCasper et al., 1994).

The advantages that a full-term fetus has over a premature, 28-week-old fetus include: (1) the ability to begin and maintain regular breathing; (2) a stronger sucking response; (3) well-coordinated swallowing movements; (4) stronger peristalsis and, therefore, more efficient digestion and waste excretion; and (5) a more fully balanced control of body temperature.

The full-term fetus has been able to take advantage of minerals in the mother's diet for the formation of tooth enamel. As the placenta begins to degenerate in the last month of pregnancy, antibodies against various diseases that have been formed in the mother's blood pass into the fetal bloodstream. They provide the fetus with immunity to many diseases during the first few months of life.

The uterus cannot serve indefinitely as the home of the fetus. Several factors lead to the eventual termination of the fetal-uterine relationship. First, as the placenta degenerates, antibodies that form in both the mother's and the fetus's blood would destroy the blood of the other. Second, because the placenta does not grow much larger than 2 pounds, the fetus, as it reaches its maximum size, cannot obtain enough nutrients to sustain life. Third, the fetal head cannot grow much larger than the pelvic opening without endangering the brain in the birth process. Even though soft connecting membranes permit the skull plates to overlap, head size is a factor that limits fetal growth.

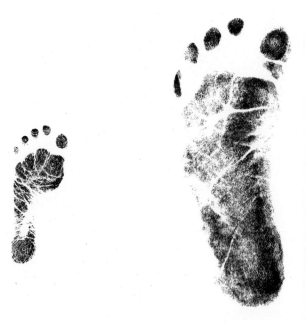

Courtesy of Stanford Hospital

These are the birth footprints of a baby born prematurely at 23 weeks, and one born at a full 40-week gestational age.

Late in pregnancy, the fetal brain begins to produce hormones that increase the production of estrogen in the placenta. This, in turn, leads to a shift from mild to strong uterine contractions, which result in dilation of the cervix, rupture of the amniotic sac, and delivery (Nathanielsz, 1996). The approximate time from conception to birth is 38 weeks. However, there is a great deal of variability in the duration of pregnancies and in the size of full-term infants, even infants born to the same mother.

The Birth Process

Objective 4. To describe the birth process and factors that contribute to infant mortality.

Birth is initiated by involuntary contractions of the uterine muscles, commonly referred to as **labor**. The length of time from the beginning of labor to the birth of the infant is highly variable. The average time is 14 hours for women undergoing their first labor (*primiparae*) and 8 hours for women undergoing later labors (*multiparae*).

The uterine contractions serve two central functions: *effacement* and *dilation*. **Effacement**, or thinning, is the shortening of the cervical canal. **Dilation** is the gradual enlargement of the cervix from an opening only millimeters wide to one of about 10 centimeters—large enough for the baby to pass through. Effacement and dilation occur without deliberate effort by the mother. Once the cervix is fully enlarged, the mother can assist in the birth by exerting pressure on the abdominal walls of the uterus. The baby, too, helps in the birth process by squirming, turning its head, and pushing against the birth canal.

Stages of Labor

The medical profession describes three stages of labor. The first stage begins with the onset of uterine contractions and ends with the full dilation of the cervix; this is the longest stage. The second stage involves the expulsion of the fetus. It begins at full dilation and ends with the delivery of the baby. The third stage begins with delivery and ends with the expulsion of the placenta. This stage usually lasts 5 to 10 minutes.

These three stages of labor do not precisely parallel the personal experience of childbirth. For example, although the expulsion of the placenta is considered a unique stage of labor in the medical model, it is rarely mentioned in women's accounts of their birth experiences. On the other hand, many of the signs of impending labor that occur in the last weeks of pregnancy are often included in women's accounts of labor.

In terms of the psychological adaptation to the birth process, labor can be viewed as having five phases: (1) early signs that labor is approaching; (2) strong, regular uterine contractions, signaling that labor has begun and generally accompanied by a move from the home to the hospital or birthing center; (3) the transition phase, during which contractions are strong, rest times between contractions are short, and women experience the greatest difficulty or discomfort; (4) the birth process, which allows the mother's active participation in the delivery and is generally accompanied by a move from the labor area to the more sterile delivery room; and (5) the postpartum period, which involves the initial interactions with the newborn, physiological changes that mark a return to the prepregnant state, and the return home. The significant events of these phases are summarized in Table 4.3.

Cesarean Delivery

Sometimes a normal, spontaneous vaginal delivery would be dangerous to the mother or the newborn (Cunningham et al., 2001). One alternative is to remove the baby surgically through an incision in the uterine wall. The procedure, called a **cesarean section**, may have gotten its name from an 8th century BC Roman law, *lex cesarea*, which required that in the case of the death of a pregnant woman, a postmortem operative delivery would be performed, so that the mother and child could be buried separately (Sehdev, 2005). Until as late as the 17th century, infants might be saved through the cesarean section but the operation was usually fatal to mothers.

The incidence of cesarean deliveries in the United States increased from 5.5% of births in 1970 to 32% in 2007 (Menacker & Hamilton, 2010). Cesarean deliveries may be planned or unplanned. The procedure may be used if labor is severely prolonged and the fetus appears to be at risk due to lack of oxygen. It may also be used when the infant is in the breech position (feet or buttocks first rather than head first) or if the mother's pelvis is too small for the infant's head to pass through. Physicians often recommend a repeat cesarean if the woman has delivered by cesarean section before. The rate of cesarean deliveries is higher for mothers age 30 and older than for younger mothers.

The cesarean delivery makes childbirth a surgical procedure, requiring anesthetics, intravenous feeding of the mother, and a prolonged recovery period. Although the procedure undoubtedly saves many infants and mothers who would not survive vaginal childbirth, there is some concern that it is being misused for the convenience of health professionals or busy mothers who want to be able to schedule deliveries and thus avoid waiting for the unpredictable onset of labor. In a national goal statement, *Healthy People 2020*, the U.S. Public Health Service calls for a reduction of the national cesarean rate for both first-time deliveries and for births following a cesarean with an overall rate of 15% (National Center for Health Statistics, 2009)—a goal implying that a substantial number of the current cesarean procedures are not required.

TABLE 4.3 Significant Events of the Five Stages of Labor

PHASE 1: EARLY SIGNS THAT LABOR IS APPROACHING

1. Lightening (about 10 to 14 days before delivery). The baby's head drops into the pelvic area.
2. Release of the plug that has kept the cervix closed.
3. Discharge of amniotic fluid.
4. False labor: irregular uterine contractions.

PHASE 2: ONSET OF LABOR

1. Transition from home to hospital or birthing center.
2. Strong, regular contractions 3–5 minutes apart.

PHASE 3: TRANSITION

1. Accelerated labor, with contractions lasting up to 90 seconds and coming 2 or 3 minutes apart.
2. Some sense of disorientation, heightened arousal, or loss of control.

PHASE 4: BIRTH

1. The baby's head presses down on the bottom of the birth canal.
2. The mother experiences a strong, reflexive urge to push to expel the baby.
3. The mother typically is moved from a labor area to a more sterile delivery room.

PHASE 5: POSTPARTUM PERIOD

1. Mother and infant have initial contact.
2. Placenta is expelled.
3. Rapid alteration of the hormone system to stimulate lactation and shrink the uterus.
4. Mother and infant engage in early learning behaviors; infant attempts to nurse; mother explores infant and begins to interpret his or her needs.
5. Return to the home and introduction of the newborn into the family setting.

Infant Mortality

The **infant mortality rate** is the number of infants who die during the first year of life per 1000 live births during that year. In 2006, the U.S. rate was estimated at 6.7 deaths per 1000 live births.

The rate for Black babies in the United States in 2006—13.3 deaths per 1000 live births—was higher than the infant mortality rates in countries such as Chile, the Czech Republic, Cuba, and Poland, which are considered economically emergent nations (U.S. Census Bureau, 2009).

Roughly two thirds of infant deaths occur during the first month after birth. Most of these deaths result from severe birth defects, premature birth, or **sudden infant death syndrome** (SIDS), in which apparently healthy babies are put to bed and are later found dead with no clear explanation, even after autopsy.

Infant mortality rates are influenced by many factors, including the: (1) frequency of birth complications; (2) robustness of the infants who are being born, which is influenced by their prenatal nutrition and degree of exposure to viruses or bacteria, damaging X rays, drugs, and other teratogens; (3) mother's age; and (4) facilities that are available for prenatal and newborn care. One fourth of infant deaths result from complications associated with low birth weight. If the conditions leading to prematurity could be altered, the U.S. infant mortality rate would be significantly improved (Kocohanek & Martin, 2004).

Infant mortality rates vary from one country and region of the world to another. In 2003, the infant mortality rate in Japan was 3.3, but in that same year, the infant mortality rate in nine other countries of the world was more than 90. The United States, with all its resources and advanced technology, ranks behind other industrialized countries, including Australia, Canada, France, Germany, Italy, Japan, the Netherlands, South Korea, Spain, and the United Kingdom. Within the United States, regional infant mortality rates range from a low of 4.7 per 1000 in the state of Washington, to a high of 11.3 in the District of Columbia (U.S. Census Bureau, 2010).

The density of low-income populations, availability of educational materials on the impact of diet and drugs on the developing fetus, and adequacy of medical facilities for high-risk newborns all contribute to the regional variations in infant death rates among populations of different incomes. Children conceived in poverty are at the greatest risk of infant mortality. Their mothers receive poorer quality prenatal care and are exposed to more dangerous environmental and health factors during the prenatal period than are mothers of children conceived in more advantaged families. The chances that any one infant will survive the stresses of birth depend on the convergence of biological, environmental, cultural, and economic influences on the child's intrauterine growth, delivery, and postnatal care (Dole et al., 2004).

The Mother, the Fetus, and the Psychosocial Environment

Objective 5. To analyze the reciprocity between the pregnant woman and the developing fetus, focusing on ways in which pregnancy affects a childbearing woman and expectant father and on basic influences on fetal growth, such as maternal age, drug use, nutrition, and environmental toxins.

The course and pattern of prenatal development are guided by genetic information that unfolds in the context of the pregnant woman's biopsychosocial environment. A woman's health, her attitudes toward pregnancy and childbirth, her lifestyle, the resources available to her during her pregnancy, and the behavior demanded of her by her culture all influence her sense of well-being. Many of these same factors may directly affect the health and growth of the fetus. In the next section, we discuss the impact of the fetus on the pregnant woman, including how the pregnancy might affect the infant's father and his relationship to the mother. The subsequent section focuses on the impact of the pregnant woman on the fetus and the many factors that contribute to the quality of the intrauterine environment.

The Impact of the Fetus on the Pregnant Woman

Consider some of the ways in which a fetus influences a pregnant woman. Pregnancy initiates sweeping hormonal changes that prepare the uterus to host the developing fetus. Over the months of pregnancy, the uterus changes in size and shape, altering the woman's physical appearance and placing new pressures on internal organs. Beginning in the second trimester, women experience fetal movement. Research that focused on the synchrony between fetal movement and maternal heart rate showed that after about 20 weeks gestational age, a regular pattern could be observed in which fetal movement is followed after 2 or 3 seconds by an increase in maternal heart rate. Fetal movement occurs about once every minute. Even when the pregnant woman is not aware of the movement, changes in heart rate following movement were observed. One can think of the fetus as making repeated and continuous signals that engage the mother's autonomic nervous system, and thereby begin a process through which the mother's level of arousal is linked to the infant's state (DiPietro et al., 2006).

Pregnancy alters a woman's body image and her sense of well-being. Some women feel especially vigorous and energetic during much of their pregnancy; others experience distressing symptoms such as nausea, backache, swelling, headache, and irritability. Some women say they have difficulty remembering things during their last trimester.

Although changes in the hormonal environment might be able to account for some of these symptoms, others are probably brought about by the convergence of the physical, cognitive, and emotional changes of pregnancy (Buckwalter et al., 1999). In some cases, pregnancy is accompanied by serious illnesses that threaten the mother's health.

Changes in Roles and Social Status

Women who become pregnant may be treated in new ways by people close to them and by the broader community. Usually, fathers become more concerned for and supportive of their pregnant partners, and pregnant women may also be viewed in a new light by their peers. In some communities, adolescent girls who become pregnant feel ashamed or guilty. In others, becoming pregnant during adolescence is viewed by the peer group as an accomplishment, a sign of maturity. At work, women who become pregnant may be given fewer responsibilities or may be passed over for promotions.

© Don Mason/CORBIS

Depending on their health, the type of work they do, and the support of family and workplace colleagues, some women can continue to work well into the last trimester of their pregnancy.

APPLYING THEORY AND RESEARCH TO LIFE

The Doula or Birth Companion

THE IDEA OF having a supportive companion available to women during childbirth has been formalized in the role of **doula**. The term *doula* comes from a Greek word for handmaiden, referring to the primary servant for the woman of the household. Before the introduction of hospital deliveries, most cultures had a role for a close female companion who accompanied a woman during childbirth. The contemporary doula is trained to offer information as well as physical and emotional support during labor, delivery, and the early weeks following childbirth. Her role is to remain at the side of the laboring mother to help her have a safe, reassuring childbirth experience. She does not take the place of the midwife, obstetrician, nurses, or the mother's partner (Doulas of North America, 1998).

The contribution of companion support to reducing complications during labor and delivery was studied with a group of Guatemalan women (Sosa, Kennell, Klaus, Robertson, & Urrutia, 1980). The hospital normally did not permit any visitors to remain with an expectant woman in the maternity ward.

Each woman in this study, however, was assigned a companion who stayed with her until delivery, talking to the woman, holding her hand, rubbing her back, and providing encouragement during labor. These mothers had fewer complications during labor than a group of women who had no companion, and their babies showed fewer signs of fetal distress. The mean length of labor was more than 10 hours shorter for those women who had a companion than for those who were alone.

A review of 15 studies involving more than 12,000 women examined additional empirical support for the contribution of the doula in childbirth (Hodnett, 2003). The studies were conducted in Australia, Belgium, Botswana, Canada, Finland, France, Greece, Guatemala, Mexico, South Africa, and the United States, under very different hospital conditions. All of the studies contrasted the childbirth experiences of women who did and did not have a supportive companion available during labor and delivery. Mothers who were accompanied by a supportive companion had shorter labors and fewer obstetrical difficulties. The presumption is that a woman who is attended by a doula has lower levels of anxiety, thus reducing the release of neurotransmitters that might contribute to obstetrical difficulties and neonatal distress (Corter & Fleming, 2002). The presence of a doula is especially valuable in cases, as in the Guatemalan study, where women would ordinarily labor alone with just the presence of the medical staff. To find out more about doulas and their role as birth companions, visit http://www.DONA .org (Doulas of North America).

Critical Thinking Questions

1. What are some possible mechanisms through which the presence of a supportive companion might shorten labor and ease the delivery?
2. What are the characteristics that would make a person an effective doula?
3. How would you design a study to evaluate the benefits of a doula in childbirth?
4. What are the characteristics of the U.S. birth culture that might prevent or support the inclusion of a doula as a component of prenatal care and childbirth?

In business settings, pregnancy may be viewed as an annoyance, something that is likely to interfere with productivity and is, at best, to be tolerated.

Within the family, a pregnant woman is likely to be treated with new levels of concern and care. Her pregnancy affects her partner, her parents and siblings, her previous children, and her partner's family. By giving birth to a first child, a woman transforms her mother and father into grandparents and her brothers and sisters into uncles and aunts. Moreover, pregnancy may strengthen the gender identity of the baby's mother or father. Just as infertility threatens one's gender identity, becoming pregnant may be viewed as confirmation of a woman's femininity and a man's virility in impregnating her (Heitlinger, 1989).

In some societies, pregnancy and childbirth confer special status on a woman. In Japan, for example, traditional values place motherhood above all other women's roles. "Only after giving birth to a child did a woman become a fully tenured person in the family" (Bankart, 1989). When they become mothers, Japanese women begin to have an impact on government, community, and public life as the people who are especially responsible for molding and shaping the next generation. For Mexican American women, childbearing is likely to be viewed within a broad religious context. "It is considered the privilege and essential obligation of a married woman to bear children, but children come 'when God is willing'" (Hahn & Muecke, 1987). Despite their difficult economic and social conditions, women who are Mexican immigrants in the United States have relatively fewer low-birth-weight babies than mothers from other low-income groups. One explanation for this is that pregnancy brings forth substantial family support, which buffers the pregnant woman from the adverse effects of poverty (Sherraden & Barrera, 1996; Sagrestano, Felman, Killingsworth Rini, Woo, & Dunkel-Schetter, 1999). See the box that discusses the positive effects for the mother of having a doula or supportive companion during the labor and delivery.

Changes in the Mother's Emotional State

Pregnancy is the 12th most stressful life change in a list of 43 life events in the *Social Readjustment Rating Scale* (Holmes & Rahe, 1967). Thus, it is no surprise that mothers and fathers have strong emotional reactions to pregnancy. The woman's attitude toward her unborn child may be pride, acceptance, rejection, or—as is usually the case—ambivalence. In most normal pregnancies, women experience anxiety and depression as well as positive feelings of excitement and hopefulness. The normal physical changes during the gestational period include symptoms that are often associated with depression, such as fatigue, sleeplessness, slowed physical movement, preoccupation with one's physical state, and moodiness (Kaplan, 1986). Moreover, throughout the pregnancy, the expectant woman has recurring worries and fears about the childbirth experience, whether the baby will be healthy, her own well-being, and the health and well-being of her family. These fears may be accentuated if the woman has heard about problems with childbirth from friends and relatives. In one study, women who had attended childbirth classes were interviewed 4 weeks after they gave birth. Thirty-four percent of the women reported that their childbirth experience was traumatic, including many who had symptoms of post-traumatic stress disorder (Soet, Brack, & Dilorio, 2003). Among women who have had previous pregnancies, worries may focus on recollections about the difficulties of delivery and the health and care of the new baby (Melender, 2002). Some women receive troubling information during an ultrasound screening about possible fetal abnormalities. This information adds to anxiety during pregnancy (Brisch et al., 2003).

Certain psychosocial factors are associated with increased anxiety and depression during pregnancy, including exposure to stressors, the absence of a supportive partner, and experiencing an unwanted pregnancy (Kalil, Gruber, Conley, & Sytniac, 1993). In a study of low-income African American and European American women, depression was high early in the pregnancy and declined in the months following the birth of the child, as the women coped successfully with their pregnancy. Self-esteem, which was higher for the African American women in the study, was associated with lower levels of initial prenatal depression. For both African American and European American women, the women who showed the greatest drop in depression over the pregnancy had relatively more financial resources, more social support, and fewer other life stressors (Ritter, Hobfoll, Lavin, Cameron, & Hulsizer, 2000). Some level of maternal anxiety may be appropriately adaptive as a woman prepares to experience labor and delivery and to make the many changes necessary to care for a newborn.

Fathers' Involvement during Pregnancy and Childbirth

Just like women, men have diverse reactions to the idea of having children. Their reproductive behaviors reflect their own psychosocial maturity, their perceptions about the quality and stability of the relationships they are in, the stability of their employment, and their readiness to embrace the responsibilities of fatherhood. Some men worry about the economic ramifications of the impending birth. If they are unemployed or underemployed, they may worry about money, have low confidence, feel they are not worth much, or be fearful that the mother's income will decrease. In a study of an ethnically diverse sample of low-income, noncustodial fathers, 171 men were aware of their responsibility for 424 pregnancies. In-depth interviews with these men revealed four levels of intentionality about conception (Augustine, Nelson, & Edin, 2009). At the two extremes, 17% of pregnancies were considered accidental and 15% were planned. But two intermediate responses illustrate the complex nature of reproductive behavior among this population. The largest group of pregnancies (47%) was described by the men as a result of "just not thinking." These men did not have an overt plan to have a child, but did nothing to prevent it. In many cases, the pregnancy actually brought about a new level of personal responsibility and self-respect.

Dante, a 38-year-old African American father who had been living a high-risk lifestyle before the birth of his child, told researchers, "I know for a fact that if it wasn't for my son and I was just a single guy [without kids] my life would be chaos!" (p. 109). Another group (19%) described their pregnancies as "unplanned but not unexpected." These men had more stable employment, and were in a relatively long-term positive relationship with the mother. As a result, even if the conception was not deliberately planned, the men felt that they were ready to become fathers and have a family.

> Interviewer: Did you think she might get pregnant?
> Respondent: Yeah, but I didn't care. It was good. I was still a young man. I wasn't wearing no protection, so it happened. (p. 109)

The many different types of relationships that are possible between a woman and her partner have implications for both the emotional state of the mother during pregnancy and the psychosocial development of the child. Research supports the idea of continuity between the quality of the relationship between the partners during the prenatal period and the quality of their parenting in the early years of childhood. This continuity in turn has implications for the child's growth and development. Partners who show high levels of negative interaction or detachment during the prenatal period may have trouble providing an emotionally secure environment for their newborn child.

Couples characterized by positive mutuality, partner autonomy, and the ability to confront problems and regulate negative affect are responsive to the needs of their infants, promote their autonomy, and have more secure and autonomous children, as seen throughout the first 4 years of life (Heinicke, 1995, p. 295).

In the first trimester, involved fathers are able to hear the fetal heartbeat amplified through the Doppler. Through the use of ultrasound, fathers are able to visualize the developing fetus. During the second trimester, a father is able to make contact with his unborn child as he places his hand on his partner's abdomen and feels the life and movement within. For many men, this is a time of great joy, as the prospect of fatherhood becomes more than abstract empathy with his partner's experiences. Investment in the new life begins to increase as the reality of the fetus becomes more concrete. These times can provide the basis for a new kind of intimacy for the expectant couple as they begin to talk about their plans and hopes for the child, share their feelings about the pregnancy and upcoming birth, and explore their feelings related to assuming responsibility for the care and protection of their child.

Sometimes, however, the first movements of the fetus stimulate a negative reaction in the father. In a longitudinal study of men during their partner's pregnancy and 8 weeks after birth, men living in stepfamilies had higher levels of depression both before and after the birth than did men in more traditional families (Deater-Deckard, Pickering, Dunn, & Golding, 1998). A father's depression may, in turn, have a negative effect on the mother, leaving her depressed and aware that she is without the support she was expecting.

Some men are not comfortable with the physical events of pregnancy, and they try to deny them by turning away from the mother. They do not want to feel the fetus's movements and are extremely uneasy or embarrassed by the pressure to understand the details of the female anatomy. Some men think that the fetus and then the baby threaten their own position with the mother, and they feel resentful and competitive toward the woman and the unborn infant. In some families, this resentment may lead to violence. For example, one study of low-income, urban women found that 38% had experienced violence from their male partner during their pregnancy (O'Campo et al., 1995). Studies focusing on pregnant adolescents report the prevalence of violence from partners ranging from 16% to 41% (Kennedy, 2006).

Trends in the United States have shifted dramatically toward greater involvement of fathers during labor and delivery (Reed, 2005). Expectant fathers often attend childbirth classes to learn to assist their partners during the delivery. The father's presence during labor and delivery is typically a great comfort to the pregnant woman. When the father is present, women tend to have shorter labors, report experiencing less pain, use less medication, and feel more positive about themselves and their childbirth experience (Grossman et al., 1980; Woollett & DosanjhMatwala, 1990). Fathers also describe their participation in the birth as a peak

Fathers are becoming increasingly involved in supporting their partner's pregnancy and delivery. This support is both an important aspect of identification with the father role, and a great emotional comfort to the mother.

Rod Morata/Getty Images

experience. First-time fathers interviewed about their child-birth experiences reported both positive and negative feelings. These fathers felt that they were most helpful to their wives during labor, and they found the birth experience to be extremely powerful (Nichols, 1993). Nevertheless, these birthing experiences are commonly set in the context of a medical environment in which fathers are typically viewed as assistants. Little attention is given to their own psychological transition as fathers. Negative experiences for men during childbirth occur when they are unsure what their role is during the delivery or when hospital personnel treat them rudely, as a disruption, or fail to provide them with the information they want during the labor and delivery process (Johnson, 2002).

CASE STUDY

A FATHER'S RECOLLECTIONS ABOUT HIS DAUGHTER'S BIRTH

The sentiments of frustration and joy are captured in this description of a father's experiences during labor and delivery. The text was taken from a bulletin board discussion about fathers' views of whether they should be present at their child's birth on Blacknet.com, a place for dialogue and communication within the Black community of the United Kingdom.

Gonna remenise about when my first child was born, I remember being dragged out of work on a Wednesday am because my then wife had gone into labour. Someone however forgot to inform me that women needed to dialate. geeez.

So after rushing to Guys hospital I'm told Baby not ready. Anyway I'm waiting for said wife to get big enough so to speak. All flippin day, All day man watching the paint dry.

I was like Donkey in Shrek 2 'Are we there yet?' every five minutes, then night falls I think ok, maybe it will be a night birth. Oh nooo, nooo such luck.

So here am i holding my wifes hand, or was that her squeezing the blood out of my hand. hmmm yes that was it. I'm giving the *'i'm in control mans'* talk you know *'come on darling its ok, breath breath'* My girl is in full contractions now about 20 mins apart. So the top half of me is trying to be firm and calm, the bottom half is trying hard not to piss mi pants.

Then the nurse mentioned Epidural, oh my days I know i nearly passed out at the sight of the needle going into the spinal column, all the while that wretch is screaming blue murder in the next room. *'get it out'.*

Anyway after waiting ALL day (do I still sound vex?) and ALL night with a hardback chair for a bed, you know I'm happy right? … next thing I know doctor come in approx 8:40 am ish. *'ok lets do it'.* Next thing I know they pull out these stirrups out of nowhere and got my wife with both legs in the air like she's riding an invisable horse whilst lying on her back.

Then a whole heap of student doctors and nurses come into the room, and I mean a whole heap. So here's the wife with legs up in the air, fanny out of door, and all these strangers peering right up it. Now you know man is about to cuss right.

Anyway before I could get into it, baby starts to be delivered and out she pops, 9 am in the morning. she pops out. can't describe how i felt but it was as close to perfection as i will ever get. bonded with her and we've been close not matter what 21 years later.

Source: Kunjufu (2004).

CRITICAL THINKING AND CASE ANALYSIS

1. Given all the stress of the situation, what might account for the very positive feelings reported by Kunjufu at the moment of birth?
2. What are some different roles that men can play during the childbirth process? What roles is Kunjufu playing?
3. What might be some reasons that men do not want to be present during labor and delivery?
4. How do hospital personnel influence the experiences of fathers during childbirth?
5. How might childbirth preparation classes influence the experiences of fathers during childbirth?

The Impact of the Pregnant Woman on the Fetus

Among the factors that influence the fetus's development are the mother's age, use of drugs during pregnancy and delivery, exposure to environmental toxins, and diet. The quality of a pregnant woman's physical and emotional health before and during pregnancy is linked to her own knowledge about, and preparation for, pregnancy as well as to her culture's attitudes and practices associated with childbearing. One of the most harmful influences of the psychosocial environment on fetal development is poverty. Embedded in the conditions of poverty are many of the individual factors associated with suboptimal prenatal development.

The Impact of Poverty

Perhaps the most powerful psychosocial factor that influences the life chances of the developing fetus is poverty (Lipina & Colombo, 2009). Women living in poverty are likely to experience the cumulative effects of many of the factors associated with infant mortality and developmental vulnerabilities. Poverty is directly linked to poor prenatal care. Women who live in poverty are likely to begin having babies at an earlier age and to have repeated pregnancies into their later adult years—practices that are associated with low birth weight. Women who have had little education are less likely to be aware of the risks of smoking, alcohol, and drug use for their babies and are more likely to use or abuse these substances. Women living in poverty are less likely to have been vaccinated against some of the infectious diseases (e.g., rubella) that can harm the developing fetus. Poverty is linked with food insecurity, lack of safe, affordable housing, lack of health insurance, higher instances of infection, and higher rates of diabetes and cardiovascular disease, which are all linked to the infant's low birth weight and physical vulnerability (MacDonald, Seshia, & Mullett, 2005).

Many of the risks that face infants born to women who live in poverty are preventable. One of the Millennium Development Goals established under the auspices of the United Nations is to reduce global maternal mortality rates by 75% by the year 2015. A key element in achieving this goal is to dramatically increase the percentage of births attended by skilled medical personnel. Impoverished and rural women are currently far less likely than their wealthier and urban counterparts to receive skilled care during childbirth. Inequality in access to skilled care between urban and rural women is especially notable in Sub-Saharan Africa where wealthier women are 6 times more likely to deliver with the assistance of skilled birth professionals than the poorest women (United Nations, 2006). Unfortunately, not much progress toward this goal has been achieved in the areas where the greatest inequities exist—Sub-Saharan Africa and southern Asia.

A well-organized, accessible system of regional medical care facilities combined with an effective educational program on pregnancy and nutritional support can significantly improve the health and vigor of babies born to women in poverty. One of the central themes in delivering effective prenatal and continuing services to women in poverty is the establishment of a caring relationship between the woman and the health care provider. This caring relationship provides emotional support to the woman, encouraging her to feel valued as a client, as a mother, and as an adult in the community (Barnard & Morisset, 1995; Massey, Rising, & Ickovics, 2005). Psychosocial factors linked to preterm births are discussed in the box that explores the rates of preterm births among African American and European American women.

Comprehensive prenatal care programs can improve birth outcomes even in a high-risk population. This kind of coordination involves more than providing prenatal checkups and information about health care during pregnancy. It recognizes the complex challenges that face women in poverty, including violence, hazardous living conditions, poor quality services, and unstable or disruptive social relationships (McAllister & Boyle, 1998). Effective interventions must include nonmedical support services, such as making sure the woman has access to food stamps; is part of the Women, Infants, and Children (WIC) food program; has the transportation needed for prenatal and postnatal health care appointments; and receives housing assistance or job training as necessary. Furthermore, resources must be provided to care for, educate, and support children whose intellectual, physical, and emotional capabilities have been restricted before birth by their mothers' poverty. The life chances and quality of survival of infants born in poverty are a reflection of the value that a society places on social justice.

Mother's Age

The capacity for childbearing begins about 1 to 1½ years after menarche (the beginning of regular menstrual periods) and normally ends at the climacteric, or menopause (the ending of regular menstrual periods). Thus, a woman is potentially fertile for about 35 years of her life. Pregnancy and childbirth can occur at various times during this period. The effects of childbirth on the physical and psychological well-being of a mother vary with her age and emotional commitment to the mother role. Similarly, these factors also contribute significantly to the survival and well-being of her infant. In later chapters, we will discuss the psychosocial consequences of childbearing for adolescents and adults. Here we simply point out that the quality of prenatal care and the degree of risk during childbirth are associated with the age of the mother during pregnancy.

Women between the ages of 16 and 35 tend to provide a better uterine environment for the developing fetus and to give birth with fewer complications than do women under 16 or over 35. Particularly when it is their first pregnancy, women over 35 are likely to have a longer labor than younger women, and the labor is more likely to result in the death of either the infant or the mother. As expected, the two groups with the highest probability of giving birth to premature babies are women over 35 and those under 16 (Behrman & Butler, 2007). In an analysis of over 180,000 deliveries, the risk of having a preterm delivery increased with age for women living in poor neighborhoods, African American women, and women who smoked (Holzman et al., 2009).

Mothers under 16 tend to receive less adequate prenatal care and to be less biologically mature. Young mothers are likely to engage in other high-risk behaviors including alcohol and drug use that have negative consequences for fetal development (Cornelius, 1996; Cornelius, Goldshmidt, Taylor, & Day, 1999). In addition, adolescent mothers are more likely than older mothers to be exposed to violence in their communities, homes, and in the context of intimate relationships, thus increasing their level of stress and an associated increased use of tobacco, alcohol, drugs, and antidepressants, all of which can have negative consequences for the developing fetus (Kennedy, 2006). As a result of these interacting factors, premature children of teenage mothers are more likely than those of older mothers to have neurological defects that will influence their coping capacities. Evidence suggests that good medical care, nutrition, and social support improve the childbirth experiences of adolescent mothers who are over 16. However, the physical immaturity of those under 16 puts the mother and infant at greater risk even with adequate medical and social supports (Behrman & Butler, 2007).

A primary risk for infants of mothers who are over 40 is Down syndrome (Moore, 1993). It is hypothesized that the relatively high incidence of Down syndrome in babies born to older women is the result, in part, of deteriorating ova. However, older women are also likely to have male partners who are their age or older. Even though new sperm are produced

HUMAN DEVELOPMENT AND DIVERSITY

Psychosocial Factors Linked to Preterm Births for African American and European American Women

THE RATE OF preterm and low-birth-weight babies has risen substantially from the mid-1980s to the present. Roughly 12.5% of all U.S. births are at less than 37 weeks of gestational age, and close to 8% have low birth weight (under 2500 grams). Preterm births and low birth weight are major causes of infant mortality (Behrman & Butler, 2007). Research about the causes of preterm births typically focuses on genetic, physiological, psychological, and behavioral factors. Much of this research has found that even when taking into account differences in income, education, health behaviors, and access to prenatal care, African American women have a higher risk for preterm births than European American women.

Researchers in North Carolina conducted a study to determine whether psychosocial factors such as stressors experienced during pregnancy, social support from the baby's father, perceptions of racial or gender discrimination, perceived neighborhood safety, and strategies for coping with stress might help predict preterm births (Dole et al., 2004). The investigators examined the hypothesis that African American and European American women differ in the kinds of environmental stressors they are exposed to and in the way they cope with these stressors, and that these differences might help account for their different rates of preterm births.

Data were gathered from more than 1800 pregnant women, 38% of whom were African American. The study examined which psychosocial factors were the best predictors for preterm delivery in the two groups when controlling for age, parity (number of previous pregnancies), education, marital status, household income in relation to the number of adults and children in the household,

prepregnancy body mass, and prenatal care.

European American women were more at risk for preterm births when they:

• Reported a large number of negative life events during pregnancy.
• Were not living with a partner.
• Used escape or avoidance as a strategy for coping with problems.
• Reported living in a dangerous neighborhood.

African American women were more at risk for preterm births when they:

• Reported using distancing as a strategy to cope with problems.
• Reported high levels of racial discrimination.
• Reported high levels of gender discrimination.
• Reported high pregnancy-related anxiety.

Not only is the nature of the psychosocial environment different for African American and European American women in North Carolina, but they experience different vulnerabilities to stress. For example, even though more African American than European American women lived in dangerous neighborhoods, this factor was a significant predictor of having a preterm infant for European American women, but not for African American women. More African American than European American women reported high levels of racial discrimination, and those who did were at greater risk for a preterm delivery. Escape and avoidance were high-risk coping strategies for European American women; distancing was a high-risk strategy for African American women. The implications of this research are that programs designed to prevent preterm births need to examine the psychosocial

contexts of the participants and take into consideration racial and cultural differences, including different perceptions of stressors and resources that help women cope with those stressors.

Critical Thinking Questions

1. The research suggests that there are different combinations of stressors that predict having a preterm infant for African American and European American women. What explanations can you think of to account for these differences?

2. The research finds certain coping strategies are less effective than others in buffering stress. Escape and avoidance coping were more likely to be associated with preterm births for European American women, whereas distancing was associated with preterm births for African American women. What might account for these differences in the effectiveness of various coping strategies for the two groups?

3. How does discrimination influence childbirth outcomes? What mechanisms can you think of that might account for this influence?

4. Do you think that gender and race discrimination act cumulatively to impact childbirth outcomes? Why is the stress associated with gender discrimination a stronger predictor of childbirth outcomes for African American women than for European American women?

5. Using the results of this research, what might you recommend regarding the development of pregnancy and childbirth support for European American and African American women? In what ways should this support differ for the two groups?

daily, some evidence suggests that among older men, the rate of genetically defective sperm increases. Thus, aging in one or both partners may contribute to the increased incidence of Down syndrome in babies born to older women. These explanations are not entirely satisfactory, however, because older women who have had multiple births are not as likely to have a baby with Down syndrome as are women who have their first child at an older age. Moreover, many babies with Down syndrome are born to women who are under 35. It is likely that in some cases, Down syndrome is a result of errors that occur during cell division and that in others, it is a result of a genetically transmitted condition.

Figure 4.8 shows the rate of live births to women in the age range from 10 to 44 between 1960 and 2007. In every age range except the youngest, fewer women are having babies today than in the 1960s. Two other observations about the data presented in this figure are relevant to our understanding of the timing of childbearing in adult life. First, since 1960 the trend has shifted from a higher birth rate in the period from age 20 to 24 to a more equal birth rate during the full decade of the 20s and early 30s. Second, in comparison to the 1980s, the current trend shows a decline in the birth rate for women in their early 20s, and an increased rate of childbearing for women during their 30s and early 40s.

Maternal Drug Use

The range of drugs used by pregnant women is enormous. Iron, diuretics, antibiotics, hormones, tranquilizers, appetite suppressants, and other drugs are prescribed for or are taken over-the-counter by pregnant women. Furthermore, women influence the fetal environment through their voluntary use of such drugs as alcohol, nicotine, caffeine, marijuana, cocaine, and other narcotics. Studies of the effects of specific drugs on fetal growth suggest that many drugs ingested by pregnant women are in fact metabolized in the placenta and transmitted to the fetus. Furthermore, although the impact of a specific dosage of a drug on the pregnant woman may be minimal, the impact on the fetus may be quite dramatic. Male-mediated effects of drugs on fetal development are also documented but less well publicized. Drug abuse among men may produce abnormalities of the sperm that can account for birth defects in their offspring (Pollard, 2000).

In reviewing the following sections about the impact of drugs on fetal development, three principles must be considered. First, evidence suggests that genetic predisposition may make some developing fetuses more vulnerable than others to the negative effects of certain drugs or toxins. Data on this genetic variability were derived from animal studies, because animals are more likely to have large litters of offspring, some of which show greater resilience to the presence of prenatal teratogens than others (O'Rahilly & Muller, 2001). Second, most teratogens do not have an all-or-none impact on the central nervous system. The consequence to the fetus of exposure to teratogens varies by the *dosage*, *duration*, and *timing* of exposure. A dosage that might be acceptable for the pregnant woman might be harmful to the developing fetus. Third, research is sparse on the ways that specific medications are metabolized during pregnancy. Because of physiological changes during pregnancy, some medications may be metabolized so quickly that they do not treat the condition for which they were prescribed. In an effort to avoid harming the pregnant woman or the fetus, some serious conditions such as asthma or depression may be left untreated, thereby placing the pregnant woman and the fetus at risk for additional complications (Lyerly, Little, & Faden, 2009).

Nicotine. Women who smoke are at greater risk for miscarriages, stillbirths, preterm deliveries, low-birth-weight babies, and infant mortality. Children born to mothers who smoke are at increased risk for developing asthma. Neurological examinations of babies exposed to nicotine during the prenatal period showed decreased levels of arousal and responsiveness at 9 and 30 days after birth. Infants of smokers have a 3 to 4 time greater risk of SIDS before 2 months of age. For mothers who smoke, 12.4% of babies are very low birth weight as compared to 7.7% of babies born to mothers who do not smoke (Pergament, 1998; ChildTrends, 2005).

Alcohol. The evidence is conclusive that alcohol is a teratogen. Prenatal exposure to alcohol can disrupt brain development, interfere with cell development and organization, and modify the production of neurotransmitters, which are critical to the maturation of the central nervous system (Sokol, Delaney-Black, & Nordsstrom, 2003). The complex impact of alcohol on fetal development has been given the name **fetal alcohol spectrum disorders** (Centers for Disease Control and Prevention, 2007). Fetal alcohol spectrum disorders

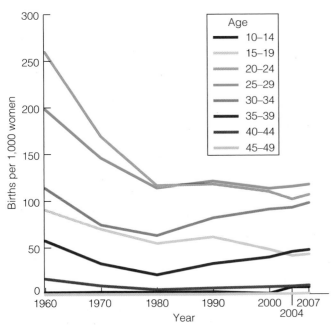

FIGURE 4.8 Live Birthrates by Age of Mother, 1960–2007

Source: U.S. Census Bureau, 1986, 1989, 1992, 2003, 2007, 2010.

(FASDs) is an umbrella term for the range of effects that can occur in an individual whose mother drank alcohol during pregnancy. These effects include physical, mental, behavioral, and learning disabilities with possible lifelong implications. FASDs include fetal alcohol syndrome (FAS), as well as other conditions in which individuals have some, but not all, of the clinical signs, which include abnormal facial features, growth deficiencies, and central nervous system (CNS) problems. People with FAS might have problems with learning, memory, attention span, communication, vision, hearing, or a combination of these. These problems often lead to difficulties in school and problems getting along with others. FAS is a permanent condition. At a rate of 0.5 to 2 infants affected per 1000 live births, fetal alcohol syndrome is the greatest source of environmentally caused developmental disruption in the prenatal CNS (O'Rahilly & Muller, 2001). For every child born with FAS, an estimated three more children are born who suffer some of the neurological complications associated with fetal exposure to alcohol.

Fetal exposure to alcohol disrupts verbal and visual learning. In a longitudinal study of the effects of prenatal exposure to alcohol, children born to mothers who consumed 1.5 ounces of alcohol (one average-strength drink) daily during pregnancy showed significantly lower IQ scores at age 4 than did children whose mothers used little or no alcohol (Streissguth, Barr, Sampson, Darby, & Martin, 1989). Alcohol use was a significant predictor of reduced IQ scores even when many other factors—the mother's educational level, the child's birth order, the family's socioeconomic level, the child's involvement in preschool, and the quality of the mother-child interaction—were taken into account. In other words, the many environmental variables that are known to have a positive effect on a young child's intellectual functioning did not compensate for the disruption in development of the CNS associated with exposure to alcohol during pregnancy.

We emphasize the risks associated with prenatal exposure to alcohol because it is so widely used in American society and because even what many adults perceive to be a safe or socially acceptable amount of alcohol during pregnancy can have a negative effect on the fetus. In 2005, the U.S. Surgeon General advised all women who are pregnant or trying to get pregnant to abstain from alcohol consumption in order to prevent fetal exposure to alcohol. Because of discoveries that even minimal alcohol consumption could result in some disruption in fetal development, the old advice of limiting one's alcohol consumption during pregnancy has been revised. In order to prevent any possible damaging effects of alcohol, the advice is to abstain from alcohol consumption entirely (Centers for Disease Control and Prevention, 2007).

Caffeine. Caffeine freely crosses the placenta. It is commonly consumed in coffee, certain sodas, and tea. An estimated 200 foods and food products contain caffeine. Caffeine raises the heart rate and acts as a diuretic, resulting in loss of fluids and the possibility of dehydration. Heavy caffeine consumption—defined in one study as more than 300 milligrams, or roughly three cups of coffee per day—is associated with an increased risk of low birth weight, and there is a modest relationship to prematurity. Babies exposed to high doses of caffeine have been found to have a higher heart rate, more startles and tremors, and are more difficult to soothe (Howell, 2005). Infants born to women who reduced the amount of caffeine they drank after the sixth week of pregnancy showed no ill effects associated with early caffeine consumption (Fenster, Eskenazi, Windham, & Swan, 1991; McDonald, Armstrong, & Sloan, 1992).

Narcotics. The use of narcotics, especially heroin and cocaine, as well as methadone (a drug used in the treatment of heroin addiction), has been linked to increased risks of

Both of these children show the facial characteristics of fetal alcohol syndrome: eyes widespread, with an epicanthic fold; short nose; small midface and thin upper lip.

© David Young-Wolff/PhotoEdit

birth defects, low birth weight, and higher rates of infant mortality (Howell, Heiser, & Harrington, 1999). Infants who have been exposed prenatally to opiates, cocaine, and methadone show a pattern of extreme irritability, high-pitched crying that is evidence of neurological disorganization, fever, sleep disturbances, feeding problems, muscle spasms, and tremors (Bard et al., 2000). These babies are at high risk for SIDS. Prenatal cocaine exposure has been linked to cortisol reactivity, a hormone that contributes to a person's ability to manage and regulate the responses to the stressors of daily life. Babies who were exposed to cocaine prenatally were observed at 7 months of age. They had elevated cortisol levels, which leads to greater reactivity to stress, and disruptions in the ability to self-regulate. The disruptive consequences of cocaine exposure were more serious when the caregiving situation was unstable, suggesting that the infants who were physiologically predisposed to having difficulties in managing arousal and stress suffered even further when they were not able to rely on a consistent context of care (Eiden, Veira, & Granger, 2009). Longer range studies found that some children who were exposed to addictive drugs in the prenatal period continued to show problems with fine motor coordination, had difficulty focusing and sustaining their attention, and, perhaps as a result, had more school adjustment problems (Ben-Dat Fisher et al., 2007).

The longer term impact of prenatal drug exposure varies. Many women who use cocaine also drink alcohol and are malnourished and often exposed to violence and to sexually transmitted diseases. Thus, the impact of cocaine alone is difficult to assess (Pollack, 2000). In one study, about one third of the babies exposed prenatally to cocaine showed deficits in tests of motor or mental development during infancy; the others scored in the normal range (Cosden, Peerson, & Elliott, 1997). Of course, it is difficult to separate the direct prenatal effects of these drugs on the nervous system from the effects after birth that are associated with being parented by a drug-using mother (Tyler, Howard, Espinosa, & Doakes, 1997). One study focused on the caregiving environment of 2-year-old children who had been prenatally exposed to cocaine. Those who were in nonparental caregiving environments were doing much better at age 2 with respect to physical development, cognitive and language skills, and social and emotional functioning than those who continued in the care of their cocaine-using birth mothers (Brown et al., 2004).

Because of the widespread abuse of cocaine, some law enforcement officials are arresting and charging women who have exposed their unborn infants to these harmful and illegal substances. In 1997, a woman in South Carolina was charged with murder by child abuse when it was determined that she had smoked crack cocaine while pregnant, which was responsible for the death of her unborn child ("Crack-Using Woman," 1997). State laws have been passed that allow criminal charges to be filed against women who give birth to babies who have illegal substances in their blood. Several states have tried taking babies away from these mothers, but this action poses an extremely difficult ethical dilemma. Those who oppose such actions argue that alcohol use, smoking, and other forms of maternal behavior also have known negative effects on the developing fetus. Should women who use these legal substances also be charged with child abuse? Moreover, can society ensure that the babies taken from these mothers and placed in foster care will do better than they would have done in the care of their birth mothers? On the other hand, some argue that the state has the responsibility to protect the well-being of the unborn child, especially during the third trimester when the fetus has reached the point of viability. According to this view, actions that result in harm or death to the fetus ought to be considered child abuse and prosecuted as such (Pollack, 2000).

Prescription Drugs. Some drugs are administered to women during pregnancy as part of the treatment of a medical condition. The tragic outcome of the use of thalidomide for the treatment of morning sickness in the 1960s alerted society to the potential danger of certain chemicals to the fetus, particularly during the period of fetal differentiation and growth in the first trimester. Thalidomide taken during the 21st to 36th days after conception can cause gross deformities of the baby's limbs.

Some drugs are administered to help sustain the pregnancy. Others are used to help control medical conditions, such as epilepsy or AIDS. Studies examining the dose and timing of these drugs suggest that they can have temporary or long-term consequences for neurological development, motor behavior, and personality (Rovet et al., 1995). The effects of some kinds of drugs may persist for a long time after birth, either by directly altering the CNS or by influencing the pattern of caregiver-infant interactions.

Obstetric Anesthetics. The study of the effects on the newborn of drugs used during delivery provides further evidence of the infant's dependence on the immediate environment. Initially, pain-relieving drugs were used for the benefit and convenience of pregnant women and their physicians, and their effects on the newborn were not noticed. However, evidence suggests that the type, amount, and timing of anesthetic use in delivery are all factors that may induce neonatal depression and affect the coping capacities of newborns. The use of anesthetic drugs during delivery has been found to interfere with the infant's ability to habituate to a stimulus (i.e., to stop responding after repeated presentations of the stimulus), to reduce the infant's smiling and cuddliness, and to reduce alert responses to new stimuli. Furthermore, the relationship between drug use and some infant behavior has been observed to last as long as 28 days (Stechler & Halton, 1982; Naulty, 1987).

Environmental Toxins

As increasing numbers of women enter the workforce and assume nontraditional work roles, concern about the hazards of work settings for fetal development continues to grow. The levels of exposure to environmental toxins that may be considered safe or acceptable for adults may still have a negative impact on fetal development. Fetal exposure to lead, mercury, and ethanol in the workplace have been found to disrupt normal immune system development (Science Daily, 2005). Wives of men who are employed in hazardous environments may also experience higher rates of miscarriage, sterility, and birth defects in their babies. In one study, fathers' exposure to specific solvents and chemicals at work was linked to higher rates of spontaneous abortions among their wives (Lindbohm et al., 1991). Recent research links men's workplace exposure to lead to reduced sperm count, sperm motility, and sperm concentration, resulting in negative consequences for fertility. Paternal exposure to lead is also associated with low-birth-weight babies (Alexander et al., 1996; Min, Correa-Villasenor, & Stewart, 1996).

The workplace is not the only setting in which pregnant women may be exposed to environmental toxins. Women who regularly ate a large amount of polluted fish from Lake Michigan for 6 years before they became pregnant had infants who showed certain memory deficits at 7 months of age (Jacobson, Fein, Jacobson, Schwartz, & Dowler, 1985). Although the level of these toxins—industrial waste products found in air, water, and soil—had no measurable effects on the mothers, it was high enough to influence CNS functioning in the fetuses. This finding makes it clear that all communities must be sensitive to the quality of their water, air, and soil. Each new generation depends on its predecessors for protection from these environmental hazards.

Mother's Diet

The notion that no matter what the pregnant woman eats, the fetus will get what it needs for growth is simply not true. Providing adequate nutrition for fetal development requires both a balanced diet for the mother and the capacity to transform nutrients into a form that the fetus can ingest, which the placenta takes care of (Tanner & Finn-Stevenson, 2002).

Because of ethical problems involved in experimentally modifying the diets of pregnant women, much of the research on the effects of maternal malnutrition on fetal development has been conducted with animal models, primarily rats. The impact of prenatal malnutrition on rats shows that when the mother is malnourished, fewer nutrients cross the placenta. The fetal brain receives comparatively more of the limited nutritional resources than the other organs; however, the CNS is disrupted. The consequences, for those fetuses that survive, include delayed skeletal development, impaired reflexes, and cognitive deficits (Galler & Tonkiss, 1998; Lukas & Campbell, 2000).

Many experts assert that for humans, prenatal malnutrition, depending on its timing and severity, has an irreparable impact on CNS development and, as a result, on intellectual performance (Morgane et al., 1993). However, this assertion is difficult to demonstrate experimentally. Most of the data on the effects of malnutrition on human fetal growth have come from studying the impact of disasters and crises—such as famines, wars, and extreme poverty—on pregnant women. For example, several studies examined the impact of the Dutch Hunger Winter of 1944–1945, when the German army blockaded food supplies to the Netherlands. In a study of men born in the famine region during that period, 21% were exposed to severe prenatal malnutrition for one or more trimesters. Malnutrition is inferred from the baby's low birth weight in comparison with the baby's gestational age (the age of the fetus from the time of conception until birth). Babies who are small for their gestational age have a higher mortality rate, more complications during post-delivery care, and a higher risk of mental or motor impairment than do babies who are of average weight for their gestational age. Prenatal malnutrition has an impact on the normal growth of all organs, normal organ functions, and the normal development of the CNS. Behavioral disorders, learning disabilities, and certain forms of mental illness have been linked to prenatal malnutrition (Morgane et al., 1993; Neugebauer, Hoek, & Susser, 1999; Tanner & Finn-Stevenson, 2002).

One of the nutrients of grave concern because of its role in the maturation of the CNS is iron. Iron deficiency is a widespread nutrient disorder, with an estimated 20% to 25% of babies worldwide suffering from **iron deficiency anemia**. Babies who have severe iron deficiencies test lower in motor and cognitive development and show evidence of fearfulness, fatigue, and wariness. Even with postnatal iron-enriched treatment, these behavioral consequences have been found to persist. The brain uses iron to help support myelination. The hippocampus, which is a key brain structure that supports recognition memory, is also very sensitive to an early lack of iron. In the United States, pregnant women who are receiving prenatal care are typically given iron supplements. However, iron is often missing in the diet of poor women, and, as a result, the cognitive deficits established in the prenatal period when the nervous system is developing are likely to be compounded by lack of access to adequate nutrition after birth (National Research Council and Institute of Medicine, 2000).

A child may be malnourished during pregnancy, after birth, or both. Although some growth retardation is hypothesized to occur if a fetus is malnourished, the most severe impact on growth occurs when resources are inadequate both before and after the child is born. This is the case in many poverty stricken areas of the world. When prenatal malnutrition is followed by postnatal malnutrition and disease, it is impossible to study the effects of prenatal malnutrition alone.

A pregnant woman's diet can be successfully modified to increase the newborn's weight. Diet supplements that are rich in protein and high in calories appear to have the most positive impact (Sigman, 1995). The rate of infant mortality declined 69% for the babies born to Guatemalan women who were given a protein-enriched supplement (Brown & Pollitt, 1996). In Mexico, a longitudinal study compared children born to women who had received nutritional supplements with those who had not, when the children were 12 and again at 18. Those without the supplement had a longer, slower period of cognitive maturity, some still showing gains at age 18. However, the prenatally undernourished children never performed at the level of those whose mothers received a supplement, even at age 18 (Chavez, Martinez, & Soberanes, 1995).

In order for prenatal nutritional intervention to have the greatest impact, it must be coupled with efforts to reduce the continued effects of poverty after birth. Children who are at risk for malnutrition are likely to experience more illness, lethargy, and withdrawal; delayed physical growth; and, in consequence, delayed intellectual growth. On the other hand, some of the negative effects of malnutrition can be offset if infants are adequately nourished after birth (Tanner, 1990). These infants show increased activity, make greater demands on their environment, and prompt more active caregiving responses (Brazelton, 1987a). This pattern of interaction may offset the initial deficits resulting from an inadequate prenatal nutritional environment.

The many factors we have reviewed, including maternal age, exposure to drugs and environmental toxins, exposure to illnesses, and inadequate nutritional resources during various phases of pregnancy, can occur singly or in combination. The greater the number of risk factors the fetus encounters, the greater the chance for disruption in neurological and behavioral development. The concept of plasticity is well illustrated as we think about the impact of the many possible disruptive factors that can occur during the prenatal period. As suggested in Chapter 2 (Figure 2.6), psychosocial processes can contribute to growth and new resources for coping or to disruption and limitations on coping. Within the prenatal environment, a child's genetic potential may encounter a supportive, healthy, optimizing environment or an environment in which one or more conditions place fetal development at risk. Even for infants who carry the genetic markers for anomalies, the expression of these conditions may be less disruptive or less severe when fetal development has taken place in a healthy, fully resourced uterine environment. In contrast, even infants who would otherwise be healthy may suffer long-term negative consequences when they are exposed to a combination of teratogens and disruptive uterine conditions.

Stress and Fetal Development

A woman's feelings about her femininity, her attitudes toward the unborn child, and her psychological stability are associated with difficulties experienced during pregnancy and labor. Women who have more stable personalities and a positive orientation toward pregnancy react more favorably to the stresses of labor. Anxious, irritable women are more likely to have longer labors and more complications during labor and delivery. During labor and delivery, women who are more fearful of childbirth and who believe that the outcomes of childbirth are outside their own control are more likely to request epidural anesthesia than are women who had a low fear of childbirth and wanted to participate actively in the childbirth process (Heinze & Sleigh, 2003).

Strong emotional reactions—such as prolonged anxiety or depression—may influence the fetal environment directly through the secretion of maternal hormones that cross the placental barrier. Research with animals has demonstrated that mothers' exposure to stress during pregnancy does have long-term negative consequences for learning, motor development, and adaptive behavior in offspring (Kaiser & Sachser, 2009). A review of existing literature suggests that among humans, prenatal stress is associated with higher rates of spontaneous abortion, preterm labor and delivery, and growth delay among babies (Mulder et al., 2002). Current studies consider the relationship between stress-related changes in endocrine levels during pregnancy and motor development, cognitive development, and immune functioning in babies. Research is focusing on ways in which stress-induced physiological changes in the mother might influence fetal growth and nervous system development (Field et al., 2003; DiPietro, 2004).

What are the sources of stress for pregnant women that can have an impact on the developing fetus? Studies have explored the role of women's exposure to psychosocial stress and racism on birth outcomes. Prenatal anxiety is higher among women who have a less positive outlook about their pregnancy, and who are undergoing a large number of challenging life events during pregnancy. In a comparison of European American, African American, and Latina women, the sources of prenatal anxiety were different for women of the different racial/ethnic groups. Income adequacy was the primary source of prenatal anxiety for European American women. For African American women, both childhood and current exposure to racism was significantly related to pregnancy stress. For Latinas, a sense of mastery and support from the baby's father were important predictors of levels of pregnancy stress (Dominguez et al., 2008; Gurung et al, 2005).

Another source of stress is related to a woman's working conditions. Although it is generally positive for women to be employed and to have work-related income, work-related strain can have a negative impact on fetal development. Women who work 32 hours a week or more early in their pregnancy and who are exposed to high levels of job strain, such as a demanding work pace, time pressures, expectations to do multiple tasks as once, and physically demanding, strenuous work are more likely to have low-birth-weight babies or babies who are small for their gestational age (Vrijkotte, van der Wal, van Eijsden, & Bonsel, 2009).

The mother's emotional state during pregnancy has an impact beyond the events of childbirth. Women who experience notable anxiety or depression during pregnancy are more likely to continue feeling depressed after giving birth and are more likely to have additional depressive symptoms in the 5 years following childbirth. Clinicians who focus on the etiology of depression in women emphasize that the period of pregnancy and childbirth should be a time for preventive intervention (Le, Munoz, Ippen, & Stoddard, 2003).

HUMAN DEVELOPMENT AND DIVERSITY

AIDS and Mother-to-Child Transmission

BY THE CLOSE of 2008, an estimated 15.7 million women and 2.1 million children were infected with HIV (human immunodeficiency virus) worldwide (Avert.org, 2010). Almost all the children under the age of 10 were infected by their mothers, and most of them live in developing countries in Africa and Asia. Children born to untreated HIV-positive mothers have about a 25% chance of developing the disease. The chances of transmitting HIV increase to 45% when mothers breastfeed—a practice that is very common in developing countries (Bassett, 2001; Rosenfield & Figdor, 2001; UNAIDS, 2006).

In North America and Europe, the transmission of HIV from mother to infant has decreased dramatically due to the availability of drugs administered to the mother for a few weeks—or once while the mother is in labor—and to the infant within 3 days after birth. However, in the developing countries of Africa and Asia, where the disease is a raging epidemic, these effective treatments are almost never available. What accounts for this failure?

Four issues prevent the translation of what is known as best practice to what is actually done in developing countries:

1. The costs of the medication to prevent mother-to-infant transmission are enormous for poor countries.

2. Voluntary counseling and testing are the cornerstones of prevention and intervention, but many women are reluctant to be tested for HIV due to the stigmatizing nature of the disease. Even though most women are infected by their husbands, the testing is done on women, and they are blamed for bringing HIV into their families. Women who test positive may risk being abandoned by their husbands, thus losing the support of their families even as they face the future of their illness.

3. The risk of transmission of HIV through breastfeeding continues even with the drug treatment. In order for women to give up breastfeeding, they need to be assured of safe water supplies and adequate availability of formula. Otherwise, an equally large number of the children will die of diarrhea and malnutrition.

4. The treatment does not benefit the HIV-infected women but prevents the spread of the disease to infants. As a result, although the infants may be spared the disease, they are highly likely to become orphans of infected fathers and mothers. In Africa alone there are an estimated 14 million children under age 18 whose mother or father has died of AIDS.

This example illustrates the broad issues underlying the topic of the influence of the mother on fetal development. The care of mothers is essential to the well-being of the developing fetus, and the cultural, societal, and family contexts figure prominently in the care of mothers.

Critical Thinking Questions

1. What are the cultural beliefs that might prevent women from seeking prenatal counseling and HIV testing and treatment?

2. What steps would you need to take in order to learn about the barriers that exist for prevention in a specific cultural group? Who would you approach as informants? What kinds of information would you gather?

3. Visit the website for Aidsmap.com to learn more about HIV and AIDS worldwide. From what you read, make a list of some of the most effective efforts to control the AIDS epidemic.

4. What are the emerging considerations for the growing number of AIDS orphans? What challenges are they most likely to face? What solutions are being considered for their safety and care?

5. In your view, what steps should international organizations such as the World Bank or the UN take to solve this health crisis?

The Cultural Context of Pregnancy and Childbirth

Objective 6: To examine the impact of culture on pregnancy and childbirth.

Julan is a Hmong, now living in Australia. She has just had a baby, and she and her family are preparing for the soul-calling ceremony on the third day after the baby's birth. Once completed, she will feel that she has done what is needed to protect the baby and link it to its living as well as its supernatural world. The Hmong believe that each of us has three souls—one that enters the body when the infant is conceived, one that enters as the baby takes its first breath during childbirth, and one that enters on the third day after birth. The soul-calling ceremony secures these souls in the infant's body and thus ensures the baby's well-being (Rice, 2000).

In order to appreciate the events surrounding the birth of a child, one must understand some of the idiosyncrasies in a culture's approach to pregnancy and birth. The beliefs, values, and guidelines for behavior regarding pregnancy and childbirth have been referred to as the **birth culture** (Scopesi, Zanobini, & Carossino, 1997; Gross & Pattison,

HUMAN DEVELOPMENT AND DIVERSITY

Couvade

SOME CULTURES OBSERVE the formal practice of **couvade**, in which the expectant father takes to his bed and observes very specific taboos during the period shortly before birth. Among the Arapesh of New Guinea, childbearing is believed to place as heavy a burden and drain of energy on the father as on the mother. Some cultures believe that by following the ritual of couvade, fathers distract the attention of evil spirits, so that the mother and baby can go through the childbirth transition more safely (Helman, 1990).

Even in groups that do not practice the ritual of couvade, it is common to find expectant fathers experiencing some couvade symptoms, such as general fatigue, stomach cramps, nausea, dizziness, or backache. Symptoms often begin toward the end of the first trimester, are noticeable again toward the end of pregnancy, and end with childbirth (Klein, 1991).

> Couvade is a crisis of faith—the faith a man has in his ability to face the unknown. As the wife increaseth, the husband decreaseth. In his despair, he is at the bottom of the barrel of his manhood. There he gropes for something new in his composition to help him to cope; and what he finds is something very, very old—an ancient technique to help man survive this very normal but very upsetting ordeal.
> Ancient tools, ancient tricks, ancient masks. What he discovers is that modern man and ancient man, different as button-down and buckskin, are quite alike in one respect—they both value their security, and are both threatened when their manly armor starts to crack. (Finley, 1984)

Trethowan (1972), one of the first to document the nature and extent of couvade symptoms in the normal population, suggested that these physical symptoms are the product of a man's emotional ambivalence toward his wife during her pregnancy. The expectant father may experience empathy and identify with his wife's pregnant state. At the same time, he may experience some jealousy of his wife, resentment of the loss or potential loss of intimacy in their relationship, repulsion by his wife's physical appearance, or some envy of his wife's ability to bear a child. These psychological conflicts, many of which are probably unconscious or unexpressed, are amplified by an expectant father's conscious worries about the health and well-being of his wife and their baby. The combination of these stresses may produce the couvade syndrome.

Critical Thinking Questions

1. See if you can find out about some societies in which couvade is routinely practiced. What are some characteristics of these societies?
2. What functions might be served by ritualized couvade behaviors?
3. Why might a woman's pregnancy create conflict for her male partner?
4. In addition to the explanations for couvade symptoms presented in this box, what other explanations can you think of?
5. Aside from couvade symptoms, what other psychological reactions are expectant fathers likely to have?

2007). The decision to have a child, the social and physical experiences of pregnancy, the particular style of help that is available for the delivery of the child, and the care and attitudes toward both mother and baby after delivery are all components of the birth culture. Not everyone in a cultural group adheres to the full script of the birth culture, but at the very least, these guidelines are part of the mythology or lore that surfaces as a woman and her partner experience the events of pregnancy. The transmission of AIDS from mother to fetus and the challenges associated with effective intervention are discussed in the box on the prior page.

Information about approaches to pregnancy and childbirth in traditional cultures are drawn primarily from the Human Relations Areas Files (Murdock & White, 1969) and from Ford's (1945) comparison of reproductive behavior in 64 cultures. In most traditional societies, men and nontribal women are not allowed to observe delivery. Furthermore, many of the events related to conception and delivery are considered too personal or private to discuss with outsiders. Thus, the data on childbearing practices are not complete.

Comparisons across cultures serve only to place the American system in a cultural context.

Reactions to Pregnancy

Many cultures share the assumption that the behavior of expectant parents will influence the developing fetus and the ease or difficulty of childbirth. Of the 64 cultures studied by Ford (1945), 42 prescribed certain behaviors for expectant parents and prohibited others. Many such restrictions were dietary.

> Among the Pomeroon Arawaks, though the killing and eating of a snake during the woman's pregnancy is forbidden to both father and mother, the husband is allowed to kill and eat any other animal. The cause assigned for the taboo of the snake is that the little infant might be similar, that is, able neither to talk nor to walk. (Roth, 1953, p. 122)

In many Asian, Mediterranean, and Central and South American cultures, pregnancy is believed to be affected by the balance of hot and cold foods in a woman's diet. Pregnant women are advised to avoid both very hot foods, such as chili peppers and salty or fatty foods, and very cold foods, such as acidic, sour, or cold fresh foods (Hahn & Muecke, 1987).

A culture's view of pregnancy determines the kinds and severity of the symptoms associated with it, the types of treatment or medical assistance sought during pregnancy, and the degree to which pregnancy is responded to as a life stressor. Attitudes toward pregnant women can be characterized along two dimensions: (1) **solicitude versus shame** and (2) **adequacy versus vulnerability** (Mead & Newton, 1967). A syndrome of fathers' reactions to a wife's pregnancy, called couvade, is discussed in the box on the prior page.

Solicitude versus Shame

Solicitude toward the pregnant woman is shown in the care, interest, and help of others. For example, it is said among Jordon villagers that "as people are careful of a chicken in the egg, all the more so should they be of a child in its mother's womb" (Grandquist, 1950). As the Chagga in Africa say, "Pay attention to the pregnant woman! There is no one more important than she" (Guttmann, 1932).

At the other end of this spectrum are the cultures that convey shame through their practices. They keep pregnancy a secret as long as possible. This custom may stem from a fear that damage will come to the fetus through supernatural demons or from shyness about the sexual implications of pregnancy.

Societies that demonstrate solicitude increase the care given to the pregnant woman and fetus. These attitudes emphasize the importance of birth as a mechanism for replenishing the group, and additional resources are likely to be provided to the pregnant woman. By keeping the pregnancy a secret, cultures that instill a sense of shame in the woman do not promote the health of the mother or the fetus and may not encourage couples to have children.

Adequacy versus Vulnerability

In many societies, pregnancy is a sign of sexual prowess and a means of access to social status. Some cultures do not arrange a wedding until after the woman has become pregnant. In a polygynous family—one in which a man has more than one wife—the pregnant wife receives the bulk of her husband's attention and may prevent her husband from taking an additional wife (Grandquist, 1950). In some cultures, women are considered more attractive after they have borne children. "Thus, the Aymara widow of South America with many children is regarded as a desirable bride" (Tichauer, 1963). "Lepcha men consider that copulation with women who have borne more than one child is more enjoyable and less exhausting than with other adult women" (Gorer, 1938).

The other end of this continuum is the view that childmaking is exhausting, pregnant women are vulnerable, and women grow more frail with each pregnancy. Among the Arapesh of New Guinea (Mead, 1935), pregnancy is tiring

for both men and women. Once menstruation stops, the husband and the wife believe that they must copulate repeatedly in order to provide the building materials for the fetus's semen and blood. Many cultures teach that during pregnancy, the woman and the fetus are more readily exposed to evil spirits. In several cultures, the forces of life and death are thought to be engaged in a particularly intense competition for the mother and the fetus around the time of delivery. See the box that discusses the Korean beliefs called **Taegyo** that assumes that the fetus is able to feel what the mother feels.

Solicitude versus shame and adequacy versus vulnerability are two dimensions that create a matrix within which the birth culture of any society or subculture can be located. Within this framework, pregnancy may be viewed as a time of great rejoicing or a time for caution and privacy; a time for feeling sexually powerful or extremely vulnerable. One might describe the U.S. medical birth culture, for example, as being characterized by solicitude and vulnerability. Pregnant women are usually treated with increased concern and care and are often placed in a medical system that increases their sense of dependency. Attitudes in the workplace also contribute to the sense of vulnerability when pregnancy is viewed as incompatible with serious dedication to the job.

In the United States, both men and women apply expectations of a sick role to pregnant women. This idea includes the view that pregnant women should not exert themselves and are excused from certain obligations; that they need special care and should seek out medical expertise to meet these health care needs; that they should do whatever is necessary to comply with the health recommendations of experts; and that their moodiness, irritability, or other symptoms are forgiven because these symptoms are attributed to their pregnant state (Myers & Grasmick, 1990).

Reactions to Childbirth

Childbirth is an important event in most societies, marked by the presence of specially designated attendants, a specified location, and certain ceremonies and rituals intended to support the miraculous emergence of the newborn into the society (Dundes, 2003). In traditional societies, the delivery is usually attended by two or more assistants with specific assigned roles. Traditional birth attendants are found in all areas of the world. They are usually women who have had children themselves and are respected members of their community. In Jamaica, the *nana*, or midwife, is one of the key figures in the village. She is called on to assist in many family crises. During pregnancy and childbirth, the nana provides assistance in the many rituals and taboos that mark the rebirth of the woman as a mother, and she usually cares for the mother and the infant until the ninth day after birth (Kitzinger, 1982).

In most traditional cultures, childbirth takes place in a familiar setting, either at home or in a nearby birthing hut. If the birth takes place at home, a woman may be separated from others by a curtain for privacy, but she knows that her

HUMAN DEVELOPMENT AND DIVERSITY

Taegyo (Fetal Education)

THE FOLLOWING DESCRIPTION of Korean prenatal care practices was written by a Korean woman who delivered her first child in Korea and her second in the United States while her husband was in graduate school. She struggled with her own ambivalence about whether the traditional Korean practices were restrictive superstitions or valuable wisdom. Writing this research paper about her own culture helped her clarify the place of traditional practices in her modern world.

> *Taegyo* has a long history. I could easily find its history and the contents transmitted from generation to generation through literature and folklore on several Korean websites. *Taegyo* dates from the Koryo dynasty (918–1392 A.D.) in Korea. The old Korean literary works, such as *Taegyohunnyo*, *Taegyosingi*, *Kyuhabchongseo*, and *Donguibogam* provide mental and attitudinal guides for pregnant women. The most important point is the behavior of pregnant women; there are guides for maintaining the emotional stability of pregnant women, including having good carriage; guides for clothes, for promot-

ing pregnant women's health, the prohibition of certain foods and medicines, and so on. In addition, paternal *Taegyo* has been considered important from old traditional times until now because it is believed to significantly influence the physical and psychological condition of the baby as well.

> According to *Taegyosingi*, which was written in the Chosun dynasty (1392–1910) and became the foremost guide for fetal education, pregnant women need peaceful and comfortable surroundings and special care from other family members. It also recommends that pregnant women read good literature, follow the teaching of sages, look at good pictures, listen to good stories, and eat beautifully shaped foods with vivid colors. There are also many prohibited points: not to sleep with your husband; not to take any medications without caution; not to sit in cold or dirty places; not to go outside when it is dark, windy, or rainy; not to wash with cold water; not to sleep on your stomach; not to sleep after eating too much; not to whisper; not to lie or deceive; not to use abusive language. These prohibitions are based on the belief that the fetus feels exactly what the mother feels;

thus pregnant women should be careful in everyday life, and listen and speak good things and behave and think properly (Kim, 2002).

Source: Kim (2002).

Critical Thinking Questions

1. How would you evaluate the belief that a fetus feels exactly what the mother feels?
2. What underlying attitudes toward pregnancy does the Taegyo philosophy and tradition suggest?
3. How does the Taegyo philosophy fit with other features of Korean culture?
4. What difficulties might a contemporary Korean American couple face in trying to follow the Taegyo philosophy in the context of the U.S. birth culture?
5. The Taegyo philosophy includes guidelines for physical, emotional, and moral care during pregnancy. Which of these guidelines do you think should be included in general prenatal care for all women? Why?
6. How would you characterize the role of fathers during pregnancy in the Taegyo philosophy?

family members are close at hand. Women typically give birth standing, squatting, or sitting and reclining against something or someone. The Western birth custom of lying on one's back with one's feet propped up in the air has no counterpart in traditional birth cultures, nor are women expected to be moved from one setting or room to another during the phases of labor (Helman, 1990). That appears to be a ritual reserved for women in modern, industrialized societies. Views about the birth itself range from an extreme negative pole, where birth is seen as dirty and defiling, to an extreme positive pole, where it is seen as a personal achievement. The view of childbirth as a normal physical event is the midpoint on this continuum.

When birth is viewed as dirty, as it is by the Arapesh of New Guinea and the Kadu Gollas of India, the woman must go to an area away from the village to deliver her child. Many cultures, such as that of the ancient Hebrews, require extensive purification rituals after childbirth. Vietnamese villagers believe that mothers should not bathe or shampoo their hair

for a month after giving birth so that the baby will not "fall apart," and that the new mother must not have sexual intercourse for 100 days (Stringfellow, 1978).

A slightly more positive orientation toward childbirth is to identify it as a sickness. This view causes a pregnant Cuna Indian woman to visit her medicine man for daily medication. The midpoint of this spectrum—what we might most appropriately describe as natural childbirth—is a setting in which the mother delivers her baby in the presence of many members of the community, without much expression of pain and with little magic or obstetrical mechanics. Clark and Howland (1978) described childbirth for Samoan women as follows:

> The process of labor is viewed by Samoan women as a necessary part of their role and a part of the life experience. Since the baby she is producing is highly valued by her culture, the mother's delivery is also commendable and therefore ego-satisfying. Pain relief for labor may well present the patient with a conflict. She obviously experiences pain

as demonstrated by skeletal muscle response, tossing and turning, and fixed body positions, but her culture tells her that she does not need medication. It is the "spoiled" palagi [Caucasian] woman who needs pain-relieving drugs. Moreover, the culture clearly dictates that control is expected of a Samoan woman, and no overt expressions of pain are permissible. (p. 166)

At the most positive end of the scale, birth is seen as a proud achievement. Among the Ila of Northern Zimbabwe, women attending childbirth were observed to shout praises of the woman who had a baby. They all thanked her, saying, "I give thanks to you today that you have given birth to a child" (Mead & Newton, 1967, p. 174).

A similar sentiment is expressed in Marjorie Karmel's (1983) description of the Lamaze method of childbirth:

From the moment I began to push, the atmosphere of the delivery room underwent a radical transformation. Where previously everyone had spoken in soft and moderate tones in deference to my state of concentration, now there was a wild encouraging cheering section, dedicated to spurring me on. I felt like a football star, headed for a touchdown. (pp. 93–94)

The American view of childbirth seems to be evolving toward an emphasis on safety for mother and child, and convenience. In comparison with the medical practices of the 1940s and 1950s, there is greater involvement of fathers or other birth coaches during labor and delivery, and more immediate contact between newborns and their parents. There are more opportunities for the baby to spend much of the day with the mother and for siblings to visit. Hospital stays are typically shorter. Many hospitals have affiliated birth centers that provide a more home-like environment, where fewer technical interventions are used, and where the birth is attended by a midwife or obstetrical nursing team.

At the same time, couples are advised that the best way to promote the healthy development and safe delivery of their child is to make early and regular visits to their obstetrician during the prenatal period, to attend childbirth instructional classes, to observe restrictions in diet and use of drugs, and to avoid exposure to certain environmental hazards that may harm the fetus. In the United States, 99% of births take place in hospitals or hospital-affiliated centers, and 91% are attended by physicians (BabyCenter.com, 2007). Despite the fact that the overwhelming majority of women giving birth are healthy and could expect an uncomplicated birth, over half of women surveyed in 2006 experienced an induced labor or cesarean delivery, thereby exposing themselves and their babies to a variety of drugs and surgical interventions that bypass spontaneous labor (Declercq, Sakala, Corry, & Applebaum, 2006).

I had a lot of pressure from the nursing staff to take Pitocin and to have an epidural. I felt like the birth experience was severely impacted by this pressure, as if the most important thing to the nurses was for me to have the baby quickly. My

© Christopher Bissell/Getty Images

The modern U.S. birth culture favors less use of obstetrical medication so that the mother is awake, the father is involved, and the medical staff are part of the support group.

doctor is a big fan of induction which is not my cup of tea. (Childbirthconnection.org, 2007)

It is reasonable to speculate that events at the time of the birth influence the mother's feelings about herself and her parenting ability. Efforts by the community—especially family members, close friends, and health care professionals—to foster a woman's competence in, and control of, parenting and to express care and support for her seem to promote a woman's positive orientation toward herself and her mothering role. On the other hand, messages of social rejection, doubts about a woman's competence, and attempts to take away control or to isolate the mother from her infant or social support system may undermine the woman's self-esteem and interfere with her effectiveness as she approaches the demanding and exhausting task at hand (Dunkel-Schetter, Sagrestano, Feldman, & Killingsworth, 1996).

The population of the United States is increasingly diverse, and attention must be given to understanding the variety of cultural norms affecting the pregnant woman and her family support system. For example, research on the birth settings in hospitals in the United States, Germany, France, and Italy found that each country had a somewhat different focus on the woman's ability to have control over the birth process, the types of emotional and technical support provided, the availability of childbirth preparation classes, and the focus given to mother-child and father-child bonding in each setting (Scopesi, Zanobini, & Carossino, 1997). Other studies of immigrants giving birth in a new country emphasize problems of communication between women, their families, and the childbirth professionals that undercut the woman's sense of confidence and control. Immigrant women are especially distressed by behaviors that they perceive to be unkind, rushed, or unsupportive during their labor and delivery (Small, Rice, Yelland, & Lumley, 1999). Efforts are needed to interpret the key elements of the birth culture for women who are not familiar with it, so that they may understand and possibly reinterpret those aspects that appear disrespectful or threatening.

APPLIED TOPIC

Abortion

Objective 7: To analyze abortion from a psychosocial perspective, including the legal context, its social and emotional impact on women, and men's views.

Abortion is the termination of a pregnancy before the fetus is able to live outside the uterus. Each year, thousands of pregnancies are terminated through spontaneous abortion, usually referred to as **miscarriage**. However, the focus of this section is on the *voluntary* termination of pregnancy. In obstetrical practice, abortions are induced differently before and after 12 weeks of gestation. Before 12 weeks, the pregnancy is aborted by dilating the cervix and then removing the contents of the uterus by suction with a vacuum aspirator or by scraping out the uterus. After 12 weeks, abortion can be induced by the injection of a saline solution or of prostaglandin, which stimulates labor. The fetus may also be removed surgically by a procedure similar to a cesarean section (Cunningham et al., 2001).

A nonsurgical approach to abortion, sometimes referred to as medical abortion, was developed in France in 1988 with the drug RU-486, now called mifepristone. This drug interrupts pregnancy by interfering with the synthesis and circulation of progesterone (Baulieu, 1989). When combined with doses of prostaglandin, it is found to be 92% effective if taken within the first 49 days after the last menstrual period. It causes the uterine lining to slough off, so there is no need for vacuum aspiration or surgical intervention (Planned Parenthood, 2000). Administration of mifepristone typically requires several clinic visits. If expulsion is not complete by the third visit, a surgical abortion is required. Studies find that 1 woman out of 100 using the drug is still pregnant at 12 days, and 2 to 4 out of 100 have had incomplete abortions ("How RU-486 Works," 1997). The drug was approved by the FDA in the United States in 2000 to be prescribed by a physician who can make a referral to a hospital or surgeon should a surgical abortion be required ("Congress and RU-486," 2001). Medical abortions using mifepristone have increased each year since 2000 when it was first distributed in the United States. In many countries of Europe and the United Kingdom, where mifepristone has been available for a longer time, medical abortions are increasingly common in the first 9 weeks of pregnancy (Guttmacher Institute, 2007).

The Legal Context of Abortion in the United States

At the heart of the abortion controversy in the United States is the conflict between society's responsibility to protect the rights of a woman and its responsibility to protect the rights of an unborn child. On one side are those who insist that a woman has the right to privacy and the right to choose or reject motherhood. On the other side are those who seek to protect the rights of the unborn fetus, which is incapable of protecting its own interests. Some argue that this is a false dichotomy and that we cannot truly separate the well-being of the mother and unborn fetus.

A major point requiring definition in the abortion controversy is the developmental age at which the embryo is considered an individual and thus entitled to protection by the state. In 1973, in the case of *Roe v. Wade*, the U.S. Supreme Court proposed a developmental model to address that issue. The court supported the division of pregnancy into three trimesters and considered abortion a woman's right in the first trimester, guarded by the U.S. Constitution's protection of privacy. The court said that in the second trimester, some restrictions could be placed on access to abortion because of its risk to the mother; however, the fetus's rights were still not an issue during this period. In the final trimester, when the fetus was regarded as having a good chance of surviving outside the uterus, states could choose not to permit abortion. This ruling endorsed a woman's right to full control over the abortion decision until the fetus reached a point of developmental viability. At that point, the Court ruled, society's responsibility to the unborn child outweighs the woman's right to freedom and privacy.

In the years since the *Roe v. Wade* decision, the Supreme Court has ruled unconstitutional the state laws that tried to regulate abortions. However, by the year 2001, the states had a wide range of regulations, some permitting and others prohibiting restrictions of various types. The main areas where restrictions have been imposed are as follows: restrictions on abortion after a specified point related to **fetal viability**, abortion reporting requirements, clinic access, parental involvement, mandatory delay and state-directed counseling, restrictions on insurance coverage of abortion, state funding of abortion for Medicaid recipients, partial-birth abortion bans, and restrictions on later abortions. For details about the restrictions that apply in each state, visit the website of the Guttmacher Institute, www.guttmacher.org.

In general, courts have ruled that states ought not to impose an undue burden on a woman by placing major obstacles in her way if she seeks an abortion before the fetus has reached viability. However, many states require counseling and informed consent, often with a mandatory waiting period, before the abortion can be performed. Restrictions also focus on the requirement for minors to get parental consent before having an abortion. Most states require reporting from physicians who perform abortions. At present, women are not required to have the consent of their husbands or the child's father before having an abortion.

The abortion controversy continues to highlight the social, political, religious, and cultural significance of the prenatal period. What do you see as the eventual resolution of this controversy in the United States?

The Incidence of Legal Abortions

The number of reported legal abortions in the United States increased dramatically after the *Roe v. Wade* decision, from 745,000 in 1973 to 1,554,000 in 1980 (U.S. Census Bureau, 1999). Since then, the trend has been a decline in the number of abortions and in the ratio of abortions to live births. A report from the Alan Guttmacher Institute placed the number of abortions in 2005 at 1,206,000 with an abortion ratio of 19.4 abortions per 1000 women ages 14 to 44, which is the lowest abortion ratio in the United States since 1975 (Guttmacher Institute, 2008). This decline is attributed to a number of factors, including changes in attitudes toward abortion, decline in access to abortion clinics, more effective contraceptive use, and a resulting decline in the number of unwanted pregnancies especially among adolescents. The public controversy and acts of violence at abortion clinics have had an impact on the number of facilities that perform abortions and on the training of physicians. One report found that first-trimester abortion education is a routine part of the training in only 46% of obstetrics and gynecology residency programs. In fact, 87% of U.S. counties do not have abortion facilities (Guttmacher Institute, 2008).

Some of the characteristics of U.S. women who had legal abortions in 2005 are summarized in Table 4.4. The data suggest that women who have abortions come from a variety of socioeconomic, developmental, and family contexts. Based on this diversity, one can assume that women have different reasons for having an abortion. The age group from 20 to 24 years old had the highest rate of abortions (32.8% of all abortions), followed by those from 25 to 29 (23.7% of all abortions) and 15 to 19 (16.2% of all abortions). White women had 54.9% of all legal abortions. Most of the abortions were performed at less than 9 weeks gestation for unmarried women, a majority of whom had no prior abortions. Roughly one in five abortions were performed for women who had experienced two or more prior abortions.

The Psychosocial Impact of Abortion

What do we know about the impact of abortions on women? Are abortions medically risky? How do women cope emotionally with the experience of abortion? In 1965, 20% of all deaths associated with pregnancy and childbirth were linked to abortion. Since the legalization of abortion, abortion-related deaths for women have decreased dramatically. The risk of death associated with abortion between 1993 and 1997 was 0.6 per 100,000 abortions, making it one of the safest surgical procedures in the United States. For comparison, the risk of maternal death from childbirth was 6.7 per 100,000 deliveries. Legal abortion, especially before 12 weeks, was over 10 times safer physically than carrying a pregnancy to term (Henry J. Kaiser Family Foundation, 2002).

Although the physical risks of abortion are less than those associated with childbirth, this still leaves unanswered questions about the emotional or psychological risks. Current research on the emotional and mental health consequences of abortion continues to be challenged with methodological criticisms and inconsistent findings (Cougle, Reardon, & Coleman, 2005; Schmiege & Russo, 2005). Methodological questions include the following:

1. What are some differences between women who have had abortions and are willing to participate in research and those who are not?

TABLE 4.4 Legal Abortions in the United States: Selected Characteristics, 2005

Total legal abortions in 2005:	1,206,000
Abortion ratio (no. of abortions per 1000 women ages 14–44):	19.4

Age of women having abortions (%)

Under 15	0.6
15–19	16.2
20–24	32.8
25–29	23.7
30–34	14.8
35–39	8.7
40 and over	3.2

Marital status of women having abortions (%)

Married	17.2
Unmarried	82.8

Race of women having abortions (%)

White	54.9
Black and other	45.1

Number of prior live births for women having abortions (%)

None	41
1	27
2	20
3	8
4 or more	4

Number of prior induced abortions (%)

None	53
1	27
2 or more	20

Weeks of gestation at time of abortion (%)

Less than 9 weeks	60.4
9–10 weeks	18.0
11–12 weeks	9.8
13 weeks or more	11.8

Source: U.S. Census Bureau, 2010, Table 100.

2. What are the appropriate comparison groups in studies of abortion?
3. What are the appropriate outcome measures?
4. When, how often, and for how long should the consequences of abortion be assessed?
5. How should differences in age, family status, and economic status be considered in this research?
6. How should differences in the reasons for having an abortion be considered in this research?

CASE STUDY

KAREN AND DON

The decision about giving birth to an infant with severe genetic anomalies.

A young couple, whom we will call Karen and Don, wanted to start a family but were troubled by a puzzling coincidence. A few years before, Don's sister had given birth to a daughter with abnormalities that matched a pattern in Don's younger brother: a heart defect, a double thumb, a club foot, and severe mental retardation. One child like this in the family could be attributed to "accident" or "fate," thought the couple, but two could not.

Karen and Don went to a human genetics clinic and began a process of discovery. With the help of a counselor, they constructed a family tree . . . identified potential carriers of the disorder in Don's family, and persuaded them to get a blood test. Don's test confirmed the young couple's worst fear: He was a carrier and potential children were at risk. . . .

The impact of these discoveries on Don's family was profound. When blood testing revealed that his mother was not a carrier, she was relieved of a burden of guilt she had secretly carried for years. She had always thought that she was the cause of her son's and her granddaughter's abnormalities. The same information implicated Don's father; his reaction to it can be gauged by his refusal to have a blood test. Don's sister, who had just given birth to a normal child, had a tubal ligation. Don himself fell into guilty silence. Not only was he the carrier of a genetic defect, he was disappointing his wife, who desperately wanted to have a baby. He thought of artificial insemination, rejected the idea, and came close to abandoning altogether the idea of having children. Then, suddenly and surprisingly, after beginning to look into adoption, Karen discovered she was pregnant. . . .

Now the process of discovery was extended one generation down, as Karen underwent amniocentesis to determine the status of her unborn fetus. . . . Karen's mother . . . would not tolerate abortion. "She kept saying, 'There is no way that you will terminate your pregnancy if you get bad news. There is just no way.' She didn't tell anyone I was pregnant." . . . A process of intervention began for Karen and Don when amniocentesis revealed that theirs was to be a child with severe abnormalities. "Maybe I should go ahead and have the child," she remembered thinking, "because it could be the only one I'll ever have." But they had already decided under what conditions they would terminate their pregnancy. "If the fetus had been a carrier, then we were going to go ahead and go full term and have the child. But we did not want to have a child that we knew would have physical deformities and be mentally retarded." They had to inform their families of their intentions, and that included Karen's mother. "When we called and said, 'It's bad news and I'm terminating the pregnancy,' she just couldn't believe it."

Karen's abortion was no easy matter for her. "It's not like I just lost the baby, I had a miscarriage. I willfully went in and terminated a pregnancy, and it was hard for people to deal with it. Some people think it was the kind of thing … you go in and you're knocked out and you wake up and you're not pregnant anymore. And that's not the way it was at all. They induced labor, and I was in labor for ten hours, and I delivered a child. I was awake. My mother called to find out how I was doing afterward, but then dropped the subject. When I went back to work, everyone acted like things should be normal, like nothing had ever happened, and I was definitely mourning.

Source: "Intergenerational Buffers: The Damage Stops Here," by J. Kotre and K. B. Kotre, pp. 367–389, in D. P. McAdams & E. de St. Aubin (Eds.), *Generativity and Adult Development: Psychosocial Perspectives on Caring for and Contributing to the Next Generation.* Copyright © 1998 American Psychological Association. Reprinted by permission.

CRITICAL THINKING AND CASE ANALYSIS

1. Try to put yourself in the roles of the main characters in this case: Karen, Don, Karen's mother, Don's mother, Don's father. How might you react?
2. How does technology enter into the case?
3. How are the biological, psychological, and societal systems involved in understanding the issues faced by Karen and Don?
4. How might Karen and Don's marital relationship be influenced by these experiences?
5. What are the ethical considerations in this case?
6. In what ways do cultural issues related to pregnancy, childbirth, and abortion come into play in this case? How might a couple living in a different cultural context approach this situation differently?

Findings of a task force convened by the American Psychological Association on Mental Health and Abortion reviewed numerous studies. After evaluating their methodological strengths and weaknesses, the task force reached the following conclusions: The majority of women who terminate their pregnancy through a legal, first-trimester abortion do not have any mental health problems. There is no systematic causal association between abortion history and mental health problems. The risks of mental health problems associated with the first trimester termination of an unwanted pregnancy are about the same as risks for mental health problems among women who deliver an unwanted child (Major, Appelbaum et al., 2009).

The typical emotional reactions of women who have had abortions are relief at having taken control over one's situation by ending an unwanted pregnancy, and regret over the loss (Lemkau, 1988; Elias, 1998; Zucker, 1999). In a study of more than 400 women 2 years after they had an abortion, 70% felt they had made the right decision. Especially when the pregnancy was unwanted and the abortion was performed within the first 12 weeks, women generally resolve any negative feelings and thoughts they may have had soon after the abortion (Adler et al., 1990). However,

roughly 30% of women experience some emotional distress as they look back on their decision (Bradshaw & Slade, 2003).

Several factors are associated with a positive abortion outcome (Alter, 1984; Miller, 1992). Women who have an androgynous gender identity—that is, a flexible view of both masculine and feminine characteristics—report less sense of loss, less anxiety, fewer physical symptoms, and fewer thoughts about death than other women (androgyny is discussed further in Chapter 10). These women tend to have a less traditional gender role orientation and expect to find a variety of sources of satisfaction in their lives in addition to or instead of childrearing.

Women differ in the reasons they give for having an abortion. In one study, 80 Norwegian women were interviewed at 10 days, 6 months, and 2 years after their abortion. Some of the reasons they gave as most important for the decision to have an abortion were: education, job, finances, being tired and worn out, having enough children, the partner does not want children, and pressure from the male partner to have an abortion. At 6 months and 2 years, the strongest predictor of women's emotional distress associated with the abortion was feeling pressure from their partners to have the abortion. Women who said they had enough children had somewhat better psychological outcomes at 2 years than others (Broen, Moum, Bodtker, & Ekeberg, 2005).

Another factor related to post-abortion adjustment is a woman's views about the acceptability of abortion within the cultural context of her family's and community's beliefs (Wang & Buffalo, 2004). Not surprisingly, women who believe that abortion is an acceptable solution to an unwanted pregnancy and that abortion is also acceptable to their friends, family, and partner are less likely to experience strong feelings of regret or emotional upset following an abortion. Religious beliefs, childbearing motives, and the woman's awareness of community opinions influence her own attitudes toward abortion.

Even though abortions can be associated with positive feelings of having taken control of one's destiny, one must not overlook the negative reactions that some women face. For women whose support systems do not sanction abortion, the decision to have an abortion is likely to be associated with strong negative emotions. Lemkau (1988) reviewed clinical cases in which abortion produced strong, unresolved negative emotions. Sometimes, when a genetic anomaly is discovered in the fetus, abortion is performed late in pregnancy. A woman who has already become attached to the fetus grieves for her loss. In other second-trimester abortions, the ambivalence that caused the delay in the decision to have an abortion is exaggerated by the physical discomfort associated with a later abortion. Some women discover that they are unable to conceive after an abortion, and guilt, anger, and regret surface. Women who are divorced, separated, or widowed at the time of an abortion appear to be more vulnerable to strong negative emotional reactions (Speckhard & Rue, 1992).

Men's Reactions to Abortion

Although abortion is often construed as a women's issue, women and their unborn babies are not the only people affected by the abortion decision. In 1976, the Supreme Court ruled that a woman did not need the consent of her husband or the child's father to have an abortion, overruling a previous requirement of the father's consent that had been legislated in 12 states (Etzioni, 1976). Since that decision, the Supreme Court has supported a woman's independence from her husband or a child's father with regard to reproductive decision making. However, questions about the legal rights of fathers to determine the fate of their unborn children are still being raised, and the laws will probably continue to be challenged as fathers become increasingly committed to participation in parenting.

Not much is known about men's reactions to their partners' abortions. Shostak and McLouth (1985) interviewed 1,000 men who had accompanied women to abortion clinics across the United States. Of these men, 93% said they would alter their birth-control methods as a result of the experience, and 83% believed that abortion was a desirable way of resolving the pregnancy problem. Many of these men expressed anxiety, frustration, and guilt in relation to the unwanted pregnancy and the abortion.

In a qualitative study of men's experiences with unintended pregnancy and abortion, a range of reactions were identified. Men differ in the degree to which they take responsibility for the pregnancy. In some cases, they view the unintended pregnancy as entirely the responsibility of their female partner. In other cases, they accept shared responsibility. Similarly, men differ in the perception of the role they played regarding the pregnancy outcome. Some believe that their female partner made the decision and excluded them entirely, others feel that the decision was reached together, and still others claim that they convinced their partner to end the pregnancy through abortion (Reich & Brindis, 2006).

Some research has focused especially on adolescent fathers who may experience feelings of anxiety, anger, and moral conflicts about abortion. Young men feel that they need to be strong for their girlfriends, even if they are feeling their own sense of confusion or loss. Just as for women, the response of men is embedded in their value system and in their relationship with the baby's mother. For young fathers, issues of secrecy and consideration for the girlfriend may prevent them from seeking support for their own feelings (Maloy & Patterson, 1992; Thomas & Striegel, 1994–1995; Holmberg & Wahlberg, 2000).

Men clearly influence the abortion decision. Research on men's influences on women's reproductive health suggests that women are concerned about their partner's attitudes, especially if they think that having a child or not having a child might result in abandonment (Dudgeon & Inhorn, 2004). Abuse by a partner may be one reason women choose to have an abortion. Women who believe that their partner will love them and their unborn child are more likely to give birth. However, most of the research on the role of men in the abortion decision is based on what women say about how they have taken their partner into account in reaching their decision. More research is needed to learn what shapes men's reactions to unintended pregnancy, their attitudes about abortion, how men contribute to the abortion decision, and how abortion experiences may influence a man's future approach to sexual relationships and paternity. This research needs to be approached from a cultural perspective, recognizing the dynamic interplay of gender roles, family structure, and religious and ethnic values.

The debate surrounding the legalization and availability of abortion services is an excellent example of a psychosocial controversy. Embedded in this controversy are key human development issues: When does human life begin? When is a fetus viable—that is, capable of life outside the uterus? What is society's responsibility to unborn children? To women of childbearing age? What is the impact of an abortion on a woman's physical health, psychological well-being, and future childbearing? What is the impact of bearing and rearing an unwanted child on a woman's physical health and psychological well-being? What is the impact of being an unwanted child? What are the rights of fathers with respect to a woman's decision to have an abortion? What are the rights and responsibilities of parents in regard to an adolescent's abortion? The politicization of the abortion controversy often overshadows the personal dilemmas that face women and men as they confront this difficult decision.

Chapter Summary

Objective 1. To describe the biochemical basis of genetic information and the process through which it is transmitted from one generation to the next.

Genetic inheritance links each new infant to a specific ancestry and to the evolutionary history of the species. The important work of the genes is to produce proteins, which then guide cellular formation and functioning. The laws of heredity explain how genetic information is passed from parents to their offspring. The genotype is the biochemical information encoded in the DNA; the phenotype is the expression of that information which can be influenced by patterns of interacting genes, or the interaction of genes and the surrounding cellular, social, or physical environment.

Objective 2. To identify the contributions of genetic factors to individuality through their role in controlling the rate of development, their contributions to individual traits, and the genetic sources of abnormalities.

Individual differences are due to a combination of the many variations in environment and experience that confront a growing person and the variability built into the biological mechanisms of heredity. Genetic factors contribute to differences in the rate and timing of development, to patterns of individual characteristics such as temperament or intelligence, and to mutations that result in abnormal development. The norm of reaction is a way of conceptualizing the probabilistic outcome of various phenotypes given a particular genotype. The more we study human genetics, the more we learn about the dynamic and ongoing interplay of genetic information with environmental factors.

Objective 3. To trace fetal development through three trimesters of pregnancy, including an understanding of critical periods when normal fetal development can be disrupted.

The 38 weeks of prenatal development, including the germinal period, the embryonic period, and the fetal period, involve a rapid differentiation of body organs and a gradual integration of survival functions, especially the ability to suck and swallow, the regulation of breathing and body temperature, and the maturation of the digestive system. Sense receptors are prepared to respond to stimulation long before they are put to use. The CNS, which begins to take shape in the third and fourth weeks after conception, continues to develop and change throughout the prenatal period and into childhood and adolescence. The newborn's neurobehavioral capacities are influenced by the quality of the prenatal environment, including potential disruptions to the CNS. During weeks 3 through 9 of the prenatal period, fetal development is especially vulnerable to the disruptive impact of teratogens, a wide range of viruses, medications, and environmental toxins that can harm organ differentiation and the maturation of the CNS.

Objective 4. To describe the birth process and factors that contribute to infant mortality.

Childbirth is described in five stages: early signs that labor is approaching, the onset of labor, transition from labor to delivery, birthing, and the postpartum period. The length of labor is quite variable with first births taking longer than subsequent births. Infant mortality rates are influenced by the quality of prenatal care, the availability of quality medical facilities for newborns, and risks associated with low birth weight often coupled with preterm births. The United States ranks behind many industrialized countries in the number of infants who die before the age of 1.

Objective 5. To analyze the reciprocity between the pregnant woman and the developing fetus, focusing on ways in which pregnancy affects a childbearing woman and expectant father and on basic influences on fetal growth, such as maternal age, drug use, nutrition, and environmental toxins.

During pregnancy, the mother and the fetus are interdependent. The fetus alters the mother's physical state, fetal movements provide an ongoing source of stimulation, and pregnancy can introduce new risks to maternal health. Pregnancy affects a woman's social roles and social status. Pregnancy influences how people treat a woman, including the baby's father, and what resources become available to her. A woman's physical well-being and emotional state along with her attitude toward her pregnancy and her developing attachment to her unborn child set the stage for the quality of her parenting after the child is born.

Characteristics of the mother, her lifestyle, and her physical and cultural environment all influence fetal development. Of special concern are the mother's age, any drugs she takes during her pregnancy, her exposure to certain diseases and environmental toxins, the use of anesthetic drugs during delivery, and the adequacy of the mother's diet. Infants conceived by women living in poverty are exposed to the cumulative effects of many of the environmental hazards that are known to result in low birth weight and congenital abnormalities.

Objective 6. To examine the impact of culture on pregnancy and childbirth.

The experiences of pregnancy and childbirth are embedded in a cultural context. The birth culture provides a set of guidelines for behavior, attitudes toward and beliefs about restrictions on the woman's activities, the availability of resources, and the treatment of a pregnant woman by others. A matrix of orientations toward pregnancy reflects solicitude versus shame and adequacy versus vulnerability. Most birth cultures can be located within this matrix.

Objective 7. To analyze abortion from a psychosocial perspective, including the legal context, its social and emotional impact on women, and men's views.

Several factors involved in the prenatal period converge in the issue of abortion. The decision to abort reflects the mother's attitude toward childbirth; her criteria for a healthy, normal child; her age and economic resources; and her access to a safe means of ending the pregnancy. Decisions about abortion are often tied to a woman's perceptions about her partner and his attitudes toward the unborn child. Decisions about abortion also reflect the culture's attitudes about the moral implications of ending a life after conception and the legal principles about when the fetus itself has a right to society's protection. Finally, the decision to abort is related to the safety, accessibility, and expense of the procedure.

The stage is now set to consider the remaining life stages in a psychosocial context. In this chapter, we have discussed the emergence of a child into an existing family, community, and cultural network. Although much attention has been given recently to the early period of childhood (birth through age 3) for subsequent cognitive, social, and emotional development, the analysis of the prenatal period suggests that the dynamic epigenetic process is already under way before birth. The care provided for expectant parents is intimately connected to the potential for optimal development in their offspring.

Key Terms

abortion, 127
adequacy versus vulnerability, 124
alleles, 90
amniotic sac, 103
artificial insemination, 100
assisted reproductive technologies, 101
birth culture, 122
cesarean section, 108
chromosomal disorders, 93
chromosomes, 89
codominance, 90
couvade, 123
cumulative relation, 90
dilation, 108
dizygotic twins, 99
dominance, 90
doula, 111
effacement, 108
embryo, 103
embryonic period, 102

environmental toxins, 103
epigenetics, 90
epigenetic marks, 91
fertility drugs, 100
fertilization, 98
fetal alcohol spectrum disorders, 117
fetal period, 102
fetal viability, 127
fetus, 103
fraternal twins, 99
gametes, 99
genes, 89
genetic counseling, 93
genome, 89
genotype, 90
germinal period, 102
heterozygous, 90
homozygous, 90
identical twins, 99
imprinting, 91

in vitro fertilization, 100
infant mortality rate, 109
infertility, 99
intelligence, 89
iron deficiency anemia, 120
labor, 108
miscarriage, 127
monozygotic twins, 99
norm of reaction, 96
nuclear transplantation, 95
phenotype, 90
placenta, 103
proteome, 89
quickening, 106
sex-linked, 91
solicitude versus shame, 124
sudden infant death syndrome, 109
surrogate mother, 101
taegyo, 124
teratogens, 103
zygote, 99

Further Reflection

1. What do you know about your genetic makeup? How would you find out more if you were interested?
2. Based on your reading, how do you evaluate the relative contribution of genetics and environment to human behavior? How do genetics and environment contribute to areas of human functioning such as intelligence, creativity, leadership, or sense of humor?
3. If you were to face the challenge of infertility, how might you cope? What alternatives would you be willing to consider? Childlessness, adoption, fertility drugs, artificial reproductive technologies? How important is it to you to have genetically related offspring?
4. Suppose your work exposed you to environmental toxins that might have a negative impact on your unborn child. What would you do?

5. Pregnancy is a powerfully gendered experience. As a man or woman, what do you imagine is the experience of pregnancy for the opposite sex?
6. What are your experiences with the cultural rituals, practices, and beliefs of the period of pregnancy? What superstitions or rituals have you encountered associated with pregnancy?
7. How do you distinguish abortion as a legal issue and as a topic in the study of human development? How much do you rely on science and technology to help inform your views about abortion?

Psychology CourseMate

To access additional course materials, including CourseMate, please visit www.cengagebrain.com. At the CengageBrain.com home page, search for the ISBN of your title (from the back cover of your book) using the search box at the top of the page. This will take you to the product page where these resources can be found.

Casebook

For additional cases related to this chapter, see the case of "Lonita and Tano" in *Life Span Development: A Case Book*, by Barbara and Philip Newman, Laura Landry-Meyer, and Brenda J. Lohman, pp. 32–37. This case introduces the challenges of supporting a healthy pregnancy for a new immigrant couple with few financial resources.

Through a process of mutual adaptation, mother and infant establish a pattern of meaningful interactions and build the foundation of trust.

© 2011 Estate of Pablo Picasso/Artists Rights Society (ARS), New York/Photo © SuperStock

Infancy (First 24 Months)

Chapter Objectives

1. To describe characteristics of newborns and the challenges facing low-birth-weight babies.

2. To identify important milestones in the maturation of the sensory and motor systems, and to describe the interactions among these systems during the first 2 years of life.

3. To describe the development of sensorimotor intelligence, including an analysis of how infants process information, organize experiences, conceptualize causality, and understand the properties and functions of objects.

4. To characterize forerunners of language competence from birth through the first 2 years of life.

5. To understand social attachment as the process through which infants develop strong emotional bonds with others, and to describe the dynamics of attachment formation during infancy.

6. To examine the nature of emotional development, including emotional differentiation, the interpretation of emotions, and emotional regulation.

7. To describe the psychosocial crisis of trust versus mistrust; the central process through which the crisis is resolved, mutuality with the caregiver; the prime adaptive ego quality of hope; and the core pathology of withdrawal.

8. To evaluate the critical role of parents and caregivers during infancy, with special attention to issues of safety and nutrition; optimizing cognitive, social, and emotional development; and the role of parents and caregivers as advocates for their infants with other agencies and systems.

INFANCY IS A period of strikingly rapid development. During the first year of life, the infant's birth weight almost triples. (Imagine if your weight tripled within 1 year at any other time in your life!) The baby seems to grow before your very eyes. Parents will remark that they go to work in the morning, and their baby seems to have changed by the time they return in the evening. Along with this extraordinary rate of physical growth comes a remarkable process of increased control and purposefulness, leading to the integration of simple responses into coordinated, patterned behavior. By the age of 2, the fundamentals of movement, language, and concept formation can be observed. Most infants are marvelously flexible, capable of adapting to any of the varied social environments into which they may be born.

At the turn of the 20th century, since many infants died before their first birthday many parents did not invest themselves emotionally in their infants. For example, they often did not name an infant right away until they were fairly sure that the infant would live. Today, with vast improvements in infant survival and smaller family size, we have seen a change in the emphasis that society places on infancy. Each child is taken much more seriously. Safety concerns have prompted laws about car seats for infants, guidelines for putting babies to sleep on their back or side, and the widespread use of monitors in the baby's room to catch signs of infant distress. The medical community is devising complex technologies for saving the lives of babies who are born weighing 1,000 grams (32 oz.) or less. The psychological community is giving attention to infant temperament and to the early origins of personality, focusing on individual differences among infants from the very first weeks of life. Some parents take classes, read books and magazines, and join support groups so that they can "get it right the first time." The Internet is replete with websites and blogs targeted to expectant and new parents. A growing baby industry offers special equipment, foods, toys, books, and other paraphernalia. Sometimes in their exuberance to make a profit from a receptive target market, companies produce infant equipment, toys, and medications that are flawed and dangerous and have to be recalled.

The story of development during infancy requires that one keep in mind a genetically guided pattern of growth and development in continuous interaction with a complex and changing social and physical environment (Plomin, DeFries, Craig, & McGuffin, 2003). The mother's personality, the father's involvement in child care, the quality of the parents' relationship with each other and their access to social support, cultural beliefs surrounding childrearing practices, and poverty or economic strain that affect the parents' psychological well-being are all factors that influence a child's vulnerability or resilience. As the infant's capacities change, they bring the baby into interaction with new facets of the environment. As daily experiences take place, they shape the infant's neural pathways into patterns of thought and behavior (Coll, 2004).

From the perspective of psychosocial development, five major developmental tasks are especially critical during infancy:

- Establishment and coordination of the sensory, perceptual, and motor systems
- Elaboration of information-processing capacities and sensorimotor intelligence
- Early communication skills
- Formation of attachments
- Differentiation of the emotional system

This chapter begins with a description of the physical status of the newborn and then discusses each of the five developmental tasks. The psychosocial crisis of infancy—trust versus mistrust—is explored as a way of thinking about the foundational orientation toward self and society. The chapter closes with an examination of the key roles that parents and caregivers can play in providing the environmental supports that promote optimal development in the infant and lay the foundation for future growth. ∎

Newborns

Objective 1. To describe characteristics of newborns and the challenges facing low-birth-weight babies.

In the United States, the average full-term baby weighs 3300 grams (7 to 7.5 pounds) and is 51 centimeters (20 inches) long. Boys are slightly heavier and longer than girls. At birth, girls' nervous systems and bones are about 2 weeks more mature than boys'.

In the first minute after birth, and then again at 5 minutes, the newborn's life signs are evaluated using the **Apgar scoring method**, named for its originator, Virginia Apgar (see Table 5.1). Five life signs are scored on a scale from 0 to 2: heart rate, respiratory effort, muscle tone, reflex irritability, and body color. A score of 7 to 10 means the infant is in good condition. Scores of 4 to 6 mean the infant is in fair condition and may require the administration of supplemental oxygen. Scores of 0 to 3 suggest an extremely poor condition and the need for resuscitation. Even among the infants who score 7 to 10, those with scores of 7 or 8 show less efficient attention and poorer cognitive processing than the higher scoring infants. The most important use of the Apgar scoring method is for evaluating the need for immediate intervention rather than as a means of assessing subsequent development (American Academy of Pediatrics,

1996). The Apgar score does not explain the source of the difficulty, but it provides an indication about whether some level of intervention is needed.

Babies differ in their physical maturity and appearance at birth. Differences in physical maturity have distinct consequences for the capacity to regulate survival functions such as breathing, digesting, waking, and sleeping. Infants who weigh less than 2,500 grams (about 5 pounds, 8 ounces) are called **low-birth-weight** babies. Low birth weight may result from prematurity (i.e., being born before the full period of gestation). It may also result from the mother's inadequate diet, smoking, or use of drugs, as discussed in Chapter 4. These factors tend to lower the fetus's weight for a given gestational age. Babies who are **small for their gestational age** (SGA) are at greater risk for health problems than those who are born prematurely but are of average weight for their gestational age.

Preterm births, that is, births before 38 weeks of gestational age, have been increasing in the United States since 1981, and now comprise 12.5% of all live births. Although many interventions have been devised to increase the survival of preterm infants, those born before 32 weeks have a high rate of infant mortality and increased risk for serious medical complications including cerebral palsy, vision and hearing impairments, and serious cognitive impairments (Institute of Medicine of the National Academies, 2006).

TABLE 5.1 The Apgar Scoring Method

SIGN	SCORE		
	0	1	2
Heart rate	Absent	Slow (less than 100 beats/minute)	More than 100 beats/minute
Respiratory effort	Absent	Slow or irregular breathing	Good crying, strong breathing
Muscle tone	Flaccid or limp	Weak; some flexion of extremities	Active motion, strong flexion of extremities
Reflex irritability	No response	Weak cry, grimace, cough, or sneeze	Vigorous cry, grimace, cough, or sneeze
Color	Blue, pale	Body pink, extremities blue	Completely pink

Source: Apgar, 1953.

APPLYING THEORY AND RESEARCH TO LIFE

Very Small Babies

MANY BABIES ARE born before they reach full gestational maturity. Modern technology has pushed back the boundary of fetal viability to about 24 weeks of gestational age, or a weight of about 500 grams (slightly more than 1 pound). These tiny babies, not much bigger than the palm of your hand, receive weeks of round-the-clock care in their struggle to survive. In the United States, 49% of babies with birth weights between 500 and 750 grams survive (NICHD, 2004). Very-low-birth-weight infants who survive are at a significantly increased risk of severe problems, including physical and visual difficulties, developmental delays, and cognitive impairment requiring increased levels of medical, educational, and parental care (Child Health USA, 2005). Hours of intensive care combined with new medical technologies increase the life chances for very tiny babies. Yet many of them are at high risk for developmental disabilities associated with their extremely low birth weight and related physical immaturity.

What do we know about the developmental progress of these very small babies? Very-low-birth-weight babies are clearly different from full-term babies. They are less physically attractive; have higher pitched, unpleasant cries; are more easily

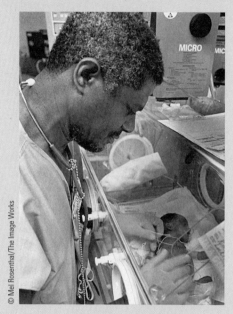

© Mel Rosenthal/The Image Works

overstimulated and more difficult to soothe; and are less able to establish rhythmic patterns of social interaction. In a longitudinal study, Ruth Feldman (2006) compared high-risk, very small babies born at less than 1,000 grams to low-risk preterm infants (1,700–1,850 grams) and full-term infants. She was interested in how the coordination of two important biological rhythms, the sleep-wake cycle and vagal tone, differed for the very small babies, and how these biological rhythms might relate to the infant's ability to orient to and react to stimuli.

Vagal tone is a process through which changes in heart rate vary during changes in environmental conditions. Typically, when you breathe in, heart rate increases, and when you breathe out, heart rate decreases. Under conditions when a task requires attention and concentration, heart rate increases, which allows for the adaptive mobilization of resources. When the situation becomes more intense or threatening, heart rate slows, leading to conservation of resources and the ability to achieve a more calm state. The vagal system contributes to regulation of arousal, reactivity, and is considered to be a basic neural component of self-regulation, information processing, and emotion (Bornstein & Suess, 2000). Feldman was also interested in whether these biological rhythms would predict the infants' ability to modify their reactions to stimuli and to engage in synchronous interactions with their mothers at 3 months.

The first comparison of the three groups was based on data collected at 37 weeks gestational age for the preterm babies and at the second day after birth for the full-term babies. The full-term babies had the most mature sleep-wake cycle and the most mature vagal tone. The low-risk preterm babies scored next, and the high-risk preterm babies had the poorest scores. Both the sleep-wake cycle and vagal tone were

---

The care for preterm infants typically takes place in a neonatal intensive care unit (NICU) of a hospital. Many interventions have been devised to improve the life chances and medical care of very small babies. Management of their breathing, temperature regulation, monitoring of heart rate, creation of appropriate stimulation, and nurturant care in the hospital all contribute to improving the chances for survival. Skin-to-skin contact between mothers or fathers and their infants, sometimes referred to as Kangaroo Care, has been shown to have benefits for the newborn as well as for parents. It provides a variety of sensory stimulation to the infant and increases the caregivers' confidence and comfort in caring for their baby. Preterm babies who receive Kangaroo Care as well as other forms of gentle touching and massage gain weight faster, have improved temperature regulation, and improved alertness as compared to babies who do not receive the systematic comfort of human touch (Feldman & Eidelman, 2003; Feldman, 2004).

A growing body of evidence suggests that certain self-regulatory functions related to self-calming in the face of unpleasant stimuli and organization of wake-sleep cycles become integrated and synchronized during the third trimester, especially between 30 and 34 weeks of gestation. Babies born before 30 weeks do not have the benefit of positive features of the uterine environment that support these aspects of **self-regulation**. The box about very small babies in this chapter discusses some of the risks for developmental disabilities among babies weighing less than 1,500 grams. Very-low-birth-weight infants are highly vulnerable to medical complications. In 2000, these infants comprised 1.4% of U.S. births but 51% of infant deaths (NIH, 2007). Renewed efforts are needed to determine the causes of low birth weight and to prevent as many preterm births as possible (Institute of Medicine of the National Academies, 2006).

related to neurobehavioral orientation. At 3 months, the infants who showed the poorest vagal tone were more likely to show distress and crying in response to a sequence of stimuli, and less likely to engage in synchronous interactions with their mothers. The study supports the important role of full gestation in allowing for the organization of critical neurobiological rhythms and their subsequent role in fostering emotional regulation, attention, and social interactions. It also helps to account for some of the difficulties parents experience in social interactions with their very small babies.

In a study of very high-risk low-birth-weight babies (average weight 1,000 grams), significantly fewer preterm babies had secure attachments at 19 months than the comparison group of full-term babies. In fact, the percentage of very small babies who showed a secure attachment *declined* from 14 to 19 months. One explanation for this decline is that the disruptive effects of neurological damage resulting from prematurity accumulate during the second year of life, introducing more anxiety among caregivers and greater difficulty in achieving mutuality in the infant-caregiver relationship (Mangelsdorf et al., 1996). Other studies find that for lower-risk preterm babies, about 60% establish secure attachments with their caregivers and 40% have

insecure or disorganized attachments, a distribution that is very similar to that for full-term infants (Goldberg & DiVitto, 1995; Brisch et al., 2005).

Extremely low-birth-weight infants are at risk for problems in subsequent cognitive development. Infants who are born weighing less than 1,500 grams are likely to suffer serious brain hemorrhages. Moreover, their undeveloped lungs cannot deliver an adequate supply of oxygen to the brain. Chronic lung disease, frequently associated with prematurity, results in breathing problems, feeding difficulties, lung infections, and disrupted flow of oxygen (Singer, Davillier, Bruening, Hawkins, & Yamashita, 1996). These insults to the nervous system have an impact on a variety of information-processing skills that can be measured in newborns, including regulation of arousal and attention, visual recognition of familiar stimuli, and reactivity to novel stimuli (DiPietro, Porges, & Uhly, 1992; Rose, Feldman, & Wallace, 1992). In a Dutch study, more than 1300 very-low-birth-weight babies born in 1983 were studied into adolescence. About 10% had very serious abnormalities. However, another 40% had disabilities and behavioral and learning difficulties that accumulated over time to impede their ability to function independently (Walther, den Ouden, & Verloove-Vanhorick, 2000). As pointed out in the research on attachment, the

consequences of neurological damage associated with prematurity are likely to have an impact on social and emotional development as well as on cognitive functioning.

Critical Thinking Questions

1. Why are very small babies at risk for impairments of cognitive and sensorimotor functioning? What might be happening with respect to neurological development in the last trimester that is disrupted by preterm birth?

2. What are some features of very-low-birth-weight infants that might disrupt the establishment of synchronous interactions with their caregivers? What kinds of interventions can you think of that could help overcome some of these difficulties?

3. Can you think of reasons that could account for a decline in the proportion of preterm babies found to have secure attachments between 14 and 19 months of age other than the one suggested in the text?

4. Why might the consequences of neurological damage due to prematurity become more evident as children get older?

5. What advice would you give to parents of premature infants about how to evaluate their child's developmental level and how to foster a developmentally appropriate set of childrearing expectations?

Developmental Tasks
The Development of Sensory/Perceptual and Motor Functions

Objective 2. To identify important milestones in the maturation of the sensory and motor systems, and to describe the interactions among these systems during the first 2 years of life.

During the first months of life, the sensory/perceptual system—vision, hearing, taste, smell, touch, motion sensitivity, and responsiveness to internal cues (*proprioception*)—is developing rapidly and functions at a more advanced level than the motor system. Because most muscle movements are not under the infant's voluntary control in the early days and months of life,

researchers have had to apply considerable ingenuity to study infants' sensory/perceptual competencies. How can you know if an infant detects the difference between the color red and the color orange, or between the mother's voice and the voice of a stranger? We cannot simply ask an infant to point to a circle or press a button to respond to a certain change in color or image. Behaviors such as gazing time, changes in heart rate, strength or frequency of sucking, facial action, head turning, and habituation are used as indicators of infants' interest or change in response to stimuli.

Habituation means that the infant's response decreases after each presentation of an identical stimulus (Schöner & Thelen, 2006). Habituation allows the infant to shift attention to new aspects of the environment as certain elements become familiar. When a new stimulus is presented, such as a new level of loudness, or the same tone presented to a different ear, the infant shows an increase in alert responsiveness. Habituation is one of the most primitive forms of learning and is observed in many other mammalian species.

Habituation is one way to determine whether an infant can discriminate between two different stimuli. The researcher first habituates the infant to one stimulus; then a second stimulus is presented. Signs of renewed interest or alertness, measured by changes in heart rate, gazing time, or eye movements, are taken as evidence that the infant has detected a difference between the two stimuli. If the infant shows no new signs of interest or responsiveness, this is taken as evidence that the differences between the two stimuli were too slight to be perceived.

For example, 16 newborns who were 48 hours old were habituated to a two-dimensional image of a normal face or a scrambled face (eyes on the bottom of the oval, nose at the top with the eyebrows). The face was moved slowly along a bar from the midline to the right and then to the left. Fixation time was measured until the baby's looking time decreased by 60% from the level of the first three trials. Then the new stimulus was introduced. No matter whether the babies were initially habituated to the normal or to the scrambled face, they all showed an increase in fixation or looking time when the novel face was presented. Habituation was a sensitive technique for demonstrating newborns' ability to tell the difference between a normal and a scrambled face (Easterbrook, Kisilevsky, Muir, & Laplante, 1999). Similar findings have been observed in infants' responses to patterns of musical notes, phonetic sounds, and complex shapes. These studies support the notion that young infants are capable of forming and retaining a scheme for sensory experiences against which they can compare new events.

Brain Development in Infancy

Most infants are born with intact sensory organs and a well-formed brain. The infant's brain contains about 100 billion **neurons**, or nerve cells, which are already connected in pathways that are designed to execute functions related to sensation, perception, and motor behavior as well as to regulate internal systems such as respiration, circulation, digestion, and temperature control. The fundamental organization of the brain does not change after birth, but details of its structure demonstrate **plasticity** (Singer, 1995; Nash, 1997; Johnson, 1999).

What is **neural plasticity**? It can be thought of in two different but related ways. First, there are all the changes in the interconnections among neurons that occur as a result of learning and experience. Because the wide range of human experiences cannot be anticipated, the human brain is genetically designed to take in information and use it to guide further thought and action through the establishment of neural pathways. Second, there are a variety of ways that the brain compensates for injury by making use of alternative resources. For example, severe damage to the left cerebral cortex, where many language-related functions have

been located, does not result in lasting language deficits if it occurs prenatally or in the very early postnatal period. As long as the damage does not impact both hemispheres, the infant's language capacities can mature without significant or noticeable disruption or delay (Bates & Roe, 2001). Although we have a growing body of research that addresses factors that can injure or disrupt brain development, some of which is discussed in Chapter 4, we do not know as much about the conditions that optimize or foster neural development. Much of the research on this topic comes from animal models where conditions can be controlled to increase or eliminate certain forms of stimulation and then examine the impact of these conditions on the number of connections among neurons, the mylenation of the neurons, and changes in the biochemistry of the brain that facilitate or inhibit nerve cells from firing.

In the prenatal period, brain cells are formed and the initial organization of the brain structures takes place. Neurons are produced at an astounding rate, and axons and dendrites are formed as the nerve cells begin to link up with each other (see Figure 5.1). **Transient exuberance** is the term given to this rapid increase in the number of neurons, dendrites, and synapses that form during the first 2 years of life. As the term suggests, the growth is exceptional, producing far more neurons than will actually be used; and the rate of growth is temporary, preparing the brain to be shaped and organized through experience. Maturational processes continue throughout infancy that alter the interconnections among neurons and the speed of firing. Maturational changes in the central nervous system that advance the infant's ability to organize and use information, and to regulate behavior include:

- The formation of neurons
- The continuing growth of axons and dendrites
- The formation of synapses, the connections between the axons of one cell and the dendrites of another
- The sculpting or **pruning** of synapses
- The production of neurotransmitters, the chemicals that stimulate or inhibit the firing of specific neurons
- Myelination, which insulates the neurons and increases the speed of firing from one neuron to the next
- The production of glial cells that provide stability for the neural network

During the first 3 years, the brain triples in weight and creates about 1,000 trillion connections among the neurons. Different areas of the brain experience an overproduction of synapses at different times, with the visual cortex taking the lead, followed by areas related to hearing and language, and the prefrontal cortex where higher level thought and problem solving take place. Then, the pathways are gradually pruned or sculpted. As a result of early experiences, sights, smells, sounds, tastes, touches, and postures activate and strengthen specific neural pathways, whereas other pathways are not used and decay. The frequency and speed with which nerves fire across a synapse strengthen the stability of

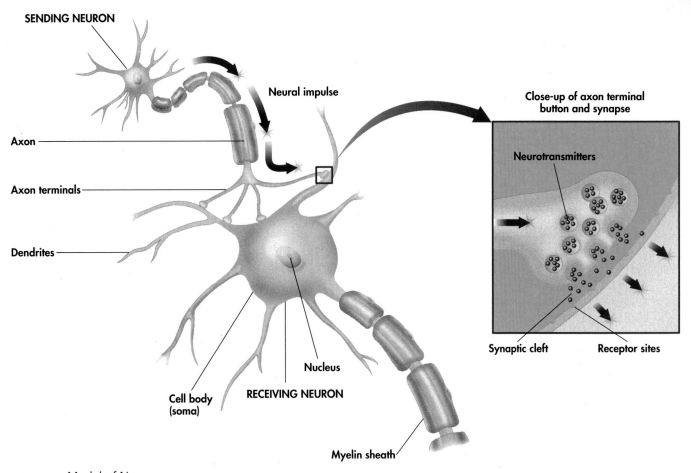

SENDING NEURON

Neural impulse

Axon

Axon terminals

Dendrites

Close-up of axon terminal
button and synapse

Neurotransmitters

Synaptic cleft

Receptor sites

Nucleus

Cell body
(soma)

RECEIVING NEURON

Myelin sheath

FIGURE 5.1 Model of Neuron

Source: Rathus, *Psychology: Concepts and Connections Brief Version*, 8E, Wadsworth/Thomson, Fig. 2.1, p. 40.

the synapse. In the visual and auditory regions, this pruning seems to be completed during the preschool and early childhood periods. In the prefrontal cortex, however, sculpting continues throughout middle to later adolescence, suggesting a much wider window for the organization of higher order reasoning capacities (Huttenlocher & Dabholkar, 1997). Thus, experiences and the infant's response to experience play a role in shaping the unique patterns of interconnections that are preserved in each individual (Johnson, 2000).

The process of pruning or sculpting leads to a reduction in plasticity. Although we do not know the exact timing for each area of sensory or motor competence, it is believed that there is much greater plasticity during the period of overproduction of synapses and reduced plasticity once the number of synapses reaches its adult level. For example, in the development of language, all infants are capable of recognizing and uttering sounds from a wide universe of languages. However, after repeated interactions with family members and caregivers, the infant develops strong neural connections for the sounds of the language(s) spoken in the home environment, and the neural connections associated with sounds from other languages decay with

disuse (Hoff, 2004). Significant injuries or deficiencies in experiences required for optimal functioning become harder to correct as the system becomes more finely organized. We understand this process most fully in the visual system, which has been a focus of research in animals as well as in human infants born with specific visual anomalies.

In addition to the production and loss of synaptic connections among neurons, brain development advances through the production of **neurotransmitters**, the chemicals that influence how the nerves grow, how they respond to stimulation, and whether they result in the firing or the inhibition of firing of the neurons. These chemicals influence the growth in dendrites and synapses in various parts of the brain, they alter synaptic strength, and they change in strength following trauma to aid in **repair**. Experiences such as skin-to-skin contact, which was described as an intervention for preterm infants, contributes to the release of certain chemicals, helping to relieve pain and reduce stress (Carter, 2003). Although it is not fully understood, there is a growing interest in how specific aspects of early nurturing might influence the neurochemical environment and thereby alter brain development.

As we continue to understand the relationship of brain development to changes in motor behavior, cognition, emotional expression and inhibition, language and communication, interpersonal or social behavior, and self-awareness, keep these two important principles in mind: First, through interactions with the immediate stimulus environment each infant shapes the organization of neural connections, creating very early patterns of familiarity and meaning (National Research Council and Institute of Medicine, 2000). Thus, infants contribute to their own brain development by repeating certain actions, attending to certain stimuli more than others, and producing responses in caregivers. Second, throughout childhood, adolescence, and adulthood, more complex cognitive functions, including organized and abstract thought; self-control; appreciation for subtle forms of communication such as sarcasm; capacities for poetry, music, and symbolic art; spatial reasoning; and cognitive flexibility will emerge (Rubia et al., 2006). Even though a lot of attention has been given to the importance of brain development in the first 3 years of life, advanced reasoning and expert knowledge require continued maturation of specific areas of the cortex as well as the synchronization of systems.

Sensory/Motor Development

Figure 5.2 provides a map of the sensory and motor areas of the brain that are related to the infant's emerging capacities. The map suggests that specific functions are guided by activity in certain areas of the brain. However, that is an oversimplification. The more complex processes such as decision making, learning and memory, emotional expression and recognition, planning, and participation in meaningful social interactions require the interaction and feedback loops among several areas, a process that unfolds over time with experience and practice (Buschman & Miller, 2007).

It would be difficult to review the full range and detail of sensory capacities that emerge and develop during infancy.

Maturation in these domains is breathtaking. Our discussion focuses on those abilities that permit infants to participate in and adapt to their social environment. From birth, sensory/perceptual capacities are vital resources that help infants establish emotional links with their caregivers, gather information about their environment, and cope with sources of stress. Although we provide information on each of the sensory modalities, it is important to realize that they typically function together in a multimodal system. Infants not only hear their caregivers, but they see, smell, and touch them. Voices are normally associated with faces; tastes are linked to smells and textures. Sensory meaning-making takes place with the benefit of information from multiple sources.

Hearing. You may be surprised to learn that hearing rather than vision is the sense that provides the very earliest link between newborns and their mothers. Research has confirmed that the fetus is sensitive to auditory stimulation in utero (Porcaro, 2006). Before birth, the fetus hears the mother's heartbeat. This sound continues to be soothing to the infant in the days and weeks after birth. Newborns show a preference for the sound of their mother's voice over an unfamiliar voice. The speed with which they recognize their mother's voice suggests both increased attention and clear memory for this type of auditory stimulus (Purhonen et al., 2005). Infants show a preference for the sound of melodies that their mother sang during the pregnancy and even for the sound of prose passages she read during the prenatal period (De Casper & Fifer, 1980; De Casper & Spence, 1986). One must assume that an infant's indication of preference for these auditory stimuli is based on familiarity with the sounds from exposure in utero.

Young infants can distinguish changes in the loudness, pitch, duration, and location of sounds. They can use auditory information to differentiate objects from one another and to track the location of objects (Bahrick, Lickliter,

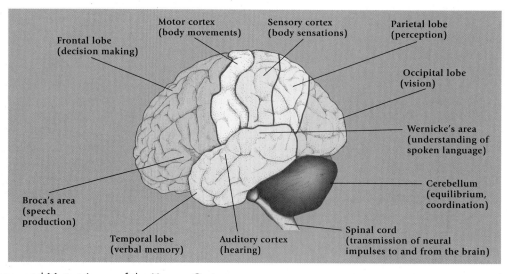

FIGURE 5.2 Sensory and Motor Areas of the Human Cortex

Source: Shaffer & Kipp, *Developmental Psychology, Childhood & Adolescence*, 7E © 2007, Wadsworth/Thomson, Fig. 6.6, p. 202.

© Ariel Skelley/CORBIS

Even in the first days of life, a new-born is taking in sensory information about his mother's face, the sound of her voice, her scent, and the way it feels to be cuddled in her arms.

& Flom, 2006; Wilcox, Woods, Tuggy, & Napoli, 2006). Many of these capacities are present among newborns but become increasingly sensitive by 6 months. In one study, babies ages 6 to 8 months were placed in a darkened room. Objects that made sounds were located within reach and out of reach, and off to the right or left of midline. The babies made reaching motions in the correct direction of the sounds, and they made more efforts to reach objects that sounded as if they were within reach than to reach objects that sounded out of reach (Clifton, Perris, & Bullinger, 1991). In another study, infants ages 4 to 6 months were exposed to a looming sound, which appeared to come closer or recede from them at a slow or rapid pace. When the sound loomed toward them quickly, the babies leaned back in a defensive strategy to escape the anticipated threat. This suggests that infants have the ability to use auditory information to detect relative speed and distance (Freiberg, Tually, & Crassini, 2001).

The human voice is one of the earliest stimuli to evoke an infant's smile; infants appear to be particularly sensitive to language sounds (Benasich & Leevers, 2003). In a comparison of newborns and babies 3 months old, the newborns were equally interested in human and monkey vocalizations, and preferred these sounds to synthetic sounds. By 3 months, however, babies showed a clear preference for human over monkey vocalizations suggesting that human auditory preferences take shape rapidly in the first months of life (Vouloumanos, Hauser, Werker, & Martin, 2010).

Very young babies are able to differentiate basic sound distinctions used in human speech throughout the world. Infants from all language environments are able to perceive and distinguish among the speech sounds that could be used in one or more of the world's languages. By 6 months of age, however, infants prefer to listen to sequences of words spoken in the mother's language rather than in a foreign language, especially if the two languages differ in their overall tone, pauses, and rhythm (Sansavini, Bertoncini, & Giovanelli, 1997). During the second 6 months of life, after exposure to a native language, the infant's ability to make some sound distinctions declines. Speech perception becomes more tied to the native language as infants begin to attach meaning to certain sound combinations, indicating a reorganization of sensory capabilities as the child learns to listen to people speaking a particular language (Bornstein, 1995; Werker & Tees, 1999). This is an example of the plasticity referred to earlier—a fine-tuning of the neural network as a result of experience.

Vision. Infants respond to a variety of visual dimensions, including movement, color, brightness, complexity, light-dark contrast, contours, depth, and distance (Slater & Johnson, 1998). The vast majority of research on sensory development in infancy has concentrated on assessing the acuity or sensitivity of vision. Visual behaviors also offer a way to assess the infant's cognitive capacities. For instance, the time an infant takes to scan an object and the length of time spent fixating on a novel object are indications of infant intelligence. Shorter fixation time indicates greater speed and efficiency in neural processing (Colombo, Mitchell, Coldren, & Freeseman, 1991; Jacobson et al., 1992).

For sighted, normally developing infants, gazing provides an early and continuing source of information that guides social interactions and learning about the physical environment (Hoehl et al., 2009). Newborns and their caregivers gaze into each other's eyes. Mutual gazing has been shown to have a calming effect on distressed babies; and babies also actively avert their gaze when they need to reduce or withdraw from stimulation. By 4 months of age, babies can follow the gaze of another person toward an object and by 9 months, they use the gaze and head turning cues of others to direct their attention. By gazing at others and following the gaze of others, babies use vision to form social connections, focus attention, and gain information from others about important objects and activities in their environment (Moore, 2008; Akhtar & Gernsbacher, 2008).

Visual acuity improves rapidly during the first 4 months. Pattern and movement perception mature as well. By 2 months, infants form an expectation of a visual sequence. As they watch a pattern of events, they show evidence of anticipating the next event in the sequence (MacMurray & Aslin, 2004). Three-month-old infants respond to wavelengths of light as though they perceive distinct hues of blue, green, yellow, and red (Bornstein, Kessen, & Weiskopf, 1976; Aslin, 1987; Teller & Bornstein, 1987). Four-month-old babies perceive objects as adults would, although they do not have the same set of cognitive associations with them that imply specific functions or categories. They recognize shapes and detect complex patterns of motion such as human walking. Infants are born with a variety of skills for detecting visual stimuli, which matures rapidly into the coordination of visual perception. However, the process of visual cognition—that is, understanding the nature of objects and their physical properties—requires further experimentation.

Faceness. Faces are a particularly salient kind of visual stimulus. Several specific areas of the brain respond specifically to faces as compared to other kinds of complex objects. Research with macaques shows that specific nerves in the region of the brain that is active in processing faces fire exclusively to faces and not to other visual stimuli. Moreover, among those neurons, some are triggered by particular features of faces such as the round shape, the arrangement and distance between the eyes, or the size of the iris (Tsao, 2006). It is as if the brain is organized to build an increasingly complex perception of faces by integrating the recognition of a variety of specific features.

Infants show preference for face-like stimuli (Nelson, 2001). In the early weeks following birth, infants have optimal focus on objects that are about 20 cm away—approximately the distance between the mother's face and her baby cradled in her arms. Newborns can shift focus to scan and keep track of a moving target, but not as easily and smoothly as older babies. Young infants focus their attention on the contours or external borders of objects rather than on the internal details. Thus, if you were holding a young baby, the child might appear to be staring at your hairline or your chin rather than at your mouth. Faces have many of the properties that infants prefer. The hairline is a type of contour; the eyes provide a light-dark contrast; and the facial expressions provide a changing, moving stimulus.

An experiment with newborns who were 25 to 73 hours old demonstrated that one aspect of a face that is important to babies is the top-heavy configuration of the features (Cassia, Turati, & Simion, 2004). Figure 5.3 shows the comparisons that support this conclusion. Fixation time to the stimulus pairs of faces was used as evidence of preference. In Experiment 1, babies preferred the upright to the upside-down face. In Experiment 2, babies preferred the top-heavy scrambled face to the bottom-heavy scrambled face. In Experiment 3, there was no difference in preference between the normal upright face and the top-heavy scrambled face. The results of the three studies together provide evidence

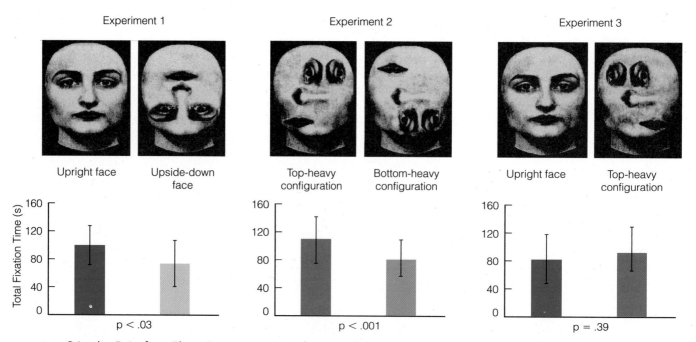

FIGURE 5.3 Stimulus Pairs from Three Experiments on Infants' Preference for Top-Heavy Configurations. For each experiment, the total fixation time toward each stimulus is shown along with the *p* value for comparison between the two stimuli.
Source: Cassia, Turati, & Simion, 2004.

of the importance of this aspect of **faceness** in capturing a newborn's attention.

Subsequent studies have demonstrated that another feature of faceness is the congruence of the inner features with the outer shape. Human faces have more features, including eyes and eyebrows, at the wider part of the head and fewer features at the narrow part of the head. When stimuli combine the two features of top-heaviness and congruency, they evoke the same level of visual preference among newborns as faces (Cassia, Valenza, Simion, & Leo, 2008). By 6 or 7 months of age, infants treat faceness as a special visual category, showing surprise when facial features are disorganized or upside down (Catherwood, Freiberg, Green, & Holt, 2001; Cohen & Cashon, 2001).

In addition to the form, shape, and movement of the human face, certain facial expressions appear to have meaning to very young babies. One- and 2-day-old babies are able to discriminate and imitate the happy, sad, and surprised expressions of a live model (Field, Woodson, Greenberg, & Cohen, 1982). This very early capacity for imitation wanes and is replaced between the ages of 1 and 2 months with a voluntary capacity for imitation of facial expressions when the model is not present. Sometime between 4 and 7 months, infants are able to recognize and classify some expressions such as happiness, fear, and anger (McClure, 2000).

Lack of motion in an adult face has a disturbing effect on infants. When adults pose with a still face, babies stop looking at the adult and, in some cases, begin grimacing or showing other signs of discomfort. This reaction suggests that infants anticipate a certain normal sequence of facial movements in a human interaction. Thus, the absence of facial movements is not simply noted as novel but distressing (Muir & Lee, 2003).

Some 2-day-old infants discriminate between their mother's face and the face of a stranger (Field, Cohen, Garcia, & Greenberg, 1984). By 3 months, almost all infants can distinguish a parent's face from that of a stranger (Zucker, 1985). These visual perceptual skills illustrate the highly developed capacities for orienting toward social stimuli that permit infants to participate readily in the social context on which their survival depends.

Of course, sights and sounds typically go together. When people speak, their mouths change shape and their faces move. By 3 months of age, infants can recognize familiar voice-face associations. They show surprise when a familiar face is paired with an unfamiliar voice (Brookes et al., 2001). By 4.5 months, they can imitate the facial expressions associated with specific spoken sounds—making different faces for the / i / sound and the / a / sound (Patterson & Werker, 1999). So while babies are making sense of their visual environment, they are also using vision as a source of information about language and communication.

Taste and Smell. Newborns can differentiate sweet, sour, bitter, and salty tastes. Facial responses to salty, sour, and bitter solutions share the same negative upper and midface response but differ in the accompanying lower face actions: The lips purse in response to a sour taste, the mouth gapes in response to a bitter taste, and no distinctive lower facial reaction is seen in response to a salty taste. Two hours after birth, an infant's facial responses to a sweet taste (sucrose) are characterized primarily by relaxation and sucking. Sucrose has an especially calming effect on newborns and appears to reduce pain. In one experiment, newborns 1 to 3 days old who were undergoing circumcision or were having their heel pricked for a blood test for phenylketonuria cried much less when they were given a small sucrose solution to suck (Blass & Hoffmeyer, 1991). The calming effect of sweet-tasting substances has been observed in both preterm and full-term infants (Smith & Blass, 1996). It is likely that the normal taste of milk, which includes this sweet flavor, has the combined effect of releasing natural opioids, thereby raising the pain threshold, and reducing heart rate and activity level, thereby conserving energy.

Breastfed babies are particularly sensitive to their mothers' body odors (Cernoch & Porter, 1985). One study found that 7-day-old babies could use the sense of smell to distinguish their own mothers' nursing pads from those of other mothers (MacFarlane, 1975). The mother's odor may play an important role in stimulating early mother-infant interactions (Porter, Balogh, & Makin, 1988).

Touch. The skin is the largest sensory organ and the earliest to develop in utero. A variety of evidence from animal and human research suggests that touch plays a central role

© Diane Rosenstein and Helen Oster (1988) / Society for Research in Child Development

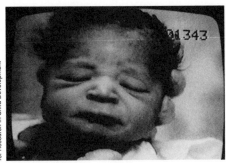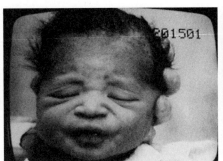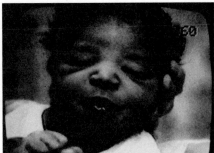

This sequence of facial expressions in a newborn was elicited by a sweet solution. The initial negative grimace is followed by relaxation and sucking.

Sucking and mouthing are important ways of exploring objects. Fists and toes are the first easy targets.

© Philip Newman

in development. Gentle handling, such as rocking, stroking, and cuddling, has soothing effects on a baby. Swaddling—the practice of wrapping a baby snugly in a soft blanket—is a common technique for soothing a newborn in many cultures. One of the effective techniques for caring for low-birth-weight babies is to introduce regular gentle stroking, rocking, and other forms of soothing touch.

Touch is an active as well as a passive sense; babies use it to explore objects, people, and their own bodies. *Sucking* is one of the earliest coping strategies infants use to calm themselves (Blass & Ciaramitaro, 1994). Sucking and mouthing are early forms of exploratory touch. Babies can recognize the qualities of objects from the way they feel in their mouths—nubbly or smooth, chewy and flexible, or rigid (Rose & Ruff, 1987). For older infants, most tactile information comes through touching with the hands and bringing objects to the face in order to take a closer look or to explore them with the mouth. By 5 or 6 months of age, infants can use their hands for the controlled examination of objects. They finger surfaces to explore small details and transfer objects from one hand to the other to detect corners, shapes, and the flexibility of surfaces as well as the object's size, temperature, and weight (Streri, 2005).

The Interconnected Nature of Sensory/Perceptual Capacities. The sensory/perceptual capacities function as an interconnected system to provide a variety of information about the environment at the same time (Calvert, Spence, & Stein, 2004). Consider the situation when an infant is being nursed. At first, the mother guides the baby toward her breast, but the baby makes use of visual, tactile, olfactory, and kinesthetic cues to find and grab hold of the nipple. If very hungry, the baby may close the eyes in order to concentrate exclusively on bursts of sucking behavior, coordinating sucking and swallowing as efficiently as possible. But as the initial swallows of milk satisfy the strong hunger pangs, the

baby pauses to take in other aspects of the situation. The baby may then gaze at the contours of the mother's face, playfully lick the milk dripping from the mother's breast, smell the milk's fragrance and taste its special sweet taste, and listen to the sound of the mother's voice offering comfort or inviting conversation. The baby may reach up to explore the mother's skin or relax in the comfort of the mother's gentle embrace. All the sensory information becomes integrated to create familiarity with this scheme, including a growing recognition of the mother and a rich mixture of sensory impressions associated with this special situation in which hunger is satisfied.

Motor Development

At birth, an infant's voluntary muscle responses are poorly coordinated. Most early motor responses appear to be reflexive, meaning that a specific stimulus will evoke a particular motor response without any voluntary control or direction. Many of these built-in responses help infants survive and lead them to develop more complicated sequences of voluntary behavior. The sucking reflex is a good example. At birth, inserting something in an infant's mouth produces a sucking reflex. This helps infants gain nourishment relatively easily before sucking behavior is under their control. Before long, infants become skillful at controlling the strength and sensitivity of sucking behavior. They use sucking and mouthing as strategies for tactile exploration. Infants have been shown to use their mouths to explore objects that they can then identify visually, thus transferring information from the tactile sense to the visual sense (Meltzoff & Borton, 1979; Gibson & Walker, 1984).

Table 5.2 describes a number of common infant reflexes, the evoking stimulus, and the response. Infant reflexes include sucking, grasping, rooting (turning the head in the direction of the cheek that is stroked), coughing, and stepping. With time, many of these behaviors make a transition

TABLE 5.2 Some Infant Reflexes

REFLEX	EVOKING STIMULUS	RESPONSE
Reflexes that facilitate adaptation and survival		
Sucking reflex	Pressure on lips and tongue	Suction produced by movement of lips and tongue
Pupillary reflex	Weak or bright light	Dilation or constriction of pupil
Rooting reflex	Light touch to cheek	Head movement in direction of touch
Startle reflex	Loud noise	Similar to Moro reflex (below), with elbows flexed and fingers closed
Swimming reflex	Neonate placed prone in water	Arm and leg movement
Reflexes linked to competences of related species		
Creeping reflex	Feet pushed against a surface	Arms and legs drawn under, head lifted
Flexion reflex	Pressure on sole of foot	Involuntary bending of leg
Grasp reflex	Pressure on fingers or palm	Closing and tightening of fingers
Moro reflex	Infant lying on back with head raised—rapidly release head	Extension of arms, head thrown back, spreading of fingers, crossing arms across body
Springing reflex	Infant held upright and slightly forward	Arms extended forward and legs drawn up
Stepping reflex	Infant supported under the arms above a flat surface	Rhythmical stepping movement
Abdominal reflex	Tactile stimulation	Involuntary contraction of abdominal muscles
Reflexes of unknown function		
Achilles tendon reflex	Blow to Achilles tendon	Contraction of calf muscles and downward bending of foot
Babinski reflex	Mild stroke on sole of foot	Fanning and extension of toes
Tonic neck reflex	Infant on back with head turned to one side	Arm and leg on side toward which head is facing are extended, other arm and leg flexed

from an *involuntary* to a *voluntary* behavior. In the process, infants may lose a response before they regain control over simple movements. Then they blend several of these new voluntary movements into increasingly coordinated and complex patterns of behavior (Fentress & McLeod, 1986). For example, very young infants can support their full weight through the strength of their grasping reflex. When propped in an infant seat, they will reach and grasp reflexively at an object, reaching their target about 40% of the time. At 4 weeks of age, this reflexive reaching behavior seems to disappear, but by 5 months it is replaced by voluntary reaching, accurate grasping, clutching, and releasing (Bower, 1987).

Reaching and Grasping. The transition from involuntary to voluntary reaching and grasping results from genetically guided maturation coupled with repeated exploration. Infants practice controlled, coordinated muscle movements, guided by visual and auditory cues—particularly cues about size, distance, and direction. In the following example, a 2-month-old girl gains control of her hands and fingers.

> She has discovered her hands, stares at them many times a day for three or four minutes at a time, watches them as she wiggles fingers, extends and flexes them, rotates wrists.

She also clasps her hands together and stares at them out in front of her at arm's length. (Church, 1966, p. 7)

Voluntary reaching begins as the child tries to make contact with objects on the same side of the body as the outstretched hand. By 4 months, babies will reach for objects placed on the same side, the opposite side, or in the middle of the body. By this age, babies have also become skilled in using both hands to hold an object, so they are more able to keep the object close enough to investigate. They may shift from exploring with their fingers to sucking and biting to find out more about the object (Rochat, 1989). Between 5 and 7 months, babies become increasingly accurate at reaching and grasping a moving object, alternating hands to intercept an object by anticipating the direction of its movement (Robin, Berthier, & Clifton, 1996).

By 12 months, babies have mastered the pincer grasp, using their index finger and thumb to pick up tiny things, such as string and thread, pieces of dry cereal, and spaghetti noodles. With this advance, they can also manipulate things by lifting latches, turning knobs, and placing small things inside bigger things and trying to get them out again. These motor skills provide new information about how objects work and how they relate to one another. The development of fine motor skills contributes to the infant's sense of mastery and can be a source for positive emotions. At the same time, they may cause new conflicts between the baby and the caregiver, who knows that tiny things shouldn't go into the mouth, and that certain objects ought not to be touched, moved, and manipulated.

Motor Sequence. Motor skills develop as a result of the physical growth and maturation of bones, muscles, and the nervous system in the context of varied environmental opportunities. Figure 5.4 shows the normal sequence of development of motor and movement skills during the first year of life; however, babies vary in the sequence and rate at which they acquire these skills. Individual children grow in spurts, interspersed with times of slow growth and some periods of regression (Fischer & Rose, 1994). Usually, however, during the first 12 months, babies begin to hold their heads up and roll over by themselves; they learn to reach for things and grasp them; they sit, crawl, stand, and

walk. Parental expectations seem to influence the timing of the onset for some of these milestones (Hopkins & Westra, 1990). During the second year, walking becomes increasingly steady; crawling may be used for play but is no longer the preferred method for locomotion. Babies explore stairs, climbing up and down using a variety of strategies. They start to slide or jump down from modest heights. Each of these accomplishments requires practice, refinement, struggle, and, finally, mastery.

The Contributions of Nature and Nurture in Motor Development. Motor development provides an excellent illustration of the interaction between the genetically guided plan for growth and experience. The unfolding of motor capacities is guided by genetics, beginning as it does with the presence of a wide range of reflexive responses that are hardwired, so to speak, into the infant's neurological system. At the same time, within this plan, one observes both

FIGURE 5.4 A Typical Sequence of Gross Motor Development and Locomotion in Infancy

Source: From W. K. Frankenberg and J. B. Dodds (1967). "The Developmental Screening Test," *Journal of Pediatrics*, 71, 181–191.

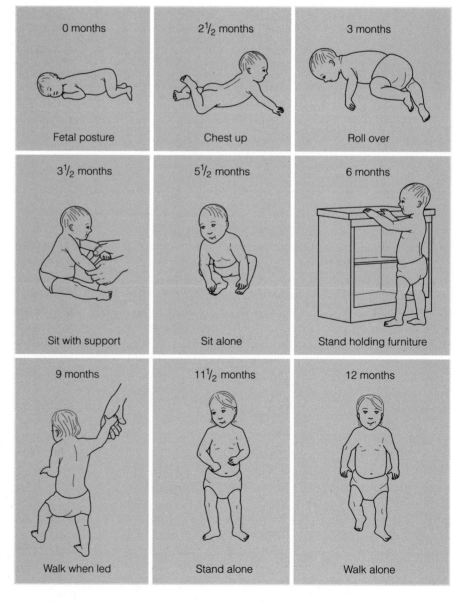

0 months — Fetal posture

2½ months — Chest up

3 months — Roll over

3½ months — Sit with support

5½ months — Sit alone

6 months — Stand holding furniture

9 months — Walk when led

11½ months — Stand alone

12 months — Walk alone

individual and group differences. Not only are babies different from one another at birth, but they also show different rates of motor advancement. For example, one study examined how babies adapted their locomotor strategy for going down a slope. Thirty-one infants, all 14 months old, were recruited for the study. Even though they were all the same age, their prior experience with walking ranged from 10 days to 137 days (Adolph & Eppler, 2002).

In addition to individual differences in the timing and tempo of motor development, cultures differ in the opportunities provided for motor exploration. In a longitudinal study of almost 16,000 infants living in the United Kingdom (England, Wales, Scotland, and Northern Ireland), cultural differences in the attainment of developmental motor milestones were noted. Black Caribbean infants, Black African infants, and Indian infants were on average more advanced in motor development than White infants. Pakistani and Bangladeshi infants were more likely to show motor delays than White infants. Whereas the delays among the Pakistani and Bangladeshi infants were explained largely by factors associated with poverty, the advantages of the babies of Caribbean, African, and Indian ethnicity could not be accounted for by these factors. The authors suggest that a combination of parental expectations and parenting practices associated with cultural tradition helped support advanced motor development in these groups (Kelly, Sacker, Schoon, & Nazroo, 2006).

Although the normative pattern of motor development suggests a preprogrammed sequence of stages that is heavily guided by genetics and neural structures, research on the process of motor development has challenged this assumption. Researchers now regard the regularities in motor behavior as the result of a dynamic process of exploration in which infants coordinate their physical actions with the demands and opportunities of the situation. The combination of a maturing central nervous system, growth in strength and coordination, opportunities for various types of movements, and the emergence of cognitions to understand and anticipate actions underlies an ongoing process of self-correcting, adaptive movement (Rutkowska, 1994).

Perception and action work hand in hand, giving the infant information about the physical properties of the situation and feedback about the consequences of a specific motor strategy. Over time and with practice in similar situations, the infant discovers the combination of action, intensity, direction, and speed that will create the desired outcome. With additional practice, this pattern then becomes most likely and increasingly efficient (Thelen, 1995). (See the featured box on the stepping reflex.)

Consider Brad's efforts to crawl. He is placed face down in the middle of a brightly colored blanket. His mother kneels at the edge of the blanket and dangles a favorite stuffed bear. She smiles and says encouragingly, "Come on, Brad. Come get Teddy." Brad looks intently, reaches toward the bear and, by kicking and squirming, manages to move forward. This snakelike movement is Brad's first accomplishment en route to well-organized crawling. Before he masters crawling, however, he must learn to raise himself on his knees, coordinate his hand and leg movements, and propel himself forward rather than backward. Most babies reach a point when they rock in a stationary position on all fours before they can crawl. In repeated observations of 15 infants as they made the transition to crawling, a key precursor was found to be the establishment of a strong hand preference. When infants fell from a seated position onto their hands, they tended to fall onto their nonpreferred hand, so that the preferred hand was available to reach out and begin crawling. Confidence in being able to maintain one's body weight on one arm and two legs while reaching out with the preferred hand is part of the motor sequence necessary for forward crawling (Goldfield, 1989). Crawling, which tends to be regarded as natural and easily performed in infancy, is in fact achieved by long and patient effort in the coordination of head and shoulder movement, reaching, and kicking. As the baby changes from crawling to walking, new strategies for navigating the environment have to be invented.

Infant motor behavior requires flexibility because of the rapid change in physical size and strength and the variety of contexts for movement. Infants gain greater motor control with each postural status from sitting and crawling to standing and walking. At the same time, each new motor capacity permits the exploration of a more varied environment. As a result, infants have to be able to make immediate assessments of the relationship between their physical abilities and the environmental conditions in order to decide whether to avoid action, take familiar actions, or try to invent some new, adapted action. The evidence for this flexibility can be seen as babies experiment with descending slopes and slides. Some try going headfirst and then slide backwards; others try to go down with a crablike crawl and then switch over to their bottoms, and still others won't go down at all (Adolph & Eppler, 2002).

Sensorimotor Intelligence: Processing, Organizing, and Using Information

Objective 3. To describe the development of sensorimotor intelligence, including an analysis of how infants process information, organize experiences, conceptualize causality, and understand the properties and functions of objects.

What is sensorimotor intelligence? Think for a moment of a familiar experience, such as tying your shoelaces. The pattern of tying shoelaces unfolds with little, if any, language involved. In fact, the task of explaining to a young child how to tie shoelaces is particularly difficult because very few words or concepts are part of the process. This kind of motor routine is an example of **sensorimotor intelligence**. When infants begin to adapt their sucking reflex to make it more effective, or when they use different techniques of sucking on the breast and the bottle, they are demonstrating

The Dynamic Development of Stepping

AT SOME POINT within the first 2 or 3 weeks of life, when you hold an infant upright under the arms, the infant makes stepping motions that look very much like walking (Barbu-Roth et al., 2009). This stepping response is evoked by a number of stimuli, including the posture in which the baby is held; tactile stimulation to the feet; and visual information about the relationship of the body to the surface below. By the age of 2 or 3 months, this stepping behavior seems to disappear. Initial explanations for this loss of the stepping response were that the reflex is inhibited by higher level cortical functions. The assumption was that the stepping reflex was a vestigial behavior from some earlier evolutionary primate period, and that true stepping and walking was a product of voluntary movement genetically programmed to emerge with more advanced cortical development.

The idea that a behavior that is so closely related to walking would disappear and then reappear was puzzling. Esther Thelen and Donna Fisher (1982) designed research to examine the relationship of the biomechanics of infant stepping and its relation to the infant's posture and physical growth. They were able to take advantage of video recordings and electromyography (EMG) of four muscle groups to capture data on patterns of muscle activation associated with various movements. Their first goal was to explore the similarities between infant stepping while held upright and infant kicking while the infants were lying on their backs. The former seems to disappear and the latter becomes stronger and more coordinated over time. Their second goal was to consider the biomechanical conditions that might constrain the stepping response and increase the kicking response.

The infants who participated in the study were all under 2 weeks old. Of 13 infants, 8 showed both stepping and kicking during the recording session.

Both the stepping and kicking showed alternating right and left leg action. The EMG data (an electronic technique for recording muscles at rest and when they are contracting) for the two types of movement were quite similar. The timing of the flexion and extension phases of the kick and the step were also similar. Thelen and Fisher argued that neonatal stepping and kicking while lying on the back are essentially the same movement patterns. The key to the disappearance of stepping and the increase in kicking is in the role of gravity as infants' legs gain mass. As the legs gain in fat, the muscle strength needed to lift the legs against the force of gravity is not sufficient to permit the stepping action. However, in the prone position, the kicking action is actually supported by the force of gravity. During the first months of life, the growth of body fat outpaces the growth of muscle mass, so the babies cannot lift their legs in the upright position. However, the action itself is not lost, and in fact is practiced actively in the prone position. When

sensorimotor intelligence. The familiar scheme for sucking is modified so that it takes into account the special properties of the breast and the bottle, depending on the situation.

How Infants Process Their Experiences

According to Piaget's (1970) theory of cognitive development, the chief mechanism governing the growth of intelligence during infancy is **sensorimotor adaptation**. From the very earliest days of life, infants use their reflexes to explore their world. At the same time, they gradually alter their reflexive responses to take into account the unique properties of objects around them. Infants do not use the conventional symbolic system of language to organize experience. Rather, they form concepts through perception and direct investigation of the environment. The notion of sensorimotor intelligence, then, encompasses the elaboration of patterns of movement and sensory experiences that the child comes to recognize in association with specific environmental events.

Information-Processing Abilities. Four basic information-processing abilities provide the cognitive resources that support the maturation of sensorimotor intelligence. They include: attention, processing speed, memory, and

representational abilities (Rose, Feldman, & Jankowski, 2009). **Attention** refers to the infant's ability to focus on an object or task as well as to shift or redirect focus from one task to another. Attention is a foundational cognitive ability that allows infants to follow the gaze of another person, track the path of a moving object, and participate in alternating interactions. Attention is typically measured by noting how long an infant looks at an object, and how often the infant shifts gaze from one object to another when comparing objects.

Processing speed is the time it takes to identify a stimulus and figure out its meaning. The faster the processing speed, the more quickly one can incorporate a stream of information. Processing speed is often assessed with reaction time tasks where the time elapsed from presentation of the stimulus to response is taken as evidence of processing speed.

Memory is a complex capacity that includes recognizing something as similar to something one has seen or experienced in the past, holding information in mind for a brief period before using it, and recalling information as needed (Flom & Bahrick, 2010). One way of studying **memory** in infancy is through the use of habituation tasks, which rely on the ability to match a stimulus with something that was experienced in the past, and to evaluate it as similar or different.

According to research on motor development, the stepping reflex remains intact and plays a role in upright walking when babies are strong enough to lift their legs against the force of gravity.

slightly older babies were submerged waist-high in water, overcoming the biomechanical constraints of body mass and gravity, the stepping pattern was observed (Thelen, Fisher, & Ridley-Johnson, 1984).

Thus, the shift from stepping to no stepping was actually a dynamic adaptation to the combination of changing physical characteristics in a particular physical context (Thelen & Smith, 1994). The results of this research led to a transformation in the way we think about development. The earlier view was that the stepping motion was a primitive reflex that falls away and is eventually replaced by a genetically guided plan for voluntary walking. However, this research shows that the stepping motion remains intact, but is not observed when the infant is in the upright position, because of a change in the ratio of fat to muscle mass. The babies' legs get too heavy to lift against the force of gravity when they are in an upright position.

Studies of infant care practices in other cultures, especially in Africa and Central America, find a more common practice of holding infants upright rather than lying them down in a cradle or crib. Infants in these cultures have been observed to walk at an earlier age than Western infants. Thelen and Fisher suggested that infants who are given more experience in an upright position have the opportunity to strengthen their leg muscles by experiencing the resistance against gravity when they flex their legs, possibly leading to an earlier use of legs for support in standing and walking.

Critical Thinking Questions

1. Why is this research on stepping important for our understanding of development?
2. What does this research suggest about the interaction of neurological, physical, and experiential aspects of motor behavior?
3. What does this research suggest about how to think about the coordination of systems in the early years of life? Can you think of other examples of behaviors that might be better understood from this systems perspective?

Representational skills refer to the ability to use symbols or signs to stand for something, and to keep a principle or feature of something in mind and apply it more generally. The ability to transfer information across modalities—for example, to use visual information to guide tactile exploration—is evidence of representational ability. Representational skills are involved when a child uses a word or a gesture to indicate an object or when a child imitates an action in pretense, like using a block to feed a doll or giving it a sip of pretend water from a pretend cup.

Taken together, these information-processing skills—attention, processing speed, memory, and representational skills—support an infant's ability to form increasingly complex schemes about objects, people, actions, and the relationships among them. Changes in the demand properties of one aspect of a task, such as processing speed or memory, may influence attention or representational competence. For example, immature memory capacities may make it difficult for infants to accurately represent and categorize new objects (Oakes, 2009).

According to an emerging view, sometimes referred to as the *Theory theory*, infants form theories about how their world operates and modify them as new information is gathered (Schöner & Thelen, 2006). The infant starts out with some basic sensory, motor, and cognitive organizational structures. With each new challenge, a process of adaptation results in the revision of basic schemes to better predict and interpret experience (Gopnik & Meltzoff, 1997). For example, Ruby, who is 12 months old, may be surprised and upset when her grandmother scolds her as she reaches for a shiny glass bowl on the table. Grandmother knows that the bowl will break if Ruby pushes it off the table. By 16 months, Ruby warily watches her grandmother's face as she reaches for the bowl and may withdraw her hand if she sees Grandma frown or hears the sharp "No!" that has come to be associated with "Don't touch." Ruby has developed a theory that she should not touch the bowl, which she cautiously tests by reaching for it and watching for the response.

Causal Schemes

One of the most important components of sensorimotor intelligence is the capacity to anticipate that certain actions will have specific effects on objects in the environment. Infants develop an understanding of causality based largely on sensory and motor experience. By 9 months of age, infants show evidence that they anticipate the direction of an action, like pouring a liquid into a glass or using a spoon to bring soup to the mouth, and are surprised when the action is not completed or takes an unexpected twist. This understanding of the goal-directed nature of behavior provides a framework for interpreting actions as reflecting intention or purposefulness (Reid et al., 2009). Babies discover that if they cry, Mama will come to them; if they kick a chair, it will move; and if they let go of a spoon, it will fall to the floor. These **predictable sequences** are learned through repetition and experimentation. The predictability of the events depends on the consistency with which objects or people in their world respond as well as on the child's initiation of the action. Babies learn to associate specific actions with regularly occurring outcomes. They also experiment with their own actions to determine the variety of events that a single behavior may cause. Eventually, they are able to work backward: They can select a desirable outcome and then perform the behavior that will produce it.

The achievement of complex, purposeful, causal behaviors develops gradually during the first 2 years of life. This achievement requires that infants have an understanding of the properties of objects in their environment and a variety of strategies for manipulating those objects. Research has shown that infants form expectations about how objects function in specific conditions (Baillargeon, 2004). For example, one object can fit inside another, but not if the second object has no opening. Another expectation is that an object can be hidden behind another larger object. Over time, infants become aware of the relevant variables that operate in a specific physical context. For example, a tall object cannot completely fit inside a shorter container. Infants appear to learn about the relationship of objects under specific conditions, but they do not generalize from one type of event to another. Therefore, they must be able to explore and experiment with objects in order to select the most effective strategies for coordinating actions to achieve specific goals.

The dynamic process of establishing a complex causal scheme is illustrated in a study of the emergence of the use of a spoon as a tool for eating (Connolly & Dalgleish, 1989). The infants were observed once a month for 6 months in their home during a mealtime. At first, actions involving the spoon appeared to focus on exploration of the spoon itself. The infants banged the spoon, sucked it, or rubbed it in their hair. Then the babies showed an understanding of the purpose of the spoon as a tool by repeating the action sequence of dipping the spoon in the dish and bringing it to the mouth. However, no food was on the spoon. In the third phase, babies began to integrate the function and the action by loading the spoon with food and then bringing it to the mouth. During this phase, they made so many errors that very little food actually got to the mouth via the spoon. Finally, babies were able to coordinate the action and the function by using the other hand to steady the bowl, altering the angle of the spoon, picking up food they had dropped, and devising other strategies to enhance the function, depending on the type of food involved. Here we see a demonstration of how one complex motor behavior becomes part of a problem-solving action sequence during the sensorimotor period of development.

Piaget and Inhelder (1966/1969) described six phases in the development of **causal schemes** (see Table 5.3). Subsequent research and related theoretical revisions have confirmed these levels of cognitive development (Fischer & Silvern, 1985). In Phase 1, *reflexes*, cause and effect are linked through the involuntary reflexive responses. The built-in stimulus-response systems of key reflexes are viewed as the genetic origin of intelligence. Babies suck, grasp, and root in response to specific types of stimulation. Piaget viewed these reflexes as adaptive learning systems. In detailed observations of his youngest child, Laurent, he noted daily changes in sucking behavior during the first month of life. Laurent became increasingly directed in groping for the breast, forming early associations between those situations in which he would be fed and those in which he would not (Piaget, 1936/1952; Gratch & Schatz, 1987).

TABLE 5.3 Six Phases in the Development of Sensorimotor Causality

PHASE	APPROXIMATE AGE	CHARACTERISTIC	EXAMPLE
1. Reflexes	From birth	Reflexive responses to specific stimuli	Grasp reflex
2. First habits	From 2nd week	Use of reflexive responses to explore new stimuli	Grasp rattle
3. Circular reactions	From 4th month	Use of familiar actions to achieve new goals	Grasp rattle and make banging noise on table
4. Coordination of means and ends	From 8th month	Deliberate use of actions to achieve new goals	Grasp rattle and shake to play with dog
5. Experimentation with new means	From 11th month	Modifications of actions to reach goals	Use rattle to bang a drum
6. Insight	From 18th month	Mental recombination of means and ends	Use rattle and string to make a new toy

In the second phase, *first habits*, the reflexive responses are used to explore a wider range of stimuli. Babies explore toys, fingers, parents' noses, and blankets by sucking on them. Gradually, they discover the unique properties of objects and modify their responses according to the demands of the specific objects. The fact that a baby can satisfy the need to suck by bringing an object to the mouth is a very early form of purposive causal behavior.

The third and fourth phases involve coordination of means and ends, first with familiar situations and then with new ones. In the third phase, *circular reactions*, babies connect an action with an expected outcome (Wentworth & Haith, 1992). They shake a rattle and expect to hear a noise; they drop a spoon and expect to hear a noise when it hits the floor; they pull Daddy's beard and expect to hear "ouch." They do not understand why a specific action leads to the expected outcome, but they show surprise when the expected outcome does not follow.

In the fourth phase, *coordination of means and ends*, infants use familiar actions or means to achieve new outcomes. They may shake a rattle to startle Mommy or pull Daddy's beard to force him to look away from the television set. The means and the outcomes have become quite distinct. There can be no question about the purposiveness of behavior at this point. At this stage, coordination of means and ends are closely tied to a specific context. For example, a baby may know how to make certain kicking motions to move a mobile or to get a toy to jiggle in the crib. But in another room with the same toy, the baby may not make the same connection. This may explain why babies perform less competently in the laboratory environment than they do at home. Many causal strategies that become part of a baby's daily repertoire are supported by the context of a familiar environment (Rovee-Collier, Schechter, Shyi, & Shields, 1992).

The fifth phase, *experimentation with new means*, begins as children experiment with familiar means to achieve new goals. When familiar strategies do not work, children will modify them in light of the situation. One can think of this stage as sensorimotor problem solving. Children will try to reach a drawer by standing on a box, fix a broken toy with a string, or make a gift by wrapping a toy in a piece of tissue.

The last phase in the development of sensorimotor causality, *insight*, involves mental manipulation of means–end relationships. Instead of actually going through a variety of physical manipulations, children carry out trial-and-error problem-solving activities and planning in their minds, anticipating outcomes. They can sort out possible solutions and reject some without actually having to try them. The result is insight: Mental experimentation brings the child to the best solution, which is the only one necessary to enact.

The capacity to perceive oneself as a causal agent and to predict the outcome of one's actions are essential to the development of a sense of competence, which involves investigation of the environment, directed problem solving, and persistence toward a goal. At later stages, the abilities

© Philip Newman

Through mouthing, Josie is gathering information about a spoon.

to formulate a plan, execute it, and evaluate its outcome depend on these skills.

Understanding the Nature of Objects and Creating Categories

Babies are active explorers of their environment (Bruner, 2001). From birth, they try to make direct sensory contact with objects. They reach for, grasp, and mouth objects. They track objects visually, altering their gaze to maintain contact with them. Certain combinations of mouthing, looking at, and manipulating objects have been categorized as a type of examining behavior that provides infants with a scheme for gathering information about novel objects (Ruff, Saltarelli, Capozzoli, & Dubiner, 1992). As products of this active engagement with the object world, two related but independent aspects of infant intelligence develop: an understanding of the nature of objects, and the ability to categorize similar ones.

The Nature of Objects. Through looking, manipulating, and examining, infants establish that objects have basic properties. In the discussion of vision, we pointed out that very young babies recognize the contours of objects and that by 4 months, they seem to perceive objects just as adults would. That is, babies see objects as separate from each other, defined by boundaries, taking up space, having depth, and having certain attributes of weight, color, malleability, texture, and the capacity to contain something else or not. All of these properties influence the types of actions that infants use to explore the objects and the ways they are eventually woven into other actions (Xu, 2003).

Object Permanence. Piaget (1954) argued that understanding the properties of objects was one of the foundations of logical thought. One of the most carefully documented of these properties is **object permanence**—the concept that objects in the environment are permanent and do not cease to exist when they are out of reach or out of view. A permanent object retains its physical properties even when it cannot be seen.

Piaget suggested that initially, the infant is aware of only those objects that are in the immediate perceptual field. If a 6-month-old girl is playing with a rattle, it exists for her. If the rattle drops out of her hand or is taken away, she may show some immediate distress but will not pursue the rattle. The attainment of the concept of the permanent object frees children from reliance only on what they can see. The ability to hold the image of an object in the mind is a critical step in the emergence of complex representational thinking.

Piaget suggested that the capacity to understand that objects continue to exist requires a level of representational or symbolic thinking, which would permit an infant to hold the idea of the object in mind while it was hidden. It also requires a combination of sensorimotor capacities that permit the infant to become actively engaged in reaching, tracking, and uncovering hidden objects and learning about the spatial properties of objects in the environment. Thus, according to Piaget, the first real evidence that infants have the ability to pursue a hidden object could not really be observed much before 8 or 9 months of age, when babies begin to crawl; and the full confidence in an object's permanence could probably not emerge much before 16 to 18 months, when infants have access to representational thinking. By this age, infants can imagine various movements and displacements of objects without actually viewing them.

A growing body of research has focused on what infants know and expect about objects well before they can crawl or pursue objects through space. In a series of experiments, Renée Baillargeon (2008) has tried to determine how infants evaluate objects that are hidden from view. One of the features of her experiments is that she has deleted the motor search component that is required in Piaget's studies of object permanence. Most of her experiments use habituation in pretest conditions and a change in looking time as evidence for infants' reactions to an unexpected outcome. You may recall from the earlier section that habituation refers to the fact that with repeated exposure to a stimulus, the infant pays less and less attention to it. Based on her studies, she has been able to demonstrate that even at very early ages, before infants can search for and retrieve objects, they appear to have a memory for the locations of objects. Baillargeon's studies demonstrate that infants can follow an object through at least three different ways of hiding it: by placing the object in a container; by moving the object behind a screen; or by covering the object (Baillargeon, 2004).

Young infants have a well-developed sense of objects as distinct, permanent structures that will be set into motion when they are pushed, knocked, or in some other way launched by another object. They also expect that, once in motion, an object will follow a prescribed trajectory (Belanger & Desrochers, 2001). The infant's ability to anticipate an object's trajectory behind a screen is an early step in a sequence of abilities that will eventually produce the complex search process that Piaget described (Wilcox, Schweinle, & Chapa, 2003).

The Categorization of Objects. Physical objects have four basic properties:

1. Objects have a location, and a path and speed of motion.
2. Objects have mechanical properties that include how they move and their relation to other objects.
3. Objects have features, such as their size, shape, and color.
4. Objects have functions; this is what objects do or how they are used (Wilcox, Schweinle, & Chapa, 2003).

As infants explore and experiment with objects, they begin to devise schemes for grouping objects together. They modify these schemes to add new items to the category and to differentiate one category from another. Categories can be based on the physical properties of objects, such as smooth and rough, or on the functions of objects, as in something to sit on and something to dig with. The classification of objects and events into categories is one method infants have of coping with the vast array of new experiences they encounter.

Categorization is an aid to information processing. By treating certain individual objects as similar because they belong to the same basic grouping, like two individual red blocks or two wiggly goldfish, the potential amount of information to process is reduced. Categories can be specific, such as cups, chairs, and cars, or abstract, such as tools, food, or animals (Minami & Inui, 2005; Freedman et al., 2001). If an item is classified as a member of a category, then all the information that has been accumulated regarding that category can automatically be applied to the specific object. This process aids in the storage and recall processes of memory, in reasoning and problem solving, and in the acquisition of new information. Classification of objects into categories is a cognitive capacity that becomes increasingly sophisticated over the childhood years.

As we pointed out earlier in the chapter, one category that has special meaning for infants is faceness. By 6 months of age, infants attribute clear expectations to faces. They expect faces to be organized in a certain pattern and to move and respond in special ways (Nelson, 2001). Six-month-old infants can categorize faces as attractive or unattractive (Ramsey et al., 2004).

A second related category that appears early in infancy is the distinction between people and inanimate objects (Ellsworth, Muir, & Hains, 1993; Rakison & Poulin-Dubois, 2001). Infants have been observed to smile, vocalize, and become more active when interacting with people as compared to things. By 3 months of age, infants show their ability to categorize stimuli as people or things by smiling almost exclusively at people. Infants may look with equal interest at inanimate objects, especially novel ones, but their smiles are reserved for people. This distinction between the social and the nonsocial realm can be considered a **foundational category**. It provides evidence for the unique role of social relationships in the process of adaptation and growth. From this basic distinction between a person and a thing, many further categories, such as father and mother, familiar and stranger, or adult and child, emerge that begin to differentiate the infant's social world.

Research on infant categorization skills typically involves sorting objects or images into groups. Using a habituation-type methodology, the earliest form of categorization can be observed. When 4.5-month-old babies see an object alone, and then placed next to a different object, they respond in a way that indicates their recognition that the two objects are different (Needham, 2001). Using visual silhouettes, 3- and 4-month-old babies were able to distinguish between images of cats and dogs, primarily through a comparison of the information in the shape and features of the silhouette heads (Quinn, Eimas, & Tarr, 2001; Quinn, Doran, Reiss, & Hoffman, 2009). Thus, at very early ages, infants are able to differentiate and group people and objects in their environment.

The categorization process advances over the first 24 months as features of objects are differentiated and linked to concepts and functions. Information about the shape and size of objects seems to guide an infant's identification and categorization of objects by 4.5 months. At 7.5 months, infants make use of information based on differences in pattern, and by 11.5 months they incorporate color and shininess as features that help guide categorization (Woods & Wilcox, 2010).

By 15 months, babies will touch all the objects that belong to one category and then touch all the objects in another category. By 18 months of age, children can perform multidimensional categorization tasks (e.g., sorting eight objects, such as four brightly colored yellow rectangles and four human-shaped plastic figures, into two distinct groups; Gopnik & Meltzoff, 1987, 1992). This kind of sorting does not require the ability to give names to the objects. However, by 20 months, infants will use both visual cues and names to categorize objects. The larger the infant's vocabulary, the more likely the baby is to use names to help group objects together (Nazi & Gopnick, 2001). Thus, categorizing and naming appear to be closely linked. By the close of the second year of life, babies know that objects have certain stable features, that some objects belong with others, and that objects have names. With these achievements, infants impose a new degree of order and predictability on their daily experiences.

The Prefrontal Cortex and Infant Intelligence

The cognitive skills that we have described in the preceding sections, particularly the ability to anticipate what actions will result in which consequences, the ability to develop a plan and follow it through in order to achieve a goal, and the ability to categorize objects and understand the rules that distinguish one set of objects from another, are all evidence of a capacity to generalize principles and devise abstract rules from experience. The human brain is ready at birth to detect a wide range of sensory stimuli, and, as we have discussed, there are also prewired reflexes that link stimuli with responses. With experience and biological maturation, all of these systems mature and become increasingly attuned to features of the environment. However, in addition to the sensory and motor systems, the hallmark of human intelligence is the ability to derive abstract concepts, rules, and generalizations from sensory and motor experiences and to apply them in new situations. The area of the brain that appears to be responsible for supporting these capacities is the **prefrontal cortex**.

The prefrontal cortex is more developed in humans than in other species, and, within humans, continues to develop into the mid twenties. It has been viewed as the brain's executive, an area of the brain that is highly interconnected with all the sensory and motor systems, and with areas of the brain associated with emotion, memory, and reward (Miller, Freedman, & Wallis, 2002). The neurons in the prefrontal cortex can be activated from all the sensory domains in anticipation of events, during actions, and during memory of past events. One of the key features of neurons in the prefrontal cortex is their ability to sustain mental activity for several seconds without additional stimulation. As a result, the neurons of the prefrontal cortex are able to guide actions for the period of time it takes to transmit signals to other related brain areas in order to accomplish a task. Neuroimaging studies of infants find that the prefrontal cortex is involved in language processing, identification of novel stimuli, working memory, goal-oriented reasoning, and an understanding of objects. From ages 6 to 12 months, infants perform increasingly better on tasks that require them to resist distractions, a capacity that has been strongly associated with frontal cortex development (Holmboe, Menoda, Fearon, Csibra, Sasvari-Szekely, & Johnson, 2010). People with damage in the prefrontal cortex can recognize objects, engage in conversation, and have no significant memory impairment. Yet, they have trouble staying on task; they have difficulty resisting impulses to act in response to environmental stimuli. They tend to act on a whim without regard for the consequences.

Communication

Objective 4. To characterize forerunners of language competence from birth through the first 2 years of life.

Many of the notable achievements in language competence occur during toddlerhood (ages 2 and 3) and will be discussed in detail in Chapter 6. However, as you have already learned, auditory experiences in the prenatal period and continuing in infancy inform babies about the sounds and rhythm of the language that is spoken by their mothers. Through visual and auditory experiences, they see and hear people talking, making gestures, and combining language with actions. So even though infants may not be active partners in the spoken language of their home and culture from birth, they begin to participate in rhythmic communication exchanges through gazing, smiling, cooing, and coordinated play. Research on language development has focused on the many forerunners of language competence that emerge from birth through the first 2 years of life.

Thought and language seem to travel independent courses that typically intersect during the second year of life. Before that time, one can distinguish meaningful communication that does not require speech, such as pointing and gesturing, and vocalizations that are not meaningful, such as babbling and cooing. A rare genetic disease, Williams syndrome, illustrates that the capacities for language and cognition are distinct. Children with Williams syndrome are typically very talkative and sociable; they develop a large vocabulary and speak in grammatically correct sentences. Although their speech indicates some developmental abnormalities, it is much further advanced than their other cognitive functions. For example, children with Williams syndrome may have difficulty with tasks that are easy for most middle-school-age children, like tying their shoes, subtracting 2 from 4, or writing their street address (Schultz, Grelotti, & Pober, 2001). This genetic condition forces one to think about language competence separate from other cognitive abilities. Of course, one does not have to go to the extreme of people with Williams syndrome to find examples of people whose speech seems disconnected from their ability to think and reason.

Language Perception

Infants are able to recognize sounds and differentiate between sound combinations long before they are able to produce language or understand word meaning. This capacity to recognize language sounds, including the phonetic combinations of letters and words and the intonation of words and sentences, is called **language perception** (Tsao, Liu, & Kuhl, 2004). Young infants are able to hear and distinguish among the major language sounds used in natural language. By 5 months of age, infants are able to differentiate words that emphasize the first syllable, like *father*, and words that emphasize the second syllable, like *begin*. By this age, they also recognize the sound of their own name (Mandel, Jusczyk, & Pisoni, 1995; Weber, Hahne, Friedrich, & Friederici, 2004).

Babbling

Babbling, initially characterized by sounds used in many languages, begins to reflect the sounds and intonation infants are most likely to hear. Sounds they do not hear drop out of their babbling and, at about this same time, their capacity to differentiate among language sounds not found in their native language diminishes (Bates et al., 1987). This environmental shaping of language competence provides another example of the plasticity of brain functions. Some networks grow and become strengthened by experience, whereas others wither and are absorbed into the neural mass.

Babbling begins to take on a special character, connecting consonants and vowels and repeating these combinations, when the baby is around 6 to 10 months. Although parents may eagerly receive this type of babbling as evidence of first words (i.e., *baba, mama, dada*), there is debate about whether these repetitions of babbling sounds have a symbolic value.

One sound that is especially important in the parenting process is "Mama." The infant word for mother has many similarities across hundreds of language groups. In a study of "Mama" sounds, a pediatrician asked 75 parents of newborns in his practice to listen for *mama* sounds (Goldman, 2001). If they heard one, he asked them to note the infant's age; the circumstances of the sound (time of day, etc.); if they could determine whether the infant wanted something, and if so, what; and if the sound was directed at anyone, to whom it was directed. Of the 75 parents, 52 spoke only English. Other languages included Spanish, Hindi, Italian, Russian, Hebrew, Ibo, Chinese, and some combination of Spanish and Greek or Italian. Fifty-five of the parents heard a *mama* sound, often as part of a cry. Thirty-two infants made the *mama* sound for the first time in the first 2 months of life. It became more distinct and more of a whine or call as it was repeated over the first 6 months. For those babies who made *mama* sounds, the sound was interpreted as an indication of wanting—especially wanting to be picked up, wanting attention, or wanting to be taken out of the crib or infant seat and entertained. An implication of this research is that by 2 months, many infants have the ability to use a noncrying vocalization to serve as a call that brings caregiver attention.

Communication with Gestures

By 8 months, infants use sounds like grunting and whining in combination with **gestures** to achieve a goal. Sounds combined with gestures and looks in a certain direction become part of purposeful **communication**—trying to get the caregiver to reach a cookie or get a certain toy off the shelf. A common first gesture is to raise the arms up toward the caregiver in a desire to be picked up (Fenson et al., 1994). Sounds may also be used to express emotion or to get someone's attention. When Jakob was about 14 months, he used the gesture of shaking his hands to signal that he was all done with his food. This was much preferred to having him throw the food on the floor!

Three other communicative strategies emerge at about 9 to 11 months. Infants begin to seek adult interest and attention by *showing* them objects and thereby initiating

Gestures, such as pointing, are forms of preverbal communication.

an interaction. Soon after showing, the infant begins *giving* objects. Adults who are willing to engage in this type of exchange will find the baby bringing them a whole variety of toys, utensils, and pieces of dirt or dust for inspection. Following giving, a common next key gesture is *pointing*. There is some debate about whether pointing is a form of reaching or a way of getting an adult's attention to notice an object. In either case, it is an example of an infant's initial ability to establish a shared reference point with respect to some object in the environment. The role of gestures in establishing intersubjectivity is an excellent example of the interdependence of motor, social, and psychological systems as they combine to support language development (Iverson & Thelen, 1999).

Gestures are a way for a nonverbal child to ask for additional information. Pointing or reaching may be precursors of asking a question like "what is this?" or "where is this?" This preverbal question-asking behavior is fundamental to the knowledge acquisition process and illustrates the child's early active role in seeking information. The way that adults respond to these gestures, by ignoring them, responding to them, or providing additional information once the initial request or question has been addressed, illustrates the parents' active role in guiding the construction of this knowledge base (Chouinard, 2007).

Baby Signs

Building on the emerging capacity of infants to invent gestures for shared communication, Linda Acredolo and Susan Goodwyn began to study the role of symbolic gestures in preverbal infants. During the second year of life, it is not uncommon for infants and their caregivers to use symbolic gestures, like waving bye-bye, putting the thumb to the mouth to request or refer to a bottle, or using a throwing motion to suggest playing ball. Infants are avid observers of such action-meaning combinations, and once established, parents seem enthusiastic about using them to enhance communication. Following these naturalistic observations of symbolic gestures, Acredolo and Goodwyn conducted experimental research to increase parents' use of symbolic gestures with their infants, and to evaluate the impact of this intervention on subsequent language development. One question their research addressed was whether exposure to an expanded capacity for symbolic gestures might replace a child's need for spoken language and thereby delay **language production**.

In one study, three groups of parent-infant dyads were compared; one received symbolic gesture training, one received training to include verbal labels in interaction with their infants but no training in symbolic gestures, and one received no special training. The verbal labeling group was created in order to rule out the potential benefit of any type of special attention or training on babies' language acquisition. The infants were all healthy, 11-month-old babies at the start of the study (Goodwin, Acredolo, & Brown, 2000). For the symbolic gesture group, the target gestures included simple movements for five object and three nonobject concepts: "fish" [SMACKING LIPS], "flower" [SNIFFING], "bird" [FLAPPING ARMS], "airplane" [SWOOPING HAND MOVEMENT], "frog" [FIST OPEN AND CLOSE], "Where is it?" [PALMS UP AND OUT], "more" [FINGER TO OPPOSITE PALM], and "all gone" [PALM DOWN, BACK AND FORTH]. For the verbal labeling group, the target words included "kitty," "doggy," "ball," "shoe," "boat," "bye-bye," "more," and "all gone." Families in the symbolic gesture group were encouraged to invent their own additional gestures, and families in the verbal labeling group were encouraged to provide other labels as they interacted with their babies. These families were also given toys to take home that corresponded to the target words in order to encourage the use of gestures or labels. Follow-up telephone interviews were conducted every 2 weeks to learn about how often and in what contexts the gesturing or labeling activities were taking place. Infants in all three groups were tested at 11 months for baseline data, and then again at 15, 19, 24, 30, and 36 months to evaluate both expressive and receptive language.

In the follow-up phone conversations it was determined that the infants in the symbolic gesture group had acquired an average of 20 gestures that were initiated by the infant and used in a regular, patterned way to refer to objects or situations that generalized beyond the object to which the gesture first referred. Babies in the verbal labeling group were compared to those in the control group to evaluate the impact of the training effect without gestures. There were no significant differences in performance between these two groups. However, when compared to the control group, babies in the symbolic gesture group showed advanced performance in expressive and receptive language as well as advances in their ability to use two-word combinations at 15, 19, and 24 months. There were no significant differences between the symbolic gesture group and the control group at 36 months.

The authors point to several processes at work that may help account for the role of gesture training for language development. First, it increases the amount of infant-directed speech between adults and infants. Second, it encourages communication around activities and objects that the infant is interested in, thereby creating more shared attention and fostering a greater motivation on the infant's part to attend to and engage in communication. Third, the gestures serve as a scaffold, allowing conversations to expand from the initial identification of an object or action of interest into more talk, new gestures, and greater appreciation for the use of language for increasing understanding and social connection. The results of this and related research has led to a new enthusiasm for teaching symbolic gestures to infants, incorporated into a program called **Baby Signs** (Acredolo, Goodwyn, & Abrams, 2002).

Early Grammar Recognition

Grammar refers to rules that guide the combination of words and phrases in order to preserve meaning. In English, for example, sentences are usually formed from nouns (people, places, or things) or noun phrases, followed by verbs (actions) or verb phrases (e.g., "The girl reads the book"). Certain cues about the way words are used in a sentence or their order in a sentence convey their meaning. For example, the word "the" is a signal that a noun will follow.

By 7 to 8 months of age, infants show the ability to recognize the specific regularities in spoken speech and to detect rules about the combination of language sounds. For example, babies were exposed to a long string of nonsense syllables for 2 minutes. In this string, certain sounds were always followed by other sounds. For example, *pa* was always followed by *biku*. In the test situation, babies recognized the difference between a sound combination that was used frequently in the string of sounds, such as *pabiku*, and a combination that was used very infrequently (Saffran, Aslin, & Newport, 1996). In other studies, babies were habituated to 2 minutes of a grammar in which sentences followed an ABA form, such as *ga ti ga*, or a grammar that followed the ABB form, such as *ga ti ti*. In the test situation, babies recognized the difference between the grammar to which they were habituated and an inconsistent grammar made up of entirely different sounds (Marcus, 2000). The implication of these findings is that long before babies can produce words, word phrases, or grammatically correct sentences, they are gathering information about the rules that hold sounds and phrases together in order to make meaning.

First Words

From infancy to toddlerhood, one of the most significant changes that takes place is that **words** emerge as more salient than gestures as a way to refer to objects (Namy & Waxman, 2002). Around the age of 8 months, infants understand the meanings of some individual words and phrases (Harris, 1992; Fenson et al., 1994). This ability to understand words, called **receptive language**, precedes language production, the ability to produce spoken words and phrases. You can direct a baby's glance by saying, "Look at the flowers," or "Do you want candy?" At this age, babies can go through their paces in the ever delightful game of "point to your nose, eyes, ears," and so on. The number of words infants understand increases rapidly after 12 months. According to one analysis, 16-month-olds have a receptive vocabulary of between 92 and 321 words (Fenson et al., 1994).

One of the first significant events in the development of language production is the *naming* of objects. With repetition, a sound or word becomes associated with a specific object or a set of related objects. For example, a child may say *ba* whenever she sees her bottle. If she is thirsty and wants her bottle, she may try saying *ba* in order to influence her caregiver to produce the bottle. Gestures, actions, and facial expressions often accompany the baby's word and help establish its meaning in the caregiver's mind. If the baby's word has meaning to the caregiver and serves to satisfy the baby's needs, it will probably be retained as a meaningful sign. The word *ba* may come to mean "bottle" and other liquids the child wishes to drink, such as juice, water, or milk.

The important characteristic of first words is their shared meaning. Even though *ba* is not a real word, it functions in the same way that any noun does—it names a person, place, or thing. These single-word utterances accompanied by gestures, actions, vocal intonation, and emotion are called **holophrases**. They convey the meaning of an entire sentence. For example, saying "ba, ba" in a pleading tone while pointing to the refrigerator and bouncing up and down conveys the meaning "I need a bottle," or "Get me the bottle." Gradually, the child discovers that every object, action, and relationship has a name. Rapid progress occurs between 12 and 16 months in the naming of objects. By 16 months a typical infant has a productive vocabulary of 26 words. Table 5.4 provides a summary of milestones in language over the first 16 months of life.

Young children first talk about what they know and what they are interested in. Common first words include important people (*Mama, Dada*, names of siblings), foods, pets, toys, body parts (*eye, nose*), clothes (*shoe, sock*), vehicles (*car*), favorite objects (*bottle, blanket*), other objects in the environment (*keys, trees*), actions (*up, bye-bye*), *yes, no, please, down, more,* pronouns (*you, me*), and states (*hot, hungry*). Lois Bloom (1993) has suggested that a "principle of relevance" guides the early acquisition of new words. Babies pay special attention to words and expressions that are most closely linked with what they are doing and thinking about at the time. For that reason, the actual vocabulary that is acquired during infancy is quite idiosyncratic, reflecting the themes and experiences of each child's everyday life.

TABLE 5.4 Milestones in Language Development from 12 Weeks to 16 Months

AT THE COMPLETION OF:	VOCALIZATION AND LANGUAGE CHARACTERISTICS
12 weeks	Markedly less crying than at 8 weeks; when talked to and nodded at, smiles, followed by squealing/gurgling sounds usually called cooing, that is vowel-like in character and pitch-modulating; sustains cooing for 15–20 seconds.
16 weeks	Responds to human sounds more definitely; turns head; eyes seem to search for speaker; occasionally some chuckling sounds. Recognizes the sound of his/her name.
20 weeks	The vowel-like cooing sounds begin to be interspersed with consonantal sounds; acoustically, all vocalizations are very different from the sounds of the mature language of the environment.
6 months	Cooing changing into babbling resembling one-syllable utterances, neither vowels nor consonants have very fixed recurrences; most common utterances sound somewhat like ma, mu, da, or di.
8 months	Reduplication (or more continuous repetition) becomes frequent; intonation patterns become distinct; utterances can signal emphasis and emotions. Produces meaningful gestures like wanting to be picked up, showing, or giving. Understands some words and phrases.
10 months	Vocalizations are mixed with sound play such as gurgling or bubble blowing; appears to wish to imitate sounds, but the imitations are never quite successful; expansion in comprehension of words.
12 months	Identical sound sequences are replicated with higher relative frequency of occurrence and early word production (mama or dada); understands about 50 words and simple commands (i.e., "Show me your eyes.").
16 months	Has a definite repertoire of about 40 words (the top 90th percentile has 180-word vocabulary); still much babbling but now of several syllables with intricate intonation pattern; no pattern; words may include items such as thank you and come here, but there is little ability to join items into spontaneous two-word phrases; understanding is progressing rapidly.

Source: Adapted from Lenneberg, 1967, and Fenson et al., 1994.

Attachment

Objective 5. To understand social attachment as the process through which infants develop strong emotional bonds with others, and to describe the dynamics of attachment formation during infancy.

Have you ever wondered how feelings of love and connectedness form between babies and their caregivers? At birth, an infant has some familiarity with the sound and rhythm of the mother's voice but a newborn does not show evidence of a specific emotional preference for the biological mother over other responsive adults. By the end of the first year of life, however, babies not only know their caregivers but also have very strong emotional preferences for these adults over all others. **Attachment** is the process through which people develop specific, positive emotional bonds with others. John Bowlby proposed the notion of the *attachment behavior system* as an organized pattern of infant signals and adult responses that lead to a protective, trusting relationship during the very earliest stage of development. The nurturing responses of the caregiver form a corresponding behavioral system referred to as *parenting* or *caregiving* (Ainsworth, 1985; Bowlby, 1988).

From an ethological perspective, the coordinated attachment and caregiving systems form a pattern of mutual regulation through which the infant alerts the caregiver to distress, and the caregiver provides protection, comfort, and care. Given the prolonged dependent status of human infants, this attachment/caregiving system is foundational to survival. It creates the social context through which infants are protected and loved, and sets the stage for the establishment of the radius of significant relationships that emerge over the next stages of life.

The Development of Attachment

Attachment theorists have described a sequence of stages in the formation of the attachment relationship, much of which takes place during the first 12 months of life (Bowlby, 1969/1982; Ainsworth, 1973, 1985; Marvin & Britner, 1999; see Table 5.5). Many of the sensory and motor competencies described earlier in this chapter contribute to an infant's ability to establish a vivid **mental representation** or scheme of the caregiver and to stimulate caregiving behaviors. In the first stage, during the first 3 months of life, infants engage in a variety of behaviors, including sucking, rooting, grasping, smiling, gazing, cuddling, crying, and visual tracking or following, which serve to *maintain closeness with a caregiver* or *bring the caregiver to the infant*. Through these contacts, babies learn about the unique features of their caregivers. Caregivers, for their part, use a variety of strategies including eye contact, touching and holding, and vocalizing as means of establishing and maintaining social engagement with their infants (Akhtar & Gernsbacher, 2008). Caregivers and infants experience repeated interactions, which result in the formation of predictable patterns. Infants begin to internalize

TABLE 5.5 Five Stages in the Development of Attachment

STAGE	AGE	CHARACTERISTICS
1	Birth to 3 months	Infant uses sucking, rooting, grasping, smiling, gazing, cuddling, crying, and visual tracking to maintain closeness with caregivers.
2	3 to 6 months	Infant is more responsive to familiar figures than to strangers.
3	6 to 9 months	Infant seeks physical proximity and contact with objects of attachment.
4	9 to 12 months	Infant forms internal mental representation of object of attachment, including expectations about the caregiver's typical responses to signals of distress.
5	12 months and older	Child uses a variety of behaviors to influence the behavior of the objects of attachment in ways that will satisfy needs for safety and closeness.

rhythmic patterns of interaction, which lays a foundation for expectations about interpersonal communication.

In the second stage, from about 3 to 6 months, an infant's attachment is expressed through preferential responsiveness to a few familiar figures. Infants smile more at the familiar person than at a stranger. They show more excitement at that person's arrival, and appear to be upset when that person leaves. During this phase, babies initiate more interactions toward the familiar caregiver. They are able to control the interaction by linking a chain of behaviors into a more complex sequence. In Stage 1, for example, the baby may look intently at the primary caregiver. In Stage 2, the baby looks intently, reaches toward the caregiver's face, and pulls the caregiver's hair.

In Stage 3, from about 6 to 9 months, babies seek physical proximity with the objects of attachment. The ability to crawl and to coordinate reaching and grasping contribute to greater control over the outcomes of their actions. In this phase, babies experiment with finding an optimal distance from the caregiver. They may crawl away, look back, and then, depending on the caregiver's perceived availability, crawl back to the caregiver or smile and continue exploring. If the caregiver is preoccupied or out of sight, the baby may cry to bring the caregiver closer or to reestablish contact.

In Stage 4, from about 9 to 12 months, babies form their mental representation of their caregivers. This mental picture provides the first robust **working model** of an attachment relationship. Specific characteristics of a caregiver and expectations about how the caregiver will respond to the infant's actions are organized into a complex attachment scheme including expectations about how the caregiver will respond when the child is frightened, hurt, or distressed.

In Stage 5, in toddlerhood and later, young children use a variety of behaviors to influence the behavior of their parents and other objects of attachment in order to satisfy their own needs for closeness. Bowlby described this new and important capacity as the creation of a **goal-corrected partnership.** Children may ask to be read to, cuddled at bedtime, and taken along on errands. These and other strategies produce caregiver behaviors that will satisfy a child's continuing needs for physical contact, reassurance, closeness, and love. As children become aware that other people have their own separate points of view, they begin to include the other person's needs and goals into their plans.

As children mature, they begin to conceptualize new risks and threats to their security. They may initiate new strategies for maintaining closeness to the objects of their attachment. Especially when they are undergoing unusual stress, as in times of illness, divorce, or rejection, children of any age may try to activate the attachment system by sending signals that are intended to evoke the caregiver's comfort and closeness.

© 2011 Estate of Pablo Picasso/Artists Rights Society (ARS), New York/Photo © Art Media/Heritage-Images/The Image Works

Close physical contact during nursing provides infants with a combination of sensory stimuli—sight, sound, smell, and touch—that contribute to the formation of an early scheme for their mother.

Stranger Anxiety. During the second half of the first year, two signs of a child's growing attachment to a specific

With Dad nearby, Jakob can begin to explore this new environment and return to his secure base as needed.

person are observed: stranger anxiety and separation anxiety. **Stranger anxiety** refers to the baby's discomfort or tension in the presence of unfamiliar adults. By 6 months of age, most babies can distinguish a picture of their mother from a picture of a stranger (Swingler, Sweet, & Carver, 2010). Babies vary in how they express their protest to strangers and in how intensely they react (Rieser-Danner, 2003). They may cling to their parents, refuse to be held, stiffen at the stranger's touch, or merely avert their eyes from the stranger's face.

The baby's response to a stranger depends on specific features of the situation, including how close the mother is, how the stranger approaches the baby, and how the mother responds to the stranger. For example, if a mother speaks in a positive tone of voice to her baby about a stranger, the baby's response to the stranger is likely to be positive. In contrast, if the mother interacts with the stranger in a socially anxious manner, the baby will be more fearful of the stranger. This effect is especially notable in infants who are temperamentally more fearful and inhibited (deRosnay, Cooper, Tsigaras, & Murray, 2006). The baby's response will also be influenced by the amount of prior experience with unfamiliar adults. Some children are in childcare arrangements where adults frequently come and go. In some parts of the world, babies rarely come into contact with anyone outside of their small village. Strangers are more unfamiliar to infants in some cultures and contexts than in others (Rothbaum et al., 2000). Normally, wariness of strangers is considered a positive developmental sign—that is, babies are able to detect the differences between their parents and adults they do not know. Wariness of strangers continues to be expressed throughout life. In fact,

one often sees stronger expressions of suspiciousness or fear among adults encountering strangers than among babies.

Separation Anxiety. At about 9 months, infants give another indication of the intensity of their attachment to their parents. They express rage and despair when their parents leave them. This reaction is called **separation anxiety**. A baby's response to separation depends on the conditions. Infants are less distressed when mothers leave them alone in a room at home than when they do so in a laboratory (Ross, Kagan, Zelazo, & Kotelchuck, 1975). They are less likely to protest if the mother leaves the door to the room open than if she closes the door as she leaves. Separation from the mother for periods of 30 minutes has been identified as a distinct source of stress for babies 9 months of age and older. Neurological and biochemical evidence of stress, including increases in adrenocortical activity and concentrations of cortisol in the saliva, were associated with 30 minutes of separation from the mother in a laboratory situation (Larson, Gunnar, & Hertsgaard, 1991; Gunnar, Larson, Hertsgaard, Harris, & Brodersen, 1992). The impact of stressful separations can be seen in the disruption of basic physical patterns, especially sleep disturbances, and in regression to more immature forms of play behavior, aimless wandering, and altered interactions with peers and teachers in the childcare setting (Field, 1991).

Babies' responses to separation also appear to be related to their temperament. Babies who have a strong negative reaction to uncertainty, those who are especially distressed when they are confined or prevented from attaining a goal, and those who are upset by novelty or who tend to withdraw from it find the experience of separation more stressful than others. Unique strategies of caregiving might be needed to buffer these babies from the stressful impact of separation (Rettew et al., 2006).

A baby's responses to separation and reunion have been used as key behavioral indicators of attachment quality. Babies who are described as having an insecure attachment are more distressed when they are separated from their mothers, and the mothers appear to be less responsive in calming their babies following separation (Harel & Scher, 2003).

Over time, most babies become more flexible in response to parents' temporary departures. Young children learn to tolerate brief separations. At 2 years of age, children are able to use a photograph of their mother to help sustain their adaptation to a new setting in the mother's absence (Passman & Longeway, 1982). By the age of 3, children may even look forward to a night with a babysitter or an afternoon at grandfather's house. Once the attachment is fully established, children can comfort themselves by creating mental images of their parents and by remembering their parents' love for them. During infancy, however, the parents' physical presence remains a focal point of attention and concern.

Formation of Attachments with Mother, Father, and Others

Most infants have more than one caring person with whom they form an attachment. Most commonly, the first object of attachment is the mother, but fathers, siblings, grandparents, and childcare professionals also become objects of attachment. Several factors have been identified as important for predicting which people will form the infant's hierarchy or radius of significant attachment figures (Colin, 1996; Cassidy, 1999):

1. The amount of time the infant spends in the care of the person.
2. The quality and responsiveness of the care provided by the person.
3. The person's emotional investment in the infant.
4. The presence of the person in the infant's life across time.

Attachments to Mothers and Fathers. Infants tend to have the same type of attachment with their fathers and their mothers, but these relationships are established independently and depend on the amount of time the infant and parent spend together as well as the quality of the interactions (Fox, Kimmerly, & Schafer, 1991). Early studies found that babies tended to have more playful interactions with their fathers—smiling, laughing, and looking—and more comforting, stress-reducing interactions with their mothers (Lamb, 1976). Recent studies confirm that infants experience positive emotions as they play with their mothers and fathers. However, the intensity and rhythm of the experiences seem to differ with each parent. In mother-infant interactions, babies seem calmer, and their happy expressions are part of a social dialogue. In father-infant interactions, the babies are more excited, showing sudden bursts of laughter

and activity (Feldman, 2003). In a study of 126 firstborn sons, 60% were found to have secure attachments with their fathers at 13 months of age (Belsky, 1996).

Attachments to Mother, Father, and Metapelet: The Israeli Case. In Israel, kibbutz-reared infants showed great similarity between their attachment to their fathers and to their specially trained caregiver (called *metapelet*). However, there was no consistent pattern of similarity in the quality of their attachments to mother and father and to mother and metapelet (Sagi et al., 1985). In subsequent research, when these kibbutz-reared children were 5 years old, the quality of their infant attachment to the metapelet was a significant predictor of their socioemotional development as observed in school and at free play in their dormitory (Oppenheim, Sagi, & Lamb, 1988). In the Israeli case, where there are multiple caregivers, it has also been observed that when one attachment relation is negative, it can negatively influence other attachment relations. For example, in a study of more than 750 Israeli infants, those who experienced poor quality care in center-based settings were also more likely to develop insecure attachments with their mothers (Sagi et al., 2002).

This research suggests that in the Israeli case, the combined contribution of multiple secure attachments, rather than the mother-infant relationship alone, is the best predictor of subsequent social competence (Sagi & van IJzendoorn, 1996). Exactly how infants synthesize the internal representations of various attachments is not well understood. Possibly, the distinct relationships have relevance for different interpersonal domains or become central as individuals assume diverse social roles as friends, parents, or supervisors and teachers of others.

Patterns of Attachment

It is important to distinguish between the presence of an attachment and the quality of that attachment. According to attachment theory, if an adult is present to interact with the infant, an attachment will be formed. However, individual differences emerge in the quality of that attachment, depending on the accumulation of information the infant gathers over many instances when the infant is seeking reassurance, comfort, or protection from threat (Weinfield, Sroufe, Egeland, & Carlson, 1999). The adults' acceptance of the infant and their ability to respond to the child's varying communications are important to forming a positive, secure attachment. The caregivers' patterns of expressing affection and rejection will influence how well babies can meet their strong needs for reassurance and comfort.

The Strange Situation. Differences in the quality of attachment have been assessed through systematic observations of babies and their caregivers in a standard laboratory procedure called the **strange situation** (Ainsworth, Blehar, Waters, & Wall, 1978; Bretherton, 1990). During an approximately 20-minute period, the child is exposed to a sequence of events that are likely to stimulate the attachment behavior system (see Table 5.6). The situation introduces several

TABLE 5.6 The Strange Situation Laboratory Procedure

EPISODE	DURATION	PARTICIPANTS*	EVENTS
1	30 seconds	M, B, O	O shows M and B into the room, instructs M on where to put B down and where to sit; O leaves.
2	3 minutes	M, B	M puts B down close to her chair, at a distance from the toys. She responds to B's social bids but does not initiate interaction. B is free to explore. If B does not move after 2 minutes, M may take B to the toy area.
3	3 minutes	M, B, S	This episode has three parts. S enters, greets M and B, and sits down opposite M without talking for 1 minute. During the 2nd minute, S engages M in conversation. S then joins B on the floor, attempting to engage B in play for 1 minute. At the end of this episode, M leaves "unobtrusively" (B usually notices).
4	3 minutes	B, S	S sits on her chair. She responds to B's social bids but does not initiate social interaction. If B becomes distressed, S attempts to comfort B. If this is not effective, M returns before 3 minutes are up.
5	3 minutes	M, B	M calls B's name outside the door and enters (S leaves unobtrusively). If B is distressed, M comforts B and tries to reengage B in play. If B is not distressed, M goes to sit on her chair, taking a responsive, noninitiating role. At the end of the episode, M leaves, saying, "Bye-bye; I'll be back."
6	3 minutes	B	B remains alone. If B becomes distressed, the episode is curtailed and S enters.
7	3 minutes	B, S	S enters, comforting B if required. If she cannot comfort B, the episode is curtailed. If B calms down or is not distressed, S sits on her chair, taking a responsive role as before.
8	3 minutes	M, B	M returns (S leaves unobtrusively). M behaves as in episode 5.

*O = observer; M = mother; B = baby; S = stranger.

Source: Data from I. Bretherton, "Open Communication and Internal Working Models: Their Roles in the Development of Attachment Relationships." R. Dienstbier & R. A. Thompson (eds.), *Nebraska Symposium on Motivation, 1988: Socioemotional Development, 36*, 60–61.

potentially threatening experiences, including the presence of a stranger, the departure of the mother, being left alone with a stranger, and being left completely alone—all in the context of an unfamiliar laboratory setting. During this sequence, researchers have the opportunity to make systematic observations of the child's behaviors, the caregiver's behaviors, and the characteristics of their interactions. These behaviors are coded and compared across varying segments of the procedure.

Four Patterns of Attachment. Four patterns of attachment behavior have been distinguished using the strange situation methodology: (1) secure attachment, (2) anxious-avoidant attachment, (3) anxious-resistant attachment, and (4) disorganized attachment.

Infants who have a **secure attachment** actively explore the laboratory setting and interact with strangers while their mothers are present. After separation, the babies actively greet their mothers or seek interaction. If the babies were distressed during separation, once the mothers return, the infants go to the mothers for comfort, and the mothers effectively reduce their distress. Then the babies resume exploring the environment.

When observed at home, babies who have a secure attachment cry less than other babies (Tracy & Ainsworth, 1981; Ainsworth, 1985). They greet their mothers more positively on reunion after everyday separations and respond more cooperatively to their mothers' requests. One can sense that securely attached babies have a working model of attachment in which they expect their caregiver to be accessible and responsive. Mothers of infants who have secure attachments are able to talk openly and coherently about their own childhood attachment figures and attachment behaviors (van Ijzendoorn, 1995).

Infants who show an **anxious-avoidant attachment** avoid contact with their mothers during the reunion segment following separation or ignore their efforts to interact. They appear to expect that their mothers will not be there when needed. They show less distress at being alone than other babies. Mothers of babies who were characterized as anxious avoidant seem to reject their babies. It is almost as if they were angry at their babies. They spend less time holding and cuddling their babies than other mothers, and more of their interactions are unpleasant or even hurtful. At home, these babies cry a lot, they are not readily soothed by contact with the caregiver, and yet they are quite distressed by separations. Mothers of infants who show an anxious-avoidant attachment are often dismissive or devaluing of their own childhood attachment experiences (Main & Solomon, 1990).

Infants who show an **anxious-resistant attachment** are very cautious in the presence of the stranger. Their exploratory behavior is noticeably disrupted by the caregiver's departure. When the caregiver returns, the infants appear to

Is There a Sensitive Period for Attachment?

A **SENSITIVE PERIOD** is a time of maximal sensitivity or readiness for the development of certain skills or behavior patterns. The particular skill or behavior pattern is not likely to emerge before the onset of the period, and it is extremely difficult if not impossible to establish once the critical time period has passed. The successful emergence of any behavior that has a sensitive period for development depends on the coordination of the biological readiness of the organism and environmental supports (Scott, 1987).

Konrad Lorenz (1935, 1937/1961) was one of the first ethologists to compare the critical periods in physical development and those in behavioral development. Lorenz described a process of social attachment among birds that he called **imprinting**. In this process, the young bird establishes a comparatively permanent bond with its mother. In her absence, however, the young bird will imprint on other available targets, including a model of its mother or a human being. For birds, the onset of the critical period coincides with the time at which they are able

© Nina Leen/Time Life Pictures/Getty Images

Konrad Lorenz inadvertently became the target of imprinting for these geese. They followed him as if he were their mother.

to walk and ends when they begin to fear strangers. After this point, no new model or species can be substituted as a target for imprinting.

Is there a time when infants are most likely to form such an attachment to the primary caregiver? Is there a point after which such attachments cannot be formed? The answer to these questions is especially relevant for policies related to foster care and adoption. We need to know about the plasticity of social

attachment in order to support optimal social and emotional development.

Evidence to address these questions has been drawn from real-life situations in which mother-infant relationships have been disrupted. Leon Yarrow (1963, 1964, 1970) observed 100 infants who were shifted from foster mothers to adoptive mothers. The infants who were separated from their foster mothers at 6 months or earlier showed minimal distress. They did not express prolonged anger or

want to be close to the caregiver, but they are also angry, so that they are very hard to soothe or comfort. Infants who are characterized as anxious-resistant have mothers who are inconsistent in their responsiveness. Sometimes, these mothers ignore clear signals of distress. At other times, they interfere with their infants in order to make contact. These infants do not know if their needs will be attended to. Although these mothers enjoy close physical contact with their babies, they do not necessarily do so in ways appropriate to the baby's needs. The result is the formation of an internal working model of attachment that is highly unpredictable. These babies try to maintain proximity and to avoid unfamiliar situations that increase uncertainty about accessibility to their caregiver. Caregivers of infants who have formed an anxious-resistant attachment are overly preoccupied with conflicts around their own childhood attachment issues.

In the **disorganized attachment**, babies' responses are particularly notable in the reunion sequence. These babies

have no consistent strategy for managing their distress. They behave in contradictory, unpredictable ways that seem to convey feelings of extreme fear or utter confusion (Belsky, Campbell, Cohn, & Moore, 1996). Observations of mothers and infants who are described as having a disorganized attachment highlight two different patterns. Some mothers are negative, intrusive, and they frighten their babies in bursts of intense hostility. Other mothers are passive and helpless, rarely showing positive or comforting behaviors. These mothers appear to be afraid of their babies, perhaps not trusting their own impulses to respond appropriately (Lyons-Ruth, Lyubchik, Wolfe, & Bronfman, 2002). The mothers often have experiences of loss or abuse in their childhood that have disrupted their own attachment experiences.

In U.S. samples, about two thirds of the children tested have been characterized as securely attached. Of the remainder, more children fall into the anxious-avoidant category than into the anxious-resistant category (Ainsworth et al.,

depression over the separation if their physical and emotional needs continued to be met. In contrast, all the infants who were transferred from foster mothers to adoptive mothers at 8 months or older showed strong negative reactions, including angry protest and withdrawal. These infants found the disruption of their earlier relationships very stressful.

Later research by John Bowlby (1980) focused on adolescents who had moved repeatedly from one foster home or institution to another. These children never had an opportunity to form an enduring, loving relationship with a caring adult. As adolescents, they were described as *affectionless* and unable to form close relationships with others. Subsequent studies of adopted children have confirmed that children who spend their infancy in institutions where the turnover in caregivers is high show disruptions in social functioning, including indiscriminate friendship formation, difficulty in forming close relationships, and difficulty in finding emotional support from peers (Rutter, 1995).

In the 1990s, a large number of orphans from Romania were adopted by families in the United States, Canada, and several European countries. While in the Romanian orphanages, these children had been exposed to a variety of neglectful conditions including: poor nutrition,

little attention or adult interaction, and long periods of time in their cribs with little opportunity for stimulation or play. Those who were adopted by 4 months of age seemed to develop quite normally. However those who were adopted at 8 months of age or older had a wide range of cognitive and affective problems that lasted into childhood. In particular, those who had longer exposure to the Romanian orphanages had disrupted social competence characterized by an overly friendly style of interaction regardless of whether the person was a familiar caregiver or a complete stranger, and a lack of close connection to their adoptive parents (Carlson & Earls, 1997; Gunnar, 2000; Rutter et al., 2010).

From these real-world examples of disruption in the mother-infant relationship, we can say that a sensitive period for attachment must begin at about 6 months of age. However, it is not clear if there is a time after which a secure attachment can no longer be established. In a study of children who spent their first years of life in an institution where the quality of care was good but staff turnover was high, children who were adopted at age 2 were able to form secure attachments to their adoptive parents. However, at later observations at ages 8 and 16, the children showed evidence of difficulty in peer relations

similar to the children who remained in the institution (Hodges & Tizard, 1989). Lack of continuity in caregiving during infancy is likely to produce long-lasting disruptions in relationship formation, even if a secure attachment with a caregiver is formed at a later time.

Critical Thinking Questions

1. From a developmental perspective, what do you conclude about a sensitive period for the formation of social attachment?

2. How would you design a research study to evaluate whether there is a sensitive period for the formation of a secure attachment? What kinds of evidence would be needed to determine whether there is a sensitive period for attachment?

3. How would you determine whether the problems arising from disruptions in early caregiving were a result of a lack of attachment or some other explanation such as poor nutrition or lack of stimulation?

4. Can you think of other aspects of infant development that might be characterized as having a sensitive period for optimal emergence?

5. Based on what you have read about attachment, what implications can you draw regarding the process of foster care and adoption?

1978). Only a small percentage of infants show the disorganized pattern (Radke-Yarrow, Cummings, Kuczynski, & Chipman, 1985; Carlson, Cicchetti, Barnett, & Braunwold, 1989; van IJzendoorn et al., 1992). Research has suggested links between the disorganized attachment and serious mental health problems in later childhood and beyond, including depression, borderline personality, and dissociative reactions (Lyons-Ruth et al., 2002; Fonagy, 2003).

Parental Sensitivity and the Quality of Attachment

How can we account for differences in the quality of the attachment? Early work on the formation of a secure attachment argued that a cornerstone in this process was maternal sensitivity (Ainsworth et al., 1978). **Sensitivity** is defined as attentiveness to the infant's state, accurate interpretation of the infant's signals, and well-timed responses that promote

mutually rewarding interactions (Isabella & Belsky, 1991). A sensitive caregiver is able to recognize the infant's emotional state, empathize with it, and make an appropriate response. A parent might recognize that the infant is distressed but be too busy or preoccupied to respond or to provide effective comfort (Leerkes, Crockenberg, & Burrows, 2004). Caregivers who are psychologically available, responsive, consistent, and warm in their interactions with their babies—especially during the first 6 months of the baby's life—are found to be most successful in establishing a secure attachment relationship that can be measured by the time the baby is 12 months old (Braungart-Rieker, Garwood, Powers, & Wang, 2001). The way caregivers respond when infants are distressed is uniquely related to the formation of a secure attachment independent of how they respond to other infant cues (Leerkes, Blankson, & O'Brien, 2009). This makes sense since the attachment system is theorized to be especially adapted to protecting infants from threat. The Applying Theory and

Research to Life box discusses the possibility that there may be a sensitive period for the development of attachment.

Four factors come into play in producing the kind of sensitivity that underlies secure attachments: (1) cultural and subcultural pathways, (2) the caregiver's personal life story, (3) contemporary factors, and (4) characteristics of the infant (see Figure 5.5).

Cultural and Subcultural Pathways. Cultural and subcultural pathways are integrated into one's mental representation of a parent or caregiver. The culture's beliefs about infants, including how fragile or vulnerable they are, how best to help infants cope with distress, and what skills or temperamental qualities are most valued, are likely to shape a caregiver's practices (Coll, 2004). For example, Japanese mothers keep close, continuous proximity to their infants. Separations are infrequent, and infants are expected to monitor their mothers' reactions in order to assess people and objects in the environment. Japanese mothers subtly direct their infants' play behavior through gestures and facial expressions. Independent play is not especially valued, and the idea that children would handle separation and reunion with the mother with little distress is not expected by Japanese caregivers (Okimoto, 2001).

Ethnographic studies (in-depth observations of behaviors central to the survival of a group, such as caregiving strategies) document the widespread practice of shared child care. When many adults and older siblings share responsibility for infant care, a child's needs can be readily met. When mothers expect to be able to share the tasks of infant care with others, they may also have a different ideal about the quality of infant attachment, a model that is less exclusive and possibly less emotionally intense. As a result, infants emerge with a more confident mental representation about the willingness of others to protect and care for them (Seymour, 2004).

The Caregiver's Personal Life Story. Aspects of the caregiver's personal life story contribute to being able to serve as a secure base for a child. Adults who recall their own parents as accepting, responsive, and available are more likely to be able to transmit those qualities as they enact the caregiver role. Adults who have experienced early loss or disruption of an attachment relationship have more difficulty providing a secure base for their offspring (Fonagy, Steele, & Steele, 1991; Belsky, 1996). Studies suggest that the internal working model of an attachment relationship may be transmitted across generations, with mothers and fathers drawing on the model of an attachment they formed as infants and young

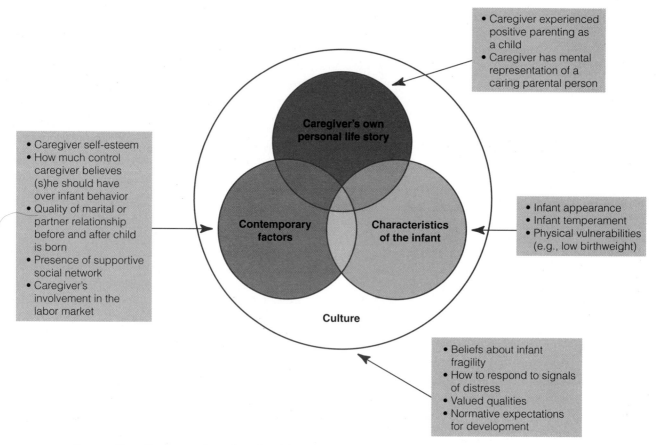

FIGURE 5.5 Factors Contributing to Caregiver Sensitivity

Source: From "Variability in Early Communicative Development," by L. Fenson et al., 1994, *Monographs of the Society for Research in Child Development, 59* (5), 38. Copyright © 1994 The Society for Research in Child Development, Inc. Reprinted by permission.

children, which then guides their perceptions of infant cues and their own responses (George & Solomon, 1999; Bornstein, 2002).

Contemporary Factors. Contemporary factors can influence the ability of an adult to provide a secure base for attachment. For example, some mothers experience high levels of postnatal depression. Depressed mothers are likely to be less attuned to their infants' signals, less playful, less verbally stimulating, more irritable, and generally less enthusiastic and happy as they interact with their infants (Edhborg, Lundh, Seimyr, & Widstroem, 2001). Attachment insecurity is more likely when infants' mothers are suffering from depression (Toth, Rogosch, Sturge-Apple, & Cicchetti, 2009). The role of the child's father, and the relationship between the mother and father or the caregiving partners are especially central. A partner who is supportive, involved in caregiving, and reassuring about meeting the challenges of parenting a newborn provides a context in which even mothers who have had insecure attachments themselves can thrive. On the other hand, some relationships are characterized by conflict and poor communication, in which the partner may even compete with the infant for the mother's care or impede the mother's efforts to care for her infant (Cowan, Cohn, Cowan, & Pearson, 1996). Other contemporary factors that influence the caregiver's sensitivity to the infant include the caregiver's self-esteem, the degree of control the caregiver believes is necessary to have over the infant's behavior, the presence of a supportive social network that validates the person's caregiving efforts, the person's involvement in the labor market, and financial worries (George & Solomon, 1999; Belsky, 2006).

Infant Characteristics. The quality of attachment can also be influenced by the characteristics of the infant. Infants born with physical abnormalities are more likely to evoke responses of rejection or neglect from caregivers (Langlois, Ritter, Casey, & Sawin, 1995). Physical conditions such as colic can test the parents' commitment to caregiving and create a cycle of anxiety and fearfulness. Babies with colic may not find comfort in their caregivers' efforts to soothe them, and caregivers may not experience a sense of efficacy in their ability to calm their child.

Certain aspects of the infant's temperament—especially fearfulness, sociability, and the intensity of negative emotions—may influence the way the attachment relationship is established (Izard et al., 1991). Studies have shown that temperament influences the kinds of caregiver responses that are most likely to create an internal sense of security or insecurity. Infants who are irritable are often difficult for parents to respond to. Over time, some parents may respond to difficult infants harshly or by withdrawing. These behaviors may produce an insecure attachment for the infant (Putnam, Sanson, & Rothbart, 2002).

The Relevance of Attachment to Subsequent Development

The nature of one's attachment and the related internal working models of attachment influence expectations about the self, others, and the nature of relationships (Shaver, Collins, & Clark, 1996). Moreover, the formation of a secure attachment relationship is expected to influence the child's ability to explore and engage the environment with confidence, knowing that the protective "other" is near at hand. Children who experience a secure attachment are less likely to be exposed to uncontrollable stress. They experience rhythmic, meaningful, and predictable interactions that contribute to their social competences. As a result, they are *hopeful* about their ability to form positive relationships with others (Weinfield et al., 1999). Securely attached infants become preschoolers who show greater resilience, self-control, and curiosity. In contrast, infants who have a disorganized attachment are very hostile, aggressive preschoolers (Hazan, Campa, & Gur-Yaish, 2006). Results of numerous studies indicate that as they get older, children who have a disorganized attachment, especially boys, are at high risk for externalizing problems (Fearon, Bakermans-Kranenburg, van IJzendoorn, Lapsley, & Roisman, 2010).

A clinical diagnosis—**reactive attachment disorder**—has been linked to serious disturbances in infant attachment. Two expressions of this disorder have been described: **inhibited type**, in which the person is very withdrawn, hypervigilant in social contacts, and resistant to comfort; and **uninhibited type**, in which the person shows a lack of discrimination, being overly friendly and attaching to any new person (DeAngelis, 1997b; Cain, 2006).

From a life-span perspective, the quality of the attachment formed in infancy influences the formation of later relationships (Ainsworth, 1989). Children who have formed secure attachments in infancy are likely to find more enjoyment in close peer friendships during their preschool years. In an analysis of the results of more than 60 studies of the relationship of parent-child attachment and peer relations, the quality of attachment with the mother was consistently predictive of the quality of close peer friendships well into middle school and early adolescence (Schneider, Atkinson, & Tardif, 2001). Children who have secure attachments are more likely to attribute positive intentions to peers, whereas children with anxious attachments are more likely to view peers with wariness.

The attachment construct has been used to help explain the nature of adolescent and adult love relationships. Romantic relationships can be characterized along many of the same dimensions as infant attachments, including the desire to maintain physical contact with the loved one, increased disclosure and responsiveness to the loved one, the effectiveness of the loved one in providing comfort and reassurance that reduce distress, and an element of exclusiveness or preferential response to the loved one (Hazan & Shaver, 1987; Reis, 2006).

The attachment construct continues to be evident in adult, loving relationships. This mother and daughter enjoy physical closeness, comfort each other, and look to each other for reassurance in times of stress.

Fears about loss and abandonment, born from anxious avoidant attachments, are likely to result in anxiety about one's contemporary romantic relationships:

I had a real problem trusting anyone at the start of any relationship. A couple of things happened to me when I was young, which I had some emotional difficulties getting over. At the start of our relationship, if P. had been separated from me, I would have been constantly thinking: "What was he doing?"; "Was he with another girl?"; "Was he cheating on me?"; all that would have been running through my head. (Feeney, 1999, p. 365)

People with insecure attachments tend to be more coercive and mistrustful. They tend to push their partners away. They may have problems establishing and maintaining romantic relationships and in meeting the demands for sexual intimacy and disclosure in these relationships (Tracy,

Shaver, Albino, & Cooper, 2003). The contribution of attachment orientation to intimate relationships will be discussed further in Chapter 11 (Early Adulthood).

The parenting relationship can also be understood as an elaboration of the attachment representation. Adults who have experienced a secure attachment in their own infancy are more likely to be able to comfort and respond to their children. Adults whose childhood attachments were unpredictable or even hostile are more likely to have difficulty coping successfully with young infants' needs (Ricks, 1985; George & Solomon, 1999). For example, in an observational study, parents were observed while their infants were having inoculations. Those parents who had an anxious-avoidant attachment style were less responsive to their infants' distress in this context (Edelstein et al., 2004).

It may be obvious that people who have a secure attachment benefit from their belief that the world is a safe place and that others can be counted on to provide help under conditions of threat. Most of the time, people who have a secure attachment are more confident, work more effectively with others, and are better able to resolve interpersonal conflicts than people who have an anxious-resistant or anxious-avoidant attachment (Rom & Mikulincer, 2003; Mikulincer & Shaver, 2007). However, under some conditions, especially conditions of real danger or threat, people who have insecure attachments may be better able to cope specifically because they are likely to see situations as threatening, and other people as unlikely to meet their needs (Ein-Dor, Mikulincer, Doron, & Shaver, 2010). Anxiously attached individuals are more likely to detect dangers and alert others. Those with an avoidant attachment are more likely to depend on themselves and to resist becoming overly dependent on others. Under conditions of real threat, they may be the first to find a way to escape, acting quickly to save themselves. Whereas a securely attached person may underestimate dangers because of a general feeling of safety, the anxiously attached person is likely to be among the first to recognize real dangers. Whereas the securely attached person is likely to reach out to others under conditions of threat, the person with an avoidant attachment may be among the first to find a way to flee the danger. Thus, the survival of the group as a whole may be enhanced by the diversity of attachment orientations of the members.

Critique of the Attachment Paradigm. The attachment paradigm and its measurement using the strange situation have significant limitations especially when viewed from a cross-cultural or comparative cultural lens. Three criticisms are discussed here; you may think of others.

1. The strange situation analyzes the child-caregiver attachment based on how the infant copes with the stressors associated with separation from the caregiver. Although one might assume that infant-caregiver separation is a universal problem, it is much more common in some cultures than others. For example, in many parts of Asia, Africa, and South America, infants sleep with their mothers

and are carried on the mother's back or side throughout the day. Close physical contact is a culture's way of conveying warmth and safety. The prolonged physical separation that would occur if a baby sleeps in a bassinet or in a separate room would be considered harsh or cruel parenting. Thus, the premise that attachment can be assessed by how well a baby copes with separation may be a poor yardstick in cultures where infant-mother separation is rare and not highly valued (Greenfield, Keller, Fuligni, & Maynard, 2003).

2. The attachment framework and the strange situation emphasize the nature of the mother-infant dyad as the prototype of an attachment relationship. Although some research has been carried out to compare attachment to mothers and fathers, or mothers and caregivers, the focus is on a dyadic attachment. However, in many cultures, the infant is cared for by a cluster or collective of older siblings, cousins, aunts, fathers, and uncles, as well as the mother and other specially designated caregivers. In these cultures, the ability of the child to feel safe and secure depends on the coordinated care of many members of the family or village, rather than exclusive care by the mother. The strange situation in particular and the attachment paradigm more generally do not capture the fluid nature of this collective caregiving context and the degree to which it is effective in supporting a child's feelings of safety and security (Lewis, 2005).

3. Infant-caregiver interactions can be understood as an introduction to the nature of valued social relationships which, over time, will contribute to the child's survival and successful integration into the social community. One of the assumptions of the attachment framework is that a secure attachment provides a safe harbor from which the child feels free to explore the environment.

From this view, attachment is a foundation for subsequent independence. However, autonomy, exploration, and self-reliance are not primary goals of socialization in all cultures. Societies marked by greater value for interdependence view the formation of infant attachment as a precursor to obedience, intragroup harmony, and acceptance of cultural norms and values. Thus, while the need to insure the survival of the young through sensitive and responsive care may be a cultural universal, the socialization goals that follow from the formation of a secure attachment may differ from one culture to the next depending upon the culture's goals, values, and traditions (Greenfield & Suzuki, 1998; Weisner, 2005).

The formation of an attachment relies on social, cognitive and emotional capacities that emerge in infancy. Attachments form as infants experience comfort when they are distressed. The sensitive caregiver may use multiple strategies, including rocking and holding, gentle touch, vocalizations, and food, to reassure and soothe a baby. The caregiver also anticipates sources of distress and tries to keep them to a minimum, while engaging the baby in positive, pleasant interactions. Over time, infants learn to regulate their own emotional reactions, and to find effective ways of conveying both positive and negative emotions in ways that will result in meaningful communication with others.

Emotional Development

Objective 6. To examine the nature of emotional development, including emotional differentiation, the interpretation of emotions, and emotional regulation.

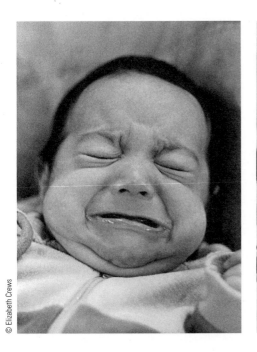 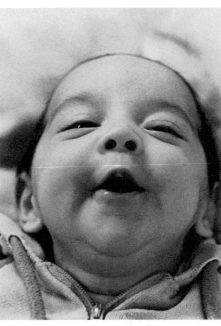

At 10 weeks of age, a baby's expression of emotion through cooing and crying provides distinct, easily interpreted messages that cue caregivers to the baby's inner states.

© Elizabeth Crews

TABLE 5.7 Age-Related Changes in Emotional Differentiation

MONTH	PLEASURE-JOY	WEAKNESS-FEAR	RAGE-ANGER
0–3	Endogenous smile; turning toward	Startle/pain; obligatory attention	Distress due to covering the face, physical restraint, extreme discomfort Rage (disappointment)
3	Pleasure		
4–5	Delight, active laughter	Wariness	
7	Joy		
9		Fear (stranger aversion)	Anger
12	Elation	Anxiety; immediate fear	Angry mood, petulance
18	Positive valuation of self	Shame	Defiance
24	Affection		Intentional hurting
36	Pride, love		Guilt

Source: From "Socioemotional Development," by L. A. Sroufe, in *Handbook of Infant Development*, J. D. Osofsky (Ed.), pp. 462–516. Copyright © 1979 John Wiley & Sons, Inc.

Because of their essential role in survival and social interaction, emotions have become an important focus of study in infant development. Emotional development during infancy can be understood along four dimensions. First, new emotions emerge over the period of infancy. Infants express their emotions at different levels of intensity—for example, from a whimper or fussy noise to a full-blown angry rage, or from a happy cooing gurgle to outright laughter. Second, with cognitive maturation, a child interprets events differently. New emotions may become attached to familiar situations. An experience that may once have caused wariness, such as a new toy or a loud noise, may become a source of excitement or joy as the child gains a new understanding of the situation. Third, children develop strategies for regulating their emotions, so that they are not overwhelmed by emotional intensity. Fourth, emotions serve as a channel for adult-infant communication.

Emotional Differentiation

Emotions gradually become differentiated during the first 2 years of life. Peter Wolff (1966) described seven states of arousal in newborn infants: regular sleep, irregular sleep, periodic sleep, drowsiness, alert inactivity, waking activity, and crying. Each is characterized by a distinctive pattern of breathing, muscle tone, motor activity, and alertness. In these states, one observes the earliest differentiation among distress (*crying*), interest (*alert inactivity*), and excitement (*waking activity*). A newborn's state of arousal influences the capacity to respond to the environment. Changes in arousal state also serve to cue responses from caregivers. Crying usually brings an effort to comfort or soothe. Visual alertness is likely to prompt social interactions with caregivers who use a variety of strategies to sustain contact such as smiling, making cooing sounds, or shaking a toy or rattle.

Crying is an especially important emotional expression that contributes to the infant's survival. Until about 6 or 7 months of age, the infant's mobility is quite limited. The cry is one of the primary signals available that will bring the caregiver to the infant. Infant cries vary in pitch as well as in tempo and duration. Adults have measurable emotional reactions to infant crying, including changes in heart rate, breathing, and perspiration, which indicate that the cry serves as a stressor (Brewster, Nelson, McCanne, Lucas, & Milner, 1998). Studies from laboratory and natural field settings and across cultures suggest that high-pitched cries are considered more upsetting to the caregiver and are treated as a signal of a more urgent need than are low-pitched cries. Moreover, information is contained in the pauses between cries. Cries that involve shorter pauses between crying sounds are perceived by adults as more arousing and unpleasant (Zeskind, Klein, & Marshall, 1992).

A broad pallet of emotions emerges gradually from the basic states of arousal and distress. The differentiation of emotions follows a regular pattern, as Table 5.7 suggests. This table describes age-related changes for three dimensions of emotion: *pleasure-joy*, *wariness-fear*, and *rage-anger*. Emotional responses during the first month are closely tied to the infant's internal state. Physical discomfort, arousal, pain, and changing tension in the central nervous system are the major sources of emotions. During the period from 1 to 6 months, emotions begin to reflect the infant's awareness of features of the environment. Babies smile at familiar faces; they show interest in and curiosity about novel stimuli. They express rage when nursing is disrupted or when they are prevented from viewing an activity they have been intently watching.

From 1 to 6 months, the intensity of emotional expression becomes more varied. For example, four different kinds of infant smiles have been observed: the simple smile in which a baby's mouth curves upward at the corner; the Duchenne smile, which involves crinkling eyes, raised cheeks, and an open, smiling mouth; the play smiles in which the jaw drops and the mouth stays open; and the duplay smiles in which the jaw drops and the cheeks are raised (Fogel et al., 2006). The simple smile is considered a signal of happy social engagement, whereas the Duchenne, play, and duplay smiles reflect different levels of intensity in play that accompany such activities as tickling, peek-a-boo, and playful interactions with familiar caregivers.

The period from 6 to 12 months reflects a greater awareness of the context of events. Emotions of joy, anger, and fear are tied to a baby's ability to recall previous experiences and to compare them with an ongoing event. These emotions also reflect ability to exercise some control over the environment and frustration when goals are blocked. Fearfulness, assessed several times from 4 to 12 months, increases steadily over the first year. Babies who are less fearful at 4 months show a steeper increase in fear than babies who are already temperamentally fearful at a very young age (Gartstein et al., 2010).

The dimension of wariness-fear becomes more differentiated during the second year. Wariness is viewed as an early feature of the attachment process, especially as it relates to stranger anxiety at about 6 months and separation anxiety at about 9 months. Anxiety of a more nonspecific form begins to be observed during the second year. Babies begin to anticipate negative experiences and express fear of objects or events that have been associated with negative experiences in the past. The construct of anxiety is included as a major dynamic in describing patterns of attachment, especially in relationships characterized by potentially rejecting or unpredictable caregivers.

By the end of the first year, the extent of an infant's negative emotions, such as irritability and fear, are influenced by the caregiver's depression and anxiety. The impact of maternal depression on infants' psychosocial development has received a great deal of attention in the literature, demonstrating that there are distinct differences in the emotional expressiveness and social engagement of infants of depressed mothers. Higher levels of maternal depression and anxiety in infancy are linked to greater increases in fearfulness at the end of infancy, and more symptoms of anxiety at age 2 (Gartstein et al., 2010). Positive emotions are not as clearly tied to the caregiver's characteristics (Pauli-Pott, Mertesacker, & Beckman, 2004).

Emotions that are observed during the second year of life—especially anxiety, pride, defiance, and shame—suggest an emerging sense of self. Infants recognize that they can operate as causal agents. They also begin to respond to the emotions of others. They can give love to others through hugs, kisses, and tender pats. They can share toys, comfort another distressed infant, and imitate another person's excitement. In becoming a more distinct being, an infant achieves a new level of awareness of the capacity to give and receive pleasure as well as the vulnerability of self and others.

Emotions as a Key to Understanding Meaning

An infant's emotional reactions provide a channel for determining the meaning the child is giving to a specific situation. Often, these reactions are studied by the systematic coding of facial expressions. One example of how emotions provide a window on meaning comes from a study of infants in an operant conditioning experiment. Infants at ages 2, 4, and 6 months were observed while they learned an operant arm-pulling task. A string was attached to the infant's wrist. When the string was pulled, it activated a switch that turned on a color slide of an infant smiling accompanied by the sound of children singing the *Sesame Street* theme song. During the learning phase, pulling the string produced the visual and auditory stimulus. During the extinction phase, nothing happened when the string was pulled. Even as young as 2 months old, the babies' expressions changed from interest and enjoyment during the learning phase to anger and sadness during the extinction phase. The findings were interpreted to illustrate that infants' anger is associated with violation of their expectations and that expressions of interest and enjoyment are associated with learning and increased control (Sullivan, Lewis, & Alessandri, 1992).

An infant's smile can have a wide variety of meanings and can be produced in response to many stimuli. The earliest smiles, observed during the first month of life, may occur spontaneously during sleep or in response to a high-pitched human voice. Gentle tactile stimulation—touching, tickling, and rocking—can produce these early smiles. A baby's first smiles are not a true form of social communication, although they are likely to produce positive feelings in the adult caregiver (Wolff, 1963, 1987).

Social smiles begin to be observed at about 5 weeks of age. These smiles are first produced in response to a wide range of stimuli: familiar faces and voices (especially the mother's), strangers, and nonhuman objects. Games such as tickle and peek-a-boo bring on open-mouth smiles and laughter (Fogel et al., 2006). The social smile conveys both recognition of familiarity and an invitation to further communication or interaction. By 4 months of age, infants smile more when the pattern of interaction is organized and predictable than when it is random and unfamiliar (Rochat, Querido, & Striano, 1999).

The *cognitive smile* develops alongside the social smile. Infants smile in response to their own behaviors, as if they were expressing satisfaction with their accomplishments or self-recognition. In a study of infants over the period from 7 to 20 weeks, babies were observed to show the coy smile—smiling while averting their gaze—when they were successful in getting attention or renewing attention from an adult (Reddy, 2000). As evidenced in the string-pulling task described previously, infants also smile elaborately when they are able to make something happen. These *mastery smiles* do not appear to have a social intention.

In the second year of life, smiling is associated with a primitive form of *humor*. Babies smile when they recognize an incongruity, such as seeing their mother drinking from a baby bottle or crawling on her hands and knees. They also smile and laugh when they violate a caregiver's expectations. These smiles suggest that the baby appreciates something about the discrepancy between what is being presented and what is normally observed (Loizou, 2005).

The Ability to Regulate Emotions

Emotional regulation refers to a variety of processes that allow infants to control the intensity of their emotional state and reduce feelings of distress. These abilities, which mature over the first 2 years of life, have important implications for a child's successful social participation in preschool and later childhood (Calkins, 2004). Infants develop a range of techniques for coping with intense emotions, both positive and negative. Even newborns have some strategies for reducing the intensity of distress, such as turning the head away, sucking on their hands or lips, or closing their eyes. As infants gain new motor coordination and control, they can move away, distract themselves with other objects, or soothe themselves by rocking, stroking, or thumb sucking (Kopp, 1989). However, there are also many instances when infants are not able to regulate the intensity of their emotions. Researchers who work with infants often note the number of babies who had to be eliminated from their study because they simply could not be calmed enough in the experimental procedure to attend to the task. The way an infant reacts to environmental stimuli, and the intensity of that reaction is often conceptualized as a reflection of the concept of temperament.

Temperament. **Temperament** is a theoretical construct that refers to relatively stable characteristics of response to the environment and patterns of self-regulation (Thomas & Chess, 1980; Putnam, Sanson, & Rothbart, 2002). Temperament is often viewed as the biological or physiological basis of personality that can be observed early in infancy. When we describe babies as active, cheerful, quiet, or fussy, we are often making reference to what scholars study as temperament. Temperament is a significant source of individual differences that emerges from a combination of genetic, environmental, and socially constructed factors. Theorists have offered different views about the specific features of temperament and what accounts for the stability of these features. However, they all tend to agree on two aspects of temperament: (1) a primary feature of temperament is the child's positive or negative reaction to environmental events, and (2) the stability of this reaction leads to a consistent response by others (Vaughn & Bost, 1999).

Dimensions of Temperament. Thomas, Chess, and Birch (1970) were able to classify infants into three temperamental groupings: *easy*, *slow to warm up*, and *difficult*. Table 5.8 summarizes the characteristics of each of these temperaments and the percentages of the sample that could be clearly identified as one of the three categories. Roughly 35% of the sample could not be classified.

Three aspects of temperament—activity level, sociability, and emotionality—are thought to be influenced largely by genetic factors (Thomas & Chess, 1977, 1986; Buss & Plomin, 1984, 1986; Goldsmith & Campos, 1986; Wilson & Matheny, 1986; Goldsmith et al., 1987; Braungart, Plomin, DeFries, & Fulker, 1992; Saudino & Zapfe, 2008). Patterns of electrical activity in the frontal cortex in infancy have been associated with individual differences in these features of temperament,

Is this baby showing evidence of a difficult temperament or is the protest a result of the father's lack of attention? What observations would you need to make in order to answer this question?

© 2010 Sporrer/Rupp/Jupiterimages Corporation

TABLE 5.8 Three Types of Infant Temperaments

TYPE	DESCRIPTION	% OF TOTAL SAMPLE
Easy	Positive mood, regular body functions, low or moderate intensity of reaction, adaptability, positive approach rather than withdrawal from new situations	40
Slow to warm up	Low activity level, tendency to withdraw on first exposure to new stimuli, slow to adapt, somewhat negative in mood, low intensity of reaction to situations	15
Difficult	Irregular body functions, unusually intense reactions, tendency to withdraw from new situations, slow to adapt to change, generally negative mood	10

Note: Some researchers prefer terms such as flexible and active, cautious, and feisty rather than easy, slow to warm up, and difficult which have judgmental connotations.

Source: From "The Origin of Personality," by A. Thomas, S. Chess, and H. Birch, 1970, *Scientific American, 223,* 102–109.

particularly distinguishing between babies who are more able to regulate their emotions, who are easily soothed, and who seem to be relatively positive as contrasted to the babies who are easily distressed, difficult to soothe, and have difficulty focusing their attention (Schmidt, Fox, Perez-Edgar, & Hamer, 2009). These dimensions—especially emotionality and activity level—show modest stability over adjacent periods of infancy and toddlerhood (Henderson, Fox, & Rubin, 2001).

Another view of temperament focuses on the construct of **behavioral inhibition,** a combination of fearfulness, a low threshold for arousal in the presence of novel or unusual stimuli, and general cautiousness. A method of assessing behavioral inhibition involves presenting infants with a set of unusual stimuli and observing their reactions. Some infants seem to think this is great fun. They smile, coo, and respond with positive excitement. Other infants get very distressed. They cry, struggle, arch their backs, and try to escape the situation. These early reactions in the laboratory setting at 4 months of age are predictors of toddler behavior. The infants who react positively to the novel stimuli are likely to become active, busy, exploratory toddlers. The infants who react with distress to the novel stimuli are likely to become fearful, shy, and socially wary toddlers (Kagan, Snidman, & Arcus, 1998).

A child's temperament influences the tone of interactions, the frequency with which interactions take place, the way others react to the child, and the way the child reacts to the reactions of others. Highly active, sociable children are likely to initiate interactions and to respond positively to the attention of others. More passive, inhibited, or fearful children will be less likely to initiate interactions and may withdraw when other children or adults direct attention to them. There is growing concern that infants and toddlers who are temperamentally shy, fearful, and readily distressed by novel or unfamiliar situations may be vulnerable to subsequent difficulties regulating anxiety and depression (Moffitt et al., 2007).

Many studies emphasize the relevance of the fit or match between the parent's temperament and that of the child (Plomin, 1990; Rettew et al., 2006). Consider the role of temperament in the case study on the Cotton family.

Although temperament shows some consistency over the period of infancy and toddlerhood, it is only modestly stable over longer periods of time, depending on culture, measurement techniques, and methods of analysis. Measures of temperament in infancy do not correlate all that highly with measures in the early and middle school years. In all likelihood, temperamental characteristics are modified as they come into contact with socialization pressures at home and at school, as well as with new internal capacities to regulate behavior. For example, Thomas and Chess (1977, 1986) found that when parents were calm and allowed their difficult children to adapt to novelty at a leisurely pace, the children grew more comfortable and had an easier time adapting to new routines. However, if parents were impatient and demanding, then their difficult children remained difficult and had a hard time adjusting to new situations as they grew older.

The kind of caregiving a child receives will depend in part on the parental context. For example, a mother's age, her economic resources, the nature of the neighborhood where she lives, and characteristics such as depression, stress, or a sense of parenting efficacy might each influence how patient and supportive a mother may be with a child who has an emotionally negative or irritable temperament (Paulussen-Hoogeboom, Stams, Hemranns, & Peetsma, 2007).

A growing body of research has expanded the idea that child outcomes are a product of child temperament and parenting strategies (Rothbart & Bates, 2006). Depending on the caregiving they receive and the environments they encounter, shy children can become sociable, fearful children can become secure explorers of their surroundings, and highly exuberant children can develop considerable self-control (National Research Council and Institute of Medicine, 2000, p. 389).

A few examples of this kind of interaction follow:

- Gentle, low-power discipline techniques are more effective in socializing infants who are relatively fearful and inhibited; these techniques do not work well with temperamentally fearless infants who respond better to socialization strategies that emphasize positive feelings between the mother and child (Kochanska, Aksan, & Joy, 2007).
- Children who are fearful are more likely to be inhibited with their peers when their mothers are overprotective, but more confident with their peers when their mothers are reassuring and supportive of the child's autonomy (Rubin, Hastings, Stewart, Henderson, & Chen, 1997).
- Parental use of harsh punishment is not predictive of aggressive behavior for children who are flexible and low in reactivity, but is strongly linked to aggressiveness among children who are inflexible and highly reactive (Patterson & Sanson, 1999).

These and other findings are creating a complex picture of differential susceptibility to the features of the caregiving environment. A modest level of parental dominance or assertiveness may be frightening and intimidating for a child with high behavioral inhibition, and completely insignificant for a child with low behavioral inhibition (Gilissen et al., 2007).

CASE STUDY

THE COTTON FAMILY

Nancy and Paul Cotton are a professional couple who gave birth to their first child, Anna, after they had been married for 7.5 years.

Nancy said, "We wanted a baby but couldn't decide when to have one. Finally we realized that we could not control everything, or time things perfectly. No one can predict the future. So we finally decided to go ahead and have a child as soon as possible. … We were both privileged, lucky, and had lived well. By the time we had Anna, I was thirty-three, and our marriage and careers were established. We felt secure.

"Being an optimistic person, I guess I expected nirvana. Anna was difficult to deliver, and breastfeeding was a nightmare. Every time she nursed, it hurt. But I didn't want to miss the opportunity. I was so determined. I used a stopwatch to make sure Anna got enough milk, and I gave her a pacifier for recreation. When she was five weeks old, I went off to our summer house on Martha's Vineyard. I wondered if it was the right decision because there was less in the way of family and friends for support. But we worked things out together that summer. She was energetic from the first, and I was constantly sleep-deprived, but we were oh! so close. I found ways to make it easier for us. I found a babysitter to give me an afternoon break; I used the "Swyngomatic" so that I could eat a warm supper every once in a while, and I learned to give Anna pacifiers or bottles to soothe herself."

Paul interjected: "She was like a miracle to me. She was fabulous! Miraculous! She even looked like me. I did as much for her as Nancy did, not out of guilt, but because I couldn't keep my hands off her. I took her with me everywhere when I was off work. At the Stop-and-Shop, all the ladies crowded around me, 'How do you do it? You're so good with her!'" As he talked of Anna, his cheeks flushed, his whole body actively described the dramatic and exciting time they had together. "I learned all about babies from her. I can bathe a kid faster than anyone in the world."

"I went back to work when Anna was three months," said Nancy. "I found full-time help. That way, I could enjoy her when I was home and get away when I needed to. I am a high-activity person, so I could understand a high-activity child like Anna. We could cycle together. I've never felt a bit of anxiety or ambivalence about her. I feel as if I've known her from the very first.

"Anna fit," said Nancy. "From the time she was born, we'd pick her up and just go. As you can see, going is pretty important in our family, and Anna thrived on it. We were not the only ones who enjoyed her; my own mother thought she was fabulous. She took care of her part-time after I went back to work. I had a chance to see my mother be loving and kind, a good mother to Anna. It was like reliving my own childhood—another kind of miracle. You see, I'd had a sister, Ginny, who had died. Anna gave my mother an opportunity to heal the pain of Ginny's death. This was true for me, too. We called her Anna Virginia after this sister. Ginny had a devastating mental illness. Ginny's spirit, intelligence, and humor seemed to live again in Anna, but without the shadow of vulnerability."

Source: From *What Every Baby Knows*, by T. B. Brazelton, pp. 11–13. Copyright © 1987 Addison-Wesley. Reprinted by permission of Perseus Books Group.

CRITICAL THINKING AND CASE ANALYSIS

1. How would you describe Anna's temperament? What problems might the Cotton family have faced if Anna had been a more passive, reserved, and inhibited child?
2. In what ways was Anna being expected to adapt to the Cotton family lifestyle?
3. What are some of the challenges Nancy and Paul faced as new parents? How did they cope with these challenges?
4. How would you describe Paul's enactment of the father role?
5. How would you describe Nancy's enactment of the mother role?
6. Anna seems to be influencing the well-being of her mother, father, and her grandmother. What impact does Anna have on each of these family members?

How Caregivers Help Infants Manage Their Emotions

One of the most important elements in the development of emotional regulation is the way caregivers assist infants to manage their strong feelings (Kopp, 1989; Tronick, 1989). Caregivers can provide direct support when they observe that a child is distressed. They may cuddle, hug, rock, or swaddle a baby. They may offer food or a pacifier to the baby or nurse her as a means of comfort. Through words and actions, the caregiver may help a child interpret the source of the stress or suggest ways to reduce the stress.

In a longitudinal study of maternal comforting strategies, mothers were observed as they tried to comfort their children following an inoculation at 2 and 6 months of age. The intensity and duration of infant crying decreased over this 4-month period. At the younger age, mothers used affection and soothing as comforting strategies when their babies cried after the shot; at 6 months, they used vocalization and distracting strategies more often, taking advantage of the infant's more developed capacities for attention and playfulness. For all levels of infant distress, the most effective method of soothing was a combination of holding/rocking and vocalizing, combining the sense of touch and the rhythmic movement of rocking with the calming features of the mother's voice. Feeding or offering a pacifier were effective as soothing strategies when the baby was moderately distressed, but not when the baby was extremely distressed. In general, caretaking strategies, like changing the baby's diaper or getting the baby dressed to leave the office, were not especially effective soothing strategies (Jahromi, Putnam, & Stifter, 2004).

Concern has been focused especially on babies who show intense negative emotionality early in infancy. Babies who show high levels of motor activity and who cry a lot at 4 months of age have been found to show high levels of wariness, fearfulness, and shyness at later ages (Park, Belsky, Putnam, & Crnic, 1997). These babies tend to be at risk for subsequent behavior problems. Studies have been directed toward analyzing individual differences in negative emotionality and the family characteristics that might be associated with changes in negativity over the first year of life (Calkins & Howse, 2004; Pauli-Pott et al., 2004). In one such study involving 148 babies and their parents, characteristics of the mothers and the fathers were examined separately to learn what might lead to increased negativity in the infants from 3 months to 9 months of age. In addition to the direct quality of interactions between the mother-infant and father-infant pairs, researchers found that high levels of marital dissatisfaction on the part of the mother or the father and the father's emotional insensitivity were tied to increases in the infant's negativity. This is significant because it suggests that the emotional climate of the parental system is communicated in ways that an infant can perceive as early as 3 to 9 months of age (Belsky, Fish, & Isabella, 1991).

Caregivers' approaches to infant emotional regulation vary with the culture (Kitayama, Karasawa, & Mesquita, 2004). In some cultures, caregivers regulate emotions by preventing a child from being exposed to certain arousing situations. Japanese mothers, for example, try hard to prevent their children from being exposed to anger by avoiding frustrating them. Furthermore, parents rarely express anger to their young children, especially in public. Thus, Japanese parents try to regulate anger by minimizing the child's experiences with it. Cultural values influence how mothers respond to infants' distress and what they teach their babies about how to regulate feelings of wariness, fear, and anxiety.

Infants achieve emotional regulation by observing emotional reactions of others. Children observe anger, pride, shame, or sadness in others, often in response to their own emotional expressions. For example, Connie stumbles and falls in trying to take a step on her own. She looks up at her mother. If her mother looks upset and frightened, Connie may begin to cry. On the other hand, if her mother laughs or speaks to her in a comforting tone, Connie may get up and try again. Children can be distracted from their sadness by seeing laughter and joy in someone else. Through empathy, they can reduce their angry feelings toward someone else by seeing how sad or frightened the other person is.

As children understand the consequences or implications of a situation, they have new motives for regulating or failing to regulate their emotions. Children may extend or expand their signals of distress if they think they will help them achieve their goals, such as special attention or nurturing. Children may try to disguise their distress if they think it will provoke additional pain. Emotional regulation, like emotional signaling, takes place in an interpersonal context.

Emotions as a Channel for Adult-Infant Communication

Emotions provide a two-way channel through which infants and their caregivers can establish **intersubjectivity**. An infant has the capacity to produce a range of emotional expressions, including fear, distress, disgust, surprise, excitement, interest, joy, anger, and sadness. Parents and other caregivers rely on the facial, vocal, and behavioral cues related to these emotions as ways of determining an infant's inner states and goals and responding to them. Babies in turn can also detect and differentiate the affective expressions of others. Young infants can differentiate facial expressions of fear, anger, happiness, sadness, and surprise. In cycles of interaction, responsive caregivers monitor changes in a baby's affect as a way of determining whether their interventions are effective (Meins, 2003).

Think of a 6-month-old baby who wants a toy that is out of reach. The baby waves her arms in the direction of the toy, makes fussy noises, and looks distressed. As her father tries to figure out what the baby wants, he watches her expressions in order to discover whether he is on the right track. Parents who are attuned to this form of communication are more likely to help babies to achieve their goals, and babies are more likely to persist in attempts to communicate because they have experienced success in such interactions. Through a shared repertoire of emotions, babies and their caregivers are able to understand one another and create common meanings. Thus, emotional expression becomes a building block of trust (Trevarthen & Aitken, 2001).

Social Referencing. One of the most notable ways that infants and adults have of co-constructing their reality is the mechanism of **social referencing** in which infants gather information about a situation or an object by assessing their parent's or caregiver's reactions. Social referencing involves three coordinated processes: (1) the infant coordinates attention between the adult and an ambiguous object or situation,

© Myrleen Ferguson Cate/Photo Edit

Emotions provide a channel of communication before speech and language. The exchange of playful laughing and smiling is an early form of conversation.

(2) the infant understands that the adult's emotional reaction refers to the specific object or situation, and (3) the infant uses the information from the adult's emotional reaction to guide behavior toward the object (Hornik & Gunnar, 1988; Feinman et al., 1992; Murray et al., 2008). By 12 months of age, infants can draw upon all of these abilities to use the emotional responses of another person to guide their own behavior (Carver & Vaccaro, 2007). They often use their mothers as a *social reference*, but other adults can serve this function as well. As infants approach an unfamiliar adult, an ambiguous situation, or a novel object, they look to their mother and use her facial expression or verbal expressions as a source of information about the situation. If the mother expresses wariness or a negative emotion, the infant is more likely to withdraw or to explore with caution. On the other hand, if the mother expresses a positive emotion, the infant is more likely to approach the situation or the unfamiliar person with confidence. By 12 months of age, infants consistently use this mechanism to try to appraise an ambiguous situation (Rosen, Adamson, & Bakeman, 1992; de Rosnay, Cooper, Tsigaras, & Murray, 2006).

In an extension of the social referencing concept, researchers wondered whether infants could gather information by observing how adults interacted with each other in relation to an object (Repacholi & Meltzoff, 2007). In an experimental situation, infants observed while one adult (the experimenter) performed specific activities with an object and a second adult (the emoter) expressed either an angry or a neutral reaction to the first adult. For example, the angry adult might say to the experimenter who was demonstrating an activity with an object: "That's aggravating! That's so annoying," while speaking in an angry tone of voice and using angry facial expressions. Then the infants were given an opportunity to touch the object while the experimenter and the emoter sat quietly in the room. Infants who observed the angry emoter were less likely to imitate the activity, slower to touch the object, and more likely to look at the angry adult who remained in the room, even though the adult was now calm and neutral in behavior. In the angry emoter condition, the infants had fewer positive facial expressions during the time when they were allowed to explore the object. The results of this research suggest that infants can gather and retain information about how to interact with objects in their environment based on what they observe of the emotional reactions of others to these objects, even when the responses are not directed toward them.

Social referencing illustrates how members of a cultural group build a shared view of reality during infancy. Infants actively request information by looking to their mothers or other adults. They also eavesdrop on adults, watching and listening to the emotional tone of their interactions. The adult's expression, either positive or negative, cues the infant about whether to approach or withdraw.

Infants reduce their uncertainty and begin to appraise their world in the context of the emotional responses of their caregivers. You can probably imagine the wide range of objects and situations that can be evaluated through this mechanism. Foods, toys, people, animals, sounds, plants, and objects of all sorts can be discerned as positive and approachable or negative and a cause for wariness. Depending on the cultural outlook, infants in different societies will begin to categorize their experiences differently based in part on these early appraisals derived from social referencing.

The Psychosocial Crisis: Trust versus Mistrust

Objective 7. To describe the psychosocial crisis of trust versus mistrust; the central process through which the crisis is resolved, mutuality with the caregiver; the prime adaptive ego quality of hope; and the core pathology of withdrawal.

The term *psychosocial crisis* refers to a state of tension that occurs as a result of the developmental needs of the individual and the social expectations of the culture. At each stage of life, the crisis is expressed as a struggle between the positive and negative poles of a critical dimension. In infancy, the specific nature of the crisis—trust versus mistrust—focuses on the fundamental nature of an infant's sense of connection to the social world.

Trust

In adult relationships, **trust** refers to an appraisal of the availability, dependability, and sensitivity of another person (Mikulincer, 1998). Trust emerges in the course of a relationship as one person discovers those traits in another person. As the level of trust grows, the partners may take some risks by disclosing information or feelings that may lead to rejection. Relationships that endure through periods of risk grow in feelings of trust. However, trust is more than a summary of the past: It is a faith that the relationship will survive in an unpredictable future. This faith begins in infancy. A trusting relationship links confidence about the past with faith about the future.

For infants, trust is an emotion—a positive experiential state of confidence that their needs will be met and that they are valued. Trust is inferred from the infant's increasing capacity to delay gratification and from the warmth and delight that are evident in interactions with family members. The sense of trust expands from immediate figures in the social environment to the supportiveness and responsiveness of the broader social and physical world. Infants also learn to trust their sensory systems in processing stimulation from the environment. In this function, the sense of trust extends to learning to trust oneself.

The sense of basic trust is related to but not identical to Bowlby's concept of attachment. Attachment refers to the behavioral system that ensures safety and security for the infant. Over time, the internal representation of the attachment relationship generalizes to other dyadic (paired) relationships, especially where issues of intimacy and protection are relevant. Trust is a broader, more abstract construct. It not only refers to the dyadic infant-caregiver relationship but includes the orientation of the infant to the wider social network of trustable and caring others. As such, it establishes the infant's first paradigm for social integration. Moreover, infants not only establish an assessment of the central social figures in their world as trustable or untrustable, but they also achieve a sense of their own value and trustworthiness. Over time, a basic sense of trust expands to a global optimism about how one expects to be treated by others and about one's ability to cope with life's challenges. Trust is an integrating force that helps synthesize emotions, cognitions, and actions under conditions of uncertainty, allowing the person to pursue goals with a belief that things will work out well.

Given the key role of trust in forming and sustaining human social bonds, it makes sense to think that there is a biological basis for trusting in interpersonal interactions. Research has shown that in nonhuman mammals, a substance called **oxytocin** acts as a hormone associated with labor and lactation and also as a kind of neurotransmitter in brain regions associated with emotional and social behaviors (Carter, 1998). Oxytocin produces a general sense of calm relaxation. In nonhuman animals, oxytocin seems to reduce wariness or resistance to the physical proximity of other animals, thereby increasing approach behavior. Recent research is beginning to suggest a similar role for oxytocin in humans—an increased willingness to accept social risks in interpersonal situations—which is essential for cooperation.

In this research, participants made monetary exchanges in the roles of investor and trustee (Kosfield, Heinrichs, Zak, Gischbacher, & Fehr, 2005). The investor and trustee both received 12 monetary units at the start of the game. The investor had to decide how many units, if any, to transfer to the trustee. Once the transfer was made, the amount was tripled by the experimenter, and the trustee had to decide how many units, if any, to give back to the investor. The investor benefits only by giving many units to the trustee if the trustee gives a substantial number back once the investment has been tripled. But the trustee can keep all the investment and return nothing. Before the interchange began, both investors and trustees received a dose of oxytocin or a placebo through a nasal spray. Investors who received the oxytocin showed more trust in the trustee and were willing to invest more money with them than investors who received the placebo. The amount returned by the trustees did not differ for the oxytocin and placebo groups. The researchers suggest that in these types of economic exchanges, oxytocin helps overcome wariness of betrayal and increases the reward value of social interactions. It did not increase reciprocal behavior on the part of the trustees, suggesting that the action of oxytocin has more to do with overcoming the initial uncertainty created by wariness than to promoting prosocial behavior.

In real life, it is likely that when a person perceives a combination of certain interpersonal cues such as facial expressions, especially smiling and laughter, rhythmic gestures, and tone of voice in a specific context, oxytocin is released. The release of oxytocin then triggers a set of neural networks that reduces wariness and fear of others, and increases willingness to trust the other person (Damasio, 2005; Kirsch et al., 2005).

Mistrust

During infancy, experiences of **mistrust** can arise from at least three sources: infant wariness, lack of confidence in the caregiver, and doubt in one's own lovableness. First, wariness, one of the earliest infant emotions, is linked initially to at least two infant reflexes, the startle response in reaction to loud noises and the Moro reflex in response to sudden loss of support (see Table 5.2). All infants are prewired neurologically to be alert to certain environmental dangers. Infants are able to use sensory information, especially the ability to interpret facial expressions and the ability to differentiate auditory cues, to assess interpersonal anger or threat. By 6 months of age, most infants show evidence of stranger anxiety, another indication of normal capacities for wariness. Two of the caregiver's functions are to minimize the infant's exposure to stimuli that evoke these responses and to comfort and reassure the infant after exposure to threatening stimuli.

Second, babies can lack confidence in the good intentions of others. Most parents contribute to experiences of mistrust because they inevitably make some mistakes in responding to their infant's signs of distress, particularly when the baby is young. They may first try the bottle, and, if the crying continues, they may change the diaper, give water, move the baby to another room, or put the baby to bed—trying a variety of things until something works. Over time, however, sensitive caregivers learn to interpret their child's signals correctly and to respond appropriately, thereby fostering the infant's sense of trust in the environment.

Some caregivers are unable to differentiate the infant's needs or respond appropriately to them. Others are indifferent or unusually harsh. Under conditions of maltreatment, seeds of doubt may grow about the trustworthiness of the environment. Abused infants become especially sensitive to cues that suggest hostility or anger in their environment, and are more likely to fixate on those cues, even when the threat has passed (Pollak, 2008).

Infants are not only aware of threats expressed toward them, but are sensitive to expressions of anger or hostility among other members of the household. Infants are attuned to angry, negative interactions which, at some level, threaten their security. Under conditions of interpersonal conflict, infants may try to intervene by crying, or by sidling up to one of the adults; or they may try to escape by crawling away. Chronic exposure to interpersonal conflict creates a level of insecurity in the child who may feel that needs cannot be met when the adults in the family, especially attachment figures, are engaged in angry interactions with each other (Davies & Woitach, 2008).

Third, babies experience the power of their own rage. In some children, self-regulatory abilities are poorly developed,

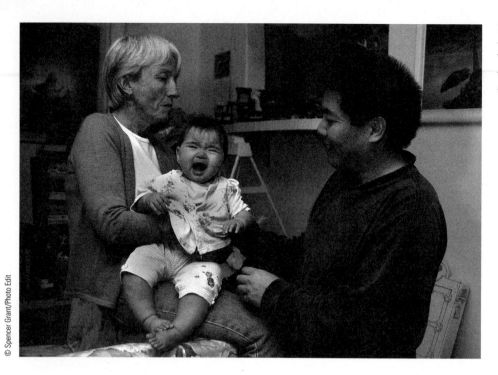

Lilly expresses her wariness as her father gives her over to the nanny. The intensity of her protest reflects the discomfort of being placed in the care of a stranger.

which leads to frequent outbursts of negativity and frustration. They can learn to doubt their own lovableness as they encounter the intensity of their own capacity for anger.

Feelings of doubt or anxiety about the bond of trust are more common than may have been expected. About one third of American infant-mother pairs who have been systematically observed show evidence of an insecure attachment. Cross-cultural research provides further evidence that a significant proportion of infants have difficulty deriving emotional comfort or security from their caregivers (van IJzendoorn & Kroonenberg, 1988; Posada et al.,1995; van IJzendoorn & Sagi, 1999).

In addition to the mistrust that emerges in the context of inconsistent, unresponsive, or harsh caregiving, there are many cases in which the mother-infant relationship is disrupted. This can happen in conditions of war, parental imprisonment, parental death due to disease or accident, or lengthy hospitalization. In all of these situations, an infant is at risk for experiencing a strong sense of mistrust.

Mistrust may manifest itself in the infant by withdrawal from interaction and by symptoms of depression and grief, which include sobbing, lack of emotion, lethargy, and loss of appetite (Field et al., 1988). It may also be revealed later on in development in the expressions of interpersonal distress observed in the angry, anxious, and resistant behaviors of children with insecure attachments or in the inability to form close, satisfying relationships with others as adolescents and adults. Mistrust may provide a foundation for the emergence of a negative scheme about the self—a scheme that is elaborated over time by defining the self with a cluster of closely related, negative attributes such as cautiousness, nervousness, or introversion (Malle & Horowitz, 1995).

All infants experience some aspects of mistrust, either as a result of mismatches between their needs and the caregiving strategies they receive or as a product of their own difficulties in modulating strong feelings of wariness or anger. Thus, the resolution of the crisis in the direction of trust reflects a real psychological achievement, in which infants are able to minimize their wariness of the environment and to regulate their own inner passions.

Over the life span, the sense of trust is transformed and matures into a framework for the understanding of life. Among older adults who have a strong sense of trust, many of life's disappointments and complexities are minimized by a growing religious faith. Their basic sense of trust evolves into a powerful belief in a great source of goodness and love in the universe, a force that can transcend the pain of daily tragedies and give integrity and meaning to their dying as well as to their living (Erikson et al., 1986).

The Central Process for Resolving the Crisis: Mutuality with the Caregiver

To resolve the crisis of trust versus mistrust, an infant must establish a feeling of **mutuality with a caregiver**. Mutuality is a characteristic of a relationship. Initially it is built on the consistency with which the caregiver responds appropriately to the infant's needs. The caregiver comes to appreciate the variety of an infant's needs, and the infant learns to expect that personal needs will be met. Within families, the establishment of mutuality differs with each child, depending on infant characteristics and parental responses (Deater-Deckard & O'Connor, 2000).

© Spencer Grant/Photo Edit

An infant influences the responses of a caregiver in many ways. Infants' irritability and soothability contribute to the kinds of responses that adults make. Infants can reject or end an interaction by fussing, becoming tense, crying, or falling asleep. They can maintain an interaction by smiling, cooing, snuggling comfortably, or maintaining eye contact. Techniques of comforting do not call forth the same responses from all babies. A pacifier helps comfort some babies, whereas others respond to being wrapped snugly in a warm blanket.

An infant and a caregiver learn to regulate the amount of time that passes between the expression of a need and its satisfaction. Bell and Ainsworth (1972) observed mothers' responses to infant crying during the first year of life. Over the course of the year, the infants' crying decreased, and the mothers tended to respond more quickly to their cries. This finding suggests a process of mutual adaptation by mothers and infants. Some mothers came quickly and ignored few cries. Other mothers waited a long time and ignored much of the crying. The longer mothers delayed in responding to their infants' cries, the more crying the infants did in later months. Babies whose mothers responded promptly in the first 6 months of life cried less often in the second 6 months.

Coordination, Mismatch, and Repair of Interactions

The study of mutuality with the caregiver has focused in some detail on patterns and rhythms of social interaction, especially coordination between the infant and trusted adults (Tronick, 2003). **Coordination** refers to two related characteristics of interaction: matching and synchrony. **Matching** means that the infant and the caregiver are involved in similar behaviors or states at the same time. They may be playing together with an object, cooing and smiling at each other, or fussing and angry at each other. **Synchrony** means that the infant and caregiver move fluidly from one state to the next. When infants are paying attention to their caregivers, the caregivers attempt to stimulate them. As babies withdraw attention, the caregivers learn to reduce stimulation and wait until the infants are ready to engage again. Normally, mother-infant interactions become increasingly coordinated (Tronick & Cohn, 1989; Isabella & Belsky, 1991). This does not mean that most of the interactions are coordinated. In fact, especially when babies are very young, matched interactions appear to become mismatched rather quickly.

A mother and infant may be engaged in a period of cooing and laughing. The mother makes a funny noise, the baby reacts by cooing and laughing, then the mother makes the noise again and the baby laughs. On the third try, the mother cannot get the baby to make eye contact. She may try shifting the baby to another position or making the noise at a different pitch, but the baby looks away and squirms. The game is over; the connection is temporarily broken.

Why is mother-infant communication so frequently disrupted? The explanation may lie partly in the infant's inability to sustain coordinated attention with the caregiver, partly in a rapid shift of need states, and partly in the inability of adults to sustain long periods of nonverbal communication. In normal mother-infant pairs, however, periods of **mismatch** are usually followed by **communication repairs**, so that infants and mothers cycle again through points of coordination in their interactions.

The coordination that occurs in the mother-infant interaction becomes a prototype for the positive feelings of connection that people enjoy in social relationships. Long before infants can use language to convey their feelings or needs, they can experience the satisfaction of social connection through these cycles of communication. They do not rely on spoken language, but on the many emotional cues that arise from rhythmic patterns of breathing, facial expressions, tone of voice, touch, and eye gaze. As mother and baby move into renewed moments of coordination, their sense of pleasure increases, leaving a memory of such moments to guide future conversations (Goleman, 2006).

At a biological level, what appears to occur through experiences of coordination, mismatch, and repair is the establishment of a neurochemical pattern: Networks of synapses are established; oxytocin is released; pleasurable feelings ensue; and the amygdala is impacted, resulting in reduced arousal and a greater sense of calm. Toward the end of infancy, as a product of experiences of receiving sustained, sensitive caregiving, the infant's complex neurological social capacity for trust is strengthened. Even though the brain is prewired to recognize and respond to certain types of social stimulation, the nature of actual caregiving experiences establish more or less likely patterns of social engagement. Infants who experience disrupted, harsh, or neglectful care do not develop the same underlying neurochemical structures for patterns of social behavior. As they grow older, these children may experience a wide range of problems in social behavior, emotional development, and even cognitive development, especially in areas of language and communication competence.

At a theoretical level, the process of coordination, mismatch, and repair can be viewed as a building block for mutuality. Infants and caregivers gain confidence in their ability to communicate. Infants have many opportunities to experience the satisfaction of shared communication and the sense of being embedded in a responsive social environment. They also experience frequent recovery from a mismatched state to a state of effective communication, so that they can be hopeful about the ability to make these repairs in the future.

Establishing a Functional Rhythm in the Family

The match or mismatch between an infant's rhythms and the family's rhythms is an important factor in the overall adjustment of a family to a new baby. Some babies are quite predictable; the timing of their sleeping, eating, playtime, and even fussy periods follows a clear pattern. Other babies are much less regular. All babies are changing rapidly during the first 24 months of life, so daily patterns are bound to change, and families must make frequent adjustments in order to continue to meet the infant's needs.

In American culture, by the end of the first year of life, babies are typically expected to modify their schedule of needs so that they sleep when the rest of the family sleeps, play when the rest of the family is awake, and eat three or at most four times a day, generally when the other family members eat. During the second year of life, the demands of parenting change. Babies become more mobile and have new capacities to initiate activities. Their attention span increases, they have new requirements for stimulation, and they have new areas of wariness and resistance—things they don't want to do (like take a nap) or people they don't want to be with (like a certain babysitter). These and other changes require adaptation on the part of parents in order to sustain the mutuality that had been achieved or to rectify problems in attachment and trust that may now be evident (Heinicke & Guthrie, 1992). The stable features in mutual relationships are the caregiver's effort to be responsive to the child's changing capacities and needs, and the child's ongoing monitoring of and responsiveness to the caregiver's cues (Masur & Turner, 2001; Robinson & Acevedo, 2001).

Parents with Psychological Problems

The importance of reciprocal interactions in building trust and hope during infancy is highlighted by studies of parents with psychological problems. Sensitivity to an infant's emotional states, the ability to respond appropriately to an infant's needs, and the quality of common, daily interactions can all be impaired by family risk factors. Studies of parents who are experiencing marital discord, who have been victims of child abuse or neglect, who are depressed, or who are mentally ill suggest that the interactional cycles of these parents and their children lack synchrony (Rutter, 1990). For example, in a comparison of mothers who had been maltreated as children and those who had not, the maltreated mothers were less involved with their children during play, made use of fewer strategies to direct their children's activities, and used a more negative tone with their children (Alessandri, 1992).

Other research has compared interactions between depressed and nondepressed mothers and their infants. The depressed mothers were found to be unresponsive, emotionally unavailable, and unable to sustain smooth communication with their babies. Depressed mothers were less likely to show animated, positive facial expressions. Typical efforts at fostering an infant's emotional regulation, commonly observed in nondepressed mothers—such as introducing stimulating toys and games, touching and talking, and the efforts at reducing arousal through appropriate soothing and comforting—were not common in depressed mothers. For their part, the infants of depressed mothers

had few expressions of interest, showed more sad and angry expressions, showed less ability to match a happy face with a happy vocal expression, and were less able to regulate their emotions. Interactions between the mothers and their infants appeared to be stressful and mutually unsatisfying (Field, 2002).

The Prime Adaptive Ego Quality and the Core Pathology
Hope

Erikson (1982) theorized that the positive resolution of the psychosocial crisis of trust versus mistrust leads to the adaptive ego quality of **hope**. As you will recall from Chapter 3, the prime adaptive ego qualities shape a person's outlook on life in the direction of greater openness to experience and information, greater capacity to identify a variety of pathways to achieve one's goals, more willingness to assert the self and to express one's wishes and views, and a positive approach to the formation of close relationships. Even in the face of difficulties and stressful life events, these qualities contribute to higher levels of functioning and well-being (Peterson & Seligman, 2003).

As the first of the prime adaptive ego qualities, hope pervades the entire life story. It is a global cognitive orientation that one's goals and dreams can be attained and that events will turn out for the best. As Erikson described it, "Hope bestows on the anticipated future a sense of leeway inviting expectant leaps, either in preparatory imagination or in small initiating actions. And such daring must count on basic trust in the sense of a trustfulness that must be, literally and figuratively, nourished by maternal care and—when endangered by all-too-desperate discomfort—must be restored by competent consolation" (1982, p. 60).

Hopefulness combines the ability to think of one or more paths to achieve a goal with a belief in one's ability to move along that pathway toward the goal (Snyder, Cheavens, & Sympson, 1997). The roots of hopefulness lie in the infant's understanding of the self as a causal agent. Each time a baby takes an action to achieve an outcome, the sense of hope grows. When babies encounter obstacles or barriers to their goals, sensitive caregivers find ways to remove the obstacles or lead them along a new path toward the goal. The infant's sense of the self as a causal agent combined with the caregiver's sensitivity create the context for the emergence of hope.

Research with adults shows that people who have a hopeful, optimistic outlook about the future have different achievement beliefs and emotional reactions in response to actual achievement than do people who have a pessimistic outlook (Norem & Cantor, 1988; Dweck, 1992). People who have higher levels of hopefulness undertake a larger number of goals across life areas and select tasks that are more difficult. Hopefulness is generally associated with higher goals, higher levels of confidence that the goal will be reached, and greater persistence in the face of barriers to goal attainment, thus leading to higher overall levels of performance (Snyder, 2002). Hopefulness is essential for behavior change in that it combines a desire to achieve new goals and a belief that one will be able to find successful paths toward those goals. Feelings of hope help people deal with their most difficult challenges, including serious illness, injury, bereavement, and facing the end of life (Sullivan, 2003).

Within the psychosocial framework, hope provides the platform from which very young children take certain leaps of faith. When an infant overcomes doubts and hesitancy in taking a first independent step, you see the dividend of hope. When a toddler clambers over the bars of her crib and lets herself drop several inches to the floor, you see the dividend of hope. As a parent, when you give your adolescent the keys to the car, you see the dividend of hope. Without hope, neither the individual nor the society could bear the weight of uncertainty in our changing world. With hope, individuals can envision a better society and come together in actions to reach the collective good (Braithwaite, 2004).

Withdrawal

As a core pathology, **withdrawal** refers to a general orientation of wariness toward people and objects. This is especially disturbing because, during infancy, healthy development is a pattern of outward motion, extension, and increasing engagement with the social and physical worlds. Infants typically reach and grasp, crawl, stand, and walk. They explore through gazing, mouthing, and manipulating objects. Their behavior is typically characterized by interest in novelty, joy in learning, and frustration at encountering barriers to goal achievement. Over the first year, babies become increasingly connected to significant figures in their social world, following them about, devising strategies to engage them in interaction, and looking to them for consolation when they are distressed.

Infants who are characterized by withdrawal may show evidence of passivity, lethargy, and neutral or negative affect. They are not readily engaged in social interaction and do not show the signs of self-directed exploration that are typical of most healthy infants. Withdrawal may have some of its roots in genetically determined temperamental characteristics. Some babies have a very low threshold for pain. They are highly sensitive to sensory stimulation and recoil from the kinds of handling that other babies find comforting or pleasurable. Some babies are more passive than others, requiring little in the way of stimulation and showing less evidence of exploratory behavior than active babies.

One of the earliest descriptions of withdrawal in infancy was provided by Rene Spitz's (1945, 1946) analysis of children who had been institutionalized before 1 year of age. The babies who suffered the most had been placed in a foundling home in which eight babies were cared for by one nurse. These babies went through a phase of initial rage, followed by a period of physical and emotional withdrawal. They lay passively in their cribs, showing limited motor exploration and little emotionality. Furthermore, they rarely smiled or showed excitement. The babies' babbling and language were extremely delayed. They deteriorated physically. Their measured developmental level dropped substantially over a year's time. These babies suffered from a combination of a loss of their attachment figure, a lack of meaningful social interaction, and an absence of appropriate sensory stimulation—all of which produced what Spitz called *anaclitic depression*.

Not all instances of withdrawal are as severe as the anaclitic depression syndrome. However, a growing literature focuses on the links between disrupted mother-infant interaction and subsequent social withdrawal (Gerhold et al., 2002). Temperamental factors including behavioral inhibition and a low threshold for sensory stimulation, an anxious-avoidant attachment, and a lack of contingent, responsive caregiving can combine to produce mistrust and the formation of the core

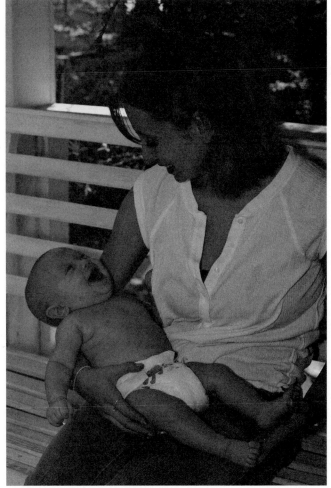

© Leroy Dickson/Alamy

As a result of mutual responsiveness in playful interactions, babies experience joy and a sense of trust. The mother's ability to love expands as she finds ways to respond to her infant and evoke these wonderful feelings of happiness.

HUMAN DEVELOPMENT AND DIVERSITY

Sensitive Care in Two Cultures

SOCIALIZATION TOWARD CULTURALLY valued goals is a primary focus of parenting. This socialization process begins in infancy and is expressed through the beliefs parents have about what children should be able to do and what they should know or understand in the period of infancy. These beliefs are translated into caregiving strategies (Lamm & Keller, 2007). A primary assumption of attachment theory is that the quality of early care, and especially sensitive caregiving, promotes attachment security, an assumption that has been supported in a large number of studies (De Wolff & van IJzendoorn, 1997). However, the behavioral components of sensitive caregiving and how it might be expressed in various cultures has not been explored in great detail. A study by German Posada and colleagues (2002), which contrasted maternal care in two middle-class samples, one in Denver, Colorado, and the other in Bogota, Colombia, was designed to clarify this topic.

Although men's and women's roles are changing in Latin America, especially among the urban middle class, the Colombian culture is considered more collectivistic and interdependent than the U.S. culture, which is viewed as more individualistic and independent. Two questions guided the research: (1) Are the features outlined in the attachment literature that define sensitive care descriptive of care in both cultures?; and (2) Are there features of care that might be unique to the specific cultures that are related to attachment security?

The researchers used an ethnographic methodology to formulate categories of maternal behaviors. Two researchers observed mother-infant pairs at home for two 2-hour visits. Following the visits, the observers used a Q-sort technique to describe the mothers' behaviors. This technique involved sorting 90 cards that describe maternal behavior into three piles: characteristic, neither characteristic nor uncharacteristic, and

uncharacteristic. Each of the three piles is then further sorted into categories rated from 1 (most uncharacteristic) to 9 (most characteristic).

From this rating process, eight categories of care were identified. Four of these categories were very similar to features of sensitive care outlined in the basic attachment research: (1) sensitive responding to infant signals and communication; (2) accessibility, which reflects a mother's ability to consider the baby's needs despite other competing demands; (3) acceptance of the infant, which is reflected in the mother's positive emotional tone when interacting with the baby; and (4) interference, a mother's intrusive or noncoordinated interactions with the baby. Two categories were observed that had not been captured in the literature as related to sensitive care: Active-animated interactions with the baby and creating an interesting environment for the baby. One category was observed in each cultural group that

pathology of withdrawal. Social withdrawal can become such a severe social deficit that it interferes with adaptive functioning and requires clinical treatment (Calkins & Fox, 2002).

APPLIED TOPIC

The Role of Parents

Objective 8. To evaluate the critical role of parents and caregivers during infancy, with special attention to issues of safety and nutrition; optimizing cognitive, social, and emotional development; and the role of parents and caregivers as advocates for their infants with other agencies and systems.

Parents have an enormous responsibility for their children's physical and psychosocial growth. In this chapter, we have portrayed infants as active, adaptive, and eager to master the environment. At the same time, the immaturity of human infants at birth necessitates a long period of dependence on adults. The

few instinctive behaviors of human infants in comparison with the infants of other species are compensated for by their enormous capacity to learn. For this potential to be realized, infants must rely on their parents to maintain their health, provide stimulation, and protect them from danger. During the period of dependence, infants become entwined in complex social systems and develop strong emotional bonds with their caregivers. The quality of these early relationships provides infants with mental representations that guide their later development of friendships, intimacy, and relationships with their own children.

Infancy, just like pregnancy and childbirth, is culturally constructed. The content of experience and the way the period of infancy is viewed depend on cultural traditions, beliefs, and technologies. Some of the ways that culture defines infancy include the infant's sleeping arrangements, the choice of clothing, the choice of the infant's name and the naming process, the selection of foods, and access to nursing from mothers and other lactating women (Valsiner, 2000). Parents transmit the culture through their care, and by enacting certain rituals and practices, they introduce and integrate their infant into the cultural community. The box, "Sensitive Care in Two Cultures," provides a contrast between features of sensitive care for U.S. mothers and

was unique to that culture: For the U.S. mothers it was close-intimate interactions involving cuddling, and close affectionate touching; for the Colombian mothers it was concern with the baby's physical appearance, including concern that the baby was getting messy during feeding and that the baby was messy or soiled during play.

Mothers from the United States and Colombia were very similar in their scores on sensitive responding, accessibility, and acceptance, and all these dimensions were predictive of infants' secure attachments. Mothers from Colombia were less interfering and more animated in their interactions than the U.S. mothers. Mothers from the United States scored higher on creating an interesting environment for the baby. Of these three dimensions, interfering was negatively related to secure attachments for the U.S. sample, but not for the Colombian sample, and animated was positively related to secure attachment for the

Colombian sample but not for the U.S. sample.

The results of this study highlight several points about the role of parents during infancy. First, certain features of parenting appear to have beneficial consequences for infants in both cultures, and, when combined with results from many other studies, these features are becoming accepted as universally supportive of the attachment process—attuned response to the infant's signals, accessibility in the face of competing demands, and acceptance or the positive emotional tone of mother-infant interactions. Second, some features of parenting are observed across cultures but not always related to attachment security in every culture. Third, some features of parenting may be culturally or contextually specific and, while important for early socialization, may not be specifically relevant for the formation of a secure attachment.

Critical Thinking Questions

1. Based on this study, what are the basic features that are essential for sensitive caregiving across cultures? Do you have any experiences with cultures where these features would not be seen as essential for sensitive caregiving?

2. How do the differences in caregiving between the U.S. and Colombian samples fit with characterizations of these cultures as more individualistic or collectivistic? Are there results of the study that do not exactly fit with these characterizations?

3. Assuming that the research has captured features of caregiving that are generally distinct between the U.S. and Colombian cultures, what implications do these differences have for infant socialization and subsequent socialization in the two cultures?

4. What is your evaluation of the Q-sort methodology for assessing features of the caregiving environment? What are the weaknesses and strengths of this approach? What other methods might be used?

Colombian mothers. Five aspects of the parental role are considered aspects of promoting optimal development in infancy: ensuring safety in the physical environment, fostering socioemotional and cognitive development, coordinating the roles of father and mother, **parents as advocates** with other societal systems, and parents as links to other sources of social support.

Safety and Nutrition

Safety

One of the central responsibilities that parents face is to ensure infants' survival by protecting them from environmental dangers. The ecology of home and neighborhood, including the society's degree of modernization, influences the kinds of dangers to which infants are exposed and the kinds of practices that families and cultures invent to protect their offspring. In addition to physical risks, some dangers are linked to superstitions, religious beliefs, and matters of the spirit world. In many parts of the world, parents take special precautions to prevent their infants from coming under the influence of an evil eye. The eye gaze may be viewed as a vehicle through which a person may deliberately or

inadvertently transmit harmful feelings of jealousy, revenge, or unbridled pride (Galt, 1991). The presence of dangers or risks in the environment usually elicits some effort to restrict a child's movement through swaddling, carrying the baby in a sling, or placing the baby in a playpen. Because of concern about dangers, caregivers also invoke certain prohibitions, such as telling the child, "No, don't touch that," or pulling the child away from something dangerous. As infants become more mobile in the second half of their first year, the need to introduce prohibitions and to monitor exploratory activities increases. Depending on the cultural values concerning independent exploration, caregivers may heighten their restrictions and prohibitions or may try to modify the environment to permit safe, unrestricted exploration.

Certain childrearing practices arise from a desire to protect young children from known dangers. For example, Robert LeVine (1977) described the practice of many African cultures of carrying infants 18 months and older on the back, even though they were able to walk around. This practice was used to prevent toddlers from getting burned on the open cooking fires at an age when they were mobile enough to walk or stumble into the fire and yet not old enough to know how to inhibit their movements. Other hazards in the neighborhood, such as falling off steep cliffs or into lakes, rivers, or wells, prompted this same carrying behavior.

In industrialized countries, infants face different types of hazards, such as electrical outlets, steep stairs, and open containers of insecticides, cleaning agents, and other poisons. Many American families protect babies from these dangers by putting gates at a doorway or at the top of a stairway, or by placing an infant in a crib or playpen to restrict exploration. In other homes, the strategy is to baby proof the home by removing as many known dangers as possible so that the baby has maximum freedom for exploration. These two different strategies reflect two different values concerning childrearing—both with the same goal of providing maximum safety and protection from danger. In the former case, parents try to preserve their adult environment. Children must modify their behavior in order to fit into the home. In the latter case, parents modify the environment to accommodate the baby's developmental needs. For more information about child safety, you may want to visit the website of the U.S. Consumer Product Safety Commission, www.cpsc.gov, which publishes reports on recalls as well as guidelines for child safety and toy safety.

Nutrition

In addition to protecting children from dangers and preventing injuries, parents are responsible for providing an age-appropriate diet that supports the infant's changing nutritional needs. In the first 4 to 6 months of life, breast milk or formula is sufficient to provide the baby's nutritional needs. Newborns may nurse every 2 to 4 hours; by 4 months of age, babies may nurse 4 to 6 times in 24 hours.

If the baby is breastfeeding, mothers have to be careful about how their own diet and medications might affect their breast milk. If they are using formula, they have to be careful about the water quality that is used. In some areas of the world, poor water quality makes the use of powdered formula a serious health risk for infants.

In making the transition to solid foods, sometime around 4 to 6 months, there are both safety and dietary concerns. Babies need to be strong enough to hold their heads up, and to sit with some support so they do not choke on solid foods. Typically, parents are instructed to introduce some type of iron-fortified rice cereal mixed with breast milk or formula as the first solid food. New foods are introduced one at a time, giving the baby a few days to become accustomed to the new taste, watching for signs that the baby is able to digest the new food, and also ensuring that the baby is not allergic to the food. Most resources on pediatric nutrition advise against giving infants honey, which can cause botulism.

The American Academy of Pediatrics recommends continuing with breast milk or formula for the first 12 months. After 12 months, most babies can drink cow's milk, and eat cheese, cottage cheese, and yogurt, which are good sources of protein, calcium, and vitamins.

Safety concerns related to food include: avoiding foods that are likely to cause choking like nuts, raisins, or large pieces of meat; avoiding giving bottles with milk, juice, or sweetened beverages at bedtime which can cause tooth decay; and putting food from a jar into a small dish or bowl rather than feeding the baby from the jar in order to prevent bacteria from the baby's saliva from contaminating unused portions of the food (Kliegman, Behrman, Jenson, & Stanton, 2007).

Infancy is culturally constructed. Cora rises early each morning, ties her infant to her back, and walks to the market to sell flowers. She expects her baby to be calm and quiet while she earns her living.

© Oliver Benn/Getty Images

Many first-time parents are unsure about how to provide adequate, safe nutrition for their babies. This is a source of some anxiety since it is an area in which the infant so obviously depends on caring adults for health, safety, and survival. Many excellent resources are available to inform parents about infant nutrition, including online resources such as the Mayo Clinic, and the MedLine Plus of the National Institutes of Health. The WIC (Women, Infants, and Children) program provides federal grants to states to make supplemental foods, health care referrals, and nutrition education available for low-income pregnant, breastfeeding, and nonbreastfeeding postpartum women, and to infants and children up to age 5 who are found to be at nutritional risk (USDA, 2010).

Fostering Socioemotional and Cognitive Development

Another component of the parents' role during infancy is their ability to promote socioemotional and cognitive development. Much of the behavior that appears to be important in the development of strong emotional bonds between infants and parents is also central to fostering intellectual growth. Three features of parenting quality have been found to support optimal development, including children's language, literacy, cognition, autonomy, self-efficacy, and school readiness. They are: parenting sensitivity, cognitive stimulation, and warmth (Lugo-Gil & Tamis-LeMonda, 2008). Parenting sensitivity refers to the way parents respond to their infant's distress, emotional expressions, interests, and abilities, effectively balancing the infant's needs for comfort and reassurance with the infant's needs for autonomy and self-control. Cognitive stimulation refers to parents' efforts to teach their child, to enrich the child's language and cognitive development, and to provide an interesting, age-appropriate environment. Warmth refers to the parents' expressions of affection, admiration, and respect for their child.

Parents foster both emotional and intellectual growth by structuring the stimulus environment to suit the infant's developmental level (Bornstein, 2002). Parents need to recognize the infant's perspective in providing toys, sounds, and visual stimulation. Part of the parents' function is to initiate interactions and not just respond to their infants' demands for attention. Parents need to create what they perceive to be a suitable environment—one that allows a variety of experiences, a reasonable amount of challenge, and adequate opportunities to experience success. Furthermore, parents should be attuned to their infant's developing skills and alter the environment appropriately. As their children mature, parents must provide more complex stimuli, more opportunities for autonomy, and more encouragement for tolerating frustration. By providing experiences that are attuned to the infant's level of cognitive functioning, parents are also supporting emotional satisfaction, confidence, and joy.

Parents use a variety of methods to help their infants regulate their emotions. Through physical and verbal play, they increase the baby's arousal and orient the baby toward objects in the environment. Through soothing and comforting, they help their infants regain a calm state after distress. As babies mature, parents increase their use of language to guide behavior and provide new problem-solving strategies. Infants are constantly watching their parents, observing the parents' emotional reactions as well as their novel behaviors. As a negative example, infants of depressed mothers become passive and inhibited in their reactions to the environment as they observe their mothers' passive or angry depressive symptoms.

Over the past 20 years, the growing interest in infant brain development has stimulated a burgeoning market to sell what is advertised as intellectually stimulating and developmentally appropriate toys for infants and toddlers. The idea that there might be a sensitive period for cognitive development during the first 3 years of life resulted in the production of special lines of toys, resources, and programming purported to promote infant intelligence. U.S. parents of infants have made enormous expenditures for special toys, music, videos, and infant stimulation programs. Research on the continuing plasticity of brain development, the subsequent pruning of synapses, and the biochemistry of brain functions suggests that brain development is fluid and continuous well into adulthood. Although early deprivation, exposure to toxins, disease or malnutrition, and harsh or neglectful parenting can have long-term disruptive consequences for cognitive development, a preoccupation with the need to provide very specifically designed resources to promote infant stimulation in the period from birth to 3 in order to ensure optimal cognitive growth is probably overdone. In their desire to support optimal development, parents need to be wary of fads and hypes that make it seem as if some specific form of stimulation is essential for their baby's growth. In fact, parents and other sensitive caregivers are the most valuable sensory and emotional assets a baby can have. Rhythmic interactions, positive tone, comfort and soothing care under conditions of distress, and playful, relaxed interactions that allow babies to initiate as well as to follow are among the most valuable forms of stimulation for promoting social, emotional, and cognitive growth in infancy.

Fathers' and Mothers' Parental Behaviors

Do fathers and mothers differ in how they enact the parent role with infants? As we noted earlier, babies form strong attachments to their fathers as well as to their mothers. Fathers may be just as involved in and sensitive to their babies' needs as mothers. However, the daily interactions between mothers and their babies and those between fathers and their babies are distinct. In a study of more than 1,500 children in U.S. two-parent families, children spent an average of 1.4 hours on weekdays with their fathers, and 3.3 hours on weekends. Mothers were the primary caregivers of infants and young children during the week, but fathers took on a more equal role on the weekends (Yeung, Sandberg, Davis-Kean, & Hofferth, 2001). A greater proportion of the time that mothers spend with their babies is devoted to caregiving. Fathers, who spend less time overall with their babies, tend to focus more on play—especially physical play. They use their strength and physical activity as a resource as they interact with their babies. When mothers play with their babies, the play tends to be with words or with toys, as opposed to rough-and-tumble activity (Laflamme et al., 2002).

Cameron, a stay-at-home father of two daughters (an infant and a two-year-old), speaks about how he thinks fathers are different from mothers: "I find I am very playful with the girls. I become the play structure you know. I will have them sitting on me. We'll sing 'the people on the bus' and *I'm the bus!* I'm the slide. I don't think I've ever really seen my wife do that. I will do it for hours at a time throughout the day. They are climbing all over me all day long" (Doucet, 2009, pp. 86–87).

Mothers more frequently respond to their babies, express affection, and follow up on behavior their babies initiate. They are also likely to be more accepting of their child's behavior and to emphasize and value emotional expressiveness. Fathers are more likely to disregard babies' cues and to direct their attention to new targets. They are more likely to emphasize control and discipline (Rosen & Rothbaum, 1993). At home, fathers are likely to continue their leisure activity, such as reading or watching television, in the presence of their babies, whereas mothers are likely to interact with their babies.

The quality of interaction between fathers and infants depends heavily on the context. When mothers are present, for example, fathers interact less with their babies. When fathers are alone with their babies, they are more engaged and sensitive play companions. When fathers are not overly stressed at work, have strong positive identification with their own fathers, and are in satisfying, harmonious marriages, they achieve greater levels of intersubjectivity with their babies. Fathers of male infants tend to interact more with them than fathers of female infants (Goldberg et al., 2002). Fathers become more effective parents the more they understand the complexity and sophistication of infant competencies.

Parents as Advocates

In addition to providing care themselves, more and more parents are responsible for arranging supplemental care for their infants. As a result, parents become **advocates** for their child. Parents must review the childcare services available to them and select a setting that will meet their infant's needs and accommodate their work requirements and economic resources. Family day care, in-home babysitting, and center-based care are three common alternatives.

To function as advocates for their children, parents may have to engage in an unfamiliar kind of thinking. They

The more involved a father is in his infant's care, the more accurate he is in reading the baby's signals.

may even feel unqualified to make the kinds of judgments required. For example, parents must evaluate the competence and motivation of the adults who will care for their child. They must estimate how successful these caregivers will be in meeting their child's needs for security and stimulation. And they must consider the degree to which alternative caregivers reflect their own parental values, beliefs, and strategies.

Even when pressures to continue a caregiving arrangement are very strong, parents must be able to assess its impact on their children. They must try to judge whether their children are in the kind of responsive, stimulating environment that will enhance their development. In the best situations, alternative care settings actually complement a parent-infant relationship. In the worst settings, infants may be neglected and abused. It is essential for parents to maintain communication with the alternative caregivers, to assess the quality of the care, and to intervene promptly when necessary to ensure their infant's well-being.

Another situation in which parents serve as advocates for their infants occurs when the children have some form of chronic illness, developmental delay, or special physical needs. These children may require coordinated health care, therapeutic interventions, mental health services, and educational supports. Most states have early intervention programs to support parents and help them understand the nature, prognosis, and treatment of the infant's condition. Early intervention case managers help build a bridge between parents and physicians or other health professionals. They also assist in the identification of appropriate community resources. However, the parents are ultimately responsible for making sure that the services match the child's changing needs.

The Importance of Social Support

The infant's physical, cognitive, social, and emotional development are fostered through the loving care of mothers, fathers, other family members, and community caregivers who are able to create supportive relationships with one another and with the infant. Infant mental health and optimal development are intimately entwined with the mental health of caregivers (Weatherston, 2001). A variety of contextual factors play a part in parents' ability to promote their child's optimal development. Adults who had difficult experiences with their own caregivers may come to the parental role with special challenges. They may not have experienced the comfort, responsiveness, or appropriate stimulation that are essential for effective parenting. Some factors, however, help to make up for these deficits. The quality of one's intimate relationship with a loving partner is important in sustaining positive parent-child relationships. Couples who experience mutuality and trust in their own relationship are better able to create a predictable, supportive, and caring family environment for their children (Crockenberg, Leerkes, & Lekka, 2007).

Sources of **social support** beyond the intimate partner may also enhance one's effectiveness as a parent. This support may come from the child's grandparents and other family members, friends, and health care and mental health professionals (Bornstein & Tamis-LeMonda, 2001).

The effective use of a social support network ensures that adults will not be isolated as parents, and that others will be available to help the parents identify and interpret childrearing problems. Often, the help is very direct—for example, child care or sharing of clothes, playthings, and furniture. Support may also take the form of companionship and validation of the importance of the parental role. However, evidence suggests that social support cannot fully compensate for the lack of partner support or for the stresses on parenting caused by economic pressures that prevent parents from meeting basic life needs (Simons et al., 1993).

In reviewing this chapter, you can begin to appreciate the demanding nature of the parents' role in promoting optimal development during their baby's infancy. The elements of effective parenting that we have identified or implied are listed in Table 5.9. As a parent, one must rely heavily on one's own psychological well-being and on the encouragement of one's spouse, caring friends, and family to sustain the ego strengths and emotional resources necessary to the task.

The way parents conceive of their role has a major influence on the direction and rate of their infants' development. Parenting also allows adults opportunities for creative problem solving, empathy, physical closeness, and self-insight. Enacting the parent role makes considerable physical, cognitive, and emotional demands, but attachment to a child also promotes the parent's own psychosocial development. These contributions to adult development are described further in Chapters 11 (Early Adulthood) and 12 (Middle Adulthood).

TABLE 5.9 OPTIMIZING AN INFANT'S DEVELOPMENT

Spend time with the child; be available when the child needs you.

Provide warmth and affection; express positive feelings toward the baby in many ways—verbally, through touching and hugging, and through playful interactions.

Communicate often, directly with the child; engage the child in verbal interaction. Provide stimulation.

Encourage the child's active engagement in and exploration of the environment. Help the child understand that he or she causes things to happen.

Help the child engage in directed problem solving. Encourage the child to persist in efforts to reach a goal.

Keep things predictable, especially when the infant is very young.

Guide language development by using words to name, sort, and categorize objects and events. Accept the child's efforts to achieve closeness.

Be sensitive to the child's state; learn to interpret the child's signals accurately; time your responses appropriately.

Find effective ways to soothe and comfort the child in times of distress.

Help the child interpret sources of distress and find ways to regulate distress. Minimize the child's exposure to intensely negative, hostile, and frightening events.

Be aware of the visual and auditory cues you send when you interact with the child. Pay attention to how the child is changing over time.

Monitor the child's emotional expressions to evaluate the success of specific actions and interventions.

Chapter Summary

Although the genetic plan plays a major role in guiding physical and sensory/perceptual maturation during infancy, there is considerable evidence for plasticity in neurological development as an infant's sensorimotor system interacts with the social and physical environment. During infancy, a child rapidly develops sensory and motor skills, social relationships, and emotional and conceptual skills. Babies are born with the capacity to perceive their environment and to evoke responses from their caregivers. They are ready to respond to a wide array of caregiving conditions. Caregivers convey cultural beliefs and values through their childrearing practices, thereby shaping the infant's experiences along particular cultural pathways. The result is a blend of many universal features of infancy, such as the reflexes, sequences of motor development, attachment process, sensorimotor reasoning, and experiences infants have in their culture of care. Some of these experiences are a result of socialization goals, such as sleeping arrangements or types of food that are given to the infant. Some of the experiences are a result of the language, communication patterns, and social interactions that accompany care. Others of these experiences are a result of individual differences in the caregivers' sensitivity and ability to meet infants' needs.

Objective 1. To describe characteristics of newborns and the challenges facing low-birth-weight babies.

Babies differ in their physical maturity and appearance at birth. Differences in physical maturity have distinct consequences for the capacity to regulate survival functions such as breathing, digesting, waking, and sleeping. The Apgar scoring method is used to evaluate the newborn's need for immediate intervention. Infants who weigh less than 2,500 grams (about 5 pounds, 8 ounces) are called low-birth-weight babies. Babies who are small for their gestational age (SGA) are at greater risk for health problems than those who are born prematurely but are of average weight for their gestational age. Babies born before 30 weeks do not have the benefit of positive features of the uterine environment that support the maturation of various aspects of self-regulatory functions.

Objective 2. To identify important milestones in the maturation of the sensory and motor systems, and to describe the interactions among these systems during the first 2 years of life.

It makes sense to think of infants as newly developing systems that require continuous support for ongoing growth and refinement. The synapses in their brains become more elaborated in the context of engagement in a stimulating and responsive environment. As regions of the brain become more organized, they influence each other, leading to new cognitive capacities and abilities for goal-oriented behavior and self-regulation. The infant brain, including capacities for social connection, sensory processing, motor behavior, and emotional regulation and expression, is emerging in an ongoing, fluid process of exchange of information with its social and physical environments. What begins as an explosion of possible meanings and connections gradually becomes sculpted into certain patterns and preferred responses, but with a continuous potential for new interconnections into childhood and beyond.

During the first months of life, the sensory/perceptual system—vision, hearing, taste, smell, touch, motion sensitivity, and responsiveness to internal cues (*proprioception*)—is developing rapidly and functions at a more advanced level than the motor system. Young infants can distinguish changes in the loudness, pitch, duration, and location of sounds. They can use auditory information to differentiate objects from one another and to track the location of objects. Infants respond to a variety of visual dimensions, including movement, color, brightness, complexity, light-dark contrast, contours, depth, and distance. By 6 or 7 months of age, infants treat faceness as a special visual category. Newborns can differentiate sweet, sour, bitter, and salty tastes. Touch is an active as well as a passive sense; babies use it to explore objects, people, and their own bodies. Over the first year, infants' voluntary motor functions mature rapidly. Many motor functions are present in a reflexive form and emerge more fully as a result of continuing muscle development, motor coordination, and practice. Stepping is one example of this dynamic emergence.

Objective 3. To describe the development of sensorimotor intelligence, including an analysis of how infants process information, organize experiences, conceptualize causality, and understand the properties and functions of objects.

Sensorimotor intelligence begins with the use of motor and sensory capacities to explore and understand the environment. Four basic information-processing abilities provide the cognitive resources that support the maturation of sensorimotor intelligence: attention, processing speed, memory, and representational abilities. Of the many schemes that are established during this period, the emergence of an increasingly complex sense of causal relationships, the establishment of the concept of object permanence, and the formation of categories of objects are achievements that impose order and predictability on experience.

Objective 4. To characterize forerunners of language competence from birth through the first 2 years of life.

Evidence of both language perception and language production can be traced to infancy. Auditory and visual cues contribute to an awareness of the structure and rhythm of spoken language. Infants are able to recognize sounds and differentiate between sound combinations. They communicate through babbling and gestures before using spoken words. Around the age of 8 months, infants understand the meanings of some individual words and phrases. By 16 months, an infant has a receptive vocabulary of between 90 and 300 words; and a productive vocabulary of about 26 words.

Objective 5. To understand social attachment as the process through which infants develop strong emotional bonds with others, and to describe the dynamics of attachment formation during infancy.

A social attachment forms between the infant and the primary caregiver, creating the basic mental representation for subsequent intimate relationships. The attachment has physical as well as social and emotional characteristics. Sensory and motor experiences with the caregiver's voice, touch, aroma, facial expressions, soothing, and playfulness are all part of what become integrated into the mental representation of the object of attachment. Depending upon the sensitivity of the caregiver, attachments can be secure, anxious-resistant, anxious-avoidant, or disorganized.

Objective 6. To examine the nature of emotional development, including emotional differentiation, the interpretation of emotions, and emotional regulation.

Emotions are an early and continuous means of achieving intersubjectivity between infants and their caregivers. Emotions become increasingly differentiated in intensity and meaning. Emotional regulation provides a critical underpinning for subsequent cognitive functioning and social competence.

Objective 7. To describe the psychosocial crisis of trust versus mistrust; the central process through which the crisis is resolved, mutuality with the caregiver; the prime adaptive ego quality of hope; and the core pathology of withdrawal.

The establishment of trust between the infant and the caregiver is significant in both intellectual and social development. Through repeated interactions with caregivers, the infant develops a concept of the adult as both separate and permanent. Parental sensitivity is an underlying factor in determining the quality of attachment. Factors that appear to influence sensitivity are the adult's past experiences, including how the parent was cared for as a young child; contemporary factors that influence the caregiver's well-being, self-esteem, and emotional availability, such as the quality of the parental dyad and experiences at work; and characteristics of the infant. Once established, the trusting relationship between the infant and the caregiver becomes a source of security for the infant's further explorations of the environment and a framework for future close relationships. Trust serves as a basis for an orientation toward hopefulness.

Objective 8. To evaluate the critical role of parents and caregivers during infancy, with special attention to issues of safety and nutrition; optimizing cognitive, social, and emotional development; and the role of parents and caregivers as advocates for their infants with other agencies and systems.

Infants are skilled at adapting to their environment, but they cannot bring about major changes in it. Parents and other caregivers are ultimately responsible for structuring the environment so that it is maximally suited to the infant. Infants count on their caregivers to create a safe environment, to provide safe and adequate nutrition, to protect them from distress, to promote their health and physical growth, and to rally appropriate social support and community resources as needed. Parents must act as advocates for their infants and for themselves in the parental role.

Key Terms

Further Reflection

1. What are some examples of how hearing and vision work together to help infants form schemes about their world?
2. What is the possible evolutionary basis of the attachment behavioral system? How might contemporary life events threaten to disrupt this system?
3. What are some ways that caregiving practices can nurture the infant's ability to develop causal schemes?
4. How might differences in temperament modify the kind of caregiving a baby receives?
5. What does it mean to say that meaning is co-constructed in infancy? How do infants and caregivers use emotional communication to create meaning?

6. How might life conditions such as poverty, the dual career family, single parenting, or having a very-low-birth-weight baby influence the role of parents as advocates during infancy?
7. What role might the sense of trust and the ego strength of hope have for the enactment of life roles such as friend, teacher, supervisor, or political or spiritual leader?
8. What are some examples of how infants influence and even enhance the lives of their family members?

Psychology CourseMate

To access additional course materials, including CourseMate, please visit www.cengagebrain.com. At the CengageBrain .com home page, search for the ISBN of your title (from the back cover of your book) using the search box at the top of the page. This will take you to the product page where these resources can be found.

Casebook

For additional case material related to this chapter, see the case of "Marcie and Mom" in *Life Span Development: A Case Book*, by Barbara and Philip Newman, Laura Landry-Meyer, and Brenda J. Lohman, pp. 54–55. The case offers a starting point for discussing a common parenting routine—bedtime—and how infant temperament, mother's parenting style, and context interact to create a parenting environment.

© 2011 Estate of Pablo Picasso/Artists Rights Society (ARS), New York /© Francis G. Mayer/CORBIS

As locomotion skills develop, toddlers find new avenues for investigating the environment, and new strategies for coping with stressful situations. With their first hesitant efforts to walk, toddlers demonstrate the combination of trust in a nurturing caregiver and an expanding passion for autonomous action.

Toddlerhood (Ages 2 and 3)

CHAPTER 6

Chapter Objectives

1. To describe the expansion of motor skills during toddlerhood, indicating their importance for the child's capacity to explore the environment and to experience opportunities for mastery.

2. To document accomplishments in language development and to describe the influence of experiences for learning to communicate.

3. To describe the development of fantasy play and its importance for cognitive and social development.

4. To examine the development of self-control, especially impulse management and goal attainment, highlighting strategies young children use to help regulate their actions.

5. To analyze the psychosocial crisis of autonomy versus shame and doubt, to clarify the central process of imitation, and to describe the prime adaptive ego strength of will and the core pathology of compulsion.

6. To conceptualize the impact of poverty on development in toddlerhood.

7. To apply a psychosocial analysis to the topic of child care, emphasizing the impact of the kind of care and the quality of care on development during toddlerhood.

TODDLERS SEEM TO bubble with unpredictable, startling thoughts and actions that keep adults in a state of puzzled amazement. Toddlers are extremely busy—talking, moving, fantasizing, and planning all the time. Their outpouring of physical activity is remarkable for its vigor, constancy, and complexity. Equally impressive is the flood of cognitive accomplishments, especially language production and unique forms of playful fantasy.

Building on a foundation of trust and optimism formed during infancy, toddlerhood brings a flowering of the sense of personal **autonomy**, an enjoyment and confidence in doing things for oneself and expressing one's will. The successful blending of these two basic capacities for trust and autonomy provides a strong, protective shield for the young child's ego system. From this foundation, children are able to venture into satisfying and meaningful social relationships, engage in playful problem solving, and face their future with an outlook of hopefulness and assertiveness.

The chances for such a positive conclusion to the period of toddlerhood rest largely on the quality of the home environment. Toddlers, with their high energy level, improbable ideas, impish willfulness, and needs for mastery, run headlong into the full range of limits in their physical and social environment. Parenting during toddlerhood is like paddling a canoe through the rapids. It requires vigilance, good communication between the bow and the stern, flexibility, and a certain *joie de vivre* that keeps the whole trip fun. A child's cognitive and social development during this period of life can be facilitated by the parents' own ego development, their style of parenting, and the quality of their relationship. The degree to which discord and conflict introduce stress into the lives of parents brings special risk for some toddlers. ∎

CASE STUDY

ALICE WALKER GOES TO THE FAIR

It is unusual to find first-person recollections of the period of toddlerhood. In this selection, Alice Walker, Pulitzer Prize–winning novelist and poet, shares an early memory.

It is a bright summer day in 1947. My father, a fat, funny man with beautiful eyes and a subversive wit, is trying to decide which of his eight children he will take with him to the county fair. My mother, of course, will not go. She is knocked out from getting most of us ready: I hold my neck stiff against the pressure of her knuckles as she hastily completes the braiding and then the beribboning of my hair. My father is the driver for the rich old White lady up the road. Her name is Miss Mey. She owns all the land for miles around, as well as the house in which we live. All I remember about her is that she once offered to pay my mother thirty-five cents for cleaning her house, raking up piles of her magnolia leaves, and washing her family's clothes, and that my mother—she of no money, eight children, and a chronic earache—refused it. But I do not think of this in 1947. I am two and a half years old. I want to go everywhere my daddy goes. I am excited at the prospect of riding in a car. Someone has told me fairs are fun. That there is room in the car for only three of us doesn't faze me at all. Whirling happily in my starchy frock, showing off my biscuit-polished patent leather shoes and lavender socks, tossing my head in a way that makes my ribbons bounce, I stand, hands on hips, before my father. "Take me, Daddy," I say with assurance; "I'm the prettiest!"

Later, it does not surprise me to find myself in Miss Mey's shiny black car, sharing the back seat with the other lucky ones. Does not surprise me that I thoroughly enjoy the fair. At home that night I tell the unlucky ones all I can remember about the merry-go-round, the man who eats live chickens, and the teddy bears, until they say: "That's enough baby Alice. Shut up now, and go to sleep."

Source: From "Beauty: When the Other Dancer Is the Self," by A. Walker, pp. 257–258. In H. L. Gates, Jr. (ed.), *Bearing Witness: Selections from African-American Autobiography in the Twentieth Century.*

CRITICAL THINKING AND CASE ANALYSIS

1. What is the spirit of toddlerhood that is captured in this case?
2. How does the case relate to the tasks of locomotion, language, fantasy play, and self-control?
3. What aspects of Alice's self-concept appear to be forming in this episode?
4. What images of her mother and father are being established at this age?

Developmental Tasks

The use of the word *toddler* to describe development for 2- and 3-year-olds is in itself a clue to the important part that locomotion plays. In fact, it is only during the first year of this stage that the child actually toddles. By age 3, the child's walk has changed from the precarious, determined, half-humorous toddle to a more graceful, continuous, effective stride. Removal of diapers probably plays an important role in the progress of a child's walk. When toddlers no longer have a large wad of padding between their legs, they quickly make the transition from ugly duckling to swan.

The developmental tasks of toddlerhood—expanded locomotion, language and communication skills, **fantasy play**, and **self-control**—all contribute to the child's emerging independence within the boundaries of the social group. Some theorists refer to this as the first individuation process (Mahler, Pine, & Bergman, 1975; Blos, 1979). Obviously, 3-year-olds are not ready to set out for life alone in the big city. But they are ready to express independent thoughts, exercise some control in making choices, and do some things independently. The psychosocial crisis during this period of life—autonomy versus **shame** and **doubt**—refers to the child's struggle to establish a sense of separateness without disrupting the bonds

of affection and protection that are critical to a young child's physical survival and emotional connection to the family. In many cultures, expectations for autonomy are brought about by the birth of the next child, requiring the toddler to achieve new levels of self-sufficiency. Typically, this takes place with the support of older siblings, neighboring children, and extended family members who model and encourage more mature behavior (Edwards & Liu, 2002).

Elaboration of Locomotion

Objective 1. To describe the expansion of motor skills during toddlerhood, indicating their importance for the child's capacity to explore the environment and to experience opportunities for mastery.

Locomotion plays a central role in the toddler's psychosocial development, facilitating the transformation of ideas into action and prompting new types of interactions with the social and physical environment. As locomotor skills develop, the child has new ways of remaining close to the object of attachment, new avenues for investigating the environment, and new strategies for coping with stressful situations. Growth in locomotion and cognition go hand in hand. An understanding of space, distance, and the relationship of one place to the next expand as children maneuver through their environment (Gibson & Pick, 2000). One study found that when people think about the future, their leg muscles react as if they are moving ahead; and when they think about the past, their leg muscles react as if they are moving backward (Miles, Nind, & Macrae, 2010). We can extrapolate that in toddlerhood, sensorimotor exploration may serve as the physical basis for subsequent thinking about the future (moving ahead through space), and thinking about the past (moving backward through space).

Locomotor skills also figure prominently in the elaboration of play during this period. To the extent that coping involves the ability to maintain freedom of movement under conditions of threat, the locomotor skills acquired during toddlerhood provide a fundamental arsenal of lifelong strategies for fight or flight. Advanced locomotor skills may also increase conflicts with caregivers, introducing new struggles of willfulness and new parental constraints (Biringen, Emde, Campos, & Appelbaum, 1995).

When Ellen was about 2½ years old, she enjoyed watching her older brother climbing up a tree in the neighbor's yard. She would beg her brother to lift her up so she could get into the tree with him. One afternoon, Ellen's brother lifted her into the tree and then ran off to play with a friend. Ellen tried to get down from the tree, but she got her foot stuck in a crack between the branches. She cried and yelled until her mom came to get her. Ellen's mom scolded her for being in the tree and warned her never to go up there again. But the next afternoon, Ellen was back trying to figure out how to climb into the tree on her own.

From this example, one can see that when locomotor skills occur early in a developmental period, before the maturation of verbal and cognitive competence, toddlers may find themselves at odds with caregivers who must limit locomotion to protect the child's safety and to secure the safety of other people and objects in the environment.

Difficulties encountered by engineers and inventors in trying to duplicate human locomotor skills with robots have demonstrated just how intricate and exquisite are the toddler's accomplishments (Meghdari & Aryanpour, 2003). The possibility that lifelong movement patterns are acquired during these 2 years extends our appreciation of toddlers' locomotor accomplishments. Qualitative changes in locomotive behavior are not simply a result of maturation of the cerebral cortex. Dynamic systems theory, as discussed in Chapter 2, has guided a more fully differentiated view of motor development. Five factors interact to support the emergence of motor skills: (1) physical characteristics of the limbs, joints, and muscles involved in the movement; (2) changes in body weight and muscle mass; (3) new capacities in the central nervous system that improve coordination of feedback from the limbs and guide the amount of effort needed to achieve a motor goal; (4) the nature of behavioral goals; and (5) opportunities for practice (Thelen & Smith, 1994; Adolph &

Berger, 2006). These factors are integrated through repeated action; as one factor changes, the others must change. As a result, although most toddlers eventually achieve the same kinds of gross motor skills, the exact path toward proficiency differs for different children and across cultural groups.

Some landmarks of motor development that are reached from ages 2 to 6—walking and running, jumping, hopping, throwing and catching, pedaling and steering—are described in Table 6.1. The development and perfection of these skills depend on opportunity and encouragement as well as on the maturation of the cognitive and motor systems (Piek, 2006).

As walking becomes a more comfortable form of locomotion, new skills are added to the child's repertoire. Running and jumping are the first to emerge. By the age of 4, children are likely to leap from stairways, porches, or ladders. They have begun to imagine what it might be like to fly. Jumping is their closest approximation to flying. The actions involved in jumping form a pattern that remains stable throughout childhood and into adulthood (Clark, Phillips, & Petersen, 1989).

Children's running abilities become more elaborated all through toddlerhood. In films used to study the emergence of running, it appears that for toddlers, running and walking are very much alike, with little increase in velocity and little or no flight (the time when both feet are off the ground) in running.

TABLE 6.1 Changes in Gross Motor Skills during Toddlerhood and Early School Age

AGE	WALKING AND RUNNING	JUMPING	HOPPING	THROWING AND CATCHING	PEDALING AND STEERING
2–3 years	Walks rhythmically; opposite arm-leg swing appears. Hurried walk changes to true run.	Jumps down from step. Jumps several inches off floor with both feet, no arm action.	Hops 1 to 3 times on same foot with stiff upper body and nonhopping leg held still.	Throws ball with forearm extension only; feet remain stationary. Awaits thrown ball with rigid arms outstretched.	Pushes riding toy with feet; does little steering.
3–4 years	Walks up stairs, alternating feet. Walks downstairs, leading with one foot. Walks in a straight line.	Jumps off floor with coordinated arm action. Broad jumps about 1 foot.	Hops 4 to 6 times on same foot, flexing upper body and swinging nonhopping leg.	Throws ball with slight body rotation but little or no transfer of weight with feet. Flexes elbows in preparation for catching; traps ball against chest.	Pedals and steers tricycle.
4–5 years	Walks downstairs, alternating feet. Runs more smoothly. Gallops and skips with one foot.	Improved upward and forward jumps. Travels greater distance.	Hops 7 to 9 times on same foot. Improved speed of hopping.	Throws ball with increased body rotation and some transfer of weight forward. Catches ball with hands; if unsuccessful, may still trap ball against chest.	Rides tricycle rapidly, steers smoothly.
5–6 years	Increased speed of run. Gallops more smoothly. True skipping appears.	Jumps off floor about 1 foot. Broad jumps 3 feet.	Hops 50 feet on same foot in 10 seconds. Hops with rhythmical alternation (2 hops on one foot and 2 on the other).	Has mature throwing and catching pattern. Moves arm more and steps forward during throw. Awaits thrown ball with relaxed posture, adjusting body to path and size of ball.	Rides bicycle with training wheels.

Source: From Berk, Laura E., *Infants, Children, and Adolescents*, 3/e. Published by Allyn and Bacon, Boston, MA. Copyright © 1999 by Pearson Education. Adapted by permission of the publisher.

© 2010 Photodisc/Jupiterimages Corporation

Toddlerhood brings tremendous advances in locomotion as children enjoy walking, running, jumping, and hopping. Leaping from steps, walls, chairs, and benches is almost like flying!

At the beginning, toddlers appear to be running because they are moving a bit faster, but their action is not similar to adult running. Over time, however, the movements smooth out as flight time and velocity increase (Whitall & Getchell, 1995). These examples of jumping and running suggest how important early locomotor activity is in establishing motor skills that become elements of more complex athletic abilities in later childhood, adolescence, and adult life.

At first, youngsters may run for the sake of running. They practice over and over again. Later in toddlerhood, running changes from a kind of game in itself to a valuable component of many other games. The absolute speed of toddlers is limited by their somewhat precarious balance and short legs. This does not discourage them, however, from devoting a great deal of time and energy to running. The goals of mastery and getting to new places for exploration are too strong to dampen their enthusiasm.

Toddlers are often exposed to a wide variety of other forms of locomotion, such as swimming, skiing, skating, sledding, and dancing. Children seem eager to use their bodies in a variety of ways, and they learn quickly (Gallahue & Ozmun, 2006). As their physical coordination improves, children engage in a new repertoire of large-muscle activities: climbing, sliding, swinging, pounding, digging, and rough-and-tumble

play. Locomotor play provides immediate benefits to children in terms of physical fitness, including increased bone density, cardiovascular fitness, and flexibility (Pellegrini, 2009). Certain forms of physical activity provide an important source of information about the physical self. They offer an avenue for mastery and are also the basis for a lot of fun. Toddlers enjoy their bodies and are generally joyful when in the midst of physical play. Thus, physical activity contributes in an essential way to the toddler's self-concept. Children who lack muscle strength or coordination experience strong feelings of frustration as they struggle to keep their balance, throw or catch a ball, or use their hands and feet to perform new tasks.

Although one might expect that children who attend preschool would have a variety of opportunities for vigorous physical activity, recent research does not support this view. The National Association for the Education of Young Children (NAEYC) recommends at least 60 minutes of outdoor activity daily for preschoolers. The National Association for Sport and Physical Education advises 120 minutes of physical activity for young children. In fact, studies of daily opportunities for physical activity suggest that children in preschool spend most of their time indoors in what is described as sedentary activity, such as sitting, standing, or lying down. Even when they are outdoors, only 17% of the children's activities were described as moderate to vigorous such as walking, running, crawling, jumping, or skipping. The amount of moderate to vigorous activity varies by the quality of the preschool environment, with higher quality settings offering more materials and equipment to encourage active play, and more instances of teacher-initiated physical activity throughout the day (Brown, Pfeiffer, McIver, Dowda, Addy, & Pate, 2009).

Language Development

Objective 2. To document accomplishments in language development and to describe the influence of experiences for learning to communicate.

Semiotic Thinking

Jean Piaget (1970) described the years from about 2 to 5 or 6 as the stage of **preoperational thought**. This is a transitional period during which the sensorimotor schemes that were developed during infancy are represented internally. The most significant achievement of this new stage of cognitive development is the capacity for semiotic or *representational* thinking—understanding that one thing can stand for another. In **semiotic thinking**, children learn to recognize and use symbols and signs. **Symbols** are usually related in some way to the objects for which they stand. The cross, for example, is a symbol of Christianity. In pretend play, a scarf or a blanket may be a symbol for a pillow or a dress. **Signs** stand for things in a more abstract, arbitrary way. **Words** are signs; there is no direct relation between the word *dog* and the animal to which the word refers, yet the word stands for the object. For adults, it seems natural to use matchsticks or little squares of cardboard to represent people or buildings, but for children, the idea that a stick may be a car or a horse is a dramatic change in thinking that emerges gradually during the preoperational period.

Semiotic thinking brings enormous flexibility to human cognition. Signs embody an idea of something separate from the thing itself. With the elaboration of various types of symbols and signs, children can begin to recount events apart from the situation in which they occurred. They can invent worlds that never existed.

Children acquire five representational skills that allow them to manipulate objects mentally rather than by actual behavior: (1) imitation in the absence of the model, (2) mental images, (3) symbolic drawing, (4) symbolic play,

and (5) language. Representational skills allow children to share their experiences with others and to create imagined experiences. These skills also free children from communicating only through **gestures** and opens up opportunities to communicate about the past or the future as well as the present. Children can express relationships they may have known in the past by imitating them, drawing them, talking about them, or acting them out in fantasy. They can also portray events and relationships that they wish would occur or that they wish to alter (Nelson, 2010). In this and the following sections, we focus on two of these representational skills, language and fantasy play, which are among the most notable achievements of toddlerhood and are foundational for psychosocial development across the life span.

APPLYING THEORY AND RESEARCH TO LIFE

How the Brain Processes Language

BRAIN DEVELOPMENT AND language capacity are intimately related. From birth to age 3, the brain increases in weight from 400 to 1,100 grams, and trillions of neural connections are formed. Furthermore, myelination increases, continuing beyond infancy and toddlerhood well into adolescence. Myelination contributes to the speed of neural firing. Thus, over the period of infancy and toddlerhood, the brain is working extremely hard, forming synapses and responding with increasing speed.

With the use of positron emission tomography (PET) and functional magnetic resonance imaging (fMRI), one can observe different areas of activity in the brain related to varying language activities, including speaking, seeing words, and hearing words. PET is a technique that begins with the injection or inhalation of a radioactive material. As this material is metabolized in the brain, gamma rays are emitted and recorded. Using PET technology, one can discern which area of the brain is active during a particular type of activity, such as hearing or reading language. In fMRI, brain areas with more blood flow and more oxygenated blood show up better on the MRI. The fMRI takes advantage of this by comparing the brain at rest to

the brain performing a series of tasks. The areas of the brain that become more visible following the task are assumed to have been activated by the task (Gregg, 2004).

In infancy, both hemispheres are involved in language perception. Research confirms that by the end of the third year, for the vast majority of right-handed children, the essential aspects of speaking and understanding spoken language typically become focused in the left hemisphere of the brain. For left-handed children and those who are ambidextrous, these aspects of language are focused in the right hemisphere (Brownlee, 1998). The nondominant hemisphere becomes important for understanding features of language such as interpreting the emotional tone of the speaker, humor, and metaphor. However, various neuroimaging studies have demonstrated that many regions of the brain are involved in language production and comprehension (Gernsbacher & Kaschak, 2003; see Figure 6.1). Studies that monitor brain activity find that nouns and verbs, the kinds of words that are especially important for conveying meaning, are associated with different patterns of activity than prepositions and conjunctions, the kinds of words that are more important for grammatical information. Delays in exposure to a language, for example among deaf individuals who begin with American Sign Language and learn English later

in life, result in little disruption in the organization of the brain related to word meaning, but significant disruption in the areas of the brain that process grammatical information (Neville & Mills, 1997; Neville et al., 1998).

Damage to these areas leads to a loss of the ability to speak, called *aphasia*. Damage to Broca's area results in an inability to produce speech, but language comprehension remains functional. Damage to Wernicke's area does not affect the ability to produce language, but understanding is lost. People with Wernicke's aphasia can produce words clearly, but they do not make sense. People who have damage to the arcuate fasciculus can understand language, but their speech does not make sense, and they cannot repeat words.

In addition to the areas identified as especially key for language, speaking involves the motor cortex; reading involves the visual cortex; and understanding spoken language involves the auditory cortex. The task of reading aloud involves the visual cortex, motor cortex, and Broca's area.

Speech is different from other cognitive functions related to communication, such as language comprehension or symbolizing an idea by drawing a picture. In a condition called *aprosodia*, people have difficulty talking about their emotions when there is damage to the area of the right

Communicative Competence

In the process of language development, children acquire **communicative competence**: They become adept at using all the aspects of language that permit effective participation in the **language environment** of their culture (Kuczaj & Hill, 2003; Tomasello, 2006). This includes producing the sounds of the language; understanding the system of meanings, the rules of word formation, and the rules of sentence formation; developing a rich vocabulary; making adjustments to the social setting that are necessary to produce and interpret communication (*pragmatics*); and acquiring the ability to express thoughts in written as well as oral form. Through the achievement of communicative competence, children become increasingly integrated into their culture. They learn the expressions, tones of voice, and gestures that link them intimately to the language environment of their home and community. They learn when to speak and when to remain silent, and how to approach communication with peers, parents, and authority figures. They learn the terms applied to kin, close friends, acquaintances, and strangers; the words that are used to disparage or devalue; and the words that are used to recognize and praise. Although much of communication is intended to create shared meaning between the sender and the receiver of messages, sometimes communicative competence is used to deceive, mislead, or intimidate (Fiedler, 2008). If nurturing is the primary vehicle for cultural socialization in infancy, communication is the primary vehicle in toddlerhood. A discussion of how the toddler's brain processes language is presented in the "Applying Theory and Research to Life" box.

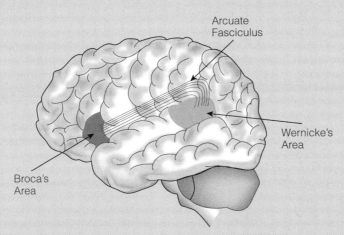

FIGURE 6.1 Three Areas of the Brain That Are Intimately Related to Speech: Broca's Area, Wernicke's Area, and the Arcuate Fasciculus, a Bundle of Nerve Fibers That Connects the Two. Damage to these areas leads to a loss of the ability to speak, called *aphasia*. Damage to Broca's area results in an inability to produce speech, but language comprehension remains functional. Damage to Wernicke's area does not affect the ability to produce language, but understanding is lost. People with Wernicke's aphasia can produce words clearly, but they do not make sense. People who have damage to the arcuate fasciculus can understand language, but their speech does not make sense, and they cannot repeat words.

in research comparing children who had congenital left hemisphere damage with adults who had left hemisphere injuries. The children scored much higher than the adults on measures of spontaneous speech, suggesting that other areas of the brain had taken over many of these functions (Bates et al., 2001).

Critical Thinking Questions

1. Based on what you have read about how the brain processes language, what are the distinct components of language competence? Which areas of the brain are associated with these components?

2. How can you explain the notion that the brain shows both sensitive periods and plasticity regarding language competence?

3. What are some differences between vocabulary and grammar that might require different brain functions? What are the unique cognitive capacities that are needed for these two aspects of language?

4. What are some differences between receptive and productive language? Why does receptive language precede productive language? Where might you look in brain development to explain this difference?

5. How does the synthesis of vocabulary and grammar take place in everyday speech of normal toddlers?

hemisphere that mirrors the area of the left hemisphere that is used for language. Studies comparing deaf users of sign language to hearing participants who use spoken language have provided evidence that injury to the left hemisphere can result in a form of language aphasia. For the deaf, this injury does not interrupt the capacity to make other types of gestures, confirming that language functions are differentiated from other symbolic and motor functions that might be involved in the communicative process (Corina, Vaid, & Bellugi, 1992).

Language production capacities of the brain demonstrate both sensitive periods and remarkable plasticity. Sensitivity is evidenced by the impact of delayed exposure to language on disruptions in grammar as well as on the ability to recognize and produce certain language sounds. Plasticity is evidenced

Communicative competence begins during infancy and develops across the entire life span. Vocabulary, grammar, and pragmatics continue to be refined as one engages in formal schooling and enters a wider range of social settings where specific words, expressions, and styles of interaction are in use. But toddlerhood appears to be the time of a dramatic expansion in verbal competence, when remarkable achievements are made in an exceptionally brief period. The following discussion of language and communication is divided into two major sections: (1) language milestones and (2) the language environment. The first section outlines the pattern of communication accomplishments of toddlerhood, including the expanded use of words with meaning, the formation of two-word sentences, more complex sentence formation, and grammar. Important physiological structures support this emerging competence. The second section identifies factors in the psychosocial environment that help facilitate and optimize communicative competence.

The text provides an overview of patterns of accomplishment in language and communication from infancy through about age 4. As you may remember, many of the precursors of spoken language, including language perception, babbling, and gesturing, were discussed in Chapter 5. Certain sequences or *developmental milestones* appear to be quite common among children from many language environments. Communicative gestures precede the production of spoken words, and the production of a substantial vocabulary of spoken words precedes the linking of words into two-word sentences. However, it is important to recognize the wide variability in the development of communicative skills. The timing of the onset of these various abilities and their rate of growth vary from child to child. For example, in a large national study of infant/toddler language, word production for 12-month-old infants ranged from the 90th percentile, who used 26 words or more, to the 10th percentile, who produced no words (see Figure 6.2). By 16 months

of age, those in the 90th percentile were using 180 words, and those in the 10th percentile produced 10 words or less (Fenson et al., 1994). All these children were healthy, normal children, with no known history of developmental delay, prematurity, or genetic disease. As you read about modal or typical patterns, try to remember that these patterns disguise important variations.

Communicative Competence in Toddlerhood

Language development in toddlerhood brings rapid acquisition of a wide-ranging vocabulary and the initial use of a primitive grammar that is quickly transformed into the grammar of the spoken language. The typical developmental progression in language competence is characterized by three common patterns: (1) an acceleration in the production of single words, followed by two-word combinations; (2) a predominance of nouns in the vocabulary followed by the addition of verbs, adjectives, and prepositions; and (3) two-word utterances followed by longer strings of words organized by use of grammatical rules that include more indicators of meaning, such as possession, plural, and past, present, and future.

Although there appears to be a universal capacity for language, which matures rapidly in the first 4 years of life, and although each of the approximately 6,000 languages spoken in the world today are capable of doing roughly the same things (conveying ideas), each language has its own vocabulary and grammar, which have to be learned specifically. Whereas there may be a universal capacity to recognize certain facial expressions as happy or sad, or even certain gestures as meaning "give me" or "pick me up," there is no universal human code that links objects, ideas, or actions to spoken words and sentences. Each human child has to learn a particular spoken language. This uniqueness of language contributes to its flexibility, leading to the creative use of language and its capacity to express novel thoughts and ideas (Wargo, 2008).

Vocabulary. During the period from 12 to 16 months, infants make significant progress in learning the names of objects and applying them to pictures or real examples. There is a rapid expansion of vocabulary during these 4 months from few or no spoken words to about 26. Sometime around 18 months, the child acquires a large number of new words, and vocabulary continues to expand at a rapid rate throughout the toddler and early school years (Booth, 2009). The average toddler of 30 months has a spoken vocabulary of about 570 words. In order to accomplish this feat, children seem to *fast-map* new meanings as they experience words in conversation. To **fast-map** is to quickly form an initial, partial understanding of a word's meaning. It is an information-processing technique in which children relate the new word to the known vocabulary by linking it to known words and concepts that are already well understood. The child has to hear the new word only a few times in a context that makes its meaning clear. In day-to-day life, children

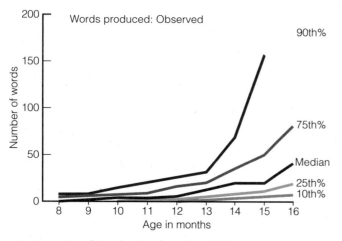

FIGURE 6.2 Word Production from 8 to 16 Months

Source: From "Variability in Early Communicative Development," by L. Fenson et al., 1994, *Monographs of the Society for Research in Child Development, 1994, 59* (5), 38. Copyright © 1994 The Society for Research in Child Development, Inc. Reprinted by permission.

hear thousands of words, many over and over again, without necessarily knowing their meaning. However, once children recognize the link between a word's sound and its meaning, they can quickly associate other familiar word sounds with their meanings (Swingley, 2007). Thus, without direct word-by-word tutoring, children accumulate numerous samples of their culture's language from the speech they hear and attach a minimally satisfactory definition to each word or phrase. This vocabulary burst is associated with speed of processing in word recognition. Young children who recognize words with greater speed also seem to have a greater vocabulary. The relationship between these two factors is not fully understood (Fernald, Swingley, & Pinto, 2001).

The early phase of vocabulary development seems to focus on broad semantic categories—animals, vehicles, fruits, clothes, and so on. New words, particularly nouns, are treated like the name of a category of things rather than of only one specific object or a part of it. For example, when a child learns the word *cup*, it is used to refer to all objects that have the general shape and function of a cup. A much slower process of vocabulary development occurs as children and adults learn the distinctions among words within categories (McDonough, 2002). You may have a very good idea about the distinction between annual and perennial flowering plants, but you may not know the difference between the many types of each group and how to recognize them. In fact, building a vocabulary of subcategories may become an entire field of study, such as botany or zoology, in which the types and subtypes of a larger category are identified, classified, and named.

Two-Word Sentences. At 16 months of age, few children make two-word sentences, but by 30 months almost all children make them (Fenson et al., 1994). These two-word sentences are referred to as **telegraphic speech.** Children merge two words into phrases that are essential to communicate what they intend to say. Just as in a telegram, however, other words—verbs, articles, prepositions, pronouns, conjunctions—are left out. A child will say, "my ball," "more juice," and "Daddy gone." Before this point, children tend to utter single words accompanied by gestures and actions. By stringing two words together, they convey more meaning through verbal communication and rely less heavily on gestures and actions. The acquisition of telegraphic speech allows a child to make greater use of the symbolism inherent in language to communicate meaning (Powers, 2002).

Children are quite innovative in using two-word sentences. They continue to understand more than they are able to say, but they appear to use their limited number of words and the newfound ability to combine them to get their point across. Children may convey different meanings with the same sentence. "Daddy go," for example, may be used to tell someone that Daddy has left, or it may be used to tell Daddy to leave. Children often indicate their meanings by tone of voice or by the words they stress. The use of two-word sentences is characteristic of toddler-age language learners in many cultures (Messer, 2000).

Martin Braine (1976) analyzed the first word combinations spoken by children in English, Samoan, Finnish, Hebrew, and Swedish. His goal was to identify the kinds of rules or patterns that governed these early combinations. Ten patterns of word combination were embedded in those early language samples:

1. Making reference to something: See +X (*see mother*)
2. Describing something: Hot +X (*hot stove*)
3. Possession: X has a Y (*Billy has a bottle*)
4. Plurality: Two +X (*two dogs*)
5. Repetition or other examples: More +X (*more up*)
6. Disappearance: All gone +X (*all gone milk*)
7. Negation: No +X (*no sleep*)
8. Actor-action relations: Person +X (*Daddy sleep*)
9. Location: X + here (*Grandma here*)
10. Requests: Have +X (*have it, ball*)

Braine found that although he could identify some common patterns of word combinations, they were not guided by the grammatical categories of the spoken language but by the meanings the child wished to express and by the variety of objects, people, and interactions in the immediate environment. The patterns of word combinations used by some children did not overlap at all with those used by other children in the same culture.

Early language is closely tied to the representation of sensorimotor schemes—the activities that dominate the child's life, such as eating, sleeping, playing games with mommy or daddy or the siblings, going places, coming back home, and so on. It expresses the properties and relationships of the objects and people that are important in a child's life. Language use emerges within a larger communication system and reflects a child's cognitive capacities. At the same time, it reflects the perceptual and functional characteristics of the environment. Vocabulary and grammar grow hand in hand; as toddlers learn more words, they use them in combination to express more complex ideas (Bates & Goodman, 2001).

Grammatical Transformations. By combining words according to the set of rules of **grammar** for a given language, a person can produce a limitless number of messages that can be understood by another person. Remarkably, by the age of 4, children appear to be able to structure their sentences using most of these rules without any direct instruction. Consider the difference in meaning between "The boy hit the ball" and "The ball hit the boy." The simple matter of word order in a sentence is critical for preserving meaning. The basic format of an English sentence—noun phrase followed by verb phrase—is a central part of its grammar. In order to ask a question or produce a negative sentence, the speaker transforms this word order according to a specific set of rules (e.g., "You are going" versus "Are you going?"). The addition of certain inflections and modifiers conveys information about time, possession, number, and relation. As children learn the grammatical transformations of their language, they become much more effective in conveying exactly what they have in mind.

A surprising observation is that children use correct transformations for the past tense of irregular verbs (*went, gave, run*) before they use correct inflections of regular verbs (*talked, walked, jumped*). It appears that children first learn the past tense of irregular verbs through rote memory. Once they learn the rule for expressing the past tense by adding *ed*, they occasionally **overregularize** this rule and begin making errors in the past tense. Thus, a 2-year-old is likely to say "I ran fast," but a 3-year-old may say "I runned fast." According to a model proposed by Gary Marcus, children recognize and have a symbolic category for words that are verbs. They establish a default rule: "To form the past tense, add *ed* to any word that can be categorized as a verb." They also memorize the past forms of the irregular verbs as they encounter them. When an irregular verb is required, its irregular past tense form is always used if the child can recall it. However, if the child cannot recall the past tense, or if the word is novel, the default rule is called into play. In a study of preschoolers, the rate of overregularization was 4.5%. This fell to 2.5% for first graders and 1% for fourth graders, suggesting that as a child's vocabulary grows, the need to apply the default rule to unfamiliar verbs declines (Marcus, 1996).

The grammatical errors that young children make alert us to the fact that they are working to figure out a system of rules with which to communicate meaning. It is unlikely that these errors result from imitation of adult speech. Children say such things as "My do it" or "Dose mines." They have certainly not copied those expressions from adults; rather, these errors suggest the beginning of a grammar that becomes more specialized and accurate as children acquire the opportunity to match their speech to that of others. One can catch toddlers in the act of building their grammar by listening to them revise their own speech. From the age of 2 to 4, as their grammar matures, toddlers will pause in mid-sentence and revise their speech to make a more complex or complete expression. Aware of linguistic alternatives, they stop to select one that best expresses their thoughts in a specific language environment (Rispoli, 2003).

The milestones in language development from 24 months to age 4 are summarized in Table 6.2. In the second year of life, babies understand words and phrases. They develop a vocabulary and begin to form two-word phrases. During the third year, language is definitely used to communicate ideas, observations, and needs. Comprehension of spoken language seems almost complete. Some of their speech may not be easily understood by people outside the family, partly because they are unable to produce clear phonetic sounds and also because their knowledge of adult grammar is limited. During the fourth year, most children acquire an extensive vocabulary. They can create sentences that reflect most of the basic rules of grammar. Their language is a vehicle for communicating complex thoughts that are usually understood by children and adults outside the family. They can use their communicative skills to participate in social exchanges with other children, talk about their experiences, make plans, and resolve conflicts.

The pattern of language milestones is very similar across languages, and appears to be similar for toddlers who are learning a second language. In an investigation of international adoptees, researchers compared English language acquisition for children who had been adopted from China and U.S.-born monolingual infants (Snedeker, Geren, & Shafto, 2007). The Chinese children were between the ages of 2½ and 5½ when they were adopted. They were compared to U.S. infants between the ages of 1½ and 2¾. Language competence was assessed every 3 months until the Chinese children had been in the United States 18 months. These adopted children were learning English in much the same way that babies of English-speaking parents learn the language—from exposure to English in the family environment. They had the advantage of more advanced cognitive maturation and experience learning a first language, and the disadvantage of delayed exposure to English during infancy.

Three features of language learning were observed among the Chinese adoptees: (1) They showed the same pattern of language production as monolingual infants, using one-word utterances at first, which were mostly nouns with other kinds of words added over time. (2) During their first 3 months in the United States, the adopted children acquired English vocabulary at a rate four times

TABLE 6.2 Milestones in Language Development from 24 Months to 4 Years

AT THE COMPLETION OF	VOCALIZATION AND LANGUAGE CHARACTERISTICS
24 months	Vocabulary of more than 300 items (some children seem to be able to name everything in the environment); begin spontaneously to join vocabulary items into two-word phrases; all phrases appear to be own creations; definite increase in communicative behavior and interest in language.
30 months	Continuing increase in vocabulary with more than 550 words; many new additions every day; no babbling at all; utterances have communicative intent; frustrated if not understood by others; utterances consist of at least two words, many have three or even five words; use of linguistic suffixes for possession, plural, and past tense; frequent use of irregular plural noun (foot/feet) and irregular verbs; intelligibility is not very good yet by those unfamiliar with the child's speech.
3 years	Vocabulary of some 1,000 words; about 80% of utterances are intelligible even to strangers; grammatical complexity of utterances is roughly that of colloquial adult language, although mistakes still occur.
4 years	Language is well established; deviations from the adult norm tend to be more in style than in grammar.

Source: Adapted from Lenneberg, 1967, and Fenson et al., 1994.

faster than comparable monolingual infants. This suggests that prior experience coupled with advanced understanding of the object-word link contributed to an accelerated process of vocabulary learning. (3) Both adopted children and monolingual infants showed the same positive correlation between vocabulary size and sentence complexity. Neither infants nor adoptees whose vocabulary was less than 300 words produced multiword expressions. Thus, despite their advanced cognitive maturation and prior exposure to another language, adoptees seemed to go through the same sequence of problem-solving steps to build grammatically complex sentences that are characteristic of monolingual infant language learners.

Language Development beyond Toddlerhood

Although the fundamentals of language are well established by age 4, there are still some things that toddlers cannot achieve with language. For example, Mary may raise a fuss about wanting the biggest piece of cake. If you allow her to make a choice, she selects a piece with lots of frosting. Clearly, the word *biggest* is not being used correctly. Even though Mary is able to memorize and repeat the words *big, bigger,* and *biggest,* she does not yet fully understand the concept to which they refer. Other observations suggest that 2- and 3-year-olds have difficulty using verbal instructions to control or guide their behavior (Tinsley & Waters, 1982). They may be able to tell themselves to "stop" or "go slow," but these commands are not effective in slowing them down. Both of these examples demonstrate that toddlers' language development can be somewhat misleading. One may assume that children fully understand the more abstract meaning of the words they use, but in fact their language continues to be very idiosyncratic throughout toddlerhood.

As the process of **fast-mapping** implies, children may add a word to their vocabulary without understanding the several meanings that this word has in different contexts. During the periods of early and middle childhood, considerable time and attention is devoted to exploring vocabulary, correcting some meanings that were incorrectly learned, and expanding the full range of meanings and underlying concepts that are linked to the many words that were acquired so rapidly during toddlerhood. One estimate is that the reading vocabulary or comprehension of dictionary entries of a 10-year-old child is close to 40,000 words, with another 40,000 proper names, places, and expressions unique to the child's own family, neighborhood, and cultural group (Anglin, 1993).

Important language functions develop more fully during early and middle childhood (Dickinson & Tabors, 2001). As their understanding of the self and the social environment expands, older children use language to plan a problem-solving strategy, guide a complex series of motor activities, or identify the relationships among objects. Vocabulary expands, and words are used more frequently in the ways they are used in adult speech. Children learn the patterns of polite speech as well as slang. Depending on the nature of their conversational partners at home and school, their sentences become more complex, including conditional and descriptive clauses. The irregular verbs and nouns are learned and used correctly. As children attend school, they learn to conceptualize the grammatical structure of their language.

Beyond the formal elements of vocabulary, grammar, reading, and writing, language becomes a vehicle for creative expression. Children write poems, essays, and stories. They begin to use sarcasm, puns, and metaphors to elaborate their speech. They create secret codes with their special friends. Children make up riddles and jokes, put on plays and puppet shows, work on school newspapers, and leave enigmatic

Toddlers can use their language to enhance play and foster cooperation.

or corny messages in their friends' yearbooks. With the widespread use of text messaging and Twitter, new forms of expression have been invented that abbreviate or condense meaning. If you participate in these modes of communication, you quickly learn the meanings of these new symbols and signs.

Language plays a critical role in the resolution of subsequent psychosocial crises, especially the establishment of group identity, intimacy, and generativity. It is primarily through the quality of one's spoken language that one achieves the levels of disclosure that sustain friendship and subsequent intimate relationships. Language also serves as a mechanism for resolving conflicts and for building a sense of cohesiveness within groups, whether of friends, coworkers, or family members.

The Language Environment

In this section, we focus primarily on the nature of the interaction between toddlers and their caregivers, with some attention to the issue of bilingualism and the relationship of the language environment at home and school. Language is a cultural tool, a means for socializing and educating young children. It is one of many inventions for creating a sense of group identity and for passing the mythology, wisdom, and values of the culture from one generation to the next. Language is a part of the psychosocial environment. Competence in the use of language solidifies the young child's membership in the immediate family and in the larger cultural group. Although there is strong evidence for genetically based origins of the capacity for language learning, the specific content and tone of a child's communication is strongly influenced by the language

HUMAN DEVELOPMENT AND DIVERSITY

Bilingualism

THE RISE IN THE NUMBER OF ASIAN AND LATINO IMMIGRANTS TO THE United States has led to a growing interest in the process through which young children manage the challenges of learning and speaking two or more languages. Studies of children in U.S. schools find that there are some children who speak primarily a language other than English, some children who speak only English, and some children who are fluent in two or more languages including English. A growing body of research documents that the children who speak mostly a language other than English have more emotional, academic, and behavioral problems than those who are bilingual (Han & Huang, 2010).

Young bilingual children are adept at switching from one language to another as the conversational situation demands. In one study of bilingual Latino children in Miami, Florida, the children had access to two vocabularies, one in Spanish and one in English. Rather than knowing two words for the same thing, these vocabularies did not overlap much. Knowing the two languages actually expanded the concepts children could use to express their thoughts in comparison to children who spoke English or Spanish only (Umbel, Pearson, Fernandez, & Oller, 1992).

Code switching begins at a very early age. Infants growing up in multilingual families begin to acquire first words in both languages and are soon able to use these words appropriately, for example, speaking Spanish to their Spanish-speaking caregiver and English to their English-speaking grandmother (Holowaka, Brosseau-Lapré, & Pettito, 2002). In a study of a bilingual English-Portuguese infant at play with his mother and father, the child switched languages to fill in the gaps in his vocabulary. If he did not know the word for something in one language, he used the other. Similarly, his parents switched codes in order to provide language that was the best match with the child's level of understanding. Thus, bilingual families can use their language environment to the child's advantage, providing alternative communication strategies to improve communication and understanding (Nicoladis, 1998; Nicoladis & Secco, 2000).

How do bilingual individuals prevent one language from interfering with another? Research using functional magnetic resonance imaging (fMRI) explored the process by which bilingual individuals inhibit one language while drawing on another. In this research, individuals who were

bilingual from infancy were compared to those who were monolingual. Participants were asked to press a button when they saw a word in one language, but not to press the button when they saw words in another language or made up words that were not really words in either language. In this type of task, bilinguals can detect when a word is not in the language they have been instructed to attend to, but they do not process the word for its meaning. None of the brain areas that are associated with word meaning were activated when the nontarget words were displayed. Instead, bilinguals had adapted a distinct path from sound properties of the words to meaning only for the words in the target language (Rodriguez-Fornells, Rotte, Heinze, Nosselt, & Munte, 2002). The implication is that early bilingualism stimulates additional plasticity in brain organization and function to accomplish tasks that require language separation. Regardless of which language is being spoken, the same regions of the cortex are used to produce and understand spoken language. However, when words from different languages are spoken or presented visually, an additional brain area is activated which is sensitive to monitoring and controlling the language that is in use

environment. In many industrialized cultures, children are separated from the world of adult work. Special educational settings are created to prepare children for the tasks of adulthood, and adults interact with children in specific ways that differ from their interactions with other adults. In other cultures, children are present in the midst of ongoing adult activities. Children are encouraged to become active listeners and observers, gradually participating in conversations and work as their abilities permit. Thus, the nature of the interactive language environment, the expectations for children to participate, and the kinds of communications that children are likely to engage in can vary based on the broad cultural orientation about the place and role of children in the larger society (Rogoff & Angelillo, 2002; Rogoff, Paradise, Arauz, Correa-Chavez, & Angelillo, 2003).

Interaction and Language Development. Probably the most important factor that caregivers contribute to a child's cognitive growth is the opportunity for interactions. Brain development in infancy and toddlerhood is stimulated by exposure to adult language through conversation, baby talk, and reading aloud. An interactive human being can respond to a child's questions, provide information, react in unexpected ways and surprise the child, explain plans or strategies, and offer praise or criticism. The frequency and quality of parent-child interactions are closely associated with children's social and cognitive competence (Hart, Newell, & Olsen, 2003). The "Human Development and Diversity" box discusses **bilingualism**, the complex learning process that takes place in children who are brought up in families that speak two languages.

(Crinion et al., 2006). You can think of this process as a low-level recognition switch that does not contribute to the interpretation of speech nor to the production of meaningful speech, but simply signals higher level brain centers that a different type of speech-related stimulus has been experienced.

There appear to be some costs as well as benefits associated with bilingualism. Bilingual children have a smaller vocabulary overall, and in controlled experiments they are a bit slower in tasks that require thinking of words that name a picture. Benefits of bilingualism are evident in many tasks that are associated with executive control, including focusing attention, resisting distractions, monitoring changes in stimuli, and changing strategies between tasks. Bilingualism is increasingly being viewed as a context that stimulates early and ongoing advantages in cognitive flexibility, selectivity, and control (Kovács & Mehler, 2009; Bialystok & Craik, 2010).

Copyright © Michael Newman/Photo Edit

The teacher, who speaks Spanish and English fluently, helps students become bilingual by encouraging them to use both languages to express their ideas.

Critical Thinking Questions

1. How would you evaluate the following statement? "The human brain has the capacity for a great deal more language competence than is typically observed."

2. Based on the information presented here, what would you advise parents who speak more than one language? How should they organize the language environment for their children?

3. What are some potential advantages and disadvantages to bilingualism?

4. How does the study of bilingualism help inform our understanding of language development?

5. How would you set up a computer program to function as a bilingual translator? What features would be needed to support the integration of two or more languages?

6. How would you develop methods and a curriculum to accomplish the goal of fostering English fluency for children who are not native English speakers while preserving and extending their fluency in their native language?

The link between the frequency of parent-child interactions and the child's verbal competence is well established. Three different explanations have been suggested to account for this link:

1. Parents and their offspring share a genetic predisposition for verbal competence, which is evident in the frequency of parent-child interactions and in the early acquisition of verbal skills.
2. Parents who interact frequently with their children provide a rich array of verbal stimuli and thereby promote high levels of verbal comprehension and production.
3. Children who are more verbally competent stimulate more interaction from their caregivers, which then establishes a more active and diverse verbal environment. Over time, research will no doubt clarify the nature of these relationships.

Certain characteristics of a language partner have been shown to facilitate a child's language acquisition and communication skills (Snow, 1984; Singh, Morgan, & Best, 2002). When talking to infants and young children, adults tend to speak in a high pitch, use shorter sentences, speak slowly, use attention-getting strategies, and speak in a friendly, positive tone. Even older children will modify their speech when interacting with toddlers to hold their attention and guide their behavior (Rice, 1989).

Caregivers have been observed to modify their speech in the following ways so that they are more likely to be understood (Mitchell, 2001):

1. They simplify utterances to correspond with the toddler's interests and comprehension level.
2. They emphasize the here and now.
3. They use a more restricted vocabulary.
4. They do a lot of paraphrasing.
5. They use simple, well-formed sentences.
6. They use frequent repetitions.
7. They use a slow rate of speech with pauses between utterances and after the major content words.

These characteristics of caregiver speech are not universal; rather they reflect cultural norms for addressing toddlers. They are most typically observed in middle-class, European American families. In one cross-cultural analysis, for example, African American adults in the rural South were observed in interaction with their children (Heath, 1989). Adults did not simplify or censor their speech for young children. They frequently did not address children directly, but expected the children to hear what they said and to interrupt if they had something to add. Adults and children directed one another's behavior with specific commands. It was just as acceptable for a toddler to command an adult as the other way around. Adults teased children, especially in the presence of others, in order to give the children a chance to show off their quick wit and to practice assertiveness. Within this language environment, children had the opportunity to hear a variety of opinions, gather information to extend their direct experience, and observe shifts in language tone and style that accompany changes in the topic or purpose of the conversation. This example illustrates the variation in communication styles that characterize American families, producing substantial differences in the language-learning environments of the home.

Other research describes variations in the nature and amount of parent-child interaction that takes place during a typical day. In one longitudinal study, 40 families (15 Black and 25 White) were observed once per month over 2½ years (Hart & Risley, 1992). The observations covered the period shortly before, during, and after the child was learning to talk. The number of words spoken to a child in an hour varied from 232 to 3,606; the percentage of time that parents were in the same room as the child ranged from 38% to 99%; and the average number of times that parents and children took turns in an interaction ranged from 1.8 to 17.4.

This observational study found that the quality of a parent's speech toward the child was positively related to the child's IQ at 37 months of age. The study also found a systematic relationship between the quality of a parent's speech toward the child and the family's socioeconomic status. Children in lower socioeconomic status families experienced less time with their parents, fewer moments of joint play, and exposure to fewer words. Children were less likely to have their speech repeated or paraphrased by their parents, less likely to be asked questions, and more likely to experience prohibitions placed on their behavior. Those parents who were most likely to place prohibitions on their child's activities during this age period were less likely to listen intently to their child's speech, repeat what the child had said, or ask the child questions.

Other studies have emphasized that it is not socioeconomic status per se that influences language development. Four features of parent-child interaction differentiate high SES and lower SES family interactions. These are: the amount of talking; the use of a varied vocabulary; the early use of gestures to convey meaning; and the use of more complex sentences. The way parents talk to their infants and toddlers is closely related to the child's vocabulary by age 4 (Rowe & Goldin-Meadow, 2009). Within socioeconomic groups, the more children experience responsive and stimulating interactions with caregivers in the home, the further advanced their language abilities are by age 3 (Roberts, Burchinal, & Durham, 1999). However, when parents have the television playing, even when it is just playing in the background, the amount of parent-child interaction is decreased. Experimental studies have shown that when the television is playing in the background at home, toddlers' social behavior declines, their parents engage in fewer conversations with them and are less responsive (Kirkorian, Pempek, Murphy, Schmidt, & Anderson, 2009). As result of a habitual reliance on having the television playing, some parents inadvertently create environments that are disruptive to their toddler's optimal language development.

One component of parent-child interaction that has been studied in detail is **question-asking** by the child. Children as young as 18 months ask questions in order to gather information and accomplish other goals, such as asking permission or clarifying a situation. In one intensive study of four children, they asked an average of 107 questions an hour while engaged in conversations with adults (Chouirnard, 2007). It appears that the ability to ask questions of parents begins early in infancy and may be a universal strategy that infants use for information gathering. However, the extent to which question-asking is encouraged depends on the nature of parental responses and the way parents, themselves, use question-asking in daily conversation. For example, Tizard and Hughes (1984) reported that middle-class children asked more curiosity-based questions whereas working-class children asked more questions about procedural matters. Mothers who asked more questions had children who asked more questions. In the study cited previously, question-asking by parents was related to other aspects of their interactive style, especially the tendency to expand on what their child has asked rather than to stop their child from speaking or acting (Hart & Risley, 1992).

In middle-class families, children are more likely to persist in sustained questioning where one question is followed by an answer, is followed by another question, and so on. This pattern is more likely to lead a child from factual information to explanations and the formation of abstract concepts. When a child asks a lot of questions and the parent answers and gives additional information, this guides how the child builds a knowledge base and understands the world. It also conveys that a relationship exists between child and parent that allows the child to keep asking questions and to expect informative answers even if a question has to be asked several times in order for the parent to understand it (Harris, 2007). The ability to ask questions allows the child to use this form of challenge to gain information and to trust that it is all right to do this rather than to be rejected or rebuked with an angry response. By creating this interactive relationship around inquiry and information sharing, the child and parent create a secure base regarding access to information that offers the emotional security from which new and more exploratory forms of curiosity can grow.

In learning vocabulary, children appear to be sensitive to the competence of their language partners. For example, in one study, 3- and 4-year-olds participated in an experiment where the experimenter appeared to be either knowledgeable and confident or uncertain about the name for a given toy. In the confident situation, the experimenter said things like: "I know right where my friend left her *blinket*." In the uncertain situation, the experimenter said, "I'd like to help my friend, but I don't know what a *blinket* is." Even though the children in both situations learned how the toy worked, they used the name of the toy only if the experimenter appeared confident (Sabbagh & Baldwin, 2001). The implication of this work is that by age 3, children are able to assess the expertise and confidence of the language partner before incorporating words into their vocabulary.

Scaffolding and Other Strategies for Enhancing Language Development. The process of language learning involves upward **scaffolding** and a process of mutual regulation. Scaffolding is a metaphor for providing assistance in helping someone reach a new, higher level of functioning. Verbal scaffolding refers to the variety of ways that adults have to help children reach a more advanced level of language competence, for example, by repeating words, offering new words, restating a child's expressions in different words, correcting a child's mistakes, or encouraging a child to say more about his or her ideas (Rodgers & Rodgers, 2004). With assistance, children can be more effective in learning vocabulary and expressing their ideas (Nelson, 1973). Sometimes a child may be misunderstood because the child's pronunciation is so discrepant from the real word (*ambiance* for *ambulance*; *tommick cake* for *stomach ache*). Adults can scaffold the child's expression by modeling the correct pronunciation. Sometimes an adult will use a word that is a little more advanced than the word the child is using, which helps the child link known vocabulary to the new word or idea. For example: "We call that kind of car that has a top that goes down a *convertible*." Scaffolding is closely related to Vygotsky's idea of the **zone of proximal development**. By interacting with a more verbally competent adult or peer, children are able to reach new levels of linguistic ability (Landry, Miller-Loncar, Smith, & Swank, 2002; Gregory, Kim, & Whiren, 2003).

Adults do not always interact with children by encouraging the child to express ideas in a more mature form. Sometimes, adults restate or simplify their expressions to make sure they are being understood. Through frequent interactions, adults encourage language development by establishing a good balance between modifying their speech somewhat and modeling more complex, accurate speech for their children. Children respond to the scaffolding by expressing themselves in more complete sentences and by using a larger vocabulary. This reflects the idea of mutual regulation.

Adults make use of several strategies to clarify a child's meaning when the speech is unclear. One is **expansion**, or the elaboration of the child's expressions:

CHILD: Doggie wag.

PARENT: Yes, the dog is wagging her tail.

Another strategy is **prompting**, often in the form of a question. Here the parent urges the child to say more:

CHILD: More crackel.

PARENT: You want more what?

In both of these interactions, the adult is helping the child to communicate more effectively by expanding on or asking the child to elaborate on something of interest to the child. The kinds of sentences that parents use help children see how they can produce new sentences that are more grammatically correct and therefore more meaningful to others.

Reading and Language Games. Socially interactive rituals, such as telling stories, playing word games, verbal joking and teasing, and reading books together, also seem to enhance language development, especially by building vocabulary and preparing children to use language comfortably in social situations. Reading aloud has been identified as an especially important language activity, not only in preparation for literacy, but also for expanding a child's language skills (Crain-Thoreson & Dale, 1992; ValdezMenchaca & Whitehurst, 1992; Hammer, 2001). During toddlerhood, an adult may start out by reading picture books and asking the child questions about the pictures. The adult may try to relate the picture to some event in the child's life or ask the child to tell something about the pictures. Thus, just as in scaffolding with respect to language, reading along with an experienced reader can scaffold the child's literacy skills (Verhoeven, 2001). Over time, the child becomes more and more the storyteller, while the adult listens, encourages, and expands the tale. Some books are read aloud so often that the toddler begins to read them from memory or retell the story in the child's own words from the pictures.

By reading aloud and pointing to pictures, parents and their toddlers create an environment for the development of literacy.

As children enter early school age, this type of ritualized reading activity provides a framework for the child's concept of what it means to be a reader. Reading aloud introduces the notion that printed letters make up words; that stories usually have a beginning, middle, and end; and that printed words and spoken words are similar in some ways. Experiences with handling books, becoming aware of the link between letters and their sounds, beginning to recognize printed words, and practicing the actions associated with reading all contribute to early reading proficiency (Hammill, 2004). Depending on the context in which children read, they may also realize that you can learn things from printed words that you cannot always know from the pictures. They discover that reading is a way to learn about the world beyond what you can know through direct experiences.

Children and parents often engage in language games that expand the child's use of words and phrases. These games are usually part of ongoing family life. They are introduced not as a separate activity but as an extension of a related activity. The quality of toys, social games, and conversation between mothers and their infants predicts the level of the child's language development at ages 2 and 3 (Lacroix, Pomerleau, Malcuit, Seguin, & Lamarre, 2001). As an example, one mother described one of her 3½-year-old son David's spontaneous games that began to build the bridge from speech to literacy. As the game developed, the object was for David to point to road signs as he rode with his mother to nursery school and for her to read as many of the signs as possible while they were driving along. David had created this game, and his mother played along willingly (Hoffman, 1985):

On the way to nursery school, David said, "Let's talk about signs! What does that sign say?" I answered, "Right turn signal."

David proceeded with, "And what does that yellow and red shell say?"

I answered him, "It says 'Shell'—that's a gasoline station."

He asked, "Does it have seashells in it?"

I answered, "No."

We proceeded to read signs. I read the majority as he requested. However, David read "Speed Limit 35," "Bike Route," and "No Parking Any Time." When we came to "No Parking This Side of Street," he thought it was "No Parking Any Time."

These were the signs that I was able to read as he requested while I was driving. They were not the only ones on the route.

Speed Limit 40	Watch Children
Bike Route (2 times)	No Parking Any Time (20 times)
Speed Limit 35 (12 times)	Signal Ahead (3 times)
No Turn on Red (3 times)	School Speed Limit (2 times)
No Littering	No Parking on This Side of
Driveway	Street (7 times)

With the achievement of language skills, children and their caregivers begin to explore a vast array of topics through spoken language. They explore their needs—hunger, thirst, sleepiness, and companionship. They travel along

© Istockphoto.com/Digital Planet Design

Copyright © Robert Brenner/Photo Edit

Cindy hopes that by talking with her son now about his feelings she will build a strong basis for communication in the years ahead when their conflicts may be more difficult.

the paths of emotions such as anger, sadness, delight, pride, and shame. They talk playfully with one another, examining new objects, discussing kinship relations, and creating fantasies. Furthermore, adults and children talk about philosophical and moral questions like lying, helping, "what ifs," and the question "how would you feel if it happened to you?" As children speak from their own inner world, revealing their own point of view, parents begin to know and appreciate their children's concerns and needs in a new way. Similarly, children begin to hear and understand their family's talk in a new way. They can question what they do not understand and expand what they know through family talk.

One area that has received special attention is the role of family conversation about feelings and its relation to a child's ability to express feelings and to identify feelings in others. Children's use of words to refer to feelings and to describe emotions increases notably at 3 and 4 years of age. At this same time, children become more skilled at recognizing feelings in others and in understanding how a person might feel in a certain situation (Brown & Dunn, 1992). Toddlers who have frequent experiences of talking with their mothers when they are in distress or conflict appear to be more effective at the age of 6 in understanding the point of view of others and in anticipating others' needs (Dunn, Brown, & Beardsall, 1991). Children who grow up in families that are open to identifying and talking about emotions are more likely to carry on this kind of talk at later ages and to show sensitivity to others in relationships outside the family (Jenkins, Turrell, Kogushi, Lollis, & Ross, 2003).

Fantasy Play

Objective 3. To describe the development of fantasy play and its importance for cognitive and social development.

Fantasy play and language are contrasting forms of representation (Copple, 2003). In acquiring language, children learn to translate their thoughts into a commonly shared system of signs and rules. For language to be effective, children must use the same words and grammar as the older members of the family, discovering how to translate their thoughts into existing words and categories. Fantasy serves almost the opposite function. In fantasy, children create characters and situations that may have a very private meaning. There is no need to make the fantasy comprehensible to an audience. There are probably many times when children have strong feelings but lack the words to express them. They may be frustrated by their helplessness or angry at being overlooked. They can express and soothe these feelings in the world of imagination, even though the feelings may never become part of a shared conversation (Erikson, 1972).

The worlds of make-believe, poetry, fairy tales, and folklore—the domains we often associate with childhood—open up to the toddler as the ability for symbolization expands. Pretend play is not possible without semiotic thinking; it underlies the capacity for imagination, for allowing objects and people to take on new identities and new meaning.

The Nature of Pretend Play

During infancy, play often consists of the repetition of a motor activity. Infants delight in sucking their toes or dropping a spoon from the high chair. These are typical **sensorimotor play** activities. Toward the end of infancy, sensorimotor play includes the deliberate imitation of parental acts. Children who see their mothers washing the dishes may enjoy climbing up on a chair and getting their hands wet, too. At first, these imitations occur only when they are stimulated by the sight of the parent's activity. As children enter toddlerhood, they begin to imitate parental activities when they are alone.

A vivid mental image of an action permits them to copy what they recall instead of what they see. This is the beginning of symbolic play. Before the period of preoperational thought, children do not really pretend because they cannot let one thing stand for something else. Once the capacity for symbolic thought emerges, children become increasingly flexible in allowing an object to take on a wide variety of pretend identities.

Two-year-olds appear to be able to understand the context of a pretend situation. Using pretend props, they can pretend to feed a hungry animal or give a drink to a thirsty animal. They can assign a pretend function to a substitute prop, treating a wooden block as if it were a banana or a piece of cake. And they can follow through with the consequences of a pretend situation, like pretending to wipe up pretend spilled tea with a towel (Harris & Kavanaugh, 1993). These young children can construct a make-believe world, in which objects are assigned a pretend meaning (toy blocks can be bananas) and words are used in pretend ways ("feed the monkey a banana" is acted out by putting a toy block up to the mouth of a toy monkey).

The Capacity for Pretense

A child's ability to pretend provides insight into the child's "theory of mind." **Theory of mind** refers to the way we account for the behaviors of others. This includes the ability to attribute beliefs, desires, and intentions to others, and to realize that these beliefs, desires, and intentions may be the cause for behaviors. Theory of mind also allows children to understand that it is possible for other people to have beliefs, desires, or intentions that differ from their own. This understanding is a *theory* because you cannot actually see the other person's beliefs, desires, or intentions; you have to infer them from your own observations and understanding of how minds work. Theory of mind is a representational extension of the capacities for causal reasoning discussed in infancy. Young babies distinguish animate and inanimate objects; they attribute intentions and goal-directedness to animate objects (Meltzoff, 1995). These very early understandings provide the platform on which more complex representations about others are built. As children mature, sometime between the ages of 3 and 5, they become increasingly accurate in predicting how another person might act, depending on that person's beliefs or knowledge. Imagine the following situation. Allison is shown a small box and asked what she thinks is in the box. Allison says she doesn't know. Then, the experimenter opens the box and shows Allison that there is a toy elephant in the box. Now, the experimenter closes the box, and introduces Allison to a Tiger puppet. The experimenter asks Allison, "What does Tiger think is in the box?" Allison's answer is evidence about how her theory of mind is operating. If Allison says, "The Tiger doesn't know what's in the box," she is demonstrating advanced reasoning about the mind of the other. If Allison says, "The tiger thinks there is an elephant in the box," she is demonstrating immature reasoning about the mind of the other, since she is not able

to separate what she knows from what the Tiger might know (Sabbagh, Bowman, Evraiar, & Ito, 2009).

Sometimes, adults wonder whether children can in fact distinguish between reality and pretense. The line between make-believe and reality may become blurred for all of us. At times, adults can encounter such confusion when watching television. Which televised images are pretend and which are real? Are the images and messages used to advertise products real or pretend? Is a television news story real or pretend? Are dramatic reenactments of historical events real or pretend?

In simplified situations, children as young as 2 can tell when someone is pretending and can follow the transformations in a pretend sequence (Walker-Andrews & Harris, 1993; Rakoczy, Tomasello, & Striano, 2004). For example, an investigator might tell a child that she is going to fill two bowls with cereal, and then pretend to fill the bowls. The investigator then pretends to eat all of the cereal in her bowl, saying something at the end to indicate that all the cereal is gone. She then asks the child to feed a doll its cereal. Many 2-year-olds and most 3-year-olds can follow this type of scenario, selecting the bowl that is still full of pretend cereal and feeding it to the doll.

Studies about pretense lead to further speculations about what toddlers understand about someone else's mental state. For example, some research focuses on what toddlers think is going on in someone else's mind as they are pretending. In judging whether someone else is pretending or not, toddlers tend to focus on the way the person is acting and the context of the situation rather than on what the person's intentions might be. Toddlers are quite accurate about judging when someone is engaging in make-believe or in a realistic activity, but they may not be able to tell you what the person is thinking about (Rosen, Schwebel, & Singer, 1997; Ganea, Lillard, & Turkheimer, 2004; Sobel, 2004).

Toddlers know the difference between what an object really is and what someone is pretending that it is (Flavell, Flavell, & Green, 1987). For example, 3-year-olds understand that a sponge is really a sponge, but they can pretend it is a boat floating in the water or a car driving along the road. Three-year-olds also understand the difference between knowing something and pretending something. If they see a rabbit, they know it is real, but they also know that they do not have to have seen a rabbit in order to imagine one. However, compared with older children, 3-year-olds are more convinced that imagination reflects reality. If they imagine something, like a fire-breathing dragon or a horse with wings, they think it may actually exist. In contrast, 4-year-olds understand that something that is imagined may not have a counterpart in reality (Woolley & Wellman, 1993).

Changes in Fantasy Play during Toddlerhood

Toddlers can direct their play in response to mental images that they have generated by themselves. At first, their symbolic play is characterized by the simple repetition of familiar activities. Pretending to sweep the floor, to be asleep, to be a dog or a cat, and to drive a car are some of the early play activities of toddlers. Fantasy play changes in four ways during toddlerhood (Lucariello, 1987; Tamis-LeMonda, Uzgiris, & Bornstein, 2002):

1. The action component becomes more complex as children integrate a sequence of actions.
2. Children's focus shifts from the self to fantasies that involve others and the creation of multiple roles.
3. The play involves the use of substitute objects, including objects children only pretend to have, and eventually the invention of complex characters and situations.
4. The play becomes more organized and planned, and play leaders emerge.

First, children combine a number of actions in a play sequence. From pretending to sweep the floor or take a nap, they devise strings of activities that are part of a complex play sequence. While playing firefighter, children may pretend to be the fire truck, the hose, the ladder, the engine, the siren, the people being rescued, and the firefighters. All the elements of the situation are brought under the children's control through this fantasy enactment.

Second, children become increasingly able to include others in their play and to shift the focus of the play from the self to the others (Howes, 1987; Howes, Unger, & Seidner, 1989). One can see a distinction here between solitary pretense, social play, and **social pretend play**. Children engaged in solitary pretense are involved in their own fantasy activities, such as pretending that they are driving a car or giving a baby a bath. Children engaged in social play join with other children in some activity. They may dig together in the sand, build with blocks, or imitate each other's silly noises. In social pretend play, children have to coordinate their pretense. They establish a fantasy structure, take roles, agree on the make-believe meaning of props, and solve pretend problems. That 2- and 3-year-olds can participate in this type of coordinated fantasy play is remarkable, especially given their very limited use of language to establish and sustain coordination.

Third, fantasy play changes as children become more flexible in their use of substitute objects in their play. Fantasy play begins in the areas closest to children's daily experience. They use real objects or play versions of those objects as props in their pretense. For example, they pick up a toy telephone and pretend to call Grandma, or they pretend to have a picnic with toy cups and plates and plastic foods. But as they develop their fantasy skills, these props are no longer essential. Children can invent objects, create novel uses for common objects, and sometimes pretend to have an object when they have nothing (Boyatzis & Watson, 1993). Despite these remarkably inventive capacities to impose meaning on neutral objects, children's toys have become increasingly more realistic, reflecting the nature of modern technology. Whereas experts in early childhood education continue to recommend the use of flexible, open-ended play materials for young children, toy makers appear to be enthusiastic about producing realistic play materials.

© Elizabeth Crews

One of the favorite forms of social pretense is "doctor." With the use of a few props, friends can explore the fascinating realm of illness, healing, comforting, and advising. Patient-doctor play allows children to gain mastery over an area of great concern and uncertainty.

Play moves away from common daily experiences to invented worlds based on stories, television programs, or purely imagined characters and situations. Three-year-olds begin to generate negative as well as positive imaginary images, including fears about supernatural creatures, witches, ghosts, and monsters. Children may take the roles of characters with extraordinary powers. They may pretend to fly, become invisible, or transform themselves into other shapes with the aid of a few secret words or gestures. Their identification with a particular fantasy hero or heroine may last for days or even weeks as they involve the characters of the story in a variety of fantasy situations.

Fourth, fantasy play becomes more planned and organized. The planning emerges as children try to coordinate their pretend play with other players. It is also a product of a new realization of what makes pretend play most fun, and of the desire to make sure that those components are included in the play. In a preschool or day care group, certain children are likely to take the lead in organizing the direction of fantasy play. They may set the play in motion or give it direction by suggesting the use of certain props, assigning roles, or working out the context of the play. In this example, a child demonstrates this kind of leadership:

STUART (climbing up on a tractor tire): This will be our shark ship, OK? Get on quick, Jeremy! The sharks will eat you!

JEREMY: No! This is my police helicopter!

STUART: Well, OK. We're police. But we need to chase the sharks, OK? I see the sharks way down there! Come on!

JEREMY: OK. Let's get 'em! (They both make helicopter noises and swat at make-believe sharks with plastic garden tools.) (Trawick-Smith, 1988, p. 53)

Some theorists distinguish symbolic role-playing from games with rules, implying that the latter are guided by a formal set of mental operations that constrain play, whereas the former is open and flexible. However, it is clear that pretend play operates within a rule-bound structure (Vygotsky, 1978; Harris & Kavanaugh, 1993). In order to coordinate **symbolic play** with a partner, children have to come to some mutual understanding about the situation, props, characters, and plot. The players have to limit their behavior in ways that conform to the unspoken or latent rules of the pretense. For example, if the children decide that certain leaves are the pretend food, then no one can use the leaves as bricks to build a house or as hats. If one player is supposed to be the mommy, that player has to act like the mommy and not like the baby. In games with rules, the rules are more readily spelled out, but in both types of play, part of what makes it fun is to function within the boundaries of certain kinds of constraints.

Dramatic role-playing, in which a child takes on the role of another person or creates a fantasy situation, increases steadily from the ages of 3 through 5. By the age of 6, however, children become involved in games with rules. They may use their fantasy skills during play by making up new games or new rules rather than by engaging in pretend play. If one is looking for the experts in diversified, elaborated fantasy, observe 4- and 5-year-olds.

Theoretical Views about the Contributions of Fantasy Play to Development

Fantasy play is not simply a diversion. Children use fantasy to experiment with and understand their social and physical environments and to expand their thinking (Pellegrini & Bjorklund, 2004). Theoretical views of the importance and value of fantasy play vary widely. Here we consider how Piaget, Vygotsky, and Erikson understood the role of fantasy play.

Piaget (1962) emphasized the assimilative value of play. He believed that through fantasy and symbolic play, children are able to make meaning of experiences and events that are beyond their full comprehension. Fantasy play is a private world to which the rules of social convention and the logic of the physical world do not necessarily apply. From this perspective, fantasy play frees the child from the immediacy of reality, permitting mental manipulations and modifications of objects and events. One cognitive benefit of fantasy play is the opportunity to engage in role reversal, taking turns playing the various characters, which helps to advance perspective taking among play companions.

Vygotsky (1978) saw fantasy play quite differently.

Play creates a zone of proximal development of the child. In play a child always behaves beyond his average age, above his daily behavior; in play it is as though he were a head taller than himself. As in the focus of a magnifying glass, play contains all developmental tendencies in a condensed form and is itself a major source of development. (p. 102)

Vygotsky used the term **zone of proximal development** to refer to the distance between the actual level of a child's performance, and the potential level that a child is capable of reaching with help from a more skilled peer or adult. When trying to assess a child's developmental level, it is important to understand not only what the child already knows and can already perform, but also the domains that are in progress, so to speak—the areas that are emerging as new fields of mastery. Normally adults—especially parents and teachers—and more advanced peers promote development by engaging children in activities and problem-solving tasks that draw children into their zone of proximal development—the new directions along which their capacities are moving. However, in play, Vygotsky saw a cognitive process that in and of itself captures a foreshadowing of the child's next higher level of functioning.

In pretend play, children address areas where they do not yet feel competent in their lives and try to act as if they were competent. They set rules for their performance, and they commit themselves to function according to them. So if a child is pretending to be a good mother, she brings forward all the ideas she has about how to be a good mother and applies them to the pretend situation. Similarly, if a child is pretending to be a superhero, she imposes all the rules of power, goodness, and helpfulness that she knows of and tries to limit her actions to those rules. Vygotsky regarded fantasy play as a window into the areas of competence that the child is striving to master but are still out of reach.

Erikson (1972) considered fantasy play vital in promoting personality and social development. He valued play as a mechanism for dramatizing the psychological conflicts that children are struggling with, such as angry feelings toward their siblings or parents, or jealousy over a friend's new toys. According to Erikson, the play often not only represents the problem but also offers a solution, so that children experience some new sense of resolution and a reduction in the tension associated with the conflict. Symbolic play provides a certain flexibility or leeway in structuring the situation and, at the same time, imposes some limits so that children may experience a new mastery of issues that are perplexing or overwhelming in real life. One way that children use pretend play to explore relationship issues and mastery of puzzling questions involves creating an imaginary companion to serve as a play partner (see the box "Imaginary Companions").

Pretend play is a form of representational thought—a way that children experiment with the relationships of objects and social roles. For children who have some forms of language delay, observations of their pretense provides insight into their cognitive capacities (Butterfield, 1994). Research suggests that pretend play actually fosters cognitive, emotional, and social development. Children who have well-developed pretending skills tend to be well liked by their peers and to be viewed as leaders. This is a result of their advanced communication skills, their greater ability to take the point of view of others, and their ability to reason about social situations. Children who have

APPLYING THEORY AND RESEARCH TO LIFE

Imaginary Companions

PROBABLY THE MOST sophisticated form of symbolic play is the creation of an imaginary friend (Singer, 1975). An imaginary friend, which may be an animal, a child, or some other creature, springs complete in concept from the mind of the child. It occupies space. It has its own personality, which is consistent from day to day. It has its own likes and dislikes, which are not necessarily the same as those of its creator. The prevalence of **imaginary companions** may be greater than one might have guessed. Although not all children who have imaginary companions will disclose this information to adults, some studies have shown that as many as 65% of young children have imaginary companions, and some children have more than one (Singer & Singer, 1990).

In one study in the United Kingdom, 1,800 children were asked about past or present experience with imaginary companions. Roughly 46% said they had one (Pearson et al., 2001). When parents were surveyed about their children, those with imaginary companions were more likely to be firstborn or only children, were judged by parents to be very imaginative in other aspects of their play, and to enjoy magical or fantasy play as compared to other forms of play. Children who have imaginary companions also report a more vivid imagery when daydreaming or engaging in pretend play, and more mythical creatures in their dreams (Bouldin, 2006). Children who have imaginary companions also tend to have more extensive language competence, which is observable in their ongoing conversations with their invisible friend (Bouldin & Pratt, 1999; Gleason, Sebanc, & Hartup, 2003). One by-product of having ongoing conversations with an imaginary companion and telling others about one's adventures with an imaginary companion is that children gain practice in storytelling. As a result, children who have imaginary companions also have advanced abilities to produce verbal narratives as evidenced in the way they retell stories, explain past situations to others, and expand on their experiences in social conversations (Trifoni & Reese, 2009).

In one study, investigators invited children who had imaginary companions to come to the laboratory and play with their companions (Taylor, Cartwright, & Carlson, 1993). The children seemed willing to talk about their companions, and they thought the investigators would be able to see and touch their companions just as they could. For most of the children, the companions remained consistent for 6 months and retained an active role in the child's fantasy life.

Several functions are served by an imaginary friend: it takes the place of other children when there are none around; it serves as a play companion for pretend play; it serves as a confidant for children's private expression; and it is often involved in their efforts to differentiate between right and wrong (Taylor & Mannering, 2006). Children can distinguish the social relationship they have with their imaginary companion from the relationships they have with parents, siblings, and best friends. Imaginary companions and real friends are viewed as similar in many ways, but children are more likely to comfort and nurture their imaginary friend than their real friend (Gleason, 2002).

Critical Thinking Questions

1. How do imaginary friends get created? What experiences, ideas, or mental states might be necessary in order for an imaginary companion to be invented?
2. Imagine that you are 3 or 4 years old. What type of imaginary companion would you create for yourself? Why? Could you have an imaginary companion now? Is there an equivalent of an imaginary companion in the lives of adults? What functions do they fill?
3. Design a study to explore the similarities and differences between imaginary friends and real friends. What approach might you take to investigate this question? What would be some challenges you would need to overcome in order to pursue this problem?
4. Suppose that a parent comes to you with a concern about the fact that their child has an imaginary companion. What information would you need in order to understand the nature of the imaginary companion and the functions it serves for the child? Depending on the information you gather, what might be the optimal approach for parents toward their child's imaginary companion?

been encouraged in a playful, imaginative approach to the manipulation and exploration of materials and objects through fantasy show more complex language use and more flexible approaches to problem solving. Children who have frequent opportunities for pretend play—especially with a more experienced play partner—are better able to express their feelings, show higher levels of empathy, and are more aware of their emotional states (Galyer & Evans, 2001; Lindsey & Colwell, 2003).

Fantasy play is essential for the full social, intellectual, and emotional development of young children. Some parents and teachers want to define a young child's cognitive growth in terms of the acquisition of words and concepts that seem relevant to the real world. They emphasize the importance of learning numbers and letters, memorizing facts, and learning to read. However, research on cognitive development suggests that gains in the capacity for symbolic thought provide essential underpinnings for subsequent intellectual abilities, such as abstract reasoning and inventive problem solving.

The Role of Play Companions

Cognitive developmental theory emphasizes the normal emergence of representational thought and symbolic play as the natural outcome of cognitive maturation during toddlerhood. However, the quality of that play as well as its content depends in part on the behavior of a child's play companions. Consider the following incident:

> In a university preschool where college students were having their first supervised experience as teachers of young children, a child of 3 made a bid for some pretend play with a student teacher. The child picked up the toy telephone and made ringing noises. The student teacher picked up another phone and said, "Hello." The child asked, "Is Milly there?" The student teacher said, "No," and hung up the phone. Rather than extending the pretense into a more elaborate social pretend situation by saying something like "Who is calling?" or pretending to put Milly on the phone, the student teacher brought the scenario to a close.

As play companions, parents, siblings, peers, and child care professionals can significantly enrich a child's fantasy play. Play companions can elaborate a child's capacity for fantasy, legitimize fantasy play, and help the child to explore new domains of fantasy. Research has shown that when mothers are available as play companions, the symbolic play of their 2-year-old children is more complex and lasts longer (Slade, 1987; Tamis-LeMonda, Uzgiris, & Bornstein, 2002). When adults are trained to engage in and encourage pretend play with toddlers, the toddlers show a higher level of ability to coordinate their responses with those of the adults. From age 16 to 32 months, toddlers become increasingly skillful in directing an adult's behavior and negotiating changes in kinds of play (Eckerman & Didow, 1989). Early and frequent opportunities to pretend with older siblings as well as with parents contribute to a young child's ability to understand other people's feelings and beliefs. As toddlers experiment with pretend roles, construct fantasy situations, and manipulate objects with a play companion, they are forced to establish new channels of shared meaning, thus fostering a new degree of awareness about self and others (Youngblade & Dunn, 1995).

In child care settings, the availability of a consistent group of age-mates results in more complex, coordinated play. In contrast, children who have had many changes in their child care arrangements are less likely to engage in complex social pretend play with other children (Howes & Stewart, 1987). Because toddlers rely so heavily on imitation and nonverbal signals to initiate and develop their social pretend play, the more time they have together, the more complex their fantasy play will be (Eckerman & Didow, 1996).

The importance of pretense and the way pretend play is nurtured depends in part on the meaning it is given in one's culture. For example, among the Ijaw of Nigeria, children under 5 are thought to have a special link with the female creator spirit. Adults may watch a young child playing alone, interacting with imaginary companions by giving out pretend food, or speaking to them in a happy tone. Rather than dismissing this activity as child's play, the adults believe that the child is interacting with the spirit world and will take care not to disrupt the activity. An Ijaw woman who wants to become pregnant might try to appeal to a small child, hoping that if she is kind to the child, the child will use this special link to the spirit world to help bring about the pregnancy (Valsiner, 2000). The nature and role of imaginary companions may be tolerated by U.S. families, but among scholars of child development, they are considered evidence of advanced symbolic representation, an emerging sense of self, and a strategy for achieving new levels of self-control.

Self-Control

Objective 4. To examine the development of self-control, especially impulse management and goal attainment, highlighting strategies young children use to help regulate their actions.

Do you ever find that you roll over for 10 more minutes of sleep even when you know you should get out of bed? Do you let your mind wander when you need to be paying attention? Do you go for that extra helping of cake when you are trying to lose 5 pounds? These are just a few examples of lapses in self-control. **Self-regulation** is frequently noted as a marker of maturity. The ability to control impulses, direct action toward a goal, express and inhibit the expression of emotions, and resist temptation are all evidence of this capacity (Heatherton, 2000; Myrseth & Fishbach, 2009). Over time, self-control becomes a foundation for moral behavior. For toddlers, self-control is the ability to comply with a request, modify behavior according to the situation, initiate or postpone action, and behave in a socially acceptable way without having to be guided or directed by someone else (Kopp, 1982). In the following sections we consider two components of self-control: (1) control of impulses, which you might think of as a form of self-control directed inward toward managing one's emotional states and drives (see the "Applying Theory and Research to Life" box below for a discussion of the expression and control of angry feelings); and (2) self-directed goal attainment, which you might think of as a form of self-control directed outward toward mastery of the environment.

Control of Impulses

Early in infancy, self-control is usually understood as the infant's ability to prevent the disorganization of behavior brought on by overstimulation and to recover from emotional distress. Babies have a variety of internal regulating strategies (Kopp, 1982). For example, by sucking or rocking, babies can soothe themselves. They can also resist overstimulation by turning away from the source of stimulation, crying, or going to sleep.

During toddlerhood, children improve their ability to modify and control their impulses. The case of Colin illustrates how toddlers may fail to control their impulses. Sometimes, they simply cannot interrupt an ongoing action, even one they know is inappropriate. Colin, age 2 years 9 months, is just starting preschool:

> In his relations with children, Colin progressed quickly from a quiet, friendly, watching relationship on the first few days to actively hugging the other children. The hugging seemed to be in an excess of friendliness and was only mildly aggressive. Having started hugging, he didn't know how to stop, and usually just held on until he pulled the child down to the floor. This was followed very closely by hair pulling. He didn't pull viciously, but still held on long enough to get a good resistance from the child. He grabbed toys from others. When stopped by an adult from any of these acts, he was very responsive to reason, would say, smiling, "I won't do it any more," would tear around the room in disorganized activity, and then return to hugging or pulling hair. (Murphy, 1956, pp. 11–12)

From age 2 to 4, most children are increasingly able to modify and control their impulses and withstand delays in gratification. They also become more willing to modify their behavior because they do not wish to cause distress to others. The ability to regulate or restrain behavior is a product of changing cognitive, social, and emotional competencies. Children become increasingly sensitive to the negative consequences of impulsive acts. At the same time, they develop new strategies to help manage feelings of frustration, such as distracting themselves and redirecting their attention to some alternative activity or toy, creating a pretend scenario in which they soothe themselves through conversation with a fantasy character, using some physical soothing or comforting strategy like thumb sucking or cuddling with a blanket, and seeking comfort or distraction from a parent or play companion (Zahn-Waxler, Radke-Yarrow, Wagner, & Chapman, 1992; Grolnick, Bridges, & Connell, 1996).

Increasing Sensitivity to the Distress of Others. Toddlers can observe and empathize with distress expressed in others, both children and adults. Moreover, they begin to understand when they have been the cause of someone else's distress (Zahn-Waxler, Radke-Yarrow et al., 1992; Zahn-Waxler, Robinson, & Emde, 1992). Often, the socialization environment helps to focus toddlers' attention on these instances when parents or teachers point out their actions and the consequences. The following observation from a study of family interaction shows how a conversation about negative consequences and a child's concern over his mother's distress contributed to the self-regulation of impulses:

> Danny is 33 months old. He and his mother are at the sink washing dishes. Danny blows a handful of suds at his mother and some gets in her eyes. Danny is laughing at this new game.
>
> MOTHER: No! Nuh uh, Danny. Danny, you got it in my eye. (mild negative affect)
> Danny stops laughing.
>
> MOTHER: Don't do that in my eye, OK? It hurts to get soap in your eye.
>
> DANNY: (very serious) I won't. (Brown & Dunn, 1992, pp. 347–348)

It takes a lot of self-control for Anna to cope with the baby's screaming. She holds her ears, grits her teeth, and shakes her leg rather than give the baby a wallop.

© Elliott Erwitt/Magnum Photos

APPLYING THEORY AND RESEARCH TO LIFE

The Expression and Control of Angry Feelings

THE EXPRESSION OF anger, which is important to the child's development of a sense of autonomy, typically generates tension between parents and children (Wenar, 1982). Toddlers get angry for many reasons, including inability to perform a task, parental restrictions on behavior, and peer or sibling rivalry. As toddlers become increasingly involved in directing the outcomes of their activities, they get angry when someone interrupts them or offers unrequested assistance. Toddlers are likely to get angry when they are tired, or when forced to make a transition from something they are enjoying to something someone else wants them to do. Studies involving observational coding of toddler behavior and mothers' reports of infants and toddlers provide evidence that during the second year of life, children begin to use physical aggression toward other children, especially when they want to get something that another child has or in retaliation if a child hits them (Baillargeon et al., 2007). The most common forms of physical aggression

at this age are kicking, biting, pushing, and hitting. Between ages 2 and 5, the frequency of physical aggression declines as children develop effective strategies for self-control.

In addition to physical aggression, some children use **relational aggression** to harm others. In toddlerhood, relational aggression involves behaviors that result in social exclusion by refusing to let a child join in a play activity, making fun of another child, telling another child that you don't want to be his or her friend, or failing to invite one child to a party when many other children in the class or group are invited (Murray-Close & Ostrov, 2009).

Some children are temperamentally more aggressive than others. Although occasional acts of aggression are not uncommon among toddlers, only a small percentage of toddlers are frequently aggressive and irritable (Tremblay et al., 2004; Paulussen-Hoogeboom, Stams, Hermanns, & Peetsma, 2007). These children have been characterized by negative emotionality and difficulties in emotion regulation. They are more frequently in a negative mood, get angry easily, have a highly intense negative reaction to any type of limit-setting, and when upset, have a hard time recovering or returning to a calm state (Calkins & Dedmon, 2000).

Children rely on their parents as models for learning how to express and control anger. The times when parents are angry are very important. Children learn as much or more about the expression of anger from watching their parents when they are angry as they do from verbal explanations or punishment (Bandura, 1977). Children are sensitive to angry expressions directed toward them through both verbal and nonverbal behavior. In some parent-child dyads, anger is a dominant theme in the parenting interactions (Aber, Belsky, Slade, & Crnic, 1999). Parents who are angry and abusive toward their children provide a model for the imitation of angry behavior. Children are also sensitive to anger between their parents, even when it is not directed at them. Parents' hostility to each other, expressed through quarrels, sarcasm, and physical abuse, increases children's sensitivity to anger and is closely related to disturbances in development (Kochanska, Aksan, & Joy, 2007).

Not all parenting efforts are directed at inhibiting the expression of anger. In an ethnographic study of the socialization of anger and aggression, three 2-year-old girls and their mothers from a working-class neighborhood of Baltimore were studied in detail. The mothers considered assertiveness

Discipline Strategies and Impulse Control. In toddlerhood, the immediate aim of discipline is to achieve compliance (Kochanska, Aksan, & Koenig, 1995). A parent typically wants children to stop doing something ("Don't touch those figurines; they might break") or to do something ("Help me put the toys away now; it's time to go to bed"). If the child complies, a parent might respond positively by smiling, patting the child or giving a hug, or complimenting the child for being good, helpful, or obedient. If the child does not comply, a parent may try some form of distraction or offer some choice ("You can help clean up now or in 5 minutes"). But if compliance is not forthcoming, some type of discipline is likely to ensue. Discipline practices have been described in three general categories (Hoffman, 1977):

1. **Power assertion**: Physical punishment; shouting; attempts to physically move a child or inhibit behavior; taking away privileges or resources; or threatening any of these things.

2. **Love withdrawal**: Expressing anger, disappointment, or disapproval; refusing to communicate; walking out or turning away.

3. **Inductions**: Explaining why the behavior was wrong; pointing out the consequences of the behavior to others; redirecting the behavior by appealing to the child's sense of mastery, fair play, or love of another person.

In addition to these three general categories of discipline techniques, parental modeling and reinforcement of acceptable behaviors are significant in the development of internal control (Maccoby, 1992). In order to correct their behavior, children must know what acts are considered appropriate as well as how to inhibit their inappropriate acts. Modeling and reinforcement aid children in directing their behavior; discipline serves to inhibit or redirect it.

The manner in which the discipline is carried out over time is associated with child outcomes, especially increases in compliance, prosocial behavior, and the eventual

and self-defense essential to survival in their neighborhood. Along with socialization strategies that focused on controlling inappropriate aggression, the mothers found many ways to model aggressiveness as they talked to others in the girls' presence and to reward certain displays of toughness and assertiveness in the girls' behavior (Miller & Sperry, 1987).

Children who can express anger without losing control make tremendous gains in the development of autonomy. Anger or conflict with parents gives toddlers evidence that they are indeed separate from their parents and that this separateness, although painful, is legitimate. Children who are severely punished or ridiculed for their anger are left in a state of doubt. They see models for the expression of anger in the way their parents respond to them, and yet they are told that anger is not appropriate for them. The goal in the socialization of angry feelings is to help children find legitimate expressions of anger without hurting themselves or others.

Several strategies help young children manage or reduce the intensity of their anger. These parenting strategies have to be coordinated with the child's temperament and the ecological context in which parenting takes place (Thompson, 1990; Brinkmeyer & Eyberg, 2003; Kochanska, Aksan, & Joy, 2007).

- Increase a child's experiences of positive, responsive interactions with caregivers, which has been found to increase a child's sense of security and willingness to cooperate with parental requests.
- Provide brief time-out periods in a nearby quiet area to help children return to a calm state.
- Arouse feelings that are incompatible with anger, especially empathy for a possible target for one's aggressive impulses.
- Minimize exposure to stimuli that arouse aggressive or fearful impulses.
- Explain the consequences of a child's aggressive actions for others.
- Suggest ideas about acceptable ways to express angry feelings.
- Model strategies for nonaggressive responses to frustration and conflict.

Critical Thinking Questions

1. What are some of the adaptive functions of anger as a basic emotion?
2. How does the expression of anger help a toddler achieve autonomy? What functions might the expression of anger serve in later stages of development?
3. Why is anger both difficult to express and difficult to control once it is expressed?
4. How does the expression of angry feelings fit in with your ideas about optimal child rearing strategies and socialization goals?
5. The research suggests that there are temperamental differences in the tendency to get angry, and these differences might be accentuated by certain parenting practices. Imagine that you are advising parents about how to respond to their child's anger. What different advice would you give if you thought that the child was especially anger-prone as compared to a child who was especially fearful and inhibited?
6. What might be some gender differences in the experiences of anger and in societal preferences for the expression and control of anger? Do you think there is a biological basis for gender differences in aggressive behavior? What evidence would you need to support your conclusion?
7. Imagine that you tried all the methods suggested at the end of the box to help reduce your child's aggressiveness and none of them was effective. What would you conclude? What would you do?

internalization of moral standards; or increases in noncompliance, aggressiveness, and low levels of moral reasoning. Three features of the approach to discipline appear to be important (O'Leary, 1995):

1. The discipline should be immediate or as close in time to the situation as possible. Laxness in discipline, such as laughing at an undesirable behavior, waiting too long to respond, reprimanding the child sometimes but not at other times for the same misconduct, or inadvertently rewarding a child for misconduct are all practices that are likely to increase rather than decrease the undesired behavior.

2. The discipline for a toddler should be brief. It is important to make sure that the toddler understands what the misbehavior was and why it was wrong, but the explanation should be concise and presented at the toddler's level of understanding. Punishment involving love withdrawal is especially likely to be carried on too long. The parent should make sure the toddler knows when the punishment is over, and not let the child spend hours thinking the parent is still angry.

3. The discipline should be appropriately firm, but not overreactive. The response to noncompliance should be coordinated with the child's behavior, focusing on expressing concern for the harm that was done, engaging the child in talking about how to repair the situation, and setting the stage for what the child might do next (Edwards & Liu, 2002). Practices that are intensely harsh, abusive, or cruel, whether they involve physical or emotional intensity, are associated with increases in problem behaviors. Infrequent use of power-assertive punishment in an overall context of a warm, nurturing relationship may be effective in fostering compliance. However, intense and frequent harsh punishment is associated with a variety of maladaptive consequences for children (Weiss, Dodge, Bates, & Petit, 1992; Repetti, Taylor, & Seeman, 2002).

Economic hardship produces emotional distress among parents, which is likely to result in harsh, neglectful, or erratic parent-child interactions (McLoyd, 1990). Mothers living in poverty are more likely than more affluent mothers to use power assertion and physical punishment as a form of discipline. Studies of the relationship of poverty to parenting practices and children's mental health have found that the amount of spanking parents use is directly related to the family's current level of poverty. This pattern has been observed in Black, Hispanic, and non-Hispanic White families. Furthermore, the more likely parents are to use spanking and harsh discipline—especially when it is used without accompanying emotional support or warmth—the more likely their children are to show signs of emotional distress (depression, fearfulness, and crying) and externally directed behaviors such as arguing, disobedience, destructiveness, and impulsiveness (McLeod & Shanahan, 1993; Conger et al., 2002; McLoyd & Smith, 2002).

Infants and toddlers whose home environments are characterized by high levels of conflict, anger, and aggression, and who are targets of harsh, cold, unsupportive, and neglectful environments are at great risk for disruptions in self-regulation. Early experiences of abuse produce repeated physiological responses of fear, anxiety, and stress. Over time, these stress responses result in greater fearfulness, dysregulation of the natural systems that are helpful in calming and controlling emotions, and difficulty regulating anxiety and depression. Emotional processing is also disrupted under conditions of harsh parenting. Toddlers have fewer chances to observe or model effective strategies for handling conflict and are more likely to behave in aggressive ways with peers. The lack of social competence that is caused by harsh parenting is likely to result in peer rejection, weak social relationship skills, and low levels of social integration (Repetti, Taylor, & Seeman, 2002).

Individual Differences in the Ability to Control Impulses.

The ability to delay gratification varies with the individual. At least three factors are associated with differences in the ease or difficulty that children have in controlling their impulses (see Figure 6.3). First, toddlers differ in their capacity to empathize with the distress of others. Empathy itself appears to have a genetic as well as an environmental basis. In a study of identical and fraternal twins who were 2 years old, the identical twins showed greater similarity in their emotional concern about and response to others' distress than did the fraternal twins. Moreover, mothers who showed a stronger concern for others in their childrearing strategies had children whose empathy was more fully developed. Furthermore, girls were observed to be more empathic than boys (Zahn-Waxler, Robinson et al., 1992). Individual differences in sensitivity to the distress of others lead to differences in how upset children might be when their behavior causes someone else's suffering and in how willing the child may be to curb that behavior in the future.

Second, differences in temperament affect self-control. Children who are more aggressive, active, or socially

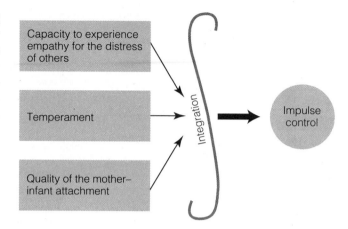

FIGURE 6.3 Factors Associated with the Ability to Control Impulses

outgoing may experience more situations in which their actions are viewed as disruptive or in need of control. In contrast, children who are more socially inhibited, withdrawn, or passive may encounter fewer expectations to curb or restrict their behavior (Kochanska & Radke-Yarrow, 1992). The temperamental characteristic described as **effortful control** refers to a child's ability to suppress a dominant response and perform a subdominant response instead. For example, even when Riley wants to shout out loud, he can talk in a whisper because he sees that grandpa is napping and he does not want to wake grandpa. Infants who are less emotionally intense in their expressions of anger or joy, and who are more cautious in a novel situation, have been found to have greater effortful control in toddlerhood (Kochanska & Knaack, 2003).

In addition, effortful control reflects the ability to slow down one's actions on request and suppress movement in response to instructions (e.g., sit still; stop fidgeting; walk, don't run). One measure of effortful control requires a child to move a toy turtle and a toy rabbit along a curved path toward a barn. Effortful control is demonstrated in the child's ability to move the rabbit quickly and the turtle slowly along the same path. Children show substantial improvement in their effortful control over the period from ages 2 to 4 (Li-Grining, 2007). Longitudinal evidence suggests that effortful control in toddlerhood provides a basis for the formation of conscience and moral development in the early school-age period. It allows the young child to respond more easily to parental requests and to interrupt or suppress undesirable behaviors (Kochanska, Murray, & Harlan, 2000).

Third, the capacity for self-regulation may depend on the quality of the mother-infant attachment. Maternal responsiveness, emotional expressiveness, and a sense of connection are associated with a child's ability to delay gratification. Sensitive caregiving, in which the mother and toddler are able to coordinate their interactions to sustain longer periods of mutually responsive interaction, is associated with an enhanced capacity for self-regulation. Toddlers who experience this rhythmic co-regulation are better able to distract themselves and deliberately guide their attention away from tempting objects that they are not allowed to touch (Li-Grining, 2007).

Since the early 1960s, Walter Mischel and his colleagues have investigated the process by which children delay gratification. To delay gratification, a child must exert willpower in order to resist a strong immediate pull or temptation. This requires shifting attention or distancing oneself from the immediate situation and redirecting attention or action in order to achieve a different goal (Mischel & Ayduk, 2002). For example, when they were at the zoo, Kelly asked for ice cream. Her mother said she could either have ice cream now or go to McDonalds for dinner when they left the zoo. Kelly agreed to wait and go to McDonalds. At age 4, children who delay gratification longer tend to be more intelligent, more likely to resist temptation, demonstrate greater social responsibility, and have higher achievement strivings.

According to Mischel's research, a 4-year-old's ability to use self-regulatory strategies to delay gratification has enduring effects. More than 10 years later, children who had waited longer in an experimental situation that required a self-imposed **delay of gratification** at age 4 were described by their parents as socially and academically more competent than their peers. Their parents rated these children as more verbally fluent and able to express ideas, using and responding to reason, and more competent and skillful. These children were more attentive and able to concentrate, plan, and think ahead, and they were also seen as better able to cope with frustration and resist temptation (Mischel et al., 1989; Morf & Mischel, 2002).

Other longitudinal studies have supported the strong link between early evidence of self-control and subsequent socialization. Children who are able to regulate their emotional reactions and resist temptations in toddlerhood are less likely to violate parental rules, they are more likely to plan as they approach new tasks, and as a result, they are more likely to be successful in school settings where cooperation and compliance are highly valued (Rothbart, Ahadi, & Evans, 2000; Tangney, Baumeister, & Boone, 2004). A growing body of research supports the relationship of children's self-regulatory competence and many positive outcomes, including: better scholastic performance; more successful social functioning; and fewer behavior problems. By adolescence, self-control is a better predictor of academic performance than IQ (Eisenberg, Fabes, Guthrie, & Reiser, 2002; Duckworth & Seligman, 2005). Children who are able to resist temptations are demonstrating that they can outwit their desires, using a variety of strategies to achieve longer-term goals that may be in conflict with immediate pleasure.

The Role of Language and Fantasy in Impulse Control.
Language and fantasy are children's most useful tools for managing impulses. Talking about feelings and needs enables adults to help children understand more about their emotions and to devise strategies for self-regulation. Although we tend to think of self-control as internally initiated and managed, there are many social prompts that foster self-control and help children manage their impulses (Fitzsimons & Finkel, 2010). Thompson (1990) identified four ways that

caregivers use talking about emotions to help young children gain impulse control. First, parents articulate the family or cultural rules of emotional expression: "Don't get so excited; calm down!" or "Stop that fussing; big boys don't whine and cry!" These lessons give young children an idea about the acceptable levels of impulses or emotional intensity and about the types of emotions that need to be regulated.

Second, adults help modify the intensity of emotions through reassuring or distracting talk. They may try to distract a child who is worried about getting an injection, or try to convince the child that the shot won't hurt or that it will be just a little sting. They may try to comfort a sobbing child by talking about some happy event that will distract the child.

Third, adults give children ideas for ways to manage their impulses. They might help by suggesting that the child think of pleasant times from the past or by singing a cheerful song. Adults teach children superstitions, rituals, and stories about how people handle their strong feelings.

Fourth, children listen to and imitate adults who talk about their own strong emotions and impulses. Toddlers who can talk to themselves may be able to control their fears, modify their anger, and soften their disappointments. They may repeat their parents' comforting words, or they may develop their own verbal strategies for reducing pain and suffering.

The development of symbolic fantasy allows children to create imaginary situations in which disturbing problems can be expressed and resolved. Through fantasy play, toddlers can control situations that are far beyond their real-world capacities (Singer & Singer, 1990). They can punish and forgive, harm and heal, fear and conquer fear—all within the boundaries of their own imagination. Children can use the context of pretense to manage strong feelings and to preserve their emotional control (Galyer & Evans, 2001). When Robbie feels bad about something, he says, "Superheroes don't cry." He is making use of fantasy and language to control his emotional state. When children are asked to resist temptation, they use a variety of verbal strategies, including talking quietly to themselves and singing songs to distract themselves (Mischel, Shoda, & Rodriguez, 1989).

Self-Regulated Goal Attainment
The second sense in which self-control develops has to do with toddlers' feelings that they can direct their own behavior and the behavior of others to achieve intended outcomes (Messer, Rachford, McCarthy, & Yarrow, 1987). During infancy, children become increasingly aware of themselves as causal agents. They make things happen. In toddlerhood, children become much more assertive about their desire to initiate actions, persist in activities, and determine when these activities should stop.

Benjamin at 27 months, 17 days:

When I put him to bed tonight he bellowed at the top of his lungs for a good five minutes from sheer rage that I wouldn't let him get down on the floor and go on playing with his car. What he wants and doesn't want he can be very noisy about—but he can also obviously be rather confused as to what he does want....This is especially true in the afternoon after his nap. He may wake up demanding a ride or a walk. By the time he gets downstairs, it has switched to "Want to pway bwocks." (Church, 1966, p. 157)

Toddlers' sense of agency—their view of themselves as the originators of action—expands to include a broad array of behaviors. Children want to participate in decisions about bedtime, the clothes they wear, the kinds of foods they eat, and family activities. They want to do things they see their parents and older siblings doing. Their confidence in their own ability to handle very difficult tasks is not modified by a realistic assessment of their own skills. According to toddlers, "Anything you can do, I can do better." When they have opportunities to do some of these new and complex things and they succeed, they gain confidence in themselves and their abilities. Toddlers feel themselves to be valuable members of the family as they contribute to routine household tasks. Their feelings of confidence and value are matched by the acquisition of a wide variety of complex, coordinated skills.

The Role of Language in Self-Directed Goal Attainment. Toddlers use what was described by Piaget (1952) as egocentric speech to accompany their behavior. They talk aloud, but do not seem to be concerned about whether anyone

In toddlerhood, children develop new skills for self-reliance. Abbie likes to brush her teeth. Sometimes she just drops into the bathroom to give them a special shine. Right now she's at her grandma's house, trying out her grandma's toothpaste.

Image copyright Raia 2010. Used under license from Shutterstock.com

can hear them or understand them. He described the talk as egocentric because it did not seem to have any social intention. Piaget suggested that the development of communication began with inner thinking of a very private, nonsocialized nature. In toddlerhood, he viewed egocentric speech as evidence of the relative absence of social life and the great extent of nonsocialized thoughts that the child is unable to express.

Vygotsky (1987) proposed a completely different developmental pathway to account for egocentric speech and its function. He represented the scheme as follows:

Social speech → egocentric speech → inner speech

Vygotsky viewed speech as beginning in the social interactions between children and adults or other children. In his view, the first and foremost function of speech is social. Egocentric speech is a transformation of this social speech inward. The child uses speech, initially acquired through interactions with others, to guide behaviors. It does not have a social intention; rather, it is a tool for problem solving. Vygotsky viewed egocentric speech and actions as part of the same problem-solving function. The more difficult the problem, the more speech is necessary for the child to find a solution. "Children solve practical tasks with the help of their speech, as well as their eyes and hands" (Vygotsky, 1978a, p. 26). Eventually, the egocentric speech of an audible nature dwindles (but does not disappear entirely) and becomes inner speech.

The kind of speech that guides problem solving emerges from the social speech that characterizes children's interactions with adults and eventually becomes **inner speech**. Often, when young children try to figure out how to work something or how to get something that is out of reach, they turn to adults for help. Vygotsky suggested that the kind of talk that adults use as they guide young children is then used by the children themselves to support and guide their own behavior. He referred to this process as the internalization of social speech. In a sense, a child's capacity for self-directed goal attainment depends on what the child has taken in of the spoken, practical advice and guidance given by adults and older peers who have tried to help the child solve problems in the past. In adulthood, these speech-like cognitions are not typically audible; they are experienced as inner talk, or self-talk, that help organize complex tasks (e.g., *first make an outline*), encourage persistence (e.g., *concentrate, stay focused*), or review and revise (e.g., *doesn't fit, try the bigger one*).

Inner speech gives children a new degree of freedom, flexibility, and control in approaching tasks and working toward a goal. They can use words to call to mind tools that are not visible. They can plan steps toward a goal and repeat them to guide their actions. They can use words like *slowly, be careful*, or *hold tight* to control their behavior as they work on a task. Language skills and self-control operate together to help children inhibit negative emotions and disruptive behavior during times of frustration (Lynam & Henry, 2001).

We have considered two rather different phenomena under the developmental task of self-control. Children's ability to control their impulses is closely linked to the psychoanalytic concept of delay of gratification, as Freud (1905/1953) used it to describe development during the oral and anal stages. Self-directed goal attainment, sometimes referred to as agency, is a general motivation that accounts for children's efforts to increase their competence through persistent investigation and skillful problem solving (White, 1960; Harter, 1982). Both abilities foster toddlers' growing awareness of themselves. To function effectively as family members, toddlers must feel confident in their ability to control the inner world of their feelings and impulses and the outer world of decisions and tasks. As toddlers discover that they can tolerate stress, express or withhold their anger as appropriate, and approach difficult tasks and succeed at them, they also lay claim to a growing definition of selfhood.

Toddlerhood is an important time in the development of a person's sense of self-efficacy—the conviction that one can perform the behaviors demanded by a specific situation (Bandura, 2000). The more toddlers can do by themselves, the more confidence they will have in their ability to control the outcomes of their actions and achieve their goals. Over time, the sense of self-control that is formed during toddlerhood is integrated into adult capacities to overcome obstacles to achieve important goals and to engage in acts of generosity and kindness even when these acts conflict with their own immediate needs.

The Psychosocial Crisis: Autonomy versus Shame and Doubt

Objective 5. To analyze the psychosocial crisis of autonomy versus shame and doubt, to clarify the central process of imitation, and to describe the prime adaptive ego strength of will and the core pathology of compulsion.

During toddlerhood, children become aware of their separateness. Through a variety of experiences, they discover that their parents do not always know what they want and do not always understand their feelings. In early toddlerhood, children use rather primitive devices to explore their independence. They may say "no" to everything offered to them, whether they want it or not. This is the period that people often refer to as the terrible twos. Toddlers seem very demanding and insist on having things done their own way.

Autonomy

The positive pole of the psychosocial crisis of toddlerhood is autonomy. During this period of life, autonomy refers to the ability to behave independently—to perform actions on one's own. In most cultures, expectations for autonomy are expressed as encouragement for children to perform daily tasks, such as dressing and feeding themselves, playing alone

or with peers, and sleeping apart from parents. The exact list of expectations and the age at which these behaviors are to be accomplished varies from one society to the next. Within U.S. society, pressures for autonomy are often expressed in early expectations for skill acquisition and verbal expressiveness. Children do not just prefer to do most things on their own, they *insist* on it. Once children begin to work on a task, such as putting on pajamas or tying shoelaces, they will struggle along, time after time, until they have mastered it. They may adamantly reject help and insist that they can manage on their own. They will allow someone else to help them only when they are sure that they can progress no further by themselves.

In many non-Western cultures, *interdependence* rather than independence is the valued goal of socialization. Children are likely to experience pressures toward autonomy with the birth of a sibling. Rather than pressing for separateness and distance from the caregiver, toddlers may hover near their mother, distressed at her new lack of availability. Through guidance from older siblings and peers, young children learn to participate in the ongoing activities of the household, watching intently, imitating others, and contributing as they can to daily tasks. Within this cultural context, expectations for autonomy may emphasize the ability to demand less of the mother, to become sensitive to the needs of others, and to function cooperatively with peers (Harkness & Super, 1995; Edwards & Liu, 2002).

The establishment of a sense of autonomy requires not only tremendous effort by the child but also extreme patience and support from parents. Toddlers' demands for autonomy are often exasperating. They challenge their parents' good sense, goodwill, and good intentions. Parents must learn to teach, cajole, absorb insults, wait, and praise. Sometimes, they must allow their children to try things that the children may not be able to do. By encouraging their children to engage in new tasks, parents hope to promote their sense of competence.

In the development of autonomy, toddlers shift from a somewhat rigid, nay-saying, ritualized, unreasonable style to an independent, energetic, persistent one (Erikson, 1963). The behavior of older toddlers is characterized by the phrase "I can do it myself." They are less concerned about doing things their own way and more concerned with doing them on their own. Toddlers demonstrate an increasing variety of skills. Each new accomplishment gives them great pride. When doing things independently leads to positive results, the sense of autonomy grows. Toddlers begin to create an image of themselves as people who can manage situations competently and who can satisfy many of their own needs. Children who have been allowed to experience autonomy should, by the end of toddlerhood, have a strong foundation of self-confidence and feelings of delight in behaving independently.

Shame and Doubt

Some children fail to emerge from toddlerhood with a sense of mastery. Because of their failure at most attempted tasks or because of continual discouragement and criticism from

---

Toilet Training

EVERY HUMAN CULTURE has some mechanism to remove waste products from close proximity to the social group. The effort to teach children how to dispose of human waste in a culturally appropriate fashion is the focus of what we in the United States refer to as *toilet training* or *potty training*. Any approach to this task reflects a combination of technology, beliefs, and practices. One of the basic issues is whether one believes that the regulation of this training should be left to the child, drawing on a sense of developmental readiness, or left in the hands of the trainers, which usually suggests a training program (Valsiner, 2000).

In Freud's psychoanalytic theory, toilet training symbolized the classic psychological conflict between individual autonomy and social demands for conformity. In this particular conflict, children are destined to lose (White, 1960). They must subordinate their autonomy to expectations for a specific routine regarding elimination. In the United States, the contemporary approach to this dichotomy between autonomy

and conformity is advocated by the American Academy of Pediatrics (1999). Their advice about toilet training combines waiting until the child is ready with introducing toileting in a guided, systematic fashion:

Autonomy/Readiness: Chances are, toilet training won't be very successful until your child is past the extreme negativism and resistance to it that occurs in early toddlerhood. He must want to take this major step. He'll be ready when he seems eager to please and imitate you, but also wants to become more independent. Most children reach this stage sometime between 18 and 24 months, but it is also normal for it to occur a little later.

Conformity/Training: The best way to introduce your toddler to the concept of using the toilet is to let him watch other family members of his sex....For the first few weeks, let him sit on the potty fully clothed while you tell him about the toilet, what it's for, and when to use it. Once he sits on it willingly, let him try it with his diaper off. Show him how to keep his feet planted solidly on the floor, since this will be important when he's having a bowel movement. Make the potty part of his routine, gradually increasing from once to several times each day.

© Margaret Miller/Photo Researchers

Spencer is able to relax on a potty just his size, taking advantage of a few quiet moments for reading as he develops his toilet habits.

The experts suggest starting with bowel training, and then moving on to urinating in the potty by allowing the child to play near the potty, dropping the contents of the dirty

---

parents, or most likely because of both, some children develop an overwhelming sense of shame and self-doubt. This is the negative resolution of the psychosocial crisis of toddlerhood (Erikson, 1963). **Shame** is an intense negative emotion that focuses on a negative evaluation of the self. Often it is accompanied by a sense of having been exposed or ridiculed and made to feel inferior to others. Feelings of shame do not have to occur in the presence of an audience; however, they usually involve at least an imagined notion of how one's behavior might look to others (Tangney, 2001).

One source of shame is social ridicule or criticism. You can probably recall feelings of shame for having had some kind of accident—you spilled your milk or wet the bed or got dirt on your new outfit. Early experiences of shaming are often linked to toilet training (see the box entitled "Toilet Training"). Shame generally originates in an interpersonal interaction in which a child is made to feel embarrassed or ridiculed for behaving in a stupid, thoughtless, or clumsy way (Tangney, Wagner, Fletcher, & Gramzow, 1992). Under

these circumstances, the child may have acted without considering the consequences, or was unable to control his or her actions. The negative reaction by others accompanies feelings of helplessness. When you are shamed, you feel small, ridiculed, and humiliated. Some cultures rely heavily on shame coupled with opportunities for restitution as a means of social control. Children in these cultures grow up with a strong concern about how their behaviors might reflect on their family or result in disrupting the social bond with their community. One of their greatest fears is to be publicly accused of immoral or dishonorable actions that would bring disgrace to their family (Scheff, 2003).

The quality of early attachment relationships can also contribute to experiences of shame. Attachment theory suggests that in the process of ongoing interactions between infants and their caregivers, children form an internal working model of self and other. If the child's working model of the parent is rejecting, indifferent, or unpredictable, this is likely to be linked to a sense of the self as unworthy or unlovable.

diaper in the potty so the child sees the connection, reminding the child to use the potty when needed, but not to show disappointment when he or she misses or forgets. Patience, reassurance, and praise are suggested while the caregiver encourages increasing compliance with toileting practices.

This approach, which you may find extremely sensible and right, can be contrasted with the practices of the Digo, a group living in coastal Kenya and Tanzania. The Digo live in huts with mud floors. The smell of urine mixed with the mud is extremely unpleasant and difficult to remove. So the Digo are eager to have their infants urinate out of the hut as early as possible. Training begins at 2 to 3 weeks of age. The caregiver sits on the ground outside the hut with feet outstretched and places the baby in the appropriate position for urinating. The baby is placed on the caregiver's feet, facing away from the caregiver but supported by the caregiver. While in this position, the caregiver makes a low sound ("shuus"), which serves as a conditioned stimulus for urination.

This is repeated frequently, day and night, until the baby urinates in this position following the sound. When this happens, the baby is rewarded with breastfeeding. By the age of 4 to 5 months, Digo babies are trained to urinate only in the culturally approved position and setting (De Vries & De Vries, 1977). In contrast to the recommendations of the American Academy of Pediatrics, this approach places a strong emphasis on training and shows a perception of readiness that is much earlier than the perception of readiness held in the United States and other Western cultures.

Critical Thinking Questions

1. Given what you have read about toddlerhood, including physical, cognitive, language, and emotional development, how do you think toilet training should occur?
2. How is toilet training related to the themes of autonomy versus shame and doubt?
3. What is the role of self-control, including self-regulation and self-directed goal attainment in toilet training?
4. How are cultural beliefs and goals expressed in the toilet training process? What cultural beliefs do you think are conveyed though the advice given by the American Academy of Pediatrics?
5. Toilet training is one area in which toddlers may experience strong feelings of shame and doubt that are a result of how they are treated by adult caregivers. Why is it so difficult for adults to deal calmly with toileting processes? How would you help adults overcome their strong emotional reactions to toileting in order to support their child's successful mastery of toileting behavior?
6. Toilet training takes place over a fairly long period. Once you have introduced the process and the child has experienced some success, there will be times when the child does not make it to the bathroom on time. What is the best way to respond when a child has accidents in order to continue effective and successful toilet training?

In toddlerhood, the child's representations of self and other become more readily observable in the way they talk about themselves, and in their fantasy play. Children whose earlier attachments were insecure are more likely to form a negative representation of the self, including expressing anger, blame, or shame about their actions or feelings (Toth, Rogosch, Sturge-Apple, & Cicchetti, 2009).

As children construct an idea of what it means to be a good, decent, capable person, they build a mental image of an ideal person. Children feel shame when their behavior does not meet the standards of their ideal, even though they have not broken a rule or done anything naughty. In general, shame is associated with feelings that the whole self is bad or worthless. It makes one want to disappear from the eyes of others.

Shame is extremely unpleasant. In order to avoid it, children may refrain from all kinds of new activities. Children who feel shame lack confidence in their abilities and expect to fail at what they do. The acquisition of new skills becomes slow and painful when feelings of self-confidence and worth are replaced by constant doubt. Children who have a pervasive sense of doubt feel comfortable only in highly structured and familiar situations, in which the risk of failure is minimal. As college students, young people who have high levels of shame were also characterized by high levels of resentment, irritability, anger, suspiciousness, and a tendency to blame others (Lewis, 1987; Kaufman, 1989). Intense feelings of shame do not generally result in restitution or prosocial behavior. Rather, shame often motivates denial, defensiveness, anger, and aggression (Tangney & Dearing, 2002; Tangney & Mashek, 2004).

All children experience some failures amid their many successes. In the process of achieving a new level of separateness, children may discover that they have harmed a loved one, broken a treasured toy, or wandered too far away and become separated from the caregiver at a crowded store or an unfamiliar park. Toddlers often exhibit periods of ambivalent dependency alternating with what appears to be unrealistic self-assurance as they try to establish a comfortable level of individuation from the loved one. The successful outcome to this process requires

Through imitation, toddlers participate in and sustain social interactions. Lacey helps her mom with her stretching exercises and gets a good workout herself.

flexibility and warmth on the part of caregivers who accept and welcome the emerging selfhood of their child while building support for appropriate levels of self-control.

The Central Process: Imitation

The primary mechanism by which toddlers emerge as autonomous individuals is **imitation**. Imitation is one of the most widely used and efficient mechanisms for learning. Along with teaching and practice, imitation is one of the basic mechanisms that support cultural transmission over generations. Children observe their more skillful parents, siblings, and peers. Each successive generation benefits from observing the skilled behaviors of the previous generation (Caldwell & Millen, 2009). Imitation plays a role in skill learning as well as in social cognition, allowing one person to observe and reproduce the actions, expressions, and gestures of others. Although imitation requires the presence of active models, its outcome is a shift of the action from the model to the imitator. In other words, once toddlers succeed in imitating a certain skill, that skill belongs to them, and they can use it for any purpose they like.

Toddlers seem driven to imitate almost everything they observe, including their parents' positions at the toilet. Toddlers' vocabularies expand markedly through their imitation of the words they hear in adult conversations, on television, and in stories. Their interest in dancing, music, and other activities stems from imitation of parents and peers. When one child in a play group makes a funny noise or performs a daring act, other children seem compelled to recreate this novel behavior.

The imitative behavior of toddlers is different from the socially induced conformity observed in older children. Toddlers are not aware of a great many social norms, and therefore feel little pressure to conform to them. Their imitative behavior is really a vehicle for learning. Every act becomes their own, even if it has been inspired by others. The primary motivation for imitation during toddlerhood is the drive for mastery and competence.

Jess liked to imitate adult tasks. When his mother cleaned the house, he followed her with a cloth, trying to dust the tables. When Mark (*Jess's older brother*) fed the dog, Jess helped him by getting the dog's dish. When his father shaved in the morning, Jess took a toothbrush to imitate his father with lathering and shaving motions. He was learning to brush his teeth, even though his span of attention was short at this job and the cleansing ineffective. (Brazelton, 1974, pp. 139–140)

Imitation is also a means of participating in and sustaining social interactions and advancing social cognition (Meltzoff, 2002). In a peer setting, imitation emerges as a dominant strategy for children to coordinate their behaviors with those of other toddlers. Before verbal communication becomes a truly useful tool for establishing or maintaining social contact, toddlers imitate one another. Through imitation, toddlers can feel connected to one another and begin to invent coordinated games. With increasing cognitive maturity, children select imitation behaviors that have relevance to their own needs for mastery, nurturance, and social interaction. Imitation advances empathy. By watching and repeating the actions of others, toddlers begin to gain insight into the other person's experiences and emotional state (Rogers & Williams, 2006). Imitation can also be a way to reestablish a sense of belonging after experiences of exclusion or rejection. By mimicking others, especially those the child wants to be connected to, the child increases the target's feelings of liking, closeness, and trust (Lakin, Chartrand, & Arkin, 2008).

The emphasis on imitation highlights the central role of culture at this period of life. In many cultures, adults orient young children toward important tasks and expect them to watch and learn in a process of imitation and shared problem solving (Rogoff, Mistry, Goncu, & Mosier, 1993). Children are surrounded by daily events that provide models for imitation, which reflect the culture of their families and communities. Toddlers rapidly accumulate the vocabulary of speech and action that belongs to their cultural group. How visitors are greeted when they arrive at the home; how adults groom themselves, dress, and speak to one another; how household tasks and chores are performed; how older children amuse themselves; how young people and older people treat each other—the thousands of words, gestures, and rituals of daily life make up the culture absorbed by watchful toddlers as they arm themselves with the resources to press toward autonomy.

Given its pervasive role in the early development of children, it is not surprising to learn that imitation is supported by specific neural mechanisms. Recent research has identified a **mirror neuron system,** which underlies a person's ability to observe and then recreate the actions of others as well as to understand the emotions and intentions of others (Iacoboni & Dapretto, 2006). The mirror neuron system in humans is a coordinated network of three areas: One area gathers visual information; one recognizes and processes the motor components of the visual information; and one processes the goal of the action. Information from the goal-oriented area is sent back through the system to match up with the original visual information to guide motor behavior. The system supports sensory and motor integration while the person is observing others, imitating others,

©2010 Thinkstock Images/Jupiterimages Corporation

and being imitated by others. These neurons show activity during observation, and even greater activity while one performs an action that was observed when watching others—in other words, when one is imitating something one is watching. The mirror neurons are sensitive to the intention of the action as well as to the actions themselves. For example, a different pattern of neural firing in the mirror neuron system is observed when a grasping action is linked to drinking from a cup and when grasping is linked to taking the cup away from the table to clean up. The mirror neuron system is considered to be a key to clarifying empathy and our ability to understand others through imitation of facial expressions, body posture, and gestures. Disruptions of the mirror neuron system may be implicated in the social deficits associated with autism (Gallese, 2006).

The Prime Adaptive Ego Quality and the Core Pathology

As a result of the resolution of the psychosocial crisis of autonomy versus shame and doubt, toddlers emerge from this period of life with the prime adaptive ego quality of will or the core pathology of compulsion. The ego quality of will provides a sense of being in control of one's thoughts and actions. It is vital to emerging capacities for self-expression, self-direction, and eventually self-fulfillment. In contrast, the core pathology of compulsion reflects pervasive anxiety. Thoughts impose themselves; actions must be carried out over and over. The will is taken hostage by unbidden impulses that must be satisfied.

Will

Erikson et al. (1986) identified the prime adaptive ego quality that emerges through the successful resolution of the psychosocial crisis of toddlerhood as **will**—the capacity of the mind to direct and control action. It is closely linked to the idea of self-directed goal attainment. Will is the inner voice, focusing attention, encouraging, and urging one on, especially in the face of obstacles. It provides the psychological energy that allows people to press harder in competition, work to surpass previous achievements, and reach for new goals. In the face of disability, it is the force that urges the person to make peace with the loss and focus on alternate goals. In the face of crisis, people often refer to their will to survive or their will to live as the fundamental strength that kept them looking for new solutions or that prevented them from giving up hope. In older people who experience potentially spirit-crushing, painful losses or disabilities, will is the force that provides buoyancy as they learn to accept their decline, look for areas of continued mastery, and reflect nostalgically on past achievements.

Sometimes, we think of will in a negative way, as associated with stubbornness or overbearing dominance, that is, bending to someone's will. But the meaning of will in the psychosocial context refers to the sense of inner determination and purpose

Will reflects an inner determination to persist toward a goal. Cody shows his will as he drags the beach equipment out to the family spot.

that permits a person to set goals freely and make persistent efforts to achieve them. It reflects the positive connotation of the term *willpower,* the ability to sustain effort and delay gratification in order to achieve a long-term goal (Mischel & Ayduk, 2004). Will leads to a positive belief in oneself as someone who can make things happen. When you see a child struggling to carry a heavy box or drag a wagon filled with toys up a steep hill, you see will in action. When you watch an older child chew and twist a pencil trying to figure out a tough math problem, you see will in action. And when you go to the high school swimming pool at 6 o'clock in the morning and see students working out or swimming laps to get ready for an upcoming meet, you see will in action.

Compulsion

Will provides a voluntary energy and focus to action. In contrast, compulsions are repetitive behaviors that are motivated by impulse or by restrictions on the expression of it. They are nonspontaneous and unchanging. Compulsions are a close relative to the *ritualization* that is developed in toddlerhood. Children at this stage typically devise some well-ordered rituals, especially around important transitions such as going to bed, getting dressed, and leaving the house. They insist that these rituals be followed precisely and threaten to become extremely angry if the rituals are violated. Rituals represent efforts to bring control and order to the environment. They are often associated with fears, such as fear of strangers or separation from loved ones for younger children, or fears of environmental threats such as burglars or illness in somewhat older children (Evans, Gray, & Leckman, 1999). Rituals help provide feelings of sameness and continuity during changes in setting or state that may threaten toddler's feelings of selfhood.

Benjamin at 27 months, 17 days:

His bedtime rituals are changing but still evident. He must be read to—as many books as the reader will stand for—and his music-box must be wound up. And I don't think he knows it's even possible to sleep any way except on the stomach. But he doesn't ask for his three old favorite stories to be told to him any more (thank heaven) and he doesn't always ask to be sung to—sometimes he wants one of three or four particular songs, but by no means always. (Church, 1966, p. 159)

Toddlers' rituals usually do not repeat adult ways of doing things; thus, they are not mere imitations of adult rituals. Their rituals, however, like those of adults, serve the important psychological function of bringing order and a sense of mastery to the unknown or the unpredictable. This in turn provides a feeling of security as toddlers pursue well-learned behaviors that work and may also have private symbolic meaning. In comparison to adaptive rituals that actually provide a sense of comfort and relief from uncertainty, compulsions must be carried out again and again, never adequately resolving the anxiety that motivates them.

Obsessive-compulsive disorder (OCD) is a clinical diagnosis that has been increasingly observed among children and adolescents. **Obsessions** are persistent, repetitive *thoughts* that serve as mechanisms for binding anxiety. **Compulsions** are repetitive, ritualized *actions* that serve the same function. Binding anxiety occurs when the person feels that the thoughts or behaviors reduce some other source of distress. For instance, a person with a compulsive neurosis may become committed to repeated handwashing to rid the self of uncleanness. The compulsive handwasher "scrubs his hands in tortured solitude, until they become raw, and yet he never feels clean" (Erikson, 1977, p. 78). Over time, a neurosis may become very disruptive to daily life because it takes a lot of time, makes it hard to concentrate on tasks, and the person feels a loss of control.

Cases of OCD have been documented as young as 4 years of age. The pattern of symptoms observed in children and adolescents tends to differ from the pattern observed in adults, and among children the number and severity of symptoms can be quite diverse. Common groups of OCD symptoms among children include: (1) mental rituals, touching and ordering, (2) contamination and cleaning, (3) superstitions, (4) obsessions/checking and confessing, and (5) somatic concerns (Ivarsson & Valderhaug, 2006). One case study described a child who had obsessive fears of choking on a big object at age 4 and needed repeated reassurances that this would not happen. By age 9, the child was diagnosed with OCD (Geffken, Sajid, & MacNaughton, 2005). There is evidence that OCD is associated with unique

brain abnormalities in an area known as the striatum. In rare instances, OCD can be brought about as a result of a strep infection, when the immune system attacks an area of the brain in its efforts to fight off the infection (U.S. Department of Health and Human Services, 1999).

In a sense, people who suffer from obsessions and compulsions have a damaged will. Their ability to willfully direct their thoughts and actions toward a goal is impaired. Rather, they feel that their thoughts and actions are being controlled by some powerful force outside their voluntary control. It is not the same as a hallucination. People with compulsions or obsessions do not think that someone from outer space or some voice from the spirit world is telling them what to do. They recognize the directive as coming from their mind, but not from their will.

Compulsions represent the ego's attempts to provide some structure to reality, but they do not work to promote further development because they are not meaningful (Erikson, 1982). The experience of the doubt-filled, shame-ridden person tends to be continuously unpleasant, uncertain, and sometimes tortuous. Life is enacted around carefully orchestrated patterns of meaningless, compulsive behaviors.

The Impact of Poverty on Psychosocial Development in Toddlerhood

Objective 6. To conceptualize the impact of poverty on development in toddlerhood.

According to the U.S. Census Bureau, approximately 20% of U.S. children under the age of 5 (4.2 million children) were living in families with incomes under the poverty level in 2007. This means that, if they lived in a three-person family, the family's annual income was $16,705 or less. In fact, this is much less than it costs to meet basic needs for housing, food, transportation, health care, and child care expenses. The United States has the dubious distinction of the highest child poverty rate among 17 developed countries, with more than 13 million children suffering from food insecurity. These children do not consistently have access to food and may have to eat substandard food, inadequate meals, skip meals, or get their food from food pantries and shelters (Lott & Bullock, 2001; Children's Defense Fund, 2005).

Poverty is often associated with conditions that are disruptive to optimal development, including poor nutrition, inadequate health care, limited parental education, lack of stimulating parent-child interactions, and harsh punishment (Ramey, Campbell, & Ramey, 1999; Bradley & Corwin, 2002). In the first years of life, the rapid growth and interdependence among cognitive, social, and physical domains mean that significant modifications in any one system can have a substantial impact on the others. Early malnutrition, iron deficiency,

Left to wait for his mother on a street corner in New Delhi, this child comes into contact with trash, pollutants, glass, dirty water, and crumbling building materials. Prolonged exposure to poverty in toddlerhood has cumulative effects that increase lifelong risks of illness, impaired cognitive development, passivity, and mistrust.

© Rachael Bowes/Alamy

exposure to environmental toxins such as lead, lack of adequate stimulation, and exposure to harsh or neglectful parenting can all impact brain development, including reactivity to stress, ability to regulate anxiety, executive control, memory, and attention (Rodier, 2004). Many children from low-income families have no regular source of health care and have not been immunized for measles and other infectious diseases. Repeated bouts of illness combined with poor nutrition detract from a child's energy. The combination of malnutrition and illness has multiple consequences, including the possibility of structural brain damage, lethargy, delayed physical growth, and, as a result, minimal exploration of the environment. All these factors taken together produce what has been observed as delayed psychomotor and cognitive development in toddlerhood (Pollitt, 1994; Brown & Pollitt, 1996). Poor health in childhood has a lasting impact on adult health (Halfon, Inkelas, & Hochstein, 2000).

Families in poverty are a diverse group, characterized by a range of conditions that could present challenges to optimal development. For example, young mothers whose education is disrupted by early childbearing, and mothers who are suffering from depression, are likely to also have reduced financial resources. However, educational level and depression are associated with different consequences for children. Mothers' educational attainment is strongly associated with their children's vocabulary and school achievement. Among low-income families, children whose mothers have had fewer years of school have lower levels of school readiness and do worse on standard measures of academic achievement. Maternal depression is a different risk factor, associated with the child's social skills. Children whose mothers are depressed are less cooperative, less compliant, and show more evidence of oppositional or defiant behaviors in preschool (Perry & Fantuzzo, 2010).

Early exposure to poverty has lasting consequences for adult outcomes, especially outcomes related to academic achievement and cognitive abilities (Duncan & Brooks-Gunn, 1997). A combination of factors tied to family poverty, including exposure to harsh parenting, disruptions in emotional regulation, and the absence of positive interactions with adults, results in a lack of school readiness and a trajectory of lower academic motivation and subsequent disengagement from school. In a long-term analysis of the relationship between early poverty and adult outcomes, a clear link was found between exposure to poverty in the first 5 years of life, and reduced income and hours of work after age 25 (Duncan, Ziol-Guest, & Kalil, 2010).

In a worldwide analysis of the developmental potential of children under the age of 5, Sally Grantham-McGregor and her colleagues estimated that over 200 million children are exposed to such extreme conditions of poverty, malnutrition, and neglectful care that they are at critical risk for disrupted developmental outcomes (Grantham-McGregor et al., 2007). Poverty for these children is associated with inadequate food supplies, poor sanitation, increased infections and illness, and growth retardation. The mothers of these children have had limited education, and the home environment is barren and unstimulating. Poor families are more likely to live in high-risk neighborhoods, where children are likely to be exposed to chaotic conditions, including disruptions in basic services such as water or electricity, violence, and family instability (Ceballo & McLoyd, 2002; Evans et al., 2005). Schools are inadequate, and there is relatively little encouragement for education. As a result, the children who live in extreme poverty will attend fewer years of school, and have less earning potential as adults. As they enter adulthood, they will have more children than adults who had more years of education, and be less able to provide the educational or economic resources for their children that will support optimal growth in the next generation. Investment in the nurturance, safety, education, health, and nutrition of young children worldwide is critical in order to alter the trajectory of an intergenerational pattern of lost developmental potential.

Child Care

Objective 7. To apply a psychosocial analysis to the topic of child care, emphasizing the impact of the kind of care and the quality of care on development during toddlerhood.

EVERY PERSON WHO expects to combine parenting and employment or schooling must give some thought to how to provide **child care**. In the United States, child care arrangements constitute a highly diverse market, especially when compared with kindergarten through 12th-grade public education (Holloway & Fuller, 1992). Child care in the United States is covered by minimal federal and state regulations. Thus, children are in the care of a wide range of caregivers with varying types of education and training, from no specific background and training at all to bachelor's and master's degrees.

Table 6.3 summarizes the child care arrangements for children under 6 who have not yet entered kindergarten (U.S. Department of Education, 2005). In 2005, 74% of children were involved in some type of nonparental care. This is an increase from 69% in 1991. The largest group, 57.2%, was in center-based care, which includes day care centers, Head Start programs, preschool, prekindergarten, and other early childhood programs. Arrangements vary by the child's age, the family's race/ethnicity, and household income. Three-year-olds are more likely than 4- or 5-year-olds to be cared for by their parents. White, non-Hispanic families are more likely to arrange for nonrelative care than other racial/ethnic groups. Hispanic families are more likely to rely on parental care than other racial/ethnic groups. African American families are more likely than other racial/ethnic groups to use center-based care. Households with higher incomes ($75,000 or more) are more likely to make some type of nonparental arrangement for their children and are the most likely to use center-based programs.

Child care settings reflect a variety of philosophies about the care of young children, wide differences in curriculum, and a wide range of physical settings. The *laissez-faire*

TABLE 6.3 Patterns of Child Care for Children Ages 3–5 in the United States Who Have Not Yet Entered Kindergarten: 1991–2005

CHARACTERISTIC	Children		Type of Nonparental Arrangement[1]			
	NUMBER (1,000)	% DISTRIBUTION	IN RELATIVE CARE	IN NONRELATIVE CARE	IN CENTER-BASED PROGRAM[2]	WITH PARENTAL CARE ONLY
1991, total	8,428	100.00	16.9	14.8	52.8	31.0
1995, total	9,232	100.00	19.4	16.9	55.1	25.9
2001, total	9,066	100.00	22.6	11.6	57.2	26.3
Age:						
3 years old	4,070	44.9	24.0	14.4	42.5	33.4
4 years old	3,873	42.7	20.8	9.2	69.2	20.6
5 years old	1,125	12.4	23.8	9.2	68.7	20.4
Race-Ethnicity:						
White, non-Hispanic	5,177	57.1	21.4	15.0	59.1	24.1
Black, non-Hispanic	1,233	13.6	25.0	5.2	66.5	19.5
Hispanic	1,822	20.1	22.7	8.1	43.4	38.0
Other	834	9.2	26.4	8.1	61.5	24.7
Household income:						
Less than $10,001	795	8.8	25.1	8.6	53.4	33.4
$10,001 to $20,000	978	10.8	26.0	7.8	49.2	27.2
$20,001 to $30,000	1,183	13.1	25.4	6.3	43.9	28.5
$30,001 to $40,000	1,124	12.4	23.8	6.9	48.7	33.4
$40,001 to $50,000	808	8.9	21.8	11.6	50.0	35.4
$50,001 to $75,000	1,849	20.4	21.1	13.3	57.1	25.5
$75,001 or more	2,329	20.7	19.8	18.0	75.1	11.4

[1]Columns do not add to 100.0 because some children participated in more than one type of nonparental arrangement.

[2]Center-based programs include day care centers, Head Start programs, preschools, prekindergarten, and nursery schools.

Source: U.S. Department of Education (2005). Early childhood program participation survey of the National Household Education Surveys Program (NHES). National Center for Education Statistics. (http://nces.ed.gov)

approach to the care of toddlers seems to reflect a cultural belief that the nurturance and socialization of young children are primarily the responsibility of the family, whereas the schooling of children over the age of 5 is a public concern. However, most early childhood experts agree that there are markers of quality care that have an impact on children's daily experiences as well as on their long-term cognitive, emotional, and social development. These markers include advanced training in the field of child development and early childhood education for the caregivers; a small caregiver-to-child ratio and smaller group size; a safe, clean environment; and sensitive, developmentally appropriate interactions between caregivers and children (Honig, 2002).

Because of the growing national need for child care and the wide choice of child care arrangements, parents, educators, and policymakers are asking such critical questions as, "How does child care influence the development of young children? What is our obligation to ensure quality child care for the children of working parents? What is our obligation as a society to meet the health, nutrition, and safety needs of the children of poor parents?"

Assessments of child care's effects on young children generally focus on intellectual abilities, socioemotional development, and peer relations. Research has tended to emphasize the impact of child care on the children of families living in poverty, because they are at a higher risk for school failure, illiteracy, and subsequent minimal employment or unemployment, even though they are less likely to be enrolled in center-based care than families with more resources. Many studies focus on Head Start—a federally funded early childhood program that has a complex mission, including education, health, mental health, and family support. However, until recently, Head Start was structured as a preschool enrichment program rather than full day care. Not all child care programs have the same educational emphasis or developmental curriculum as Head Start. Many studies that investigate the impact of child care do not systematically control for the differences in program focus, services, and hours of service that exist among public and private child care and preschool programs.

Efforts to assess the impact of early child care arrangements on subsequent development are often discussed as causal relationships (e.g., participation in quality early child care results in cognitive benefits). However, these causal statements should be treated cautiously. Very few studies randomly assign children to early childhood programs. Even in a recent study where children were randomly assigned to Head Start programs or to a non–Head Start control group, some of the children who were assigned to Head Start did not enroll, and some who were assigned to the control group managed to get into a Head Start program on their own (Puma et al., 2005). About 15% of young children experience a combination of care arrangements including parental and family member care as well as center-based and nonrelative care, and these arrangements may change from year to year. Experiences with multiple care arrangements, and frequent changes in arrangements, have been found to be associated with behavioral difficulties even when the settings are of good quality (Morrissey, 2009). The quality of care a child experiences can be assessed, but the many factors that might account for why some children are in high-quality care and others are in poor-quality care, or why some children are in care for many hours a day and others are in care for few hours a day cannot be fully measured or controlled. As a result, it is best to think of studies that evaluate the impact of early child care arrangements as associational rather than causal.

The Impact of Child Care on Intelligence, Cognition, Academic Achievement

Results of a growing body of research suggest that the effect of quality day care on toddlers' cognitive development is positive but modest (Azar, 1997; Ludwig & Phillips, 2007). Data from model programs show that quality child care contributes to intellectual achievement, as reflected in higher IQ scores, both during the preschool years and during the first grade (Burchinal et al., 2000). Because of the questionable validity of IQ scores for very young children and for children from various racial and ethnic subgroups, the focus on IQ as an indication of program impact may be inadequate. Thus, recent studies have focused on more specific competencies such as language ability, prereading and prewriting skills, vocabulary, cognitive problem solving, and motivation for school and school achievement as evidence of the long-term impact of child care on intellectual development (Yoshikawa, 2005).

The National Institute of Child Health and Human Development (NICHD) has been conducting a longitudinal study of the effects of early child care (Owen, 1997; National Institutes of Health, 2000). The primary aim of the study is to learn what impact child care has on developmental outcomes above and beyond the influence of family and home environment. In this study, 1,300 children under 1 month of age and their families were identified as participants from 10 sites across the United States. The study, initiated in 1991, has now followed children into early adolescence, ages 14 and 15. Families varied by race, income, family structure, mother's education and employment status, and the number of hours children spent in nonparental care. The kinds of care included: care provided by grandparents and other relatives; by a nonrelative in the home; in a home-based setting; and in a center. The quality of care was measured with a focus on caregiver interactions that are expected to promote positive emotions, social competence, and cognitive and language skills.

Positive caregiving is measured by observing and documenting the frequency of interaction, and then rating the quality of the interaction. The child care settings were also measured both in terms of their regulable characteristics, or guidelines recommended by governments, such as group size, child to adult ratio, and physical environment; and of the caregiver's characteristics, such as formal education, specialized training, child care experience, and beliefs about child rearing.

The research team found that child care situations with safer, cleaner, more stimulating physical environments and smaller group sizes, lower child/adult ratios, and caregivers who allowed children to express their feelings and took their views into account, also had caregivers who were observed to provide more sensitive, responsive, and cognitively stimulating care—quality of care that was expected to be associated with better developmental outcomes for children. (Retrieved July 29, 2001, from www.nichd.nih.gov/publications /pubs /early_child_care.htm)

For more detailed information about this national longitudinal study, visit the NICHD website at http://secc.rti.org.

Findings from this research suggest that family variables were *more important* predictors of the child's development than the quality of child care in infancy, toddlerhood, and even in middle school. "Higher levels of parenting quality predicted greater levels of tested reading, math, and vocabulary achievement in fifth grade, and lower levels of teacher-rated externalizing problems and conflict and high levels of social skills, social-emotional functioning, and work habits in the sixth grade" (Belsky et al., 2007, p. 693). However, after all these family factors were taken into account, the quality of language stimulation directed to the child in the child care setting made a significant additional contribution to children's language and cognitive competence measured at ages 2 and 3 (NICHD Early Child Care Research Network, 2002). Children in higher quality care had higher scores on measures of infant development and school readiness. After controlling for quality of child care settings, the research found that children who did not attend any type of formal child care and were cared for at home performed just as well as those who attended quality care programs. Those who were cared for in family day care in their infancy performed better at age 3 than did those in other types of nonfamily care (National Institutes of Health, 2000).

Follow-up studies have found indications of long-term consequences of exposure to early child care. By the sixth grade, a positive relationship was observed between experiences in quality care and measured vocabulary (Belsky et al., 2007). By age 15, there was continued evidence of a benefit to high-quality care as measured in adolescents' academic performance (Vandell et al., 2010).

Focusing on children from low-income families, experiences in high-quality child care offset the negative associations between poverty and subsequent math and reading skills. For children from low-income families, high-quality child care proved to be a benefit with regard to school readiness at age 3, which was then strongly associated with higher scores in measures of math, reading, applied problem solving, and language skills in grades 5 and 6 (Dearing, McCartney, & Taylor, 2009).

In addition to test score benefits, children who have participated in model programs and Head Start are less likely to be placed in special education classrooms or to be held back a grade. These advantages are of significance in thinking about the tradeoff in costs and benefits of providing early educational experiences to children at risk of school failure (Ludwig & Phillips, 2007).

The Perry Preschool Project, a model program that has carried out extensive longitudinal research on its participants, has seen a number of indications of academic success. In the mid-1960s, 123 African American children from very-low-income families were selected to participate in this program. They were randomly assigned to a quality preschool intervention or to no preschool. At age 19, children who had attended a quality preschool program had higher grades, fewer failing grades, a more positive attitude toward school, and a higher literacy rate than a comparable group of young adults living in poverty who had not participated in a quality child care program (Schweinhart & Weikart, 1988; Schweinhart, Montie, Xiang, Barnett, Belfield, & Nores, 2005). Most (95%) of those who had participated in the study were reinterviewed at age 27. The group that had the preschool experience continued to show evidence of the benefits of their early childhood education. Those who had attended the quality preschool were 30% more likely to have graduated from high school or received their GED. They were 4 times more likely to be earning $2,000 or more per month, and three times more likely to own their own homes (High/Scope, 2003).

The Impact of Child Care on Social Competence

Quality care is also associated with higher levels of social competence, self-esteem, and empathy. Children who interact positively with adults in their day care settings are more likely to continue to interact positively and comfortably with their teachers and classmates in the elementary grades (Vandell, Henderson, & Wilson, 1988). Some studies have found that children with more hours of child care experience are less compliant with their parents' wishes than children who have not been in day care. The study conducted by NICHD helps explain these findings. The more time children spent in nonmaternal care, the less responsive mothers were to their children at ages 15 and 36 months, and the less affectionate the child was to the mother at 24 and 36 months (Owen, 1997; NICHD Early Child Care Research Network, 2002). These findings were strongest for children who were in low-quality care for the longest time periods. Even when children were adolescents, the consequences of experiences in poor quality care and long hours of care continued to be observed. By age 15, the more hours a child spent in nonfamily care as a toddler, the more they were observed to have difficulties controlling their impulses as an adolescent (Vandell et al., 2010).

Recent studies suggest that some children are more affected by the quality of their early child care experiences than others (Pluess & Belsky, 2010). Children who were characterized as having a difficult temperament in

Toddlers' social competence is enhanced in quality child care settings through daily opportunities for sharing, taking turns, helping, and coordinating their play with others.

infancy, especially high levels of negativity and irritability at 6 months, were compared to children who were characterized as low in negativity at 6 months. In 6th grade, these two groups of children were rated by teachers on behavior problems and teacher-child conflicts. For the children who had low levels of negativity, there was no relationship between their experiences in high- or low-quality child care and the way teachers rated their behavior in 6th grade. For the children who had high levels of negativity as infants, the experiences in high- or low-quality child care made a big difference. If these children who had a more difficult temperament also experienced low-quality child care in toddlerhood, they had many more behavior problems and teacher-child conflicts. If the children who had a more difficult temperament were in high-quality child care, they had fewer behavior problems and teacher conflicts than the low-negative children, even those who had been in high-quality care. The point is that when evaluating the long-term consequences of early child care experiences, it is important to take into account variations in children's susceptibility to environmental conditions.

Quality child care also has an impact on peer relations. Children benefit from opportunities to interact with a variety of peers in settings where adults are readily available to help them make choices and resolve differences. The quality and complexity of social play are especially enhanced when children remain in the same child care setting rather than moving from one arrangement to another. In stable conditions, toddlers, whose verbal skills are limited, expand their strategies for coordinating their play with others and for exploring shared fantasies. Children who are growing up in difficult and impoverished life circumstances are especially likely to benefit from stable, consistent caregiving practices, where they can form a secure attachment to the caregivers and experience calm, friendly interactions with peers (Ritchie &

Howes, 2003). Long-term benefits for peer relations were observed for the participants of the Perry Preschool Project when, at age 19, they were more likely to report that they provided help to their friends and family than were comparison participants, but less likely to volunteer without pay for community service (Schweinhart & Weikart, 1988; Schweinhart et al., 2005).

Few of the evaluations of model programs or Head Start have addressed long-term social consequences. However, results from the Perry Preschool Project showed that by age 19, fewer of the children studied had committed delinquent acts or had been processed by the courts, fewer had been on welfare, and more had been employed (Barnett, 1996). In the follow-up at age 27, those who had been enrolled in the quality preschool program were less likely to have been arrested for drug dealing, men had been married longer, and women were more likely to be married and less likely to have had a child out of wedlock (High/Scope, 2003).

Benefits Associated with Head Start

Head Start is more comprehensive than most preschool or child care programs. As a result, it has the potential for a broader range of benefits to children and families than other programs. The Head Start program standards include requirements for the staff to provide children and families with comprehensive services related to health and nutrition. Staff must assist parents in using available resources for immunization; regular checkups; screening for health, vision, and behavioral problems; and regular preventive dental care (U.S. Code of Federal Regulations, 2002). In 30 studies that reported on the health impact of Head Start, the data showed that participating children are more likely to get a wide variety of examinations and assessments covering medical and dental health, speech and hearing, vision, and nutrition. Because Head Start provides meals, young children in the program have a much higher daily nutritional intake than similar children who are not in the program (Zigler & Styfco, 2004). All of these opportunities allow a direct response to young children's physical needs when their parents may not be aware of emerging problems or are unsure how to address them.

Head Start's overall impact on the health of young children is 6 times greater than the average effect of schooling on health found across hundreds of studies (Grott & van den Brink, 2005). Thus, Head Start succeeds in bringing to young children essential benefits that they are not receiving through their families or other school settings.

As an additional benefit, Head Start has had a positive impact on families and communities. A key area of Head Start programming is parent education and parent involvement. Results of the national Head Start Impact Study show that parents whose children are in Head Start are less likely to spank their children, and spend more time reading to their children, than parents whose children are in other kinds of child care programs (Puma et al., 2005). Head Start has provided education, training, and career development for millions of parents and community members. It has mobilized over a million community volunteers to assist in Head Start classrooms, and most of these volunteers were once Head Start or Early Head Start parents. Head Start has created hundreds of thousands of jobs, the majority of which are held by people who live in the low-resource communities where the programs are located. Thus, Head Start contributes to the advancement and engagement of community adults, drawing on their talents to contribute to the quality of education in their communities (NHSA.org, 2007).

Recent changes in professional standards for Head Start teachers have included expectations for a bachelor's degree. In our experience in Rhode Island, this has led to a new relationship between Head Start and the University of Rhode Island in order to facilitate attainment of bachelors' degrees in child development for many Head Start teachers. As part of this program, Head Start is providing some tuition assistance, classroom space, and resources for study. Thus, through its commitment to improve the quality of the teaching staff, Head Start is building a pool of college-educated early childhood professionals in a population that might otherwise never complete a college degree.

Directions for the Future of Child Care in the United States

The United States faces a critical gap between the demand for *affordable, quality* child care and its availability. Although the number of child care settings appears to be ample, those that meet the standards of high quality are comparatively scarce. In a study conducted by the U.S. Consumer Product Safety Commission, 220 licensed child care settings were evaluated for the presence of possible safety hazards. The safety hazards monitored in this study included: unsafe cribs, soft crib bedding, improper playground surfacing, poorly maintained playground surfacing, absence of child safety gates at the top of stairs, loops hanging from the window blind cords, drawstrings around the necks in children's clothing, and recalled children's products. The study reported that two-thirds of the settings showed at least one of these hazards (Consumer Product Safety Commission, 1999).

Concern about the need for affordable, quality child care is expressed by parents who are in the labor market as well as by those who would like to be in the labor market. The United States now has a national parental-leave policy, so that parents can take time off to care for their newborns without risking the loss of their jobs. But concerns about child care continue throughout toddlerhood and well into the elementary school years, when children need adult companionship and supervision before and after school hours. Services for certain groups, including children with disabilities, those whose parents have evening work schedules, children who are ill, and those who need year-round programs, are in short supply. Furthermore, the supply of quality centers is unevenly distributed, so that many families in low-income communities do not have access to quality care (Fuller, Kagan, Caspary, & Gauthier, 2002). Changes in national welfare policies place new pressures on the need for affordable, quality child care services. In the past, for example, Head Start programs, which have been an important resource to children in low-income families, have not offered full day care. However, because mothers of young children who were previously receiving welfare benefits are required to enter the labor market, they need to find full day care for their children. Consider the dilemma of a woman who was trying to locate quality care for her child:

> I called child care agencies. . . . And I interviewed all the people they [the state] gave me with licenses. I sat in some of the places for quite a while. I saw drugs being sold in and out of those places. I found one place I thought my daughter would be secure. She was sexually abused. I think that was the thing that really gave it to me then: I quit my job and went fully back on the welfare system. (Scarbrough, 2001, p. 267)

Quality, affordable child care is one of the primary resources that single parents rely on in order to stay off welfare. Without some form of child care subsidy, women cannot support themselves and their families on what they are typically able to earn in jobs that pay a minimum wage. Even with such a subsidy, the likelihood of finding a high-quality setting are low, and the risks of spending time in a poor-quality setting are great.

Chapter Summary

Objective 1. To describe the expansion of motor skills during toddlerhood, indicating their importance for the child's capacity to explore the environment and to experience opportunities mastery.

The developmental tasks of toddlerhood support children's ability to express themselves through action, language, fantasy, and self-directed goal attainment. Locomotive skills heighten toddlers' sense of mastery and expand their boundaries of experience. Advanced motor skills highlight the dynamic interaction of brain development, physical growth, opportunity, and practice.

Objective 2. To document accomplishments in language development and to describe the influence of experiences for learning to communicate.

Language is both a tool for the expression of feelings and concepts and a primary mechanism of socialization. Communicative competence relies on both genetically based capacities for symbolic representation and exposure to a language system. Certain language skills are more vulnerable to the timing of exposure than others, illustrating an important feature of plasticity. Toddlers' use of language gives us clues as to their cognitive development and their needs. Through language, children influence others, gain access to worlds of information, and learn new strategies for the control and expression of their impulses.

Objective 3. To describe the development of fantasy play and its importance for cognitive and social development.

The emergence of fantasy provides toddlers with an internal, personal form of symbolic representation. Fantasy allows a pseudomastery in which barriers are overcome and the limitations of reality are less important. Conflicts can be acted out, and pretend solutions can be found. Fantasy may be enhanced by language, but it thrives even in the absence of words.

Objective 4. To examine the development of self-control, especially impulse management and goal attainment, highlighting strategies young children use to help regulate their actions.

Efforts at self-control—both impulse regulation and self-directed goal attainment—begin in toddlerhood and continue through life. Temperamental differences in negative emotionality, anger-proneness, fearfulness, and activity level can all influence the child's ability to achieve self-control. At the same time, these differences are shaped by parenting practices that help or disrupt children's capacities for regulation.

Objective 5. To analyze the psychosocial crisis of autonomy versus shame and doubt, to clarify the central process of imitation, and to describe the prime adaptive ego strength of will and the core pathology of compulsion.

The psychosocial crisis of autonomy versus shame and doubt reflects the child's needs for self-expression and mastery. Young children develop individuality by exercising the skills that develop during toddlerhood. Self-doubts result from repeated ridicule, shame, and failure. The adaptive ego quality of will, directly linked to self-directed goal attainment, emerges in a positive resolution of this crisis. In the context of shame and doubt, the child is likely to rely more and more on compulsive, ritualized behaviors.

Autonomy and individuation are given different values across cultures. Within the context of parent-child relationships, children learn in what ways they are expected to become self-sufficient and self-expressive, and to what extent they are expected to fit in or blend in with others. Toddlers are avid observers, imitating and incorporating parental behaviors and values into their own routines. Parental interaction, acceptance, and discipline all contribute to a child's emerging sense of individuality and connection.

Objective 6. To conceptualize the impact of poverty on development in toddlerhood.

Living in poverty begins to pose challenges to optimal development during the prenatal period, and these risks continue throughout toddlerhood. Poor nutrition, lack of health care, harsh or neglectful parenting, and exposure to chaotic neighborhoods can all influence the direction of cognitive development, emotional regulation, and sense of control. Growing up in a very poor community increases the likelihood that parents will be psychologically unavailable or will use harsh, restrictive disciplinary strategies that produce shame or unexpressed rage in their young children.

Objective 7. To apply a psychosocial analysis to the topic of child care, emphasizing the impact of the kind of care and the quality of care on development during toddlerhood.

Increasing numbers of young children are being cared for in group settings. The impact of child care depends largely on the quality of the personnel, the nature of the program, and an appropriate physical environment. The most important predictor of children's social and cognitive maturation is the quality of parenting they receive. Nonetheless, many studies find a consistent relationship between quality child care and cognitive development, especially in the area of language acquisition. It might be fair to conclude that whereas the contributions of quality child care are modest but positive, the consequences of poor quality care can be seriously disruptive. A major policy concern is how to expand affordable, high-quality care for those families that need it.

Key Terms

autonomy, 196
bilingualism, 207
child care, 230
code switching, 200
communicative competence, 201
compulsions, 228
delay of gratification, 221
doubt, 197
effortful control, 220
expansion, 209
fantasy play, 197
fast mapping, 205
grammar, 203
imaginary companions, 215
imitation, 226
inductions, 218

inner speech, 222
language environment, 201
language perception, 202
language production, 204
locomotion, 197
love withdrawal, 218
mirror neuron system, 226
obsessions, 228
obsessive-compulsive disorder, 228
overregularize, 204
power assertion, 218
preoperational thought, 199
prompting, 209
question-asking, 209
receptive language, 194

scaffolding, 209
self-control, 197
semiotic thinking, 199
sensorimotor play, 211
shame, 197
signs, 199
social pretend play, 213
symbolic play, 214
symbols, 199
telegraphic speech, 203
theory of mind, 212
will, 227
words, 199
zone of proximal development, 209

Further Reflection

1. What do you recall from your childhood about the emergence of locomotor activities? In what ways do motor skills continue to contribute to your sense of autonomy and mastery as an adult?
2. Reflect on the words *language*, *thought*, and *speech*. What are the differences among these three? How are they interconnected?
3. How does the capacity for pretense contribute to development in childhood? How would you evaluate our contemporary U.S. society with respect to the value it places on fantasy play in childhood? In adulthood?
4. Why is self-control emphasized as a primary developmental task in toddlerhood? How does it relate to the theme of autonomy versus shame and doubt? How do individual differences in self-control play out in later stages of childhood and adolescence?
5. How does culture influence the expression of the psychosocial crisis of autonomy versus shame and doubt? What are the societal forces that foster the sense of autonomy in toddlerhood? What are the forces that create a sense of shame and doubt?
6. Imagine that you have to decide about child care arrangements for your child. Given what you have read about the developmental tasks and the psychosocial crisis of toddlerhood, what are some of the features of the child care arrangement that would be most important in your decision?

Psychology CourseMate

To access additional course materials, including CourseMate, please visit www.cengagebrain.com. At the CengageBrain .com home page, search for the ISBN of your title (from the back cover of your book) using the search box at the top of the page. This will take you to the product page where these resources can be found.

Casebook

For additional case material related to this chapter, see the case of "Little Raymond" in *Life Span Development: A Case Book*, by Barbara and Philip Newman, Laura Landry-Meyer, and Brenda J. Lohman, pp. 77–80. The case illustrates ways in which a toddler uses language and fantasy to cope with frustration when his mom's boyfriend interferes with his play.

Claude in Blue, 1950/© 2011 Estate of Pablo Picasso/Artists Rights Society (ARS), New York

Starting school brings an expansion of the child's social world: encounters with new adults and peers, new social norms, higher expectations, and new information. Each of these changes has an effect on the child's self-concept.

Early School Age (4 to 6 Years)

Chapter Objectives

1. To describe the process of gender identification during early school age and its importance for the way a child interprets his or her experiences.

2. To describe the process of early moral development, drawing from theories and research to explain how knowledge, emotion, and action combine to produce internalized morality.

3. To analyze changes in the self-theory, with special focus on the theory of mind and self-esteem during the early-school-age years.

4. To explore the transition to more complex play and the process of friendship development in the early-school-age years.

5. To explain the psychosocial crisis of initiative versus guilt, the central process of identification, the prime adaptive ego quality of purpose, and the core pathology of inhibition.

6. To analyze the construct of school readiness, its relation to the developmental tasks of early school age, and the obstacles that may prevent children from being able to adapt and learn in the school environment.

THE PERIOD OF **early school age** brings children face to face with new and complex socialization forces. By the age of 6, virtually all children in the United States are enrolled in school. Children today are encountering school or school-like experiences at earlier ages than in the past. In 2007, 65% of 3- to 5-year-olds were enrolled in public or private pre-primary schools, not including the 5-year-olds who were enrolled in kindergarten. This is an increase from 37% in 1970 (U.S. Census Bureau, 2010). It is *normative* for children to be enrolled in some type of schooling before the age that the law requires. School brings new information and experiences, new opportunities for success and failure, and new settings for peer group formation. School is a new source of influence on the child beyond the family. Beliefs and practices followed at home may come under scrutiny

and be challenged by teachers or classmates. Parents' personal hopes and aspirations for their children may be tempered by the reality of their children's school performance.

Most early-school-age children exhibit wide-ranging curiosity about all facets of life. "How does this work?" "Why is that the rule?" "Why can't I do that?" The child's self-concept is transformed in coordination with exposure to new socialization voices. In addition to family and school, the peer group, neighborhood, and television all influence children's self-concept during early school age. Once children become aware of alternatives to their own families' rules and patterns, they begin to question familiar notions. The press toward *independence of action* seen in the toddler is now accompanied by a new *independence of thought* in the early-school-age child. ■

Developmental Tasks

During the early-school-age period, between the ages of 4 and 6, children are constructing a broad overview of how their interpersonal world is structured and where they fit in. They are devising a scheme for self in society. Because children's life experiences are limited and they are still highly impressionable, the nature of this initial worldview is likely to be very compelling, permeating their outlook in the years ahead. The lessons from early childhood about what it means to be a good person, to be a good boy or girl, man or woman, to be cherished or despised are established at a deep emotional and cognitive level. These ideas are intertwined with feelings of being safe, loved, and admired or neglected,

rejected, or abused. As a result, the basic beliefs about oneself and others that are formed at this time are often difficult to review or revise.

In this chapter, four developmental tasks are discussed that contribute to the child's capacity to construct a worldview: gender identification, moral development, self-theory, and peer play. The topic of **gender identification** includes a discussion of the physical, cognitive, emotional, and social domains as they become integrated into an early scheme for thinking of oneself as male or female. Issues of right and wrong surface constantly as a result of the child's newly acquired abilities for independent thought and exposure to a much wider range of social influences. These experiences provide the basis for early **moral development**.

In early school age, children's worlds expand as they spend more time at school and in their neighborhoods. Marta loves this time, hanging out with the big girls while she waits for the school bus to bring her home at the end of the day.

Understanding and experiencing the self expand markedly during early school age. This developmental task centers on the acquisition of a personal **self-theory** that becomes increasingly complex because it is being stimulated by expanding social influences. Accompanying the development of the self-theory is the development of a set of complex feelings about the self called **self-esteem**. A fourth area involves new levels of participation in **peer play**. Through the process of learning the rules and playing cooperatively with others, children begin to form meaningful friendships and mental representations of ways of participating in groups.

Gender Identification

Objective 1. To describe the process of gender identification during early school age and its importance for the way a child interprets his or her experiences.

Every human society has patterns of organization based partially on gender. Male and female individuals are often assigned different roles, engage in different tasks, have access to different resources, and are viewed as having different powers and attributes. The specific content of these gender roles varies widely from one culture to another. As children form their concept of gender identity, they must integrate their own physical experiences, knowledge, and observations with the socialization messages coming to them from parents, siblings, peers, and other salient voices of the culture.

In this and other discussions of gender identification, you will want to differentiate among three concepts: sex, gender, and sexual orientation. **Sex** refers to a person's biological maleness or femaleness determined by chromosomal information. An infant's external genitalia are typically used as the evidence to determine sex. In most cases, the chromosomes and the hormones that are produced in the prenatal period converge to produce an unambiguous sex. However, there are exceptions of chromosomally male (XY) individuals who have undeveloped male genitalia and are identified as female at birth; and chromosomally female (XX) individuals who have hormonal imbalances that result in the appearance of male genitalia (Crooks & Bauer, 2005).

Gender refers to the integrated cognitive, social, emotional, and behavioral patterns associated with being a boy or girl, man or woman in one's culture. In childhood, gender identification includes learning to identify oneself as a boy or girl in one's family, friendship group, and community; learning and internalizing the community's expectations for how boys and girls ought to behave; and sensing how well one meets the social expectations for a boy or girl.

Sexual orientation refers to one's preference for and attraction to sexually intimate partners. Four sexual orientations discussed in the literature are *heterosexual*, *homosexual*, *bisexual*, and *asexual*. Sexual orientation is not a primary topic of discussion in this chapter. However, it is common for men and women who are homosexual to recall evidence of their gender nonconformity in early childhood, suggesting some childhood precursors of sexual orientation (Bailey & Zucker, 1995; Zucker, Drummond, Bradley, & Peterson-Badali, 2009).

CASE STUDY

GENDER IDENTIFICATION IN EARLY CHILDHOOD

Lee, a mother of six children, recalls with warmth and humor her early childhood years growing up in New Mexico in the 1920s and 1930s.

I was born in the southern part of New Mexico in Ruidoso. The town was up in the pines in the mountains and was mostly just a main street that followed the river. There was a meadow on one side of the river with a lot of Indian arrowheads and shards and the biggest grasshoppers in the world. I used to go catch grasshoppers and find arrowheads, and my cousin Bob and I would wander around by ourselves.

My father was a carpenter and my mother had planned to be a nurse until she stopped and got married. I think my father must have really wanted a son because I was quite a tomboy and grew up as his only son. I helped him dig and move rocks instead of learning how to cook and sew. We had a large family, uncles and aunts and a grandmother and great aunt, with houses right next to each other and big, traditional holiday dinners with everybody there.

My cousin Bob was two years younger than I was and we were inseparable. . . . He was a rough, tough little kid. We ran around without coats in the winter and hardly ever got sick, and he and I grew up together. It was almost like two boys because we used to go to the river and fish with our hands and churn the fish over a little fire and try to eat it. We just grew up like little wild things. My parents expected me to be on the premises by nightfall, but that was about it. We played cowboys and Indians with the other kids in the neighborhood, and we never played with girls at all; they were really something to be scorned. But he was allowed to cuss and have good tantrums that I wasn't allowed to have.

My mother always provided books and she would tell stories about Huckleberry Finn. The river in our town was much too small for a raft; it was rocky and was just a stream, but we'd pretend rafts and imagine running away. One time I got tied up on an Indian raid and left there, and I was too stubborn to call for help, so I was there past supper time and my mother found me and brought me in. I was always tearing up my clothes, and my mother was always tearing me up about that. I think she would have liked to have a daughter. It wasn't until my sister Barbara was born that she had a daughter. Barbara had long curls and was pretty feminine. That way mother had the daughter to play with and daddy had the son and everything was all right.

Source: Excerpt from *Dignity: Lower Income Women Tell of Their Lives and Struggles*, by F. L. Buss, pp. 173–174. Copyright 1985 University of Michigan Press.

CRITICAL THINKING AND CASE ANALYSIS

1. What aspects of the formation of gender identification are captured in this narrative?

2. What are the salient images of mother and father that Lee may have identified with?
3. What role might the rural, small-town environment have played in Lee's experiences of gender identification in early childhood?
4. How much of Lee's preference for rough-and-tumble play do you attribute to her desire to be "the son" for her father? How much do you attribute to her temperament and other aspects of her personality?
5. From what you have read, and drawing on your own experiences, how might Lee's gender identification at this period of her life influence her later relationships with male and female peers, and her capacity to form intimate relationships in later adolescence or early adulthood?

A Framework for Thinking about Gender Identity

Our goal in the discussion that follows is to explore how young children begin to conceptualize gender as a dimension of their self-concept, an organizing principle of social life, and a guide to their behavior. We do not expect a lifetime's work on gender identity to have been completed by 6 years of age. During this stage, however, significant conceptual and emotional changes give gender greater clarity and highlight the relevance of one's gender in a child's overall self-concept. Gender is among the very early social categories that result in stereotyped thinking upon which children base inferences about others. The establishment of gender identity links a child to others of their same group (boys or girls), and influences their interests, preferences, and social interactions (Ruble et al., 2004).

Biological factors including brain organization and physical capacities converge with socialization pressures and a child's own understanding of the demands of the situation to create attractor states or experiences of positive, enjoyable action. So, in one culture, a 4-year-old girl may feel happy and competent when she is playing with a toy loom, learning to weave as her older sisters and her mother do; and in another culture a 4-year-old girl may feel happy and competent when she is playing pretend school with a friend. These gendered states are emotionally and behaviorally satisfying. They draw on cognitive and motor skills that are well developed for girls, and are socially encouraged by adults and peers in the community. As a result, there is a desire to replicate them. Over time, attractor states become increasingly more likely, and draw the child into a pattern of gendered interpersonal interactions, play, and learning activities. However, they are not fixed. The girl who most enjoys playing pretend school with friends can engage in rough and tumble play if her male cousins come over for a visit or when her dad comes home from work. As in the case of Lee, a girl can experience rough and tumble play as the attractor state and still know that she is a girl. The process of moving toward gendered action is revised whenever one or more of the constraints, including biological factors, socialization norms, and situational demands, are modified.

Our analysis of gender identification focuses on four components: (1) understanding the concept of gender, (2) learning gender role standards and stereotypes, (3) identifying with parents, and (4) forming a gender preference.

As you read about gender identification, try to keep in mind that each child is actively working to make sense of gender in light of his or her body, unique talents, preferences, temperament, and the gendered behaviors of others. Children of this age are asking a lot of questions about reproductive and sexual topics, taking great interest in the nature of household and family roles, and trying to figure out how their status as a male or female fits in to their self-theory. The outcome of this work will be distinct and differ from child to child. Most of the literature on gender differences acknowledges that differences within groups of males or females are greater than the average differences between males and females (Hyde, 2005). We believe that these intragroup variations have their origin in the unique ways that boys and girls create personal representations of gender during the early-school-age period.

Understanding Gender

Understanding one's gender involves four components that emerge in a developmental sequence from toddlerhood through early school age (Kohlberg, 1966; Martin, Ruble, & Szkrybalo, 2002): (1) applying the correct gender label to themselves and others, (2) understanding that gender is permanent, (3) understanding gender constancy, and (4) understanding the genital basis of gender (see Figure 7.1). According to this analysis, children construct the meaning of gender, including the stability and constancy of their own gender and the gendered nature of their society, in much the same way that they form other cognitive schemes such as object permanence, which was discussed in Chapter 5 (Infancy) or

conservation of matter, which will be discussed in Chapter 8 (Middle Childhood).

The correct use of **gender labels** is the earliest component of gender identification to be achieved. The categorization of people as male and female is a natural category, much like the distinction between the familiar person and the stranger or between people and inanimate objects, as discussed in Chapter 5. Even before the abstract categories *male* and *female* are understood, children learn to refer to themselves as boys or girls by imitating their parents. From infancy, parents make continual reference to a child's gender in such statements as "That's a good boy" or "That's a good girl."

As early as 21 months, a majority of infants produce at least one gender label, such as boy or girl. By the age of 2½ children can accurately label other children as boys or girls, and by the age of 3, they can accurately sort photographs of boys and girls. They can also apply gender labels such as *Mommy* and *Daddy*, *brother* and *sister*, and *boy* and *girl* accurately. These verbal labels become useful for guiding a child's attention to important distinctions between males and females (Gelman, Taylor, & Nguyen, 2004; Baron, Dunham, Banaji, & Carey, 2007). Once they know these labels, children seek out cues to help them make these distinctions correctly, like hair style, clothes, or body shape. Their attention is directed to the differences between male and female individuals. Having the words or labels for gender categories, the use of these words stimulates a child's further conceptualization about the categories and their appropriate applications, resulting in new understandings about the nature of gender (Nelson, 2005; Waxman & Lidz, 2006). What is more, when infants begin to use gender labels, they are also observed to increase their gender-typed play, suggesting that the representation of oneself

1. Correct use of the gender labels.

2. Gender is permanent.

3. Gender is constant.

4. Gender has a genital basis.

FIGURE 7.1 Four Components for Understanding Gender

Source: © Cengage Learning.

as a boy or a girl motivates and guides their gender-typed behaviors (Zosuls, Ruble, Tamis-Lemonda, Shrout, Bornstein, & Greulich, 2009).

Understanding **gender permanence and constancy** emerges somewhat later, usually between ages 4 and 7 (Serbin, Powlishta, & Gulko, 1993; Levy, 1998). Permanence refers to an appreciation that a boy grows up to be a man and a girl grows up to be a woman. One's sex is permanent over time, even though many things about one might change. Constancy refers to an appreciation that one's sex is unchanged by clothing, hairstyle, play activities, and other day-to-day alterations. Even if a boy puts on a wig and dresses up in a fancy dress, he is still a boy. Even if a girl puts on a helmet and shoulder pads and pretends to be a football player, she is still a girl. Understanding the **genital basis of gender** provides a fundamental context for understanding that gender is permanent and constant. In research involving 3-, 4-, and 5-year-olds, the majority of children who understood the genital differences between the sexes could also tell that a child's sex did not change simply because the child was dressed up to look like a member of the opposite sex. These young children understood that sex is a constant feature of a person, no matter how the person is dressed or whether the hair is long or short. In contrast, the majority of the children who had no knowledge of genital differences were unable to respond correctly to questions about constancy (Bem, 1989).

Gender Role Standards and Stereotypes

Gender role standards are cultural expectations about appropriate behavior for boys and girls and for men and women. One might consider these *sex stereotypes*. If you had no information about a person other than whether the person was male or female, what qualities would you attribute to that person? How would you expect the person to behave? Gender role standards tell us what the culture considers typical and admirable for girls and boys, men and women (Eagly, 2009). For young children, this usually means the kinds of toys, clothes, and activities that would be preferred by boys or girls.

In research on gender role standards, children are typically asked to identify whether certain activities, occupations, or traits are more frequently associated with male individuals, female individuals, or both. For example, in the *Sex-Role Learning Index*, children are shown drawings of 20 objects traditionally associated with gender roles—10 for the male gender role (such as a hammer, a shovel, and a fire helmet) and 10 for the female gender role (such as an iron, a stove, and dishes). By age 7, most children make a perfect score on this type of test, illustrating that they know how their society links a person's sex to activities or occupations (Beere, 1990; Serbin et al., 1993; Levy, 1998). Knowledge of gender-typed personality traits, such as gentle and affectionate or adventurous and self-confident, emerges somewhat later. In one study of more than 550 children, sixth graders answered about 90% of these types of questions correctly (Serbin et al., 1993).

An early-school-age child's knowledge about gender role standards shapes the child's preferences and behaviors. For example, once children identify certain toys as more appropriate for girls and others as more appropriate for boys, their own toy preferences are guided by these standards. Conversely, when they like a toy that is not obviously sex-stereotyped, they are inclined to think that other children of their sex would like that toy as well (Martin, Eisenbud, & Rose, 1995). One consequence of this gender-typed thinking is that it limits a child's willingness to play with certain toys and games, and therefore reduces the child's opportunities to learn from a variety of play experiences.

Although early-school-age children are familiar with gender stereotypes, they are also likely to be flexible in their gender role-play.

© ROB & SAS/CORBIS

The nature of parental influences on children's gender role stereotyping is very complex (Turner & Gervai, 1995). Some parents believe that boys should be assertive and fight for their rights. Others believe that boys should think carefully about what is right and wrong and guide their actions by reason rather than by impulsive aggression. Each of these sets of parents has a conception of male attributes that is communicated to their sons by a variety of means over a long period. The toys that parents give their children, the experiences to which they expose them, and the activities in which they encourage their children's participation all reflect dimensions of the parents' gender role standards. By the time children reach school age, they have been encouraged to adopt those standards and disciplined for what their parents have viewed as gender-inappropriate behavior. Young girls may be shamed for their assertiveness by being told that they are acting bossy, and young boys may be warned to stop acting like a sissy.

As the cognitive underpinnings related to the concept of gender mature, children form **gender schemes**, or personal theories about cultural expectations and stereotypes related to gender. Children look for clues about gender, seeking information from their social environment about what activities they should or should not engage in ("Boys don't dance," "Girls don't play with trucks"), whom they should play with, and what information is especially relevant for them as boys or girls. They use this information to organize their perceptions, focus their attention, and interpret information in such a way as to be consistent with their gender scheme (Levy, Barth, & Zimmerman, 1998; Martin & Ruble, 2004).

Gender schemes play a role in the recollection of behavior (Bauer, 1993). By the kindergarten years, both boys and girls recall information that is consistent with their gender stereotypes better than information that is counter to the stereotype or that is more relevant to the opposite sex (Liben & Signorella, 1993). Among children ages 5 to 12, those with more knowledge of gender role standards also have a stronger preference for same-sex peers and for gender-typed adult activities and occupations (Serbin et al., 1993).

Not all children are equally rigid in applying gender role standards to themselves or to others. Flexibility in the application of gender role standards to oneself and others appears to be influenced by both cognitive factors and socialization. Children learn the stereotypes and expectations related to their own gender before learning the expectations for the opposite gender (Martin, Wood, & Little, 1990). Preschool-age children are likely to see gender role transgressions (e.g., boys playing with dolls or girls pretending to be firefighters) as more permissible than are older children, ages 6 and 7 (Smetana, 1986; Lobel & Menashri, 1993). In particular, young children who have more advanced abilities to differentiate between moral norms (e.g., telling the truth) and social norms (e.g., saying "please" and "thank you") are also less stereotyped in their play activities and toy choices (Lobel & Menashri, 1993). Among 5- to 10-year-olds,

training in multiple classification skills (sorting objects into more than one category) is associated with more egalitarian, less stereotyped responses to gender-related tasks (Bigler & Liben, 1992).

Variations in family environment and socialization influence children's thinking about gender role norms. Girls are generally more flexible about gender roles than boys. Young boys whose fathers live in the home typically have an earlier knowledge of gender-typed roles. However, if these fathers participate in nontraditional activities in the home, the boys' gender role knowledge is delayed. Children whose mothers perform nontraditional tasks develop a more flexible attitude, seeing more activities and occupations as appropriate for both men and women (Serbin et al., 1993).

Identification with Parents

The third component of gender identification involves **parental identification**. Identification is the process through which one person incorporates the values and beliefs of another. To identify with someone is not to become exactly identical to that person, but to increase one's sense of allegiance and closeness with that person. Through the process of identification, ideals, values, and standards of the family and community are **internalized** so that they become a part of the individual's own belief system.

During early school age, most children admire and emulate their parents. Young children are avid observers of their parents as models, they are emotionally invested in their parents' reactions to them, and they are eager to internalize parental values. Young children integrate parental values and behaviors as part of their gender scheme. Children identify with both parents, not just with the parent of the same sex. However, same-sex parental identification can provide important information for a child's gender identity, including the tasks and roles that the parent enacts at home and in the community, the way to behave with members of the opposite sex, and traditional or flexible views about gender.

Individual differences in children's gender-typed preferences in toys and play activities as well as their gender role knowledge are linked to their parents' attitudes and behaviors. Parents who have more traditional gender-typed attitudes tend to have children who are more stereotyped in their play preferences and whose knowledge of sex stereotypes develops at a younger age (Weinraub et al., 1984; Fagot & Leinbach, 1989). Parents can make deliberate efforts to encourage more flexibility in gender role conceptualization and preferences by deliberately modeling counterstereotyped activities—fathers making dinner or mothers mowing the lawn—and including more counterstereotypical comments in conversations with their children (Friedman, Leaper, & Bigler, 2007). Parents can also balance their children's play activities so that both boys and girls have opportunities for independent play that does not require collaboration (e.g., playing with toy trucks and cars on a track) and opportunities for cooperative, social-relational play (e.g., playing pretend school) (Leaper, 2000).

Parents devise their beliefs and parenting practices out of their own internalized cultural script about gender. So even if they endorse gender flexibility, they may not be able to carry through entirely with their beliefs. For example, many studies focus on how parents talk to their children. The results of this work suggest that mothers are generally both more supportive and more negative with their children—that is, more expressive—whereas fathers are more directive, or task oriented. Furthermore, daughters receive more verbal interaction than do sons, especially from mothers. Finally, fathers are more assertive than mothers, and children are more assertive with their mothers than with their fathers (Leaper, Anderson, & Sanders, 1998). Thus, the family environment is *gendered* through patterns of communication that give children different role models for the behavior of mothers and fathers and provide boys and girls with opportunities to develop different approaches to social interaction.

In addition to the enactment of scripts for how to interact, most adults have deeply held standards about how men and women, boys and girls ought to behave. Consider the following:

> [A family] with three children (5-year-old Dan, 7-year-old Lyle, and 3.5-year-old Amy) in which the mother had always believed that her children should be exposed to all types of experiences, with no distinction indicated between "boy's kind" and "girl's kind." She encouraged her older son's play with dolls. . . . The boys were not allowed to play "aggressive" sports (American football) and were redirected by parents toward ballet and soccer. Yet the mother herself reported being "taken to the limits":

> . . . watching her [the mother] play with Amy, the mother was painting Amy's fingernails, Dan asked his mother to paint his fingernails too. "I could only bring myself to paint two [nails]. I knew it was ridiculous, but it just bothered me." (MacKain, 1987, p. 120)

This example illustrates how strongly internalized the standards about gender distinctions can be. Even for parents who want to minimize gender distinctions, some

APPLYING THEORY AND RESEARCH TO LIFE

Children Raised by Gay or Lesbian Parents

A GROWING NUMBER of gay and lesbian couples are rearing children. In many cases, the children were conceived in heterosexual marriages. Then one parent established a lesbian or gay relationship and continued to raise the child. Some couples have children conceived through artificial insemination or other assisted reproductive technologies, and both lesbian and gay couples have assumed the parent role through adoption (Bailey, Bobrow, Wolfe, & Mikach, 1995; Flaks, Ficher, Masterpasqua, & Joseph, 1995). The emergence of this unique family structure provides an opportunity to better understand the process of gender role socialization and the development of sexual orientation. Many questions about child-rearing environments and child outcomes can be posed. Do parents who have a homosexual orientation differ from heterosexual parents in their parenting strategies or parental role behaviors? How relevant is a parent's sexual orientation in shaping a child's gender role identification?

Research suggests that the sexual orientation of parents is not a powerful predictor of their child's gender identification or future sexual orientation.

Over 20 years of research has addressed the adjustment and development of children raised by gay and lesbian parents. Several studies have reported that when compared to heterosexual couples, lesbian couples exhibit more sensitive parenting and more egalitarian role relationships. Open disclosure of the lesbian relationship, the ability to maintain ties with the rest of the child's family, and a perception that the partners share equally in the tasks associated with household and child care all contribute to the child's emotional well-being (Patterson, 1995).

In general, studies of the well-being, cognitive levels, and emotional adjustment of children growing up with lesbian mothers find no differences between these children and those growing up in heterosexual families (Fitzgerald, 1999; Patterson, 2006). The children have gender role preferences that are very similar to those of children growing up in heterosexual families (Patterson, 2009). One study reviewed findings from 23 studies of children of lesbian and gay parents (Anderssen, Amlie, & Ytteroy, 2002). Of these studies, most were conducted in North America, but four focused on European samples. Twenty studies reported on children of lesbian mothers; three on children of gay fathers. The results of these studies were discussed in terms of seven outcomes: emotional functioning, sexual preference,

prohibitions or constraints are difficult to disregard (Valsiner, 2000).

The contribution of parental identification to a child's gender identity is not all that well understood (Fagot, 1995). On balance, mothers spend much more time than fathers in the care and rearing of young children. Thus, much of what children learn about the male role is likely to be interpreted through interactions with their mothers, and by watching their mothers and fathers, other male companions, or observing men on television. In a study of 3- to 6-year-olds in which the fathers were the primary caregivers, children had higher levels of a sense of internal control and scored higher on verbal ability than children in more traditional families. However, there were no differences in the children's gender identification between traditional and father-caregiver families (Radin, 1982, 1988). In a follow-up study, when the children were adolescents, the children who had experienced primary care by their fathers endorsed more nontraditional employment arrangements and role sharing by men and women. They also were more favorable about nontraditional child care arrangements where fathers spent more time caring for their young children (Radin, 1993). Thus, based on findings from this research program, the impact of father involvement on gender identity was more evident as the children got older, rather than during early childhood.

The Applying Theory and Research to Life box discusses children raised by gay or lesbian parents. The research finds no differences in gender role behavior, gender identity, or emotional well-being between children raised by heterosexual or homosexual parents.

Gender Preference

The fourth component of gender identification is the development of a personal preference for the kinds of activities and attitudes associated with masculine or feminine roles. Preferences for gender-typed play activities and same-sex play companions have been observed among preschoolers as well as older children (Hoffmann & Powlishta, 2001). Egan and Perry (2001) conceived of **gender preference** as a

---

stigmatization, gender role behavior, behavioral adjustment, gender identity, and cognitive functioning. Not all studies measured all of these variables, and even when studies focused on common outcomes, they used a variety of methods to measure the same variables. The studies of children of gay fathers focused only on sexual preferences and stigmatization.

Despite the variations in approaches to sampling, measurement, and design, the studies reported quite similar results. Children of lesbian mothers did not differ from other children with respect to emotional or behavioral problems, gender identity, gender role behavior, or cognitive functioning. Children's sexual preference was not related to their parents' sexual orientation. There was some greater sensitivity to stigmatization among children of lesbian and gay parents, with children in some studies reporting being teased about being gay or lesbian. Also, children gave more thought to whom they would tell about their parents' sexual orientation. However, these experiences were not associated with higher rates of emotional or behavioral difficulties. The authors concluded that the research, with its many flaws,

provides a picture of basic similarity between children reared in gay or lesbian families and those reared by heterosexual families.

The results of this and subsequent research suggest that the sexual orientation of parents is not a significant predictor of a child's gender identification or of future sexual orientation (Herek, 2006). Future research might focus more on the unique nature and experience of children growing up in gay and lesbian families, with a particular need to include more studies of gay fathers and their approaches to parenting. Rather than examining vulnerabilities or potential deficits in comparison to children raised in heterosexual families, future research might shed new light on the approaches to gender socialization and the interpersonal worldview that emerge in this family form (Lambert, 2005).

Critical Thinking Questions

1. The research discussed previously finds no systematic relationship between a child's sexual orientation or gender identification and the sexual orientation of the parents. How do you explain this null finding?

2. If you were asked to design research to study the child-rearing practices and gender socialization of gay and lesbian parents, what factors would you want to take into account? What would you measure? Who would be your comparison group? Why?

3. What do you think might be some particular strengths of the parenting process for lesbian or gay parents? What might be some weaknesses? How might these strengths and weaknesses differ from those of heterosexual parents?

4. Based on what you have read about gender identification, what role would you expect a parent's sexual orientation to play in the way gender identification is formed?

5. What do you think is the likely relationship between gender preference in childhood and gender preference in adolescence or adulthood? Perhaps the association of a parent's sexual orientation to a child's gender identification or sexual orientation is not observed in childhood, but might be observed in later adolescence or adulthood. What do you think of that idea?

combination of gender typicality and gender contentedness. **Gender typicality** refers to whether a child fits in with others of the same sex, likes to do the same kinds of things as others of the same sex, is good at the same kinds of things as others of the same sex, and in general displays the typical traits of being a girl or a boy. **Contentedness** means that a child likes being the sex proscribed at birth, does not think it would be more fun to be the opposite sex, and does not spend time wishing to do things that members of the opposite sex can do. In their research, Egan and Perry found a strong and consistent relationship between gender typicality and measures of self-esteem, social competence, and acceptance from both male and female peers. With respect to gender contentedness, they found that the greater social pressure children felt to conform to gender role norms, the more important gender contentedness was in sustaining self-esteem and perceived social competence. Those children who were not content about being a boy or a girl and also perceived a lot of pressure to conform to gender stereotypes experienced lower self-esteem.

Generally, there is more latitude or flexibility around the behaviors that are viewed as acceptable for young girls than for young boys. Little boys are more frequently stigmatized for acting in what is considered girlish ways, and are more likely to experience peer rejection if their behaviors are deemed gender atypical. As a result, a nonconforming gender preference is more likely to be a source of distress for boys (Wallien, van-Goozen, & Cohen-Kettenis, 2007; Hegarty, 2009).

Both boys and girls can have experiences, like those described by Lee in the case study on Gender Identification in Early Childhood, when their personal preferences for play behaviors, friends, and interests do not seem to fit with the cultural standards or stereotypes for their sex. In most cases, children and adults recognize these preferences as expressions of a child's unique temperament or personality. However, some children have a strong aversion to some or all of the physical characteristics or social roles associated with their own biological sex, a condition called **gender dysphoria**, and express a desire to be the opposite sex (APA Task Force on Gender Identity and Gender Variance, 2009).

Gender preference can be influenced by environmental cues as to the value of one sex or the other. The cues may emanate from the family, ethnic and religious groups, the media, social institutions (such as the schools), and other culture carriers. Many cultures have traditionally valued men more than women and have given men higher status. For example, among Japanese immigrants who came to the United States between the 1890s and early 1900s, a strong value was the commitment to a hierarchical and male-head-of-household view of the family (Ishii-Kuntz, 1997):

The Issei (*first-generation immigrant families*) customarily designated their eldest son the successor to the family business. . . . Accordingly, the eldest Nisei (*second-generation*) son usually received special treatment and privileges from his parents. In many Issei families, he was the second to be served at meals, after his father, and he was generally indulged by his mother. . . . Younger siblings were instructed to obey his directions, and even older sisters were expected to defer to him. (Ishii-Kuntz, 1997, p. 138)

To the extent that a cultural preference for males is communicated to children, boys are likely to establish a firmer preference for their sex group, and girls are likely to experience some ambivalence toward if not rejection of their sex group. It is easier to be happy and content with oneself if one feels highly valued than if one feels less valued. The attainment of gender preference is a more complex and dynamic accomplishment than might be imagined. In fact, one's gender preference may fluctuate at different stages of life particularly as one perceives gender-based changes in access to roles, resources, and social status (Maccoby, 2002).

Some families develop a strong preference regarding the sex of an expected child. In a longitudinal study of Swedish children from birth to age 25, the parents' prenatal preferences for a son or daughter were related to perceived problems in the mother-child and father-child relationships (Stattin & Klackenberg-Larsson, 1991). Mothers' perceptions of problems in the parent-child relationship—especially the relationship between fathers and their nonpreferred daughters—were significantly related to the fathers' disappointed hopes for a son.

Looking back on their relationship with their parents at age 25, nonpreferred daughters were especially likely to note problems, saying that their mothers did not have time for them, their fathers were stricter with them and had less time for them, and their relationships with their fathers were, in general, worse than the relationships described by preferred daughters. Research among families in India found that mothers' preferences for sons were positively correlated with their sons' IQ scores and negatively correlated with their daughters' IQ scores (Raina, Malhi, Malhotra, & Jerath, 2003). These kinds of studies suggest that parental preference for one sex over the other can influence the quality of parent-child interactions and the resources, interactions, and opportunities available to boys and girls as they are growing up.

Table 7.1 summarizes the four components of the acquisition of gender identification: (1) developing an understanding of gender, (2) learning gender role standards, (3) identifying with parents, and (4) establishing a gender preference. What was once viewed as a predominantly biological process of sex role differentiation is now viewed as a product of the interaction of biological, cognitive, and social factors. The outcome of the process for an individual child depends on the interaction of biologically based sex characteristics, the parents' approaches to gender role socialization, the child's personal capacities and preferences, and the cultural and familial values that create gender-linked expectations for behavior.

TABLE 7.1 Dimensions of Gender Role Identification

DIMENSION	GENDER ROLE OUTCOME
Developing an understanding of gender	I am a boy; I will grow up to be a man.
	I am a girl; I will grow up to be a woman.
Acquiring gender role standards	Boys are independent; they play with trucks.
	Girls are interpersonal; they play with dolls.
Identifying with the same-sex parent	I am a lot like Daddy. I want to be like him when I grow up.
	I am a lot like Mommy. I want to be like her when I grow up.
Establishing a gender role preference	I like being a boy. I'd rather be a boy than a girl.
	I like being a girl. I'd rather be a girl than a boy.

Source: © Cengage Learning.

A child's gender identity becomes a basic cognitive scheme that influences the interpretation of experiences. Children learn that people are grouped into two sexes—male and female. In our society, this dichotomy imposes itself on a wide array of social situations, including work, play, and politics—arenas where one's genital sex is not especially relevant. Once children learn this powerful category, they go about the business of figuring out how to apply it. They recognize people as men and women, boys and girls, and they identify themselves as members of one of these two groups. They form expectations based on this categorization—that certain toys, interests, and behaviors are appropriate for boys and others are appropriate for girls; that certain activities, dispositions, and occupations are appropriate for men and others for women. These expectations are generally reinforced by the beliefs of the older children and adults with whom children interact. Thus, the gender schemes that are conceived during childhood play a significant role in guiding a child's daily activities and in shaping a preliminary vision of oneself in the future. Gender-based beliefs may become integrated into moral development, so that children begin to believe that it is morally right to adhere to certain gender role standards and morally wrong to violate these standards.

Early Moral Development

Objective 2. To describe the process of early moral development, drawing from theories and research to explain how knowledge, emotion, and action combine to produce internalized morality.

The moral dilemmas facing young children are not about plagiarism or cloning or abortion. Rather, they are about understanding that lying, cheating, stealing, hurting others, or making fun of other children's differences are morally wrong, and that telling the truth, playing fairly, being helpful, and respecting people's differences are morally right. The following analysis of moral development focuses on how children learn moral standards and apply them to their own behavior as well as the behavior of others. For early-school-age children, achievements in moral development include changes in three interrelated domains:

1. *Emotions.* (a) Experiencing the array of emotions that foster caring about others and that produce anxiety, guilt, and remorse when a moral standard has been violated; and (b) recognizing these emotions in others.
2. *Knowledge.* Learning the moral code of one's community and making judgments about whether something is good or bad, right or wrong.
3. *Action.* Taking appropriate actions to inhibit negative impulses, to act in accordance with rules and requests, to obey parents and other authorities, or to act in a caring, helpful manner, depending on the situation.

Early moral development involves a process called **internalization**, which means behaving according to parental standards, rules, and values without external monitoring and constant reminders. This process, sometimes referred to as the formation of a conscience, requires that the child experience moral emotions, understand the community's moral code, and be able to take appropriate actions to either inhibit bad behavior or enact good behavior (Aksan & Kochanska, 2005). During toddlerhood, a child's attention is focused on limits of and standards for behavior. Toddlers typically feel that demands for proper behavior do not come from within themselves but emanate from the external world. In contrast, during early school age, standards and limits become part of a child's self-concept. Specific values may be acquired primarily from parents, but they become integrated elements of the child's worldview.

Internalized morality includes inhibiting harmful or socially unacceptable impulses and striving to do what is right. This is often characterized as the want vs. should conflict. A child *wants* to indulge impulses for immediate expression or pleasure, but knows that there *should* be a consideration for the consequences of those behaviors (Milkman, Rogers, & Bazerman, 2008). For example, a 3-year-old boy may take great delight in teasing his dog by threatening it with a stick. During one of these attacks, his mother scolds him. She insists that he stop and explains that it is cruel to hurt or frighten the dog. She may have to remind the boy on several other occasions that hitting the dog is not permitted. As the boy internalizes this standard, he begins to experience internal control over his own behavior. He may see the dog lying calmly in the sun and, with a gleam in his eye, begin to pick up a stick. At that moment, his behavior is interrupted by a feeling of tension, which is accompanied by the thought that it is wrong to hit the dog. If the standard has been successfully internalized, the emotional tension and the thought will be sufficient to inhibit the boy from hitting the dog.

Five Theoretical Perspectives on Moral Development

A variety of theories explain how the domains of emotion, knowledge, and action converge to produce the internalized moral behavior considered appropriate for the early-school-age child. The five theoretical approaches presented here—learning theories, cognitive developmental theory, psychoanalytic theory, object relations theory, and evolutionary theory—each offer distinct views about the way morality becomes internalized. You may find it helpful to refer back to Chapter 2 (Major Theories for Understanding Human Development) to review the basic concepts of these theories.

These theories focus on the *process* of moral development, not the content. Each culture or subcultural group has its own set of moral standards. For example, in many Asian cultures, children are taught that teachers are highly revered. Children learn to show respect to a teacher and to view their teachers as important role models. Children who are disrespectful of a teacher would be shamed. In the United States, the role of teacher does not have especially high status in comparison to many other occupations. Parents may express criticism of teachers openly in front of their children. They may write excuses for children's absences or failure to complete their homework, even though both the children and parents know these excuses are fabrications. Children may learn that some teachers are fair and helpful, but others are not. They may not believe that it is immoral to ignore a teacher's request or to make fun of a teacher with the other children. The theories that follow suggest how children internalize moral standards; they do not explain what the standards are or suggest what they should be.

Learning Theories. The focus of learning theories is on the conditions that support moral behaviors or actions. Moral behavior and the process of internalization are viewed as a response to environmental reinforcements and punishments (Aronfreed, 1969). Moral behaviors can be shaped by the *consequences* that follow them. A positive, prosocial behavior, like offering to help put the toys away or comforting another child who is distressed, is likely to be repeated if it is rewarded. In contrast, if a behavior is ignored or punished, it is less likely to occur again. If a child performs a misdeed or defies an authority and suffers negative consequences, these consequences ought to reduce the likelihood that such behavior will recur. If a child is in an unpleasant or painful environment and performs a behavior that reduces or eliminates the unpleasantness, the child is more likely to perform this same behavior again in similar situations. For example, if a child says, "I'm sorry. I'll try to do better next time," and this apology reduces the parent's anger or irritability, this behavior is likely to be repeated at other times when the parent is angry at the child. According to learning theory, internalization results as the behaviors that lead to a more comfortable, less threatening environment become more common and the behaviors that produce parental anger or conflict disappear.

The special case of **avoidance conditioning** is viewed as a paradigm for understanding how internalization is sustained. Having been disciplined in the past for wrongdoings, a child contemplating a misdeed should feel tension. Avoiding or inhibiting the impulse to misbehave reduces the tension and is therefore reinforcing. This process may occur even when the person who was involved in administering the discipline is absent. In other words, the scenario of thinking about a wrong or naughty action, feeling the anxiety that is associated with past discipline, and reducing that anxiety by exercising restraint may take place mentally, without any observable behavior. Over time, the reinforcement of **tension reduction** that is linked to controlling a wrongful impulse strengthens the tendency to inhibit it, and the child's behavior becomes less impulsive.

Social learning theory adds another mechanism for moral learning: the **observation of models**. By observing and imitating helpful models, children can learn prosocial behavior. When a child observes someone else perform a kind, generous, or selfless act, it produces an uplifting emotional response.

© 2010 Jon Feingersh/Jupiterimages Corporation

According to learning theory, Martin's willingness to do his chores and help around the house is strengthened because he receives a reward for his efforts. According to this theory, what would happen if Martin's father stopped giving him the reward?

If the opportunity for positive or altruistic actions occurs, the child who has observed someone else's generosity is likely to be more caring or helpful as a result of having observed this positive action by others (Schnall, Roper, & Fessler, 2010).

By observing the negative consequences that follow the misdeeds of models, they can also learn to inhibit their own misbehavior. Their moral behavior is not limited to the actions they have performed—it may be based on expectations formulated from observations of how the conduct of relevant models has been rewarded or punished (Bandura, 1977, 1991). For example, early-school-age children are more likely to judge an act of televised violence as *right* if the act goes unpunished. Having viewed such unpunished acts, children formulate abstract rules, concepts, and sets of proposition about when aggressive behavior is justified (Kremar & Cooke, 2001).

Cognitive learning theory describes how moral behavior is influenced by *situational factors* and by the child's *expectations, values,* and *goals* (Mischel, 1973). For example, some people place great value on success in athletics and may be more tempted to lie or cheat in order to succeed in an athletic competition than in an academic setting. Another situational factor is the presence or absence of monitoring. The expectation that a misdeed will be observed and punished leads to greater resistance to temptation than does the expectation that a misdeed will go unnoticed. Similarly, the belief that positive, prosocial behaviors are expected and will be noticed influences a child's generosity and helpfulness (Froming, Allen, & Jensen, 1985). According to this theoretical perspective, the specific situation will influence the extent to which moral behavior is displayed (Carroll & Rest, 1982). According to the learning theories, moral character is built on the accumulation of many experiences across different situations day after day where children learn which behaviors are acceptable and which are not.

Cognitive Developmental Theory. In comparison to the learning theories, cognitive developmental theorists focus more on **moral reasoning** than on moral behavior. They place emphasis on the child's active construction of moral meaning, focusing on developmental changes in the ways children make judgments and reason about morally relevant situations. Piaget (1932/1948) described the major transition in moral judgment as a shift from heteronomous to autonomous morality. In **heteronomous morality,** rules are understood as fixed, unchangeable aspects of social reality. Children's moral judgments reflect a sense of subordination to authority figures. An act is judged as right or wrong depending on the letter of the law, the amount of damage that was done, and whether or not the act was punished.

In **autonomous morality,** children see rules as products of cooperative agreements. Moral judgments reflect a child's participation in a variety of social roles and in egalitarian relationships with friends. Give-and-take with peers highlights mutual respect and mutual benefit as rewards for holding to the terms of agreement or abiding by the law. Piaget posed situations like the following to young children in order to help clarify the difference between heteronomous and autonomous morality.

Mark rushes into the kitchen, pushing open the door. Although he did not realize it, his mother had left a set of 10 cups and saucers on a stool behind the door. When he pushed the door open, the cups and saucers fell off the stool and broke.

Matt was climbing up on the kitchen counter to reach some cookies that his mother told him he was not supposed to eat. While climbing on the counter, he broke one cup and saucer.

Who committed the more serious moral transgression? Which boy should be more severely punished?

Hannah got in trouble in school today for talking back to her teacher. Now her mother is trying to explain that it is wrong to be disrespectful to teachers. At the preconventional level of morality, Hannah just thinks it's wrong if you get punished. Lots of other kids are disrespectful to the teacher and nothing ever happens to them.

© 2010 Image Source/Jupiterimages Corporation

Children operating with a heteronomous morality believe that the child who breaks 10 cups by accident has committed a much more serious transgression than the child who broke only one. Children who have achieved an autonomous morality believe that the child who disobeyed and violated his mother's trust committed the more serious transgression. In general, younger children are likely to judge the moral seriousness of an action based on the magnitude and nature of the consequences. If an action, no matter what the intent, produced harm, it should be punished. Older children are able to consider both the intention and the consequences in making a moral judgment. If an action was intended to harm and produced harm, it should definitely be punished (Helwig, Zelazo, & Wilson, 2001).

Expanding on the distinction between heteronomous and autonomous morality, cognitive developmental theorists have described a sequence of stages of moral thought (Kohlberg, 1976; Gibbs, 1979; Damon, 1980). As children become increasingly skillful in evaluating the abstract and logical components of a moral dilemma, their moral judgments change. At the core of this change is the mechanism called **equilibration**—efforts to reconcile new perspectives and ideas about basic moral concepts, such as justice, intentionality, and social responsibility, with existing views about what is right and wrong. Children's reasoning may be thrown into disequilibrium by external sources, such as their parents' use of explanations and inductions regarding a moral dilemma or encounters with friends who reason differently about a moral conflict. Children's own cognitive maturation, especially the ability to think abstractly and hypothetically about interrelated variables, determines how their reasoning about moral dilemmas will be structured (Piaget, 1978/1985; Walker, Gustafson, & Hennig, 2001).

Kohlberg (1969, 1976) described three levels of moral thought, each characterized by two stages of moral judgment (see Table 7.2). At Level I, **preconventional morality**, Stage 1 judgments of justice are based on whether a behavior is rewarded or punished. Stage 2 judgments are based on an instrumental view of whether the consequences will be good for "me and my family." The first and, to some degree, the second stage of Level I characterize children of early school age. Level II, **conventional morality**, is concerned with maintaining the approval of authorities at Stage 3 and with upholding the social order at Stage 4. Level III, **postconventional** morality, brings an acceptance of moral principles that are viewed as part of a person's own ideology rather than simply being imposed by the social order. At Stage 5, justice and morality are determined by a democratically derived social contract. At Stage 6, a person develops a sense of universal ethical principles that apply across history and cultural contexts.

According to this theory, the stages form a logical hierarchy. At each new stage, individuals reorganize their view of morality, realizing the inadequacy of the preceding stage. For example, once a person sees morality in terms of a system that upholds and protects the social order (Stage 4), then the reasoning that argues for an act as moral because it was rewarded or immoral

---

TABLE 7.2 Stages in the Development of Moral Judgment

LEVEL I: PRECONVENTIONAL

Stage 1 Judgments are based on whether behavior is rewarded or punished.

Stage 2 Judgments are based on whether the consequences result in benefits for self or loved ones.

LEVEL II: CONVENTIONAL

Stage 3 Judgments are based on whether authorities approve or disapprove.

Stage 4 Judgments are based on whether the behavior upholds or violates the laws of society.

LEVEL III: POSTCONVENTIONAL

Stage 5 Judgments are based on preserving social contracts based on cooperative collaboration.

Stage 6 Judgments are based on ethical principles that apply across time and cultures.

Source: Based on Kohlberg, 1969, 1976.

---

because it was punished is seen as inadequate. The stages form an invariant sequence, moving from a very idiosyncratic, personal view of morality to a view in which rules and laws are obeyed because they have been established by an authority or a society, and finally to an understanding of rules and laws as created to uphold basic principles of fairness, justice, and humanity (Boom, Brugman, & van der Heijden, 2001).

Consistent with this theory of moral development, early-school-age children can be expected to reason about moral situations at Level I, preconventional morality, which is dominated by concerns about the consequences of their behavior. At Stage 1, children's judgments of good and bad, right and wrong, are based on whether a behavior has been rewarded or punished or is expected to be rewarded or punished. At Stage 2, children's moral judgments are based on whether the behavior will bring about benefits for them or for other people they care about. Thus, young children's moral outlook has a *utilitarian* orientation (Kohlberg, 1976). Research with first graders confirms that this preconventional outlook is quite common, whether children are discussing hypothetical or real-life moral dilemmas (Walker, 1989).

However, children understand that not all misbehavior involves a moral transgression (see the Applying Theory and Research to Life box for a discussion of moral transgressions, social convention, and personal choice). Moreover, a child's moral reasoning can be altered by exposure to an environment that encourages children to participate actively in creating the moral climate. For example, in the preschool and early primary grades, children can function at a more flexible, autonomous level when the moral atmosphere consistently emphasizes mutual respect. Classrooms where children are involved in rule making and conflict resolution give children an opportunity to appreciate each other's perspectives and to construct a social order that is largely regulated by the children themselves (DeVries, Hildebrandt, & Zan, 2000).

APPLYING THEORY AND RESEARCH TO LIFE

Moral Transgressions, Social Convention, and Personal Choice

NOT ALL SOCIAL RULES or prohibitions have to do with moral concerns. There is a difference between **morality**, which usually involves the rights, dignity, and welfare of others, and **social convention**, which involves socially accepted norms and regulations (Turiel, 1983; Smetana, 1985). For example, in the preschool context, stealing another child's toy would be a moral transgression; a transgression of social convention would be getting up and wandering away during circle time. Preschool-age children are consistently able to differentiate between moral and social convention transgressions. They understand that moral transgressions are wrong because they affect the welfare of others and that social convention transgressions are wrong because they are disruptive or create disorder (Turiel, 2002).

Social convention transgressions depend on the situation. At home, it may be permissible to get up from the table during dinnertime before everyone has finished and go somewhere to play, whereas it is not permissible to get up from the snack table at preschool until the teacher says everyone may leave. Moral transgressions apply more consistently across settings: It is morally wrong to steal at home, at preschool, or at a friend's house. Children as young as 3 and 4 make this distinction when they evaluate transgressions. In contrast to social convention transgressions, young children tend to judge moral transgressions to be more serious, deserving of greater punishment, and independent of the rules or authority in a situation (Smetana, Schlagman, & Adams, 1993).

In addition to moral and social convention, some behaviors fall within the domain of **personal choice**. Within the boundaries of fairness and social reciprocity, children recognize a domain

© Christina Kennedy/Alamy

Ryan has a closet where he keeps his clothes. He can select whatever he wants to wear to school; this is a common domain of personal choice.

of personal freedom. Whereas moral and social decisions are often guided by adult authority and regulations, personal choices are typically guided by a child's own preferences (Nucci & Turiel, 2000). These choices might include preferences for certain toys or play activities, foods, or choice of friends. Children perceive that they have more latitude for expressing their personal preferences at home than at school, where social convention and teachers' authority may restrict some of their choices (Weber, 1999). Studies of Colombian and Chinese preschool-age children suggest that even in cultures that are considered strongly hierarchical or collectivist, young children perceive that they have a legitimate role in certain personal decisions, such as which foods or toys they prefer, so long as these decisions are coordinated with consideration for others (Ardila-Rey & Killen, 2001; Yau & Smetana, 2003).

Critical Thinking Questions

1. What are the distinguishing features of morality, social convention, and personal choice? Is it reasonable to differentiate these

three domains? Can you think of a behavior that might be considered an aspect of personal choice in one culture, but a moral imperative in another?

2. The discussion of moral development begins with a summary of five theories. How does each of these theories distinguish between the domains of morality, social convention, and personal choice?

3. In certain totalitarian dictatorships, children have been urged to report on the behaviors and political views of their parents, especially any behaviors or views that might be critical of the ruling party. What are the moral implications of this kind of expectation? What should a child do under these conditions?

4. What kinds of experiences and socialization messages might help a child to identify areas of personal choice? How might families differ in the extent to which they create room for children to have and express personal preferences? What are the likely consequences of a socialization environment that allows wide or narrow avenues for personal choice?

The notion that people move through a hierarchical sequence of stages of moral reasoning prompted by a process of cognitive disequilibrium has been challenged on a number of fronts. The direction of development over the stages has been viewed as too linear, valuing justice over social cooperation. It has been criticized as embodying a Western cultural orientation, and a male-oriented value system, which places the individual good and individual freedoms above the good of the group or community (Arnold, 2000). However, cross-cultural comparisons have found support for the idea that as people mature, they find increasingly sophisticated ways of approaching moral situations. A study of more than 500 high school and university students in Taiwan found that the students showed evidence of high levels of postconventional reasoning, even though they adopted a culturally collectivist Chinese moral ethic (Gielen & Miao, 2000). Longitudinal studies in a variety of countries have observed an evolution of moral thought much like that proposed by Kohlberg, in which the reasoning shifts from an idiosyncratic to a more principled approach to evaluating moral conflicts (Gielen & Markoulis, 2001).

Psychoanalytic Theory. The psychoanalytic theorists focus on the ability of children to control their impulses and resist temptation, rather than on their cognitive reasoning about what constitutes a moral transgression. This theoretical perspective addresses moral emotions, especially guilt about having harmful or naughty impulses, and pride in behaving in accord with one's ideals, as they contribute to moral behavior. According to psychoanalytic theory, a moral sense develops as a result of strong parental identification. Classical psychoanalytic theory viewed a child's conscience, or **superego,** as an internalization of parental values and moral standards. It holds that the superego is formed during the phallic stage, between the ages of about 4 and 7, as a result of the conflict between a child's sexual and aggressive impulses and the ways in which the parents deal with the behavioral manifestations of those impulses.

According to psychoanalytic theory, the more severely a parent forces a child to inhibit impulses, the stronger the child's superego will be. Freud (1925/1961) assumed that boys would develop more highly differentiated and punitive superegos than girls because he believed that boys' impulses are more intense. He also believed that because of the greater impulsive energy demonstrated by boys, boys are treated more harshly by their parents than are girls. Finally, Freud suggested that boys identify with their fathers for two reasons: fear of losing the father's love and fear of the father as an aggressor. This identification with the father is intense and typically leads to a fully incorporated set of moral standards. According to Freud, a girl identifies with her mother for a single reason: fear of losing her love. As Freud considered this motivation for identification less intense than that of the boy, he believed that the girl's superego would be correspondingly weaker.

Research on the development of conscience has failed to support Freud's hypotheses. Studies that have investigated the ability to resist temptation or to confess after wrongdoing

According to the psychoanalytic view, young children act on their impulses. As the superego develops, they are more successful at resisting temptation.

© JLP/Jose L. Pelaez/CORBIS

have found that young girls are *better* able to resist temptation than boys and show a pattern of decreasing moral transgressions over the toddlerhood and early school years (Mischel et al., 1989). Studies that have attempted to assess the relative contributions of mothers and fathers to their children's moral behavior have found that mothers' values and attitudes are strongly related to the moral behavior of their children, whereas the values and attitudes of fathers have little relationship to such behavior (Hoffman, 1970). Finally, research has found that the children of parents who use harsh physical punishment do not have higher levels of internalization. These children are likely to inhibit impulsive behaviors in the presence of their parents, but when they are observed with their peers away from home, they tend to be physically aggressive and do not control their behavior well (Pettit, Dodge, & Brown, 1988; Hart, Ladd, & Burleson, 1990). Parental warmth, limited use of power assertion, involving children in decision making, and modeling resistance to temptation contribute to high levels of prosocial behavior and social responsibility (Maccoby, 1992).

Object Relations Theory. In contrast to Freud's views on the formation of conscience, **object relations theory** views the critical time for moral development as infancy rather than the early-school-age years (Klein, 1932/1975; Winnicut, 1958; Mahler, 1963; Kohut, 1971). Infants develop an awareness of three domains: the body and its physical experiences and needs; the existence of others; and the relations between the self and others (Beit-Hallahmi, 1987). All subsequent psychological growth must be assimilated into these three domains. According to this view, the origins of moral reasoning and behavior have links to early feelings about the self and its needs, especially the feelings of pleasure and pain, and the way these feelings are mirrored or accepted by the loving caregiver.

Morality has a basis in a young child's awareness of valued others and in behaviors that strengthen or threaten the bonds between the self and these others. All humans are seen as confronted by a dynamic tension between positive and negative emotions—love and hate, kindness and cruelty. One basis of early morality lies in the child's own sense of self-love, a wish to enhance and not harm or violate the self. Another basis is the extension of this self-love to the other and the wish to preserve feelings of connection, trust, and security that have been established in the early parent-infant relationship. Through experiences with sensitive caregiving, infants become increasingly aware of the loved object as an integrated whole with feelings, motives, and goals as well as a physical reality. At the same time, this realization about the other fosters the child's own awareness of his or her inner mental life. When a child is distressed, for example, a calm, reassuring caregiver will use a certain tone of voice, facial expressions, and comforting strategies to help the child cope with the difficulty. This gives the child a chance to feel safe about experiencing the inner world of painful emotions. The loving caregiver allows the child an intimate context in

which to encounter these impulses, emotions, and fears. As a result, the child does not have to split off from his or her angry, vengeful self or project it onto others. By seeing the loved other as both good and bad, and the self as both good and bad, the child's capacity for caring and empathy expands (Fonagy, 1999).

Longitudinal studies have provided support for the link between experiences of mutually responsive care in infancy and later moral emotion and behaviors (Kochanska, Forman, Aksan, & Dunbar, 2005). Children whose relationship with their mothers was characterized as mutually responsive in infancy showed stronger moral emotions, that is, greater distress over another person's pain and distress, and greater remorse after having damaged a valued toy. These children also showed greater restraint in resisting temptation and higher levels of compliance with requests from a parent or an experimenter when they were left alone. The early experiences of mutuality with a caregiver is transformed over time into enjoyment during child-caregiver interactions, greater willingness for compliance, and less need for the use of power assertion or monitoring to ensure compliance.

Evolutionary Theory. The evolutionary perspective emphasizes an emotional or affective as well as a cognitive aspect to morality. Haidt (2007, 2008) characterizes these components as **moral intuition** and moral reasoning. The emotional or intuitive component is a more primitive, immediate, almost automatic system that evaluates experiences as positive or negative, good or bad, without going through steps of searching for more information or weighing evidence. The moral reasoning component is thought to have evolved later, along with language, and is used to reach a moral judgment or decision. According to the evolutionary view, the moral reasoning component is slower than moral intuition, and is often used to justify the initial moral intuition.

Certain areas of the brain, especially the amygdala and insula, produce emotional alarms, signaling fear or danger, as well as positive responses to stimuli. Social emotions, including lust and disgust, pride, humiliation, and guilt, which are processed in the insula, contribute to moral intuition. These affective areas operate to produce an orienting emotion that colors subsequent judgments. When people are told a moral story or dilemma, they typically have an immediate emotional reaction. They then begin to use reason to justify this reaction. Sometimes, they can override the initial intuitive reaction, most commonly when they interact with others who might stimulate a different, alternative emotional reaction to the situation.

According to an evolutionary view, morality, especially altruism and care for others, and fairness and reciprocity in social interactions help to bind members of groups together. Early human groups that were able to create a moral code that rewarded and increased behaviors beneficial to the group and that punished or reduced selfishness would have been more successful in attracting new members, and fighting off competing groups. Thus, morality is thought to have co-evolved with the formation of larger human communities in which individuals are tied together beyond the basis of immediate kinship. As part of this process, rites, rituals, and institutions have emerged that link emotions, motor behaviors, and states of consciousness of large groups of people such that they are more attuned to one another than to members of out-groups and more willing to share resources, behave in a caring way, and exhibit loyalty to others in their group (Hauser, 2006).

Whereas the cognitive developmental and psychoanalytic perspectives focus on individuals and how they manage to control their antisocial impulses, the evolutionary emphasis is on the benefit of moral emotions for the protection and preservation of the group. Most of the focus on the evolution of morality has emphasized two components: (1) protection from harm, caring and altruism toward kin, and, by extension, to the salient in-group or community; and (2) reciprocity, fairness, or justice toward members of one's group. Haidt (2007) added three more content areas that he has found to be salient in the moral codes of a large number of cultures: in-group loyalty; respect and obedience to authority; and bodily and spiritual purity and the importance of living in sacred or sanctioned, not a disgraceful or disgusting, way (p. 1001). These content areas are elaborated to varying degrees by each cultural group, given more or less prominence in various religious teachings, and passed along from generation to generation through parental socialization, stories, and rituals. All five of these moral domains operate to build and strengthen communal bonds, creating a framework for how people should treat others, how they expect others to treat them, and how they should function in a larger social group.

CASE STUDY

EARLY LEARNING ABOUT OBEDIENCE

Jung Chang describes the moral environment to which she was exposed in her early childhood years through interactions with her grandmother.

For my grandmother, all flowers and trees, the clouds and the rain were living beings with a heart and tears and a moral sense. We would be safe if we followed the old Chinese rule for children, *ting-hua* ("heeding the words," being obedient). Otherwise all sorts of things would happen to us. When we ate oranges my grandmother would warn us against swallowing the seeds. "If you don't listen to me, one day you won't be able to get into the house. Every little seed is a baby orange tree, and he wants to grow up, just like you. He'll grow quietly inside your tummy, up and up, and then one day, Ai-ya! There he is, out from the top of your head! He'll grow leaves, and bear more oranges, and he'll become taller than our door. . . ."

The thought of carrying an orange tree on my head fascinated me so much that one day I deliberately swallowed a

seed—one, no more. I did not want an orchard on my head; that would be too heavy. For the whole day, I anxiously felt my skull every other minute to see whether it was still in one piece. Several times I almost asked my grandmother whether I would be allowed to eat the oranges on my head, but I checked myself so that she would not know I had been disobedient. I decided to pretend it was an accident when she saw the tree. I slept very badly that night. I felt something was pushing up against my skull. (Chang, 1991, pp. 208–209)

CRITICAL THINKING AND CASE ANALYSIS

1. What is the moral lesson of this case?
2. How does the case illustrate the themes of moral emotion, knowledge, and action?
3. How does each of the theoretical perspectives discussed earlier contribute to an understanding of this case?
4. How does this case illustrate the particular orientation of early-school-age children to moral dilemmas?
5. How generalizable is this case? Can you imagine similar moral conflicts among non-Chinese children?

These theoretical views about moral development have been expanded through research in several directions. The research on empathy and perspective taking focuses on how children come to know and understand others. These abilities are essential for moral action. The research on parental discipline highlights the socialization process that supports self-regulation and internalization of moral values, including the passing on of a moral code from one generation to the next. The research on television illustrates the co-evolution of morality and culture.

Empathy, Caring, and Perspective Taking

The following sections focus on empathy, caring, and perspective taking. They consider how the child understands the emotional state and the intention or motivation of others. These are both factors that contribute to a child's ability to care about another person's distress and to consider the other person's needs and intentions when judging a moral act (Eisenberg, 2000).

Empathy. **Empathy** has been defined as sharing the perceived emotion of another—"feeling with another" (Eisenberg & Strayer, 1987, p. 5). This definition emphasizes one's emotional reaction to the observation of another person's emotional condition. By merely observing the facial expressions, body attitudes, and vocalizations of another person, a child can identify that person's emotion and feel it personally. The range of emotions with which one can empathize depends on the clarity of the cues the other person sends and on one's own prior experiences. Research on the mirror neuron system discussed in Chapter 6 suggests that humans are neurologically and psychologically prepared to synchronize their feelings and movements with others, thus enhancing the capacity for empathy.

The capacity for empathy changes with development. Hoffman (1987) described four levels of empathy, especially in reference to the perception of another person's distress.

1. Global empathy: You experience and express distress as a result of witnessing someone else in distress. Example: A baby cries upon hearing the cries of other infants.

2. Egocentric empathy: You recognize distress in another person and respond to it in the same way you would respond if the distress were your own. Example: A toddler offers his own cuddle blanket to another child who is crying.

3. Empathy for another's feelings: You show empathy for a wide range of feelings and anticipate the kinds of reactions that might really comfort someone else. Example: A child sees another child crying because his favorite toy is broken. She offers to help fix the toy.

4. Empathy for another's life conditions: You experience empathy when you understand the life conditions or personal circumstances of a person or group. Example: A child learns of children in another town who have become homeless after a flood. The child asks his mother if he can send some of his clothes to those children.

The capacity for empathy begins in infancy. Infant imitation, observed in the first months of life, provides an initial link between the observation of emotional expressions in another person and the expression of that emotion (Meltzoff,

Young children can be very caring and supportive in comforting others, especially if they understand the reason behind another child's distress.

2002). Infants appear to be able to recognize and interpret auditory and facial cues that suggest emotional expressions in others. In the newborn nursery, when one infant starts to wail, the other infants begin to cry (Sagi & Hoffman, 1976; Martin & Clark, 1982). Following from object relations theory, the intimate infant-caregiver relationship forms an early framework for empathy. The coordination of rhythmic interactions, the creation of joint attention, and the achievement of intersubjectivity through early gestures and words provide infants with an understanding of their caregiver's state. In a study of 125 firstborn girls, empathic concern for their mothers' distress was observed to increase from 16 months to 22 months of age. In contrast, empathic concern for a stranger was observed to decrease. In infancy, empathy for others appears to be situational, requiring an ability to overcome wariness or fearfulness in order to offer comfort to another person (van der Mark, van IJzendoorn, & Bakermans-Kranenburg, 2002).

Early-school-age children can usually identify the circumstances that may have produced another child's emotional response, especially anger and distress, and they can understand and empathize with another child's feelings. Children are most likely to think that external events produce emotional reactions: "The teacher made her put her toys away," or "He tripped over the blocks." But they can also think about internal states that may produce strong emotions: "He's mad because he didn't get a turn," or "She's sad because her stomach hurts" (Fabes, Eisenberg, McCormick, & Wilson, 1988; Fabes, Eisenberg, Nyman, & Michealieu, 1991; Dunn, Cutting, & Demetriou, 2000). The ability to understand the emotions and mental state of another person allows children to justify someone's moral behavior and perhaps to forgive a transgression: "The dad just spilled juice on his paper, so he yelled at his daughter. He was upset; he didn't really mean it."

The ability to identify pleasurable and unpleasurable emotions in others and to empathize with them makes the child receptive to moral teachings. Experiences of empathy can result in **sympathy**, a concern for the other person that may motivate the child to help relieve the other person's distress. It can also serve a reactive function, where the child experiences personal distress by recognizing the distress of the other (Eisenberg et al., 1999). The child may wonder: "What did I do to cause this unhappiness?" In the case of social attitude formation, empathy has been engaged in efforts to help children develop more compassion and acceptance of stigmatized groups (Batson et al., 1997).

Caring. It is one thing to feel sympathy for someone else, and yet another to take action to help that person. The **principle of care** refers to a sense of duty or obligation to help someone who is in need. Caring may build upon the emotions aroused by empathy. However, the principle of care also requires a cognitive evaluation of the other person's situation and an action component—the desire or intention to do something to help. From a developmental perspective, the principle of care reflects a greater degree of cognitive awareness than empathic distress, and an internalized moral standard that one should do what one can to reduce another person's distress (Eisenberg & Fabes, 1998; Wilhelm & Bekkers, 2010).

Perspective Taking. The terms *empathy* and *perspective taking* are sometimes confused. Empathy typically refers to the ability to identify and experience the *emotional* state of another person. **Perspective taking** refers to the *cognitive* capacity to consider a situation from the point of view of another person. This requires a recognition that someone else's point of view may differ from one's own. It also requires the ability to analyze the factors that may account for these differences (Piaget, 1932/1948; Selman, 1971; Flavell, 1974).

Imagine a child who wants to play with another child's toy. If the first child thinks, "If I had that toy, I would be happy, and if I am happy, everyone is happy," then that child may take the toy without anticipating that the other child will be upset. This is evidence of a lack of perspective taking. Whereas empathy provides an emotional bridge that enables children to discover the similarities between self and others, it does not teach them about differences. Recognizing these differences requires perspective taking. The capacity to take another person's perspective is achieved gradually through parental inductions, peer interaction, social pretend play, conflict, and role-playing.

Children at ages 4 and 5 frequently exhibit prosocial behaviors that evidence an understanding of others' needs. The most common of these behaviors are sharing, cooperating, and helping. Two examples illustrate the nature of this kind of social perspective taking:

> The path of a child with an armload of play dough was blocked by two chairs. Another child stopped her ongoing activity and moved the chair before the approaching child reached it.
>
> A boy saw another child spill a puzzle on the floor and assisted him in picking it up. (Iannotti, 1985, p. 53)

Robert Selman (1980) studied the process of social perspective taking by analyzing children's responses to a structured interview. Children watched audiovisual filmstrips that depicted interpersonal conflicts. They were then asked to describe the motivation of each actor and the relationships among the various performers. Four levels of social perspective taking were described. At Level 1, the youngest children (4 to 6 years old) recognized different emotions in the various actors, but they assumed that all the actors viewed the situation much as they did. The children at Level 4 (about 10 to 12 years old) realized that two people were able to take each other's perspective into account before deciding how to act. Furthermore, they realized that each of those people may have viewed the situation differently from the way they did.

Many moral dilemmas require that children subordinate their personal needs for someone else's sake. To resolve such situations, children must be able to separate their personal wants from the other person's. Selman's research suggests that children under 10 can rarely approach interpersonal conflicts with this kind of objectivity (Selman, 1994).

One longitudinal study followed children from the ages of 4 and 5 into early adulthood. Those children who showed spontaneous sharing, helping, and other prosocial behaviors in the early childhood years continued to exhibit prosocial behavior, sympathy, and perspective taking over the course of adolescence and early adulthood (Eisenberg et al., 1999). Some combination of a genetically based social orientation, an ability to regulate or inhibit one's impulses, and a consistent socialization environment contribute to a young child's sympathetic response toward others' distress. Over time, this outlook combines with a more mature capacity for moral reasoning and deepening social ties that help sustain a prosocial orientation.

Parental Discipline

Another contribution to an understanding of moral development comes from the research on parental discipline, which was introduced in Chapter 6 in relation to self-control. Parents are the child's first teachers about the content of the moral code the child will be expected to internalize. Parents must make a stand for certain values, beliefs, and behaviors that embody the foundation of a moral way of life. When disciplining a child, the parent emphasizes that certain behaviors are wrong and should be inhibited; other behaviors are right and should be repeated. This distinction between good and bad behaviors and the accompanying parental approval or disapproval forms the content of the child's moral code. Ideally, the socialization process as well as the specific moral teaching should support a child's belief in a caring, just, and fair community. Discipline strategies that are unduly harsh or erratic are likely to undermine these values and produce a set of moral beliefs focusing on power, domination, and self-interest (Arsenio & Gold, 2006).

Parents use specific discipline techniques to bring about compliance with the moral code. Four elements are important in determining the impact of these techniques on the child's future behavior. The discipline should:

1. Help the child interrupt or inhibit the forbidden action.
2. Point out a more acceptable form of behavior, so that the child will know what is right in a future instance.
3. Provide some reason, understandable to the child, why one action is inappropriate and the other more desirable.
4. Stimulate the child's ability to empathize with the victim of the misdeed. In other words, children are asked to put themselves in their victim's place and to see how much they dislike the feelings they caused in the other person.

In considering discipline as a mechanism for teaching morality, one becomes aware of the many interacting and interrelated components of a moral act. The discipline techniques that are most effective in teaching morality to children are those that help children control their own behavior, understand the meaning of their behavior for others, and expand their feelings of empathy. Discipline techniques that do not include these characteristics, such as power assertion, may succeed in inhibiting undesired behavior but may fail to achieve the long-term goal of incorporating moral values into future behavior.

The child's temperament is often overlooked in determining the likely effectiveness of certain disciplinary techniques. For example, children who are especially fussy and irritable as infants are more likely to be spanked by their parents (Berlin et al., 2009). Children who are temperamentally fearful and inhibited in response to novel stimuli, and who choose to stay close to their mothers during toddlerhood, are especially sensitive to messages of disapproval. For these children, a small dose of parental criticism is adequate to promote moral internalization, and too much power assertion appears to be counterproductive. In contrast, children who are highly active and who are insensitive to messages of disapproval require more focused and directive discipline, especially a consistent program of recognizing and rewarding good behaviors and minimizing the situations and stimuli that may provoke impulsive or aggressive actions (Kochanska, 1997).

In addition to the use of discipline, parents guide moral development by modeling positive, prosocial behaviors and by talking with their children about moral issues. In Chapter 6, we discussed the use of scaffolding to promote more effective communicative competence. In the same way, parents can scaffold their child's moral reasoning by talking with their children, raising questions about moral decisions their children are facing, and introducing new arguments or alternative views as their children think about moral conflicts (Walker & Taylor, 1991).

For example, Beth's mother asks her to help pick up the toys and put them away. Beth says that her brother made the mess, and he should pick up the toys. Beth's mother might acknowledge Beth's frustration about picking up after her little brother. But then she could point out that Beth would be helping her by picking up the toys, and that at some time in the future, she will want her brother to help clean up a mess that Beth made. Meanwhile, it is important to pick up the toys so they do not get broken and so no one trips or falls over them. The idea that helping in a family is not just about what each person does, but about what is good for the family as a whole, challenges Beth's moral reasoning and encourages her to move to a new level of moral reasoning.

Security in the child-caregiver attachment, the expression of warmth and affection in the relationship, and a parent's willingness to talk about feelings and moral concerns all contribute to a child's early moral development (Laible & Thompson, 2000). Children and parents encounter many examples when children behave well and show signs of kindness, caring, and truthfulness. They also encounter many examples when children misbehave, exhibiting selfishness, anger, or cruelty. Especially at times when children are experiencing emotional distress, parents teach and model positive moral behavior through their tone of voice, their willingness to hear a child's explanations, their willingness to provide explanations for their rules, and their ability to maintain open communication, even during conflict. They convey a sense that we are all imperfect, that we continue to strive toward a moral ideal, and that we can forgive and try again.

The Impact of Television and Video Games on Moral Development

Moral influences extend beyond the family to include schools, religious institutions, and the community. One of the societal influences that is of great concern is the impact of the media, especially television, video games, and Internet play on children's attitudes and behavior. Some people suggest that the television has become a part of the family system. In about 80% of homes, the television is often on even when no one is watching. Family interactions are different in the presence of the television, involving less talking and more touching. Images, information, and dramatic situations

Image copyright EZoom Team 2010. Used under license from Shutterstock.com

Steven is completely engrossed in his video game. Even though he is an active child, he can sit like this for long stretches. His mother has to set the timer to limit his play.

portrayed on television influence family members, resulting in new kinds of behaviors, shared experiences, points of discussion, and exposure to distressing images that may require comforting or interpretation (Gentile & Walsh, 2002).

A primary focus of research has been on exposure to *violence* on the beliefs and behaviors of young children (Huesmann & Skoric, 2003). Concern about media violence is particularly meaningful in the context of the child's growing moral consciousness. More than 30 years of laboratory experiments, field experiments, and analyses of naturally occurring behaviors have led to the conclusion that televised and video game violence have definite negative consequences for young children's behaviors and beliefs.

Those who monitor contemporary television estimate that a typical child, watching an average of 27 hours of TV a week, will view "8,000 murders and 100,000 acts of violence from age 3 to age 12" (Silver, 1995, p. 62). An analysis of music television videos found that almost one fourth of the videos included images of violence and carrying weapons. Video games are especially permeated with violent themes. Many video games require children to become increasingly adept at killing off characters with the use of special weapons or superpowers. Studies suggest that long-term exposure to violent video game play is associated with lower empathy for others, increased aggressive behavior, and desensitization to real-life violence (Carnagey & Anderson, 2004; Funk, Baldacci, Pasold, & Baumgardner, 2004; Swing & Anderson, 2007).

The American Academy of Pediatrics issued a policy statement on television viewing in which they make the following recommendations (American Academy of Pediatrics, 2001):

1. Discourage television viewing for all children under age 2.
2. Remove televisions from children's bedrooms.
3. Limit children's total entertainment media time (television, video games, Internet play) to no more than 1 to 2 hours per day.
4. Focus on programs and games that are informational, educational, and nonviolent.

These recommendations are based on research evidence suggesting that about two thirds of current television programming contains a great amount of violence, and portrayals of violence are often glamorized and go unpunished. As a result, watching television and playing video games that have violent content have a strong impact on a child's willingness to engage in real-life violence or they may be frightened by these violent images (Federman, 1998; Wilson et al., 2002).

Studies of children in the United States and in other countries have provided evidence that at least three processes are at work that may increase the level of aggressiveness in children who are exposed to media violence (Huesmann & Eron, 1986; Huesmann & Malamuth, 1986; Josephson, 1987; Liebert & Sprafkin, 1988; Comstock & Paik, 1991; Huston et al., 1992; see Table 7.3). First, children observe role models who perform aggressive actions. Especially when the hero

TABLE 7.3 Three Processes That May Increase the Level of Aggression in Children Who Watch Televised Violence

PROCESS	POSSIBLE CONSEQUENCE
Observing role models who engage in aggressive actions.	Imitation of violent action is likely when: Hero is provoked and retaliates with aggression. Hero is rewarded for violent actions. New violent behaviors added to repertoire.
Viewing aggressive actions leads to heightened level of arousal.	Brings network of aggressive thoughts, feelings, memories, and action tendencies into consciousness. Repeated stimulation strengthens this network. Stimulation interacts with aggressive temperament to increase the likelihood of aggressive action.
Viewing aggression affects beliefs and values.	Aggressive behavior is seen as an acceptable way to resolve conflicts. Viewers are hardened to the use of aggression in peer interactions. Aggression is used as a response to frustration. Viewers expect others to be aggressive toward them. Viewers worry about being victims of aggression. Viewers see the world as a dangerous place.

Source: © Cengage Learning.

is provoked and retaliates with aggression that goes unpunished, the child is likely to imitate the aggressive actions. Thus, viewing media violence adds new violent behaviors to the child's repertoire. Moreover, when the hero is rewarded or viewed as successful because of violent actions, children's tendencies to express aggression are increased (Bandura, 1973).

Second, exposure to media violence produces a heightening of arousal (Simons et al., 2003). The fast action that usually accompanies televised violence captures the viewer's attention. The violent incident raises the child's level of emotionality, bringing to the fore other aggressive feelings, thoughts, memories, and action tendencies. The more frequently this network of elements is activated, the stronger will be their association. In some video games, the child selects a character and is encouraged to identify with that role. Violent acts are repeated over and over, with the possibility that the child increases the character's aggressive behaviors after each encounter, thereby escalating the level of emotional intensity and angry feelings as the play continues (Bushman & Anderson, 2002). Particularly for children who are temperamentally aggressive, watching violent television or playing violent video games increases their inclination toward aggressiveness in real-life situations (Wittman, Arce, & Santisteban, 2008).

Finally, exposure to media violence affects a young child's beliefs and values. Children who are exposed to frequent episodes of televised violence are more likely to believe that aggressive behavior is an acceptable way to resolve conflicts, and they become hardened to the use of aggression in peer interactions. They are also more accepting of the use of aggression as a response to frustration. Children (and adults) who are exposed to media violence are more likely to expect that others will be aggressive toward them, to worry about being victims of aggression, and to see the world as a dangerous place (Huesmann & Skoric, 2003).

Exposure to media violence has long-lasting effects. For example, in a longitudinal study, TV viewing habits in childhood (ages 6 to 10) were related to adult aggressive behavior 15 years later. The study found a significant relationship between extensive exposure to televised violence in childhood and later aggressive behavior for both men and women, even after controlling for mitigating factors such as intelligence, parenting characteristics, and family's socioeconomic status. The more children identified with aggressive TV characters, the stronger this relationship to adult aggressive behavior (Huesmann, Moise-Titus, Podolski, & Eron, 2003).

Researchers have barely begun to scratch the surface of television's uses to promote prosocial development. There is clear evidence that children who are exposed to prosocial programming are influenced toward more positive social behavior. One study recontacted more than 500 adolescents whose television viewing had been studied when they were in early childhood. Watching educational programming in the early years was associated with many positive characteristics in adolescence, including higher grades, reading more books, greater creativity, and less aggression (Anderson, Huston, Schmitt, Linebarger, & Wright, 2001).

Many programs—some developed for children and others intended for a broader viewing audience—convey positive ethical messages about the value of family life, the need to work hard and sacrifice in order to achieve important goals, the value of friendship, the importance of loyalty and commitment in relationships, and many other cultural values. A number of contemporary programs include characters of many races and ethnic backgrounds. Many feature women in positions of authority or performing acts of heroism. Increasingly, programs include characters with physical disabilities who play important roles. Through exposure to these programs, children learn to challenge social stereotypes and develop positive images of people from many ethnic groups (Rosenkoetter, 1999).

Review of Influences on Moral Development

In early school age, children are developing an initial moral code. The approaches to this issue are summarized in Table 7.4. Each contribution highlights an essential element of the larger, more complex phenomenon. *Learning theory* points out that an external reward structure inhibits or reinforces behavior. Children also learn about how to behave morally by observing the behaviors of others and noting whether those behaviors are rewarded or punished. *Cognitive theory* suggests that in early childhood, children are most likely to take a pragmatic view about whether something is right or wrong, based largely on the consequences. However, children can distinguish between moral transgressions and social convention transgressions and do not regard them with the same degree of seriousness. *Psychoanalytic theory* is especially concerned with the relationship between parental identification and the development of conscience. Drawing on *object relations theory*, the importance of early, loving relationships with a sensitive caregiver is emphasized as the path through which a child comes to value the self and to care about others. *Evolutionary theory* suggests that the human brain has both a rapid, seemingly automatic intuitive moral response system that provides the emotional basis for moral judgments as well as a capacity for more deliberate moral reasoning. The evolutionary benefits to groups that were able to create moral codes for altruism, caring, and reciprocity suggest that these social orientations are highly likely to be supported at the genetic and neurological levels and readily expressed under conditions of appropriate nurturance.

The research on *empathy* and *perspective taking* shows that moral behavior requires an emotional and cognitive understanding of the needs of others. These prosocial skills help children appreciate how other children or adults may be experiencing reality. With this insight, children can modify their own actions to benefit others. Theory and research on *parental discipline* suggest that parents promote moral development when they establish clear standards, involve their children in

TABLE 7.4 Contributions to the Study of Moral Development

CONCEPTUAL SOURCE	SIGNIFICANT CONTRIBUTIONS	RELEVANCE FOR A PARTICULAR ASPECT OF MORAL DEVELOPMENT
Learning theory	Relevance of an external system of rewards and punishments.	Moral behaviors. Internalization of a moral code.
	Imitation of models.	
	Formation of expectations about the reward structure.	
Cognitive theory	Conceptual development of notions of intentionality, rules, justice, and authority.	Moral judgments.
	Stages of moral reasoning.	Distinctions between moral transgressions, social convention transgressions, and personal choice.
Psychoanalytic theory	Parental identification.	Internalization of parental values and moral standards.
	Formation of the superego and the ego ideal.	Experiences of guilt.
Object relations theory	The origins of morality in infancy with the development of object relations.	Moral emotions.
	The extension of self-love to love of the other and the desire to maintain connection with loved others.	Formation of strong ties between self and others. Willing compliance with adult requests.
Evolutionary theory	Adaptive nature of moral intuition and moral reasoning.	Moral emotions.
	Morality as co-evolving with large cultural groups.	Content of moral principles and their relationship to group survival.
	Moral standards promoting the cohesiveness and stability of the group.	
Research on empathy and perspective taking	Ability to experience another's feelings begins very early and changes with age.	Empathy heightens concern for others and helps inhibit actions that might cause distress.
	Ability to recognize differences in point of view emerges slowly during early-school-age and middle childhood years.	Perspective taking can foster helping and altruism.
	Peer conflict, peer interactions, and specific role-taking training all increase perspective-taking skills.	
Research on parental discipline	Parents define moral content.	Standards for moral behavior.
	Parents point out the implications of a child's behavior for others.	Moral reasoning.
	Parents create a reward structure.	Internalization of moral values.
	Differential impact of power, love withdrawal, warmth, and inductions.	Empathy, shame, and guilt.
Research on media violence	Observing aggressive role models.	New repertoire of aggressive behaviors.
	Arousal of aggressive emotions, memories, and action tendencies.	Lower threshold for aggressive actions.
	Formation of beliefs and values about the use of aggression to resolve conflict.	Expectations of aggression from others. Desensitization to acts of violence.

Source: © Cengage Learning.

dialogue, and try to increase children's understanding of the effects of their behavior on others. Research on *television and video game violence* shows that children who are exposed to many hours of violent programming or who engage in many hours of violent video game play are more likely to act aggressively, accept violence as a method for resolving conflicts, and interpret the behavior of others as having an aggressive intention. Early exposure to high doses of media violence has long-term consequences for a person's tendency toward aggressive behavior.

Self-Theory

Objective 3. To analyze changes in the self-theory, with special focus on the theory of mind and self-esteem during the early-school-age years.

The development of the self-concept is at the heart of psychosocial development. Psychosocial theory provides a framework for understanding how the ego is transformed through ongoing interaction with society over the life span. It describes the creative process through which very rudimentary experiences of the physical self in infancy are transformed into self-consciousness, self-control, a sense of self—other relationships, a personal identity, a style of life, and finally a sense of integrity about the life one has lived.

The self-concept can be viewed as a theory that links the child's understanding of the nature of the world, the nature of the self, and the meaning of interactions between the two (Epstein, 1973, 1991, 1998). The function of the **self-theory** is to make transactions between the self and the world turn out as positively and beneficially as possible. One's theory about oneself draws on such inner phenomena as dreams, emotions, thoughts, fantasies, and feelings of pleasure or pain. One's self-theory is also based on logical thoughts and information processing such as assessments of one's abilities, comparisons with others, and analysis of experiences with the environment (Epstein, 2003, 2008). When I tell my mother that I had a dream about monsters, does she tell me not to be ridiculous—that there are no monsters? Or does she ask me to tell her all about the monsters—what they looked like, how they smelled, what they ate? As I share my inner world with others, do they confirm or disconfirm my reality? Do they validate or invalidate my inner experiences?

The complexity and logic of the self-theory depend on the maturation of cognitive functions, which is tied in part to the maturation of the brain. Furthermore, because the self-theory is based on personal experiences and observations, one would expect it to be modified over the life course as a result of changing physical, cognitive, and socioemotional competencies as well as by participation in new roles.

The Neuroscience of the Self

While one group of neuroscientists has focused on social cognitive functions that support social interaction and the ability to understand and predict the behaviors of others, another group has been searching for the specific regions of the brain that create a sense of self. Work by Uddin, Iacoboni, Lange, and Keenan (2007) has begun to integrate these research areas, suggesting that two separate but interrelated brain areas support the capacity for distinguishing the self and others, self-representation, and the ability to understand and learn from others. The right frontoparietal area of the brain is active when individuals view their own face as compared to faces of familiar others. This same area is also active in response to images of one's body and sounds of one's voice. This area of the brain overlaps with an area of the mirror neuron system that was described in Chapter 6. The mirror neuron system supports the ability to understand and replicate the actions and goals of others. Thus, in a self-recognition task these brain areas are operating in synchrony to intensify the experience of the sense of oneself as both the perceiver and the perceived (Neiworth, 2009).

Other brain regions are associated with self-representations including self-recognition, use of personal pronouns, expression of ownership ("Mine!"), self-appraisal, judging one's personality traits, and making judgments about the mental states of others. Advances in self-representational thought in infancy are associated with the maturation of these brain regions (Lewis & Carmody, 2008).

Uddin et al. suggest that just as the mirror neuron system maps the behaviors of others onto the self, the cortical midline structures map the attitudes and mental states of others onto the self. The cortical midline structures are activated in a variety of tasks involving self-referential processing, suggesting that this area of the brain contributes to the integration of information that is involved in the formulation of a self-concept (Northoff & Bermpohl, 2004). As one might expect, the frontoparietal motor neuron system and the cortical midline structures are connected, facilitating a multidimensional understanding of self-other representations. These brain areas contribute to the ability for self-recognition, self-other distinctions, the ability to replicate another person's actions and understand the intentions of those actions, and the ability to reflect upon another person's experiences and perceptions in comparison to our own (Ruby & Decety, 2001, 2004). This line of research supports the underlying principle from psychosocial theory of an ongoing interaction between the person and the social environment. At the neural level there are a variety of mechanisms for connecting information about the self and the other. As self-awareness and self-understanding mature, so does awareness of and understanding of the other.

In the sections that follow, the self-theory is discussed in relation to the distinction between the *me* and the *I*, a general description of how the self-theory changes from infancy through middle childhood, and the nature of self-esteem—the evaluative aspect of a child's sense of self.

© Pixel Shepherd/Alamy

Sophia is fascinated by her image. She likes to gaze at her face in the mirror, changing her expression, making funny faces, and thinking about who she is. The capacity for self-evaluation is beginning to emerge.

The Me and the I

One of the earliest psychological analyses of self-theory was provided by William James (1892/1961). He described two elements of the self, the *me* and the *I*. The *me* is the self as object—the self one can describe—including physical characteristics, personality traits, social roles and relationships, thoughts, and feelings. The *I* is the self who is aware of one's own actions. It can be characterized by four fundamental features: (1) a sense of agency or initiation of behaviors; the self that experiences a sense of voluntary action or free will; (2) a sense of uniqueness; (3) a sense of continuity from moment to moment and from day to day; and (4) an awareness of one's own awareness (i.e., metacognition) (Damon & Hart, 1988).

Building on these ideas, Damon and Hart (1988) devised a model of self-understanding that includes both the *me* (*self as object*) and the I (*self as subject*) changing over time. This model is presented in Figure 7.2 as two adjoining charts. Along the bottom of the left hand chart—the self as object—Damon and Hart identified four domains of the *me*: *physical self* (my physical appearance and observable characteristics), *active self* (my behaviors and actions), *social self* (my social bonds and social skills), and *psychological self* (my personality, emotions, and thoughts.) Along the bottom of the right hand chart—the self as subject—they identified three domains of the *I*: *continuity* (experiences that allow me to know that I am the same person from day to day), *distinctiveness* (experiences that illustrate how I differ from others and perceive myself to be a unique individual), and *agency* (experiences that allow me to believe that I have an impact, that I am a causal agent). The height of the charts reflects the four stages of development during which the *me* and the *I* mature in each domain: early school age, middle childhood, early adolescence, and later adolescence.

Characteristics of the self as *me* and *I* at a particular stage of life can be understood by following along one row around the cube. Development over time, shown by the vertical changes in each of the seven domains, is traced from early school age through later adolescence. According to Damon and Hart, one can recognize evidence of self-understanding in each domain even in early childhood. Development of the self is not viewed as a shift in awareness of the physical self in childhood to an awareness of the social self at a later age. Rather, each domain of the self changes according to the general organizing principle around which all aspects of the *me* and the *I* are synthesized. Self-understanding is transformed from a categorical and concrete assessment of the self in early school age to a comparative assessment of self and others in middle childhood. This is followed by a shift to an understanding of the social implications of one's self-characteristics in early adolescence. In later adolescence the organizing principle becomes the formulation of a personal and social identity that integrates the characteristics of the self into a set of beliefs and plans that guide future actions. By later adolescence, a dynamic relationship is formed, which links aspects of the self-theory, including personal values, experiences, and interpretations of life events, to interpersonal relationships and moral choices.

Developmental Changes in the Self-Theory

At each stage, the self-theory is the result of a person's cognitive capacities and dominant motives as he comes into contact with the stage-related expectations of the culture (Stipek, Recchia, & McClintic, 1992). In infancy, the self consists of a gradual awareness of one's independent existence. The infant discovers body boundaries, learns to identify recurring need states, and feels the comfort of loving contact with caregivers. Basic needs to maximize pleasure and avoid pain and to preserve closeness to the loving caregiver serve as organizing principles for the infant's behavior. Many theorists emphasize the close connection of the infant's internal working model of the self with the responsiveness of the other (Bretherton & Munholland, 1999). The infant relies on the other to be accessible, to permit exploration, and to comfort and reassure. During the second year of life, self-recognition and the sense of the self as a causal agent add new dimensions to the self-theory. Gradually, these experiences are integrated into a sense of the self as a permanent being who has an impact on the environment, existing in the context of a group of other permanent beings who either do or do not respond adequately to the infant's internal states.

In toddlerhood, the self-theory grows through an active process of self-differentiation. Children explore the limits of their capacities and the nature of their impact on others. Because of toddlers' limited ability to entertain abstract concepts and their tendency toward egocentrism (the perception of oneself as the center of the world), their self-theories are based largely on the accumulation of daily experiences of competence, self-directed goal attainment, and praise or disapproval. There is little recognition of social comparisons (being better or worse than someone else), but an increasing sensitivity to the positive and negative reactions of others.

In order to collaborate on a project, children need to be able to take the point of view of the other person. As the self-concept matures, so does the ability to think about how situations may appear to someone else.

Developmental Level	General organizing principle	Domains of the "me"				Domains of the "I"		
		Physical self	Active self	Social self	Psychological self	Continuity	Distinctiveness	Agency
4. Later adolescence	Systematic beliefs and plans	Physical attributes reflecting volitional choices or personal and moral standards	Active attributes that reflect choices, personal or moral standards	Moral or personal choices concerning social relations or social-personality characteristics	Belief systems, personal philosophy, self's own thought processes	Relations between past, present, and future selves	Unique subjective experience and interpretations of events	Personal and moral evaluations influence self
3. Early adolescence	Interpersonal implications	Physical attributes that influence social appeal and social interactions	Active attributes that influence social appeal and social interactions	Social-personality characteristics	Social sensitivity, communicative competence, and other psychologically related social skills	Ongoing recognition of self by others	Unique combination of psychological and physical attributes	Communication and reciprocal interaction influence self
2. Middle childhood	Comparative assessments	Capability-related physical attributes	Abilities relative to others, self, or normative standards	Abilities or acts considered in light of others' reactions	Knowledge, cognitive abilities, or ability-related emotions	Permanent, cognitive, and active capabilities and immutable self-characteristics	Comparisons between self and other along isolated dimensions	Efforts, wishes, and talents influence self
1. Early school age	Categorical identifications	Bodily properties or material possessions	Typical behavior	Fact of membership in particular social relations or groups	Momentary moods, feelings, preferences, and aversions	Categorical identifications	Categorical identifications	External, uncontrollable factors determine self
		The self as object				**The self as subject**		

FIGURE 7.2 A Developmental Model of Self-Understanding

Source: From *Self-Understanding in Childhood and Adolescence*, W. Damon & D. Hart, p. 56. Copyright 1988 by Cambridge University Press. Reprinted by permission.

During early school age, the self-theory becomes more differentiated. Children can distinguish between the real self (how one actually is) and the ideal self (how one would like to be). They recognize some discrepancies between how they describe themselves and how their parents or friends may describe them (Oosterwegel & Oppenheimer, 1993). They can differentiate among various areas of activities like math, reading, and music, indicating perceptions of strength in certain areas and weakness in others (Eccles, Wigfield, Harold, & Blumenfeld, 1993).

According to Damon and Hart (1988), in early school age the self is understood as an accumulation of **categorical identifications**. No additional linkage or significance is taken from these categorical statements—simply a recognition that they exist.

> EXAMPLES: What kind of person are you? *I have blue eyes.*
>
> Why is that important? *It just is.*
>
> What kind of a person are you? *I'm Catholic.*
>
> What does that say about you? *I'm Catholic, and my mother is, and my father is, and my grandmother, and my grandfather, and I'm Catholic too.*
>
> (pp. 59–60)

In middle childhood, the organizing principle shifts to **comparative assessments**. Self-understanding relies on comparisons of oneself with social norms and standards or with specific other people.

> EXAMPLES: What are you like? *I'm bigger than most kids.*
>
> Why is that important? *I can run faster than everybody.*
>
> What are you like? *I'm not as smart as most kids.*
>
> Why is that important? *It takes me longer to do my homework.*
> (pp. 62–63)

The period of early school age brings with it the beginnings of self-consciousness. Through conversations, stories, photographs, and rituals, early-school-age children begin to understand that their experiences have a uniqueness. They realize that they exist in a specific time, not in the long ago of dinosaurs or pioneers, nor in near past of their grandmother's or their mother's childhood (Nelson, 2000).

Culture and the Self-Theory

Certain aspects of culture are thought to influence the nature of **self construal**. In many Western countries, values given to characteristics such as self-reliance, autonomy, and distinctiveness shape a relatively more *independent* view of the self. In many Asian cultures, values given to fitting in with the group and preserving harmonious relationships shape a relatively more *interdependent* view of the self (Markus & Kitayama, 1991; Martin & Ruble, 1997). In both cultural views, individuals are able to differentiate a sense of self and other. They are aware of a continuous self who is the same today as yesterday, and can make distinctions between a view of an inner or private self and a public self. However, in the independent orientation, greater emphasis is placed on an inherent distinctiveness in which the self is the figure and others are the ground. In the interdependent orientation, a greater emphasis is placed on the inherent interconnectedness of members of the group and an appreciation that one's thoughts, feelings, and behaviors fluctuate based on the desire to fit in to the larger social unit.

For example, one study reported on U.S. and Chinese college students' earliest childhood memories (Wang, 2001). The average age for these first memories was 3½ years for U.S. students, and 4 years for the Chinese students. The U.S. students' memories tended to be discreet events where they had the lead role in a drama of some emotional event or moment. The Chinese students' memories tended to be more routine events involving family and neighborhood. Students were asked to produce something that they actually remembered, not something someone had told them.

The following is a U.S. college student's response to a request to think of her earliest memory and to describe it as precisely as possible. This memory comes from a time when the student was about 3.

> I remember standing in my aunt's spacious blue bedroom and looking up at the ceiling. Then something caught my eye—it was the white wainscoting that bordered the top of the wall with the ceiling. I remember staring, fixated with its intricate design. And while I was doing this, all of sudden, I had an epiphany, a sort [of] realization. It was almost my first realization of a sense of "self." Because, as I was staring at the ceiling, I realized that no one else was around. I remember being taken aback by the ability to amuse myself without any toys. (Wang, 2001, p. 220)

The next childhood memory was told by a Chinese female college student from the time when she was about age 5.

> I was 5 years old. Dad taught me ancient poems. It was always when he was washing vegetables that he would explain a poem to me. It was very moving. I will never forget the poems such as "Pi-Ba-Xing" one of the poems I learned then. (Wang, 2001, appendix)

Cultural worldviews are preserved in each society's view of the self. In the United States, the self is valued as a unique, bounded, autonomous being. Self memories and narratives are told to preserve a sense of the self that guides the life history through choices and action. In China and in other Asian cultures, the self is viewed as an interdependent, relational being. In these cultures, children are encouraged to show restraint in their interactions with certain others, particularly in public situations, in order to preserve social cohesion. Whereas self-expression may be encouraged in private, self-control is valued in public (Raeff, 2010). As we think about the emergence of a self-theory in early school age, it is important to keep in mind that cultures not only shape the value placed on certain attributes, but also influence whether children are likely to think of the self as relatively stable and enduring across settings or relatively fluid and attuned to the demands and expectations of the social situation.

Theory of Mind

From ages 4 to 6, children become more aware that people have different points of view. Work on the **theory of mind** focuses on the natural way children understand their own mental states and the mental states of others. In day-to-day functioning, the theory of mind suggests that children attribute beliefs, knowledge, and desires to others, and that they begin to understand that a person's mental state is a cause or explanation for their behavior (Wellman, 1990; Doherty, 2009). With development, children gradually discern that another person's mental state can be different from their own. They can begin to appreciate that someone else's behaviors might be based on a set of beliefs that are erroneous, or desires that are in conflict with their own desires.

Research on the theory of mind typically poses situations to children to see what they understand about someone else's beliefs and desires. For example, in the early research, children watched a character named Maxi put a chocolate candy in one location. Then, when Maxi leaves, children watched while another character moved the chocolate to a new place. Children were asked what Maxi thinks or what Maxi will do when he comes back into the room. Where will Maxi *think* the chocolate is located? Where will Maxi *look* (action) for the chocolate? Three-year-olds typically said that Maxi will look for the chocolate where *they* know it is—in the new location. Older children, ages 4 and 5, realized that Maxi has an incorrect belief and predicted that Maxi will look for the chocolate in its old location (Wimmer & Perner, 1983; Wellman, Cross, & Watson, 2001).

Subsequent research using similar scenarios has found that children as young as 3 are very good at considering what a character *wants*, even if it is different from what they might want. However, they have trouble thinking about what someone else might *believe*, especially disconnecting their own knowledge of the situation from the point of view of another. By the time children are 5, however, they are quite facile at detecting the possibility of false or incorrect beliefs. They can separate what they know about a situation from what someone else may know, and they expect that a character's actions will be based on the character's beliefs, even when those beliefs are incorrect (Ziv & Frye, 2003).

The ability to appreciate that what you know or believe to be true is different from what others know and believe to be true is a salient feature of self-awareness. It allows children to begin to speculate about what others may think about them, and how their behavior may be understood or misunderstood. Gender role standards are especially important in this regard. Children are very sensitive to any implication that they are not living up to the expectations of how a boy or girl ought to act. Children are also aware of moral imperatives that define good and evil. These cognitive gains make a child more sensitive to social pressure, more likely to experience feelings of guilt or failure, and more preoccupied with issues of social comparison, self-criticism, and self-evaluation. For these reasons, the issue of self-esteem becomes especially salient during early and middle childhood.

Self-Esteem

For every component of the self—the physical, active, social, and psychological self—a person makes an evaluation of worthiness. This self-evaluation, or **self-esteem**, is based on three sources: (1) messages of love, support, and approval

Experiences of success build confidence and contribute to positive self-esteem. Gloria is thrilled to be able to ride her big two wheeler even though it has training wheels. She feels competent, proud of her accomplishment, and happy to be riding. What other kinds of accomplishments are likely to contribute to self-esteem at this age?

Copyright © Myrleen Ferguson Cate/Photo Edit

from others; (2) specific attributes and competencies; and (3) the way one regards these specific aspects of the self in comparison with others and in relation to one's ideal self. The need to protect and enhance one's self-esteem is considered a basic psychological motive that drives behavior (Greenberg, 2008). Views of the self as being loved, valued, admired, and successful contribute to a sense of worth. Views of the self as being ignored, rejected, scorned, and inadequate contribute to a sense of worthlessness. These early affective experiences build a general sense of pride or shame, worthiness or worthlessness, that is captured in the global statements children make about themselves even as early as age 3 or 4 (Eder, Gerlach, & Perlmutter, 1987; Eder, 1989).

Information about specific aspects of the self is accumulated through experiences of success and failure in daily tasks or when particular aspects of one's competence are challenged. A young child may develop a positive sense of self in athletics, problem solving, or social skills through the encouraging reactions of others as well as through the pleasure associated with succeeding in each of these areas (Harter, 1985a, 1998).

With experience in a variety of roles and settings, each specific ability takes on a certain level of importance for a person. Not all abilities are equally valued at home, at school, and by friends. Children may believe they have abilities in some areas but not in those they consider highly important. Others may believe they have only one or two areas of strength, but they may highly value those areas and believe them to be critically important to their overall success. Self-esteem is influenced by the value one assigns to specific competencies in relation to one's overall life goals and personal ideals. Thus, it is possible to be a success in the eyes of others and still feel a nagging sense of worthlessness. Similarly, it is possible to feel proud and confident even when others do not value the activities and traits in which one takes satisfaction.

Feelings of positive self-worth provide a protective shield or buffer against anxiety that is associated with insecurity or conditions that threaten to expose one's lack of value or meaning. If a person has a positive, optimistic self-evaluation, then messages that are negative and incongruent with it will be deflected. People with high self-esteem will explain a failure by examining the task, the amount of time needed for its completion, the other people involved, or the criteria for evaluating success and failure. They use a variety of strategies to minimize the importance of negative feedback. They do not permit a failure to increase doubt about their basic worth. Rather, their high self-esteem functions to protect their positive self-evaluation by coping effectively with negative feedback and reclaiming their view of the self as someone who has socially valued qualities (Brown, Dutton, & Cook, 2001).

By contrast, people with low self-esteem feel worse after a failure, tend to view failure as new evidence of their lack of worth, and are less likely to cope effectively with the negative feelings that accompany failure (Heimpel, Wood, Marshall, & Brown, 2002). People with low self-esteem appear to accept negative moods that follow a failure experience and are less likely to take action to try to improve their mood. Because negative feedback is so painful for those with low self-esteem, they avoid unfavorable comparisons with others, leading them to be more cautious in situations that might expose them to criticism (Bernichon, Cook, & Brown, 2003).

Despite the many positive correlates of high self-esteem, some scholars have questioned whether high self-esteem is necessarily a universally positive quality. Some researchers have suggested that there is such a thing as unrealistic or fragile high self-esteem (Kernis, 2003). For example, people with high self-esteem seem to deflect failure messages in one area by emphasizing their abilities in another area (Brown & Smart, 1991). When employed consistently, this strategy can be perceived as a defensive reaction that allows the individual

By the age of 5 or 6, children are trying hard to gain acceptance from adults and peers. Even mild criticism from a teacher is often enough to arouse feelings of guilt or remorse. What kind of teacher criticism do you imagine might be taking place in this photo?

Copyright © Elena Rooraid/PhotoEdit

to preserve a sense of self-worth rather than to address underlying feelings of inferiority or shame (Jordan et al., 2003).

A different criticism concerning self-esteem is that the emphasis on high self-esteem is a value that reflects the individualist nature of Western culture. In contrast, Eastern cultures are less concerned with affirming the positive qualities of the individual, valuing instead self-discipline and self-improvement (Marku, Mullally, & Kitayama, 1997). A pancultural or universalist perspective suggests that it is a universal tendency for humans to strive for and protect their self-regard. However, the norms for what one considers evidence of self-worth and the strategies that human beings use to advance their self-regard are shaped by culture (Brown, 2003; Sedikides, Gaertner, & Toguchi, 2003; Sedikides, Gaertner & Vevea, 2005).

Self-Esteem and the Early-School-Age Child. At each life stage, as individuals set new goals for themselves or as discrepancies in competence become apparent, temporary periods of lowered self-esteem may be anticipated. Although we tend to think of self-esteem as a stable trait that characterizes individuals across settings, there are periods of life when self-esteem is more vulnerable to fluctuation, especially as individuals encounter dramatic changes in roles, environments, and normative expectations for behavior (Trzesniewski, Donnellan, & Robins, 2003). Early childhood appears to be one of those periods.

As early-school-age children mature, they move into new social and physical environments where they encounter new threats to their sense of safety and new sources of evaluation about their value and meaning. They have a new awareness of the limits of their parents' ability or willingness to protect them. Moreover, they are increasingly aware of the discrepancies between their own competencies and what they recognize as the skills expected of them by their teachers and parents or exhibited by older children. They are able to view themselves as objects of evaluation by others. They are also aware of the importance of acceptance by adults and peers outside the family, especially their teachers and classmates. These newly valued others may not be as proud of their skills or as understanding about their limitations as are their family members. At school, for example, young children often make critical comments about one another's work. Criticisms tend to outnumber compliments, and boys tend to be more critical than girls of their peers' work (Frey & Ruble, 1987). The combination of open peer criticism and a heightened emphasis on peer competition may make school an environment in which one's self-esteem is frequently challenged.

For all these reasons, early-school-age children are likely to experience feelings of depression and worthlessness. This decrease in self-esteem may be a temporary fluctuation. However, it may endure. In research with kindergartners, children were faced with a challenging task. The way they approached the task, their hopefulness about succeeding, and their general expression of positive or negative attributes were combined to reflect a measure of helplessness. Five years later, the expressions of helplessness assessed in kindergarten proved to be a good predictor of depression and a low sense of self-worth. The implication is that a scheme for low self-esteem and helplessness may begin to be crystallized in the early childhood period and, unless challenged through positive intervention, may color one's sense of mastery and competence in the years ahead (Davis-Kean & Sandler, 2001; Kistner, Ziegert, Castro, & Robertson, 2001). Young children need frequent reassurance from adults that they are competent, safe, and loved. They need numerous opportunities to discover that their unique talents and abilities are useful and important, and that they can have a positive impact on others. As competencies increase, as thought becomes more flexible, and as the child makes meaningful friendships, self-esteem is expected to increase.

Peer Play

Objective 4. To explore the transition to more complex play and the process of friendship development in the early-school-age years.

Although experiences in the family provide the primary information that guides a young child's construction of the social world, interactions with peers contribute important opportunities for physical, cognitive, social, and emotional development. The quality of play expands during the early-school-age period, introducing more complex games with larger numbers of participants. Children form friendship groups that allow them to sustain more elaborate fantasy play, experience group conflict, participate in group problem solving, and encounter varying ideas about the topics discussed previously: gender, morality, and the self. Developmental scholars generally acknowledge the value of child-initiated, freely chosen play for the young child's cognitive and social development. Nonetheless, playtime at school and at home is dwindling. One estimate suggests that young children have 8 fewer hours a week of unstructured play time today than did children 20 years ago (Elkind, 2007; Miller & Almon, 2009). What is more, the toys and play resources that are marketed for young children are becoming increasingly oriented toward specific educational objectives such as vocabulary building and math facts. Through the insertion of computer chips, the play value of many modern toys is controlled in advance by the manufacturers rather than invented through the child's active exploration (Winerman, 2009).

Group Games

The early-school-age child continues to use vivid fantasies in play. During this period, a new form of play emerges. Children show interest in **group games** that are more structured and somewhat more oriented to reality than play that is based primarily on imagination. Duck-Duck-Goose, London Bridge, and Farmer-in-the-Dell are examples of early group play. Hide-and-Seek, Hopscotch, and Statue-Maker are more complex games of early school age. They involve more cognitive complexity, physical skill, and ritual. These games combine fantasy with an emphasis on peer cooperation. Group play is a transitional form between the fantasy play of the toddler and the team sports and other games with rules of middle childhood (Erikson, 1977).

Group games usually include a few rules that are simple enough so that a child can use them effectively to begin a game and determine a winner without the help of an adult. Usually, no team concept is involved. A game is played repeatedly, so that many children have an opportunity to win. The particular pleasure that children derive from these games seems to result more from peer cooperation and interaction than from being a winner. Many of these games permit children to shift roles. A child is the hider and then the seeker, the catcher and then the thrower, the statue-maker and then the statue. Through group play, children experience the reciprocal nature of role relationships. Whereas many of their social roles are fixed—son or daughter, sibling, student—in play with peers, children have opportunities to experience a variety of perspectives. The Human Development and Diversity box presents a discussion of hopscotch, an extremely popular and enduring children's game that can be played by a group and by an individual child.

Media Play

From a psychosocial perspective, development is a product of the ongoing interaction of the changing person in a changing environment. The media environment is an excellent example of this idea, with children being exposed at younger and younger ages to electronic media, including television programs and videos designed specifically for infants and toddlers, video games, handheld game players and computer software for toddlers and preschoolers, and Internet sites for the very young. A research literature is accumulating about the scope and extent of use of these

electronic media by very young children and its impact on their social and cognitive development (Dill, 2009; Strasburger, Wilson, & Jordan, 2009).

A national survey sponsored by the Kaiser Family Foundation was designed to provide descriptive information to address a variety of questions such as: How much time do children spend with electronic media? How much autonomy do they have in the use of these media? How much do these media activities replace traditional childhood activities, such as playing outside or reading and being read to (Rideout, Vandewater, & Wartella, 2003)? The study was a random, national telephone survey of families with children ages 6 months to 6 years old. The parent who spent the most time with the child was asked to complete the survey. When both parents spent equal amounts of time, one parent was chosen at random to reply.

Almost all the children (99%) had TVs in their homes, with 50% having three or more TVs. Children spent on average 2 hours a day with some type of screen media, about the same amount of time playing outside, and about 39 minutes reading or being read to. About two thirds of the children lived in homes where the TV is on at least half the time, even if no one is watching.

Children are not just passive consumers of electronic media—they are making choices and affecting their media environment: 77% turn on the TV by themselves, 67% ask to watch specific shows, 62% can use a remote to change the channel, and 71% ask for their favorite DVDs or videos. By the time they are 4 to 6 years old, 70% have used a computer, and of those who use a computer, 64% can point and click with a mouse, and 40% can load a CD or DVD and start it playing.

Some homes were characterized as heavy TV households where the TV was on always or most of the time. When children grow up in homes where the TV is on most of the time, they begin watching at a younger age (before the age of 1), they watch TV longer, and they read less often and for

Eric is playing an adventure video game while his sister looks on. She gives him suggestions about what to do, and they plan their strategy together. We do not yet have good data about the developmental outcomes associated with long hours of computer gaming among young children.

© Red Images, LLC/Alamy

HUMAN DEVELOPMENT AND DIVERSITY

Hopscotch

AN ANCIENT GAME played around the world, hopscotch takes children from earth to heaven and back again. A hopscotch diagram is inscribed into the floor of the Forum in Rome. As the Roman empire expanded, soldiers copied this or similar diagrams on the cobblestone roads in Europe. Children have improvised on the Roman diagrams, but they usually have some type of fantasy theme. Across the continents, hopscotch has been described in 16 countries, including the United States, Great Britain, Russia, India, Aruba, and Nepal, each with their own regional variations. Children toss their markers, hop over boxes, avoid danger areas like hell, moon, water, or boxes marked by other players, and return to home base (Grunfeld, 1975; Lankford, 1996; see Figure 7.3). The widespread appeal of the game reflects many of the competencies and challenges of the early-school-age period.

The game symbolizes the perils of early childhood, as children try to move ahead in their lives without stepping on lines, going outside the boxes, or stepping into forbidden areas. Children in all cultures must balance carefully in order to stay within the parameters of their socialization.

At the same time, the game provides an opportunity to exercise mastery. Children are the creators of their hopscotch world, and they have the skills to conquer it by being careful, agile, and having a bit of luck. Erikson (1982) would emphasize the link in language and thought between hopping and hoping. Children take a leap of faith as they hop from box to box, facing perils, overcoming some, failing sometimes, and starting over.

Critical Thinking questions

1. What are some of the elements of the game of hopscotch that might appeal to a child in the early-school-age years?
2. What aspects of development are fostered through this kind of play? How is physical, cognitive, and emotional development stimulated through this game?
3. What are some other games that 4- to 6-year-olds like to play? What aspects of development are enhanced by these games?
4. Hopscotch is a game that can be played alone or with others. What are some other games that have this same kind of flexibility? What is the value of this aspect of a game?
5. Hopscotch is an example of a game that young children play that has rules, and many of the rules are subject to interpretation. Is the marker in the box or out of the box? Did you step on a line when you jumped? Did you remember to jump in every open box? How is this process of playing a game with rules and making judgments about these rules related to early moral development? What are some moral issues that are likely to be confronted in games of this type?
6. What do you remember about playing group games when you were young? Why do you think you have these specific memories?

FIGURE 7.3 Hopscotch

Eric Schnakenberg/Getty Images

Hopscotch combines fantasy, mastery, and a bit of strategy as children hop from earth to heaven and back again.

shorter amounts of time. Among 4- to 6-year-olds, 34% of those in heavy TV viewing households can read, compared to 56% in households where TV is on less often. Thirty percent of children under 3 and 43% of those ages 4 to 6 have a TV in their rooms. Many of these children have their own VCR or DVD player and video game console as well. DVDs and videos are a common part of many children's lives, with 25% watching at least one video daily.

Many videos, computer programs, and video games are marketed to parents as having an educational value. However, manufacturers argue that their first concern is that the materials have to be fun. They believe that if children don't experience the materials as fun, then the media won't be used and the educational value will never be realized. Parents appear to have confidence in the educational value of these resources, seeing them as very important for their child's cognitive development. However, a systematic review of the evidence suggests that there are few if any published studies that document the advertised educational claims associated with these resources (Garrison & Christakis, 2005).

Children's computer programs and video games seem to share certain features. The most popular video games are action or combat scenarios, sports, and adventure games. At every age, boys spend more time playing video games than girls (Cherney & London, 2006). That may be explained in part by the fact that 73% of the player-controlled characters in the most popular video games are male. In the seven top-selling games designed for children, all the human characters were white (Children Now, 2001).

Studies that focus on the design features of interactive games find that experience with these games contributes to spatial visualization, visual attention, manual dexterity, and early readiness for computer literacy (Subrahmanyam, Kraut, Greenfield, & Gross, 2001). Most of the video games require some reading skills. Speed of response is a feature of many games. This rewards children who can think quickly, analyze the situation, and make a rapid fine motor response. When you lose or the turn ends, it is easy to start over and try to do better the next time. Many of the games provide immediate reinforcement through increasing points, sounds, accumulation of virtual rewards, and access to new screens or levels. In some games, children can play with or against each other.

Studies of video game use among young children suggest that children integrate their experiences with television, videos, and video games into other areas of imagination and creativity. The media themselves are often linked so that characters from a movie or television program are integrated in computer software or a video game. In role-playing videos, children may be able to choose a favorite character or switch characters as part of the play. Children use images from these media in their written narratives, their imaginative play, and their conversations with friends (Singer & Singer, 2008; Wohlwend, 2009).

Given the extensive exposure to electronic media at young ages, additional research is needed to help clarify the impact of these media. Concerns about the relationship of extensive TV viewing to childhood obesity, possible interference with social communication and language development, and exposure to noneducational content deserve empirical study. The media environment may also contribute to the emergence of self-directed goal attainment, new capacities for managing multiple stimuli at once (multitasking), and new appreciation for music, art, poetry, and the natural environment through early exposure.

Friendship Groups

In early school age, friendships are based on the exchange of concrete goods and the mutual enjoyment of activities. Young children are sensitive to the norms for fairness and cooperation among friends, and are more likely to be generous with their friends than with children they know who are not friends (Moore, 2009). Friendships are maintained through acts of affection, sharing, or collaboration in fantasy or constructive play. By the age of 4 or 5, children who have stable friendships become skilled at coordinating their interactions with their friends, creating elaborate pretend games, and being willing to modify their play preferences so that both members in the friendship have a chance to enjoy the kinds of play they like best (Park, Lay, & Ramsay, 1993; Vaughn, Colvin, Azria, Caya, & Krzysik, 2001). Children may build snow forts together, play dolls or space adventures, or sleep over at one another's homes. Friendships may be broken by taking away a toy, hitting, or name-calling. The opportunity to form friendships benefits young children by enhancing their interpersonal sensitivity, social reasoning skills, and conflict resolution skills (Volling, Youngblade, & Belsky, 1997).

Conflicts among Friends. Young children tend to evaluate situations on the basis of outcomes rather than intentions. Therefore, they are often harsh in assigning blame in the case of negative outcomes. For example, children were asked how much they should be blamed for another child getting hurt. The injury took place in six different hypothetical situations. In the case of the lowest level of responsibility, the child was accidentally hurt by someone's toy, but the owner did not actually cause the injury. At this level, 6-year-olds were more likely than older children or adults to blame themselves for the outcome (Fincham & Jaspars, 1979). Because of this rigid approach to social responsibility, peer play is frequently disrupted by quarrels, tattling on others, and hard feelings about injustices.

Even though children appear to be drawn into the active world of peer friendships, it is an uneven, difficult, and often extremely frustrating terrain for many early-school-age children. For example, many 5- and 6-year-olds participate in play fighting. In a study of children's perceptions of play fighting, Italian and British children of ages 5, 8, and 11 were surveyed about the differences between real fighting and play fighting (Smith, Hunter, Carvalho, & Costabile, 1992).

About half the children liked play fighting—a somewhat larger number of boys than girls. But about 80% thought there was a risk that play fighting could lead to a serious, real fight. This might happen if there was an accidental injury, if the play fighting got carried away into mean name-calling, or if, when one child accidentally hurt the other, the second child mistook the injury as purposeful and hurt the first child back. Five-year-olds said that if play fighting turned into real fighting, they would tell an adult. No matter whether the other child was a friend or not, they believed that such a transgression had to be handled with a serious intervention by a grown-up. The older children were more likely to forget about it, especially if the other person was a friend.

Sex Segregation Among Friends. One of the most noticeable characteristics of young children's friendship groups is that they are likely to be segregated by sex. When boys and girls are free to choose play companions, they tend to choose others of their own sex. This pattern of same-sex social groupings among children is found not only in the United States but also in most other cultures (Edwards & Whiting, 1988). In one longitudinal study, children at age 4½ were found playing with same-sex friends about three times more often than with opposite-sex friends. By age 6½, they were *eleven* times more likely to be playing with same-sex friends (Maccoby & Jacklin, 1987).

Sex segregation is promoted by both cognitive and behavioral factors (Barbu, Le Maner-Idrissi, & Jouanjean, 2000). Based on the earlier discussion of gender identification, it is clear that children expect others of the same sex to like similar activities, toys, and forms of play. Children form internal representations of what boys and girls are like as friends and playmates. These internal models guide the inferences they make as they engage in peer interaction (Markovits, Benenson, & Dolenszky, 2001). Thus, children are likely to seek others of the same sex because they believe these other children will have the same play preferences they have.

At the same time, boys and girls do appear to play differently, especially when in same-sex and mixed-sex groups. Thus, a preference for same-sex play groups may be fostered by feelings of comfort or discomfort as children accumulate play experiences. Finally, some cultures discourage girls and boys from participating in the same types of play. For example, when children in a Brazilian tribal culture play family, the boys (husbands) go off to pretend to be hunting and fishing, returning with leaves that are then given to the girls (wives), who pretend to cook them and pass them out to the boys to eat (Gregor, 1977).

The significance of the formation of same-sex social groups is that boys and girls grow up in distinct peer environments (Maccoby, 1988, 1990). They tend to use different strategies to achieve dominance or leadership in their groups. Boys are more likely to use physical assertiveness and direct demands; girls are more likely to use verbal persuasiveness and polite suggestions. The verbal exchanges in all-boy groups are apt to include frequent boasts, commands, interruptions, heckling, and generally playful teasing. Boys try to top one another's stories and to establish dominance through verbal threats. The interactions in all-girl groups, on the other hand, tend to include agreeing with and acknowledging the others' comments, listening carefully to one another's statements, and talking about things that bind the group together in a shared sentiment or experience (Leaper, Tenenbaum, & Shaffer, 1999). In mixed-sex groups, boys may be less controlling and dominating than they would be in all-boy groups, but this may still be more than girls find acceptable or comfortable. As a result, girls' negative views of boys are reinforced and their tendency to seek all-girl peer interactions increases.

At this age, boys and girls tend to prefer same-sex play companions. Boys enjoy rough-and-tumble play; girls enjoy fantasy-based, relational play.

Of course, many young children do form friendships with children of the opposite sex. These friendships may begin as early as infancy or toddlerhood between children who live in the same neighborhood or attend the same child care center. They are sustained by a compatibility of interests and play preferences and may survive the trend toward seeking same-sex friendships, even during early and middle childhood (Howes & Phillipsen, 1992). However, the general preference for same-sex friendship groups is an important aspect of social development that is established during the early childhood years and continues into adolescence (Bukowski, Gauze, Hoza, & Newcomb, 1993). Although a boy and a girl grow up in the same culture, the same neighborhood, and even the same family, the tendency to establish separate play and friendship groups fosters the development of distinctive gender-linked communication strategies and makes the achievement of mutual understanding between boys and girls difficult.

Groups and Dyads. In addition to the preference for same-sex friends, boys and girls tend to prefer to interact in groups of different sizes. Early-school-age girls seem to enjoy **dyadic** (two-person) interactions over larger groups, whereas boys seem to enjoy larger groups (Benenson, 1993; Markovits, Benenson, & Dolenszky, 2001). This is not to say that boys and girls cannot function effectively in both dyadic and larger peer group situations, but when given the choice, boys prefer the group and girls the dyad. These two configurations, the group and the dyad, provide different opportunities for intimacy, different needs to exercise dominance and control, and different problems in the coordination of action. They provide models for different forms of adult social relationships—the dyad being associated with intimacy between partners or in parent-child relationships, and the group being associated with sports teams, work groups, and families.

The Psychosocial Crisis: Initiative versus Guilt

Objective 5. To explain the psychosocial crisis of initiative versus guilt, the central process of identification, the prime adaptive ego quality of purpose, and the core pathology of inhibition.

As children positively resolve the toddlerhood crisis of autonomy versus shame and doubt, they emerge from that stage with a strong sense of themselves as unique individuals. During early school age, children shift their attention toward investigation of the external environment. They attempt to discover the same kind of stability, strength, and regularity in the external world that they have discovered within themselves.

Initiative

Initiative is an expression of agency—an outgrowth of early experiences of the self as a causal agent that continues to be demonstrated as children impose themselves and their ideas and questions onto their social world. It is a manifestation of the *I*, the executive branch of the self that was discussed earlier in the section on self-concept (Damon & Hart, 1988). Initiative is the active, conceptual investigation of the world, in much the same sense that autonomy is the active, physical manipulation of it (Erikson, 1963). It can be recognized in a child's curiosity, exploratory behavior, and active coping strategies in the face of obstacles (Frese, 2001).

The child's motivation for and skill in investigation depend on the successful development of a strong sense of autonomy in toddlerhood. Having acquired self-control and self-confidence, children can perform a variety of actions and observe the consequences. They discover, for example, what makes parents or teachers angry and what pleases them. They may deliberately perform a hostile act in order to evoke a hostile response. Children's curiosity about the order of the universe ranges from the physical to the metaphysical. They may ask questions about the color of the sky, the purpose of hair, the nature of God, the origin of babies, or the speed at which fingernails grow. They take things apart, explore the alleys and dark corners of their neighborhood, and invent toys and games out of odds and ends.

One expression of initiative is children's playful exploration of their own bodies and sometimes of their friends' bodies. It is not uncommon to find 5- and 6-year-olds intently involved in a game of doctor in which both doctor and patient have their pants off. Boys of this age may occasionally be observed in a game that is won by the individual who can achieve the longest urine trajectory. Girls report occasions on which they have attempted to urinate from a standing position, attempting to imitate how a boy does. Both boys and girls engage in some form of masturbation. These behaviors are evidence of children's growing curiosity about and pleasure in their bodies and their physical functioning.

Children may express initiative while they are alone, by attempting to discover how things work and by building or inventing novel devices.

> Donald kicked and knocked over an endless variety of things at hand. He put a block on top of a toy car, a leaf on top of that, then knocked the leaf off. Then he turned a truck over on its side, put a block on top of it, moved over to the car, stacked three blocks on top of it, and knocked the whole structure over. He took the car again, spanked it as if it were a doll, knocked it upside down, placed a leaf on top of it, then swept the leaf off. He played a little longer in this way, then ran out of the garage. (Murphy, 1962, p. 102)

Children may also express initiative in social situations by asking questions, asserting their presence, and taking leadership. In one study of social competence, children described the strategies they used to enter a peer play group (Dodge,

Pettit, McClaskey, & Brown, 1986). Two children were playing a game (they were referred to as the *hosts*), and a third child was asked to enter the room and try to initiate play with the others. The entry episode was videotaped and coded. The child who tried to initiate play and the two hosts were interviewed about the episode and asked to evaluate how successful the entry child had been. Three strategies for initiating interaction were judged to be effective and were associated with other evidence of social competence:

1. Children established common ground by giving meaningful information in response to questions.
2. Children engaged in a positive, friendly interchange with the others.
3. Children did not show evidence of negative, irritable behaviors. The children who were least successful in initiating entry into the play "were disruptive, . . . made nagging, weak demands, . . . engaged in incoherent behaviors, or . . . disagreed with hosts without citing a rule or reason" (Dodge et al., 1986, p. 25).

Children who experience a positive sense of initiative can apply this orientation to investigation of the physical as well as the social world. They innovate through the creation of magic potions mixed together with soap, perfume, pinecones, leaves, and other powerful ingredients. They create plays, stories, puppet shows, dances, and ceremonies. They dress up in costumes, entertain company by standing on their heads, engage in daring acts by hanging from tree limbs or walking on the tops of high ledges, and impose themselves in any and all curious and private discussions. They spend time trying to figure out ways to catch a glimpse of Santa Claus on Christmas Eve or the Tooth Fairy when she comes at night to collect her treasures. These are the *Little Rascals* years, when a sense of initiative is associated with a naive, exuberant, entrepreneurial spirit and a desire to discover, direct, and dominate. All manner of investigation and inquiry is fair game.

Guilt

Guilt is an emotion that accompanies the sense that one has been responsible for an unacceptable thought, fantasy, or action (Izard, 1977). It is recognized as a fundamental moral emotion that is usually accompanied by remorse and a desire to make reparation for real or imagined wrongdoing. It has the adaptive function of promoting social harmony, because it disrupts or inhibits aggressive actions and leads people to ask for forgiveness or to compensate for wrongs they may have done. In comparison to *shame*, which often is accompanied by strong feelings of anger or resentment, guilt is typically tied to constructive efforts to repair the harm done to others (Tangney, 2001).

Three theories offer different explanations for the dynamics that underlie feelings of guilt (Zahn-Waxler & Kochanska, 1990). The psychoanalytic perspective views guilt as an emotional reaction to one's unacceptable sexual and aggressive impulses. These impulses are especially threatening during the phallic stage, when hostility and feelings of sexuality toward one's parents become a focus of the child's wishes and must be repressed.

Second, research on empathy suggests that guilt may be awakened at a very early age through emotional arousal and sensitivity to another person's emotional distress. This view of guilt based on empathy is not defensive; it is closely linked to prosocial feelings and the basic emotional ties between infants and their caregivers (Hoffman, 1982).

The third, cognitive perspective suggests that guilt occurs when one fails to act in accord with one's own personal standards and beliefs. This view supposes a more advanced level of self-reflection and the ability to compare one's behaviors against personal standards. In this theory, guilt begins to be experienced in early and middle childhood as children begin to be more comparative in their organization and evaluation of self.

Every culture imposes some limits on legitimate experimentation and investigation. Some questions may not be asked; some acts may not be performed. Adults' reactions

© Laura Dwight/Photo Edit

Saniosa made her sister cry by calling her a bad name. Now she is in her room, thinking things over. For most children, occasional feelings of guilt lead to wanting to set things right and regain positive feelings with their family or friends.

determine whether the child will learn to view specific behaviors, such as aggressiveness, sexual play, or masturbation, as wrong or acceptable. Children gradually internalize cultural prohibitions and learn to inhibit their curiosity in the taboo areas. One taboo shared by most cultures is the prohibition of incest. Most children learn that any behavior that suggests sexual intimacy between family members is absolutely forbidden. Even the thought of such a relationship comes to generate feelings of anxiety and guilt.

The child's curiosity in other domains is limited to the extent that the family and the school impose restrictions on certain areas of inquiry or action. The psychosocial crisis of initiative versus guilt is resolved positively when children develop the sense that an active, questioning investigation of the environment is informative and pleasurable. Inquiry is tempered by a respect for personal privacy and cultural values. However, the dominant state of mind is curiosity and experimentation. The child learns that, even though certain areas are off limits, efforts to understand most aspects of the world are appropriate.

Guilt, like other negative poles of the psychosocial crises, can have an adaptive function. As children grow in their sense of empathy and ability to take responsibility for their actions, they are able to acknowledge when their actions or words may have caused harm to someone else. Normal levels of guilt have been associated with positive levels of prosocial behavior and high levels of empathy (Tangney, 1991). Feelings of guilt generally lead to remorse and some attempt to set things right again, to restore the positive feelings in a relationship.

Girls and boys may show different patterns in the experience of guilt, based on different patterns of socialization and relationships (Maccoby, 1990). Girls tend to have higher levels of empathy and boys higher levels of aggression. Girls are socialized to be concerned about others and to pay attention to preserving connections with them. Thus, they are more likely to experience guilt when they have lied or been inconsiderate to others. They are also more likely to experience guilt when they blame themselves for unhappiness or conflict among others. In contrast, boys are socialized to be assertive and control the expression of their emotions. They are more likely to experience guilt over overt actions like fighting, victimizing other children or animals, or damaging property (Williams & Bybee, 1994).

Some children suffer from overwhelming guilt. They feel that each of their questions or doubts about the world is inappropriate. They may experience guilt about their own impulses and fantasies, even when they have taken no actions and no negative consequences have resulted. Moreover, these children begin to believe that their thoughts and actions are responsible for the misfortune or unhappiness of others. They do not seem to take any enjoyment in play, and their play is often characterized by negative or sad themes. Excessive guilt is one of the symptoms associated with early identification of depression in preschoolers (Luby, 2010).

Young children of depressed mothers express unusually high levels of distress, concern, and feelings of responsibility for others' unhappiness. Mothers who are consistently sad set an example of blaming themselves for most of the bad things that happen. Depressed mothers are likely to withdraw love when the child has misbehaved—a discipline technique associated with high levels of guilt and anxiety (Zahn-Waxler, Kochanska, Krupnick, & McKnew, 1990). In this environment, children learn to restrict new behaviors out of fear that they may cause harm or unhappiness to someone else. Children who resolve the crisis of initiative versus guilt in the direction of guilt are left to rely almost totally on their parents or other authorities for directions on how to operate in the world.

The psychosocial crisis of initiative versus guilt highlights the close tie between intellectual curiosity and emotional development. During this stage, parents and the school transmit the cultural attitudes toward experimentation, curiosity, and investigation. They also make demands that direct the child's curiosity away from familial, subgroup, and cultural areas of taboo. Children are expected to develop the ability to control their own questions and behavior. Whereas violations may bring disapproval and punishment, successful self-control may attract no notice whatsoever. Children must develop a strong internal moral code that will help them avoid discipline. They must also develop the ability to reward themselves for correct behavior. The more areas of restriction that are imposed on children's thinking, the more difficult it is for children to distinguish between legitimate and inappropriate areas of investigation. The only way that children have of coping with this problem is to develop a rigid moral code that restricts many aspects of thought and action.

The Central Process: Identification

The discussion of the developmental tasks during early school age points directly to **identification** as the central process in the resolution of the conflict between initiative and guilt. We have introduced the concept of identification in discussions of gender identity and moral development. Self-theory and self-esteem also develop in the context of social interactions. As a result of identification, children internalize salient cultural values. Children at this age actively strive to enhance their self-concepts by incorporating into their own behavior some of the valued characteristics of their parents. Through a variety of processes, including watching the behavior of others, imitating others, engaging in activity where others are watching, and participating in play, conversation, and problem solving with others, children form an internal representation of the self that is coordinated with the representation of the other (Sherkow, 2001; Decety & Chaminade, 2003).

There appear to be four substantially different theories about the motives for identification (see Table 7.5). The *fear of loss of love* is founded on a child's initial realization

TABLE 7.5 Four Motives for Parental Identification

MOTIVE	DEFINITION
Fear of loss of love	A child behaves like a parent in order to Ensure a continued positive love relationship.
Identification with the aggressor	A child behaves like a parent in order to protect himself or herself from the parent's anger.
Identification to satisfy needs for power	A child behaves like a parent in order to achieve a vicarious sense of the power associated with the parent.
Identification to increase perceived similarity	A child behaves like a parent to increase a perceived similarity to the parent and thereby to share in the parent's positive attributes.

Source: © Cengage Learning.

of dependence on the parents. A child behaves like a parent in order to ensure a continued positive relationship. Eventually, the child incorporates aspects of the loved one's personality into the self-concept. The child can then feel close to the loved person even when they are not physically together (Jacobson, 1964). If a child can be like a loved parent, the parent's continuous presence is not required to reassure the child about that parent's love.

Identification with the aggressor is aroused when children experience some fear of their parents. In order to protect themselves from harm, they perform behaviors that are similar to those they fear. Children identify even with parents who are extremely brutal. Because most of the behaviors that these children incorporate are aggressive, they often tend to be aggressive toward others. This kind of identification may give children a magical feeling of power and decrease the parents' tendency to mistreat them. Parents who see great similarity between themselves and their children are less likely to threaten or harm them (Freud, 1936).

A third motive for identification is the *need for status and power* (Bandura, 1977, 1986). Studies of modeling show that children are more likely to imitate the behavior of a model who controls resources than they are the behavior of a model who is rewarded. The imitative behavior is motivated by a vicarious feeling of power experienced when they behave in the same way as the powerful model. Within a family, children are likely to have personality characteristics similar to those of the more dominant parent.

A fourth motive for identification results from the *children's need to increase the perceived similarity with their parents* (Kagan, 1958). Children attribute a number of valued characteristics to their parents, including physical size, good looks, special competencies, power, success, and respect. Children more readily share these positive attributes when they perceive a similarity between themselves and their parents. They experience this sense of similarity in three principal ways: by (1) perceiving actual physical and psychological

similarities, (2) adopting parental behaviors, and (3) being told about similarities by others. Increasing perceptions of similarity promote stronger identifications.

These four motives apply to the process of identification at all ages and regardless of the sex of the identifier or the model. For a particular child, one of these motives may dominate, but all four motives are involved in the process. Parental identification allows children to feel that their parents are with them even when they are not physically present. This feeling of connection with parents provides an underlying sense of security for children in a wide variety of situations.

Viewed from another perspective, identification allows children a growing sense of independence from their parents (Jacobson, 1964). Children who know how their parents would respond in a given situation no longer need the parents' physical presence to direct their behavior. Children who can praise or punish themselves for their actions are less dependent on their parents to perform these functions.

Parental identification affects children's development in two different ways. On the one hand, the closeness with parents provides the basis for the incorporation of parental sanctions and prohibitions. Once children have integrated these guidelines for behavior, they are bound to feel guilty whenever they anticipate abandoning them. On the other hand, the security that results from strong parental identification allows children increased freedom when they are away from their parents. The child whose parental identification is strong is more likely to engage the environment, take risks, and initiate action.

Identification with parents results in a strengthening of the child's personality. An important outcome of early-school-age identification is the formation of an ideal self-image, which psychoanalytic theorists sometimes refer to as the **ego ideal** (Freud, 1909/1955; Sandler, Holder, & Meers, 1963). The conscience not only punishes misdeeds but also rewards actions that bring children closer to some aspect of their ideal self-image. The ideal self is a complex view of the self as it may be in the future, including skills, profession, values, and personal relationships. It is a fantasy, a goal that is unlikely to be attained even in adulthood. Nonetheless, the discrepancy between the real self and the ideal self is a strong motivator. As children strive to achieve their ideal, they attempt new activities, set goals that strain the limits of their abilities, take risks, and resist temptations that might interfere with their desired goals.

The ego ideal is more unrealistic during early school age than at later stages. Young children fantasize anything they wish about themselves in the future. They take their parents' values literally and use them to project an ideal person of mythic proportions. The ideal self may include the strength of Hercules, the wealth of Queen Elizabeth II, the wisdom of Confucius, and the compassion of Jesus. The lack of realistic constraints on the ego ideal allows children to investigate and vicariously experience certain human qualities that may always be beyond their reach. As people grow older, it is important that the fantasy of the ideal self-image becomes

Identification is the central process through which children develop an ego ideal.

increasingly attainable, although still beyond what has been attained. People who find it difficult to modify their ideal self-images become vulnerable to personal frustration and psychological despair because they are unable to be what they wish. Many 6-year-old children may wish to become president of the United States. This largely unrealistic fantasy is exciting and, for some, ennobling. However, few people actually achieve this position. By the time one reaches early adulthood, it is important to have developed an occupational ideal that is closer to what is actually attainable.

Identification with parents is the process by which the ideal self-image and moral prescriptions are blended into the child's personality. When children are unable to control their behavior so that it corresponds to the sanctions and ideals that they have internalized, they will experience guilt. In contrast, when children's behavior approaches their ideals and conforms to internalized sanctions, they will experience feelings of self-confidence that allow them to take initiative. The balance between guilt and self-confidence determines the eventual resolution of the psychosocial crisis of initiative versus guilt.

The crisis of initiative versus guilt captures the child's need to question existing norms and the emerging feelings of moral concern when these norms are violated. This crisis does not focus specifically on intellectual development; however, one may assume that the level of questioning that takes place during this stage is possible only because of an increase in cognitive complexity. The process of positive parental identification promotes the incorporation of cultural norms and strengthens the child's sense of competence. Socialization during this stage may either foster a creative openness or an anxious dread of novelty.

The Prime Adaptive Ego Quality and the Core Pathology

As a result of efforts to resolve the crisis of initiative versus guilt, children emerge from the period of early school age with the benefit of the prime adaptive ego quality of purpose or the core pathology of inhibition. These predispositions suggest an orientation that leaves a child with coping resources that will support directed, action-oriented problem solving or a more passive, self-protective approach to stress, in which the child is more likely to allow others to guide the course of behavior.

Purpose

Purpose is thought or behavior with direction, and therefore, with meaning. "Purposefulness is the courage playfully to imagine and energetically to pursue valued goals" (Erikson, 1978, p. 29). It is a cognitively more complex extension of the will gained in toddlerhood, in that it combines a sense of agency with a plan. In contrast to the toddler, who exercises the will through the mere delight in action, the early-school-age child imposes intention and goals on action. This is the difference, for example, between running around the yard, laughing and shouting—typical behavior for toddlers—and saying to a friend, "Let's play tag," which is more likely for early-school-age children. Toddlers may enjoy stacking blocks or splashing in water, whereas early-school-age children want to turn materials and toys into a story or a project. Their actions are going in a direction; their play has a plan. Behind the process of planning is a complex sense of the situation, the creation of a goal, strategies to achieve it, and monitoring success in realizing the goal (Scholnick, 1995). The sense of purpose, expressed in planning and enacting plans, reflects a significant expansion of the ego into the realm of the present and the future.

A sense of purpose suggests not only that the action does have meaning, but also that the person initiating it has meaning. Ricky enters a play situation and says, "I have an idea. Let's play trains." This kind of suggestion reflects Ricky's sense of a goal-directed plan, and a sense of confidence about introducing his idea into the ongoing activities of the group.

Inhibition

Inhibition refers to the restraint or suppression of thoughts and behavior. Inhibition is assumed to emerge when parents or caregivers use high levels of love withdrawal and guilt-inducing interactions with their children. These kinds of interactions suggest to the child that the parent's love, affection, and approval are conditional on the child matching certain specific parental standards. In order to adapt in this kind of environment and avoid risking loss of love, the child becomes self-conscious and restrained in action. In contrast to the sense of confidence and agency implied in the notion of purpose, a child who is inhibited does not want to take the risks associated with imposing a plan or suggesting a direction, for fear that suggestions will result in parental disapproval.

Lois Murphy (1972) proposed that inhibition has early origins in the mother-infant relationship. She suggested that in healthy mother-infant interactions, mothers take care to provide meaningful feedback and consequences for their babies' actions. When mothers are very depressed or psychologically unavailable, they may be unable to engage in the kinds of consistent, rhythmic behaviors that produce early experiences of cause and effect. Their babies do not

have opportunities to participate in the typical give-and-take exchanges that provide a model for cause-effect interactions. These babies do not participate in the goal-corrected partnership with their caregiver in infancy as part of the attachment process. As a result, by early school age some children have a very passive orientation toward play and social interactions. According to Murphy, their inhibition is due to a lack of basic early structures or schemes for how to direct the flow of play or have a positive impact on the course of social interactions. These children do not impose organization on toys or integrate sensory and motor play into a more complex scenario. They remain focused on the sensory activity itself, like digging in the sand, or on the imitation of basic behaviors, like feeding the baby.

Inhibited children are likely to emerge as shy, withdrawn, and often lonely during the subsequent period of middle childhood. Without some form of social intervention, they become increasingly withdrawn, not knowing how to impose their ideas into the ongoing activities of the group, and not experiencing the confidence-building effects of making suggestions and having them accepted. Consequently, by the end of the early-school-age period, their inhibition produces new deficits in social skill development.

Coach Carl is guiding Billy to overcome his doubts and to keep trying to make a basket. Goal-directed play becomes increasingly important in early school age, and requires a sense of purpose. A few successes will make a big difference in his confidence.

© Gabe Palmer/Alamy

APPLIED TOPIC

School Readiness

Objective 6. To analyze the construct of school readiness, its relation to the developmental tasks of early school age, and the obstacles that may prevent children from being able to adapt and learn in the school environment.

IN 1989, PRESIDENT George H. W. Bush and the state governors created an educational agenda for the United States. The first goal was that by the year 2000, all children in the United States would start school *ready to learn*. This goal identified the importance of the first years of schooling in setting the long-term course for school achievement and entry into adulthood as an educated person ready to undertake the roles and responsibilities of adult life. This goal, which seems positive and appropriate on the face of it, has resulted in important dialogue about what is meant by **school readiness**, how to measure it, what obstacles stand in its way, and who should be responsible for achieving it (Wesley & Buysse, 2003).

Defining Readiness

The concept of readiness is a familiar idea in the study of development. Typically, the term is used to refer to a time when the child's physical, cognitive, social, and emotional maturation are at a level to undertake new learning or to engage in a more complex, demanding type of activity or relationship. It is sometimes referred to as a critical or sensitive period or a teachable moment. The idea of a *sensitive period* was identified in Chapter 5 in relation to attachment relationships, in Chapter 6 in relation to language use and toilet training, and in this chapter in relation to gender role identification. Vygotsky's concept of a *zone of proximal development* is another way of conceptualizing readiness; it is the next higher level of performance one can achieve with the help of more competent teachers.

When thinking about the goal that all children should come to school ready to learn, the concept of readiness becomes somewhat more complicated. Does it refer to readiness to learn or readiness to start school? One might argue that all children—except perhaps those with severe neurological damage—are both ready and eager to learn. However, not all children have the combined physical, cognitive, emotional, and social skills that allow them to adapt to the demands of the kindergarten environment or to succeed at the academic challenges of its curriculum without support (Bowman, Donovan, & Burns, 2000; Early, Pianta, Taylor, & Cox, 2001).

Measuring Kindergarten Readiness

In the past, kindergarten readiness was established largely by chronological age. School districts typically established a birthday cutoff. For example, if a child was 5 by December 1 of a given year, the child could start kindergarten in September of that year. Those who missed the December 1 date had to wait until the following year. In the 1980s, concern about the quality of education in the United States led to an upgrading of the elementary school curriculum. As part of this school reform, academic demands for school performance were raised, and children were exposed to a more challenging curriculum in earlier grades. Many skills that had been introduced in first grade are now part of the kindergarten curriculum, and more children are having trouble meeting the expectations for school performance. In efforts to prevent early school failure, some states began to administer school readiness tests. However, there is no agreement or universal acceptance of a measure of kindergarten readiness, and some educators dispute whether any test given to 5-year-olds can accurately predict a child's ability to learn in the school environment (American Academy of Pediatrics, 1995; Pyle, 2002). Intelligence is not a stable construct for young children whose cognitive abilities are changing in an uneven pattern across many domains. When it comes to school readiness, norm-referenced assessment techniques typically fail to include the role of motivation, temperament, social and cultural factors that may influence the various strategies and processes that young children use for learning.

Most 5-year-olds do not read or write, so mass testing is not feasible. Any approach to measuring kindergarten readiness must involve one-on-one evaluation. Many early childhood educators emphasize that cognitive skills in reading, mathematics, and general knowledge are not enough to understand the child's readiness for school. Physical development and motor coordination, social skills,

These children are learning a fundamental skill for success in school: walking in line.

© Bill Aron/Photo Edit

communication skills, and a child's enthusiasm for learning all play a part in how well a child will adapt to the school environment. Increasing attention is being given to social and emotional resources that support children's learning and ability to cope with the demands of the school environment (DeAngelis, 2010). The way a child approaches learning, such as task persistence, attentiveness, and organization; a child's capacity for self-control and behavioral regulation; and a child's interpersonal skills, such as getting along with others, and being able to express one's feelings and ideas in a positive way are all aspects of social and emotional competence that contribute to school success (Ponitz, McClelland, Matthews, & Morrison, 2009; Galindo & Fuller, 2010).

To address the question of what kindergartners are able to do at the start of school, the U.S. Department of Education initiated the Early Childhood Longitudinal Study, Kindergarten Class of 1998–1999 (Zill & West, 2000). A national sample of more than 19,000 kindergartners who were attending their first year of regular school were evaluated in one-on-one assessments. Information about the children was also gathered from parents and teachers. Children were evaluated in reading, mathematics, and general knowledge as well as physical health, motor development, social skills, problem behaviors, and the child's approach to learning. The hope was that these assessments would provide norms for what most children can do when they come to kindergarten, and a look to the future for how these early abilities may predict subsequent school success. A report of how kindergartners performed on each of the areas assessed can be found in *America's Kindergartners* (West, Denton, & Germino-Hausken, 2000). Four specific skills provide an indication of the level of competence that was measured: recognizes all the letters in the alphabet; counts to 20 or higher; writes (prints) own name; and reads or pretends to read. Thirty-nine percent of children ages 3 to 5 who had not yet started school had three or four of these skills (U.S. Census Bureau, 2003).

Given the lack of an objective, accepted measure or screening test, what do parents and teachers think are essential markers of school readiness? How can a parent judge if a child is ready or should wait a year before beginning kindergarten? In two separate national surveys, parents and teachers were asked what characteristics a child needs to be ready to start school. Teachers emphasized that children need to be physically healthy, well rested, and well nourished as the most important aspects of readiness. Beyond that, they emphasized the ability to communicate effectively, demonstrate enthusiasm and curiosity, follow directions, not be disruptive, and show sensitivity to the feelings of other children as important indicators (Lewit & Baker, 1995). From the teachers' perspective, many of the components of readiness focus on social aspects of learning

and cognitive skills that support self-regulation. Parents tended to emphasize the importance of specific skills—such as using a pencil or scissors, knowing the alphabet, or counting to 20—more frequently than the teachers (Lewit & Baker, 1995).

Typically, the teachers' opinions about kindergarten readiness placed greater emphasis on social and emotional competence than on skills and knowledge, although these expectations differed by geographic region and by teachers' years of experience. Children need to be ready to separate comfortably from their parents, interact in a positive way with other children, and engage in the appropriate behaviors associated with the student role: following directions, being quiet when asked, and asking and answering questions. School success relies more on being able to focus one's attention, express one's needs and thoughts, and exercise what has been described as effortful control than it does on being able to count to 20 or name the colors (Blair, 2002; Lin, Lawrence, & Gorrell, 2003).

Obstacles to School Readiness

Success in kindergarten is based on a combination of intellectual and social skills, enthusiasm for learning, and the motivation to succeed. Most children are excited about going to kindergarten and doing well. However, certain demographic characteristics are associated with the likelihood of poor school adjustment, even in kindergarten. According to the national study of America's kindergartners, four family risk factors are (1) parents who have not graduated from high school, (2) low income or welfare dependence, (3) single-parent families, and (4) families where a language other than English is the primary language spoken at home (Zill & West, 2000).

Forty-six percent of U.S. kindergartners have one or more of these risk factors. Having one or more risk factors was associated with lower scores in reading and mathematics, and poorer health. Children with multiple risk factors were more likely to show aggressive behavior in school and were judged as having somewhat more difficulty making friends, listening to other children's ideas, and comforting other children than those with no risk factors. Children with multiple risk factors were more likely to be described by teachers as having difficulty paying attention or persisting in the completion of a task and were more likely to be described as sometimes or never eager to learn, in contrast to children with no risk factors.

Figure 7.4 shows the trajectory of reading scores for children from the fall of their first kindergarten year (1998) to the spring of their third-grade year (2002) as it relates to the number of family risk factors (Rathbun, West, & Haausken, 2004). As the figure illustrates, risk factors are associated with measurable differences in reading at kindergarten. All groups improve

FIGURE 7.4 Mean Reading Scale Scores for Fall, 1998 First-Time Kindergartners, by Time of Assessment and Number of Family Risk Factors: Fall 1998, Spring 1999, Spring 2000, and Spring 2002

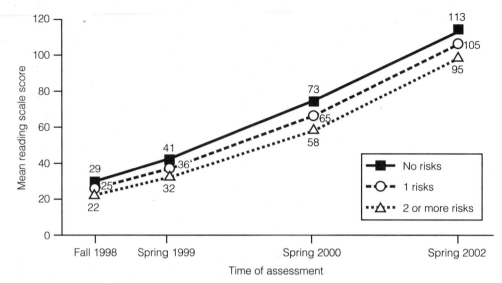

Note: Family risk factors included living below the federal poverty level, primary home language was non-English, mother's highest education was less than a high school diploma/GED, and living in a single-parent household. Values range from 0 to 4. Estimates reflect the sample of children assessed in English in all assessment years. The ECLS-K assessment was not administered in 2001, when most of the children were in second grade.

Source: U.S. Department of Education, National Center for Education Statistics, Early Childhood Longitudinal Study, Kindergarten Class of 1998-99 (ECLS-K), Longitudinal Kindergarten-First Grade Public-Use Data File and Third Grade Restricted-Use Data File, fall 1998, spring 1999, spring 2000, and spring 2002.

in their reading scores from kindergarten through third grade, but the presence of risk factors is associated with an increasing gap in reading as children progress through school.

Who Is Responsible for Meeting the Goal for School Readiness?

In establishing a national goal for children to start school ready to learn, we are faced with the question, "Whose responsibility is it to meet this goal?" Do we need to place more responsibility on families to provide the early experiences that will foster health, confidence, motivation, and cognitive and social development during the first 4 years of life? Do we need to place more responsibility on schools to work with children where they are by providing the environment, services, curriculum, and methods of instruction that will facilitate learning for an increasingly diverse group of students? Do we need to place more responsibility on local, state, and federal government to sustain and expand programs such as Head Start, so that more children can participate in early educational experiences that help offset the negative effects of poverty?

A psychosocial perspective suggests action on all three fronts. The child's chances of success in school can be improved if *all* interacting systems support one another and keep the goal of academic success for the widest range of students in focus. Schools need to be attuned to the characteristics of their incoming kindergartners and become ready schools. Professionals need to identify the cognitive, social, and motivational factors that support school success and find ways to support development in those domains

during the infancy and early childhood years. Parents need to foster a home environment that supports their child's interest and motivation for learning as well as providing specific opportunities for the acquisition of school-related competences. Educators and parents must become partners for the optimal development of children, identifying those children who are at risk for school failure and making plans for integrated, multiyear, multiservice programs to support their success.

One such model, described as the *CoZi schools*, integrates the philosophies of James Comer, a psychiatrist, and Edward Zigler, a developmental psychologist (Hornblower, 1996; Zigler, Kagan, & Hall, 1996). In these schools, the staff members reach out to families as early as the last trimester of pregnancy. They visit the homes of families, encourage interest in books and educational activities, and talk with parents about child development and child rearing. The schools involve parents in school-based activities that meet their own needs (e.g., exercise classes, adult education classes) as well as the needs of their children. The schools are sites for child care, before- and after-school care, and summer programming. Staff members take the responsibility of mentoring specific children who suffer from neglect or are going through unusual family disorganization. These schools have redefined their role to be a community resource. The goal of each child's educational success is reached by addressing the child's and the family's broader social, emotional, and physical needs at the earliest possible moment (Dryfoos, 1999). See the Human Development and Diversity box for a discussion of how to support school readiness for children with disabilities.

HUMAN DEVELOPMENT AND DIVERSITY

Supporting School Readiness for Young Children with Disabilities

ABOUT 5% OF young children ages 3 through 5 have been identified as having moderate to severe disabilities. For the 2002 to 2003 school year, over 600,000 children of ages 3 to 5 were being served under the Individuals with Disabilities Education Act (U.S. Department of Education, 2003). By definition, these children are performing at or below the 50th percentile of their age-mates in one or more domains, including motor skills, speech and language, social and emotional competence, and learning and memory (Siegel, 1996). In the national longitudinal study of the kindergarten class of 1998 to 1999, about 10% of the children were identified by their parents as having a developmental difficulty. For that study, a child with a developmental difficulty was defined as one whose parents noted by first grade "obtaining a diagnosis from a professional for problems related to attention, activity, communication, hearing, or sight that could not be corrected with eyeglasses" (Malone, West, Flanagan, & Park, 2006).

The term **disability** can refer to a wide variety of possible functional challenges. The two most common impairments are speech and language delays (55% of those receiving services) and developmental delays (25% of those receiving services). In the study of American kindergartners, parents reported that "substantial minorities of children are already experiencing risks for developmental difficulties, with one in five being described as overly active, one in six having problems concentrating for sustained periods, and one in nine not articulating words clearly or fluently" (Zill & West, 2000).

Preschool and kindergarten programs that include children with disabilities face a significant task—to ensure that the inclusion benefits the child both socially and academically. Many children with disabilities are mainstreamed in a classroom without any provision for encouraging social interaction with the other children. One of the major concerns facing teachers is the ability to promote positive social skills, including appropriate levels of assertiveness, self-control, and cooperation among students of varying abilities (U.S. Department of Education, 2002). The school setting makes specific demands on children to function in more constrained, regulated ways than might be required at home. Some children benefit from the routine and predictability of the school setting, whereas others have difficulty regulating their behavior to comply with teacher and peer expectations.

Effective **inclusion** requires strategies for promoting contact between students with and without disabilities and creating an accepting social climate among students. The interventions must be tailored to address the unique areas of deficit. A child with autism, for example, may need to be taught how to imitate a model and may have difficulty cooperating with peers, but might be able to play successfully with puzzles or to listen to the teacher read a story. A child with moderate neurological deficits may have difficulty with tasks that require fast reaction time, such as competitive games among students, but could perform well if speed of response is not a concern. Children with speech and language difficulties may find it difficult to express themselves or to engage in conversation with peers. As a result, they may withdraw from social interactions. Teachers need to find ways to build on each child's level of performance so that the child is not stigmatized for a disability and continues to make progress toward an appropriate academic standard.

Critical Thinking questions

1. What kinds of accommodations do schools have to make for children who have been identified as having serious, moderate, and mild disabilities? You may want to contact someone at a local elementary school or the school you attended to find out what they are required to provide. How might this have changed since you were in elementary school?

2. What might be some of the advantages and disadvantages of mainstreaming early-school-age children as compared to placing these children in special education classes?

3. What are some of the challenges to effective inclusion? How might a course in human development help teachers meet these challenges?

4. What ideas do you have about how to support the social and academic goals of inclusion while still meeting the unique needs of children who have specific disabilities? What might be some specific ways to support children with the following disabilities: autism, developmental delays, speech and language difficulties, and motor or sensory difficulties.

5. How might parents of children who have developmental difficulties work with school professionals to help support their child's academic and social development?

Chapter Summary

Early school age marks the beginning of work on developmental tasks that will persist well into adulthood. The four tasks of early school age are closely interrelated.

Objective 1. To describe the process of gender identification during early school age and its importance for the way a child interprets his or her experiences.

The complex process of gender identification has cognitive, affective, physical, and interpersonal elements. As young children clarify the content of their gender identity, they create a set of beliefs about the self, including their self-worth, relationships with other children, and the kinds of activities and interests that are appropriate for them, not only in the present but also in the future. The gender identity of the early-school-age child will be revised and reintegrated as it becomes a core element of personal identity in adolescence.

Objective 2. To describe the process of early moral development, drawing from theories and research to explain how knowledge, emotion, and action combine to produce internalized morality.

The development of conscience, with its capacity to reward and punish, brings an internalization of moral standards. Moral development is accompanied by a heightened sensitivity to violating basic cultural standards, many of which relate to interpersonal behavior, especially toward adults and peers. The child's experiences with transgressions, guilt, or praise for prosocial behavior have implications for the elaboration of the self-theory and particularly for the establishment of self-esteem.

Objective 3. To analyze changes in the self-theory, with special focus on the theory of mind and self-esteem during the early-school-age years.

Although the self-theory is continuously revised with entry into new roles and the emergence of new cognitive capacities, the establishment of a positive sense of worth in early school age brings an important tone of optimism as the child faces new challenges. Competence and social acceptance are the essential antecedents of self-esteem.

Objective 4. To explore the transition to more complex play and the process of friendship development in the early-school-age years.

Play takes on new complexities including games with rules and multiple roles, exposure to diverse forms of media, and participation in friendship relationships. Increased involvement with peers brings about an appreciation of others' perspectives, social acceptance, and delight in the intimacy of friends as well as new experiences with conflict and conflict resolution. Children's sense of initiative and purpose are reflected in the ways they actively create their social environment through their choice of games, media entertainment, and friends. The social worlds of boys and girls become notably distinct as gender preferences are expressed in different patterns of play and play companions.

Objective 5. To explain the psychosocial crisis of initiative versus guilt, the central process of identification, the prime adaptive ego quality of purpose, and the core pathology of inhibition.

The psychosocial crisis of initiative versus guilt has direct implications for such essential personality characteristics as self-esteem, creativity, curiosity, and risk taking. The child who resolves this crisis positively will be fortified with an active, exploratory approach to the environment. Guilt plays an important role in orienting children toward the implications of their actions for others. In moderation, guilt is an essential ingredient in preserving social bonds. In the extreme, however, guilt restricts creative thought and limits action.

Objective 6. To analyze the construct of school readiness, its relation to the developmental tasks of early school age, and the obstacles that may prevent children from being able to adapt and learn in the school environment.

The applied topic of school readiness illustrates the potential conflict between development and socialization. The society has determined that 5-year-old children will attend school. At the same time, 5-year-olds are at a wide array of developmental levels, bringing them to the door of the school with substantial differences in physical, cognitive, social, and emotional competence. Factors such as disabilities, poverty, and a non-English-speaking home environment may all complicate the child's ability to adapt to the school environment.

Key Terms

autonomous morality, 251
avoidance conditioning, 250
categorical identifications, 266
comparative assessments, 266
contentedness, 248
conventional morality, 252
disability, 283
dyadic, 274
early school age, 240
ego ideal, 277
empathy, 256
equilibration, 252
gender, 241
gender constancy, 244
gender contentedness, 248
gender dysphoria, 248
gender identification, 240
gender labels, 243
gender permanence, 244

gender preference, 247
gender role standards, 244
gender schemes, 245
gender typicality, 248
genital basis of gender, 244
group games, 269
guilt, 275
heteronomous morality, 251
identification, 276
inclusion, 283
inhibition, 279
initiative, 274
internalization, 249
morality, 253
moral intuition, 255
moral reasoning, 251
object relations theory, 255
observation of models, 250
parental identification, 245

personal choice, 253
perspective taking, 258
postconventional morality, 252
preconventional morality, 252
principle of care, 257
purpose, 278
school readiness, 279
self construal, 266
self-esteem, 267
self-theory, 263
sex segregation, 273
sex, 241
sexual orientation, 241
social convention, 253
superego, 254
sympathy 257
tension reduction, 250
theory of mind, 267

Further Reflection

1. What are some examples of the interconnections among the developmental tasks of this stage? Think about how gender identification, moral development, and peer play influence a child's self-theory, and how the self-theory might influence these other areas.

2. How might the biological system, including physical appearance, disabilities, motor development, and health, affect a child's ability to master the developmental tasks of this age?

3. What are your earliest recollections about your own moral development? What factors were most important in shaping what you believed to be right and wrong? Did you develop a sense of yourself as a good or a naughty child? What difficulties did you face in trying to comply with the standards for good behavior?

4. Think about the crisis of initiative versus guilt. What does it mean to you? What would you look for in a child's behavior or conversation that would indicate a strong sense of initiative or guilt? How do you distinguish initiative from autonomy? How is the concept of initiative related to challenges for coping and adaptation that are required in adulthood?

5. Consider the role of the media as part of the child's family environment. What is the bidirectional nature of influence between children and the media? What role did the media play in structuring your own childhood? How did you make use of the media to meet your own needs?

6. What would you do to foster a child's sense of initiative and purpose in the transition to kindergarten? How does a caring community promote early school achievement for diverse learners? How can you conceptualize the biological, psychological, and societal factors that interact to shape the transition to kindergarten?

Psychology CourseMate

To access additional course materials, including CourseMate, please visit www.cengagebrain.com. At the CengageBrain .com home page, search for the ISBN of your title (from the back cover of your book) using the search box at the top of the page. This will take you to the product page where these resources can be found.

Casebook

For additional case material related to this chapter, see the case entitled "Delaney Goes to Kindergarten" in *Life Span Development: A Case Book*, by Barbara and Philip Newman, Laura Landry-Meyer, and Brenda J. Lohman, pp. 87–94.

This case illustrates some of the challenges that children face in the transition to kindergarten and how home, preschool, and kindergarten systems can work together to foster a child's continuing school success.

© 2011 Estate of Pablo Picasso/Artists Rights Society (ARS), New York/Photo © Réunion des Musées Nationaux/Art Resource, NY

Under the guidance of parents and other adults, in middle childhood children gain confidence in their ability to master new skills and perform valued work. Friendship formation is another domain that requires children's attention, effort, and persistence as the required social skills become more complex.

Middle Childhood (6 to 11 Years)

Chapter Objectives

1. To clarify the role of friendship in helping children to learn to take the point of view of others, be sensitive to the norms and pressures of the peer group, experience closeness in relationships, and clarify the negative consequences that result from social rejection and loneliness.

2. To describe the development of concrete operational thought, including conservation, classification skills, mathematical reasoning, and the child's ability to understand and monitor his or her own knowledge and understanding.

3. To analyze the nature of skill learning, including the presentation of a model for the process of acquisition of complex skills such as reading and examination of societal factors that provide the context in which skill learning occurs.

4. To examine the development of self-evaluation skills, including feelings of pride, self-efficacy, and ways that social expectations of parents, teachers, and peers contribute to a child's self-evaluation.

5. To describe a new level of complexity in play as children become involved in team sports and athletic competition, and form more enduring in-group and out-group attitudes.

6. To explain the psychosocial crisis of industry versus inferiority; the central process through which the crisis is resolved; education; the prime adaptive ego quality of competence; and the core pathology of inertia.

7. To explore the impact of exposure to violence on development during middle childhood.

THE THEORIES OF Jean Piaget and Erik Erikson stimulated developmental research focusing on children ages 6 through 11. These theories emphasize intellectual growth and a growing investment in mastery and competence. During this time, children are learning the fundamental skills that are valued in their culture, whether those are reading, writing, and arithmetic or hunting, fishing, and weaving. As children gain confidence in their abilities, they begin to have more realistic images of their potential contributions to the larger community.

For many children, this is a joyful, vigorous time. The fears and vulnerabilities of their early school days are behind them. Energized by ego qualities of hope, will, and purpose, most children are able to enjoy many of the resources and opportunities of their communities. Even as the presence of their family members continues to be a comfort to them, they begin to explore more complex social relationships with their peers and other significant adults.

In some parts of the world, however, life in middle childhood is marked by extreme disorganization and exploitation. Children are vulnerable to the **violence** of war as victims of terrorist attacks, civil wars, injury from explosions of abandoned land mines, and forced enlistment as soldiers among warring tribes (Pearn, 2003; Beah, 2007). Slavers travel through impoverished areas, kidnapping, buying, or luring children into forms of slave-like labor where they are often beaten or sexually abused. Children of impoverished families are being sold or given away as slaves or bonded laborers. An estimated 60 million children worldwide are involved in the harshest forms of slave labor and bondage, used in armed conflicts and in the service of drug trafficking, as well as in all forms of hazardous work (Human Rights Watch, 2004). Tens of thousands of young children in West Africa have been kidnapped and sold into slavery to work in cocoa farms, where their labor contributes to the production of the chocolates that children worldwide love (Bess, 2001). With the signing of the Optional Protocol to the Convention on the Rights of the Child on the involvement of children in armed conflict by X countries, the documented forced participation of children in armed conflicts was reduced from 27 wars in 2004 to 17 wars in 2007. Nonetheless, even now tens of thousands of children are forced into armed conflicts in which they not only witness bloodshed, but may be used as soldiers, spies, messengers, informants, and soldiers' "wives" (Smith, 2001; Human Rights Watch, 2006; Coalition to stop the use of child soldiers, 2008; Annan, Brier, & Aryemo, 2009).

In such circumstances, the opportunity for children to work on the developmental tasks of friendship formation, concrete operational reasoning, skill learning, self-evaluation, and team play may be viewed as a great luxury. We do not know much about the developmental outcomes for these children. Having the time, resources, and security to promote areas of cognitive, social, and emotional development is possible only in the context of communities that are economically and politically stable and ideologically committed to the intellectual and interpersonal future of their children. ∎

Developmental Tasks

New developmental tasks emerge as children become focused on friendship formation, concrete mental operations, skill learning, self-evaluation, and team play. This mix of tasks coupled with new capacities for complex social, emotional, and intellectual activity produce a remarkable synergy. Whereas play dominates the behavior of early-school-age children, middle childhood is characterized by more purposeful, industrious behavior such as earning money for completing chores, planning and building toys, gardens, or play spaces, or participating in competitions, performances, and community events. This is not to say that play is lost. New thrills and excitement accompany the capacity to engage in more complex forms of play and games, and to take new risks—riding one's bike farther from home, jumping and then diving into a pool from the high board, or riding on the big, fast rollercoasters without a parent.

Friendship

Objective 1. To clarify the role of friendship in helping children to learn to take the point of view of others, be sensitive to the norms and pressures of the peer group, experience closeness in relationships, and clarify the negative consequences that result from social rejection and loneliness.

Can you remember some things about a friend you had when you were 9 or 10 years old? Friendships of middle childhood are often quite memorable. At this age, children describe close friends as people who play together, like the same activities, share common interests, enjoy each other's company, and count on each other for help. Peer relationships include forming meaningful dyadic and group relationships, participating in larger peer networks, and experiencing peer acceptance or rejection (Gifford-Smith & Brownell, 2003).

Friendships clearly provide social and developmental advantages (Berndt & Murphy, 2002; Hruschka, 2010). Human beings are social animals whose development is intricately dependent on a network of close, supportive social relationships. In middle childhood, the radius of significant relationships expands to include classmates, teammates, and close friends. According to ethological theory, being a member of a group has protective advantages. Group cooperation gives a selective advantage to many social species, especially in tracking and hunting for food. Therefore, the skills of cooperation and sociability may advance the species as a whole as well as the individual. On an individual level, children who are able to participate in positive peer friendships are embedded in an intellectually and socially stimulating environment. For children who have caring, responsive relationships with their family members, friendships provide additional reassurance about being integrated into the social community.

Family Influences on Social Competence

Not all children enter middle childhood with the same capacity to make friends and enjoy the benefits of close peer relations. Early family experiences, including the quality of a child's attachment, the family's approach to discipline, and the nature of family conversations, all contribute to a child's **social competence**. By social competence, we mean all the skills involved in the child's ability to form and maintain positive relationships with others (Bloom, 2009). Social competence includes the ability to alter one's behavior to conform to the norms and expectations for interactions in various settings, and with different social partners. For example, a socially competent child can be friendly but not overly friendly with an unfamiliar child, or respectful but not overly intimidated with an unfamiliar adult. Social competence includes strategies for initiating an interaction as well as for sustaining and building an ongoing relationship. Social competence also involves the ability to manage occasional social difficulties, such as being teased, excluded, or ignored. The features of social competence change as children mature, because the expectations for social behavior change with a child's age, and the social settings a child is likely to encounter become more diverse.

Children who have secure attachments in infancy appear to be more socially competent in preschool as evidenced by their greater popularity and their ability to engage more freely in social interactions. They are perceived as more helpful and better able to consider the needs of others (Sroufe & Fleeson, 1986; Park & Waters, 1989). By age 10, the children who were securely attached in infancy have more friends than those with insecure attachments, indicating greater levels of social competence. Various studies have suggested that when two children with histories of secure attachments are friends with one another, those friendships are likely to be more responsive, less critical, and offer more companionship than friendships between children whose attachment history is mismatched (e.g., secure-insecure) (Berlin & Cassidy, 1999).

A mother's discipline techniques, the way she speaks to her child, and her parenting values are all linked to a child's development of social competence. Children whose mothers interact with them in positive, agreeable ways and openly express their feelings are likely to have more positive friendship relations than children whose mothers are harsh or neglectful. These patterns are observable as early as preschool and continue to be found in the elementary grades (Youngblade & Belsky, 1992). In contrast, mothers who use power-assertive discipline techniques and who believe that aggression is an acceptable way of resolving conflicts have children who expect to get their way by asserting power in peer conflicts (Dishion, Patterson, Stoolmiller, & Skinner, 1991; Haskett & Kistner, 1991; McCloskey & Stuewig, 2001). Observations of the social relationships of 8- to 12-year-old children who had been physically abused indicate that these children demonstrate impaired social competence. These children had lower ratings of social status among their peers and were described by their peers as being aggressive and uncooperative, and by their teachers as showing noticeable behavior problems (Salzinger, Feldman, Hammer, & Rosario, 1993). A parent's discipline technique may influence what a child expects in a social interaction. Children who have been exposed to aggressive parenting or violence between their parents may believe that these same strategies will work to establish control and compliance with their peers. As a result, these children are more likely to have conflicts with their friends and to experience social rejection because of their aggressiveness.

Children may directly imitate their parents' interpersonal communication styles and positive or aggressive behaviors. If parents ask a lot of questions and invite their child's opinions, for example, the child may be more likely to show interest in others' ideas and opinions. One study asked children and parents to describe characteristics of parental conflict, and related this to the child's friendship quality (Kitzmann & Cohen, 2003). Children who perceived their parents' conflicts as poorly resolved (e.g., "Even after my parents stop arguing, they stay mad at each other") also had difficulty resolving conflicts in their own close friendships. Children's perceptions of poor parental conflict resolution were correlated with lower friendship quality, including seeing their friends as less of a source of companionship, help, or intimacy.

Parents who are highly restrictive and who try to control their children's behavior are less likely to permit their children to have frequent or diverse peer social interactions. Thus, these children may arrive at the middle childhood years with less experience in peer play (Hart, Ladd, & Burleson, 1990; McCloskey & Stuewig, 2001).

Although parent-child relationships play an important role in the development of social competence, sibling relationships are also important. When asked about their close friends, many adolescents mention their siblings. Sibling relationships provide opportunities for social interactions. Younger siblings are likely to be exposed to the toys, play companions, and play activities of their older siblings, bringing them into contact with more mature play partners at a young age. Depending on the age differences among siblings, many older siblings are expected to play a nurturing or protective role for their younger siblings, thereby advancing their own sense of responsibility and competence. Some families deliberately try to foster close sibling friendships by planning family activities and encouraging at-home play time.

The study of sibling relationships is extremely difficult given the many possible configurations of sibling order, sibling spacing, sex composition of siblings, and family values regarding sibling relationships. There are few consistent results linking birth order to personality characteristics. What is more, relationships among siblings change over time as siblings develop new levels of social understanding. However, it makes sense to consider that children learn patterns of peer interaction with their siblings that they bring to the larger arena of peer relationships at school or in the neighborhood. For example, firstborns are more likely to be self-assured in their position in the family whereas laterborns, having less power or authority, need to devise unique strategies to get their needs met or opinions heard. The more positive the quality of a sibling relationship, the more likely the siblings are to use compromise or reconciliation to resolve conflicts; conflicts between siblings who do not like each other are more likely to result in aggression or submission, often with one child in tears (Recchia & Howe, 2009). In contrast to children with siblings, only children have less experience handling the day-to-day conflicts that arise among siblings, leaving them less prepared to manage peer conflicts outside the family (Kitzmann, Cohen, & Lockwood, 2002). Results from two large studies find that in adulthood, people are likely to form close friendships and romantic relationships with other people of the same birth order (Hartshorne & Salem-Hartshorne, 2009). This is an indication that people learn patterns of social interaction in their sibling relationships that contribute to their social competence and provide a foundation for the establishment of intimacy.

Three Contributions of Friendship to Social Development

Children learn at least three lessons from daily interactions with their peers. The first lesson is an increasing appreciation of the many points of view represented in the peer group. As children play together, they discover that there may be several versions of the same song, different rules for the same game, and different customs for the same holiday. In learning about others through the friendly exchange of ideas, children also learn about themselves. The second lesson teaches children to be sensitive to the social norms and pressures of their peer group. The third lesson is the value of emotional closeness to a peer (Bukowski, 2001).

Perspective Taking and Cognitive Flexibility. The behavior of well-adjusted, competent children is maintained

Courtesy of the Authors

These brothers are starting the first day of the new school year. The older brother, who has been to this school before, will be there to reassure his younger brother. The younger brother will be comforted to know that his older brother is nearby. After a few weeks, they will each form their own sphere of friends, but at the beginning it's reassuring to have sibling support.

in part by a number of social cognitive abilities, including social perspective taking, interpersonal problem solving, information processing, and communicative competence. These cognitive abilities foster a child's entry into successful peer interactions. At the same time, active participation with peers promotes the development of these social cognitive abilities. In a longitudinal study of the influence of friendship on motivation and school adjustment, students who had a reciprocated friendship in sixth grade showed greater prosocial behavior, higher academic achievement, and less emotional distress than those who had no reciprocated friendship. The children whose friends had high levels of prosocial behavior in sixth grade were more likely to express prosocial goals for themselves in eighth grade (Wentzel, Barry, & Caldwell, 2004).

You may recall the discussion of **perspective taking** from Chapter 7 as one of the key factors that contributes to moral development, especially moral reasoning. As children interact with peers who see the world differently, they begin to understand the limits of their own points of view. Piaget (1932/1948) suggested that peers have an important influence in diminishing one another's self-centered outlook precisely because they interact as equals. Children are not forced to accept one another's ideas in quite the same way as they are with adults. They argue, bargain, and eventually compromise in order to maintain friendships. The opportunity to function in peer groups for problem solving and for play leads children away from the egocentrism of early childhood and closer to the eventual flexibility of adult thought.

The benefit of these interactions is most likely to occur when peers have differences in perspective that result in conflicts that must be resolved. The benefits are especially positive for children who interact with slightly more competent peers who can introduce more advanced or flexible approaches to problem solving (Tudge, 1992).

Perspective-taking ability improves other social skills that contribute to the quality of a child's social relationships. Such skills include the ability to analyze social problems, empathize with the emotional state of another person, understand that others may construe a situation differently because of their own information or beliefs, and accept individual differences in personality or abilities (Chalmers & Townsend, 1990; Wellman, 1990; Pillow, 1991; Montgomery, 1993). Children who are sensitive to the variety of perspectives that coexist in a social situation are also likely to be more positively evaluated and trusted by their peers. Those who are perceived as more trustworthy and attuned to the concerns of others are likely to form more friendships (Rotenberg, McDougall, Boulton, Vaillancourt, Fox, & Hymel, 2004). An interactive process is thus set in motion. Children who have opportunities to participate in peer friendships make progress in achieving new levels of interpersonal understanding. As interpersonal understanding grows, children acquire the skills and sensitivity with which to be more effective with—and usually more valued by—their peers.

Social Norms and Peer Group Pressure. The peer group evolves **norms** for acceptance and **rejection**. As children become aware of these norms, they begin to experience pressure to conform to the peer group. Adults, particularly teachers, then lose some of their power to influence children's behavior. In the classroom, the early-school-age child focuses primarily on the teacher as a source of approval and acceptance. By age 9 or 10, children perceive the peer group as an equally significant audience. Children often *play* to the class instead of responding to the teacher. The roles of class joker, class snob, and class hero or heroine emerge during middle childhood and serve as ways of gaining approval from the peer group.

The need for **peer approval** becomes a powerful force toward **conformity**. Children learn to dress, talk, and joke in ways that are acceptable to their peers. They learn to inhibit the expression of certain emotional reactions—especially sadness, vulnerability, and anger—in order to present a cool, competent public image to their peers (Salisch, 2001). Heterosexual antagonism, which is common at this stage, is perpetuated by pressures toward conformity. If all the fifth-grade boys hate girls, Johnny is not very likely to admit openly that he likes to play with Mary. There are indications that perceived pressures to conform are stronger in the fifth and sixth grades than at later times, even though the importance of specific peer groups has not yet peaked (Gavin & Furman, 1989).

Close Friends. Peer acceptance is not the same thing as close friendship (Gifford-Smith & Brownell, 2003). To gain peer acceptance, children may need to conform to group norms for dress, action, and attitude; they may have to conceal certain strong feelings (Lansford & Parker, 1999; Salisch, 2001). With close friends, there is a more intimate level of disclosure, trust, and supportiveness. Close friendships are often measured through a *mutual nomination*

strategy. Children are given a roster of the names of their classmates and asked to circle the names of children who are their friends. When two children circle each other's names, they are identified as friends. **Close friendships** are then identified by the children as those characterized by high levels of shared activity, companionship, help or guidance, and ease of conflict resolution (Asher & Paquette, 2003). In the context of these friendships, children share private jokes, develop secret codes, tell family secrets, set out on adventures, and help each other in times of trouble. They enjoy spending time together. They also fight, threaten, break up, and reunite.

Sullivan (1949) pointed out the significance of these early friendships as building blocks for adult relationships. Intimacy in best friend relationships provides a degree of understanding and openness that is often not possible with parents or family members. Within these friendships, private thoughts and fantasies are shared without the worry of being judged as silly, gross, or impractical. It is significant that the child experiences love for and closeness to a peer rather than an adult. The relationship is more likely to allow for mutuality of power, status, and access to resources (Youniss, 1980). Conflicts in a relationship may be worked out in terms that the children control. One child cannot take away another child's allowance or send the other child out of the room when a conflict arises. The children must resolve their differences within the framework of their commitment to each other.

The stability of close friendships is quite variable, with some children remaining friends over several years, despite changes in classrooms and schools, whereas other children seem to be in different friendship relationships every few months (Kindermann, 1996). The structure of a school or classroom influences friendship formation and stability.

Carly and Michelle have been best friends since first grade. They love to spend time together whether they're washing the dog, going for bike rides, or listening to music. They depend on each other for fun, support, and problem solving.

Copyright © Nancy Sheehan/PhotoEdit

Close friends often see each other during the school day in classes and extracurricular activities. In schools that promote stable classroom groupings, where children remain in the same homeroom or class group from one grade to the next, friendship groups also remain more stable (Neckerman, 1996).

Close friendships are influenced by attractiveness, intelligence, classroom social status, and satisfaction with and commitment to the best friend (Clark & Ayers, 1988). In a study of more than 800 children in grades 3 to 5, 78% had at least one reciprocating best friend (i.e., one child named another as one of three best friends, and that other child named the first child high on the list as well), and 55% had a *very* best friend. More girls than boys had best friends, and the quality of their best friendships was somewhat different. Girls and boys described their best friend relationships quite similarly with respect to having low levels of conflict or betrayal and high levels of companionship and shared recreational activities. However, girls described their best friend relationships as having higher levels of caring and personal validation ("makes me feel good about my ideas"), intimacy ("we always tell each other our problems"), help and guidance ("help each other with schoolwork a lot"), and conflict resolution ("we make up easily when we have a fight") (Parker & Asher, 1993).

Loneliness

With the increased emphasis on friendship and peer acceptance comes the risk of peer rejection and feelings of loneliness. In the period from preschool to middle childhood, issues of shyness, social anxiety, and peer victimization become increasingly salient. Experiences of social rejection or dissatisfaction in friendship quality become linked to a more general sense of anxiety in the school environment and a decline in self-worth (Asher & Gazelle, 1999; Asher, Parkhurst, Hymel, & Williams, 1999; Fordham & Stevenson-Hinde, 1999). By third grade, some children are characterized as anxious and solitary. They are shy, typically watching their peers without joining in, wanting to interact with their peers but afraid that they will be socially awkward or will not be accepted (Rubin, Coplan, & Bowker, 2009).

Three social characteristics combine to increase a child's experiences of **loneliness**. First, children who are anxious and solitary have trouble forming close friendships that provide emotional closeness and companionship; they are more likely to feel lonely. It is not necessarily important to have many friends. However, children who have at least one enduring, high-quality friendship are less likely to experience loneliness (Nangle, Erdley, Newan, Mason, & Carpenter, 2003). Second, some children are systematically excluded. When they ask if they can play, other children say no. They don't get invited to children's parties or are the last to be chosen for teams. Peer rejection is especially powerful in producing feelings of loneliness. Children who experience a generally positive level of peer acceptance feel less alone than those who are rejected by their peers. This relationship between peer rejection and loneliness has been found across countries and grades from kindergarten through middle school (Crick & Ladd, 1993; Asher & Paquette, 2003). Third, among the children who are anxious and solitary, those who experience exclusion or are rejected by peers become increasingly socially helpless, anticipating rejection and being unwilling to take new risks to reach out or initiate social exchanges (Gazelle & Druben, 2009). Children who tend to blame themselves for their lack of social acceptance feel more lonely and are possibly less likely to believe that they can do anything to improve their situation. Those who are withdrawn, victimized, or bullied report higher levels of loneliness than other unpopular children (Kochenderfer-Ladd & Wardrop, 2001).

What can lonely or socially anxious children do to increase their sense of closeness to friends? **Cognitive restructuring** techniques have been used to help children deal with social anxiety (Marini, Dane, & Volk, 2010). The central feature of cognitive restructuring is to identify thoughts that increase strong emotions such as anger, anxiety, or sadness, challenge their accuracy, and replace them with interpretations that are more realistic and less disruptive to adaptive behavior (Dombeck & Wells-Moran, 2010). With regard to social anxiety, students learn to monitor changes in their anxiety level, and to become aware of the thoughts that accompany this increase in anxiety. For example, a student may recognize that his anxiety rises in class when he thinks about answering a question out loud, because he assumes that his classmates would think he is stupid if he were to give an incorrect answer. Once these assumptions have been identified, the student may be guided to look for evidence that these assumptions are correct, and to consider alternative interpretations. The student may be encouraged to take a more accepting view, recognizing that everyone makes mistakes. When other students make mistakes, he does not usually think badly of them. To strengthen this perspective and remain calm, the student might practice self-talk, such as "It's OK to make mistakes; that's how we learn." Through cognitive restructuring, socially anxious students learn to recognize the sources of their anxiety and practice strategies for redefining the situation so that they can be more confident about taking initiative in peer situations.

Some children have discovered that online communication provides an environment where they can experience greater levels of self-disclosure and depth of communication with friends. The Internet is increasingly being used as a way to supplement face-to-face friendship interactions through Instant Messaging (Peter, Valkenburg, & Schouten, 2005). Many children use the Internet to participate in chat with strangers, most use it to maintain their existing network of friends, and some form friendships with strangers through chat who then become face-to-face friends (Walther & Parks, 2002). In a study of Dutch children, 61% of the participants who were 10 and 11 years old used the Internet for online communication. Almost 90% of those children communicated with preexisting friends (Valkenburg & Peter, 2007). Children who described themselves as either lonely or socially anxious were more likely to perceive online communication as facilitating greater breadth and depth of communication. Those socially anxious children who perceived the Internet as offering a way to achieve greater intimacy in communication used the Internet more often and described their friendships as closer than socially anxious children who used online communication infrequently. The authors suggest that socially anxious children have more difficulty with face-to-face self-disclosure. For these children, the value of the Internet is not for increasing general social interaction or for forming new relationships but for allowing greater levels of intimacy with existing friends, unencumbered by the difficult visual and auditory cues that may disrupt disclosure in face-to-face interactions. Unfortunately, online technologies and text messaging can also be used in a hostile way to send messages of rejection. Youth can use electronic media to embarrass, harass, or threaten their peers.

Rejection

Rejection hurts. Studies of rejection find different patterns of reaction, including emotional numbness, changes in mood reflecting new levels of sadness or feeling bad, and decreases in self-esteem. Two basic needs appear to be thwarted when a child experiences social rejection—the need for control and the need for belonging. Under some conditions, children protect themselves from the negative feelings associated with rejection by withdrawing from social interactions; in other conditions they may act aggressively to try to reassert control (Gerber & Wheeler, 2009; Baumeister, DeWall, & Vohs, 2009).

Research has identified three types of children who experience peer rejection. Some children who are rejected are disruptive and aggressive with their peers; others are socially withdrawn but do not exhibit aggressive tendencies; a third group has been described as both aggressive and withdrawn (French, 1988, 1990; Hymel, Bowker, & Woody, 1993). Children who are physically aggressive are identified as early as toddlerhood. Aggressiveness has been noted as a feature of personality that is linked to difficulties in emotional regulation, exposure to power assertive or harsh parenting, and reduced levels of empathy. Genetic and environmental factors combine to support a child's aggressive and oppositional behavior (Burt & Neiderhiser, 2009). **Aggressive-rejected** children, often referred to as *bullies*, are more likely than nonaggressive children to attribute hostile intentions to others. They see peer interactions as threatening and say they would be likely to use aggressive strategies in response to negative peer behaviors (Quiggle, Garber, Panak, & Dodge, 1992; Waldman, 1996). Aggressive-rejected children tend to have an exaggerated idea of their competence and social status. They are less accurate in reading their own social status among their classmates, although they are just as accurate as other children in reading the social status of others (Zakriski & Coie, 1996). The Applying Theory and Research to Life box on page 298 discusses bullying and a school program designed to prevent it.

Children as young as 8 or 9 can share information with others on social networking sites. They can be in contact with friends from school, the neighborhood, or summer travels or form new friendships as penpals and Facebook friends with children they have never met face to face. Sadly, some children become targets of cyberbullying, which creates a new context for teasing and experiences of peer rejection.

© David Lichtneker/Alamy

However, not all aggressive children are rejected. One study looked at the relationship of antisocial and prosocial characteristics of young children and their social standing in the classroom (Farmer & Rodkin, 1996). Children in four different types of classroom groups were compared: academic giftedness, emotional and behavioral disorders, general education, and learning disabilities. Across all four types of classrooms, the most popular and socially central children were more athletic, cooperative, and studious and were rated as having more leadership skills than the less popular children. Aggressive, disruptive characteristics were strongly associated with peer rejection or isolation for girls. For boys in the general education classes, however, aggressive behavior was positively associated with popularity. Thus, one is led to consider person-environment fit in evaluating the relationship between aggressiveness and peer rejection. In some classroom contexts, aggressiveness, particularly among boys, may be a viable path toward bonding with other boys and asserting one's leadership, especially for boys who cannot achieve notice through their academic performance (Poulin & Boivin, 2000). Subsequent studies have found that in many cases, bullies deliberately choose targets who are already rejected by their peers, thus minimizing the risk of social rejection from other children. Moreover, boys who bully other boys are admired by some girls who are possibly being attracted to this gender-stereotyped dominant male behavior (Dijkstra, Lindenber, & Veenstra, 2007; Veenstra, Lindenberg, Munniksma, & Dijkstra, 2010).

Children in the **withdrawn** group tend to be inhibited, anxious, and interpersonally reserved. They have a negative self-concept and tend to interpret negative peer reactions as resulting from their own personal failings (Hymel et al., 1993). They have difficulty dealing with stress. These children may exhibit inappropriate emotions and display various unusual behavioral mannerisms that are likely to draw ridicule from their peers (French, 1988). For example, studies of children with developmental disabilities and language disorders suggest that these children begin to have more relationship problems in the upper elementary school grades. Their social status among classmates is likely to decline, they may become targets of bullying, and they are less likely to be involved in reciprocal friendships. Over time, children who experience a combination of anxiety, lack of a close friend, and peer victimization are likely to continue to be targets of victimization (Asher & Gazelle, 1999; Goldbaum, Craig, Pepler, & Connolly, 2003; Gazelle, 2008).

Children in the **aggressive-withdrawn** group tend to be the least well liked of all three types of rejected children. They exhibit anxiety, poor self-control, and social withdrawal in addition to aggressive behavior. They are rated by other children as incompetent in school ability; unattractive; showing the poorest skills in leadership, cooperation, or sense of humor; and the most likely to behave inappropriately in school. Aggressive-withdrawn children are similar to the bully-victims described in the box on bullying (Marini, Dane, Bosacki, & YLC-CURA, 2006). Having been excluded or rejected by their peers, they respond by lashing out against children who are more vulnerable than they. Despite high levels of peer rejection, aggressive-withdrawn children do not have the same low self-concept and negative view of their abilities as the withdrawn children. They are likely to have future adjustment problems and often require psychiatric treatment in adolescence or adulthood (Coie & Krehbiel, 1984; Hymel et al., 1990).

Although we tend to think of peer rejection as having significant implications for the formation of interpersonal relationships, a substantial body of research points to links between peer group acceptance or rejection and school adjustment. Beginning in the early school grades, peer rejection is associated with school problems, including school avoidance, negative attitudes about school, less engagement with school-related tasks, and a less cooperative orientation toward teacher requests and group activities. The longer this peer rejection lasts, the more impact it seems to have on a child's engagement with the learning environment and the academic challenges of school (Ladd, Herald-Brown, & Reiser, 2008).

Concrete Operations

Objective 2. To describe the development of concrete operational thought, including conservation, classification skills, mathematical reasoning, and the child's ability to understand and monitor his or her own knowledge and understanding.

Children's abilities to analyze and manage social relationships, including friendships, are linked to their ability to solve other kinds of problems. Advances in reasoning about the physical world may stimulate new ways of handling complex social situations; similarly, engaging in complex social situations may enhance the child's ability to bring flexibility and perspective to problems of the physical world.

Thinking back to the period of infancy, the discussion of infant intelligence focused on the establishment of sensory and motor patterns used to explore the environment, manipulate means-end relationships, clarify the nature of physical objects, and begin to form simple categories. During toddlerhood, cognition moves beyond the experiential domain as children develop a variety of representational skills that free them from complete reliance on their immediate physical environment. Toddlers create novel situations and solve problems by using thought, fantasy, and language. Piaget (Piaget & Inhelder, 1969) suggested that at about age 6 or 7, a qualitatively new form of thinking develops, which he referred to as **concrete operational thought**. This type of reasoning guides thought by imposing logical rules on one's judgments, leading to the acceptance of certain inferences that adhere to the logic as more compelling or convincing than others (Moshman, 2004).

Bullying

BULLYING IS A common and long-standing problem for children in many cultures. A child is considered to be bullied when repeatedly exposed to negative actions by peers, including physical contact, harsh and degrading words and gestures, exploitation, and exclusion. Dan Olweus (1995), who has been studying aggression and bullying since the 1970s, has estimated that roughly 9% of children ages 7 through 16 have been victims of bullying, and 7% of school-age children have bullied others. This suggests that as many as 5 million children in the United States are involved in problems of bullying or peer intimidation each year.

What are the characteristics of bullies and their victims? Bullies typically are physically stronger than their peers. They have strong needs for power and enjoy being in control. They have been reared in a family environment characterized by indifference, low involvement, and lack of warmth. This context results in little sense of personal empathy and a high degree of hostility toward others.

Bullies are often aggressive toward teachers and other authority figures as well as toward peers. It is not uncommon for aggressive boys to have best friends who are also aggressive. Within these relationships, the boys encourage each other toward rule breaking (Bagwell & Coie, 2004). Finally, bullies often find some reward or reinforcement for their behavior, especially when they coerce their victims into giving them money, taking things of value, and being treated with respect by other peers.

Bullies often use their size to intimidate their victims.

Our understanding of the nature of bullies has been expanded by research by Jaana Juvonen and her colleagues (Juvonen, Graham, & Schuster, 2003). In research involving over 1900 middle school children, peer nominations were used to identify bullies (those who start fights, use put-downs and make fun of other kids, and those who spread mean rumors about others) and victims (those who get pushed around, are made fun of, and about whom nasty rumors are often started). Children were asked to nominate up to four classmates who fit the description of bullies and victims. These peer nominations were accompanied by teacher ratings, and self-report measures of psychological distress, including depression, social anxiety,

and loneliness. Several of the results were unexpected. First, there were two kinds of bullies, those who were identified by their peers as higher than average in aggression and low in victimization (bullies); and those who were both high in aggression and high in victimization (bully-victims). Second, the bullies had few psychological problems and were perceived as being cool by their classmates although the classmates did not want to spend time with them. The fact that bullies enjoy both high social status and report few psychological problems helps explain why bullying is so hard to modify. Bullies enjoy their social reputation and, although feared by others, do not seem to be bothered by the fact that many of the children avoid them.

In contrast, bully-victims were more depressed and lonely than bullies, had lower social status than bullies, were less popular than bullies, and were more likely to be avoided by their classmates than any other group. They were described by their teachers as having the most conduct problems and being the most disengaged from school of any of the groups. These bully-victims are most like the aggressive-withdrawn children described previously. They are likely to be children who have been victimized by others and subsequently lash out as a result of shame, rage, and a desire for revenge.

Victims of bullying commonly have low self-esteem. They are anxious, cautious, and fit into the withdrawn category of rejected children. In comparison to the bullies, the victims, especially boys, are physically weaker.

The word **operation** refers to an action that is performed on an object or a set of objects. A **mental operation** is an action that is carried out in thought rather than in behavior. Piaget argued that such mental operations are built on some physical relationship that the younger child can perform but cannot articulate. For example, a toddler can arrange a graduated set of circles on a stick so that the largest circle is at the bottom of the stick and the smallest circle is at the top. The child does not have a verbal label for the ordering operation but can perform it. With the emergence of concrete operations, children begin to consider a variety of actions that can be performed on objects and can do so mentally without having to do them physically. Thus, a mental operation is a representation or scheme for an alteration in the relationships among objects. One of the most powerful mental operations is *reversibility*. One can imagine an action, such as filling a glass with water, and then undoing the action by emptying the glass. One can even imagine adding salt to water and then removing the salt, even though this would be difficult in practice. In contrast to sensorimotor

When attacked, they do not retaliate. As a result, the abuse continues and often escalates. In Juvonen's research, children who are perceived by their peers as victims also report the highest levels of depression, social anxiety, and loneliness; have the lowest social status as rated by peers; and are described by teachers as the least popular of the children. They are the most marginalized of the children, and, as a result, may be additionally vulnerable because they have no classmates who will defend them or intervene when they are being attacked.

Sexual orientation and race/ethnicity are two factors that are commonly intertwined with bullying. Gay, lesbian, and bisexual students are targets of frequent bullying. Surveys of LGBTQ youth find that 80% say that their teachers never or rarely intervened to stop homophobic joking or bullying (SPLC Report, 2010). Children who are members of a numeric ethnic minority in their school are more vulnerable to harassment than children who are in the ethnic majority. When a school is ethnically diverse and no group is in a clear numeric majority, children who are victims of bullying are more likely to attribute the problem to the bullies or to conditions of the school environment that allow this kind of harassment than to blame themselves (Graham & Juvonen, 2002; Graham, 2004).

The complex social dynamics surrounding bullying call for a multidimensional approach to intervention. Olweus has designed a school-based intervention program to reduce bullying and prevent children from feeling harassed and degraded at school (Olweus, Limber, & Mihalic, 1999). The program, which has been implemented in Norway, the southeastern United States, England, and Germany, calls for intervention at three levels: the school, the classroom, and the individual. Intervention begins with awareness of the extent of bullying and victimization within the school through the use of an assessment survey. Once the nature of the problem and the seriousness of its impact on students have been identified, interventions are implemented that focus on five basic principles:

1. Create an environment in which children experience warmth, interest, and frequent involvement with adults.
2. Set clear, firm limits about unacceptable behavior that are endorsed at school and home.
3. When rules and limits are violated, sanctions should be nonhostile and nonviolent, but consistently enforced.
4. Student activities during and after school must be monitored through the presence of adult supervision. The topic of monitoring and appropriate adult supervision must be discussed with parents during PTA meetings and parent conferences.
5. Students need to meet regularly with teachers to discuss problems associated with the social environment of the school and to work on ways of improving the school climate.

For more information about 12 programs that have been reviewed and positively evaluated to result in violence prevention, visit the Web site for the Center for the Study and Prevention of Violence at the University of Colorado.

Critical Thinking Questions

1. Why do you think that some bullies are popular and have high status among their peers? What are some implications of having popular bullies for the students' social structure?
2. What might be some consequences of being a victim of bullying? How might being a victim affect subsequent school achievement? Peer relationships?
3. What might be the negative consequences of bullying for the school environment more generally, beyond the impact on specific victims?
4. What do you think are the likely trajectories for bullies as they move into adolescence and adulthood? Do you think being a bully is a "stable" trait that will continue to be expressed in some fashion in later stages of life?
5. What strategies can you think of that would improve the school environment for gay, lesbian, or bisexual students?
6. If you were to evaluate a school-based program to prevent bullying, what outcome measures would you select? In other words, what would you consider evidence that a program to prevent bullying was effective?

---

schemes, which unfold in a behavior sequence, operations can be done and undone in the mind (Lerner, 2002).

Piaget (1972a) used the term **concrete** to contrast this quality of thinking to the more hypothetical reasoning of adolescents and adults. The child reasons about objects and the relations among them but has difficulty entertaining hypothetical statements or propositions. Thinking is typically focused on real objects that exist in the world, even if the child is not seeing or manipulating these objects at the moment. For example, children can reason about problems involving the grouping of trees into different categories and identifying the features of these categories. However, if you pose a problem involving trees that migrate from North to South with the seasons, a child in the concrete stage of thinking will have difficulty even entertaining the problem, because trees do not migrate. Piaget's characterization of intelligence in middle childhood as concrete operational thought is only one perspective. In the Applying Theory and Research to Life box on page 306, three theoretical views about the nature of intelligence are compared.

Tony has created a plan, and is focusing seriously to implement his plan as he builds his brick structure. The combination of fine motor skills, computational skills, and logical reasoning come together in the design of his project. For many children, materials that offer opportunities to design and build new structures are a source of satisfaction throughout middle childhood.

During the stage of concrete operations, the three conceptual skills that have received the most attention are (1) conservation, (2) classification, and (3) computational skills. Over the period of middle childhood, children apply these skills to achieve a clearer understanding of the logic, order, and predictability of the physical world. As children take a new approach to problem solving through the use of the logical principles associated with concrete operational thought, they generalize these principles to their thinking about friendships, team play and other games with rules, and their own self-evaluation.

As the order of the physical world becomes more apparent, children begin to seek logic and order in social and personal domains as well. Sometimes, this search for order is frustrated by the unpredictability of the social world. At other times, children use their enhanced capacities for reasoning to solve interpersonal problems and to arrange their daily life so that it better meets their interests and needs. A hallmark of this period is an increase in logical, focused problem solving. Children are able

to consider two competing explanations, look at a problem from another person's point of view as well as their own, and, using this information, plan a strategy to reach a goal.

Conservation

The basic meaning of **conservation** is that physical matter does not magically appear or disappear despite changes in form, shape, or container. The concept of conservation can be applied to a variety of dimensions, including mass, weight, number, length, and volume. A child who conserves is able to resist perceptual cues that alter the form of an object, insisting that the quantity remains the same despite the change in form. One of the most common problems of this type that Piaget investigated involves *conservation of mass*. The child is presented with two clay balls and is asked to tell whether or not they are equal. Once the child is satisfied that the balls are equal, one of them is flattened out into a pancake. The child is then asked, "Which has more—this one [the pancake] or this one [the ball]?" Sometimes, the child is also asked whether the clay pieces are still the same. The child who does not conserve might say that the pancake has more clay because it is a lot wider than the ball. This child is still in the preoperational stage of thought: She is using personal perceptions to make judgments rather than logic. In contrast, the child who conserves knows that the two pieces of clay are still identical in mass and can explain why.

Children eventually use the three concepts illustrated in Figure 8.1 to ascertain that equality in any physical dimension has not been altered. First, the child may explain that the pancake has the same amount of clay as the ball; no clay has been added or taken away. This is an example of the concept of **identity**: The pancake is still the *same* clay, and nothing has been changed except its shape. Second, the child may point out that the experimenter can turn the pancake back into a ball. This is an example of the concept of **reversibility**. The child becomes aware that operations can be reversed, so that their effects are nullified. Third, the child may notice that, although the pancake has a larger circumference, the ball is much thicker. When the child can simultaneously manipulate two dimensions, such as circumference and thickness, we observe the concept of **reciprocity**. In the

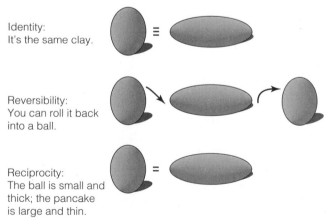

Identity:
It's the same clay.

Reversibility:
You can roll it back
into a ball.

Reciprocity:
The ball is small and
thick; the pancake
is large and thin.

FIGURE 8.1 Three Concepts That Contribute to Conservation

Image copyright Dmitry Naumov 2010. Used under license from Shutterstock.com clay ball example, change in one dimension is compensated for by change in another; the total mass remains the same. With consolidation of the concepts of identity, reversibility, and reciprocity, the child is able to conserve in any physical dimension. There appears to be a developmental sequence in the capacity to conserve. Children generally conserve mass and number earliest, weight later, and volume last.

Conservation may not generalize across all of the physical modes. For example, children who are unable to conserve quantity in an unfamiliar object, such as poker chips, can do so with a more familiar one, such as M&M's (Gulko, Doyle, Serbin, & White, 1988). In one study, girls were able to perform a conservation of liquid task when it was presented in the standard manner of comparing the experimenter's glass and their own. However, when the task was embedded in a story where juice had to be divided between two dolls, their performance declined. Evidence of a lack of generalizability of knowledge from in-school to out-of-school contexts is found in other areas of reasoning, especially mathematical codes and scientific principles (Perret-Clermont, Perret, & Bell, 1991).

Extensions of Piaget's Ideas about Conservation. Researchers have raised questions about the meaning of conservation tasks, the timing of the emergence of conservation, and the possibility of teaching children to conserve. The way the task is presented and the kinds of questions asked may influence a child's responses. For example, the task may emphasize identity or equivalence. In an *identity* task, the child is asked to judge whether a single clay ball has the same amount of clay after it has been rolled into a sausage. In an *equivalence* task, there are two balls of clay. The child is asked to judge whether the ball that is rolled into a sausage has the same amount of clay as the standard, comparison ball. Some studies have shown that children can perform the identity task earlier than the equivalence task; others have shown the opposite; and still others have argued that identity and equivalence are achieved at the same time (Silverstein et al., 1982). In a study of 5- to 7-year-olds, children were asked to tell how the materials looked, and then to tell how they really were. Giving the child this distinction between appearance and reality resulted in more correct answers than the standard procedure, in which this distinction was not made (Bijstra, Van Geert, & Jackson, 1989).

In a study of fifth graders, half the students were identified as being in the preoperational stage, even at age 10. This finding in itself suggests that Piaget's view that children will enter the stage of concrete operational reasoning through active construction and experimentation around the age of 6 or 7 is not universally true. The study examined strategies for enhancing concrete operational reasoning through guided intervention. Half the children received training involving special activities intended to promote logical problem solving and abstract thinking. Children received the training in English or Spanish depending on their language competence. This intervention was found to be successful in promoting concrete operational thought (Bakken, Thompson, Clark, Johnson, & Dwyer, 2001).

Theoretically, Piaget's view of development suggests that there is a period of maturational readiness for the application of logical operations to physical objects. Left to their own process of exploration and experimentation, Piaget argued that children would discover the regularities and operations that underlie conservation. Showing a child a conservation problem and then explaining and reinforcing the correct answer should not be very effective if the child is not ready to assimilate this information. However, research has shown that it is possible to train young children of preschool age to conserve (Brainerd, 1977). These early training studies have both theoretical and practical implications. The training studies suggest that it is possible to introduce such concepts as identity and reversibility so that children as young as 4 can achieve conservation. They also transfer conservation from the tasks involved in training to other materials and dimensions (Field, 1981; May & Norton, 1981).

An important element in modifying a child's approach to conservation is being confronted by someone else's reasoning that contradicts one's own. For this contradiction to be effective, however, the child must be approaching a level of readiness to reorganize his thinking, and the gap between the child's current level of reasoning and the new ideas must not be too great. This reminds us of Vygotsky's concept of the zone of proximal development. The implication here is that entry into a new stage of thought may emerge earlier and may be more readily influenced by the social environment than Piaget's cognitive developmental theory predicts. However, Piaget himself was not especially impressed by faster and sooner. He believed in the enduring benefits of personal discovery.

Practically speaking, research has demonstrated that preschool and kindergarten-age children can integrate and apply more abstract concepts than educators once believed they could. For example, studies of children as young as 3 and 4 have shown that they understand the idea that materials are made of tiny particles that retain their properties even when they are invisible. They can use this notion of particles to explain how a substance, such as sugar, continues to exist in a solution and retain its sweetness even when it is invisible (Au, Sidle, & Rollins, 1993; Rosen & Rozin, 1993). In a study focused on estimating volume, many children in kindergarten and first grade were able to consider the integration of three dimensions—height, width, and depth—to guess how many small cubes would be needed to build a larger cube. Their estimates suggest that at even this young age, children can integrate information from three dimensions (Ebersbach, 2009). Early childhood educators have found that, through a planned program of exploring, experimenting, and describing the transformation of materials, young children can be guided to conceptualize the physical world in a systematic, logical manner.

Classification Skills

Classification was first discussed in Chapter 5, describing infants' basic **categorization** skills. **Classification** is the ability to identify the properties of categories, to relate categories or classes to one another, and to use categorical information to solve problems. Two components of classification provide the essential ability to apply knowledge from a known or familiar instance to a new instance: categorization and induction. Categorization simply means that if one apple belongs to the category of fruit, then *all* apples are fruit. You do not need to learn this categorization label for each type of apple. Induction refers to the realization that whatever holds true for one member of a category is likely to hold true for other members as well. For example, water and juice are both liquids. If you can pour water, you can pour juice. Other substances classified as liquids should also have this property—even substances one has never seen. The value of classification skills is not merely to organize objects or experiences into classes, but to take advantage of what is known about these categories to make inferences about the characteristics and dynamics of members of the same categories, members of hierarchically related categories, and objects that are not members of a specific category (Kalish & Gelman, 1992; Lopez, Gelman, Gutheil, & Smith, 1992; Farrar, Raney, & Boyer, 1992).

One component of classification skills is the ability to group objects according to some dimension that they share. The other component is the ability to order subgroups hierarchically, so that each new grouping will include all previous subgroups. Vygotsky (1962) suggested a method for studying classification in young children. Children are presented with a variety of wooden blocks that differ in shape, size, and color. Under each block is a nonsense syllable that is hidden from view. The children are instructed to select, one at a time, all the blocks that have the same syllable. The youngest children, who would be characterized as preoperational in Piaget's stage theory, tend to select blocks by their color. Their technique for grouping is highly associative. They choose each new block to match some characteristic of the previous selection, but they do not hold in mind a single concept that guides their choices.

Children who have entered the stage of concrete operations tend to focus on one dimension at first, perhaps shape, and continue to select blocks until they discover that they have made an incorrect choice. They use this discovery to change their hypothesis about which characteristics of the blocks are associated with the nonsense syllable. This classification task demonstrates the child's ability to hold a concept in mind and to make a series of decisions based on it. It also demonstrates that during the stage of concrete operations, children can use information from their mistakes to revise their problem-solving strategy.

Piaget studied reasoning about class hierarchies or class inclusion by asking questions about whether a group of objects included more members of one subtype than of the group as a whole (Piaget, 1941/1952; see also Chapman & McBride, 1992). Thus, when a set of pictures shows three ducks, six sparrows, and two robins, one might ask, "Are there more sparrows or more birds in these pictures?" This is an unusual kind of question, one that children are rarely asked. By the age of 8 or 9, however, many children can respond correctly because they recognize the distinction between classes and subclasses. In order to handle such

Masterfile (Royalty-Free Div.)

Laura loves to sit and sort her change into piles (categories) of coins and then to see how high she can stack each type of coin.

problems, children have to inhibit their tendency to reinterpret the question in line with a more common comparison, such as, "Are there more sparrows than ducks?"

In one study of class inclusion reasoning, an intriguing pattern was found. Children of ages 3 and 4, who could not repeat the question and clearly had not learned any rules about classes, were more likely to answer correctly than children of ages 5 and 6. Children of ages 7 and 8 performed better than any of the younger children. The 5- and 6-year-olds, who answered quickly and confidently, were consistently incorrect. They seemed unable to inhibit the more obvious comparison in order to consider the actual question (McCabe, Siegel, Spence, & Wilkinson, 1982).

Two processes appear to contribute to classification judgments among young children. First, perceived similarities among target objects guide judgments about whether the objects belong to the same category. Second, verbal labels play an important role in cuing children into the similarities among objects. When no verbal labels are available, children judge whether two objects are members of the same category based on the number of similar features. In comparison to adults, who rely less on verbal labels than on similarity of features, young children expect the labels to provide important information about objects, but they do not rely solely on these labels to guide their judgment (Sloutsky & Fisher, 2004).

From ages 6 to 12, children's knowledge of categories and of the information associated with them expands dramatically. Moreover, children have a broad range of categories available into which to incorporate a novel observation. The capacity for classifying and categorizing has been explored in relation to specific domains, such as health and illness or concepts of the family. For example, children were told about 21 different human groupings and asked to say whether these groupings were a family: "Here are Mr. Mead and his son, Tom. They live together, just the two of them. Are they a family?" The youngest participants (4- to 6-year-olds) had trouble accepting examples involving single parents or biologically related people who did not live in the same home as instances of a family. Principles of biological relatedness and shared physical residence were both important to these children's view of a family. By middle childhood, the children were able to accept a wider variety of groups as meeting certain essential criteria of a family, usually biological relatedness and emotional closeness. Emotional closeness was endorsed by 80% of the participants as a defining feature of a family and was used repeatedly as a basis for judging whether a specific instance of a grouping could be considered a family or not (Newman, Roberts, & Syre, 1993).

Categorization skills can be used in an active way to construct and constrain behavior. Butler and Weatherall (2006) observed the natural use of categorization in the play sequences of 6- and 7-year-olds. Children systematically mapped participants to categories of play roles, and used these categories to establish appropriate behaviors within the play sequence. The use of membership categories, such as good and bad pirates, provides a guide toward the kinds of actions, props, and strengths or vulnerabilities children are allowed within the pretense. These categories are used to include new players to the situation, and to guide the initiation of new play sequences that will fit with the established categories.

Computational Skills

A third characteristic of concrete operational thought is the development of **computational skills**. The number symbols (1, 2, etc.) can provide three types of information: nominal, cardinal, and ordinal. *Nominal numbers* are used like names, such as the number on a football player's jersey or a home address. They do not refer to an amount. *Cardinal numbers* refer to a quantity (e.g., two siblings or 5 minutes). *Ordinal numbers* refer to the position or progression of things in a set (e.g., first, second, third) rather than to a specific amount. In the transition from preoperational to concrete operational thought, children shift from using numbers in a nominal way (knowing and reciting the names of numbers, or reciting their street address) to the ordinal and cardinal nature of numbers.

Conservation of number is achieved around age 6 or 7 (Halford & Boyle, 1985). Once they have acquired the operations underlying conservation of number, children understand that certain physical transformations will not alter the number of units in a set. If 10 poker chips are lined up in a row, the number remains constant whether they are spread out, squeezed tightly together, or stacked. Children can use counting to answer a "how many" question sometime between the ages of 3 and 4. For example, they can assign one number to each item in a set of four poker chips and tell you that there are four chips in all. However, young children have more difficulty selecting a set of six chips from a larger pile, or establishing that two sets of chips are equal in number. They also have trouble solving verbal story problems when no concrete objects are present (Jordan et al., 1992; Sophian, 1998).

Young children differ widely in their mathematical knowledge and problem-solving skills. Success in doing addition and subtraction requires counting knowledge, working memory, understanding of part-whole relationships, familiarity with the language and features of specific problems, and experience with a variety of strategies for estimating answers, solving problems, and checking one's answers (Canobi, Reeve, & Pattison, 2003; Ginsburg & Pappas, 2004). The ability to solve addition problems begins with an understanding that cardinal numbers refer to quantities and that there is a relationship between counting objects and adding or subtracting them as part of a larger set or whole (Canobi, 2004; Zur & Gelman, 2004). Early number competence includes an understanding that each number is one more than the number preceding it and one less than the number following it. This understanding allows children to make quick and accurate judgments about the value of small quantities, and to understand the logic behind joining or separating of sets (e.g., 5 and 2 makes 7; 7 take away 2 leaves 5). During the first few elementary grades, most children acquire the complementary operations of addition, subtraction, multiplication, and division and learn to apply these operations no matter what specific objects or quantities are involved. Longitudinal studies show that children's number competence and rate of growth in understanding numbers in kindergarten and first grade are strong predictors of their mathematics achievement by third grade, a point at which many children are required to take mathematics assessment tests (Jordan, Kaplan, Ramineni, & Locuniak, 2009).

There is a difference between the cognitive understanding of single computational operations, such as addition and subtraction, and the coordination of computational abilities to solve mathematics problems (Montague, 2006). As the problems become more complex, involving larger numbers, more numbers, or numbers embedded in story problems, same-grade children demonstrate notable differences in the speed and accuracy of their solutions. The explanation for these differences may rest with the interaction between teachers and their students. Teachers differ in their confidence about their own mathematical abilities, as well as their ability to assess children's understanding of mathematics and to select appropriate approaches to mathematics instruction.

In a detailed policy report on mathematics education for young children, the researchers concluded that early childhood mathematics instruction is poor, failing to build upon the basic capacities of mathematics understanding that most children bring to the preschool or kindergarten setting. "The typical situation is that (teachers) are poorly trained to teach the subject, are afraid of it, feel it is not important to teach, and typically teach it badly or not at all" (Ginsburg, Lee, & Boyd, 2008, p. 1). More research is needed to clarify factors that support the cognitive basis of computational skills and factors that support more advanced computational problem solving (Newcombe et al., 2009).

At the beginning of the stage of concrete operational thought, children's performance on tests of cognitive maturity is inconsistent. For example, children can conserve mass (using the clay balls task) but may make errors in conservation of weight, volume, or space. They may be able to perform a classification task correctly when they sort by one dimension, such as color, but they may make errors when asked to sort objects that have more than one dimension in common. Computational operations involving addition and subtraction are applied to simple, one-digit problems at first, and are gradually extended to larger, more complex problems. The variety of concrete operations that emerge during middle childhood may not be fully integrated and available for purposeful problem-solving analyses until adolescence or adulthood (Flavell, 1982).

As concrete operational intelligence develops, children gain insight into the regularities of the physical world and the principles that govern relationships among objects. Perceptions of reality become less convincing than a logical understanding of how the world is organized. For example, even though it looks as if the sun sinks into the water, we know that what we see is a result of the earth's rotation on its axis. Table 8.1 summarizes the components of concrete operational thought.

Metacognition

As Piaget began his method of inquiry into concrete operational thought, he pointed the way to the study of metacognition. Rather than being concerned solely with the exact answers that children gave to the questions he asked, he was interested in how they explained their answers. How do children know what they know? What reasons do they give to justify or support their answers? **Metacognition** refers to a range of processes and strategies used to assess and monitor knowledge. It includes the feeling of knowing that accompanies problem solving—the ability to distinguish those answers about which we are confident from those we doubt (Butterfield, Nelson, & Peck, 1988). One element of this feeling of knowing is understanding the source of one's beliefs. For example, we can be told about sand, we can see pictures of it for ourselves, or we can feel and touch it. All three of these sources of information may coincide to create a single belief, or we may discover that there are inconsistencies between what someone says is true and what we perceive through sight or touch. By the ages of 4 and 5, children are able to understand how all three sources of information have contributed to their understanding of an experience (O'Neill & Gopnik, 1991).

Metacognition includes the ability to review various strategies for approaching a problem in order to choose the one that is most likely to result in a solution. It includes the ability to monitor one's comprehension of the material one has just read and to select strategies for increasing one's comprehension (Currie, 1999): "I need to reread this section." "I need to underline and take notes to focus my attention on new information." "I need to talk about this with someone in order to understand it better." Recent research has considered psychological mindedness as an aspect of metacognition. This refers to the ability to think about what might be accounting for one's own or another person's behavior. It requires building a link between experiences, emotions, and behaviors. For example, a child who is feeling sad may think about what happened in the recent past that is producing this feeling. This would be a type of reflection on one's psychological state (Lagattuta & Wellman, 2001).

Metacognition develops in parallel with other cognitive capacities. As children develop their ability to attend to more variables in their approach to problems, they simultaneously increase their capacity to take an executive posture in relation to cognitive tasks. They can detect uncertainty and introduce strategies to reduce it. They can learn study techniques that will enhance their ability to organize and

TABLE 8.1 Components of Concrete Operational Thought

COMPONENT	NEW ABILITIES
Conservation	Ability to apply the identity operation
	Ability to apply the reversibility operation
	Ability to apply the reciprocity operation
Classification	Ability to categorize objects according to some common dimensions
	Ability to induce that properties of one member of a class apply to others
	Ability to order subclasses in a hierarchy
Computational Skills	Ability to understand that numbers represent quantities
	Ability to manipulate quantities using the operations of addition, subtraction, multiplication, and division

recall information. These capacities continue to develop as the child becomes a more sophisticated learner (Veenman, Wilhelm, & Beishuizen, 2004). They are also quite amenable to training, both at home and at school. Metacognition appears to be a natural component of cognitive development. However, just like first-level cognitive capacities, it is constructed in a social context. Interactions between children and adults or peers may nurture and stimulate metacognition by helping children to identify sources of information, talk about and recognize the differences between feelings of certainty and uncertainty in their knowledge, and devise effective strategies for increasing their feelings of knowing (Stright, Neitzel, Sears, & Hoke-Sinex, 2001; Teong, 2003).

Skill Learning

Objective 3. To analyze the nature of skill learning, including the presentation of a model for the process of acquisition of complex skills such as reading and examination of societal factors that provide the context in which skill learning occurs.

Concrete operational thought refers to an approach to reasoning about the physical world that is guided by the compelling logic of certain mental operations. In addition to this general cognitive achievement, middle childhood brings impressive growth in the acquisition of skills. **Skills** are the basis of intellectual competence. They combine knowledge (knowing *about*) and practice (knowing *how*) directed toward identifying and solving significant, meaningful problems (Gardner, 1983; Kuhn, Garcia-Mila, Zohar, & Andersen, 1995). Typically, a person moves through a developmental progression within a skill area, starting off as a **novice**, becoming more proficient, and then, depending on a combination of aptitude, training, and practice, becoming an **expert.**

Cultures differ in the kinds of abilities that are valued (Greenfield, Keller, Fuligni, & Maynard, 2003). In some societies, like ours, symbolic skills focusing on reading, mathematics, and abstract reasoning are highly valued. In other cultures, reading and mathematics are of less use and value than agricultural skills, hunting, or food preparation. In some cultures, parents consider social skills (knowing how to behave appropriately with peers and teachers), practical skills necessary for adjustment to school (completing one's homework), and motivation (working hard to understand a problem) as more important indications of intelligence than cognitive accomplishments (Neisser et al., 1996; Sternberg, 2007). In many African cultures, parents emphasize social intelligence, the ability to be attuned to the social intentions of others and the ability to anticipate the social impact of one's actions and the actions of others. In a study of concepts of intelligence in rural Kenya, four different concepts were used: *rieko* (knowledge and skills), *luoro*

(respect), *winjo* (comprehension of how to handle practical problems), and *paro* (initiative) (Sternberg, 2007, p. 149). Parents are likely to view the acquisition of technical skills and academic knowledge as important primarily insofar as these skills can enhance social intelligence, social harmony, and social acceptance (Dasen, 1984; Nsamenang, 1992).

In the United States, one observes the emergence of a wide range of valued skills during middle childhood, including mathematics, science, writing, computer operation, sports, mechanics, music, dance, theater, art, cooking, sewing, crafts, and reading. The nature and diversity of these skills and the fact that individual children can function at high levels in some but not in others raises the question of exactly what is meant by *intelligence*. The debate about intelligence is especially relevant in middle childhood, because this is when intelligence tests are administered and school placement decisions are made. As children discover the results of these tests, they make personal attributions about their ability or potential. Thus, IQ tests have a direct impact on the kind of educational experiences that children encounter and on their sense of academic self-efficacy. Three theoretical approaches to the definition of intelligence are discussed in the box entitled "What Is Intelligence?"

Features of Skilled Learning

Skills are actions that take place in specific contexts (Fischer & Bidell, 2006). One uses the skill of manipulating a fork for eating, not to type on a computer. Skills can be of varying levels of complexity, from whistling a tune to playing poker. In each case, they have a developmental trajectory—the skill begins in some rudimentary form of action, which may mature to increasingly high levels of performance. Skills are both context specific and culturally guided. The skill of managing a fork for eating is valued in most western cultures; however, chopsticks are the preferred tool in many eastern cultures.

Skills are changing as they become more advanced; they are also integrated with other skills that may permit new, more complex skills. Each skill is comprised of systems that must work together in order for the skill to be effective. For example, the use of a fork for eating requires hand-eye-mouth coordination, judgments about the consistency and size of the food, and understanding cultural practices for eating. Once the basic skill of using a fork becomes well established, it can be integrated into more complex skills such as cutting food with a knife and a fork, or the use of a fork in food preparation. The systems that contribute to one skill, such as hand-eye coordination, may contribute to more than one skill. These contributing systems may develop at different rates, thus explaining why a skill may change slowly and then seem to advance to a new level rather suddenly.

Skills are self-organizing. Skills, by their very nature, are goal-oriented actions designed to perform specific functions in a particular environment. As the goals or the contexts for skill performance change, the skills may be modified or integrated with other skills to produce new behavior.

What Is Intelligence?

THE TERM **INTELLIGENCE** is used in many contexts, with a variety of meanings. Informally, it may refer to the ability to solve difficult problems, to draw on scholarly research or literature in defending an argument, or to adapt to environmental conditions. At a psychometric level, it may refer to the score on a standardized test composed of one type of item (such as *Peabody's Picture Vocabulary Test*) or many kinds of items (such as the *Stanford-Binet Intelligence Test*). Some theorists emphasize a general underlying factor, *g*, that reflects what many different types of test items have in common (Spearman, 1927). Other models suggest multiple intelligences with distinct areas of specialization. The remarkable adaptive and inventive capacities that human beings exhibit suggest a diversity of intellectual abilities, which are captured in the three theories of intelligence described here.

Jean Piaget (1972b) analyzed intelligence from a developmental perspective. He described four types of intelligence, each emerging at a different period of life: (1) *sensorimotor intelligence* (the ability to know through direct observation and manipulation of objects); (2) *representational intelligence* (the ability to distinguish between the real and the pretend; to think about and represent objects and events that are not present); (3) *concrete operational intelligence* (the ability to detect the logical relationships among objects; to place objects in sequences; and to comprehend and manipulate numbers); and (4) *formal operational intelligence* (the ability to use experimental techniques and hypothetical reasoning to solve problems, to generalize observations from one situation to another, and to relate cause and effect in complex, multidimensional problems). These approaches to problem solving are not lost as one moves from stage to stage. Rather, each is integrated into the next level, with lower levels of reasoning being viewed as inadequate as the person achieves new capacities.

Howard Gardner's (1983) theory of multiple intelligences identifies at least eight distinct intelligences, each with its own content and unique contribution

Materials designed to foster spatial reasoning have become increasingly diverse, allowing children to explore new areas of creativity and problem solving. Lee is really concentrating on this project, and seems quite pleased as she figures out how these blocks fit together.

For example, think about playing the piano as a skill. The original goal is to create music through the use of this specific instrument. Many components are required in order to play, including: memory, auditory perception, manual dexterity, rhythm, and the ability to read music. As one area improves, the level of playing may improve so that the notes are smoother, more rhythmic, and more musical. At some point, simple tunes are replaced by more complex compositions requiring new fingering, more complex rhythms, faster speed, and coordinated use of right and left hands. As the technical challenges of playing the piano are mastered, the person begins to build a repertoire of pieces and introduces emotion, interpretation, liveliness, and a personal voice into the music. Now, the skill of playing the piano becomes a means of self-expression, and possibly the entertainment of others.

Four principles have been identified for understanding how complex behavioral skills are achieved. First, the development of a skill depends on a combination of sensory, motor, perceptual, cognitive, linguistic, emotional, and social processes. In sports, for example, a child must learn to coordinate specific sensory information and motor activities, understand the rules of the game, be able to communicate with the coach and the other players, gain control over emotions such as fear or anger that might interfere with performance, and sustain motivation to keep trying despite errors or defeat.

Second, skills are attained through the simultaneous integration of many levels of the component behaviors. They are not acquired in strict sequence from simple to complex. Instead, children work on the simple and more complex components of the skill at the same time. For example, as children learn the game of baseball, they practice simple skills like throwing and catching, and at the same time, they have to learn more complex skills like fielding a ground ball and throwing it accurately to the first baseman in order to make an out.

Third, the limits of the human system place constraints on an individual's capacity to perform skilled behavior. With practice, lower level processes begin to function automatically, so a person can attend to higher order processes. In writing, for example, young children struggle with the physical act of printing and writing, concentrating largely on the motor skills necessary to make each letter, word, and sentence. A skilled writer can write with little effort, focusing attention on the meaning of the writing, the plot, or the

to solving important, meaningful problems. These include *linguistic, musical, logical-mathematical, spatial, naturalist, bodily-kinesthetic,* and two forms of personal intelligence—one directed toward understanding one's own internal feelings (*intrapersonal*) and the other directed toward identifying and differentiating among the characteristics of others (*interpersonal*). This theory recognizes domains of human functioning that show evidence of high levels of achievement that are not necessarily related to scientific, mathematical, or verbal reasoning. They cover a broader range of skills than are normally included in tests of intelligence, validating the variety of individual differences in competence typically observed among school-age children (Gardner, Kornhaber, & Wake, 1996).

A third view, devised by Robert Sternberg (1985; Sternberg, Castejon, Prieto, Hautamäki, & Grigorenko, 2001), describes three kinds of intelligence— analytic, creative, and practical. According to Sternberg, only the first is systematically measured by tests of intelligence, but the latter two are often required in job performance or adaptation to the demands of daily life. Practical intelligence is knowledge about how to do something, how to assess a situation and get a desired outcome. In two studies involving children in third and eighth grades, a classroom approach that focused on analytic skills was compared with an approach that included activities that called on analytic, creative, and practical intelligence. Children in the latter groups showed higher levels of performance, reflecting the effectiveness of drawing on the three kinds of intelligence for more fully embedded learning (Sternberg, Torff, & Grigorenko, 1998).

Critical Thinking

1. Compare the three theories of Piaget, Gardner, and Sternberg. What, if anything, do they have in common? What are their distinguishing features?
2. What are some implications of the three theories of intelligence for educational practice? How might teachers approach the teaching/ learning process differently depending on which of these three views of intelligence they endorsed?
3. Many scholars support the idea of a single underlying factor, often referred to as *g*, which refers to basic intelligence. Do you think there is such a thing as *g*? What evidence do you have for your belief? How does the idea of *g* fit with the three theories presented here?
4. How does culture influence intelligence? Do you believe there can be such a thing as a culture-free test of intelligence?
5. What role does intelligence play during middle childhood? Using the three theories presented here, how might you characterize the aspects of intelligence that are likely to be prominent at this stage of life?

Image copyright Alexey Fursov 2010. Used under license from Shutterstock.com

By the age of six, Kim has already reached a very high level of skill development in rhythmic gymnastics. Although we tend to think of children as novices in skill development, individual children can become very accomplished in particular domains such as music, drama, art, sports, mathematics, and invention.

character development rather than on the physical aspects of the task.

Fourth, skilled behavior requires the use of strategies. Skillful people operate with purpose and continuously monitor their performance. They perceive breakdowns in performance, are selective in focusing attention on various aspects of what they are working on, and refine higher order processes as they perform the skill. This model of skill development focuses on the elements that are necessary in order to move from what might be considered a novice level to a more advanced level in skill performance.

One must keep in mind that children vary widely in their rate of intellectual development and in their capacities to perform skills. For example, by grade 1 or 2, children have been identified as mathematically gifted, normal, or mathematically disabled (Geary & Brown, 1991; Geary, Hoard, ByrdCraven, & DeSoto, 2004). These designations relate to children's abilities to perform relatively simple mathematical operations, such as addition.

Studies of children who have experienced early and prolonged deprivation, for example children who have spent 12 months or more in institutional care before adoption, show evidence of neurological deficits in certain areas by the age of 8 or 9, even when they have been adopted by stable, well-educated families who provide supportive parenting and adequate resources. By the stage of middle childhood, the impact of early deprivation is evidenced in specific cognitive domains but not others. For example, the children who experienced prolonged institutionalization perform less well on tests of visual memory, attention, and inhibitory control, but about the same as children who were adopted before 8 months, and those who were never institutionalized on tests of auditory memory or executive function (Pollack, Nelson et al., 2010). The impact of early deprivation may be masked in the early years, when expectations for skill development are at a novice level for these children. However, by age 8 or 9, these neurological deficits may have a more noticeable impact on a child's ability to reach a more advanced, sustained level of competence or mastery.

In each distinct area of skill development, a combination of maturational factors, aptitude or talent, opportunities for exposure and training, and the value placed on the skill by the family, school, or larger society all play a role in how rapidly and how well a skill will be developed. In the sections that follow, we look at reading as a specific case of skill development, and at the social and cultural contexts within which learning reading as a skill occurs.

Reading

Reading may be the most significant skill that develops for children in the United States, because it opens the door to all the others. **Literacy** transforms children, just as the advent of the written alphabet transformed civilization. Reading provides access to new information, new uses of language, and new forms of thinking. Children are limited in their ability to learn mathematics, social studies, and science if they cannot read. However, once they can read fluently, the possibilities for independent inquiry expand significantly.

Children begin to read in a variety of ways. Recall from Chapter 6 how David and his mother used a game with street signs along the road to build the bridge from language to literacy. At first, David would ask his mother to tell him what every sign said. After a while, David began to sight read the signs by memorizing words and phrases that were linked to certain shapes and patterns in the signs. Other children begin to read by learning letters and the sounds linked to them, and by experimenting with sounding out the letters when they are strung together. At first, most children are bewildered and confused by these experiences. This is a time when they require a good deal of support and encouragement for their efforts. Gradually, through a process of trial, feedback, and repetition, children learn to read simple words and sentences (Knight & Fischer, 1992). At some point, a child begins to articulate the concept "I can read" or "I am a reader." Once this idea is part of the self-concept, efforts to read increase and are energized by a confidence in one's potential for success.

Reading is a complex skill that involves the acquisition and integration of several abilities, and which improves greatly with practice. In order to read, children have to translate the printed word into the spoken word they recognize and link it to its meaning. Young children have a large spoken or oral vocabulary. They understand the meaning of many words. However, in order to read, they have to realize that each spoken word is comprised of sounds which are represented in English by letters or letter combinations. **Phonemic awareness**, that is, knowing the sound of a letter and being able to hear it as one reads, is a key to reading. Children with **dyslexia** frequently have trouble with this process of connecting letters and their sounds. Another component of reading is the rapid naming of objects, referred to in the literature as RAN (rapid automatized naming). To measure RAN, children are asked to name 40 items including colors, objects, numbers, and letters as fast as possible. RAN, measured before children have begun formal reading instruction, is a predictor of reading fluency. Scholars who study reading argue that RAN is a general capacity for object recognition that is enlisted into the reading process, so that as a child learns to read the brain treats printed words as if they are objects to be recognized (Lervåg & Hulme, 2009).

Reading involves more than recognizing one word at a time. **Reading fluency** refers to the accuracy and speed with which children can read words in a text. Those children who struggle with figuring out each word may find it difficult to capture the meaning of a sentence or paragraph. Over time, children who have difficulty reading are less willing to practice reading outside of class, and this lack of practice confounds their problems with fluency (Gabrieli, 2009). Certain interventions have been shown to be successful for children who are having difficulties with reading, especially when these interventions occur early in kindergarten or first grade, and involve intensive, small group lessons with active,

Children who enjoy reading books outside of school show the greatest gains in reading achievement between second and fifth grades. Reading opens up limitless sources of information, new experiences, and fun.

engaging interactions between students and their teachers (Cirino, Vaughn et al., 2009).

Parents Influence Their Child's Reading Abilities.

Parents affect their children's reading in at least six ways (Tudge, Putnam, & Valsiner, 1996).

1. The value they place on literacy
2. The emphasis they place on academic achievement
3. The reading materials they make available at home
4. The time they spend reading with their children and listening to their children read
5. The way they read with their children
6. The opportunities they provide for verbal interaction in the home

There are many different ways to approach the social occasion of reading. Some parents ask their children about the story as they read along to make sure the child understands. Some try to expand on the story, talking with their children about other things they notice in the pictures or experiences related to the story. Some parents point out words and specifically teach about the sounds of letters as they read (Reese & Cox, 1999; Justice & Ezell, 2000).

In a study of parents' contributions to their children's literacy development in the United States and Japan, family members in both countries were found to employ a wide range of strategies both at home and away from home to encourage their children's ability to read. These included reading and telling stories, discussing stories, teaching vocabulary, writing about their experiences, playing board games, and watching certain types of television programs (Saracho & Shirakawa, 2004). Parents who value the ability to read do some direct teaching to promote reading, urge their children to do well in school, provide resources for reading, take turns reading and listening to their children read, and talk with them about what they are reading. All these strategies produce children who are more skilled readers (Bus, van IJzendoorn, & Pellegrini, 1995; Haney & Hill, 2004).

Parents also have an indirect effect on how well a child will learn to read by influencing the child's placement in a school reading group. Ability grouping for reading instruction is practically universal in elementary schools. Teachers depend on their perceptions of a child's ability, work habits, and behavior when they assign students to reading groups (Haller & Waterman, 1985). The higher the level of the children's reading group, the better they learn how to read. Parents need to understand the school's approach to ability grouping and help their child understand it (National Association of School Psychologists, 2002). Parents who encourage good work habits and appropriate classroom behavior are likely to influence a teacher's perception of their child and, as a result, influence the child's assignment to a more advanced reading-level group.

The Social and Cultural Contexts of Reading.

Recent attention has been given to the social and cultural contexts in which many skills, especially school-related abilities such as reading, emerge (Eccles, 1993). Progress in skill development is influenced by parental and school expectations regarding levels of performance in a specific culture. The analysis of reading provides many good examples of the importance of context.

First, societies differ in their level of literacy. For example, in Afghanistan, 43% of men and 12.6% of women age 15 and older are literate (Central Intelligence Agency, 2007). In Finland, a country with a population of more than 5 million, compulsory public schooling does not begin until age 7, and 100% of the population is literate. Expectations that children should be read to, should be able to read, and the level of skill development they are expected to reach at a certain age depends on cultural norms for literacy. The Progress in International Reading Literacy Study (PIRLS) assessed reading activities of fourth graders in 40 countries. In the United States, 35% reported reading for fun daily or almost every day; this was lower than the average of 40% across all the countries. The more children

© Jose Luis Pelaez, Inc./CORBIS

read for fun, the higher their reading achievement scores. In the United States, 43% of children said they read for fun twice a month or less. This was a higher percentage than the international average of 32% across all 40 nations (Mullis, Martin, Kennedy, & Foy, 2007).

Second, the purpose of literacy varies from one culture to the next. For example, missionaries introduced literacy to the Kaluli of New Guinea primarily as a way to teach the Bible. Among the Kaluli, reading is viewed as having limited purpose for daily life, and as too difficult for children (Schieffelin & Cochran-Smith, 1984). In many societies, the ability to read the Bible, the Koran, or the Torah is the principal reason for literacy, and that one book has been the primary written resource.

Third, the mark of a literate person varies by context. In the United States, we have age-graded expectations for reading and tests to measure reading ability. By the time they are applying to college, students are expected to be able to analyze a complex text for meaning, to know advanced principles of grammar, and to write a well-organized essay under time constraints. In other cultures, a good reader might be someone who can read a letter for someone else, someone who can keep track of business accounts, or someone who can accurately make a copy of a text. The point is that the achievement of literacy is a product of cultural expectations, individual capacity, and opportunities to learn (Tudge, Putnam, & Valsiner, 1996).

The emphasis on skill building and the energy that children ages 6 to 12 bring to the acquisition of new skills suggest a strong parallel to toddlerhood. At both stages, children's motives for competence and mastery are directed

HUMAN DEVELOPMENT AND DIVERSITY

Cross-National Comparisons of Mathematics Ability

IN 1980, COMPARATIVE studies showed that first- and fifth-grade children in Minneapolis, Minnesota, were substantially behind their age-mates in Sendai, Japan, and Taipei, Taiwan, in tests of mathematics achievement. In a 10-year follow-up, U.S. children still lagged behind, and by the eleventh grade, the gap in achievement had widened (Stevenson, 1992; Stevenson, Chen, & Lee, 1993). Even the top 10% of the Minneapolis students scored at about the average level of the Taipei and Sendai students.

Beginning in 1995, and then again in 1999, 2003, and 2007, the U.S. National Center for Education Statistics sponsored the Trends in International Mathematics and Science Study (TIMSS), which examined mathematics and science teaching practices and student accomplishment for eighth graders in 48 countries. Analysis of the 2007 data indicated some improvement in U.S. students' scores from 1995. Eighth graders in five countries had average scores statistically greater than the U.S. average: Taiwan, Korea, Singapore, Hong Kong, and Japan (National Center for Education Statistics, 2010).

It is difficult to account for these cross-national comparisons on the basis of ability. All these countries have practically universal enrollment of school-age children. Moreover, when children were compared in their knowledge of general information of the type not included in the school curriculum, the U.S. children in first and fifth grades scored higher than the Japanese and Chinese children.

At least four sociocultural factors interact to contribute to the advantage that Japanese and Chinese children show in mathematical skill development. First, there is a difference in parents' views about what they should expect of their children. U.S. parents appear to be satisfied with their children's level of mathematics performance and do not expect their children to do better. In contrast, Japanese and Chinese parents have high expectations for their children's performance.

Second, parents differ in how they evaluate their children's schools. U.S. parents are generally satisfied with the school curriculum and think that the schools are doing a good job. Far fewer Japanese and Chinese parents view the schools as good or excellent. The public pressure in these cultures is for greater improvement in the quality of education. They are more critical of their schools. Even though Japanese and Chinese children spend more time on homework than do U.S. children, their parents are more likely to encourage them to spend even more time on homework.

Third, there are cultural differences in the emphasis given to ability as compared to effort. U.S. parents and teachers highlight the importance of natural ability as a major factor in accounting for individual differences in mathematical ability. Japanese and Chinese parents and teachers are more likely to see outstanding performance as a result of studying hard. On the one hand, if you believe that skill depends on natural ability, you might conclude that not much can be done to improve performance. On the other hand, if you believe that skill depends on effort, you may be more inclined to devote additional time and focused application to reach a new level of performance.

Finally, there are notable differences in the approach to mathematics instruction across countries. In Japan, for example, the classroom teaching approach is quite distinct from that in the United States. Based on videotapes of U.S. and Japanese classrooms, one can observe Japanese teachers spending more time introducing new concepts and less time reviewing

outward to the environment. At both stages, children appear to be delighted by the potential for learning that almost every new encounter offers. However, as a result of children's cognitive capacities and their awareness of social expectations, skill learning during middle childhood is embedded in a much more complex framework of continuous monitoring and self-assessment. Children's beliefs and attitudes about which skills are important, what they should expect of themselves, what others expect of them, and what kinds of competing demands should influence their dedication to skill development all contribute to the levels of performance they are likely to achieve. The Human Development and Diversity box (starting on page 310) presents a cross-national comparison of mathematics mastery and performance in the United States, Japan, and Taiwan.

Self-Evaluation

Objective 4. To examine the development of self-evaluation skills, including feelings of pride, self-efficacy, and ways that social expectations of parents, teachers, and peers contribute to a child's self-evaluation.

During middle childhood, the emphasis on skill building is accompanied by a new focus on **self-evaluation**. Children strive to match their achievements to internalized goals and external standards. Simultaneously, they receive feedback from others about the quality of their performance. Some children may be asked to sit at one table to receive help; others may be told to go down the hall for tutoring.

Japanese mathematics classes involve two teachers, one who gives instruction to the whole class, and one who meets individually with students to help them in areas where they may be having difficulties. In this way, all the students are able to move ahead at the same pace and "no child is left behind."

previous content, focusing more on complex problems that require four or more steps to reach a solution, and spending more time on problems that are mathematically related but not simply a repetition of the previous problem (National Center for Education Statistics, 2004b).

Critical Thinking Questions

1. Were you surprised to learn that children in the United States lag behind children in other industrialized countries with regard to their mathematics and science test scores? What are some implications of these findings for the U.S. economy? For career opportunities in adulthood?

2. What were your experiences in mathematics and science instruction in elementary and secondary school? Did you leave high school feeling confident about your ability in these domains? What role did teachers, parents, and peers play in your interest and achievement in mathematics and science?

3. Three of the four sociocultural differences between the Japanese and Chinese cultures and that of the United States have to do with parental attitudes and beliefs. In general, what role do parents in the United States play with respect to their children's education? Are they as passive with regard to their children's mathematics and science achievement as the research suggests?

4. What are the differences between the U.S. and the Japanese and Chinese cultures that you believe make the greatest difference with respect to science and mathematics achievement? How do concepts of individualism and collectivism enter into your thinking?

5. Do you tend to favor the explanation that differences in achievement are a result of differences in basic ability or differences in motivation and effort? Why?

6. How would you go about studying the relationship between beliefs in ability versus beliefs in effort on school achievement in mathematics and science?

Some children are designated as peer tutors who assist their classmates. These and many other signs are sources of social evaluation that children incorporate into their own self-evaluations.

In middle childhood, the process of self-evaluation is further complicated because the peer group joins the adult world as a source of social comparison, criticism, and approval. Toddlers and early-school-age children are likely to observe and imitate their peers in order to learn new strategies for approaching a task, or out of curiosity to see how their peers are doing a particular project. But in middle childhood, pressures toward conformity, competition, and the need for approval feed into the self-evaluation process. At this age, children begin to pay attention to the work of others in order to assess their own abilities (Butler & Ruzany, 1993). Their athletic skills, intellectual abilities, and artistic talents are no longer matters to which only teachers and parents respond. Peers also identify others' skills and begin to generate profiles of one another: "Oh, Rafael is good in math, but he runs like a girl"; "Jane is kind of fat, but she writes great stories"; "I like Rashidah best, because she's good at everything." Depending on their resolution of the crises of toddlerhood and early school age, children approach the process of self-evaluation from a framework of either self-confidence or self-doubt. They may expect to find tasks easy to accomplish and approach them vigorously, or they may anticipate failure and approach tasks with hesitation.

In research involving children in the 8 to 13 age range, Susan Harter (1985b, 1993) devised a method for assessing children's perceptions of competence in five specific domains: scholastic competence, athletic competence, likability by peers, physical appearance, and behavioral conduct. She also measured general or global self-esteem. Her research was guided by the idea that by the age of 8, children not only differentiate specific areas of competence, but view certain areas as more important than others. She found that self-esteem is highest in those children who view themselves as competent in domains that they judge to be important. Competence in relatively unimportant domains is not strongly related to overall self-esteem.

Feelings of Pride

Feelings of pride are typically associated with positive self-evaluations. In general, children as well as adults feel happy when they succeed at an achievement-related task. However, the experience of **pride** depends in part on the child's perceptions about the cause of their success. As children mature, their feelings of pride after a success become increasingly linked to whether they attribute the success to internal factors such as their own ability or effort as compared to external factors such as the poor preparation of the other children or a teacher who is an easy grader (Graham & Weiner, 1986). In experimental tests of these relationships, young children ages 5 and 6 felt about the same degree of pride whether the success was due to internal or external

factors. However, by ages 8 to 10 children were making a clearer distinction. They felt greater pride when success was due to internal factors and less pride when success was due to external factors (Graham & Weiner, 1991). By middle childhood, children are engaged in a complex process of self-evaluation that includes several sources of information including their past performance, task difficulty, the reactions of others, and their assessment of their ability and effort.

Self-evaluation takes place in relation to internal frames of reference, as a child compares how well he can perform in one domain versus another. The internal frame of reference includes an assessment of both ability and effort. Self-evaluation also takes place in relation to external frames of reference, as a child evaluates her own performance in light of parent, teacher, or peer feedback and observations of the performance of other children (Skaalvik & Skaalvik, 2004). In the sections that follow, we focus on two different paths toward self-evaluation: *self-efficacy*, which reflects a child's personal judgment of ability, and *social expectations*, which reflect the impact of the expectations of others on a child's performance.

Self-Efficacy

How do children assess their competence in a specific ability area? Albert Bandura (1982) theorized that judgments of self-efficacy are crucial to understanding this process. **Self-efficacy** is defined as the person's sense of confidence that she can perform the behaviors demanded in a specific situation. Expectations of efficacy vary with the specific ability. In other words, a child may view efficacy in one way in a situation requiring mathematical ability and in another way when the situation requires physical strength.

Bandura theorized that four sources of information contribute to judgments of self-efficacy (see Figure 8.2). The first source is **enactive attainments**, or prior experiences of mastery in the kinds of tasks that are being confronted. Children's general assessment of their ability in any

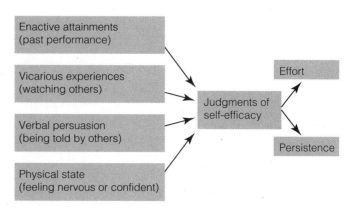

FIGURE 8.2 Four Components of Self-Efficacy

istockphoto.com/ManoAfrica

Three fifth grade boys are celebrating their success at winning the Olympics of the Mind competition for their school.

area (e.g., mathematics, writing, or gymnastics) is based on their past accomplishments in that area. There is a bidirectional relationship between achievement in a domain and one's confidence about being able to perform well in that domain. High confidence will lead to better performance, and better performance will increase one's confidence. Over time, children compare their performance across various domains and begin to establish a more stable view of areas where they expect to do well and areas where they anticipate greater difficulty (Denissen, Zarrett, & Eccles, 2007). Success experiences increase self-efficacy, whereas repeated failures diminish it. Failure experiences are especially detrimental when they occur early in the process of trying to master a task. Many boys and girls are diverted from mastering such sports as tennis and baseball because they have made mistakes early in their participation. They develop doubts about their abilities, which then prevent them from persisting in the task.

The second source of information is **vicarious experience**. Seeing a person similar to oneself perform a task successfully may raise one's sense of self-efficacy; seeing a person similar to oneself fail at a task may lower it.

Verbal persuasion is the third source. Children can be encouraged to believe in themselves and try a new task. Persuasion is likely to be most effective with children who already have confidence in their abilities, and it helps boost their performance level.

The fourth source is **physical state**. People monitor their body states in making judgments about whether they can do well or not. When children feel too anxious or frightened, they are likely to anticipate failure. In contrast, children who are excited and interested but not overly tense are more likely to perceive themselves as capable of succeeding.

Self-efficacy judgments are related to children's perceptions of their likelihood of success. These judgments also determine the factors to which children attribute their success or failure (McAuley, Duncan, & McElroy, 1989; Pajares, 1996). In the face of difficulty or failure, children who have confidence in their abilities and high self-efficacy will work harder to master challenges. They will attribute their difficulties to a failure to try hard enough, and they will redouble their efforts. Children who have a low sense of self-efficacy tend to give up in the face of difficulty because they attribute their failure to a basic lack of ability (Bandura & Schunck, 1981). The level of self-efficacy also affects how children prepare to handle new challenges. In their thoughts, emotions, and preparation for action, those who are preoccupied by self-doubts differ from those who believe in themselves.

Children with high levels of self-efficacy related to academic achievement are likely to set challenging goals for themselves. They are also likely to regulate their learning behaviors by deliberately enlisting a number of strategies, including concentrating, organizing their work, finding a good place to study, taking notes in class, and completing their homework assignments so that they have the best chances of reaching their goals (Zimmerman, Bandura, & Martinez-Pons, 1992; Bandura, Barbaranelli, Caprara, & Pastorelli, 1996). The following case study of Becca illustrates the behaviors and thoughts of a middle school student whose sense of self-efficacy has been declining.

CASE STUDY

BECCA

Becca, an eighth grader, is disengaging from school.

Under the weight of her family burdens, Becca's academic confidence has begun to falter.... In sixth grade, Becca was an A student; at the end of seventh grade, she asked to be removed from the advanced math class; and by the middle of eighth grade, her grades in all of her classes were drifting to low C's.

A quiet girl, Becca says she has never spoken much in class ("unless I'm really, really sure of an answer, and sometimes not even then"), but with her self-esteem flagging, she stops volunteering entirely. She even begins to see her silence as an advantage: As long as she's perceived as shy, her teachers won't notice that she has, in truth, disengaged from school.... In a sense, Becca is invisible. Her teachers don't see her as someone in need of counseling or special help because, although her grades have dropped, she is never combustible: She never, for instance, yells in class, pounds desks, fights with other children, or conspicuously challenges authority. Becca's is a passive resistance—a typically feminine resistance. By opting out rather than acting out, Becca still conforms to the image of the ideal female student—quiet, compliant, obedient; as such she is easily overlooked, or seen as making choices rather than expressing psychological distress. "Becca is so quiet," her math teacher admits, "she gets lost in the crowd. I don't like that to happen, but it has happened with her. She doesn't disrupt. She always looks like she's paying attention, but maybe she's not. I don't know."

"Maybe she thinks she'll be more cool as a C student," her history teacher says. "But she doesn't even get it together after she gets the bad grade. I'll say, 'Becca, you have a D, you may fail,' but then she doesn't turn in the next homework assignment, which is really easy. But I think of her as someone who's responsible for her own grade, and I let her be responsible for that."

Source: Orenstein, 1994, pp. 80–81.

CRITICAL THINKING AND CASE ANALYSIS

1. How would you describe Becca's level of academic self-efficacy?
2. Using Bandura's model, how are the four factors of enactive attainments, vicarious experiences, verbal persuasion, and physical states contributing to her self-efficacy?
3. What would you say is missing from Bandura's theory of self-efficacy that is illustrated in the case of Becca?
4. What are some gender issues that may underlie this case? In what ways is Becca's situation made possible because of gender stereotypes?
5. How might teachers intervene to reverse this decline in self-efficacy?
6. What might be the likely outcome for Becca if this pattern of disengagement continues?

Social Expectations

Several theories of the self suggest that the appraisals and expectations of significant others become incorporated into one's own self-concept and become a source for self-evaluation (Chen, Boucher, & Tapias, 2006). Self-esteem is based on the general positive regard and approval of others and on the specific expectations they have for one's ability and achievement in certain areas of performance (Jussim, 1990a; Harter, 1993). In attempting to assess their own abilities, children rely on many external sources of evaluation, including school grades, teachers' comments, and parent and peer evaluations (Hergovich, Sirsch, & Felinger, 2002). If feedback from important adults suggests to children that they are cooperative, intelligent, and creative, these attributes are likely to be incorporated into their self-evaluations. Children who see themselves as cooperative and intelligent are likely to approach social and intellectual tasks with optimistic expectations about their performance. Conversely, feedback suggesting lack of cooperation, intelligence, or creativity can produce a pessimistic or antagonistic approach to the challenges of skill development. Even one's self-efficacy can be influenced by how a relevant other has evaluated one's performance in the past.

Repeated failure information or remarks that imply lack of ability tend to make children less confident of success in subsequent tasks. This pattern of expectations appears to crystallize during grades 2 and 3. Preschoolers do not make systematic use of success or failure feedback in predicting their next success (Parsons & Ruble, 1977). Even in the first grade, children's expectations about the grades they will receive on their first report cards are not clearly related to their IQs or to parents' or teachers' expectations, nor are they closely related to the children's later estimates of their grades. By the end of the first grade, however, children begin to be more accurate predictors of their performance (Alexander & Entwisle, 1988; Entwisle, Alexander, Pallas, & Cadigan, 1987). By middle childhood, children are more aware of their teachers' expectations for their performance and are likely to mirror those expectations in their own attitudes about school, academic achievement, and school behaviors (Weinstein et al., 1987; Alexander, Entwisle, & Kabbani, 2001).

Teachers' Expectations: The Self-Fulfilling Prophecy. The feedback that students receive from their teachers is not wholly objective. Teachers' expectations about their students' abilities may be based on objective assessments, but they may also be derived from stereotypes about certain types of children or from biases based on prior experiences, like having a child's older siblings in class in prior years or hearing unfavorable comments from other teachers. Merton (1948) suggested that problems may arise through a process that he called the **self-fulfilling prophecy**. This concept refers to the idea that false or inaccurate beliefs can produce a personal reality that corresponds with them.

In the original study on the effect of teacher expectations on student performance, teachers were led to believe that certain students were late bloomers who would show major gains in IQ later on in the school year. These children, chosen at random from among first and second graders, actually did show increases in IQ of 10 to 15 points by the end of the school year in comparison to the control group (Rosenthal & Jacobson, 1968).

Subsequent studies of the self-fulfilling prophecy in classroom settings have shown that it has a consistent but comparatively small effect on student performance (Rosenthal, 1994, 1995). In one longitudinal study, students' math achievement and mathematics self-concept data were collected at the end of fifth grade, early in sixth grade, and at the beginning of seventh grade. Teachers' expectations about student performance were assessed early in sixth grade as well. Both student achievement at the end of fifth grade and teachers' expectations in sixth grade were predictive of students' achievement at the beginning of seventh grade. In the analysis of these data, the researchers found that the self-fulfilling prophecy (the impact of teacher expectations separate from prior student achievement scores) was observable only for those students who were in the low achievement group. Both overestimates and underestimates of these students' abilities in sixth grade were predictive of the students' achievement in seventh grade. There was some tendency for overestimates to have a greater impact in boosting these students' performance than for underestimates to depress the students' performance (Madon, Jussim, & Eccles, 1997).

Teachers' expectations for a student's performance are influenced by their assessments of both the student's ability and effort. In a study of elementary school teachers, a relationship was found between the teachers' explanations for students' success and failure and the emotions that teachers felt under the various conditions. These emotional reactions were assumed to be the major cues that teachers sent to students about their performances.

When teachers believed that students' poor performances were due to a lack of effort, they were likely to feel angry toward the students, particularly if they believed the students were capable of good work. Children make attributions about what might make a teacher angry at a student. According to studies by Graham and Weiner (1991) when children observe that a teacher is angry, they are likely to infer that the student did something or failed to do something that was within their control, which interfered with their performance. They may conclude that if the teacher is angry, the student did something wrong such as fooling around instead of studying for a test, or watching television instead of finishing their homework.

When children of low ability suddenly begin putting forth a great deal of effort, teachers were likely to take pride in their own accomplishments, believing they had really helped these children become more motivated. If low-ability students who were trying hard failed, teachers felt a sense of guilt. Teachers were more willing to accept personal responsibility for certain configurations of student success and failure than for others. The students who made teachers the angriest were the bright ones who did not try hard (Prawat, Byers, & Anderson, 1983).

Research on teacher expectations illustrates how social expectations influence both perceptions of others and the quality of interpersonal communication. Intervention programs to improve the reading performance of first graders in low-income minority schools have built on this line of research. Specific strategies were designed to help teachers recognize their assumptions about student ability and effort and to convey encouragement and positive attainment messages to students (Good & Nichols, 2001).

Certain conditions make children more or less vulnerable to internalizing false expectations. Children who are unsure about their abilities and children who are learning something for the first time may be more likely to rely on the information they receive from others to assess their

Students react to teachers' interactions with their classmates. While Ms. White is correcting Lin's work, Eric, Stephanie, and Amy are watching or listening. What do you think they may be feeling in this situation?

© Tom McCarthy/Photo Edit

Parents' Specific Beliefs
and Perceptions

Parents' Specific Actions
and Behaviors

Child Outcomes

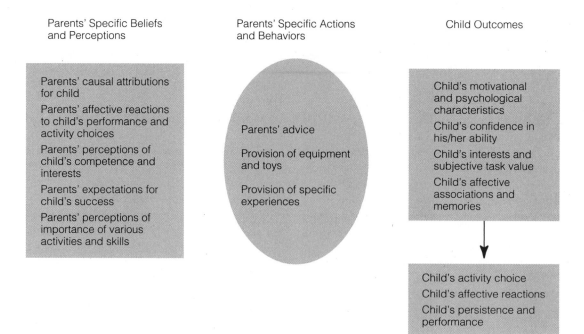

FIGURE 8.3 The Relationship of Parents' Gender Role Stereotype Beliefs and Perceptions to Parental Actions and Behaviors and Child Outcomes

Source: Data from I. Bretherton, "Open Communication and Internal Working Models: Roles in the Development of Attachment Relationships," R. Dienstbier & R. A. Thompson (Eds.), Nebraska Symposium on Motivation, 1988; *Socioemotional Development, 36,* 60–61.

abilities. Being in a new situation, like moving to a new school or changing from elementary to middle school, may increase a child's dependence on social expectations for performance. In middle childhood, when many new domains of skill development are first being introduced, children may be more vulnerable to the effects of biased perceptions and erroneous expectations than are older children (Jussim, 1990b).

Some children appear to monitor their social environment more self-consciously than others (Musser & Browne, 1991). High **self-monitoring** children are more aware of the emotional and nonverbal behavior of others and make more use of social information to evaluate and regulate their own behavior. These children are more responsive to subtle forms of feedback about their performance, taking in more information about social expectations for their performance than do the children who are comparatively oblivious to the intricacies of the social environment.

Parents' Expectations. Parents' as well as teachers' expectations influence children's perceptions of their abilities. This process was demonstrated in a study of parents' and children's attitudes toward mathematical aptitude (Parsons, Adler, & Kaczala, 1982). Children in Grades 5 to 11 and their parents were asked about their attitudes toward the children's mathematics achievement. Parents had lower expectations for their daughters' math achievement than for their sons'. They believed that mathematics is more difficult and requires more effort for girls than for boys. Their expectations about their children's aptitude were better predictors of the children's self-assessments than were the children's own past performances in mathematics.

Expanding on the relationship between gender role bias and the socialization of children's competencies and interests, Eccles (1993) proposed the following model (see Figure 8.3).

The evidence suggests that general (parental) gender role beliefs influence perceptions of individual children's competencies and interests, which in turn affect the kinds of experiences parents provide.... Essentially, we believe that parents' gender role stereotypes, in interaction with their children's sex, affect the following mediators: (1) parents' causal attributions for the children's performance; (2) parents' emotional reaction to their children's performance in various activities; (3) the importance parents attach to their children acquiring various skills; (4) the advice parents provide their children regarding involvement in various skills; and (5) the activities and toys parents provide. In turn, we predict that these subtle and explicit mediators influence the development of the following child outcomes across the various gender-role-stereotyped activity domains: (1) children's confidence in their ability; (2) children's interest in mastering various skills; (3) children's affective reaction to participating in various activities, and as a consequence of these self and task perceptions, (4) the amount of time and type of effort the children devote to mastering and demonstrating various skills. (p. 170)

A number of studies support the underlying dynamics of this model. Independent of actual gender differences in specific domains, including math, sports, and English, parents' stereotypes about which gender is more talented in a particular area influence their perceptions of their own child's competence in that area. Parents' perceptions of competence are directly related to their children's perception of competence (Eccles, Jacobs, & Harold, 1990).

A longitudinal study followed a cohort of children, starting when they were in first grade, in 1982, through to the end of high school. Data were collected from these children, who were from various socioeconomic and family backgrounds; from their parents; and from school records. The study examined factors that placed children from this group at risk for dropping out of school. Parental attitudes about their children's school success and school completion were significant predictors of children's school achievement starting in first grade and continuing through middle school and high school. Although socioeconomic status was a powerful predictor of dropping out of school, parental attitudes about their child's ability and promise moderated the impact of social class for students in low, middle, and high resource groups, but especially in the higher resource groups (Alexander, Entwisle, & Kabbani, 2001).

Illusions of Incompetence and Competence. Some children who perform well on tests of academic achievement (at the 90th percentile or above) perceive themselves as below average in academic ability, a phenomenon described as the **illusion of incompetence**. These children expect lower levels of success, are less confident, attempt less challenging tasks, and say that their schoolwork is more demanding than peers of similarly high ability who have more positive self-evaluations. It appears that parents play a central role in establishing these children's low assessments of themselves. Children who have an illusion of incompetence think that their parents have a low opinion of their abilities and expect little of them. They see their fathers, in particular, as having rigorous standards that they are not expected to meet (Phillips, 1984, 1987).

The parent-child dynamics that underlie this negative assessment were observed in a study involving children with high academic ability who had varying levels of perceived academic competence. Children worked with their mothers and fathers on solvable and unsolvable tasks. The fathers of children who had low perceptions of their own academic competence were found to interact with their children in more critical or unsupportive ways than did the fathers of children who had high perceptions of their academic competence. The children who had illusions of incompetence were more emotionally upset and dependent when they approached the unsolvable tasks (Wagner & Phillips, 1992).

Cross-sectional research suggests that children may infer messages of incompetence from parental control. In a comparison of children in grades 2 through 5, the older children interpreted parental helping, monitoring, and decision making as evidence that the parents thought they were incompetent. As children get older and their desire for autonomy, initiative, and industry increases, they may interpret parental monitoring as evidence of a lack of confidence in their ability to make good decisions or to function competently (Pomerantz & Eaton, 2000).

In contrast to illusions of incompetence, some people have **illusions of competence**. In four separate studies, researchers found that those participants who scored in the lowest 12% of test takers on measures of grammar, logic, and humor substantially overestimated their own abilities. The extreme lack of ability in an area is accompanied by the inability to distinguish accurate from inaccurate responses, thus leading to a misconception of competence. In contrast to illusions of incompetence, where children underestimate their abilities, illusions of competence occur when people have such deficiencies that they do not even realize the extent of their limitations (Kruger & Dunning, 1999).

The discussion of self-evaluation highlights children's sensitivity to their social environment. They become aware of existing roles and norms and of the sanctions for norm violation. Direct experiences with success and failure are important, but they are also embedded in the context of social expectations. In this age period, with the skills of metacognition and perspective taking, children come to understand that people may alter their behavior in order to project an image that will receive a favorable evaluation from others. They can recognize that under certain circumstances they may wish to alter their own self-presentation in order to receive positive social evaluation from parents, teachers, or peers. This kind of motivated modification of self-presentation is sometimes referred to as brownnosing or kissing up. Even though this behavior can be a subject of critical taunts from peers, the motivated student may realize that this strategy is necessary in order to receive positive evaluations or high grades. For example, Perry notices that his English teacher is especially nice to a friend of his who reads poetry during their free time. Perry knows that his friend is not at all interested in poetry, but that the friend has received positive grades from the teacher, who believes that the child is really interested in English literature. Taking a cue from this strategy, Perry begins to bring a book of poetry to class and makes frequent eye contact with the teacher to convey interest. He finds that the teacher now smiles at him more often, shows new interest in his ideas, and gives his written work a more positive evaluation. Perry concludes that the image he is presenting of himself as one who likes English literature is influencing his teacher's evaluation of his work. Thus, the notion that self-evaluation is shaped by the reflected appraisal from others becomes more complicated as children become skilled in image management (Banerjee, 2002; Hergovich, Sirsch, & Felinger, 2002).

By the end of middle childhood, children have had enough school experience that they can detect favoritism, bias, and unfair treatment and can devise strategies to protect themselves from the impact of negative biases. They are able to judge their abilities by considering their mastery level and the amount of effort they have to exert in order to do well.

They are also able to decide when someone else might be a better judge of their abilities than they are (Burton & Mitchell, 2003). The more children are embedded in strong, supportive social relationships, the more confidence they will have in their general worth, and the more likely they will be to arrive at accurate assessments of their own abilities.

Team Play

Objective 5. To describe a new level of complexity in play as children become involved in team sports and athletic competition, and form more enduring in-group and out-group attitudes.

During middle childhood, a new dimension is added to the quality of a child's play. Children begin to participate in team sports and, as a result, gain a sense of team success as well as personal success. Team sports are generally more complicated than the kinds of games described as group play in Chapter 7. The rules are so complex that they may require a referee or an umpire if they are to be followed accurately. In these sports, children join together into teams that remain together for the duration of the game. Some children join teams that play together for an entire season, such as Little League. A growing interest in physical activity and fitness in adulthood has shed new light on the importance of involvement in team sports in childhood and early adolescence. In a study of adult men ages 32 to 60, researchers found a strong link between voluntary participation in team sports in the middle childhood period and continued physical activity in adulthood (Taylor, Blair, Cummings, Wun, & Malina, 1999).

In addition to its contribution to fitness and enthusiasm for physical activity, participation in **team play** provides a context for preworking—the skills and orientations that will apply to the world of work and to functioning in the family group (Van der Vegt, Emans, & Van De Vliert, 2001). Participation on a team may create a climate for collectivist values such as cooperation, interdependence, and the subordination of the individual's goals to the team's success (Kernan & Greenfield, 2005). Team participation raises issues of moral judgment and moral behavior, especially regarding cheating, sportsmanship, and prosocial or antisocial behaviors (Lee, Whitehead, & Ntoumanis, 2007). In addition to mastery of skills and knowledge about a particular sport, team participation provides opportunities to spend time with friends and to celebrate together (Mowling, Brock, & Hastie, 2006). Three significant characteristics of the experience of team membership are relevant to development during this stage: (1) interdependence, (2) the division of labor, and (3) competition.

Interdependence

Team membership carries with it an awareness that one's acts may affect the success or failure of the entire group. There is a definite emphasis on winning and losing, and children may be ostracized or ridiculed if they contribute to a team loss (Mowling, Brock, & Hastie, 2006). Although team sports do provide opportunities for individual recognition, it is quite clear that team success casts a halo over even the poorest players and team failure a shadow over even the best. Participation in team sports provides lessons in **interdependence**. All of the team members rely on one another, and ideally, it is to everyone's advantage to assist the weaker members

After a hard-fought game, the winners experience the positive emotions that are a result of winning after a rough competition, while the dejected losers absorb the negative emotions associated with defeat.

© Lori Adamski Peek/Getty Images

in improving the quality of their play. Over time, the team provides what is sometimes referred to as a **superordinate group identity**, such that the individual members who bring their own individual racial/ethnic, cultural, or socioeconomic group differences are willing to suppress these differences and work together for the success of the group (Jackson et al., 2002). The best coaches are noted for inspiring this sense of interdependence and mutual support among team members. They urge team members to work together to improve their skills. Often, when teams are closely matched, it is the unexpected success of the weaker players that contributes to a victory.

Division of Labor

Through participation with peers on teams, children discover that **division of labor** is an effective strategy for attaining a goal. Children learn that each position on a team has a unique function and that the team has the best chance of winning if each player performs her specific function rather than trying to do the work of all the other players. The concept of the team encompasses the variety of activities in which each of the team members actually engages.

A team becomes an experiential model for approaching other complex organizations. Once children learn that certain goals can best be attained when tasks are divided among a group of people, they begin to conceptualize the principles behind the organization of social communities. They recognize that some children are better suited to handling one aspect of the task and others to handling another. Some children enjoy the skill development associated with team play; others enjoy learning the rules and devising strategies; others especially value peer companionship; and still others have a strong inner motive to compete and win (Ntoumanis, Vazou, & Duda, 2007). The distribution of roles to fit the children's individual skills and preferences is a subtle element of the learning that is acquired through team play.

Competition

Team play teaches children about **competition**. In team sports, both sides cannot win; success for one side must result in failure for the other. If the team experience is a laboratory for learning lessons about the larger social community, this characteristic promotes a view of social situations in competitive terms. Some adults think of business, politics, popularity, and even interpersonal conflicts as win-lose situations, in which the primary goal is to beat one's opponents. The idea of a win-win strategy to resolve conflict is very foreign in this context.

Winning is a great high. Many young adults have fond memories associated with winning an important game or a big match. They hope to reexperience the energy that occurs as a result of winning as they approach their adult activities. The metaphor of playing on a winning team is deeply interwoven into the world of work, helping to give focus and drive to day-to-day work-related obligations and tasks. When adults look back on their childhood play experiences, many recall the excitement associated with competition and continue to long for this excitement in their daily life. In one study of women in traditional and nontraditional professions, for example, more professional businesswomen and other women in nontraditional fields remembered experiences playing in competitive sports and being on teams with both boys and girls during their childhood (Coats & Overman, 1992).

In contrast to those who are energized by the challenges of competition, some children are especially sensitive to the pain of failure. The public embarrassment and private shame that accompany failure are powerful emotions. Some children will go to remarkable extremes to avoid failing. In team sports, each game ends with a winning and a losing side. Children who have a low sense of self-esteem are more likely to experience intense anxiety about losing in a competitive situation (Brustad, 1988). Involvement in team sports is guaranteed to bring with it the bitterness of losing and the commitment to avoid it at all costs—experiences that drive some children away from sports and into other domains of competence.

Cooperation

A complementary concept is cooperation: Team members learn that if the team as a whole is to do its best, the team members must help one another. Rather than playing all the roles, a team member tries to help every other member play his role as well as possible. **Cooperation** takes many forms: Members share resources, take time to help other team members improve their skills, plan strategies together, work together on the field, encourage each other, bring out the equipment, or clean up after the game. In many sports, there is a dynamic tension between competition and cooperation. Team members may compete with each other for a more desirable position or for the status of being the top player. At the same time, the team members know that they have to support each other, especially when they play against another team.

Cooperation is a fundamental feature of evolution. Selection favors families and groups whose members are cooperative. In the evolutionary past warfare between competing groups was common. Those groups that were able to foster greater cooperation among members had a better chance of survival (Pennisi, 2009). It appears that the human brain has evolved so that the individual acts to defend the group against threat, even if such efforts result in exposure to danger to the self. Under conditions of intergroup competition, the brain produces oxytocin, a hormone that enhances empathy, generosity, cooperation, and trust. The adaptive value of cooperation is supported by this hormonal activity, which strengthens the individual's positive sentiments toward the group and willingness to promote the group's welfare (De Dreu, Greer et al., 2010).

In-Group and Out-Group Attitudes

Team membership provides a microsystem for observing the formation of in-group and out-group attitudes and behaviors. All human societies observe distinctions between in-group and out-group attitudes and behaviors (Haidt, 2007). The **in-group** members share common norms, goals, and values. They also share a common fate—in sports, for example, the team wins or loses as a team. Feelings of cohesiveness with and similarity to members of an in-group prompt behaviors that are supportive of that group's survival. Typically, individuals distribute resources so that members of their in-group receive more and members of the out-group receive less. However, when in-group norms emphasize fairness and reject discrimination, members are more likely to treat members of the out-group with fairness. Thus, in-group norms can influence the degree to which out-group hostilities are encouraged and expressed or suppressed (Jetten, Spears, & Manstead, 1996).

The **out-group** is any group whose goals are either in opposition to or inconsistent with the goals of the in-group. Any group may be perceived as an out-group, even though it does not actually pose any physical threat to members of the in-group. Students at one university may perceive students at another university as an out-group (e.g., the longstanding football rivalry between Ohio State University and the University of Michigan). Students enrolled in one program or major may view students in a similar but competing major as an out-group (e.g., chemical engineers vs. electrical engineers). In experimental studies, in-groups and out-groups have been formed based simply on wearing a blue or yellow badge, or based on those with blue eyes and those with brown eyes (Bigler, Spears, & Brown, 2001; Verkuyten & De Wolf, 2007). Children as young as age 5 are aware of the status of their group. If they believe that their group has positive qualities and is valued, they are more likely to want to remain in the group and to see themselves as similar to other group members (Nesdale & Flesser, 2001; Bigler, Brown, & Markell, 2001).

Children learn to see the outcome of competition as a win-lose situation. For sports teams, the out-group's goal of winning is in direct competition with the in-group's similar goal. The other team is seen as the enemy, and there is no alternative to trying one's hardest to defeat it. Antagonism toward the out-group is valued in team sports, and any attempt to assist the other team is seen as unethical. Moving to the level of interethnic or intertribal conflict, children may learn that moral principles that apply to members of the in-group do not necessarily apply to members of the out-group (Triandis, 1990). In the extreme, adults may justify killing a member of an out-group under conditions of terrorism or war.

Children may belong to more than one team. Depending on the situation, children can view one another as members of their in-group in one sport and as members of an out-group in another sport. For example, Ryan and his friend Tom were on the school soccer team together, but they belonged to different summer baseball leagues. During the summer, they had to compete against each other, so it usually turned out that they spent more time together and were closer friends during the school year than they were during the summers. Categorizing a peer as a member of an in-group or an out-group will lead to different attitudes and behaviors toward that person.

As children get older, their tendency to show unquestioning favoritism for their in-group is tempered by social reality and their experiences of participating in multiple groups (Verkuyten & De Wolf, 2007). They can evaluate information that suggests that one team or nationality or ethnic group is better than another, and use that information to temper their in-group favoritism or their out-group prejudices. At the same time, functional messages that highlight the benefits of being in one group over another can strengthen in-group bias. For example, research on gender identity suggests that young children are especially likely to attribute positive qualities to their own sex and to exaggerate the differences between their sex and the opposite sex. When sex is used as a functional category, for example, comparing boys' and girls' conduct or school performance, these in-group preferences are likely to be strengthened (Egan & Perry, 2001). Table 8.2 shows the in-group and out-group attitudes that may result from experiences in team play.

TABLE 8.2 In-Group and Out-Group Attitudes That Develop Through Team Play Experiences

IN-GROUP ATTITUDES	OUT-GROUP ATTITUDES
The child learns:	The child learns:
1. To value and contribute to team goals	1. To view the goals of the opponent as inconsistent with the goals of the in-group
2. To subordinate personal goals to team goals	2. To view the outcome of competition as a zero-sum game, in which only one team can win
3. To receive and use feedback and help from team members	3. To recognize that helping the other team is unethical
4. To value one's role as an element in a larger system and the interdependence of the team members	4. To accept the necessity for antagonism between members of opposing teams
5. To recognize that team members share a common fate	5. To devise strategies that will exploit the weaknesses of the opponent

Team Play as a Context for Development

Participation in team sports provides socialization experiences that have both positive and negative consequences. For most children, belonging to a team, making friends, learning new skills, and enjoying the sense of success associated with a collaborative effort are positive experiences of middle childhood. For example, in a study of what young people value about their sports experiences, most children placed the greatest emphasis on enjoyment and personal achievement, and the least emphasis on winning (Lee, Whitehead, & Balchin, 2000). However, we all know of instances where rivalries escalate into peer hatreds, children from neighboring schools turn against each other, and coaches humiliate and degrade children in order to instill a commitment to the team and a determination to win. Perhaps the question is whether—particularly in team sports—the focal point of the activity is to enhance children's natural impulses for competence and skill elaboration, or whether the team activity becomes a way for adults to vent their own frustrated needs for domination and power.

Team play has implications for both social and intellectual development. Children who play team sports see themselves as contributors to a larger effort and learn to anticipate the consequences of their behavior for the group. Team play creates a valuable context for the formation of interpersonal relationships. Inclusion in a positive team experience often results in a child's identification with the coach and other team members. These new emotional investments can expand the child's sense of well-being and social support (Blanchard, Perreault, & Vallerand, 1998; Wylleman, 2000). In a comparison of seventh-grade children who were or were not involved in organized team sports, teachers rated the children who were involved in sports as more socially competent, and less withdrawn. There were no differences between the groups in aggression. However, among the boys, those involved in sports also reported a broader range of delinquent behaviors (McHale et al., 2005).

Games that involve teams are generally so complex that children are called on to learn many rules, make judgments about those rules, plan strategies, and assess the strengths and weaknesses of the other players. All of these characteristics of participation in team sports can stimulate cognitive growth. In one study, for example, children were divided into soccer experts and soccer novices (Schneider & Bjorklund, 1992). The experts had an impressive depth of knowledge about the game of soccer and, when given a memory task involving soccer-related items, were able to use their expertise to perform at a high level.

Interest in sports and competitive team play has been used as a motivational hook to promote other areas of school ability. For example, children diagnosed with attention deficit/hyperactivity disorder (ADHD) were recruited for a basketball camp. Many of these children had difficulties regulating their impulses and showed poor social skills. The camp focused on athletic competence and sportsmanship.

The combined efforts resulted in improved communication skills, reduced aggressiveness, increased interest in basketball as an activity, and some improvement in sports ability (Hupp & Reitman, 1999). Well-designed sports programs can have a broad impact on intellectual and social development by combining increased competence in physical activity with related emphasis on the cognitive and social components of team play.

The Psychosocial Crisis: Industry versus Inferiority

Objective 6. To explain the psychosocial crisis of industry versus inferiority; the central process through which the crisis is resolved; education; the prime adaptive ego quality of competence; and the core pathology of inertia.

According to psychosocial theory (Erikson, 1963), as a result of the resolution of the psychosocial crisis of industry versus inferiority, a person's fundamental attitude toward work is established during middle childhood. As children develop skills and acquire personal standards of evaluation, they make an initial assessment of whether or not they will be able to make a contribution to the social community. They also make an inner commitment to strive for success. Some children are keenly motivated to compete against a standard of excellence and achieve success. Other children have low expectations about the possibility of success and are not motivated by achievement situations. The strength of a child's need to achieve success is well established by the end of this stage (Atkinson & Birch, 1978).

Supporting the psychosocial perspective, results of the American Psychological Association's *Stress in America* survey indicate that children in middle childhood experience a variety of worries linked to the themes of industry and inferiority (Munsey, 2010). Among children ages 8 to 12, 44% worry about doing well in school; 28% worry about whether their family will have enough money; and 22% worry about getting along with their friends. Their worries are associated with physical symptoms including headaches, sleep disturbances, and upset stomachs. The survey found that parents tended to underestimate the extent to which their children were worrying about family finances or doing well in school, and were often unaware of the physical symptoms their children were experiencing. These findings illustrate the domains in which the conflict of industry versus inferiority are being played out for children in the United States. They suggest that children are keenly attuned to themes of evaluation and competence, not only in their academic lives, but in social relationships and in the adult world of work and family financial well-being.

Industry

Industry is an eagerness to acquire skills and perform meaningful work. During middle childhood, many aspects of work are intrinsically motivating. The skills are new. They bring the child closer to the capacities of adults. Each new skill allows the child some degree of independence and may even bring new responsibilities that heighten her sense of worth. In addition to these self-motivating factors associated with increased competence, external sources of reward promote skill development. Parents and teachers may encourage children to get better grades by giving them material rewards, additional privileges, and praise. Peers also encourage the acquisition of some skills, although they may have some negative input with regard to others. Certain youth organizations, such as scouting and 4-H, make the acquisition of skills a very specific route to success and higher status.

Kowaz and Marcia (1991) described the construct of industry as comprising three dimensions:

1. The *cognitive* component of industry was defined as the acquisition of the basic skills and knowledge that are valued by the culture.
2. The *behavioral* component of industry was defined as the ability to apply the skills and knowledge effectively through characteristics such as concentration, perseverance, work habits, and goal directedness.
3. The *affective* component of industry was defined as the positive emotional orientation toward the acquisition and application of skills and knowledge, such as a general curiosity and desire to know, a pride in one's efforts, and an ability to handle the distresses of failure as well as the joys of success.

Inferiority

What experiences of middle childhood might generate a sense of **inferiority**? Feelings of worthlessness and inadequacy come from two sources: the self and the social environment. Alfred Adler (1935) directed attention to the central role that organ inferiority may play in shaping a person's perceptions of his abilities. **Organ inferiority** is any physical or mental limitation that prevents the acquisition of certain skills. Children who cannot master certain skills experience some feelings of inferiority. Individual differences in aptitude, physical development, and prior experience result in experiences of inadequacy in some domain. No one can do everything well. Children discover that they cannot master every skill they attempt. Even a child who feels quite positive toward work and finds new challenges invigorating will experience some degree of inferiority in a specific skill that she cannot master. For example, students who are born just after the age cutoff date for a particular sports competition may find that they have a hard time competing with the slightly older children in their age group. Especially at younger ages, children who are matched with others who are 10 to 12 months older may experience disappointment when they cannot compete successfully (Musch & Grondin, 2001). For many children who have developmental delays or motor impairments, the challenge of experiencing mastery in school-based skills can be very frustrating. Disorders of childhood that influence school success are discussed in the Human Development and Diversity box on page 324.

If success in one area could compensate for failure in another, we would be safe in minimizing the effect of individual areas of inadequacy on the overall resolution of the psychosocial conflict of industry versus inferiority. However,

In many countries, children in middle childhood are expected to contribute to their families' economic well-being. This family is picking vegetables. Each child's sense of industry is tied to being able to work efficiently at a difficult task that is essential for the family's survival.

Indeed/Jupiter Images

the social environment does not reinforce success in all areas equally. During middle childhood, success in reading is much more highly rewarded than success in tinkering with broken automobile engines. Likewise, success in team sports is more highly valued than success in operating a ham radio. It is difficult for a child who does not excel in culturally valued skills to compensate through the mastery of others.

The social environment also generates feelings of inferiority through the process of *social comparison*. Particularly in the school setting, but even in the home, children are confronted by statements suggesting that they are not as good as some peer, sibling, or cultural subgroup. Children may be grouped, tracked, graded, or publicly criticized on the basis of how their efforts compare with someone else's. The intrinsic pleasure of engaging in a task for the challenge it presents conflicts with messages that stimulate feelings of self-consciousness, competitiveness, and doubt: "I like playing ball, but I'm not as good as Ted, so I don't think I'll play." As children become increasingly sensitive to peer acceptance and peer rejection, they may refuse to try a new activity because they fear the possibility of being bettered or embarrassed by their peers.

Finally, the social environment stimulates feelings of inferiority through the negative value it places on any kind of failure. Two types of failure messages that may contribute to feelings of inferiority have been described. One type consists of criticisms of the child's motivation or effort. Such criticisms imply that, if the child had really tried, he could have avoided failure. The other type refers more specifically to a lack of ability. Here, the implication is that the child does not have the basic aptitude to succeed. This type of failure message is associated with a pattern of attitudes about the self that has been described as learned helplessness.

Learned helplessness is a belief that success or failure have little to do with one's effort and are largely outside one's control (Seligman, 1975; Nelson, 1987). In a study of fourth, fifth, and sixth graders, children were asked to verbalize their thoughts as they worked on various tasks. The children's verbalizations following failure showed a clear difference between the mastery-oriented children and the helpless ones. The mastery-oriented children were able to keep a positive attitude, increase their problem-solving efforts, and use their past mistakes to correct their approach. The helpless children began to blame themselves ("I never did have a good memory"). They emphasized the negative aspects of the task or criticized their own abilities and tried to find ways to escape from the situation (Diener & Dweck, 1980).

Helpless children tend to discount their successes and, in response to even a few remarks about their lack of ability, generate a self-definition that leads them to take a pessimistic view of their future success. When faced with a difficult or challenging situation, children described as helpless experience a negative mood while working on the task, give up quickly, blame their failures on a lack of ability, and expect to fail in the future (Cain & Dweck, 1995). Messages about failure usually suggest that there is an external standard of perfection—an ideal that the child did not meet. A few failures

© 2010 Brand X Pictures/Jupiterimages Corporation

In the modern classroom, children are encouraged to help one another solve complex problems.

may generate such strong negative feelings that the child will avoid engaging in new tasks in order to avoid future failure. Longitudinal research suggests that children who are identified as helpless in their approach to tasks in kindergarten continue to show evidence of these same behaviors, expectations, and emotions as first graders and as fifth graders (Ziegert, Kistner, Castro, & Robertson, 2001).

When children resolve the psychosocial crisis in the direction of inferiority they do not conceive of themselves as having the potential to contribute to the welfare of the larger community. This is a serious consequence. It makes the gradual incorporation of the individual into a meaningful social group difficult to achieve. The irony of the psychosocial crisis at this stage is that the social community, which depends on the individual's motives for mastery for its survival, is itself such a powerful force in negating those motives by communicating messages of inferiority.

The Central Process: Education

Education is a culture's process for transmitting valued knowledge and skills from one generation to the next. Every culture must devise ways of passing on the wisdom and skills of past

HUMAN DEVELOPMENT AND DIVERSITY

Disorders of Childhood That Interfere with School Success

WHAT HAPPENS WHEN children have real difficulty accomplishing the tasks associated with basic areas of school achievement? The centrality of success in school-based learning for a positive resolution of the psychosocial crisis of industry versus inferiority brings the problem of childhood disorders to our attention. Three groups of disorders are described here, each one posing significant challenges for academic and social success during middle childhood and beyond. Typically, these disorders become more disruptive as children encounter the increasingly complex demands of the school curriculum.

LEARNING DISORDERS

Learning disorders are diagnosed when a child's skills and measured abilities in reading, mathematics, or written communication are well below the child's grade level and the level expected from the child's measured IQ (National Center for Learning Disabilities, 2001). Learning disorders have been identified in approximately 5% of public school children in the United States. These children are differentiated from others who show low performance because of mental retardation, poor teaching, or cultural factors that interfere with school performance. Typically, **learning disorders** are linked with deficits in the primary processing system, including speed and accuracy of information processing, attention, and memory. These deficits may be a result of genetic disorders, neurological damage during the prenatal period, or lead poisoning during childhood, but not all children with learning disorders have a history of these conditions. Children who have learning disorders commonly also suffer from low self-esteem and are more likely than other children to drop out of school.

MOTOR SKILLS DISORDERS

Approximately 4% to 6% of children in the 5 to 11 age range have a developmental problem in the area of motor skills. **Motor skills disorders** may manifest themselves in a variety of ways, including difficulty with large or small muscle coordination, speed of movement, muscle tone and strength, motor planning, and sensory integration (Floet & Maldonado-Durán, 2006). Children with these disorders may appear clumsy and delayed in the typical acquisition of early motor skills such as walking, running, tying their shoes, or using scissors or a knife. In later school years, they have trouble writing with a pencil or pen, are slow to develop skills in putting together puzzles or models, and their athletic skills, such as throwing and catching a ball, are delayed. These children are distinguished from others who have some broader medical diagnosis such as cerebral palsy. Their delay in motor skills interferes with academic achievement to the extent that these children struggle with any kind of written assignment and have difficulty completing projects that require manual dexterity. They lack the satisfaction of excelling in physical activities because even simple motor skills such as running or playing catch are sources of frustration.

---

generations to its young. This is the meaning of **education** in its broadest sense. It is also the process through which standards are established for exemplary, acceptable, or unacceptable performance. As a result, education is the central process through which children experience the sense of mastery and accomplishment associated with industry and the critical feedback or negative evaluations that are associated with inferiority.

Education is different from schooling. The term *education* can have different meanings across cultural groups. For example, in Spanish the word *educación* refers to the internalization of proper, respectful social behavior. The goal of *educación* is character development. For children growing up in indigenous communities of north and central America, the cultural tradition for education emphasizes learning by keenly observing the activities of the adults around them, and then participating as they feel ready (López, Correa-Chávez, Rogoff, & Gutiérrez, 2010). In the United States, the term *education* focuses on an individual's acquisition of knowledge and skill development, typically gained within the context of school or a formal program of instruction (Greenfield, Keller, Fuligni, & Maynard, 2003).

The practice of separating formal educational experiences from the direct, intimate, hands-on activities of home and community is only about 200 years old. Before the industrial revolution, most children were educated by participating with their parents in the tasks of home life, farming, commerce with neighbors, and participation in religious life (Coleman, 1987). In the case of the nobility, children often had tutors who supervised their education at home. Today, however, schools bear the primary responsibility for education. Teaching, which began as an extension of the parental role, has become a distinct profession. In our culture, education is not the kind of continuous interplay between the skilled and the unskilled that it is in more traditional cultures. Formal learning takes place in a special building during certain hours of the day. To be sure, the success of that experience in promoting a child's skills and a sense of the self as a learner

COMMUNICATION DISORDERS

Some children experience a developmental delay in effective social communication. Difficulties may include delays in acquiring new vocabulary; oversimplified grammatical expressions; limited variation in sentence types and structures; problems in sound production, such as lisping, omitting certain sounds in spoken speech, or stuttering; and problems in understanding certain types of words, expressions, and grammatical constructions. About 3% to 5% of children have some type of developmental communication disorder that is distinct from mental retardation or a hearing impairment that influences speech (National Dissemination Center for Children with Disabilities, 2004). These difficulties interfere with academic performance especially because school learning involves the ongoing communication of information and ideas. Children who have **communication disorders** are also likely to be the target of peer teasing and social ridicule, leading to a pattern of social withdrawal or inappropriate social participation.

Learning disorders, motor skills disorders, and communication disorders are three of the more common childhood disorders among a variety of mental, emotional, and physical disabilities that young children may face as they struggle to resolve the crisis of industry versus inferiority. Each of these conditions makes it more difficult for children to succeed in the daily tasks of schooling. Children who experience these disorders may find it difficult to carry out projects or to complete assignments that others view as simple. They may also become targets of peer teasing, bullying, or rejection. As a result, they may define themselves as incompetent, inferior, or unable to learn (Valas, 2001). With appropriate diagnosis and effective intervention, however, children can learn strategies to overcome or compensate for their disabilities.

Success in coping with a disability may, in fact, strengthen a child's self-confidence and provide a basis for beliefs of self-efficacy. Many children use the experience of coping with a disability as evidence that they can face and overcome other difficult challenges in their lives.

Critical Thinking Questions

1. Compare and contrast the kinds of problems children with each type of disorder described in this box might experience in school.
2. What are some implications of each of these disorders for peer relationships and friendship formation?
3. What steps might a family take to help support a child with each of these disorders? What role might family members play with regard to school? Peers? The child's own self-evaluation?
4. What is the responsibility of schools for meeting the needs of children with these kinds of disorders? What might be the best approach for supporting children with these various special needs?
5. What might be some coping strategies that children use to sustain their positive self-regard and to pursue high levels of achievement despite these challenges?

depends heavily on the ongoing involvement and commitment of family members (Hill & Taylor, 2004). However, schools play a key role in providing opportunities for skill development and mastery, contexts for assessment, social comparison, and self-evaluation, and socialization for the behavioral characteristics—including focus, persistence, and organization—that contribute to the formation of a personal sense of industry.

During the elementary school years, the goal of education is to help children develop the basic tools of learning. Central to this process is an introduction to the language of concepts, theories, and relationships that will allow them to organize their experiences. Schools strive to develop verbal and analytic problem solving. Instruction focuses on rules, descriptions, and abstract concepts (Tharp, 1989). Children are exposed to a range of disciplines and methods of inquiry for dealing with complex problems. Throughout the educational process, children are presented with problems of increasing difficulty. They are given many opportunities to

practice their newly developing skills, receiving continuous feedback about their level of competence.

In addition to the acquisition of skills and knowledge, schools emphasize an approach to behavior that can be described as a combination of *citizenship, social competence*, and *study habits*. Schools impart a code of conduct that is intended to facilitate the teacher's ability to guide students' attention, help children organize and focus on the tasks at hand, and foster a respectful, cooperative attitude toward adults and peers. Within this framework, all of these qualities become part of the sense of industry for those children who adapt well to the culture of schooling. Some children do not do well in this culture of schooling; they do not bring the expected social behaviors or study habits; they do not demonstrate the desired qualities of cooperation, self-regulation, or rule compliance. As a result, they receive negative evaluations, which contribute to feelings of inferiority, leading to a gradual disengagement from the educational experiences of school. Low school-engagement behaviors in the early elementary grades are as strong predictors of dropping out of school as are grades and test scores (Alexander, Entwisle, & Kabbani, 2001).

Schools, as institutions of the larger communities they serve, may not have the same expectations for success for all the students who attend; and children and their families do not all bring the same degree of trust in the educational process to their schooling. In some cases, parents find that they have no access to or voice in decisions affecting their children. They and their children experience barriers to achieving success in the skills that schooling values. For example, in a study of Latino immigrant families, parents experienced language barriers, an inability of teachers to explain their children's school difficulties, and constraints in making contact with teachers. Even though parents expressed a desire to support their children's school success, they felt helpless and dismissed as they tried to make contact with the school (Ramirez, 2003). The sense of inferiority can be provoked for children when they perceive that the school devalues or disrespects their parents.

In some cases, inferiority is inflicted on children through abusive treatment by school adults. In the United States, in a single school year over 200,000 children were victims of corporal punishment in their schools, a practice that is legal in 20 states. African American children and children with disabilities were overrepresented in the percentages of groups who were punished by paddling and other physical means (Murphy, Vagins, & Parker, 2010).

Failure in school and the public ridicule that it brings play a central role in the establishment of a negative self-image, which can be readily linked to the sense of inferiority. Sometimes, children defend themselves against the threat of failure messages by blaming others for their failures or by bragging that they can succeed in other ways. Much as it may appear that these children do not care about school or the school's goals, the school remains a symbol of cultural authority. Children in these groups may conclude that the only way to retain a basic sense of self-confidence is to withdraw from school and try to establish their competence among their peers by accelerating their transition to adulthood through more risky paths (Ogbu, 1987; Clark, 1991; Gregory, 1995; Alexander, Entwisle, & Kabbani, 2001).

The Prime Adaptive Ego Quality and the Core Pathology

Competence

Erikson's (1982) notion of **competence** as the prime adaptive ego quality is a belief in one's ability to make sense of and master the demands of a situation.

> Competence, in turn, is the free exercise of dexterity and intelligence in the completion of tasks, unimpaired

by infantile inferiority. It is the basis for cooperative participation in technologies, and it relies, in turn, on the logic of tools and skills. (Erikson, 1978, p. 30)

Competence provides the child with a deep confidence in his ability to engage in new situations and do well. This idea is illustrated by a study that monitored children's perceptions of competence during school transitions from grade 5 to 6 and from grade 6 to 7. The children who had the highest levels of perceived competence also had the strongest positive feelings about how they were doing in school and showed the highest scores on a measure of intrinsic motivation. They wanted to be challenged by their schoolwork and they liked working independently and figuring things out for themselves. They expressed curiosity about the tasks, saying they would work hard because of their own interest rather than to please the teacher or to get good grades (Harter, Whitesell, & Kowalski, 1992).

As she conceptualized the relationship of competence and self-esteem, Harter (1993) described two distinct paths of development that emerge during middle childhood: daily monitoring of self-esteem and stable self-esteem. For one group, day-to-day self-esteem is based on current experiences of competence and social approval. For these children, feelings of self-worth vary depending on how people who are important to them treat them that day and on whether the child is comparing her accomplishments with someone who is quite a bit better, about the same, or not really as competent. The second group of children tends to have had many positive experiences of approval and competence in the past, which lead to a stable, positive sense of self-worth. As a result, these children are not as dependent on changing day-to-day conditions to sustain a positive feeling of worth. They tend to feel good about themselves, and thus enter new situations with a more positive, optimistic expectation of being liked and doing well. Sensing that they are competent, they leave this stage capable of using mastery and the resulting coping strategies to add to their repertoire of adaptive ego qualities—hope, will, and purpose—as they begin to encounter the new demands of early adolescence.

Children who have internalized a sense of competence love to learn and work. They are excited about developing new skills and are optimistic about being able to achieve success. These children are the ones who sign up for new activities or start neighborhood clubs, want to be on two or three sports teams, look forward to field trips and school projects, and take pleasure in being asked to help with difficult tasks like planting trees along the highway, building a new playground, or raising money for earthquake victims. In contrast, some children feel a powerful sense of apathy or disinterest, which Erikson referred to as *inertia*.

Inertia

Inertia is the core pathology of middle childhood: "The antipathic counterpart of industry, the sense of competent mastery to be experienced in the school age, is that inertia

Erika is an excellent student who enjoys teaching others. Here she is demonstrating her reading and spelling competence as she guides the class in a word-recognition activity.

that constantly threatens to paralyze an individual's productive life and is, of course, fatefully related to the inhibition of the preceding age, that of play" (Erikson, 1982, pp. 76–77).

Children who leave early school age with a sense of inhibition fail to participate and engage much during middle childhood. These are not the students who try and fail repeatedly, nor are they the ones whose sense of competence must be reconfirmed daily. Instead, they are students who tend to be passive and withdrawn, never engaging psychologically with the demands of their schools or their communities. Children who leave middle childhood with a sense of inertia continue to be withdrawn and passive. They will have trouble instigating actions or changing the course of events in their lives. As a result, they will not be likely to address challenges or problems by formulating plans of action, evaluating them, and then executing them. Children with a sense of inertia will not believe that they can master the challenges they face, and thus, they are likely to be swept along by the tide of events.

We all experience periods of inertia—times when we cannot muster the energy, enthusiasm, or confidence to take action. We may become besieged by doubts about our competence and worth—doubts that can produce work blocks, writer's block, waves of fatigue, boredom, procrastination, or aimlessness. Typically, one can survive a few days or even weeks on automatic pilot, doing the bare minimum to survive. And children may be able to get by for quite a while without exercising much energy or direction, especially if they are being sustained by parents and teachers. Eventually, however, life brings demands for change and expectations to meet new challenges that have never been faced before. At those times, children who are burdened with a pervasive sense of inertia may be unable to cope.

Violence in the Lives of Children

Objective 7. To explore the impact of exposure to violence on development during middle childhood.

IN RECENT YEARS the problem of violence in families, schools, and neighborhoods has threatened to undermine the quality of the psychosocial development and educational attainment of many American children. Each year, an estimated 5 million children in the United States are exposed to violence in the form of direct physical abuse, domestic violence between their parents or other members of their household, and exposure to violent crimes in their neighborhood or school. In the terrorist attacks of September 11, 2001, thousands of U.S. children lost one or both parents in an act of violence; thousands more were evacuated from their homes and schools; and continuing threats of violence have raised new levels of fear about unpredictable harm. Since the start of the U.S. military engagement in Iraq in 2003, Iraqi children have been exposed to unpredictable violence on a daily basis as a result of suicide bombings, roadside explosions, rocket and machine gun fire, military actions, and executions of targeted civilians (www.Iraqbodycount.org, 2007). Estimates by the United Nations have been as high as 100 civilian deaths a day. The topic of violence in the lives of children illustrates the interaction of the biological, psychological, and societal systems as they contribute to developmental trajectories.

Every 15-year-old boy in this Ethiopian village of cattle breeders is expected to know how to defend his herd from raids from competing tribes. Children are exposed to frequent violence and are trained at a young age to use assault weapons to protect their homes and property.

© Ton Koene/ANP/Newscom

Consequences of Exposure to Violence

Three consequences of exposure to violence are of especially grave concern: children are harmed, children become more violent, and exposure to violence disrupts cognitive functioning and mental health.

First, as a result of the violence in their families and neighborhoods, large numbers of children and youth are victims of violent crimes. Homicide is the third leading cause of death for children ages 5 to 14, and the second leading cause of death for adolescents and young adults ages 15 to 24 in the United States (U.S. Census Bureau, 2010). Children who live in low-income neighborhoods are especially vulnerable to exposure to violence. According to a report issued by the National Center for Educational Statistics, in 2003 roughly 740,000 violent crimes were committed at schools against students (DeVoe et al., 2005). In a survey of fifth graders who live in a very poor urban district in the Northeast, 82% reported being victimized at school, including being hit by another student, kicked or pushed by a student, threatened with a knife or other weapon, verbally threatened, or robbed. Ninety-three percent of the children had observed one of these forms of violence being directed to other students at their school (Cedeno, Elias, Kelly, & Chu, 2010). Neighborhoods that are centers of illegal drug trade are also often the sites of violence, including stabbings, shootings, and gang raids. In these communities, the loss of a legitimate economic base, with few people in stable or high-status occupations, leads to takeovers by gangs and other organized criminal activities. Children are lured into dangerous forms of drug-related transactions, which make them targets of violence on the streets as well as victims of abuse by drug-addicted family members and youth (National Research Council, 1993; Okundaye, 2004).

A second consequence of exposure to violence is the number of children who are themselves aggressive and violent. Many studies report a significant relationship between victimization or witnessing violence and carrying out violent actions on others. The accumulation of exposure to violence across several settings, including community, school, and home, coupled with low parental monitoring and the likelihood of being a victim of violence, create a context in which children exhibit serious violent behaviors (Garbarino, 2001; Preski & Shelton, 2001; Weist & Cooley-Quille, 2001).

A third consequence of exposure to violence is the disruption it produces in children's cognitive functioning and mental health (Osofsky, 1995). Children who have been severely abused or exposed to intense violence are now viewed as suffering from symptoms similar to post-traumatic stress disorder (Hamblen, 2003). **Post-traumatic stress disorder** can result from direct experience of a grave threat to personal safety or injury, witnessing the injury or death of another person, or learning about the violent death or injury of a family member or someone close. The response usually includes "intense fear, helplessness, or horror," and the person typically has recurrent vivid recollections or dreams of the event with accompanying strong emotional reactions. Children may have recurring nightmares, repeat the same play sequences that reenact some part of the traumatic event, withdraw interest from activities they used to enjoy, and show physical symptoms that they did not have before the event, such as stomachaches or headaches. School-age children may believe that there were warning signs that would have allowed them to avoid the trauma if they had been alert enough to recognize them. As a result, these children maintain a type of **hypervigilance** or increased arousal, directing their attention to threat-related stimuli (Dalgleish, Moradi,

Taghavi, NeshatDoost, & Yule, 2001). These symptoms may last for more than 1 month and often interfere with sleep, schoolwork, concentration, and normal social life (American Psychiatric Association, 1994).

Symptoms of post-traumatic stress disorder can be long lasting and, in some cases, can emerge long after the event has passed. For example, one study focused on 69 children who had lived within 100 miles of Oklahoma City in 1995 when the federal building was bombed. These children, studied in 1997, did not see the explosion, they did not live near the explosion, and no one they knew personally was injured or killed in the explosion. Yet 2 years after the event, many of these children showed evidence of post-traumatic stress disorder symptoms and related difficulties in functioning. Their symptoms were attributed to experiences of the event through the media and indirect loss through friends or family members who know someone who was killed (Pfefferbaum et al., 2000).

Evidence suggests that children preserve sensory and motor memories of the conditions associated with their trauma, which are then released under contemporary conditions of fear. In boys, these symptoms commonly reflect **hyperarousal**, including startle response, increases in heart rate, sleep disturbance, anxiety, and motor hyperactivity. In girls, the symptoms are more likely to be dissociation, gastrointestinal symptoms, and pain. Under threatening conditions, children who have been traumatized in the past automatically return to these disruptive states, making it difficult to access higher order problem-solving and reasoning skills.

According to the neurobiology of aggression, simple regulatory and impulsive functions are governed by the more primitive, reactive areas, including the brain stem and the midbrain. More complex functions of language and abstract reasoning develop later and are located largely in the subcortical and cortical areas. The ability to modify and regulate impulses involves the coordination of two neurological pathways, one which provides intense signals about threats or dangers emerging from the brain stem, and the other which provides ideas about alternative coping strategies emerging from the cortex (Perry, 1994). An overreactive brain stem that produces intense and frequent impulses may result from any one or a combination of factors, including fetal exposure to alcohol and drugs, environmental exposure to lead, hormonal abnormalities, head injuries, or exposure to child abuse. Children reared in a socialization environment of chaos, violence, parental aggression, and harsh and abusive discipline lack the opportunity to develop empathy, self-control, and higher order problem-solving skills that might allow them to modulate their strong impulses. Exposure to severe trauma may produce long-lasting changes in the way a child's brain regulates emotional reactions, the ability to concentrate, and the ability to inhibit impulses (American Psychological Association, 1996; *Science Daily*, 2007).

Preventing Violence

The prevention of violence in society and the reduction in exposure to violence among children have become significant public health issues (Dorfman, Woodruff, Chavez, & Wallack, 1997). Rather than focusing solely on the criminal justice definitions and strategies for deterrence, a public health perspective emphasizes the need to understand the contexts of violence from which strategies for prevention can be devised and evaluated, and invites collaboration in identifying many layers of prevention. We must learn more about what predisposes young children to respond to events in their lives with violence. We must try to determine what kinds of socialization environments can help children control their aggressiveness. Furthermore, we must discover strategies to reduce violence in neighborhoods, schools, and the media (Sampson, Raudenbush, & Earls, 1997; Henrich, Brown, & Aber, 1999). Several directions for prevention have been identified and require coordination:

1. Prevent prenatal and perinatal conditions that cause neurological damage and increase the biological vulnerability for violent behaviors.
2. Develop effective techniques for educating parents and teachers about socialization practices that help develop self-control, empathy, and perspective taking.
3. Develop effective techniques for teaching children alternative, nonaggressive strategies to handle and respond to insults, threats, and frustration.
4. Devise educational experiences that help children to reframe cognitions and beliefs that lead them to interpret the behaviors of others as threatening.
5. Reduce exposure to violence at home, in the neighborhood, and on television.
6. Decrease children's access to guns.
7. Increase the sense of social control and cohesion in neighborhoods, so that mutual trust is higher, people help one another more, and people are more willing to take steps to intervene when children are acting destructively.

A wide variety of school-based programs are being implemented to help reduce violence. Some focus on providing information about the problem and strategies for avoiding violence; some use role-playing, modeling, feedback, and reinforcement to alter students' behaviors; and some go beyond the classroom and the school environment by involving parents and community leaders to create a safe community where people are encouraged to practice positive behavioral interactions (Task Force on Community Preventive Services, 2007). In a review of 53 studies that evaluated universal school-based programs, researchers found that these programs were generally effective in decreasing violence. This research found that school-based programs that are delivered to all the children in the school rather than targeted to children who are at special risk for exposure to violence not only succeed in reducing violence, but are often associated with reduced truancy, improved school achievement, and improved social skills among students. To learn more about strategies that are designed to reduce violence in schools and support a positive school climate, visit the Web site of the Center for the Prevention of School Violence at www.ncdjjdp.org/cpsv.

Chapter Summary

During middle childhood, cognitive and social skills develop that are crucial to later life stages. Remarkable synergies occur across the cognitive domains, bringing new levels of skill development, expanded access to information, and complex strategies for approaching and solving problems. Children apply their cognitive abilities not only in academic, school-related domains, but also in an increased capacity for social cooperation, self-evaluation, and peer group participation. As a result of the combination of cognitive and social skill development, children are able to make significant contributions to the social groups to which they belong. They are also likely to seek approval and acceptance from these groups.

Objective 1. To clarify the role of friendship in helping children to learn to take the point of view of others, be sensitive to the norms and pressures of the peer group, experience closeness in relationships, and clarify the negative consequences that result from social rejection and loneliness.

The family environment provides the early context in which social competence emerges. The child's ability to establish and preserve friendships in middle childhood is built upon earlier capacities including temperament, attachment, sibling interactions, and the family's orientation toward peer relationships. Three important lessons are gained through participation in friendship: increasing appreciation for various points of view; awareness of peer norms and expectations; and a growing capacity for intimacy. As the role of friendship increases, problems tied to loneliness, rejection, and peer victimization become increasingly distressing.

Objective 2. To describe the development of concrete operational thought, including conservation, classification skills, mathematical reasoning, and the child's ability to understand and monitor his or her own knowledge and understanding.

In early and middle childhood, new cognitive capacities focus on mental operations that provide a logical system of relationships among objects. Three achievements of this stage of reasoning include the scheme for conservation, classification, and combinatorial skills. A hallmark of this period is an increase in logical, focused problem solving. Children are able to consider competing explanations, look at a problem from another person's point of view as well as their own, and use information to plan a strategy to reach a goal.

Objective 3. To analyze the nature of skill learning, including the presentation of a model for the process

of acquisition of complex skills such as reading and examination of societal factors that provide the context in which skill learning occurs.

An understanding of skill development combines an appreciation of the child's intellectual maturity with a sense of the significant motives that may influence willingness to learn. Skilled action takes place in a cultural context. Skill development involves the integration of multiple domains that may mature at different rates. Skilled behavior involves the coordination of simple and complex elements as well as overarching strategies to achieve specific goals. Reading is discussed as an example of a skill that begins as a focus of its own (learning to read) and then becomes integrated into the achievement of many other skills (reading to learn).

Objective 4. To examine the development of self-evaluation skills, including feelings of pride, self-efficacy, and ways that social expectations of parents, teachers, and peers contribute to a child's self-evaluation.

The combination of advanced reasoning through concrete operational thought and engagement in a more complex peer environment contribute to new approaches to self-evaluation. The themes of pride, self-efficacy, and sensitivity to the social expectations of others are all relevant to understanding how children evaluate their competence or incompetence, and their willingness to strive toward new levels of achievement.

Objective 5. To describe a new level of complexity in play as children become involved in team sports and athletic competition, and form more enduring in-group and out-group attitudes.

Team sports offer a new and more complex form of play, which combines the need for advanced levels of skill, cognitive capacities to understand rules and strategies for success, and interpersonal skills related to interdependence, cooperation, division of labor, and competition. Experiences regarding the formation of in-group and out-group attitudes are part of team sports. Team sports provide a microcosm of intergroup and intragroup relations that will be repeated in various contexts through adult life.

Objective 6. To explain the psychosocial crisis of industry versus inferiority; the central process through which the crisis is resolved; education; the prime adaptive ego quality of competence; and the core pathology of inertia.

Industry focuses primarily on building competence. The family, peer group, and school all play their part in the support of feelings of mastery or failure, industry or inferiority. In our society, school is the environment in which continuous attention is given to the child's success or failure in basic skill areas. The child's emerging sense of industry is closely interwoven with the quality of the school environment and the extent to which the child encounters experiences that foster enthusiasm for new learning and provide objective feedback about levels of mastery.

Objective 7. To explore the impact of exposure to violence on development during middle childhood.

The applied topic illustrates the biological, psychological, and societal contexts of violence. Children can be exposed to prenatal and perinatal risks that disrupt their neurological development. They may be embedded in a family system in which abusive or disorganized parenting reduces their ability to cope with threats or stress. Violence in the neighborhood, media, and school strengthens impulsive, reactive responses and makes it increasingly difficult for children to draw on their higher order reasoning skills to reinterpret or interrupt their sense of anger and threat. Access to weapons, especially guns, leads to new heights of destructive expression for these children.

The achievements of middle childhood contribute in key ways to coping and adaptation in adulthood. Issues of industry, mastery, achievement, social expectations, social skills, cooperativeness, and interpersonal sensitivity are all salient themes during this stage. A person's orientation toward friendship and work—two essential aspects of adult life—begin to take shape.

Key Terms

aggressive-rejected, 296
aggressive-withdrawn, 297
bullying, 298
categorization, 301
classification, 301
close friends, 294
cognitive restructuring, 295
communication disorders, 325
competence, 326
competition, 319
computational skills, 303
concrete operational thought, 297
conformity, 294
conservation, 300
conservation of number, 303
cooperation, 319
division of labor, 319
dyslexia, 308
education, 324
enactive attainment, 312
friendship, 291
hyperarousal, 329
hypervigilance, 328

identity, 300
illusion of competence, 317
illusion of incompetence, 317
industry, 322
inertia, 326
inferiority, 322
in-group/out-group attitudes, 320
intelligence, 306
interdependence, 318
learned helplessness, 323
learning disorders, 324
literacy, 308
loneliness, 295
mental operation, 298
metacognition, 304
motor skills disorders, 324
norms, 293
novice/expert, 305
operation, 298
organ inferiority, 322
peer approval, 294
perspective taking, 293
phonemic awareness, 308

physical state, 313
post-traumatic stress disorder, 328
pride, 312
reading fluency, 308
reciprocity, 300
rejection, 293
reversibility, 300
self-efficacy, 312
self-evaluation, 311
self-fulfilling prophecy, 314
self-monitoring, 316
skill learning, 305
skills, 305
social competence, 291
social expectations, 314
superordinate group identity, 319
team play, 318
verbal persuasion, 313
vicarious experience, 313
violence, 290
withdrawn, 297

Further Reflection

1. Think back on your middle childhood years, between the ages of 6 and 11. What are some examples of experiences that made you feel competent and self-assured? What are examples of experiences that led to feelings of inferiority or self-doubt?

2. Consider the role of friendship during this period of life. How might friends contribute to skill development? Self-evaluation? Cognitive problem solving?

3. How does the environment of school change from age 6 (grade 1) through age 11 (grade 6)? How well do changes in the school environment match the developmental changes that take place during this period of life?

4. Think about school success and failure in middle childhood. What personal, family, cultural, and environmental factors might contribute to school success? To school failure? Suppose that you were asked to provide guidance to a local school board about improving their elementary schools. What ideas from this chapter might inform your recommendations?

5. The psychosocial crisis of industry versus inferiority is closely linked to one's attitude about work in later stages of life. What is your view about how young adults view entry into the world of work? What contribution might events from middle childhood make to this outlook?

6. What are the primary factors that promote violence among children in middle childhood? What steps are needed to buffer children from the negative impact of violence and to promote a cooperative, peaceful resolution of conflicts?

Psychology CourseMate

To access additional course materials, including CourseMate, please visit www.cengagebrain.com. At the CengageBrain .com home page, search for the ISBN of your title (from the back cover of your book) using the search box at the top of the page. This will take you to the product page where these resources can be found.

Casebook

For additional case material related to this chapter, see the case entitled "Ayesha and the Dinosaurs" in *Life Span Development: A Case Book*, by Barbara and Philip Newman, Laura Landry-Meyer, and Brenda J. Lohman, pp. 100–104. The case suggests how new cognitive skills, skill learning, and a sense of competence come together to promote new levels of leadership and problem solving in middle childhood. The case also illustrates some of the challenges that children face in the transition to kindergarten and how home, preschool, and kindergarten systems can work together to foster a child's continuing school success.

© The Metropolitan Museum of Art/Art Resource, NY/© 2011 Estate of Pablo Picasso/Artists Rights Society (ARS), New York

In early adolescence, physical changes of puberty are accompanied by alterations in the self-concept. These alterations are prompted, in part, by the realization that one is making a transition from childhood toward adulthood, and, in part, by changes in the way one is perceived and treated by others.

Early Adolescence (12 to 18 Years)

Chapter Objectives

1. To describe the patterns of physical maturation during puberty for female and male adolescents, including an analysis of the impact of early and late maturing on self-concept and social relationships.

2. To characterize the development of romantic and sexual relationships, including a focus on the transition to coitus, the formation of a sexual orientation, and factors associated with pregnancy and parenthood in adolescence.

3. To introduce and critically evaluate the basic features of formal operational thought, highlighting the new conceptual skills that emerge in early adolescence and the factors that promote the development of advanced reasoning at this period of life.

4. To examine patterns of emotional development in early adolescence, including three examples of emotional disorders: eating disorders, delinquency, and depression.

5. To describe the further evolution of peer relations in early adolescence, especially the formation of cliques and crowds, and to contrast the impact of parents and peers during this stage.

6. To describe the psychosocial crisis of group identity versus alienation, the central process through which the crisis is resolved, peer pressure, the prime adaptive ego quality of fidelity to others, and the core pathology of isolation.

7. To review the patterns of adolescent alcohol and drug use and the factors associated with their use and abuse within a psychosocial framework.

AT THIS POINT in our discussion of life stages, we depart again from Erikson's conceptualization. His psychosocial theory viewed adolescence as a single stage, unified by the resolution of the central conflict of identity versus identity confusion. Erikson's approach attempted to address the tasks and needs of children and youth ranging in age from about 11 to 21 years within one developmental stage. Based on our own research on adolescence and our assessment of the research literature, we have come to the conclusion that two distinct periods of psychosocial development occur during these years—early adolescence (12 to 18 years) and later adolescence (18 to 24 years). This chapter discusses the stage of early adolescence; Chapter 10 discusses later adolescence.

Early adolescence begins with the onset of puberty and ends with graduation from high school (or roughly at age 18). This stage is characterized by rapid physical changes, significant cognitive and emotional maturation, newly energized sexual interests, and a heightened sensitivity to peer relations. We have called the psychosocial crisis of this stage **group identity** versus **alienation**. Later adolescence begins at approximately age 18 and continues for about 6 years. This stage is characterized by new advances in the establishment of autonomy from the family and the development of a personal identity. The psychosocial crisis of this period is **individual identity** versus **identity confusion**.

The elaboration of adolescence into two stages is closely tied to social and historical changes. At the beginning of the 20th century in the United States, few youths in the 12 to 18 age range were in school; at the turn of the 21st century, almost all of them were. The time between entry into puberty and entry into the self-sustaining roles of adulthood has expanded. In contrast to life 100 years ago, we have a longer period of required education and training, fewer opportunities to enter the full-time labor force without a high school education, laws restricting the employment of children under the age of 16, and a workplace that requires more advanced technical, representational, and interpersonal skills for success. At the same time, occupational choices are much more diverse, and the process of selecting a career path has become increasingly difficult. Thus, adolescence has stretched out as a period of life. Young people reach the biological capacity to reproduce and the physical stature of an adult at an earlier age, but they do not yet have the education, skills, training, or sense of purpose to create a sustainable lifestyle independent of their family of origin.

For adolescents, the challenge and even the joy of the period is to construct a sense of self that is at once connected to meaningful individuals and groups and, at the same time, authentic and autonomous. Adolescence is a thrilling time of life, a time of lasting memories about first experiences. Young people emerge into a wider, more varied social environment. Their social relationships take on a new intensity and complexity. New and more intricate thoughts are possible, accompanied by new insights about the self as well as the physical, social, and political environments. Many adolescents experience new levels of emotional intensity, including positive feelings such as romantic sentiments, sexual desires, tenderness, and spirituality, as well as the negative emotions of jealousy, hatred, and rage.

In many cultures, adolescence is a period of transition from the relatively weak and protected status of childhood to a more equal position in relation to adults and authority figures. As a result of their new physical stature, intellectual abilities, and social skills, adolescents can take on many of the tasks and roles of adult life. In some cases, as adolescents strive to express their views and preferences, they are met with a strong resistance by adults who still treat teens as if they were young children who are not mature enough to make important decisions. Adolescents who are treated this way may display strong feelings of anger, rebellion, or depression. These are the problems that the media, television, and movies tend to highlight. However, this is not an accurate portrayal of most teens. According to a special report by *U.S. News and World Report* in 2005, "adolescents now are less likely than their parents were to smoke, do hard drugs, get pregnant, commit violent crimes, . . . and drive drunk" (Baxter, 2009). Given a supportive environment in which adults are able to balance autonomy-granting and warmth, most young people make important new strides toward maturity during this time. They reach new levels of mastery and a new appreciation of their interdependence with family, friends, community, and culture. ■

Developmental Tasks

Physical Maturation

Objective 1. To describe the patterns of physical maturation during puberty for female and male adolescents, including an analysis of the impact of early and late maturing on self-concept and social relationships.

Coming on the heels of a period of gradual but steady physical development in middle childhood, early adolescence is marked by rapid physical changes, including a height spurt, maturation of the reproductive system, appearance of **secondary sex characteristics**, increased muscle strength, and the redistribution of body weight. At the same time, the brain continues to develop, with changes that increase emotionality, modify memory, and gradually improve connections among areas of the brain that regulate emotion, impulse control, and judgment (Brownlee, 1999; Spear, 2000). Variability in the rate and sequence of development is well documented (Brooks-Gunn & Reiter, 1990; Tanner, 1990). The time from the appearance of breast buds to full maturity may range from 1 to 6 years for girls; the male genitalia may take from 2 to 5 years to reach adult size. These individual differences in maturation suggest that during early adolescence, the chronological peer group is biologically far more diverse than it was during early and middle childhood.

Puberty encompasses a group of interrelated neurological and endocrinological changes that influence brain development, changes in sexual maturation, cycles and levels of hormone production, and physical growth. Puberty starts when the hypothalamus begins releasing a hormone called gonadotropin-releasing hormone (GnRH). GnRH then signals the pituitary gland to release two more hormones—luteinizing hormone (LH) and follicle-stimulating hormone (FSH)—to start sexual development. This system—the hypothalamus, pituitary gland, and the gonads, often referred to as the HPG axis—is responsible for the production and regulation of the sex hormones that result in the growth and maturation of the reproductive organs (NICHD, 2007). The hypothalamus and pituitary glands are also linked to the adrenal gland (the HPA axis), which controls reactions to stress, regulates digestion, and influences the immune system, mood, energy use, and the sleep-wake cycle (see the Applying Theory and Research to Life box for changes in the sleep needs of adolescents). The HPA axis establishes a feedback system that integrates the brain, glands, and hormones to support adaptation. During adolescence, both the HPG axis and the HPA axis are emerging into new patterns of regulation and growth.

There is a great deal of individual variation in the timing, rate of change, and coordination of these changes. Some changes, such as the maturation of the adrenal glands, occur very early, at around ages 6 to 9, and some changes, such as continuing growth in height, can continue well into the late teens and twenties. Thus, from a psychosocial perspective, one must think of pubertal development as a gradual transformation in which internal states and external appearance are coordinated with social expectations and a changing self-image (Dorn, Dahl, Woodward, & Biro, 2006).

Adaptation at puberty requires an integration of biological, psychological, and social changes. A young person may be responding to noticeable physical changes, such as a height spurt or the growth of pubic hair. Some changes in behavior may be due to less readily observable biological

APPLYING THEORY AND RESEARCH TO LIFE

Sleep Loss in Adolescence

ALONG WITH MANY changes in physical stature and appearance, puberty brings changes in **sleep patterns**. Research carried out in sleep labs suggests that when allowed to sleep as long as they wished, adolescents would sleep about 9 hours. However, as they get older, the quality of the sleep changes, with less time spent in deep sleep, leaving adolescents more tired during the day even when they get the same amount of sleep as younger children (Dahl & Caskadon, 1995). In actuality, as adolescents make the transition to high school, they get less sleep than younger children, leaving them more tired and more likely to fall asleep during the day. The pattern of later bedtime and fewer hours of nighttime sleep in adolescence has been observed in studies conducted in Germany, Greece, New Zealand, and Taiwan as well as the United States.

The study of sleep and its relation to psychosocial outcomes is a growing field (Johnson, 2004). Questions of interest include how the biological changes of puberty contribute to changes in sleep quality, sociocultural factors that contribute to sleep deprivation, and the impact of sleep habits on moodiness, self-esteem, depression, substance abuse, and school achievement. A combination of factors contributes to sleep deprivation in adolescence. Middle school tends to start earlier than elementary school,

and high school starts earlier still. Many adolescents are in activities that involve before-school preparation. Adolescents are likely to stay up late on school nights doing homework, talking with friends, using the computer, or watching television. Some adolescents have jobs at restaurants and stores where they stay until closing time.

The family environment has also been studied as a factor that influences sleep time. For younger children ages 5 through 11, parental warmth is associated with more hours of sleep during the weekdays. However, for older children in the age range 12 to 19, those adolescents whose families had stricter rules actually got more sleep (Adam, Snell, & Pendry, 2007).

In addition to these contextual factors, there is some evidence that the natural biorhythm for adolescents shifts toward a preference for a later sleep phase. In comparison with younger children, who sleep about the same amount during the weekdays as on weekends, adolescents tend to sleep much later on the weekends (Gaina, Sekine, Chen, Hamanishi, & Kagamimori, 2004). When they have a choice, as on the weekends, older adolescents stay up later at night, when they feel alert and energized, and sleep later in the morning. This shift is tied to pubertal status; those teens who are in a more advanced pubertal status show a greater tendency toward this delay and a greater difference between weekend and weekday sleep (Laberge, Petit, Simard, Vitaro, Tremblay, & Montplaisir, 2001).

In a longitudinal study of more than 2,000 children, the amount of sleep that children said they got on a typical school night was tracked for 3 years, in sixth, seventh, and eighth grades (Fredriksen, Rhodes, Reddy, & Way, 2004). The amount of sleep for both boys and girls declined from sixth to eighth grade. In the sixth grade, children who got fewer hours of sleep also had lower self-esteem, lower grades, and more depressive symptoms. Those students who experienced the greatest decline in hours of sleep over the 3 years also showed greater increases in depressive symptoms and lower self-esteem by eighth grade. Given the strong associations of depression and self-esteem with risky health behaviors, the role of sleep deprivation clearly deserves greater attention in family and school contexts.

Critical Thinking Questions

1. How do biological maturation and social environment interact to alter the amount of sleep adolescents get?
2. What are some implications of not getting enough sleep for adolescents' academic and social life?
3. What could schools do to alter their schedules so that adolescents get the sleep they need?
4. How might learning be influenced by sleep needs? What might be happening while a person sleeps that contributes to learning?
5. Why do you think that children who get fewer hours of sleep have lower self-esteem and more signs of depression?

---

changes in hormone production associated with new levels of arousal and emotionality. Psychological changes may be due to age as well as pubertal status and the changes that are associated with age. For example, some children make a school transition into seventh grade at age 12, leading to new status, a new sense of responsibilities, and new expectations for school performance. Some responses to puberty are cued by the way other people, including parents, teachers, siblings, and peers, respond to a child whose physical appearance has changed. In many cultures, **rites of passage** occur with entry into puberty, giving the young person new roles and new status within the community. Finally, some

responses to puberty have to do with the timing of these changes—whether pubertal changes are perceived to be early, on time, or late in relation to their peers. Thus, puberty is not one event, but a *biopsychosocial* transition that takes on meaning in the context of a child's culture and community.

The degree to which one's body matches the desired or socially valued body build of the culture influences social acceptance by peers and adults. This match between body shape and cultural values also influences the future course of psychosocial development. The European American culture gives self-esteem advantages to muscular, well-developed boys and petite, shapely girls. In contrast, it detracts from the self-esteem of thin, gangly boys, underdeveloped girls, and overweight boys and girls. Changes in body size and shape at puberty can bring advantages or disadvantages, depending on the context (see the case study on Carly Patterson).

CASE STUDY

CARLY PATTERSON, OLYMPIC GYMNAST

At age 16, Carly Patterson was an all-around gold medal Olympic champion in gymnastics.

Carly was born February 4, 1988, in Baton Rouge, Louisiana, the first of two children to Ricky and Natalie Patterson. She was a straight-A high school student and enjoyed things almost all teenagers enjoyed: shopping, movies, the beach. But Carly was far from normal. She worked with coaches Yevgeny Marchenko and Natasha Boyarskaya at the World Olympic Gymnastics Academy in Plano, Texas. Marchenko called her "Harley Davidson" because of her power. She trained twice a day, 6 days a week, for about 32 hours a week. She balanced her training and competition schedule with a regular high school workload. On a typical day, she was at the gym from 8 to 11: 30 a.m., then at school in the middle of the day, and then at the gym again from 4 to 7:30 p.m.

Carly began gymnastics in 1994, after attending a cousin's birthday party at Elite Gymnastics in Baton Rouge. Less than a decade later, she made her debut at the senior international elite level, winning back-to-back American Cup titles in 2003 and 2004, as well as the title of 2004 U.S. Co-National Champion. Carly was also a part of the 2003 World Championship team where she won a silver medal in the all-around and helped lead the United States to their first ever World Championship team gold medal. It was also at this competition that Carly's signature beam dismount (an Arabian double front) was officially named the Patterson. A year later, Carly achieved her ultimate goal in gymnastics by earning a trip to the 2004 Olympic Games in Athens, Greece.

Carly came home from Athens with three Olympic medals. The U.S. women won silver in the team competition—the first medal for the U.S. women in 8 years, as well as the second highest finish for the Americans in a fully attended Olympic Games. Carly also earned a silver medal on her specialty, the beam. However, it was on August 19 that all of Carly's hard work, dedication, and love for gymnastics paid off. She won the most prestigious title in gymnastics, the title of 2004 Olympic All-Around Champion. Carly was the U.S.A.'s first Olympic all-around champion in 20 years, as well as the first American woman to win an Olympic all-around title in a fully attended Olympic Games.

We cannot fully predict how puberty will transform a child's body into that of an adult. Often, adults focus on the challenges and difficulties that youth face, such as **eating disorders** or high-risk behaviors. For many young people, however, puberty opens up expanded opportunities for athletic achievement. With her small stature and slight build,

Carly's ability as a gymnast was enhanced by a significant increase in musculature that occurred at puberty. We do not know what might have happened to Carly's gymnastic career if her puberty had been accompanied with a greater height spurt or more breast development. There is concern that competitive events in which athletes are punished for weight gain or encouraged to manipulate their weight in order to compete may contribute to serious health risks, especially during adolescence (Brown University, 2004).

Source: Retrieved on November 28, 2004, from www.acepeople.com/c/Carly-Patterson.asp.

Critical Thinking and Case Analysis

1. Thinking about the world of competitive athletics, what are some examples of how the physical changes of puberty might open up new opportunities for adolescents? How might the physical changes of puberty reduce such opportunities?

2. How does Carly's case illustrate the interaction of biological, psychological, and societal systems?

3. How might a training program interact with the changes of puberty to promote athletic ability? What might be the risks of too much training or poor training at this age?

4. What personal, emotional, and intellectual attributes do you think are necessary in order to function as a world-class athlete? How likely is it that a person in early adolescence has these attributes?

5. What messages might someone like Carly be able to convey to other adolescents about health and physical development in early adolescence?

Physical Changes in Girls

The window for the transition into puberty appears to be expanding for girls in the United States. When European American, African American, and Latina girls of the same socioeconomic background were compared, the average age at menarche was about age 12 for European American and African American girls. Latina girls reached menarche slightly earlier than the African American girls (Obeidallah, Brennan, Brooks-Gunn, Kindlon, & Earls, 2000). However, menarche is not one of the first events in the transitions of puberty. A study of more than 17,000 girls ages 3 to 12 found that roughly 15% of European American girls and 50% of African American girls were showing evidence of secondary sex characteristics, including breast buds and pubic hair, by age 8 (Herman-Giddens et al., 1997; Lemonick, 2000). There are speculations about the cause of this early onset of puberty. Some consider **obesity** in children as a stimulus for early puberty; others point to the breakdown of insecticides in the soil, or hormones given to cattle that eventually make their way into a child's diet. Family disruption and father absence, as well as the presence of fathers who have significant symptoms of psychopathology, are all associated with earlier age of menarche (Tither and Ellis, 2008). Finally, some argue that exposure to sexual stimulation in television, movies, advertisements, and overt behavior plays a role in promoting the production of hormones that stimulate puberty. None of these speculations has been accepted as the determining factor (Lemonick, 2000).

For girls, the earliest evidence of puberty is usually breast bud development and the beginning of the height spurt, which occur on average between ages 10 and 11—almost 2 years sooner than the parallel experiences for boys (see Table 9.1). Initially, the increase in height may be embarrassing when a girl finds herself towering above her male classmates. To compensate, girls often slouch or wear baggy clothes.

Generally, girls are more dissatisfied than boys with their physical appearance and their overall body image. For girls, self-consciousness and dissatisfaction with their appearance reach their peak between the ages of 13 and 15. The cultural, family, or community emphasis on a thin ideal, combined with the view that thinness can be achieved through effort, lead many girls to experience dissatisfaction with their body. Body dissatisfaction is associated with lower levels of self-esteem and increased likelihood of depression among early adolescent girls (Jones, 2004; Moore & Rosenthal, 2006).

Concerns About Obesity. The greatest concern that adolescent girls express about their bodies is the perception that they are too fat. This concern is not so much that being overweight is unhealthy, but that it results in peer rejection from both boys and girls.

Lisa is a seventh grader who attends a White, upper-middle-class, middle school. She is clearly overweight. As a newcomer to her school, she found that her weight was the major factor in determining her social and academic experiences.

> At first I thought if I got good grades and tried to fit in it wouldn't matter how I looked. But I still got teased; it didn't make a difference. All the good things about me—like that I was smart—it was just, "You don't fit. You don't look good. You're fat." I felt like I was doing all the good things for no reason. So I just said, "Fine, if it's going to be that way, then I don't care." And I don't try at all anymore. I don't care about school. (Orenstein, 2000, pp. 100–101)

In a review of research on body dissatisfaction and eating pathologies, Stice and Shaw (2002) found support for a relationship between body image disturbances and eating disorders (see Figure 9.1). Three factors appear to contribute to **body dissatisfaction** among adolescent girls: social pressures to be thin, an internalized thin ideal body type, and higher than average body mass. Those girls who have higher body dissatisfaction are likely to start dieting and also to experience negative emotional states, especially depression. In a longitudinal study of adolescents in grades 7 through 12, symptoms of depression predicted obesity 1 year later. The link between depression and obesity may be due to a decrease in physical activity, or for some, an increase in hunger eating and weight gain (Goodman & Whitaker, 2002; Needham Epel, Adler, & Kiefe, 2010). The combination of these factors can lead to future eating pathologies. In an attempt to attain a thin ideal and to reduce negative feelings about themselves, many early adolescent girls begin a

TABLE 9.1 The Development of Primary and Secondary Sex Characteristics for Girls and Boys

GIRLS	AVERAGE AGE OF OCCURRENCE	BOYS
Onset of height spurt	10–11	**Growth of testes**
Initial breast development	11	Development of pubic hair
Increased activity of oil and sweat glands (acne can result from clogged glands)	11–12	Increased activity of oil and sweat glands (acne can result from clogged glands)
Development of pubic hair	12	**Growth of penis**
Onset of menarche (age range is 9–17)	12–13	Onset of height spurt
Earliest normal pregnancy	14	Deepening of the voice
Completion of breast development (age range is 13–18)	15–16	**Production of mature spermatozoa** **Nocturnal emissions**
		Growth of underarm and facial hair
Maturation of skeletal system	17–18	Maturation of skeletal system
		Development of chest hair

Note: Primary sex characteristics are in boldface type.
The **primary sex characteristics** relate to the development of genitalia and reproductive organs. **Secondary sex characteristics** are other physical changes associated with puberty, such as body hair or breast development.

Source: Adapted from Turner and Rubinson, 1993.

FIGURE 9.1 The Relationship of Body Image to Eating Disturbances
Source: Based on Stice and Shaw, 2002.

process of strict and often faddish dieting. This strategy is ill-timed, because their bodies require well-balanced diets and increased caloric intake during the period of rapid growth (Stice & Shaw, 2004).

Concern about being overweight is culturally linked. For example, studies have found that girls who have strong religious backgrounds have a heavier real and ideal weight than less religious girls. Black girls view a slightly heavier body image as ideal in comparison to White girls. With Black youth, one does not see the relationship of obesity and low self-esteem that is often observed in studies of White adolescents (Martin et al., 1988; Abell & Richards, 1996; Flynn & Fitzgibbon, 1996).

Concern about being overweight is also linked to the day-to-day experiences girls have with peers at school. Girls who are overweight are more likely to try to lose weight if other girls at their school of similar body type are also trying to lose weight. Girls who are underweight are also more likely to try to lose weight if other underweight girls at their school are trying to lose weight. The implication is that even though girls are aware of a broad, cultural ideal about thinness, their own behavior regarding weight control or weight loss is influenced to a great extent by what other girls in their immediate social world are doing (Mueller, Pearson, Muller, Frank, & Turner, 2010).

Obesity is related to activity level. For girls, one of the compounding factors in obesity is that they tend to reduce their activity level with age. One longitudinal study monitored common physical activities for children from grades 3 through 10. During grades 6 through 8, those girls who were more advanced in their pubertal status were less active than the girls who were less physically mature. Pubertal status was not a factor that predicted activity level for boys in those same grades (Bradley, McMurray, Harrell, & Deng, 2000). In an ethnically diverse sample of more than 550 girls in grades 5 to 12, only 36% met the national goal for strenuous activity (15 minutes of strenuous activity at least three times per week; Wolf et al., 1993). The amount of overall activity and strenuous activity decreased with age, and obesity was negatively correlated with activity. The study also revealed differences in exercise patterns across ethnic groups. Hispanic American and Asian American girls had significantly lower scores on activity level than African American and European American girls. Two cultural hypotheses were formulated to explain this pattern, but neither one was tested: First, strenuous physical activity may be viewed as especially unfeminine by Asian Americans and Hispanic Americans. Second, it is possible that the slender body type is not seen as desirable by these ethnic groups; thus, there is less motivation to do strenuous exercise.

Reactions to Breast Development and Menarche. For girls, two of the most noticeable events of puberty are the development of breast buds and the onset of the menstrual cycle (**menarche**). Breast development is one of the early aspects of pubertal growth, and often serves as a signal for the need to begin dialogue about puberty. To the average girl, the development of breast buds is a welcome sign of her growing maturity and femininity (Brooks-Gunn & Warren, 1988). Some girls begin to wear brassieres early in puberty in anticipation of the onset of breast development. However, the trend toward earlier breast development has parents and mental health experts concerned about the compression of childhood. Eight-year-old girls with breasts are still emotionally and cognitively like their undeveloped 8-year-old peers. Their physical development may result in new expectations for more mature behavior and new sexualized attention from older boys (Lemonick, 2000).

Menarche is a comparatively late event in a girl's pubertal development. Breast development and the growth of pubic hair are earlier evidence of pubertal growth and may provide the signal that a conversation about menarche is in order. Although most girls are prepared by their mothers for menstruation, the topic is often handled as a matter of hygiene rather than as a sexual transition. Many girls do not understand the relation of menstruation to reproduction. They simply accept their monthly periods as another sign of their femininity. The process of learning about menarche may be somewhat more anxiety producing for girls who are not living with their mothers or with a female caregiver. In a

© Michael Newman/PhotoEdit

Selecting the first bra is a sign of a girl's transition from childhood to adolescence.

qualitative study of girls who were living without their mothers, the girls were often embarrassed to ask questions of their fathers and experienced more distress around this issue if they did not have access to a woman who could answer their questions (Kalman, 2003). This has special implications for the health of girls who may be separated from their mothers due to maternal death, war, or imprisonment.

Most girls seem to react to menstruation with a mix of positive and negative feelings. The positive feelings reflect their pride in maturing and the confirmation of their womanliness. The negative feelings reflect the inconvenience, some unpleasant symptoms, and the possible embarrassment of menstruation (Brooks-Gunn & Reiter, 1990). Girls rarely tell their male peers or their fathers about the onset of menarche, but they do discuss it with their female friends and their mothers. Negative feelings are especially likely if a girl matures early, at age 9 or 10. In a retrospective study involving more than 1,500 Chinese American junior high school girls, students were asked about their knowledge and attitudes about menarche and their emotional responses to their first menstruation. Although 85% reported feeling annoyed and embarrassed by their first menstruation, about 66% also reported positive feelings, especially feeling more grown up. The more adequate their preparation for menarche and the more they saw menarche as a natural, healthy event, the more positive were their emotional responses (Tang, Yeung, & Lee, 2003).

Physical Changes in Boys

Boys generally welcome the changes involving increased height and muscle mass that bring them one step closer to adult maturity. Nonetheless, some ambivalence is likely as boys experience the transitions of puberty. On the one hand, a mature physique usually brings well-developed physical skills that are highly valued by peers and adults alike. On the other hand, the period of rapid growth may leave a boy feeling awkward and uncoordinated for a time. This awkwardness results because growth does not take place at the same rate in all parts of the body. One particular discrepancy is the time lag between the height spurt and the increase in muscle strength. For boys, the increase in the rate of growth in height starts at about 12.5 years and reaches a peak around age 14. The peak increase in muscle strength, however, usually occurs about 12 to 14 months after the peak height spurt (Brierley, 1993). This time lag results in a temporary period during which a boy simply cannot accomplish what he might expect given his height. Psychologically, this awkward period poses challenges to a boy's self-esteem. For boys, body image dissatisfaction is typically associated with frustration about not looking muscular or strong—a concern that is magnified by the lag between the height spurt and the increase in muscle mass (Cohane & Pope, 2000).

The onset of the growth of the testes and the penis also poses important challenges for early adolescent boys. Testicular growth is one of the first signs of puberty in boys. A somewhat controversial study of U.S. boys reported that genital

© Michael Newman/Photo Edit

Shaving is a symbol of a boy's transition into adolescence and continues to be an element of a young man's masculine identity throughout young adulthood.

growth was observed to begin sometime between ages 9 and 10—more than 2 years before the estimate given by prior studies (Associated Press, 2001). The median age for sperm production is about 14. Thus, like menarche, spermarche occurs rather late in the pubertal process (Dorn et al., 2006). In contrast to girls, boys are generally not well prepared by their parents with information on the maturation of their reproductive organs (Bolton & MacEachron, 1988). Specifically, they are not taught about spontaneous ejaculation and may be surprised, scared, or embarrassed by it. The sexual connotation of the event may make it difficult for boys to seek an explanation from their parents. They are left to gain information from friends and reading material or to worry in private about its meaning. For many boys, spontaneous ejaculation provides an important clue to the way in which physical adult sexuality and reproduction are accomplished. The pleasure of the ejaculation and the positive value of the new information that it provides are counterbalanced by a mild anxiety (Gaddis & Brooks-Gunn, 1985; Marsiglio, 1988; Adegoke, 1993). This is only one of the developments that arouse ambivalence in many boys during early adolescence.

A third area of physical development that has psychological and social meaning for boys is the development of secondary sex characteristics, particularly the growth of facial and body hair. In many societies, the equipment and ritual behaviors associated with shaving are closely linked to the masculine gender role. Most boys are eager to express their identification with this role, and they use the slightest evidence of facial hair as an excuse to take razor in hand. The ritual of shaving not only provides some affirmation of the boy's masculinity, but it also allows him an acceptable outlet for his narcissism. As he shaves, it is legitimate for him to gaze at and admire his changing image. In some societies, the ability to grow a mustache or a beard is a sign of one's masculinity. In these cultures, boys cultivate and admire their mustaches or beards as evidence of their enhanced male status.

Cultural Contexts of Puberty

The way adolescents react to the physical changes of puberty depends in part on the cultural context. For example, studies of Mexican youth find that girls become somewhat more depressed as they go through puberty, whereas boys experience an improved sense of body image and well-being (Benjet & Hernandez-Guzman, 2002). These gender differences may reflect the greater status and new responsibilities given to male children in Mexican culture, and the new restrictions that apply to female children as they enter puberty in order to protect their chastity. In another cultural comparison, several studies comparing African American and European American adolescent girls were summarized. In general, African American adolescent girls are more satisfied with their body image and less inclined toward eating disorders than European American girls. Furthermore, early pubertal onset and weight increases were not particularly strong predictors of negative body image and depression among African American girls, as they are for European American girls (Franko & Streigel-Moore, 2002).

The Secular Growth Trend

Along with the genetic influence that guides the timing of pubertal growth and sexual maturation, the environment plays an important role in the eventual attainment of one's growth potential. A **secular growth trend** is a change over time in the average age at which **physical maturation** takes place (Godina, 2009). All over the world, changes in hygiene, nutrition, and health care have contributed to an earlier entry into puberty and earlier growth spurt over the past century (Richter, 2006). In the United States, children ages 10 to 14 increased in height by an average of 2 to 3 centimeters every decade from 1900 to 1960. Adult height is not necessarily greater due to this increase; it is simply attained at an earlier age.

Other evidence of a secular trend is the decrease in age at menarche. Data reported by Tanner (1990) showed a decrease in the average age at menarche from the 1950s (13.5 to 14 years) to the 1970s (12.5 to 13 years). At present, the mean age at menarche for girls in the United States is 12.3, but the range is from 9 to 17. There is no evidence for a continuing decline in age at pubertal development for non-Hispanic girls, in the period from 1966 to 1994; but there is some evidence for earlier pubertal development for Mexican American boys and girls over these years (Sun et al., 2005).

Age at menarche varies among countries and even among socioeconomic groups within a country. Evidence from two rural counties in China illustrates the impact of improved living standards on age at menarche. In a survey of over 12,000 females, age at menarche decreased from an average of 16.5 to 13.7 over an approximate 40-year interval. Improvements were associated with a variety of environmental conditions, including reduced pesticide exposure before age at menarche, the source of drinking water, the amount of physical labor the girls were required to perform, and improved nutrition (Graham, Larsen, & Xu, 1999).

What is the relevance of the secular trend for understanding the development of contemporary adolescents in post-industrialized societies? Reproductive capacity and physical adult stature occur at a younger age than at the turn of the 20th century, but full engagement in the adult society requires more training, education, and complex preparation than in the past. Thus, adolescence is prolonged, with more time to experience the risks of unwanted pregnancy, the sense of being in a marginal social status, and disruptions in the transition from childhood to adulthood.

The concept of the secular trend alerts us to the importance of the psychosocial context of physical development. Not only are peers experiencing diverse patterns of growth, but parents and grandparents may also be reacting to a discrepancy between their children's development and their own timetable for growth. Moreover, because the period of reproductive capacity starts earlier than it did 50 years ago, young people must cope with special challenges in the expression and regulation of their sexual impulses. One consequence of the earlier onset of puberty is that adolescents may find themselves in potentially high-risk situations at a relatively young age. Given the risks inherent in a technological society, it is no wonder that adolescent exposure to risk behaviors is a major contemporary health concern.

Individual Differences in Maturation Rate

The age at onset of puberty and the rate of change in physical maturation vary. Early and late maturing have psychological and social consequences for both boys and girls. Recent research about the effects of pubertal timing has challenged the view that was established by researchers in the 1950s and 1960s. In those studies, boys who matured early experienced positive consequences, including greater opportunities for leadership and social status, and as a result, they had higher self-esteem (Mussen & Jones, 1957; Clausen, 1975). A similar advantage for early maturation for fifth- and sixth-grade boys was reported in the early 1990s. The boys who were more physically mature described more positive daily emotions, better attention, and feelings of being strong (Richards & Larson, 1993). The explanation for these advantages was that early maturing boys are likely to be given increased responsibility by their parents and teachers. They are generally more satisfied with their bodies, feel more positive about being boys, and are likely to be more involved in school activities by the tenth grade than are late-maturing boys (Blyth, Bulcroft, & Simmons,

1981). In contrast, boys who mature later than their age-mates may experience psychological stress and develop a negative self-image. Late-maturing boys are treated as if they were younger than they really are. They may become isolated from their peers or behave in a silly, childish manner to gain attention.

Recent research has painted a somewhat different picture of the consequences of early maturing for boys, especially those who mature in grade 7 or before. These studies show that early maturing boys have more hostile feelings, greater levels of anxiety and depression, more problems with **drug and alcohol use**, and more deviant activities and problems in school than boys who mature at a more average time (Alasker, 1995; Ge, Conger, & Elder, 2001; Wichstrom, 2001). The association of early maturation and heightened rates of violent and non-violent delinquent behavior has been observed for African American, Mexican American, and European American youth (Cota-Robles, Neiss, & Rowe, 2002). In a longitudinal study of over 3,000 South African children born in the early 1990s, early maturing boys and girls were found to be more involved in high-risk behaviors such as smoking, experimenting with drugs, and sexual behavior than their less physically mature age-mates (Richter, 2006).

How can we account for these differences? Is early maturing a benefit or a risk for boys? Explanations for this new view of the impact of early maturation for boys vary. One explanation is that we are looking at a cohort effect. Maturing early in the 1950s may have been a more positive experience, whereas maturing early in the 1990s may expose adolescent boys to more stressors. Another explanation is that in today's society, physical maturation at age 12 and earlier converges with other stressful life events, especially school transitions, disruption of the peer network, more challenging expectations for school performance, and the related risk of failure. More stressful life events coupled with the pubertal transition increase uncertainty and may leave boys feeling out of control. A third explanation is that boys who mature early have not had time to fully master the tasks of the middle childhood period. With an early height spurt and a more

mature physical appearance, they may be accelerated into situations where they are faced with expectations for a level of self-control, decision making, and leadership for which they are not prepared. Too much, too soon produces overload (Ge, Conger, & Elder, 2001; Ge & Natsuaki, 2009).

These different views of the impact of early maturing may all be correct. For example, it may be true that early maturing boys do experience greater opportunities for leadership and social status. The advantages of an earlier height spurt and related increases in muscle mass and endurance can make a significant difference as boys engage in athletic competitions with their age-mates (Gladwell, 2008). At the same time, because they look older, they may begin to engage in some of the high-risk behaviors of slightly older boys.

Several studies suggest that early pubertal onset is also a source of stress for girls (Kornfield, 1990; Caspi & Moffitt, 1991). Because pubertal changes occur about 2 years earlier for girls than for boys, the early maturing girl stands out among all her male and female age-mates. Early onset of menstruation is especially stressful, resulting in heightened self-consciousness and anxiety (Hill, 1988). Early maturing girls are less likely to have been prepared for the onset of menstruation, and they are less likely to have close friends with whom they can discuss it. Early pubertal maturation may result in feelings of social isolation for girls.

Early maturing girls experience higher levels of conflict with their parents and are more likely to report depression and anxiety (Wierson, Long, & Forehand, 1993). Early maturing girls who are dissatisfied with their physical appearance are especially vulnerable to low self-esteem (Williams & Currie, 2000). There is some evidence that early maturing girls earn lower grades and lower scores on academic achievement tests. They are also more likely to be identified as having behavior problems in school (Blyth et al., 1981). Early maturing girls start dating earlier and perceive themselves as more popular with boys than do late-maturing girls. Some studies report that early maturing girls are more likely to engage in high-risk, promiscuous sexual behavior. In general, however, the timing of the transition to puberty in and of itself is not a strong predictor of a girl's emotional well-being. Rather, this timing interacts with other events, including school transition, family conflict, or peer acceptance, to influence how girls construct the meaning of this physical transition (Booth, Johnson, Granger, Crouter, & McHale, 2003).

Romantic and Sexual Relationships

Objective 2. To characterize the development of romantic and sexual relationships, including a focus on the transition to coitus, the formation of a sexual orientation, and factors associated with pregnancy and parenthood in adolescence.

During adolescence, romantic relationships, sexual fantasies, and sexual behaviors increase, partly as a result of biological

© 2010 Jon Feingersh/Jupiterimages Corporation

By grade 8, the physical diversity of the peer group is quite noticeable. Differences in height, weight, and body shape have implications for popularity, leadership, athletic success, and self-confidence.

changes and partly as a result of social, cultural, and historical contexts. One of the earliest signs of puberty is the gradual release of hormones from the adrenal gland. DHEA and other adrenal hormones are associated with the growth of pubic hair, body odor, acne, and prepubertal growth (Shirtcliff, Dahl, & Pollack, 2009). The amount of this hormone that is absorbed in the blood reaches a peak between the ages of 10 and 12—a time when both boys and girls begin to be aware of sexual feelings toward others (Herdt & McClintock, 2000; LaFreniere, 2000). The way these sexual feelings are expressed depends largely on cultural factors.

The Transition into Sexualized Relationships

Most young people are involved in a variety of romantic relationships during adolescence, including dating, feelings of tenderness and love, and deepening commitments (Moore & Rosenthal, 2006). Components of both gender identity and sexual orientation are formulated during this period of life. Some adolescents are reticent about sexual behavior. Others are sexually permissive and regularly active in sex play, from petting to intercourse. The manner in which early adolescents think about sexual relationships varies. Some are preoccupied by thoughts of very romantic, idealized relationships. They can become infatuated with rock stars, athletes, movie stars, or other sex symbols. Some have crushes on boys or girls in their school or neighborhood, and still others have obsessions with sexual material but do not have any tender or caring relationships with peers. Early adolescents' sexual awakenings represent a system that is just being started up and tested out. As a result of these sexual experiences, adolescents begin to think of themselves as sexual, develop scripts and schemes for how to act sexually with others, and begin to formulate ideas about the kinds of people they find sexually attractive.

Dating. Dating relationships provide the initial context for most sexual activity. Pubertal changes may increase a young person's interest in sexual ideation, but the timing and rituals or *script* of dating depends heavily on the norms of the peer group and the community (Garguilo, Attie, Brooks-Gunn, & Warren, 1987). Young people learn the art of flirtation, practice how to approach and how to coyly refuse, and learn the rules of engagement between the sexes, which vary from culture to culture and from cohort to cohort. The following description of dating in the United States in the 1920s reflects the values regarding gender, sexuality, and economics of the time.

> Boys or young men asked for the company of a girl or young woman to some public amusement—dance, movie, party, or other social event. They went without adult supervision or interference. The male member of the couple paid and frequently in the 1920s provided transportation. After the main event, the couple often went out to eat and frequently would try to find some private place for necking. Whereas physical intimacy became an expected element of dating, the limits of sexual experience depended on the girl and to a large extent on her [social] class. (Spurlock & Magistro, 1998, p. 26)

© 2010 Radius Images/Jupiterimages Corporation

Romance begins to stir in the halls of the high school.

Involvement in romantic relationships increases over the middle school and high school years, and the quality of these relationships becomes increasingly intimate. Furman and Wehner (1997) suggested that four types of needs are met in these romantic relationships: *affiliation*, *attachment*, *caregiving*, and *sexual gratification*. As suggested by Sullivan's (1953) interpersonal theory, the ability to engage in close and confiding friendships during middle childhood lays the groundwork for the capacity to have romantic relationships. Those children who have close friendships in middle childhood are more likely to have romantic relationships in adolescence (Neeman, Hubbard, & Master, 1995). Participation in mixed-sex friendship groups is also likely to provide the context for the formation of romantic pairing, which becomes more exclusive and less group oriented over time (Dunphy, 1963; Connolly, Furman, & Konarski, 2000).

First Intercourse. The sexual transition may take place in very different contexts for adolescents. It may be a planned event or an unplanned impulse, often combined with alcohol use or a drug high. The sexual encounter may be viewed as a marker of independence or as an act of rebellion against and defiance of the family. It may take place in the context of an ongoing close relationship or as part of a casual encounter. Usually, the earlier the transition into sexual activity and intercourse, the more likely the act is to be part of a profile of high-risk behaviors, including alcohol use, drug use, and delinquent activity. For girls 14 years old and younger, 27% said that they did not want their first sexual experience (Terry-Humen, Manlove, & Cottingham, 2006). For many of these young teens, their first sexual experience was a result of being sexually assaulted (Haffner, 1998). The later the transition, the more likely it is to be seen as a marker of the transition into adulthood or as a planned aspect of the deepening commitment to an ongoing relationship (Terry-Humen, Manlove, & Cottingham, 2006).

In the United States, the recent trend has been toward a delay in sexual experience from 1988 to 2009, especially notable among adolescent boys. Data from a national survey of students in grades 9 through 12 conducted in 2009 reported that 46% of students surveyed had had sexual intercourse during their lifetime. The prevalence of sexual intercourse increased with grade level, such that by twelfth grade, 62% of females and 64% of males were sexually experienced. Eleventh grade seems to be the tipping point, by which time more than half the students (51%) are sexually experienced (Centers for Disease Control and Prevention, 2010c).

Boys are more likely to report being sexually active than girls at the younger ages; 8.8% of boys and 3.7% of girls report having sexual intercourse before age 13. By grade 12, boys and girls are equally likely to be sexually active and report about the same likelihood of having had sex with four or more partners (20% of females and 22.6% of males). A significant percentage of U.S. adolescents (roughly one third) have not had sexual intercourse by twelfth grade. This does not mean that they have had no experience with intimate behavior. In a study of 11- and 12-year-old girls, 46% of 12-year-old girls had hugged a boy. Other intimate behaviors that were reported at this age were spending time alone with a boy, holding hands, and kissing (Hipwell, Keenan, Loeber, & Battista, 2010). Roughly 75% of U.S. teens have engaged in what they describe as heavy petting by the age of 18 (Haffner, 1998). It is not uncommon for teens to experience oral sex, even if they have not had sexual intercourse. Figure 9.2 compares teens ages 15 to 17 from three race/ethnic groups, non-Hispanic Whites, Hispanics, and non-Hispanic Blacks with respect to their sexual behavior. Three categories of sexual behavior are included: sexual intercourse, oral sex only, and neither intercourse nor oral sex. Hispanic and non-Hispanic Black teens are more likely to report having had sexual intercourse than non-Hispanic White teens. Non-Hispanic White teens are more likely to report having oral sex only than the other two groups (Terry-Humen, Manlove, & Cottingham, 2006).

There are at least five reasons why data regarding entry into sexual activity and age at **first intercourse** must be interpreted with caution (Savin-Williams & Diamond, 2004). First, teens who are uncomfortable or whose parents are uncomfortable participating in research on this topic will not be included. Second, studies rarely include questions about same-sex sexual activity that might be comparable to first intercourse. Third, the reporting is retrospective (i.e., asking adolescents to think back to when they first engaged in sexual activities) and thus is vulnerable to inconsistencies and memory errors. Fourth, cultural and social contexts may influence reporting. It may be socially desirable to exaggerate one's sexual experiences in some communities, and socially

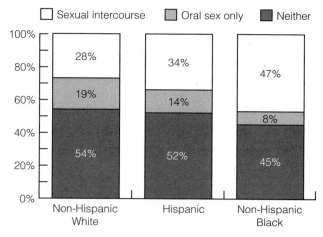

*Numbers may not equal 100% due to rounding

FIGURE 9.2 Sexual Behavior Among Teens Ages 15 to 17 by Race/Ethnicity

Source: Child Trends (2005). Child Trends' analyses of the National Survey of Family Growth, 2002.

responsible to conceal one's sexual experience in others. Finally, most studies focus on individual reports and do not gather data to confirm reported sexual experiences by participating partners.

Factors Affecting the Initiation of Sexual Intercourse. Udry and Billy (1987) devised a model that is very useful for conceptualizing the transition to coitus in early adolescence (see Figure 9.3). In that model, three basic dimensions account for the adolescent's initiation of sexual activity: *motivation*, *social controls*, and *attractiveness*.

The first dimension, **sexual motivation**, includes the biologically organized drives associated with sexual arousal and sexual pleasure, and a range of social motives such as achieving new levels of intimacy in a relationship, pleasing one's partner, impressing one's peers, gaining sexual experience, or preventing conflict or dissolution by providing sexual satisfaction (Impett & Tolman, 2006). Some sexual motives can be considered approach motives in that sexual activity is viewed as a way of achieving a positive outcome, like increasing one's physical pleasure or enhancing intimacy. Some sexual motives can be considered avoidance motives if sexual activity is viewed as preventing a negative outcome, like reducing conflict in a relationship. In a study of positive sexual motives among ninth graders, females valued achieving intimacy more than males and sexual pleasure less than males. Adolescents expected that sexual experience would most likely satisfy motives for sexual pleasure, then for intimacy, and least for social status. Those ninth graders who were sexually active had greater expectations that sexual activity would result in greater intimacy in the relationship than those who were not sexually active (Ott, Millstein, Ofner, & Halpern-Felsher, 2006).

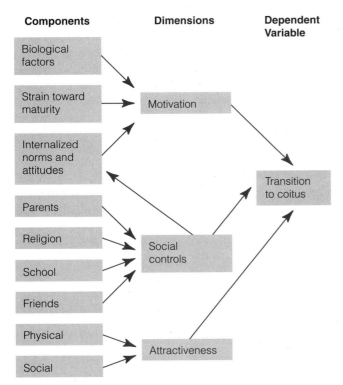

Components   **Dimensions**   **Dependent Variable**

Biological factors

Strain toward maturity

Internalized norms and attitudes

Parents

Religion

School

Friends

Physical

Social

Motivation

Transition to coitus

Social controls

Attractiveness

FIGURE 9.3 A Model of the Transition to First Coitus in Early Adolescence

Source: Adapted from Udry & Billy, 1987.

The second dimension, **social controls,** provides the normative environment in which sexual activity is embedded. According to the model, these controls are a product of parental socialization and practices, school achievement and educational aspirations, and the attitudes and sexual experiences of friends. We have added the important influence of religious beliefs and values to the model's list of social controls.

The third dimension, **attractiveness,** influences the availability of partners. Attractiveness is defined in part by pubertal maturation, social acceptance or popularity, and also by whether one is judged to be pretty or handsome.

In an effort to assess this model, researchers found that the transition to sexual intercourse for White boys was most strongly predicted by hormonal levels and by popularity with the opposite sex. In contrast, there was no clear relationship between hormone levels and girls' sexual activity (Udry, Billy, Morris, Groff, & Raj, 1985; Katchadourian, 1990). For girls, various social controls—including parents, school achievement, friends' attitudes and behaviors, and religious values—all play an important part in predicting sexual intercourse. A girl's decision to become sexually active is influenced by her own self-esteem, her personal aspirations, her parents' values, her educational expectations, and the capacity of her parents to exercise appropriate control over her social and school activities, and the norms of her peer group (Crockett,

Bingham, Chopak, & Vicary, 1996; Meschke, Zweig, Barber, & Eccles, 2000; O'Sullivan, Meyer-Bahlburg, & Watkins, 2000). Another reason that the link between hormonal levels and sexual debut is unclear for girls is that for many young girls their early sexual experiences were unwanted.

The Effects of Religious Beliefs on Sexual Behavior. One of the clearest cultural influences on adolescent sexual behavior is religious participation. Adolescents who frequently attend religious services and church-related activities and who value religion as an important aspect of their lives have less permissive attitudes toward premarital sex. However, an adolescent's attitudes toward premarital sex are shaped by many factors in addition to religious beliefs. By the time young people are making independent decisions about religious participation, they also have opinions on premarital sex. Thus, those young people who have more permissive views on sex may be less likely to attend religious services and may find less satisfaction in religious participation (Thornton & Camburn, 1989).

As an example of how religious beliefs can affect sexual behavior, the Southern Baptist Church initiated a program that encouraged teens to make a public virginity pledge. Since 1993, more than 2.5 million youth have taken this pledge, in which they vow to abstain from sex until marriage. In a study of those who participated in the program, the pledge was found to be most effective in delaying the age of first intercourse when taken by younger teens. It is also more effective for pledge takers who are a minority among their peers. Taking the pledge is then viewed as an act of independent decision making and identity commitment rather than as compliance to peer norms (Bearman & Brueckner, 2001). Findings based on the National Longitudinal Study of Adolescent Health suggest that one of the hazards of taking the pledge is that when it is broken, youth are less well prepared to engage in protected sex and are therefore at risk for sexually transmitted diseases (USA Today, 2004). In a study reported by Rosenbaum (2009), 5 years after making their pledge, 82% of teens denied having ever made this pledge. Those who had pledged were no different from matched nonpledgers in the percentage who had premarital sex, sexually transmitted diseases, or lifetime sexual partners.

Sexual Orientation

Although one might assume that **sexual orientation**—heterosexual, homosexual, or bisexual—begins to take shape in early adolescence, the research on this point is limited and suggests a more differentiated path. Although 6% to 8% of youth responding to the National Longitudinal Study of Adolescent Health said that they had experienced same-sex attractions or same-sex relationships, only a small number acknowledged same-sex behaviors, and even fewer identified themselves as gay, lesbian, or bisexual. Many teens who have self-identified as gay or lesbian have also had cross-sex experiences. In studies of adults, many people who consider themselves heterosexual have had same-sex attractions and experiences (Savin-Williams & Diamond, 2004). For sexual minority youth, two aspects of a sexual orientation have been identified: **self-labeling** and **disclosure** (Savin-Williams, 1996). Self-labeling refers to applying a label such as gay, lesbian, or bisexual to oneself. Disclosure refers to sharing this information with others.

Self-Labeling. In one study of 77 gay men, most recalled having an awareness of gay feelings as early as middle school or early adolescence, but they did not label themselves gay until later adolescence (D'Augelli, 1991). The majority (75%) knew they were gay *before* their first sexual experience. However, once they had labeled themselves gay, they waited an average of 8 years to disclose their homosexuality to someone else.

Self-labeling may begin with experiences in early childhood when boys or girls recall feeling different from their peers. These feelings, typically captured in retrospective studies of gay or lesbian young adults, may include a general sense that they did not share the same interests as others of their same sex. Boys may recall being more sensitive than their peers or being drawn to more artistic and aesthetic interests. Girls may remember passionate, mysterious friendships in the prepubertal and early adolescent period (Diamond, 2000). In many instances, these feelings of being different are associated with confusion and a sense of isolation or lack of belonging.

Often, at puberty, the implications of these earlier childhood experiences become more evident. A growing awareness of one's own sexual interests and fantasies, coupled with new information about the variety of sexual orientations that may exist in the peer group or community, leads to new insights about one's own sexual preferences. In some ways, this may be

a shocking realization. In other ways, it may help focus and clarify feelings of uncertainty and dissociation that had been difficult for the child to understand at an earlier age. Not all young people who eventually recognize their same-sex sexual orientation reach the point of self-labeling in adolescence. However, with the greater visibility, openness, and acceptance of differences in sexual orientation and the presence of homosexual role models, it is increasingly likely that this will happen.

Disclosure. Disclosure may be a prolonged process in which young people carefully decide which individuals can be trusted with this information, or it can be a very open, obvious statement of personal identity. Reports of adolescents who are openly gay suggest that disclosure can be very stressful when it is accompanied by negative reactions from parents and friends and by acts of open hostility from school peers (Remafedi, 1987). Anticipating the strong social censure attached to an unconventional sexual orientation, adolescents may deny or mask it by functioning as heterosexuals during this period of life.

> I feared not being liked and being alienated. I was president of various school clubs, and once I beat up a guy for being a faggot. I was adamant that fags should be booted out of the Boy Scouts. Other kids asked me why I was so rough on them. I did not say. No one suspected me because I did sports and had several girlfriends. (Savin-Williams, 1996, p. 169)

Disclosure typically occurs first with close friends, and later, if at all, with family members. Studies of gay, lesbian, and bisexual youth suggest that parental acceptance and the ability to maintain closeness and autonomy with parents after disclosure are very important to their continued identity development and well-being (Floyd, Stein, Harter,

A group of several hundred people demonstrate in support of a new high school for lesbian and gay students in New York City. The Harvey Milk High School opened for the first day of school with 100 students. What might be some developmental outcomes of attending a gay high school?

© Jeff Christensen/Reuters/CORBIS

Allison, & Nye, 1999). Most mental health professionals suggest that even when disclosure is accompanied by negative reactions, it has many emotional and social advantages. By disclosing, the young person has a greater sense of authenticity and freedom. Once adolescents disclose to their friends and family, they can be more readily integrated into the gay community and find others who will help support their emerging identity. They can direct more of their effort to the task of integrating their gender identity, sexual identity, and social relationships and figuring out how to cope with the challenges that their minority sexual orientation poses. Despite growing societal awareness of the diversity of sexual orientations, sexual minority youth continue to face negative attitudes from teachers, peers, and community members; possible social rejection; and difficulty finding age-appropriate, nonexploitive sexual partners.

Problems and Conflicts Associated with Sexuality

The sexual system is one of the most problematic components of psychosocial development for young people in the United States. Most parents do not feel comfortable discussing sexuality with their children. In addition to private thoughts, impulses, and fantasies, which may result in feelings of guilt or confusion, young people confront conflicting messages about sexual behavior from their peers, the mass media, and the religious community. For example, in the late 1990s, the U.S. Congress authorized funding to support programs that taught **abstinence** as the primary approach to sex education. These programs were required to teach about the social, psychological, and health benefits of abstinence; the risks of sex outside of marriage; and the importance of monogamy. At the same time, adolescents recognize that nonmarital abstinence is not being practiced now and was not practiced by their parents' generation. National studies show that the vast majority of both men and women are not virgins when they marry. In a congressional review of 13 government-funded abstinence-only curricula, 11 presented information that included "unproved claims, subjective conclusions, or outright falsehoods regarding reproductive health, gender traits, and when life begins" (Connolly, 2004, p. AO1).

Perhaps in part because of the scarcity of well-integrated, scientifically based educational programs to help students understand and cope with their sexual growth and desires for intimacy, three problems arise that are discussed in the following: unwanted sexual attention, inconsistent contraceptive use, and sexually transmitted diseases.

Unwanted Sexual Attention. Many adolescents, especially girls, are exposed to **unwanted sexual attention**. In a national survey, 7.5% of students in grades 9 to 12 reported being forced to have sexual intercourse (Centers for Disease Control, 2006). In a sample of seventh-, ninth-, and eleventh-grade girls, 21% reported unwanted sexual contact, ranging from unwanted touching and fondling to unwanted or forced intercourse (Small & Kerns, 1993). In many of these instances, unwanted sexual intercourse occurred on the first date or in a dating relationship. This pattern illustrates the problematic nature of sexual contact in early adolescence. The boundaries for acceptable sexual contact are unclear; the sexual agenda for boys and girls is likely to be very different; and other risk-taking behaviors, including alcohol and drug use, may create an unwanted sexual encounter.

In an effort to learn more about adolescents' reactions following their involvement in sexual intercourse, Australian researchers surveyed students in secondary schools in seven of the eight Australian states and territories (Donald, Lucke, Dunne, & Raphael, 1995). Students were asked about the context of their most recent sexual experience and how they felt about it. The majority of boys and girls said they felt good about their most recent sexual experience, with older students (ages 16 and 17) more likely to be positive about it than the younger students (15 and under). For girls, five factors were significantly associated with feeling good about their most recent sexual experience: believing that there was a low risk for contracting a sexually transmitted disease; having a steady relationship with the partner; having talked with their partner about avoiding pregnancy; having talked with their partner about ways of having sexual pleasure without having intercourse; and not being drunk or high. For boys, two factors were significantly associated with feeling good about their most recent sexual experience: having sex with a steady partner and not being drunk or high. Larger percentages of girls than boys were likely to say they felt used or bad after their most recent sexual experience, and the younger girls were more likely than older girls to say they felt bad or used. About equal percentages of girls and boys said they felt guilty after their most recent sexual experience.

The lack of supervision and monitoring by adults, as well as the lack of opportunity to talk about sexuality with them, can place adolescents at risk for early sexual experiences that are abusive or associated with negative feelings. The sex-linked problems that many people encounter—unintended pregnancy, marital infidelity, rape and other forms of unwanted sexual contact, child sexual abuse, pornography addiction, and sexually transmitted diseases—are evidence that the socialization process—including efforts by parents, teachers, and religious leaders—is failing to promote mature sexuality in significant numbers of adolescents and adults in the United States.

Inconsistent Contraception. Despite the fact that many parents and teachers do not provide information about the use of contraceptives as part of their education about sex and sexual behavior, the use of contraceptives by U.S. teens has increased. In 2005, 63% of the sexually active students in grades 9 through 12 reported that they or their partner used a condom during their most recent sexual intercourse (Centers for Disease Control and Prevention, 2006). Although contraceptive use has increased among adolescents, their use continues to be inconsistent. In part, this is because sexual activity among many adolescents is sporadic. In addition, studies of contraceptive use among adolescents have identified a number of explanations for inconsistent use: lack of knowledge about the need for **contraception**; lack of skills in the use of contraceptives and a desire to avoid embarrassment; barriers to acquiring contraceptives including cost, lack of anonymity, and religious or cultural barriers; lack of communication among the partners about who is responsible for contraceptive use; a view that contraceptives intrude on the spontaneity of sexual activity; and the involvement of drugs and alcohol with sexual activity, which may increase impulsiveness and reduce reasoned decision making (Centers for Disease Control and Prevention, 2006; Moore & Rosenthal, 2006).

In a study about adolescents' views on contraceptive use it was clear that many adolescents were confused about the difference between contraception for the prevention of pregnancy and contraception for the prevention of STIs. For example, girls might say that they were more likely to expect a boy to use a condom if this was a casual sexual relationship, but that it wasn't necessary if it was a steady relationship.

> Jane answered unequivocally "yes" to the question whether young people she knew would use condoms every time they had sexual intercourse. But she added: "Depending on whether they didn't want to—and whether the girl's on the pill and they were in a steady relationship and they didn't want to use one. But otherwise most people would use them." (Kirkman et al., 1998)

Sexually Transmitted Infections. About 25% of sexually active teens contract a **sexually transmitted infection** each year. Teens are especially at risk for chlamydia, genital herpes, and gonorrhea. In the year 2000, of those cases of chlamydia where the age of the person was reported, 75%

were between the ages of 15 and 24 (Weinstock, Berman, & Cates, 2004). Untreated, chlamydia and gonorrhea can produce pelvic inflammatory disease, leading to infertility and abnormal pregnancies (Alan Guttmacher Institute, 1999).

A major focus of AIDS and HIV education has been directed toward adolescents. The number of AIDS cases reported among U.S. adolescents increased from 53 in 1986 to 4,428 in 2001; 52% among males and 48% among females. Most of these cases are a result of sexual transmission (Centers for Disease Control and Prevention, 2006). Although adolescents believe that they have a strong understanding of AIDS as a disease, including its transmission and prevention, studies have shown that their knowledge is often confused or incorrect (Meschke, Bartholomae, & Zentall, 2002). At the same time, adolescents express little interest in learning more about AIDS. Many young people overestimate how well they understand this health problem. Others are cynical about getting the specific information they need from typical school-based sex education courses. These courses are often unable to provide the practical information that is needed to resolve questions about contraception, sexual intimacy, and specific patterns of physical contact that might lead to transmission of the disease. For example, many state and federal policies *prohibit* teaching about correct condom use as part of their sex education program, even in programs intended to focus on HIV/AIDS prevention (Alan Guttmacher Institute, 2002).

Parenthood in Early Adolescence

One of the consequences of early entry into sexual activity and inconsistent use of contraception is adolescent pregnancy. In 2007, 451,000 infants were born to women age 19 or younger in the United States. The birth rate was 42.5 births per 1,000 girls ages 15 to 19, up slightly from the low of 40.4 in 2005 (U.S. Census Bureau, 2010). In efforts to

In this classroom the teacher is showing students wrapped condoms as part of her instruction about safe sex. This is not always permitted as part of sex education, especially in programs that promote abstinence only.

Copyright © Mary Kate Denny/Photo Edit

explain the decline in birthrates to young mothers during the 1990s, data were collected that focused on sexual activity and contraceptive use. Both delays in the initiation of sexual activity and more effective contraceptive use were important factors that contributed to the decline in teen pregnancy (Santelli et al., 2004).

Predictors of Teenage Pregnancy. Are there any characteristics of teenage girls or their family and community contexts that are systematically linked to the likelihood of becoming pregnant? Using two national samples, Mollborn and Morningstar (2009) compared teenage girls who were pregnant to similar age girls who did not become pregnant, and to women who became pregnant at age 20 or older. The teenage mothers were more distressed; that is, they had higher scores on a measure of depression, than the other two groups, and these young mothers continued to be more distressed into their early and middle adulthood than women who were mothers at an older age. However, the study found that these differences in distress were already evident before the girls became pregnant, and that when other factors were taken into consideration, depression was not a significant predictor of becoming pregnant. The risk factors for becoming a teenage mother included: low parental education, having low grades in school, being in a single mother or stepparent family, and having had sexual intercourse. For those girls who lived in very low-resource households, being poor coupled with high levels of distress combined to predict the increased likelihood of teen pregnancy.

Consequences of Teenage Pregnancy. The phenomenon of teenage parenthood is complex, touching the lives of the adolescent mother and father, the child or children born to them, their parents, and the schools, counseling services, and family planning services that have been created to help young parents cope with parenthood. The consequences of teenage pregnancy and parenthood for the young mother and her infant depend on the psychosocial context of the pregnancy. Within the time period of early adolescence, there is a big difference between becoming a mother at 14 or at 18. For the younger teens (i.e., those younger than 14), the pregnancies are typically unplanned and often a result of involuntary or forced sexual encounters. Younger teens are more likely to end their pregnancy by abortion. For the older teens, the girl's partner is usually within 2 years of her age, and even if the pregnancy was unplanned, the majority of girls go ahead with the birth. Overall, 27% of pregnancies among those 15 to 19 years old ended in abortion in 2006 (Alan Guttmacher Institute, 2010). Overall, fewer than 2% of unmarried pregnant teens choose to allow the baby to be adopted (Moore, Miller et al., 1995; Moore & Rosenthal, 2006).

Two common consequences of early pregnancy are its association with poverty, and the increased risk of birth complications associated with a lack of prenatal care. The most significant measurable impact of early pregnancy is its association with subsequent poverty. Teens growing up in high-poverty neighborhoods are at greater risk for teenage pregnancy and dropping out of school, both of which contribute to continuing poverty in adulthood (Harding, 2003; Hao & Cherlin, 2004). The relation between age at first pregnancy and family income by age 27 was studied in a sample of African American, Hispanic American, and European American women (Moore et al., 1993). This effect is mediated through a number of other personal and family factors that unfold following the first birth, such as continuing in school, the chances of getting married, the kind of work one does and one's personal earnings, and the earning capacity of other family members. For African American women, the poverty level is high regardless of age at first birth. However, the earlier African American women begin childbearing, the more children they are likely to have—a factor that increases their level of poverty. For Hispanic American women, delaying childbearing resulted in higher educational attainment, a factor that predicts higher personal income by age 27. For European American women, delaying the age of childbearing was associated with older age at first marriage, fewer children, and higher personal earnings. For all three ethnic groups, but especially for European Americans and Hispanic Americans, each year of delayed childbearing had a substantial impact on reducing the chances of ending up in poverty by age 27.

Complications during labor and delivery may be devastating to the newborn's health. Are young mothers more likely than older ones to experience such complications? Mothers under 19 are less likely than older mothers to initiate prenatal care during the first trimester of pregnancy. Infants born to mothers under 17 are at greater risk than those born to women in their twenties and thirties. They have a higher risk of dying during the first year, of being born prematurely or with a low birth weight, and of suffering neurological damage as a result of complications associated with delivery (McCarthy & Hardy, 1993; U.S. Census Bureau, 2003). Thus, young parents are more likely to have to cope with the special needs of a child with developmental disabilities. However, these risks arise from converging socioeconomic factors rather than from any biological inadequacies of being young. Studies involving large numbers of births at urban hospitals have found that younger mothers (i.e., those under 20) who are not poor are actually *less likely* to experience complications of pregnancy and negative birth outcomes than older mothers of similar economic standing (Roosa, 1984; McCarthy & Hardy, 1993).

Complications of pregnancy and negative birth outcomes for adolescent mothers are linked to the contexts of pregnancy. One study found that in a sample of 170 African American teens, the pregnancy was unplanned or unwanted in about half the cases (Crosby, DiClemente, Wingood, Rose, & Lang, 2003). Other studies have linked sexual abuse in childhood with earlier sexual activity and **teen pregnancy** (Cinq-Mars, Wright, Cyr, & McDuff, 2003; Brown, Cohen, Chen, Smailes, & Johnson, 2004). When pregnancy occurs in these abusive or exploitive contexts, it is likely to be accompanied by alcohol or drug use, cigarette smoking, and heightened anxiety, all of which may contribute to low birth weight and neurological impairments for the infants. Teens who become pregnant under these circumstances are more likely to be socially isolated and to become psychologically disengaged from their infants. In contrast, when teen pregnancy occurs in the context of family, peer, and partner support, teen mothers are likely to receive encouragement for their caregiving, greater financial support, and opportunities to engage in appropriate social and educational activities that contribute to their own psychosocial maturity (Bunting & McAuley, 2004).

For some teens, the experience of motherhood has an enhancing or self-righting impact. In a comparison of adolescent mothers who ended their pregnancies through abortion and those who kept their babies, the latter group demonstrated some important changes in their behavior. Rates of delinquency declined in this group, and they reduced their cigarette smoking and marijuana use (Hope, Wilder, & Watt, 2003). Young mothers may be inspired by their infant to make a better future for themselves and their baby. This often means completing their education, creating a more stable home environment, and taking better care of their own health.

Not much is known about the impact of teen fathering on a boy's psychological development. What factors might influence whether the boy becomes committed to nurturing and supporting his child or leaves the parenting entirely to the mother and her family?

Adolescent Fathers. Although the focus of studies on adolescent pregnancy has been on girls, there is growing interest in factors that predict early fatherhood, as well as concerns about the impact of early fatherhood on subsequent development. Data from the National Longitudinal Study of Youth provided information about approximately 1,500 boys ages 13 or 14 who were studied over a period of 8 years. Participants reported their age at the birth of their first child. Overall, 140 participants or slightly over 9% became fathers before the age of 20. A combination of individual, family, peer, and environmental factors predicted early age of fatherhood in this sample. Boys who were involved in more delinquent behaviors and more substance use were more likely to become fathers. Boys who started dating at a younger age were more likely to become fathers. Boys whose mothers had less education, and who had their sons while they were adolescents, were more likely to become fathers. Boys who were living in a single parent home or not living with their biological father were more likely to become fathers. And boys who were living in more dangerous neighborhoods were more likely to become fathers. After taking all these factors into account, sons of adolescent fathers were at greater risk for becoming fathers themselves in adolescence than were boys whose fathers were 20 or older at their birth. These findings suggest an intergenerational pattern of early fathering in which young boys learn about early sexual activity as a pathway into adulthood as part of the family socialization process (Sipsma, Biello, Cole-Lewis, & Kershaw, 2010).

Most studies of adolescent pregnancy find that—contrary to the stereotype—many fathers remain in contact with the mother and the child in the first months after the child is born.

However, by the time the children are in school, contact drops off. In one study, half of the new adolescent fathers had weekly contact with their child, but by the time the children were in school, only 25% were still seeing the child weekly (Lerman, 1993). Some adolescent fathers marry the mothers; others live with them for a while. Often, the couple continues to date. In some instances, they actually marry several years after the child is born. In many cases, the father contributes financial support to the mother and child, even when the couples do not marry. Many adolescent fathers, however, have little education and are minimally employed, so the material support they can provide is limited (Bunting & McAuley, 2004).

Fathering a child is bound to stimulate conflicting feelings of pride, guilt, and anxiety in the adolescent boy. He must struggle with the fact that he contributed to a pregnancy that may bring conflict and pain to someone for whom he cares. Also, he must confront the choices that he and his girlfriend have in coping with an unplanned pregnancy. Furthermore, he may feel excluded from the birth of a child he has fathered. Feeling obligated to provide financial support for his girlfriend and child may lead him to drop out of school and enter the labor market, even though he can only hope to be minimally employed (Hendricks & Fullilove, 1983; Paschal, 2006).

Little systematic research has been done on the attitudes, knowledge, or behaviors of adolescent fathers or the impact of fatherhood on a teenage boy's subsequent development. One study followed a large sample of adolescent boys through their teen years. Those who became fathers were characterized as having lower self-esteem and a lower sense of internal control than their age-mates who did not become fathers. Shortly after fatherhood, these boys experienced a boost in self-esteem, but in the next several years, their self-esteem declined to its prefatherhood level (Pirog-Good, 1995).

Researchers who have studied the topic of unwed fathers argue that much stronger emphasis should be placed on the father's responsibility, not only for financial support of the mother and child, but also for his continued interaction with his child. School counselors, for example, tend to have a much clearer idea about how to support the continuing psychosocial development of teen mothers and their children than about how to support the continuing development of teen fathers (Kiselica, Gorcynski, & Capps, 1998). Efforts to include young fathers in family planning programs, parent education, and employment training initiatives would help strengthen the social context for the young mother and her child and would contribute to the young father's psychosocial development (Armstrong et al., 1999).

For both girls and boys, a key to the prevention of early pregnancy requires the building of greater confidence in and commitment to the consistent use of contraception as part of any sexual relationship and comfortable, user-friendly access to reproductive health care (Cicatelli, 2004). For girls, fostering a sense of self-efficacy and investment in academic goals leading to postsecondary education or professional training is an especially important area for intervention. For boys, building greater social expectations and commitment to assuming the financial and social responsibilities associated with fatherhood—including sending clearer messages from family and community that boys have responsibilities in these areas and devising specific opportunities for them to enact these responsibilities—seem promising directions for future intervention. For more information on pregnancy prevention programs, visit the website of the Centers for Disease Control and Prevention and go to the Unintended Pregnancy home page.

Formal Operations

Objective 3. To introduce and critically evaluate the basic features of formal operational thought, highlighting the new conceptual skills that emerge in early adolescence and the factors that promote the development of advanced reasoning at this period of life.

As the body undergoes significant changes during puberty, so too does mental activity. Early adolescents begin to think about themselves and their world in new ways that reflect a broadening of consciousness. This includes greater introspection or monitoring of their thoughts, greater integration of information from various sources, and more focused planning and control of behaviors guided by goals and strategies. Young people are able to think about several dimensions at once rather than focusing on just one domain or issue at a time. They are able to generate hypotheses about events that they have never perceived and to use logical reasoning to evaluate evidence to support or disconfirm these hypotheses (Keating, 2004).

Brain Development in Adolescence

You will recall from Chapter 4, which is about the prenatal period, that the brain is comprised of **gray matter,** the cell body of neurons and the nonmyelinated sections of axons and dendrites, and **white matter,** the myelinated axons that connect gray matter and carry messages between nerve cells and brain regions. **Myelin** is a substance that forms around the axons, acting as an insulator that speeds signals from one neuron to the next. Gray matter volume and distribution are associated with competence in that region of the brain. White matter is associated with speed and efficiency of processing.

Brain development is ongoing throughout the prenatal period, infancy, childhood, adolescence, and adulthood. Like physical maturation, it is very individual, reflecting an ongoing interaction between genetics and environment. Brain development is characterized by periods of intense production of neurons and synapses followed by a process of sculpting and pruning when some connections are strengthened and others drop away. One of the most important discoveries related to adolescent brain development is that various areas of the cerebral cortex reach their peak in gray matter production during early adolescence, followed by a process of sculpting and pruning. The timing for these peak periods of gray matter production vary quite a bit from one person to the next, but the average is around ages 10 to 12 for the parietal lobe, ages 11 to 12 for the frontal lobe, and ages 16 to 17 for the temporal lobe (Lenroot & Giedd, 2006).

The process of sculpting and pruning that occurs during the course of the high school years strengthens certain neural networks while others fall into disuse. Whatever a young person does frequently will be woven into a strong, well-integrated network of neural signals; neural functions that are infrequently or rarely stimulated will weaken. Thus, the high school years provide a truly irreplaceable opportunity to shape a person's neural landscape, creating areas of unique competence and mastery that develop as a result of active engagement in certain thoughts and behaviors.

In contrast to the gray matter, which shows an inverted U-shaped pattern, increasing from childhood through adolescence and declining in the late teens and early adulthood, there is a steady increase in the volume of white matter from ages 4 through the twenties. The prefrontal cortex, which is responsible for the full range of executive functions, is not fully myelinated until the twenties.

Executive functions, sometimes called cognitive control functions, include:

Working memory. The memory system used for temporarily storing and managing the information required to carry out complex cognitive tasks such as learning, reasoning, and comprehension.

Planning and organizing. Devising an approach to a complex task, including following a sequence of steps to task completion and using feedback to revise one's plan.

Impulse control. Including resisting distractions, self-regulation, and behavioral inhibition.

Peak 1. Ages 1–6. Rapid brain growth across several areas. Associated with ability to form images, use words, place things in serial order, development of problem-solving tactics.
Peak 2. Ages 6–10. Peak growth in the sensory-motor regions. Associated with operational functions such as determining weight and reasoning about mathematical problems.
Peak 3. Ages 10½–13. New growth in the visual and auditory regions of the brain. New abilities to perform calculations and to perceive new meanings and functions for familiar objects.
Peak 4. Ages 13–17. New growth in the visuoauditory, visuospatial, and somatic systems of the brain. New ability to review mental operations, find flaws in their reasoning, and use information to revise their problem-solving strategies.
Peak 5. Ages 17–21. New growth in the frontal executive region. New capacities to question and evaluate information, form new and original hypotheses integrating their own experiences with information taken from other sources.

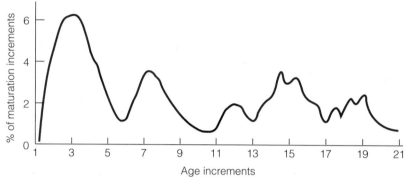

FIGURE 9.4 Peak Periods of Cerebral Maturation
Source: From "The Effects of Neurologic Injury on the Maturing Brain," by M. Allison, *Headlines*, October/November, pp. 2–4.

The combination of changes in gray matter and white matter in the frontal, parietal, and temporal lobes and the resulting improvements in executive functions are associated with the following potential changes in mental competence during adolescence (see Figure 9.4).

Ages 10.5 to 13: New growth in the visual and auditory regions of the brain; new ability to perform calculations; increasing ability to perceive new meanings and functions for familiar objects.

Ages 13 to 17: New growth in visuoauditory, visuospatial, and somatic systems; new ability to review mental operations (metacognition), especially the ability to find flaws in one's reasoning and to use information to revise problem-solving strategies.

Ages 17 to 21: New growth in prefrontal cortex: new abilities to question and evaluate information; new abilities to formulate hypotheses based on new information from a variety of sources.

The relationship of the brain and behaviors is bidirectional. Many studies have shown a relationship between maturation in the prefrontal cortex and improvements in executive functions including working memory and response inhibition (Paus, 2005). At the same time, studies have shown that repeated activity, such as musical training, can alter brain structure. For example, a 3-month period of juggling practice was found to be related to an increase in gray-matter density in the motion-processing region of the brain (Draganski et al., 2004). In other words, the maturing brain makes new accomplishments possible for adolescents; and, at the same time, the effort and persistence an adolescent exerts toward advanced skill building stimulates new neural growth.

Piaget's Theory of Formal Operational Thought

Without the benefit of brain scans, Jean Piaget proposed a qualitative shift in thinking during adolescence from concrete to **formal operational thought** (Inhelder & Piaget, 1958; Piaget, 1970, 1972a). In the period of concrete operational thought, children use mental operations to explain changes in tangible objects and events. In the period of formal operational thought, young people use operations to manipulate and modify thoughts and other mental operations (Piaget, 1972b). A central feature of formal operational reasoning is the ability to separate and distinguish between *reality* and *possibility*. For example, in thinking about trying to get a part-time job, adolescents may consider the possibilities about work related to the kind of work they would like to do and the kind of work they think they are qualified to do. They may also consider certain realities such as the specific jobs that are available in their town, the number of hours they can work given other school and family commitments, and their access to transportation. They are able to create different scenarios about working, based partly on what they want and partly on what they learn in the process of applying for jobs. Some of the possibilities they may have considered are no longer realistic; and some of the information suggests new possibilities that they may not have considered.

The opportunity to manipulate variables in an experimental situation stimulates formal operational thought. At the same time, the capacity for hypothesis testing makes it possible for students to evaluate the results of their experiments. How might you design chemistry experiments so that they are most likely to foster formal operational reasoning?

In the maturation of scientific reasoning, the ability to distinguish between reality and possibility results in the formal operational process of hypothesis testing. **Hypotheses** are tentative propositions or *possible* explanations about the causes of events or the systematic associations among factors that explain events. In the scientific process, one raises hypotheses to explain an event, and then follows the chain of evidence to determine whether the reality supports the hypothesis. One of the classic experiments that Piaget and Inhelder designed to demonstrate the development of hypothetical deductive reasoning involves the explanation of the swing of a pendulum. The task is to find out what variable or combination of variables controls the speed of the swing. Four factors can be varied: the mass of the object, the height from which the pendulum is pushed, the force with which it is pushed, and the length of the string. To investigate this problem, it is necessary to begin by isolating the separate factors and then varying only one factor at a time while keeping the others constant. As it happens, only the length of the string influences the speed of the pendulum. The challenge, then, is to demonstrate that the length of the string accounts for the speed of the pendulum and that the other factors do not. Children at the stage of concrete operational thought have difficulty coordinating the interaction among four separate variables and may lose track of what is being varied and what is held constant. After trying one or two strategies, they may simply give up. In contrast, being able to use formal operational thought, a child can create a matrix of variables and test each factor separately to evaluate its contribution (Inhelder & Piaget, 1958; Flavell, 1963).

Six Characteristics of Formal Operational Thought.
Formal operational thought is not a specific skill or expertise;

rather, it is a way of approaching and solving problems based on new capacities for abstract, probabilistic thinking. Six conceptual skills emerge during the stage of formal operations that have implications for how adolescents approach interpersonal relationships and the formulation of personal plans and goals and for how they analyze scientific and mathematical information (see Table 9.2; Neimark, 1982; Demetriou & Efklides, 1985; Gray, 1990). First, adolescents are able to mentally manipulate more than two categories of variables at the same time; for example, they can consider the relationship of speed, distance, and time in planning a trip (Acredolo, Adams, & Schmid, 1984). They can draw on many variables to explain their behavior as well as that of others. Second, they are able to think about things changing in the future. They can realize, for instance, that their current friendships may not remain the same in the years ahead.

TABLE 9.2 New Conceptual Skills That Emerge During the Stage of Formal Operational Thought

1. Ability to mentally manipulate more than two categories of variables simultaneously.
2. Ability to think about the changes that come with time.
3. Ability to hypothesize logical sequences of events.
4. Ability to foresee consequences of actions.
5. Ability to detect logical consistency or inconsistency in a set of statements.
6. Ability to think in relativistic ways about self, others, and the world.

Third, adolescents are able to hypothesize about a logical sequence of possible events. For example, they are able to predict college and occupational options that may be open to them, depending on how well they do in certain academic coursework in high school. Fourth, they are able to anticipate the consequences of their actions. For instance, they realize that if they drop out of school, certain career possibilities will be closed to them.

Fifth, they have the capacity to detect the logical consistency or inconsistency of a set of statements. They can test the truth of a statement by finding evidence that supports or disproves it. They are troubled, for example, by the apparent contradiction between statements such as "all people are equal before the law" and the reality that people who have more money can afford better legal representation and are likely to have different experiences with the legal system than those who live in poverty.

Sixth, adolescents are able to think in a relativistic way about themselves, other individuals, and their world. They know that they are expected to act in a particular way because of the norms of their community and their culture. Adolescents also know that in other families, communities, and cultures, different norms may govern the same behavior. As a result, the decision to behave in a culturally accepted manner becomes a more conscious commitment to their cultural group. At the same time, it is easier for them to accept members of other cultures, because they realize that these people are the products of societies with different sets of rules and norms.

These qualities of thought reflect what is *possible* for adolescents rather than what is typical. Most adolescents and older adults approach problem solving in a practical, concrete way in their common, daily functioning. However, under the most supportive conditions, more abstract, systematic, and self-reflective qualities of thought can be observed and bring a new perspective to the way adolescents approach the analysis of information and the acquisition of knowledge (Lee & Freire, 2003).

Factors That Promote Formal Operational Thought.

Neurological development alone is not enough to foster formal operational thought. Healthy brain development must be coupled with a social environment that encourages hypothetical, abstract reasoning; opportunities to investigate and explore alternative solutions; and a well-developed symbolic capacity for carrying out mental representations and operations. The affective components of interest, motivation, and self-efficacy are also involved in sustaining engagement with complex problems and the emotional regulation that allows one to stay focused despite frustrations and failures.

Several environmental conditions facilitate the development of formal operational thought and reduce egocentrism. First, early adolescents begin to function in a variety of role relationships that place both compatible and conflicting demands on them. Among these role relationships are son or daughter, worker, student, friend, dating partner, religious believer, and citizen. Early adolescents experience firsthand the pressures of multiple expectations for behavior. Participating in a variety of roles also facilitates relativistic thinking by demonstrating that what is acceptable and valued in one situation may not be in another. A second environmental factor is the adolescent's participation in a more heterogeneous peer group. When children move from their community elementary school to a more centralized junior high and high school, they are likely to meet other students whose family backgrounds and social

Conversations with parents often force adolescents to rethink their assumptions or come up with support for their decisions. Although this is not always pleasant, these kinds of interactions are an important stimulus for more advanced reasoning.

Copyright © Robert Brenner/Photo Edit

class are different from their own. In working and playing with these friends, they realize the extent to which their expectations for the future differ from those of their new acquaintances because their values are shaped by the families and neighborhood from which they come. In research involving Mexican high school students, those who were identified as leaders, especially those with cross-cultural contact and those who were of high socioeconomic status, reasoned at higher stages than those who were not (Commons, Galaz-Fontes, & Morse, 2006).

The use of formal operational skills can be observed in adolescent discussions of peer-related issues and in the formation of intimate or romantic relationships—domains that require a wide range of hypothesis raising and testing. An example of a conversation between a 15-year-old girl and her best friend follows.

CINDY: I'm so frustrated I can't stand it. Before Sean and I started to date, he was nice to me. I enjoyed being with him. He said hello to me in the halls; we'd walk along together. We talked about all kinds of things. Now that we're going out, he seems rude and uncaring. When we're with other people, he jumps in when I start to talk, and his eyes say "be quiet." He breezes by me in the halls sometimes, and when we talk about things (if we talk), he acts as if he is always right. I don't think he cares about me anymore. What's going on?

DONNA: I know he likes you because he tells me. Maybe you should talk to him and tell him what he does and how it makes you feel.

CINDY: No, if I do that he'll get mad and he won't like me anymore. Why don't you talk to him?

DONNA: No, that wouldn't do any good, because then he would know you talked to me about this and he would not like it, or he would just say what he thinks would make him look good.

As this conversation continues, many possible scenarios are proposed about why this behavior is occurring, and many hypotheses are raised about what could be done. The girls propose likely outcomes of each set of possible actions and attempt to evaluate the results of each. Finally, a tentative conclusion is reached: Boys treat girls differently when they are involved in a boyfriend-girlfriend relationship than when they are not. In the just-friends situation, there is a tendency to treat the girl as an equal, but in the boyfriend-girlfriend situation, there is a tendency for the boy to expect that he should dominate the girl. A solution is derived: Cindy must shape up Sean. Because she still likes him and wants to go out with him, she must try to tell him how she feels and hope he will change his behavior so that it is supportive and comfortable for her.

The context of friendship between Cindy and Donna allows Cindy to trust discussing her problem with Donna so that they can examine it fully. It also allows Donna to disagree with Cindy without terminating the conversation. Thus, Cindy can get a somewhat different point of view on her situation and the two friends together can explore a personal problem on a more objective, rational basis than Cindy probably could have done on her own.

The third condition that fosters the development of the cognitive skills of early adolescence is the content of the high school curriculum. Guided by Vygotsky's theory of a zone of proximal development, we assume that an adolescent's capacities for formal operational reasoning are ready to be nurtured and advanced through exposure to educational experiences that promote systematic logical reasoning and problem solving. Courses in science and mathematics formally introduce students to the logical relationships inherent in these disciplines, and give them practice in a hypothetical deductive style of reasoning. Courses in the social sciences, such as child development, psychology, anthropology, or sociology introduce students to the organization of societies, individual differences in perspective, and psychological mindedness. The fine arts and the humanities advance students' conceptions of ways the world has been or might be. They expand the repertoire of representational thought. According to Gardner's model of multiple intelligences (discussed in Chapter 8), the visual arts provide a means of integrating and innovating spatial intelligence with interpersonal intelligence. Many high schools involve students in community service learning, an experience that helps promote a greater sense of connection to the community and appreciation for the diverse perspectives on community improvement. The more complex, differentiated academic environment of the high school can bring substantial gains in conceptual skills for those students who become actively engaged in its academic programs (Gehlbach, 2006; Yamauchi, Billig, Meyer, & Hofschire, 2006; Cohen & Sandy, 2007).

The following examples illustrate how high school course experiences contributed to students' formal operational reasoning.

"In my senior physics class we would learn new concepts then apply them by building something. For example we were learning about inertia so then we had to build a cart to hold a pumpkin and it had to go straight and travel a certain distance."

"An assignment that enhanced my logical reasoning and critical thinking was to design a school playground using specific software. I had to think about dimensions of my playground and logically think about safety issues in the design."

"In high school I took a money matters course that talked about saving money, stocks, loans, debt, and every other aspect of money. It made me think in a much more logical way because hearing it from someone other than my parents made it more real."

"In my AP art class my senior year my teacher gave us a topic and we had to do 20 pieces of artwork with that one topic/object. Mine was a seashell and water. It broadened my thinking to think of 20 different things to do with a seashell." (Newman, 2010)

Although schooling can be a vehicle that promotes formal operational reasoning, not all school experiences are equally effective in promoting abstract, hypothetical reasoning. Keating (1990) described the following characteristics that are important in creating a cognitively stimulating school experience.

Students need to be engaged with meaningful material; training of thinking skills must be embedded in a knowledge of subject matter, for acquisition of isolated content knowledge is likely to be unproductive; serious engagement with real problems has to occur in depth and over time; students need experiences that lead to placing a high value on critical thinking, to acquiring it as a disposition, not just as a skill; and many of these factors occur most readily, and perhaps exclusively, when students have the opportunity for real, ongoing discourse with teachers who have reasonably expert command of the material to be taught. (p. 77)

One does not expect to see a mature scientist or a profound philosopher by the end of early adolescence. A young person's formal operational reasoning awaits further encounters with a specific discipline and its full range of significant problems. However, the opportunity for cognitive growth during this period is extensive. Adolescents are able to generate novel solutions and apply them to current life challenges. They also are able to be increasingly objective about the problem-solving process and to gain insight into their own mental activity (Lee & Friere, 2003).

Criticisms of the Concept of Formal Operational Thought. In Piaget's theory, formal operational reasoning is viewed as the final stage in the development of logical thought. A number of scholars have pointed to limitations in this construction. Three criticisms are discussed here. First, some scholars question whether there really is a qualitative, stage-like consolidation in the use of formal reasoning. Although most researchers agree that formal operational thinking exists and does characterize the nature of mature, scientific reasoning, many studies show that adolescents and adults typically do not function at the formal operational level, and that their use of formal reasoning is inconsistent across problem areas (Bradmetz, 1999). For example, Neimark (1975) followed changes in the problem-solving strategies of adolescents over a 3½-year period. Even the oldest participants in her study, who were 15, did not apply formal operational strategies across all problems. Research has not been able to confirm Piaget's claims that thinking becomes consistently more propositional across problem areas or that formal operational reasoning is a universal characteristic of adolescent reasoning in a variety of cultures. At the same time, the evidence does suggest that adolescents become more aware of the need to coordinate logic and evidence as they evaluate propositions (Keating, 2004). Even Piaget speculated that people were most likely to use formal operational reasoning primarily in the area of their greatest expertise.

A second criticism of formal operational reasoning is that it is not broad enough to encompass the many dimensions along which cognitive functioning matures in adolescence. Information processing, another aspect of cognitive science, focuses on specific mechanisms for perceiving, encoding, and retrieving bytes or units of information. Increases in speed, efficiency, and capacity of information storage and retrieval have been documented during the period from ages 11 to 16 (Kwon & Lawson, 2000). These capacities can be applied to hypothetical reasoning, but are not the same as formal operational thought. Improvements in logical reasoning may result in part from the ability to handle greater quantities of information more quickly and efficiently.

In addition to development in basic processing, there are gains in knowledge, both as a result of schooling and experience. Knowledge in each specialized subject, such as mathematics, language, or science, expands, bringing not only increases in logic but increases in understanding the procedures or strategies that are most likely to work for a given problem. Complementing changes in specialized knowledge, adolescents demonstrate increases in self-monitoring and conscious control of mental activity, such as the ability to hold conclusions in abeyance while they examine alternative solutions or gather new information. These capacities for cognitive flexibility contribute to the potential for more mature solutions (Donald, 2001).

Finally, some scholars claim that formal operational thought does not represent the apex or endpoint of adult thought and reasoning. As adults mature, they face many problems in which abstract, logical-mathematical reasoning must be integrated with the special emotional and social demands of the circumstances. The problem may need to be reframed to suit the situation. The solution may need to be evaluated for its impact on many interrelated parties. The cognitive processes associated with psychotherapy, diplomacy, and spiritual leadership are all examples of what might be considered **postformal reasoning** (Richards & Commons, 1990; Torbert, 1994).

Egocentrism and Decentering

The term **egocentrism** refers to the child's limited perspective at the beginning of each new phase of cognitive development (Piaget, 1926; Inhelder & Piaget, 1958). In the sensorimotor phase, egocentrism appears as an inability to separate one's actions from their effects on specific objects or people. As the scheme for causality is developed, the first process of **decentering** occurs. Infants recognize that certain actions have predictable consequences and that novel situations call for new, relevant behaviors. For example, one cannot turn the light on by turning the knob on the radio. At each developmental stage, decentering allows the person to approach situations from a more objective, analytic point of view.

In the phase of preoperational thought, egocentrism is manifested in an inability to separate one's own perspective from that of the listener. When a 4-year-old girl tells you about something that happened to her at the zoo, she may explain events as if you had seen them too. When a

3-year-old boy is explaining something to his grandmother over the phone, he may point to objects in the room, unaware that his grandmother cannot *see* over the phone lines.

The third phase of heightened egocentrism occurs in the transition from concrete to formal operational thought. As children develop the capacity to formulate hypothetical systems, they begin to generate assumptions about their own and others' behavior that will fit into these systems. For example, an early adolescent boy may insist that cooperation is a more desirable mode of interaction than competition. He argues that cooperation ought to benefit each participant and provide more resources for the group as a whole. This boy may become angry or disillusioned to discover that teachers, parents, and even peers seek competitive experiences and appear to enjoy them. He may think, "If the cooperative system is so superior, why do people persist in their illogical joy in triumphing over an opponent?" This kind of egocentrism reflects an inability to recognize that others may not share one's own hypothetical system.

In early adolescence, decentering requires an ability to realize that one's ideals are not shared by all others. We live in a pluralistic society, in which each person is likely to have distinct goals and aspirations. Adolescents gradually discover that their neat, logical life plans must be constantly adapted to the expectations and needs of others. As they develop the flexibility of thought that accompanies formal operational perspective taking, their egocentrism usually declines.

Early adolescent egocentrism has two characteristics that may affect adolescents' social interactions as well as their problem solving: (1) preoccupation with their own thoughts, and (2) a belief that others are also preoccupied with their thoughts. First, adolescents may become withdrawn and isolated as the domain of their consciousness expands. Thoughts about the possible and the probable, the near and the distant future, and the logical extension of contemporary events to future consequences all flood their minds. David Elkind (1967) described one aspect of this process as the formation of a **personal fable**—an intense investment in one's own thoughts and feelings, and a belief that these thoughts are unique. Adolescents may conclude that they alone are having certain insights or difficulties and that no one else could understand or sympathize with their thoughts. This tendency to withdraw into their own speculations may cut off access to new information or ideas and inhibit social interaction.

Second, early adolescents may assume that they are the center of interest of others' thoughts and attentions. Elkind (1967) referred to this as an **imaginary audience**. Instead of considering that all people are equally wrapped up in their own concerns and plans, early adolescents may envision their own thoughts as being the focus of other people's attention. This subjectivity generates an uncomfortable self-consciousness that makes interaction awkward. There is some question about the outcome of this heightened self-consciousness. On the one hand, a preoccupation with the idea that others are watching your every move may be an important element in decentering, directing attention to others and how you may be viewed in their eyes. Thus, self-consciousness may stimulate cognitive perspective taking. On the other hand, an increased ability to consider the point of view of others and their expectations for your behavior may increase self-consciousness.

Egocentrism is a problem not only during the adolescent years. At each new phase of expanding awareness, people rely heavily on their own experiences and perceptions in order to minimize the anxiety associated with uncertainty. Part of the progress of formal thought implies a reliance on reason over experience, placing greater confidence in what is known to be true than in what is seen or heard. This can lead to becoming confined to the world of one's familiar beliefs. We may interpret new experiences as examples of familiar concepts rather than as novel events. We may reject evidence for an argument because it does not support an already carefully developed explanation. The business of casting around for new evidence and explanations is a lifelong challenge. It is much easier to rely on earlier assumptions than to continually question one's perspective.

Emotional Development

Objective 4. To examine patterns of emotional development in early adolescence, including three examples of emotional disorders: eating disorders, delinquency, and depression.

Descriptions of adolescence often refer to new levels of emotional variability, moodiness, and emotional outbursts. However, evidence suggests that this is also a time of increased emotional complexity, with new capacities to identify, understand, and express a wider range of emotions (Kang & Shaver, 2004). These capacities illustrate the close interdependence of cognition and emotion, especially as reasoning about the consequences of expressing emotions may result in the control or management of emotional expression (Hoeksma, Oosterlaan, & Schipper, 2004). Given the likelihood of a more differentiated range of emotions during adolescence, a major task during this time is to gain insight into one's emotionality, and to expand one's capacity for empathy with the emotional state of others (Weissberg & O'Brien, 2004). This means accepting one's feelings and not interpreting them as a sign of going crazy or being strange. Adolescents who are highly sensitive to social expectations or overly controlled about expressing or accepting their feelings probably experience a sense of shame about their emotional states. Attempts to rigidly control or defend oneself against feelings are likely to result in social alienation or maladaptive behaviors. In contrast, those who experience a diverse and well-differentiated range of emotions are also more likely to be characterized by greater openness to experience, empathy, and interpersonal adaptability (Kang & Shaver, 2004).

The Interplay of Emotion and Cognition

A key feature of the human's adaptive capacity is the ability to detect and respond quickly to situations that threaten our survival. Some areas of the brain, especially the limbic system, detect threats, react intuitively to information, and produce quick emotional reactions to situations. The limbic system produces signals that identify the immediate situation as threatening, or link the immediate situation to other previously experienced dangers. The sound of an explosion, being hit or threatened with violence, or the experience of being caught in a raging storm are all examples of situations that could trigger an immediate threat reaction in the limbic system. These reactions are referred to as bottom-up processing. Other areas of the brain, especially the prefrontal cortex, are more analytic. Information from a variety of sources is evaluated, decisions are made, and a logical plan is formulated. The frontal cortex receives information from the limbic system, evaluates this information in light of the context, and makes an assessment of possible consequences of action. Information is then transmitted back to the limbic system to modify emotional signals and to the sensory-motor cortex to guide subsequent behavior. The frontal cortex control is referred to as top-down processing. The coordination of the limbic system and the frontal cortex is referred to as vertical control (Greenberg, Riggs, & Blair, 2007).

The vertical control system undergoes a process of maturation that is usually not complete until the twenties. In adolescence, there is evidence of some changes in the level of neurotransmitters in the limbic system. Adolescents are more emotional, more reactive to stressors, and less responsive to rewards than older adults. They need a more intense reward to have the same positive or pleasurable impact that might be experienced from a milder stimulus by an older person. At the same time, the frontal cortex and the myelination of neural pathways connecting the frontal cortex to the limbic system are not fully developed. The prefrontal cortex is the site of a variety of executive functions, some of which serve to manage strong emotions through monitoring one's internal state, interpreting the emotions, and finding acceptable ways for expressing or, if needed, inhibiting the expression of emotions. Other executive functions are useful for planning a course of action, evaluating possible consequences, and adapting to changing circumstances as the situation requires. The combination of these aspects of brain development may result in adolescents' need for greater stimulus seeking and the willingness for more risk taking. With a less fully developed prefrontal cortex, adolescents may have difficulty suppressing the immediate, emotional responses of the limbic system. At the same time, they may engage in more intensely stimulating activities, some of which adults would judge to be highly risky, in order to achieve the desired experience of pleasure or arousal.

Compared to adults, adolescents are nearly equally able to understand information about the negative consequences of risky behavior. In early adolescence, they may even overestimate the likelihood of their exposure to risk since they have relatively little life experience upon which to base their assessment of risks. However, if the negative consequences rarely happen, or if they engage in these behaviors frequently, they are likely to conclude that the consequences are not as harmful as they were led to believe. What is more, the risks and rewards of certain behaviors are not the same for adolescents as they might be for adults. For example, the risk of being bullied, socially isolated, or embarrassed might be more serious for adolescents than for an adult. Imagine that a young person has to choose between calling his parents for a ride home from a party or getting a ride home from a friend who is intoxicated. While the parent may view the risk of riding with an intoxicated friend as a great risk, the adolescent may view the risk of being seen by peers as overly dependent upon his parents as the greater risk.

In contrast to the vertical control system, through which the frontal cortex exerts control over the limbic system, there is also a horizontal control system that plays a role in risk taking and responses to threat. This horizontal system refers to the flow of information between the right and left hemispheres of the brain. For right-handed children, the left hemisphere of the brain is the primary area involved in understanding spoken language, speech production, and the expression of positive emotions. The right hemisphere is involved in recognizing nonverbal expressions, processing positive and negative emotions, and expressing uncomfortable or negative emotions. The effective flow of information between the two hemispheres provides teens with the ability to use verbal skills to identify and regulate their emotional states. With maturity, adolescents are increasingly able to use language to gain greater control over their behavior and to explain their internal states to themselves and to others. Although executive control and verbal behavior are two separate cognitive capacities, they can work together to manage strong emotional states as well as to guide effective action. Given the state of their brain development, the challenge that adolescents face is how to use their maturing executive functions under conditions of intense emotional arousal in order to avoid unnecessary risk taking.

The Diversity of Emotions in Adolescence

Adolescents are more aware than younger children of gradations in their emotional states and are able to attribute them to a wider range of causes. However, some researchers have questioned whether adolescence really brings the peaks and valleys of emotional intensity that are stereotypically linked to this time of life. In an attempt to assess this question, researchers gave an electronic paging device to children and adolescents ages 9 to 15 and asked them to describe their emotional state every time they were paged (Larson & Lampman-Petraitis, 1989). Over 1 week, each participant responded about 37 times. The variability of emotions was not found to increase with age. However, both the boys and the girls in the older group expressed fewer extremely positive emotions and more mildly negative emotions than did

Sporting events provide settings where adolescents can express their exuberant and wild emotions, including joy, pride, and anger.

the children in the younger group. In a subsequent study using similar methods, daily emotions were monitored in relation to children's pubertal status (Richards & Larson, 1993). Boys and girls with a more mature body shape at each age reported more frequent thoughts and feelings about love. Pubertal development was slightly related to heightened feelings of anger in girls, but in general, physical maturation was not closely linked to patterns of specific emotions in girls. In boys, the relationships between pubertal development and emotions were much stronger. Those boys who were more physically mature reported more experiences of feeling frustrated, tense, and hyper. They also reported a more positive mood, a greater ability to focus their attention, and more feelings of strength. Thus, in boys, pubertal changes were associated with both positive moods and a restless irritability.

After puberty, boys and girls show noticeably different levels of aggression and depression, with girls showing more problems coping with depression and boys showing more problems managing and controlling their aggressive impulses (Leadbeater, Kuperminc, Blatt, & Hertzog, 1999). These differences are often expressed in terms of **internalizing problems**, such as feelings of hopelessness or worthlessness, in which the adolescent's conflicts are directed inward on the self; and **externalizing problems**, sometimes referred to as conduct problems, such as aggression or delinquency, in which the adolescent's conflicts are directed outward toward property or other people (Achenbach, 1991). Three topics are discussed below, two of which are considered examples of internalizing problems—eating disorders and depression— and one that is considered an example of an externalizing problem, delinquency.

Eating Disorders

Eating disorders are an example of internalizing problems— turning one's frustration, anger, or fear inward on the self. Eating disorders are typically diagnosed in adolescence, and

primarily but not exclusively among girls. Three eating disorders have been described in the medical literature, but each one can be expressed in more severe or less severe patterns of symptoms (Liburd, 2006). **Anorexia nervosa** is characterized by a fear of gaining weight, refusal to maintain a minimally normal body weight, and perceptions of one's body as overweight in general or in specific areas (Herzog et al., 1999). Weight loss is viewed as an important accomplishment and is accompanied by increased self-esteem. Anorexia is found primarily in girls, with symptoms beginning either shortly after the weight spurt that accompanies puberty or at about age 18. Adolescents with this condition focus their behavior on weight loss. They take an obsessive, determined position in rejecting most foods, accompanied by dieting, fasting, or excessive exercise. They also tend to have a distorted perception of their body image, seeing themselves as much fatter than they really are. Only about half the patients who are treated for anorexia recover completely. A potentially life-threatening consequence is extreme starvation (Liburd, 2006).

Bulimia involves spurts of binging and overeating, followed by the use of different strategies to prevent the absorption of food, such as induced vomiting, the use of laxatives, or strenuous exercise. Bulimia has an incidence of between 1% and 3% in the female adolescent population and is experienced somewhat more commonly by male adolescents than is anorexia. Individuals who suffer from bulimia are usually ashamed of their eating and often eat in secret. Their eating is often experienced as a frenzy or an intense loss of control, followed by self-criticism and depression (Moreno & Judd, 2006).

The origins of eating disorders are not fully understood. Many authors implicate the cultural infatuation with thinness as a stimulus of this condition. Support for this view comes from evidence that anorexia and bulimia are almost nonexistent in nonindustrialized countries where there are often food shortages and where thinness is not a cultural ideal. A combination of parent, peer, and media idealization of thinness, coupled with a tendency for girls to experience body dissatisfaction during puberty, leads teens to restrict their food intake and engage in faddish diets (Dunkley, Wertheim, & Paxton, 2001; McCabe & Ricciardelli, 2001; Stice & Shaw, 2004).

Evie tells me that she learned how to throw up in school, in fact in health class, from a one-day lesson designed to discourage eating disorders. . . . Evie says she vomited after dinner three to five times a week off and on for almost a year. She didn't do it over the summer, she says, just when school was in session; and never during lunch—only after dinner, especially when her mother's boyfriend, a frequent guest at the table, urged her on to extra helpings of Tater Tots or dessert. On those nights, she'd wait until the dishes were done, then, a little while later, she'd mosey into the kitchen and pilfer a spoon. (Orenstein, 2000, p. 91)

A preoccupation with body appearance may be provoked by the relatively rapid physical changes associated with

AP Photo/Jack Plunkett

puberty. The psychoanalytic view is that eating disorders link back to fear of sexual maturity and are an unconscious strategy to delay entry into adulthood. The family system perspective emphasizes the parents' control or overcontrol of their child's actions and preferences. Eating disorders, in this view, are a way for a child to exert control or power over one key area, eating, in a context where little power is permitted. In addition to these theories, some clinicians describe the adolescents who suffer from anorexia as having difficulty accepting and expressing their emotions. Compared with adolescents who have other types of emotional disorders, adolescents with anorexia show less emotional expressivity, greater timidity, and more submissiveness. Adolescents with anorexia have been described as "duty bound, rigidly disciplined, and moralistic with underlying doubts and anxious hesitancy" (Strober, 1981, pp. 289–290).

Recent investigations have implicated certain genetic factors as associated with eating disorders. Twin studies provide evidence of a hereditary component to eating disorders. Three groups of genes have been shown to be associated with eating disorders, especially through their role in emotional regulation, anxiety, and appetite suppression and weight gain or loss. The first group of genes influences the receptors and transporters of serotonin, which functions in the brain to control appetite, mood, sleep, memory, and learning. The second group of genes is related to brain-derived neurotrophic factor (BDNF), a protein that supports the growth of neurons in the brain. BDNF is also associated with appetite and weight gain or loss. Finally, genes associated with estrogen receptors have been tied to food intake as well as to depression and anxiety (Klump & Culbert, 2007). The exact role of each gene group in contributing to eating disorders or the severity of symptoms is not known. One hypothesis is that a few genes make the person vulnerable to eating disorders when they are exposed to certain environmental conditions. For example, girls who are engaged in specific types of activities such as ballet, gymnastics, or modeling, where weight is very important and where they are likely to be exposed to the stresses of competition and control, may be especially likely to develop eating disorders if they also have the genetic vulnerability that supports this condition.

Studies of long-term outcomes following the diagnosis of anorexia find that appropriate treatment can restore normal body weight. However, a large number of young people who suffered from anorexia as adolescents continue to have social and emotional difficulties, especially problems in empathy, difficulty recognizing and identifying their emotions, obsessive-compulsive disorders, and anxiety (Herpertz-Dahlmann, Wewetzer, Hennighausen, & Remschmidt, 1996; Hsu, 1996). Over a 10-year period, an estimated 5.6% of people with anorexia die from the disorder (DeAngelis, 1997a).

Because of the seriousness and widespread nature of eating disorders, public health experts are working to create a more positive acceptance of people of various body types and shapes, with less focus on thinness. Advertisers are being urged to regulate ads promoting weight loss programs and products to children and adolescents and to disclose more accurately the amount of weight that can be lost. Physicians are being encouraged to rely less on height-weight tables as they discuss health with adolescents, because those tables do not take into account body type and the range of individual differences in healthy weight (DeAngelis, 1997a). The Academy for Eating Disorders has tried to encourage the fashion industry to support the health of models by setting minimal body mass index (BMI) guidelines for models. They oppose the trend of presenting design collections on extremely thin models. The Council of Fashion Designers of America has resisted endorsing specific weight and height requirements, arguing that fashions change as standards of beauty change (Wilson, 2007).

Depression

There is growing concern about the number of adolescents who experience **depression** (Graber, 2004). Depression is used in at least three different contexts: depressed mood, depressive syndrome, and a depressive disorder (Petersen et al., 1993). *Depressed mood* refers to feeling sad or despondent, a loss of hope, a sense of being overwhelmed by the demands of the world, and general unhappiness. Almost everyone experiences this kind of depression at some time or another, describing it as the blues, feeling down in the dumps, or feeling low. Related symptoms include worrying, moodiness, crying, loss of appetite, difficulty sleeping, tiredness, loss of interest in or enjoyment of activities, and difficulty concentrating. Depression may range from mild, short-lived periods of feeling sad and discouraged to severe feelings of guilt and worthlessness. A depressed mood may be predictive of more serious emotional disorders, but it is not in itself a clinical diagnosis. Depression appears to increase for both boys and girls during adolescence, with a peak at about ages 17 or 18 (Petersen et al., 1993). One estimate is that about 35% of adolescents—a higher percentage for girls than for boys—have experienced a depressed mood in the previous 6 months.

The second use of the concept of depression is the notion of a *depressive syndrome*. This term refers to a constellation of behaviors and emotions that occur together. The syndrome usually includes complaints about feeling depressed, anxious, fearful, worried, guilty, and worthless. Roughly 5% of the normal population experiences this syndrome.

The third use of the concept of depression is its central role in clinical diagnosis. For a diagnosis of *major depressive disorder*, the adolescent must have experienced five or more of the following symptoms for at least 2 weeks: "Depressed mood or irritable mood most of the day; decreased interest in pleasurable activities; changes in weight or perhaps failure to make necessary weight gains in adolescence; sleep problems; psychomotor agitation or retardation; fatigue or loss of energy; feelings of worthlessness or abnormal amounts of guilt; reduced concentration and decision-making ability; and repeated suicidal ideation, attempts, or plans of suicide" (Petersen et al., 1993, p. 156).

Copyright © David Young-Wolff/Photo Edit

Ironically, the fact that girls are likely to try to comfort and support their friends during periods of emotional turmoil makes them more vulnerable to negative moods and depression. How might adolescent girls protect themselves from this negative consequence of close friendships?

Factors Associated with Adolescent Depression.

Adolescents face a number of challenges that make them vulnerable to depression. At present, no single theory is accepted as the explanation for depression. Some research points to genetic factors associated with the clinical diagnosis of depression. Neuroimaging of the brains of individuals with major depressive disorder has identified an area of the prefrontal cortex that is reduced in size and shows reduced functional links with the amygdala, a region of the brain that is associated with the regulation of emotions. This observation of a disruption in the link between a higher-order system that evaluates information, and a lower-order system that recognizes and reacts to threat coincides well with the symptoms of major depressive disorder that combines cognitive deficits and difficulties in emotion regulation (Insel, 2007).

Recalling the research on the interaction between depressed mothers and their infants discussed in Chapter 5 (Infancy), it is hard to separate genetic and environmental factors in the etiology of clinical depression. Having a depressed mother increases the risk of depression during adolescence. Teens whose mothers are depressed are characterized by more anxious attachments, more suicidal thoughts, and more frequent episodes of depression than teens whose mothers are not depressed (Essau, 2004). The direction of influence between brain and behavior is difficult to establish. Are some children more vulnerable to the negative impact of disrupted parenting because of some genetic neurological abnormality, or does the disrupted parenting produce a change in emotional regulation that eventually results in structural and functional abnormalities in the brain?

Parental loss or rejection has been found to increase an adolescent's vulnerability to depression (Robertson & Simons, 1989). In one longitudinal study of the consequences of economic pressures on families, a connection was shown between the family's economic stresses and increased parental depression. Economic strain is associated with heightened marital conflict, increased hostility, and less nurturance toward the children, resulting in subsequent adjustment problems in adolescent daughters, especially problems with hostility and depression (Conger et al., 1993; Tomarken, Dichter, Garber, & Simien, 2004). Even though scholars no longer view adolescence as a unique period of emotional turmoil, they recognize that adolescents are often exposed to more negative events than are younger children. Adolescents are more aware of what other people are experiencing, and because more is expected of them, there is more to worry about. School is more demanding, and there are more instances of high-stakes testing; selection or rejection in teams, clubs, and activities; and new performance standards (Locker & Cropley, 2004). Teens have a wider circle of relationships than younger children, through which they are exposed to more problems, expectations, and disappointments.

Adolescents report experiencing hassles in the following domains: social alienation (disagreements with teachers, disliking other students); excessive demands (not enough time to meet responsibilities, not enough time for sleep); romantic concerns (dissatisfaction in a romantic relationship); decisions about one's personal future (important decisions about a future career); loneliness and unpopularity (being ignored); assorted annoyances and concerns (money problems, disagreement with a boyfriend or girlfriend); social mistreatment (being taken advantage of, having one's trust betrayed); and academic challenge (struggling to meet other people's standards of performance at school; Kohn & Milrose, 1993). In this list, peer relations, including romantic relations and the elements of interpersonal experience that are part of being a member of a friendship group, play a central role.

Depression is linked to experiencing negative peer comparisons in areas that are considered to be important to others, such as good looks, athletic ability, having money, or having good social skills (Thwaites & Dagnan, 2004). Problems with peer relations can be a source of stress that triggers depression. At the same time, depression can lead to disruptions in peer relationships. Adolescents who are depressed may make more negative meaning of social interactions, feel more dependent on others to confirm their sense of self-worth, and have less energy or emotional resources for coping with experiences of rejection. Whereas having close friends who are not depressed may be a protective factor against depression, having friends who are depressed may actually induce a depressed mood. Depressed teens may ruminate about their problems, focus largely on negative experiences, experience more conflicts with each other, and generally convey dissatisfaction in their relationships (Brendgen, Lamarche, Wanner, & Vitaro, 2010). There is some evidence that girls who are depressed at age 15 are more likely to enter long-term romantic relationships with partners who are coercive, nonsupportive, and physically violent (Hammen, 2009). The implication is that depression plays a role in continuing to be exposed to stressful interpersonal relationships that, in turn, create new sources of depression.

Adolescents are relatively inexperienced in coping with these kinds of stressors. They may not have developed strategies for interrupting or reducing the feelings of grief or discouragement that accompany stressful life events. The combination of pressures on parents, especially marital conflicts and economic pressures that affect youth, plus exposure to their own failures, disappointments, and loss of relationships with peers and in school, are clearly linked to a negative mood in adolescents, especially sadness and depression (Larson & Ham, 1993). Feelings of depression may be intensified by accompanying hormonal changes (Hartlage, Brandenburg, & Kravitz, 2004). Young people may become convinced of their worthlessness, and this distortion of thought may lead them toward social withdrawal or self-destructive actions.

Gender Difference in Depression. Most studies find no differences in depression between prepubescent boys and girls; however, during the period from about age 11 to 15, gender differences are systematically noted and continue to be evident into adulthood (Jones-Webb & Snowden, 1993; Crawford, Cohen, Midlarsky, & Brook, 2001). Experiences of depression appear to be more common in adolescent girls than in boys. This gender difference has been found in comparisons of the depression scores of European American, African American, Mexican American, and other Hispanic American adolescents (Roberts & Sobhan, 1992).

Several ideas have been offered to explain this gender difference (Nolen-Hoeksema & Girgus, 1994; Murakumi, 2002). First, the estrogen cycle has been linked to changes in mood, with periods of low estrogen production linked to negative feelings and low self-esteem. Second, at puberty, girls become critical of their bodies and especially have concerns about being overweight and unattractive. This attitude may lead to prolonged feelings of dissatisfaction with the self and a consequent depression. When coupled with restricted dietary intake, girls may feel listless and drained of energy. Third, girls tend to look within for explanations of their failures and problems, blaming them on their own lack of ability; in contrast, boys tend to focus on factors outside the self, blaming other people or unfair conditions for their failures.

Fourth, even when girls receive strong social support from their parents and friends, they are also somewhat more sensitive to the problems that people in their support network are having. Girls who have higher levels of caring and are involved in the problems of their close friends are more vulnerable to depression (Gore, Aseltine, & Colten, 1993). Any negative experiences that a girl's best friend or members of her family are going through tend to add to her own negative mood. For example, one study found a significant link between mothers' emotional distress and their daughters' internalizing symptoms over the period from age 11 to 22. The same association was not found for adolescent boys and their mothers (Crawford et al., 2001).

Finally, adolescent girls may begin to experience numerous micro-aggressions spawned by the sexist views of teachers, male peers, and even their parents. These negative messages create a picture of a world in which the adolescent girl is viewed as less important, less competent, and less entitled to her own independent views than her male peers. The result is increased feelings of insecurity, lack of confidence, and new feelings of worthlessness.

Depressed mood is of special concern during early adolescence for several reasons. First, it is associated with adolescent suicide. (For further discussion of adolescent suicide, see the Applying Theory and Research to Life box.) Although depression is not always a precursor to suicide, there is a link between depression and suicidal thoughts. Second, depression is linked to alcohol and drug abuse. Adolescents who are struggling with strong feelings of depression may turn to alcohol or other drugs to try to alleviate or escape from these feelings. Third, adolescents who are depressed may be unable to participate effectively in the classroom, so their academic performance deteriorates. Finally, depression during adolescence may be a forerunner of severe depression later in adulthood.

Delinquency

Delinquency is an example of externalizing problems, related to difficulties in controlling or regulating one's impulses. *Delinquent offenses* are actions for which an adult could be prosecuted. Then there are offenses such as truancy, running away, or underage drinking that are known as *status offenses*, which are illegal for adolescents. Many adolescents commit some type of delinquent act that goes undetected. For most young people, the fear and guilt that follow a delinquent act are usually enough punishment to prevent further violations.

Delinquency, especially acts against property or other people, is an expression of externalizing behavior. At his sentencing hearing, Trevor apologizes to the court and to the victim's family for his assault on a five-year-old girl.

AP Photo/*The Idaho Press-Tribune*, Mike Vogt

APPLYING THEORY AND RESEARCH TO LIFE

Adolescent Suicide

I thought how easily you could kill yourself when you were drunk. Take a bath, fall asleep, drown. No turtle would come floating by to rescue you, no spotter plane would find you. I took my mother's knife and played johnny johnny johnny on the play-house floor. I was drunk, stabbed myself every few throws. I held my hand up and there was satisfaction at seeing my blood, the way there was when I saw the red gouges on my face that people stared at and turned away. (Fitch, 1999, pp. 184–185)

SUICIDE AT ANY age is deeply troubling, but adolescent suicide is cause for special anguish and soul searching. Why would a young person, with all of life ahead with its endless possibilities and opportunities, choose death? Is it possible that the prospect of becoming an adult is so threatening and terrifying that some young people would rather die than grow up?

Public concern over adolescent suicide has been increasing in response to the rise in the suicide rate among adolescents since the early 1960s. Suicide, which is the third leading cause of death among adolescents ages 15 to 24, rose from 5.2 per 100,000 in 1960 to 13.3 per 100,000 in 1995. By 2006, the rate had declined to 9.9 per 100,000. In that age group, there were approximately 4,000 suicides—one death by suicide every 2 hours and 15 minutes (U.S. Census Bureau, 2010). Some claim that these suicide rates are underestimated, as there is a social stigma to reporting a death as suicide, and there are financial consequences to identifying a death as a suicide rather than as an accident. It is suspected that a significant number of adolescent deaths involving automobile accidents were actually suicides. According to the Youth Risk Behavior Surveillance System reports (2010), 14% of high school students had seriously considered suicide in the preceding 12 months, and 6.3% attempted suicide in the preceding 12 months. Girls are twice as likely as boys to attempt suicide, but boys are 5 to 6 times as likely as girls to die in a suicide attempt (Irwin, Burg, & Cart, 2002). The rate of adolescent suicide differs by racial and ethnic groups. The risk of suicide

death is substantially higher among American Indian and Alaskan Natives, especially the boys, than among other racial/ethnic groups. Suicide attempts are highest among American Indian and Alaskan Native girls. Differences in rates of suicide and suicide attempts across racial and ethnic groups suggest different risk and protective factors tied to culture, acculturation strains, exposure to stresses of poverty and community disorganization, the stigma of discussing mental health problems, and the strength of ties to a supportive community (Goldston, Molock, Whitbeck, Murakami, Zayas, & Hall, 2008).

Instances of suicides prompted by widely publicized suicides, copycat suicides, and clusters of friends who commit suicide as part of a pact suggest that suicidal ideation can be triggered by a variety of external events as well as by internal depression or as a reaction to humiliation or loss. In attempting to understand the causes of suicide, primary risk factors have been identified (Garland & Zigler, 1993; King et al., 2001; Russell & Joyner, 2001). These factors were reconstructed by studying the lives of adolescents who committed or attempted suicide. However, they may not be very useful in predicting whether a particular individual will commit or attempt suicide. Although depression and low self-esteem are often included in the profile of those who attempt suicide, they are usually coupled with other issues. The risk factors include:

- Drug and alcohol abuse
- Mood disorders, especially depression
- A prior suicide attempt
- A history of psychiatric illness
- A history of antisocial, aggressive behavior
- A family history of suicidal behavior
- Low parental monitoring
- A high number of stressful life events
- A minority sexual orientation
- The availability of a firearm

In addition to these factors, there is usually some precipitating event. A shameful or humiliating experience, a notable failure, and rejection by a parent or a romantic partner are all examples. Use of drugs that alter cognitive functioning and decrease inhibitions,

coupled with easy access to a gun, suggest one likely path from suicidal ideation to suicidal action.

The national Substance Abuse and Mental Health Services Administration (SAMHSA, 2001) has issued a monograph, the *National Strategy for Suicide Prevention: Goals and Objectives for Action*. A key premise of this monograph is that suicide is a public health problem that is preventable. Two action components of prevention include broadening community support for mental health education and reducing the stigma associated with seeking mental health services. A study of the impact of the Signs of Suicide (SOS) program in 92 schools demonstrated the potential impact of effective intervention. Students who participated in the program showed an increase in help seeking of 60% in the month following the introduction of the curriculum. School coordinators found no negative reactions among students who were exposed to information about suicide and suicide prevention, and some improvement in student and teacher communication following this intervention (Aseltine, 2003). To learn more about suicide prevention, visit the website of the American Foundation for Suicide Prevention, or the Substance Abuse and Mental Health Services Administration of the U.S. Department of Health and Human Services.

Critical Thinking Questions

1. Why might the number of reported suicides be an underestimate?
2. How do you account for the fact that girls are more likely than boys to attempt suicide, but that boys are much more likely than girls to die as a result of their attempts?
3. Imagine that someone you knew well started talking to you about different ways people might kill themselves and then you read an essay he wrote for class about teen funerals. What would you do?
4. Why might people resist the implementation of an SOS program in their schools? What resources should schools and communities have available for teens and their families if they do implement such a program?

In an examination of a 10-year arrest trend, from 1996 to 2005, the number of males under the age of 18 who were arrested decreased by 28.7% and the number of females under the age of 18 who were arrested decreased by 14.3%. Overall, in the 10-year period, juvenile arrests for violent crime decreased by 25% (Federal Bureau of Investigation, 2005).

In a longitudinal study of more than 4,500 high school seniors and high school dropouts in California and Oregon, more than half the sample reported being involved in violent behavior—65% of the boys and 41% of the girls. A subset of these youth, the repeat offenders, were persistently involved in violent acts and were also significantly more likely to be involved in other high-risk delinquent behaviors such as selling drugs, committing felonies, and using alcohol, marijuana, or other drugs. These extremely violent youths were also more likely to drop out of school and to have other mental health problems. The findings of this study suggest that efforts to curb youth violence must pursue a differentiated approach—creating programs that are appropriate for the large number of youth who engage in an isolated act of violence, and other interventions focusing on the serious offenders who have multiple problems and are likely to be involved in both aggressive behavior and antisocial delinquency (Ellickson, Saner, & McGuigan, 1997).

Weapon carrying has increased dramatically over the past 20 years. As part of the National Longitudinal Study of Adolescent Health, students in grades 7 through 12 were asked about their involvement in weapon-related violence. Among seventh and eighth graders, 22% of European American teens, 30% of Hispanic American teens, and 39% of African American teens responded that they had some type of involvement (Blum et al., 2000). Because many young people carry some type of weapon with them—especially knives and guns—questions are raised about the emotional correlates of this type of behavior.

Are children who carry weapons primarily preoccupied with fear and motivated by self-defense, or are the weapons an extension of their aggressive motives? In one analysis, teens who carried guns were found to differ from those who carried knives (Webster, Gainer, & Champion, 1993). For girls, the more people they knew who had been victims of violence, the more likely they were to carry a knife. For boys, the two strong predictors of carrying a knife were having been threatened with a knife and having been frequently involved in fights, although not usually as the one who started them. Carrying a knife is linked to self-protective motives.

Too few girls carried guns for the researchers to identify predictors for that group. For the boys, however, the correlates of carrying a gun included having been arrested before, having been involved in many fights and being one of the people who started them, and believing that shooting people was justifiable in certain circumstances. Gun carrying was linked to a much more violent, aggressive orientation, and could not really be construed as a strategy for self-protection. Subsequent studies support the picture of boys who carry guns as being motivated by the desire to gain respect or to

In an effort to protect students and staff, many schools have installed metal detectors or security guards at the entrance to the school. What might be some positive and some negative consequences of this kind of monitoring?

Copyright © Cleve Bryant/Photo Edit

frighten others. These boys are likely to be bullies, whose friends also engage in high-risk activities.

Recall from the discussion in Chapter 8 that chronic exposure to violence has a disruptive impact on neurological development. Youth who are exposed to violence experience higher levels of symptoms associated with post-traumatic stress disorder, including difficulties regulating emotional reactions, difficulties concentrating, and difficulties inhibiting aggressive impulses. Exposure to violence also increases aggressive cognitions and the attribution of aggressive motives to others while, at the same time, lowering one's sensitivity to the pain and suffering of others. Some authors suggest that many boys who commit violent crimes are suffering from a form of post-traumatic stress disorder that leaves them angry, disconnected from their feelings, and unable to anticipate or control overwhelming images of violence that surge up with minimal provocation (Cunningham, Henggeler, Limber, Melton, & Nation, 2000; Slovak & Singer, 2001; Allwood, 2007).

Membership in the Peer Group

Objective 5. To describe the further evolution of peer relations in early adolescence, especially the formation of cliques and crowds, and to contrast the impact of parents and peers during this stage.

The importance of peer interaction for psychosocial development is a continuous theme across the life span. During early adolescence, the peer group becomes more structured and organized than it was previously (Newman, 1982). The implications of the individual's relation to the peer group become more clearly defined. Before the adolescent period, it is important to have friends but not so important to be a member of a definable group. The child's friends are often found in the neighborhood, local clubs and sports teams, community centers, or classrooms. In early adolescence, young people spend more time away from home. In middle school and high school, students are more likely to interact with each other across classroom boundaries, leading to the formation of larger, more loosely affiliated friendship groups. Dyadic friendships become an increasingly important source of social support, and the quality of these friendships changes. In addition to dyadic friendships, adolescents form small groups of friends, sometimes referred to as *cliques*, and in most communities they also become identified with a larger constellation of teens who have a common social identity, usually referred to as a *crowd* (Brown, 2004).

Cliques and Crowds

Cliques are small friendship groups of 5 to 10 friends (Ennett & Bauman, 1996). Usually, these groups provide the framework for frequent interactions both within the school and in the neighborhood. Adolescents usually do not refer to their group of friends as a clique, but the term is used to

connote a certain closeness among the members. They hang out together, know about each other's families, plan activities together, and stay in touch with each other from day to day. Within cliques, intimate information is exchanged and, therefore, a high degree of loyalty is expected. In the transition from middle school or junior high school to the larger, more heterogeneous environment of the high school, there is a reordering of students according to a variety of abilities and a corresponding reordering of friendship groups. It may take some time for adolescents to find their clique, the members of which may change from time to time over the first year or two of high school. There is quite a lot of variability in the stability of the cliques; some dissolve over the course of a school year, and others remain intact throughout high school.

Crowd refers to a large group that is usually recognized by a few predominant characteristics, such as their orientation toward academics, involvement in athletics, use of drugs, or involvement in deviant behavior. Crowds are more reputational than cliques, reflecting students' values and attitudes, preferred activities, and school and nonschool engagement. Students can typically name the crowds at their school, but when asked, not all students clearly fit with a specific crowd, and some students are in more than one.

Membership in a crowd at the high school may be based on one or more of the following characteristics: good looks; athletic ability; social class; academic performance; future goals; affiliation with a religious, racial, or ethnic group; special talents; involvement with drugs or deviant behavior; or general alienation from school. Although the criteria for group membership may not be publicly articulated, the groups tend to include or exclude members according to consistent standards. In a racially diverse sample of more than 600 middle school and high school students, some of the most common crowds mentioned were floaters (belonging to more than one group), nice or regulars, populars, middles (related to income), jocks, nerds/unpopulars, preps, skateboarders, and misfits/alternatives. Roughly 20% of the students said they did not belong to any group (Lohman, 2000).

In racially and ethnically diverse schools, it is not uncommon for students to identify crowds based specifically on ethnic categories, such as the Asian American group, the Mexican Americans, and the African Americans. Given the language diversity of some communities, adolescents may be drawn to peers who have a common home language. Banding together with other students who speak one's native language can provide a buffer from the direct or inadvertent stigma of limited English proficiency in a predominantly English-speaking school (Hill & Torres, 2010).

Crowds can be identified in a school setting by their dress, their language, the activities in which they participate, and the school settings in which they are most likely to congregate. For example, in one school, the peer groups take their names from the place in the school where they hang out: "the fashionable 'wall people' who favor a bench along the wall outside the cafeteria, and the punkish 'trophy-case' kids who sit on the floor under a display of memorabilia" (Adler, 1999, p. 57). The peer culture in any high school is determined largely by the nature of the peer groups that exist and their characteristic patterns of interaction (Youniss, McLellan, & Strouse, 1994). These large, visible groups provide an array of prototypical identities. Although many adolescents resist being labeled as part of one crowd or another, they usually recognize that these categories of students exist in their school.

In one analysis of more than 3,000 students in grades 9 to 12 in nine different high schools, nine crowd types were identified with a high degree of regularity across the schools. The crowds were labeled by the students as jocks, populars, popular nice, average-normal, brains, partyers, druggies, loners, and nerds (Durbin, Darling, Steinberg, & Brown, 1993). These crowds had distinct profiles with respect to their school grades, use of alcohol and drugs, involvement in delinquent acts, involvement in fights and carrying weapons to school, and perceptions of how involved they were in the social life at the school. Thus, the youth culture, as it is sometimes called, actually comprises a number of subcultures, each endorsing somewhat different attitudes toward adults and other authority figures, school and academic goals, and drugs and deviant behavior, and expressing different orientations toward partying and social life (Brown, Mounts, Lamborn, & Steinberg, 1993).

The relationship of crowd affiliation to behavior and especially behavior problems has been established in research in the United States and Australia (Prinstein & LaGreca, 2002). In an effort to expand this picture to adolescents in Europe, researchers carried out a study of crowd affiliation in the Netherlands (Delsing, ter Bogt, Engles, & Meeus, 2007). The sample included over 2,000 adolescents ages 12 to 19 from 12 schools who self-identified as Dutch, Antillean, Moroccan, and Turkish. Adolescents were asked to rate how much they identified as a member of one of 10 crowds: punks, metal heads, Gothics, rural youth, Christian youth, normals, hip-hoppers, Rastas, elites, and brains. They also completed measures of aggression, delinquency, anxiety, and depression. The crowds could be differentiated on the basis of four dimensions—namely, their orientation toward: conventional or adult values, achievement and financial independence, urban youth culture, and rebelliousness, nonconformity, and enthusiasm for rock music. Crowds whose members had a stronger conventional or achievement orientation also had lower levels of aggression and delinquency. Crowds whose members had stronger urban or alternative orientations also had higher levels of depression, delinquency, and aggression.

Group Boundaries and Norms

Membership in cliques is relatively stable but always vulnerable to change. One description suggests that these groups have some central members who serve as leaders, others who are regularly included in clique activities, and still others who are on the periphery. At the same time, there are the wannabes, who would like to be part of the clique but

Groups of high school students are easily identifiable by their style of dress and the place in the school where they hang out.

for one reason or another are never fully included (Hansell, 1985). Some students try to push their way into a certain group; others may fall out of a group. Dating someone who is a member of a clique or getting involved in a school activity (such as athletics or cheerleading) may be a way of moving into a new peer group. A more likely scenario is that through gossip, refusal to adhere to **group norms**, or failure in heterosexual relationships, individuals may slip outside the boundaries of their clique. Even when the specific members of a clique change, new members tend to have some common characteristics. Cliques of druggies find new friends who do drugs; cliques of jocks find new friends who excel in sports.

Changing one's crowd identity may be more difficult than changing from one clique to another. When the school population is relatively stable, it is more difficult to lose the **reputational identity** one has already established. In some schools, specific crowds have strong animosity toward each other. Members of the opposing crowds may occupy different areas of the school, participate in different activities, mock or ridicule each other, or articulate their differences in symbolic ways through dress, art, and music. When these differences are widely known, it becomes even more difficult to shift crowd identities. More research is needed about the contexts that permit changes in crowd membership and the motives that students might have for wanting a new crowd affiliation (Brown, 2004).

Important skills that are learned by becoming a member of a peer group are the assessment of group structure and the selection of the particular group or groups with which one would like to affiliate. As one begins to develop a focused peer group affiliation, one becomes aware of that group's internal structure and norms. In adolescence, the structure may include patterns of dominance, dating, and relationships with others outside the group. Associated with each of these dimensions of social structure are sets of norms or expectations for the behavior of the peer group members. As adolescents discover their positions in the dominance hierarchy of the group, they learn how they may advance within it and what behaviors are expected at various levels. On the basis of all this information, they must decide whether their personal growth is compatible with the peer group affiliation they have made.

Membership in an adolescent peer group is a forerunner of membership in an adult social group. Adolescent peer groups are somewhat less organized than their adult counterparts, but they are considerably more structured than childhood friendship groups. Through **peer group membership**, adolescents begin to learn techniques for assessing the organization of social groups and their own position within them. They develop aspirations for advancing their own social standing. Also, adolescents gain some insight into the rewards and costs of extensive group identification. Although the actual friends made during adolescence may change as one grows older, the social skills learned at this time provide a long-lasting basis for functioning in a mature social group.

Parents and Peers

How does involvement with peers during early adolescence relate to one's closeness to family members? Do adolescents abandon family interactions and values for peer interactions and values? Can closeness to peers compensate for a lack of closeness to parents, or does the intimacy achieved with parents extend outward to a circle of friends? To what extent do parents continue to have an influence on adolescent peer relationships?

In the transition from childhood to adolescence, the child's radius of significant relationships changes. One study looked at the structure and function of social support among African American, European American, and Hispanic American children in three age groups: 7-, 10-, and 14-year-olds (Levitt, Weber, & Guacci, 1993). In the transition from age 7 to 10, extended family members became increasingly important to children as a source of support. This pattern was found in all three ethnic groups, but the African American and Hispanic American children were more likely to identify extended family members as sources of support than were the European American children. From age 10 to 14, friends become an increasingly important source of support. The number of people mentioned as friends increased notably from age 7 to 14. However, at all three ages and in all three ethnic groups, family members were mentioned as the most central in these children's lives—"the people who are the most close and important to you—people you love the most and who love you the most" (Levitt et al., 1993). Moreover, at each age, support from this close, inner circle made up largely of family members was an important correlate of well-being and sociability.

Under optimal conditions, the increasingly important role of peer relationships in early adolescence takes place against a background of continuing close, supportive relationships with family members. Adolescents describe a variety of overt signs of independence from their families: They may make decisions about clothes, dating, and so on; they may drive cars; they may stay out late; and they may earn their own money. However, they continue to maintain an emotional attachment to their families and to family values.

What is the nature of parent-adolescent interaction? How do differences in its quality influence the adolescent's well-being? Using the attachment paradigm as a frame of reference, one can think of adolescence as a time when young people strive to expand their range of exploration with reduced needs to return to the secure base. Adolescents try to decrease their dependence on their parents for setting goals, establishing patterns of tastes and preferences, and making decisions. This does not mean that the sense of closeness and connection with parents is less important. For example, adolescents may not want to seek help from parents when they are experiencing difficulty in their social relationships, but at the same time, if a serious problem arises, they want to know that their parent is available to be supportive and understanding. Adolescents who continue to experience parental warmth also report lower levels of emotional distress than those who report more distant relationships with parents and turn more to peers for support (Operario, Tschann, Flores, & Bridges, 2006). Adolescents can take the point of view of their parents. They realize when their behavior has been a source of distress to their parent, of if they have tested the limits of previously agreed-upon rules or boundaries. Within the context of a secure attachment, these times lead to a goal-corrected revision in the balance of autonomy and closeness. In many ways, the parent's desire to foster a child's self-reliance and a child's goal to reduce the parent's authority over day-to-day behaviors are compatible. In the process of achieving these goals, some loss of emotional closeness is likely (Allen & Land, 1999; Collins & Laursen, 2006).

As adolescents go through puberty, conflicts with parents are likely. One way of understanding this conflict is to view it as a way for adolescents to achieve new levels of individuation and autonomy while still preserving bonds of closeness and connection (Collins & Laursen, 2006). A meta-analysis of patterns of conflict in White, middle-class families found that frequency of conflict and intensity of conflict were two distinct dimensions. The meta-analysis found that the frequency of parent-adolescent conflict decreased from early adolescence (ages 10 to 12) to middle adolescence (12 to 16), but that the intensity of those conflicts increased (Laursen, Coy, & Collins, 1998). Typically parent-adolescent conflicts are about daily issues, like household chores, cleaning up their room, how money will be spent, whether the child is spending enough time on schoolwork, or curfews, rather than about basic value issues like political ideology or religious beliefs. This same pattern has been observed in African American and White middle-class families (Smetana, Daddis, & Chuang, 2003).

With age, adolescents and their parents expand the range of issues that are considered personal issues that should be decided by teens and not subject to parental authority, like how they spend their free time, how they dress, or the kind of television shows they watch. Nonetheless, certain areas of morality or safety, like using drugs or smoking cigarettes, still fall under parental authority. Some issues, such as hanging around with people your parents disapprove of, may be topics that require negotiation. They are not clearly in the parental authority or the personal preference domain. Even though the trend is for the domain of personal preference to increase with age, families differ both within cultures and across cultures in how likely they are to view decisions as legitimately governed by parental authority, personal adolescent preferences, or shared control (Cumsille, Darling, Flaherty, & Martinez, 2009). These differences in perceptions about who has legitimate authority around issues of concern to adolescents is relevant for the extent to which parents and children experience conflict, the extent to which adolescents try to deceive their parents, and the opportunities that parents have to influence their children's decision making. Consider the following narrative written by a Chinese adolescent whose family had recently immigrated to Canada (Li, 2009).

> My parents said we brought you to Canada because student life in China is too hard. But now I don't think my life has changed except for the place. I am still being pushed very hard. . . . They always press me like, "you should study, you should study, you should study. . . like this." If I just watched TV for 10 minutes, by the 11th minute, they would say "go study, don't watch it" or they would say "if you are tired, you can rest for 5 minutes, then go back to your study." They say this to me almost every day. (Li, 2010, p. 488)

In European American families, as children get older, they are less likely to concede to their parents, and parents are increasingly likely to concede to their children. In African American families, most conflicts end with the child conceding to the parents, preserving the cultural value of obedience and respect for elders (Smetana, Daddis, & Chuang, 2003). In a study of Chinese American adolescents, expectations for personal autonomy seemed to be expressed at a somewhat later age. Urban Chinese American youth were more accepting of open disagreements with their parents than rural youth, and described their relationships with parents as less cohesive and more conflictual than rural youth (Wenxin, Meiping, & Fuligni, 2006). Mild, periodic conflicts reflect a changing balance of power or control within the family, as adolescents give voice to their own opinions and defend their choices. The acceptability of these conflicts, their intensity and frequency, and the ways they are resolved appear to be shaped by the cultural context and values regarding individuation and interdependence.

One area that has been studied recently is parent-adolescent conflict about peer relationships. Parents use a variety of techniques to manage, monitor, and possibly control their adolescent children's peer interactions (Mounts, 2004). Whereas adolescents may seek parental advice from time to time about peer issues, they also view peer friendships, clique membership, and time spent with peers to fall into the category of personal choice. As they get older, adolescents are likely to defend their right to choose their friends and to spend time with friends as they see fit. In a study of an ethnically diverse sample of seventh and eighth graders, high levels of parent-adolescent conflict over peer relationships was associated with greater amounts of delinquent behavior, more drug use, and lower grades (Mounts, 2007). Because this was a correlational study, we do not know whether the parent-adolescent conflict is a result of the parents' assessment that the child's friends are antisocial and engaging in high-risk behaviors, or if the parent-child conflict about peers leads the child to seek out friends who are similarly distressed at home and resort to antisocial, high-risk behaviors.

The quality of the home environment, especially the nature of parenting practices, has implications for the adolescent's peer relationships as well as for the quality of parent-child interactions. Recall from the discussion in Chapter 8 that high levels of power assertion by parents are associated with a greater likelihood of peer rejection during middle childhood. Studies of the relationship of parenting practices to adolescent peer group membership are extending this analysis. A model was proposed to examine the relationship of parenting practices to adolescent behaviors and ultimately to crowd affiliation (Brown et al., 1993; Durbin et al., 1993). Parenting practices were operationally defined as the extent to which parents emphasized academic achievement, parental monitoring of adolescent behaviors, and the degree to which parents involved adolescents in decision making. Three adolescent behaviors were measured: the students' grade point averages, drug use, and self-reliance. Finally, the students were identified as members of one of six crowds: popular, jocks, brains, normals, druggies, or outcasts.

Results of the research found that parenting practices had both direct and indirect impacts on adolescents' crowd memberships. Parenting practices were linked to the children's behavior, which in turn was a strong predictor of their crowd affiliation. Parents who emphasized academic achievement were likely to have adolescents who had high grades and who were self-reliant, factors that also predicted being popular and not being members of the druggie or outcast groups. Low parental monitoring and little joint decision making were associated with drug use, low self-reliance, and membership in the druggie crowd. Even though adolescents may perceive their involvement with their peers as a domain that is separate and distinct from their family life, this research suggests that parental socialization practices influence peer relations.

The Psychosocial Crisis: Group Identity versus Alienation

Objective 6. To describe the psychosocial crisis of group identity versus alienation, the central process through which the crisis is resolved, peer pressure, the prime adaptive ego quality of fidelity to others, and the core pathology of isolation.

Throughout life, tensions arise between the desires for individuality and for connection. Certain cultures emphasize connection over individuality, whereas others put individuality ahead of connection. However, all societies must deal with both aspects of the ego: the *I* as agent, originator, and executive of one's individual thoughts and actions, and the *we* as agent, originator, and executive of collective, cooperative enterprises that preserve and further the survival of the group (Triandis, 1990). During the early years of adolescence, one confronts a new psychosocial conflict, in which pressures to ally oneself with specific groups and to learn to be comfortable functioning as a member of a group are major preoccupations. This conflict is called *group identity versus alienation* (Newman & Newman, 2001).

Group Identity

In early adolescence, young people form a *scheme*—an orchestrated, integrated set of ideas about the norms, expectations, and status hierarchy of the salient groups in their social world, building these representations from groups of which they are members or in which they aspire to hold membership (**reference groups**; Gurin & Markus, 1988). Associated with these schemes are strong emotional investments, cognitions, and possibly behavioral patterns. As a young person prepares to engage in the larger social world, a positive sense of group identity provides confidence that she is meaningfully connected to society, has a cognitive map of the characteristics of the social landscape, and the skills or tools to navigate the terrain. Perceiving oneself as a competent member of a group or groups is fundamental to one's self-concept as well as to one's willingness to participate in and contribute to society. The formation of social commitments in early adolescence provides a foundation for the capacity to establish meaningful ties to groups at the personal, community, national, and international levels in adult life (Lawler, Thye, & Yoon, 2009).

Early adolescents experience a search for membership—an internal questioning about the groups of which they are most naturally a part. They ask themselves, "Who am I, and with whom do I belong?" Although membership in a peer group may be the most pressing concern, questions about other group identifications also arise. Adolescents evaluate the nature of their ties to immediate and extended family members, and they begin to understand the unique characteristics of their racial, ethnic, cultural, and sexual identities. They may become identified with various organizations (e.g., religious, political, civic). Research confirms that in the most positive pattern, peer group membership does not replace attachment to parents or closeness with family. Rather, the adolescent's network of supportive relations is anchored in the family and expands into the domain of meaningful peer relationships. Adolescents who show strong signs of mental health and adaptive coping strategies have positive communication and trusting relationships with parents or other close family members as well as strong feelings of trust and security among their friends (Raja, McGee, & Stanton, 1992; Levitt et al., 1993).

In the process of seeking group affiliation, adolescents are confronted by the fit—or lack of fit—between their personal needs and the norms and values of relevant social groups in the environment. The process of self-evaluation takes place within the context of the meaningful groups whose members are available for comparison and identification. Individual needs for social approval, affiliation, leadership, power, and status are expressed in the kinds of group identifications that are made and rejected during the period from age 12 to 18. In a positive resolution of the conflict of group identity versus alienation, adolescents discover one or more groups that provide them with a sense of group belonging, meet their social needs, and allow them to express their social selves. They become psychologically connected to social life.

Cognitive Processes That Support the Formation of Group Identity

Adolescence is not the first time that children are aware of being a group member or claiming an affiliation with a group. Young children may be on sports teams, play in an orchestra or band, or belong to a dance group. They tend to define groups on the basis of common activities. In comparison, adolescents begin to have a mental representation of the social groups in their school or community and the relationships among these groups. They are able to analyze the norms and expectations associated with various groups. They can assess the status or prestige of being a member of a particular group, and the ways that group membership affects attitudes and values, shapes interests, and influences one's self-concept through acceptance and rejection (Bettencourt & Hume, 1999). For example, in a high school, teens can identify various crowds such as the populars, the druggies, the athletes, and the outcasts. They can describe distinctions among these groups with regard to their dress, where they hang out at the school, and behaviors or values that are associated with these crowds. Further, adolescents can characterize what it would take to be a member of one of these crowds, the possibility of being in more than one of these crowds, the possibility for interactions among members of these crowds, and the advantages or disadvantages linked to being associated with each of these crowds.

There are three cognitive capacities necessary for an adolescent to establish a group identity: group representations, which refers to the conceptualization and labeling or classification of groups; group operations, which refers to the processes through which groups are formed, maintained, or dissolved; and reflective thinking about groups, which includes an ability to analyze the array of groups and their relationship to one another.

Group Representations. Group representations provide the earliest forms of group identity, reflecting the ability to use words and symbols to signify membership in a group. Infants and young children have a wide variety of group experiences and are able to represent their group membership using verbal labels and drawings. The capacity for representing groups and the relationships among groups expands in early adolescence, so that youth are able to map more groups simultaneously, including those in their immediate family, school, and peer environments. The expansion of this representational ability may be stimulated by exposure to a greater variety of groups, by increases in representational skills, and by new social demands to establish one's place within the range of existing groups. It may also be a product of neurological changes that accompany puberty.

Group Operations. Group operations include such diverse processes as joining a group, forming in-group and out-group attitudes, stereotyping, quitting or rejecting a group, and exercising leadership in a group. Some of these operations can be observed among toddlers and early-school-age children. They recognize the common members of a group, use fantasy play to coordinate roles with other members of a group, and talk about themselves as part of a family, school, or friendship relationship. Group operations can be observed in neighborhoods, with some children experiencing exclusion and others experiencing acceptance and support. Children as young as 5 or 6 may join sports teams and learn lessons of team spirit, teamwork, and team pride. Research has shown that by the fourth and fifth grades, some children have already begun to experience social isolation and social rejection (Hymel, Bowker, & Woody, 1993; Farmer & Rodkin, 1996).

In early adolescence, teens develop more advanced skills for connecting to their groups, experiencing bonding and acceptance, participating in leadership and team building, and detecting evidence about the possibility of rejection by their significant groups. These skills are refined and extended as teens confront a wider array of groups with varying degrees of associational closeness.

Reflective Thinking About Groups. The level of conceptualization necessary for the formation of group identity involves reflective and comparative thinking. It requires decentering from one's own groups to consider how these groups may be perceived by others, evaluating the strengths and weaknesses of a group, and considering the implications of group membership for how one is treated in the community. Early adolescence is characterized by a new consciousness about one's membership in groups, the boundaries and barriers that separate groups or limit membership in groups, and the social implications of being in one group or another. The emergence of formal operational reasoning may help produce new capacities for reflection and speculation about social relationships and complex social systems.

Four Types of Experiences That Build a Group Identity

Given the three cognitive capacities that permit the conceptualization of a group identity, we hypothesize that the actual formation of a group identity requires four types of experiences: (1) categorizing people into groups and recognizing the distinguishing features that define members, (2) experiencing a sense of history as a member of a group, (3) having an emotional investment in the group, and (4) detecting the social evaluation of one's group and its relation to other groups.

Categorizing People and Recognizing Distinguishing Features of Group Members. Beginning in toddlerhood, young children use social categories related to gender and age to group people (Leinbach & Fagot, 1986; Martin et al., 1990; Lobel & Menashri, 1993; Hirschfeld, 1994). Toddlers have a sense of the family group and understand that some people are in the family, whereas others are not (Newman, Roberts, & Syre, 1993). With a broadening of exposure to social settings, children learn to recognize a wider variety of groups. By middle childhood, they can appreciate their simultaneous membership in a variety of groups such as family, sports team, and friendship groups (O'Brien & Bierman, 1988).

Groups typically have *boundaries* that limit membership and *shared markers* that bind the members together. In early adolescence, young people learn to read, categorize, and relate to informal peer networks where clique structures provide a comparatively egalitarian learning environment, determine social status, and help define a person's feelings of belonging and worth. Language use, nonverbal gestures, style of dress, use of certain spaces, behaviors such as cigarette smoking or drug use, and participation in specific activities may become markers that delineate group membership and provide a sense of group identification. Friends may invent expressions or unique ways of speaking that help define a group and strengthen members' commitment. Over time, the similarities among members of a peer group are strengthened, thereby clarifying their commitment to certain values and behaviors. Although much of the literature that explores this process has focused on deviant or risky behaviors, such as cigarette smoking, alcohol use, or truancy, the process can support prosocial commitments as well (Dielman, 1994; Berndt & Keefe, 1995).

Experiencing a Sense of History as a Group Member. In a gym class, one may be assigned to the red team one day and to the gray team another. These assignments do not foster a meaningful sense of group identity. However, if one joins the band and practices every day, goes to games, travels on the bus, and parties with the band members, the sense of being a bandie begins to take shape. Group identity emerges out of continuous interactions, through which one becomes visible and known to other group members while they become visible and known to you (Reicher, Levine, & Gordijn, 1998). What was done in fun last year may become next year's tradition as a group selects rituals to symbolize how important they all are to each other.

Of course, memberships in groups change. One may transfer to a new school, join a new team or club, or become part of a group that gets together only in the summers. In

Charlene is showing the friends in her clique a photo that she took of them at a party the night before. Their sense of a shared history increases their emotional investment in the group.

each case, the formation of a sense of group identity requires the accumulation of interactions and the sense of having a history of shared experiences (Worchel, 1998). Here one sees the interconnection of the *I* and the *we*. One may think of the *I* as the agent that seeks out group membership, choosing to join one group or avoid another. At the same time, as one participates in a group and experiences a sense of shared history, one begins to internalize values, beliefs, and practices held in common by the group, thus leading to a revision of the *I* and strengthening of the *we*.

Emotional Investment in the Group. The intensification of emotions that occurs with puberty and early adolescence is often evidenced in a deepening dedication and commitment to one's groups, including family and kinship groups (Bettencourt & Hume, 1999). One sees here the seeds of nationalism and patriotism—a redirection of narcissism to the group and a binding of energy to the group as an extension of oneself (Markovsky & Chaffee, 1995; Coats, Smith, Claypool, & Banner, 2000). As evidence of this emotional investment, one finds the expression of pride about one's group, a tendency to idealize the members of the group in comparison to others outside the group, and a willingness to make personal sacrifices in order to support or advance the group's goals (Reicher et al., 1998). The emotional investment can be expressed as positive feelings of attraction to other members of the group and negative feelings of depression or jealousy associated with betrayal. New levels of intimacy are possible, as are new levels of hurt.

Social Evaluation of One's Group and Its Relation to Other Groups. Adolescents become aware of the status hierarchy of the groups in their school and neighborhood. They recognize how their groups are viewed by others, and they form their own views of each group's value and importance to them (Dunbar, 1997). Adolescents spend a good deal of time analyzing and evaluating the groups in their lives. Studies of racial and ethnic identity clearly show that

adolescents are able to differentiate between being viewed negatively by others or being a target of discrimination, and expressing personal pride in their racial group (Williams & Thornton, 1998; Valk, 2000). The important point is that the group identity established during early adolescence occurs in the context of a social reality in which one's own group can be located in a status hierarchy leading to judgments about the merits of the group and about oneself as a member of the group (Luhtanen & Crocker, 1992).

Ethnic Group Identity

One of the most challenging aspects of establishing group identity facing many adolescents is the formation of an **ethnic group identity** (Spencer & Markstrom-Adams, 1990). Ethnic identity is not merely knowing that one is a member of a certain ethnic group, but recognizing that some aspects of one's thoughts, feelings, and actions are influenced by one's ethnic identity. One's ethnic group becomes a significant reference group, whose values, outlook, and goals are taken into account as one makes important life choices. Ethnic identity varies across ethnic groups and among individuals within groups. For example, some young people have had more exposure to the cultural norms and values of their ethnic group than others. Some have had more guided parental socialization about the existence of prejudice and ways of coping with discrimination. Thus, ethnic identity is more aptly viewed as a psychosocial rather than a demographic variable. It is based upon socially constructed meaning rather than biological or genetic differences (Phinney, 1996b; Smedley & Smedley, 2005; Quintana et al., 2006).

In the United States, a history of negative imagery, violence, discrimination, and invisibility has been linked to African Americans, Native Americans, Asian Americans, and Hispanic Americans. Young people in each of these groups encounter conflicting values as they consider the larger society and their own ethnic identity. They must struggle with the negative or ambivalent feelings that are linked with their own ethnic group because of the cultural stereotypes that have been conveyed to them through the media and the schools and because of the absence of role models from their own group who are in positions of leadership and authority.

Issues of ethnic group identity may not become salient until early adolescence. As children of color grow up, they are surrounded by members of their own ethnic group and socialized to internalize the values and beliefs of that group. At the same time, through participation in school, exposure to the media, and exploration of their community, they incorporate many of the ideals and values of European American culture. Several longitudinal studies demonstrate that there is a significant trajectory of development of racial/ethnic identity across adolescence (Altschul, Oyserman, & Bybee, 2006; Pahl & Way, 2006). As we have discussed, in adolescence peer groups become more structured. Sanctions against cross-race/cross-ethnic friendships and dating relationships may become more intense.

In the transition to high school, adolescents may encounter more evidence of discrimination through overt rejection, academic hassles, being ignored, being harshly punished, or experiencing fewer opportunities to be recognized for school leadership roles (French, Seidman, Allen, & Aber, 2000; Seaton, Yip, & Sellers, 2009). The nature and extent of racial or ethnic hostilities are related in part to the composition of the high school. Students who are in a racial or ethnic minority within their school are more likely to experience intergroup hostilities than those who are in a more diverse, well-balanced school (Graham, 2004). Students may find that their family and ethnic group values conflict with the values of the majority culture. Acculturation strain may stimulate new levels of exploration and ethnic commitment, or new sentiments of alienation. During the high school years, most youth are in the process of exploring what their ethnic group membership means to them, not yet having made a clear commitment to embracing or crystallizing an ethnic identity (Yip, Seaton, & Sellers, 2006). In a longitudinal study of Latinos' ethnic identity over a 4-year period, girls showed a steady growth in exploration of their ethnic identity, increased clarity about what their ethnic identity meant to them, and increasingly positive feelings about their Latina identity. For boys, there was little evidence of exploration or increased clarity, but there was growth in the positive feelings about being Latino. For both boys and girls, affirmation of their Latino ethnicity was positively associated with self-esteem (Umaña-Taylor, Gonzales-Backen, & Guimond, 2009).

In the wake of the terrorist attack on the World Trade Center in New York on September 11, 2001, Muslim adolescents became a focus of some attention. The nature of their ethnic identity and their divided allegiances were highlighted. Students at a Muslim high school in Brooklyn, New York, were interviewed about their feelings and their conflicts:

> "We have a burden on us," said Andira Abudayeh, who is 16 and attends Al Noor. "We're Muslims, and we feel like other Muslims around the world do. And we're Americans." . . .

For these Chinese teens, their ethnic identity is integrated into their personal identity as they form friendships and make commitments to their families and community.

The students also said the Koran, which Muslims consider the literal word of God, provides a perfect blueprint for their lives. Their ideal society would follow Islamic law and make no separation between religion and state. In the meantime, they said, they want to become doctors and lawyers and teachers in the United States. (Sachs, 2001, p. B1)

In a study of Muslim adolescents ages 12 to 18, 84% said they experienced one or more acts of discrimination in the previous year, and 10% reported daily discrimination (Sirin & Fine, 2008). Many of these experiences take place in school. Layered on to these overt acts are experiences of being watched, talked about, or treated with suspicion. Thus, while they claim to feel totally American, these Muslim youth feel misunderstood and judged, experiencing a sense of being outsiders which, in its own way, strengthens their ethnic identity. In the face of difficulties in trying to explain their Muslim faith to their non-Muslim peers, strong bonds of peer support form with other Muslim teens who have made similar commitments regarding everyday behaviors:

> "You are not going to hang out with somebody who drinks if you don't drink. Someone who parties if you don't party. You need to find people to get that base and who can give you support when you are away from home. And most likely, by choice the ones you can identify yourself with most, that's Islam for us." (Sirin & Fine, 2008, p. 109)

In the transition from early to late adolescence, most minority youth experience some critical evaluation of the values and beliefs of the dominant culture and how they conflict with the values and beliefs of their own ethnic group. The more fully immersed young children are in the values and traditions of their ethnic heritage, the more likely it is that they will experience a *dual* or *multiple identity*—for example, seeing themselves as both American and African American or American and Chinese American (Phinney, 1997). Over time, and with the benefit of exposure to reading, conversations, and interactions with people from other subgroups, young people begin to synthesize a sense of how their ethnic identity fits into their overall personal identity and how it will influence the quality of their relationships with members of their own and other ethnic groups (Cross, 1991; Phinney, 1989, 1996; Yip, Seaton, & Sellers, 2006).

Most research on ethnic identity has focused on African American, Latino American, and Asian American youth. Relatively little attention has been given to the ethnic identity of the racially/ethnically privileged European American youth. Considerable evidence suggests that there are substantial benefits to being a member of a racially/ethnically privileged group for social status, access to resources, and social expectations. Not much is known about how these benefits and their link to being a member of a privileged racial/ethnic group are conceptualized by European American youth, and how the experiences of adolescence shape a racial or ethnic group identification that might persist into the future (Spencer, 2006).

© 2010 Huntstock/Jupiterimages Corporation

Alienation

Alienation refers to a sense of social estrangement, an absence of social support or meaningful social connection (Mau, 1992). Alienation can be viewed as deriving from dilemmas associated with issues of **common identity**, **common bond**, or both. Alienation associated with issues of common identity may occur when young people are forced to take on roles or are expected to comply with group expectations to which they do not subscribe. This might occur as a result of stereotyping, racism, or elitism within a school or community. Under these conditions, adolescents perceive that their opinions, beliefs, and values differ substantially from those of the groups they are viewed as belonging to. In many schools, some subsets of students are marginalized due to some marker such as minority status, physical abnormalities, or developmental delays, or as a result of poor social skills and low academic motivation. These students are often typed as nobodies, loners, disengaged, or outcasts. In a longitudinal study of crowd identity, Strouse (1999) found that not all students in the uninvolved crowd remained so over the 4 years of high school. Many changed to the average crowd orientation, usually by finding new friends, engaging in social activities, and placing more emphasis on getting good grades.

Alienation associated with issues of common bond occurs when adolescents are unable to form interpersonal ties that provide feelings of acceptance and emotional support. This type of alienation may arise from several different sources. Under conditions of parental coldness, distancing, neglect, or rejection, children find that they cannot count on the family to serve as a source of emotional or instrumental support (Dishion, Poulin, & Medici-Skaggs, 2000). They lack a template for experiencing the foundational benefits of belonging that are associated with group identity. As a result of harsh parenting, some adolescents have poor social skills—they are either overly aggressive and domineering, or overly withdrawn and socially inept (Poulin, Dishion, & Haas, 1999). Over time, children with poor social skills are less likely to form satisfying social relationships with friends and are more likely to engage in delinquent behaviors that reflect their sense of alienation from family and peers.

In some families, children are exposed to a pattern of hostile, aggressive parenting in which the custodial parent insists in the most assertive and unkind way that their other parent is someone to be mistrusted; an enemy to be avoided and disrespected. These efforts to alienate a child from a parent are frightening, confusing, and a source of emotional distress. The child, exposed to this kind of emotional abuse, may experience a variety of symptoms such as anxiety, withdrawal, self-inflicted injuries, or uncontrolled aggression, any of which may make the establishment of effective peer relationships difficult. As the child gets older, he may question or challenge the hostile, aggressive parent, asserting his independent view about the absent parent, and defying the custodial parent. The child may reach adolescence, alienated from both the noncustodial parent and the custodial parent, and lacking the social skills needed to form satisfying peer friendships (hostile-aggressive-parenting.com, 2010).

Alienation may result from personality characteristics, such as shyness, introversion, or lack of sociability. Some young people experience social anxiety, mistrust in others, or cautiousness in interactions that prevent them from forming interpersonal connections. Others are overly self-conscious, becoming so preoccupied with their own feelings and thoughts that they withdraw from social interactions (Kochanska, Murray, & Coy, 1997). Feelings of shame over an illness, disability, or perceived inadequacy may lead to perceptions of peer rejection or an unwillingness to form social bonds (Fife & Wright, 2000).

Finally, alienation may result from a combination of problems with common identity and common bond. For example, friendships across racial groups may be very difficult to preserve in a neighborhood but are supported in the school environment. If an African American and a European American adolescent become close friends at school, both may feel alienated from the same-race peers in their community. Youth who are recent immigrants may experience this conflict as they become acculturated. They may become increasingly distant from their families as they take on U.S. language and practices, but they may still be unable to form close, supportive relationships with U.S. adolescents who view them as outsiders. Nataša, an immigrant from Bosnia, described her experiences of alienation as a high school student:

> I was so different and so odd. I ended up in an all-girls Catholic school in the middle of Ohio where everyone is blond and everyone wants to get married and have babies. . . . And no one wanted to talk to me; *no one even wanted to talk to me.* I was the only person in the class that no one ever talked to because I'm so different, and they all made a point of seeing me as different. (Mosselson, 2009, p. 463)

In this case, Nataša's alienation is in part a result of her cultural displacement and the related lack of common identity and in part a result of the lack of common bond with other students in her school.

The Contribution of Alienation to Group Identity and Individual Identity

To some degree, experiences of alienation are important for the continued formulation of both group and individual identity. A period of feeling alone and lonely may help teens to appreciate how good social acceptance feels and how important it is for their well-being. Moreover, experiences of alienation within a group may help a young person see the *I* against the backdrop of the *we*. The discomfort of not fitting in helps one recognize the distinctiveness of one's point of view. In the extreme, however, the lack of social integration that may result from a negative resolution of this crisis can have significant implications for adjustment to school, self-esteem, and subsequent psychosocial development. Chronic conflict about one's integration into a meaningful reference group can lead to lifelong difficulties in areas of personal health, work, controlling anger, and the formation of intimate family bonds (East, Hess, & Lerner, 1987; Spencer, 1982, 1988; Weigel, Devereux, Leigh, & Ballard-Reisch, 1998).

The Central Process: Peer Pressure

Adolescents' family backgrounds, their interests, and styles of dress quickly link them to subgroups of peers who lend continuity and meaning to life within the context of their neighborhoods or schools. The peer group social structure is usually well established in most high schools, and members of that structure exert pressure on newcomers to join one peer group or another. **Peer pressure** refers to demands for conformity to group norms and a demonstration of commitment and loyalty to group members. At the same time, young people outside the groups form expectations that reinforce adolescents' connections to specific peer groups and prohibit their movement to others. Likewise, an individual who becomes a member of a group is more acceptable to the social system than one who tries to remain unaffiliated and aloof.

The term *peer pressure* is often used with a negative connotation, suggesting that young people behave in ways that go against their beliefs or values because of a fear of peer rejection. However, we suggest an alternative meaning that highlights the emerging role of the peer group in the radius of significant others. The pressure from those close by—those with whom a young person interacts each day—is not necessarily perceived as oppressive or coercive. It is, more often, the subtle co-adaptation of those who interact in the same social space, shaping and guiding one another toward intersubjectivity, much as an infant and a caregiver achieve mutual regulation. In a process of give and take, friends adapt to each other's preferences and interests, leading to a shared outlook on their world. For example, Ellen is very shy, but it's Friday night and her good friend Pam wants to go to the basketball game and then to a party afterward. Ellen is reluctant. She knows there is often a lot of drinking at these parties, and she is not in with the popular crowd that usually goes to these parties. Pam promises her that she won't drink at the party and that if Ellen is really not having a good time Pam will leave with her. Ellen decides to go along with Pam and they end up having a very good time. Pam keeps her promise of no drinking, and at midnight they leave so they are home by their curfew. Pam and Ellen are now thinking about having a party at Ellen's house next week, since this turned out to be a lot of fun.

Brown (2004) suggested four modes of peer influence, all of which may serve to encourage some behaviors and discourage others. The most overt mode is the direct suggestion that a teen should perform a behavior (e.g., smoke marijuana) or risk group rejection. This is the usual connotation of peer pressure, and parents or educators are often focused on helping teens resist this type of influence. A second type of peer influence occurs through modeling. Teens who spend time with one another watch each other's style of dress, gestures, and use of language, and imitate those behaviors in an effort to consolidate their sense of group membership. A third type of influence is more subtle normative regulation, where peers use teasing, gossiping, or sarcasm to influence each other's attitudes and behavior. Finally, peer influence occurs when friends create opportunities for unsupervised activities—having parties where beer is served, cruising in cars, or arranging to meet at a park or mall when adults are not likely to be present.

Affiliating with a Peer Group

The process of affiliating with a peer group requires an adolescent to accept the pressure and social influence imposed by it. This process provides the context in which the crisis of group identity versus alienation is resolved. Adolescents are at the point in their intellectual development when they are able to conceptualize themselves as objects of expectations. They may perceive these expectations as forces urging them to be more than they think they are—braver, more outgoing, more confident, and so forth. These expectations help define the zone of proximal development for group skills and social competencies. Peer pressure may have a positive effect on the adolescent's self-image and self-esteem, serving as a motive for group identification. Those dimensions of the self that are valued by one's own peer group become especially salient in each young person's self-assessment.

As members of peer groups, adolescents have more influence than they would have as single individuals; they begin to understand the value of *collective enterprise*. In offering membership, peer groups expand adolescents' feelings of connection and protect them from loneliness. When family conflicts develop, adolescents can seek comfort and intimacy among peers. For adolescents to benefit in these ways from their affiliation with a peer group, they must be willing to suppress some of their individuality and find pleasure in focusing on the attributes they share with those peers.

Conflicts Between Belonging and Personal Autonomy

Peer groups do not command total conformity. In fact, most peer groups depend on the unique characteristics of their members to lend definition and vigor to the roles that emerge within them. However, the peer group places importance on some level of conformity in order to bolster its structure and strengthen its effectiveness in satisfying members' needs. Indeed, most adolescents find some security in peer group demands to conform. The few well-defined characteristics of the group lend stability and substance to adolescents' views of themselves. In complying with group pressure, adolescents have an opportunity to state unambiguously that they are someone and that they belong somewhere (see the box on gangs).

Adolescents may also find that some peer expectations conflict with their personal values or needs. For example, they may feel that intellectual skills are devalued by the peer group, that they are expected to participate in social functions they do not enjoy, or that they are encouraged to be more independent from their families than they prefer to be. In most cases, adolescents' personal values are altered and shaped by peer group pressure to increase their similarity with the other group members. If, however, the peer group's expectations are too distant from the adolescents' own values, establishing a satisfying group identification will become much more difficult. As a result, adolescents experience tension and conflict as they try to balance the allure of peer group membership with the cost of abandoning personal beliefs.

Susceptibility to coercive peer pressure seems to peak at age 13 or 14, when adolescents are most sensitive to peer approval and make the initial transition toward new levels of behavioral autonomy and emotional independence from parents (Urberg, Shyu, & Liang, 1990; Lamborn & Steinberg, 1993). During the years from 14 to 16, adolescents become more adept at resisting peer pressure. Through encounters with peer pressure and opportunities to see how it feels to conform or resist, they develop a growing appreciation for the content of their personal values against the backdrop of peer expectations. However, if the emotional costs of identifying with the peer group become too great, adolescents may not open themselves up to group pressures. Therefore, they will be unable to establish the sense of group identity that is so central to psychosocial growth. An inability to reduce the tension and conflict between group pressure and personal values produces a state of alienation, in which the individual is unable either to identify with social groups or to develop personal friendships.

The Prime Adaptive Ego Quality and the Core Pathology

Fidelity to Others

A positive resolution of the psychosocial crisis of group identity versus alienation results in the achievement of the prime adaptive ego quality referred to as **fidelity to others**—a capacity to freely pledge one's loyalty to a group and to sustain one's faithfulness to the promises and commitments one makes to others. Fidelity to others produces the sentiments that are necessary to preserve small groups and larger communities alike: dedication to family, civic pride, and patriotism. One of the by-products of fidelity to others is *mattering*, a "feeling that others depend upon us, are interested in us, are concerned with our fate" (Rosenberg & McCullough, 1981, p. 163). Mattering is a relational aspect of the self-concept that reflects an assessment of how aware others are of you, how important you are to others, and how much others rely on you (Elliott, Kao, & Grant, 2004). When we pledge ourselves to others, we also become salient for them. We make a difference in their lives, and that, in return, contributes to our sense of well-being (Taylor & Turner, 2001). Adolescents who perceive that they matter to their parents and friends report higher levels of well-being than those who matter only to their parents, or to neither group (Marshall, 2004). The box on gangs illustrates how the desire for mattering may lead a young person to make an affiliation with a dangerous or deviant group where they feel valued and protected, needs that are not being met by family, school, or other community groups.

Looking ahead to subsequent life stages, one can anticipate the significant role that this ego quality plays in pledging long-term faithfulness to friends, marital partners, children, one's aging parents, and other groups. Research on factors that buffer the effects of stress often cite the contribution of social support to the long-term abilities of individuals to cope with change and to adapt positively to life challenges. Social support implies a capacity for fidelity. People who function as sources of support have the ability to remain compassionately connected to others during periods of hardship and loss as well as during periods of success and prosperity. When one thinks of a true friend, one pictures someone who stands by you even when it is not especially advantageous to do so. A true friend is someone who cares about you and supports you during moments of adversity as well as in times of joy.

Fidelity to others becomes a source of family solidarity as family members age and adults are called on to meet the needs of their own aging parents—a topic we will cover in Chapter 12 on middle adulthood. The role one plays in caring for one's aging parents is largely voluntary. It is based on one's own definition of filial obligation, a sense of duty and responsibility for one's parents. Surely the way adults enact this role reflects their capacity for fidelity to others.

Dissociation

Dissociation refers to a sense of separateness, withdrawal from others, and an inability to experience the bond of mutual commitment. It does not mean a preference for being by oneself, but rather a tendency toward social distancing and a reluctance to make the kinds of commitments to others that are required for the establishment and maintenance of enduring friendships. The following is an example of an adolescent who describes herself as floating along,

Gangs

IN THE LATE 1920s and 1930s, the study of delinquency included an analysis of the role of gangs. Early on, it was understood that delinquent behavior was typically group behavior, involving two or more boys in some type of criminal activity. Gangs were viewed as social groups, not unlike the kinds of groups that boys in more stable, prosperous neighborhoods create. The motives for joining a gang—"desires for recognition, approbation, and esteem of his fellows, for stimulation, thrill, and excitement, for intimate companionship, and for security and protection" (Burgess & Bogue, 1967, p. 300)—do not differ much from the motives that adolescents have for joining any number of social groups and clubs. However, the focus of these gangs developed a delinquent emphasis and tradition that was passed from one generation of gang members to the next in a neighborhood. The ethical standards and values of these groups were often contrary to conventional values. In fact, actions that might bring a nondelinquent boy dishonor or shame—such as being arrested, appearing in juvenile court, or being sent to a correctional institution—would be viewed as a source of pride

Copyright © A. Ramey/Photo Edit

Four Cambodian gang members are flashing hand signals. These signs can be used to identify their gang membership, send messages to each other, and taunt rival gangs. To learn more about gangs and gang behavior, you may want to go to the website www.knowgangs.com.

and distinction to a gang member (Burgess & Bogue, 1967).

This analysis of the nature of gangs has not changed much over the years. Gangs continue to thrive in communities all across the United States. According to a survey carried out by the National

Youth Gang Center, 3,330 jurisdictions experienced gang problems in 2008. This is an increase of 15% from 2002. Based on this survey, there are 774,000 gang members in 27,900 gangs across the United States. The biggest increases have been in small cities and suburban

disconnected from reality. Dissociation may be a symptom of more serious mental health problems such as schizophrenia, or an acute reaction to stress such as exposure to violence, rejection, or loss.

> What can I tell you about that time in my life? Hunger dominated every moment, hunger and its silent twin, the constant urge to sleep. School passed in a dream. I couldn't think. Logic fled, and memory drained away like motor oil. My stomach ached, my period stopped. I rose above the sidewalks, I was smoke. The rains came and I was sick and after school I had nowhere to go. (Fitch, 1999, p. 201)

Dissociation may occur as a result of rejection, abuse, or neglect. It may be a symptom of a more serious mental disorder, such as schizophrenia or depression. Adolescents who experience dissociation are likely to mistrust their peers and may even develop an attitude of hostile resentment toward the amiability and companionship they observe in others. Over time, dissociation results in the formulation of a mental world that is not well coordinated with social reality. A young person who experiences dissociation is likely to feel misunderstood and to lack confidence in her ability to communicate with or connect to others.

At a basic level, any sense of *we*-ness requires a shared understanding between at least two people and a recognition that they experience some bond of investment in or identification with a common reality. This common reality could involve facing a common enemy, encountering a common crisis, or embracing a common goal. The core pathology of dissociation occurs when the young person is unable to experience the level of mutual understanding or symbolic connection that creates such bonds of *we*-ness.

jurisdictions. Forty-five percent of agencies describe their gang problems as getting worse; 10% say their problems are getting better. Overall, in cities of 250,000 and more, gang-related crimes, including aggravated assault, drug-related crimes, and homicides, have increased since 2002 (Egley, Howell, & Moore, 2010).

Gangs actively recruit new members, engage in violent acts of initiation, and are becoming increasingly associated with drug trafficking and violent crime. Experts say that what drives young people to gangs are poverty, the desire to belong, and the desire to be loved and recognized (Howell, 1994). One teenager said that his mother was hooked on crack cocaine. He joined the gang looking for love. Another one had an eye that was a little crossed. He said that some people at school made fun of him, but that members of his gang did not make fun of him.

Young people seek love, money, protection, and prestige from gang membership. Adolescents who join gangs are often unsuccessful in school and may have been suspended or expelled. School failure leads to periods of unsupervised time in the community

and an inability to find work. Modern gang activities are supported by a growing and spreading drug trade, easy access to guns, and the communication technology of beepers, cell phones, and voice mail, which allow gang members to coordinate their activities and preserve control over a wider area with increased mobility.

The concept of gangs is closely linked to the theme of **group identity**. Although gangs have a violent, criminal, and antisocial value system, they provide a highly organized social group for identification. Gangs have clothing, colors, symbols, and signs that provide recognition across settings. Young people are recruited into gangs, making them feel valued and protected by the older gang members. Despite the great risks associated with gang activities, the pervasive presence of gangs in cities and larger towns suggests that gangs address a number of needs of today's youth—needs that are not being met by communities, schools, and families.

To learn more about gangs and ideas about preventing adolescent involvement in gangs, visit the website sponsored by the U.S. Office of Juvenile Justice and Delinquency

Prevention or the National Youth Gang Center.

Critical Thinking Questions

1. Are gangs cliques or crowds? Why do you think so?
2. What might be some differences between being a gang member and being part of a clique or friendship group that is involved in delinquent activities? In what ways are gangs similar to other kinds of tough or antisocial peer groups? In what ways are they different?
3. What functions are served by gang membership? Are the effects of gang membership only negative?
4. How do concepts presented in the chapter related to peer group membership and group identity versus alienation inform your understanding of gang membership?
5. Imagine that you are a school counselor and a student has been brought to your attention as someone who is suspected of being involved in criminal activity. How might you work differently with a student who you know to be a member of a gang than with someone who is not a gang member?

APPLIED TOPIC

Adolescent Alcohol and Drug Use

Objective 7. To review the patterns of adolescent alcohol and drug use and the factors associated with their use and abuse within a psychosocial framework.

American high-school-age youth show a higher level of illicit drug use than those of any other industrialized nation. By their senior year in high school (typically ages 17 and 18), almost half of American high school students have tried an illegal drug—whether marijuana, amphetamines, heroin or other opiates, cocaine, or barbiturates (Johnston, O'Malley, Bachman, & Schulenberg, 2007).

Figure 9.5 provides a historical overview of the lifetime prevalence of illicit drug use for eighth, tenth, and twelfth graders from 1975 to 2009 based on the *Monitoring the Future* national survey sponsored by the National Institute on Drug Abuse (Johnston, O'Malley, Bachman, & Schulenberg, 2009). Following a period of decline in drug use from 1981 through 1992, drug use among adolescents increased over the 1990s and is now beginning to decline again, though not to its 1992 low. In 2008, 37% of twelfth graders had used an illicit drug, and 17% of twelfth graders had tried an illicit drug other than marijuana. The authors, who have been following trends in teen drug use and attitudes toward drugs for 30 years suggest that the early and growing use of marijuana can account for the substantial number of youth who have used an illegal drug during the high school years.

Alcohol use has remained at a stable and relatively high level since 1975. In 2008, 39% of eighth graders

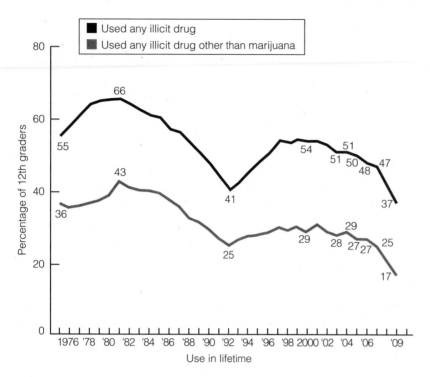

FIGURE 9.5 Trends in Lifetime Prevalence of an Illicit Drug Use Index for Twelfth Graders

Source: Johnston, O'Malley, Bachman, & Schulenberg, 2010.

had tried alcohol, and 18% said that they have been drunk at least once in their lives. By the twelfth grade, 72% had tried alcohol and 55% had gotten drunk. About 22% of twelfth graders had experienced binge drinking (five or more drinks in a row) in the past month (Johnston et al., 2009). Binge drinking and drunkenness among twelfth graders has declined since their peak in the early 1980s.

Physical Effects of Alcohol

Alcohol depresses the central nervous system. Although many people think that alcohol makes one high, at its highest levels of concentration in the body it can cause death by suppressing breathing. Although this outcome is extremely rare, it may occur after chugging large quantities of alcohol, a practice that is sometimes included in certain adolescent initiation rites and demonstrations of attention seeking. Deaths associated with fraternity initiation activities on college campuses have brought the practice of *chugging* to heightened attention ("Parents Should Talk to College Students," 1997). There are two other situations in which alcohol use has potentially lethal consequences. One is the use of alcohol in combination with other drugs, especially barbiturates. The other is its use in combination with driving.

The physical development accompanying puberty leads to a heightened awareness of body sensations. In small quantities, alcohol has a relaxing effect that may accentuate

pleasurable bodily sensations. Adolescents may use alcohol in an attempt to increase their sense of physical arousal, reduce sexual inhibitions, and minimize the self-consciousness that is a barrier to social interactions. In larger quantities, alcohol may alter reality in such a way that adolescents are willing to take risks or ignore certain physical limitations. When adolescents are intoxicated, the barriers of physical appearance, height, weight, or sexual immaturity may be minimized. Thus, dissatisfaction with one's body image may contribute to an inclination to drink heavily in social situations.

Information from the National Institute on Alcohol Abuse and Alcoholism provides information about the potential harm alcohol can have for health and brain functioning (NIAAA, 2004). The following information about health risks associated with alcohol is taken from that source.

1. Alcohol can result in memory impairments after only a few drinks and, as the amount of alcohol increases, so does the degree of impairment. One consequence of binge drinking, especially on an empty stomach, is blackouts, a time for which the intoxicated person cannot recall key details of events, or even entire events. Blackouts occur more often among social drinkers than was previously assumed; they are not a risk only for those who are addicted to alcohol.

2. Because alcohol consumption interferes with normal eating patterns, a common consequence of alcoholism is thiamine deficiency. Thiamine, also known as vitamin

B1, is an essential nutrient required by all tissues, including the brain. The cerebellum, an area of the brain responsible for coordinating movement and some forms of learning, appears to be particularly sensitive to the effects of thiamine deficiency and is the region most frequently damaged in association with chronic alcohol consumption.

3. Long-term drinking can damage the liver, the organ chiefly responsible for breaking down alcohol into harmless by-products and clearing it from the body. Prolonged liver dysfunction, such as liver cirrhosis resulting from excessive alcohol consumption, can harm the brain, leading to a serious and potentially fatal brain disorder known as hepatic encephalopathy. Hepatic encephalopathy can cause changes in sleep patterns, mood, and personality; psychiatric conditions such as anxiety and depression; severe cognitive effects such as shortened attention span; and problems with coordination such as a flapping or shaking of the hands. In the most serious cases, patients may slip into a coma (i.e., hepatic coma), which can be fatal.

Factors Associated with Alcohol Use

Let us look at some of the factors associated with the use of alcohol and the part it plays in the adolescent's life. We are especially concerned about understanding the relationship between alcohol use and the major themes of early adolescence—cognitive development, parent-child relationships, and peer relations.

Assessment of Risk

Many adolescents do not view alcohol consumption as especially risky. In a national survey, about 30% of high school seniors saw daily drinking as involving great risk, and 47% of high school seniors saw binge drinking (five or more drinks once or twice over a weekend) as involving great risk (Johnston et al., 2007). In a summary of research about adolescent decision making and risk taking, Reyna and Farley (2006) describe some of the characteristics of children and adolescents that may influence their behaviors:

> Compared to adults, children and adolescents have been found to be less able to delay gratification, inhibit their behavior, plan for or anticipate the future, spontaneously bring consequences to mind, or learn from negative consequences; and adolescents do not view consequences as being as harmful as adults do, especially if risky behaviors are engaged in only once or twice. (p. 29)

In contrast to what is often said of adolescents, they typically see themselves as more vulnerable to negative consequences than do adults, and overestimate their exposure to risks. However, after early adolescence, these overestimations

decline, most likely because they have had more experiences, explored more, and have rarely encountered the negative consequences or have judged the consequences to be less serious than they expected. As a result, in the case of binge drinking, adolescents view the behavior as less risky as they get older.

In addition to the assessment of risk, some adolescents can be characterized by high levels of *sensation seeking,* including thrill seeking, adventure seeking, disinhibition, and susceptibility to boredom. Youth who have a great need for novel, complex sensory experiences may be willing to take physical risks in order to satisfy this need (Tang, Wong, & Schwarzer, 1996). Teens who have difficulty conceptualizing the future impact of their behaviors and who have a strong need for thrill seeking are more likely to become involved in frequent and heavy alcohol use (Robbins & Bryan, 2004).

The Social Contexts for Understanding Alcohol Misuse

Adolescent alcohol use takes place in a complex social environment comprised of family, friends, school, and neighborhood. Within each of these settings, three processes come into play: the extent to which adolescents are exposed to models who drink; the strength of the bond between the adolescent and those who either encourage or discourage drinking in each context; and exposure to stressors that might increase an adolescent's feelings of distress and magnify the inclination to use alcohol. A study of over 6,000 adolescents ages 11 to 17 explored the importance of these four contexts in predicting alcohol misuse, and how these contexts might interact to influence drinking among teens (Ennett et al., 2008). Each context made an independent contribution to the likelihood that adolescents would misuse alcohol. The nature of the family environment was closely tied to an adolescent's alcohol misuse. High levels of family conflict and alcohol use by parents were associated with a teen's drinking. Family closeness and parental supervision were associated with less drinking. In the peer context, peer modeling of drinking was associated with teens' drinking when the peer relationships were close and reciprocated. In the school and the neighborhood contexts, the most important factor was the frequency of alcohol use by students or neighbors. There was also evidence of some interaction among contexts. When family supervision was high, teens were less likely to misuse alcohol even if their friends and schoolmates were drinking. When family conflict and family alcohol use were high, teens were more likely to be influenced by their friends' and schoolmates' drinking.

Given the significance of social contexts and the **socialization forces** that may encourage or reward risky behavior, it is important to keep sight of the role of self-selection in alcohol and drug use as well. **Selection forces** refer to the fact that some adolescents seek out friends who will support their involvement with alcohol or drugs as part of a more general pattern of deviance or thrill seeking, whereas other teens, who do not drink alcohol or use drugs, find friends who support this position. Both factors—socialization pressures toward alcohol and drug use and willingness to seek out peers who misuse drugs and alcohol—increase over the high school years, with a consequent increase in the likelihood that adolescents will become involved in the misuse of alcohol and drugs themselves (Schulenberg & Maggs, 2001).

A combination of biological, psychological, and societal factors converge to make alcohol and drug use a part of the life of normal adolescents during the high school years. Experimentation with alcohol is relatively easy to understand in the context of the adolescent's psychosocial needs and the modeling of alcohol use in the family, peer group,

and community. Although alcohol and drug use may be considered a normative rite of passage for most adolescents, it appears that children who begin to drink or use drugs early in adolescence—that is, before ninth grade—are especially vulnerable to more serious involvement with alcohol and drug use later (Murray, 1997). They experience some combination of family, peer, and psychosocial pressures that increase their willingness to engage in deviant behavior and to ignore or minimize the risks. The risk factors associated with early alcohol and drug use are linked to social class and culture. Control over the sale of alcohol to minors, its cost, and the efforts of parents and other adults—including school officials and the police—to monitor its use among adolescents are all community factors that influence the use of alcohol in early adolescence.

Chapter Summary

Early adolescence provides vivid evidence of the interaction of the biological, psychological, and societal systems during a period of rapid growth and development.

Objective 1. To describe the patterns of physical maturation during puberty for female and male adolescents, including an analysis of the impact of early and late maturing on self-concept and social relationships.

The period is characterized by biological changes of puberty, new cognitive capacities, and a new range and intensity of emotional life. Rapid changes in height, weight, muscle strength, endurance, and reproductive capacities are accompanied by new roles, and new responses from others. The timing of puberty has important and long-lasting implications for personal and social development.

Objective 2. To characterize the development of romantic and sexual relationships, including a focus on the transition to coitus, the formation of a sexual orientation, and factors associated with pregnancy and parenthood in adolescence.

Physical maturation is accompanied by new romantic feelings and sexualized experiences, some desirable, and some unwanted. Most adolescents find ways to express sexual impulses in the context of socially acceptable practices. The majority of adolescents engage in forms of sexual behavior, including intercourse, with its accompanying risks and rewards, by the end of high school. The transition into sexual activity involves individual motivations, family and peer influences, attractiveness, and religious values and beliefs. Teens face a variety of challenges associated with early

sexuality, including unwanted sexual attention, identification and disclosure of an alternative sexual orientation, inconsistent contraception, sexually transmitted diseases, and unwanted pregnancy.

Objective 3. To introduce and critically evaluate the basic features of formal operational thought, highlighting the new conceptual skills that emerge in early adolescence and the factors that promote the development of advanced reasoning at this period of life.

The physical changes of adolescence are taking place in a context of new and more complex cognitive capacities. Adolescence marks a period of brain development and sculpting leading to more advanced, abstract reasoning, and greater capacity to address complex, multidimensional problems. During this stage of life, the quality of experiences and the demands for higher-order thinking can play a significant role in advancing a young person's cognitive abilities.

Objective 4. To examine patterns of emotional development in early adolescence, including three examples of emotional disorders: eating disorders, delinquency, and depression.

Emotional development is characterized by a more diverse range of emotions, greater awareness of one's emotions, and for most teens, a growing capacity to express and control the expression of emotions. After puberty, boys tend to have more problems coping with anger and aggression, girls have more problems coping with anxiety and depression.

Objective 5. To describe the further evolution of peer relations in early adolescence, especially the formation of cliques and crowds, and to contrast the impact of parents and peers during this stage.

The radius of significant relationships expands as adolescents enter new roles and new settings. Parents continue to be an important source of reassurance and support. However, the period is characterized by strong desires to find membership and acceptance among peers. Within this context, adolescents seek like-minded peers and are open to peer influence.

Objective 6. To describe the psychosocial crisis of group identity versus alienation, the central process through which the crisis is resolved, peer pressure, the prime adaptive ego quality of fidelity to others, and the core pathology of isolation.

The crisis of group identity versus alienation involves a potential tension between the *I* and the *we*, the desire to feel meaningfully connected to a valued group and, at the same time, to have an authentic, autonomous sense of self. Leadership, mastery of complex knowledge, success in social

relationships, and new respect from parents, teachers, and peers reflect some of the positive consequences of effective coping. In the process of resolving this conflict, most adolescents experience moments of alienation, a sense of separateness and disconnection, out of which can grow a new personal confidence or a deep well of resentment and rage. The threat of peer rejection may push those adolescents who lack confidence in their own worth to violate essential values in the pursuit of acceptance.

Objective 7. To review the patterns of adolescent alcohol and drug use and the factors associated with their use and abuse within a psychosocial framework.

Teenage pregnancy, drug addiction, drunkenness, and serious delinquent behavior all reflect adolescents' capacity to engage in high-risk behaviors that have a great potential for modifying the life course and exposing them to new and serious physical and emotional hazards. Alcohol misuse, which is common among U.S. teens, takes place in a context of family, peer, school and community forces that constrain or encourage drinking and drunkenness.

Key Terms

alienation, 336
anorexia nervosa, 361
attractiveness, 347
body dissatisfaction, 340
bulimia, 361
cliques, 367
common bond, 375
common identity, 375
contraception, 350
crowds, 367
decentering, 358
delinquency, 364
depression, 362
disclosure, 348
dissociation, 377
drug and alcohol use, 344
eating disorders, 339
egocentrism, 358
ethnic group identity, 373

executive functioning, 353
externalizing problems, 361
fidelity to others, 377
first intercourse, 346
formal operational thought, 354
group identity, 336
group norms, 368
hypotheses, 355
identity confusion, 336
imaginary audience, 359
individual identity, 336
internalizing problems, 361
menarche, 341
obesity, 339
peer group membership, 369
peer pressure, 376
personal fable, 359
physical maturation, 343
postformal reasoning, 358

puberty, 337
reference groups, 371
reputational identity, 368
rites of passage, 338
secondary sex
     characteristics, 337
secular growth trend, 343
selection forces, 381
self-labeling, 348
sexual motivation, 346
sexual orientation, 347
sexually transmitted
     infections, 350
sleep patterns, 338
socialization forces, 381
teen pregnancy, 351
unwanted sexual
     attention, 349

Further Reflection

1. Think back on your early adolescence, from the age of about 12 to the end of high school. How would you characterize that time of your life? What are some examples of experiences that made you feel competent and self-assured? What are examples of experiences that led to feelings of inferiority or self-doubt?

2. Consider the role of friendship during this period of life. How did your friendships change from middle childhood to adolescence? Can you recall being part of a clique? A crowd? How would you describe those groups in terms of attitudes, values, dress, orientation toward school, or involvement in high-risk

behaviors? What are some lessons learned from high school peer relations that continue to be meaningful to you today?

3. What happens in the context of schooling that supports the development of formal operational reasoning? How well does the high school environment match the cognitive developmental changes that take place during early adolescence?

4. Think about the impact of physical development, including the emergence of sexuality and sexual interests, on adaptation during early adolescence. What personal, family, cultural, and environmental factors help adolescents cope effectively with these changes? What factors lead to dissatisfaction with body image, risk taking, and harmful or unhealthy behaviors?

5. Suppose that you were asked to provide guidance to a parents' group about how to improve health among adolescents. What ideas from this chapter might inform your recommendations?

6. The psychosocial crisis of group identity versus alienation is closely linked to the issue of intergroup relations. What factors in school or community foster positive intergroup relations among adolescents? What factors promote intergroup hostilities? What is your view about how to promote positive intergroup relations at the middle school and high school levels?

Psychology CourseMate

To access additional course materials, including CourseMate, please visit www.cengagebrain.com. At the CengageBrain .com home page, search for the ISBN of your title (from the back cover of your book) using the search box at the top of the page. This will take you to the product page where these resources can be found.

Casebook

For additional case material related to this chapter, see the case entitled "The Early Bloomer" in *Life Span Development: A Case Book*, by Barbara and Philip Newman, Laura Landry Meyer, and Brenda J. Lohman, pp. 120–123. The case focuses on the challenges of early maturing for girls and how pubertal timing influences social relationships.

Portrait of the Artist's Wife, Jacqueline Kneeling. 1954/Private Collection/Index/The Bridgeman Art Library International/© 2011 Estate of Pablo Picasso/Artists Rights Society (ARS), New York

Engaged in the active resolution of the identity crisis, young people make commitments that will shape the structure of their adult lives. In this portrait, Picasso suggests the balance, focus, and purposefulness of a young woman who is striving to achieve a sense of personal identity.

Later Adolescence (18 to 24 Years)

Chapter Objectives

1. To examine the concept of autonomy from parents and the conditions under which autonomy is likely to be achieved.

2. To trace the development of gender identity in later adolescence, including a discussion of how the components of gender role identification that were relevant during the early-school-age period are revised and expanded.

3. To describe the maturation of morality in later adolescence, with special focus on the role of new cognitive capacities that influence moral judgments and the various value orientations that underlie moral reasoning.

4. To analyze the process of career choice, with attention to education and gender role socialization as two major influential factors.

5. To define and describe the psychosocial crisis of later adolescence, individual identity versus identity confusion; the central process through which this crisis is resolved, role experimentation; the prime adaptive ego quality of fidelity to values and ideals; and the core pathology of repudiation.

6. To examine some of the predictors and consequences of dropping out of college.

There is general agreement among human development scholars that the years from about 18 through 24 are a distinct stage of development, separate from early adolescence and from early adulthood. Studies from a variety of industrialized countries confirm the idea that young people in these societies have characteristics that distinguish them from younger teens, especially advanced cognitive reasoning abilities, intensive personal identity exploration, a feeling of being somewhere in between childhood and adulthood, and a preoccupation with future possibilities. These features are tied to cultural conditions, including a prolonged period of education and training before entry into and investment in an occupational role, delayed age at marriage and childbearing, and difficulties becoming financially self-sufficient (Arnett, 2006; Sirsch, Dreher, Mayr, & Willinger, 2009).

What should we call this stage of life? Despite a growing trend in the field of human development to refer to this as the stage of emerging adulthood, we prefer the term later adolescence for the following reasons:

1. Adulthood, a status that is socially and culturally constructed, is becoming an increasingly elusive state, difficult to define or achieve. The adult transition is considered to be completed when three or more of the following five criteria have been achieved: leaving home, completing one's education, becoming financially independent, getting married, and, for most, having children (Furstenberg, 2010). Figure 10.1

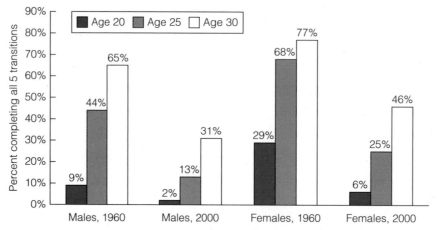

FIGURE 10.1 The Percentage Completing Five Criteria of the Adult Transition, 1960 and 2000, by Age and Gender

Source: Data are from the Integrated Public Use Microdata Series extracts (IPUMS) of the 1960 and 2000 U.S. Censuses. Men are defined as financially independent if they are in the labor force; women are defined as financially independent if they have completed all transitions except employment in the labor force. Table reprinted, with permission, from: Furstenberg, F.F., Kennedy, S., McLoyd, V.C., Rumbaut, R.G., & Settersten, R.A. (2003). *Between Adolescence and Adulthood: Expectations about the Timing of Adulthood*. (Working Paper No. 1). Philadelphia, PA: Network on Transitions to Adulthood. Used by permission of Frank Furstenberg, Jr.

provides a comparison of the percentage of men and women at three ages who completed all five of these markers of adult status by age 20, 25, and 30 in 1960 and 2000. In 1960 this transition into adulthood was very unusual for men and women aged 20, but common for young men aged 25 and normative for young women aged 25. By 2000, it was no longer normative for all five markers of adult status to be achieved by men or women at age 25 or 30. These data illustrate that adulthood is not emerging in the period of 18 to 24 years, but in fact, is further away than it was 40 years ago.

2. In contemporary industrialized or post-industrialized countries, young people are enrolling in postsecondary education at greater rates than ever before. This includes associates degree, bachelor's degree, and professional degree programs. The student status has been extended, a status that is by definition transitional as one moves toward a level of new knowledge and expertise. Typically the student status delays full-time entry into the labor market, and fosters a prolonged period of transitional or temporary residential identification with a community.

3. The age at first marriage is approaching 30. Although the majority of young people in the age range 18 to 24 are sexually active, their relationships are temporary. Relatively few young people in the age range 18 to 24 are involved in relationships that they expect will result in marriage.

4. The economic recession of the last 3 years has resulted in a growing number of young people who are out of work, underemployed, or working at jobs that are viewed as temporary. The percentage of young people in this age group who can support themselves is declining even further than it was in 2000.

5. Almost half of people ages 20 to 24 years who are not married live with their parents. One of the recent changes in the U.S. health policy was a provision to allow young people to remain on their parents' health insurance policies until age 26. These are just two indications of the continued financial dependence of young people on their parents.

The prospects of making a behavioral, psychological, or social transition into adulthood is not emerging in the age period of 18 to 24 years. We prefer the term later adolescence because it connotes a process of continued growth and maturation prior to adulthood. The executive decision-making capacities of the frontal cortex are still maturing, suggesting that later adolescents have new abilities for reflection, problem solving, and planning. For many, this is a period of exploration, experimentation, and self-development. As one author described it, "between the late teens and late 20s . . . young Americans experience their 'odyssey years,' a time of wandering on the path to maturity" (Boonstra, 2009, p. 13).

Others, an estimated 15% of youth ages 16 to 24, are disconnected; they are not in school, and they are not employed. Some are in jail, others are homeless or disabled, and others have been released from foster care but are having difficulty achieving independent lives (Hair et al., 2009).

Later adolescence is a time of fewer constraints and greater self-determination than early adolescence. Young people in the age range 18 to 24 do not have to be in school even though many are. New legal rights and privileges become available. This is a time when life paths become increasingly divergent as young people make choices and pursue their goals. But, by and large, these paths are experimental and temporary, reflecting the flexibility of the stage and the lack of urgency to make long-term commitments.

The years from 18 to 24 are characterized by a heightened sensitivity to the process of identity development. Personal identity is developed as an individual struggles to answer the questions, "What is the meaning of my life? Who am I? Where am I headed?" Most young people are cognitively complex enough to conjure up alternative scenarios about their own future, including possible kinds of work and various meaningful relationships. They struggle with the uncertainty of having to choose many of their own life's directions. This period is often characterized by a high level of anxiety. Even though most young people are energetic and capable, they are also troubled by the lack of certainty about their future. Some worry whether they will be able to succeed in a chosen direction; others may be anxious because they do not even know what direction they wish to take. ■

Developmental Tasks
Autonomy from Parents

Objective 1. To examine the concept of autonomy from parents and the conditions under which autonomy is likely to be achieved.

Achieving a psychological sense of autonomy from one's parents is a multidimensional task that is faced gradually over the course of later adolescence and early adulthood. **Autonomy** from parents is the ability to regulate one's behavior and to select and guide one's decisions and actions in order to achieve meaningful personal goals without undue control from or dependence on one's parents. Autonomy suggests that decisions and behaviors are guided by personal will; they are voluntary rather than imposed or controlled by others (Ryan & Deci, 2000). Autonomy is not the same as rejection, alienation, or physical separation from parents. Rather, it is an independent psychological status in which parents and children accept each other's individuality. Many areas of similarity between parents and children may provide bonds for a continued close, supportive relationship into adulthood. However, those bonds are re-created in later adolescence and early adulthood through a process of self-definition. Adolescents who achieve autonomy can recognize and accept both the similarities and the differences between themselves and their parents, while still feeling a sense of love, understanding, and connection with them.

Autonomy may refer to independence of behavior, thoughts, and emotions (Steinberg, 2005). Much of the psychosocial development that has occurred before this stage can be understood as preparing the individual for behavioral independence from his parents. Such skills as dressing oneself, handling money, cooking, driving a car, reading, and writing have been mastered. Many of these skills are incorporated into the concept of Activities of Daily Living (ADLs), a measure that is used to assess the self-sufficiency of older adults. Although it is easy to take these skills for granted, they are essential for someone who is living independently. The physical maturation that has taken place also contributes to the possibility of autonomy. Daily survival requires a certain amount of physical strength, coordination, and endurance—qualities that accompany the physical maturity of adolescence.

Beyond these physical requirements, autonomy involves a psychological sense of confidence about one's unique point of view and an ability to express opinions and beliefs that may differ from those of one's parents (Herman, Dornbusch, Herron, & Herting, 1997). In early school age, the process of identification and the accompanying internalization of parental values allow the young child to function with a sense of what is appropriate behavior. In early adolescence, the child's ability to emerge from the intimacy of the family may also be promoted by a growing involvement with the peer group. In early adolescence, a young person's autonomy is expressed in personal preferences and tastes that are considered legitimate domains for decision making. In later adolescence, a young person's cognitive maturity provides problem-solving abilities, the ability to consider multiple perspectives and to evaluate information from multiple sources, and a capacity to plan for the future, all of which support new levels of autonomous reasoning about important life choices. As later adolescents become more autonomous in thought, they are able to reflect upon their parents' opinions and advice, and to set these views next to their own as well as the views of peers or other mentors or authorities in order to decide what makes sense for them.

The concept of **differentiation**, which emerged from family systems theory, has been associated with emotional maturity and a healthy emergence of individuality in adolescence. Differentiation is the extent to which a social system encourages intimacy while supporting the expression of differences (Bomar & Sabatelli, 1996). Within the family context, identity exploration is facilitated by an open exchange of ideas and a certain level of challenge. Adolescents must have opportunities to express their separateness within the boundaries of the family. They must feel that their parents accept and understand their need to have distinct opinions and views. This takes place as parents support their child's quest for autonomy and encourage their child to express new ideas and differing points of view without making them feel guilty when they disagree (Best, Hauser, & Allen, 1997). Adolescents who experience high levels of parental control and frequent exposure to parental conflict are likely to have difficulties in achieving a comfortable sense of autonomy (Taylor & Oskay, 1995). Ideally, individuality is achieved in a context of mutual caring and emotional support. A secure attachment to parents, based on a perception of them as committed to their child's well-being, is essential for growth toward independence (Palladino-Schultheiss & Blustein, 1994; Perosa, Perosa, & Tam, 1996; Buhl, 2007).

The meaning a young person gives to achieving autonomy from parents varies depending on personal, family, and cultural values, such as commitment to education, financial independence, and marriage. For example, some cultural groups are more accustomed to living in multigenerational families and place great value on the filial bond between children and their parents. Parents in these cultures may be more comfortable with the idea of having their later adolescent children living in their home without paying rent, and the children may perceive it as part of their obligation to stay near their parents and grandparents in order to provide them with social and instrumental support. In contrast, in some cultures, families expect their later adolescent children to achieve residential separateness. They may expect that children ages 18 to 24 who are living at home will contribute to the cost of housing. Paths toward autonomy are also influenced by the young person's family context. For example, children living with their two biological parents are likely to leave home later than are children living in a stepfamily. Three components of achieving autonomy from parents are discussed in the following sections: leaving home, attending college, and self-sufficiency.

Autonomy and Leaving Home

Living away from one's parents' household may be a symbol of independence; however, it is not as readily achievable in the age range from 18 to 24 as it was in the past. Before about 1960, marriage was the most traditional reason for moving to a new residence, other than leaving temporarily for college or the military. Since that time, however, the median age at marriage has increased, so that in 2008 87% of males and 79% of females in the age range from 20 to 24 have never been married (U.S. Census Bureau, 2010). Of those who have never married, almost half live at home with one or both parents. Few later adolescents live alone, but a large number, almost 25%, live in group arrangements with nonfamily members including housemates, close friends, or intimate partners (U.S. Census Bureau, 2009).

Parents and adolescent children have different views about the age at which children are expected to leave home. Parents tend to expect children to leave home at an older age—more closely tied to the expected age of marriage—than do adolescent children. Also, parents expect daughters to live at home longer than sons. However, these differences are not reflected in the expectations of the adolescents themselves. Thus, this issue is a potential source of family conflict. Family structure is also associated with the age of leaving home. Children in single-parent families and girls in stepfamilies leave at an earlier age (Cooney & Mortimer, 1999).

Economic factors and social norms play a significant role in the timing of leaving home. A child's ability to live away from home may depend on whether the family is willing and financially able to provide support during this period. This, in turn, depends in part on the family's values and the later adolescent's values. For example, many families are strongly committed to having their children complete college and are willing to provide financial support while the child is away at school. However, if the child gets married while still in college, some families may feel that their financial obligation to support the child is over. Some parents are willing to support their children who are away from home if the child is in college, but not willing to provide support if the child wants to live away from home but not attend school (Goldscheider, Thornton, & Yang, 2001). Imagine that, after 1 or 2 years of college, a child wants to move to a new city, live with a same-sex partner, and seek opportunities in the entertainment industry. Some parents might encourage this path toward self-discovery; others might consider it risky, immoral, or frivolous. When children and parents disagree about the appropriate path toward self-reliance and adulthood, parents may be unwilling to provide the financial resources that would make this level of autonomy possible.

Given the variety of living arrangements that are now common in later adolescence, questions are being raised about the relationship of living arrangements to well-being. Do young people who continue to live at home with their parents have the same sense of well-being and life satisfaction as young people who live in some type of group situation with other friends or who live independently? There are some conflicting views about this. Some studies show that later adolescents who live with peers or on their own have a more adult-like view of themselves, and get along better with their parents than those who live with their parents (White, 2002). Other studies show that later adolescents who have a good relationship with their parents are more likely to live with them for a longer period (Lanz & Tagliabue, 2007). When there is a stepparent involved or frequent conflict with parents, later adolescents may feel pushed out into independent living. In a study of Belgian later adolescents, three types of living arrangements were related to well-being: living at home with parents, living with other students but returning home frequently, and living independently with a partner or alone. In this study, the most important factor was the young person's sense that the living arrangement was of their own choosing. In addition, later adolescents whose parents supported their autonomous decision were most confident about their decision and had the greatest sense of well-being, regardless of whether they lived at home with their parents, with friends, or on their own (Kins, Beyers, Soenens, & Vansteenkiste, 2009).

Autonomy and the College Experience

Going away to college is an intermediate step between living at home and establishing a permanent residence in early adulthood. The mere act of going to college does not in itself bring a sense of leaving home or of psychological autonomy from one's parents. In fact, most students do not go far from home when they enter college as freshmen; roughly 80% attend college in their home state (*Chronicle of Higher Education*, 2009). Many students continue to live at home while they attend college, and most still request and receive both emotional and instrumental support from their parents.

Some college-age students are more ready than others to embrace the demands for new levels of independence and responsibility. College freshmen express a variety of attitudes that suggest different views about their desire to be independent from their family. Of students entering college in the fall of 2004, 21% said that an important reason for deciding to go to college was to get away from home, whereas 42% said that an important reason was that their parents wanted them to go. When asked about reasons that were important in selecting the specific college that they ended up attending, 20% of those attending their first-choice college said they wanted to live near home (CIRP, 2006). As they enter college, students differ markedly in how much work they have

Students who go away to college use their group identity skills to form new relationships while creating a physical environment that preserves a connection to family, friends, and home.

already done toward achieving autonomy from their parents, how much they desire autonomy, and what evidence they use to determine whether they have achieved autonomy.

Revision of Attachment to Parents

The experience of entering college focuses new attention on the changing quality of the attachment relationship between college students and their parents. Students who live at college are more likely to rely on the mental representations of their attachment figures, whereas students who live with their parents continue to be involved daily with concrete interactions. Issues of autonomy and control, establishing new guidelines and limits related to participation in family life, involvement in relationships with peers, and management of time and money are resolved in the absence of direct input from parents for most students who live at college, but these decisions continue to involve parental input for students who live at home.

For students who live on campus, preoccupation with thoughts and concerns about their parents tend to diminish over the course of the first semester, while new relationships form and a new confidence in their independent decision making builds. The attachment scheme or representation, rather than the actual interactions with parents, is what becomes modified. Many students who attend college away from home begin to have more positive thoughts and feelings about their parents. At the same time, they begin to detect a new level of confidence and respect from their parents, who appreciate that their children are managing to take on new responsibilities and to make good decisions on their own.

> Over the past year I have become very close with my dad. Before college there was a definite parent-child relationship with my father. Now he is more like a mentor or friend.

Overall, the relationship between my parents and I has been a growing mutual respect. (Arnett, 2004a, p. 215)

In other cases, going to college represents a move toward upward mobility and a decision to seek a life path quite different from one's parents. Even when parents are supportive of a child's college attendance, the experiences of college may introduce their child to new ideas, values, and interests that create conflict. Parents who have not attended college may not understand what their child is doing, why it is important or valued, or how their child's involvement in certain classes or campus activities will lead to economic betterment. For some, this distance is gradually bridged as parents become familiar with their children's lives, and children become more skilled at giving parents ways of understanding what

Moving to college often brings a revision to the parent-adolescent relationship.

they are doing. For others, as in the case of Mary, the distance widens over time:

> I go home, we talk about the weather, talk about people in the family, people in the neighborhood. . . . The stuff I would like to talk about, [my mother] can't. She doesn't understand it. Stuff she'd like to talk about I think would be incredibly boring. . . . I learned very early on that they couldn't discuss [school]. To try to discuss it with them would be very frustrating to me, and embarrassing for them. . . . I realized I had far educated myself past my parents. (Roberts & Rosenwald, 2001, p. 102)

Students who live at home while attending college tend to continue to be preoccupied by concerns and thoughts about their parents based on their actual daily interactions, and the quality of their relationships involves more conflict (Sullivan & Sullivan, 1980; Berman & Sperling, 1991).

The relationship between emotional closeness and living at home appears to be culturally shaped. For example, in the United States, later adolescents who live at home and have frequent daily interactions with their parents tend to be *least* close to them. In comparison, studies of European later adolescents find that young people who live at home are quite happy with their living arrangements, find their parents to be an important source of emotional support, and experience considerable autonomy in the context of their parents' household (Arnett, 2000). The box on attachment and identity formation provides more detail on the relationship of **parental attachment** to identity formation in later adolescence.

The delay in age at marriage also has implications for the revision of the parental attachment relationship. When the majority of young people in the 20 to 24 age range were married, it was normal to expect that some of the emotional investment in one's family of origin would shift to the new intimate marital bond. Thus, emotional distancing from one's parents made sense in the context of forming a culturally approved marital commitment. Today, many young people have deeply valued love relationships, but they are not married and are not ready to make lifelong commitments to these relationships. This results in lengthening the period when both children and parents may feel that the child's primary emotional attachment is to the family of origin.

Autonomy and Self-Sufficiency

Despite the variety of life paths and demographic characteristics of those in the period of later adolescence, most young people can recognize when they have achieved a sense of autonomy from their parents. One important underlying theme is a sense of **self-sufficiency**, which is expressed by making independent decisions, taking responsibility for one's actions, and achieving a degree of financial independence. In order to gain a clearer idea of how college students and their parents view issues related to financial self-sufficiency, researchers asked students and their parents to select a question from a survey about autonomy and write why

they might disagree about this issue. One of the items was: "My parents will give me money when I ask for it." The following responses illustrate the point of view of a student who would like to be as financially self-sufficient as possible, and the point of view of a parent who wants her daughter to know that there are some limits to the kind of support she can expect (Kenyon & Koerner, 2009, p. 307).

> 18-YEAR-OLD FEMALE: I think one of the things we would disagree about is money. My father is helping me with rent, and both of my parents are helping me financially, when I need it. They want me to come to them if I need money, but I want to be able to do things on my own, without having to run to mommy or daddy whenever I need money. They don't mind helping me out, but I would like to try and get by on my own as much as I can. It will be easier when I get a job.
>
> 44-YEAR-OLD MOTHER: She will think that I will give her money for 99% of the things that she thinks is important and that is not going to be the case. I will give her money when she needs it for the important things that you need to live on or with. No shopping sprees for the heck of it!

With respect to financial independence, roughly 50% of college students who are enrolled full time are also employed. In a comparison of young people in the age range 22 to 26 in six countries including the United States and Canada, evidence suggests that over the past 20 years there has been a decline in the percentage of later adolescents who are able to support themselves as defined by wages and salary above 50% of the national adjusted disposable personal income for their country (Bell, Burtless, Gornick, & Smeeding, 2007). In 2007, 17.3% of those in the 18 to 24 age range had incomes below the poverty level. This rate varied by race/ethnicity: 15% of White adolescents, 28% of Black adolescents, 14% of Asian and Pacific Islanders, and 22% of Hispanics (U.S. Census Bureau, 2010). All these data contribute to the pattern of delays in self-sufficiency and the postponement of an independent lifestyle.

One obstacle to the sense of financial self-sufficiency is the increasing burden of debt faced by many college students. In addition to their student loans, 84% of students have credit cards. According to a survey conducted in 2009 by Sallie Mae, half of all college students have four credit cards or more. The median balance on these cards was $1,645. Seniors were graduating with an average balance of $4,100 and 20% of seniors owed $7,000 or more. Over 90% of college students reported charging educational expenses including books, supplies, and tuition on their credit cards (Sallie Mae, 2009; Woolsey & Schulz, 2010). Many students with credit card debt feel forced to put jobs ahead of school in order to keep up with payments, and when faced with academic hearings, some students mention working multiple jobs to pay on debts as reasons for poor academic performance. Consequences of credit card debt among college students may include working multiple jobs; dropping out of school; postponing graduate school; starting off careers

Attachment and Identity Formation

IDENTITY FORMATION IS usually viewed as a process that requires young people to distance themselves from the strong expectations and definitions imposed by parents and other family members. To achieve an individual identity, one must create a vision of the self that is authentic—a sense of having taken hold of one's destiny in an effort to reach goals that are personally meaningful. Yet research has demonstrated that the quality of family relationships contributes significantly to a young person's ability to achieve a personal identity (Allen & Land, 1999).

The relationship can be compared with the contribution of a secure attachment in infancy to a subsequent willingness to explore the environment. Securely attached infants will move away physically from their caregiver, confident that the caregiver will be available when they are in need of help. For later adolescents, autonomy-seeking behaviors can be interpreted as a more advanced form of the exploratory activities observed in infancy.

Later adolescents who have a secure relationship with their parents and who are comfortable in loosening these ties can begin to explore the ideological, occupational, and interpersonal alternatives that will become the content for their own identities.

Attachment to parents has been measured in later adolescence and adulthood using the *Adult Attachment Interview* (AAI), which asks participants to describe their relationship with their parents when they were younger, including specific memories of that relationship; recall incidences of distress in the relationship; and discuss factors that have influenced their relationship (George, Kaplan, & Main, 1996). The interview is then coded to characterize the attachment state of mind as (1) *autonomous*, which is reflective of an open, coherent narrative about the parent-child relationship; (2) *dismissive*, which is reflective of minimizing the importance of the parent-child relationship, inability to recall many details, and a tendency to idealize one's parents; or (3) *preoccupied*, which is reflective of continuing anger toward one's parents and a confused, vague, or passive narrative (Bernier et al., 2004). Interviews with students at the beginning and end of the first year of college found that the preoccupied students had the most difficulty adapting to college and actually did worse with respect to adjustment and grades as the year went along. These students had the greatest difficulty transferring their emotional investment from parents to peers, even if that investment was negative (Bernier et al., 2004).

Male and female college students who have a positive attachment to their mothers are more likely to have an achieved identity and are less likely to be in a moratorium or identity-confused status than are students who have insecure, mistrustful relationships with their mothers. On the other hand, those who are still emotionally dependent on their parents and require constant reassurance of their affection show a greater tendency to experience identity confusion (Benson, Harris, & Rogers, 1992).

By the time young people reach later adolescence, those who are securely attached to their parents are confident about parental affection and

with high debts; poor credit ratings leading to an inability to obtain loans, continue education, or acquire a job; and bankruptcy (Mannix, 1999; Norvilitis & Santa Maria, 2002; Lyons, 2004).

A sense of self-sufficiency goes beyond personal income. It is a subjective experience that is distinct from a person's living arrangement, student status, having a steady job, or being in a serious love relationship. A subjective sense of self-sufficiency is achieved gradually as young people face and meet important challenges of school, work, and family life and build a degree of confidence in their capacity to make good decisions.

The process of achieving autonomy from parents opens the door to new considerations of basic ego structures, including gender identity, morality, and career aspirations. In each of these areas, a young person has the opportunity to *decenter*—to step back from the close socialization pressures of family and neighborhood—and construct her own point of view. After a period of role experimentation and **introspection**, some may choose to adopt the framework that was in place at the end of the high school years. Others may invent novel and nontraditional perspectives. The growth that takes place during the period of later adolescence in each of these areas reflects a willingness to evaluate multiple perspectives and to integrate personal commitments with societal expectations and resources.

Gender Identity

Objective 2. To trace the development of gender identity in later adolescence, including a discussion of how the components of gender role identification that were relevant during the early-school-age period are revised and expanded.

In later adolescence, new and important revisions and elaborations of the child's earlier work on gender identification are taking place (see Chapter 7). The formulation of **gender identity** refers to the acquisition of a set of beliefs, attitudes, and values about oneself as a man or a woman in many areas

support. At the same time, they trust in their own worth and in their ability to make decisions (Blain, Thompson, & Whiffen, 1993). In a study comparing university students who lived with their parents with those who lived away from home, those who lived away from their parents experienced more daily life challenges, but they also used more effective problem-solving strategies to address those challenges. In comparison to students who lived at home, those who lived away from their parents had made more progress in the formation of their personal identity, suggesting that the pressures toward self-reliance may contribute to the clarification of values and commitments (Jordyn & Byrd, 2003). Later adolescents may make a point of *not* seeking parental support, but in a secure relationship, they know that help is available if needed. By imposing emotional distance and achieving greater self-reliance, later adolescents are able to reach a more objective evaluation of their parents as figures for identification and, thereby, to create the needed space for the emergence of their own identity (Kobak, 1999).

A secure parental attachment fosters identity formation in the following ways:

- It fosters confidence in the exploration of social relationships, ideologies, and settings.
- It establishes positive expectations in regard to interpersonal experiences outside the family.
- It fosters the formation of group identities apart from the family, thus providing a transitional context for work on individual identity.
- It provides a basic layer of self-acceptance, permitting the young person to approach the process of identity formation with optimism.

Critical Thinking Questions

1. How does the typology of *preoccupied* attachment correspond to the attachment styles described in the section on infant attachment in Chapter 5? What do you think the psychology of the preoccupied students is like? Why might they have the greatest difficulty adjusting to college?
2. What is the relationship between a secure attachment in infancy and an autonomous attachment in later

adolescence? What kinds of behaviors and attitudes would you expect to see among students who have an autonomous attachment style?
3. How might the formation of an anxious avoidant, an anxious resistant, or a disorganized attachment in infancy relate to work on identity in later adolescence?
4. What might be some trade-offs between living at home with parents and living on campus with respect to identity formation and self-acceptance? How might cultural differences with regard to the values of independence and interdependence influence the outcomes of this decision?
5. How would you describe the optimal balance between autonomy from parents and connection to parents during the college years? What should parents do to try to achieve this balance? What should students do to try to achieve this balance? What should colleges and universities do to help families achieve this balance?
6. What might be the impact of the three different attachment styles—autonomous, dismissive, and preoccupied—on later adolescents' efforts to establish romantic relationships?

of social life, including intimate relations, family, work, community, and religion. The developmental task of forming one's gender identity reflects the need to integrate and synthesize the three basic components of gender—its biological, psychological, and social meanings—into a view of oneself as a man or a woman entering the complex social world of adult life.

The Role of Culture

As discussed in Chapter 3, according to social role theory, *roles* are basic building blocks of social organizations. Every organization, including a family, a workplace, a community, and a culture, can be described by its roles. Individuals learn the roles of their social system throughout their lives. Through the socialization process, people internalize the expectations associated with many life roles and apply the socially shared norms and standards linked to these roles to their own behaviors. This process occurs with respect to gender-related roles as well as to kinship, age, occupation, and other socially constructed roles. For example, when a person becomes a parent, a man is called a *father* and a

woman is called a *mother*. Both are parenting roles, but gender is identified, and each role is associated with somewhat different expectations.

All cultures construct gender-differentiated roles, and people expect one another to behave in certain ways because they are male or female. Perhaps more important, they form expectations of how men and women ought to act when they are together, so that the distinctions between the genders are demarcated (Freud, 1994). These expectations are taught and learned, beginning early in life. For later adolescents, the gendered nature of the family is an especially important factor in shaping gender identity. Family experiences from the past provide the gender script with which they are most familiar. The family life they envision for themselves in the future creates many of the priorities that shape their current commitments and goals (Valsiner, 2000).

In the United States, many people argue that gender-based role distinctions are inappropriate, at least as a part of public life. They believe that men and women should be considered equal and treated identically in all public matters. But in many cultures, there are distinct, agreed-upon norms

Cultures construct gender-differentiated roles. In the United States, the traditional attire of the bride and groom symbolize ideal images of feminine beauty and masculine respectability to which many young people aspire.

prescribing differences in how men and women are treated, which tasks they are expected to perform, and what status they hold in their family and community. Often, these norms establish specific power differences as part of the gender distinctions. Typically, men have more power than women, but this is not always the case.

Others argue that men and women should be considered equal, but that they should be treated in ways that take into account the differences in their needs and capacities. For example, a bill introduced in the U.S. Congress required that all public places, such as auditoriums, stadiums, and theaters, have twice as many public bathroom facilities for women as for men to take into account the physiological and social differences in women's toileting practices.

In the United States, and in many other industrialized nations, people are engaged in a wide-ranging dialogue about the scientific, legal, and sociohistorical bases of gender roles that is leading to a revision—perhaps even a revolution— in how gender serves as an organizing social structure. Although this dialogue takes place across many groups and in many contexts, there is still powerful pressure on young people to achieve their own personal gender identity. They may be influenced by voices and views in the larger society; however, later adolescents must decide for themselves about

the meaning they will make of their own designation as male or female. The box on human development and diversity introduces the concept of the third gender, an idea that illustrates alternative pathways toward gender identity that exist in many cultures.

Reevaluating Gender Constancy

Each of the components of gender identification discussed in Chapter 7 undergoes some transformation as work on gender identity continues. Later adolescents can appreciate that the use of gender labels is a social convention and that, apart from the genital basis of this label, there are wide individual differences *within* gender groups in most traits and abilities. Moreover, information about genetic anomalies and medical technologies may lead later adolescents to realize that it is possible to have a conflict between one's genetic **sex** and one's external genitalia.

Transsexuals develop a gender identity that is opposite to their biological sex. They feel certain of their gender, which is at odds with their genital features. In these cases, the possibility of a sex-change operation provides an alternative to the notion of gender constancy (Crooks & Bauer, 2005). One study followed the adjustment of 20 adolescent transsexuals who had experienced sex-reassignment surgery. In the 1 to 4 years following treatment, these young people were functioning well, and none of them expressed regrets about their decision (Smith, van Goozen, & Cohen-Kettenis, 2001). Later adolescents may realize that one's sex is not quite as fixed and constant as they may have believed. Furthermore, those who experience psychological conflict about their gender may learn that a new designation is not only possible but desirable.

Reevaluating Earlier Gender Role Standards and Learning New Ones

Gender role expectations exist at the cultural, institutional, interpersonal, and individual levels. As later adolescents learn about these expectations, they must integrate and synthesize them with their assessments of their personal needs and goals. The content of gender role standards—that is, the cultural and subcultural expectations concerning the appropriate behavior of male and female individuals—is different for later adolescents than for young children. This content changes as a result of changing age-related expectations and social change. For a 6- or 7-year-old boy, it may have been important to learn to be tough and not to cry or whimper, to stand up for himself, and not to hit girls. For a young man in later adolescence, the gender role expectations may include holding a steady job, demonstrating sexual prowess, or being competitive. For a 6- or 7-year-old girl, on the other hand, the emphasis may have been on taking turns, not being too bossy, and staying clean. For a young woman in later adolescence, gender role expectations may focus on being a caring, supportive friend; expressing maternal, nurturant behavior; or having an attractive figure and knowing how to dress well.

© Philip Newman

In later adolescence, young men and women begin to develop an analysis of what it takes to get ahead in their social world, whether success is defined as finding a mate, getting a good job, being a good parent, or being popular. They may learn to be more flexible in their interpersonal behavior, modifying their strategy to suit their goals. They discover that such traits as assertiveness, goal-directed behavior, competitiveness, being a good communication partner, personal disclosure, and negotiation are all required in social situations, and they learn to develop and apply them as required. In previous generations, some of the aforementioned traits were considered masculine and some feminine. Today, however, they are perceived as helpful to both men and women to be able to succeed in work and family life.

Gender role standards may change from one generation to the next, so that parents who are socializing their children may have grown up with one set of gender-role expectations, but their children may enter later adolescence with a very different set of norms and expectations. For example, in a national survey of college freshmen, students were asked to respond to a number of statements about attitudes and values. One of those statements was, "Activities of married women are best confined to home and family." In 1970, 48% of freshmen agreed with that statement; in 2004, only 21% of freshmen agreed (U.S. Bureau of the Census, 1996; *Chronicle of Higher Education*, 2005). One could speculate that many of the parents who were college freshmen in the 1970s had more traditional gender role attitudes than their children have today. Historical trends modify the outlook of both men and women on their appropriate and normative roles.

As one considers the contemporary context of gender role expectations, it appears that the main U.S. culture is moving toward more flexible standards. For example, it is recognized that it benefits both men and women in the workplace to be appropriately assertive and to be sensitive communicators. Many gender-stereotyped expectations about behaviors that are appropriate for men or women have been relaxed and replaced by a greater diversity of behavior that is considered acceptable for both men and women in our society. The greatest impact of this revision is on the later adolescent population as they formulate their gender identities. There are more options, choices, and goals, and fewer obstacles to expressing personal preferences.

Within this context of greater freedom from gender role stereotypes, however, certain ethnic groups face new conflicts between adhering to traditional cultural expectations and embracing gender roles that are less scripted. For example, Latinas experience a strong cultural emphasis on the role of women as mothers who are nurturant, virtuous, and devoted to their husbands and children. This gender role standard places pressure on them to restrict their occupational aspirations and to remain close to their family of origin, particularly when it comes to thinking about going to college or planning a career (Chilman, 1993). In later adolescence, Latinas must review these expectations, weighing the benefits they have had from this kind of close, attentive mothering with their own changing desire for higher levels of educational and occupational attainment. As economic demands and educational opportunities have expanded, Latinas have found ways to satisfy their community's traditional expectations while still claiming some space for their own personal goals (Denner & Dunbar, 2004).

Revising Childhood Identifications

The component of parental identification that contributes to gender identity is also reviewed and revised in later adolescence. During this time, young people begin to encounter a wide range of possible targets for identification. In the college environment, students meet teachers, residence hall counselors, and older students whose views and values may differ widely from those of their parents. Outside the college environment, workers meet supervisors, other workers, and social companions whose views and values may differ widely from those of their parents. Later adolescents may admire public figures, such as religious leaders, political leaders, artists, or scholars whose work and ideas are especially inspiring. In the process, later adolescents revisit the content of their parental identifications. They analyze those beliefs, attitudes, and values that they may have swallowed whole as children, evaluating which of them are still relevant to their own personal vision of themselves functioning as a man or a woman in their current situation. They try to determine whether the lessons they learned as children about how husbands and wives, fathers and mothers, and men and women treat each other and think about each other remain applicable.

Adding a Sexual Dimension to Gender Identity

In addition to revisions in parental identifications, later adolescents add a sexual dimension to their gender identity. Biological changes of puberty, including changes in reproductive capacities, secondary sex characteristics, body shape, height, weight, and strength, must be incorporated into one's gender identity.

Satisfaction with one's physical appearance provides an important basis for approaching social relations with a positive, optimistic outlook (Abell & Richards, 1996). Furthermore, it may influence one's attractiveness or initial desirability as a sexual partner. In contrast, dissatisfaction with one's physical appearance as integrated into the self-concept may interfere with the formation of positive social relationships, causing the person to approach interpersonal contacts with self-consciousness and a pessimistic expectation that he will be rejected.

Maturation of the hormonal system, which influences emotional arousal as well as sexual urges, contributes to the development of one's gender identity. The hormonal changes of puberty bring new sexual impulses as well as the capacity

HUMAN DEVELOPMENT AND DIVERSITY

Third Genders

BIOLOGICALLY, HUMANS MAY be sexually dimorphic, but in many cultures there is evidence of alternatives that expand on the dualistic perspective of male and female gender. Three examples of cultural traditions that have *third gender* categories are provided here as a way of illustrating the potential diversity of gender concepts. Many more examples can be found in anthropological writings (Nanda, 2001). Even as cultures differ in the norms that are associated with the male and female gender roles, many cultures include alternatives to the traditional male and female categories. These alternatives broaden the possibilities for pathways that individuals may follow as they crystallize their gender identity.

In Oman, a country in the Persian Gulf, *Xanith* is a term used to refer to biological males who function mostly as women (Nanda, 1998). In some Middle Eastern countries, this term is used as insulting slang for effeminate men. When asked, *Xanith* say they are women, but they are not entirely like women according to Omani standards. *Xanith* behavior falls in between that of men and women. Under Islamic law, *Xanith* have all the rights of men and are allowed to worship with the men at the mosque, yet they are allowed to visit with women, eat with women, and walk arm in arm with women. The facial expressions, voice, laugh, movements, and swaying walk of the *Xanith* imitate those of women, but they wear clothing that is a mixture of men's and women's styles. *Xanith* are prohibited by law from wearing some women's clothing, including the mask and veil that all adult women must wear. A *Xanith* wears the ankle-length tunic typical for men, but it is belted tightly at the waist as a woman might do. In Oman both men and women cover their heads, but *Xanith* go bareheaded. Unlike women, *Xanith* move around freely outside their houses, though only during the day. Most importantly, *Xanith* are openly prostitutes, an activity that is not acknowledged for Omani woman. Thus, the *Xanith* demonstrate a third gender role in many aspects of their public self-presentation.

In India and Pakistan, the *Hijra* provide another example of a third gender. The *Hijra* have an ancient tradition, inspired in part by the Hindu deity, Shiva. Shiva is sometimes portrayed as half male, half female. The Sanskrit name for this form of the deity, *Ardhanārīśvara*, is best translated as "the lord who is half woman." This image is used to symbolize the idea that the sacred powers of the universe are both feminine and masculine (Pettis, 2004). Thus, Hindu thought allows for overlapping and even contradictory categories that support flexibility in

The *Hijra* of India are men who think of themselves as both male and female.

---

for reproduction. Hormonal changes may also contribute to changes in the basis of relationships. These changes call attention to new emotions, such as jealousy, love, depression over loss of love, sexual arousal, and passion. Individual differences in hormone levels are linked to gender role characteristics.

The general term for male sex hormones is **androgens**, the most prevalent of which is *testosterone*. Androgens, especially testosterone, are associated with sexual arousal, interest, and behavior. This relationship is observed in both men and women. For men, higher levels of androgens are associated with both increased sexual motivation and increased involvement in sexual activity. For women, higher levels of androgens are associated with increased sexual motivation, but **estrogens** appear to be implicated in their willingness to engage in sexual activity. This may be a result of the fact that estrogens contribute to the maturation of primary and secondary sex characteristics that make women more sexually attractive. In general, hormone levels are not as good a predictor of sexual activity for women as are the social contexts of family and peer group and the woman's own internalized standards about sexual behavior (Savin-Williams & Diamond, 2004).

The domain of sexual activity is one of the few remaining vestiges of the double standard for male and female gender roles. As we pointed out in Chapter 9, it has become normative for both males and females to engage in sexual intercourse during their adolescence. However, there is a persistent set of social norms that advantages males who are sexually active, and places sexually active females at risk for damaging their reputation. A male who is known to have multiple sexual partners may be viewed as a stud, whereas a female who is known to have multiple sexual partners may be viewed as easy, fast, or a slut.

gender roles. In general, *Hijra* are men who dress in women's clothing, but do not try to hide their masculine features. When asked, they say they are not trying to be women, but view themselves as both male and female. In some writings, the *Hijra* are described as eunuchs; and some do undergo surgeries to have their male genitalia removed. They appear at weddings, usually uninvited, to sing and dance and bring wishes for fertility. They expect to be paid for these performances, and usually they are. *Hijras* refer to themselves using feminine pronouns and expect others to do so. They typically live together in a commune arrangement of five or more chelas (disciples), supervised by a guru.

Among American Indian tribes, the two-spirit person is a native tradition that anthropologists have associated with some of the earliest discoveries of native artifacts. Before colonization and contact with European cultures, Native people believed in the existence of three genders: the male, the female, and the male-female gender, or what is now called the two-spirit person, a term derived from interpretations of Native languages used to describe people who displayed both male and female characteristics (Project Interaction, 2010). In the religious views of many Native people, humans are seen as minor relatives of goddesses and gods. When a human person is born, only one or the other spirit usually comes into substance, into life on Earth—the other half remains in the spirit world as a higher self. A woman may have her hidden male side, and a man may have his female side. Traditionally, the two-spirited person was one who had received a gift from the Creator, the privilege to house both male and female spirits in the body. Being given the gift of two spirits meant that this individual had the ability to see the world from two perspectives at the same time. This greater vision was a gift to be shared with all, and as such, two-spirited beings were revered as leaders, mediators, teachers, artists, seers, and spiritual guides. They were treated with the greatest respect, and held important spiritual and ceremonial responsibilities (Warren, 1998).

These examples extend our thinking about gender. They illustrate cultural strategies for formalizing alternative understandings about gender. In some cultures and at certain times in history, people who embrace these alternatives have been persecuted or reviled; but in other cultures and at other times, people who claim a third gender identity have been recognized as having special powers or insights.

Critical Thinking Questions

1. What are your reactions to the idea of a third gender? How does the concept of a third gender fit with your own understanding of gender identity? Is it possible to be neither male nor female? Or both male and female?

2. Why might many indigenous people or cultures have conceived of a social identity for people who combine male and female qualities?

3. Whereas third gender individuals were respected and acknowledged as having their own social space in many non-Western cultures, individuals who exhibit these characteristics have been ostracized and stigmatized in many Western societies. Why is that?

INTERVIEWER: What do you think about girls or boys who sleep around?

BOY RESPONDENT: (Girls?) Sluts, basically. Because they have a mattress on their back, they like having sex. That's the way I look at it, no two ways about it. Boys? A stud. Good luck to him. It's OK for a guy to be like that. I don't have to have sex with a guy, so I don't care. That's what the difference is.

GIRL RESPONDENT: (Girls?) I think they are sluts basically. (Boys?) They are different to girls because they like competing against others, like [a] peer group pressure type of thing. When a guy does something, the other guys do it, too. They also like bragging, I think. (Moore & Rosenthal, 2006, p. 143)

There is growing concern about the sexual and reproductive health of young people in their early twenties (Boonstra, 2009). Later adolescents are more likely than those in their late twenties and thirties to be involved in multiple sexual relationships, with little intention of permanency or desire for having children. The birthrate to unmarried females in the age range 20 to 24 increased from 1990 to 2006. In 2006 there were 636,000 births to unmarried women in this age range, and approximately 400,000 abortions (U.S. Census Bureau, 2010). Roughly 25% of males under age 25 have fathered a child (Sonfield, 2002). Later adolescent males are at especially high risk for sexually transmitted infections (STIs), with 500 to 600 new cases of chlamydia and gonorrhea each year per 100,000 men in their early twenties. In 2007, there were 1,927 documented cases of AIDS and 4,907 newly diagnosed cases of HIV among those 20 to 24 years of age in the United States (Centers for Disease Control and Prevention, 2010b). As a group, later adolescents are more on the move, less connected to a specific community, and therefore less linked to health care services that might meet their needs. Until the recent change in health care policy in the United States, which allowed children to remain on their parent's health insurance policy until age 26, later adolescents have been an especially vulnerable group when it comes to having a health provider and health insurance. This results in reduced access to reproductive health care and delayed treatment for STIs.

Sexual Orientation

Sexual orientation refers to the erotic, romantic, and affectionate attraction to people of the same sex, the opposite sex, or both sexes (Sexuality Information and Education Council of the United States [SEICUS], 2001). Sexual orientation can be understood along a continuum from completely heterosexual to bisexual to completely homosexual preferences. Regardless of their biological sex or gender identity, people can be sexually attracted to men, attracted to women, attracted to both, or attracted to neither.

Gender identity refers to the meaning a person makes of being male or female and to the internalization of attitudes, beliefs, and values associated with male and female behaviors. Four terms that are often used in discussing gender identity are masculinity, femininity, androgyny, and transgendered. **Masculinity** is typically associated with being instrumental and *agentic* (i.e., having leadership abilities, being assertive, taking control); **femininity** is typically associated with being expressive and *communal* (i.e., valuing interpersonal and spiritual development, being tender, sympathetic, and concerned about the well-being of others). **Androgyny** refers to the capacity to express both masculine and feminine characteristics as the situation demands. Androgynous men score high in both masculine and feminine characteristics in comparison to other men; androgynous women score high in both masculine and feminine characteristics in comparison to other women (Bem, 1993). **Transgendered** refers to people who do not identify with or present themselves as reflecting the sex they were born with and who move across or combine gender boundaries. Knowing a person's gender identity does not allow one to predict sexual orientation.

Research on sexual orientation suggests that later adolescence is a common time for the crystallization of a sexual identity. During this time, young people begin a more active process of integrating their sexual fantasies, experiences of sexual arousal, and understanding about sexual behavior into a sexual identity (Herold & Marshall, 1996). Later adolescents who may have struggled with acknowledging and accepting their homosexual orientation during the high school period are likely to resolve these inner conflicts and disclose their sexual orientation to others. This process is fostered by support from at least one close person and by increasing involvement in the gay community. Although disclosure has its risks, failure to disclose or trying to continue to pass as heterosexual is typically associated with strong feelings of isolation and self-repudiation (Troiden, 1993).

The crystallization of gender identity requires the integration of one's sexuality, including physical appearance, primary and secondary sex characteristics, sexual drives, and fantasies. One's sexual identity is as much a mental representation as a physical reality.

Much of the progress on identifying one's sexual orientation takes place in the context of romantic relationships. In many early writings about the nature of homosexual couples, the concepts of gender identity and sexual orientation were blurred. One stereotype about homosexual relationships is that they are gendered like traditionally imagined heterosexual relationships—one partner playing the dominant role and the other partner playing the submissive role. Studies of same-sex couples reject this view. Lesbian and gay couples tend to have more equality in their relationships and greater flexibility than comparable heterosexual couples. Because the partners are of the same sex, they cannot rely on traditional gender role stereotypes to define their functions in the household. Rather, they have to find solutions that meet their personal preferences and competencies and try to adapt to the constraints of other work or school commitments (Kurdek, 1995). In one study comparing gay and lesbian couples with cross-sex cohabiting couples, same-sex and mixed-sex couples who lived together appeared to be quite similar with respect to their satisfaction as a couple. One noted difference was that the lesbian couples and the heterosexual men were more satisfied with the emotional expressiveness in their relationships and the amount of leisure time they spent together than were the

Girl Before a Mirror, 1932/Pablo Picasso/© 2011 Estate of Pablo Picasso/Artists Rights Society (ARS), New York/SuperStock

gay men or the heterosexual women (Means-Christensen, Snyder, & Negy, 2003).

When viewed through a gendered lens, men tend to be more instrumental, achievement oriented, autonomous, and assertive than women; women tend to be more expressive, interpersonally oriented, and caring than men. Based on these gender differences, another misconception is that lesbian relationships are more likely to be *fused*, suffering from too great a need for connection, and gay relationships are more likely to suffer from *disengagement* and disruption. Research suggests that this description is overly simplistic. Just like heterosexual men and women, lesbians and gay men differ in their gender identities. As later adolescents engage in intimate relationships, the nature of their gender identity is clarified. Within the context of lesbian or gay relationships, the interaction between the partners helps each person clarify gender identity. The conflicts that gay and lesbian partners experience with respect to power, decision making, sharing of responsibilities, disclosure, and closeness are not unlike the conflicts that heterosexual couples face as they take on roles and responsibilities in their relationship (Green, Bettinger, & Zachs, 1996).

Integrating One's Gender Identity

During later adolescence, young men and women formulate their gender identities as they encounter diverse and sometimes competing social messages, role relationships, sexual motives and activities, and dyadic interactions. These gender identities are situated in interpersonal, institutional, and cultural contexts. One of the salient factors contributing to the emergence of gender identity is **gender role preference**. This preference is based on an assessment of two factors: how well one can meet the cultural and social expectations associated with one's gender, and how positively one views the status associated with it. The idea of **gender typicality** was introduced in Chapter 7. As the norms for gender-related expectations shift, later adolescents may revise their view of whether their own traits, preferences, and talents are typical for their gender. Their view of gender typicality may become more differentiated. For example, Laura realizes that she has personal ambitions for career success and the accumulation of wealth that are not typical of other women in her friendship group or her family. Yet, she still sees herself as fitting in with her female friends and spending time in shared activities, including shopping for new clothes, volunteering at the senior center, and playing tennis. Her friends tease her about wanting to make her first million dollars by the age of 25, but they admire her for it as well. As her personal identity becomes clearer, she can accept that she is similar to other women in many respects and different from them in others.

Later adolescents can view themselves as personally and socially typical of their gender, and still not be satisfied with their gender if the culture or context assigns a low status to their gender. If later adolescents become aware that their gender prevents them from having access to resources, influence, and decision-making authority, they are likely to experience a decline in their gender role preference. This could happen to men as well as women, depending on the paths they choose to pursue and the gender biases they encounter. For example, in general, we tend to think of career aspirations as being stifled for women as a result of attitudes on the part of men who think that women are not suited to certain types of work. However, the reverse situation may apply to men who are interested in fields such as early childhood education or nursing.

If later adolescents perceive that, apart from real differences in ability, one gender group is treated with greater respect, given more opportunities, and responded to with more attention or greater rewards, then their gender role preferences are likely to be recalibrated. During the high school years, adolescent girls are likely to encounter stereotyped expectations that restrict their behavior, judge their appearance, or label them as sluts. Sometimes, these stereotypes intersect with race and social class, especially as they encounter negative expectations from teachers or suspiciousness from shopkeepers (Abrams, 2003). Strict cultural norms regarding femininity, especially about body type and sexual behavior, can result in negative affect and alienation. Although some young women give in to these pressures, others resist, refusing to give up their voice or their autonomy in the face of adult judgments:

> Well, a lot of adults—they look at me kinda like, "ooh, she's like really crazy looking," or something like that. And my mom always says "oh, people are gonna think you're a bad girl." And I'm like "Whatever. I don't care." (Abrams, 2003, p. 71)

It appears that college students do not see much of this type of gender discrimination or preference. They tend to view the college environment as providing many opportunities and equal access to resources for both male and female students. Moreover, both male and female students feel equally oppressed by the stressors of college life and the uncertainties associated with the decisions they are trying to make. Typically, it is not until they enter the world of adult employment that they begin to experience the power differential that continues to operate to the benefit of White men in U.S. society (Heilman, 2001).

Later adolescents who enter the world of work at the end of high school are confronted by the power differential immediately and may experience intimidation that forces them to accept it. For example, a woman who makes $2 per hour less than a male counterpart may be afraid to say anything because she needs the job. She will have to integrate the reality of what she experiences into the formulation of her gender identity. One strategy is to accept that this is the way things should be according to gender role norms—that women should defer to men, and their contributions should be treated as less worthwhile. Another strategy may be to look for a different kind of work, in a setting where women and men are paid equally.

The college population tends to set social trends by according more variety and less rigidity to sex-linked role expectations. Most studies find that during the college years, students become more flexible in their gender role attitudes and more egalitarian in their views about how men and women ought to function in school, work, family, and community life. On the other hand, the noncollege population tends to set employment trends by breaking down barriers in many male-dominated areas of work, such as construction, trucking, and public safety. Individuals can shape and strengthen the nature of their gender identity by spending time with other people who support their views and values about how men and women ought to behave toward one another and what life paths are most desirable for them.

Internalized Morality

Objective 3. To describe the maturation of morality in later adolescence, with special focus on the role of new cognitive capacities that influence moral judgments and the various value orientations that underlie moral reasoning.

The development of morality was introduced in Chapter 7. In early school age, morality consists primarily of internalizing parental standards and values, recognizing the difference between right and wrong, and learning to control one's behavior in anticipation of its moral consequences. As young people achieve new levels of autonomy from their parents and encounter new situations, they discover that some of the moral principles they learned as 6- or 7-year-olds neither apply to the new situation nor provide much of a rationale for why they should behave one way and not another. Later adolescents explore the distinction between *social conventions* and *moral issues*. Behaviors that may have been viewed as moral issues during childhood may be reevaluated as social conventions. The domain of personal preference or personal choice expands, resulting in a reorganization of one's moral thinking.

Within the overall process of formulating a personal identity, later adolescents begin to see themselves as moral beings whose actions have implications for the well-being of others. They make moral commitments and judge their behavior and the behavior of others according to new moral standards (Damon, 1996, 2000). In the framework of forming a moral identity, the three elements of morality—judgment, caring, and action—come together in an increasingly complex political, social, and interpersonal environment (Nucci & Turiel, 2009). Morality may be expressed in a variety of behaviors, including acts of consideration and kindness; resistance to temptation; opposition to unfair laws, rules, or practices; and contributions of time, money, or other resources to enhance the well-being of others. The following sections examine Kohlberg's analysis regarding advances in **moral reasoning**, experiences that promote moral reasoning, and the expansion of research on moral development, which includes prosocial behavior and the ethics of care.

New Cognitive Capacities

Later adolescents bring new cognitive capacities to the arena of moral decision making. They are able to use abstract reasoning to consider the logical consequences of their actions, both for themselves and for others. They can project alternative paths in a probabilistic future. They are also able to consider the multiple perspectives that are possible in a moral situation. Most societies are structured around certain group inequalities in power, resources, and freedoms. Later adolescents can consider how resistance against certain laws, rules, or normative practices by a subordinated group, such as women or ethnic minorities, might be viewed as morally justified by the less powerful group and morally wrong by the dominant group (Turiel, 2006). Later adolescents are increasingly aware of the rights and needs of others, and they are able to step outside the situation in order to examine how an action may satisfy their own needs but harm others. Later adolescents can reflect about how principles of social responsibility, human rights, and justice can be preserved in a moral decision.

Stages of Moral Reasoning. Building on Piaget's theory of cognitive development, Kohlberg (1964, 1969; Colby & Kohlberg, 1987) suggested that a qualitative change in a person's ability to reason about moral issues is expected from early school age to later adolescence. With age and exposure to moral conflicts, moral reasoning advances in much the same way that other domains of logical reasoning mature, from an early reliance on direct perceptions and immediate consequences to more complex, abstract, and relativistic judgments. Kohlberg's theory includes three levels of moral reasoning divided into six substages (see Chapter 7, Table 7.2).

At Stage I, the **preconventional level**, from about age 4 to 10, children judge an action as morally justifiable based on the immediate consequences of the behavior and the approval of powerful authority figures. Stage II, the **conventional level**, from about age 10 to 18, reflects a concern about the maintenance of the existing rules and laws, and a respect for legitimate authority. Stage III, the **postconventional level** of moral reasoning, from about age 18 into adulthood, brings an awareness of social, cultural, and political processes that result in the formulation of rules and laws. Morality is viewed as a system of rules that are agreed upon in order to preserve human rights and social order. These rules are understood as having been created in cultural and historical contexts, and can be altered as the norms of the community change. Beyond this appreciation for the **cultural relativism** of moral principles, there may emerge a commitment to overarching universal moral principles, including greater concern for the value of human life, human dignity, and justice for all members of society.

The proportion of people who reach this final level of moral reasoning is small, but it increases during early and middle adulthood.

Longitudinal data provide evidence of the sequential nature of these stages during childhood and adolescence (Nisan & Kohlberg, 1982; Colby, Kohlberg, Gibbs, & Lieberman, 1983; Snarey, Reimer, & Kohlberg, 1985; Colby & Kohlberg, 1987). The sequence of stages proposed by Kohlberg is noted in a variety of cultures outside the United States. Research confirming this has been done in Israel, Turkey, the Bahamas, Honduras, Mexico, India, Kenya, Nigeria, and Taiwan. Participants in these studies used forms of reasoning similar to those used by U.S. samples. The adults and adolescents in every culture used levels of reasoning that were higher than those used by the children (Nisan & Kohlberg, 1982; Rest, 1983; Snarey et al., 1985; Colby & Kohlberg, 1987; Dawson, 2002). The stages reflect qualitatively distinct ways of reasoning about moral dilemmas that are supported by increasingly complex cognitive capacities (Dawson, 2003).

Experiences That Promote Moral Reasoning. Later adolescents must formulate an integrated value system with which to guide their behavior, particularly in the face of strong pressures to violate their moral beliefs. Young people encounter situations that they have never faced before—situations that require moral evaluation, judgment, and decisions about action. College students may be asked to lend a paper that they have written so that another student can turn it in as her own work. Dilemmas about using illegal drugs, stealing books and journals from the library, or maintaining religious traditions and practices may confront a young person who is away from home for the first time. In these situations, the young person has the opportunity to envision the self as a moral actor and take a course of action most congruent with other facets of his personal identity.

Although the *sequence* of moral stages appears to be well established, the level of moral reasoning that an individual actually attains depends on the kinds of moral challenges and situations encountered. For college students, like the one in the following example, the academic curriculum itself often creates a degree of cognitive disequilibrium that promotes a revision in moral reasoning:

I was taking a theology class as a freshman in college and was presented with "bold" alternatives to understand and interpret the creation story—primarily to understand it as a myth. My life up to that point was characterized by asking many questions but arriving at few answers. To those in my fundamentalist background, those questions were annoyances but not insurmountable problems. In my shift to some answers to those questions, I moved away from fundamentalism to a more broadly based and responsible manner of critical thinking. The professor was very bright and responsible, yet in a sophisticated way he was somewhat irreverent. I was troubled by the dilemmas that this posed for me in terms of my belief structures, but something

about the information and the self-assurance of the professor encouraged me to embrace this new way of thinking. (Chickering & Reisser, 1993, p. 240)

Through participation in thought-provoking discussions or challenging life experiences, moral reasoning can advance to the next higher level. Social and educational experiences tend to promote moral reasoning when they draw on existing constructs, but they also challenge those constructs by making their inadequacies clear. During later adolescence, young people are exposed to a broader social context at work, in their college courses, or through greater involvement in community and national affairs.

Many young people participate in community service, such as volunteering at a soup kitchen or tutoring younger children in reading or math (Seider, 2007). These experiences can stimulate discussions about differing points of view and a more complex analysis of the many interdependent factors that contribute to the social order. Many communities have established youth development programs that involve adolescents in community service. As a result, a growing number of young people are likely to have new insights into moral situations (Yates & Youniss, 1996; Nasir & Kirshner, 2003). In a study of 12,000 college students, Sax & Astin (1997) found that participation in community service during college had long-term consequences for adult involvement in volunteering, community activism, and helping others. A student at UCLA described her experiences:

As a volunteer for the UCLA Medical Center, my conversations with chronically ill patients made me realize the profound emotional drain caused by long-term hospitalization. With each visit, I wished there was something more than my compassion that I could use to bring vibrancy and warmth back into these patients' lives. In 2004, I used my background playing the piano and flute to create the volunteer organization, Music to Heal, through which I arrange for student musicians to bring music into the lives of hospital patients. (Mahanian, 2008, p. 27)

Exposure to a diversity of information, relationships, and worldviews stimulates moral reasoning. The change from **conventional** to **postconventional morality** that begins during adolescence involves a rethinking of traditional moral principles. During this period, there may be a loosening of ties to the family of origin and an increase in encounters with an expanding network of friends, students, and coworkers. Through interactions with diverse reference groups, there is an increasing recognition of the subcultural relativity of one's moral code. There may also be a degree of conflict over which moral values have personal meaning.

Expansions of Kohlberg's View of Moral Development

Kohlberg's view of moral development focuses on reasoning or moral knowledge, not on the emotional or behavioral aspects of morality. One criticism of the theory is that studies do not find a consistent relationship between a person's level of moral reasoning and that person's willingness to behave in a morally caring way. For example, several studies have taken the approach of identifying **moral exemplars**—people who have dedicated themselves to improving the lives of others—and comparing them to others who are not especially exemplary (Hart & Fegley, 1995). The moral exemplars are not more complex or advanced in their *reasoning* than the comparison group. What the exemplars demonstrate is a **moral identity**—a sense in which they define themselves in moral terms and evaluate their behavior against moral standards. Moral identity reflects an integration of parental socialization about caring for others, an appreciation for the cultural and social contexts of moral actions, and experiences that have required moral action (Colby & Damon, 1999; Reimer, 2003).

A second criticism of Kohlberg's approach to understanding moral development is that his theory is based on a specific method that emphasizes **prohibitive moral judgments**, in which a person is asked to reach a decision about violating a law or breaking a promise in order to achieve some other goal. A typical example is the case of Heinz, a man who is faced with the dilemma of having to steal a drug from a pharmacist if he is to save his wife's life. These dilemmas place justice—usually framed in terms of the legitimate needs or rights of the individual—in conflict with rules, laws, authority figures, and the obligations associated with adhering to these rules or laws.

Not all moral dilemmas are of this type, however. Some moral judgments involve a conflict between doing something helpful for someone else and meeting one's own needs. An example would be stopping to help a person whose car has stalled on the highway at the risk of being late for a very important job interview. These dilemmas are described as **prosocial moral judgments**. The prosocial aspect of morality includes a concern for the welfare and rights of others and a willingness to act in order to benefit or enhance the lives of others. Just as society depends on people adhering to rules and laws in order to preserve order, it also depends on a commitment to caring. People seem to be able to think more flexibly about a prosocial moral dilemma than about a prohibitive one. Moral decisions that draw on empathy and concern for the well-being of another person tend to evoke a higher level of moral reasoning than those that would require breaking a law (Eisenberg & Strayer, 1987; Eisenberg & Fabes, 1998).

Expanding on the theme of prosocial morality, Carol Gilligan (1977, 1982/1993, 1988) challenged Kohlberg's perspective, arguing that his description of the developmental course of reasoning about moral dilemmas is incomplete because it is based largely on the reasoning of male respondents about hypothetical rather than real-life situations. She claimed that men and women have distinct orientations toward moral dilemmas. According to Gilligan, women approach moral decisions with greater sensitivity to the

context of the problem and a strong sense of **caring**, focusing on one's responsibility for others and feelings of connection to them. Gilligan asserted that men, in contrast, emphasize abstract principles, rules, and laws, and the conflicts between the rights of the parties involved in the conflict. A woman, for example, might ask which outcome of a moral dilemma would result in the least harm for all concerned, whereas a man might ask whether one person has the right to infringe on the rights of others (Friedman, Robinson, & Friedman, 1987). These differences, according to Gilligan, are the product of different socialization patterns and result in different orientations to values, family life, and the basis of self-worth.

Several investigators have examined the claims of consistent differences between men and women in moral orientation. The literature is inconclusive regarding the strength and consistency with which men and women differ in their use of what have come to be called the **justice orientation** and the **caring orientation**. It appears that experiential and situational issues, as well as concerns about interpersonal obligations and caring, are more dominant in open-ended responses from both men and women than are issues of justice and individual rights. However, with age, both men and women add more autonomous, justice-oriented reasoning to their repertoire (Walker, de Vries, & Trevethan, 1987; Galotti, 1989; Galotti, Kozberg, & Farmer, 1991; Colby & Damon, 1994). The tendency of men and women to approach a moral dilemma using a justice-based or a care-based form of reasoning is dependent on the social distance between the self and the other person involved. Regardless of gender, a caring orientation is more likely when the other person is viewed as a close friend or a member of one's relevant social group; a justice orientation is more likely when the other person is viewed as a member of an outgroup, a stranger, or when the nature of the relationship to the other person is not specified (Ryan, David, & Reynolds, 2004).

In studies of prosocial behavior and empathic response to others, gender differences are commonly observed. Women report more caring behaviors, are rated as being more kind and considerate than men, emphasize the importance of helping others as a value, and exhibit more personal distress when faced with the distress of others (Eisenberg & Morris, 2004). In many cultures, family socialization practices emphasize the importance of prosocial behavior and social responsibility for female children. As a result of this focus, perhaps women are more likely than men to integrate a prosocial orientation into their gender identity (Froming, Nasby, & McManus, 1998).

The process of achieving a moral identity is made more difficult in a pluralistic society, where one's moral concerns may be at odds with others' social concerns. Certain groups are consistently wronged by deeply ingrained inequalities in the social structure. Acts of resistance or subversion by groups in positions of less power may be labeled as immoral by those in higher positions and as heroic by those in the disenfranchised groups (Turiel, 2003). In later adolescence,

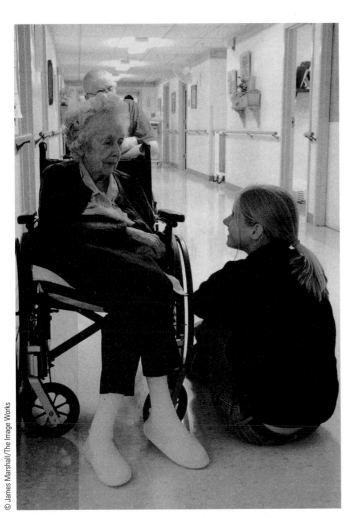

The caring orientation is evidenced when Alison volunteers to spend time visiting with older adults in a nursing home in her university community.

young people begin to appreciate the moral ambiguities of their communities and may take action to express their commitments to justice and care through individual or group efforts.

Whereas some young people appear to be characterized by self-indulgence and social indifference, others are intensely engaged in actions fueled by the passion of indignation about social injustice and commitments to moral goals. In 2009, a record number of college freshmen (roughly 31%) indicated that they expected to engage in community service or volunteer work during their college years. Those who already had a community service experience in high school were more likely to expect to continue this type of commitment during college. Volunteering has been found to be strongly associated with two aspects of moral commitment, social agency, or a personal goal of being politically and socially active in the community, and valuing and respecting other groups' points of view (Higher Education Research Institute, 2010). This large and growing group of college students provides a very hopeful indication about the willingness of the new generation of young people for combining

a caring and a justice orientation in order to make contributions to their communities.

Career Choice

Objective 4. To analyze the process of career choice, with attention to education and gender role socialization as two major influential factors.

The choice of occupation sets the tone for one's early adult lifestyle. The world of work determines one's daily routine, including the time one wakes up, daily activities, expenditures of physical and mental energy, and conditions for both immediate and long-term rewards. Because one's occupation has implications for income and earning potential, one's **career choice** will influence one's personal financial resources and opportunities. Occupation confers social status and provides varying opportunities for advancement. Finally, it represents a direct or indirect expression of one's value system. In subsequent chapters, we will discuss socialization in the work setting and the management of a career. Here, we focus on the process of career choice and its impact on development during later adolescence.

Work Experiences in Early Adolescence

Later adolescence is not the first time young people encounter the world of work. Many early adolescents hold part-time jobs while they attend high school. In 2008, 40% of 16- to 19-year-olds were in the labor force, and 19% were unemployed—meaning that they were recently fired or had been unsuccessful in looking for work during the preceding 4 weeks (U.S. Census Bureau, 2010). There is some controversy about the benefits of working during high school and the extent to which these work experiences actually make a positive contribution to the occupational component of identity development. A number of investigations have found that high school students who work long hours in stressful jobs are more likely to evidence increased cigarette smoking, marijuana and alcohol use, receive lower grades, earn fewer course credits, and are more likely to drop out of high school (Entwisle, Alexander, & Olson, 2005; Marsh & Kleitman, 2005). Students who work long hours have less time for school activities, socialization with friends, or the development of other areas of interest. The kinds of work opportunities that are available to adolescents are usually minimally skilled jobs with high turnover, low pay, little decision-making responsibility, and little stimulation of skill development. These kinds of jobs are likely to produce depression and low self-esteem and may contribute to feelings of alienation from the school environment. For some adolescents, the time spent in these kinds of work settings is associated with the development of cynical attitudes toward work and greater acceptance of unethical practices by workers.

Other researchers have emphasized the diversity of work experiences and the potential benefits of certain kinds of work. Students who are able to find and keep a good job may feel more confident about themselves and their promise for future employment. When the work does not involve too many hours, and when it involves skill development that young people see as related to their future career direction, the experience is likely to be associated with higher levels of well-being and less involvement in problem behaviors. For girls, the perception of continuity between school and work and the feeling that work improves one's school performance had an especially positive relationship with mental health and well-being (Mortimer, Finch, Shanahan, & Ryu, 1992; Mortimer & Johnson, 1999).

Factors Influencing Career Choice

As Figure 10.2 suggests, career choice is influenced by six major factors: individual, psychosocial-emotional, socioeconomic, societal, familial, and situational (O'Neil et al., 1980). These same factors contribute to gender role socialization. It is important to see the interrelationship of these two domains for young people in our culture. Gender role socialization creates a powerful filter through which choices related to career development are made. Gender role stereotyping may apply to certain occupational fields, thereby limiting their desirability to those with traditional gender role expectations. Over time, as the process of identity formation unfolds, involvement in careers and exposure to nontraditional role models can also modify one's gender identity.

Of the six factors described in Figure 10.2, high school and college students reported that the individual factors, such as abilities, achievement needs, attitudes, and self-expectancies, most strongly affected their career decision making. They perceived familial, societal, and socioeconomic factors as having little or no impact (O'Neil et al., 1980). This is contrary to social science research evidence. Family factors play a key role in shaping educational aspirations and occupational goals. Societal and socioeconomic conditions are major factors influencing the job market and the chances of both employment and advancement. Students who have a clearer understanding of the critical social and economic factors that influence the labor market are better able to consider career alternatives and to analyze the steps they need to take in order to achieve their career goals (Diemer & Blustein, 2006).

Family Background and Career Opportunities. Family background characteristics, including parents' occupation, educational background, income, culture, and community, are associated with educational opportunities,

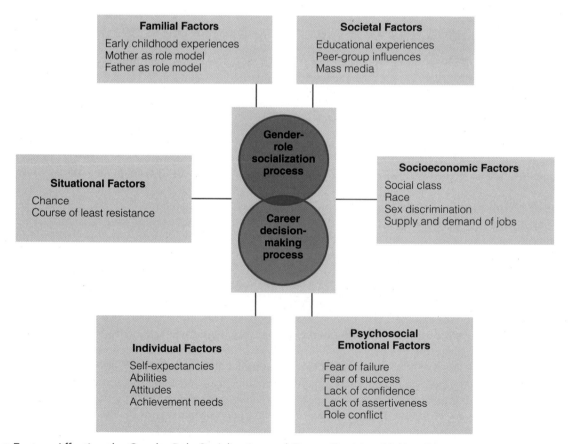

FIGURE 10.2 Factors Affecting the Gender Role Socialization and Career Decision-Making Process
Source: O'Neil, Ohlde, Barke, Prosser-Gelwick, and Garfield, 1980.

aspirations, and academic achievement from early school age through the high school and college years. Differences in family resources result in diverging educational backgrounds, which have direct implications for the kinds of careers one is prepared to enter. In the period of early adolescence, children from low-income families and from families in which the parents did not graduate from high school are more likely to drop out of high school and less likely to be enrolled in postsecondary education. Of the seniors graduating from high school in 2008, 72% of European American, non-Hispanic students went on to college, compared to 56% of African Americans and 64% of Latino students (National Center for Education Statistics, 2010). Children whose parents are in the top 25% of family income are more than 7 times more likely to graduate from college (61%) than children from families in the lowest 25% of family income (8.5%) (Mortenson, 2001). Differences in families' ability to support occupational exploration, the parents' own occupational attainments, and their ideas about ideal career paths influence their children's career decision-making process. For example, in a comparison of Chinese American and European American youth, the Chinese Americans emphasized the importance of entrepreneurial opportunities in their career interests, whereas the European Americans emphasized the importance of social features (Marjoribanks, 1997–1998; Leong, Kao, & Lee, 2004).

Education and Career Choice. It is well documented that career advancement and the associated earnings are closely linked to levels of educational attainment. For those who do not graduate from high school, career development is a bumpy path. In 2008, the unemployment rate for high school dropouts was 25.8%. (U.S. Census Bureau, 2010). In 2007, 67% of high school graduates in the United States were enrolled in some type of postsecondary institution, 66% of men and 68% of women. This compares to 49% of high school graduates in 1980 (U.S. Census Bureau, 2010). College is becoming an increasingly essential aspect of career development. Despite the large number of students who attend some type of college, many do not complete a degree. In 2008, 29% of the population ages 25 and older had a college degree or more. This percentage varies greatly by race/ethnicity: African Americans, 19.6%; Asian Americans and Pacific Islanders, 52.6%; European Americans, 29.8%; and Hispanic/Latinos, 13.3% (U.S. Census Bureau, 2010).

Table 10.1 shows the mean earned income on the basis of educational level for men and women who were 25 to 34 years old in 2007. Educational attainment has a significant relationship to annual income. As the data indicate, however, educational achievement does not result in the same economic advantages for men and women. Women with 1 to 3 years of college but no degree earned less on average than men who were high school graduates (U.S. Census Bureau, 2010).

TABLE 10.1 Mean Annual Income of Men and Women 25–34 Years, 2007, by Level of School Completed and Sex

EDUCATION	MEDIAN ANNUAL INCOME ($)	
	MEN	WOMEN
Grades 9–12, not a high school graduate	28,475	28,099
High school graduate	35,995	30,092
Some college, no degree	41,551	34,561
Bachelor's degree or more	66,731	49,966

Source: U.S. Census Bureau, 2010.

For youth who leave high school or who graduate but do not go on to college, the job market has several unattractive features:

> Most of the jobs available at this level of educational attainment are routine, menial, temporary, more likely to be part time and to provide reduced monetary and nonmaterial rewards compared with jobs held by older workers. . . . Moreover, jobs within this sector are unusually unstable and may be supervised by rigid, autocratic employers, many of whom, particularly in the fast food industry, are not much older than the novice worker. (Borman & Hopkins, 1987, p. 136)

The impact of school experiences on subsequent career development goes beyond whether one plans to attend college or not. Vocational coursework of a specific nature, such as agricultural training, an emphasis on math and science courses, and frequent conversations with teachers about one's work-related decisions are all associated with higher income and more stable work records after high school. Identity formation, self-insight, and active clarification of work values are all related to greater career confidence and more mature career decision making (Schulenberg, Vondracek, & Kim, 1993; Vondracek, Schulenberg, Skorikov, & Gillespie, 1995).

Gender Role Socialization and Career Choice. Gender role socialization shapes career decisions through two significant psychological factors: (1) perceptions of ability, and (2) career-related values and goals. First, as a result of socialization, men and women are likely to form different expectations about their ability to succeed at various career-related skills. Self-expectancies about the ability to fulfill the educational requirements and the job duties of specific careers are a major factor in determining career choices. Recall from Chapter 8 (Middle Childhood) the discussion of parents' expectations about their children's competence in certain skill areas and its relation to the child's own perceptions of competence. In a longitudinal study, mothers' gender-stereotyped beliefs about their young child's math and science abilities predicted their child's self-perceptions of math and science self-efficacy 2 years after high school. Mothers' predictions of their child's ability to succeed in a math-oriented career was a significant predictor of their college-age child's career choice (Bleeker & Jacobs, 2004). In the process of career decision making, strong gender-typed conceptualizations of the job demands of specific careers intervene to screen out some alternatives and highlight others (Stromquist, 1991; Gati, Osipow, & Givon, 1995). For example, there is a clear path from belief in one's competence in math to aspirations about careers in math, science, and engineering (Correll, 2001). Gendered beliefs about mathematics competence, influenced in part by parental expectations, may contribute to the persistent gender divide with respect to women enrolling in university and graduate programs in mathematics, physics, and engineering. Studies of career choice or career aspirations find that women with a strong sense of their own goals, an awareness of their personal needs, and an ability to cope realistically with stress have been more likely to adopt a nontraditional career choice.

Second, as a result of socialization, women and men are likely to establish different value hierarchies, reflecting different long-range life goals. Among later adolescents, young men have been found to prefer "jobs characterized by high salaries, power or influence over others, opportunities for advancement or achievement, risk taking, challenging tasks, a high level of responsibility, and a high level of prestige" (Weisgram, Bigler, & Liben, 2010, p. 779). Young women have been found to prefer "jobs that allow them to work with or help others, develop their knowledge or skills, and spend time with family" (Weisgram, Bigler, & Liben, 2010, p. 779). For example, one study compared what college students wanted from their careers, referred to as work goals,

with what they thought certain careers might allow them to achieve, called *goal affordances*. The study found that students who thought a career would help them achieve their work goals were also more interested in those careers (Morgan, Isaac, & Sansone, 2001). Women rated interpersonal goals as more important and high pay and high status goals as less important than men. Both men and women viewed careers in physical and mathematical science as offering less in the way of interpersonal goals and more in the way of salary and status. As a result, women were less interested in careers in physical and mathematical science and less likely to identify those fields as career choices. The internalization of gender-related goals is directly related to how motivated a young man or woman is in pursuing a career that promises to allow her to attain those goals (Evans & Diekman, 2009).

The consequences of gender role socialization for career choice can be seen in distribution of men and women in the labor force (U.S. Census Bureau, 2010). Although there are many areas where men and women are equally involved, patterns of gender differentiation are quite notable. For example the large majority of those working in fields of preschool education, elementary or middle school teaching, special education, nursing, and office/administrative support are women. The large majority of those working as firefighters or police, or in engineering, computer programming, transportation, construction, and natural resources, are men.

Gender identity is shaped by cultural values that may determine one's career goals and related choices. In a study of the educational and occupational attainment of low-income, rural Appalachian women, the importance of family socialization influences was highlighted (Wilson, Peterson, & Wilson, 1993). These families tend to have strong kinship ties and high levels of consensus about norms for appropriate

After high school, Rick decided to work in a local fish market. He will probably quit when he has earned enough money to buy the truck he has been wanting. Then he'll travel for a while and get a job in another town.

© Paul A. Souders/CORBIS

behaviors. They endorse traditional gender roles in which the men are the dominant decision makers and the women are expected to be homemakers and also hold low-paying jobs to help support the family. Educational and occupational aspirations are generally higher for male than for female children in these families, but both are encouraged to restrict their aspirations to career options that will keep them close to their childhood homes.

Career Decision Making

The idea of **career decision making** must be evaluated in light of rapid changes in the nature of work, the pervasiveness of the two-earner family lifestyle, the increased likelihood of multiple job and career changes over the life course, and the constant reconfiguration of the job market—especially the trends toward downsizing, workforce reductions, retraining, and outsourcing. The idea of occupational choice should not be confused with choice about labor market participation. Although they may have a wide choice in the kind of work they will do, most people in the United States do not have a choice about whether to work or not. In fact, about 6% of young people in the 20 to 24 age range have more than one job (U.S. Census Bureau, 2007).

Career choice reflects a central component of a person's emerging identity. For some young people, occupational choice is a reflection of continued identification with their parents. They may select the same job or career as that of one of their parents, or they may select a career because it reflects their parents' aspirations for them. Little personal choice is involved. For some young people, primarily women, there continues to be a path of primary identification with the roles of wife and mother, with only secondary investment in the labor market. Many of these women, especially those who marry and have children after high school, return to school or to technical training in their thirties and forties in order to pick up the thread of career development, either as a result of divorce or when their children get older. Increasing numbers of men and women realize that their occupational career will need to be coordinated and integrated with that of their spouse. In anticipation of a dual-earner lifestyle, young people begin to screen their career aspirations through the lens of the compatibility of job demands with family commitments and personal aspirations.

Concerns about future educational and career decisions constitute a major source of worry for college students. Of the students entering college as freshmen in 2004, 72% said that an important reason for going to college was to be able to get a better job (*Chronicle of Higher Education*, 2005). Many people assume that the younger a person is when he makes a career choice, the better. Most career development professionals, however, advise that a decision about a career be delayed until later adolescence or early adulthood. The concept of **career maturity** suggests that with increased cognitive and affective development, a person develops decision-making strategies, gains access to information,

Most colleges have resources to help students with their career decision making, including advisors, online software, and career fairs.

and achieves a degree of self-insight that permit a realistic and consistent choice (Schmitt-Rodermund & Silbereisen, 1998). A person who delays the decision has a clearer sense of her adult interests and goals. By delaying the career decision, one also has more opportunities to explore alternative work scenarios and to understand more about the labor market.

Nonetheless, high schools, colleges, and various industries urge young people to make career choice decisions as early as possible. Thus, some of the tension that later adolescents experience in connection with a choice of career is a product of the lack of fit between socialization pressures and their own developmental timetable. With the increased likelihood of living to be 80 years old, there is no great rush to decide on a career by age 20. In the United States, the average person with a bachelor's degree has 11 jobs between the ages of 18 and 32 (U.S. Census Bureau, 2007). In this context, selecting the first career ought to be viewed as an extension of one's occupational education, not a decision that has to last a lifetime.

Phases of Career Decision Making. Once a person begins to accept certain elements of his self-concept related to the occupational aspect of identity, the process of career decision making begins. Tiedeman (Tiedeman & O'Hara, 1963; Tiedeman & Miller-Tiedeman, 1985) developed a model of the **phases of career decision making**. This model illustrates how making career-related decisions helps to clarify one's occupational identity and, at the same time, uses the context of work to promote new learning about other aspects of the self (see Figure 10.3). A career decision depends on the outcomes of several tasks during early and later adolescence and early adulthood. With effective problem solving, the person gains increased control over life events and is better prepared to meet the challenges of the next phase of decision making. Tiedeman identified seven phases; the first four emphasize planning and clarification, while the last three emphasize implementation. The model reflects an individual's capacity for ongoing adaptation and change. At

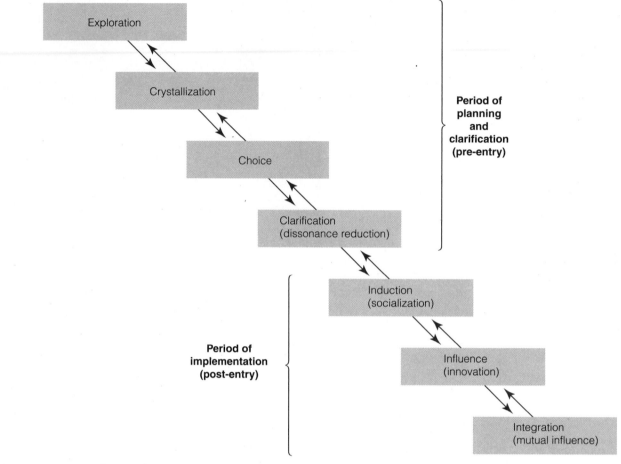

FIGURE 10.3 Seven Phases of Career Decision Making
Source: Based on Tiedeman and O'Hara, 1963.

each phase in the process, people can redefine the self and transcend the conditions of the work environment to change their minds (Miller-Tiedeman, 1999).

In the **exploration phase**, the person realizes that a career decision must be made and therefore begins to learn more about those aspects of the self and the occupational world that are relevant to the impending decision. The person begins to generate alternatives for action. Uncertainty about the future and the many possible alternatives is accompanied by feelings of anxiety.

In the **crystallization phase**, the person becomes more aware of the alternatives for action and their consequences. Conflicts among alternatives are recognized, and some are discarded. The person develops a strategy for making the decision, in part by weighing the costs and benefits of each alternative.

In the **choice phase**, the person decides which action alternative to follow. The decision is solidified in the person's mind as she elaborates the reasons why the decision is beneficial. There is a sense of relief and optimism as the person develops a commitment to executing the decision.

In the **clarification phase**, the person more fully understands the consequences of the commitment to the decision

that has been made. He plans definite steps to take and may actually take them or may delay them until a more appropriate time. A person's self-concept is modified by the commitment to a career path, and by the desire to create congruity between one's decision and the demands that are likely to accompany that decision.

During the **induction phase**, the person encounters the new career environment for the first time. She wants to be accepted and looks to others for cues about how to behave. The person identifies with the new group and seeks recognition for her unique characteristics. Gradually, the self-image is modified as the person begins to believe in the values and goals of the new group.

In the **influence phase**, the person is very much involved with the new group. He becomes more assertive in asking that the group perform better. The person also tries to influence the group to accommodate some of his values. The self is strongly committed to group goals. During this phase, the group's values and goals may be modified to include the orientation of the new member.

Finally, in the **integration phase**, group members react against the new member's attempts to influence them. The new member then compromises. In the process, she attains a more objective understanding of the self and the group. A true collaboration between the new member and the group is achieved. The new member feels satisfied and is evaluated as successful by the self and others.

This model emphasizes continuous interaction between the individual and the work context. At first, interaction is necessary to clarify the person's talents and choice of career. Later, it is necessary to achieve a satisfactory level of adaptation to the work environment. At each juncture, whether the decision relates to college major, occupation, job change, or career redirection, effective decision making involves all seven phases.

The concept of **career decision-making self-efficacy** is widely used in the field of vocational education and development to highlight the role of a person's emerging confidence in her ability to make an effective career choice. You may recall from Chapter 2 that Albert Bandura introduced the concept of self-efficacy to refer to the confidence that a person has that he can meet the standards for performance in a particular domain. We discussed self-efficacy in some detail in Chapter 8, as a component of the developmental task of self-evaluation. Judgments of self-efficacy stem from four sources: prior experiences of success or failure in a specific domain; encouragement or discouragement from others (verbal persuasion); vicarious experiences of watching others succeed or fail; and the physical state of arousal that accompanies being engaged in the task. Career decision-making self-efficacy includes assessments about whether one can make an accurate self-appraisal of one's abilities, gather relevant occupational information, formulate appropriate goals, make plans to achieve those goals, and solve the problems that pose barriers to the achievement of goals (Betz, 2001). In each of these areas, a student can be expected to monitor all four sources of information to reach a level of confidence that she can make effective career choices. For college students, the sense of career decision-making self-efficacy is closely tied to confidence in other domains, the most important of which is leadership. Students who believe that they have strong leadership abilities and who have had positive leadership experiences are also more confident about their ability to make effective career decisions. In addition, confidence in science, math, writing, using technology, and cultural sensitivity all contribute to career decision-making self-efficacy (Paulsen & Betz, 2004). Many courses and programs are introduced on college campuses to help support students' career decision making. The idea that self-efficacy about career decision making can be enhanced through deliberate interventions has guided many of these programs, resulting in measurable improvements in career confidence, especially for students who are unsure or highly anxious about their career direction (Betz, 2007).

The Impact of the Labor Market on Career Decision Making

Each birth cohort faces unique labor market conditions as they enter the career search process in later adolescence and

New technologies result in new approaches to training. Carl is using a 3D screen as part of his training to perform eye surgery.

early adulthood. Characteristics of the contemporary labor market may be contributing to new difficulties that later adolescents encounter as they attempt to move through the first four phases of Tiedeman's model.

- The increasing number of jobs and careers available make the exploration phase more difficult.
- As a result of changes in technology and organizational structure, some skills become obsolete and some job markets dry up. A career may become obsolete in the time it takes a young person to prepare for it.
- As established firms lose their identities in corporate mergers, identification with a particular company ceases to be appropriate.
- As most large companies go through restructuring and downsizing, the people who are left are asked to do more tasks of a greater variety. In addition to one's special area of training, it is important to develop support skills, such as word processing, data management, literature search skills, and verbal and written communication skills.
- New careers emerge at a rapid pace. From the time one enters the choice phase to the time one enters the influence phase, new kinds of work roles may become available.
- Career paths are less clear than they once were. Young people are being advised to expect three or four career changes in their lifetime. They may end up moving from the private to the nonprofit sector, from business to education, from service provider to entrepreneur.
- The cost of living—especially the costs of housing, health care, and education—introduces concerns about the amount of money that will be needed to live comfortably. Worries about making money may interfere with effective career decision making.

Given the complexity of the world of work, **career indecision** is common in later adolescence. In contrast to those college students who know what career they plan to enter, there are two different patterns of career indecision. One is considered a developmentally normal state that results from a lack of work experience and information about the world of work coupled with continuing emergence of personal identity. The other is considered to reflect chronic indecision, related to a pervasive lack of self-efficacy, dependency, and more serious identity confusion (Guay, Ratele, Senécal, Larose, & Deschênes, 2006).

Ideally, one's choice of occupation is the result of personal experimentation, introspection, self-evaluation, fact finding, and intuition. This process becomes intimately interwoven with one's psychological development. In order to make a career choice, people may first choose to pose difficult questions to themselves about their skills, temperament, values, and goals. When they make a decision based on this kind of personal evaluation, they are likely to see their careers as a well-integrated part of their personal identities rather than as activities from which they are alienated or by which they are dominated.

The Psychosocial Crisis: Individual Identity versus Identity Confusion

Objective 5. To define and describe the psychosocial crisis of later adolescence, individual identity versus identity confusion; the central process through which this crisis is resolved, role experimentation; the prime adaptive ego quality of fidelity to values and ideals; and the core pathology of repudiation.

The basic conflict of the psychosocial crisis of later adolescence is individual identity formation versus identity confusion. It results from the enormous difficulty of pulling together the many components of the self—including changing perspectives on one's inner sense of beliefs and values as well as new and changing social demands—into a unified image that can propel the person toward positive, meaningful action. As part of this process, a young person struggles to formulate a worldview, an outlook on those goals and values that are personally important and to which the person is willing to make a commitment. Over the period of later adolescence, whether in the context of college or in other work and community settings, young people begin to examine the beliefs and goals they may have internalized from childhood. Through self-reflection, role experimentation, and feedback from significant others, later adolescents make decisions about whether these beliefs and goals are still meaningful as they look ahead to the future.

Individual Identity

Erik Erikson provided a comprehensive treatment of the meaning and functions of **individual identity**, from his inclusion of this concept in the theory of psychosocial development in 1950 to his analysis of American identity in 1974. His notion of identity involves the integration of past, present, and future. From the past, young people undertake a process of reexamination of childhood identifications. From the present, young people identify and evaluate their talents, interests, and abilities. From the future, there is an articulation of valued life goals and aspirations. These three sources of identity content have to be woven into a meaningful sense of a purposeful self. The major works in which he discussed identity are the article "The Problem of Ego Identity" (Erikson, 1959) and the book *Identity: Youth and Crisis* (Erikson, 1968). Our discussion, which is grounded in these works, is broadened to include the ideas of others who have begun to extend and operationalize the concept of identity (Schwartz, 2001; Kroger, 2004; Crocetti, Rubini, & Meeus, 2008; Lawler, 2009).

Later adolescents are preoccupied with questions about their essential character in much the same way that early-school-age children are preoccupied with questions about their origins. In their efforts to define themselves, later adolescents must take into account the bonds that have been built between them and others in the past as well as the direction they hope to take in the future. Identity serves as an anchor point, providing the person with an essential experience of continuity in social relationships:

> The young individual must learn to be most himself where he means the most to others—those others, to be sure, who have come to mean most to him. The term identity expresses such a mutual relation in that it connotes both a persistent sameness within oneself (self-sameness) and a persistent sharing of some kind of essential character with others. (Erikson, 1959, p. 102)

The Private and Public Faces of Identity

As the preceding quotation suggests, identity achievement is associated with an internal sense of individual uniqueness and direction accompanied by a social or community validation about the direction one has chosen. Thus identity includes both a private and a public self. The **private self**, often described as a *sense of self*, refers to one's inner uniqueness and unity, the subjective experience of being the originator of one's thoughts and actions and of being self-reflective. Through the private self, one recognizes the range of values and beliefs to which one is committed, and one can assess the extent to which certain thoughts and actions are consistent with those beliefs. The private, subjective sense of self, which develops over the course of the life span, includes four basic elements (Blasi, 1991; Glodis & Blasi, 1993):

- A sense of *agency*—Being the originator of thoughts and actions.
- A sense of *unity*—Sensing that one is the same basic self from one moment or one situation to the next.
- A sense of *otherness*—Recognizing the boundaries between the self and others.

- A sense of *decentering* or *distancing*—Reflecting on oneself so that one can recognize and own one's thoughts and actions.

The elements of the **public self** include the many roles one plays and the expectations of others. As young people move through the stage of later adolescence, they find that social reference groups—including family members, neighbors, teachers, friends, religious groups, ethnic groups, and even national leaders—have expectations of their behavior. A young person may be expected to work, attend college, marry, serve the country in the military, attend religious services, vote, and provide economic support for family members. Persistent demands by meaningful others result in decisions that might have been made differently, or not made at all, if the individual were surrounded by a different configuration of social reference groups. In the process of achieving personal identity, one must synthesize the private sense of self with the public self derived from the many roles and relationships in which one is embedded.

The Content and Evaluation Components of Identity

The structure of identity has two components: content and evaluation (Breakwell, 1986; Whitbourne, 1986). The *content* includes what one thinks about, values, and believes in, and the traits or characteristics by which one is recognized and known by others. Erikson suggested that identity was achieved by finding one's sense of direction with respect to salient roles and values, especially vocational decisions, political and religious ideologies, sexual expression, and gender role or interpersonal values. In many measures of identity formation, these domains comprise the foundational content areas (Kroger, 2003). The second structural component of identity, *evaluation*, refers to the significance one places on various aspects of the identity content. Even though most people play many of the same roles, their identities differ in part because they place different values on some of these roles. Some people are single-minded, placing great value on success in one domain, such as their vocational goals, and little value on the others. Other people strive to maintain a balance in the roles they play; they consider themselves successful if they can find enjoyment in a variety of relationships and activities.

A person's assessment of the importance of certain content areas in relation to others influences the use of resources, the direction of certain decisions, and the kinds of experiences that may be perceived as most personally rewarding or threatening. College students, for example, may differ in whether academic success and professional preparation or interpersonal success is most central to their sense of identity. Students who are more concerned about academic success take a different approach to the college environment, become involved in different kinds of activities, and have a different reaction to academic feedback than do students who are more concerned about making friends

and having new kinds of social and interpersonal success (Green & Hill, 2003).

Both the content and evaluation components of identity may change over the life course. In later adolescence, the focus

This image captures a contemporary sense of the search for individual identity: a young woman with a broad-rimmed hat, hair flowing, one eye looking outward to the world, and one turned inward on the self.

For later adolescents who are in military training, being a soldier becomes part of one's public identity. However, each young person has a private identity attached to specific values, beliefs, and goals.

Woman with a Hat, Picasso, Pablo (1881-1973)/Private Collection/Photo © Bonhams, London, UK/The Bridgeman Art Library International/ © 2011 Estate of Pablo Picasso/Artists Rights Society (ARS), New York

Bob Peterson/Getty Images

is on integrating the various sources of content and determining which elements have the greatest salience. This is a major accomplishment that requires self-awareness, introspection, and the active exploration of a variety of roles and relationships. Insight into this process is provided in the case study of Houston A. Baker, Jr. However, the identity that is formed at the end of this period is often very abstract, because later adolescents have not yet encountered many of the responsibilities, pressures, and conflicts of adult life. The ideological framework of identity has not yet been forged in the flames of reality.

CASE STUDY

HOUSTON A. BAKER, JR.

A poet and literary scholar tells of the impact of one of his college professors on his personal identity.

He intrigued us. Slowly puffing on the obligatory pipe, he would chide us for the routineness of our analyses of revered works in the British and American literary canons. He wore—always—a tie and tweed of Ivy provenance, and at the end of the first session of his "World Literature" course at Howard University in the fall of 1963, I had but one response—I wanted to be exactly like him.

The task was to prove myself worthy. I labored furiously at the beginning assignment—an effort devoted to Marvellian coy mistresses and pounding parodies thereof. The result was a D and the comment: "This is a perfunctory effort. You have refused to be creative. There are worlds on worlds rolling ever. Try to make contact with them." I was more than annoyed; I was livid. Who did he think he was? I'd show him. My next essay would reveal (cleverly, of course) that I didn't give a tinker's dam for his grade or his comments. "Creative"— indeed!

My second essay might properly have been entitled: Love's labor loosed on William Blake. I strained to see every nuance of the "Songs of Innocence." I combed the poems for every mad hint that would help forward my own mad argument. I never turned my eyes from the text as I sought to construct the most infuriating (yet plausible) analysis imaginable. I felt my feet dancing to Muhammad Ali rhythms as I slaved away, darting logical jabs at Professor C. Watkins who would (I was certain) be utterly undone when I threw my irreverent straight right. The paper came back with the comment: "This is a maverick argument, but stubbornly logical—A–" Bingo! The grade in itself gave me almost enough courage to seek him out during office hours—but not quite. I corralled a friend to make the pilgrimage with me.

He was extraordinarily gracious on the mid-autumn afternoon when we had our first long talk. "Come in, Mr. Baker—Miss Pierce. How are you?" His tie was loose; he was reared back in his desk chair. There was a clutter of papers and blue books, and they provided a friendly setting for a two-hour conversation. . . . We were thrilled that he considered us (potentially) enough like him to invite us to visit him and his wife two weeks hence—for dessert.

The evening surprisingly took on (in my youthful imagination) the cast of Greenwich Village "Beats" and verboten revelations. The greatest stimulation, however, came when he played the Library of Congress recording of T. S. Eliot reading "The Wasteland." In that moment, I became, willy-nilly, a party to "modernism" in its prototypical form. I was surprised and delighted. I had heard nothing like it before. The Eliotian reading initiated my habit of "listening" for poems rather than "looking" for them. . . . I stepped into a late fall evening with an entirely new sense of myself and of "worlds on worlds rolling ever."

Source: From "An Apple for My Teacher: Twelve Writers Tell About Teachers Who Made All the Difference," by H. A. Baker, Jr., pp. 317–319. In H. L. Gates, Jr. (Ed.), *Bearing Witness: Selections from African-American Autobiography in the Twentieth Century.* Copyright © 1991 Pantheon Books.

CRITICAL THINKING AND CASE ANALYSIS

1. What elements of the identity process are evident in this case?
2. What are some of the characteristics of Professor Watkins that may have made him a target for identification for Houston Baker?
3. What aspects of the college environment are likely to stimulate the identity process?
4. Have you ever had an intellectual experience that gave you a "new sense of yourself"? What combination of factors came together to permit that to happen?

Identity Status

The **identity process** takes place in a historical and cultural context. During early and later adolescence, young people are aware of the age-graded expectations that exist in their families and communities, typically structured around specific tasks and roles, including educational attainment, occupation, intimacy, marriage, and childrearing. In most modern societies, each of these areas presents a variety of opportunities or possible paths as well as some constraints about which paths are possible given certain personal, financial, and cultural resources. In later adolescence, the identity work includes selecting goals in these domains and preparing for the achievement of these goals (Nurmi, 2004).

Identity formation is a dynamic process that unfolds as young people assess their competencies and aspirations within a changing social context of expectations, demands, and resources. A variety of potential resolutions of the psychosocial crisis of individual identity versus identity confusion have been described. At the negative pole of the crisis, identity confusion or diffusion, the person is not able or possibly not willing to make any commitments to adult roles and values. At the positive pole, identity achievement, the person has made commitments to a defined set of values and goals. Between these two outcomes, other identity resolutions have been described, including premature resolution, identity foreclosure, postponement of resolution, psychosocial moratorium, and negative identity (Kroger, 1993, 2003).

One of the most widely used conceptual frameworks for assessing **identity status** was devised by James Marcia

(1980; Waterman, 1982). Using Erikson's concepts, Marcia assessed identity status on the basis of two criteria: *crisis* and *commitment*. **Crisis** in this context refers to a period of role experimentation, exploration, and active decision making among alternative choices. **Commitment** consists of a demonstration of personal involvement in the areas of occupational choice, religion, political ideology, and interpersonal relationships. On the basis of Marcia's interview, the status of respondents' identity development is assessed as **identity achievement**, **foreclosure**, **moratorium**, or **confusion** (see Table 10.2). People who are classified as identity achieved have already experienced a crisis time and have made occupational and ideological commitments. People who are classified as foreclosed have not experienced a crisis but demonstrate strong occupational and ideological commitments. Their occupational and ideological beliefs appear to be close to those of their parents. The foreclosed identity is deceptive. A young person of 18 or 19 who can say exactly what she wants in life and who has selected an occupational goal may appear to be mature. This kind of clarity of vision may impress peers and adults as evidence of a high level of self-insight. However, if this solution has been formulated through the wholesale adoption of a script that was devised by the young person's family, it may not actually reflect much depth of self-understanding.

People who are classified as being in a state of psychosocial moratorium are involved in an ongoing exploration and experimentation. Their commitments are diffuse. The moratorium status is typically an active, open time for gathering information and discovering how one fits in certain roles. Finally, people who are classified as identity confused may or may not have experienced a crisis, and they demonstrate a complete lack of commitment. Marcia described the identity-confused group as having a rather cavalier, party attitude that allows members to cope with the college environment. He suggested that the more seriously confused persons (such as those described by Erikson, 1959) may not appear in his sample because they are unable to cope with college.

Sometimes, a young person develops a **negative identity,** because the society has labeled the person in a negative way (Erikson, 1959). *Failure*, *good-for-nothing*, *juvenile delinquent*, *hood*, *gangster*, and *loser* are some of the labels that the adult society applies to certain adolescents. Terms such as *illegal alien* or *terrorist* define individuals as without value to society, and as such, impose a negative identity (Lawler, 2008). These labels disconnect individuals from meaningful social bonds or valued roles. The society creates a negative identity as other or to be feared. The young person accepts such negative labels as a self-definition and proceeds to validate this identity by continuing to behave in ways that will strengthen it. Some young people grow up admiring people who have become very successful by following antisocial or criminal paths. Drug lords; gang leaders; leaders of groups that advocate hate, violence, and vengeance; and people who use elected political positions for personal gain are all examples of possible role models around which a negative identity may be formed.

A negative identity may also emerge as the result of a strong identification with someone who is devalued by the family or the community. A loving uncle who is an alcoholic or a clever, creative parent who commits suicide may stimulate the crystallization within the adolescent of a self-construal as one who may share these undesirable characteristics. Linda, for example, established the negative identity of a person going crazy:

> Her father was an alcoholic, physically abusive man, who terrified her when she was a child. . . . Linda, herself a bright child, became by turns the standard bearer for her father's proud aspirations and the target of his jealousy. Midway through grade school she began flunking all her courses and retreating to a private world of daydreams. . . . "I always expected hallucinations, being locked up, down the road coming toward me. . . . I always resisted seeing myself as an adult. I was afraid that at the point I stopped the tape [the years of wild experimentation] I'd become my parents. . . . My father was the closest person I knew to crazy." (Ochberg, 1986, pp. 296–297)

Identity Confusion

The foreclosed identity and the negative identity both resolve the identity crisis in ways that fall short of the goal of identity achievement. Yet both still provide the person with a concrete identity. The more maladaptive resolution of the crisis is **identity confusion**. Young people in this state are unable to make a commitment to any single view of themselves. They may be unable to integrate the various roles they play. They may be confronted by opposing value systems or by a lack of confidence in their ability to make meaningful decisions. Within the private, subjective self, some young people may reach later adolescence having difficulty accepting or establishing clear ego boundaries, or they may not experience feelings of agency. Individuals with identity confusion have been shown to have low self-esteem; they are more likely than individuals with other identity statuses to be influenced by peer pressures toward conformity, and they approach problem solving with tendencies toward procrastination and avoidance, which contribute to difficulties in adjusting to the college environment (Berzonsky & Kuk, 2000; Kroger, 2004). At an unconscious level, they may have incorporated two or more conflicting ideas about the self—for example, an abusive, harsh, rejecting powerful father and a wise, loving, nurturant, powerful grandmother—that stand

TABLE 10.2	Relationship of Crisis and Commitment to Identity Status	
STATUS	**CRISIS**	**COMMITMENT**
Identity achievement	+	+
Foreclosure	−	+
Moratorium	+	−
Identity confusion	+/−	−

Source: © Cengage Learning.

in opposition to each other. Under any of these conditions, the demands for integration and synthesis of a personal identity arouse anxiety, apathy, and hostility toward the existing roles, none of which they can successfully adopt.

In comparison to the moratorium group, young people with a confused identity status are less conscientious, more likely to experience negative emotions, and more disagreeable (Clancy & Dollinger, 1993). They are generally not outgoing; rather, they describe themselves as self-conscious and likely to feel depressed. Their relationship with their parents is described as distant or rejecting. Several studies have found that some young people who are characterized as identity confused have had a history of early and frequent involvement with drug use and abuse (Jones, 1992). Difficulties in resolving earlier psychosocial crises—especially conflicts related to autonomy versus shame and doubt and initiative versus guilt—leave some young people with deficits in ego formation that interfere with the kind of energy and playful self-assertiveness that are necessary in the process of identity achievement.

Dolores, an unemployed college dropout, describes the feeling of meaningless drifting that is associated with identity confusion:

> I have two sisters, and my father always told me I was the smartest of all, that I was smarter than he was, and that I could do anything I wanted to do . . . but somehow, I don't really know why, everything I turned to came to nothing. . . . I had every opportunity to find out what I really wanted to do. But . . . nothing I did satisfied me, and I would just stop. . . . Or turn away. . . . Or go on a trip. I worked for a big company for a while. . . . Then my parents went to Paris and I just went with them. . . . I came back . . . went to school . . . was a researcher at Time-Life . . . drifted . . . got married . . . divorced . . . drifted. [Her voice grew more halting.] I feel my life is such a waste. I'd like to write, I really would; but I don't know. I just can't get going. (Gornick, 1971)

The theoretical construct of identity status assumes a developmental progression. Identity confusion reflects the least defined status. Movement from confusion to foreclosure, moratorium, and finally identity achievement reflects a developmental progression. Movement from any other status to confusion suggests regression. A person who has achieved identity at one period may conceivably return to a crisis period of moratorium. However, those who are in a moratorium or achieved status can never be accurately described as foreclosed, because by definition they have already experienced some degree of crisis (Waterman, 1982; Meeus, 1996). A number of studies, both cross-sectional and longitudinal, have shown that over time, more young people are characterized as having the mature identity statuses of moratorium and achievement, and fewer are in foreclosure or identity confusion (Yip, Seaton, & Sellers, 2006).

In the process of evolving an individual identity, everyone experiences temporary periods of confusion and depression. The task of bringing together the many elements of one's experience into a coordinated, clear self-definition is difficult and time consuming. Adolescents are likely to experience moments of self-preoccupation, isolation, and discouragement as the diverse pieces of the puzzle are shifted and reordered into the total picture. Thus, even the eventual positive identity formation will be the result of some degree of identity confusion. The negative outcome of identity confusion, however, suggests that the person is never able to formulate a satisfying identity that will provide for the convergence of multiple identifications, aspirations, and roles. Such individuals have the persistent fear that they are losing their hold on themselves and on their future.

Identity Formation for Men and Women

Questions have been raised about whether the theory of identity formation, including the ideas of identity content, identity status, and the process of crisis and commitment, apply equally well to men and women. Some have argued that the concept of identity as it has been formulated is a reflection of a male-oriented culture that focuses heavily on occupation and ideology rather than on interpersonal commitments as the foundation for identity content. These critics suggest that the construct of personal identity places greater value on self-sufficiency and autonomy, characteristics associated with the traditional male gender role, and less value on the building of close relationships and connections to the group, characteristics associated with the traditional female gender role (Archer, 1992; Sorrel & Montgomery, 2001).

Some evidence of gender differences has been found in the *content* of identity. Erikson's (1968, 1982) work suggests that ideological and vocational commitments are central to identity formation. Gilligan (1982/1993) criticized this orientation, arguing that interpersonal commitment may be more central for women, and that its clarification opens the way for more advanced exploration of vocations and ideology. Research findings lend some support to this concept. The quality of interpersonal relations and the establishment of satisfying social commitments are more central to the content of personal identity, particularly for women who endorse more traditional gender role expectations (Kroger, 2003).

Research comparing the *identity status* of males and females finds that the kinds of ego strengths associated with identity achievement are equally important to the adaptive functioning of men and women (Ginsburg & Orlofsky, 1981). Few sex differences in identity status have been discovered (Kroger, 1997, 2002). Men and women are equally likely to be distributed across the four identity statuses. Over the period of later adolescence, they show the same pattern of increasing frequencies in the moratorium and achievement categories and decreasing frequencies in the foreclosed and confused categories (Marcia, 1993; Horst, 1995). For both sexes, identity achievement is associated with positive ego qualities: "Identity achieved youths generally exhibit higher levels of self-esteem, greater cognitive and ego complexity, postconventional levels of moral reasoning, and a strong capacity for inner-directed behavior" (CraigBray, Adams, & Dobson, 1988, p. 175).

Young men and young women do appear to handle the *process* of role experimentation and identity achievement somewhat differently. The uncertainty of the identity crisis is more likely to be accompanied by anxiety in women than in men (Ollech & McCarthy, 1997). This anxiety may be linked to concerns about achievement strivings. Many women experience conflict between their image of femininity and their desire to set ambitious personal goals (Ginsburg & Orlofsky, 1981).

Anxiety may also be a product of the general distress that women feel when they focus on their own agendas rather than on facilitating the agendas of others, as society seems to expect them to do. The family context is especially important for young women who need to experience continued attachment with parents in the process of individuation (Schultheiss & Blustein, 1994). The moratorium status, which is considered a positive interlude on the path toward achievement, has been found to be linked to higher levels of self-doubt in women than in men. This finding may be explained by feelings of guilt that women experience when they attempt to assert their self-sufficiency or when they try to disconnect from demanding relationships in order to focus on their own ideas and needs.

The Central Process: Role Experimentation

The concept of identity status, which has dominated the research on identity development, implies steps or levels of attainment in one's identity work. This approach may obscure the important question of how adolescents go about the task of figuring out their values and commitments. The central process of **role experimentation** suggests an answer to this question. Later adolescents experiment with roles that represent the many possibilities for their future identities. They may imagine themselves in a variety of careers in an effort to anticipate what it would be like to be members of specific occupational groups. They may take a variety of summer jobs, change their college major, read extensively, and daydream about success in several occupations. They consider whether to marry, and they begin to define the ideal qualities they are looking for in a long-term intimate partner. Dating is one form of role experimentation; it allows for a different self-presentation with each new date. Friendship is another important context within which young people begin to clarify their interpersonal commitments. Later adolescents may also evaluate their commitment to their religion, consider religious conversion, or experiment with different rationales for moral behavior. They may examine a variety of

political theories, join groups that work for political causes, or campaign for candidates.

Some researchers have conceptualized the process of role experimentation as a cycling of commitment formation and commitment reevaluation (Klimstra, Luyckx et al., 2010). Early in the identity formation process, this cycle may occur frequently, possibly daily, as young people vacillate between certainty about their values or commitments and uncertainty about whether these commitments make sense. For example, as a freshman in college Sam tells his parents that he wants to major in political science and become a lawyer. Then, after a few weeks he tells his folks that he wants to go into the field of foreign service and be a diplomat. By the time Sam comes home for Thanksgiving, he is talking about getting more involved in the student government, and thinks that when he graduates from college he would like to go into politics. By his senior year, Sam has changed his mind about his future career five or six times, but each time he comes back to his interest in the law, and ends up applying to law school. Over time, as commitments become more stable, the young person will experience greater confidence and fewer episodes of reevaluation.

During later adolescence, people have few social obligations that require long-term role commitments. They are free to start and stop or to join and quit without serious repercussions to their reputations. As long as no laws are broken in the process of experimenting, young people have the opportunity to play as many roles as they wish in order to prepare themselves for the resolution of the identity crisis without risking serious social censure.

Psychosocial Moratorium

The process of role experimentation takes many forms. Erikson (1959) used the term **psychosocial moratorium** to describe a period of free experimentation before a final identity is achieved. Ideally, the moratorium allows individuals freedom from the daily expectations for role performance. Their experimentation with new roles, values, and belief systems results in a personal conception of how they can fit into society so as to maximize their personal strengths and gain positive recognition from the community. The idea of being able to disconnect from daily demands and experiment with new roles may be more difficult for some later adolescents than for others. For example, young people who marry early and who go into the labor force right after high school may not have the luxury of a moratorium.

The concept of the psychosocial moratorium has been partially incorporated into some college programs that permit students to enroll in pass-fail courses before they select a major. The concern is to eliminate the problems of external evaluation during the decision-making process. Some high school students take a year off for work, travel, or volunteer service before deciding about college or a career. College students often express a need for a moratorium by leaving school for a while, disrupting the expected path of educational and career development. They assert their autonomy by imposing their own timetable and agenda on a socially prescribed sequence. Travel abroad is another strategy for experiencing moratorium. The time spent in another culture can give students an opportunity to demonstrate their self-sufficiency, examine many of their assumptions about values and goals, express their individuality, and break out of whatever social environment they may feel is constraining or overshadowing their sense of self. The moratorium offers temporary relief from external demands and an opportunity to establish their identity.

As parents observe the process of role experimentation, they may become concerned because their adolescent son or daughter appears to be abandoning the traditional family value orientation or lifestyle. The adolescent talks of changing religions, remaining single, or selecting a low-status career. The more vehemently the family responds to these propositions, the more likely the young person is to become locked into a position in order to demonstrate autonomy rather than being allowed to continue the experimentation until a more suitable personal alternative is discovered. Many adolescents seem to want to take a shocking stand or to question the unquestionable so that they have a feeling of control—a feeling that they have chosen their own path rather than simply followed the one carved out for them by their family, culture, and time in history. Parents are well advised to understand role experimentation as the expression of an appropriate developmental process in which a young person is trying on various roles, beliefs, and philosophies to see how they fit. If at all possible, parents need to trust in this process, giving their opinions and reactions when appropriate, but encouraging the young person to find the combination of roles, values, goals, and commitments that bring her the greatest feelings of enthusiasm and optimism about her own future.

Individual Differences in Role Experimentation

Not all young people approach the process of role experimentation with the same degree of openness to new

For some later adolescents, the psychosocial moratorium allows them to explore the wonders of nature and to test the limits of their physical capabilities.

experiences and new information. Michael Berzonsky (1989, 1993, 2003; Berzonsky & Sullivan, 1992) hypothesized that in later adolescence, individuals differ in how they select, process, and apply self-relevant information. Three types of approaches to identity-related information processing were described, each with a somewhat different implication for the place of role experimentation in the resolution of the identity search. The *informational types* "actively seek out and evaluate self-diagnostic information when negotiating identity issues and making decisions" (Berzonsky, 1993, p. 289). The *normative types* are "relatively more defensive and closed to feedback that may threaten hard core areas of the self" (Berzonsky, 1993, p. 290). The *diffuse-avoidant types* "procrastinate and delay dealing with self-relevant issues as long as possible. When push comes to shove, they tend to be influenced by immediate rewards and operate in a situation-sensitive fashion" (Berzonsky, 1993, p. 290). The three identity-processing styles are associated with distinct patterns of defense mechanisms that come into play when later adolescents encounter conflicts or threats to their identity. The informational types use cognitive strategies to minimize anxiety. The diffuse-avoidant types use defenses that turn aggression inward toward the self or outward, blaming others. The normative types use mechanisms of denial, distortion, and negation to defend against threatening information (Berzonsky & Kinney, 2008).

An implication of this theory of styles of identity-related information processing is that the path toward identity status depends in part on how willing a young person is to engage in role experimentation. The informational types are most likely to initiate role experimentation as a means of clarifying existing beliefs and values. The normative types have to process contradictions among the demands and expectations of the varying roles they play, but if possible, they will probably avoid novel experiences that would challenge their views. The diffuse-avoidant types may engage in role experimentation if it is viewed as cool or is positively regarded among others in their peer group, but they probably would not take the initiative to seek out new experiences as a conscious, proactive strategy. Figure 10.4 shows the relationship between the three information-seeking styles and the four identity statuses described earlier. In this model, exploration or seeking information is associated with both the moratorium and the achieved statuses (White, Wampler, & Winn, 1998).

Role experimentation implies an active process by which later adolescents sort through various identifications, scripts, and social pressures in order to find their niche. For some young people, however, a turning point or critical incident marks the point of commitment. Often, a dramatic loss, an unexpected victory, or an experience of victimization can help crystallize a young person's vision of how the self can fit in with the community or transcend the community. Two examples of turning points are illustrated in the following case study.

Image copyright Ben Heys 2010. Used under license from Shutterstock.com

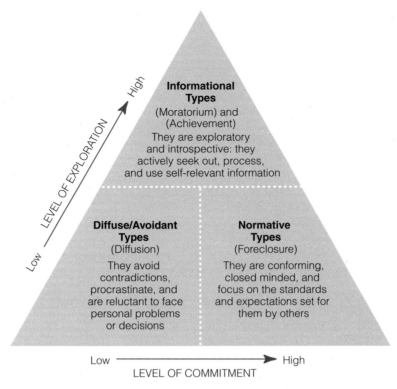

FIGURE 10.4 Relations Among Identity Status, Level of Exploration, and Level of Commitment
Source: White, Wampler, and Winn, 1998, p. 226.

CASE STUDY

TURNING POINTS IN THE IDENTITY PROCESS

The following two examples illustrate how a critical life event can refocus personal identity toward a new consolidation of energy, purpose, and commitment. In the first example, Sullivan experiences personal losses that lead to a new occupational and value commitment. In the second example, Rachel experiences a national tragedy that reorients her political ideology.

SULLIVAN

With her mother, Sullivan was living in a housing project. In high school, when life got very hard, she began drinking and using drugs. She often stayed out late "to all hours" without her mother knowing or caring. Her father stepped in, put his foot down, and tried to teach her better habits. Soon after high school, she eloped with a young man who tried to control her and keep her from going to college. . . . The marriage ended after two years, then tragedy followed. An old boyfriend of Sullivan's committed suicide, and shortly thereafter her sister was hospitalized because of a suicide attempt.

The near-death of her sister changed Sullivan. She did not want to be a "loser"—someone who could not pull her weight—so she enrolled in a local community college. She went on to earn a bachelor's degree and then a master's degree, and she became a licensed social worker. Now Sullivan's work is aimed at helping people who are like she was. (Levine & Nidiffer, 1996, pp. 122–123)

RACHEL

When I was 19, I moved to New York City to be a musician. The first thing I did was get a tattoo on each hand: One was a treble clef, the other was the insignia for Silvertone guitars. . . .

If you asked me to describe myself then, I would have told you I was a musician, a poet, an artist and, on a somewhat political level, a woman, a lesbian, and a Jew. Being an American wouldn't have made my list.

I'm a junior at a Manhattan college. In my Gender and Economics class earlier this semester we discussed the benefits of socialism, which provides for all members of society, versus capitalism, which values the self-interests of businesspeople. My girlfriend and I were so frustrated by inequality in America that we discussed moving to another country. On September 11, all that changed. I realized that I had been taking the freedoms I have here for granted. Now I have an American flag on my backpack, I cheer at the fighter jets as they pass overhead, and I am calling myself a patriot.

I had just stepped out of the shower when the first plane crashed into the North Tower of the World Trade Center. I stood looking out the window of my Brooklyn apartment, dumbfounded, as the second plane barreled into the South Tower. In that moment, the world as I had known it was redefined. (Newman, 2001, p. 9)

CRITICAL THINKING AND CASE ANALYSIS

1. How are turning points different from role experimentation?
2. What might determine whether a turning point leads to identity achievement or identity confusion?
3. What is the difference between the events that Sullivan experienced and those that Rachel experienced? How might the differences in these two kinds of events relate to subsequent identity work?
4. What factors might be necessary to preserve the focus and sense of purpose that are evoked in these critical life events? For example, how might family support, the response of close friends, or opportunities for enacting new roles influence whether these changes are sustained?

Role Experimentation and Ethnic Identity

In Chapter 9 (Early Adolescence), we introduced the idea that group identity precedes individual identity. One component of group identity is an orientation toward one's ethnic group. Efforts to understand one's **ethnic identity** and to clarify one's commitment to a particular ethnic subculture lead to self-definition that facilitates work on personal identity as well (Yip, Seaton, & Sellers, 2006). Part of forming a clear sense of personal identity requires an understanding of one's ancestry, especially one's cultural and ethnic heritage and the values, beliefs, and traditions that may have shaped one's childrearing environment as well as one's vision of the future. Ethnic group identity typically involves the incorporation of certain ideals, values, and beliefs that are specific to that ethnic group; a sense of how this ethnic group is regarded by outsiders; and the way in which one orients oneself with respect to this group—that is, whether one seeks out other members of the group, feels proud of one's membership in it, and has positive attitudes about it (Cross, 1991).

As you might imagine, young people make the transition from early to later adolescence having done different amounts of work in exploring their ethnic group identity. One theory of ethnic minority identity development offers a five-stage model (Atkinson, Morten, & Sue, 1983):

1. *Conformity*. Identification with the values, beliefs, and practices of the dominant culture.
2. *Dissonance*. Recognition and confusion about areas of conflict between the values, beliefs, and practices of the dominant culture and those of one's own ethnic group.

3. *Resistance and immersion*. Rejection of many elements of the dominant culture; education about and involvement in one's own ethnic group and its beliefs, values, and practices.
4. *Introspection*. Critical examination of the values, beliefs, and practices of both the dominant culture and one's own ethnic group's views.
5. *Articulation and awareness*. Identification of those values, beliefs, and practices from the dominant culture and from one's own ethnic group that are combined into a unique synthesis that forms a personal, cultural identity.

In this model, one recognizes the interaction between ethnic identity and personal identity (Rotheram-Borus & Wyche, 1994; Cross & Fhagen-Smith, 2001). Not all young people experience all of these stages. Some children are raised in families where ethnic socialization begins at a young age, and they never experience a sense of accepting the dominant culture. In fact, if they are raised in a racially segregated community, they may not encounter members of the dominant culture as significant figures during their early childhood years.

For many people, the stage of articulation and awareness may not occur until sometime later in adulthood. But for many, later adolescence is the period when exploration about ethnic identity is highlighted (see the box "Ethnic Identity and Adjustment"). The transitions from Stage 1 (conformity) to Stages 2 and 3 are commonly stimulated by the college experience. Ethnic identity exploration and commitment typically increase over the college years (Sayed & Azmitia, 2009). The student body is usually much more diverse than one's high school. Young people of many racial, ethnic, social-class, regional, and religious backgrounds come together in college and are expected to live together in the residence halls, learn together in the classrooms, and collaborate in college organizations, social activities, sports, and cultural events. Exposure to this diversity may be accompanied by experiences of racial and ethnic prejudice, cultural ethnocentrism, and intergroup conflict. At the same time, racial diversity often contributes to more divergent thinking, introduces new perspectives, and, as a result, promotes more complex thinking about social issues (Antonio, Chang et al., 2004). Exposure to the college curriculum offers an intellectual framework for understanding the historical, psychological, and sociological foundations of racism, prejudice, and cultural conflict (Phinney, 1996b).

For young people who remain in low-income, urban communities and do not attend college, the interaction of ethnic identity and personal identity can serve as an adaptive process for coping with high-risk environments. Identification with the history, struggles, and heroism of one's people serves as an anchor of dignity and hope in communities that are disrupted by unemployment and violence (Spencer, Cunningham, & Swanson, 1995). Through interaction with other members of their ethnic group, young people build competence and a set of strategies for managing the poverty and hostility that they face.

© Jim Sugar/CORBIS

The college environment provides an opportunity for students to learn about their cultural identities and the history of their ethnic groups.

The Prime Adaptive Ego Quality and the Core Pathology

In the process of resolving the crisis of identity versus identity confusion, later adolescents have to examine their values and goals. This process relies upon more advanced executive functioning, including the capacity to take a step back from one's current commitments and reflect on their meaning as well as an ability to deliberately seek out new sources of information and ideas that can inform personal decisions (Klimstra et al., 2010). As a result of this reflective work, later adolescents who achieve a sense of personal identity are also likely to benefit from a clearer, more confident sense of their values and beliefs. In contrast, later adolescents who experience identity confusion are likely to leave this stage of life with the core pathology of repudiation—a rejection or standing *against* rather than standing *for* specific beliefs and values.

Fidelity to Values and Ideologies

Fidelity to values and ideologies is closely linked with the notion of *commitment*. In later adolescence, the ego strength of **fidelity** refers to "the ability to sustain loyalties freely pledged in spite of the inevitable contradictions and confusions of value systems" (Erikson, 1978, p. 28). Fidelity incorporates the trust and hope of infancy and directs it toward a belief in values and ideologies. Fidelity may be fostered by identification with inspirational role models or by participation in meaningful institutions. It is also achieved as a result of the new cognitive capacities of adolescence that permit self-reflection, relativistic thinking, and insight. Fidelity to values and ideals provides evidence of a reflective person who has taken time to struggle with opposing views and to select those that best reflect personal convictions (Waterman, 1992).

The emergence of fidelity to values provides a channel for guiding strong passions and drives toward the achievement of meaningful goals. At the close of later adolescence, young people who articulate specific values and goals, such as making a contribution to their community, gaining new levels of expertise in their chosen field, or establishing a loving, caring relationship, are more likely to experience a sense of subjective well-being in the years ahead as they take deliberate steps toward goal attainment (Bauer & McAdams, 2010). Fidelity to values strengthens one's ethical resolve, especially in the face of the many pressures and temptations of adult life. It also creates a bond of belonging with others who share the same loyalties. At the same time, fidelity in the individual strengthens the society by drawing on the commitments of those who share a common set of values to sustain and support basic institutions, such as religious organizations, political parties, educational institutions, and social service agencies.

Fidelity to values and ideologies is closely linked to the developmental tasks of autonomy, gender identity, moral development, and career choice. In each of these domains, the young person faces challenges that may undermine self-respect, or that may foster in-group favoritism over out-group derogation. When individuals perceive their own personal or group identity to be threatened, they are more likely to withdraw, lash out, or reject the values of others. On the other hand, when individuals perceive a context of acceptance, inclusion, and fair treatment, they are more likely to be open to dialogue and cooperation. We do not know which values a young person will embrace. However, the more individuals are treated in a humane, respectful, and inclusive manner, the greater the likelihood that these values will be reflected in their outlook toward others (Andersen, Downey, & Tyler, 2005).

Repudiation

Repudiation refers to a rejection of certain values, beliefs, and roles. In the diverse and pluralistic society of the United States, some degree of repudiation may be necessary in order to forge an integrated identity. One cannot embrace all ideologies and

HUMAN DEVELOPMENT AND DIVERSITY

Ethnic Identity and Adjustment

ETHNIC IDENTITY HAS been studied for individual ethnic groups as a component of the self-concept, usually focusing on how important people's ethnicity is to them, how often they think about themselves as members of their ethnic group, and how close they feel to other members of their ethnic group (Sears, Fu, Henry, & Bui, 2003). Ethnic identity has also been measured as a general concept, allowing one to compare the strength of ethnic identity across groups. The *Multigroup Ethnic Identity Measure* (MEIM) is one such measure, which consists of two subscales (Phinney, 1992; Roberts et al., 1999):

1. *Affirmation, belonging, and commitment*, which assesses one's feelings of connection and pride in membership.
2. *Ethnic identity search*, a developmental and cognitive component, which assesses a person's efforts to be involved in activities and practices associated with their ethnic group, and to increase their understanding of the group and its history and traditions.

The MEIM allows one to characterize individuals along a continuum from an unexamined ethnic identity acquired with little exploration or commitment (*low ethnic identity*) to a well-developed, achieved ethnic identity (Yasui, Dorham, & Dishion, 2004). The parallels with personal identity status are striking, capturing the two processes of exploration (crisis) and commitment.

Ethnic identity, as measured by the MEIM, has been positively associated with self-esteem across middle childhood, early adolescence, and later adolescence. Individuals with positive ethnic identity have been found to deal more effectively with threatening social situations involving discrimination and stereotyping (Roberts et al., 1999). A sense of belonging to one's ethnic group may be important as part of one's social identity for all groups. However, the *salience* of ethnic identity is not the same for all groups. The establishment of a clear acceptance of their ethnic identity may be especially relevant for those who face discrimination or oppression on the basis of their ethnic membership.

Critical Thinking Questions

1. The MEIM has two scales: ethnic identity search; and affirmation, belonging, and commitment. How well do you think these scales capture the meaning of ethnic identity? What other dimensions would you add if you were going to modify this measure?
2. What are the parallels between ethnic identity achievement and personal identity achievement? How might they relate to each other as the person matures? Can you imagine having an achieved personal identity without a clear ethnic identity? What about vice versa?
3. Do you think ethnic identity is equally important for all ethnic groups? For all members of an ethnic group? What factors might determine how important or salient ethnic identity is for an individual or for an ethnic group?
4. What implications might one's ethnic identity achievement have for the developmental tasks of autonomy from parents, gender identity, moral development, and career choice?

roles; each commitment brings some boundaries to one's values and limits one's investment to a certain vision of the self continuing into the future. Repudiation can serve as a mechanism for intergenerational change. For example, a young person may decide that he will reject the characteristics of an unloving or abusive parent. In this context, the young person will form his identity around suppressing certain negative qualities and learning to enact and endorse opposing positive qualities.

In the extreme case, repudiation results in a hostile rejection of all the ideas, values, and groups that do not adhere to one's own beliefs (Erikson, 1982). It fosters a rigid worldview that does not admit to the contributions of others' ideas. The roots of militancy, prejudice, and terrorism lie in the formation of the core pathology of repudiation. Imagine young people who, on the threshold of adulthood, see their future as grim or hopeless. They may perceive themselves as subjugated victims, rejected by the mainstream. They may believe that their culture, their ethnic identity, or their religion is mocked or berated. They may transform the mistrust and shame of childhood into fury against the other. The energy of youth that can mobilize noble, courageous acts of fidelity can also crystallize around hate, turning against one or more groups in acts of violence.

APPLIED TOPIC

Dropping Out of College

Objective 6. *To examine some of the predictors and consequences of dropping out of college.*

THERE IS GROWING national concern about the large percentage of students who attend college and then leave

Tracy Whiteside/Shutterstock.com

Sitting in an alley outside of his dorm, Jason thinks about his low grades and wonders if being in college is just a waste of money.

without a degree. In general, the percentage of the U.S. population with advanced degrees has not grown much over the past 10 years. Data from the U.S. Census Bureau (2010) show that among those ages 25 to 34, about 30% have a bachelor's or advanced graduate or professional degree. Although the majority of high school graduates (67% in 2007) attend some type of postsecondary institution in the year following high school, many do not graduate. According to a report of the National Center for Higher Education Management Systems (NCHEMS, 2010), in 2008 the national graduation rate for 4-year colleges was 56% after 6 years. The graduation rate for 2-year colleges was 27.5% after 3 years. These rates differ by state, type of institution (public or private, research university or liberal arts college), and by students' race/ethnicity and family economic resources. Degree completion is notably lower for students entering college whose families have limited economic resources, and for certain ethnic minorities, who tend to be overrepresented among low-income families.

Models of student retention and persistence suggest that degree completion is a result of the interaction of four classes of factors: financial factors, academic preparation, personal factors, and characteristics of the college environment (Newman & Newman, 1999).

Financial Factors

The cost of tuition, room, board, and fees increased 21.6% at public universities and 20% at private universities (adjusted for inflation) from the 1999–2000 academic year to the 2007–2008 academic year (NCES, 2010). These increases far outpaced the average increase in family income over the same period. Among college freshmen, about two thirds state that they are either somewhat or very concerned about their ability to finance their college education (Marchand, 2010). It is no surprise that college students in the lowest quartile of family income are less likely to graduate than those in the higher quartiles. Students from poor families are more likely to be working several jobs to pay for school. Often they are troubled by the burden of growing debt and are

uncomfortable about borrowing more. Many students have financial responsibilities for their family members. Unexpected fees, and textbook and laboratory costs associated with college courses, are more difficult to cover for students from poor families, because they have less access to supplemental financial resources. These students' parents have fewer resources, and cannot help them meet unanticipated expenses. Students who dedicate their summer earnings to paying for tuition and fees do not have enough discretionary income to cover unanticipated costs.

In order to manage the financial requirements of attending college, many students from low-income families make a combination of decisions that put them at risk for **dropping out of college**. They decide to save money by living at home, and they work more hours a week at jobs to help defray expenses. Both of these factors, living off campus and working long hours, are associated with an increased likelihood of dropping out of college (Bozick, 2007). Because they are not living on campus, they are less likely to feel a part of the college community, and less likely to benefit from the friendship and social and academic support of other students. In addition, working 20 hours per week or more makes it just about impossible to become involved with campus activities or informal friendships that might increase feelings of belonging and help provide resourceful ideas about how to cope with the academic and career preparation demands of college. When demands from classes conflict with demands from work, students from low-income families are less likely to be able to cut back on work hours.

In many cases, students from low-income families have had to establish independent financial status, and do not receive any funds from parents. Students from very poor families may also have attended high schools that did not provide adequate academic preparation, resulting in a requirement to take additional developmental coursework that does not count toward a college degree (Stinebrickner & Stinebrickner, 2006). Over time, students who are working at a job many hours a week just to keep up with tuition payments may find that life in college is more stressful and less enjoyable than it seems to be worth.

Academic Preparation

The following factors that precede college enrollment have all been found to relate to college retention and graduation:

- Attendance at a college-oriented high school
- Participation in a college-preparatory curriculum
- Parents' educational background
- Family's educational values and goals
- The student's intention to attend college
- Clarity of career goals
- High school coursework and grades

High school GPA and SAT and ACT scores have been identified as strong retention predictors (Astin, Korn, & Green, 1987). A rigorous high school curriculum is the strongest predictor of postsecondary persistence and success (Adelman, 1999). Students with inadequate academic preparation and lack of familiarity with the college environment are more likely to leave before graduating.

There is growing concern among college faculty that students are not prepared to meet their expectations for writing, mathematics, independent work, critical thinking, detailed examination of information, and complex problem solving (Sanoff, 2006). Early failure experiences in college courses can result in a decision to drop out of college. Michael Van Adams' story illustrates this process:

> Van Adams . . . told himself that the University of Maine wasn't for him. He dropped out a couple of weeks before completing his first semester. "Frankly, I wasn't properly prepared for college," he says. "I didn't go into my freshman year with the right attitude. At age 18, I thought I had the world figured out; I thought I could ace my college classes like in high school. I couldn't have been more off. I was failing three classes, and I didn't see the point of sticking around." (Whitbourne, 2002)

College mathematics and science courses are prerequisites for many majors. Students who fail an early mathematics or science course may realize that they will not be admitted to the major of their choice and decide to leave school. Students who have been accustomed to ranking in the top 10% of their high school class may be shocked to receive grades of C or D in college courses, and they may assume that they do not have the ability to do college work. Many colleges have cut back on offering precollegiate or developmental courses in writing, mathematics, and science, thereby removing the support for students whose high school curriculum did not prepare them adequately for college-level work.

Personal Factors

The theme of personal identity and its salience in later adolescence is central to the decision to remain in college or leave. For many students, the decision to go to college is a commitment to a view of oneself in the future as a person who is more accomplished, prepared to function at a higher level, earning a better income, and being in a better position to direct the course of one's life. Within the college environment, identity work can be fostered as one is supported by others who validate the sense of a future self that is taking shape. It can be reassuring to be surrounded by others who have similar academic aspirations. Interacting and identifying with faculty and graduate students who are pursuing interests as models for the future, the young person begins to see how personal goals may be attained. College coursework and interactions with peers can result in growth in worldview and exposure to new models of organizing, analyzing, and representing experience.

A variety of personal factors can interfere with this process. Once in college, the level of a student's social and academic integration, along with his intent to complete college, can affect decisions to stay in school. Factors that can contribute to dropping out of college may include:

- An inability to cope with the new demands for autonomy, time management, and competition
- Disillusionment with the environment of college
- Discouragement or confusion about one's ability to achieve important goals
- The onset of mental health problems
- Alcohol or drug abuse/use
- Victimization

The college environment presents new challenges to mental health. Many students suffer from mental health problems that were managed satisfactorily in high school, but that become more challenging in the college environment. Away from family, friends, and familiar medical resources, students may stop taking their medication, become overwhelmed by anxiety or depression, or engage in new risky behaviors that impede their ability to concentrate. Being away from home may result in unexpected feelings of loneliness and isolation. The college environment typically introduces new opportunities to make decisions about daily life, and, as a result, brings new demands for time management. Students may feel unable to succeed at the academic or social demands of the environment. They may feel overwhelmed by the number of tasks or the social stimulation. Students who are participating in competitive athletics may have difficulty meeting expectations to perform at a new, high level. Feelings of being overwhelmed or overloaded may result in poor academic performance or low levels of life satisfaction that can lead to dropping out of school (Larson, 2006).

African American and Hispanic American students leave college at a higher rate than European American students, even when controlling for family income. This pattern is often attributed to a lack of a sense of connection or belonging in the college environment. Students who are doing well academically may decide to leave an environment where they are alienated, targets of discrimination, or disconnected from faculty and students (Schwitzer & Thomas, 1998; Murtaugh, Burns, & Schuster, 1999).

Characteristics of the College Environment

Characteristics of the college environment have also been associated with student retention. In a study of student retention at colleges and universities with large numbers of low-income students, the Pell Foundation compared schools with higher than average and lower than average graduation rates (Muraskin & Lee, 2004). School structure was associated with graduation rates. Universities characterized as Research I, where there were more graduate students and a greater emphasis on faculty research, had higher retention and graduation rates than the bachelor's degree/specialized colleges. Those institutions with higher graduation rates had more full-time students, a larger student enrollment, and more graduate students. These schools enrolled more students from the top half of their high school graduating classes. They had more full-time faculty, lower student/

faculty ratios, and smaller classes. As a related factor, they spent more money per student full-time equivalent (FTE), and tuition and fees were higher, but these colleges were able to offset these costs with more grants to students.

Beyond these structural features, colleges and universities that were successful in graduating their low-income students focused on five aspects of the college environment (Muraskin & Lee, 2004):

- Building academic skills
- Providing financial support
- Working with students to help them clarify their academic direction
- Fostering a personalized environment for instruction and academic support
- Encouraging campus participation

At the colleges that are successful in graduating relatively large numbers of low-income students, one is likely to find pre-college or pre-enrollment courses to prepare students for the tone and tempo of college courses; supplemental services such as focused, proactive academic advising, study groups, and writing centers; and special housing groups, affinity groups, and interest groups to support students of common interest or background. Many of these campuses offer undergraduates research experiences with encouragement to consider graduate school. They create learning communities, and organize students into social and academic groups in order to create a more personalized educational environment. These institutions express their commitment to retention and graduation through the ways faculty and staff interact with students, the care that is taken to create a supportive environment, and the encouragement that students experience to achieve their goals.

The Consequences of Dropping Out of College

In comparison to the research that has been done to predict student retention, relatively little is known about how students who drop out of college cope with this disrupted educational trajectory and its impact on their transition into adulthood. Dropping out of college does not necessarily solve the young person's problems, and may introduce new ones. Abandoning the set of goals and activities that are linked to college attendance leaves the student in a directional vacuum. Formulating another set of goals and becoming involved in the activities required to achieve these goals may be difficult. There may be new pressures on the college dropout as people ask, "What are you going to do now?" While enrolled in college, students can cover some of their uncertainty by saying, "I'm in college." Dropping out means losing this protective, if somewhat ambiguous, role. This decision brings a need to recalculate and reorganize one's trajectory for the transition into adulthood. This task may be difficult and confusing because the identity work needed to flourish outside of college is different than the identity work required of the college student.

Dropping out has an impact on short- and long-term earnings. Leaving college has significant financial implications that will impact the young person's autonomy and capacity for financial self-sufficiency. As presented in Table 10.1, the median income for a person who has some college but no degree is only slightly more than for a person who has graduated from high school. In some states, like California, New York, and New Jersey, the difference in median annual income between college graduates and high school graduates who are in their twenties is $12,000 to $13,000 (NCHEMS, 2007). This difference in earning capacity increases as people move into their middle adulthood because opportunities for advancement are associated with higher levels of education. Moreover, those who attend college for a year or two and then leave are likely to have debts from tuition, fees, and other costs that they carry with them without hope of the increase in salary that might help them repay those debts.

Reduced educational attainment will have an impact on occupation. This in turn may have consequences for one's social status in the community. Dropping out of college may be accompanied by the loss of a peer group and the need to create a new social network, and the possibility of disappointing family members. The lack of a college degree may make one a less desirable life partner and reduce one's marriage prospects.

Given the flexibility of the higher education system in the United States, there are many opportunities to reengage the college environment, including online enrollment, part-time status, evening and weekend courses, and continuing education. We do not know much about the process through which students who leave college without a degree decide to return or how they make meaning of their disrupted college years. One might wonder whether the experiences leave a person with a feeling of regret about unrealized promise, or if they are able to identify a more authentic set of life goals that can be achieved without benefit of a college education. There are many instances of people who do not graduate from high school or college, but who become engaged in creative, productive lives. A number of successful actors, singers, models, athletes, inventors, entrepreneurs, and authors have taken the noncollegiate route, choosing to use these years to become clearer about their life goals and to develop their talents (collegedropoutshalloffame.com, 2010).

Chapter Summary

At the close of later adolescence, most young people are making the transition from childhood to adulthood. However, the process is gradual for most and increasingly prolonged into the decades of the twenties and thirties.

Objective 1. To examine the concept of autonomy from parents and the conditions under which autonomy is likely to be achieved.

Later adolescents are striving for self-sufficiency in a complex culture. Many have achieved a new degree of independence from their parents, so that ties of love, trust, and support are expressed within a framework of mutual respect and autonomous decision making. The process of achieving autonomy from parents opens the door to new considerations of basic ego structures, including gender identity, morality, and career aspirations. In each of these areas, a young person has the cognitive ability to reflect on the earlier socialization pressures of family and neighborhood and to construct a personal point of view.

Objective 2. To trace the development of gender identity in later adolescence, including a discussion of how the components of gender role identification that were relevant during the early-school-age period are revised and expanded.

The formulation of gender identity requires an integration of the biological, psychological, and societal meanings associated with being a man or a woman. It is a powerful lens through which many other aspects of personal identity are interpreted, including the content of values, commitment to family relationships, preferences and expectations for career choice, and beliefs about one's role in an intimate relationship.

Objective 3. To describe the maturation of morality in later adolescence, with special focus on the role of new cognitive capacities that influence moral judgments and the various value orientations that underlie moral reasoning.

Exposure to a diversity of information, relationships, and worldviews stimulates moral reasoning. The change from conventional to postconventional morality that often occurs during later adolescence involves a rethinking of traditional moral principles. During this period, there may be a loosening of ties to the family of origin and an increase in encounters with an expanding network of friends, students, and coworkers. Through interactions with diverse reference groups, there is an increasing recognition of the subcultural relativity of one's moral code. There may also be a degree of conflict over which moral values have personal meaning.

Objective 4. To analyze the process of career choice, with attention to education and gender role socialization as two major influential factors.

The process of career choice, often accompanied by periods of uncertainty and confusion, is influenced by interacting factors, including personal abilities and attributes, emotional and motivational factors, family and societal factors, educational background, gender identity and gender role socialization, and the situational realities of the current labor market. Ideally, one's choice of occupation is the result of personal experimentation, introspection, self-evaluation, fact finding, and intuition. As such, this choice becomes intimately interwoven with one's psychological development.

Objective 5. To define and describe the psychosocial crisis of later adolescence, individual identity versus identity confusion; the central process through which this crisis is resolved, role experimentation; the prime adaptive ego quality of fidelity to values and ideals; and the core pathology of repudiation.

Those who have resolved the psychosocial crisis of individual identity versus identity confusion have an integrated identity that includes a definition of themselves as sexual, moral, political, and career participants. Identity achievement represents a private sense of unity and confidence in one's beliefs as well as a more public integration of roles and commitments to specific values.

The strain of this stage is felt in the tension between the person's need to question and experiment and the society's expectations for closure on significant themes, particularly occupation, gender identity, and political ideology. The expansion of roles and relationships exposes many young people to new views that require evaluation. The crisis of individual identity versus identity confusion suggests a new synthesis of earlier identifications, present values, and future goals into a consistent self-concept. This unity of self is achieved only after a period of uncertainty and open questioning. Role experimentation during this time is an essential strategy for coping with new information and new value orientations. Once young people know what they stand for, they can commit themselves more deeply to others.

The prime adaptive ego quality of fidelity reflects the capacity to commit oneself to an ideology or belief system. The core pathology of repudiation suggests an intense rejection of certain values and beliefs. Although most later adolescents are forming a positive vision of the self that is connected to a shared community, some are defining themselves in opposition, as rebels, terrorists, or avengers.

Objective 6. *To examine some of the predictors and consequences of dropping out of college.*

The applied topic, dropping out of college, illustrates the fluidity of this period. Identity work, which requires an integration of one's biological, psychological, and social selves, takes place in concrete settings where daily demands and expectations must be met. Societal expectations set many young people on a path toward college that they cannot follow, whether for financial, academic, personal, or situational reasons. The disruption of this academic trajectory poses significant challenges for establishing a life structure into adulthood. At the same time, it may invite more serious and considered reflection about what a person wants out of life and the activities and resources that will be required to achieve those goals.

Key Terms

androgens/estrogens, 398
androgyny, 400
autonomy, 390
career choice, 405
career decision making, 409
career indecision, 411
career maturity, 409
caring, 404
caring orientation, 404
choice phase, 410
clarification phase, 410
commitment, 415
confusion, 415
conventional level, 402
crisis, 415
crystallization phase, 410
cultural relativism, 402
differentiation, 390
dropping out of college, 423
ethnic identity, 420
exploration phase, 410
femininity, 400

fidelity, 421
foreclosure, 415
gender identity, 394
gender role expectations, 396
gender role preference, 401
gender typicality, 401
identity achievement, 415
identity confusion, 415
identity foreclosure, 414
identity process, 414
identity status, 414
individual identity, 412
induction phase, 410
influence phase, 410
integration phase, 410
internalized morality, 402
introspection, 394
justice orientation, 404
masculinity, 400
moral exemplars, 404
moral identity, 404
moral reasoning, 402

moratorium, 415
negative identity, 415
parental attachment, 393
phases of career decision
   making, 409
postconventional level, 402
postconventional morality, 403
preconventional level, 402
private self, 412
prohibitive moral judgments, 404
prosocial moral judgments, 404
psychosocial moratorium, 417
public self, 413
repudiation, 421
role experimentation, 417
self-sufficiency, 393
sex, 396
sexual orientation, 400
third gender, 396
transgendered, 400
transsexuals, 396

Further Reflection

What distinguishes the stage of later adolescence from early adolescence and early adulthood?

1. How is the process of achieving autonomy from parents related to identity development?
2. What changes would you expect to see in gender identity over the college years? Do you think men and women become more traditional or more nontraditional in their views about gender roles during college? Why?
3. What aspects of the college experience influence moral development? What is the direction of that influence?
4. Consider the bidirectional influence of career decision making and identity development. How do the two influence each other?
5. What are some contemporary factors that may make it difficult to resolve the conflict of individual identity versus identity confusion during the period from ages 18 to 24?
6. What is ethnic identity? How does it contribute to adjustment and identity achievement in later adolescence?

Psychology CourseMate

To access additional course materials, including CourseMate, please visit www.cengagebrain.com. At the CengageBrain.com home page, search for the ISBN of your title (from the back cover of your book) using the search box at the top of the page. This will take you to the product page where these resources can be found.

Casebook

For additional case material related to this chapter, see the case entitled "Life Turning Points and Career Choice" in *Life Span Development: A Case Book*, by Barbara and Philip Newman, Laura Landry-Meyer, and Brenda J. Lohman, pp. 153–156. The case illustrates how a young person's encounter with a difficult personal situation leads to a revised sense of self and a new focus on meaningful goals for the future.

Family of Acrobats with Monkey, 1905/© 2011 Estate of Pablo Picasso/Artists Rights Society (ARS), New York

The major themes of early adulthood—work, intimacy, marriage, and parenting—are all captured in this image of the Young Harlequin Family. The challenges of adulthood often emerge in efforts to balance and integrate diverse life roles.

Early Adulthood (24 to 34 years)

Chapter Objectives

1. To identify and define selected concepts that are especially relevant for understanding development during adulthood, including social roles, the life course, and fulfillment theories.

2. To analyze the process of forming intimate relationships, including initial attractions, mate selection, and commitment to a long-term relationship; the role of cohabitation in forming close relationships; and the challenges that one faces in adjusting to the early years of marriage.

3. To describe the factors associated with the decision to have children, the impact of childbearing on the intimate relationship, the developing parental relationship, and the contribution of childbearing to growth in adulthood.

4. To explore the concept of work as a stimulus for psychosocial development in early adulthood, with special focus on the technical skills, authority relations, demands and hazards, and interpersonal relations in the work environment.

5. To examine the concept of lifestyle as the expression of individual identity, with consideration for the pace of life, balancing competing role demands, building a supportive social network, and adopting practices to promote health and fitness.

6. To define and describe the psychosocial crisis of intimacy versus isolation, the central process through which the crisis is resolved, mutuality among peers, the prime adaptive ego quality of love, and the core pathology of exclusivity.

7. To analyze divorce as a life stressor in early adulthood, including the factors contributing to it and the process of coping with it.

WELCOME TO THE study of adulthood. All that has gone before can be seen as preparation; all that follows can be viewed as actualization. We have considered psychosocial development through seven preparatory stages of life, encompassing approximately 24 years. During these stages, an individual undergoes rapid physical, cognitive, social, and emotional development. In the United States, life expectancy at birth is currently about 78 years. Thus, more than 50 years remain after the seven preparatory stages. In our conceptual scheme, four stages of psychosocial development unfold during these 50 years. In this chapter, we discuss a few theoretical concepts about development in adulthood, and then we address the period of early adulthood.

Major Concepts in the Study of Adulthood

Objective 1. To identify and define selected concepts that are especially relevant for understanding development during adulthood, including social roles, the life course, and fulfillment theories.

In Chapter 2 (Major Theories for Understanding Human Development) and Chapter 3 (Psychosocial Theory) we introduce a variety of theoretical concepts that explain the processes of continuity and change over the life span. In this chapter, we expand the discussion of theoretical constructs that help account for the directions of growth in adult life. The biological, psychological, and societal systems continue to interact, but the nature of lives becomes increasingly diverse and more difficult to characterize as stage-like over time. Life stories are guided by historical events, unexpected crises and opportunities, and personal choices. New levels of mastery and autonomy allow individuals to make decisions and choices about the kinds of environments in which they participate. In addition, the autonomy of adult life allows individuals to express their genetic predispositions to a greater degree than when their parents, teachers, and other authority figures were creating their environments, and constraining their choices. The bidirectional nature of development is increasingly obvious in adulthood as interests, beliefs, and goals guide the direction and focus of actions, and these actions and their consequences in turn create the context for the revision of interests, beliefs, and goals. In the following sections, we review the concepts of social roles, the life course, and personal fulfillment, ideas that help explain the psychosocial dynamics of adulthood.

Social Roles

Social role is one of the concepts most frequently used for understanding adulthood. The major concepts of social role theory, which were introduced in Chapter 2, are summarized in Table 11.1. We consider this concept numerous times in the analysis of childhood and adolescent life stages, including Chapter 7 (Early School Age) when we discuss gender role identification, and again in Chapter 10 (Later Adolescence) when we examine individual identity versus identity confusion. Clearly, many roles are learned and enacted during childhood. In adulthood, however, people assume multiple roles that expand their opportunities for self-expression and bring them into contact with new social demands. Adulthood can be seen as a series of increasingly differentiated and complex roles that the individual plays for substantial lengths of time. The salient roles of adulthood, such as worker, spouse, friend, parent, teacher, mentor, volunteer, or community leader, give structure to adult identity and meaning to life.

Social roles link individuals to their social environments. The roles that an individual plays exist as socially shared patterns of expectations for behavior. All roles can be characterized by costs and benefits that accumulate over time. For example, by assuming the role of worker, one has access to the benefits associated with the role, such as social status, social support, or financial resources. One also becomes responsible for meeting the expectations of the role, such as working for a certain number of hours each week or completing one's work to a certain standard of quality. Over one's life, the costs and benefits of the roles accumulate, influencing the ease or difficulty with which new roles and role transitions can be managed (Jackson, 2004). For example, if a person's worker role involves many short-term jobs with no retirement benefits, the transition to retirement may be more difficult financially, but the person may have less

Image copyright iofoto 2010. Used under license from Shutterstock.com

Maureen is already off to an early morning meeting. Cheryl is eating the breakfast that her mother left out on the counter for her. Bert is checking materials online for his first meeting while he talks to Cheryl's preschool to let them know that she will be picked up at noon by Suzie, her babysitter. The roles of husband, father, worker, and household manager are difficult for Bert to cope with, but he does his best.

identification with a specific worker role and find the transition into retirement psychologically easier.

Roles are *reciprocal*, requiring complementary role identities—such as teacher-student, mother-child—in order to be enacted and sustained. Thus, participation in multiple roles brings with it a form of social integration and social support

TABLE 11.1 Major Concepts of Social Role Theory

CONCEPT	EXPLANATION
Social role	Parts or identities a person assumes that are also social positions: kinship roles, age roles, gender roles, occupational roles
Role enactment	Patterned characteristics of social behavior generated by a social role
Role expectations	Scripts or shared expectations for behavior that are linked to each role
Role gain	Addition of roles
Role strain	Stress caused by too many expectations within a role
Role conflict	Conflict caused by competing demands of different roles
Role loss	Ending of a role; may result in stress and disorientation
Dimensions of life roles that vary from person to person	Number of roles
	Intensity of involvement in roles
	Time demands of each role
	Structure or flexibility of the role

Source: © Cengage Learning.

(Thoits, 1999; Wethington, Moen, Glasgow, & Pillemer, 2000). Involvement in multiple roles allows adults to help socialize younger generations. Only in adulthood do individuals experience the behavioral requirements of many of their roles, which in turn provide a basis on which to socialize their children for the demands of adulthood (Kite, 1996).

The expectations associated with adult roles provide a frame of reference within which individuals make their own personal decisions. For example, a man may know what is expected of him in the worker role, but he may choose to ignore those expectations and strive for greater responsibilities, more power, or more autonomy. People can conform to role expectations, revise them, or reject them altogether. In addition to the tensions produced by role conflicts and role strain, some of the stresses of adulthood result from the need to redefine certain role expectations in order to preserve an authentic sense of self.

Life Course

Life course refers to the integration and sequencing of phases of work and family life over time. Glen Elder (1985, 1996; Elder & Shanahan, 2006), who has been a leader in the elaboration of the life course perspective, described the two central themes of trajectories and transitions. A trajectory is the path of one's life experiences in a specific domain, particularly work and family. The family trajectory might include marriage, parenthood, grandparenthood, and widowhood. A transition is the beginning or ending of an event or role relationship. In the work trajectory, for example, transitions might be getting one's first job, being fired, and going back to school for an advanced degree. Transitions are the events that make up a lifelong trajectory. A person's work and family trajectories are embedded in a sociohistorical context. For example, for people born in the early 1920s, the events of World War II, occurring during their twenties, influenced their work and family formation. For many young men, the planned work trajectory was interrupted by military service, and many young women entered the labor market unexpectedly. At the close of the war, in the late 1940s and early 1950s, many couples who had delayed parenting started their families, which gave rise to the baby boom generation.

The life course concept can be applied to the content of individual life histories as they are expressed in a social and historical time period. Each person's life course can be thought of as a pattern of the adaptations to the configuration of cultural expectations, resources, and barriers experienced during a particular time period. One form of cultural expectations is what Bernice Neugarten and her colleagues (Neugarten, Moore, & Lowe, 1965) termed the social clock. This term refers to "age norms and age expectations [that] operate as prods and brakes upon behavior, in some instances hastening behavior and in some instances delaying it" (p. 710). Neugarten and her associates suggested that social class groups tend to agree on the appropriate age for significant life events, such as marriage, childrearing, and retirement. This consensus exerts social pressure

on individuals in the group, pushing them to assume a particular role at an expected age. Age norms may also suppress behaviors that are considered inappropriate for one's age. Adults are aware of existing norms regarding the timing of certain behaviors and evaluate their own behaviors as being on time, too soon, or too late. Implied in the notion of the social clock are expectations about the sequencing of entry into new roles and age-related role transitions. For example, European-American adults in the United States tend to view an ideal sequence as work, marriage, and parenting, in that order. Research indicates that for women, following this sequence is associated with better mental health, including less depression and greater happiness in adulthood. Among African Americans, however, the sequence of work, parenting, and then marriage is associated with less depression and greater happiness. This suggests that different social norms for role sequencing may be operating in the respective ethnic communities (Jackson, 2004). The social clock is constantly being reset as people confront the challenges, demands, and new structures of modern society. In contemporary society, with the lengthening of the life expectancy and the increasing vitality of older adults, there are fewer and fewer domains in which a person is considered too old to participate (Neugarten, 1990).

Figure 11.1 provides a view of the age-linked changes in occupational and family careers. The figure maps the convergence of transitions across the occupational and family trajectories, illustrating periods of potential harmony and conflict between the demands in the two trajectories. The bottom line shows a model of transitions in a family career. The line above shows a model of transitions in an occupational career. Sometimes these transitions occur around the same time in life. For example, in Figure 11.1, marriage occurs during a period of job experimentation when a person may be changing jobs. This could create tension in the marriage if it results in economic insecurity. Occupational experimentation might be cut short in order to establish financial stability for the marriage. The conflicts that arise in coordinating these family and occupational careers may contribute to the high divorce rate in the first year following marriage. Looking at Figure 11.1, you could consider many other examples where the demands of the family and occupational careers influence each other.

In considering adult lives in contemporary society, one can see that this is only one possible map of the interconnections between work and family in the course of a life. The occupational and family careers look quite different for the following people: a woman who extends her educational preparation to include a professional degree, works before marriage, and delays childbearing into her middle to late 30s; a woman who remains single and dedicates her energy to excellence in a career; and a woman who marries right after high school, begins having children at 18, works during her childbearing years, and then retires at 55 to enjoy her grandchildren and her personal freedom.

The pattern of the life course is influenced by the *historical era* (Schaie & Elder, 2005). The life course of a person

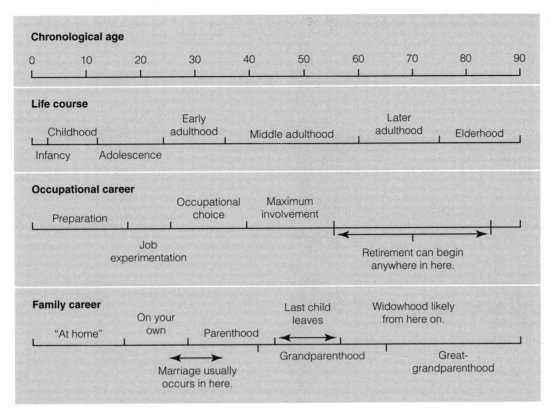

FIGURE 11.1 A Hypothetical Life Course
Source: Adapted from Atchley, 1975.

who was born in 1900 and died in 1975, including the ages of completion of educational attainment, entry into the labor market, marriage, and retirement, would look quite different from that of a person born in 1930 and reaching age 75 in 2005. The two people would have gone through the same chronological ages, but during different periods of history, with different opportunities, expectations, and challenges. The first person would have been 30 at the time of the Great Depression. Her family could have been seriously influenced by loss of employment, difficulty in finding work, and loss of savings for retirement. The second person would have been 30 in 1960. Having served in the military during the Korean War, he would have been eligible for the GI Bill benefits to go to college, resulting in new occupational opportunities that contribute to occupational advancement during a booming economy (MacLean & Elder, 2007). There are many other possibilities of historical impact, but these examples illustrate how historical factors might affect the life course.

All the people who are roughly the same age during a particular historical period are referred to as a cohort. Differences in medical advances, occupational opportunities, educational resources, and the number of people in the cohort are four factors that may affect the pattern of life events for cohort members. Moreover, major crises, such as war, famine, and political unrest, may alter a trajectory by introducing unanticipated transitions—for example, closing off certain activities, as when young men interrupt their education to go to war, or opening up new opportunities, as when women enter the labor market because many of the men are in the military (Elder, 1986; Elder, Caspi, & van Nguyen, 1986; Elder, Shanahan, & Clipp, 1997).

The study of the life course focuses not only on the sequencing of events but also on the psychological growth that occurs as adults strive to adjust to changing and sometimes conflicting role demands. At different ages, people bring a distinct perspective to these events. For example, a crisis such as widespread unemployment may have a direct impact on the work trajectory of an adult, and also on the family environment or educational opportunities of a child. The person's developmental level and the particular developmental tasks and psychosocial crises that are most salient at the time will determine how a specific event will influence the life course.

Fulfillment Theories

As the norms and cultural expectations of modern life become more flexible, there is renewed interest in personal fulfillment and self-actualization as concepts that guide individual choices and directions for growth. The *humanistic* or *fulfillment* theorists emphasize the purposive, goal-oriented strivings that characterize adult life. People do not always act to reduce tension, achieve equilibrium, or avoid risk. Over the course of adult life, people seek out new challenges, impose new and difficult standards on their behavior, and put themselves in unfamiliar situations in order to seek fulfillment. In its recent transformation, the fulfillment theories have become integrated into the field of *positive psychology*, the scientific study of the strengths and virtues that enable individuals and communities to thrive (Seligman, Parks, & Steen, 2006).

Charlotte Buhler was one of the earliest and most continuously productive of the humanistic or fulfillment theorists. Her work emphasized the centrality of life goals and intentionality through the life course (Buhler & Massarik, 1968). In her view, each person experiences life within a complex orientation to past, present, and future time. It is the hope for meeting future goals and for achieving a sense of fulfillment that prompts psychological growth. Buhler saw the years of early and middle adulthood as a time of setting definite goals and striving to achieve them. Toward the end of middle adulthood, there is focused preoccupation with the assessment of goals and the analysis of successes and failures. This process ends with a sense of fulfillment, partial fulfillment, or despair.

The last phase of life is seen as a reaction to this assessment. People may resign themselves to their successes and failures (as Erikson suggests in the concept of integrity). However, some people may be motivated to return to an earlier phase of striving to achieve unfulfilled goals or to undo past failures. Some people end their lives in a despondent state of unfulfillment, concluding that their existence has not been meaningful (as we suggest in the concept of immortality versus extinction). Three concepts from fulfillment theory are especially relevant for understanding the directions of growth in adulthood: competence, self-acceptance, and self-actualization.

Competence

Robert White (1960, 1966) introduced the term **competence motivation** to explain behaviors that are motivated by a desire for new levels of mastery. People strive to increase their competence through repetition and practice of skills, by gaining new information, through education and training, and through feedback from earlier efforts at mastery. The competence motive can be seen in an infant's efforts at self-feeding even when those efforts result in less food making its way from dish to mouth. The competence motive can be seen in the determination of an adult to learn to ski despite the cold, the expense, and the sore muscles. It can be seen when retired persons enroll in adult education courses to expand their knowledge. Over the course of adulthood, competence is expanded through a deepening of interests, by pursuing information and experiences that contribute to what we often term expert knowledge.

Self-Acceptance

According to Carl Rogers' theory of personality development, an essential component of continued growth is to experience and accept the authentic self (Rogers, 1959, 1961). This means achieving a sense of trust in one's ideas and impulses rather than denying or constantly disapproving of them. It means fostering acceptance and trust in relationships with others, so that people bring their most authentic selves into interactions. **Self-acceptance** is a product of the positive feelings that come from being direct and from the acceptance one receives from others.

In Rogers' view, barriers to self-acceptance come largely from conditions that others place on their love or approval. If significant others give approval based only on meeting certain conditions, then the person learns to modify his behavior so that it conforms to those conditions. However, these modifications are made at the price of self-acceptance. They lead a person into a pattern of inhibiting or rejecting new thoughts and relying more and more on the opinions of others. The greater the discrepancy between the authentic self as one perceives it and daily experience, the more one is likely to experience life as threatening and stressful. The greater the harmony between the authentic self and experience, the more likely one is to experience a sense of trust, freedom, and creativity in daily functioning. An implication of this theory is that well-being is a product of person-environment coadaptation. In the search for self-acceptance, the person seeks social settings where her thoughts, beliefs, and actions are highly valued and where the social setting can be modified to value and endorse the talents of those who participate in it.

Self-Actualization

According to Abraham Maslow's theory, human beings are always in a state of striving (Maslow, 1968). **Self-actualization** is a powerful, growth-oriented motive that sits atop a pyramid of needs (see Figure 11.2). In Maslow's view, the primary human motives concern physiological needs, such as hunger, thirst, and a need for sleep. The second level focuses on safety and security—the need to find protection from dangers and threats. At this level, one might include security of employment, safety for oneself and one's family, and concerns about one's health and the health of one's family. As those needs are satisfied and maintained at a relatively stable level, people direct their energy to satisfying needs for belongingness and love, including friendship, intimate relationships, family and kinship ties, and desired group belonging. At the next level, one is motivated to enhance and protect self-esteem by building confidence in oneself, achieving valued goals and gaining the respect and admiration of others. Finally, if those needs can be met and sustained, the person directs energy to self-actualization, a motive that urges the person to make optimal use of his full potential, to become a fully effective, creative participant in daily life. The need for self-actualization, like White's idea of competence, becomes a driving force, urging the person to seek new levels of insight and personal fulfillment. People who are characterized as self-actualized are described as authentic, having a reality-based orientation about themselves and others. They are spontaneous, interested in solving problems, and accepting of others. They lack prejudice. These qualities result from a continuous force toward growth as the richness of a person's human capacities are allowed to flourish (Maslow, 1943).

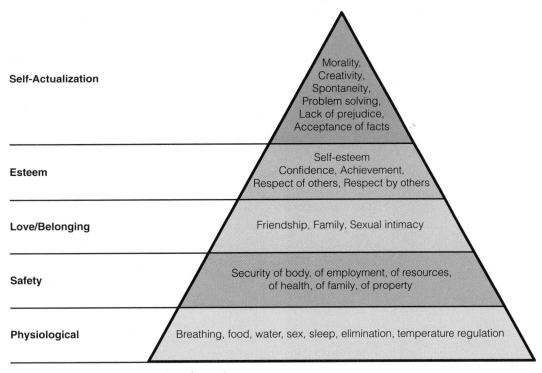

FIGURE 11.2 Maslow's Hierarchy of Needs

The fulfillment theories suggest that growth and maturation in adulthood are characterized by successful encounters with life challenges that result in a sense of purpose, meaning, and mastery. Questions have been raised about the possible negative impact of prejudice and discrimination on the mental health and sense of personal self-worth of members of minority groups. A study of a national sample called "Midlife in the U.S." examined this issue (Ryff, Keyes, & Hughes, 2003). Psychological well-being was defined in terms of constructs basic to fulfillment theory, including a sense of autonomy, environmental mastery, personal growth, positive relations with others, purpose in life, and self-acceptance. The results showed that individuals who were members of minority groups, including African Americans and Hispanic Americans, had higher levels of well-being than comparable European American participants, even after perceived discrimination was taken into account. With regard to the sense of purpose of life, this advantage was especially noteworthy among the more highly educated participants, where the more highly educated African Americans had a greater sense of purpose in life than the highly educated European American participants. The study found that perceived discrimination was negatively associated with psychological well-being for women but not for men. Thus, two processes seem to be at work simultaneously: (1) perceived discrimination undermines psychological well-being for women, and (2) minority status is associated with many indicators of psychological strength for both women and men.

In summary, the concepts of life roles, the life course, and fulfillment theories extend an understanding of psychological development in adulthood. Childhood is over. One addresses life with great expectations and exhilaration. After the initial excitement of the period subsides, one comes to realize that there is serious work to be done. Young adults engage in intense and meaningful relationships in marriage or with intimate partners, friends, and coworkers. They attempt to cope with the complex challenges of daily life by balancing multiple roles. At the same time, they put into action the practices that express the values and beliefs to which they became committed at the close of later adolescence. They establish and revise goals, setting new standards for competence and self-acceptance. Over the course of adulthood, people return periodically to reflect on the meaning of their life and the value of their accomplishments. The expanding period of later adulthood and very old age provides new opportunities to seek self-actualization and moments of joy through intense dedication to personal and interpersonal achievements.

Developmental Tasks

We have identified the period from ages 24 to 34 as early adulthood. For many, this is a time of continued uncertainty as people begin to make essential commitments to work, relationships, and ideologies that express the content of their personal identities. The nature of early adulthood has changed dramatically over the past 40 years, from a time when young people moved with some deliberate focus into roles that they expected would be stable and long-lasting, to a time of many more transitions and temporary commitments. Recall the figure in Chapter 10 that compares the percentage of young people who completed the transition to adulthood in 1960 to those

Oprah Winfrey personifies Maslow's theory of self-actualization. She has overcome the challenges of her early childhood to found a massive business empire that has made her one of the wealthiest women in the world. Along the way she won an Oscar for her performance in the movie, *The Color Purple*, and she became a model of integrity, dignity, generosity, and compassion for American television audiences as she connected with viewers of her afternoon talk show.

who completed this transition in 2000. The five criteria for the transition to adulthood as defined in this figure are: leaving home, finishing school, becoming financially independent, getting married, and having a child. By 2000, only 31% of men and 46% of women had made this complete transition by the age of 30. It is certainly possible to feel like an adult even if one has not completed all of these behaviors. Yet, for most young people, they capture the essence of a cultural definition of adult status, and, as such, provide a framework for the psychological sense of maturity. In the 10 years from age 24 to 34, most young adults are striving to enact the key life roles of worker, intimate partner, community member, and parent that will reflect their ability to take responsibility for themselves, make important decisions about their lives, and begin to care for others (Arnett, 2000, 2004b, 2006).

By and large, the developmental tasks of this period have a lot to do with the person's ability to form effective relationships. The establishment of a sense of intimacy with a marital partner or cohabiting adult requires movement toward a greater sharing of personal feelings, secrets, and ways of looking at the world. In addition, one is often called upon to hear and respond to these same highly personal expressions from another person. Sometimes the demand is to listen; sometimes to listen and offer advice; sometimes to be understanding and helpful. Another set of behaviors that develop during this period involves establishing effective relationships in the world of work. Getting along with associates, responding to authority figures, and having respectful relationships with clients or customers are the keys to success. For those who decide to be a parent, parenting is another type of relationship of considerable responsibility. Becoming a parent is a role that most people are not terribly well prepared for, and as a result, there is a great deal of learning by doing. Becoming a parent means creating a new relationship that is distinct from any role in one's past—blending the caregiver, planner, and disciplinarian in a balance that changes frequently as the child matures. These three key relationships—intimate partner, worker, and parent—form the basic structure of the lifestyle that is enacted in early adulthood.

The pathway into adulthood is taking longer and is more diverse today than it was 40 years ago. Some young adults who did not go to college directly after high school, later enroll in college. Some later adolescents enter the military and return to civilian life to begin their early adulthood as veterans of war. The period of job experimentation is lasting longer today with many young adults making multiple job and career changes before settling into their career. The average age of entry into marriage is now the late twenties for women and the early thirties for men. A significant percentage of early adults are in cohabiting relationships that do not end in marriage. Many marriages end in divorce. This means that for many, early adulthood is a time of multiple intimate relationships. Later age at marriage is associated with an older age for first childbearing. All of these factors reflect a lifestyle in early adulthood that is more fluid and transitional than it has been in the past. At the same time, one must keep in mind the diversity of life stories. Some young adults assume significant role responsibilities, autonomy from their family, and self-sufficiency at relatively young ages. Others delay the typical commitments of adulthood well into their thirties.

Exploring Intimate Relationships

Objective 2. To analyze the process of forming intimate relationships, including readiness to form intimate relationships, initial attractions, mate selection, cohabitation, commitment to a long-term relationship, and the challenges one faces in adjusting to the early years of marriage.

The period of early adulthood is a time when men and women explore the possibility of forming relationships that combine emotional closeness, shared interests, a shared vision of the future, and sexual intimacy. The nature of these relationships differs for various couples. Some young adults engage in a form of serial monogamy—a sequence of dyadic pairings with no commitment to marriage. Others find a same-sex partner with whom they make a long-term commitment even though formal marriage is not possible because of laws restricting marriage to a man and a woman. Most young people become involved in romantic relationships that involve both sexual and emotional intimacy. Many forms of intimate relationships in addition to marriage are established during early adulthood, including serious dating, cohabitation with or without the intention of marriage, and commitments between gay or lesbian couples.

Marriage is one context in which work on intimate social relationships takes place. In 2008, 86% of men and 99% of women had been married at least once by the ages of 45 to 54. Among those between 65 and 74 years old in 2003, 96% of men and women had been married at least once (U.S. Census Bureau, 2010). The main change in the marriage pattern in the United States over the past 50 years is that more young adults postpone marriage until the end of their twenties. The percentage of single, never-married women between the ages of 20 and 24 rose from 28% in 1960 to 79% in 2008. The comparable increase for single men was from 53% in 1960 to 87% in 2010 (U.S. Bureau of the Census, 1976, 2010). In the United States, it is now normative for men to be single throughout their twenties and for women to be single in the first half of their twenties.

Delaying the age at marriage is related to several other social trends, including having children at a later age, smaller projected family size, and, therefore, fewer years devoted to childrearing. Delaying age at marriage is also related to increased sexual exploration for single people. The 1980s brought the uncoupling of sexual activity, marriage, and childbearing. Younger age at entry into sexual activity and increases in rates of affairs and cohabitation suggest that even though many young adults do not marry, they become involved in intimate relationships during their twenties.

Readiness to Form Intimate Relationships

What factors are important in determining a person's readiness for a long-term commitment? From a psychosocial perspective, one can hypothesize that work on personal identity must be far enough along so that the possibility of a deep, emotional involvement with another person will be regarded as exciting rather than frightening. In studies of college students, a relationship has been found between identity status and the quality of intimacy. Students who had an achieved identity also reported the most genuine intimate relationships. In contrast, those who were characterized as identity confused were the least intimate and the most isolated (Dyk & Adams, 1990; Montgomery, 2005).

Early and later adolescents are likely to be thinking about intimacy issues long before their work on identity is completed. Thus, it makes sense to think that the capacity for intimacy emerges alongside identity work (Adams & Archer, 1994). However, when faced with dilemmas in which needs for identity and intimacy conflict, young men and women tend to give identity issues higher priority. The following example and others like it were presented to adolescents to determine whether identity or intimacy would be the primary developmental issue guiding an important decision.

> Allison has been accepted to a very prestigious college with a reputation for a high-quality English department. She knows she wants to major in English. The main drawback to this college is that it is a 6-hour driving distance from her boyfriend. She also has been accepted to a college located within an hour away from her boyfriend, which has an average English department. She is unsure of which one to choose. How much consideration should be given to each of the following issues in resolving this dilemma?
>
> a. The quality of the program
> b. The distance from her boyfriend
>
> Why? (Lacombe & Gay, 1998, p. 801)

In this study, young people placed greater emphasis on the identity-oriented solutions, those that relate to the quality of the program and the importance of a high-quality education, rather than on the intimacy-oriented solutions. However, women were more likely than men to try to balance the two, seeking ways to meet identity and intimacy needs in the same solution (Lacombe & Gay, 1998).

In addition to identity achievement, school enrollment as well as educational and occupational attainments are linked to relationship commitment. Young adults who are still in school are less likely to make a serious long-term commitment to an intimate partner, either through marriage or through cohabitation, than those who have completed school (Thornton, Axinn, & Teachman, 1995). The combination of educational and occupational goals and cultural views about the value of marriage create community expectations about the ideal age at marriage. The ideal age for marriage is likely to be younger in a working-class community than in a middle-class community, because expectations for continued education are not as great (Teachman, Polonko, & Scanzoni, 1987). In contrast, young people who attend college tend to have a later timetable for marriage. Advanced education delays marriage more frequently for women than for men, perhaps because young women who have had more years of education have alternative means to secure economic resources (Qian & Preston, 1993). Nonetheless, college graduates are more likely to marry and less likely to intend to remain single than those who have never graduated from high school (Mahay & Lewin, 2007).

In addition to educational goals, readiness for a long-term intimate relationship may be determined by other aspects of one's personal agenda, such as reaching a certain level of achievement in one's career, completing military service, or earning a certain income. In each case, a person with this kind of ambition is less likely to seek a long-term partner or to be receptive to expressions of love from someone than he may be once the goal is achieved.

Cohabitation. In contemporary society, cohabitation has become a common expression of a committed relationship. In 2007 there were 6.2 million unmarried-couple households in the United States, not including people living in dormitories, group housing, or other institutions (U.S. Census Bureau, 2010). As the number of cohabiting couples has increased so has the number of children growing up in the context of cohabiting relationships (Heuveline & Timberlake, 2004; Timberlake & Heuveline, 2005). These two trends raise new questions about the nature and meaning of cohabitation. Is it an informal alternative to marriage, or is it more like singlehood, except that it involves a bond of connection with a partner?

In a cross-national comparison of heterosexual couples, six types of cohabiting relationships were described that reflect a couple's decisions to live together, have children, and stay together (Heuveline & Timberlake, 2004, pp. 1216–1218):

1. *Marginal.* Cohabiting is infrequent, its duration short, and few children are born within this relationship, because the cultural norms strongly discourage this kind of union.
2. *Prelude to marriage.* In the face of high divorce rates, cohabiting may be viewed as a way for couples to test the relationship prior to marriage. The duration of cohabitation should be relatively brief, frequently transition into marriage, with few children born to cohabiting couples.
3. *Stage in the marriage process.* Couples in this type of relationship may see some disadvantages to marrying immediately, but they do intend to marry. Childbearing in the context of this relationship is more common, because the partners expect to marry. The relationships are of longer duration than in type 2, more often involve childbearing, and end in transition to marriage.
4. *Alternative to being single.* Couples want to postpone marriage and family formation, perhaps because they think they are too young to marry. These couples are more like single, dating couples than like married couples. These relationships should be relatively short in duration, end in separation, and few children are born in these relationships.
5. *Alternative to marriage.* Couples view cohabiting as an alternative to marriage. These relationships are often established in the context of cultural support for children born outside the bonds of marriage. These relationships are of long duration, less likely to transition into marriage, and more likely to involve children.
6. *Indistinguishable from marriage.* Because of the cultural acceptability of unmarried couples and institutional support for all parents, couples consider cohabitation versus marriage on pragmatic grounds. These relationships are not a conscious alternative to marriage based on attitudes or values. The relationships are likely to involve children, but they may be of shorter duration than in the alternative to marriage, if only because many of them do transition into marriage.

Andy and Jennifer take a moment to celebrate their decision to move in together. What factors will influence the future of this cohabiting relationship?

© Ingram Publishing/Alamy

The cross-national comparison was based on data from 14 European countries plus Canada, New Zealand, and the United States. Cohabitation among never-married women is comparatively rare in Spain, Italy, and Poland (less than 15%) and quite common in France, Finland, New Zealand, and Sweden (more than 60%). The median duration of cohabiting relationships is 3 years or longer in France, Sweden, and Canada; and comparatively short in the United States, where the median duration is 1.2 years. Across 11 countries where there are substantial numbers of cohabiting relationships, 61% of these relationships end in marriage. In comparison, 64% of Canadian cohabitation relationships end in separation, as do 52% of cohabitation relationships in the United States.

Using the indicators of incidence of cohabitation, proportion ending in marriage, and incidence of children born to mothers in a cohabiting relationship, the researchers tried to match countries with the six types of cohabitation most characteristic of their population. In Italy, Poland, and Spain, cohabitation was considered marginal. In Belgium, the Czech Republic, Hungary, and Switzerland, cohabitation was most likely a prelude to marriage. In Austria, Finland, Germany, Latvia, and Slovenia, cohabitation was a stage in the marriage process. In New Zealand and the United States, cohabitation was an alternative to being single. In Canada and France, cohabitation was an alternative to being married. In Sweden, cohabitation was indistinguishable from being married. The authors warned, however, that these national patterns may not reflect all the differences that are present within a culturally diverse society such as the United States (Heuveline & Timberlake, 2004). These comparisons do provide a frame of reference for interpreting the meaning of cohabitation in national contexts. They illustrate differences in cultural support for varying patterns of family formation by highlighting the frequency, duration, and path of cohabiting relationships.

Consensual union without a civil or religious marriage has been practiced in Latin America for centuries and is regarded as a form of marital union. The practice is becoming less common on the island of Puerto Rico itself, but it is regarded as legitimate among mainland Puerto Rican women. Women who had a child within such a relationship were more likely to describe it as informal marriage than as cohabitation. Women who had been married before were also more likely to describe their current relationship as informal marriage rather than cohabitation. It appears that consensual unions were perceived by women to be more like marriage than like singlehood. Long-term cohabiting couples are very similar to legally married couples with regard to the frequency of conflict, perceptions of equity, and relationship satisfaction (Willetts, 2006).

Even though cohabitation has become increasingly common in the United States, there is a consistent finding of a negative relationship between cohabitation and marital quality and stability. Individuals who have cohabited in the past have more conflict in their marriages, less marital happiness,

and a greater probability of divorce. These findings have been repeated for cohorts of couples who married between 1964 and 1980 when cohabitation was less common, and those who married between 1981 and 1997 when cohabitation became more frequent (Dush, Cohan, & Amato, 2003). The relationship was observed in a meta-analysis involving numerous studies of premarital cohabitation and marital stability (Jose, O'Leary, & Moyer, 2010). However, the relationship of cohabitation and marital instability was not found for couples who married their cohabiting partner, suggesting that for these couples, the cohabiting experience was in fact a stage in the marriage process. More research is needed to understand why those who cohabit and then go on to marry someone else experience less marital satisfaction and greater marital instability.

Close Relationships between Partners of the Same Sex. Gay men and lesbians are a diverse group with respect to their interests, talents, educational backgrounds, family backgrounds, careers, and other important aspects of adult roles. In many respects, the same dynamics that influence the formation of close relationships among heterosexual couples apply to same-sex couples. Nonetheless, gay and lesbian couples face certain unique challenges that are not typically present for heterosexual couples: they often have to establish their relationship in a context of secrecy, they often experience disapproval from their family, and in many states they lack access to legal recognition of their union should they desire it (Kurdek, 2005; Herek, 2006).

One of the common themes in the literature on gay and lesbian couples is the impact on the relationship of coming out to parents and other family members. In comparison to heterosexual couples, this is a specific challenge that may place strain on the relationship. In one study of 20 gay couples, all those who had come out to their parents had experienced ongoing disapproval from their own parents and their partners' parents (LaSala, 2000). The following reflections from the mother of a gay man suggest some of the strains that are likely to arise as gay couples disclose to family members.

Annette E. Brenner remembers joking when her oldest son was 4 that she'd approve his marrying outside the family's faith as long as he married a woman. When he came out to her and her husband at 17, one of her first reactions was to try to negotiate him out of his gayness. She offered him a car, a house, if only he would wait and try marriage. He was at boarding school in Connecticut at the time, and she was convinced it was just a stage. She remembers thinking, "Sure, this week you're a homosexual. Enjoy the experiment, have fun. Next week you'll be a Hare Krishna." Then she became enraged. "What is this kid doing to me?" she'd ask herself. "What was he doing to his grandparents, his brother and sister?" (From "Born or Bred: The Origins of Homosexuality," by D. Gelman, *Newsweek*, February 24, 1992, pp. 46–53. © 1992 Newsweek, Inc. All rights reserved. Reprinted by permission.)

As two professional women creating a life together, Jen and Rachel have to invent many aspects of their relationship, but they do not have to invent the wonderful feelings of being in love.

Courtesy of Philip Newman

Gay and lesbian couples may have to establish their relationship in a climate of secrecy and social stigma, especially fears about parental rejection. Gay and lesbian couples often perceive less social support from family members and seek out other members of the gay or lesbian community to validate and encourage their relationship (Kurdek, 2004). Even when they are in committed relationships, gay and lesbian young adults are likely to manage the negative impact of family rejection by keeping the nature of their homosexual relationship a secret from family members. Although this image management might seem to place a strain on intimate relationships, research shows no significant relationship between the couples' satisfaction in their relationship and the extent to which they are out to family members (Green et al., 1995; LaSala, 2000).

Lesbian and gay relationships are similar in many respects and distinct in others. Lesbian and gay couples who are in a committed relationship tend to give great priority to maintaining and enhancing their relationship for several reasons. First, they share the conflicts around coming out and the complications that this poses in family and work settings. This provides a common bond and a need to protect the relationship from detractors. Second, because of the nontraditional nature of same-sex relationships, the partners have to invent many of the details of their relationship, thus making it more salient and less scripted than heterosexual relationships. Finally, they face ongoing challenges, such as the complexities associated with the decision about whether and how to have children and how to ritualize their commitment to one another (Metz, Rosser, & Strapko, 1994).

In a comparison of gay and lesbian couples, the two types of couples were similar in many respects (Kurdek, 2003).

They had similar approaches to conflict resolution, similar experiences with support from their social networks, and similar rates of dissolution or instability in their relationships. The same variables predicted relationship dissolution for gay and lesbian couples. Lesbian couples were more alike than gay couples at the start of their relationship and scored higher on measures of liking their partners, trusting their partners, and perceiving equality in their relationship. Overall, lesbian couples had higher rates of relationship satisfaction. This finding is puzzling given that lesbian and gay couples had the same degree of stability.

Lesbian relationships often emerge out of close, same-sex friendships. Lesbians are somewhat more likely to be able to establish long-term relationships than gay men. Most lesbians describe their relationships as stable, sexually exclusive, and extremely close. They also describe their relationships as closer and more flexible than do gay men or heterosexual couples (Green et al., 1995). Greater levels of satisfaction in the relationship are associated with greater levels of equality and shared decision making. Equality in the relationship depends on equal resources and commitment to the relationship (Eldridge & Gilbert, 1990). In comparison with heterosexual wives, women in lesbian relationships are more likely to describe greater satisfaction in their sexual activity and greater dissatisfaction with inequalities in the relationship. These women place a strong value on companionship and on confiding in one another, but they also expect to experience high levels of autonomy within their relationships.

Gay men are also interested in long-term relationships. However, they are less likely than lesbians to be sexually exclusive, and there is less consensus among them about the importance of sexual exclusiveness (Deenen, Gijs, & van Naerssen, 1994; Kitzinger & Coyle, 1995). In comparison to lesbian relationships, gay men often find partners in the context of a more active, competitive social scene that involves multiple short-term relationships. In comparison to men in heterosexual couples, gay men are likely to be emotionally intimate. In the practical matters of household work, gay couples are more likely than heterosexual couples to divide tasks so that each partner does an equal number (Peplau & Beals, 2004). Gay couples report higher levels of closeness and flexibility than do heterosexual couples. Moreover, the combination of flexibility and closeness is strongly associated with couple satisfaction (Kurdek, 2006b).

Many of the same factors are associated with relationship quality across all types of couples: valuing security, permanence, and closeness; expressiveness; perceived rewards for being in the relationship; trust in the partner; good problem-solving and conflict resolution skills; egalitarian decision making; openness to the expression of differences; and perceived social support (Huston, 2000; Kurdek, 2006b). Factors that are likely to lead to the dissolution of a gay or lesbian couple are a lack of investment in the relationship, a decline in expressions of positive affect and emotional support, an increase in conflicts, and an increased desire for personal autonomy. Interdependence sustains the relationships, and power inequalities disrupt them. Given that the stabilizing forces such as support from family members, community recognition, and legal rights and privileges are often missing for gay and lesbian couples, it is remarkable that they are as stable as they are.

Readiness to Marry

What determines whether an intimate relationship will end in matrimony? A basic factor is the person's underlying desire to marry. In the United States, most people hope to marry. In a national sample of individuals ages 18 to 89 in U.S. households, people who were single, heterosexual, and not in a steady romantic relationship were asked the following question: If the right person came along, would you like to be married? Over 3,000 respondents were categorized into five age groups: 18–24, 25–34, 35–44, 45–54, and 55–69. Answers were coded as yes or no. Overall, only 5% of respondents were single and had no desire to marry. This percentage was higher in the youngest age group (about 7%) and the oldest age group (about 10%), and lower in the three middle age groups (about 3% to 4%). In addition to age, having been divorced, having children, and not being employed were all associated with a lack of intention to marry (Mahay & Lewin, 2007).

In the United States, most individuals have a great deal of freedom to choose their time of marriage and their marriage partner. Cultural values of individualism and autonomy provide support and justification for addressing personal goals prior to making a commitment to an intimate relationship. Although expectations that one will marry are strong, young adults have the freedom to follow their own timetables. The increased independence of young adults from their parents is associated with decreased parental influence on one's choice of marriage partner. With greater geographic mobility, young adults are more likely to make nontraditional partner choices, including interracial and same-sex unions (Rosenfeld & Kim, 2005). However, in some ethnic groups, such as Asian Indians and Arab Americans, there is still a strong expectation that parents will guide the selection of a marriage partner. In other groups, such as the Mormons, the high value placed on sexual abstinence prior to marriage results in an earlier age at marriage than for other groups (DeGenova, 1997).

Phases in the Selection of a Partner

In the United States and other individualist cultures, most people believe that romantic love is the central reason for choosing a marriage partner. In societies with a more collectivist orientation, however, love is not necessarily relevant to the selection of a partner. In these cultures, the choice may be made by family members, based on religious, financial, or family background factors believed to contribute to a good match, not only for the person but also for the extended family system. In these cultural groups, the principle of **endogamy**, or marriage within one's well-defined group, is encouraged. An Asian Indian college student of Muslim faith describes her orientation toward marriage:

> A few years ago I fell in love with a Hindu guy, but after a while I realized I had to end the relationship. My mom, it would have broken her heart. I care too much about my family. People would look down on my parents if I married outside of our religion. . . . Muslims are good people. We are very focused. We have morals. I want to give my children that sense of identity. So I'm comfortable waiting until I meet an acceptable Muslim man. (Belsky, 1997, p. 279)

Figure 11.3 provides a theoretical model including four phases of increasing involvement in the mate selection process (Adams, 1986). At each phase, the relationship may be terminated if the key issues produce undesirable information or negative assessment of the partner. Also, the relationship may end if an alternative attraction becomes so strong that it reduces investment in the first relationship. The alternative attraction may be another person, a job, school, or the desire to achieve a personal goal. In contrast, investment in the relationship may increase if no attractive or acceptable alternatives are available (Bui, Peplau, & Hill, 1996).

Phase I: Original Attraction. Phase I, original attraction, captures the early process of partner identification. *Initial impressions* are formed in the first few seconds of an interaction. Many of these cues are captured through eye contact and a scan of a person's face (Jones et al., 2010). For example, in an experimental study, women were shown pictures of men's faces. These same men had been assessed as to whether they preferred pictures of adults or pictures of infants. Their testosterone levels were assessed using a saliva sample. Women were shown the photographs of these

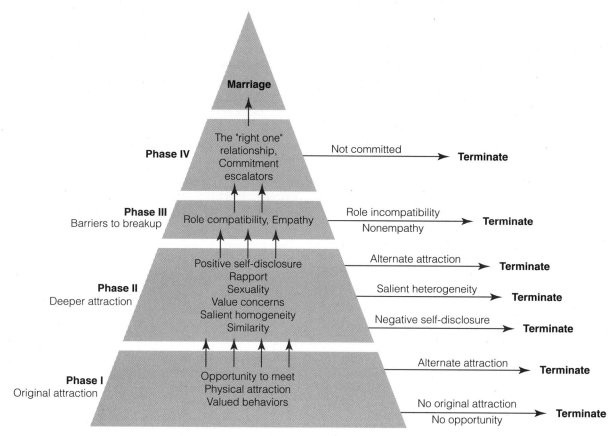

FIGURE 11.3 The Mate Selection Process in the United States
Source: Based on Adams, 1986.

men and asked to rate them on four dimensions: likes children, masculine, physically attractive, and kind. They were also asked to rate each man's attractiveness as a short-term romantic partner and as a long-term partner in a committed relationship. Based on facial cues alone, women were able to differentiate the men who preferred the pictures of infants from those who preferred pictures of adults. From these photographs women also rated the men who had higher testosterone levels as more masculine. In their assessment of short- and long-term relationships, the photos that women rated as more masculine and physically attractive were the ones they rated most highly for a short-term relationship. The photos women rated as kind, likes children, and physically attractive were most highly rated for a long-term relationship; masculinity was no longer a salient feature for these ratings. This and other research support the view that for women, initial attraction can be based on facial cues, and that the importance of various cues depends on the kind of relationship the woman is seeking (Roney, Hanson, Durante, & Maestripieri, 2006).

The principle of **homogamy** suggests that people are attracted to others who share important areas of similarity. Three of the salient similarities that have been studied are race, religion, and educational level. In a study of three levels of relationship commitment—sexually intimate partners, cohabiting couples, and married couples—the researchers found that at each level of relationship the couples showed high levels of similarity (Blackwell & Lichter, 2000, 2004). However, similarity extends beyond these basic demographic characteristics. For example, in a study of dating and mating preferences among college students, women preferred to date men who were similar to them in education and occupational level, and preferred to marry someone who was also similar in religious values and desire for children (Knox, Zusman, & Nieves, 1997). Other studies show that couples are similar in their preferences for leisure, their political orientation, and whether their parents had been divorced or not (Wolfinger, 2003).

In a study of 12,000 Dutch couples, partners were found to be significantly similar with regard to health indicators. Individuals whose partners were in poor health were significantly more likely to report being in poor health themselves than individuals whose partners were in good health. Although there were patterns of accumulated health problems within households, the young couples who had been together only a short time were just as similar in their health as older couples who had been together for years. Thus, the researcher concluded that the similarity in health status was more a result of initial similarities than a product of the impact of shared circumstances over years of marriage (Monden, 2007).

Partners are selected from among those who are available for interaction. Many of the choices one makes during adolescence and young adulthood—such as where to go to college, where to work, which activities and social functions to attend, and where to take a vacation—determine who one meets. People who occupy similar settings such as neighborhoods, college environments, work settings, or religious institutions are likely to be similar in certain characteristics that contribute to the observed homogamy in couples (Kalmijn & Flap, 2001).

Some early adults are in situations in which it is difficult to find suitable mates. They might move to a new town for a job or return home after serving in the military. The problem they face is how they are going to meet people and begin the dating process. Online dating is one strategy; speed dating is another. When there are many alternatives, the process of selecting the small number of people to follow up with or pursue requires a strategy. Studies have shown that when a person is faced with a large number of alternatives, for example, a speed dating experience in which one encounters over 25 possible partners, people tend to focus their attention on certain key, readily assessable features such as age, weight, or height. In contrast, when there are fewer possible partners, people tend to focus their selection efforts on two or three more complex, less obvious criteria such as occupation, educational background, or religious beliefs (Lenton & Francesconi, 2010).

Demographic realities influence the possibility of meeting suitable partners. In each community, for each age group of women, the number of suitable, available partners may differ, depending on such characteristics as the educational level, employment opportunities, and racial composition of the men in that community. For example, declines in the marriage rates for African Americans appear to be closely linked to the decline in the availability of appropriate African American male partners. Single, never-married African American women increased from 17% of the total female African American population 18 years old and older in 1970 to 40% in 2008 (U.S. Census Bureau, 2010). This pattern is related in part to the high rates of mortality and imprisonment of African American men and in part to their economic marginality. The decline in employment opportunities in the manufacturing industries, where African American men had made earlier gains, coupled with increased crime and drug use in the urban communities, contribute to the decline in the number of marriageable African American men (Taylor, Chatters, Tucker, & Lewis, 1990; Raley, 1996).

Once two people meet, what factors support their continued involvement? One's style of interaction—for example, whether one is shy and withdrawn or expressive and outgoing—influences the number and kinds of interactions one has with others. In the most general sense, the choice of a partner depends on the network of interactions in which one is involved. Among the people one encounters, some attract attention and others do not. For many young adults, online dating has become a way to expand contacts and reach a wider network of potential partners (Merkle & Richardson, 2000; Habib, 2001). According to a survey paid for by Match.com, in a sample of over 2,500 people who earned

$30,000 or more, roughly 20% of those in a committed relationship met in an online dating site (datingsites-reviews .com, 2010).

In contrast to the principle of homogamy, which emphasizes the role of similarity in the attraction process, **social evolutionary theory** suggests that men and women differ in the features they emphasize in evaluating someone as a desirable partner. The evolutionary perspective highlights the reproductive potential and the reproductive investment of one's partner. *Reproductive potential* refers to the physical, material, and social resources that a partner may be able to contribute to one's fertility and childrearing. *Reproductive investment* refers to the willingness of a potential partner to commit these resources to one's children. Men tend to emphasize the biological or physical resources of a potential partner, valuing youth and physical appearance in a partner more than do women. Women tend to emphasize the social status and economic resources of a potential partner, valuing earning potential and job stability in a partner more than do men (Geary, Vigil, & Byrd-Craven, 2004). In a cross-national study of heterosexual mate preferences in samples collected in Africa, Asia, Australia, Europe, New Zealand, and North and South America, David Buss (1994) found that men placed more emphasis on a partner's youth and physical appearance, whereas women placed more emphasis on a partner's financial prospects, dependability, and industriousness. In addition to physical appearance and social status, people who behave in an admirable, effective manner may be viewed as attractive or desirable. People seek others who will support their goals, who can be encouraging and positive, and who appear to be able to collaborate effectively in shared experiences (Sanders, 1997).

Phase II: Deeper Attraction. Phase I, *original attraction*, moves on to Phase II, *deeper attraction*, as the partners begin to disclose information about themselves, interact in ways that deepen the relationship, and discover areas of important similarity. In Phase II, the discovery of basic similarities and a feeling of rapport are central to continuing the relationship. Each person has key values and background characteristics that serve as a filter for assessing whether the other person is an eligible partner. Of course, eligibility is defined differently by different people. For some, any person who is conscious is eligible. Others have criteria that limit the choice of a marriage partner to someone of a certain age range, religion, race, educational background, and family history. For example, some adults would not consider marriage to someone who does not share their religious faith. For these people, only members of their own religious group are perceived as eligible partners. Research conducted on religious homogamy finds a consistent relationship between the extent to which partners have similar religious beliefs and participate together in religious practices and their marital quality. However, over the past 20 years, this relationship has been weakening. Agreement about gender ideology, partner participation in the labor market, and agreement about the balance of work and family roles have emerged as salient value positions that rival religious values in predicting marital quality and marital satisfaction (Myers, 2006).

Many individuals may not even be aware of their own criteria for the eligibility of potential partners. For example, most men expect to marry women who are a few years younger than they are. Although they do not deliberately state this as a criterion for marriage, they simply do not interact with or feel drawn to a partner who is perceived as too old (Buunk et al., 2001).

Most people seek marriage partners who will understand them and provide a sense of emotional support. There are many dimensions along which two people may recognize similarities or differences. They may seem quite different on some dimensions, such as religion and social class, yet discover that they are quite similar on others, such as life goals and political ideology. For example, partners who have similar ideas about gender roles and how men and women ought to function in a marriage are likely to be drawn to one another. The more aware individuals are of the themes that are central to their own sense of personal identity, the better they can recognize the dimensions of similarity and difference in other people that will contribute to intimate relationships.

In addition to the preferences that individuals express about potential partners and the availability of those partners in a particular community, third parties can play a role in the progression or termination of a relationship during Phase II (Kalmijn, 1998). Parent and family support can help enhance a partner's attractiveness if family members are enthusiastic about the partner and encourage the relationship. As the earlier example of the Muslim college student illustrated, parent and family reactions can also interfere with a deepening attraction if the potential partner meets with family disapproval.

Research on interethnic dating has identified the role of social network diversity as a factor that contributes to the likelihood of college students dating across ethnic boundaries (Clark-Ibanez & Felmlee, 2004). Students who had an ethnically diverse group of friends were significantly more likely to have had one or more experiences with interethnic dating relationships. Students of color and male students were more likely than White or female students to have had experiences of interethnic dating. Those students whose parents had a diverse group of friends were most likely to respond that they had experienced interethnic dating more than once or twice. In the open-ended responses, students were asked how easy or how difficult it might be to date someone of a different ethnic group. The majority mentioned social pressures and social networks in their responses. For most of the students, the social network exercised pressures against interethnic dating. As one Korean American student wrote, "My parents, just as most Korean parents that I have contact with, banish the idea of interracial dating." However, those who say it would be easy to date across ethnic lines often mention the role of friends and associates: "It is easy to

As role compatibility and empathy grow, the relationship takes on a new degree of intimacy and the couple begins to conceptualize a future together.

date interethnically. I see people of different ethnicities every day. I'm used to them" (male Latino American).

Phase III: Role Compatability and Barriers to Break Up. The relationship is likely to proceed from Phase II to Phase III if the partners extend the domains in which self-disclosure occurs, including sexual needs, personal fears, and fantasies. With each new risk taken, the discovery of a positive, supportive reaction in the partner deepens the level of trust in the relationship. The discovery of **role compatibility** and empathy begins to give the relationship a life of its own. Role compatibility is a sense that the two partners approach a situation in ways that work well together. Whether it is a visit to a relative's home, an office party, a casual evening with friends, or running out of gas on the highway, the two people discover that they like the way each behaves and that their combined behavior is effective. Empathy builds through these observations, enabling each partner to know how the other responds and how to anticipate the other's needs.

One aspect of this new level of intimacy is the special way in which romantic partners interact with one another. In affectionate and playful exchanges, partners often use baby talk, a type of gentle, high-pitched register, in which features of words are altered and new vocabulary may be created. Partners may give one another affectionate nicknames and create unique signals for communication. The establishment of this intimate communication system acts as another bond between the couple, creating a personal environment that is not shared with and often not even known to others (Bombar & Littig, 1996). At some point in Phase III, partners may begin to think that they are in love. They may even tell each other, "I love you." As described in the following case study, this is more difficult for some couples than for others.

Case Study

How Love Makes Its Way into a Relationship

Gail and Dick talk about how love entered their relationship as they made the transition from living together to deciding to get married.

Dick: We never mentioned love in our relationship. And that's for at least 3 years. We never committed ourselves to loving each other until well into the fourth year, although I don't know *why*. We'd ask each other if we like each other and placed a great deal of significance on that, but just as significantly we avoided the word "love," and all I remember about the first time we did mention love was that it was kind of a trauma.

Gail: I can remember everything. I think we were arguing about us. And Dick was trying to tell me, without telling me, that he was leaving me. You know, saying there's this problem and that it's stale and it's . . . and so on. And I'm all ready to change and work it out and then he just got frustrated and he said, "But I love you and I really care for you," and then he walked out. That I really couldn't understand. You told me you loved me and walked out and left me! I thought, "Well, that's crazy." I thought that was just the nuttiest thing I ever heard. I thought, "Well, does he feel guilty about hurting me and is that why he's saying it? And if he is all that crazy about me, he wouldn't have been walking out to somebody else!" And he didn't tell me, you know, he never told me he had another girlfriend, which bugged me a lot because I thought he could at least do that. And I had to go through this whole painful thing of finding out, when somebody said they saw Dick with this little blonde. And I thought, "Well, if that's true, he's probably at her house," and so I went over there and there they were and Dick was mortified. I was bitchy and I wouldn't go away. I just sat there making small talk—and I know now that I loved every minute of it. And so I really didn't believe it.

Dick: You mean you didn't believe it when I said I loved you. . . .

Gail: Yeah. But I guess I sort of had it in the back of my mind that we would get back together.

Dick: I was very dissatisfied with this other girl after a very short period of time, and it was interesting, because she outwardly seemed to have everything. I could, you know, I could list off consciously what I wanted and she had it, but it wasn't enough. I think one thing that I was very impressed about was that in comparing the two girls, this girl seemed not to have an independent life of her own. She seemed to be tied to whoever she was with. When we'd be talking with somebody else, she'd voice *my* opinions, and Gail doesn't do that hardly at all. She forms her own opinions and sticks to them. And I found that this really takes a great burden off me in a relationship. And I don't have to be carrying the emotional stability, or the opinions, for two people. It's really like having a burden lifted off yourself when you're not living with a mirror image of yourself but actually another person. At that point I realized that for me Gail was another individual whom I did care for.

Source: From *Becoming Partners: Marriage and Its Alternatives*, by Carl R. Rogers, copyright © 1972 by Carl R. Rogers. Used by permission of Dell Publishing, a division of Random House.

CRITICAL THINKING AND CASE ANALYSIS

1. What does love mean for Dick and Gail; in what ways might love be different from liking?
2. How is the relationship between Dick and Gail transformed when love is mentioned?
3. What are the qualities of an intimate relationship that you see illustrated in the case of Dick and Gail? What elements of an intimate relationship appear to be missing in this relationship?
4. How does the case illustrate the concept of homogamy? How does the case illustrate the concepts from social evolutionary theory?
5. What challenges do you imagine Dick and Gail might face in the first few years of marriage? What resources might help them cope with these challenges?

In addition to the growing sense of compatibility, barriers to breaking up help consolidate the relationship. First, the partners have disclosed and taken risks with each other that they probably have not taken with others. Second, they have achieved comfortable feelings of predictability and empathy that make them more certain about each other than about possible alternative attractions. Third, they have been identified by others in their social network, including family and friends, as a couple. Support from one's social network provides a stabilizing force that may be especially important for couples in nontraditional relationships. Other barriers include procedures needed to end the relationship, such as moving to a new apartment or dividing up or selling off shared purchases, and the feelings of obligation that may have accompanied earlier expressions of love and sexual intimacy (Kurdek, 2006a). At this point, the costs of breaking up begin to be quite high, including loss of a confidant, a companion, and disruption or even disapproval in their social network.

Phase IV: The Right One Relationship. Once the partners enjoy role compatibility and empathy, they move on to Phase IV, *the right one relationship*. Two processes appear to unfold that contribute to the intensification of this romantic attachment: the positivity bias and the similarity bias. The **positivity bias** refers to the tendency to view one's romantic partner in an overly positive light. This bias contributes to the perceiver's belief that he has indeed found the absolutely perfect partner. It also makes the partner feel valued and cherished (Rusbult, VanLange, Wildschut, Yovetich, & Verette, 2000). The **similarity bias** refers to the tendency to exaggerate perceptions of similarity between partners, thereby increasing feelings of closeness and being understood (Kenny & Acitelli, 2001). Both the positivity bias and the similarity bias are associated with the perceiver's satisfaction in the romantic relationship, thereby reducing the likelihood that an alternative attraction will deter the person from making a long-term commitment (Luo & Snider, 2009).

The right one relationship is characterized by both romantic love and friendship. The intensity of romantic love has been documented in studies that contrast romantic love and friendship (Davis, 1985; Hatfield, 1988). Lovers describe their relationships as characterized by *fascination*, *exclusiveness*, and *sexual desire*: "I would go to bed thinking about what we would do together, dream about it, and wake up ready to be with him again" (Davis, 1985, p. 24). They also express more intense caring for their loved ones than for friends. This caring includes giving their utmost, even to the point of self-sacrifice. The intensity of these characteristics accounts for some of the specialness and unsettling euphoria associated with being in love. It may also explain the relative instability of love relationships. Intense emotion is difficult to sustain. In contrast, friendship or companionate relationships reflect a high level of disclosure and a sense of having shared many life experiences. This leads to a sense of truly knowing the person, experiencing mutual understanding, and being concerned about each other's welfare.

Even with the help of this model, the final step of commitment to marriage is not easy to understand. In today's society, many young couples agree to live together and make a commitment to their partnership without marriage. The step from cohabitation to marriage is still not well understood.

Adjustment During the Early Years of Marriage

What are the defining characteristics of a high-quality relationship and how are they sustained during the early years of marriage? Two different theories have been advanced by family scientists. One view, sometimes referred to as the **communal norm**, is that each person should pay close attention to the partner's needs and act in ways that will support the partner's welfare. In a communal relationship, each partner tries to meet the needs of the other within reason, without regard for or without keeping track of what has been received in return. Couples that are characterized as flexibly supportive are likely to view their relationship as positive and satisfying. A second view, sometimes referred to as the **exchange norm**, is that each person expects to satisfy the needs of the partner and to have needs met in about the same amount. The exchange norm includes a sense of obligation so that what one receives from the partner should be returned in similar value. Partners keep track of the benefits given or received, so that there is a continuous sense of equity or balance in the relationship. Couples who perceive that what is given is equal to what is received will view their relationship as positive and satisfying (Clark & Lamay, 2010).

In a study of couples prior to their weddings and 2 years after they were married, most couples thought that the communal norm was ideal and preferable to the exchange norm. Over time, the couples that relied more on the exchange norm were also less satisfied in their relationship. An interesting finding in this study was that individuals who were characterized by an anxious or avoidant attachment became increasingly reliant on the exchange norm 2 years into their marriage as compared to individuals who were characterized by a secure attachment. Even though they viewed the communal norm as ideal, those who had an anxious or avoidant attachment had difficulty establishing a communal, mutually beneficial supportive relationship. The communal norm depends more on trust and reciprocity as compared to the exchange norm that reflects some doubt about the partner's ability to care for and respond to one's needs (Clark, Lemay, Graham, Pataki, & Finkel, 2010). People who have an insecure attachment are likely to be mistrustful of the good intentions of their partner. As a result, they pay very close attention to the value of what they are receiving from their partner in relation to what they give to the partner. Unfortunately, this preoccupation with a fair exchange seems to be associated with more marital conflict and lower levels of marital happiness.

Once the choice has been made and the thrill of courtship has passed, the first few years of a committed relationship involve a process of mutual adaptation. They can be extremely difficult, particularly because the couple does not anticipate the strains. The partners may be quite distressed to find their home become riddled with the tensions that are a normal part of carving out a life together. In one study of 1,000 newlywed husbands and wives, the researchers found that problems appear for many couples in the first few months of marriage. Results revealed that 8% of newlyweds scored in the distressed range on measures of marital satisfaction and 14% scored in the distressed range on measures of marital adjustment after the first few months of wedlock.

For both husbands and wives, the most problematic areas in the early months of marriage were balancing employment and marriage, and debt brought into marriage (Schramm, Marshall, Harris, & Lee, 2005). Furthermore, confirming the difficulties of adjustment in the early years of marriage, data suggest that the probability of divorce is highest during the first years of marriage, peaking between 2 and 4 years. Among marriages that end in divorce, the median time to separation is 6.6 years; the median time to divorce is about 8 years (Kreider & Fields, 2002).

There are many additional sources of tension in a new marriage. If the partners do not have similar religious, educational, or social class backgrounds, they will have to compromise on many value decisions. Assuming a shared value orientation, certain lifestyle decisions can generate tension. The couple must establish a mutually satisfying sexual relationship. They must work out an agreement about spending and saving money. They must also respond to each other's sleep patterns, food preferences, work patterns, and toilet habits. The couple may find the demands of their parents and in-laws to be an additional source of conflict. Often, it is the number of demands rather than any single one that makes the adjustment process so difficult.

As part of the adjustment to marriage, the partners must achieve a sense of psychological commitment to each other. The marriage ceremony is intended to make that commitment public and binding. It is safe to say that most people probably do not fully accept the reality of their marriage vows until they have tested the relationship. There is a period of testing in every marriage, during which each partner is likely to put strain on the relationship to see how strong it really is. The question of trust may be posed as, "Will you still love me even if I do . . . ?" or, "Am I still free to do what I did before we were married?" Every marriage relationship is different. The partners must discover the limits of their particular relationship, but both partners must feel that they still have some freedom within these limits. They must also believe that the limits are balanced by the love, respect, and support they gain in return. As each test is successfully passed, the partners grow closer. They trust each other more and become increasingly sensitive to each other's feelings. Eventually, the tests diminish in number as the question of trust is resolved. In the study of newlyweds mentioned previously, the factors that worked to protect the marriages included respect, appreciation, commitment, mutual affection, and trust (Schramm et al., 2005).

Communication and Marital Adjustment.
Intimacy and a high level of satisfaction require effective communication and the capacity to cope effectively with conflict. Happy couples enjoy being together. They start out their marriages being very much in love, and they also view one another as responsive. They value the companionship aspects of their marriage, such as spending time together with friends or having dinner together (Kamo, 1993). In a comparison of American and Japanese couples, the latter were significantly less likely to share time together in these ways. However, for both the American and Japanese couples, those who spent more leisure time together had higher levels of marital satisfaction. The causal nature of this relationship is not fully understood. One might assume that happy couples choose to spend more time together, but it may also be that couples who have opportunities to spend more time together come to feel more positive about their marriage as a result.

Partners who have a high level of marital satisfaction report frequent, pleasurable interactions and a high degree of disclosure (Lippert & Prager, 2001). High levels of *disclosure* and *disclosure reciprocity* (i.e., you tell a person what you are thinking about, and that person tells you what she is thinking about) are associated with greater relationship satisfaction among marital partners (Finkenaure, Engles, Branje, & Meeus, 2004). Self-disclosure and partner disclosure both contribute to high levels of intimacy as well as relationship satisfaction. Perceptions of responsiveness from one's spouse also contribute to daily feelings of intimacy. It is likely that the positive impact of self-disclosure and partner disclosure in strengthening intimacy and satisfaction is accompanied by simultaneous increases in perceived partner responsiveness (Laurenceau, Barrett, & Rovine, 2005).

The Two Saltimbanques, 1901/© 2011 Estate of Pablo Picasso/Artists Rights Society (ARS), New York/Photo © Superstock

To sustain a marriage, the partners must be able to interact even during periods of conflict. Withdrawal, rejection, and distancing are common reactions to conflict. These strategies may be effective during a brief cooling-off period, but they do not replace direct communication for exploring or resolving differences.

The sense of intimacy is a psychological process in its own right that involves sharing an open, tender relationship with another person. Emotional expressiveness, especially by husbands, and a lack of ambivalence about expressing one's feelings are important elements in this communication process. In contrast, declines in affectionate and pleasurable interactions, lack of intimacy, and increases in ambivalence about the union predict a high probability of divorce (Huston et al., 2001).

In contrast to factors such as self-disclosure, partner disclosure, and a sense of partner responsiveness, which predict marital satisfaction, negative interactions and conflict are associated with marital distress. Conflict can be a product of the interaction of two well-developed identities, each with a distinct temperament, values, and goals. Conflict can result from the simple day-to-day need to make decisions that the couple has never made before. It can be a reflection of one or both partners' personalities, a tendency toward irritability, mistrust, or an aggressive temperament. It can be a product of disillusionment, as one or both partners perceive that the relationship fails to meet critical expectations. Much of the research on marital distress points to differences in power between the partners, especially differences in the control of resources and ongoing disagreements about the allocation of resources as an underlying source of **marital conflict**. Whatever the source, marital stability and satisfaction are closely tied to how couples manage conflict (Huston, Niehuis, & Smith, 2001).

Three dimensions of conflict seem especially important in differentiating happy and distressed marital relationships. First, instances of **negative communication**—especially nonverbal negative expressions and hostile put-downs—are more frequent in distressed than in happy couples, even in the first few years of married life.

Second, distressed couples show a pattern of **coercive escalation**—a style of interaction in which the probability that a negative remark will be followed by another negative remark increases as the chain of communication gets longer and longer (Gottman & Levenson, 1986). This pattern has been observed at the behavioral level by coding the verbal and nonverbal characteristics of an interaction and at the physiological level by monitoring heart rate, blood pressure, and release of stress hormones during communication (Markman & Notarius, 1987; Schrof, 1994). As the communication becomes increasingly negative, the partners become so physiologically disorganized that they lose access to their more rational ego functions. Over repeated instances, they become sensitive to this physiological state, reaching it sooner. In comparison, happy couples become more effective in soothing each other and in finding ways of preventing conflicts.

Third, distressed couples have different perceptions of the approach that their partners are taking to resolve a conflict. For example, one partner may think that he is acting in a constructive way to find a solution, but the other partner may view the behavior as patronizing or minimizing the importance of the issue. **Congruence** between the partners in how they think they and their partners are approaching the resolution of conflict is significantly related to marital satisfaction, whereas **lack of congruence** is significantly related to marital dissatisfaction and distress (Acitelli, Douvan, & Veroff, 1997).

In an analysis of effective problem solving among newly married couples, partners were asked to identify the areas where they had their most significant disagreements (Tallman & Hsiao, 2004). The four most common issues were money, who does what around the house, communication, and time spent with the spouse (p. 177). The premise of the study was that couples who were able to resolve problems so that both partners were satisfied with the outcome would experience greater levels of marital satisfaction. Another assumption was that both trust in one another and cooperative approaches to problem solving were needed in order to come to mutually satisfying solutions. Over time, the couples who were able to use cooperative problem-solving strategies had greater marital satisfaction, which in turn contributed to improved cooperative behavior in subsequent problem-solving efforts. Moreover, those couples who exhibited cooperative, mutually respectful problem solving were able to maintain their relationship quality in the face of economic distress.

Communication Styles of Men and Women. A growing body of literature suggests that men and women communicate differently and have different perceptions of the process. This idea has mixed empirical support. In many ways, men and women are alike. For example, both perceive the value of affective or emotional skills in promoting and sustaining friendships and romantic relationships. They both expect close friends—and especially romantic partners—to have the ability to encourage, soothe, reassure, and validate one another (Burleson, Kunkel, Samter, & Werking, 1996). When faced with upsetting problems, both women and men are most likely to offer suggestions for how to solve the problem or to take some action, rather than simply empathize and identify with the person's problem (Goldsmith & Dun, 1997). When asked about their preferred mode or style of interaction as a couple, husbands and wives both prefer interactions that are **contactful**—that is, open to the other person's point of view—and that also clearly express the speaker's own position. They least prefer **controlling interactions**, in which one person expresses her point of view and does not take the other person's point of view into consideration (Hawkins, Weisberg, & Ray, 1980). These similarities suggest that men and women approach the process of establishing intimate relationships with many common skills and values.

A great deal of empirical research has demonstrated that couples' communication in conflicts is associated with, and predictive of, marital satisfaction and stability (Weiss & Heyman, 1997; Noller & Feeney, 2002). One pattern of communication that has been documented in the marital interaction literature is the **demand-withdraw pattern,** in which one member (the demander) nags, criticizes, and makes demands of the other to change, while the partner (the withdrawer) avoids confrontation, becomes silent, and withdraws. In a review of numerous studies by different investigators, using a variety of methodologies and samples, the demand-withdraw pattern has been found to be consistently associated with relationship dissatisfaction (Eldridge & Christensen, 2002). Further, research has demonstrated that the demand-withdraw pattern is associated with several central aspects of marriage, such as power differences and violence (Sagrestano, Heavey, & Christensen, 1999), differences in desire for closeness and independence, femininity and masculinity, gender roles, and division of labor (Eldridge & Christensen, 2002). The demand-withdraw pattern occurs most often in distressed marriages. The pattern is also extremely resistant to change in these relationships (Eldridge et al., 2007).

Although both men and women can be in either role, research demonstrates that women are more often in the demanding role and men more often in the withdrawing role. These gender distinctions have been observed in a wide variety of samples, including dating couples, cohabiting couples, married couples, clinic couples seeking therapy, violent couples, and divorcing couples (Eldridge & Christensen, 2002). Findings from recent research by Eldridge and colleagues demonstrate that the demand-withdraw pattern increases with the length of the marriage. The gender disparity in roles seems to be associated with a specific element across problem discussions: The person who needs to change is the husband. Because women are more often seeking change in the marriage (Kluwer, Heesink, & van de Vliert, 2000; Margolin, Talovic, & Weinstein, 1983), women are more often in the demanding role and men are more often in the withdrawing role. When the discussion was centered on the husband changing, whether the change was desired by the wife (wife relationship problem discussion) or by the husband himself (husband personal problem discussion), there was a gender-stereotyped difference in roles. If the discussion was about change in the wife, there was little or no gender disparity in roles (Eldridge et al., 2007). It is unclear whether the greater disparity is because husbands are more resistant to change than wives, because wives are more insistent on change than husbands, or both.

Some differences in the ways men and women approach communication have implications for the quality of an intimate relationship. The socialization of both sexes in U.S. culture is still sufficiently distinct to result in differences in expectations and competencies. For example, when faced with a problem, men are more likely to want to deny it or to spend time analyzing and defining it in comparison with women (Goldsmith & Dun, 1997). Similarly, men tend to value the skills of being a good conversationalist or storyteller and being able to laugh and joke as well as to argue and defend a position somewhat more than do women (Burleson et al., 1996). They tend to be more ambivalent than women about expressing emotions and withdraw to avoid escalating conflict. Women, on the other hand, tend to want to talk things out so that everyone feels comfortable with the situation. In conflicts, these styles can become incompatible, especially if the woman is trying to reach consensus and the man withdraws. In general, women expect and desire a degree of closeness that is often not reciprocated. Men, on the other hand, are more likely to be satisfied with the degree of intimacy that they find in marriage and have fewer expectations of or less desire for greater closeness (Dindia & Allen, 1992).

Adjustment in Dual-Earner Marriages. One of the greatest changes in U.S. families in the second half of the 20th century was the increase in the number of married women who were employed. It is now normative for married women, including those with young children, to be in the labor market. The percentage of employed, married women whose husbands are present was 32% in 1960 and 61% in 2008. The number of women with young children who work outside the home has also grown substantially. In 2005, 61% of married women with children under 6 years of age were in the labor force, compared with 39% in 1960 (U.S. Census Bureau, 2010). Rather than drop out of the labor force and return to work after their children are grown, the majority of women now remain in the labor force throughout the early years of parenthood.

There is no question that the involvement of both husband and wife in the labor market requires a departure from traditional family roles and a dialogue about the division of labor. Uncertainty about the expectations and behaviors of the spousal roles must be worked out between the partners. Sometimes, this uncertainty helps to produce greater intimacy by generating interactions that lead to greater self-disclosure by each partner. Personal preferences and habits must be examined if the partners are to arrive at an effective division of labor that is mutually satisfying. Sometimes, however, this process is threatening. The partners may not really be aware of their expectations of themselves or of the other person until they are married.

One analysis of the potential conflicts for dual-earner couples focused on the relative balance of power and demands for household labor for the two partners (Rosenfeld, 1992). In the traditional male-breadwinner, female-homemaker family model, the husband has more power as a result of his access to financial resources and participates little in the low-status household tasks. The wife, in contrast, has little power and carries the majority of responsibility for the household tasks. As women have entered the labor market, their access to financial resources has increased. To the extent that their husbands also help in sharing the household tasks, women's well-being and mental health improve.

For men, especially in families where there is a relatively high family income, as their wives' income matches or surpasses their own and they have to take on a greater role in domestic tasks, their well-being declines and their mental health suffers. This is true primarily for men who have traditional views about the importance of men as breadwinners

(Brennan, Barnett, & Gareis, 2001). Men who feel demeaned or threatened by demands to participate in household labor are likely to experience depressive symptoms that are similar to the reactions that women have when they try to carry the full responsibility of household tasks while also participating in the labor market. Finding the balance of power and of household responsibilities that preserves mutual respect and support is a major challenge in the early years of the marriage and has to be fine-tuned and renegotiated throughout the marriage.

Evidence from a variety of sources suggests that in contemporary U.S. society, there are a number of benefits for couples when husbands and wives have multiple roles that include marriage, career, and parenting (Barnett & Hyde, 2001). Four benefits are summarized here:

1. Involvement in multiple roles means that both partners are likely to be more fully integrated into meaningful social support systems.
2. Participation of both partners in the labor force increases financial resources and buffers the couple against fluctuations in each person's job situation.
3. Success in one role can buffer each person against negative experiences in other roles. For example, negative work experiences can be offset by marital happiness and the centrality of parenting.
4. Involvement in similar roles provides husbands and wives with a shared frame of reference. Thus, partners are more likely to appreciate one another's point of view and to empathize with each other's struggles and accomplishments.

However, there are limits to the benefits of the dual-earner arrangement. The advantages of the dual-earner, multiple-role lifestyle can be offset when one or both partners experience role overload—for example, if the care of an ill parent is added to an already full basket of responsibilities. The quality of the roles can undermine the benefits, as when a person is in a terrible job with inadequate wages and oppressive work conditions. Chronic stressors at home that create feelings of overload or lack of control can make the daily hassles of home or work life seem even worse. These ongoing stressors, which result in frequent but unpredictable demands, can cause psychological distress in the individual and disrupt relationship satisfaction (Serido, Almeida, & Wetherington, 2004). Multiple roles can be disruptive if a partner holds traditional gender role values that are in conflict with the enactment of multiple roles. Finally, couples may find that their actual work schedules do not fit well together, leaving too little time to be together or too little control over their nonwork life (Barnett, Brennan, & Gareis, 1999).

Roughly 100 years of social science research has established that satisfaction in the relationship of marriage contributes significantly to psychological well-being, including a greater sense of social integration and protection from other life stressors. For most adults, happiness in life depends more on having a satisfying marriage than on any other domain of adult life, including work, friendships, hobbies, and community activities. Longitudinal studies of adults who either remained single or got married and remained married over a 7-year period found that those who were married had higher levels of well-being and fewer mental health problems (Horwitz, White, & Howell-White, 1996; Williams, 2003). The research suggests that the benefits of being married for mental health and life satisfaction accrue primarily in the context of happy marriages, where the partners describe their relationship as one in which their spouse makes them feel valued and cared for (Williams, 2003).

Childbearing

Objective 3. To describe the factors associated with the decision to have children, the impact of childbearing on the intimate relationship, the developing parental relationship, and the contribution of childbearing to growth in adulthood.

One central commitment of early adulthood is parenthood. During early adulthood, the issue of reproduction is confronted many times. Young adults make choices to delay parenting, have an abortion, have a child, wait before having another child, or stop having children altogether. As discussed in Chapter 4 (The Period of Pregnancy and Prenatal Development), many couples undergo difficult and expensive procedures to conceive a child. Others who are unable to conceive decide to adopt children. Some adults become foster parents, whether or not they have children of their own. Even unplanned pregnancies are products of some kind of decision making—whether to have sexual relations knowing that pregnancy is possible, to avoid using effective means of birth control, to abort the pregnancy, or to carry the child to term (Lydon, Dunkel-Schetter, Cohan, & Pierce, 1996). In all of these decisions, many powerful themes are reflected: one's sense of fulfilling a masculine or feminine life purpose by having children; one's childhood socialization and identification with parental figures; religious beliefs about sexuality, contraception, or abortion; and ideas about carrying on a family's ancestry and traditions. Reproduction is the means by which the species perpetuates itself. As people reflect on their lives, the birth of their children is commonly recalled as a life-story high point (McAdams & Bowman, 2001). Regardless of the decisions one reaches, this issue cannot help but heighten the sense that the decisions of adulthood make a difference.

Fertility Rate

The average number of births required for the natural replacement of a population is estimated at 2.1 births per adult woman. This number is calculated by assuming that for every adult woman in a population, a female child must be born who will reach reproductive maturity and have children. Because slightly more male than female children are born, and because not all children reach childbearing age, the estimate for a replacement reproductive rate is 2.1 children (Bachu & O'Connell, 2001).

The fertility rate in the United States has fluctuated from the late 1950s, when the rate was 3.5 births per woman, to a low of 1.8 in the 1970s. In 2007, the rate was 2.1, just at the replacement estimate. Fertility rates in the United States vary by race and ethnicity, and socioeconomic status. Hispanic women have the highest fertility rate; Asian or Pacific Islanders and American Indians have the lowest (Hamilton, 2004; U.S. Census Bureau, 2007). Women who have graduated from high school have a higher fertility rate than women who graduated from college. Women who are not in the labor force have a higher fertility rate than those in the labor force. Women whose family income is below $25,000 have a higher fertility rate than those above $25,000 (U.S. Census Bureau, 2010).

Decisions About Childbearing

In contemporary society, decisions about childbearing are made in the context of other personal and family goals and commitments. Factors such as religious beliefs, career aspirations, ideals about family life, and social expectations in the family and culture all contribute to a couple's commitment to bearing children and the timing of first and subsequent pregnancies. Cultures differ in the norms and expectations they convey about the value of having children and the appropriate timing and frequency of pregnancies (see the box entitled "The Reproductive Career of the Gusii").

In a study of 4 decades of trends in attitudes toward marriage, divorce, cohabitation, and childbearing, Thornton and Young-DeMarco (2001) compared responses from men and women as well as adolescents from five different national U.S. samples. Data were collected in the 1960s, 1970s, 1980s, and 1990s, with the most recent data coming from adolescents surveyed in 1997–1998. Over time, two themes emerged. First, in the 1980s and 1990s, people viewed childbearing within marriage as more of an option than an obligation. Over that time, respondents increasingly disagreed with the idea that all married couples who can have children ought to have children. This concept was positively endorsed by 84% of mothers in 1962, but by only 41% of mothers and 22% of their adult daughters in 1993. Similarly, in the 1980s and 1990s, the majority of people disagreed with the idea that having children is the main reason for getting married, or that people who did not have children led meaningless lives.

In light of the changing sense of social obligation to have children, one might think that people would be less enthusiastic about the meaning of parenting and less likely to want to become parents, but this did not happen. The second trend was a steady endorsement of the value of parenting. The majority of high school seniors who were surveyed from the mid-1970s through the late 1990s agreed that fatherhood and motherhood are among the most fulfilling experiences of adulthood; roughly 60% of these students (both male and female) said they were likely to want to have children.

Although the majority of married couples intend to have children, the timing of their entry into parenthood varies. The age of entry into parenthood has been getting older, accompanying an older age at marriage. Between 1980 and 2007, the birth rate for women ages 20 to 24 decreased (from 115/1,000 to 106/1,000), and increased for women between the ages of 30 and 34 (from 62/1,000 to 100/1,000; U.S. Census Bureau, 2010). Both the social and biological clocks come into play in this decision. The social clock refers to expectations from family and friends that it is time to start a family. Children who grew up in large families where their own mothers began parenting at a young age may experience both social pressure and social support from their families to have children early (Barber, 2000). Couples who wait to begin their families may be pressured by parents who are eager to become grandparents or by friends who have already experienced the lifestyle changes that accompany the birth of their first child.

In recent years, many couples have decided to postpone childbearing until after the first years of their marriage. This decision is related to several other aspects of adult life and needs to be understood in the context of competing goals, including education, career aspirations, and a desire to experience the intimacy of the marriage. Couples who have a dual-earner marriage have to consider the effect of children on their family income. They may try to anticipate the best timing for childbearing in relation to job security or career advancement. Some couples set certain material goals for themselves as a prerequisite to having children. For example, they may decide to wait until they can buy a home, establish a certain amount of savings, or travel together before they have children. Given the high divorce rate, couples are likely to want to feel confident that their relationship is strong before deciding to have children.

Delayed entry into parenthood has typically been studied in relation to the characteristics of the woman. It has been found to be related to a woman's level of education, her career commitment, and the family's income.

> Zine Magubane (age 32) and her husband, Patrick McCabe, married in June. She's got a tenure-track university teaching job; he's a sports agent who travels constantly. They want to wait at least a year before beginning a family "to get a little more stability," says Magubane, whose mother delivered her at 36. Today she works hard to stay healthy, knowing she'll be an older mom. (Kalb, 2001, p. 43)

In a study of the timing of entry into fatherhood, men who were characterized as late-entry fathers (30 years old or older) were more involved with their children and had more positive feelings about them than did the on-time or early fathers (Cooney, Pedersen, Indelicato, & Palkovitz, 1993). Older fathers may feel that they have less conflict between their commitments to work and to family. They may feel that they have already demonstrated their ability to succeed in

HUMAN DEVELOPMENT AND DIVERSITY

The Reproductive Career of the Gusii

ROBERT LEVINE (1980) described the patterns of adulthood among the Gusii, a tribe living in the Kisii highlands of western Kenya, about 50 miles south of the equator. The Gusii lived in a well-protected, fertile area where they were able to expand their communities and grow their crops. LeVine characterized their adult life course as being composed of three interdependent spheres: reproductive, economic, and spiritual. His description of the reproductive career illustrates how personal and societal expectations influence the childbearing decisions of young adults.

The reproductive career seems to be the most salient for both sexes. Its goal is to become the ancestor of a maximally expanding genealogy. For women, this means to have children as frequently between marriage and menopause as is consistent with child health, which the Gusii believe to be every 2 years. A man who fails to impregnate his wife that often will be publicly accused by her of neglect. The woman must have at least one son to take care of her in her old age and whose wives work with her; to have nothing but daughters (who move away at marriage) is second only to barrenness as a disaster. If her husband dies, it is her right as well as her obligation to have a leviratic husband to impregnate her regularly so she will continue to bear children "for the dead man." For men, the goal means not only maximizing his wife's offspring but taking additional wives as he can afford them and so appending their reproductive careers to his. If a man has been a monogamist, he might take a younger second wife when his first wife reaches menopause, for that would extend his reproductive career by a decade or more. The reproductive career as I see it, however, is not limited to the individual's own procreation but includes that of his or her offspring. Grandchildren are as fervently desired as one's own children and, not incidentally, play an essential role in the burial of the grandparents. (Levine, 1980, p. 94)

The value placed on having children, the practice of child spacing, and the practice of extending the father's reproductive career by adding a second, younger wife all contribute to the high fertility rate of the Gussi (LeVine et al., 1996). However, current conditions threaten the reproductive career of the Gusii. The level of mortality for children under 5 years old is 122/1,000 births in the western region of Kenya. Kenya is among 16 countries in which the mortality rate for children under 5 was higher in 2004 than it was in 1990. According to the Republic of Kenya Ministry of Health (2004), the following issues impact the survival of children under the age of 5:

- Decline in levels of immunization coverage against the six childhood diseases, a key indicator of use of child health services. Children ages 12 to 23 months receiving full vaccination against vaccine-preventable diseases fell from 65% in 1998 to 60% in 2003. Children receiving no vaccination at all increased from 3% in 1998 to 6% in 2003.
- Recurring incidences of hunger and the resultant child protein-energy malnutrition (PEM) among children. Although chronic undernutrition among children under age 5 declined from 33% in 1998 to 30% in 2003, micronutrient deficiencies still affect large numbers of children and women.
- Widespread incidences of malaria, diarrhea, and acute respiratory infections, which mainly impact children. These diseases currently contribute to about 50% of all reported morbidity and about 25% of all reported deaths.
- HIV/AIDS scourge and its related opportunistic infections—increasing HIV infection rates among pregnant mothers.
- Lack of comprehensive obstetrics, neonatal care services, and emergency obstetrics in many hospitals, particularity in rural areas.
- Widespread poverty levels in the country, particularly in rural areas.

- Literacy levels and low mothers' education levels in many parts of the country. Children of mothers with little or no education have had the largest risk of mortality.
- Delivery complications arising from many deliveries done outside health care facilities and not supervised by skilled health workers.
- Lack of access to Preventing Mother to Child Transmission (PMTCT) services to all HIV-positive mothers.
- Poor infant feeding and weaning practices.
- Inadequate access to sustainable clean water sources and sanitation facilities.
- Lack of access to health services in many parts of the country due mainly to their maldistribution.
- Insufficient resources (e.g., trained health workers, equipment, drugs).

These factors illustrate the potential disruptive forces of modernization on traditional cultural systems and practices.

Critical Thinking Questions

1. What are some differences in the orientation toward childbearing between the Gusii and young adults in the United States?
2. What do you think is the impact of greater contact with the more industrialized, commercial world on the Gusii and their reproductive, economic, and spiritual spheres, including both values and behaviors?
3. How might the goal of becoming an ancestor of an expanded genealogy affect women's health and reproductive practices?
4. How might taking a second, younger wife in order to continue a man's reproductive career be perceived by his first wife?
5. The Gusii are the focus of a growing human rights protest. Can you find out more about it? How does this influence your understanding of the reproductive goal of the Gusii and the status of women in this culture?

This couple's affection for and commitment to each other is expanding to include love for their unborn child. How might the quality of the parent's relationship influence the experience of pregnancy?

the breadwinner role and, therefore, can approach parenthood with more confidence and a greater sense of self-efficacy. Older fathers may have more emotional resources to bring to their marriage and their parenting relationship.

Decisions to postpone childbearing are also constrained by the *biological clock*. Despite the number of highly publicized late pregnancies, the biological limits on age of childbearing are still significant. After age 30, women's fertility rates decline, and by age 40, miscarriages increase. Reproductive technologies that involve fertilizing a woman's own eggs decrease from 40% effectiveness for women in their late twenties to less than 10% for women in their forties. However, new ideas are being introduced that may push back these constraints, such as transferring the cell nucleus from an older woman's egg, transplanting it into the cytoplasm of a younger woman's egg, and implanting the new, improved egg into the older mother so that she can experience pregnancy and childbirth (Kalb, 2001).

The patterns discussed previously may lead one to believe that couples are making very deliberate and strategic decisions about the timing for their childbearing. However, data from the National Survey of Family Growth indicate that slightly more than one third of all pregnancies are described by mothers as unintended. Moreover, among women who have had one unintended child, about one third have another unintended birth (Wildsmith, Guzzo, & Hayford, 2010).

In addition to one's intentions about childbearing, certain other experiences feed into fertility decisions. For example, some research finds that the characteristics of the firstborn child influence a couple's decision about having another child. When the firstborn child has a sociable temperament, has relatively few behavioral problems, and shows a readiness and eagerness for learning, families are more likely to be enthusiastic about having another child (Jokela, 2010). Sometimes the conditions leading up to pregnancy, such as sexual abuse, or unusually difficult experiences of pregnancy result in a reluctance to have additional children (Sperlich & Seng, 2008). Social policies, such as the one-child policy in China, or the welfare policy in the United States, which emphasizes labor force participation for mothers of young children, can have an impact on childbearing decisions.

Problems in Adjustment During Pregnancy and Childbearing

Although most women are healthy and happy about being pregnant, there is growing concern about how to treat mood disorders among women during pregnancy and after childbirth. Numerous studies document the disruptive impact of maternal depression on the infant's cognitive and emotional development and the associated mother-infant relationship (Pearson et al., 2010). Some women are chronically depressed prior to pregnancy and are being treated with psychotropic drugs. Other women become anxious or depressed during pregnancy. The challenge is whether to continue the use of these therapeutic drugs, weighing the risks of potential harm to the fetus and the risks of untreated or increased depressive symptoms for the pregnant woman (Cohen et al., 2010). Approximately 13% of women experience mild to moderate depression in the first 3 months following childbirth (Bick & Howard, 2010). Many cases of depression go undiagnosed and untreated, resulting in maternal distress, negative affect, reduced sensitivity to the infant's signals, and disengagement from the mothering role.

The Dual Roles of Intimate Partner and Parent

In contrast to the elation that usually accompanies the anticipation of and preparation for the newborn, the arrival of the first child often brings a period of stress to the relationship (Newman, 2000). Belsky and Rovine (1990) found clear evidence of individual differences in how couples adapted to the transition to parenthood. In their longitudinal study of 128 families, they observed four patterns of change in the assessment of marital quality: (1) Some couples showed a

© Bill Aron/Photo Edit

rapid decline in marital quality after the first baby was born. (2) Others showed a slow, steady decline. (3) A third group showed no significant change. (4) A fourth group showed slight increases in marital quality. These findings caution us not to overgeneralize group trends to individual cases.

The quality of marital adjustment during the transition to parenthood is closely related to marital quality before the child was born (Heinicke, 1995). Couples who are in close, confiding, satisfying marriages before their children are born tend to show higher levels of marital adjustment 3 months after childbirth than do couples in conflictual marriages. However, many studies find that couples experience increased conflict after the birth of their first child. If the relationship was negative and the partners had high levels of conflict prior to the baby's birth, these difficulties are likely to increase (Crohan, 1996). In some couples, this conflict escalates to physical violence. An estimated 4% to 8% of pregnant women experience violence from their intimate partner during the pregnancy. The risks of intimate partner violence are greater in low-income households, especially in communities where people feel trapped in a life of poverty and disorganization. A wide range of negative consequences are associated with this violence, including miscarriages, abortions, injury or death to the pregnant woman, and continued abuse after the child is born (Li et al., 2010; Silverman et al., 2010). Research suggests that several characteristics of the partner relationship, especially shared involvement of the partners in household tasks and commitment to the relationship, reduce the likelihood of such violence.

In an attempt to clarify the effects of many factors on marital satisfaction during the transition to parenthood, researchers compared marital activities and evaluations of the marriage by parents and nonparents who had been married the same number of years (MacDermid, Huston, & McHale, 1990; Huston & Vangelisti, 1995). They found that over the first 3 years of marriage, couples' ratings of love and satisfaction declined somewhat. There were no differences in the magnitude of the decline for parents and nonparents. Having children did not account for a greater drop in love or satisfaction than appeared to occur as a result of adjusting to marriage in general. This is an important observation that provides new insight into much of the earlier research on marital satisfaction and the transition to parenthood.

Having children did have an impact on **marital companionship**. The percentage of leisure activities shared by the husband and wife dropped sharply after the baby was born, but it declined only slightly for the couples without children. During the third year of marriage, parents had a greater number of shared activities per day than nonparents, but few when the child was not present. Figure 11.4 shows the number of minutes of joint leisure time per day without the child for two groups of parents in comparison with joint leisure time for nonparents in the first, second, and third years of marriage. After the birth of their child, couples have only about one third as many minutes together alone as they had when they were childless. The nature of companionship in

FIGURE 11.4 Duration of Joint Husband-Wife Leisure without Child for Parents and Nonparents
Source: Based on MacDermid, Huston, and McHale, 1990.

marriage changes to incorporate a baby and therefore may become less intimate.

For most couples, coping with the early months of childrearing strengthens the bond between the partners. The partners begin to respect each other's competence in caring for their child. They also begin to conceptualize their roles as parents and to view the increasing complexity of their family structure as a challenge rather than a burden. The new baby adds a degree of energy to the family through expressions of satisfaction, pleasure, and affection.

As the roles of mother and father are added to the adults' repertoire of role relationships, adults face new challenges in balancing their work, intimate partner, and parent roles. A variety of factors influence adults' ability to achieve a positive sense of role balance. Access to financial resources helps couples enjoy leisure time, and purchase services that can reduce some degree of role strain. When partners are equally highly invested in their parental roles, they are more readily able to make the trade-offs and compromises that parenting requires, including modifying their leisure time to incorporate each other's interests and the presence of their young child. In contrast, when partners have to work long hours, especially on the weekends, or try to pursue individual leisure interests that do not include their partner or child, they may have more difficulty achieving a comfortable sense of role balance (Marks, Huston, Johnson, & MacDermid, 2001; Claxton & Perry-Jenkins, 2008).

The daily demands of the child help the parents define their own roles more realistically. Instead of wondering what parents should do, they are occupied with the actual demands of parenting. Through this experiential learning, young adults formulate their own definitions of parental roles. Assuming that the early experiences are successful and the parents are able to meet their child's needs, they gradually achieve a new level of self-efficacy in the parenting role, gaining new confidence in their ability to provide a nurturing environment for their child.

The process of social attachment and its impact on the infant were discussed in Chapter 5 (Infancy). The theme of mutuality as the central process for the establishment of trust was stressed. Mutuality also has an impact on parents. Infants actively engage their parents, evoke unique responses, and, through their differential behaviors, begin to shape parenting behaviors. Infants respond to their parents with shrieks of delight, elaborate smiles, and the active pursuit of them. They are unrestrained in their loving. They mouth, bite, grab, laugh, smile, squeal, and coo in response to pleasure. Through their open demonstrations of affection, infants teach adults about the expression of love and increase their parents' ability to demonstrate it. As parents and children begin to engage in playful interactions, the capacity to establish and maintain reciprocal interactions expands. Children learn how to initiate a play sequence by bringing a toy or making a playful gesture. Parents then learn how to respond by complying to the request for play, sitting down on the floor, bringing out the box of favorite play materials, or tickling and tumbling. As children and parents experience mutual, congruent playful interactions, the bond of affection is strengthened and communication is enhanced (Lindsey, Mize, & Pettit, 1997).

Nonmarital Childbearing

In 2006, over 1.6 million babies were born to women in the United States who were not married. This represents 38.5% of all births to women ages 15 to 44 (U.S. Census Bureau, 2010). Although the majority of births to unmarried women occur at younger ages, about 22% were births to unmarried women ages 25 to 29. The decision to have children outside of a marriage relationship at this age may be a result of recent divorce or widowhood, a decision reached in the context of a lesbian or a cohabiting relationship, or a decision to start a family without a partner. The website of Single Mothers by Choice (http://singlemothersbychoice.com) provides some insights into the motivations and resources of women who deliberately choose to have a child without a partner.

Adoption

Adoption is an alternative to childbearing for individuals who want to start a family or expand their family. Overall, adoption is relatively rare today, with fewer than 1.5% of married women having ever adopted a child (Jones, 2008). Adoption can occur between related family members, or between unrelated individuals. Roughly half of adoptions involve family members who adopt, for example, when adults with children remarry and their children are adopted by their new partner, when adults adopt the children of siblings who have died, or when grandparents adopt their grandchildren because the adult children are not able to parent. Infertility is the most common reason that adults adopt unrelated children. Other reasons that adults give for adoption include religious or philosophical convictions, for example, a belief that it is more responsible to care for otherwise parentless children than to reproduce, to prevent passing an inheritable diseases (e.g., Tay-Sachs disease), to avoid contributing to perceived overpopulation, and health concerns relating to pregnancy and childbirth.

Over the past 30 years, the context of adoption has changed in a variety of ways that has resulted in fewer children available for adoption. The fertility rate in the United

© Ariel Skelley/CORBIS

Couples with children find new ways to spend time together that includes their child. Rather than a romantic ski weekend for two, this family goes sledding together.

States has declined, and teen births, which were a source of many adoptive babies, has also declined. Social welfare practices have become increasingly focused on family preservation, emphasizing the importance of keeping children with their birth parents. International adoptions have also decreased. Countries including Vietnam, Guatemala, China, and Russia have taken steps to try to arrange for local adoption rather than sending their children to the United States (Seabrook, 2010).

The adoption process can be implemented to support the best interest of children; however, it requires a clear understanding of the unique dynamics of this bond. Parents may experience some continued feelings of sadness as a result of not having a biologically linked child. This sadness or disappointment might be conveyed to their adoptive child. Adopted children may also experience feelings of loss as they learn of the separation from the birth mother, or in the case of international adoption, as they begin to understand the separation from their cultural heritage (Grotevant, 2009). When children have been in foster care for 2 years or longer, the lack of continuity in the attachment process, and harsh or unstimulating conditions of care can have significant negative consequences for children's emotional and cognitive development. Adults who adopt older children need to be prepared to provide unique supportive parenting in order to compensate for their child's early experiences of neglect. At present, the preparation and training for adoptive parents to help them address these concerns are not adequately developed (Palacios & Brodzinsky, 2010).

Open adoptions, which are becoming increasingly common, strive to preserve the sense of family origins and connections so that children have a clearer picture of their developmental history as they mature. The success of this openness depends on the willingness of the birth mother to share information, and on the skill of the adoptive parents to incorporate this information into the narrative for the child about how their family was formed (Neil, 2009).

Two American moms are in China to meet their adoptive daughters.

The Decision Not to Have Children

Not all couples choose to have children. In 2006, 20% of women ages 40 to 44 were childless, twice as many as were childless 30 years ago (Dye, 2008). Fewer Hispanic women are childless than White non-Hispanic and Black women. Much like attitudes toward remaining single, attitudes toward a lifestyle in which a couple chooses not to have children are becoming more accepting. As discussed earlier, childbearing is increasingly viewed as a choice rather than an obligation. This shift is evidenced in part by a change in the sociological jargon from the term *childless* to the newer term *voluntarily childfree*. The decision not to have children is becoming increasingly common, not only in the United States but also in other industrialized nations, especially as women's educational attainment and occupational commitments reach new levels (Giles, Shaw, & Morgan, 2009). Nonetheless, resisting social expectations that married couples ought to bear children requires a high level of personal autonomy and less need for social support from a wide range of reference groups. It may also require a competing positive identity, such as commitment to one's career goals, or a redefinition of gender roles to sustain and validate this decision. In comparison to women who have children, those who are voluntarily childfree have higher income, more work experience, and are less religious (Park, 2002; Abma & Martinez, 2006).

The U.S. culture continues to be *pronatalist*, placing a high value on the meaning of parenthood in adult life. Women who are making childbearing decisions are often influenced by their own mothers' religiosity and their childhood religious teachings (Pearce, 2002). In some ethnic and religious groups, having children is considered a sacred trust. For example, within the Mormon Church, children are highly valued. "Mormon doctrine states that children are the spirit sons and daughters of heavenly parents, and that God holds parents responsible for their stewardship in raising them in righteousness" (Lambert & Thomasson, 1997, p. 90).

Through a pronatalist lens, motherhood is viewed as the symbol of a woman's ultimate identity, regardless of her other talents or accomplishments. Mary Blair-Loy (2001) describes a powerful family devotion schema among women—a view that the ideal mother should be committed full-time to her children and the well-being of her family. This view is contrasted to the work devotion schema, which suggests that an ideal employee should devote all time to the work setting. In comparison to people in many European countries, workers in the United States work longer days, take less vacation, have no paid maternity leave, and have limited access to quality infant care. The tensions between pronatalist cultural values, the devotion to the work ideal, and the lack of policies that support parenting result in many women leaving the labor market during their childbearing years or reducing their labor participation to part-time employment (Williams & Cooper, 2004). From 1998 to 2004, the labor force participation of women who had a child in the previous year dropped from 59% to 55%, reversing the trend of rising labor force participation of new mothers since it was first tracked by the Census Bureau in 1976 (Dye, 2005).

Work

Objective 4. To explore the concept of work as a stimulus for psychosocial development in early adulthood, with special focus on the technical skills, authority relations, demands and hazards, and interpersonal relations in the work environment.

Within the life course framework, the occupational career is a major trajectory in each person's life story. In combination with intimate relationships and parenting, efforts to balance and coordinate work and family life produce some of the greatest challenges of adult life. Work is the primary means of accumulating financial resources. It is the focus of attention for much of the waking day. One's work determines in large part the activities, social relationships, challenges, satisfactions, and hassles or frustrations of daily life. Finally, work is the context in which many adults express their personal identity and experience a sense of personal value and social status.

In Chapter 10 (Later Adolescence), we discussed the developmental task of career choice, emphasizing the link between career decision making and other aspects of individual identity. Here we focus on adaptation to the world of work, where the demands of work present new challenges and opportunities for development.

The concept of work is complex. The following discussion considers very general characteristics of work and their potential impact on one's cognitive, social, and emotional development and on one's sense of self in adulthood. This type of analysis is necessary because occupational roles in U.S. society are so varied. Each job role places the individual in a somewhat different psychosocial context, with a unique combination of expectations, resources, and strains.

The World of Work

To gain an appreciation for the variety of career paths and their associated impact on daily life, you may want to consult the *Occupational Outlook Handbook*, which has projections for jobs in hundreds of industries for the period 2008 to 2018 (www.bls.gov/oco). For each career, the handbook provides information about: the training and education needed; earnings; expected job prospects; what workers do on the job; and working conditions.

The case study of Jay Crowe, which was retrieved from www.wetfeet.com provides an excerpt from an interview with an elementary school social worker in Albuquerque, New Mexico. He describes what he does, what it takes to do well in his type of work, and how a person can get a job like the one he has. Then he describes his daily schedule. According to the *Occupational Outlook Handbook*, "demand

for school social workers will continue and lead to more jobs as efforts are expanded to respond to rising student enrollments, as well as the continued emphasis on integrating children with disabilities into the general school population. There could be competition for school social work jobs in some areas because of the limited number of openings. The availability of Federal, State, and local funding will be a major factor in determining the actual job growth in schools" (U.S. Department of Labor, 2010).

CASE STUDY

JAY CROWE

Jay Crowe is an elementary school social worker. This interview provides a glimpse of the demands, rewards, and daily requirements of that occupation.

Question: What do you do?
As a school social worker, my formal caseload consists of special-needs children who are in the special education program. They have psychiatric diagnoses ranging from clinical depression to thought disorders to character disorders. My job is to work with the children on an individual and group basis during regular school hours. I have a classroom, and in that classroom I've got therapeutic games, as well as basic kid games, and I also do a lot of outdoor activities, such as baseball, football, soccer, tag, and chasing games. In an individual situation, I use one-on-one play therapy. We use a play environment to build trust and acceptance. Then the therapist can open up important topics.

Question: What kinds of people do well in this business?
Empathetic types with the understanding that the generations who are coming after them make a difference in the long run do well. People who generally care about other people do well. You can't see the shady side of life and internalize it and take it home every day and become self-destructive. That's an easy trap to fall into. People who do well have a lot of self-awareness and understand their own needs.

Question: What do you really like about your job?
Something new comes up every day because people are not machines. You can't make absolute predictions, and that's what I like.

Question: What do you dislike?
I dislike the paperwork and the administrative double standards. Our school is defined as being site-based, meaning that the principal and the staff have autonomy. That's fine, until the site decides to do something that the district wants to do. Then the district will pull it away from the site. But it could be a lot worse. For the most part, we're able to implement programs as we see fit.

Question: How can someone get a job like yours?

After you get the education, there are a couple of things you can do. You can write queries to the heads of human resources at school districts and ask them if they have social work positions. State governments also often have listings for educational jobs on the Internet. You can also look at the classified ads in the newspaper. I've been able to get the vast majority of my jobs by talking to people who are already in the positions. As tempting as it may be at the time, don't burn any bridges. Keep all your options open, personally and professionally.

Question: Can you describe a typical day?

8:30 I've already arrived and I'm typically in the bus parking lot waiting to supervise the first busloads of students coming to school. The duty teachers are not supposed to be out there until 8:40, but the first buses come in around 8:30, so the principal asked me to supervise the bus embarking and debarking in the morning and afternoon. I stay until the duty teachers arrive.

8:40 I'm in my classroom, looking at messages that came in the day before. I follow up on urgent calls. I often get messages from parents wanting to discuss the events of the day before. Maybe their child came home with a complaint about something that happened on the bus and the parents want to make me aware of it. For children in my caseload who get write-ups, the parents and the principal might ask me to intervene and help determine consequences. If there's any information I need to pass on to teachers, I do it before 8:55, because that's when classes start.

9:00 I might have a group meeting. For instance, this past year, I met with a group of third-grade boys every Tuesday at nine. First we sit down together and do what we call the roundtable. We go around the table and check in with each other. That includes me checking in with the boys, because I work from an equality model. The groups have basic rules, which are all phrased in a positive way. Instead of "Don't interrupt," the rule is "One will wait one's turn." Other rules are "One will raise one's hand," "Use polite phrases like 'excuse me,'" and "All conversation is to be respectful." Once we do our check-in, we talk about old business that was unfinished from the week before. We review what game we decided to play for this week. If we didn't pick an activity, we have a vote to choose one. Then we play the game, focusing on social skills and problem solving.

9:45 We end the group session by reviewing the game and how everybody did, not in terms of winning or losing, but in terms of their ability to get along and share.

10:00 I have sessions for much of the day, and each lasts between 45 and 55 minutes. In an individual session, we use one-on-one play therapy. For instance, I might play chess with a child, or the child might teach me a new game. After we build up trust and acceptance, I can bring up topics such as the child's family situation.

11:00 This year, the school counselor and I started something we call "lunch bunch." Each grade level has a 45-minute lunch, with 15 minutes to eat and 30 minutes on the playground, where there are two teachers on duty at the most. Some children do not do well with such limited supervision, and they're able to come to my classroom at lunch. The school counselor and I are there to engage them in games, discussion, and arts and crafts. We have, at the most, 15 children at one time, and a total of 50 kids signed up for lunch bunch.

1:30 The school counselor and I go into classrooms and do 30 to 35 minutes of class meetings. There are classrooms that the principal has targeted as being almost leaderless—the teachers are just not competent at maintaining balanced discipline. We team up and work with the children so that, by the end of the school year, they give more respect both to each other and to the teacher. Also, the teacher learns new ways to manage the classroom.

2:00 I take care of emergencies or do some follow-up calls. This is my case-management work.

2:30 I start up with direct services again. The afternoon is mostly taken up with group sessions.

3:30 I take 10 minutes to put chairs on the tables and get ready for the custodian. When the bell rings at 3:40, I'm out there helping maintain discipline in the bus lines.

3:55 The buses are gone, and I have 5 minutes to go in and check for any messages that might have come in and make sure everything's in order. I leave at four o'clock, but most of the time, there's more work to be done and more calls to be made. There are some parents I call every week, no matter what. I make those calls from my classroom or from home in the evenings.

Source: Jay Crowe, *Jay Crowe—Elementary School Social Worker*. Retrieved December 18, 2001, from www.wetfeet.com. Reprinted with permission.

CRITICAL THINKING AND CASE ANALYSIS

1. What are some features of Jay Crowe's work that have implications for his lifestyle? How might the requirements of his work impact other aspects of his adult roles, including time for intimate relationships, the decision to have children of his own, or leisure time?

2. How much of his work involves bureaucratic tasks like filling out forms, and how much is actual client contact?

3. How would you characterize the skills required for this work? What talents or abilities might be fostered as a result of this work?

4. Even though Jay Crowe's primary role is to support special-needs students, he says that some of his work involves shoring up incompetent teachers who cannot manage their students. What is your opinion about whether this is a good use of his time? What should be done with teachers who are not able to manage their classroom in order to provide an effective learning environment?

5. How might Jay Crowe develop as an adult because of the kind of work he does?

6. Projecting ahead, how might the nature of this career change over the period from early to middle adulthood? Can you imagine that Jay Crowe might want to make a midlife career change after doing this work for 10 or 15 years? What might he do next?

7. Based on your reading and knowledge of child development, how important is it to have school social workers in elementary schools, middle schools, or high schools?

The nature of the workplace is changing rapidly. Many factors have introduced new levels of uncertainty into the process of choosing a career, finding work, and staying employed. These factors include the transformation from agricultural to manufacturing to service and information industries, the increasingly global nature of business, the higher educational standards required for entry into many careers, the expectation that workers will be able to perform across a variety of tasks, and the rapid evolution and extinction of specific types of work brought on by new technologies.

In many fields, there are now a few huge global organizations and a large number of small innovative companies that do the exciting, creative work of the industry (Handy, 2001). Neither type, the huge global organizations nor the small, innovative companies, offers what used to be known as job security, but the work environment of these two kinds of settings is likely to be vastly different. Because economic, technical, and social conditions are changing so rapidly, young adults face two related challenges as they navigate the world of work. First, they cannot expect that strategies or patterns that led to success in the past will necessarily lead to success in the future. Second, they need to be more proactive in designing or inventing an occupational identity (Patton & McMahon, 2006; Handy, 2008).

The early phases of career decision making, presented in Tiedeman's model in Chapter 10, focus on self-understanding; career exploration; identifying a good match between personal interests, skills, and values, and particular careers; and learning as much as possible about the specific job opportunities in a career domain. However, because of the wide variety of possible occupational choices and associated work settings, one can make only limited progress in preparing to enact a specific occupational role during later adolescence. Even though many employers consider educational attainment a selection criterion, they often use it more as an element in determining one's eligibility for the job rather

iStockphoto.com/LisaFX Photographic Designs

Jeneen is just out of engineering school. She is working with a civil engineering firm to explore a career in the building and construction field. Here, she works with Ted, a master engineer with many years of experience on the job. He is teaching her how to read a blueprint and translate the plan into a reality in this partially constructed building. While she explores this field in order to determine if she enjoys this work, the firm observes how well she learns and performs in order to determine whether she should be encouraged to continue in this field.

than as a detailed assessment of whether one has the background and skills to perform it.

Most jobs require a period of training for the entry-level employee, which varies from a few weeks in the case of an assembly-line worker to 10 years in the case of a physician. This is the induction phase in Tiedeman's model. Most people do not stay at their first job. A national longitudinal study followed the work experiences of people who were 18 years old in 1978 through their 32nd birthday. During this period, the average number of jobs they held was 10.3 (U.S. Census Bureau, 2010). This figure disguises a great deal of variability, with 30% having been at their current job 1 year or less, and 30% having been at their current job more than 6 years (U.S. Census Bureau, 2004). These data suggest that job mobility is to be expected in early adulthood, and the formation of what has been called an attachment to one's job takes most young adults a while to establish. Therefore, the training phase is not only about acquiring the specific knowledge and skills necessary to carry out the work, but also about developing the personal, interpersonal, and transferable skills that will be important as one moves around the labor market (Posner, 2001).

The training period involves a process of socialization of the new worker. During this time, the individual must evaluate the match between her personal characteristics and goals and four central components of the work situation: (1) technical skills, (2) authority relations, (3) unique demands and hazards, and (4) interpersonal relations with coworkers. These are the major arenas for new learning in early adulthood.

Technical Skills. Most jobs require a certain degree of technical expertise, which varies greatly from one occupation to another. The job training phase involves learning new skills. Over 33% of all workers participated in work-related education and training, with the most hours of training reported by those with a college degree, performing professional and technical work (U.S. Census Bureau, 2010). Among those ages 25 to 44, 39% participated in work-related educational programs. In addition to specific training, over half of all workers are expected to use a computer at their work, with greater percentages in some fields than others (U.S. Census Bureau, 2006). Thus, specific skill training and general technical competence are part of the job demands. The success of individuals in learning and applying new skills determines to some extent whether they will become attached to the occupation. At the same time, the opportunity to learn new skills is part of what permits new workers to advance and seek new employment.

As a result of the recession of 2007–2008, a large number of workers were forced to seek new skills through job retraining in the wake of massive firings and downsizing. The Trade Readjustment Allowance is a government program for workers who were laid off as a result of shifting industry to Canada or Mexico and who enroll in new training programs. Workers have taken advantage of this program to return to school and learn new skills in fields that have growth potential. Some colleges and universities have made a special effort to reach out to adult returning students to offer retraining to those whose jobs were lost as a result of the economic downturn. For example, Beverly Berndt was laid off from her job as a computer programmer for a cabinet hardware distributor. With help from the Trade Readjustment Act, she went back to school to earn her nursing degree. "I hate to say it, but getting laid off from Belwith was probably the best thing that ever happened to me—getting help from the state for tuition and books, and drawing unemployment—I couldn't have done it without it" (Bauer, 2010).

Authority Relations. Each job role specifies status and decision-making relationships among people. One aspect of job training is learning which people evaluate one's work, the criteria they use, and the limits of one's autonomy in the job. In today's organizational environment, career ladders are less obvious, and the authority hierarchy may be difficult to identify. Young workers may be assigned to a number of projects with different leadership, they may be asked to take on significant leadership roles early in their careers, and they may need to form interdependent, collaborative teams (Collin & Young, 2000). New workers must attend to both the authority structure and the people who occupy positions in it. They must also assess the channels for decision making and the ways in which they can influence decisions. With respect to the people who occupy positions of authority, new workers must be able to deal with a variety of personalities in positions of higher and lower status. Having a good relationship with one's supervisor is a key element in job satisfaction.

Roughly one third of American workers report that they experience some form of hostility from their supervisor at work in the form of being belittled, yelled at, or undermined. Typically, people in positions of authority are supposed to encourage and support those who work for them. However, when people in positions of power perceive threats to their competence or feel incompetent in a domain in which they are supposed to have authority, a likely reaction is to become aggressive. When bosses feel inadequate, they may lash out at those who are less powerful (Fast & Chen, 2009). Under these conditions, it may not be possible for a new worker to achieve a good working relationship with a boss who is defensive.

Demands and Hazards. Each job has unique occupational demands, including norms for self-preservation, productivity, and availability. In some work settings, the worker comes into contact with clients, patients, or customers who are very stressed, anxious, rude, or aggressive. The worker has to manage the hostile outbursts or attacks in a professional way in order to avoid escalation, but exposure to this type of negative affect can be very distressing for the worker who is trying to carry out a job as effectively as possible. A

© 2010 Ciaran Griffin/Jupiterimages Corporation

Vic is a designer with a fashion magazine. He loves leading a relaxed, creative group of young designers as they prepare the next edition of the magazine. Part of his value to the firm is his ability to develop a creative team of designers to reach optimal productivity.

licensed vocational nurse described the tensions that come with being berated by a patient's family members:

> If you are working in an office and someone comes in and they're having words with you and maybe they're rude and you can say, "Listen, you've gone too far and you need to leave," whereas we have family members who come up to us and say, "How come you . . . ? How dare you . . . ?" And they can just be rude and say terrible things and we cannot, we really cannot, we really are not expected to, nor are we really allowed to answer back." (Bullock & Morales Waugh, 2004, p. 775)

Occupational hazards include a broad range of potential physical and psychological risks associated with the workplace, including exposure to toxins, work-related injuries, and exposure to diseases, reproductive hazards, and working conditions that have negative psychological consequences, such as noise or shift work. The rate of work-related deaths and disabling injuries has decreased substantially since the 1960s. Nonetheless, in 2007, there were 4,689 deaths and 3.5 million disabling injuries among U.S. workers (U.S. Census Bureau, 2010). Settings differ in the kinds of pressures or hazards they impose on workers. For example, mining is one of the most dangerous occupations. In a recent mine disaster, 29 workers died. This disaster shocked Americans as they realize how many workers continue to face hazardous conditions such as exposure to intense heat and humidity, exposure to toxic minerals and gases, poor air quality, and long hours underground (Donoghue, 2004). Just as occupations vary in their risks, individuals differ in their vulnerability to occupational pressures and hazards, their willingness to risk certain potential dangers, and their evaluation of the payoff for enduring some degree of stress. The individual must

ultimately decide whether the particular vulnerabilities are tolerable in light of the rewards.

Interpersonal Relationships with Coworkers. Although the potential for friendships in the work setting is usually not advertised as a central component of job satisfaction, it is clearly a dominant feature in the decision to be committed to a particular work setting. The need for friends with whom one can share the anxieties of learning the new job provides a strong motive for seeking comradeship on the job. The presence of congenial coworkers who can relax together and share feelings of accomplishment greatly enhances any work setting. In fact, the spirit of friendship on the job may compensate for many stressful situational demands. A workplace that creates space for collaboration and social interaction is likely to promote friendship formation and foster a more positive interpersonal environment.

Some work settings stress competition among coworkers; incentives are arranged to stimulate competition rather than cooperation. In such settings, new workers often must shoulder the strains of their new learning independently. Some settings create both competitive and cooperative norms by creating teams or production units that compete with one another for incentives. Under these arrangements intergroup relations tend to be more distrustful, whereas individual relations among team members tend to be more trusting and cooperative. The greater the commitment to the team's goal, especially under conditions of supportive leadership and encouragement for interdependence, the greater the team's effectiveness and the participants' sense of the team effort as a high-quality experience (Aubé & Rousseau, 2005).

Workplace bullying has become a growing concern for managers who recognize that bullying results in increased illness and absences, as well as decreases in productivity (Meyers, 2006). Workers who have been bullied may be afraid or embarrassed to say anything about it. However, when interviewed about their experiences they describe the impact in powerful terms. "I feel that I have been maimed . . . I've been beaten, abused, broken, scared. . . . I feel like I have 'kick me' tattooed on my forehead" (Tracy, Lutgen-Sandvik, & Alberts, 2006). The presence of egotistical, narcissistic, and aggressive coworkers can quickly disrupt the interpersonal climate of the workplace, making it harder to solve problems or collaborate on new initiatives. People who are exposed to insults or bullying at work are likely to suffer feelings of exclusion and depression, which may result in lashing out against other coworkers, thereby adding to the hostile climate.

Poverty and Career Opportunities

A number of factors limit the range of occupational opportunities open to a person during the work search phase. Among the most obvious limiting factors are educational attainment, ability, and location. Discrimination on the basis of race and gender also continues to thwart the full participation of women and minorities in the workforce.

The recession that began in 2007–2008 has had a major impact on jobs, earnings, and unemployment. The unemployment rate, which was about 5% throughout 2007 increased to 9.9% in May 2010. In addition to the 15.3 million who were out of work, others were cut back to part-time, some had not searched for work in the past 4 weeks and were therefore not counted among the unemployed. As a result of these changes, the official poverty rate increased from 12.5% in 2007 to 13.2% in 2008, an increase of 2.5 million people. From December 2007 to February 2010, the number of people receiving food stamps increased by 44% (Davis, 2010).

These recent economic conditions have added to a societal context in which relatively few resources are allocated to support low-income families. In a comparison of 21 rich nations, the overall poverty rate for all persons ranged from a low of 5.4% in Finland to a high of 20.2% in Mexico. The United States was second highest on the list, after Mexico. This dubious honor can be explained by a combination of two factors: (1) The United States has the highest proportion of workers in poorly paid jobs, and (2) the United States spends much less than most other countries on benefits that provide cash supplements, health, education, child care, or housing for low-wage workers (Smeeding, 2008).

A study of low-income, single mothers provides an example of the dilemma facing low-wage workers. Edin and Lein (1997) found that cash from welfare, food stamps, and social security supplements covered only about three fifths of the women's expenses. Those in paid jobs were earning about $8 per hour and could not meet their expenses with these earnings. Jobs in the secondary labor market involve working in "factories producing cartons, lightbulbs, dog bones, sneakers, turkey parts, doorstops, and manhole covers. [Women] worked as waitresses or caregivers, in 'basement jobs' leading nowhere, in which they hit the 'cellar ceiling' and were vulnerable and powerless. In such jobs, a worker is expendable, can be easily replaced, receives the lowest possible wages, typically works part-time, receives no benefits, has no upward mobility, and has no job security" (Lott & Bullock, 2001, pp. 200–201).

Analyses of successful programs that try to prepare individuals and families for self-sufficiency show that they typically emphasize some combination of basic education, job skills training, and adaptive work orientation with supports such as child care subsidies and medical benefits. Some programs put more time and resources into improving the conditions of the jobs and fostering employee skills. Programs that combine work with career counseling, earnings supplements, health insurance, and child care subsidies have the combined benefits of decreasing poverty rates in a community, increasing long-term employment, and fostering children's well-being and school performance (Duncan, Huston, & Weisner, 2007).

Career Phases and Individual Development

In an attempt to synthesize career and individual development, Kathy Kram (1985; Ragins & Kram, 2007) proposed a developmental model of career issues (see Table 11.2). In this model, careers are delineated in three phases—early career, middle career, and late career—which correspond roughly to the phases of career exploration, career establishment and advancement, and career maintenance and disengagement (Osipow, 1986; McAuliffe, 1997). In each phase, career development reflects *concerns about self*, including questions of competence and identity; *concerns about career*, including questions of occupational commitment, advancement, and the quality of relationships in the work setting; and *concerns about family*, especially family role definition and possible conflicts between work and family life. Typical issues facing the person at each phase are suggested in Table 11.2.

Issues of greatest concern during the early career phase reflect the need to demonstrate competence and also to establish a satisfying lifestyle. Career development is never a completely rational process. As organizational loyalty gives way to a free agent orientation to career development, individuals have to take a more assertive, risk-taking approach to their career development. In this process, one confronts many myths and uncertainties about the meaning of work, worries about financial self-sufficiency, and conflicts between work and other spheres of life, especially intimate relations and family responsibilities. In a survey conducted by the American Psychological Association, men and women in four age groups were asked about various sources of stress in their lives (APA, 2010). Even though about two thirds of the sample reported feeling satisfied with their jobs, 41% said they typically feel tense or stressed out during the workday.

TABLE 11.2 Characteristic Developmental Tasks at Successive Career Stages

	EARLY CAREER	MIDDLE CAREER	LATE CAREER
Concerns about self	Competence: Can I be effective in the managerial/professional role? Can I be effective in the role of spouse and/or parent?	Competence: How do I compare with my peers, with my subordinates, and with my own standards and expectations?	Competence: Can I be effective in a more consultative and less central role, still having influence as the time to leave the organization gets closer?
	Identity: Who am I as a manager/professional? What are my skills and aspirations?	Identity: Who am I now that I am no longer a novice? What does it mean to be a "senior" adult?	Identity: What will I leave behind of value that will symbolize my contributions during my career? Who am I apart from a manager/professional, and how will it feel to be without the role?
Concerns about career	Commitment: How involved and committed to the organization do I want to become? Do I want to seriously explore other options?	Commitment: Do I still want to invest as heavily in my career as I did in previous years? What can I commit myself to if the goal of advancement no longer exists?	Commitment: What can I commit myself to outside of my career that will provide meaning and a sense of involvement? How can I let go of my involvement in my work role after so many years?
	Advancement: Do I want to advance? Can I advance without compromising important values?	Advancement: Will I have the opportunity to advance? How can I feel productive if I am not going to advance further?	Advancement: Given that my next move is likely to be out of the organization, how do I feel about my final level of advancement? Am I satisfied with what I have achieved?
	Relationships: How can I establish effective relationships with peers and supervisors? As I advance, how can I prove my competence and worth to others?	Relationships: How can I work effectively with peers with whom I am in direct competition? How can I work effectively with subordinates who may surpass me?	Relationships: How can I maintain positive relationships with my boss, peers, and subordinates as I get ready to disengage from this setting? Can I continue to mentor and sponsor as my career comes to an end? What will happen to significant work relationships when I leave?
Concerns about family	Family role definition: How can I establish a satisfying personal life? What kind of lifestyle do I want to establish?	Family role definition: What is my role in the family now that my children are grown?	Family role definition: What will my role in the family be when I am no longer involved in a career? How will my significant relationships with spouse and/or children change?
	Work/family conflict: How can I effectively balance work and family commitments? How can I spend time with my family without jeopardizing my career advancement?	Work/family conflict: How can I make up for the time away from my family when I was launching my career as a novice?	Work/family conflict: Will family and leisure activities suffice, or will I want to begin a new career?

Source: From *Mentoring at Work: Developmental Relationships in Organizational Life*, by K.E. Kram. © 1985 Scott Foresman.

The younger workers, those in the age range 18 to 30, were most likely to report some lost productivity due to stress at work. Fears of the unknown—of taking on new responsibilities, of discovering the limits to one's abilities, and of disappointing important people in one's life—must all be faced and reframed if one is to achieve the adaptive flexibility necessary in today's world of work.

Lifestyle

Objective 5. To examine the concept of lifestyle as the expression of individual identity, with consideration for the pace of life, balancing competing role demands, building a supportive social network, and adopting practices to promote health and fitness.

Lifestyle is a social psychological construct that integrates personality characteristics, goals, convictions, and inner conflicts with social opportunities and resources into an organizing pattern of actions and choices (Slavick, 1995; Lombardi, Melchior, Murphy, & Brinkerhoff, 1996). Simply put, a lifestyle is the self in action (Richman, 2001). Central components of the lifestyle include the tempo or pace of activities, the balance between work and leisure, the focus of time and energy in specific arenas, and the establishment of social relationships at varying degrees of intimacy. One's lifestyle guides decisions about how to organize time and prioritize the use of resources. One can think of lifestyle as the first translation of the values and commitments of individual identity into action through the devotion of time and energy to certain tasks and relationships and the development of domains of competence. In the United States, a strong cultural assumption is that individuals are active agents who make choices (Savani et al., 2010). These choices reflect one's preferences and values. In early adulthood, the desire to create a life that is satisfying and meaningful is expressed through the system of choices and decisions one makes about work, leisure, living arrangements, relationships, health, and fitness. In general, the more one perceives that there is freedom of choice about these decisions, the greater one's sense of happiness and satisfaction with life (Inglehart, Foa, Peterson, & Welzel, 2010).

Even though a person may experience considerable social pressure to build an identity around an occupational focus, the concept of lifestyle reinforces the idea that a person's work or career is not the same as a meaningful life. Because career choices can have such an impact on other aspects of life, it is important to select a career that supports a life, not the other way around. The following discussion illustrates some ways in which the overlapping systems of early adulthood—intimate relationships, parenting, and career—interact to organize characteristics of the lifestyle.

Pace of Life

Some counselors use the metaphor of a three-dimensional space to describe the lifestyle (Amundson, 2001). *Length* is the length of life, or where one is along a developmental continuum. For example, in early adulthood one is likely to view life as stretching out for many years into the future, as compared to middle adulthood when one is likely to think that one's life is about half over. *Width* is the busyness of life, including multiple role demands and how much activity one tries to jam into each day. *Depth* is the sense of purpose and meaning in life and the experiences of satisfaction or fulfillment that come with it. This three-dimensional configuration changes over the course of life, both as a result of personal changes in goals or developmental needs and as a result of situational changes in demands or resources.

The pace of life, or the busyness of life, is shaped by work, family, personality, and environmental context. For most young adults, the work setting largely determines the

structure of time, including when one goes to work and returns, what one feels energetic enough to do after work, how much time is free for leisure or vacations, and the amount of preparation required during nonworking hours to prepare for the next day. People who are trying to combine parenting with a long workday experience the greatest time bind. Schedule control, rather than reducing the number of hours of work, seems to be especially important for helping people maintain a sense of lifestyle balance (Tausig & Fenwick, 2001).

Activity level, or the pace of life, is influenced in part by one's temperament, health, and fitness. This is a circular issue. Adults whose lives are very sedentary are likely to have lower levels of endurance and to feel the strain of daily exertion. Those who are more active and who include physical activity in their lifestyle are likely to have more energy and to be able to handle the demands of an active life.

The pace of life is also influenced by the climate and community. In northern climates, for example, there may be fewer social events away from home during the winter, and life may therefore revolve primarily around the home. In spring and summer, neighborhood activities become a more important stimulus for social life as people emerge and renew their friendships. Rural communities often provide a calmer pace of life than urban communities. People often choose to live in rural or rural-like communities, even when they work in the city, to escape from the hectic pace of urban life.

Social Network

As a result of participation in multiple roles, most people expand their social network during early adulthood. They form friendships in the neighborhood and at work. In some work settings, coworkers help each other balance their work and family life by taking shifts for one another, covering special family holidays, or carpooling to save expenses. Young adults may become involved in the social life of their religious community or civic associations. They may engage in community volunteer projects with friends and become more invested in the social needs of their neighborhood. If they have young children, the parents of other young children at the child care center or preschool may become important sources of social support. When options are possible, individuals often look for housing in neighborhoods where there are others in their same life stage and lifestyle orientation. For example, when couples with young children live in a community with other young families, they tend to rate the community more favorably than couples living in the community who do not have children (Swisher, Sweet, & Moen, 2004). The contribution of friendships to personal satisfaction and lifestyle differs widely during this time, with single adults and couples without children typically having more time for adult friendships than do parents.

The rapid and continuously expanding growth in the use of online social networking sites including Facebook, Twitter, and LinkedIn reflects the important role of social networks in the lives of contemporary young adults. There are an estimated 700 million users worldwide of online social networking sites (ComScore, 2008). About 14% of the users on Facebook are ages 25 to 34 (Kiser, 2010). Similar percentages are observed for Twitter and LinkedIn. These social networking sites have a variety of functions, including staying connected with the activities of friends and relatives, sharing information and opinions about products or experiences, gaining recognition for accomplishments, and encouraging participation in upcoming events (Back et al., 2010; Boyd and Ellison, 2007). The online social networking sites function as mass communication vehicles powered by individual users who share their experiences and ideas with friends and associates. As these sites have grown, the possibility of making personalized contact with a wide and diverse audience has changed the nature and meaning of social networks so that they are now potentially quite vast, fluid, and include individuals who are not really known.

Competing Role Demands

A challenge that must be faced in early adulthood is the competition of role demands. One part of role learning involves a widening circle of competencies and relationships. Another part involves balancing the conflicting expectations of simultaneous role responsibilities. Adults struggle with the conflict between the demands of the work setting and the demands of building an intimate relationship; with the tension between the desire to have children and the desire to achieve in the workplace. For both men and women, the world of work is likely to provide the most rigorous test of commitment and the greatest pressures for productivity during the early adult years. For example, researchers have documented the impact of daily workplace events and the way men and women behave when they come home at the end of the day. At the end of a negatively arousing and stressful day of work, women are more likely to be angry at home whereas men are more likely to be withdrawn (Schulz, Cowan, Pape Cowan, & Brennan, 2004). Pressure in the work setting may come from a number of sources such as unpleasant interpersonal interactions, being bullied, increased pace and demands of work, feelings of incompetence, or frustration at being undervalued. The emotional spillover from these negative experiences competes directly with needs for intimacy and also with the time and energy needed for parenting. The lower the level of marital satisfaction, the more these workplace stressors are likely to diminish the quality of partner interactions at home.

In an analysis of the role demands of dual-earner families, researchers identified three distinct dual-earner lifestyles—high status, low stress, and main-secondary—each with its own pattern of role relationships, costs, and benefits (Crouter & Manke, 1997; Crouter, 2006). In the *high-status* couples, both partners had high-prestige careers, earned comparatively high salaries, and were involved in their work. In these couples, the division of household work was more equal than in the other two types. They experienced the greatest amount of role overload, had lower levels of love and marital satisfaction, and more marital conflict than the other two groups.

The social network for young mothers often includes other young mothers.

Michele-Salmieri/Getty Images

The *low-stress* couples worked about the same amount of hours as the high-status couples, but their jobs were in less prestigious categories. Examples were a mechanic and a secretary, and a salesman and a substitute teacher. Although the couples had levels of involvement similar to the high-status group, they had the lowest amount of role overload. This group had the highest scores in marital satisfaction and love for their spouse, and the lowest scores in marital conflict. These couples monitored their children more closely and seemed to be more accurate in describing their children's daily activities.

The *main-secondary* couples reflected a lifestyle in which husbands were the primary workers, with higher occupational prestige, more hours worked, and more work involvement than their wives, who typically worked part time. Women in these relationships had less education and tended to have more household responsibilities. A gender-typed division of labor was reflected in the pattern for female children, who performed more household tasks than girls in the other family types, whereas male children in these families performed fewer household tasks than boys in the other family types.

The more involved one is in the competitive demands of work, the less likely one is to feel comfortable about spending time away from it. Conversely, the more engrossed one is in a variety of activities away from work, including hobbies and family events, the more time one will find for leisure. In some occupations, the time schedule leaves little room for personal choice. In others, the income from a single job may not suffice to support the family. Time that might otherwise be spent in leisure must be spent in earning additional income through extra work.

The balance of work and leisure is a result of one's disposition toward them and the demands of the work setting. For some people, time with the family is more important than time at work. They highly value the time they have at home with their families and make it a priority when they choose a career. For other people, advancement in work through the expenditure of large amounts of time supersedes commitments to home and leisure. For them, the lifestyles of partners may evolve somewhat separately, because the amount of leisure time they share may be limited. Couples who are able to enjoy leisure activities together that provide opportunities for relaxed, open conversation find that these contribute substantially to the strength of and satisfaction in their intimate relationship (Kalmijn & Bernasco, 2001).

Health and Fitness

The contemporary emphasis on health and fitness indicates the importance of lifestyle decisions for illness prevention and longevity. Research on health and health-related risks has begun to identify characteristics of a healthy lifestyle, including factors that operate at an individual level and those that reflect community commitment (Healthy People, 2000, 2010, 2020). Leading health indicators include such practices as the use of preventive health services, regular exercise, eating a well-balanced diet high in fruits and vegetables and low in fat, avoiding smoking, limiting the number of sexual partners, and using contraceptives.

An aspect of lifestyle that is often overlooked is the daily pattern of sleep and waking hours. A growing concern focuses on the large number of people who do not get the nightly sleep they require. This can lead to serious health problems, deficits in performance and alertness, increased risk of motor vehicle accidents, and impaired memory and cognitive functioning. In addition to problems with disrupted sleep or inadequate sleep, shifting one's bedtime by more than 2 hours can cause difficulties in falling asleep, staying asleep, or waking up on time and feeling restored by sleep (Vital Signs, 2010). Conditions of one's lifestyle including living arrangements, the time one has to be at work or return from work, the noise level of the neighborhood, and one's involvement in leisure activities including television viewing, online social networking or gaming, and the use of drugs or alcohol, can all influence the amount and quality of one's sleep.

The concept of encouraging young adults to adopt a lifestyle that promotes health is becoming a focus for preventive health care. Much of this research suggests that lifestyle patterns established in early and middle adulthood, including one's diet, activity level, exercise, encounters with challenging and intellectually stimulating tasks, and reduced involvement with cigarette smoking and alcohol, all influence health and vitality in later life.

Although the establishment of a healthy lifestyle can be viewed as an individual's responsibility, healthy communities are shaped by adults who share a common vision about the lifestyle they want for themselves and their families. Although many aspects of fitness can be achieved at the individual or family level, some, such as environmental quality, access to health care, reduction of violence, or access to safe settings that promote physical activity require a community commitment. Adults may join together to create resources and programs that increase the involvement of children and adults in regular physical activity. They may form a coalition of parents, health care professionals, educators, business leaders, and law enforcement agencies to devise a plan to decrease incidents of violence in their community. Commitment to a healthy lifestyle may be enacted through efforts to improve air and water quality, reduce exposure to second-hand smoke, improve availability and access to health care services and health education, or increase support for environmental resources that sustain physical activity. For example, a benchmark report on walking and biking provides information about patterns of biking and walking in the 50 states, infrastructure that supports safe biking and walking, the relationship of biking and walking to health and well-being, and funding for projects that improve opportunities and resources for walking and biking (Steele, 2010). Figures 11.5 and 11.6 provide international comparisons for the percentage of individual trips that are carried out by walking

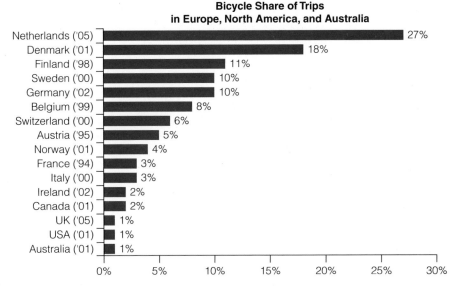

FIGURE 11.5 Comparison of the Percentage of Trips Made by Bicycle in 16 Countries

Source: © Cengage Learning.

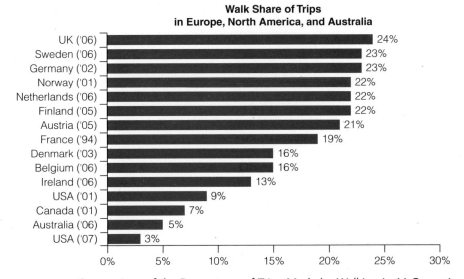

FIGURE 11.6 Comparison of the Percentage of Trips Made by Walking in 16 Countries

Source: © Cengage Learning.

or biking in Europe, North America, and Australia. As the data show, people in the United States are at the bottom with respect to the frequency with which they walk or bike to their destinations. The relationship of limited physical activity to significant health concerns, especially obesity, diabetes, and high blood pressure, is well documented. Efforts by communities to improve the infrastructure to support walking and bicycling can have important benefits for public health, as well as improvements in pedestrian safety and reduced traffic and air pollution.

Lifestyle is an umbrella concept for the variety of patterns of activities, commitments, and satisfactions that make up adult experience. The cultural expectations and personal aspirations for establishing committed relationships, childbearing, and work are confronted, evaluated, and accepted or rejected during these early adult years. In the process of

deciding about each of these life tasks, the person begins to crystallize a life pattern that reflects personal vision of a meaningful path toward maturity.

The Psychosocial Crisis: Intimacy versus Isolation

Objective 6. To define and describe the psychosocial crisis of intimacy versus isolation, the central process through which the crisis is resolved, mutuality among peers, the prime adaptive ego quality of love, and the core pathology of exclusivity.

Here in San Francisco, healthy and environmentally conscious young adults ride to work, school, and recreational activities in their own traffic lane. The fact that the city has provided a separate lane of traffic for bicyclists encourages residents to adopt this active lifestyle choice.

We have seen the importance of a sense of belonging in every stage of the lifespan, including a sense of belonging to one's family, belonging in a friendship group, belonging and feelings of inclusion at school, belonging in one's community, belonging to one's religious or ethnic group, and belonging to the variety of groups that are especially important in the high school and college years. Accompanying these feelings of belonging, a sense of mattering emerges that helps a person experience the psychological and physiological benefits of social support. In early adulthood a special and fundamental sense of belonging surfaces when two people disclose the most important characteristics of their being with each other. Within this intense dyadic context, the partners experience the openness to communicate their innermost feelings and are rewarded with the responsiveness and excitement with which the other person accepts these gifts of trust. What comes to life are special feelings of tenderness and devotion for another person, and feelings of being cherished and treasured by the other person. In contrast, some people are unable to engage in the trusting, open, mutually responsive relationships implied by intimacy. They may experience rejection, exclusion, or an inability to accept the affection of others, resulting in a sense of isolation.

Intimacy

Intimacy is defined as the ability to experience an open, supportive, tender relationship with another person without fear of losing one's own identity in the process. An intimate relationship has both cognitive and affective components. The partners are able to understand each other's point of view. They usually experience a sense of confidence and mutual regard that reflects their respect as well as their affection for each other.

Intimacy in a relationship supports independent judgments by each partner. It also permits the disclosure of personal feelings, as well as the sharing and developing of ideas and plans.

There is a sense of mutual enrichment in intimate interactions. Each person perceives enhancement of well-being through affectionate or intellectually stimulating interactions with the other (Erikson, 1963, 1980). Coming as it does after the establishment of personal identity, the possibility of establishing intimacy depends on individuals' perceptions of themselves as valuable, competent, and meaningful people. In an intimate relationship, the partners are aware of one another's aspirations. Under the best of circumstances, in a truly intimate relationship the partners interact in such a way as to promote one another's self-fulfillment, reassuring their partner about the possibility of achieving their most important goals and encouraging their self-actualization (Rusbult, Finkel, & Kumashiro, 2009).

It is not difficult to understand that a person would be on intimate terms with parents and siblings. The family is a central context for sharing confidences, expressing love, and revealing weaknesses and areas of dependence. In fact, there is growing evidence that the nature of one's parental attachment orientation influences the ability to form new intimate relationships (see the box on attachment styles and relationship formation). The unique task of young adulthood is to establish an intimate relationship with someone outside of one's family. Two people who eventually establish intimacy may begin as complete strangers who have very few, if any, common cultural bonds. Although an extreme degree of difference is unusual, it represents the greatest challenge that may confront two people.

Whether they are established in the context of marriage, friendship, or work, intimate relationships are often

Image copyright CAN BALCIOGLU 2010. Used under license from Shutterstock.com characterized by an atmosphere of romantic illusions, such as, "Together we can conquer the world." The romance of an intimate relationship is a reflection of the energy and sense of well-being that come from the support and understanding that are shared within it (Murray, Homes, & Griffin, 1996). There is a deep sense that intimate relationships are not replaceable.

Interaction Styles of Men and Women

Men interact less intimately than women. They generally demonstrate more competitiveness, less agreement, and lower levels of self-disclosure than women. However, levels of self-disclosure are not related to loneliness for men as they are for women. It appears that men have the same capacity for intimate interaction as women, but they do not choose to exercise it with other men. Whereas women consider intimacy appropriate for both same-sex and opposite-sex relationships, men tend to restrict their intimate interactions to women (Bank & Hansford, 2000).

In a national sample of more than 2,500 adults, men's and women's relationships were compared (Umberson, Chen, House, Hopkins, & Slaten, 1996). Women were shown to have more support from friends, they experienced higher levels of social integration (involvement in personally meaningful relationships), and were more likely to report having a confidant than were men. Married women received more support from their adult children than did men, whereas men received more support from their spouses than did women. In fact, almost 50% of men said that their confidant was their wife, whereas only 20% of women said that their confidant was their husband.

Intimacy in the Work Setting

A common context for the establishment of intimacy is the work setting. Affiliation and close friendships are likely to develop among coworkers. Workers may express devotion to an older leader or teacher. Through conversations, correspondence, conferences, or informal interaction on the golf course or at the bowling alley, coworkers can achieve an affectionate, playful, and enriching relationship. This kind of intimacy is demonstrated in the following reflection about a coworker.

> Alan was very influential. I respected him as being pretty sharp and pretty astute. He had a lot of guts to tackle the problems that existed in the area and that was the union-management business. I was really identifying with him in terms of what and how you run something, how you manage something. You would sit down and talk about or debate how you do certain things, what should we do in this kind of situation. We would be right in line. I think it was the way I came at a problem; it might be similar to the way he would come at a problem. (Kram, 1985, p. 33)

The increased presence of men and women as coworkers in the work setting has introduced new difficulties in the establishment of intimacy among coworkers. Problems with sex discrimination and sexual harassment at work are evidence that many men and women have not developed mature strategies for forming mutually respectful, close relationships with adults of the opposite sex. Often, men and women find it difficult to establish an egalitarian relationship at work. They have a hard time engaging in the kinds of informal interactions that bring a sense of closeness to same-sex coworkers, like going to lunch together, stopping for a drink at the end of the day, or going to the gym to work out. Many men find it difficult to establish a style of interaction with women that is forthright but not sexual in tone. Many women find it difficult to be adequately assertive with men so that their ideas are taken seriously and their views are given full consideration.

Isolation

The negative pole of the psychosocial crisis of early adulthood is **isolation**. As social beings, people have a deep need for a sense of connection and belonging. Isolation, and the accompanying feeling of being unable to experience intersubjectivity or shared meaning, is a major source of psychological distress (Jordan, 1997). As with the negative poles of other psychosocial crises, most people experience some periods of this extreme. The more fully developed the ego becomes, the more it is characterized by clear boundaries. One by-product of individuality and independence is a heightened sense of separateness from others. During a period of intense personal growth and discovery, a person may experience interpersonal isolation, feeling preoccupied by thoughts and emotions that cannot be easily shared with others (Rokach & Neto, 2001).

The obstacles to attainment of an intimate relationship are many. Some arise from childhood experiences of shame, guilt, inferiority, or alienation, which undermine the achievement of personal identity. Others result from incompatibility between partners. The number of adjustments that intimacy requires may overwhelm some young adults. Obstacles to intimacy derive from environmental circumstances that may erode the person's feelings of self-worth or interfere with the establishment of mutuality. These obstacles may be embedded in the socialization process, as children learn distinct gender roles that introduce antagonism between men and women and foster interpersonal styles that stand in the way of forming open, caring interpersonal relationships. Seven themes discussed in the following sections illustrate experiences of isolation: loneliness, depression, fragile identity, sexual disorders, situational factors, divergent spheres of interest, and enmeshment.

Loneliness

Feelings of **loneliness** can be separated into three categories: transient, situational, and chronic (Meer, 1985). *Transient loneliness* lasts a short time and passes, as when you hear a song or an expression that reminds you of someone you love

Attachment Styles and Relationship Formation

ATTACHMENT THEORY HAS become an important framework for understanding the process of relationship formation (Fraley & Shaver, 2000). One's attachment style, established in infancy, provides a template for orienting toward intimate relationships in adulthood. Anxiety over abandonment, comfort or discomfort with closeness and emotional disclosure, and the level of self-esteem associated with a secure or insecure attachment can all contribute to the type of partner one seeks and one's ability to sustain an intimate relationship (Brennan & Shaver, 1995; Jones & Cunningham, 1996; Brennan & Morris, 1997). The threat of loss of access (both physical and emotional access) to an intimate partner is likely to produce anxiety, protest, and steps to regain proximity.

Bartholomew (1990) developed an attachment typology based on one's attachment experiences in infancy and toddlerhood. One can have a positive or negative assessment of the self, and a positive or negative assessment of others (see Table 11.3).

Secure individuals have a positive model of themselves and of others: "It is easy for me to become emotionally close to others. I am comfortable depending on them and having them depend on me."

Preoccupied individuals have a positive model of others, but a negative model of the self: "I want to be completely emotionally intimate with others, but I often find that others are reluctant to get as close as I would like. I am uncomfortable being without close relationships, but I sometimes worry that others don't value me as much as I value them." When one or both partners are characterized by a preoccupied attachment, the likelihood of abuse in the relationship increases (Henderson, Bartholomew, Trinke, & Kwong, 2005).

Dismissing avoidant individuals have a positive model of self, but a negative model of others: "I am comfortable without close emotional relationships. It is very important to me to feel independent and self-sufficient, and I prefer not to depend on others or have others depend on me."

Fearful avoidant individuals have a negative model of both self and others: "I am uncomfortable getting close to others. I want emotionally close relationships, but I find it difficult to trust others completely, or to depend on them" (Crowell, Fraley, & Shaver, 1999, p. 451).

The secure and the dismissing individuals have high self-esteem; however, they differ markedly in the value they place on intimacy and in their interpersonal style. Secure individuals value relationships and are viewed as warm and nurturing. In contrast, dismissing individuals minimize relationships in favor of self-reliance and are viewed as cold or competitive. The fearful avoidant and the preoccupied individuals lack the self-esteem of the secure or dismissing groups. However, the fearful individuals avoid social contact, whereas the preoccupied individuals try hard to engage in relationships.

Interestingly, individuals seek out partners with similar attachment styles. Not everyone is looking for a partner with a secure attachment. Fearful avoidant individuals, for example, prefer other anxious partners over dismissing or secure ones—perhaps because they are better able to interpret and predict the relationship behaviors of those who have a similar attachment orientation (Frazier, Byer, Fischer, Wright, & DeBord, 1996).

The context of the relationship may also alter one's characteristic attachment responses. When a close romantic relationship is perceived to be deteriorating, insecure avoidant behaviors may increase, even among those who have a secure attachment style (Gillath & Shaver, 2007).

Critical Thinking questions

1. What are some similarities and differences between the attachment styles described in infancy and those described here regarding adult romantic relationships?

2. Imagine that people have been set up on a blind date. How might the following couples get along?
   - Secure and Dismissing
   - Secure and Preoccupied
   - Preoccupied and Fearful Avoidant
   - Dismissing Avoidant and Fearful Avoidant

3. Critically evaluate the model proposed in this analysis of adult attachment style. What are some strengths and weaknesses of creating a typology based on these two dimensions? What aspects of the attachment construct are omitted in this approach?

4. Invent your own model for characterizing adult orientations to romantic relationships. How much would you rely on the attachment paradigm for this model? What other conceptual themes might you draw on to classify how people approach intimate relationships?

5. How could you take account of culture in conceptualizing the way people orient toward intimate relationships? How might people with more independent or interdependent views differ in the type of partner they seek?

TABLE 11.3 The Attachment Typology

		WORKING MODEL OF OTHERS	
		POSITIVE	NEGATIVE
WORKING MODEL OF THE SELF	POSITIVE	Secure	Dismissing Avoidant
	NEGATIVE	Preoccupied	Fearful Avoidant

Source: Based on Bartholomew, 1990.

who is far away. *Situational loneliness* accompanies a sudden loss or a move to a new city. *Chronic loneliness* lasts a long time and cannot be linked to a specific stressor. Chronically lonely people may have an average number of social contacts, but they do not achieve the desired level of intimacy in these interactions (Berg & Peplau, 1982). Many chronically lonely people are highly anxious about all types of social activities (Cacioppo et al., 2000). They believe that success in social relationships is important, but expect social encounters to be difficult and to end poorly. People who have high levels of *social anxiety* tend to use interpersonal strategies that place barriers in the way of intimacy. They are likely to be self-deprecating and obsessed by the possibilities of negative outcomes of social interactions. These people tend to let others establish the direction and purpose of interpersonal activities. There appears to be a strong relationship between social skills and loneliness. People who have higher levels of social skills, including friendliness, communication skills, appropriate nonverbal behavior, and appropriate responses to others, have more adequate social support systems and lower

istockphoto.com/Guillermo Perales

Sarah feels like she can not go on any further. She stops to sit down and cry after having been laid off from her job as a marketing manager in an event production company. She is at the beginning of a sense of depression that will take all of her coping resources to overcome.

levels of loneliness (Rokach, Bacanli, & Ramberan, 2000). In contrast, those who are lonely are more angry and anxious, have greater fear of negative evaluation, and a more pessimistic outlook about the future of a relationship (Cacioppo et al., 2006). Although it may seem logical to suggest that the lonely person should try harder to meet new people or develop new social skills, it is possible that the sense of isolation interferes with more active coping strategies.

Depression

Depression is a worldwide health problem (Moussavi et al., 2007). When combined with one or more other chronic diseases such as arthritis, asthma, or diabetes, it substantially worsens a person's health conditions. As a result, people who have a chronic health problem and depression are less able to engage in the kinds of social activities and pleasurable interactions that are likely to result in the formation of intimate relationships. Isolation may be a cause as well as a consequence of depression. For some women, clinical depression appears to be linked to an orientation toward intimacy in which the self is systematically inhibited and devalued (Jack & Dill, 1992). They have a rigid view of how they should act in an intimate relationship, which is characterized by four major themes:

1. They judge themselves by external standards, feeling that they never quite measure up to what other people expect of them.
2. They believe that they should build a close relationship with a man by putting his needs ahead of their own, and that to do otherwise is selfish.
3. They try to maintain a relationship by avoiding conflict and repressing their own views, if they think those views may lead to disagreement.
4. They perceive themselves as presenting a false front, in which they appear happy and satisfied on the outside although they are angry or resentful inside.

Over time, women who endorse this outlook lose contact with their authentic self, and even if the relationship remains stable, they become increasingly depressed. Longitudinal studies find that depression in one of the partners and relationship distress occur together. Depression has a negative impact on relationship quality; and poor relationship quality increases depression (Papp, 2010).

For some, the roots of depression may begin in adolescence. Those young people who tend to internalize their feelings under conditions of stress are likely to experience feelings of loneliness, lack of self-worth, anxiety, and depression. People who develop internalizing disorders in adolescence are at greater risk of continuing to experience depression as adults (Pine, Cohen, Gurley, Brook, & Ma, 1998). One of the most common stressors that may set off a bout of depression in adolescence is the breakup of a romantic relationship (Monroe, Rohde, Seeley, & Lewinsohn, 1999). As adolescents move into early adulthood, they may be more inclined to isolation as a way of protecting themselves from the depression that they have learned to associate with risks of rejection in romantic relationships.

Fragile Identity

According to the psychosocial perspective, work on personal identity precedes the capacity for adult intimacy. Longitudinal research that followed a group of adolescents from ages 15 to 24 supported this developmental sequence, demonstrating a clear relationship between the ego strengths associated with personal identity in middle and later adolescence with the capacity for mature intimate relationships in early adulthood (Beyers & Seuffge-Krenke, 2010). For some people, the possibility of closeness with another person seriously threatens the sense of self. They imagine intimate relationships to be a blurring of the boundaries of their own identities and cannot let themselves engage in them. People who fear a loss of identity continually erect barriers between themselves and others in order to keep their sense of self intact. Their fragile sense of self results from accumulated experiences of childhood that have fostered the development of personal identities that are either rigid and brittle or else totally confused. Such a tenuous sense of identity requires that individuals constantly remind themselves who they are. They may not allow their identities to stand on their own strength while they lose themselves, even momentarily, in others. They are so busy maintaining their identities or struggling to make sense out of confusion that they cannot attain intimacy.

Sexual Disorders

Isolation may be linked to sexual disorders. Two widely cited desire disorders are *hypoactive sexual desire*, a decrease or absence of interest in sexual activity, and *compulsive sexual behavior*, a compulsive need to relieve anxiety through sex (Coleman, 2003). A loss of sexual desire is usually accompanied by physical withdrawal from the partner and by feelings of guilt and dread about losing intimacy. At the same time, the unafflicted partner often feels angry and guilty about imposing sexual needs on an unresponsive and uninterested partner, as in the following example.

> At first it was fun: feverish kisses in his red Chevy, giggly nights of passion in the apartment. But then came marriage, two kids, and suddenly her husband's hands on her flesh felt like tentacles, and the sight of him approaching made her body stiffen with revulsion. Then the disagreements began, hurtful scenes ending with each of them lying wedged against opposite sides of the bed, praying for sleep. (From L. Rosellini, 1992, "Sexual Desire," *U.S. News & World Report*, 113(1), p. 62. Reprinted by permission.)

In the case of compulsive sexual behavior, as in the following anecdote, sex is disconnected from pleasure or intimacy. Satisfaction of sexual drives is often accompanied by shame and disgust.

> Gary's pattern was always the same: First, the unbearable anxiety, never feeling good enough to handle the latest stress at his architect's job. Then, the familiar response—a furtive scanning of newspaper ads, a drive to a strip show, two straight Scotches to catch a buzz, and finally a massage parlor. . . . Afterward, he'd sit naked on the edge of the bed, his thought roiling in disgust: "I must be sick . . . I can't change." But a few days later, the anxiety would begin again and he'd pore over the ads." (From L. Rosellini, 1992, "Sexual Desire," *U.S. News & World Report*, 113(1), p. 64. Reprinted by permission.)

Some psychologists view compulsive sexual behavior as an anxiety-based disorder, like other compulsions. Others argue that it is an addiction, like alcoholism. All agree that those who suffer from this disorder are not able to integrate sexual behavior as a meaningful component of an intimate relationship.

Situational Factors

Isolation can also result from situational factors. A young man goes off to war in Afghanistan and returns after being seriously wounded, resulting in the amputation of his left leg. As a result of his injuries, he doubts whether he could be an attractive or effective partner, and he is reluctant to engage in social activities to pursue romantic interests. A young woman rejects marriage in order to attend medical school and finds little time for the formation of intimate relationships. By the time she completes her internship and residency, she has many fewer options for finding an intimate partner. Under these and other similar circumstances, desires for intimacy may not be met.

Divergent Spheres of Interest

Isolation can arise even within an ongoing relationship as a product of diverging spheres of interest and activity. In a traditional marriage, for example, the husband and wife may participate in distinct roles and activities. Marriages characterized by such a division of life spheres are sometimes referred to as *his-and-her* marriages (Bernard, 1972). The wife stays home most of the day, interacting with the children and the other wives in the neighborhood. The husband is away from home all day, interacting with his coworkers. When the partners have leisure time, they pursue different interests: for instance, the woman likes to play cards and the man likes to hunt. Over the years, the partners have less and less in common. Isolation is reflected in their lack of mutual understanding and lack of support for each other's life goals and needs.

Enmeshment

Although Erikson thought of the construct of intimacy in tension with the construct of isolation, some family therapists offer another tension: between healthy intimacy and enmeshment (Minuchin, 1978). Within this framework, a family is viewed as a structured system that contains individuals grouped into subsystems linked by patterns of communication, boundaries, alliances, and rules. As individual family members change and grow, the adaptive family experiences transitions that alter the structure. Families are characterized along a continuum from *disengaged* to *enmeshed*. The disengaged relationships are characterized by infrequent contact and a sense that the members of the family do not really seem to care about one another. This pattern may be viewed as similar to Erikson's concept of isolation within a family group. The enmeshed relationships, in contrast, are characterized by over-involvement in one another's lives, to the extent that any change in one family member is met by strong resistance by the others; individuality is viewed as a threat to the relationship. Individuals in an enmeshed relationship may fear isolation to such a degree that they prevent one another from any movement toward autonomy.

Clark and Maria are very much in love as they gaze, smiling, into each other's eyes to celebrate their engagement.

The Central Process: Mutuality Among Peers

The central process through which intimacy is acquired is **mutuality among peers**. Mutuality refers to empathic awareness of one another, understanding of self and other, and the ability and willingness to regulate one's needs in order to respond to the needs of one's partner (Skerrett, 1996). One must be able to give and receive pleasure within the intimate context (Jeffries, 1993). The two young adults must bring equal strengths and resources to the relationship. Their intimacy is built on their ability to meet each other's needs and accept each other's weaknesses. When one partner needs to be dependent, the other is strong and supportive; at other times, the roles may be reversed. Each partner understands that the other is capable of many kinds of relationships. Mutuality facilitates the couple's ability to meet each other's needs in different ways over time rather than producing a static, unitary relationship. In fact, mutuality should enhance both individual and couple development. In the process of supporting each other, both partners perform in ways that they might not have adopted had they been alone.

The concept of mutuality has been used in previous chapters to describe the development of a sense of basic trust during infancy. In that context, the distribution of resources, experience, and strength is quite uneven. Mutuality is possible only because the caregiver is committed to the infant's well-being. Through caregivers' consistent efforts, children eventually learn to regulate their needs to fit the family pattern. However, children at this stage are not expected to be sophisticated enough to assess and meet their caregivers' needs. In young adulthood, the partners are responsible for fulfilling each other's needs. In most cases, there is no benevolent, superordinate caregiver. Just as the infant learns to trust the caregiver's ability to meet personal needs, each adult partner learns to trust the other's ability to anticipate and satisfy the partner's needs. By expressing trust and commitment to one another, each partner strengthens the other's ability to

believe in and invest in the relationship (Avery, 1989). The partners may also realize that they depend on each other to solve the problems that they face as a couple.

Mutuality in relationships has been studied by asking participants to read brief descriptions of relationship styles and to say which style characterizes their relationship with their mother, father, best friend, and romantic partner (Neff & Harter, 2003). Three relationship styles were described: one that emphasized autonomy and one's personal needs, one that emphasized connection and the needs and feelings of the other person, and one that described an effort to balance autonomy and connection by reflecting on what would be an effective response to the other person as well as meeting one's own needs. This last style was considered evidence of mutuality. Mutuality in a romantic relationship was associated with the most ideal outcomes, including relationship satisfaction, relational self-worth, and lack of relational depression.

Mutuality is strengthened as the two partners learn to rely on each other and as they discover that their combined efforts are more effective than their individual efforts would be. Mutuality, like attachment, is a characteristic of the dyadic relationship rather than of the individual members in it (Rusbult & Arriaga, 1997). It is formed as two individuals, each of whom has a well-defined identity, discover that they can have open, direct communication, hold each other in high regard, and respond effectively to each other.

The Prime Adaptive Ego Quality and the Core Pathology

Love

For thousands of years, the nature of love and the qualities of a loving relationship have been described in songs and stories. In the resolution of the crisis of intimacy versus isolation in early adulthood, the ego quality of love emerges as the capacity for mutuality and devotion that transcends the secure attachment of infancy. Robert Sternberg (1988) has described love as a set of feelings, thoughts, and motives that contribute to communication, sharing, and support. According to his theory, almost all types of love may be viewed as a combination of three dimensions: *intimacy*, the emotional investment in a relationship that promotes closeness and connection; *passion*, the expression of physical and psychological needs and desires in the relationship; and *commitment*, the cognitive decision to remain in the relationship. These dimensions form a triangle that helps characterize the different types of love (see Figure 11.7). Each of these dimensions changes over time. Passion is the most fleeting and, without commitment, is likely to result in a short-lived love. Intimacy and commitment can grow stronger over time. However, if passion and intimacy both decline, commitment may dwindle as well (Belsky, 1997). An important aspect of this theory is that it helps account for loving relationships that do not follow the romantic ideal of U.S. culture. The factor of commitment, which may originate from valued kinship obligations or economic practicalities, can sustain a relationship and foster an enduring love with or without intimacy or passion.

Conceptions of love usually include four aspects: ideas about the beloved, feelings that are associated with love, thoughts associated with love, and actions that are likely to occur between the lover and the beloved (Beall & Sternberg, 1995). The exact content of these feelings, beliefs, and actions differs from culture to culture, based on the culture's ideals about human nature, relationships, and cultural roles, especially courtship, marriage, childrearing, and religion.

In Western cultures, 10 components of a loving relationship have been identified:

1. Promoting the welfare of the loved one
2. Experiencing happiness with the loved one
3. Highly regarding the loved one
4. Being able to count on the loved one in time of need
5. Mutually understanding the loved one
6. Sharing oneself and one's possessions with the loved one
7. Receiving emotional support from the loved one
8. Giving emotional support to the loved one
9. Communicating intimately with the loved one
10. Valuing the loved one in one's own life

These 10 dimensions are present in relationships with parents, siblings, friends, and lovers. The weighting of the 10 components, however, may vary. Also, some love relationships include a dimension of sexual attraction, and others do not.

Romantic love has a motivational quality that is similar to other basic drives such as thirst and hunger. In brain imaging studies, people who have recently fallen deeply in love are shown photographs of their loved one (Aron et al., 2005). Although participants experience a variety of emotions, both positive and negative, as they gaze at the photo, they all typically show activation of the area of the brain associated with motivation and reward, areas that are rich in dopamine production. In addition to other cognitive and affective characteristics of love, there is a neurological response associated with focused attention, new levels of energy, and feeling that a deep need is being satisfied. The association with dopamine-rich areas of the brain helps explain feelings similar to other types of craving, including mental preoccupation with the loved one, anxiety when separated from the loved one, and a desire to maintain contact with the loved one.

From an evolutionary perspective, it makes sense to think that features of love have adaptive value. The passionate and romantic features of love open a person up to including another person in one's life. In order to form a long-term relationship, a person has to reorganize activities, alter existing relationships, and modify living arrangements. All these changes require a lot of energy and time. The passionate and romantic feelings of love probably contribute to a person's willingness to make all these changes. In contrast, the dimensions of intimacy and commitment contribute to the ability to sustain a relationship over long periods of time. Love between partners must be sustained in order to have and rear children, accumulate resources, fend off competitors, and preserve the social bonds of the family and community. The feelings of companionate love help motivate a person to remain devoted to one's partner in order to maintain the family system (Reis & Aron, 2008).

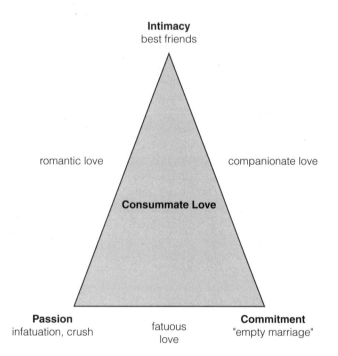

By combining the different types of love, we get the relationships seen in life.

FIGURE 11.7 Sternberg's Triangle of Types of Love

Source: © Cengage Learning.

Exclusivity

The core pathology of this period is **exclusivity**—a shutting out of others. To some extent, exclusivity is a natural element in intimate relations. For example, sexual exclusivity tends to be valued in monogamous, sexual relationships. From an evolutionary perspective, women value their male partner's sexual exclusivity in order to insure that his resources will be directed toward her and her offspring. Men will value their female partner's sexual exclusivity in order to insure their paternity. At some level, however, exclusivity can become destructive to one's ability to have relationships. Exclusivity of this type is characterized by intense jealousy, a rivalrous orientation toward anyone who shows an interest in one's loved one, and preoccupation with intense feelings of anger and resentment, both toward the loved one and toward others (Firestone, Firestone, & Catlett, 2006). The person has to expend tremendous energy monitoring the activities of the loved one. As a result, the person is cut off from relationships and ends up isolated. Ideally, the experiences of intimacy and love should broaden one's sense of connection and social integration. Through exclusivity, however, one's social support network is limited.

Exclusivity may be extended to the overestimation of one's family, religious group, and national group. As the result of a belief about one's superiority, individuals become unwilling to seek out new people or new experiences. Exclusivity may limit one's willingness to entertain new ideas. In order to preserve the belief in the value of one's exclusive world, one has to distort reality, limit access to new information, and restrict movement in the social environment. Thus, exclusivity becomes a substantial impediment to coping.

APPLIED TOPIC

Divorce

Objective 7. To analyze divorce as a life stressor in early adulthood, including the factors contributing to it and the process of coping with it.

AMERICANS HAVE ONE of the highest rates of marriage among modern industrial societies. Almost everyone in the United States wants to get married, and does. However, the divorce rate is also high. In 2008, 7.3% of those ages 30 to 34 had been divorced; another 3% had separated (U.S. Census, 2010). In international comparisons, the divorce rate in the United States is higher than that of 34 other countries including the United Kingdom, Canada, New Zealand, and Australia. After 5 years of marriage, 23% of marriages in the United States end in separation or divorce. The next highest rates were 12% in what was West Germany, and 11% in Austria and Sweden (Cherlin, 2009). An analysis of the marriage history of a nationally representative sample of women ages 15 to 44 in the United States provided an estimate of

the duration of first marriages and the probability that they will end in separation or divorce in 6-month intervals from 6 months to 20 years (Bramlett & Mosher, 2002). This study found that 20% of all first marriages have dissolved through separation or divorce at the end of 5 years; 33% have dissolved after 10 years; and 43% have dissolved after 15 years. These data are especially accurate for understanding the marital trajectory for women who married at younger ages, because a woman who married at age 30, for example, would be 50 after 20 years of marriage, and she would not have been included in the study. This study does not include information about the rate of dissolution of cohabiting couples, which would add another dimension to our understanding of relationship instability.

The focus of the following section is on the experiences of adults who are going through divorce rather than on the impact of divorce on children. The median age at first marriage is about 24 for women and 26 for men, and the median length of marriage is 7 years; therefore, one can expect that many individuals experience the divorce process during their early adulthood.

Factors Contributing to Divorce

How can we explain the high divorce rate? Here are some of the many hypotheses offered to account for the high divorce rate in the United States:

- We have an overly romantic idea about marriage; the reality of married life cannot live up to our expectations.
- We are overly individualistic and unprepared to make the commitment to achieve a collective goal.
- Men and women are socialized to fear and mistrust or devalue one another.
- We are an overly secular culture with too little commitment to religious values.
- The need for both partners to be involved in the world of work interferes with the establishment and nurturing of intimate relationships.
- Marriage is an outmoded institution, perpetuated by a patriarchal power structure.
- Women who work do not need to remain in unsupportive marriages.
- Men whose wives work do not feel obligated to remain in a marriage to support their wives.
- Smaller family size means less time devoted to childrearing, and more opportunity for nonparental, adult exploration.
- The longer life span makes it unrealistic that marriages can endure throughout adulthood.
- Children who experience insecure attachments and marital instability grow up to be young adults who are unable to sustain intimate relationships.
- Marriage is a status that requires access to financial resources; lack of equitable employment opportunities and high risks of unemployment threaten the stability of marriage among low-income populations.

For couples who are dissolving a distressed marriage, hostility and resentment that have been characteristic of their relationship are likely to escalate during the divorce process. Despite the fact that attorneys are present, negotiations are likely to be riddled with angry interactions and communication failures.

© Michael Newman/Photo Edit

A large number of variables have been examined as correlates or predictors of divorce. The scope of these analyses encompasses cross-national studies, historical cohort analyses, multicounty comparisons, and cross-sectional comparisons of couples. At the societal level, countries where there are fewer women than men and where women marry at a later age have lower divorce rates. In traditional patrilineal societies, such as many Arab cultures, the social order is organized around families linked through ties of blood and marriage. Relationships are organized in a hierarchy of obligations and privileges that are maintained through an interdependence of family ties. Divorce rates are low in traditional Arab cultures, where the stigma of disrupting a marriage is not only felt at the individual level but results in harming important kinship bonds that are critical to the larger social structure (Savaya & Cohen, 2003). In countries or regions where traditional gender attitudes are combined with traditional division of labor, that is where men are in the labor market and women are responsible for the home, the divorce rate is lower. In countries or regions where women endorse more emancipatory gender values, divorce rates are higher regardless of women's participation in the labor market (Gelissen, 2003; Kalmijn, De Graaf, & Poortman, 2004).

In a comparison of divorce rates across more than 3,000 counties in the United States, another important construct was identified—social integration, or the degree to which "people are tied or connected to one another, shared values being an important element in such integration" (Breault & Kposowa, 1987, p. 556). The characteristics of a community influence this sense of connectedness. Among the most significant of these characteristics are *population change*, the number of people who move in or out of a community each year; *religious integration*, the percentage of the population

that belongs to a religious organization; and *urbanity*, the percentage of people in each county who live in an urban area. Divorce rates are significantly linked to each of these characteristics: They are higher in counties with high population change, low religious integration, and high urbanity. These findings suggest that the difficulties that individual couples experience in their marriages may be aggravated by the community context. In contrast, marriages may be buffered and supported by a sense of community identity and shared destiny (Rosenfeld, 2007).

At the level of couple-to-couple comparisons, four variables have been associated with the likelihood of divorce: age at marriage, socioeconomic level, differences in socioemotional development of the partners, and the family's history of divorce.

Age at Marriage

In the United States, the incidence of divorce is especially high for couples who marry before the age of 20. For women who marry younger than age 18, 48% have experienced marital disruption within 10 years following the marriage. In contrast, for women marrying at age 25 and older, only 24% have experienced marital disruption within 10 years (Bramlett & Mosher, 2002).

Both for couples who marry young and for those who marry at an older age, dissatisfaction with role performance is a significant factor in marital instability. For young couples, dissatisfaction centers on sexual infidelity and jealousy. For older couples, it focuses on interpersonal conflict, a domineering style, and lack of companionship. Age at marriage is associated with different developmental needs and varying threats to marital stability. Of course, age at marriage is not a single explanatory dimension. For those who marry young, there is also a greater incidence of premarital pregnancy, dropping out of school, and lower-paying employment—all of which contribute to the likelihood of divorce.

Socioeconomic Level

The concept of **socioeconomic level** is complex. It may be thought of as a combination of education, occupation, and income. Each of these components is uniquely related to the divorce rate (White & Rogers, 2000). Men with more education have lower divorce rates. Women with more education also have lower divorce rates, except that those with 5 or more years of college are somewhat more likely to divorce than those who have had only 4 years (that is, have graduated from college). Within this overall pattern, there is also evidence of the **Glick effect**: Men and women who have dropped out of high school or college have higher divorce rates than those who have completed high school or college. Furthermore, those who have graduated from high school have a lower divorce rate than those who have had 1 to 3 years of college. Glick (1957) explained this pattern as evidence of lack of persistence. Those who are not able to complete a unit of schooling may also lack the resources to work at resolving the problems they encounter in marriage.

Many people believe that divorce is a privilege of the rich, but the evidence suggests that the opposite is true. The divorce and separation rates are generally higher among couples with minimal education and low incomes. Total family income is related to marital stability in some distinct ways. First, an erratic income and a high level of debt are more strongly associated with marital disruption than a low, steady income. Second, the relationship between income and marital instability is different for men and women. For men, higher income is associated with low divorce rates. For women, when wives contribute 50% to 60% of the total family income, and when they express low to moderate marital happiness, divorce is more likely. This explanation suggests that when both partners bring about equal economic resources to the marriage, there is less of a sense of obligation to remain in an unhappy relationship (Rogers, 2004).

Socioemotional Development of the Partners

Socioemotional development is reflected in such dimensions as the partners' self-acceptance, autonomy, and expressiveness. Personality factors associated with emotionality and constraint have been linked with the risk of divorce. Both positive and negative emotionality increase the risk of divorce, whereas constraint decreases it. The genetic basis of these personality factors and the study of the link between personality factors and marital history among twins have led some researchers to argue that genetic factors play a role in the risk of divorce (Jockin, McGue, & Lykken, 1996).

Problems in communication are frequently cited by men and women as a major cause of divorce. Couples who are characterized as conflicted in their relationship during the premarital period, who have frequent disagreements, and who have different perceptions of how to resolve arguments are more likely to be separated or divorced 3 years after marriage (Fowers, Montel, & Olson, 1996). Generally, women experience more stress and reported more problems in adjusting to marriage than men (Cotten, 1999). They tend to be more dissatisfied with the level of intimacy in their marriage than are men. These factors were examined earlier in the discussion of adjustment to marriage. Mutual satisfaction in marriage depends heavily on the husband's qualities. The stability of the husband's masculine identity, the happiness of his parents' marriage, his educational level, his social status, and his ability to be comfortable with the expression of emotions all affect marital happiness. Many husbands, however, enter marriage with a deep need to be nurtured and to continue the pattern of care that they received in childhood. The stability of a marriage depends on both partners' achieving a sense of their own identity. This achievement helps to establish the balance of power and mutual respect that is so central to emotional and intellectual intimacy.

Family History of Divorce

The partners' family history of divorce is yet another factor that contributes to marital instability. Children of divorced parents are more likely to get divorced themselves than are children of intact marriages. A number of large national studies find that parental divorce markedly increases the chances that an adult child's marriage will end in divorce. For example, Amato (1996) reported that "the odds of divorce increased by 69% if the wife's parents had been divorced and by 189% if both the wife's and the husband's parents had been divorced" (cited in Amato & DeBoer, 2001, p. 1038).

There are many interpretations of this *intergenerational transmission of divorce* (Amato & DeBoer, 2001). One interpretation is that, having seen their parents voluntarily end their marriage, children of divorce do not view marriage as a lifelong commitment and hold more favorable attitudes toward divorce as a reasonable strategy for resolving marital conflict (Greenberg & Nay, 1982). Another explanation is that children from single-parent and remarried families are likely to marry at an earlier age than children in intact marriages, thus increasing the probability of divorce. A third explanation is that children whose parents are in low-quality, high-conflict marriages are exposed to high levels of negative affect and parental hostility. This may create insecure attachment relations and result in poor relationship skills, which in turn make it difficult to form and sustain intimate adult relationships (Amato & Booth, 1996).

In a 17-year longitudinal study of marital stability, Amato and DeBoer (2001) were able to link the quality of the parents' marriage to the probability that their children's marriage would end in divorce. Of 335 married children, 20% had experienced a divorce or separation. Discord in the parents' marriage was not a strong predictor of divorce among the children. Rather, the study found that children who divorced were in families in which there was relatively little conflict, but which nonetheless ended in divorce. This lends support to the explanation that these children are not as committed to a lifelong view of marriage. When marital unhappiness occurs, these children have less inhibition about ending the relationship, especially if a more attractive alternative is likely.

Coping with Divorce

Divorce is not a single event, but a relatively long process starting with thoughts about the possibility of divorce, through possible steps of marital counseling, reconciliation, mediation, trial separation, and legal action. It is an understatement to say that divorce is stressful. Divorce is associated with numerous losses, including the loss of financial resources, emotional support, one's marital and parental role, social support, and social integration (Demo, Fine, & Ganong, 2000). Loss of income may result in other kinds of material loss. For example, a divorced woman and her children may have to move to less expensive housing, sell many of their possessions, and leave the community where they have established a network of friends and social support.

Divorce can also bring role loss and social isolation. Even when a divorce is viewed as a desirable solution, the period from the suggestion of divorce to its conclusion involves a variety of decisions and conflicts that may be painful. In an analysis of a large national sample, researchers found that people experience increases in depression after divorce, regardless of whether they are leaving a negative marriage with high levels of conflict or a marriage that was not as unpleasant (Kalmijn & Monden, 2006). Divorced partners may lose contact with family and friends as each person's social support system takes sides in the split (Kunz & Kunz, 1995). In communities where there is high disapproval of divorce, men and women who decide to continue to live in their neighborhood following divorce are likely to suffer social rejection and loss of contact with neighbors and former friends (Kalmijn & Uunk, 2007).

Many people who experience divorce go through a time of intense self-analysis. They try to integrate the failure of their marriage with their personal definition of masculinity or femininity, competence as loving people, and long-held aspirations to enact the role of husband or wife, father or mother. The stress-related correlates of divorce include increased health problems, a higher incidence of suicide, and the overrepresentation of divorced adults in all forms of psychiatric settings (Stack, 1990).

The process of leaving a marriage is different for the partner who initiates the divorce than for the partner who is being left. The initiators view the process as more voluntary and tend to be more aware of support services and feel more in control, even if they experience some sentiments of self-doubt and redefinition. On the other hand, those who do not initiate the divorce are more likely to experience a period of shock and disbelief. They, too, must go through a process of identity redefinition, which often takes longer and may

be associated with stronger feelings of emotional turmoil (Duran-Aydintug, 1995; Vannoy, 1995).

Attachment to a Former Spouse

One challenge in coping with divorce is that many divorced people retain a strong attachment to their former spouse. Grief in divorce has been compared to bereavement in widowhood. In both cases, there is a loss and a need to adjust to it. Although the loss due to death may be more intense, especially if it is sudden, the loss due to divorce may be more bitter. If an affectionate bond has been established, there is certain to be ambivalence about losing it even when the divorce is desired. Attachment to a former spouse may be positive or negative (one may wish for a reconciliation or blame the spouse, respectively) or both.

In a study of more than 200 divorced people, 42% expressed moderate or strong attachment to their former spouse. Some people wondered what their former spouse was doing, spent a lot of time thinking about them, expressed disbelief that the divorce had really taken place, and felt that they would never get over it. The attachment was stronger for those who had not initiated the divorce. The lingering feelings of attachment were associated with greater difficulties in adjustment to divorce, especially problems of loneliness and doubt about being able to cope with single life (Kitson, 1982). The stronger the positive or negative postdivorce attachment, the more difficult the adjustment in the years following the divorce (Tschann, Johnston, & Wallerstein, 1989).

In contrast to mental preoccupation or rumination about a former spouse, many former spouses continue to have contact with each other. In a Dutch study of almost 1,800 former spouses, almost half continued to have contact 10 years after the divorce (Fischer, DeGraaf, & Kalmihn, 2005). Over time, contact with a former spouse decreases, especially antagonistic contact. Yet, even 10 years after divorce about 5% of the sample reported antagonistic contact; women reporting threats of physical harm from their former husbands and men reporting verbal aggression from their former wives. Contact was most frequent for couples who had children together before the divorce. For couples who did not have children, about 60% no longer had any contact with a former spouse 10 years after divorce. For couples with children, about 70% have contact with each other 10 years after divorce. For these couples, antagonistic contact declined and friendly contact increased over this time.

The fact that divorce is stressful and that people have lingering attachments to their former spouse does not mean that they consider the divorce undesirable. Studies that ask divorcing people what went wrong in the relationship suggest that for many, the conditions of the marriage were demeaning, exploitive, or oppressive.

Common complaints by wives include their husband's authoritarianism, mental cruelty, verbal and physical abuse, excessive drinking, lack of love, neglect of children, emotional and personality problems, and extramarital sex. . . . More men than women describe themselves as having problems with alcohol, drugs, or physical abuse that contributed to the divorce. (Demo, Fine, & Ganong, 2000, pp. 283–284)

Many divorced parents report that, despite the difficulties of single parenting, life is more manageable than it was in the midst of the arguments and hostility that preceded the divorce.

Coping Strategies

Most people who experience divorce are determined to cope with the stresses it brings. Unfortunately, many adults do not anticipate the specific kinds of stressors that they will encounter. Of course, they have different coping strategies, some of which may not be effective for the special demands of divorce. In a longitudinal study that focused on how people adjusted to divorce, the researchers emphasized (1) the *kinds of stressors* that the individuals encountered, (2) the *resources* they had to help them cope, and (3) the *meaning* they gave to the divorce situation (Wang & Amato, 2000). The major stressors were large losses in income, losing friends, and having to move. Those whose post-divorce adjustment was judged most positive had higher income levels, were dating someone steadily or remarried, were most favorable about the marital dissolution before the divorce, or actually initiated the divorce.

The magnitude of the stressors was not as important in predicting adjustment as were the coping strategies (resources and meaning).

In another study comparing widowed and divorced women, the contribution of social support to coping was examined in more detail. Those women who were most stressed by their loss received increased social support from friends and relatives in the following year. For the two groups, the most beneficial type of support differed. For widows, practical support, such as transportation or help with household chores, was positive; for those who had been divorced, having someone who would listen to their personal problems was especially helpful. For both groups, receiving monetary support was associated with an increase in distress. Thus, some types of social support appear to foster recovery, whereas others may serve to highlight the extent of one's loss (Miller, Smerglia, Gaudet, & Kitson, 1998).

The process of coping with divorce requires strategies devised to deal with the aspects of it that are perceived as most troublesome. Further, many coping strategies, including becoming involved in new activities, spending more time with family and friends, gaining new skills, or taking a new job, may promote new levels of functioning. Human service professionals can be effective in helping adults develop coping skills for resolving some of the stresses of divorce and transforming a difficult life event into an opportunity for personal growth.

Chapter Summary

Objective 1. To identify and define selected concepts that are especially relevant for understanding development during adulthood, including social roles, the life course, and fulfillment theories.

Three theoretical concepts were introduced to help consider the challenges and directions of growth in adulthood: social roles, the life course, and fulfillment theories. Adulthood comprises a series of increasingly complex and demanding roles, role gain and role loss, and the challenges of balancing multiple roles. The life course perspective is a framework for examining adulthood as the interface of family and occupational careers against the backdrop of chronological age, historical period, and societal norms and expectations. Through the life course lens, one gains appreciation for the developing person and the changing historical context. Fulfillment theories emphasize the ability of adults to go beyond meeting daily needs and achieving equilibrium to make plans, strive toward goals, and seek personal meaning in life.

The developmental tasks of early adulthood require that individuals apply the many competencies they have acquired in childhood and adolescence to solving new and complex challenges. They may marry or make a commitment to an intimate partner, have children or decide to delay or forgo childbearing, and choose work roles. Gradually, they evolve a style of life. In this process, their commitment to social institutions and to significant others expands. Their worldview becomes more diverse, and their appreciation of the interdependence of systems increases. One of the major sources of stress at this life stage is the need to balance and integrate multiple roles.

Objective 2. To analyze the process of forming intimate relationships, including initial attractions, mate selection, and commitment to a long-term relationship; the role of cohabitation in forming close relationships; and the challenges that one faces in adjusting to the early years of marriage.

The exploration of intimate relationships requires a readiness to engage in the complex set of dyadic interactions that move a relationship from initial attraction to deeper levels of disclosure, role compatibility, mutual support, and commitment. These close relationships can take a variety of forms, some of which appear to set the stage for long-term commitment, and others that seem to be more marginal or temporary. A major theme in the establishment and maintenance of satisfying intimate relationships is the quality of communication and the ability of couples to coordinate their interactions, particularly under conditions of conflict or role strain.

Objective 3. To describe the factors associated with the decision to have children, the impact of childbearing on the intimate relationship, the developing parental relationship, and the contribution of childbearing to growth in adulthood.

The decision to have children is becoming increasingly one of choice rather than obligation. Age at childbearing is delayed in line with later age at marriage. At the same time, there is an increase in nonmarital childbearing and in voluntarily child-free couples. Having children alters the adults' intimate relationship, especially the amount of time parents spend with one another when the children are not present. Couples differ in the ways they balance their roles as parents and intimate partners; some couples grow closer and more companionate, whereas others experience new levels of conflict and declines in marital satisfaction.

Objective 4. To explore the concept of work as a stimulus for psychosocial development in early adulthood, with special focus on the technical skills, authority relations, demands and hazards, and interpersonal relations in the work environment.

In the period of occupational training, many new areas of intellectual awareness are stimulated. Self-understanding is integrated with social expectations and historical opportunities as men and women embark on their career paths. Four components of the work environment must be mastered: technical skills, authority relations, interpersonal relations with coworkers, and ways of coping with the hazards and risks of the workplace. One of the most challenging aspects of career development in this early phase is the coordination of work with the establishment of meaningful intimate relationships.

Objective 5. To examine the concept of lifestyle as the expression of individual identity, with consideration for the pace of life, balancing competing role demands, building a supportive social network, and adopting practices to promote health and fitness.

Lifestyle is the translation into action of the values, goals, and personal preferences that were crystallized into a personal identity in later adolescence. Components of lifestyle that impact the sense of well-being and personal life satisfaction include the pace of life, the quality of one's social network, the ability to balance competing role demands, and behaviors that contribute to one's fitness and overall health.

Objective 6. To define and describe the psychosocial crisis of intimacy versus isolation, the central process through which the crisis is resolved, mutuality among peers, the prime adaptive ego quality of love, and the core pathology of exclusivity.

The psychosocial crisis of intimacy versus isolation emphasizes the evolution of adult sexuality into an interpersonal commitment. This crisis requires that needs for personal gratification be subordinated to needs for mutual satisfaction. Success is comparatively difficult to achieve in our culture because of the basic tension between the norm of independence and the desire for closeness. The research on marriage suggests that willingness to make a personal commitment to another adult is one of the key aspects of success. The elaboration of communication skills, the ability to engage in and resolve conflict, and the ability to find time for companionate, leisurely interaction are emphasized as central to marital stability.

Objective 7. To analyze divorce as a life stressor in early adulthood, including the factors contributing to it and the process of coping with it.

The high rate of divorce suggests that many societal, community, and interpersonal factors work against the support of stable intimate relationships. In the process of coping with divorce, there is a clear need for daily problem solving and emotional expression to manage the grief, loss, and role transitions that accompany the disruption in an intimate relationship.

Key Terms

authority relations, 460
career phases, 462
childbearing, 450

coercive escalation, 448
cohabitation, 438
cohort, 433

communal norm, 446
companionship, 447
competence motivation, 434

Further Reflection

1. What are some of the developmental tasks of infancy, toddlerhood, early and middle childhood, and early adolescence that contribute to the capacity to form intimate relationships in adulthood?

2. What are some of the ways that success in the world of work competes with success in an intimate relationship? How might success in the world of work enhance one's success in an intimate relationship?

3. What characteristics are important to you in a romantic, long-term partner? What characteristics are important to people in your family who might influence your choice? On what dimensions is homogamy important to you in the choice of a mate?

4. What are your own views about the importance of having children? Where does childbearing fit into your view of yourself as an adult?

5. Describe your current lifestyle. How do you use your time? What are your priorities for work or school, intimate relationships, parenting or other family roles, leisure activities, and involvement in religious, political, and charitable organizations? As you think about yourself in the period of life from ages 24 to 34, what do you envision as the pillars (the essential structure) of your lifestyle?

6. How does culture contribute to the way adulthood is defined? What are the cultural markers of the transition into adulthood? What cultural expectations shape your decisions about marriage, childbearing, and work? Imagine a society in which commitment to family and intimate relationships would be valued ahead of work. What policies and practices would provide evidence of this priority?

7. How do you account for the high divorce rate in the United States? Give five different answers to that question, focusing on different levels of analysis: societal, historical, cultural, developmental, and interpersonal.

Psychology CourseMate

To access additional course materials, including CourseMate, please visit www.cengagebrain.com. At the CengageBrain.com home page, search for the ISBN of your title (from the back cover of your book) using the search box at the top of the page. This will take you to the product page where these resources can be found.

Casebook

For additional cases related to this chapter, see the case entitled "To Marry or Not" in *Life Span Development: A Case Book*, by Barbara and Philip Newman, Laura Landry-Meyer, and Brenda J. Lohman, pp. 163–170. The case focuses on the development of Jonah's and Abby's dating relationship, their decision to marry, and the early years of their married life as they are influenced by work and extended family relationships.

© 2011 Estate of Pablo Picasso/Artists Rights Society (ARS), New York/Photo © Francis G. Mayer/CORBIS

Gertrude Stein was Picasso's friend and mentor. She provided an environment where creative people could get together and share ideas. This portrait was the only one that Stein felt represented her true sense of self. Middle adulthood is the period when one's energy and talent are directed toward building and maintaining the structures upon which future generations depend. It is the stage when self-fulfillment is integrated with caring for others.

Middle Adulthood (34 to 60 Years)

CHAPTER 12

Chapter Objectives

1. To examine the world of work as a context for development, focusing on interpersonal demands, authority relations, and demands for the acquisition of new skills; considering midlife career changes; examining the interaction of work and family life; and examining the impact of joblessness in middle adulthood.

2. To examine the process of maintaining a vital, intimate relationship in middle adulthood, especially a commitment to growth, effective communication, creative use of conflict, and preserving passion.

3. To describe the expansion of caring in middle adulthood as it applies to two specific roles—that of a parent and that of an adult child caring for one's aging parents.

4. To analyze the tasks required for effective management of the household and the diversity of households, including blended families, single-parent families, and adults who live alone.

5. To explain the psychosocial crisis of generativity versus stagnation and the central processes through which the crisis is resolved: person-environment interaction and creativity.

6. To define the primary adaptive ego strength of care and the core pathology of rejectivity.

7. To apply a psychosocial analysis to the issue of discrimination in the workplace, with special focus on the cost to society and to the individual when discrimination operates to restrict career access and advancement.

MIDDLE ADULTHOOD LASTS from about age 34 to 60. According to psychosocial theory, a new reorganization of personality occurs during middle adulthood that focuses on the achievement of a sense of generativity—a concern about the well-being of future generations. This new stage integrates the skills and perspectives of the preceding life stages with a commitment of energy to the future. During this period, individual and societal developments are intimately interwoven. In order for societies to thrive and grow, adults must dedicate their energy and resources to preserving the quality of life for future generations. In order for individuals to continue to thrive and grow, societies must provide opportunities for adults to express and fulfill their generative strivings.

Because middle adulthood covers a relatively long period, there are opportunities to review and revise one's commitments and goals along the way. People experience many transitions in their work and family roles during this time, encountering a widening circle of relationships and new responsibilities for the care and guidance of others. Over the course of adulthood, many situations call for decisions that have no single correct answer. Several alternatives are possible, and adults must rely on their ability to gather and evaluate information to determine which choice is best for them and their loved ones. Flexibility coupled with a good sense of humor and creative problem solving emerge in this stage as key coping strategies. ■

Developmental Tasks

Every adult typically engages in all of the following developmental tasks during middle adulthood: managing a career, nurturing an intimate relationship, expanding caring relationships, and managing the household. Through their roles in the family, at work, and in the community, middle adults have broad responsibilities for the nurturance, education, and care of children, adolescents, young adults, and older adults. The strains of middle adulthood result largely from difficulties in balancing many roles and striving to navigate through predictable as well as sudden role transitions. The emotional well-being of the society as a whole rests largely on the capacity of middle adults to succeed in the developmental tasks of their life stage.

Managing a Career

Objective 1. To examine the world of work as a context for development, focusing on interpersonal demands, authority relations, and demands for the acquisition of new skills; considering midlife career changes; examining the interaction of work and family life; and examining the impact of joblessness in middle adulthood.

Work is a major context for adult development. Every person who enters the labor market has an occupational **career**. However, this career may not appear to be orderly or progressive. It may involve changes in the kind of work performed over time, short- or long-term exit from the labor market due to unemployment or family responsibilities, and periodic return to school for new training. One can argue that as long as a person is involved in an effort to make use of skills and talents, there will be significant interactions between the world of work and the person's individual development.

Using the framework of systems theory, one can appreciate that the microsystem of work is embedded in a larger societal macrosystem. Each society has an economic orientation that influences policies and practices related to work. The climate for the U.S. worker is one that encourages a relatively long work week and few benefits. For example, there is no law requiring companies to provide paid vacation. In comparison to European countries, the labor union structure is less powerful in the United States and often cannot protect workers from new demands for productivity. According to data gathered by the Organization for Economic Cooperation and Development, the average U.S. worker works over 1,750 hours a year. This is over 250 hours a year more than in Italy, Austria, France, or Sweden, but less than in Korea, Japan, Mexico, or Poland (OECD, 2010). In 2009, over 5 million employed workers ages 25 to 54 were working more than one job (U.S. Bureau of Labor Statistics, 2010). The demands for time commitment on U.S. workers are substantial and result in significant role strain as middle adults strive to balance work with their other important life roles, especially those of parent, carer of aging parents, intimate partner, and community member.

The buying power of wages has declined, so that most families find it necessary for both partners to work in order to meet a reasonable standard of living. The costs of housing, education, and health care have increased dramatically; and the projection of a longer life expectancy has placed new pressures on workers to save for a more diverse set of needs in retirement. The costs of medical expenses adds to the financial worries of many middle adults, both out of concern for their ability to pay for their own immediate family's medical expenses and for their ability to support their aging parents, whose health care costs are often not fully covered by insurance. All these features of the macrosystem in the United States have implications for the way individuals orient to the world of work and for the potential conflicts between work and family life (Warren, 2003, 2007).

There is reciprocity between work experiences and individual growth. We expect that people with certain kinds of experiences, abilities, and values will enter certain kinds of work roles (Holland, 1997). Once those roles have been entered, the work environment and the kinds of activities that the person performs also influence intellectual, social, and value orientation. One's lifelong occupational career is a fluid structure of changing activities, ambitions, and sources of satisfaction. As people move through middle adulthood, the management of their occupational career becomes a task of central importance to their sense of personal effectiveness, identity, and social integration. Four themes in the management of a career are discussed for their contribution to adaptation and individual development: achieving new levels of competence, midlife career changes, balancing work and family life, and the impact of joblessness.

istockphoto.com/Yuri Arcurs

Dr. DeMarco is showing his team the plan for the major project they will be working on next. He's explaining the goals and strategies for achieving these goals. The team members are clearly motivated to assume their assigned roles, and they know that DeMarco will ask for their feedback about the plan. They are comfortable with his leadership, and they respect his expertise and competence.

Achieving New Levels of Competence in the World of Work

Middle adulthood brings new challenges, a reformulation of ambitions and goals, and new levels of competence in the workplace. Three areas are emphasized here as they relate to the interpersonal and cognitive components of career development: understanding and managing leadership and authority relationships, expanding interpersonal skills and relationships, and achieving new levels of mastery in critical skill areas.

Understanding and Managing Leadership and Authority.

Authority relations encompass all the hierarchical relationships that give people decision-making power and supervisory responsibility for others. Returning to Tiedeman's model, which was introduced in Chapter 10 (Later Adolescence), in the *induction* phase of career development one must identify the authority structure operating in the work setting and begin to establish one's position in it. In the *reformation* phase, which typically occurs in middle adulthood, advancement in a career inevitably involves taking on positions of increased responsibility and power to make decisions. Career advancement means assuming authority in some areas, while recognizing the authority of others. However, not everyone in a position of authority provides effective leadership. A common complaint among workers is that their organization lacks leadership, or that their boss or supervisor does not provide adequate leadership.

What is **leadership**? Current organizational theory suggests that leadership is not a quality of personality as much as it is a relationship among people. Woyach (1991) defined leadership as "the process of helping a group shape a vision of its purpose and goals and of getting people, both inside and outside the group, to commit and recommit themselves to accomplishing that vision" (p. 7).

This definition embodies three basic assumptions: (1) leadership is a relationship among people, (2) leaders provide a sense of vision or direction, and (3) leaders motivate the group to work toward achieving its vision. Building on this view of leadership, Woyach (1991) argued that effective leaders try to balance the good of the group with their own self-interest. They try to take into account the best interests of individuals, groups, and communities, while they also participate and lead.

The requirements of leadership may change as the group develops, and as the team or organization faces new, emerging challenges. Groups may go through phases when everyone is overloaded and distracted. During those times, leaders help the group return to its mission and recommit to working together. At other times, the group members may understand their roles and tasks so clearly that the primary acts of leadership involve delegating responsibilities and removing obstacles to the group's success. Effective leadership involves the ability to assess the changing needs and challenges faced by the team or organization, and to adapt to those changes

through the use of flexible problem-solving strategies. **Adaptive leadership** is required when the organization faces new conditions or complex problems that cannot be solved with the current use of technologies or techniques. Under these conditions, leaders need to help frame new ways of defining problems, and engaging workers, consumers, or clients in a search for solutions (Heifetz, Grashow, & Linsky, 2009).

Some requirements of leadership are perceived differently across cultures. For example, in a study comparing full-time, white collar workers in China and Australia, participants were asked to rate traits that were important for effective leadership. The Australians, who expect their leaders to be able to work collaboratively with employees, rated friendly and respectful traits higher than did the Chinese workers. For the Chinese workers, a hierarchical authority structure is valued. A person in a leadership position might be perceived as weakening authority through friendly interactions with subordinates (Casimir & Waldman, 2007).

Other aspects of leadership appear to be universally effective. Leaders who are described as charismatic or visionary are more likely to be rated as highly effective by their subordinates. **Charismatic leaders** are typically viewed as exceptional people who are able to convey a vision by distilling complex ideas into a simple message and linking their message through symbols, analogies, or stories, to experiences that are personally relevant to their followers. Charismatic leaders are confident and optimistic. They can be seen as idiosyncratic or theatrical in their approach, and inspirational in their delivery. They are willing to take risks and often suggest a new direction that is a noticeable departure from the way the organization has been heading. Charismatic leaders are sensitive to the needs of their members and actively monitor and listen to people at all levels of an organization in order to retain rapport with their group members and to stay attuned to changes in the organizational climate (Conger & Kanungo, 1998). Across many types of groups and different degrees of organizational complexity, charismatic leaders encourage followers to become deeply committed to the organizational mission, to make personal sacrifices for this mission, and to perform above expectations (Fiol, Harris, & House, 1999). They do this in part through their positive and encouraging emotional messages and their ability to form constructive relationships with workers. Under the guidance of this positive leadership, workers are happier, less likely to miss work, and more willing to engage in training and development activities (Den Hartog, De Hoogh, & Keegan, 2007; Campbell, Ward, Sonnenfeld, & Agle, 2008; Erez, Misangyi, Johnson, LePine, & Halverson, 2008; Rowold & Laukamp, 2009).

The reorganization of many large companies has resulted in fewer employees, who are then asked to be more productive. In this context, leaders need to develop adaptive leadership to accompany their technical expertise. This involves communicating a clear view of the challenges, mobilizing and guiding the direction of innovation, coordinating people and projects, and increasing workers' willingness and readiness for change. Adaptive leadership may involve increasing employees' sense of confidence in their ability to initiate changes, as well as increasing their commitment to the organization during a period of uncertainty or transition (Heifetz, Grashow, & Linsky, 2009; Strauss, Griffin, & Rafferty, 2009).

The idea that leaders are able to motivate others is explored in detail by Rosabeth Moss Kanter (2004) in her analysis of how organizations are able to turn a losing streak around. Kanter (2004) highlighted the role of leaders in inspiring confidence. Based on hundreds of interviews and a national survey of more than 1,000 companies, Kanter identified strategies that successful leaders use to encourage members of their organization to reach new, higher levels of performance. When leaders believe in the goals of the organization and in the ability of people to achieve those goals, people will rise to meet those expectations. In inspiring confidence, leaders set high standards and are role models for these standards. They establish systems for individual and system accountability. They foster collaboration through mutual respect and effective communication. They recognize and encourage initiative, imagination, and innovation. They are able to convince others outside the organization to invest in the goals of the organization, which makes their success more attainable. Thus, it falls to the leader of a group to embrace a vision of success and to build commitment to that vision rather than to be caught up in all the many obstacles that prevent success.

The focus on leadership highlights the importance of ego strengths for middle adults in positions of authority, not only for their own personal occupational achievements, but for the future of organizations and the well-being of workers.

Especially during periods of uncertainty and transition, middle adults who are optimistic, flexible, open to new ideas, and confident of their competence can create environments where people are able to address their work in a productive, proactive manner. Through effective leadership, middle adults convey a vision about the possibilities for their organization, and guide others toward the achievement of this vision. Success in this enterprise contributes to the sense of meaning and mattering, essential elements of subjective well-being in adulthood.

Expanding Interpersonal Skills and Relationships. Many occupations place a great deal of emphasis on the development and use of **interpersonal skills**—especially the ability to interact well with customers and coworkers and the ability to communicate effectively—as underlying criteria in the selection and promotion process. The concept of interpersonal skills is complex and includes at least three components: self-presentation, or how a person introduces oneself to others and conveys openness to further interactions; social scanning, or the ability to read the social cues in the situation; and social flexibility, or the ability to respond adaptively to the social demands of the situation, for example by being assertive or cooperative as the circumstances require (Wu, 2010). Even if these skills are not mentioned explicitly in the job description, success in career management requires the ability to influence others, appear credible, develop a fluent conversational style, and learn to work effectively in groups or teams. Problems in interpersonal relationships can have a negative impact on employees, on the image of the organization, and on overall productivity.

Alan has been with the company for a long time, and has been very successful as a manager. His team is creating a mission statement for their department. Team members are pleased that he respects their ideas and provides this mechanism for them to express their ideas as they build the vision for the future.

An essential feature of many work environments is the ability to work in teams or groups. Teams that work well together are able to maintain positive social relationships among the members as they work to complete their group's tasks, all the while supporting the personal and professional development of team members. Eight features of effective teams, many of which reflect the importance of interpersonal skills and relationships, have been identified in the literature (Marquardt, Seng, & Goodson, 2010):

> Clear and meaningful goals
> Clearly stated expectations for positive interpersonal behavior
> Strong interpersonal and communication skills
> Competence and commitment to solving problems and performing tasks
> Trust, openness, and group cohesiveness
> The ability to manage conflict to preserve positive relationships among members
> Shared leadership
> Continuous individual and team commitment to learning and improvement

When individuals work in teams, especially when there is frequent interaction, there is a tendency toward **social comparison**. One may learn that a colleague has made a lot of sales, received recognition for an accomplishment, or solved an important work-related problem. This might be viewed as an *upward* comparison—a person believes that the colleague performed better than others. In contrast, one may learn that a colleague made a lot of errors, worked too slowly, or failed to make a sales quota. This might be viewed as a *downward* comparison—a person believes that the colleague performed worse than others. This type of social comparison is an ongoing aspect of the interpersonal environment at work, with some people being more likely to base their self-evaluation on comparisons with others (Buunk et al., 2005).

Thinking about reactions to social comparisons, one could observe that others are doing better than oneself and be happy for them, or one could be jealous or envious of others' success. One could observe that others are doing worse than oneself and be relieved or proud that one is doing so well, or one could feel bad about others' failures. In a cooperative work environment, people view the fate of their colleagues as directly affecting each member of the team. In such a setting, one can imagine a positive interpersonal dynamic, where people feel proud of those who are doing better than they are and are encouraged to seek out these high performers to learn from. People who feel bad when others are not doing as well as they are may be willing to help them raise their skills or improve their performance.

In middle adulthood, those in leadership positions have an opportunity to foster a cooperative or competitive work climate, and to manage the process of social comparison in the interest of productivity or effectiveness. Even if they are not in positions of authority as more senior workers, those in middle adulthood are often in a position to influence the interpersonal atmosphere, serving as models for others, demonstrating pride in their achievements, providing encouragement for appropriate work-related behavior, and fostering respect and trust among coworkers.

Meeting New Skill Demands. The characteristics of the occupation and the work setting determine what kinds of work-related skills will dominate the adult's energies. It makes sense to expect that the actual tasks a person performs from day to day will influence intellectual development. The *Dictionary of Occupational Titles* (U.S. Department of Labor, Employment and Training Administration, 1993) was updated and converted to a Web-based resource called *O*NET* (www.onetcenter.org), which is maintained by the U.S. Department of Labor, Employment and Training Administration. O*NET describes over 800 occupational titles and periodically updates each occupation with regard to skills, abilities, knowledge, tasks, work activities, work context, experience levels required, job interests, and work values and needs. Each of these dimensions has implications for workers' adaptation to their work setting. It is likely that in the process of adapting to these dimensions, adults will carry over aspects of work-related competence to family and community roles.

The idea that social structure influences personality through occupational demands was developed in some detail by Melvin Kohn (1980, 1999). One of the strongest relationships he identified was between the *substantive complexity* of the job and *intellectual flexibility*. **Substantive complexity** is the degree to which the work requires thought, independent judgment, and frequent decision making. Those whose work is characterized by substantive complexity also tend to have relatively low levels of supervision, and their work is not overly routinized. As a result of these work conditions, they tend to value self-direction, encourage self-direction in others—including their children—and show evidence of **intellectual flexibility,** the ability to handle conflicting information, grasp several perspectives on a problem, and reflect on one's own values and solutions.

This relationship between substantive complexity at work and personal intellectual flexibility was found among workers in the United States, Poland, and Japan (Kohn, 2006). In the cross-national comparison, U.S. workers whose jobs were characterized as substantively complex also had greater personal satisfaction and a sense of well-being, whereas those whose work was highly routinized and supervised had a lower sense of well-being. In contrast, in Poland, when these data were collected in 1978, the workers who had the more substantively complex work were also more distressed. The workers at the more routinized jobs were more confident of job security and less threatened by instability. Therefore, although the Polish workers at the routinized jobs had the least self-direction of all the three countries, they felt a high sense of satisfaction about their current and future employment. However, the managers, whose jobs were more substantively complex, were also at greater risk. They were held accountable for productivity with little opportunity to influence rewards or working conditions.

One of the most frequently cited areas of skill development in the contemporary labor market is *creative problem solving*. The combination of increasingly complex technology, instant international communication, and continuing reorganization of the network of interrelated businesses results in the emergence of a new and changing array of problems. These problems may relate to the need to recruit and train the workforce, bring together changing teams of workers depending on the task, find new strategies for the manufacture and delivery of products, or integrate technologies. The concept of **managerial resourcefulness** is sometimes used to capture the nature of this problem solving. Managerial resourcefulness combines three critical features: a cognitive capacity to gather and analyze information, sensitivity to the emotional and motivational aspects of change, and a readiness to take appropriate actions (Kanungo & Misra, 1992; Kanungo & Menon, 2004).

By middle adulthood, individuals have accumulated a deep knowledge of the specific tasks and routines associated with their work. At the same time, they have either tried or observed a variety of problem-solving strategies. Thus, the challenge for the middle adult worker is to synthesize these two bodies of knowledge to create a flexible approach to emerging problems. Successful development in this area requires recognizing when conditions have changed such that past solutions will not be adequate. At the same time, it requires confidence in one's ability to find new solutions and remain creative under stressful conditions.

Midlife Career Changes

Management of a career does not necessarily mean remaining within the same occupational structure throughout adult life. Recall from the discussion of work in Chapter 11 (Early Adulthood) that between the ages of 18 and 32, the average number of jobs held was 10.3. Although the rate of job turnover slows down after age 30, people still need to remain flexible about their attachment to a specific job. Descriptions of the changing nature of organizations suggest that the segment of workers employed full-time by corporations is a shrinking percentage of working-age adults. As today's working-age labor force moves through middle adulthood, from 34 to 60, the nature of the labor market is also changing to a more decentralized, fee-for-services model. This requires individuals to create what has been described as a portfolio approach to their career—developing a document that is more detailed and three-dimensional than a resume; one that highlights one's products, skills, talents, and experiences (Handy, 1996). The portfolio approach assumes that people need to market themselves, whether in hopes of advancement within a company, or as they seek new employment opportunities. People who change jobs relatively often or who work as consultants and project managers can take this approach in order to convey the range of skills they have developed, and the diverse products or activities in which they have played a major role.

Work activities or work-related goals may change for at least five reasons during middle adulthood. First, some careers end during middle adulthood. One example is the career of the professional athlete, whose strength, speed of reaction time, and endurance decline to the point where the athlete can no longer compete.

Second, some adults cannot resolve conflicts between job demands and personal goals. Some workers recognize that the kinds of contributions they thought they could make in the workplace are simply not possible within their

Image copyright Michael Rubin 2010. Used under license from Shutterstock.com

Al Franken made a dramatic midlife career change. He left his role as a comedian and ran for the United States Senate. He won a hard fought contest and has become a respected Senator.

chosen work structure. Others feel like outsiders within their corporations:

> Trish Millines Dziko didn't discover her affinity for computers until she attended college on a basketball scholarship. Later, while she was rising through the mostly White, male ranks at Microsoft, she felt uncomfortable being one of the few African Americans in Redmond. At age 39, she retired as one of many Microsoft millionaires and used $100,000 of her kitty to establish the Technology Access Foundation, designed to bring more kids of color into the game....."I want to change the dynamics of the [corporation] club," says Dziko, "by changing the demographics." (Schultz, 2001, pp. 68–69)

A third explanation for midlife career change is the realization that one has succeeded as much as possible in a given career. Adults may realize that they will not be promoted further or that changing technology has made their expertise obsolete. Consequently, they may decide to retrain for new kinds of work or return to school to move in new career directions. In 2004 to 2005, roughly one third of middle adult workers were enrolled in work-related courses to gain new skills (U.S. Census Bureau, 2010).

Fourth, family transitions may prompt career changes. In some instances, adults leave the labor market or move to part-time work in order to care for their children or their aging parents. In other cases, adults enter the labor market following divorce or widowhood. According to a U.S. Department of Commerce report (Dalirazar, 2007), over 6 million adults ages 24 to 44 said they were not working because they were taking care of children or others.

Fifth, with the restructuring of the workforce, some workers are laid off and cannot be rehired in the same field. They have to retrain for a new line of work or for similar work in a new industry. Other workers may remain with the same company but find that they are being asked to perform new tasks that require a new set of skills and responsibilities.

One must be cautious not to idealize midlife career change. It is not uncommon to experience a variety of fears or worries about leaving one occupation and starting something new: fear of making an unfavorable discovery about one's abilities as a result of the change; fear of failing to satisfy the expectations of important others; fear of taking on new responsibilities; and fear of giving up a known present for an unknown future (Patterson, 1997).

The ease or difficulty of work transitions depends in part on the extent to which workers perceive that they have control over the conditions of the change. Voluntary transitions usually occur with some control over the timing of the change, and the opportunity to prepare both financially and with the acquisition of required skills. What is more, in the case of voluntary work transitions, the person has the sense of agency about making decisions that advance desired goals. Involuntary transitions often occur with little chance to select the optimal time or to save up for the possibility

of a period of unemployment or reduced income. There is less opportunity to consider the impact of the transition on family members. The person who is making an involuntary transition may feel compelled to take a position in order to support the family or to meet existing financial obligations even if the position is not a very good fit with personal values or goals (Fouad & Bynner, 2008).

The Impact of Joblessness

Even though the workplace can be a major source of stress, **joblessness** can be even more disruptive to personal mental health and family functioning. As a result of the restructuring of the labor market, plant closings, downturns in the e-conomy, and workforce reorganizations, many workers who had a history of steady employment, including increased responsibility and advancement, have recently faced job loss in their middle adulthood. Unemployment in middle adulthood has a major psychological impact on an individual's sense of self-worth and hope for the future. Among middle-aged workers, job loss is associated with material deprivation, disruption in family life, and increases in marital conflict. Children and spouses are commonly acutely involved in the effects of job loss on a middle-aged parent, and often the entire family experiences new feelings of alienation from social institutions as a result of the experience (Lobo & Watkins, 1995; Perrucci, Perrucci, & Targ, 1997).

Job loss has been associated with both physical health and mental health consequences, such as self-doubt, passivity, and social withdrawal. Depression is a common consequence, and the associated family strains may also lead to new levels of conflict and family violence. In some instances, adjustments that families make to a husband's unemployment result in a further reduction of his sense of importance and accentuate the decline in his self-respect. Social support—especially family strengths and marital satisfaction—are important buffers for the negative effects of unemployment (Blustein, 2008; Bambra, 2010).

In 2004, the U.S. unemployment rate was 4.4%, slightly higher for men than for women. The modal period of unemployment was less than 5 weeks, but about 22% were unemployed for 27 weeks or more. By the end of 2009, the rate was 10%, and 40% of those who were unemployed, or 6.1 million people, had been jobless 27 weeks or more. Table 12.1 summarizes the unemployment rates in 2009 by race and educational attainment for individuals from 25 years old and older. Those with less education were at especially high risk for unemployment during this difficult economic period (U.S. Bureau of Labor Statistics, 2010).

There is a difference in how people cope with seasonal or short-term (less than 5 weeks) unemployment and chronic unemployment. Because of the cultural emphasis on productive work, people are especially likely to experience guilt about being unemployed. Moreover, for men, unemployment disrupts the self-concept of the traditional definition of the adult male role as breadwinner for the family. As a

TABLE 12.1 Unemployment Rates by Ethnicity and Educational Attainment, 2009

| | EDUCATIONAL LEVEL | | | |
RACE	LESS THAN HIGH SCHOOL	HIGH SCHOOL GRADUATE	SOME COLLEGE, NO DEGREE	COLLEGE GRADUATE
European American	13.9	9.0	7.9	4.2
African American	21.3	14.0	12.1	7.3
Asian American	8.4	7.5	8.9	5.6
Hispanic/Latino	13.7	10.4	9.6	5.7

Source: U.S. Bureau of Labor Statistics, 2010.

result of guilt, shame, and anger, men may find it hard to direct their energy toward creative solutions to life problems. Thus, the inability to work can be expected to become a serious hurdle to the resolution of the psychosocial conflict of generativity versus stagnation for men (Hopper, 1990). In a comparison of men and women who had both breadwinner and childrearing responsibilities, the men were more likely to view unemployment as a defeat, whereas the women were more likely to view unemployment as an opportunity (Forret, Sullivan, & Mainiero, 2010).

The threats of job loss and job insecurity can create stress for those who remain employed as well as for those who become unemployed. For example, in a study of employment conditions on job-related distress, workers in industries that were experiencing high levels of unemployment had a higher incidence of depression than did workers in industries where unemployment was low. Similarly, studies have shown that workers who are spared during downsizing and mergers show signs of anxiety and depression.

These observations highlight the salience that work has in middle adulthood and the role that meaningful work plays in supporting well-being. At its best, work provides resources for survival, creates a context for social relatedness, and offers opportunities for self-determination. As such, involuntary long-term or chronic unemployment or underemployment can undermine a middle adult's sense of mattering, and establish conditions for alienation or self-loathing (Blustein, 2008; Garrett-Peters, 2009).

Balancing Work and Family Life

Almost everyone manages a career while juggling commitments to spouse, children, parents, other household members, and friends. A decision to assume more authority, work longer hours, accept an offer with another company, quit a job, accept a transfer to a new location, or start up one's own business will touch the lives of other household and family members.

In thinking about balancing work and family life, it is useful to consider three interrelated concepts: role overload, role conflict, and role spillover. **Role overload** occurs as a result of too many demands and expectations to handle in the time allowed. For example, a parent with three children ages 8, 11, and 15 may find that the demands of getting the

As a result of the recent economic recession, people from all levels of career attainment wait in long lines to collect their unemployment checks. Job loss and unemployment are significant sources of stress that challenge people's self-concepts and feelings of self-worth. In addition, they may lead to family stress and tension.

© Frances Roberts/Alamy

children ready for school, attending functions at three different schools, picking children up and dropping them off at various places, and trying to be emotionally available for the problem of the day are exhausting. Role overload can be experienced in one or more adult roles.

Role conflict occurs when demands and expectations of various roles conflict with each other. For example, role conflict occurs when a worker is expected to stay late at the job to finish a project, but that same night is a spouse's birthday or a child's performance.

Role spillover occurs when the demands or preoccupations about one role interfere with the ability to carry out another role. For example, a person may be disrupted at work by worries about an ill parent or distracted at home by a work assignment that is due the next day.

The combination of role overload, role conflict, and role spillover can lead to reduced satisfaction at work and in family roles, and a decline in the person's sense of well-being (Kinnunen, Feldt, Mauno, & Rantanen, 2010). In contrast, multiple role involvement has also been shown to contribute to health and well-being. Spousal support for the partner's involvement in work can increase work satisfaction, and feelings of success and pride in one's accomplishments at work can contribute to marital satisfaction (Dreman, 1997). In a large, longitudinal study of British women born in 1946, those women who had participated in multiple work and family roles over the course of their adulthood were found to be healthier at age 54 than women from the same birth

cohort who were long-time homemakers (McMunn, Bartley, Hardy, & Kuh, 2006).

The domains of work and family, both central to adult lives across cultures, are likely to conflict under certain circumstances and complement each other in other circumstances. In order to understand the nature of this relationship, researchers have identified the elements of work and the elements of family life that appear to be most central to this conflict. A model of how job characteristics and family characteristics might contribute to work-family conflict and family-work conflict is presented in Figure 12.1.

The basic assumption is that there are role pressures from work and family that are mutually incompatible, so that meeting the expectations in one domain makes it very difficult to meet expectations in the other. Moreover, there may be interactions such that conflicts from work make it difficult to meet role expectations in the family, but then the disruptions in the family make it difficult to meet role expectations at work (Frone, 2003). Despite these tensions between work and family obligations, people strive to find ways for the two roles to work together (work-family fit), which leads to greater job satisfaction. Job flexibility, for example, a workplace policy that supports taking hours off to carry out family-related responsibilities, is viewed as a factor that can contribute to this successful adaptation.

In a study of the interface between work and family roles, the model presented in Figure 12.1 was tested in 48 countries (Hill, Yang, Hawkins, & Ferris, 2004). The characteristics of

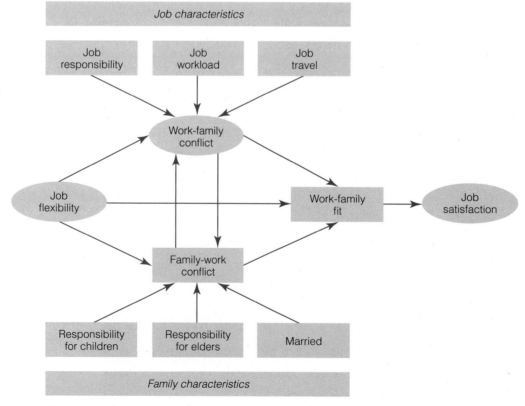

FIGURE 12.1 A Model of the Work-Family Interface
Source: Hill, Yang, Hawkins, and Ferris, 2004, Fig. 1, p. 1302.

a job that were hypothesized to produce work-family conflict were job responsibility, job workload, and job travel. The characteristics of the family that were hypothesized to produce family-work conflict were responsibility for children, responsibility for elders, and being married. The model was tested by analyzing survey responses of more than 25,000 IBM workers, whose average age was 39. The countries were divided into 11 Eastern countries with a collectivist orientation, and 3 groups of countries with a more individualist orientation: Western developing countries, Western affluent countries, and the United States.

The results of this study showed that the model was a good fit for all four groups of countries. The three job characteristics were significantly related to work-family conflict across all 48 countries, although the strength of the relationship was greater in the three individualist groups of countries. Responsibility for children and elders was related to family-work conflict across all the countries, but this relationship was stronger for women than for men. Contrary to expectations, marriage was related to less family-work conflict across all the countries. Job flexibility was associated with less work-family conflict in the Eastern countries and the Western developing countries, but not in the Western affluent countries or the United States. Across all the countries, work was much more likely to create conflict in family life than family life was to be disruptive for work. The general model was a good predictor of job satisfaction across these very different work environments. One might ask whether the global corporate environment of IBM might have smoothed out some of the cultural variations that would have been observed had workers been drawn from a greater diversity of businesses. However, this research is a very exciting beginning in trying to understand the dynamics of work-family interactions at a global level.

This cross-national study also adds to a growing literature documenting that women are more distressed by family-work conflict than are men, possibly because responsibilities for household and child care continue to rest more on the shoulders of employed women than on those of employed men (Voydanoff, 2004). Nonetheless, trends in the United States are moving toward a more egalitarian model. Men and women increasingly agree on the value of having women in the labor market and the importance of family-friendly workplace policies. Employed men are spending an increasing amount of time on household and child care tasks, both on workdays and nonworkdays.

Between 1977 and 2002, the gap between the amount of time women and men spent on household tasks decreased from 3 hours to 1 hour on nonworkdays and from 2.5 hours to 1 hour on workdays. As men spend more time on child care tasks, the result is that children actually have more time with a parent than they did in 1977 (Barnett, 2004).

Balancing work and family life is challenging; it involves the interface of multiple, interacting systems—each partner's work environment, each partner's role demands within the family, and the partners' relationships with one another and with their children. For example, one study found that for professional couples with children, when husbands were required to work long hours at their job, the probability of the wife quitting her job increased (Cha, 2010). Another study demonstrated the impact of workload on parents and their children. When mothers worked long hours and felt overloaded, they were less warm and accepting toward their adolescent children. When fathers worked long hours

After the birth of her twins, Karen decided to try working from home. She balances work and family life by having a babysitter 3 half days and trying to work on small projects for a half hour here and there while the twins are awake. The twins love their mom's computer and are eager to help.

LWA-JDC/CORBIS

and felt overloaded, they experienced more conflict with their adolescent children. Husbands' negative work-related stressors also increased their wives' sense of overload beyond what the wives were experiencing because of their own work situation (Crouter & Bumpus, 2001). Thus, for wives, balancing work and family life required coping with their husband's experiences of work-related strain as well as their own.

The ability to bring positive energy from work to family and vice versa is a product of individual and workplace characteristics. Taking the individual perspective, Ellen Galinsky (2007) has coined the term *dual-centric* to describe people who put the same emphasis and priority on their work and their personal lives. These people are equally likely to be men and women. They are more likely to have children at home, and they spend an average of about 5 hours a week more at home than those who place a higher priority on work than on their personal lives. These dual-centric individuals feel more successful at work and at home, and by objective measures such as their level in the organization or their salary, feel equally successful as those who place a greater priority on their work. In comparison to those who place a higher priority on either their work or their personal lives, fewer dual-centric people experience moderate or high levels of stress, and fewer say that they find it difficult to manage their multiple roles. In interviews with these dual-centric adults, Galinsky found that they were very clear and intentional about having both domains as priorities in their lives, they set some clear boundaries between the domains, they practiced being emotionally as well as physically present in the sphere where they were functioning at the time, and they took time to rest or redirect their energy away from work from time to time.

Although much of the responsibility for managing multiple roles falls to individuals, **work-family facilitation** is also supported by resources in the workplace that make it easier for employees to address pressing family demands within the scope of their daily work (Voydanoff, 2004). When the workplace is organized to recognize and sustain the multiple role responsibilities of employees, people are likely to experience an increase in their sense of self-worth, competence, and fulfillment, resulting in a more positive outlook on their interpersonal relationships at home and greater productivity at work. For example, policies that allow workers to take family-related leaves without risking their job security, or to take time off during the day to take a child to the doctor or meet with a teacher, reduce work-family conflict. A supportive work climate in which supervisors help workers feel comfortable about using these family-flexible policies and accommodating significant family obligations contribute to work-family facilitation. Given that most people in middle adulthood are expected to be functioning in multiple roles, it makes sense that the responsibility for success in achieving an effective balance between work and family demands should rest not only on the coping strategies of individuals but on the policies and climate of the work setting.

Nurturing an Intimate Relationship

Objective 2. To examine the process of maintaining a vital, intimate relationship in middle adulthood, especially a commitment to growth, effective communication, creative use of conflict, and preserving passion.

Although people derive a significant sense of personal identity from their jobs and may worry a lot about them, happiness in an intimate relationship is a stronger predictor of overall well-being in adulthood than is satisfaction with work. According to a survey conducted by the AARP (American Association of Retired Persons, 2010), over 90% of men and 86% of women in middle adulthood reported that having a good relationship with a spouse or partner was very important to their quality of life. Marriage and other long-term intimate bonds are salient, dynamic relationships. They change as the partners mature, as the family constellation changes, and in response to changing events, including family crises and historical events. Focus and effort are required to keep these relationships healthy and vital throughout middle adulthood.

What is a **vital marriage**? Drawing on a variety of studies of long-lasting marriages, four themes have been identified as contributing to long-lasting, happy marriages: the characteristics of the individual partners, the nature of the partners' interpersonal interactions, the partners' commitment to nurturing the future of the relationship, and the preservation of passion in the relationship (Crooks & Bauer, 2005).

Characteristics of the Partners

Happy marriages are built on love and affection between two people who are basically even tempered and warm hearted (Huston & Melz, 2004). They are not overly anxious, depressed, or impulsive. They are nurturing, expressive, gentle, understanding, and conscientious. They care about each other, rather than being self-absorbed or indifferent to one another's fate. These individuals also contribute other types of social capital that help sustain the relationship. For example, they may have a supportive network of family members and friends, they may contribute financial resources to the family, they are cooperative rather than domineering in the way they participate in decision making, or they bring unique competencies to the tasks of household maintenance (Edin, 2000).

Partners' Interpersonal Interactions

The couple must develop an effective communication system. This requires adequate opportunities for interaction. If competing life roles, including work and parenting, dramatically reduce opportunities for interaction, the couple will risk drifting apart. They will have increasingly fewer shared experiences and be less readily influenced by each other's observations and reactions. Studies of the correlates of marital happiness find that there is a reciprocal relationship between interaction and happiness. In a longitudinal study, couples who were happier early in their marriage showed higher levels of interaction in later years (Zuo, 1992). After a number of years of marriage, the two variables were strong predictors of each other: Those who were happy were involved in more frequent interactions, and, similarly, those who were involved in frequent interactions were happier.

John Gottman and his colleagues have conducted a number of studies to examine the nature of interactions among heterosexual married couples. Their technique involves videotaping couples as they discuss a difficult issue in their marriage. At the same time, they gather physiological data, including changes in heart rate and blood pressure. The couples are followed in later years of their marriage using surveys and interviews. Based on their research, they have been able to predict with a high degree of accuracy whether couples will separate in the first few years of their marriage or stay together (Gottman, Coan, Carrere, & Swanson, 1998; Gottman & Silver, 2000; Driver, Tabares, Shapiro, Nahm, & Gottman, 2003).

Gottman found that enduring relationships are characterized by a high ratio of positive to negative interactions. Couples in satisfied marriages did argue, but the balance of five positive statements to one negative statement was an important constant in predicting relationship stability. In stable, satisfied heterosexual couples, the woman tends to use a gentle, diplomatic beginning when she introduces a problem or concern, and the man accepts his wife's influence. When the woman expresses contempt, is overly negative, or aggressive, and the man is overly domineering or defensive in the face of conflict, the relationship is less likely to endure.

For couples that do not have an effective communication system, resentments tend to accumulate with no opportunity to resolve them. A common pattern is that the wife wants to talk things over, but the husband does not see what good this will do. Harmonious, satisfied couples listen to and consider each other's problems. They validate each other's concerns by expressing understanding, even if they cannot offer solutions. Dissatisfied couples, on the other hand, avoid problems or engage in counterattack. Instead of validating the spouse's concern, the partner raises complaints and criticisms, or withdraws. Over the years, expressions of affection, enjoyment, laughter, and support decline. Even if negative or critical interactions do not increase, they are embedded in a less positive overall context. The ideal 5 to 1 ratio may drop to 3 or 2 to 1, making the negative interactions more salient. This takes the couple along the path to marital disruption.

Partners' Commitment to Nurturing the Future of the Relationship

In order for a marriage to last over the long period of middle and later adulthood, the partners have to see a long-term commitment as one of their values. Research on cohabitation and research on marriage stability among children whose parents divorced both illustrate contexts in which adults may view

Omar and Vidya have been married for ten years, and they have two young children. He works as a field agent for the gas company. She works from home as a copywriter for a catalog company. This allows her to devote time and attention to caring for the children and managing the household. They are still deeply in love and delight in sharing a few moments to cuddle and laugh together.

marriage as a more temporary alliance than as a lifelong relationship. Assuming that couples share this view of their relationship as long term, the partners must learn to work toward change in areas where it is possible, and to accept one another and the characteristics of the relationship in areas where change cannot be accomplished. By expanding their tolerance for differences and admiration for their strengths, couples can achieve new levels of intimacy. Research by Wallerstein and Blakeslee (1995) on long-lasting, satisfying marriages identified a set of psychosocial tasks that couples have to master. Salient in this list are the following challenges:

- Preserving a balance between intimacy in the couple and autonomy for the individuals
- Expanding the bonds of affection to include children while preserving and nurturing the couple relationship
- Shifting the focus of energy from the family of origin to the newly formed family while preserving relationships with the extended kinship network

Image copyright Monkey Business Images 2010. Used under license from Shutterstock.com

- Managing the adversities in life, such as serious illness, death, or disaster, in ways that strengthen the relationship
- Sharing laughter and delight in daily life

The partners must be committed to growth both as individuals and as a couple. This means that they accept the idea that they will change in important ways and that the relationship, too, will change. Within any enduring relationship, each person experiences a dynamic tension between pressures and desires for personal growth on the one hand and the pressures and desires to preserve the relationship on the other hand. Both of these forces have the potential to overwhelm or dominate the sense of mutuality, as is illustrated in the case study on the struggle for commitment to growth in a vital marriage. A vital marriage requires both partners to be open to the need to be themselves (as they continue to discover new dimensions of self) and an energizing, interpersonal chemistry that is resilient even in the face of the harshest challenges.

CASE STUDY

THE STRUGGLE FOR COMMITMENT TO GROWTH IN A VITAL MARRIAGE

One common example of the need to permit individual growth within a marriage occurs when a woman who has been primarily responsible for child care and household management expresses an interest in entering or returning to the paid labor force.

Annette, who had worked as a nurse before she married, decided that it was time to go back to work. Her three children were in elementary and middle school, and her husband had a full-time job, so she was by herself for long hours during the day. She began to feel depressed and jealous of everyone else's active lives, so she took a position at a local hospital, working three afternoons and on Saturday each week.

At first, her husband, Gary, fussed and resisted. "Why did she need to go to work?" he asked. They didn't really need the money, and Gary liked to know that she would be at home when he came back from work. He wasn't used to having to take the kids to their activities after school. Plus, Saturday used to be his day to hang out with his friends from work. The kids fussed at being asked to get dinner ready. But Annette insisted that she had to get back to work—her mental health and happiness depended on it.

The first months were terrible. Annette wondered if she were doing the right thing, and Gary used every trick in the book to lure her back to the house. But there was no denying the value of this new job for Annette's self-confidence, her renewed feeling of personal identity, and her ability to return to the home with new energy and enthusiasm for her husband, children, and family life. Gary began to get more involved in the children's lives and actually looked forward to the Saturdays they spent together. Soon the children began to see their mother in a new light, as a professional who took

care of other people as well as them. They also felt a new surge of independence in being able to handle the dinner meal on their own. Gary and Annette felt closer to each other as a result of Annette's self-confidence and Gary's new level of involvement in the lives of the children.

CRITICAL THINKING AND CASE ANALYSIS

1. What features of a vital marriage are evident in this case? What features of a vital marriage are missing?
2. What are the obstacles to continued growth for Annette in this case?
3. How might childrearing responsibilities prevent new growth for women or men in middle adulthood?
4. How does Annette's decision lead to new opportunities for growth for Gary and her children?
5. What are some alternatives that Annette might have considered that could have satisfied her needs for continued growth and perhaps been less disruptive for her family?
6. Imagine that Gary had been the one looking for a new structure—perhaps going into business for himself or going back to school for a new profession. What types of changes might this have caused in the family system? On the marital relationship?

Preserving Passion in a Long-Term Relationship

According to Sternberg's three-dimensional model of love presented in Chapter 11, passion is the first thing to go. However, preserving an erotic and sexual aspect to intimacy continues to play a role in fostering long-term intimate relationships throughout adulthood. Relationship satisfaction is associated with openness about sexual needs, satisfaction with sexual frequency, and experiencing a playful enjoyment of sexual pleasure (Crooks & Bauer, 2005). This means coping with the physiological changes in sexual responsiveness that accompany aging and finding new ways to enjoy sexual contact in the context of parenting demands, chronic illness or disability, or other stressful life events that interfere with one's sexual interest. Results of a recent AARP survey found that having a satisfying sexual relationship was somewhat more important to men than to women in middle adulthood. However, for both men and women, those who had a satisfying sexual relationship had higher life satisfaction than those who did not (AARP, 2010).

Changes in sexual responsiveness over the middle adult years have been well documented (Masters & Johnson, 1966; Crooks & Bauer, 2005). For men, erections take longer to develop, orgasm is less intense, and the erection fades more quickly in midlife than in early adulthood. With age, it may take a longer period, from several hours to days, to experience a new erection. Even though the sexual response changes, orgasm continues to be a source of pleasure. Although there is a reduction in sperm production, most men remain fertile well into very old age. Most men are able to enjoy sexual activity throughout their life, provided that they continue to have a partner.

For some men, periods of illness, certain medications, heart disease, or high blood pressure can interfere with the ability to have an erection. Anxiety about being able to have an erection or a preoccupation with the quality of sexual performance may interfere with the ability to become aroused. The introduction of a variety of new drugs to treat erectile disorders has increased openness and awareness of this problem and provided new avenues for couples to discuss changes in their sexual vitality. One study estimated that 30 million men in the United States have erectile disorder (Levine, 2003). Although the incidence increases with age, usually it is not age itself but the chronic illnesses that are associated with aging and the accompanying medications that account for this relationship.

One of the common changes experienced by men in midlife is inflammation or increased size of the prostate gland. This gland produces fluids that are released during ejaculation. When the prostate becomes enlarged, it may put pressure on the urethra and restrict the flow of urine. A significant number of men experience prostate cancer. Although treatments for prostate cancer vary, they can interfere with sexual functioning (Ofman, 2004).

Physical changes that affect the sexual response also occur for women. At some time during their late forties or in their fifties, women experience the **climacteric**, or the involution and atrophy of the reproductive organs. Many physiological changes accompany the close of fertility, including the cessation of menstruation (*menopause*), gradual reduction in the production of estrogen, atrophy of the breasts and genital tissues, and shrinkage of the uterus (Carroll, 2010). The most commonly reported symptom is a frequent hot flash, a sudden onset of warmth in the face and neck that lasts several minutes. Sometimes it is accompanied by dizziness, nausea, sweating, or headaches. About 75% to 85% of women going through natural menopause report this symptom. Other physiological symptoms are related to the reduction of vaginal fluid and loss of elasticity, sleeplessness, and increased anxiety (Nelson, 2008). The symptoms appear to be closely related to a drastic drop in the production of estrogen. Postmenopausal women produce only one sixth as much estrogen as do women who regularly menstruate.

Several studies on the use of estrogen treatment have found that the administration of this hormone to menopausal women alleviates or even prevents menopausal symptoms. Results of research from the Women's Health Initiative found a relationship of hormone replacement therapy to decreased risk of osteoporosis, cardiovascular disease, and colorectal and lung cancers, but an increased risk of breast cancer. As a result, many physicians have stopped prescribing hormone replacement therapy, and have begun to seek alternative therapies to help reduce severe symptoms of menopause for those women who experience them (Beck, 2008).

The reduction in estrogen is associated with changes in the sexual response cycle. The most noticeable change is decreased lubrication and less expansion of the vagina during the excitement phase. This can cause pain during intercourse and reduced sensitivity, which interfere with sexual pleasure. Although the number of orgasmic contractions may be fewer, orgasm remains a very important and pleasurable experience for postmenopausal women. Without the risk of pregnancy, many women are more enthusiastic about sexual relations after menopause than they were before. As discussed in the box on menopause, the impact of menopause for women is determined in part by its cultural meaning. As with other aspects of an intimate relationship, preserving the sexual dimension requires good communication and a sense of humor.

Nurturing vitality in an intimate relationship throughout adulthood is a long-term challenge. The partners must strive to create continued interest, nurturance, and appreciation for each other even after they have achieved high levels of security, trust, and empathy, so that the components of a loving relationship operate continuously in the relationship. At the same time, they have to encourage and support one another's continuing growth as individuals. The significance of this task is relevant for the ongoing nature of the relationship and the social support it provides as the couple enters later life. The quality of the parents' marital relationship during middle adulthood has significant consequences for the well-being of children in the family and provides the context for the children's emerging understanding of intimacy and marital roles. As children mature into middle childhood and early adolescence, they pay attention to and try to make sense of the quality of their parents' interactions with each other. As children observe their parents, they acquire a sense of how they function as intimate partners as well as parents. Of course, children will not perfectly replicate their parents' marriages. However, the degree of egalitarianism, the approach to conflict resolution, and the expression of affection that children observe can influence their ideas about the kind of partner they seek, their ability to manage conflict in an intimate relationship, and their expectations about marital interaction (Schulz, Pruett, Kerig, & Parke, 2010).

Expanding Caring Relationships

Objective 3. To describe the expansion of caring in middle adulthood as it applies to two specific roles—that of a parent and that of an adult child caring for one's aging parents.

Middle adults have opportunities to express caring in many roles. This section focuses on two of those: parenting, and the care of one's own aging parents. Both domains offer numerous challenges to the intellectual, emotional, and physical resources of the adult caregiver.

Parenting

In parenting, we see the critical intersection of adult development and child development. As parents, adults bring a psychosocial

HUMAN DEVELOPMENT AND DIVERSITY

Menopause

IT IS WELL established that menopause causes recognizable physical changes that an adult woman may view as unpleasant. The severity of symptoms is determined by both the biological changes related to decreases in estrogen production and by the attitude of the culture toward the infertile, older woman. In cultures that reward women for reaching the end of the fertile period, menopause is associated with fewer physiological symptoms. In a study describing the reaction of women in India, menopause was associated with increased social status: "The absence of menstrual flow signaled an incredible elevation of stature for these women. Women were released from a veiled, secluded life in a compound to talk and socialize (even drink) with menfolk. They then became revered as models of wisdom and experience by the younger generation" (Gillespie, 1989, p. 46).

Recent studies support this view that women from different cultural groups have diverse attitudes about menopause that may create a more or less positive context for the end of the reproductive stage of life (Lerner-Geva, Boyko, Blumstein, & Benyamini, 2010).

A woman's attitudes toward aging and her involvement in adult roles influence the ease or difficulty with which she experiences menopause. In U.S. society, for example, a woman who is going through menopause at age 50 may also be experiencing the severe illness or death of her parents and the marriage of her youngest child. The severity of menopausal symptoms and the extent to which women experience changes in their sexual motivation may depend largely on their involvement in a satisfying intimate relationship (Hinchiff, Gott, & Ingleton, 2010).

The majority of publications dealing with menopause focus on issues such as the treatment of symptoms and the pros and cons of hormone replacement therapy (Utian, 2003). Comparatively few studies have focused on the social and psychological correlates of menopause. The tendency in the U.S. medical culture is to treat menopause as an illness or a deficit leading to the loss of reproductive capacity rather than as a normative transition into a new phase of adult life (Rostosky & Travis, 1996).

Women differ in how they interpret the meaning of menopause. Some are embarrassed by the hot flashes when they occur in a public setting. Others see the symptoms of menopause as a reminder that they are aging in a culture that values youth and physical attractiveness in women above other characteristics. An emerging group has recast hot flashes as power surges, suggesting the beginning of a new, competent period of life. In a

---

history of ego strengths and core pathologies, coping skills and defenses, and adequate or inadequate resolutions of previous psychosocial crises to the task of nurturing a child. They have scripts from their own childhood, modified by information from friends, relatives, and experts about how to approach the task. With all this, they have to adapt to the unique temperament, developmental level, and strengths or vulnerabilities of each of their children and to the work, family, cultural, and community contexts in which childrearing is taking place.

Parenting takes place over a long period of time. In a two-parent family, the partners have many opportunities to observe and appreciate each other's approaches to the care, nurturing, and guidance of their children. The concept of a **parenting alliance** has been introduced as a way to capture the importance of the working relationship between the partners as they engage in parenting behaviors. The parenting alliance is defined as "the capacity of a spouse to acknowledge, respect, and value the parenting roles and tasks of the partner" (Cohen & Weissman, 1984, p. 35). As adults establish their parenting alliance, they benefit from knowing that their partner values, trusts, and respects the way they enact their parenting role. The confidence and sense of appreciation that come with this knowledge help adults to engage more joyfully in their parenting and to weather periods of

stress. It also provides a context of reassurance for children who observe the way their parents encourage and sustain each other (Hughes, Gordon, & Gaertner, 2004; McHale, Kuersten-Hogan, & Rao, 2004).

Being a parent is a difficult, demanding task that requires a great deal of learning. Because children are constantly changing and are often unpredictable, adults must be sensitive and flexible in new situations in order to cope successfully with their demands. Each period of the child's development calls for new and innovative parenting strategies. Childrearing experiences are different with each child, and the changing family constellation brings new demands for flexibility and learning. With each successive child, however, there seems to be less anxiety about parenting skills. Children help adults learn about parenting through their responses to their parents' efforts and their own persistence in following the path of development.

Fathering

In the history of the field of family science, the research on parenting has focused almost exclusively on mothers. Most research involved interviews or surveys of mothers, and even when the study used the term *parent*, the informant was typically a mother. In an effort to balance this one-sided view

recent online survey, women from four ethnic groups were asked to describe their menopausal symptoms (Im, Lee, Chee, Dormire, & Brown, 2010). Asian American women reported the fewest symptoms; European American women reported the most. Among African American women, there was a cultural theme of being strong, accepting menopause as a natural process, and keeping silent or downplaying their symptoms. Individual variability was noted, with sensitivity to symptoms linked to the woman's health and concurrent life stressors, as well as her cultural beliefs about the meaning of this transition in her life.

The North American Menopause Society (NAMS) sponsored a Gallup poll of postmenopausal women in the United States. The respondents were divided about equally, with half seeing menopause as a medical condition that required treatment and half seeing it as a natural transition that could be weathered without medical intervention (NAMS, 2010). Another survey sponsored by NAMS found that women had significant misunderstandings about the health risks associated with menopause, but relatively few received information to address their concerns from their health care providers (NAMS, 2010).

For more information about menopause, see the North American Menopause Society website (www .menopause.org).

Critical Thinking Questions

1. What might account for the ways that women differ in their interpretation of the meaning of menopause?
2. What might be some implications of the fact that gynecologists and women patients differ in what they view as the most important concerns or worries associated with menopause? How might these differences influence doctor-patient rapport, treatment strategies, and treatment outcomes?
3. How does menopause relate to the developmental tasks of middle adulthood?
4. Design a study that focuses on either the psychological or social correlates of menopause. How would you approach these research questions? What might be some difficulties about doing research on this topic?
5. Why do you think Indian women experience an increase in status after menopause? What aspects of a culture might be related to attributing higher status and more respect to postmenopausal women than to premenopausal women?

of parenting, a growing literature is clarifying the multidimensional nature of the father role and fathering in middle adulthood (Pleck & Masciadrelli, 2004). Paternal involvement has been characterized along a variety of dimensions, including how men perceive their connection with their children; the frequency and nature of their one-to-one interactions with their children; their responsibility for specific child care needs such as taking children to school, caring for them when they are ill, or helping with homework; and their accessibility when the child wants to initiate interactions. Research has also focused on men's views and values regarding fatherhood, the impact of fathers on children, and the relationship of marital quality to men's competence as fathers.

Most men find personal meaning and emotional support in their roles as husband and father. For many men, the positive quality of their marital and parental roles helps them cope more effectively with the stresses of work (Palkowitz, 2002). In many instances, specific lessons from home—including the patience and communication necessary to be an effective parent, willingness to plan and work out alternative strategies for managing daily tasks with his wife, and the admiration he has for his wife in her paid labor force activities—actually help a man function more effectively at work.

In some families, fathers face a particularly difficult challenge in finding the time to interact effectively with their children. For example, one naturalistic observational study focused on the quality of family interactions in dual earner families when parents returned home from work, and in the evening when everyone was at home. Fathers typically returned home from work later than mothers. When mothers came home from work, they were usually greeted positively by the children who then filled them in on the day's activities. When fathers returned from work, they were greeted positively, but often the children then resumed their activities, and little conversation took place about the events of the day. Over the course of the evening, mothers were more likely to spend time with their children; fathers were more likely to spend time alone (Campos, Graesch, Repetti, Bradbury, & Ochs, 2009). One can infer from this pattern that fathers who want to have a more detailed picture of their children's daily lives may have to develop deliberate strategies for engaging their children in conversations when they are together.

As children get older, fathers and mothers modify their caregiving roles. Fathers tend to become more involved in their children's care, and mothers' involvement decreases somewhat. This is especially true when there are more boys than girls in the family. The more hours mothers work, the more responsibility fathers have for their children. Within the context of a loving marital relationship, the traits associated with a competent, caring parental role are learned and practiced so that fathers become increasingly involved and attuned to their child's needs (Wood & Repetti, 2004; Bradford & Hawkins, 2006; Jacobs & Kelley, 2006).

Developmental Stages of the Family

At each stage of a child's life, the demands on parents change. Infants require constant care and attention. Preschoolers require educational toys and interaction with peers. They can spend a great deal of time in independent play, but they require mindful supervision. Early and middle school-age children require parental reassurance about their skills, talents, and fears. The early adolescent requires less in the way of physical care but needs continuing emotional support and guidance, faces new financial demands, and needs help clarifying academic and personal goals, and facilitating participation in athletics, after-school activities, peer relations, and social life.

For the purposes of this discussion of parenting, we have chosen to consider the potential influences of the phases of family development on adult development. This approach illustrates the links in psychosocial development across generations. It highlights the processes through which the development of children may prompt new growth among parents. Although middle adults might be parenting children of any age, we will focus on the following four periods, which correspond to the most likely transitions that take place as parents age from 34 to 60:

1. The years when children are in early and middle childhood.
2. The years when children are adolescents.
3. The years when children are adults.
4. Grandparenthood.

The Years When Children Are in Early and Middle Childhood. School-age children tap parents' resources for ideas about things to do, places to go, and friends to meet. They seek new experiences in order to expand their competence and investigate the larger world outside the home. The role that parents play in exposing their children to cultural resources such as music, art, travel, theater, and science contributes positively to the children's school achievement, even beyond the impact of the parents' own educational background, beliefs, and expectations (Roscigno & Ainsworth-Darnell, 1999). Parents become active as chauffeurs, secretaries, and sometimes as buffers between their children and the rest of the community.

During this time, parents have many opportunities to function as educators for their children. They actively contribute to their children's academic success through such activities as reading with them, helping them with homework, praising them for school success, and school involvement, including talking with teachers, visiting the school, and participating in school projects. Research on academic success makes it clear that parents' aspirations for their children, their overall parenting skills, and their involvement in their children's education make a substantial contribution to their children's progress (Gutman & Midgley, 2000). Parents who combine appropriate challenges with warmth and support typically have children who are highly motivated, think of themselves as academically capable, and want to do well in school (Bronstein et al., 1998).

Parenting during this period has the potential for boosting an adult's sense of pride in the skills and knowledge already accumulated. Parents are gatekeepers to the resources of the community. They come to see themselves through their children's eyes, as people who know about the world—its rewards, treasures, secrets, and dangers.

Dad is pointing his finger at his adolescent daughter, Roseanne. He is telling her that she needs to change her top because it is inappropriate for her to go to school with this off the shoulder look. She is thinking, "but everyone is dressing like this," but she is afraid to say anything because she doesn't want him to get angrier. Mom is thinking, "Oh, here he goes again." Neil, the son, is looking down and trying to stay out of the interaction. Is this appropriate limit setting? What are the communication problems the family is having?

© Catchlight Visual Services/Alamy

The Years When Children Are Adolescents. Parents tend to view the years of their children's adolescence as extremely trying. Adolescents are likely to seek new levels of behavioral independence. They spend most of the day away from home and apart from adult supervision. As adolescents gain in physical stature and cognitive skills, they are likely to challenge parental authority. During this time, the principles that parents have emphasized as important for responsible, moral behavior are frequently tested. Children are exposed to many voices—including the media, popular heroes and heroines, peers, and school adults—that suggest there may be more than one ideal way to behave and more than one definition of success. Successful parents of adolescents attempt to balance autonomy granting (opportunities for their children to make their own decisions), responsiveness, warmth and support, communication about high standards, and limit setting in the needed proportions so that their children can grow increasingly independent while still being able to rely on an atmosphere of family guidance and reassurance (Steinberg, 2001).

Adolescent children are the front line of each new generation. The questions they raise and the choices they make reflect not only what they have learned, but also what they are experiencing in the present and what they anticipate in the future. Parents of adolescents are likely to feel persistent pressure to reevaluate their own socialization and their effectiveness as parents. Questions are raised about their preparation for their own future as well as their children's. The ego boost parents experienced from being viewed as wise and resourceful when their children were young is likely to be replaced by doubt as they and their children face an uncertain future. Parents who can respond to their adolescents in an open, supportive way can benefit by finding opportunities to clarify their own values. They can begin building new parent-child relationships that will carry them and their emerging adult children into later adulthood.

The Years When Children Are Adults. The period during which children make their own transitions into adulthood results in new patterns of interaction between parents and children and in new opportunities for the middle adult parents. Alternative patterns are clearly evident in current U.S. families, as children take a variety of paths toward self-sufficiency and entry into adult roles. In 2009, 59% of those ages 20 to 24 and 36% of those ages 25 to 29 who were unmarried lived at home with their parents (U.S. Census Bureau, 2010). By the time adult children marry, they are almost always ready to leave the parental home.

Family roles change during this time. Most women enter menopause during this period, bringing a close to the couple's natural childbearing years. The relationship between the parents also changes as parenting activities diminish. Some couples become closer—closer than they have been since they first fell in love. However, divorces also occur after the children leave home. Parents are likely to begin a review and evaluation of their performance as parents as they see the kinds of lives that their children have established for themselves. Erikson (Erikson et al., 1986) found that during this period, many parents continue to build their identities on the accomplishments of their children.

The transitional period during which children leave home does not seem to be a negative time for adults. A woman who was anticipating her children leaving home described her feelings this way:

> From the day the kids are born, if it's not one thing, it's another. After all these years of being responsible for them, you finally get to the point where you want to scream, "Fall out of the nest already, you guys, will you? It's time." It's as if I want to take myself back after all these years—to give me back to me, if you know what I mean. Of course, that's providing there's any "me" left. (Rubin, 1980, p. 313)

Parents are usually pleased as they follow their children's accomplishments. Furthermore, children's independence may permit parents to use their financial resources to enhance their own lifestyle.

Of course, adults maintain certain parental functions during this stage. Many children remain fully or partly financially dependent on their parents during their twenties. If the children are in college or in postgraduate study, their parents may experience greater financial demands than at any earlier period in their parenting history. In many families, parents take on additional jobs and additional loans to meet the financial requirements of their children's education. Children who have left home may not have resolved decisions about occupation and marriage. For them, their parents may remain a source of advice and support as they go through periods of identity and intimacy formation and consolidation. Parents begin to feel the pressure of challenges to their value orientation as their children experiment with new roles and lifestyles. During this stage, parents may serve as sounding boards or as jousting partners in young people's attempts to conceptualize their own lifestyle.

As less time is taken up with direct parenting responsibilities, parents may begin to alter their roles and redirect their energies. However, some parents experience resistance from their children, who expect their parents to remain the same as they themselves change and grow. In many cases, young adult children return home for intervals when they look for a new job, find a new roommate, recover from a love relationship that has ended, return from military service, or drop out of college (Thornton, Young-DeMarco, & Goldscheider, 1993). Throughout these transitions, young adults look to their parents as a source of stability and to their home as a safe harbor while they try to establish their own life structure.

One of the major family events that may occur during this period is the child's decision to cohabit or marry. Parents are expected to accept a new person into their family—their child's intimate partner. Along with this new relationship comes a connection to an entirely new network of relationships, the partner's family. In the United States, most parents have little influence on their child's decisions in this matter. They may find themselves associated through marriage or intimate partnership with a family kinship group that differs significantly from their own or with one that shares many of their own family's beliefs and values.

The first few years of marriage (as discussed in Chapter 11) can be somewhat precarious. Parents may have to reintegrate an adult child into the family at this stage if the marriage is not successful. It can be assumed that a child who leaves a marriage needs some temporary parental reassurance and support in order to regain confidence in the ability to form an intimate relationship. Thus, at times of crisis, middle adults may need to practice parenting skills they have not used for a while and develop new skills in helping their children deal with new challenges.

Grandparenthood. Grandparenthood—the time when an adult witnesses the birth of a new generation—might be considered the beginning of an additional stage in family development. However, the transition to grandparenthood is outside one's own control. Whenever one's children have children of their own, the grandparent becomes alerted to a new sense of ancestry, lineage, and membership in an expanding kinship network. With grandparenthood, adults begin to observe their children as parents. As people reflect on their own roles 20 to 30 years earlier, they may attribute some of their children's successes to their own parenting techniques and may take responsibility for some of the failures, too (Erikson et al., 1986). In Chapter 13 (Later Adulthood), we consider in greater detail the role of grandparenthood and its significance to the adult. Suffice it to say that as grandparents, adults have the opportunity to relate to small children as an expression of the continuity of their lives into the future. Of course, not all grandparents relate to their grandchildren from this philosophical point of view. However, the attainment of the grandparent role has the potential for bringing with it a new perspective on time, purpose, and the meaning of life that may serve as a source of reassurance during later adulthood.

Adults differ in how they define the role of grandparent. They may see themselves as carriers of the family traditions and dispensers of wisdom, as needed experts in child care, as convenient and trusted babysitters, or as admirers from afar. As grandparents, adults are asked to reinvest energy in small children. The quality of the relationship that develops between grandparents and their grandchildren depends not so much on the fact that they are relatives as on the kinds of experiences that the two generations share. Grandparents may also find that the quality of their relationship with their grandchildren is mediated by the child's parents. Especially when the grandchildren are little, the amount of time they spend with their grandparents and the way the grandparents view them are filtered through the quality of the adult relationship that their parents have with their own parents, the grandparents (Brubaker, 1990; Erber, 2005).

Parenting can be stressful. It is full of conflicts and challenges, demanding time that the partners might otherwise spend with each other or in pursuit of their own interests and ambitions. However, parenting generates the kind of conflict that promises an enormous potential for personal growth. By providing a meaningful, responsive context for children, parents have the opportunity to articulate their own value systems and to observe the consequences of their efforts in the continuous development of their children. Psychosocial growth requires a willingness to engage in tasks that may temporarily increase stress, uncertainty, and complexity. Thus, it does not mean turning away from or minimizing tension. It frequently means choosing the challenge that is noticeably difficult or intriguingly complex in hopes of growing while struggling to meet it.

Caring for One's Aging Parents

People tend to regard middle adulthood as a time devoted to future generations. However, another test of one's capacity for generativity comes in the form of commitment to one's aging parents. One of the significant challenges of middle

Grandpa remembers his playing days, and he looks forward to teaching Kyle how to hit, field, and throw.

© 2010 Steve Mason/Jupiterimages Corporation

adulthood is the struggle to respond effectively to one's parents as well as one's children and grandchildren. That is why middle adults are sometimes referred to as the *sandwich generation*, tucked in the middle between caring for one's children and caring for one's aging parents. As one ages from 30 to 50, one's parents may age from 60 to 80. The number of adults over the age of 65 increased from more than 25 million in 1980 to 38.8 million in 2005. The number of adults age 75 and over was about 18.7 million, an increase of 88% since 1980 (U.S. Census Bureau, 2010). It is becoming increasingly likely that middle adults will be involved in meeting the needs of their own aging parents and grandparents. It is also increasingly probable that their aging parents will survive through a period of vigorous and independent later adulthood into a period of frail later life.

What Is Filial Obligation? What is the nature of filial obligation as it is viewed from the perspectives of adult children and their aging parents? Who provides what kinds of help? What characterizes optimal parent-child relationships during this phase of life? **Filial obligation** is a feeling of responsibility to care for one's parents. One way of thinking about filial obligation is that it is a sense of responsibility that adult children have to help their parents as they get old and their physical or mental health declines. Another view is that the sense of filial obligation is a moral sense of duty that arises as one realizes and acknowledges the sacrifices one's parents have made and the sense of indebtedness for those sacrifices. This view is more compatible with the observation that a sense of filial obligation can be very salient in adolescence or early adulthood, not only in middle adulthood when one's parents are aging (Stein, 2009).

What can aging parents expect of their adult children? How do adult children define their responsibilities for their parents? One measure of filial obligation included five components: providing needed assistance, maintaining frequent contact, avoiding conflict, sharing appropriate personal information, and maintaining appropriate levels of self-sufficiency (Stein, 2009). Using this measure with a sample of middle adults whose parents were all living in assisted living communities, researchers found that the kind of help adults provided depended in part on their assessment of their parents' physical and mental health. The healthier the parents, the less sense of obligation the middle adults felt. When middle adults evaluated their parents' mental health as better than average but their physical health as worse, they were more inclined to provide more sharing of personal information. When they evaluated their parents' physical health as better than average but their mental health as worse, they were more inclined to provide assistance. Thus, the adults' sense of obligation was tailored to support their parents' strengths.

The expression of filial obligation is affected by one's culture as well as by the aging parent's well-being. A cross-national study of filial obligation compared responses from 1,200 adults in each of five countries: Norway, England, Germany, Spain, and Israel (Lowenstein & Daatland, 2006). Across all countries, most respondents acknowledged some

© 2010 Rolf Bruderer/Jupiterimages Corporation

Robyn derives a great deal of satisfaction from taking a walk with her mother. Because of physical frailty, her mother lives with her now. Robyn thinks about all the things her mother has done for her and all the sacrifices she made so that Robyn could go to college and have the life she now has. Robyn is very happy to take care of her mother and to still have her mother's company and wisdom.

level of filial obligation, although the extent of support was greater in Spain and Israel than in the northern European countries. The nature of the obligation was varied, more prescriptive in Spain and Israel, and more open to negotiation in the northern countries. Across countries, more help was given to older parents when they were unmarried and suffering from some kind of physical disability. Across countries, help was bidirectional, with aging adults providing emotional and financial support to their adult children as well as receiving support from them.

In fact, studies of intergenerational economic transfers find that, on average, older adults (i.e., those 65 and older) give more in cash and gifts than they receive from younger generations and that it is more likely that an adult child will live in the household of an older parent than the reverse (Litwin, Vogel, Kunemund & Kohli, 2008; Fingerman, Miller, Birditt, & Zarit, 2009).

Who Provides Help? The evidence suggests that daughters assume much more of the responsibility for their aging parents than do sons—including care for their spouse's parents as well as their own (Allen, Blieszner, & Roberto, 2001). This involvement is one element of the basic kin-keeping tasks that have traditionally been incorporated into women's socialization. Daughters are more likely than sons to provide care for their aging parents even when the daughters are employed. However, several structural aspects of an adult child's employment may influence this gender difference (Sarkisian & Gerstel, 2004). Women typically earn less than men, and more men than women are self-employed. Both of these factors predict how much time an adult child will spend helping their aging parents. Adult children who earn lower wages are more likely to take time off to help their aging parent, and adults who are self-employed are less likely to take time off to help their aging parent. Thus, some of the gender difference in caregiving is interdependent with the nature of workplace commitments and demands.

In addition to the amount of time that adult children spend helping their parents, daughters also provide somewhat different kinds of help. Daughters provide more direct care, such as bathing or dressing a parent, as well as emotional support, such as listening to a parent's concerns or helping the parent feel important and loved. However, both sons and daughters are about equally likely to assist in some of the tasks involving relations with health and human service organizations, scheduling medical checkups, and reviewing insurance and other financial matters. Research shows that aging adults who have three or more children—whether they are sons or daughters—are more likely to end up living with one of them than are adults with fewer than three children. However, for other forms of support, such as receiving telephone calls, visiting, and help in daily tasks, older adults who have one daughter receive more support than those who have only sons (Spitze & Logan, 1990).

Although adult children provide much of the family support to aging parents, young adult grandchildren also report a sense of filial obligation and participate in the caregiving role (Fruhauf, Jarrott, & Allen, 2006). In a qualitative study of 17 grandchildren ages 21 to 29 who were actively involved in their grandparents' care, some began to take a more active role when another family member was no longer able to help. Eleven said that they respected and valued the time their grandparents spent with them as children, and this was a way for them to reciprocate.

Josh, who has been caring for his paternal grandparents since he started driving, voiced the sentiment of several grandchildren when he stated, "It just felt like it was what I was supposed to do. They helped me out … helped raise me and so now they need us…. Now it is time to give back" (Fruhauf et al., 2006, p. 899).

What Factors Promote an Optimal Relationship Between Adults and Their Aging Parents? The
nature of the continuing relationship between adult children and their aging parents is not focused solely on caregiving. The norms of independence and self-sufficiency are strong among the current aging population, many of whom state that they do not need assistance from their adult children. However, when asked whom they view as their preferred source of assistance should they need it, aging parents mention their children first, before their friends, siblings, or other relatives. Likewise, adult children view themselves as being primarily responsible for meeting their parents' needs; however, most do not expect to have to meet a variety of such needs (Zarit & Eggebeen, 2002).

In adulthood, preserving and building a positive parent-child relationship is a dyadic process in which both middle adults and aging parents may need to gather new information and change old behaviors (Lyons, Zarit, Sayer, & Whitlach, 2002; AgriLife Extension, 2010). Thinking back to later adolescence and early adulthood, children may feel a sense of obligation to their parents, but they may not be in a position to reciprocate for the many ways their parents have helped them. During those stages of life, they continue to be dependent on their parents for emotional and instrumental support. However, sometime during early and middle adulthood, a socioemotional transition occurs. Now, in middle adulthood, adult children are likely to have achieved a greater sense of independence from their parents, and to have the experience and resources needed to assist them in some valued ways.

However, the relationship of adults and their aging parents has a history. For some, this history is one of a positive attachment, mutual positive regard, and experiences in which parents skillfully balanced autonomy-granting and closeness to create a family environment in which the children could emerge with the resources needed to form a strong personal identity. In other families, children formed an insecure attachment, they feel rejected or undermined by their parents, and they emerge into adulthood with strong feelings of resentment or rebellion toward their parents. Their relationships with their parents are never close as children go off on their own, and interactions become increasingly infrequent. These antecedents will influence the quality of filial obligation and the context in which any kind of relationship between an adult child and their aging parent can take shape.

Building on the past, adult children and aging parents may find that they have predictable areas of conflict. In a desire to reduce conflict, adults and aging parents may need to improve their approach to communication, or redefine the problem so that it does not continue to disrupt a caring relationship. Similarly, adult children and aging parents need to identify the activities they enjoy together, and talk openly about how much time they want to spend together. For some parent-child bonds, a few hours a week or a weekend visit every so often may be all that is desired; for others, daily contact may be pleasant and satisfying. Adult children need to learn more about the changes associated with aging, and begin to identify specific aspects of their parent's mental or physical health that may be impacted by aging. Aging parents need to learn more about the demands and stressors their children are facing in order to appreciate the constraints these demands place on their child's helping behaviors.

Adult children are sometimes in a position of trying to supplement the care and support they provide their parents by coordinating social services and interacting with various public agencies. Many feel unprepared for this aspect of the caring relationship (Zarit & Eggebeen, 2002). They are not comfortable dealing with hospitals, insurance agencies, social service agencies, or residential treatment facilities. However, when older adults require the services of these organizations, their adult children typically know their parents' unique needs and are among the best people to interpret them for service providers. Through such contacts, middle adults have the opportunity to modify and improve the services offered by these agencies, making them more effective for future generations of aging adults.

Research on caregiving within the family has begun to examine the rewards as well as the costs in this relationship (Robertson, Zarit, Duncan, Rovine, & Femia, 2007). Although quite a bit of attention has been given to caregiver strain, caregivers experience both positive and negative aspects of this role. The costs may include feelings of exhaustion, never having time for oneself, feeling overwhelmed by the demands of multiple roles, or experiencing the physical strain of caregiving. Rewards of the caregiving role may include feelings of being appreciated, putting life's demands into a new perspective, or feeling closer to the care recipient. In some cases, the care recipient is able to exchange resources with the caregiver, for example, by providing babysitting time for help with the grocery shopping. In a study of the costs and rewards experienced by children and spouses who were caring for an aging parent or partner, adult children experienced more rewards in their caregiving role than did spouses, and women experienced more caregiving costs than did men. An unexpected finding was that for women, companionship from their spouse was an especially rewarding response from the care recipients (i.e., their husbands). Thus, the research underscores the reciprocal nature of caregiving, with rewards and costs flowing in both directions (Raschick & Ingersoll-Dayton, 2004). These ideas are reflected in the case study of a daughter caring for her ailing mother.

CASE STUDY

A DAUGHTER CARES FOR HER AILING MOTHER

Lois Lyles reflects on what she learns from her mother as she provides care during her mother's last days of life.

Mama is down, I am up. Up, and up, and up. She wants Vaseline for her char-dry lips, her St. Francis church bulletin, her rosary. The vase on the dresser must be moved out of the way of the black-faced digital clock. Two twenty-five, New

Year's afternoon. She stares at the red numerals each like an imp or an infernal flame, as the five becomes a six; the six, a seven. "Water the plants, Lois."

Nervously, I dribble water into the flower pots. I work fast. She has approximately one request every three minutes.

"Thank you, darling. I feel so worthless and useless. Why can't I do anything?"

"Mama, you are not worthless. You are a beautiful person. You still look beautiful to me," I say, and mean it. She was my childhood idol. Her soulful-eyed, smooth-haired beauty was my first acquaintance with romance.

"No, I'm not," she whimpers; then says, "Thank you, darling."

"Mama, whatever happens, I'm with you, and I'm for you." She cries. Her misery makes me recall how my fear of death had once made me, to my mortal shame, abandon a sick woman I loved. I am the namesake of Mama's sister Florence, who died of cancer four summers ago. Florence is my middle name. Mama must be thinking of Aunt Flo, too, for she says, "I took care of Sister when she went up to her bedroom three days before she died and never came downstairs again. I remember she was amazed that I would wash her down there, you know, her private parts. She didn't want me to have to do that." After pausing, my mother adds, "I thought, Lois, it would help you after this is over, to be with me now when I need you, and do things for me."

I am astonished at her, the good mother. She has called me to her sickbed, not so much as to help her as to help *me*. I, in childhood, was never hungry, never homeless, never seriously ill; and was never exposed to the sight of physical suffering. My parents had made sure of all that. But an easy ride of a life is only a half-truth. Now, Mama's gift is to let me know her pain. She is letting me see if I am strong enough to grapple, by proxy, with Death (Lyles, 1991, p. 242).

CRITICAL THINKING AND CASE ANALYSIS

1. How would you describe the costs of caregiving in this case?
2. How would you describe the rewards of caregiving in this case?
3. From what you can gather, what is the quality of the mother-daughter relationship in this case?
4. What role might caring for her dying mother play in Lois's development as an adult?

Managing the Household

Objective 4. To analyze the tasks required for effective management of the household and the diversity of households, including blended families, single-parent families, and adults who live alone.

Household is a term that describes an entity that is created by people for a particular style of living. Households are bounded units that pool their resources, earn and spend

HUMAN DEVELOPMENT AND DIVERSITY

The Hindu Joint Family

THE ORGANIZATION of the joint family, including the special role of the man as head of the whole family and the woman as head of the household, is internalized as children grow up and is transformed into a commitment to daily activities in the transition to adulthood.

A Hindu joint family involves the sharing of the same household territory by the parallel kin and their offspring (brothers or sisters, their spouses, and their children). Two lines of dominance—male and female—are mutually intertwined, both honoring the age of the participants. . . . Under the traditional pattern of authority, the eldest male member of the joint family was considered the head of the whole family. He had authority over others—yet not unlimited authority. He could not use the power arbitrarily, without collectively coordinating his decisions. In the second generation, the eldest son used to hold a superior position among the other male members of the family, yet had a position subordinate to the head and the elder women. Thus, decisions within a joint family relied on making of coalitions between less and more powerful members of the family. The age-respecting dominance system allowed the older members of the family—particularly the older women—remarkable power. . . .

The particular system of social relations within a Hindu joint family created a collective cultural meaning system of attributing high value to becoming a mother-in-law. . . . Becoming a mother-in-law meant takeover of the running of the whole joint family system in the sphere of home life. Becoming a mother-in-law obviously required passing through the phase of being a daughter-in-law in the joint family of one's husband. Despite the heavy workload involved in the phase, women in the daughter-in-law phase of their lives internalize the value and positive expectations for the "promotion" to the upcoming role of mother-in-law, which is the state of "mature adulthood" in the Hindu life course. (Valsiner, 2000, p. 89)

As the female elders in a joint household, women are expected to supervise their daughters-in-law, and daughters-in-law subject themselves to the power and guidance of their mothers-in-law. Daughters-in-law make all the meals, sweep the house, make the bread, serve each person as he or she arrives at the home for each meal, and wash the dishes. In response to real and symbolic acts of service, the mother-in-law makes sure her daughter-in-law's needs are met, allows her time to visit her own family, buffers her from any jealousy or bickering from other family members, and gives her blessings. A daughter-in-law's status increases when she gives birth to a son (Gardiner & Kosmitzki, 2005).

Critical Thinking Questions

1. In this description of the Hindu joint family, the oldest male is referred to as the head of the family. What do you imagine is his role? What are his rights and responsibilities? What kinds of socialization experiences might prepare a man to become head of his family?

2. What might be some challenges to the social system of the Hindu joint family if an Indian family immigrates to the United States?

3. How might modernization and the increased involvement of women in the labor market alter the balance of gender roles in the Hindu joint family?

4. What are some similarities and differences between the organization of the Hindu joint family and the family in which you grew up? What was the power hierarchy in the family? How were men and women's roles defined and coordinated?

5. The decisions in a Hindu joint family require the family to form coalitions across gender and age categories. How might such a coalition form? How might it operate, for example, around the selection of a marriage partner for an oldest son or a decision about sending a son or daughter to college?

6. How might the organization of the Hindu joint family influence gender role preference for Hindu males and females?

---

money, interact with the labor market, and engage in social interaction with their neighbors (Wallerstein & Smith, 1991). The household provides a basic life structure for people in all cultures. The box on the Hindu joint family illustrates the way that household management is culturally constructed, based on norms for gender, age, and kinship ties. The demands and tasks of household management call forth responses that stimulate cognitive, social, and personal development during adulthood. The household is not only a physical setting, but also a shared psychological context for a group of people. In nomadic tribal groups, for example,

the continuity of the household is preserved by the group of people and their shared belongings even though the location of the household changes. The capacities to maintain a household and to nurture household members reflect the leadership skills, creativity, and self-reliance that are characteristics of maturity in middle adulthood.

Management of the household refers to all the planning, problem solving, and activities adults undertake in order to take care of themselves and others who are entrusted to their care. At present, society's ability to recognize and value the accomplishments linked to the management of the household is poorly developed. At the same time, more emphasis is being placed on the centrality of the home environment in fostering intellectual development, social competence, health, and emotional well-being.

The household system has the potential for providing an environment that facilitates human growth and mental health. Learning to create such an environment is a developmental task of the middle adult years. Households have the potential for much greater variety and flexibility than most work settings. However, many of the tasks required for household maintenance are tedious, physically demanding, repetitive, and time consuming. Over the past 40 years, as women have become more intensively involved in the labor market, research has focused on how much time people spend at the tasks of household maintenance and who is performing those tasks.

Managing Resources and Meeting Needs

Data gathered through daily time diaries provide a picture of the amount of time devoted to various household tasks and the involvement of men and women in those tasks (Bureau of Labor Statistics, 2010). These data help clarify the diversity of household tasks, the amount of time devoted to those tasks, and the way the division of labor between men and women is played out in the management of the household. Table 12.2 shows the average percentage of men and women who are engaged in various household-related activities each day. Table 12.3 shows the average number of hours spent in each activity per day by those who perform the activity. With the exception of lawn and garden care, a greater percentage of women than men are engaged in household activities, purchasing services and goods, caring for and helping household members, and communicating through telephone, mail, and e-mail. However, when men are involved in these activities, they spend almost the same amount of time at them as do women.

In comparison to patterns of time use from the 1960s, fewer hours are devoted to household tasks overall, and

TABLE 12.2 The Average Percentage of the Respondents Who Engaged in the Activity Per Day

	MEN	WOMEN	TOTAL
Eating and drinking	96.1	96.8	96.4
Household activities	66.6	85.0	76.1
Housework	20.2	51.3	36.3
Food preparation and clean up	39.9	68.3	54.6
Lawn and garden care	11.5	7.4	9.4
Household management	16.4	21.6	19.1
Purchasing goods and services	39.2	49.2	44.4
Caring for and helping household members	20.2	29.9	25.2
Telephone calls, mail and e-mail	19.6	31.4	25.7

Source: Bureau of Labor Statistics, 2010. American Time Use Series, 2009 results.

TABLE 12.3 The Average Hours Per Day for People Who Engaged in the Activity

	MEN	WOMEN	TOTAL
Eating and drinking	1.31	1.23	1.27
Household activities	2.0	2.63	2.36
Housework	1.27	1.79	1.65
Food preparation and clean up	.73	1.13	.99
Lawn and garden care	2.42	1.67	2.11
Household management	.67	.72	.70
Purchasing goods and services	1.63	1.78	1.71
Caring for and helping household members	1.81	2.34	2.13
Telephone calls, mail and e-mail	.71	.80	.77

Source: Bureau of Labor Statistics, 2010. American Time Use Series, 2009 results.

more time is devoted to child care by both men and women. Dual-career couples are more likely to purchase services for household tasks, and are especially likely to order in meals or to eat out as a way of saving time. The drop in the number of hours dedicated to household tasks among women is not solely due to women's participation in the labor market; the decline in hours of household work was greater over time for those who were not employed than for those who were (Casper & Bianchi, 2002).

The challenge of household management is to create an environment that supports both individual and group functioning. The significance of the household can be appreciated by thinking about the consequences of its absence, especially in the case of homeless individuals and families (see the box on homelessness), or in crises such as hurricanes, fires, or floods when people are displaced from their homes. Management of the household, much like the workplace, requires leadership in order to set priorities and goals, manage resources, and operationalize plans. The scarcer the resources, the greater the pressure on the adult to make careful decisions and to find creative solutions to the daily challenges of meeting the household's physical and psychological needs. Leadership begins as adults model the process of shared decision making and children (if there are any) learn to participate in problem solving. Household members discover ways to work together to achieve a shared vision of the future. The home environment is the first place where many children discover that they can have a voice. Parents can create a family atmosphere in which the spirit of democracy comes alive through a careful balance of freedom and responsibility, respect for individuality, and commitment to the welfare of others.

Building Networks and Coalitions

One of the most difficult and subtle kinds of new learning that occurs during middle adulthood is the development of an understanding of how the structures of other organizations affect one's life and the lives of family members. These other organizations may include (1) members of the extended family (e.g., one's in-laws), (2) other families, (3) business or work-related associations, (4) religious groups, (5) educational groups, and (6) community groups. This concept was introduced briefly in Chapter 2 in describing Bronfenbrenner's (1979) model of the *mesosystem*. The family is interconnected with other social systems that can expand its resources. Its contact with social groups must include the maintenance of goodwill and some evidence of group identification and commitment. Social groups also generate norms that may make demands on the family. Hence, adults must be able to protect the family from excessive external demands, while retaining valuable and satisfying external relationships.

Families differ in their investment in relationships outside the family unit. In some households, the nuclear family is more important than any other group. Such households expend little energy outside the family boundaries. At the other extreme are families who are involved in a number of community groups and who incorporate their extended families into frequent group activities. In some families, each person is encouraged to establish a group of close friends. In others, each person's friends are screened or evaluated by the other family members. The adult's task is to define the family's preferred stance toward other social groups and to create opportunities to build desired relationships.

APPLYING THEORY AND RESEARCH TO LIFE

Homelessness

THE TERM **HOMELESS** refers to people who have no permanent resting place and no private space (Nunez, 2004). Although many estimates focus on individuals who are living on the streets, in emergency shelters, or in transitional housing, there are also individuals who are living with friends or relatives, moving from one location to the next every few weeks. It is very difficult to assess the exact number of people who experience homelessness; the numbers often reflect a specific point in time rather than a lifetime estimate. In 2007, the National Alliance to End Homelessness reported a point in time estimate of 744,313 people experiencing homelessness in January 2005 (National Coalition for the Homeless, 2009). This count did not include people who were in shelters for abused women, people who were living in outdoor areas typically inhabited by the homeless, people who may have avoided the shelter on that day in order to prevent being counted, and people who were housed in some other form of temporary housing with family and friends. In some locations, many people who seek shelter cannot be accommodated. A survey by the U.S. Conference of Mayors (2008) reported that in 12 of 23 cities surveyed, emergency shelters and transitional housing units had to turn people away due to lack of capacity. Thus, efforts to count the homeless,

even on a specific day, are likely to be inaccurate. Since homelessness is usually temporary, another approach is to make annual projections. The Urban Institute (2000) estimated that each year about 2.5 million people are homeless in October and 3.5 million in February. Roughly 38% of those who are included in this count are children. The National Coalition for the Homeless provides information about this and other aspects of homelessness on its website (www.nationalhomeless.org).

The majority of the homeless population, roughly three fourths, is single men. However, the fastest growing segment of the homeless population is families with children. A survey of 23 U.S. cities in 2007 found that families with children comprised 23% of the homeless, with another 5% who were unaccompanied minors (U.S. Conference of Mayors, 2008). The proportion of families with children who are homeless is estimated to be higher in rural areas.

A combination of three major factors contributes to the continued risk of homelessness for families with children in the United States: (1) the decline in the value of the minimum wage, coupled

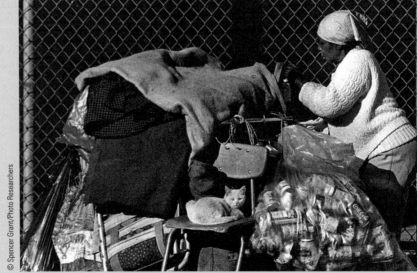

© Spencer Grant/Photo Researchers

Louise earns a bit of money by redeeming aluminum cans. Because of her cat, she cannot be admitted to a shelter, so she keeps her belongings close by in her cart and sleeps outdoors.

Preserving relationships within the extended family is a delicate matter. This is the realm of family politics. In close family relations, it is likely that positive feelings of warmth and affection are coupled with negative feelings of irritation and aggravation (Fingerman, Hay, & Birditt, 2004). Failed expectations about courtesies and obligations or thoughtless insults and slights from family members are typical stressors that occur within the family network. Family members may have opposing political, religious, or childrearing views; they may have competing motivations; or they may try to form alliances among family subgroups. When children decide to marry, they bring two family networks together that may or may not get along. Parents may or may not convey support to their child's partner or spouse; sisters and brothers have partners who may or may not support each other. Likewise, parents may divorce and remarry, bringing one family system into contact with another. All these transitions introduce challenges to sustaining valued coalitions within the extended family and protecting the family from disruptive forces.

Much of this chapter has focused on two-adult families, especially those with children, often in the dual-earner arrangement. In the following sections, three alternative forms of households are described: remarriage and blended families, one-parent families, and single person households, each of which poses unique opportunities and challenges for household management.

with the prevalence of insecure jobs with few or no benefits (an estimated 22% of homeless people are employed); (2) the decline in the availability and value of social welfare benefits; and (3) shortages in low-income housing and public-assistance housing (National Coalition for the Homeless, 2009). The recent increase in foreclosures has placed even more families at risk for homelessness.

Paths toward homelessness for families are diverse. Some of the most common precursors are job loss, domestic violence, substance abuse, mental illness, and divorce. Although some homeless individuals are in a sudden crisis, many have stumbled from one temporary living situation to the next, and others have never been able to establish a permanent home. Some of these people are singularly alone and unable to develop minimal social relationships. This is an unusual phenomenon, because most people have some ability to have meaningful social relationships. Among homeless mothers, for example, many have friends or family, but cannot count on them for housing support. For some, the nature of their housing crisis may disrupt their social network, making it impossible to ask for help from family or friends. Following an episode of homelessness, some families are relocated far from their social network, making it likely that they will become vulnerable to homelessness in the future (Toohey, Shinn, & Weitzman, 2004). As a result

of victimization earlier in their lives, some women suffer from a degree of emotional dysfunction, exacerbated by the use of alcohol and drugs. An estimated 10% to 15% of homeless parents have a problem with drug addiction, making it difficult for them to hold a job, sustain a relationship, or be approved for low-cost housing (Nunez, 2004).

In homelessness, society confronts a painful example of psychosocial stagnation—the inability of mature adults to meet their basic needs for shelter, food, and clothing—combined with its own failure to prevent their condition from reaching this degree of vulnerability. In the face of the cultural value placed on independence, self-sufficiency, and hard work, U.S. society has difficulty making effective public responses. In fact, national policies have operated to increase homelessness and the stressors of living on the streets. Since 1975, there has been a steady and dramatic decrease in the funding for low-income rural and urban housing accompanied by the loss of low-cost units that qualify for public assistance (WRAP, 2007). Over this time, a growing number of cities have enacted laws that criminalize homelessness. These laws make it illegal to sleep, camp, eat, beg, or store personal belongings in public places. The police make periodic sweeps of areas known as gathering places for the homeless, forcing them to leave their personal belongings and to move to

outlying areas (National Coalition for the Homeless and the National Law Center on Homelessness and Poverty, 2006).

Critical Thinking Questions

1. What are the challenges of managing a household that may stimulate cognitive, social, and emotional development in adulthood? How might the experiences of homelessness interfere with development in adulthood?

2. What are the physical, psychological, and social needs of people who are homeless? What kinds of societal responses might be appropriate to address these needs?

3. What factors place an individual at risk for homelessness? How are these risk factors related to psychosocial development? How are these risk factors related to societal conditions? What is the interaction of these factors?

4. As a student of human development, what two suggestions would you give to policy makers regarding reducing homelessness in the United States?

5. Look up the approach to homelessness in one of the following major cities: Los Angeles, New York, Boston, Atlanta, and Miami. What are the primary strategies being implemented in this city? Who is responsible for the success of these programs? How are they funded? How do these programs address basic themes of human development in middle adulthood?

Remarriage and Blended Families

According to a national survey of marriages and divorce in the United States in 2001, roughly 16% of men and women had been married two or more times (Kreider, 2005). The psychosocial reality of **remarriage** is unique. Partners come to the remarriage with different marital histories. One or both have a former spouse and in-laws from a previous marriage. In some cases, the relationships with the former spouse or the in-laws may involve unresolved conflicts. In other cases, relationships with the former spouse or in-laws from a previous marriage may continue to be close. If either partner has children, the remarriage involves not only a family formation between the adult partners, but may involve the establishment of new parental roles and the negotiation of ties with noncustodial parents and grandparents. Custody arrangements may require that the parents remain in the same state or community in order to facilitate visitation. As a result, the remarried couple's life choices are constrained. As the new, blended family approaches traditional holidays, celebrations, and transitions, the complexities of considering these extended family bonds can become difficult (Portrie & Hill, 2005).

One of the significant sources of ambiguity in a blended family is the relationship of stepparents to their nonbiological stepchildren. The most common blended family is one in which a man marries a woman who has custody of her children, thereby entering into the role of stepfather. What determines whether a man will embrace this role, investing in another man's children as his own? William Marsiglio (2004) has provided a glimpse into the complexity of this process as men approach the social, personal, and interpersonal nature of becoming invested in their stepfather role. For some men, like Monty, the role is continuously ambiguous:

> I never really understood what I was to her; I still don't. I felt, I've always felt, like I should have been her father, but I never was, and I never will be…. I was always there for her, in positive ways, and he never was; I mean, never. (Marsiglio, 2004, p. 28)

For others, like Terry, there is an openness to the possibility of sharing the role with the biological father:

> Look, it's OK to have two dads. You have a couple sets of grandparents and whatever. It's OK to have two different fathers. I'm the one that's here with you all the time and he's the one up there. If he gets more involved in your life, then great! If he doesn't, nothing changes. I'm still here. I'm the one that's going to be here every day. (Marsiglio, 2004, p. 30)

For still others, like Doug, there is no room for ambiguity:

> I told her, I'll marry you, but that's my son legally. No step involved, nothing like that. That's my son. She said, "Fine; I don't see anything wrong with that." So that's when she went back to him [biological father] and said she don't want any alimony, child support, nothing. Just want you out of the picture. He signed the papers; he said, "No problem. I won't cause any trouble." So when the papers came back,

In this blended family, Tony is Berta's stepfather and Andrew's biological father. The children mean everything to Tony and they both adore him.

Copyright © Michael Newman/Photo Edit

they just simply read my name, didn't say stepfather or nothing else. (Marsiglio, 2004, p. 33)

In remarriage, partners must find ways to create boundaries around the blended family, so that children can benefit from the love and support of their parents, grandparents, and other relatives, while protecting the new family from unwanted intrusions and pressures for competing loyalties. Blended families have to find new traditions and rituals to mark their distinctiveness while preserving links to valued relationships from the past.

One-Parent Families

In 2008, about 30% of all families with children under the age of 18 were one-parent families: 80% were headed by women, 20% by men (U.S. Census Bureau, 2010). This compares to 22% of all U.S. families in 1980.

The greatest stressor for single mothers is the lack of financial resources. Roughly 40% of children living in single-mother families had family incomes less than 100% of the poverty level in 2009 (U.S. Census Bureau, 2010). To put this figure in context, 11% of children in two-parent families had family incomes at 100% of the poverty level or less. Thus, children in single-mother families are 4 times more likely to live in poverty than children in two-parent families. Poverty in these families is the result of a number of factors: single mothers tend to have a lower earning capacity, they work fewer hours, and even when they receive some support from the child's father, they bear a substantial portion of their children's expenses.

In addition to stresses associated with poverty, single parents may suffer from social isolation, continuous pressure to meet the needs of their children, and experiencing overload in trying to combine work, parenting, and household decision making without a partner. How well can single mothers manage their parenting role in the face of their many role demands? Some studies emphasize a deficit perspective—for example, identifying factors that place children or adolescents from single-parent families at risk for antisocial behavior and delinquency (Bank, Forgatch, Patterson, & Fetrow, 1993). Other studies focus on adaptation and coping within the single-parent structure. They consider factors that help sustain a positive parent-child relationship, such as sharing a strong emotional connection with other family members, being able to help one another in concrete ways, talking with one another and listening, and spending time together as parent-child and with other family members (Simons, Beaman, Conger, & Chao, 1993; McCreary & Dancy, 2004). Retrospective studies show that many children who are identified as having psychological problems, especially temper tantrums, bullying, cheating, stealing, and fighting, are from divorced, single-mother families. However, prospective studies—those that look at childrearing practices and subsequent child outcomes—show that poor parenting practices, especially emotional unavailability, ineffective discipline, minimal supervision, and a dominating, hostile style of interaction, produce these negative child outcomes in both single-parent and two-parent families (Patterson, 1992). Although single-parent families face many additional problems, it is clearly inaccurate to label all of them as problem families.

Among single-mother families, one of the fastest growing subgroups is low-income women who have never been married (Casper & Bianchi, 2002). These women may be in cohabiting or serious romantic relationships, but for a variety of reasons they have rejected the idea of getting married. It is not that marriage is devalued; in fact, some argue that it is the high standards that these women have for marriage that makes them decide to stay single (Edin, Kefalas, & Reed, 2004). Women want to be able to find a partner whom they can trust to be faithful—someone who is not addicted to drugs or alcohol, who will treat them and their children with kindness, and who will be able to contribute financially to their family. In many communities, this type of partner is difficult to find. Rushing into a marriage with someone who does not have these qualities just because one has a child seems foolhardy. These women know of too many instances of couples who start out with great expectations and then run into job loss, infidelity, abuse, drunkenness, or criminal behavior. Thus, for many

© 2010 Reggie Casagrande/Jupiterimages Corporation

Jolene is very pleased to be able to spend time with her daughter, Karen, and granddaughter, Margaret. As a single mom, she knows how important it is for Karen to have someone to help her and to spend time with her. When Ray walked out, Karen was devastated financially and depressed emotionally. Jolene helped Karen get a lawyer who was able to get Ray to fulfill his obligation to provide child support. She also babysat with Margaret while Karen pursued her MFA. With the new degree, Karen was able to get a good job and to regain her joie de vivre.

women, being an unmarried, single parent is a deliberate strategy for avoiding a difficult and potentially costly divorce.

People Who Live Alone

In the discussion of household management, we have assumed that the household consists of two or more people whose lives are intertwined. Questions about decision making, consensus, and shared responsibilities are all raised in the context of a group of people living together. However, in 2007, about 31 million people in the United States lived alone. These one-person households were more likely to consist of men in the younger age groups (under 44) and women in the older age groups (45 and older; U.S. Census Bureau, 2010). Single-person households include people who have never married, are divorced or separated, and are widowed. The reasons for living alone and the backgrounds for this life pattern vary considerably.

Little is known about the differences in psychosocial development between adults who live alone and those who live with others. Some of the aspects of household management, including organizing time, planning for the future, making decisions, and establishing relationships with other social groups, pose challenges to the person living alone. On the other hand, assigning responsibility and establishing a pattern for group decision making clearly are not required. People who live alone may not feel the need to engage in elaborate planning and evaluation when they are the only ones who will be immediately affected by their choices. Therefore, they may be freer to decide spontaneously as each opportunity presents itself.

In summary, the developmental task of household management draws on many leadership skills in order to build a home environment that is comfortable, adaptive to changing demands, and responsive to the needs and goals of those who live together. The realm of the household is unique because it allows adults to perform with maximum flexibility, creativity, and adaptability in response to the daily needs and long-term goals of the household members.

The Psychosocial Crisis: Generativity versus Stagnation

Objective 5. To explain the psychosocial crisis of generativity versus stagnation and the central processes through which the crisis is resolved: person-environment interaction and creativity.

The psychosocial crisis of *generativity versus stagnation* can be understood as a pressure on the adult to be committed to improving the life conditions of future generations (Erikson, 1963). Generativity is critical to the survival of any society. At some point, adult members of the society must begin

to feel an obligation to contribute their resources, skills, and creativity to improving the quality of life for the young (de St. Aubin, McAdams, & Kim, 2004). To some degree, this motive is aroused as one recognizes the inevitability of mortality—that one will not be around forever to direct the course of events. Therefore, one must make contributions to the society, on both personal and public levels, that will stand some chance of continuing after one's death.

There is an old story about three men who were observed laying bricks for the wall of a church. When asked what they were doing, the first man said he was laying bricks, the second said he was building a wall, and the third said he was building a church. As the story implies, during middle adulthood one must arrive at a philosophy of life that will impart significance to daily activities. One part of generativity lies in the actual attainment of creative goals. The other part lies in the perspective one brings to one's lifework, an outlook that appreciates the relationship of one's life and one's efforts to promoting well-being for the next generation. In contrast, stagnation reflects an outlook dedicated to preserving or embellishing one's power and resources without regard for the impact of this self-centeredness on the long-term well-being of the larger community.

Generativity

Generativity "encompasses procreativity, productivity, and creativity, and thus the generation of new beings, as well as of new products and new ideas, including a kind of self-generation concerned with further identity development" (Erikson, 1982, p. 67). According to Erikson's observations (Erikson et al., 1986), generativity is formed as a result of experiences of maintaining the world, nurturing and being concerned, and caring.

Cal shares is carpentry skills with these college students as they all work as volunteers building a house for a family in their community whose house was destroyed in a fire. He is experiencing something very wonderful emotionally as a result of seeing that his skills will continue to be used by younger people to help others. What is he experiencing? How would you describe these feelings?

© 2010 Hill Street Studios/Jupiterimages Corporation

It is worth pausing to consider what it means to *generate*. A basic dictionary definition is "to bring into existence." Through generativity, adults may change the world by introducing new things, ideas, beings, or bonds of relationship—all of which had not existed before. Although Erikson directed us to the heightened importance of generativity for development in middle adulthood, it makes sense to view this critical capacity as emerging over the life course. Stewart and Vandewater (1998) suggested that generativity arises through three phases: (1) generative desire or motivation, (2) a belief in one's capacity for generative action, and (3) a subjective sense of generative accomplishment.

Those adolescents whose parents have strong generative motives and who exhibit generative actions are likely to identify with these values and express generative concern in their own goals (Pratt, Norris, Hebblethwaite, & Arnold, 2008). This motive might be expressed in the formation of caring relationships with friends or siblings, as well as in the articulation of broader generative goals (Pratt, Arnold, & Lawford, 2009). For example, young people who want to promote better interracial understanding or to improve the educational experiences of young children might be said to have generative motives. As adolescents and young adults begin to realize opportunities for generative action they are likely to experience a growing confidence in the capacity to have an impact on the world.

Although there is an obvious link between generativity and the parenting role, parenting is by no means the only path to a sense of generativity. In a comparison of parents and childless adults, the link between generativity and psychological well-being was equally strong for both groups (Rothrauff & Cooney, 2008). Generativity may be expressed through a wide variety of actions, including procreation, parenting, invention, teaching, mentoring in the workplace, expanding the knowledge base, improving the physical or social environment, and artistic creation (Kotre, 1995a; Clark & Arnold, 2008). Generativity may be expressed by making a success of a remarriage involving children who have been neglected in their early childhood. It may be expressed through innovations in the workplace; in the scientist's lab; in poetry, art, music, or literature; or in creating some splendid form of recreation, like a theme park, or a refreshing new food like frozen yogurt. In looking back on one's life, one can assess these actions and make a judgment about whether one's generative aspirations or motives have been realized.

Erikson suggested that the outcome of the crisis of generativity versus stagnation has implications for adults at the next life stage in the form of *grand-generativity*:

> The reconciling of generativity and stagnation involves the elder in expressing a "grand-generativity" that is somehow beyond middle age's direct responsibility for maintaining the world. The roles of aging parent, grandparent, old friend, consultant, adviser, and mentor all provide the aging adult with essential social opportunities to experience grand-generativity in current relationships with people of all ages. In these relationships, the individual seeks to integrate outward-looking care for others with inward-looking concern for self. As a complement to caring for others, the elder is also challenged to accept from others that caring which is required, and to do so in a way that is itself caring. In the context of the generational cycle, it is incumbent upon the aged to enhance feelings of generativity in their caregivers from the younger generations. (Erikson et al., 1986, pp. 74–75)

Measuring Generativity

The meaning of generativity is being clarified through attempts to measure it (Peterson & Stewart, 1993; Hawkins & Dollahite, 1997; McAdams & de St. Aubin, 1998). In a cross-sectional comparison of dimensions of generativity among participants in early (22–27), middle (37–42), and later (67–72) adulthood, four aspects of generativity were measured (McAdams, de St. Aubin, & Logan, 1993):

- Generative concern—A sense that one is making a difference in the lives of others
- Generative commitment—Personal strivings or goals that have a generative nature
- Generative action—A checklist of actions that the person has performed in the past 2 months that involved creating, maintaining, or offering
- Generative narrative—Autobiographical recollections coded for generative meaning

Based on these measures, the results suggest the following trends:

1. Across all age groups, generative concern was significantly correlated with happiness and life satisfaction.
2. When all four measures of generativity were combined, the middle adults scored higher than the young or older age groups.
3. The measures of generative commitment and generative narration were higher for the middle adult group.
4. The pattern of responses showed significant differences between the middle adult and the younger adult groups, but the middle adults and the older adults were not significantly different.

One implication of these results is that once the generative orientation emerges, it appears to endure in the life goals and activities of a person into later adulthood.

The concept of generativity suggests a commitment to social involvement and community engagement. In a study designed to examine this relationship, generativity was assessed in a sample of African American and European American adults ages 34 to 65. Individual differences in generativity were associated with social support from family and friends, involvement in religious activities, and political participation. Those individuals who scored higher in measures of generativity were also more likely to emphasize prosocial values in raising their children and were especially conscious of the way they served as role models for their children. Within this sample, the African American adults were found to score significantly higher on measures of generative concern and generative action than the European American adults, suggesting a cultural context for the support and value of generativity within various ethnic communities (Hart, McAdams, Hirsch, & Bauer, 2001).

Another approach to the measurement of generativity takes its inspiration from the construct of identity status, which was introduced in Chapter 10. In this view, generativity is defined as a commitment to "establish and guide the next generation through one's acts of care" (Bradley, 1997; Bradley & Marcia, 1998). Using a semistructured interview, individuals are characterized along two dimensions: a person's level of involvement and active concern for the growth of the self and others, and a person's level of tolerance for differences in values, ideas, and traditions, which reflects the inclusivity of their generative concern. Using these two dimensions, generative status was described as fitting into one of five types:

- Generative: Vital involvement in growth for self and others, and tolerance for a wide range of ideas
- Pseudogenerative-agentic: Active involvement in one's own growth, and openness to a wide range of ideas for oneself but not for others
- Pseudogenerative-communal: Active involvement to promote growth and tolerance for ideas in others, but not for oneself
- Conventional: Active involvement in growth for oneself and others, but low tolerance for different ideas and values
- Stagnant: Low involvement in growth for oneself and others and low tolerance for different ideas and values

This model expands the definition of generativity by making a distinction between people who are committed to growth for their own immediate circle and those who are committed to growth for humanity or a wider and more diverse population. It recognizes a group of middle adults who are generative toward those who are part of their in-group, but not toward people whose ideas and values differ from their own.

The theme of generativity versus stagnation permeates the psychological dynamics of adult life. In the following section, we discuss the negative pole, stagnation, and its expression in narcissistic self-preoccupation and depression. Since the mid-1980s, the severity of problems related to depression in adulthood have been documented, and several different patterns have been described. Although much has been written about the negative side of adult life, including people who commit crimes or betray their families, it is important to recognize that the positive forces of generativity are equally dominant in guiding the lives of most adults and that they produce acts of creative leadership and caring.

CASE STUDY

MY LEADERSHIP JOURNEY

Lourie Campos describes how a leadership training experience transformed her generative strivings into action.

In the fall of 1999, I was encouraged to apply to the Women's Health Leadership program by my former boss. At that time, my job was a hodgepodge of responsibilities, although I was beginning to focus more and more on policy work. I felt that I lacked direction and the tools to make changes in my job. I didn't consider myself a "leader" even though my colleagues saw me as one. I wanted to be proactive in making positive changes in my job, so I decided to apply to WHL. What I didn't expect was to learn as much about myself as I did about women's health issues.

In 1997, I was diagnosed with metastatic cancer. Years earlier, I saw my father lose his battle with colon cancer, which he courageously fought for 12 years, and in 1999 my brother was diagnosed with the same cancer. It has changed the way I think about my future. While work was important to me, I needed to set limits. While it may seem that participating in the WHL program would have added more stress to my life, it was just the opposite. Through WHL, I worked on an individual leadership development program that not only allowed me to be effective at my job by sharpening my skills and learning new ones but [also included] activities that I wanted to concentrate on outside of work. I spent more time having fun, learning new things, and spending quality time with my family and friends. WHL encourages personal and professional growth as well as teaching women to be advocates for themselves and other women in their community.

My major accomplishment was the creation of the *Women's Health Advocacy Guidebook*. The guidebook is specific to Santa Clara County and is full of information on the gaps and barriers low-income, medically underserved women face in Santa Clara County. It is a tool to help women's health advocates understand the legislative process and how they can participate in the process. I distributed 40 guidebooks to women in my community and I have had such a positive response from them. The guidebook is something I wish I had when I began doing policy work.

Prior to WHL, I had never spoken about my experience with cancer. I did not fully understand or recognize the positive impact my story could have. I was always afraid that if I spoke about my cancer and my family's experience with cancer people would just feel sorry for me, and that is the last thing I wanted. But WHL has taught me to take risks and to find my voice. This past year, I have been a featured speaker in a "Living with Cancer" series in Santa Cruz; I submitted my cancer story to the *San Jose Mercury News* and it was printed with a picture of me and my dog on the front page; I was a panelist on assembly member Elaine Alquist's "Women's Health Forum"; and I was selected as one of 8 people to represent California and to provide testimony to the President's Cancer Panel. Many people, especially women, have shared their experiences with me and I have felt so honored to listen to their stories.

Source: Littlefield, Robison, Engelbrecht, Gonzalez, & Hutcheson, 2002, p. 579.

CRITICAL THINKING AND CASE ANALYSIS

1. What kinds of changes did Lourie Campos experience as a result of the Women's Health Leadership training experience?

2. What evidence does the case provide about generative concern? Generative commitment? Generative action? Generative narrative?

3. How did the experience of expanding her social network of professionals outside of her job contribute to Lourie's psychosocial development?

4. What lessons can be learned from this case about how to support and nurture a sense of generativity in middle adulthood and how to overcome feelings of stagnation?

5. What role does the environment play in promoting generativity? Can you think of some examples of community programs or workplace initiatives that may foster psychosocial development in adulthood?

Stagnation

Stagnation suggests a lack of psychological movement or growth. Those unable to cope with managing a household, raising children, or managing their career are likely to feel psychological stagnation at the end of middle adulthood. As suggested in the model of generativity statuses discussed previously, stagnation has been operationalized as an absence of investment in the growth of self or others and a rejection of ideas and values that differ from one's own. Stagnation has been found to be a distinct construct, not simply the absence of generativity. Stagnation is positively associated with the personality characteristic of neuroticism, indicating high levels of worry, and negatively associated with the personality characteristics of extraversion and openness to experience, indicating difficulties in social relationships, problems achieving a sense of social acceptance, and being highly controlled. Taken together, these characteristics suggest a person who is not only closed off to experiences with others, but is also lacking in the kinds of experiences that would promote self-development (Van Hiel, Mervielde, & DeFruyt, 2006).

The experience of stagnation may differ for the narcissistic adult and the depressed adult. **Narcissistic people**—adults who devote their energy and skills to the sole end of self-aggrandizement and personal satisfaction—are likely to have difficulty looking beyond their own needs or experiencing satisfaction in taking care of others. They are self-serving and defensive, expending energy to accumulate wealth and material possessions. They relate to others in terms of how people can serve them. Narcissistic people can exist quite happily until the physical and psychological consequences of aging begin to make an impact. At that point, and continuing toward old age, self-satisfaction is easily undermined by anxieties related to death. It is not uncommon for such people to undergo some form of religious or humanitarian "conversion" after a serious illness or an emotional crisis forces them to acknowledge the limitations of a totally self-involved lifestyle.

Consider the case of Bernie Madoff, who suddenly confessed to years of money laundering that had resulted in the accumulation of billions in personal wealth.

So who was the real Bernie Madoff? And what could have driven him to choreograph a $50 billion Ponzi scheme, to which he is said to have confessed?

An easy answer is that Mr. Madoff was a charlatan of epic proportions, a greedy manipulator so hungry to accumulate wealth that he did not care whom he hurt to get what he wanted.

But some analysts say that a more complex and layered observation of his actions involves linking the world of white-collar finance to the world of serial criminals.

They wonder whether good old Bernie Madoff might have stolen simply for the fun of it, exploiting every relationship in his life for decades while studiously manipulating financial regulators. (Creswell & Thomas, 2009)

Chronically depressed people do not feel a sense of accomplishment during middle adulthood—they think of themselves as worthless. They are unable to perceive themselves as having sufficient resources to make any contribution to their society. These people are likely to have low self-esteem, doubt their opportunities for future improvement, and are therefore unwilling to invest energy in conceptualizing future progress. Adults who lack a belief in their own inner resources are vulnerable to chronic feelings of envy of others, which may be transformed into devaluation of others, and feelings of resentment or vengeance (Navaro & Schwartzberg, 2007).

One of the most commonly noted sources of stagnation in middle adulthood is *role stagnation* associated with employment. People who have been in their job a long time may be threatened by younger workers, stuck in a routine, or passed over for recognition and leadership. Rather than taking up the challenge to mentor new employees or to invent new approaches to their work, they become resentful, avoidant, and withdrawn, and may develop physical or emotional symptoms associated with the stress of their frustration (Clark & Arnold, 2008). The case of Lourie Campos illustrates how important the encouragement of professional development can be in forestalling stagnation and promoting continued generative growth in the workplace.

Middle adulthood extends over many years. During this stage, people encounter many complex challenges for which they may not be fully prepared. Promotion to an administrative position, the need to care for an aging parent, and the negotiation of a divorce are examples. Brim (1992) argued that both success and failure force people to redefine and reexamine their goals. At many points, adults doubt their ability to move ahead, achieve their goals, or make meaningful contributions. Feelings of stagnation surge temporarily.

People may recognize that unless they redefine their situation or take some new risks, the quality of their lives will deteriorate. They face the possibility of feeling outdated by new technology, outmoded by new lifestyles, overburdened by role demands, or alienated from meaningful social contacts. At these moments of crisis, adults may become entangled in a process of self-protection and withdrawal that results in permanent stagnation. However, they may also be able to muster new resources and see things from a new perspective that will permit continuing growth and the expansion of generativity.

The Central Process: Person-Environment Interaction and Creativity

Two aspects of the central process that lead to the development of generativity in middle adulthood are person-environment interaction and creativity. The first refers to ongoing experiences between the individual and the social environment, which includes the family, work setting, neighborhood, and larger political community. Day-to-day interactions, the expectations for behavior, the available resources, and the social supports that are necessary for the growth of self-confidence are elements of the social environment. The second part of the central process in the establishment of generativity is personal creativity. Although creativity has been defined in many ways, for our purposes we will define it as the willingness to abandon old forms or patterns of doing things in favor of new ways. This requires the production, evaluation, and implementation of new ideas.

Person-Environment Interaction

Successful personality growth depends on the interaction between the demands of a person's immediate environment and one's own needs, skills, and interpersonal style. The concept of interaction suggests a potential for reciprocal influence between individuals and settings. Consequently, the structure and demands of settings may alter a person's behavior, values, goals, and self-worth. People also have an impact on the settings in which they participate.

People have multiple identities and, as a result, participate in a variety of settings within their community. Adults do more than maintain or respond to their environments; they shape them. Those with higher status—that is, more resources and power—are more able to influence the quality of interactions they have with others in their environment. In turn, they are more likely to create conditions in which they receive validation for their identities because they are treated with greater respect and recognition from others for the roles they play (Stets & Harrod, 2004).

In creating their environments, adults decide whom they will marry, whether to have children, which occupation they will follow, and where they will live. To the degree that they have a choice in these matters, they are able to influence

Some Chinese Americans choose to live and work in a Chinese ethnic community. They experience a sense of acceptance and support while contributing to the continuity of their cultural heritage.

Copyright © Vicki Silbert/Photo Edit

the kinds of transactions that occur between their personality and their social milieu. They build families with lifestyles that suit the members. Making good decisions about social settings requires that they understand themselves, the nature of other people, and the social institutions that are part of their social environment. The degree of fit between family needs and community characteristics helps support the essential functions of middle adulthood, including caring for children or aging parents, coordinating work and family life, and sustaining a vital marriage. When the community consists of other families facing similar tasks, the resources, mutual support, and validation for one's life choices are likely to be greater (Swisher, Sweet, & Moen, 2004).

Although participation in some settings is a matter of choice, many others are the result of chance. Some settings can be abandoned or altered if they do not meet the individual's needs; other settings are permanent and difficult to alter. If one is in an unsuitable setting, one must be willing to leave it if possible or discover a way to influence it so that it meets one's needs more adequately. Some people, however, find themselves in social settings that can be neither abandoned nor altered. For example, a group of workers in Michigan were trained for employment in an automotive plant. When the economy slumped, they were laid off. These workers did not have enough money saved to move to another town, there were no new jobs, and they did not have the resources or the incentive to retrain for other types of employment.

When one is forced to remain in social settings that are contrary to one's needs, the possibility of developing generativity is seriously diminished. If one is unable to experience a personal sense of effectiveness at home, at work, or in the community, then one is unlikely to feel capable of contributing to future growth in these spheres. Fortunately, the social environment is so multifaceted that individuals are likely to experience satisfaction in their participation in at least one setting, even if they are dissatisfied in others. For example, people are likely to experience a sense of validation in their relationships with friends and close family members even when they have difficulty experiencing recognition at work. Under these conditions, individuals can compensate for their inability to be generative in some settings by placing increased effort and investment in those in which they can more easily attain satisfaction. This may require that individuals reorder their priorities. If there is little opportunity to find satisfaction in work, for example, one might begin to reinvest in contributions to one's family, religion, or community. Creativity is required in order to find a new balance among competing role demands while retaining a sense of joy and optimism.

Creativity

The importance of a creative response, no matter how small, is that it redefines the world and opens the door to new possibilities. Although the idea of **creativity** tends to be associated with the arts, we are using the term in a broader sense to suggest a novel transformation in any of a variety of domains from the practical to the theoretical—from creating a new recipe to creating a painting, a dance, or a theory of human behavior. Through creative effort, adults impose a new perspective on the organization, expression, or formulation of ideas.

Creative adults are not dominated by social forces but are able to direct the course of events themselves. They are at a point in their development at which their own creative responses can become a source of influence on others. Think about the menopausal woman who referred to her first hot flash as a power surge. Imagine the person who invented wheelchair basketball, or the person who invented Post-Its. Consider the influence of parents who, by creating a flexible, open, and loosely structured home environment, nurture the self-expression of their children. Through the process of creative problem solving, adults help reshape the social and physical environments in order to meet both personal and social needs more satisfactorily.

Throughout middle adulthood, adults are faced with situations in family, childrearing, and work settings that provide stimuli for creative problem solving. In their efforts to take

Picasso, who never fit into traditional society, created a vibrant world of his own. Here, in his studio, he has even created companions who entertain him while he works.

Hulton Archive/Getty Images

into account the requirements of the social setting and to be productive in it, people must develop creative plans. They must also attempt to carry out those plans—a task that may require further creativity. The essence of creative problem solving is to think outside the box—to resist defining the situation as it has been defined for you by others, then to formulate a new plan and translate the plan into action.

The roots of creativity can be found in childhood, in the semiotic, representational, playful thinking of toddlerhood. As-if thinking—the ability to imagine a situation in some different configuration, to use objects to stand for something else, to give new names to familiar objects, to devise private symbols for common experiences, to take on imagined roles—all these capacities of symbolic play are the foundational building blocks of creativity. In our view, all humans are creative in the sense that they can pretend. All humans are creative when they cope effectively in a changing, unpredictable environment. All humans are creative in that they can invent games, songs, tools, artifacts, or messages that are new to them. It is not so important that the creative act is new to the world, but that it is new to the person who is inventing it (Sternberg, Grigorenko, & Singer, 2004).

From the outset, the creative process involves frustrations and risk. Typically, a creative solution is required because the standard way—the scripted way—is not working. In order to try new things, people must give up some old, reliable ways of thinking or behaving. In this process, people must anticipate the possibility that their efforts will fail. They may flounder for a seemingly long period, unable to identify the solution that will allow forward movement. They may worry about public embarrassment or humiliation. Given one's embeddedness in many demanding social roles, it is often difficult to step aside and view one's situation from a fresh perspective. For some, the anxiety and self-consciousness associated with prolonged uncertainty and possible failure may be so great that creative solutions are never realized. Their creativity is blocked by a fear of the unknown, or by an inability to violate conventional norms of behavior.

For those who are not inhibited by the fear of failure, the achievement of a creative solution is invigorating. For the great creative geniuses—such as Sigmund Freud, Albert Einstein, Isadora Duncan, or Pablo Picasso—a breakthrough or a profound creative insight fueled their commitment to pursue the creative path with increased energy (Gardner, 1993). Personal talent combined with an appreciation of the inadequacies of the current situation can lead to a significant creative act, which then promotes future efforts. Creativity provides an outlet for caring for something that has not yet been defined or experienced. Repeated efforts to generate creative solutions eventually result in the formulation of a transforming philosophy of life. Through risk taking, occasional failure, and a predominance of successful creative efforts, adults achieve a sense of what they believe in and what gives meaning to life. With this remarkable integration of experience and information, people enter later adulthood.

The Prime Adaptive Ego Quality and the Core Pathology

Objective 6. To define the primary adaptive ego strength of care and the core pathology of rejectivity.

Implied in the concept of generativity is a moral directive to *take care of* and to *care for and about* the development of others. As generativity is fully achieved and expressed in action, it will be linked to the prime adaptive ego quality of care (Leffel, Fritz, & Stephens, 2008). In contrast, experiences of stagnation are likely to be accompanied by the core pathology of rejectivity—a defensive, self-protective outlook. The person who develops rejectivity blames the target of envy and possibly justifies expressions of vengefulness or rage.

Care

The ego strength associated with the achievement of generativity is **care**. Care "is a widening commitment to take care of the persons, the products, and the ideas one has learned to care for. All the strengths arising from earlier developments in the ascending order from infancy to young adulthood (hope and will, purpose and skill, fidelity and love) now prove, on closer study, to be essential to the generative task of cultivating strength in the next generation, for this is indeed the 'store' of human life" (Erikson, 1982, p. 67).

Parenting contributes to the expansion of caring. Seven aspects of emotional development can be identified as potential consequences of parenting. First, parenting brings a depth of commitment that is tied to the responsibility for the survival of a child. This depth of commitment is strengthened through the reinforcing nature of the child's responses to attempts to meet his or her needs. Second, parenting brings adults into contact with new channels for expressing affection. Third, it requires that adults achieve a balance between meeting their own needs and those of others. Fourth, parenting enhances adults' feelings of value and well-being through the significant role they play in the child's life. Fifth, parents achieve a degree of empathy for their child that widens the array of their emotional experiences. Sixth, parents may experience new levels of emotional intensity in reaction to their child's behavior. Finally, many parents learn to help their children express and understand emotions. By playing a therapeutic role for their children, parents may become more effective in accepting and expressing their own emotions.

Not all adults experience the expansion of caring through parenting. The psychosocial achievement of middle adulthood is to identify the domains in which one has opportunities to influence the quality of the social environment, so that it becomes more hospitable, humane, nurturant, or supportive of one's own visions for the future. Caring expands in different domains for different people, but it always leads to having the welfare of people and enduring things (including ideas) deeply at heart. There is an action component to caring, in that people work to care for what they can. As the crisis of generativity versus stagnation is resolved in a positive direction, adults find new energy and innovative ways to express their capacity for care.

Rejectivity

Caring strongly for certain people, products, and ideas can cause people to reject any person or group that appears to threaten them. **Rejectivity** refers to an unwillingness to embrace certain individuals, groups, or ideas in one's circle of care and, at an extreme level, to view these threats as appropriate targets for hostility, even annihilation. Ironically, one may exhibit great courage and dedication to protect the objects of one's care by directing intense aggression toward the objects that one rejects.

Erikson (1982) referred to this process as pseudospeciation, in which one defines another group as different, dangerous, and potentially less human than one's own. Under the rubric of pseudospeciation, family members can become scapegoats, neighboring communities can establish intense rivalries, racial or religious groups can terrorize others, and regions or countries can go to war. Thus, rejectivity goes beyond an intellectual selectivity of certain ideas and groups as more central to one's identity than others, taking on an aggressive energy, drawn from the power and authority of one's status in middle adulthood. The risk of rejectivity for the society is that certain groups will become so powerful that they can cause the extermination or domination of other groups. As each subgroup falls out of the circle of caring, the society as a whole reaches a new level of stagnation.

APPLIED TOPIC

Discrimination in the Workplace

Objective 7. To apply a psychosocial analysis to the issue of discrimination in the workplace, with special focus on the cost to society and to the individual when discrimination operates to restrict career access and advancement.

THE UNITED STATES has been characterized as an achieving society. As a cultural group, we value individual achievement, usually expressed through accomplishments in the world of work. Thus, in the United States, for men and increasingly for women the mark of successful adulthood is frequently equated with success in the labor market, which is typically attributed to personal characteristics of ability, intelligence, and motivation. Conversely, a lack of success in the labor market is attributed to deficiencies in personal characteristics—lack of ability, low intelligence, and poor motivation. Individuals are unlikely to attribute their successes to conditions of the workplace, vagaries in the economy, luck, or conditions of society that give them a special advantage and others an unfair disadvantage. Yet many Americans face serious and persistent disadvantages in the workplace that are linked to race, ethnicity, age, cultural practices, national origin, gender, sexual orientation, disability, or religion (MacLean, 2006).

Sex Discrimination
Promotion
Marilyn has worked as a sales clerk at a retail store for 10 years but has been repeatedly denied the opportunity to advance. Men with less experience, including men that she trained and/or supervised, received the promotions instead.

Pay
Carla worked her way up from the position of cook's helper to chef. Now another chef has been hired. He has similar training and work experience, but she finds out that he is being paid more than she is.

Sexual Harassment
Rita's boss is the vice-president of the company. He repeatedly makes unwelcome comments about her body and routinely puts his arm around her waist when discussing work-related matters. Rita tells him his behavior makes her uncomfortable and asks him to stop. He says, "Maybe you are too uptight for this job. I probably should never have hired you." Now Rita is afraid of losing her job if she doesn't "loosen up" (equalrights.org, 2010)

Race Discrimination

Hoping to become lieutenants, 77 New Haven firefighters took a promotion test—but when none of the 19 Black firefighters qualified, the city jettisoned the results. Their hopes dashed, 17 White firefighters sued the city for racial discrimination, and the case went to the Supreme Court (newser.com, 2009).

Age Discrimination

Two years ago I worked at a nonprofit organization and was the oldest person employed in that facility as a teacher. It was an experience that will stay with me for the rest of my life. Working with people that thought of you as being too old to work with 3- to 5-year-old children was a nightmare. I endured being called an old lady that had no business being there and why would they hire someone that old? (about .com, 2010).

Overview of Discrimination

In the past, women and minority workers in the United States were restricted to low-paying jobs in the agricultural, service, or factory sectors. In 1964, the Civil Rights Act made it illegal to refuse to hire a person or discriminate in compensation, firing practices, or any other employment benefits based on race, color, religion, sex, or national origin. This act made the practice of restricting access to employment opportunities illegal and opened up many arenas for professional development that had previously been denied to minorities (Hodson & Sullivan, 1995). With additional legislation, other groups were included in the umbrella of legal protections. Currently, the U.S. Equal Employment Opportunity Commission (EEOC) lists types of discrimination to include: age, disability, national origin, pregnancy, race, religion, and sex-based factors. This office also addresses cases of retaliation against individuals who file charges of discrimination and cases of sexual harassment. The Civil Rights Act prohibits both intentional discrimination and otherwise neutral workplace policies that disproportionately disadvantage persons of a certain age, race, disability, and so on (EEOC, 2007).

Nonetheless, barriers to full and equitable involvement in the labor market for women, minorities, and persons with disabilities as well as persons in other protected groups continue to exist (Robert & Harlan, 2006). For example, some women find that their workplace sets limits on their achievement through gender-stereotyped assumptions about the woman's commitment to her family role (Ridgeway & Correll, 2004). In these settings, women do not tend to be promoted to high-level administrative or managerial positions in which work demands would begin to invade family commitments. Some companies are reluctant to put married women in positions in which they may have to be transferred, for fear that their husbands will refuse to make the move.

In addition to blatant discrimination in hiring practices, working conditions, salary, and dismissals, individuals have to cope with subtle acts of discrimination such as marginalization, harassment, and rumors or fictionalized stories that are embarrassing or imply that they are incompetent. In 2006, over 23,000 charges of sex-based discrimination, including cases of sexual harassment and pregnancy discrimination were filed with the EEOC. In that same year, 27,000 charges of race-based discrimination and over 15,000 charges of disability-based discrimination were filed with the EEOC.

Workplace discrimination is an exceedingly costly problem for the society as a whole. Discriminatory practices that lead to the disaffection of individuals from the world of work is costly in economic terms—in lower levels of productivity, high turnover, high levels of irritability and conflict among workers, lawsuits, and less identification with the company and its goals. It is costly in personal terms as well: Feelings of frustration about not being recognized for one's competence or being passed over for promotion by less competent workers interfere with the development of a generative orientation. These experiences may lead to a more self-serving orientation, focusing exclusively on self-protection or to a pervasive sense of futility about the future.

Disparities in Income and the Occupational Structure

In 2003, the median income of people who received an income, in constant 2003 dollars, was $17,422 for White women and $30,732 for White men; $16,581 for Black women and $21,986 for Black men; $13,642 for Hispanic women and $21,053 for Hispanic men. Women with bachelor's degrees had median salaries that were 61% of those of men with the same degrees (U.S. Census Bureau, 2006). In 2003, 24.4% of Blacks, 22.5% of Hispanics, and 10.5% of Whites had incomes below the poverty level. Unemployment patterns showed that African Americans were more than twice as likely as European Americans to be unemployed (U.S. Census Bureau, 2006).

One explanation for the racial, ethnic, and gender differences in salary, rates of poverty, and rates of unemployment is that workers from different groups are distributed unevenly in the occupational structure. Jobs continue to be gender stereotyped, with women being socialized and encouraged to work in vocations that involve helping and serving others. For example, women were 46% of those employed in 2004. However, they made up 64% of those working in sales, office work, and administrative support, and 57% of those in service occupations such as child care, food preparation, and service. On the other hand, women made up only 23% of chief executives, 14% of architects and engineers, and a small segment of the skilled trades where strong unions can protect salary scale and benefits (U.S. Census Bureau, 2006).

Group differences in occupational position that result in different salary structures and risks of layoffs are not necessarily evidence of discrimination. Discrimination exists when two people doing the same job are paid substantially different wages. It occurs when factors other than merit prevent a person from being hired, promoted, or rewarded through various forms of compensation or increase a person's risk of being fired. Specifically, discrimination occurs when a person is evaluated on the basis of group membership rather than individual performance. In the workplace, this process operates as an in-group versus out-group dynamic, in which members of the in-group view members of the out-group as deficient and, at some level, possibly threatening to their own continued success and well-being.

AP Photo/Don Wright

These blue collar workers have lost their jobs, and they are angry about it. Their jobs have been outsourced to other countries. They do not forsee new jobs that would be right for them emerging in the recovery. They have banded together in an organization through which they are asserting their right to work.

How Discrimination Perpetuates Itself

Employers, supervisors, and others in positions of power typically establish a normative profile for their employees and judge each new employee against it. In some work settings, the judgment about competence is equated with a willingness to dedicate long hours to the job, to be available at a moment's notice, and to keep one's cell phone on at all times, including evenings and weekends. Against this norm, women who are mothers are expected to direct their time and energy toward their parenting role and, thus, are often judged to be less committed and less competent workers than women who are not mothers or than men who are fathers (Ridgeway & Correll, 2004). For example, in one study, participants rated women who were mothers as less competent—and thus less worthy of investing in hiring them, training them, or promoting them—than women who did not have children. Participants also rated women as less competent after they had children than before they became mothers (Cuddy, Fiske, & Glick, 2004).

These highly internalized norms about the ideal worker may include deeply held beliefs and values on the part of men about women. Men may wonder whether women can perform the same kinds of jobs as men and can effectively assume responsibility to supervise men, whether clients will place their trust in female executives, or whether women will be dedicated to their work when conflicts between work and family arise. In the same vein, these norms may include deeply held beliefs and values on the part of Whites about people of color—especially beliefs that they are superior to people of color in ability, that the cultural characteristics of people of color will be disruptive or damaging to productivity in the workplace, or that people of color are better suited to some types of jobs than others (Feagin & McKinney, 2003). In many organizations, one can observe what has been called racial segmentation—the creation of specific kinds of administrative positions that were created to carry out affirmative action agendas, community relations with specific racial or ethnic communities, or to promote the recruitment of minority employees (Forman, 2003). Because of the historical and continuing separation of neighborhoods, schools, and churches on the basis of race, few White adults have firsthand, personal relationships with people of color. Decisions about promotions or assignments to positions of increased responsibility are often made in situations where senior employees, mostly White, make decisions that do not take into account the values, beliefs, and practices of non-White groups.

Consider the following situation: "FedEx's prohibition against individuals involved in customer contact from wearing dreadlocks, beards, ponytails or braids had been company policy for years but it was not enforced until 1999 when the Memphis, Tenn.-based company gave at least seven couriers who wore dreadlocks and worked in New York an ultimatum to cut them off or lose their jobs" (Cukan, 2001).

The employees were Rastafarians, who wear dreadlocks for religious reasons. They all offered to cover their hair with a hat or some other businesslike attire. However, FedEx refused this arrangement. The men were placed on a 90-day unpaid leave and then fired because no noncustomer contact positions could be found. These men had worked for FedEx for 5 years and had excellent service records with the company. The state of New York sued FedEx for violation of antidiscrimination laws, arguing that they fired the employees based on their religious observances. In response, FedEx changed its policy, allowing individuals to request an exception to the company's policy regarding hairstyles in order to respect their religious beliefs. This example illustrates the continuing need for examination of workplace practices that create hostile or disrespectful environments for workers.

Psychosocial Analysis: Discrimination and Coping

In general, in discussing psychosocial development, one examines the outcome for the individual in achieving a positive resolution of the psychosocial crisis. But when considering discrimination in the workplace, one must also look at the consequences for a society. Discrimination in the workplace is one expression of *societal stagnation*. It is a defensive posture, in which those in power try to protect their own status and profits by preventing members of less powerful groups from gaining a foothold. Rather than treating diversity as a factor that can improve productivity in the work setting, discrimination operates to reduce it.

Over time, the fate of individuals who have been discriminated against becomes a great cost to the society at large. Perceived discrimination in the workplace has been associated with lower job satisfaction, reduced life satisfaction, health problems, depression, and general anxiety (Feagin & McKinney, 2003). Some targets of discrimination give up and become chronically unemployed or underemployed, resulting in a loss of human capital. Others remain in a discriminatory workplace, trying to get by, not making trouble, and yet operating behind a veil of caution. African American middle-class adults tell the same stories repeatedly about how much effort and energy they spend trying to help European American people feel comfortable with them (Whitaker, 1993). Over time, this expenditure is both exhausting and deeply frustrating. One outcome of the various forms of discrimination is the development within a person of an unspoken resentment of work that may be communicated in some form to children, thus transmitting a cross-generational, cynical outlook on work.

However, the history of the United States is also filled with many cases of individuals who succeed against the odds. These adults recognize the risks of staying in a setting that does not fit well with their healthy desire to create, produce, and care. They may strike out on their own by setting up their own companies, they may challenge unfair practices through the courts, and they may mentor younger workers to help them cope with the conflicts they face in the workplace. The responsibility for coping with discrimination does not rest entirely on its victims. There are also examples of work settings that have taken active steps to challenge their own practices. Companies have been cited for their policies to support the hiring and promotion of women into senior positions, and for their innovations in weaving new levels of understanding about diversity into all aspects of employee development. Companies are recognizing that by being more visibly attuned to the interests and needs of culturally diverse communities, they can increase their brand reputation and increase their client base (Rodriquez, 2006).

The American workforce of the 21st century is becoming increasingly diverse. Women and ethnic minorities are the fastest growing groups of new employees. An estimated 13% of the workforce is composed of legal and illegal immigrants. In 2003, 24% of U.S. resident children under the age of 5 were children of color (U.S. Census Bureau, 2004b). Their preparation for and participation in the labor market will be a determining factor in the quality and productivity of the U.S. economy in the 21st century. The psychosocial approach, which highlights the interdependence of the individual and the society, is dramatically illustrated in the connection between contemporary workplace policies and practices and their implications for the maturation of a sense of initiative and industry during childhood. Children who believe that their parents and other adult members of the community are thriving in work environments that respect and value them are more likely to make the commitment to schooling that is needed to participate fully when it is their turn to enter the labor market.

Chapter Summary

During the middle adult years, people have an opportunity to make significant contributions to their culture. Through work, home, childrearing, and other caring relationships, people express their own value orientations, moral codes, personalities, and talents. They grow more sensitive to the multiple needs of those around them and more skillful in influencing the social environment.

authority relations, and demands for the acquisition of new skills; considering midlife career changes; examining the interaction of work and family life; and examining the impact of joblessness in middle adulthood.

The developmental tasks of middle adulthood are complex and require long-term persistence. During middle adulthood, people gauge their self-worth largely in relation to their contributions to complex social units, especially work, family, and community. Each task calls for a new level of conceptualization of the interaction of the self with immediate and more remote social systems and an increased ability to balance one's individual needs with

Objective 1. To examine the world of work as a context for development, focusing on interpersonal demands,

system goals. In the process of managing a career, one observes the bidirectional influence of individuals and their work settings. Occupational environments have an impact on the cognitive, interpersonal, and emotional development of middle adults; and middle adults influence work settings through their positions of authority, leadership, and the achievement of new levels of expertise. One of the significant challenges of middle adulthood is the effective balancing of work and family life.

Objective 2. To examine the process of maintaining a vital, intimate relationship in middle adulthood, especially a commitment to growth, effective communication, creative use of conflict, and preserving passion.

Happiness in an intimate relationship is a cornerstone of well-being in middle adulthood. The establishment and preservation of close, nurturing relationships require ego strengths of the partners, effective communication strategies, a commitment to the future of the relationship, and creative strategies for preserving passion and excitement within a framework of close companionship.

Objective 3. To describe the expansion of caring in middle adulthood as it applies to two specific roles—that of a parent and that of an adult child caring for one's aging parents.

The maturity and commitment to care of those in middle adulthood are closely linked to the psychosocial well-being of children as well as the elderly. Through parenting, adults create the supportive environment for children's safety, health, and development. The quality of the parental alliance provides the model that children observe and internalize as they conceptualize the nature of adult relationships. Through their relationship with their aging parents, adult children can support their parents' optimal functioning and, at the same time, grow in their understanding of the challenges of aging.

Objective 4. To analyze the tasks required for effective management of the household and the diversity of households, including blended families, single-parent families, and adults who live alone.

Management of the household involves the creation of a safe, stimulating, and comforting environment for those who live there. The capacity to maintain a household and nurture those who live there is linked to the middle adult's ability to identify needed resources, and to create the network of relationships that will support the members of the household. The skills that are needed to achieve these goals will differ depending on the structure of the household and the ages, abilities, and relationships of the household members.

Objective 5. To explain the psychosocial crisis of generativity versus stagnation and the central processes through which the crisis is resolved: person-environment interaction and creativity.

The psychosocial crisis of the middle adult years—generativity versus stagnation—is really a moral crisis of commitment to a better way of life. The well-being of the community as a whole rests largely on the effectiveness of people in middle adulthood in reaching new levels of psychosocial maturity. The society must encourage adults to care for others besides themselves. The egocentrism of toddlerhood, early school age, and adolescence must eventually come to an end if the social group is to survive. In the same way that intimacy (giving oneself to another) requires identity, generativity (giving oneself to the next generation) requires love of specific others. Interpersonal sources of satisfaction are the primary forces propelling people toward a generative approach to society as a whole.

Objective 6. To define the primary adaptive ego strength of care and the core pathology of rejectivity.

As generativity is fully achieved and expressed in action, it will be linked to the prime adaptive ego quality of care, a capacity to look after and promote the optimal development of others. In contrast, experiences of stagnation are likely to be accompanied by the core pathology of rejectivity—a defensive, self-protective outlook in which self-interest and self-aggrandizement are heightened by devaluing or degrading others.

Objective 7. To apply a psychosocial analysis to the issue of discrimination in the workplace, with special focus on the cost to society and to the individual when discrimination operates to restrict career access and advancement.

The applied topic of discrimination in the workplace provides evidence of societal stagnation. Often, it is middle adults in leadership positions who, by deliberate practice or informal example, set a tone that promotes the exclusion of certain workers on the basis of age, gender, racial or ethnic group, or other group characteristics. At the same time, others in middle adulthood suffer from discriminatory policies and are unable to reach the levels of achievement and contribution that their talents merit. Social policies and practices that interfere with individuals' abilities to perform meaningful work or to achieve recognition and respect for their work pose a hazard to individual psychosocial development and to the future of the social group. These practices, born from the core pathology of rejectivity, act in opposition to the fundamental needs of a society to care about its members and foster the most optimistic ambitions and goals possible in younger generations.

Key Terms

Further Reflection

1. How do the demands of managing a career change from early to middle adulthood?
2. What are some examples of historical changes over the past 50 years that have increased strain on adults in their middle adult years?
3. How might the challenges of balancing work and family roles contribute to new directions for development and growth in middle adulthood?
4. How might generativity be expressed among people with limited education and few financial resources?
5. Why is creativity an especially important process for the resolution of the psychosocial crisis of middle adulthood?
6. What evidence do you see of workplace discrimination in the settings where you work? Where you go to school? Where you shop or do business? What are the psychosocial resources of earlier stages of life that might help a person cope with workplace discrimination?

Psychology CourseMate

To access additional course materials, including CourseMate, please visit www.cengagebrain.com. At the CengageBrain .com home page, search for the ISBN of your title (from the back cover of your book) using the search box at the top of the page. This will take you to the product page where these resources can be found.

Casebook

For additional case material related to this chapter, see the case of "Annie and Career Contemplation," in *Life Span Development: A Case Book*, by Barbara and Philip Newman, Laura Landry-Meyer, and Brenda J. Lohman, pp. 176–179. In this case, Annie evaluates her current work situation in light of health concerns and a desire for greater personal satisfaction.

1909/Pablo Picasso/© 2011 Estate of Pablo Picasso/Artists Rights Society (ARS), New York/SuperStock

The integrating theme of later adulthood is a search for personal meaning. When older adults achieve a sense of integrity, it leads to inner peace and serves as a source of reassurance to the next generation.

Later Adulthood (60 to 75 Years)

Chapter Objectives

1. To explore the construct of life satisfaction in later adulthood and the factors associated with subjective well-being.

2. To describe factors that promote intellectual vigor, with a focus on memory, postformal operational thought, and crystallized and fluid intelligence; and to consider the interaction of heredity and environment on intelligence in later life.

3. To examine the process of redirecting energy to new roles and activities, with special focus on role gain, such as grandparenthood; role loss, such as widowhood; and new opportunities for leisure.

4. To describe the development of a point of view about death.

5. To explain the psychosocial crisis of integrity versus despair, the central process of introspection, the prime adaptive ego quality of wisdom, and the core pathology of disdain.

6. To apply theory and research to understanding the process of adjustment to retirement in later adulthood.

IN THIS CHAPTER and the next, we consider the challenges, changes, and new avenues for development in later life. This chapter focuses on the period from 60 to 75; the next chapter focuses on the years from 75 to the end of life. The French refer to the years from 60 onward as the troisième age, the third stage of life (Rubenstein, 2002). One can think of the first 30 years of life as a period of construction and learning, when many avenues are open and the person is building the skills and knowledge to engage in the roles of adulthood. The second 30 years, from 30 to 60, are a period of enactment, when commitments established during identity formation are translated into roles and relationships. In this period, life is shaped by the interaction of work, family, and community demands and expectations. The individual strives to achieve personal ambitions and goals, and to meet cultural expectations for maturity while coping with planned and unexpected changes in adjoining systems. The final 30 years are a period of reinvention. For many, this stage of life brings a gradual release from the daily demands of work and family and, depending on one's health and resources, provides the opportunity to invent a new life structure. This is a time when one faces both significant adversity and great joy.

Psychosocial theory assumes that new opportunities for growth emerge at each life stage. In strong contrast to the stereotype of aging as an undesirable process associated with accumulated deficits and decline, these chapters highlight continuous growth through coping and adaptation. Like each of the preceding stages, later adulthood is marked by stressors, risks, and forces that can disrupt growth.

However, the epigenetic principle implies that one cannot understand the full unfolding of human life without appreciating the beliefs, practices, and social relationships of those in later adulthood and old age. Moreover, the interdependence of the stages in a human life story suggests that the ways in which older adults function and are treated will have immediate impact on the psychosocial development of individuals in all the earlier periods of life. The courage and vitality of older adults are sources of inspiration that motivate children and younger adults to continue facing the challenges of their daily lives with optimism.

The integrating theme of later adulthood is a search for personal meaning. On entering this stage, adults draw on the competence and creativity attained during middle adulthood to invent solutions to their changing conditions. As life progresses, motivation for achievement and power may give way to a desire for understanding and experimenting with new roles and relationships. The toddler's need to know why and the later adolescent's need to challenge and experiment with life roles provide earlier models for the coping skills required in later life. The individual continues to be confronted with essential problems of definition and explanation during later adulthood. At this stage, adults apply the wealth of their life experiences, their perspective on time, and their adaptation to life crises to construct personally satisfying answers to the questions of life's meaning.

Physical, social, emotional, and intellectual developments are intricately interrelated during later life. The more research is carried out on aspects of aging, the greater the appreciation for the fact that patterns of aging are neither universal nor irreversible. For example, although many older adults become more sedentary and lose aerobic capacity, others continue to perform strenuous labor and remain free from heart disease and respiratory difficulties. Many life conditions, especially poverty, malnutrition, poor sanitation, and limited health care, can accelerate the aging process. Other life conditions, such as access to a stimulating social environment, participation in a program of physical activity, and a well-balanced diet, can increase physical and intellectual functioning (Rowe & Kahn, 1998). It is essential to keep in mind individual differences in physical and mental health when thinking about patterns of growth in later adulthood.

For people in the United States who were 65 years old in 2006, the average life expectancy was an additional 17 years for men, and an additional 19.7 years for women (U.S. Census Bureau, 2010, Table No. 103). Major improvements in hygiene, nutrition, preventive medicine, and medical treatments and technologies have allowed more people to experience a vigorous later adulthood today than was true 70 years ago. As a result, more and more people are facing the developmental tasks of later adulthood and elderhood. ■

Developmental Tasks

The tasks discussed here reflect major themes that are likely to be confronted in the later years of life: **accepting one's life** and achieving a sense of **life satisfaction**; promoting intellectual vigor; redirecting energy to new roles and activities; and developing a point of view about death. These themes suggest new barriers to adaptation as well as new opportunities. Changes in memory and speed of neural processing may make the accomplishment of daily tasks more difficult. Role loss and the death of loved ones stimulate needs for new kinds of support and changes in daily lifestyle. They also convey a concrete message that a new period of life is under way. Success in these tasks requires considerable psychological effort. As the more structured roles of parent and worker become less demanding, a person has to find new sources of personal meaning and a new pattern to daily life. In some cultures, aging takes place in a context of reverence and high regard, which makes the loss of certain instrumental activities less significant. In other cultures, emphasis on autonomy, instrumentality, and achievement form a challenging context for the preservation of dignity in late life.

Accepting One's Life

Objective 1. To explore the construct of life satisfaction in later adulthood and the factors associated with subjective well-being.

One of the significant challenges of aging is learning to accept the reality of one's life and formulate a vision of this new phase of later adulthood.

"Weren't you ever afraid to grow old?" I asked.

"Mitch, I *embrace* aging."

"Embrace it?"

"It's very simple. As you grow, you learn more. If you stayed at twenty-two, you'd always be as ignorant as you were at twenty-two. Aging is not just decay, you know. It's growth. It's more than the negative that you're going to die, it's also

the positive that you *understand* you're going to die, and that you live a better life because of it." (Albom, 1997, p. 118)

By later adulthood, evidence about one's successes and failures in the major tasks of middle adulthood—marriage, childrearing, and work—has begun to accumulate. Data by which to judge one's adequacy in these areas are abundant. The process of accepting one's past life as it has been may be a difficult personal challenge. One must be able to incorporate certain areas of failure, crisis, or disappointment into one's self-image without being overburdened by a sense of inadequacy. Individuals also must be able to take pride in areas of achievement, even when those accomplishments fall short of personal expectations. At the same time, older adults face the work of defining new goals for the future. The discussion that follows provides a model for conceptualizing how older adults establish a satisfying approach to achieving important goals in light of changing resources.

The SOC Model

Over the life span, people confront the challenges of balancing and matching a variety of opportunities with fluctuations in resources (Freund & Baltes, 1998). At every period of life, there are limited resources—whether time, energy, or money—to address all the opportunities that present themselves. For example, in later adulthood, a person may want to continue to work (an opportunity) but find that a chronic heart condition makes it difficult to bring the required energy and resilience to the task (loss of a resource). According to the **SOC model**, adaptation requires the integration of three processes:

Selection: Identifying the opportunities or domains of activity that are of the greatest value or importance.
Optimization: Allocating and refining resources in order to achieve higher levels of functioning in the selected domains.
Compensation: Under conditions of reduced resources, identifying strategies to counteract the loss and minimize the negative impact on functioning in the selected domains.

In later life, adults are inevitably faced with changes in resources. They may have more time but less physical stamina and fewer financial resources. Life satisfaction and a sense of well-being are linked to selecting specific goals as important areas of functioning and then effectively directing both internal (e.g., energy, thought, planning) and external (e.g., hiring help, taking classes, technical assistance) resources in order to maximize their level of functioning. Demographic factors alone—such as gender, race, age, and income—are not adequate predictors of life satisfaction. Instead, well-being rests on an ability to manage or reduce the impact of stressful life events by directing resources in order to continue engaging in valued roles and activities (Hamarat et al., 2001; Salvatore & Sastre, 2001).

Life Goals and Life Satisfaction

Many older adults have high levels of life satisfaction even though they face serious stressors and physical limitations (Brandtsadter, 2002). In part, this is due to their ability to achieve or realize important personal goals, and in part it is due to the ability to modify or adjust their goals in light of changing resources. Goals are characterized as linked to daily actions, related to desired states in the present or the future, and controllable, at least in so far as the person can choose to invest resources in certain goals or not (Mayser, Schelbe, & Riediger, 2008).

In later adulthood, individuals continue to aspire to new goals and strive to achieve new levels of optimal functioning. A person's life goals and needs may change over the course of later adulthood, depending on life circumstances. Rather than viewing satisfaction in later adulthood in terms of wrapping things up and facing a roleless, undifferentiated future, older adults continue to formulate personal goals and assess their current life satisfaction in light of how well they are able to achieve those goals. In order to appreciate the link between life goals and life satisfaction, it is important to consider three aspects of life goals: goal domains, goal orientation, and goal-related activities that are aligned with achieving valued goals (Figure 13.1).

Goal Domains. What are the achievements that stand out as important areas of accomplishment in later adulthood? Studies of life goals and life satisfaction present different typologies of life goals. In one international study that compared older adults in the United States and Holland, four domains were relevant to both groups: job or daily activity goals; social contact and family goals; health goals; and income goals. Across the two cultures, attainment of social contact and family goals were the strongest predictor of overall life satisfaction (Kapteyn, Smith, & van Soest, 2010). Other studies include self-reliance or autonomy goals, and leisure time and physical activity goals in their analyses of the link between life goals and life satisfaction (Straechen, Brawley, Spink, & Glazebrook, 2010; Wong & Lou, 2010).

Individuals show different patterns of investment in these **goal domains**, and in the specific activities or achievements within domains. To some extent, a person's profile of meaningful goals takes shape in the stages of later adolescence and early adulthood. At that time, individuals are crystallizing their identity and creating a lifestyle. The combination of one's culture and life experiences shapes an imagined self, moving into the future. As a person begins the process of accepting one's life in later adulthood, there is a tendency to return to the personal goals that were envisioned at that earlier time of life in order to assess the extent to which they were realized, and perhaps to reevaluate their importance given the 40 years or more of life that have transpired since these goals were formed (Cappeliez, 2008).

Goal Orientation. In addition to the specific goals one aspires to, the literature suggests that people differ in their goal orientation. Some people are more agentic in their goal strivings. Their important goals focus on achievement, power, and the expression of personal abilities. Other people

Life Goal Domains
    Social relationships and Family
    Work and daily activities
    Finances
    Health/Fitness
    Leisure Activities
    Self-reliance
Life Goal Orientation
    Agentic
    Communal
    Self-preservation
    Well-being of others
Goal-Related Actions
    Coping
    Intentional self-development
    Cascading facilitation of related goals
    Matching goals and activities

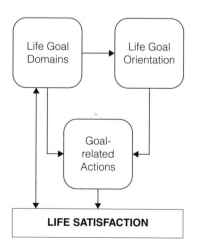

FIGURE 13.1 Life Goals and Life Satisfaction
Source: © Cengage Learning.

are more communal in their goal strivings. Their goals focus on intimacy, affiliation, and contributions to the moral community (Pohlmann, 2001). Other studies have contrasted goals that seem to emphasize self-preservation with those that focus on the interest in and well-being of others. One might look back at the psychosocial crisis of middle adulthood, generativity versus stagnation, and consider that the profile of goals emerging from that period of life might differ for those who resolved the crisis in the direction of generativity compared to those who resolved it in the direction of stagnation (Lapierre, Bouffard, & Bastin, 1997).

Goal-Related Actions. As people make progress on the developmental task of accepting their life, they are able to integrate their goals and their goal-related activities in order to experience a sense of personal fulfillment. For those in later adulthood who have a strong sense of self-directed goal attainment, sentiments of life satisfaction feed back into life goals, strengthening their sense of purpose and providing renewed energy. Activities that are not satisfying or that bring negative social exchanges will be abandoned in favor of activities that are enjoyable and that contribute to feelings of confidence or well-being. With age, it appears that a person's goals become more supportive of each other, so that one activity, for example, joining a book club, can provide support for both intellectual goals and social goals; spending time with grandchildren can be an opportunity to experience family support and physical activity. Older adults find that their goals support each other, and that they can invest more energy into personal goal pursuits as their obligations to other competing roles and role demands decline (Riediger, Freun, & Baltes, 2005). The more closely a person is able to match activities with valued goals, the greater the person's life satisfaction (Halisch & Geppert, 2001). As the case of

Orville Brim's father illustrates, many of the basic motives for goal pursuits may remain the same over time, but the implementation of specific activities may change as a person's physical health or endurance declines with advanced age.

CASE STUDY

GOAL ADJUSTMENT IN LATER ADULTHOOD

Orville Gilbert Brim, who contributed to the field of human development through his work on social role theory (see Chapter 3), became increasingly interested in ambition and self-directed goal attainment in adulthood. He describes his father's successful adaptations in later life as an example of this process (Brim, 1992).

Brim's father, also named Orville, lived to be 103. He was born in a small farming community in a rural area of Ohio in 1883. After receiving his bachelor's degree in education at Valparaiso University, he taught school in a one-room schoolhouse for 2 years and then became principal of a high school in Indiana. Eventually he left the rural Midwest to attend Harvard and then Columbia to get his PhD. He was a professor at Ohio State University until he retired at age 60. Then Orville and his wife, Helen, bought an abandoned farm of several hundred acres in Connecticut, remodeled the farmhouse, and settled into farming. In the early years of retirement, he cleared and thinned the trees on the hills and mountains of his farm. After a while, he stopped working the hillsides and planted a large vegetable and flower garden. Orville tilled the garden with a power tiller. When he was 90, he bought a riding tractor. When he could no longer manage the large garden, he focused on a small border garden and four large window boxes that he planted with flowers. As his eyesight

Ray and Carla have more time for each other now that they are getting closer to retirement. Their happiness as a couple is an important source of life satisfaction.

became more impaired, he shifted from reading to listening to "talking books," and when he had to give up actually planting the window boxes, he enjoyed watering them and looking at the flowers. Orville approached each new challenge of physical decline by correctly assessing his abilities, investing in a new project, and taking pride in his achievements within that domain.

CRITICAL THINKING AND CASE ANALYSIS

1. In this case, Brim's father drew on early life experiences growing up on a farm to guide his goals in later adulthood. What are some other examples of how earlier life roles might be integrated into a satisfying lifestyle in later adulthood?
2. Based on the information provided, what do you think Orville Brim Sr.'s goals were in the later part of his life?
3. What are some of the resources Brim's father had that allowed him to achieve new goals for mastery?

A basic element in life satisfaction is the sense of belonging, a fact that has been supported by a wide range of research across life stages (Baumeister & Leary, 1995). In later life, social relationships are a primary source of pleasure and meaning, and are an avenue for active engagement. People who experience loneliness or an inadequate social network are much less satisfied with life than those who perceive themselves to be positively connected to a meaningful circle of loved ones and friends (Gow et al., 2007). In the context of marital relationships, high levels of conflict are associated with depression and lower life satisfaction for both men and women (Whisman et al., 2006). Even though social connection is a source of life satisfaction in later adulthood, negative relationships and ongoing exposure to interpersonal conflict can disrupt feelings of satisfaction.

In a longitudinal study, men who had participated in the Terman Study of Gifted Children when they were in early childhood were interviewed about their life satisfaction at ages 58 to 72. Four styles of adaptation emerged: (1) poorly adjusted, (2) career focused but socially disengaged, (3) family focused, and (4) well rounded. Three family experiences from early childhood and adolescence, including parent-child attachment, family socioeconomic status, and early parental divorce, were associated either directly or indirectly with life satisfaction in later life (Crosnoe & Elder, 2004). In addition, contemporary factors including health and socioeconomic resources were generally predictive of life satisfaction for the group as a whole. Goals related to family life and religious life provided a greater sense of meaning, social benefits, and emotional support than occupational goals, especially for the family-focused and well-rounded groups (Crosnoe & Elder, 2002b). The family-focused and well-rounded groups had many areas of similarity, as did the career-focused and poorly adjusted groups. There is some suggestion that people who place too great a priority on occupational attainment during middle adulthood may find it difficult to reorient toward satisfying life goals in later adulthood.

Personality and Well-Being

We all know people who have lived difficult lives yet appear to be full of zest and enthusiasm. We also know people who appear to have had the benefits of many of life's resources yet are continually complaining about problems. Whether specific events will contribute to feelings of satisfaction or dismay depends in part on how they are interpreted. Some people are more likely to be grumblers; others are more likely to be celebrants of life. In response to this reality, some researchers have looked to personality factors to predict subjective life satisfaction in later adulthood (Ryff, Kwan, & Singer, 2001). The construct of **personality**, which is typically viewed as stable across situations, provides ways of understanding individual differences in coping, goal orientation, and self-evaluative processes. Personality dimensions interact with changing life tasks to produce individual differences in the ways these tasks are interpreted.

A number of personality characteristics have been linked with life satisfaction in later life, including extroversion, openness to experiences, lack of neuroticism, usefulness/competence, optimism, a sense of humor, and a sense of control. **Extroversion** includes such qualities as sociability, vigor, sensation seeking, and positive emotions. People who are outgoing and enjoy social interaction tend also to report high levels of life satisfaction (Costa, Metter, & McCrae, 1994). **Openness to experience** includes characteristics such as curiosity, imaginativeness, and enthusiasm about exploring different music, art, foods, travel, or points of view. Older adults who are open to ideas and to feelings are more likely to have a high level of life satisfaction, because they seek and take advantage of the novelty and unpredictability of their lives (Stephen, 2009). A personality dimension described as **neuroticism** is characterized by anxiety, hostility, and impulsiveness. People who are neurotic experience discouragement, unhappiness, and hopelessness. For them, real-life events are screened and interpreted through a negative filter, resulting in low levels of satisfaction.

A personality factor associated with **well-being** and high self-esteem in older adults is **usefulness/competence**. This quality is associated with informal volunteer work, higher levels of involvement with others, and a greater sense of purpose and structure in the use of time (Ranzijn, Keeves, Luszcz, & Feather, 1998). Continuing to work in later adulthood may also contribute to this sense of usefulness/competence, or perhaps those who have a high sense of usefulness/competence choose to work longer. Those older adults who take on the role of mentor for new or younger workers can enhance their sense of life satisfaction through this role to the extent that it creates opportunities to feel useful, to be involved as a valued resource, and to achieve their own career goals in this relationship (Stevens-Roseman, 2009).

Optimism is another predictor of life satisfaction. **Optimism** is a belief that one's decisions will lead to positive consequences and that uncertain situations will turn out well. Under conditions of uncertainty and stress, adults who are optimistic have less depression, greater hopefulness, and, as a result, a greater sense of well-being (Chang & Sanna, 2001). In contrast, those who are pessimistic experience more social strain, have lower social support, and as a result, are likely to have lower life satisfaction (Luger, Cotter, & Sherman, 2009).

Along with optimism, a sense of humor has been found to predict life satisfaction. Given the many changes associated with aging, it helps to see events as amusing rather than embarrassing or demeaning. Older adults who have a good sense of humor are likely to experience life in a more playful, engaged way, even if they view life as somewhat more absurd (Ruch, Proyer, & Weber, 2010).

A **sense of control** is systematically associated with life satisfaction (McConatha, McConatha, Jackson, & Bergen, 1998). Life experiences such as engaging in physical activity, the opportunity to select one's leisure activities, or the ability to decide when to retire are all examples of factors that can improve an older adult's sense of control. Loss of financial resources and social support or reduced physical resilience can diminish this sense. Taken together, one might infer that people who are extroverted, open to new experiences, optimistic, experience a sense of usefulness, have a good sense of humor, and feel that they are in control of events in their life will also express high levels of satisfaction.

Illness and Health

Experiencing a sense of well-being and acceptance of one's life is associated with physical health. In addition to an increase in vulnerability to acute illnesses, such as influenza, more than 80% of people over the age of 65 have at least one chronic condition such as arthritis, hypertension, coronary heart disease, diabetes, or cancer. **Chronic illnesses** are long-lasting and can be characterized by periods of intense illness followed by periods of remission or progressive decline. The most common chronic conditions in the 65 to 74 age range are arthritis, hearing impairments, heart conditions, and high blood pressure (Warshaw, 2006).

Heart disease is the leading cause of death for men and women in the United States. However, it begins about 10 years earlier for men than for women. After menopause, the risk of heart disease for women increases. Moreover, women are less likely than men to be accurately diagnosed as suffering from a heart attack, less likely to recover from it, and more likely to suffer the complications of stroke. The lifestyle factors associated with heart disease are about the same for men and women. However, men are more likely to be at risk because they do not get the physical activity they need, eat more meat and fat and less fruit and fiber than women, are less likely to go to the doctor for regular checkups, and are generally more likely to deny being sick (Guttman, 1998; Harvard Health Publications, 2007).

Longitudinal studies of men consistently find that current health status and functional autonomy are significant predictors of life satisfaction (Berger, Donoho, & Wayment, 2009). However, the relationship of health to life satisfaction is mediated by personality, resources, and personal goals.

A chronic illness, such as arthritis, may result in a significant loss of control and reduced opportunities for physical activity or social interaction. A person who is characterized by a neurotic personality may be more discouraged and embittered by these losses than one who is optimistic or agreeable. A person whose leisure activities have focused on physical activities, such as skiing or running, may find the restrictions of arthritis more frustrating than someone whose hobbies and lifestyle are more sedentary. In a study of more than 3,000 U.S. adults, the personality traits of **conscientiousness** and neuroticism were found to be associated with mental and physical health. Adults who were more conscientious had reduced risks of health problems, whereas those who were more neurotic had increased risk. Among adults with diagnosed physical illnesses, those who were conscientious were less likely to be limited by these conditions. One explanation for this association is that the more conscientious a person is, the more likely the person will follow a recommended plan of treatment and to incorporate recognized healthy behaviors into daily life (Goodwin & Friedman, 2006). Another interpretation is that those who are more neurotic are also more likely to alienate their social support system, thereby losing the important functions of social support that are associated with health and life satisfaction (Berger, Donoho, & Wayment, 2009).

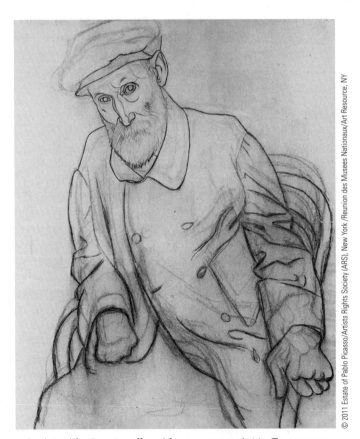

© 2011 Estate of Pablo Picasso/Artists Rights Society (ARS), New York /Reunion des Musees Nationaux/Art Resource, NY

In his later life, Renoir suffered from severe arthritis. To compensate, he tied paintbrushes to his hands so that he could continue to function in this highly valued domain.

Erikson on Accepting One's Life

Erikson et al. (1986) highlighted the importance of trust in the acceptance of one's life and the challenge of accepting support as it becomes needed.

> Maples and aspens every October bear flamboyant witness to this possibility of a final spurt of growth. Nature unfortunately has not ordained that mortals put on such a fine show. As aging continues, in fact, human bodies begin to deteriorate and physical and psychosocial capacities diminish in a seeming reversal of the course their development takes. When physical frailty demands assistance, one must accept again an appropriate dependence without the loss of trust and hope. The old, of course, are not endowed with the endearing survival skills of the infant. Old bodies are more difficult to care for, and the task itself is less satisfying to the caretaker than that of caring for infants. Such skills as elders possess have been hard won and are maintained only with determined grace. Only a lifetime of slowly developing trust is adequate to meet this situation, which so naturally elicits despair and disgust at one's own helplessness. Of how many elders could one say, "He surrendered every vestige of his old life with a sort of courteous, half humorous gentleness"? (p. 327)

Promoting Intellectual Vigor

Objective 2. To describe factors that promote intellectual vigor, with a focus on memory, postformal operational thought, and crystallized and fluid intelligence; and to consider the interaction of heredity and environment on intelligence in later life.

Memory, reasoning, information processing, problem-solving abilities, and mental rigidity or fluidity all influence an adult's capacity to introspect, select meaningful goals, manage changing resources, and plan for the future. These intellectual capacities also influence the adult's ability to remain involved in productive work, advise and guide others, and invent new solutions to the problems of daily life. The person's capacity to cope with the challenges of later adulthood, and thereby preserve a high level of life satisfaction, depends on the ability to promote and sustain **intellectual vigor**.

How can one understand cognitive functioning and change in later life? The study of intelligence and cognition in later adulthood is plagued by practical and theoretical challenges that make it difficult to make broad generalizations. In the following section, we review four problems associated with the study of intelligence and aging. Specific topics are then discussed, including memory, postformal operational reasoning, and an overview of age-related changes in various mental abilities. The focus then shifts to an analysis of the impact of heredity and environment on intelligence, and factors that help to sustain high levels of intellectual functioning in later life.

Problems in Defining and Studying Intelligence in Later Adulthood

The primary goals in the study of development are to describe and explain patterns of change and continuity over time. Four problems arise in evaluating the research on intelligence in later life (Stuart-Hamilton, 1996). First, one must differentiate between **age differences** and **age changes**. Suppose that in a cross-sectional study conducted in 2000, 70-year-olds performed less well on tests of flexible problem solving than 40-year-olds. The difference may be clear, but it may not be a result of age alone. The 70-year-olds would have been born in 1930, and the 40-year-olds in 1960. Differences in performance may be a product of different educational opportunities, varying experiences with standardized tests, or other cohort-related factors. Educational opportunities increased markedly during the 20th century, so that younger cohorts are much more likely to have benefited from formal schooling at both the high school and college levels (U.S. Bureau of the Census, 2000). For example, only 10% of people ages 65 to 74 in 2000 had completed a bachelor's degree, whereas 18% of adults ages 35 to 44 had attained this level of education. In the older cohort, 26% had not graduated from high school, compared to 11% in the younger cohort. Advanced education is associated with greater reflectiveness, flexibility, and relativistic thinking. People who have attended college have been exposed to the scientific process as a way of gaining knowledge and, as a result, are more likely to consider that their understanding of the world is tentative pending new information or new technologies (King & Kitchener, 1994; Labouvie-Vief & Diehl, 2000).

In cross-sectional studies of cognitive functioning, historical factors may be confounded with developmental or aging factors that may contribute to observed differences in performance. In longitudinal studies that follow change over time, if only one cohort is sampled, it is impossible to tell whether changes from one period to the next are products of age and development or a result of fluctuations in resources and challenges faced by that particular generation.

A second problem is the *definition of abilities*. Cognitive functioning is a broad term that encompasses such varied abilities as vocabulary, problem solving, and short-term memory. It is possible that the pattern of change in abilities with age depends on which abilities are tested. Some abilities are frequently used and have been developed to a high level of efficiency. For example, an architect is more likely to retain abilities in spatial relations and reasoning than is someone whose work is not intimately connected with the construction and organization of spatial dimensions.

A third related problem is the *relevance of the tasks* used to measure adult cognitive functioning. The definition of intelligence that is used in the design and application of most intelligence tests refers to capacities that are predictive of school-related success. The criteria for assessing adult intelligence are necessarily more varied than the ability to succeed in a school curriculum. Furthermore, motivational factors come into play in the measurement of intelligence. This raises the distinction between *ability* and *performance*. If a test is perceived as irrelevant or unimportant, an adult may not give much effort to performing well (Dixon, 1992).

Finally, *factors associated with health* are intertwined with the functioning of older adults, although they are often not directly measured. A number of age-related diseases impact an individual's ability to learn and retain new information. However, the boundaries between what might be considered normal cognitive changes associated with age and disease-related changes are not easy to detect, especially in the early stages of an illness (Albert, 2002). In a longitudinal study of intelligence, Riegel and Riegel (1972) found clear declines in performance among participants who died before the next testing period. Vocabulary skills, which normally remain high or continue to show increases with age, are especially likely to decline in older individuals who will die within the coming few years (White & Cunningham, 1988). Adults who are in the early stages of dementia but have not yet been diagnosed as suffering from the disease are often included in samples described as normal or normative. This inclusion lowers the mean of the total group and overestimates the negative association of age and intelligence (Sliwinski, Hofer, Hall, Buschke, & Lipton, 2003). At each older age, the inclusion of adults who are in an early phase of a progressive illness lowers the average performance of the group as a whole.

Memory

Several aspects of cognitive functioning, including **reaction time**, visual-motor flexibility (the translation of visual information into new motor responses), and memory show evidence of decline with age. The exact nature of changes in memory with age is a topic of active and ongoing research (Giambra, Arenberg, Zonderman, & Kawas, 1995; Johnson, 2003). A common model of memory functions breaks memory into three forms: the sensory register, short-term memory, and long-term memory. In this model, the **sensory register** is the neurological processing activity that is required to take in visual, auditory, tactile, and olfactory information. **Speed of processing**, which is most closely linked to the sensory register, can be slowed as a result of illness. Illness does not seem to affect higher order aspects of memory, particularly the recall of past life events (Rosnick et al., 2004). **Short-term memory** is the working capacity to encode and retrieve five to nine bits of information in the span of a minute or two. This is the scratch pad of memory that is used when someone tells you a telephone number or gives you an address. **Long-term memory** is a complex network of information, concepts, and schemes related by associations, knowledge, and use. It is the storehouse of a lifetime of information. Remembering something for more than a few minutes involves moving the information from short-term to long-term memory, storing it in relation to other associated knowledge, and being able to recognize, retrieve, or reconstruct it at a later time (Hoyer & Verhaeghen, 2006).

The **memory** functions most relevant to an understanding of cognitive ability in aging have to do with the ability to transfer information from short-term to long-term memory and then retrieve it. Studies that compare the short-term memory abilities of older and younger adults find that age is not associated directly with the capacity of short-term memory but with the ability to transfer newly learned information to long-term memory and then retrieve it on demand. Older adults are just as effective as younger adults in recognizing information that was learned in the past, but they have difficulty summoning up a specific name or number when they want to find it (Rowe & Kahn, 1998).

Furthermore, older adults find that their memory functions are especially likely to be disrupted under conditions in which information is presented rapidly and contextual cues are absent. Older adults rely on meaning to store and retrieve new information. With each passing year of life, there is more to remember. We do not really know the limits of the storage capacity of long-term memory. Studies of memory focus on different kinds of tasks, each with its own trajectory of growth and decline. **Semantic memory** focuses on basic knowledge, such as recalling the meaning of words like *vegetable*, *democracy*, or *insect*. Once learned, semantic memory seems very resistant to loss. People continue to grow in the accumulation of new ideas and information over adulthood.

Episodic memory focuses on specific situations and data. Measures of episodic memory may ask people to recall words from a list or remember what they had for breakfast 3 days ago. With age, so many daily events and bits of information are encountered that unless the events have some particular importance, they may not be encoded, or may become difficult to retrieve in the accumulated network of memories.

A third type of memory task is called **prospective memory**. This is memory about events or actions taking place in the future. An example would be remembering to take pills at 4 p.m. or to call a spouse when arriving at a hotel after traveling on a business trip. This type of memory task requires recalling that something needs to happen at a future time or under some future condition, and also remembering specifically what needs to be done. Older adults do not do as well as young adults on prospective memory tasks in laboratory conditions. However, in naturalistic studies, the older adults do better than the young adults (Henry, MacLeod, Phillips, & Crawford, 2004). Prospective memory is a critical component of adaptive coping, and older adults use a variety of strategies to help stay attuned to their functional future.

Research using the narrative method suggests that people construct memories that make sense of their past. They tell a story about the past that puts events in a chronological sequence, highlighting events that, in retrospect, are important achievements or turning points. For example, in one study, participants were asked to provide a narrative about a time when they said, thought, or did something wise.

Adolescents and young and old adults were all able to retell experiences where wisdom helped them to turn a negative experience into something positive. Adults were also able to describe how the wisdom experience helped shape their outlook or life philosophy (Bluck & Gluck, 2004). Memory may be used in a new way in later adulthood in order to resolve the conflict of integrity versus despair. Memory is used to recall and evaluate certain life events that may preoccupy one's attention until the role of these events can be integrated into a meaningful sense of one's purpose. This process may interfere with an adult's ability to attend to current minutiae or to rehearse and recall new information.

There is wide variability in people's memory skills. Measurement of changes in memory across different types of tasks suggests more stability than change over much of adulthood (Zelinski & Lewis, 2003). Some people pay great attention to details and are more able to recall them. Others ignore many details and are not able to retrieve them. A salesman or politician may have a knack for remembering the names of friends, acquaintances, and family members. A historian may have a memory for historical events and personalities. A police detective may pay great attention to the details of the physical environment from specific cases. As the demands of work and family life accumulate, people adapt by focusing attention on the details and events that are most salient for their success. Over time, the differences in people's approaches to what they have learned, recalled, and found useful in coping with life shape the context for whether and how new information is encoded and retrieved.

In addition to actual declines in some kinds of memory performance, older adults complain of memory problems. Anxiety and frustration over memory loss nag many, even those older adults whose memory performance has not dramatically declined. However, memory complaints may reflect the person's accurate subjective assessment of a slowing in the retrieval process (Jonker, Launer, Hooijer, & Lindeboom, 1996). The seriousness of the memory complaints and people's assessment of whether they can do anything to improve their memory combine to influence older adults' worries about memory loss and their general sense of well-being (Verhaeghen, Geraerts, & Marcoen, 2000).

Postformal Operational Thinking

Research based on the standard Piagetian tasks has been criticized for its lack of relevance and familiarity to older participants. The traditional tasks are dominated by the role of pure logic, disconnected from the situation. They emphasize problems that have a scientific rather than a pragmatic focus. Although the solution to most formal operational problems requires the manipulation of multiple variables, there is typically only one correct solution. In adult life, most problems involve multiple dimensions with changing or poorly defined variables and more than one solution. For example, given my limited resources, should I buy more life insurance, put cash in a certificate of deposit, or invest in the stock and bond market to best protect my family's financial future?

As a result of these limitations or criticisms of formal operational reasoning, scholars have formulated a view of **postformal thought**, which has been characterized in the following ways:

- A greater reliance on reflection on self, emotions, values, and the specific situation in addressing a problem
- A willingness to shift gears or take a different approach depending on the specific problem
- An ability to draw on personal knowledge to find pragmatic solutions
- An awareness of the contradictions in life and a willingness to try to include conflicting or contradictory thoughts, emotions, and experiences in finding a solution
- A flexible integration of cognition and emotion so that solutions are adaptive, reality oriented, and emotionally satisfying
- An enthusiasm for seeking new questions, finding new problems, and new frameworks for understanding experience

Noel Hendrickson/Getty Images

In later adulthood, people with academic backgrounds in science and engineering use their formal operational problem-solving skills combined with postformal reasoning to find new solutions to recurring problems.

People who operate with postformal thought do not do so in every situation. When a problem has clear parameters and needs a single solution, concrete or formal operations will work. However, when a problem is value laden, ambiguous, or involves many interpersonal implications, postformal thinking comes into play (Sinnott & Cavanaugh, 1991; Labouvie-Vief, 1992; Commons & Richards, 2003).

Given the complexity of adult life, adaptive problem solving requires flexibility, differentiation of positive and negative aspects of a single alternative, and the ability to consider the implications of a course of action. Increasingly, problem solving becomes a social task, whereby several people or groups of people work together to arrive at solutions. A component of postformal reasoning includes the ability to collaborate with others, balancing the interpersonal and analytical aspects of the work. Because members of groups are vulnerable to pressures toward conformity or groupthink, it is important for individuals to retain their capacity to differentiate or distance themselves from the group in order to examine the group's product in a more objective light.

Patterns of Change in Different Mental Abilities

There has been growing interest in assessing the extent of cognitive plasticity in later life. How readily can older adults improve their skills or learn new skills? This question seems to produce two different kinds of answers. One line of research finds evidence of DNA damage in the human brain with reduced capacity for repair beginning after about age 40. Damage of this kind has negative consequences for synaptic plasticity leading to declines in learning and memory. Certain brain areas are more vulnerable to the accumulated stressors of aging than others, and certain individuals are more vulnerable to the neurological diseases of aging than others (Lu et al., 2004; Erraji-Benchekroun et al., 2005; Mattson & Magnus, 2006). In contrast, other researchers find that among people in their sixties and seventies, continuing improvement in performance is possible through training and practice. Improvement has been observed in tasks involving memory, reasoning, perceptual-motor speed, and visual attention, as well as specific areas of expertise (Krampe & Charness, 2006; Yang, Krampe, & Baltes, 2006). One possible way to reconcile these opposing observations is to consider how different types of mental abilities might change with age.

Cognitive functioning involves the coordination of a variety of mental abilities that change as a result of experience and aging. John Horn (1979) proposed that the course of mental abilities across the life span is not uniform. Some areas are strengthened, and others decline. Horn suggested differentiating **crystallized intelligence** (Gc) and **fluid intelligence** (Gf). Gc is the ability to bring knowledge accumulated through past learning into play in appropriate situations. Gf is the ability to impose organization on information and generate new hypotheses. Both kinds of intelligence are required for optimal human functioning.

Gc and Gf can be identified as integrated structures in both early and later adulthood (McArdle, Ferrer-Caja, Hamagami, & Woodcock, 2002). However, Horn argued that these two kinds of thinking draw on somewhat different neurological and experiential sources. Gc reflects the consequences of life experiences within a society. Socialization in the family; exposure to the media; and participation in school, work, and community settings all emphasize the use and improvement of Gc. Gc increases with age, experience, and physical maturation, and remains at a high level of functioning throughout adulthood.

Gf is characteristic of what is meant by someone having common sense. Finding a general relationship and applying it without having been schooled in that problem-solving area is an example of Gf, as is being able to approach new problems logically, systematically, and quickly. Horn hypothesized that Gf depends more on the specific number of neurons available for its functioning than does Gc. Thus, neurological loss would be more damaging to Gf than to Gc. Subsequent research has supported the notion that neural efficiency, often recognized through changes in sensory functioning and speed of response, is closely related to fluid intelligence and shows an age-related decline, independent of disease (Baltes & Lindenberger, 1997). However, the extent of this decline may be related to the domain in which it is studied. For example, one study focused on men who had different levels of expertise in playing the game of Go. Measures of reasoning, memory, and cognitive speed were developed to apply specifically to that game. Older players generally showed the expected decline in deductive reasoning and cognitive speed. However, for those older men who were very expert players, no decline was observed (Masunaga & Horn, 2000). The implication is that in areas where there is highly developed expertise, aging is not necessarily accompanied by declines in either Gf or Gc.

In an analysis of the pattern of cognitive abilities across the life span, Tucker-Drob (2009) gathered data from a nationally representative sample of over 6,000 individuals from ages 4 to 101. He looked at age groupings, comparing high and low scoring individuals at different ages, to address two basic questions: (1) How do various abilities change with age? (2) Do abilities cluster together (e.g., people who are good at visual-spatial thinking are also good at short-term memory), or is there differentiation among abilities with age (people can be very good in one area, and average or not so strong in another)? Seven broad areas of cognitive ability were measured: comprehension knowledge (similar to Gc), fluid reasoning (Gf), visual-spatial thinking (e.g., identifying the pieces needed to complete a pattern), processing speed (e.g., quickly identifying two identical numbers in a row of numbers), short-term memory (e.g., repeating a list of unrelated words), long-term retrieval (e.g., naming as many examples as possible from a specific category of places or objects), and auditory processing (e.g., identifying a word when it is presented against a competing background of distracting sounds). As illustrated in Figure 13.2, all the abilities with the exception

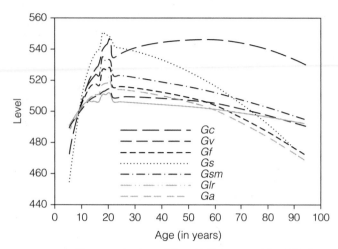

FIGURE 13.2 Changes in Cognitive Abilities over the Life Span

Source: Tucker-Drob, 2009, Figure 5, Page 1107.

Legend: *Gc* = comprehension knowledge; *Gv* = visual spatial thinking; *Gf* = fluid reasoning; *Gs* = processing speed; *Gsm* = short term memory; *Glr* = long-term retrieval; *Ga* = auditory processing.

of *Gc* increased in childhood and adolescence, peaked in later adolescence and early adulthood, and then declined through adulthood and aging. In contrast, crystallized intelligence continued to increase throughout adulthood, until about age 60, and then declined slightly into later life. Among those of higher general intelligence, there was less commonality in the scores across the various cognitive abilities suggesting that with greater intelligence comes a greater capacity to express certain abilities to a uniquely high level. Over the life span, the abilities were more differentiated; that is, people in middle adulthood and later life showed more variability in their cognitive capacities than did younger children and adolescents.

The Interaction of Heredity and Environment on Mental Functioning

For years, it was assumed that the environment played an increasingly major role in intellectual functioning over time. The accumulation of life experiences, education, and socialization were expected to introduce new bases of knowledge and problem-solving structures. Recent work suggests that the construct of the norm of reaction, introduced in Chapter 4 (The Period of Pregnancy and Prenatal Development), provides a more appropriate framework for understanding intelligence in adulthood. Genetic factors, early childhood family environment, and contemporary work and family environments all contribute to adult cognitive functioning (DeFrias & Schaie, 2001; Schaie & Zuo, 2001). Research on identical and fraternal twins who were 80 years old or older found that the heritability of general cognitive ability was about 60% (McClearn et al., 1997). In other words, genetic factors substantially contribute to the stability of cognitive capacities over the life span.

Given the strong contribution of heredity to cognitive ability, its expression in observable behavior depends on the nature of the environment. Roughly 30% of the variability

between twins was accounted for by their environment—both the shared environment reflected in growing up in the same family and community and the unshared environment, including the different interactions they had with their parents, other siblings, and friends, and their participation in different types of educational and social settings. The stimulating or stifling nature of the environment—including access to social support, the quality of health care, exposure to disease, and opportunities for continuing involvement in challenging work—transforms the genotype into an observed phenotype (Gottesman, 1997; Shanahan & Hofer, 2005).

The noted learning theorist B.F. Skinner (1983) described some possible environmental qualities that fail to reinforce systematic thinking or new ideas in aging people. Many people who live alone, for example, lack the diversity of social interaction that produces cognitive discrepancy and new concepts. Older people may be reinforced for talking about the past. Their recollections of early memories are interesting to students and younger colleagues. However, preoccupation with these reminiscences does not encourage thinking in new directions.

Skinner claimed that one is more likely to repeat oneself as one ages. He suggested that it may be important for older adults to move into new areas of work in order to prevent the repetition of old ideas. Skinner believed that it is possible to analyze how the quality of one's thinking is influenced by the circumstances of aging and also to identify interventions that will prevent the deterioration of cognitive abilities. These interventions include attempts to be sensitive to the signs of fatigue, planning for regular opportunities for stimulating verbal interactions with others, making careful outlines of written work to avoid distraction, and acting on ideas as they come to one's mind rather than counting on remembering them later.

Cognitive functioning in later adulthood is multidimensional, with substantial differences among individuals as well as differences among cognitive domains within the same person (McArdle et al., 2002). Adults experience tremendous growth in domain-specific areas of knowledge. Within these domains, many complex networks of information, strategies, and frameworks of meaning are elaborated that result in high-level, flexible functioning. The overall level of functioning is subject to environmental influences that promote particular specialization and cognitive organization based on the demands of the situation, the stresses and challenges of daily life, and the opportunities for mastery in particular areas of competence. At the same time, certain aspects of the processing base that are dependent on neural functioning may decline with age. This decline, however, is not always great, and studies have shown that capacities described as elements of fluid intelligence, such as speed of response, inductive reasoning, and spatial orientation, can benefit from targeted interventions (Van Boxtel, Paas, Houx, & Adam, 1997; Saczynski, Willis, & Schaie, 2002). The implications of age-related changes in cognitive functioning are discussed in the box about age and workplace productivity.

On the basis of extensive longitudinal research, Schaie (1994) identified seven factors that are associated with retaining a high level of cognitive functioning in later adulthood:

1. Absence of cardiovascular and other chronic diseases
2. Favorable environment linked to high socioeconomic status
3. Involvement in a complex and intellectually stimulating environment
4. Flexible personality style at midlife
5. High cognitive functioning of spouse
6. Maintenance of a high level of perceptual processing speed
7. Rating oneself as being satisfied with life accomplishments in midlife

This list illustrates the interplay of the biological, psychological, and social systems that contribute to cognitive functioning in the later years. Retaining one's intellectual complexity and creative problem-solving skills are closely linked to the ability to cope with the inevitable role transitions that occur in later life.

Redirecting Energy to New Roles and Activities

Objective 3. To examine the process of redirecting energy to new roles and activities, with special focus on role gain, such as grandparenthood; role loss, such as widowhood; and new opportunities for leisure.

Role transition, role gain, and role loss occur in every period of the life span. In later adulthood, however, a convergence of role transitions is likely to lead to a revision of major life functions and a reformulation of one's lifestyle. Roles are lost through **widowhood**, retirement, and the death of friends. At the same time, new roles, such as grandparent, senior adviser, or community leader, require the formation of new patterns of behavior and relationships.

Grandparenthood

Becoming a grandmother or grandfather brings a psychological transformation as well as a change in the family system. With the birth of a first grandchild, an adult may begin to reflect on one's own life phases of childhood, parenthood, and **grandparenthood**, revisiting earlier personal and interpersonal themes, and possibly revising earlier understandings of the parent-child relationship. Depending on one's level of engagement in the grandparent role, grandparenthood may require a renewal of parenting skills that have been stored away along with the bottle sterilizer and potty chair. Grandparents begin to rekindle their acquaintance with the delights of childhood, including diapering the baby, telling fairy tales, taking trips to the zoo, or having the pleasure of small helping hands with baking, gardening, or carpentry.

A person's parenting skills, patience, and knowledge come into play in a new configuration and may be more in demand in the grandparent role than they were in the parent role.

Grandparenting Styles. Grandparenthood involves a three-generational family system. The average age for becoming a grandparent is in the decade of the fifties, resulting in the potential of a 20- to 30-year relationship with one's grandchildren (Giarrusso, Silverstein, & Bengston, 1996). The enactment of the grandparent role depends on the timing of entry into this role and on the outlook or interest of each generation in having interactions and access to one another. The quality of the grandparent-grandchild relationship is negotiated through the adult child and is likely to change as the grandchildren mature (Smith & Drew, 2002).

People differ in the way they enact the grandparent role. In one of the first empirical studies of grandparenthood, Neugarten and Weinstein (1964) interviewed the grandparents in 70 middle-class families. The following five grandparenting styles were identified, each expressing a distinct interpretation of the role:

1. *Formal.* This type of grandparent was interested in the grandchildren but careful not to become involved in parenting them other than by occasional babysitting.
2. *Funseeker.* This type of grandparent had informal, playful interactions with the grandchildren, enjoying mutually self-indulgent fun with them.
3. *Surrogate parent.* This style was especially likely for grandmothers who assumed major child care responsibilities when the mother worked outside the home.
4. *Reservoir of family wisdom.* This style was an authoritarian relationship in which a grandparent, usually the grandfather, dispensed skills and resources. Parents as well as grandchildren were subordinate to this older authority figure.
5. *Distant figure.* This type of grandparent appeared on birthdays and holidays but generally had little contact with the grandchildren.

More than 35 years later, Bengston (2001) offered a revised picture of the nature of multigenerational family bonds. His research was based on the Longitudinal Study of Generations (LSOG), begun in 1971, and continuing with data collection every 3 years. This study is based on more than 2,000 members of three-generational families, enabling the assessment of relationship characteristics between parents and their adult children, adult children and their children, and grandparents and grandchildren. The study highlights that the way a person enacts the grandparent role is not only a product of a personal definition of the role, but also a result of how the interconnected family members permit and support intergenerational interactions.

The LSOG identified five aspects of **intergenerational solidarity**—a construct that reflects closeness and commitment within the parent-child and grandparent-grandchild relationships. These dimensions are as follows:

1. *Affectional solidarity*: Feelings of affection and emotional closeness
2. *Associational solidarity*: Type and frequency of contact
3. *Consensual solidarity*: Agreement in opinions and expectations
4. *Functional solidarity*: Giving and receiving emotional and instrumental support
5. *Structural solidarity*: Geographic proximity that would allow for interaction

Based on these measured dimensions, five intergenerational family types were identified, which closely resemble the grandparenting roles characterized by Neugarten and Weinstein. The *tight-knit* families were emotionally close, lived near one another, interacted often, and both gave and received help. The *sociable* families were emotionally close and had frequent contact, but did not offer much functional help. The *intimate but distant* families had high levels of agreement and felt emotionally close but did not interact often, lived far apart, and offered little functional help. The *obligatory* families lived near one another and had frequent contact, but were not emotionally close and did not share much in the way of common opinions or expectations. Finally, the *detached* families had low levels of all measures of solidarity.

Looking at the adult children's views of their parents, the sample was divided rather evenly across the five groups. Tight-knit and sociable families were each about 25% of the sample, obligatory and intimate but distant families were each about 16%, and detached families were about 17%. When ethnic groups were compared, European Americans were more likely than African Americans or Hispanic Americans to describe their relationship with their mother as obligatory or detached. Cultural dimensions including the emphasis on filial obligation, immigration or acculturation status, and the symbolic meaning of linkages to one's ancestry all influence the emphasis that various cultures place on the grandparent role (Ikels, 1998).

Two important ideas emerge from these descriptions. First, contemporary U.S. families are characterized by a variety of intergenerational relationships. No single type is normative. Second, about two thirds of these relationships can be characterized as showing high levels of affectional and consensual solidarity. This has been observed in repeated measurements between 1971 and 1997. Thus, despite many changes in family characteristics, including decreased family size, increased involvement of mothers in the labor force, parental divorce, and increasing educational attainment of the parent generation, sentiments of intergenerational closeness are strong. This implies an important stabilizing role for the grandparent generation—a role that may become increasingly important for the large number of children growing up in single-parent and dual-earner parent families.

The Meaning of the Grandparent Role. Grandparenthood has a variety of personal meanings that contribute to the grandparent's overall sense of purpose and worth (Kivnick, 1988; Gattai & Musatti, 1999; Scraton & Holland, 2006). Grandchildren symbolize an extension of personal influence that will most assuredly persist well beyond the grandparent's death. To this extent, grandchildren may help older adults feel more comfortable about their own death. Grandchildren offer concrete evidence that some thread of their lives will persist into the future, giving a dimension of immortality to themselves and the family ancestry that they represent. Active grandparenting can also promote a process of life review, stimulating a revisitation of one's own parenting role and possibly supporting the achievement of a psychosocial sense of integrity. For some, the lack of importance or attention given to grandparents or the difficulty in creating a meaningful way of interacting with grandchildren can create new tensions and ambivalence about aging and role transitions.

In an analysis of the sources of vitality in later life, Erikson, Erikson, and Kivnick (1986) found that relationships with grandchildren played the following critical role:

> The major involvement that uniformly makes life worth living is the thought of and participation in their relationships with children and grandchildren. Their pride in their own achievement in having brought up their young, through thick and thin, and their satisfaction in the way these young have developed gives them, for the most part, deep gratification. With the arrival of grandchildren, they may identify themselves as ancestors, graduated to venerability. Listen to their voices as they trace their own ancestry and that of their children's traits: "She has her mother's fire, that first girl of ours. She has more energy and more projects than anyone. Come to think of it, my mother had that fire, too. And my wife's two grandmothers." "My son is a perfectionist, like me." "The kids are innately smart, like their father." (p. 326)

Grandchildren also stimulate older adults' thoughts about time, the changing of cultural norms across generations, and the patterning of history. In relating to their grandchildren as they grow up, grandparents discover elements of the culture that remain stable. Some familiar stories and songs retain their appeal from generation to generation. Certain toys, games, and preoccupations of children of the current generation are remembered by grandparents from their own childhood. Grandparents may become aware of changes in the culture that are reflected in new childrearing practices; new equipment, toys, games, and forms of entertainment; and new expectations for children's behavior at each life stage. By maintaining communication with their grandchildren, older adults keep abreast of the continuities and changes in their culture that are reflected in the experiences of childhood. Through their grandchildren, adults avoid a sense of alienation from the contemporary world. The more involved grandparents are in the daily care and routines of their grandchildren, the more central they become to a child's sense of security and well-being. This kind of importance is a benefit not only to the child but also to the older

Jakob invited his grand-mother to come to school with him. First she read a story to the class; then Jakob read one. Reading aloud is one of the things they have enjoyed doing together ever since Jakob was small.

Courtesy of the Author

adult's assessment of personal worth. Over time, the grand-parent-grandchild relationship has the potential for becoming increasingly meaningful as grandchildren mature into adulthood. This relationship, typically sustained through mutual personal choice, combines love, respect, mutual support, and a unique form of shared as well as diverging history (Crosnoe & Elder, 2002a; Kemp, 2005).

Some adults interpret the role of grandparent as an opportunity to pass on to their grandchildren the wisdom and cultural heritage of their ancestry. In the process of fulfilling this role, older adults must try to find meaning in their experiences and communicate it in meaningful ways to their grandchildren. Grandparents select many avenues to educate their grandchildren, influencing their thoughts and fantasies. Storytelling, special trips, long walks, attending religious services, and working on special projects are all activities that allow grandparents moments of intimacy with their grandchildren. Educating one's grandchildren involves a deep sense of investment in experiences and ideals that one believes to be central to a fruitful life.

The many ways in which grandchildren can contribute to an adult's feelings of well-being have been replicated in studies conducted in European countries (Smith, 1991). A German grandmother addressed the meaning that her grandson gave to her life:

Yes, he is the most important thing in my life, because I have nothing else at the moment. They all say I spoil him. I don't know. Mama is a little bit strict, and so I always am careful not to spoil him too much. And it is actually Carsten this and Carsten that; he means so much to

me. Since I am a pensioner, I have time for him. (Sticker, 1991, p. 39)

Grandparent Caregivers. Roughly 6.6 million children under the age of 18, or 9% of all U.S. children, live in households with at least one grandparent present. In comparison to other ethnic groups, African American and Asian American children are more likely than Anglo or Latino children to be living in households with one or both grandparents (U.S. Census Bureau, 2010). For about one third of these children, their parents are the primary householders and one or more grandparents live at home with them (U.S. Census Bureau, 2010). These grandparents are likely benefiting from some types of support or care from their adult children. They may also provide direct and indirect support for their grandchildren, including being home when the children return from school, taking care of the children when they are ill and the parents have to work, and taking over household tasks so that parents and children can have time together.

In the other two thirds of this group, the grandparents are the householders, suggesting that many grandparents are using their resources to help support their adult children and grandchildren. About 1.5 million children live with their grandparents with no parents in the household. These children are more likely to be living in poverty, without health insurance, and receiving some type of public assistance than are children who live in their grandparents' household with their own parents present (Fields, 2003). Among grandparents who have custody of their grandchildren, an estimated 40% cared for their grandchildren for 5 years or more (Abel,

HUMAN DEVELOPMENT AND DIVERSITY

Intergenerational Relationships in Various Ethnic Groups

MUCH OF THE research about the grandparent role has been carried out by European American investigators with European American families. As a result, the work tends to begin from an individualist perspective, in which the nuclear family and the autonomy of the generations are highly valued. The results of this research suggest that grandparents play a variety of roles in U.S. families, and that these roles can vary from remote and minimally involved to actively engaged. This picture misses the qualitatively different ways that grandparents are viewed in ethnic groups that emerge from a more collectivist orientation, and the central role that grandparents play in the socialization process and family support systems. Although the majority of U.S. families do not have three generations living together in one household, the presence of grandparents living with their grandchildren is more than twice as likely in African American, Asian American, and Hispanic American families than in European American

families. This may, in part, be a result of the financial pressures on ethnic families, but it is also a result of a more collectivist outlook, in which family and kinship relationships are more central to the value system and priorities of many ethnic groups.

In an interview study of African Americans, Latin Americans, Filipino Americans, and Cambodian Americans, older adults (ages 50 and up) described the importance of mutual assistance and its critical role in fostering a sense of continuity across the generations. This can be especially important for immigrant families. Older adults provide care, guidance, and instrumental assistance for families, especially when there are young children in the home and the parents have to work (Becker et al., 2003).

Even when grandparents and their adult children are not living together in the same home, there is an intensity and frequency of involvement that are not as obvious in European American families. In many ethnic groups, the grandparent generation is highly

revered. In others, the intimacy of the family's daily concerns extends to grandparents, aunts and uncles, and other kin (Lockery, 1991; Burnett, 1999).

The following brief descriptions suggest the outlook of five U.S. ethnic groups on intergenerational relations. Each has a slightly different flavor, but each suggests a more integrated role for the grandparent generation than is characteristic of European American families (DeGenova, 1997; Contreras et al., 1999; King et al., 2006).

African Americans value strong kinship bonds and a supportive extended family system. Caregiving responsibilities are shared among kin as needed. Grandparents tend to support working parents by providing care to young children, and are cared for in return. Their active role in the family often contributes a strong moral and religious strength and provides emotional support to the parent generation, which reduces stress in the household.

Arab American families have elaborate and intensive networks of

2010). In other words, this is a long-term commitment when the adult children are unable to parent.

Many grandparents play an especially important role in supporting the development of their grandchildren during times of family stress (Landry-Meyer, 1999; Goodman, 2003; Mills, Gomez-Smith, & DeLeon, 2005). In contemporary American society, one can view grandparents as a potential resource that is called into active duty when certain difficulties arise for parents. In cases of parental divorce, grandparents often assume a central role in the lives of young children. Some custodial mothers move back home with their parents. Grandparents often assume more child care responsibilities during this time.

Following divorces in which the mother has primary custody of the children, the grandchild's relationship with maternal grandparents is more likely to be enhanced, whereas the relationship with the paternal grandparents is likely to decline. Several studies have shown that having positive ongoing relationships with grandparents during the years following the parents'

divorce is associated with a child's ability to manage school demands, maintain positive relationships with peers and teachers, and have fewer behavior problems (Heatherington, Cox, & Cox, 1985; Heatherington, Stanley-Hagan, & Anderson, 1989).

Grandparents also play a key role when their young, unmarried daughters become pregnant. The pattern of unmarried teen mothers living with parents is especially common in African American families (Minkler & Fuller-Thomson, 2005). African American grandmothers are likely to perceive themselves and to be perceived by their daughters as actively involved in childrearing. Among young adult African American parents, the grandmother is most often viewed as the person to count on for child care assistance, advice, and emotional support (Hunter, 1997). These grandmothers may be young themselves, just entering middle adulthood, when they assume the grandparent role. The presence of grandmothers appears to affect the family atmosphere as well as the childrearing environment. Having a grandmother in the home allows the mother to be more flexible in managing family members with a strong value for reciprocity, mutual protection, and care. Intimate family relationships extend to commitment to care for older family members.

Chinese Americans place a strong value on bringing honor to the family. Filial piety is one of the highest values, evidenced in a great sense of obligation, respect, and responsibility for parents.

Japanese Americans demonstrate strong feelings of respect and commitment to parents. They have a deep sense of obligation for the care of aging parents. Retired parents may live with their adult child who takes on the leadership role for the family.

Puerto Rican and many other Latino cultures embrace the value of familialism, a sense of closeness and interdependence among members of the nuclear and extended family, which includes a deep respect for elders. Family members serve many functions, including socialization, protection, companionship, social and business contacts, and economic support. Puerto Rican families create a formal intergenerational link through the role of the *compadrazgo*, or godparent, who has a responsibility for the child's well-being through life.

Critical Thinking Questions

1. If you have a living grandparent, what is your relationship like? What impact have your grandparents had on your development at different stages? Describe your relationship with grandparents in infancy, toddlerhood, early school age, and middle childhood.

2. Thinking about the idea of different styles of grandparenting, how do you think your grandparents conceptualize their role? Talk to them and ask if they have a sense of the kind of grandparent they are and how they would like to be. How does their sense of themselves compare with how you think of them in their grandparent role? What are the implications of the similarities and differences in these conceptualizations?

3. Thinking about the five different ethnic group families described in the box, consider how grandparents in each of these types of families might influence the psychosocial development of a male and a female child through the stages. Remember, you are discussing people from these ethnic groups who are also Americans.

4. For each American ethnic group, consider some likely tensions between the grandparent and the grandchild generation. What problems might arise in each family if the adult children and the grandchildren identify with American individualistic values and grandparents identify with more collectivist values?

5. Try thinking about yourself as a grandparent. How would you conceptualize your role as parent? As grandparent? What kind of grandparent would you like to be? Why? How do you think having a grandchild would influence your psychosocial development?

---

daily demands, thereby reducing much of the stress that characterizes single-parent families.

Maternal employment is another condition in which grandparents are likely to give direct support. Increasingly, parents of young children call on grandparents to provide all or part of daily child care (Brandon, 2000; Goodfellow & Laverty, 2003). These grandparents are intimately involved in the lives of their grandchildren, directing significant energy, talent, and time to this role. For more information on model programs for grandparents who are raising their grandchildren, visit the website on grandparenting developed by the AARP (www.aarp.org/families/grandparents).

Grandparents who take on primary responsibility for their grandchildren face challenges as well as experiencing satisfactions in this off-time role. Many grandparents are working as well as caring for their children. They may have to support their grandchildren with little access to the social and financial services that would be available to other low-income families or foster families because they do not have legal guardianship of their grandchildren. Caregiver stress is associated with poverty, absence of social services or financial support for child care, loss of freedom, and lack of involvement with friends and interests outside their family circle. When the grandchildren have been exposed to chaotic or neglectful parenting, they may have physical and mental health problems that place additional strain on grandparent caregivers (Longoria, 2010).

On the other hand, grandparent caregivers perceive that they are expressing their generative motives in caring for their grandchildren. They are in a unique position to form a close emotional bond with their grandchildren, helping their grandchildren to cope during periods of family disruption and preserving kinship and community ties (Bullock, 2005; Landry-Meyer, Gerard, & Guzell, 2005; Minkler & Fuller-Thomson, 2005; Dolbin-MacNab & Keiley, 2006).

Bill and Sharon Hicks were interviewed about the experiences of raising their granddaughter, Brittany:

"It has not been easy. Sometimes we feel a little bitter because our anticipated freedom has been taken away." But when asked if he and his wife would open their home to Brittany

Increasingly, more grandparents fall into the involved category, taking on parenting responsibilities for their grandchildren on a daily basis.

again, he answered: "Positively, yes! Brittany has been a shining light in our lives. She has forced us to stay young at heart. And that's not such a bad thing to happen." (Abel, 2010)

Loss of Grandparent-Grandchild Contact. In contrast to the picture of an increasing role for grandparents in caring for their grandchildren, a growing number of grandparents are losing contact with their grandchildren as a result of parental divorce, conflict between the parents, death of an adult child, or adoption of a grandchild after remarriage. Disruption in the grandparent-grandchild relationship is especially great when the grandparent's adult child is not named as the custodial parent after a divorce. In the 1980s, most states created statutes allowing grandparents to file for a legal right to enforced visitation with their grandchildren, even over parental objections. The laws differ from state to state, establishing different conditions under which grandparents may be granted visitation. In 1998, a law was passed to ensure that grandparents who have visitation rights in one state may visit their grandchildren in any state. However, in some states, earlier visitation laws have been overturned, finding that they interfere with parental rights regarding the rearing of their children. Legal recourse is not very effective given that it tends to increase the hostilities between grandparents and their adult children, making normalized visitation even less likely (Drew & Smith, 1999). For more information about grandparent visitation rights, visit the website of the Foundation for Grandparenting (www .grandparenting.org/) (Kornhaber, 2004).

Widowhood

Among those ages 65 to 74, 7% of men and 25% of women describe their marital status as widowed; by the ages 75 and over, these rates increase to 23% for men and 59% for women (U.S. Bureau of the Census, 2010). For many adults,

the psychosocial consequences of widowhood include intense emotional grief, loss of social and emotional support, and loss of material and instrumental support. Emotions of depression, anger, shock, and overall grief as well as yearning for the deceased partner are observed 6 and 18 months after the loss (Carr, House, Wortman, Neese, & Kessler, 2001). Most older widowers remarry, whereas the majority of widows remain unmarried and live alone.

Widows. Widows must learn to function socially and in their own households without the presence of a marriage partner. Adaptation to this role requires resilience, creative problem solving, and a strong belief in one's personal worth. A woman who is widowed at age 60 can expect more than 20 years of life in which to create a new, single head-of-household lifestyle.

In addition to the bereavement itself, a number of stressors challenge the coping resources of widows. Studies of economic changes among widows show that many experience increased expenses just prior to widowhood, as well as marked decreases in their financial resources for years following widowhood (Fan & Zick, 2006; Gillen & Kim, 2009). Women who have never participated in the labor market during their married years may have no marketable skills and feel insecure about entering the labor force. They may be uninformed or uneasy about using social service agencies to meet their needs. For most women, the loss of their husband is most keenly felt as a loss of emotional support, as expressed in the following example: "He is most apt to be mentioned as the person the widow most enjoyed being with, who made her feel important and secure" (Lopata, 1978, p. 221). The transition to widowhood may be especially difficult for those who have been caring for an ill partner, hoping for recovery yet observing constant decline (Bass & Bowman, 1990).

Despite the extreme pain and prolonged grief that accompany widowhood, most women cope with it successfully. In a study of women ages 60 through 98 who had recently become widows, there was a high degree of self-sufficiency (O'Bryant & Morgan, 1990). The majority of respondents said they performed a variety of daily tasks, including transportation, housekeeping, shopping, preparing meals, personal care and hygiene, financial and other decisions, and providing financial support, without help from others. More than 30% said they managed their own home repairs, yard work, and legal questions without help. From this study, a picture emerges of older, widowed women functioning at a high level of independence and autonomy yet benefiting from assistance from others, especially their children, in specific domains, depending on where help is needed. Research from other national samples in the United States, Australia, and Hong Kong confirm this picture. Resilience, which may be expressed in a variety of ways, including recovery of positive mood, engaging in new activities, or experiencing new levels of efficacy are commonly observed in the months and years following widowhood. Women report that widowhood is a very difficult negative life event, but that after a period of bereavement they find themselves making a shift to a new, positive phase of adult life in which they both receive and provide social support to others (Feldman, Byles, & Beaumont, 2000; Dutton & Zisook, 2005; Cheng & Chan, 2006; Ha, Carr, Utz, & Nesse, 2006).

Widows are likely to find support from their siblings, children, and friends. Over time, a widow's siblings, especially her sisters, may become a key source of emotional support and direct, instrumental assistance with home repairs and shopping (O'Bryant, 1988). In an exploratory analysis of the responses of widows in a support-group discussion, comments about the positive and negative contributions of their social support network were analyzed (Morgan, 1989). The widows described their nonfamily, reciprocal friendship relationships as somewhat more positive than their family relationships. In many cases, widows found that as a result of their own sense of family obligation, they were drawn into negative events occurring in their families, especially divorce, illness, and the death of other family members. These negative events added to their distress and prevented them from receiving the support they felt they needed at the time of their own loss.

The analysis also concluded that the most positive form of immediate support from family, especially children, was a willingness to accept the widow's feelings of grief and to talk openly about their father. Social support from friends included a similar willingness to allow the widow to take her time in finding a new identity. These women did not want to be forced to mourn too quickly or be told how strong they were and how well they were handling their grief: "The fact that you're using the strength that you have, just to cope, and to stay alive (another voice: "to survive") is a big job and they don't recognize that, you know it makes you angry" (Morgan, 1989, p. 105). The widows wanted to have their anger, grief, and the disruption in their lives acknowledged and accepted by their friends. In this way, they felt they could begin to come to terms with their loss and build a new life.

Widowers. Widowers suffer greater increases in depression following the loss of their spouses than do widows (Umberson, Wortman, & Kessler, 1992; Lee, DeMaris, Bavin, & Sullivan, 2001). Perhaps because men in traditional marriages rely heavily on their wives for both the instrumental support of managing daily household tasks and the emotional and social support of companionship and social activity, their lives are more intensely disrupted when their wives die. This may result in an immediate search for a new marriage partner. In a 2-year follow-up study of dating and remarriage after widowhood, 61% of men and 19% of women had remarried or were in a new romantic relationship by 25 months after the death of their spouses. For men, a higher monthly income and level of education were the best predictors of being remarried. For both men and women, involvement in a new relationship was positively associated with psychological well-being and interpreted as a positive coping strategy (Schneider, Sledge, Shuchter, & Zisook, 1996).

Widowhood also results in increased death rates among surviving spouses. In a longitudinal study of married couples in the United States, the death of one spouse from any of a variety of causes, such as cancers, infections, and cardiovascular diseases, was associated with an increased risk of death for the surviving spouse (Elwert & Christakis, 2008). The process of bereavement seems to accelerate the course of preexisting diseases, and leads to increased rates of suicides, accidents, and alcohol-related deaths. To some degree, the relationship of widowhood to mortality is tied to the well-known health effects of marriage. Depending upon the way that spouses support each others' health, the loss of a spouse may result in less effective adherence to medical care, less adequate diet, and less social interaction and social stimulation, all of which are known to support physical and mental health in later life (Elwert & Christakis, 2006). Most adults cope successfully with widowhood, either by forming a new, intimate relationship or establishing a new, independent lifestyle; however, others find it difficult to recover from the impact of their loss. The "Applying Theory and Research to Life" box illustrates the variety of patterns of adaptation to widowhood.

Leisure Activities

Whereas widowhood brings role loss, one way of coping is to become more involved in new kinds of activities and interests. As the role responsibilities of parenthood and employment decrease, older adults have more time and resources to devote to leisure activities. Involvement in leisure activities is associated with higher levels of well-being and lower stress. In a study of adaptation to widowhood, such activities were most commonly social activities with family and friends.

APPLYING THEORY AND RESEARCH TO LIFE

Patterns of Adaptation During Widowhood

IN A PROSPECTIVE, longitudinal study of widowhood, researchers surveyed married couples where the husband was 65 years old or older. Following the death of one partner, the surviving spouse was surveyed again at 6 and 18 months following the loss (Bonanno, Wortman, & Nesse, 2004). Five patterns of adjustment following the death of a spouse were described:

1. Common grief
2. Chronic grief
3. Chronic depression
4. Depression followed by improvement
5. Resilience

The most common patterns, for 56% of the sample, were common grief and resilience. These two groups had no signs of depression before the loss. The common grief group had evidence of depression at 6 months, but returned to pre-loss levels at 18 months. The resilient group had low levels of depression even at 6 months following loss. Although these groups experienced fond memories and moments of yearning for their partners, they did not experience long-term grief at 18 months. A second, unexpected pattern, characteristic of about 10% of

the sample, was a group that showed a change for the better following widowhood. The participants in this group had high levels of depression before the loss, and lower levels at 6 and 18 months following the loss. Participants in this group were in unhappy marriages, and many of them had been caring for chronically ill partners. They reported being more confident and having found a new sense of personal strength in coping with the events of widowhood.

Two other groups were described as chronically grieving and chronically depressed. The chronically grieving group was not depressed before the death of their spouse, but continued to show high levels of depression at 6 and 18 months following the death. These widows and widowers were often coping with the sudden loss of a healthy spouse and had trouble finding meaning in the death of their partners. The chronically depressed were already depressed prior to the death of their spouse. The death added a new stressor that increased their levels of depression at 6 and 18 months after the loss.

Subsequent studies of the transition from caregiver to widow support the idea that the conditions that surround the caregiving role, and the quality of the marital bond, as well as the physical and mental health of the surviving spouse, will influence the coping process (Pruchno, Cartwright, &

Wilson-Genderson, 2009). The majority of adults are able to cope effectively with the loss of a spouse. An understanding of the context of the loss and the emotional well-being of the surviving spouse before the loss are important factors that influence the bereavement process. Those striving to support widows and widowers need to be mindful of these differences in order to offer appropriate interventions.

Critical Thinking Questions

1. What are the contexts of widowhood that might determine how a person adjusts to loss?
2. Imagine that a person has spent several years caring for a dying spouse. What aspects of role loss might occur upon the death of the spouse?
3. Consider the case of couples who have been happily married for 40 years or more. What might be some challenges of widowhood when one spouse dies? What are the resources that might be useful to support adjustment under these conditions?
4. How might widowhood influence the resolution of the psychosocial crisis of integrity versus despair for the surviving spouse, either positively or negatively?
5. What are some cultural practices or beliefs regarding widowhood that might impact the process of grief or bereavement?

Recent widows and widowers who were more involved in leisure activities had lower levels of stress than those who did not participate. This does not mean that they were less bereaved, but perhaps social activities helped them to feel less isolated and gave them a sense of continuing social value (Patterson, 1996).

Different types of leisure activities are available that meet a variety of psychosocial needs. Table 13.1 shows the percentage of older adults, ages 55 to 64, 65 to 74, and 75 and older, who participated in five types of leisure activities at least once in the prior year: exercise programs, playing sports, charity work, home improvement and repair, and gardening (U.S. Census Bureau, 2009). Gardening tops the

list in each of these age groups, with relatively little difference between those 55 to 64 and those 65 to 74.

A range of needs may be met through leisure pursuits, including companionship and social integration, experiencing something new and unusual, opportunities to enhance one's competence and mastery, finding solitude and relaxation, opportunities for creativity and self-expression, opportunities for intellectual stimulation, and opportunities for community service.

Gardening. There is growing awareness of the health and therapeutic value of gardening. Gardening provides regular physical activity, including stretching, coordination, and

Two old friends provide social support for each other. After they became widows, they moved in to an apartment together to help manage costs. They're reviewing a box of bills and receipts as they get ready to do their income taxes. This also helps them reminisce about what they did during the past year.

weight resistance. Depending on the size and demands of the garden, gardening can help an older adult meet the recommendations for half an hour of physical activity each day. Gardening requires planning, research, and problem solving. Preparing a garden, evaluating plants and their care, and monitoring their health and growth are natural forms of cognitive stimulation, which can be enhanced with classes, books and magazines, and online resources. Gardening is a stress-reducing activity, especially when approached in an appropriate pace and with tools that are well adapted to one's physical capacities. The sensory components of the garden, including smells, colors, and textures, can have a soothing, reassuring impact. Gardening can be an expression of generative motives, providing a lasting contribution to the community through the planting of public gardens or the enhancement of public spaces. Gardens are increasingly incorporated into senior centers and nursing homes to encourage cognitive, sensory, and motor activity, and to provide a positive opportunity for exercising mastery. Master Gardener programs are sponsored by many universities where adult volunteers learn about up-to-date research-based information on horticulture to share with home gardeners and implement in the beautification of their communities (Morgan, 2005).

Volunteerism. **Volunteerism** is a salient area for activity among older adults. In the United States, among those 65 and older, about 25% volunteer, giving a median of 90 hours annually of unpaid time (U.S. Bureau of Labor Statistics, 2009). Especially in the year or two following retirement, individuals who are not already involved in volunteer service are especially open to considering it (Caro & Bass, 1997). Volunteering provides a meaningful structure to daily life, especially when other significant work and family roles are becoming less demanding. High rates of volunteering are associated with increases in life satisfaction and improved perceptions of physical health (Van Willigen, 2000). At the same time, certain types of volunteer work have been shown to have a positive impact on cognitive complexity and memory functions. The opportunities to assume new responsibilities and learn new skills are two of the rewards of volunteering in later adulthood (Newman, Karip, & Faux, 1995).

TABLE 13.1 Participation in Various Leisure Activities by Age, 2002

AGE	ACTIVITY* (% PARTICIPATION)				
	EXERCISE	PLAY SPORTS	CHARITY WORK	HOME IMPROVEMENT	GARDENING
55 to 64	48	16	28	45	57
65 to 74	47	14	29	38	57
75 and older	31	6	21	22	48

*Respondent has participated in the activity at least once in the last 12 months.

Source: U.S. Census Bureau, *Statistical Abstract of the United States, 2003*. Table No. 1239.

Exercise. Physical exercise is becoming a focus of leisure activity for increasing numbers of older adults because the benefits are linked to better health, positive self-esteem, and a new zest for life. Almost 50% of adults ages 65 to 74 reported being involved in an exercise program during the prior 12 months. Research suggests a relationship between physical fitness—especially a regular pattern of aerobic exercise—and the improvement of certain visual-spatial cognitive abilities that typically decline with age. In the past, professionals were reluctant to encourage vigorous activity for older adults. They believed that a person who was unaccustomed to active physical exercise might be harmed by it. However, research on exercise in adulthood suggests that adults profit from a program of exercise, and that through systematic exercise, some of the negative consequences of a sedentary lifestyle can be reversed (Riebe, Burbank, & Garber, 2002). For example, Hopkins and her associates described a program in which women ages 57 to 77 participated in a low-impact aerobic dance class three times a week for 12 weeks. The program included stretching, walking, dance movements, large arm movements, and major leg muscle movement. After 12 weeks, the group showed improvement in cardiorespiratory endurance (walking half a mile as fast as possible), flexibility, muscle strength, body agility, and balance. A comparison group of women who did not participate showed stability or decline in all of these areas (Hopkins, Murrah, Hoeger, & Rhodes, 1990).

Physical exercise has been identified as a component of optimal aging. Regular participation in moderate activity, such as walking, biking, or gardening, for 30 minutes a day may provide protection from certain chronic diseases and ease the discomfort of arthritis (DiPietro, 2001). Exercise is associated with increased muscle tone, strength, and endurance, which build confidence about one's body movement, coordination, and stamina. Exercise also increases perceptions of self-control and self-efficacy in meeting one's own needs. As a result, people who exercise tend to have a generally more positive self-evaluation and higher levels of self-confidence than their inactive peers (Fontane, 1996; Clark, Long, & Schiffman, 1999). Fitness training has also been shown to contribute to improved cognitive functioning in older adults, especially in the area of executive control processes such as decision making, problem solving, and emotional regulation (Kramer & Willis, 2002).

Redirection of energy to new roles in later adulthood requires a degree of flexibility and resilience that often goes unnoticed in observations of older adults. Try to imagine what life might be like for you 30 or 40 years from now. Will you be prepared to embrace the technology, lifestyle, or age role expectations that you will encounter during your own later adulthood? We are impressed by how readily most older adults adapt to new roles, especially those of retiree and widow, for which there is little early preparation or social reward.

Developing a Point of View About Death

Objective 4. To describe the development of a point of view about death.

During later adulthood, it is inevitable that serious, possibly frightening, preoccupations about death will fill the individual's thoughts. In middle adulthood, most people experience the death of their parents. During later adulthood, one's peers, including siblings and spouses, may die. These deaths are sources of psychological stress and require the emotional process of grief and mourning and the cognitive strain of trying to accept or understand them. At the same time, these deaths stimulate a more immediate recognition of one's own mortality.

Changing Perspectives About Death

The development of a perspective on death is a continuous process that begins in childhood and is not fully resolved until later adulthood. The earliest concern with death, which occurs during toddlerhood, reflects an inability to conceive of an irreversible state of lifelessness. Toddlers are likely to think that a person may be dead at one moment and "undeaded" the next. By middle school age, children have a rather realistic concept of death, but they are unlikely to relate that concept to themselves or to others close to them (Kastenbaum, 1992). Thoughts about one's death and the formulation of a conceptualization of death become increasingly well articulated from early through later adolescence (Noppe & Noppe, 1997). In the process of forming a personal identity, young people ask new questions about mortality, the meaning of life, and the possibility of life after death.

During middle adulthood, people recognize that they have already lived more than half of their lives. There is more time in the past than in the future. The issue of death becomes increasingly concrete as parents and older relatives die. At the same time, adults begin to have a larger impact on their families and communities. Increased feelings of effectiveness and vitality lessen the threat of death. The degree to which individuals gain satisfaction from their own contributions to future generations determines the extent of their anxiety about death during this stage. The achievement of a sense of generativity usually allows adults to accept that their impact will continue to be felt even after death.

Ideally, during later adulthood, ego concerns about death decrease. Individuals come to accept their own lives as they have lived them and begin to see death as a natural part of the life span. Death no longer poses a threat to personal value, the potential for accomplishment, or the desire to influence the lives of others. As a result of having accepted one's life, one can accept its end without discouragement. As the case of Morrie Schwartz suggests, coming to terms with death does not imply a desire for but an acceptance of the fact of death. Along with this acceptance may come a greater appreciation for life itself. It takes great courage to face the fact of one's own death and, at the same time, to live out the days of one's life with optimism and enthusiasm. Older adults who achieve this degree of acceptance of their death appreciate that the usefulness of their contributions does not necessarily depend on their physical presence (Kübler-Ross, 1969, 1972).

The notion that one's understanding of the concept of death changes with development is complemented by the idea that people go through a process in coming to terms with their own death. In the 1960s, Elisabeth Kübler-Ross engaged in groundbreaking work to understand the thoughts, feelings, and needs of patients who were dying. Through her interviews with more than 400 patients, she began to clarify a process of coping with one's death. She identified five stages that are likely to occur between the awareness of a terminal illness and ultimate acceptance of one's death: denial; anger and resentment; bargaining for a reprieve; depression and mourning one's death; and acceptance or a willingness to face the reality of one's death. She also discovered how eager most people were to have someone who would listen to their thoughts and how grateful they were to interact with someone about their death rather than have it treated as a taboo or unmentionable topic (Kübler-Ross, 1969, 1981).

Subsequent research has suggested that there is no single, typical path in the dying process. Some people alternate between accepting and denying their death. They understand their situation, yet fall into periods of disbelief. Some people are able to bring what they view as an acceptable close to their life, saying good-bye to family and friends, and finding comfort in the support of others. Others die while still in a state of fear or denial (Kastenbaum, 1981, 1985). Kübler-Ross's stages are neither a universal nor fixed sequence but they do serve as a useful model for considering the dynamic ego processes that are engaged as one faces death. The capacity to confront the reality of death can be seen as a profound occasion for new insight.

CASE STUDY

MORRIE SCHWARTZ REFLECTS ON HIS VIEWS ABOUT DEATH

Mitch Albom, in his forties, rediscovered his former college professor, Morrie Schwartz, who was dying from amyotrophic lateral sclerosis (ALS), a progressive neurological disease that attacks body muscles and leaves one increasingly paralyzed. Mitch and Morrie met every Tuesday for the last 4 months of Morrie's life.

"Everyone knows they're going to die," he said again, "but nobody believes it. If we did, we would do things differently."

"So we kid ourselves about death," I said.

"Yes. But there's a better approach. To know you're going to die, and to be *prepared* for it at any time. That's better. That way you can actually be *more* involved in your life while you're living."

"How can you ever be prepared to die?"

"Do what the Buddhists do. Every day, have a little bird on your shoulder that asks, 'Is today the day? Am I ready? Am I doing all I need to do? Am I being the person I want to be?'" He turned his head to his shoulder as if the bird were there now.

"Is today the day I die?" he said. . . .

"The truth is, Mitch," he said, "once you learn how to die, you learn how to live." I nodded.

"I'm going to say it again," he said. "Once you learn how to die, you learn how to live." He smiled, and I realized what he was doing. He was making sure I absorbed this point, without embarrassing me by asking. It was part of what made him a good teacher.

"Did you think much about death before you got sick?" I asked.

"No." Morrie smiled. "I was like everyone else. I once told a friend of mine, in a moment of exuberance, 'I'm gonna be the healthiest old man you ever met!'"

"How old were you?"

"In my sixties."

"So you were optimistic."

"Why not? Like I said, no one really believes they're going to die."

"But everyone knows someone who has died," I said. "Why is it so hard to think about dying?"

"Because," Morrie continued, "most of us all walk around as if we're sleepwalking. We really don't experience the world fully, because we're half-asleep, doing things we automatically think we have to do." . . .

"Mitch. Can I tell you something?"

"Of course," I said.

"You might not like it."

"Why not?"

"Well, the truth is, if you really listen to that bird on your shoulder, *if you accept that you can die at any time*—then you might not be as ambitious as you are." I forced a small grin. "The things you spend so much time on—all the work you do—might not seem as important. You might have to make room for some more spiritual things."

"Spiritual things?"

"You hate that word, don't you? 'Spiritual.' You think it's touchy-feely stuff."

"Well," I said.

He tried to wink, a bad try, and I broke down and laughed. "Mitch," he said, laughing along, "even I don't know what 'spiritual development' really means. But I do know we're deficient in some way. We are too involved in materialistic things, and they don't satisfy us. The loving relationships we have, the universe around us, we take these things for granted."

He nodded toward the window with the sunshine streaming in. "You see that? You can go out there, outside, anytime. You can run up and down the block and go crazy. I can't do that. I can't go out. I can't run. I can't be out there without fear of getting sick. But you know what? I *appreciate* that window more than you do."

Source: From *Tuesdays with Morrie: An Old Man, a Young Man, and Life's Greatest Lessons* by Mitch Albom, pp. 81–84. Copyright © 1997 Doubleday.

CRITICAL THINKING AND CASE ANALYSIS

1. What is the point of view about life and death that Morrie is developing?
2. Why is it difficult for most people to listen to a dying person express his or her thoughts about death?
3. What does this conversation suggest about Morrie's psychosocial development? To what extent are issues of intimacy, generativity, and integrity reflected in this dialogue?
4. How might the conditions of Morrie's illness influence his outlook on death?
5. What issues would you want to discuss if you had a mentor like Morrie who was willing to help you learn about living and dying?

The formulation of a **point of view about death** requires the capacity to absorb the loss of one's close relatives and friends and to accept one's own death. The former task may be even more difficult than the latter, in that the death of peers begins to destroy one's social group. Losing one's friends and relatives means losing daily companionship, a shared world of memories and plans, and a source of support for values and social norms. The circumstances surrounding the deaths of others may also be very frightening. Older adults observe their peers suffering through long illnesses, dying abruptly in the midst of a thriving and vigorous life, or dying in absurd, meaningless accidents. After each death, the surviving adults must ask themselves about the value of these lives and subsequently about the value of their own life.

Death Anxiety

Fear of personal death, or **death anxiety,** is natural and normal. Death may be feared for a variety of reasons, some of which relate to the actual process of dying and others to the consequences of it. Concerns about the process of dying include fears of being alone, being in pain, having others see one suffering, or losing control of one's mind and body. Concerns about the consequences of dying include fears of the unknown, loss of identity ("People will forget about me"), the grief that others will feel, the decomposition of the body, and punishment or pain in the hereafter (Tomer & Eliason, 2000).

Several researchers have considered the sources of personal anxiety about death and the changes in preoccupation with death at various ages. Although older adults seem to think about death more frequently than do young adults, they do not appear to feel more threatened by it. In comparison to middle-aged adults, older adults experience lower death anxiety (Sinoff, Iosipovici, Almog, & Barnett-Greens, 2008). Among the elderly, it appears that those who have higher levels of self-worth and sense of mastery also have lower levels of death anxiety (Ron, 2010). In comparison to those in early or middle adulthood, those in later adulthood know more people who have died and are more likely to have visited a cemetery or attended a funeral. Those in later adulthood are more likely to have made some specific arrangements related to their death, including purchasing cemetery space, writing a will, or making plans for their funeral. Their concrete experiences with the events of death, coupled with their own sense of mastery in preparing for their death may allow them to cope more effectively with their fears (Cicirelli, 2001).

What factors help older people cope with fears about death? Several resources have been identified. Psychosocial theory predicts that through acts of generativity, people experience satisfaction in guiding and nurturing future

The ritual of a graveside service helps mourners separate from their loved one before the burial. Many elements of a traditional U.S. funeral are depicted here: the casket and flowers, and the mourners gathered with a religious leader in a grassy, tree-lined cemetery.

© Spencer Grant/Alamy

generations. Achieving a positive resolution to the psychosocial crisis of generativity versus stagnation should help reduce death anxiety. One study designed to test this hypothesis found that the relationship of generativity to the fear of death was mediated by ego integrity, the positive pole of the crisis of later adulthood. Among those who were described as generative, the older adults who also had high levels of ego integrity had the least fear of death, supporting the theoretical notion of a progressive integration of ego strengths from one stage of life to the next (Bringle, 2007).

In addition to the achievement of a generative orientation, people who describe themselves as religious, those who have a strong social support system, and those who have a strong sense of self-worth are less likely to be preoccupied with the fear of death (Tomer & Eliason, 2000). Frey (2003) extended this perspective by focusing on the relationship of self-beliefs to death anxiety. Older adults who have a positive sense of self-efficacy have less fear of the unknown following death and less fear of the pain and suffering associated with dying. In particular, the sense of spiritual self-efficacy—one's perceived ability to generate spiritually based faith and inner strength—was strongly associated with low levels of death anxiety.

The Psychosocial Crisis: Integrity versus Despair

Objective 5. To explain the psychosocial crisis of integrity versus despair, the central process of introspection, the prime adaptive ego quality of wisdom, and the core pathology of disdain.

The conflict of integrity versus despair is resolved through a dynamic process of life review, **introspection,** and self-evaluation. Contemporary factors, such as health, family relationships, and role loss or role transitions, are integrated with an assessment of one's past aspirations and accomplishments. Thoughts of the past may be fleeting or a constant obsession. Memories may be altered to fit contemporary events, or contemporary events may be reinterpreted to fit memories. The achievement of integrity is the culmination of a life of psychosocial growth. Psychologically speaking, it is the peak of the pyramid, in that it addresses the ultimate question, "How do I find meaning in life given the ultimate reality of death?" Achievement of integrity in later adulthood inspires younger age groups to continue to struggle with the challenges of their own life stages.

Integrity

The term **integrity,** as it is used in psychosocial theory, refers to the ability to accept the facts of one's life and face death without great fear. As people get older, they need to step back and find a way to integrate or reconcile the events of their life with the hopes and dreams they may have had in their early or middle adulthood. This process of meaning making involves an assessment of one's life and the extent to which worthwhile goals were sought and achieved. In a search for life's meaning, a person looks for a way to assemble a coherent story of order, purpose, and value out of the complex puzzle pieces of a life (Reker, 1997; Krause, 2004). The attainment of integrity is ultimately a result of the balance of all the psychosocial crises that have come earlier, accompanied by all the ego strengths and core pathologies that have accumulated along the way. Integrity comes only after some considerable thought about the meaning of one's life. Older adults who have achieved a sense of integrity view their past in an existential light. They appreciate that their lives and individuality are due to an accumulation of personal satisfactions and crises. Integrity is not so much a quality of honesty and trustworthiness—as the term is used in daily speech—as it is an ability to integrate one's past history with one's present circumstances and to feel content with the outcome.

Most people have some regrets. One may look back and wish that one had taken advantage of certain opportunities, been smarter about saving or investing money, or spent more time with one's children while they were young (Baum, 1999). The challenge in achieving integrity is to face the decisions and experiences of the past with acceptance. In this process, a person seeks to find an integrative thread that makes sense of the life one has led without belaboring past mistakes.

Given the very abstract and subjective construct of integrity, how can it be measured? One approach was devised by Neil Krause (2007) who created a four-dimensional measure of *meaning in life.* These dimensions included: (1) having a system of values, (2) having a sense of purpose, (3) having goals to strive for, and (4) reflecting on the past to reconcile one's accomplishments with one's goals. Taken together, these four dimensions comprised a meaning in life scale. In a longitudinal study of older adults, Krause examined how various forms of social support as well as anticipated social support related to meaning in life over a 4-year period. Those older adults who received high levels of emotional support had higher meaning in life, but those who received tangible social support had lower meaning in life. Anticipated support, that is believing that you could call upon close family and friends for help if it were needed, was the strongest predictor of meaning in life. Over time, anticipated support was also a significant predictor of changes in a person's sense of meaning. When older adults are confident that they will be able to count on others for help in the future, their sense of meaning in life is bolstered. This finding speaks to the role of the radius of significant relationships in predicting and sustaining a sense of integrity in later adulthood. It also suggests a continuing role for trust and hope, the very earliest psychosocial concepts of infancy, in fostering integrity in late life.

Despair

The opposite pole of integrity is **despair**. It is much more likely that adults will resolve the crisis of integrity versus despair in the negative direction than that infants will resolve the crisis of trust versus mistrust in the negative direction. For infants to experience trust, they must depend on the benevolence of a responsible caregiver who will meet their essential needs. In most cases, this caregiver is present, and the infant learns to rely on others. In order to experience integrity, however, older adults must incorporate into their self-image a lifelong record of conflicts, failures, and disappointments, along with accomplishments. They must confront what is sometimes referred to as the "death of dreams"—a realization that some of their most cherished hopes for themselves or their children cannot be accomplished in their lifetime (Oates, 1997).

Older adults may also face some degree of **ageism**—devaluation and even hostility from the social community. The negative attitudes expressed by family members, colleagues, and younger people toward the perceived lack of competence, dependence, or old-fashioned ways of older people may lead many of them to feel discouraged about their self-worth. The gradual deterioration or loss of certain physical capacities—particularly hearing, vision, and motor agility—contribute to an older person's frustration and discouragement. Older adults recognize that they cannot perform certain tasks as well as they did in the past or that their domains of independent functioning and mastery have diminished.

Furthermore, there is a general cultural sentiment that the death of an older person—in contrast, for example, with the death of a child or youth—though sad, is not a great loss to society, because that person had already contributed to society and lived a full life. Thus, older adults may perceive that society is already letting go of them, even before they are ready to let go of life (Jecker & Schneiderman, 1994).

All of these factors are likely to create a feeling of regret about one's past and a continuous, haunting desire to be able to do things differently, or of bitterness over how one's life has turned out. People who resolve the crisis of later adulthood in the direction of despair cannot resist speculating about how things might have been or what actions might have been taken if conditions had only been different. They are preoccupied with the if-only's of their past, disrupting a calm acceptance of death. Despairing individuals either seek death as a way of ending a miserable existence or desperately fear death because it makes impossible any hope of compensating for past failures.

Depression

The theme of **depression** has been treated in several sections of this text. Given the close link between the concepts of depression and despair, it should come as no surprise that depression has been a topic of research in the study of adulthood and aging. Contrary to stereotypes, the population with depression is composed largely (61%) of younger adults between 18 and 44 years old (National Academy on an Aging Society, 2000). About 5% of older adults living independently are experiencing depression at any one time; about 15% experience depression sometime in later life (Castleman, 2001).

Many of the same factors that are associated with depression in younger age groups are also associated with depression in older age groups: poverty, poor physical health, lack of social involvement, and being single, divorced, or widowed. The risk of depression in later life cannot be attributed to the aging process itself. The negative physiological changes associated with aging—such as high blood pressure, reduced breathing capacity, reduced muscle strength, slower reaction time, memory loss, and loss of visual or auditory acuity—are not associated with depression in and of themselves (Hinrichsen & Clougherty, 2006). However, among older adults, those who rate their own health as fair to poor and those who have a chronic condition are more likely to be depressed than those who say their health is good to excellent. Whether the illness contributes to the depression or the depression leads people to be more discouraged by their physical limitations is difficult to say. Thus, depression as a complex affective and cognitive syndrome does not automatically come with the territory of aging, but it occurs in a subset of older adults. It is especially likely among those who have experienced a decreased activity level; have reduced access to a significant, close, confiding relationship; and have accumulated physical health problems that limit their independence and dampen the sense of enthusiasm for pleasant activities (U.S. Department of Health and Human Services, 1999).

The Central Process: Introspection

In order to achieve a sense of integrity, the individual must engage in deliberate self-evaluation and private thought. The final achievement of a sense of integrity requires the ability to introspect about the gradual evolution of life events and to appreciate their significance in the formation of the adult personality (Walasky, Whitbourne, & Nehrke, 1983–1984). This state can be reached only through individual effort. It may even require temporary isolation, shutting out the influences of potentially competitive or resentful associates. One mode for engaging in self-evaluation is reminiscence.

Reminiscence has been defined as the recollection of "long-term memories of events in which the reminiscer is either a participant or an observer" (Ross, 1989, p. 341). This process of nostalgic remembering allows adults to recapture some of the memorable events in their life histories. Reminiscence may be a playful recalling of a life adventure or a painful review of some personal or family crisis. The process of simple reminiscence has been described as comprising four elements: the *selection* of an event or story to retell or review; *immersion* in the details of the story, including the strong emotions linked to the event; *withdrawal* from

The process of nostalgic remembering allows adults to recapture some of the memorable people and events in their life histories.

the past by distancing oneself from the event or comparing past and present; and bringing *closure* to the memory by summing up, finding some lesson, or making a general observation. Through this kind of process, a person builds a mental and emotional bridge between the past and the present (Meacham, 1995).

Reminiscence is linked to positive adjustment in later life, especially better health, a more positive outlook, and a better ability to cope with the challenges of daily life. However, not all forms of reminiscence are of equal benefit. In particular, reminiscences of the integrative or instrumental type tend to be associated with high levels of well-being, whereas obsessive reminiscences are not. Integrative reminiscence involves reviewing one's past in order to find meaning or to reconcile one's current and prior feelings about certain life events. *Instrumental reminiscence* focuses on the past, on accomplishments, efforts to overcome difficulties, and experiences to help cope with current difficulties. *Obsessive reminiscence* suggests an inability to resolve or accept certain past events and a persistent guilt or despair about them (Wong & Watt, 1991). Contrast the following two narratives:

> When I was a teenager, my parents broke up and both remarried. I was very resentful because they did not seem to care about my feelings or needs. But as I grow older and look back, I understand that they were really not compatible with each other. They had suffered for many years before their divorce. [Integrative reminiscence]

> My husband died when I was away for two days visiting my friends in the West. He fell in the bathtub and eventually died because there was no one there to help him. It has been years now, but I still cannot forgive myself for leaving him home alone for two days. [Obsessive reminiscence] (Wong & Watt, 1991, p. 276)

Reminiscence appears to lend continuity to older adults' self-concepts. They can trace the path of their own development through time and identify moments that were of central importance in the crystallization of their personal philosophies. Through reminiscence, older adults can revise the meaning of past events by using current wisdom to understand or accept what took place in the past. For example, reminiscence was encouraged in a group of veterans who had been involved in the Normandy invasion at the end of World War II. The veterans retold their experiences of loss, grief, and shock, and how those experiences influenced their lives over the subsequent 50-year period. Formulating their experiences in a story-like format and retelling their stories to others provided a means of coping with the stressors of this past experience (Harvey, Stein, & Scott, 1995).

Reminiscence serves as an integrating process that has positive value in an eventual attainment of integrity. In a review of 20 studies with older adults who suffered from depression, guided reminiscence was found to be as effective as drug treatment or psychotherapy for alleviating depressive symptoms (Bohlmeijer, Smit, & Cuijpers, 2003). In excess, however, reminiscence can dominate reality, taking over the time and energy that might be directed toward more appropriate active social involvement. Some adults tend to dwell on sad events and allow earlier disappointments to preoccupy their current thoughts. In that case, their past lives take precedence over their current circumstances. No new events can compete successfully with past memories for their attention. The focus of reminiscence depends on personality, the specific nature of stressful life events, and the degree to which the older person is searching for new levels of self-understanding (Cappeliez & O'Rourke, 2002).

The Prime Adaptive Ego Quality and the Core Pathology

Wisdom

When people are asked about the positive goals of later life, they frequently mention wisdom, which they expect to emerge in later adulthood and to grow with increasing age. **Wisdom** is defined as the "fundamental pragmatics of life"—a type of expert knowledge that reflects sound judgment and good advice about "planning, managing, and understanding a good life" in the face of typically high levels of uncertainty (Baltes & Staudinger, 2000). Erikson identified wisdom as the prime adaptive ego quality of later adulthood, in that it reflects a detached concern for life and a desire to learn and communicate essential lessons from experience in the face of impending death (Erikson et al., 1986).

Wisdom has been characterized by five basic features (Baltes, Smith, & Staudinger, 1992, p. 272; Kramer, 2003; Ardelt, 2004; Staudinger, Dorner, & Mickler, 2005):

1. *Factual knowledge* about fundamental life matters, such as general knowledge about the human condition and specific knowledge about life events, their age-related occurrence, and their expected and unexpected course.

2. *Procedural knowledge*, composed of strategies for approaching the management and interpretation of life matters, including linking past, present, and future.

3. *Life-span contextualism*, approaching problems with the realization that events are embedded in a multidimensional context—including age-related, culturally defined, role-related, and sociohistorical frameworks—and that events take their meaning from certain distinct domains, especially family, work, and leisure.

4. *Relativism of values and life goals*, allowing the person to appreciate differences among individuals and societies with respect to the priorities they place on certain values, as well as the ability to preserve a certain core of universal values.

5. *Recognition and management of uncertainty*, incorporating the realization that the future cannot be totally predicted and that many aspects of the past and present are not fully known, plus an ability to manage and cope with this uncertainty.

One of the concepts that helps link the idea of intelligence in later adulthood with the ego strength of wisdom is **expertise**. With age, individuals who focus their intelligence in intensive study, training, and repeated opportunities for problem solving within a domain become *experts*. A variety of intellectual processes support expertise, including deductive reasoning, a rich and complex working memory, and the ability to organize large amounts of information for storage and subsequent recall. We rely on experts to help inform important and difficult decisions. In that sense, we come to see experts as having wisdom in their particular specialization. Although we may be inclined to look to experts in one field to help us solve a wide range of problems, the assumption behind expertise is that it is discipline specific. In that sense, expertise and wisdom are not identical (Horn & Masunaga, 2000; Masunaga & Horn, 2001).

Not all people who live to old age function at a high level of wisdom. However, when older people are asked to focus their responses on excellence and virtue, they appear to be able to generate solutions that are characterized by higher levels of wisdom. Moreover, people interacting together or even reflecting on the inner voice of those whom they consider wise are better able to produce rich, contextualized, and subtle responses (Baltes & Staudinger, 2000).

Three dimensions that have been hypothesized to promote wisdom are (1) opportunities to experience a wide variety of life situations and circumstances; (2) encouragement by a mentor or guide to expand one's capacity for thinking about problems from a multidimensional, psychohistorical perspective; and (3) a strong generative orientation or desire to continue to gain insight into how people meet the challenges of life (Baltes & Smith, 1990).

Joseph looks forward to these quiet talks with his father. He knows he will always come away with new insight about planning, managing, or understanding the challenges he is facing in his own life.

Copyright © Jose Galvez/Photo Edit

Disdain

Wisdom reflects flexibility of thought, openness to new interpretations, and a willingness to accept the complexity of life. In contrast, **disdain** conveys a rejection of ideas and persons and an arrogance that implies one's own opinions and views are superior. It can be understood as a defensive response to the repulsion for one's physical self and failed past. Rather than becoming more patient, more compassionate, and less critical in their later life, older adults who develop disdain are more likely to express contempt for others and detach from the world around them (Erikson et al., 1986).

APPLIED TOPIC

Retirement

Objective 6. To apply theory and research to understanding the process of adjustment to retirement in later adulthood.

RETIREMENT IS A social and psychological construct that has a variety of definitions. One definition of retirement is that the person works less than full-time year round and receives income from a retirement pension earned during earlier periods of employment. Some people define retirement as the time at which people begin to receive social security or other pension benefits, regardless of their employment status. However, retirement also refers to a psychosocial transition—a predictable, normative change that involves preparation, redefinition of roles and role behaviors, and ongoing psychological adjustment as the structure and significance of paid employment are replaced by other activities (Atchley, 2003).

Of course, some people never retire; some die before they reach retirement age, and others continue to work on a part-time schedule. Some people of retirement age leave their primary job and take another full-time or part-time job in a related field or in a totally different one. Many adults who are self-employed or whose work involves creative skills, such as acting, music, painting, or writing, simply continue to work into their late adulthood (Herzog, House, & Morgan, 1991). In fact, from a historical perspective, retirement is a relatively new concept. At the turn of the 20th century, almost 70% of men over the age of 65 were in the paid labor force.

Projections from the U.S. Bureau of Labor Statistics indicate that in the coming 10 years there will be an increasing involvement of older adults in the labor force. Table 13.2 shows the percentage of men and women at two ages, 65 to 74 and 75 and older, who were in the labor force in 1988, 1998, and 2008 as well as projections for 2018. The rate of labor force participation was relatively stable for those in later adulthood and elderhood between 1988 and 1998. However, by 2008, rates increased substantially, especially for women, and by 2018 about one third of men and close to 30% of women in later adulthood will be working. Thus, although retirement will still be normative in later life, a growing segment of the older population will be working (U.S. Senate, Special Committee on Aging, 1986; U.S. Bureau of Labor Statistics, 2009).

Adjustment to Retirement

Adjustment during the retirement transition is an individual process. Most older adults cope effectively with the changes associated with retirement, viewing it as a desired transition. In retrospect, however, they often realize that preparation for retirement should have included more emphasis on the psychosocial aspects of this change rather than focusing so exclusively on its financial impact. Retirement is a major life change; those who cope successfully with it tend to be more optimistic, actively confronting new challenges and remaining physically active in the transition (Sharpley & Yardley, 1999; Rosenkoetter & Garris, 2001).

Weiss (1997) described a longitudinal study of men and women who were over age 63 and intended to retire in the coming year or had recently retired. Most anticipated that retirement would bring a reduction in stress, especially in coping with the challenges and crises of the workplace. Workplace conditions such as lack of challenge, reorganization, and downsizing (with its accompanying increased demands on the remaining employees) are stressors that workers are glad to leave behind when they retire (Henkens & Tazelaar, 1997). In a study of young retirees ages 51 to 59, the most commonly mentioned positive aspects of retirement were the lack of pressure, more time with their spouse, and the ability to relax. In contrast, their greatest concerns were financial (not being able to keep up with inflation) and health concerns (National Academy on an Aging Society, 2001). In contrast to those who are adjusting easily, a subset

TABLE 13.2 Civilian Labor Force Participation Rates by Age and Sex for 1988, 1998, 2008, and Projections for 2018

	1988		1998		2008		2018	
	MEN	**WOMEN**	**MEN**	**WOMEN**	**MEN**	**WOMEN**	**MEN**	**WOMEN**
65–74	21.3%	11.9%	22.6%	13.7%	29.7%	21.1%	34.4%	27.1%
75+	7.4%	2.4%	7.5%	2.9%	10.4%	5.2%	13.9%	7.7%

Source: © Cengage Learning.

of retirees report declines in life satisfaction, especially those who experience significant income loss, poor health, or death of a spouse, events that are age-related and may not be attributed specifically to retirement. Approximately one third of adults report significant difficulty during this process (Pinquart & Schindler, 2007).

From a systems perspective, it makes sense to think about adaptation to retirement in the context of the other life roles one is playing. One of the most relevant is the marital relationship. With the large number of married women in the labor market, it is important to consider the impact of retirement for a couple as well as for the individual. Retirement transitions can involve one partner remaining in the labor market when the other retires, both partners retiring at about the same time, and one or both partners retiring from their primary work and becoming involved in secondary work after retirement. These configurations can have consequences for the couple's marital satisfaction because the change in work status affects their relationship.

The Cornell Retirement and Well-Being Study focused on workers and retirees ages 50 to 72. Participants were interviewed once in 1994–1995 and again in 1996–1997. Among the people in this sample, 25% were not yet retired and their spouses were also not yet retired. For another 36%, both the respondent and the respondent's spouse were retired. In the remainder, one spouse was working and the other spouse was retired. Several observations were made about marital quality during this transition. First, both men and women reported decreases in marital quality when they moved from work to retirement. The role transition from work to retirement appears to have a short-term negative impact on the marriage. Second, if one spouse remains in the labor market and the other retires, the retired partner reports more marital

conflict. In this case, the stress of the role transition from work to retirement seems to be compounded by the lack of synchrony between the partners in the structure of their daily lives (Moen, Kim, & Hofmeister, 2001).

Difficulties with Retirement

Perceptions of retirement involve a person's enthusiasm, positive anticipation, or resentment about it. This is linked to the important ways in which work structures one's lifestyle throughout early and middle adulthood. In addition to the obvious functions of paid employment—especially income and social status—a number of latent functions provide important psychological benefits (Jahoda, 1982; Lo & Brown, 1999). Work provides a structure for the use of time; a context for social contact; a content for self-identity; regular, predictable activities into which one can channel intellectual, physical, and emotional energy; and a sense of participation in a collective effort. Retirement may be perceived as resulting in deprivation in each of these areas and therefore presents a threat to psychological well-being.

Several measures have been devised to assess the stresses associated with retirement and the anxiety that people feel as they anticipate it. Sharpley (1997) found that when retirees reflected on factors that caused them stress in everyday living, three areas emerged: missing work, problems with personal health, and relationship issues. Fletcher and Hansson (1991) constructed a measure of **retirement anxiety** that captures some of the apprehensions that adults have as they anticipate retirement. It illustrates how people come to rely on work as a primary social structure and highlights the difficulties they face as they confront the transition to retirement. For those who suffered from retirement anxiety, two

After 35 years of working for the postal service, Freda missed the structure and companionship of her job when she retired. But now she has taken up ceramic painting, and the days seem to fly by. She doesn't understand how she ever had time for work.

Manchan/Jupiter Images

factors were especially troubling. First, people who had high levels of retirement anxiety worried about the loss of structured social involvement and connection. This concern was linked to worry about losing friendships, being lonely, and having little in common with former coworkers after retirement. Second, people worried about having to be assertive or proactive in finding new relationships and activities that would meet their needs. This concern was linked to a general difficulty in handling life transitions, a high level of uncertainty about the future, and a general feeling of loss of identity. Although one might think that people who have high levels of retirement anxiety would use services that help people plan for retirement, this was not the case. They may try to deny this transition by avoiding planning and counseling sessions.

In addition to worries about being unable to meet social needs following retirement, some adults find the transition difficult because they feel a lack of control. When people perceive that they are working or not working by their own choice and that they determine how much work to do, they have higher levels of health and well-being. However, when they perceive that their level of involvement in work is being decided by someone else and have little say in it, they are likely to have more difficulty adjusting to retirement, more health problems, and a greater incidence of depression (Gall, Evans, & Howard, 1997; Schultz, Morton, & Weckerle, 1998).

People whose work has brought them little satisfaction and those who are ready to become involved in new activities may feel more effective and independent after they retire (Floyd et al., 1992). They are likely to find new sources of enjoyment, new opportunities to spend time with family and friends, a sense of relief at not having to deal with the stressors of their job, and a new feeling of freedom to develop their interests or to exert more control over their daily life.

CASE STUDY

ANNA QUINDLEN WRITES ABOUT RETIRING AS "STEPPING ASIDE" FOR THE NEXT GENERATION OF WRITERS

Anna Quindlen, who has written "the last word" for Newsweek *for 9 years, explains why it's time for her to move on.*

The baby-boom generation has created an interesting conundrum for this country. Born between 1946 and 1964, boomers take up more room than any other generation in American History. They now account for about a quarter of the population. And so, inevitably, they have created a kind of bottleneck, in the work world, in politics, in power. The frustration this poses for the young and talented should be obvious. In my personal life it was reflected powerfully on the day when, talking of the unwillingness of my friends to retire, my eldest child noted, "You guys just won't go.". . .

Today we have an entire generation of Americans who seem dedicated to the proposition that they will fight aging to the death. Quite literally. And that means staying front and center professionally. The unspoken synonym for "emeritus" is "old." And old is a word we don't even use anymore in polite conversation, a modern obscenity. . . .

I believe that many of our old ways of doing things are out of date, including some of our old ways of looking at, and reporting on, the world around us. Since the day he delivered his Inaugural Address, when I was 8 years old, people have been quoting the youthful John F. Kennedy saying that the torch had been passed to a new generation. But torches don't really get passed very much because people love to hold on to them. . . .

If I had any lingering doubts about giving it up after almost nine years, they were quelled by those binders on my desk, full of exemplary work by reporters young enough to be my children. Flipping through their pages, reading such essential and beautifully rendered accounts of life in America and around the world, I felt certain of the future of the news business in some form or another. But between the lines I read another message, delivered without rancor or contempt, the same one I once heard from my own son: It's our turn. Step aside. And now I will.

Source: Quindlen, 2009.

CRITICAL THINKING AND CASE ANALYSIS

1. How are the developmental tasks of later adulthood reflected in this narrative?
2. How is the psychosocial crisis of integrity versus despair reflected in this case?
3. How is the psychosocial crisis of generativity versus stagnation reflected in Ms. Quindlen's decision to retire?
4. What challenges do you believe Anna Quindlen might face in retiring from *Newsweek*?
5. How accurate is Ms. Quindlen's analysis about the reluctance of the baby boom generation to retire? What factors might account for the baby boom cohort's approach to retirement?

Adjustment to retirement is expected to change with time. Atchley (2001) proposed phases of anticipation, transition, and eventual adaptation. Four markers in this process include: (1) a *honeymoon* period, which is busy and positive; (2) a *disenchantment* or letdown phase, in which the meaning and structure of work are missed; (3) a *reorientation* phase, in which a more realistic lifestyle is created; and (4) a *stable* period, which may last 10 or 15 years until changes in health, financial resources, or one's social support system require a significant revision.

In an attempt to assess this model, one study grouped retired men into six 6-month intervals from the date of retirement. In the period 13 to 18 months after retirement, men were significantly more dissatisfied with life and had lower levels of physical activity than did those in the first 6 months after retirement. Later periods showed lower levels of satisfaction than the first 6 months but not the marked depression of the 13- to 18-month period (Ekerdt, Bosse, & Levkoff, 1985). These findings support the idea of an early euphoric phase followed by a later letdown phase and reorientation. The pattern and degree of recovery are not as clearly described in this research.

Income Loss

Adjustment to retirement is especially difficult when it is associated with a dramatic reduction in income. There is about a 25% to 30% reduction in income after retirement, which is somewhat greater for those who retire before age 65. Although work-related expenses, taxes, and child care expenses may decrease, health and recreational expenses may increase. In addition to reduced income, not all the sources of income are adjusted to keep pace with inflation. Thus, the value of retirees' fixed income declines over time.

Older householders' annual income is derived from five primary sources: social security, property and other assets, pensions, earnings, and supplemental security income (see Figure 13.3, Fisher & Trenkamp for the Social Security Administration, 2010). Access to these various resources varies by race and ethnicity, with older Whites having greater access to personal assets and pensions, and Asian Americans and Hispanics drawing more on supplemental security income due to their poverty status. In 2007, the median income for households headed by someone 65 years old and older was $28,305. This can be compared to a median household income of $65,476 for a household headed by someone ages 45 to 54. About 10% of individuals 65 years

and older had incomes below the poverty level. Poverty is greater for older minorities and older adults who live alone (U.S. Census Bureau, 2010).

The Future of Retirement

The ongoing dialogue among older workers, retirees, and industry is creating more varied, flexible alternatives to full retirement. Certain social forces are influencing continuing involvement in the labor market after age 65. An increasing number of businesses are eliminating a mandatory retirement age. In 2000, the earnings limit for receiving full social security benefits after age 65 was lifted. Finally, the age for full eligibility for social security retirement benefits will be rising to 67 for those born in 1960 or later. At the same time, movements toward reducing labor force participation for older workers include the development of early retirement plans, phased retirement, part-time work, and reduced or redefined job expectations. Innovation in retirement options seems to be taking two directions at the same time: how to retain older workers in meaningful work roles, and how to permit more flexible earlier retirement programs (AARP, 2000).

Several long-range concerns suggest a need to reexamine the right to retirement concept. First, prospects for a longer, healthier adulthood mean that a large proportion of the population will be out of the labor force for nearly one third of their adult lives if people continue to retire fully at age 65. Between 2010 and 2030 the large baby boom generation will reach retirement age, placing new demands on the

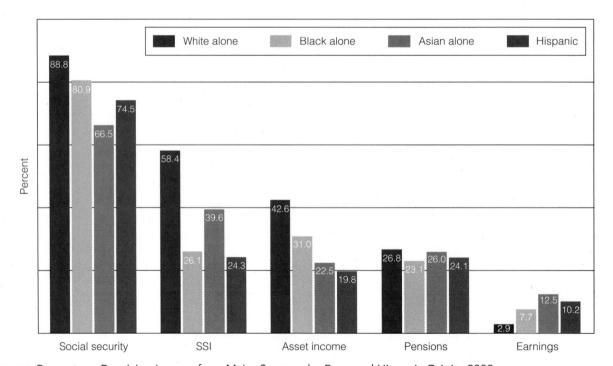

FIGURE 13.3 Percentage Receiving Income from Major Sources, by Race and Hispanic Origin, 2008
Source: Social Security Administration, 2010.

social security system and new expectations for services to support quality of life. With a reduced fertility rate, there may not be enough younger workers available to support this large nonworking population. Furthermore, it is becoming increasingly difficult to earn and save enough during the 40 or so years of employment to pay for 20 or more years of retirement.

Second, among older adults who are well educated and have enjoyed working, many want to continue some of their positive experiences through constructive work. They do not want to retire, and with the lifting of the mandatory retirement age, they do not have to. It is not uncommon for men and women to take new jobs, perhaps with fewer or more flexible hours, after they retire from their primary work. Projections suggest that by the year 2012, 21% of men and 12% of women over the age of 65 will be in the labor force. A great majority of these older workers remain in the labor market by choice. In a national telephone survey of people ages 50 to 70 sponsored by AARP, 70% of those who had not yet retired said that they expected to work after retirement or never retire. Almost half of those who had not yet retired said they expected to work into their seventies and beyond. Although many of those who were interviewed said that they would be working for financial reasons, other motives were also important, including enjoyment in the work they were doing, a desire to have something interesting to do, and wanting to stay physically active and mentally stimulated (Brown, 2003).

Third, people who reenter the labor force during midlife or make major career changes then want to persist in these new activities in order to fulfill both personal and societal expectations of achievement. Many women who delayed their entry into the labor market or achieved a professional degree after their spouse had completed his degree want to extend their work life into their late sixties and seventies (Carp, 1997). The current cohort of workers who are now in their fifties and sixties have become used to a more fluctuating work history, moving from one company or employer to another. They are more accustomed to taking charge of their occupational career rather than relying on the built-in career ladder of a single occupation or employer. Thus, just as the past few generations have begun to grow accustomed to retirement, new generations of older adults are finding ways to prolong their productive work lives, negotiating new and innovative ways of making transitions in and out of the paid labor force.

Chapter Summary

Variability in the patterns of adjustment during later adulthood results from the interaction among biological, psychological, and societal factors, including personality characteristics, health, coping strategies, ego strengths, social support, and the range of life circumstances. Certain regularities can be anticipated in the termination of old roles and the establishment of new ones. The tasks of later adulthood—accepting one's life, promoting intellectual vigor, redirecting energy to new roles and activities, and developing a point of view about death—require a balance among investments in past, present, and future.

Objective 1. To explore the construct of life satisfaction in later adulthood and the factors associated with subjective well-being.

There is an expectation that energy will be spent in the evaluative process of reviewing and accepting one's past achievements. However, this focus on the past must be complemented by the enactment of new roles, the resolution of new problems, and efforts to find new, engaging challenges in the present. People who are extroverted, optimistic, experience a sense of usefulness, and feel they are in control of events in their life are also likely to experience high levels of satisfaction. Development in this period of life requires an ability to selectively direct resources to optimize functioning in the areas of life that are of primary value and satisfaction.

Objective 2. To describe factors that promote intellectual vigor, with a focus on memory, postformal operational thought, and crystallized and fluid intelligence; and to consider the interaction of heredity and environment on intelligence in later life.

Genetic factors contribute to the stability of cognitive capacities over the life course, whereas the impact of the environment, including access to social support, engagement in challenging work and social relationships, health, and education all contribute to variability in cognitive functioning. Certain abilities, especially general knowledge and verbal abilities, remain relatively unchanged with age, whereas speed of processing and numeric abilities tend to decline.

These patterns differ depending on overall intelligence of the person, the career focus and expertise of the individual.

Objective 3. To examine the process of redirecting energy to new roles and activities, with special focus on role gain, such as grandparenthood; role loss, such as widowhood; and new opportunities for leisure.

The nature of the grandparent role differs across cultures, and within cultures across families. No single type of grandparent-adult child-grandchild relationship is normative in the United States, but most are characterized by feelings of affection, and agreement about basic opinions and values.

Adaptation to widowhood also varies across individuals, and between men and women.

Men are more likely to remarry, women to live alone after the death of their spouse. The pattern of adjustment depends heavily on the quality of the relationship before the partner died, and the conditions surrounding the partner's death. Leisure time represents another domain in which there can be both role gain and role loss. Leisure activities can serve a wide range of physical, cognitive, and interpersonal goals. Through volunteerism, later adults also make substantial contributions to their communities.

Objective 4. To describe the development of a point of view about death.

In later adulthood, people's thoughts about death tend to become more practical, focusing on the preparation of a will and planning for one's burial. However, anxiety about death seems to diminish with age. A strong sense of generativity and integrity contribute to the ability to face death with less fear, while continuing to find joy in the satisfactions of daily life.

Objective 5. To explain the psychosocial crisis of integrity versus despair, the central process of introspection, the prime adaptive ego quality of wisdom, and the core pathology of disdain.

The psychosocial crisis of integrity versus despair captures the courage and creative synthesis required in later adulthood. In the face of an increasingly evident mortality, experiences in physical changes, role loss, and the death of peers, most older adults are able to define and articulate the thread of meaning in their lives. They are able to look back with satisfaction at past achievements and with acceptance of past failures. In this process, they find a certain practical wisdom that is shared with others and becomes their legacy for the future.

Objective 6. To apply theory and research to understanding the process of adjustment to retirement in later adulthood.

The role transitions that accompany retirement illustrate the challenge of later adulthood. Retirement usually results in leaving a major life structure—one that provided social status, focus, purpose, and economic resources. The potential loss of daily stimulation poses threats to both cognitive and social functioning. Because so much of one's social status is linked to occupational attainment, leaving a work role is almost like giving up a social identity. Older adults face numerous adjustments after retirement, including role loss. They must restructure their lives so that they continue to feel pride in past achievements without dwelling on the past, and so that they seek new and realistic opportunities for making use of their talents in the present. With the prospect of a long, healthy later adulthood, many in the current cohort of older adults expect to continue participation in the paid labor force even if they intend to change jobs or shift their occupational focus.

It is critical to be sensitive to the image that children, adolescents, young and middle-aged adults, and older adults themselves have of later adulthood. One should not underestimate the impact that one's perceptions of later life have on well-being and optimism at every earlier life stage. If the later years hold no promise, all earlier stages will be tainted with a sense of desperation. On the other hand, if the later years can be anticipated with optimism, people will be free at each earlier stage to experience life in a more confident, accepting manner.

Key Terms

accepting one's life, 529
age changes, 534
age differences, 534
ageism, 552
conscientiousness, 533
crystallized intelligence, 537
death anxiety, 550
depression, 552
despair, 552
disdain, 555
episodic memory, 535
expertise, 554
extroversion, 532
fluid intelligence, 537
goal domains, 530
goal orientation, 530

goal-related activities, 531
grandparenthood, 539
integrity, 551
intellectual vigor, 534
intergenerational solidarity, 539
introspection, 551
life satisfaction, 529
long-term memory, 535
memory, 535
neuroticism, 532
optimism, 532
personality, 532
point of view about death, 550
postformal thought, 536
prospective memory, 535
reaction time, 535

reminiscence, 552
retirement, 555
retirement anxiety, 556
semantic memory, 535
sense of control, 533
sensory register, 535
short-term memory, 535
SOC model, 529
speed of processing, 535
usefulness/competence, 532
volunteerism, 547
well-being, 532
widowhood, 539
wisdom, 553

Further Reflection

1. What are some of the new directions for growth in later adulthood? How are they reflected in the developmental tasks of this stage?
2. What are some strategies that older adults might use to preserve and extend intellectual vigor during this period?
3. What might be some barriers to achieving a sense of integrity in later adulthood? How do the primary adaptive ego qualities of earlier stages contribute to the successful resolution of this crisis?
4. What is the relationship between developing a point of view about death and achieving a sense of integrity?
5. How do ethnic and cultural factors influence the grandparent role? What have you observed in your own family and community about cultural differences in how this role is enacted?
6. What are your thoughts about retirement? If you were promised a full pension that would allow you to stop working, would you continue to work? Is age a relevant factor in deciding about when a person should retire? If not, what factors should be considered?

Psychology CourseMate

To access additional course materials, including CourseMate, please visit www.cengagebrain.com. At the CengageBrain.com home page, search for the ISBN of your title (from the back cover of your book) using the search box at the top of the page. This will take you to the product page where these resources can be found.

Casebook

For additional case material related to this chapter, see the case of "Lola" in *Life Span Development: A Case Book*, by Barbara and Philip Newman, Laura Landry-Meyer, and Brenda J. Lohman, pp. 209–212. This case focuses on the role of reminiscence in resolving the psychosocial crisis of integrity versus despair and the opportunity for earlier expertise to be used in redirecting energy to new roles.

At the age of 91, shortly before his death, Picasso painted this remarkable self-portrait. He faces his death with eyes wide open— no pretenses, some fear, some wonder.

© 2011 Estate of Pablo Picasso/Artists Rights Society (ARS), New York

Elderhood (75 until Death)

Chapter Objectives

1. To identify elderhood as a unique developmental period for those of unusual longevity—a stage with its own developmental tasks and psychosocial crisis.

2. To describe some of the physical changes associated with aging, including changes in fitness, behavioral slowing, sensory changes, and vulnerability to illness, and the challenges that these changes pose for continued psychosocial well-being.

3. To develop the concept of an altered perspective on time and history that emerges among the long-lived.

4. To explore elements of the lifestyle structure in elderhood, especially living arrangements and gender roles.

5. To identify and describe the psychosocial crisis of immortality versus extinction, the central process of social support, the prime adaptive ego quality of confidence, and the core pathology of diffidence.

6. To apply research and theory to concerns about meeting the needs of the frail elderly.

PABLO PICASSO, WHOSE works illustrate this book, lived to be 91 years old. When he was 79, he married Jacqueline Roque, with whom he enjoyed 12 years of married life. During the last 20 years of his life, he remained productive and energetic, persistently experimenting with new art forms and ideas.

Here are some other examples of people who achieved major accomplishments after the age of 80 (Wallechinsky & Wallace, 1993; Wallechinsky, Wallace, & Wallace, 1977):

At 100, Grandma Moses was still painting.

At 99, twin sisters Kin Narita and Gin Kanie recorded a hit CD single in Japan and starred in a television commercial.

At 94, George Burns, who won an Oscar at age 80 for his role in *The Sunshine Boys*, performed at Proctor's Theater in Schenectady, New York, 63 years after he had first played there.

At 93, George Bernard Shaw wrote the play *Farfetched Fables*.

At 91, Eamon de Valera served as president of Ireland.

At 91, Hulda Crooks climbed Mount Whitney, the highest mountain in the continental United States.

At 89, Arthur Rubenstein gave one of his greatest piano recitals in New York's Carnegie Hall.

At 88, Konrad Adenauer was chancellor of Germany.

At 87, Mary Baker Eddy founded the *Christian Science Monitor*.

At 81, Benjamin Franklin provided leadership for the political compromises that led to the adoption of the U.S. Constitution. ■

The Longevity Revolution

We are entering a period in which increasing numbers of people are living into old age. As the previous examples illustrate, it's not that we have no models of the long-lived in earlier periods of history, but that so many more adults are living into their eighties and nineties than ever before. In 2008, 6% of the U.S. population was 75 and older, and as the baby boomers (those born between 1946 and 1964) mature this age group is expected to reach 11.6% of the population. In 1980, more than 2 million people were 85 and older; by 2008, this group had grown to 5.7 million. Of these, 92,000 were 100 years and older. The 85-and-older population, which is the fastest-growing age group in the United States, is expected to reach 6.2 million in 2015 (U.S. Census Bureau, 2010).

The 20th century was unique in human history in the large percentage of people who lived well beyond their reproductive and childrearing years into later adulthood and elderhood. This new facet of life raises questions about the pattern of mortality after achieving reproductive success and about what, if any, limit there might be to the human life span. Current projections suggest that in the United States the average life expectancy at birth will be 80 by the year 2020 (U.S. Census Bureau, 2010). Genetically based diseases that emerge only in the second half of life, such as breast and colon cancer or adult-onset diabetes, become more common as larger numbers of people reach advanced age. At the same time, the mapping of the human genome along with medical and technical innovations hold the promise of preventing some of the diseases now associated with later life. Life expectancy is most influenced by interventions that prevent infants and children from dying, ensuring that more people will reach advanced ages of 70 or older. Interventions that influence the life expectancy at ages 70 and older, however,

AFP/Getty Images

Jeanne Calment, who died in 1997 at the age of 122, was the world's longest living person whose birth date could be verified. Mme. Calment liked chocolates, smoked cigarettes, and had a wonderful sense of humor. Here she displays her Guinness certificate acknowledging her record-winning longevity.

will increase overall life expectancy by only a few years. Nonetheless, significant discoveries that might prevent death from cancers or cardiovascular diseases could affect large populations and continue to extend human longevity.

From an evolutionary perspective, the human species is a highly complex organism, designed to survive over a relatively long period in order to find a mate, reproduce, and rear and nurture the young until they are old enough to reproduce. The adaptive value of life after this sequence is not well understood. One hypothesis is that the extended family—composed of grandparents as well as parents—provides more resources for the support of the young, and forms an added protective layer against crises that might leave the younger generation vulnerable. It is clear that there is a genetic basis to longevity, suggesting that for some subgroups being long-lived has proven adaptive (Olshansky, Carnes, & Grahn, 1998).

Each new cohort of the very old will benefit from the information and technology that have been developed. The more knowledge is gained about the biological processes of aging and the genetic basis of diseases that emerge in later life, the more likely it is that human longevity can be extended.

Those adults in the current baby boom generation (born between 1946 and 1964) are quite likely to be high school graduates, to have benefited from many of the health-related innovations of the late 20th century, and to be even more vigorous than our current older population. The projections of increased numbers of people reaching advanced age are due to increases in longevity due to improvements in health care and fitness and to the size of the baby boom cohort.

In an attempt to learn the secrets of longevity, Jim Heynen (1990) interviewed 100 people who were 100 years or older. He found wide variations in their lifestyles and philosophical perspectives. Some of the advice they offered on how to live a long life follows:

> "Mind your own business, have a good cigar, and take a shot of brandy." *Brother Adelard Beaudet, Harrisville, Rhode Island*
> "I've lived long because I was so mean." *Pearl Rombach, Melbourne, Florida*
> "I always walked several miles a day. I'd talk to the flowers." *Mary Frances Annand, Pasadena, California*
> "Don't smoke before noon. Don't drink or smoke after midnight. The body needs 12 hours of the day to clear itself." *Harry Wander, Boise, Idaho*
> "I've been a tofu eater all my life; a mild, gentle man, never a worrier." *Frank Morimitsu, Chicago, Illinois*
> "I picked my ancestors carefully." *Stella H. Harris, Manhattan, Kansas*
> "Regular hours, taking it easy, smiling, whistling at the women when they walk by." *John Hilton, Fort Lauderdale, Florida*

A team of nutritionists, psychologists, physicians, and gerontologists interviewed 12 Cuban men and women who were reported to be more than 100 years old about their daily diets and lifestyles. The one theme they all agreed upon was the importance of an optimistic outlook on life. The coordinator of the meeting, Dr. Eugenio Selman, said that the six basic elements to longevity are (1) motivation to live, (2) appropriate diet, (3) medical attention, (4) intense physical activity, (5) cultural activities, and (6) a healthy environment. In this analysis, one sees the interaction of the biological, psychological, and societal systems (CNN .com, 2005). Surprisingly absent from this list is the role of social integration and social support. A growing literature highlights the contribution of a sense of belonging to overall health and resilience in the face of crisis (Gow et al., 2007).

The Gender Gap Among the Very Old

A discussion of aging in the United States must acknowledge the shifting sex composition of the population at older ages. In 2008, 54% of those between 65 and 74 were women, 61% of those 75 and older were women, and 67% of those 85 and over were women (U.S. Census Bureau, 2010). This **gender gap** in longevity is observed in virtually all countries of the world, but the differences are accentuated in the developed countries (U.S. Bureau of the Census, 2000). The imbalance in the sex composition is much more noticeable today than it was 50 years ago, when there were about as many men as women in the older-than-65 category (U.S. Bureau of the Census, 1983). Because those currently at the stage of very old age are predominantly women, many of the social issues of aging—especially poverty, health care, the future of social security, and housing—are also viewed as women's issues.

A New Psychosocial Stage: Elderhood

Objective 1. To identify elderhood as a unique developmental period for those of unusual longevity—a stage with its own developmental tasks and psychosocial crisis.

The fact that an increasing number of people are reaching advanced years and that they share certain personal and behavioral characteristics leads us to hypothesize a new stage of psychosocial development that emerges at the upper end of the life span, after one has exceeded the life expectancy for one's birth cohort. This is the stage of life that is experienced by the long-lived in a community who have outlived most of their age-mates. Drawing on the concept of village elders who share their wisdom and help resolve community disputes, we call this stage **elderhood**. Although it was not specifically identified in Erikson's original formulation of life stages, in the book *Vital Involvement in Old Age* (Erikson et al., 1986), Erikson began to characterize the dynamics of psychosocial adaptation in this period of life. Throughout this chapter, we have drawn on Erikson's insights to enrich our appreciation of the courage, vitality, and transformations that accompany elderhood.

We have formulated a psychosocial analysis of development in elderhood based on research literature, firsthand reports, and personal observations to describe the developmental tasks, psychosocial crisis, central process, prime adaptive ego quality, and core pathology of this stage. We approach this formulation of a new stage realizing that in many domains—especially physical functioning, reaction time, memories, and cognitive abilities—variability increases significantly with age. With advanced age, a person is less constrained by pressures of institutionalized roles and social demands. As a result, personal preferences and genetically based sources of individuality are freer to be expressed. In addition, individual differences reflect the diversity of educational experiences, health or illness, exposure to harsh conditions, and patterns of work and family life.

The concept of *norm of reaction* introduced in Chapter 4 (The Period of Pregnancy and Prenatal Development) offers a framework for understanding the enormous variability in vitality and functioning during elderhood. The quality of functioning in elderhood is a product of the interaction between genetic factors and environmental supports. Genetic factors influence longevity, vulnerability to illnesses, intelligence, and personality factors that contribute to coping (Pollack, 2001). Support for a genetic basis to longevity is provided from observations from the New England Centenarian Study that found that half the centenarians had grandparents, siblings, and other close relatives who also reached very advanced ages (Perls, Kunkel, & Puca, 2002). Environmental conditions including poverty, discrimination, social alienation, and lack of social support are associated with lower levels of functioning in relation to one's potential. In contrast, adequate finances,

Morris Dees is a co-founder and chief trial lawyer of the Southern Poverty Law Center (SPLC), a nonprofit civil rights organization dedicated to fighting hate and bigotry. Dees has represented SPLC in a number of high-profile cases against extremist groups, propelling the organization into the national spotlight. These included lawsuits against the Ku Klux Klan, the United Klans of America, and the White Aryan Resistance. Dees continues to be active raising money for SPLC, and taking on controversial cases on behalf of victims of bigotry and discrimination.

social integration, social support, and access to appropriate services are linked to higher levels of functioning in relation to one's potential and to greater resilience in the face of illness.

The variations in life experiences and outlook among the very old are great. As a result, chronological age becomes less useful as an indicator of aging. Neugarten (1981) offered a distinction that helps clarify the functional differences among the very old. She described two groups: the **old-old** and the **young-old**. The old-old have "suffered major physical or mental decrements," which increase their dependence on health and social services. This group will grow as the number of adults over 75 increases. Currently, it forms a minority of the very old. The majority of people over 75 can be described as young-old. They are competent, vigorous, and relatively healthy. They live in their own households and participate in activities in their communities. For example, among the New England centenarians studied, 90% were functionally independent and relatively healthy up until age 92 (Perls & Terry, 2007).

Our intention is to discuss some of the most salient characteristics of life after age 75 and to articulate what appears to be a psychosocial crisis specific to this period. We report evidence of common challenges and successful strategies for coping amid the great diversity of individual experiences.

Developmental Tasks

Despite the wide variability in capacities, lifestyles, and worldviews in later life, three themes characterize the challenges that face individuals in elderhood. First, they must adapt to *physical changes*, monitoring their health and modifying their lifestyles to accommodate these changes. Second, they must conceptualize their lives within a new *time frame*, realigning their thoughts about past, present, and future in order to stay connected to the present in a meaningful way. Third, they must develop new **life structures**—especially living arrangements and social relationships—that provide comfort, interest, and appropriate levels of care.

Coping with the Physical Changes of Aging

Objective 2. To describe some of the physical changes associated with aging, including changes in fitness, behavioral slowing, sensory changes, and vulnerability to illness, and the challenges that these changes pose for continued psychosocial well-being.

There is no way to avoid the realization that with advanced age one's body is not what it used to be. Erikson described it as follows:

> With aging, as the overall tonus of the body begins to sag and innumerable inner parts call attention to themselves through their malfunction, the aging body is forced into a new sense of invalidness. Some problems may be fairly petty, like the almost inevitable appearance of wrinkles. Others are painful, debilitating, and shaming. Whatever the severity of these ailments, the elder is obliged to turn attention from more interesting aspects of life to the demanding requirements of the body. This can be frustrating and depressing. (Erikson et al., 1986, p. 309)

Aging, which is a continuous process over the life span, includes both development and decline. In later life, some physical changes are considered to be normal or expected, and not especially related to disease. People who are well educated, have access to health care and other resources, and have observed healthy lifestyle practices in earlier stages of life are still going to experience some of the normative changes of aging when they reach advanced age, such as some loss of muscle strength or difficulty returning to normal respiration after periods of exertion. However, certain lifestyle practices including smoking cigarettes, alcohol and drug abuse, poor diet, and a sedentary life are likely to accelerate these patterns of normal decline. Other changes are disease related and not a result of normal aging. Some genetic factors appear to increase vulnerability to these diseases, but so do lifestyle factors, exposure to toxins, and stress. Thus, we want to emphasize that the **physical changes of aging** are multidimensional

and variable across individuals. Some people who have observed a healthy lifestyle in early and middle adulthood still experience diseases whereas others who have led a more risky lifestyle do not experience these diseases. We do not fully understand the extent to which genetic, environmental, social, and lifestyle factors help support continued health or vulnerability to disease in elderhood.

The theme of the physical changes of aging can be approached much like its counterpart in early adolescence. Although the rate of change may be slower, older adults notice changes in a wide range of areas, including appearance, body shape, strength and stamina, and the accumulation of chronic illnesses. Just as in adolescence, the rate and sequence of changes vary from person to person. This section will identify major areas of physical change. The patterns of change described here are average trends. Not all adults experience all of these changes, nor to the same degree. The important issues are the meaning that adults attribute to their physical condition and the coping strategies they invent to adapt to these changes.

Most of us know older adults who are vigorous and zestful. On the other hand, we also know older adults who are painfully limited in their ability to function because of physical disabilities. Many factors influence the progression of physical changes associated with aging, not the least of which is the level of fitness that was established and maintained during early and middle adulthood. The topics of fitness, sleep and rest, behavioral slowing, sensory changes, health, illness, and functional independence combine to provide a picture of the physical changes of aging.

Fitness

There is a great deal of variation in **fitness** among people after age 75 as patterns of activity or inactivity, endurance or frailty, and illness or health take their toll. What is described here might be thought of as the usual patterns of aging. However, these changes are not inevitable and, in many instances, are reversible or modifiable with appropriate intervention (Dobek, White, & Gunter, 2007).

What are the elements of physical fitness that are typically assessed in older populations? Seven components are often included in measures intended to assess fitness among the elderly: coordination, reaction time, balance, muscle strength, muscle endurance, flexibility, and cardio-respiratory endurance (Hilgenkamp, van Wijck, & Evenhuis, 2010). Among those 75 and older, elders who exhibit high levels of fitness are also likely to report a better overall quality of life, higher cognitive functioning, lower levels of depression, and a lower likelihood of encountering physical disabilities as they age (Tainaka, Takizawa, Katamoto, & Aoki, 2009; Takata et al., 2010; Voelker-Rehage, Godde, & Staudinger, 2010).

Most people begin to notice declines in their physical health and fitness in their late twenties and early thirties. As those who love baseball are likely to claim, "The legs are the first to go." On a more positive note, most people's strength and capacity for moderate effort are about the same at age 70 as they were at age 40 (Stevens-Long & Commons, 1992). However, older people are less resilient after a period of prolonged exertion. The respiratory and circulatory systems usually degenerate to some extent and are less capable of providing the heart and muscle tissue with oxygenated blood as quickly as they once could. One result is that sudden changes in posture can cause an older person to feel lightheaded. In order to adapt successfully to this kind of bodily change, an older person may find it necessary to move more slowly and to change positions more deliberately. This observable change in the tempo of movement may be incorrectly interpreted as fatigue or weakness when, in fact, it is often a purposeful strategy for preventing dizziness.

Slowed metabolism reduces the need for calories, but there are new risks. Blood sugar levels are likely to rise after eating, and body fat increases. These conditions increase the risk of type 2 diabetes. Reduction in food intake—particularly the elimination of foods such as milk—may result in the lack of essential vitamins and minerals in an older person's diet. The resulting malnutrition may then contribute to osteoporosis and iron deficiencies, which produce feelings of weakness, fatigue, and a lack of resilience (Klesges et al., 2001). Many health concerns of later adulthood that may have been attributed to the aging process itself are in fact a direct or indirect result of malnutrition. In order to cope successfully with a diminished appetite, a very old person must become more conscientious in selecting foods that will provide the nutritional elements necessary for healthy functioning.

An increasing number of factors make it difficult to maintain a high level of physical fitness in later life. Some aspects of aging that impact fitness are a result of the body's natural process as cells replicate again and again and, through metabolism, produce by-products that can be harmful to the body itself. Some aspects of aging that reduce fitness are a result of choices and circumstances such as a sedentary lifestyle, smoking, a diet heavy in fats, too much time in the sun, exposure to environmental toxins, and lack of health care.

Commitment to physical fitness is important for adults in order to face their later years in the best possible physical condition. In its report *Healthy People 2010*, the U.S. government placed inadequate physical activity at the top of the list of health concerns (U.S. Department of Health and Human Services, 2001). A primary goal is to promote regular, daily physical activity for at least 30 minutes per day. Regular physical activity is associated with decreased rates of death from heart disease, lower risk of diabetes and colon cancer, and prevention of high blood pressure. Physical activity also improves muscle and bone strength, contributes to weight control, and improves strength, flexibility, and balance. Despite these advantages, 55% of those ages 75 and older do not engage in any leisure time physical activity, and 87% say that they never engage in vigorous physical activity (National Center for Health Statistics, 2010).

With advancing age, some people tend to become more sedentary and lose interest in physical activity. In order to maintain optimal functioning and to retard the degenerative effects of aging, very old adults must continue to have frequent and regular opportunities for physical exercise. A regular program of walking or other aerobic exercise can enhance cardiovascular functioning and reverse some of the effects of a sedentary adult lifestyle. Research on weight, or resistance, training shows that even among the very old, a steady program of exercise builds muscle strength, which contributes to agility and an overall sense of well-being (Ades, Ballor, Ashikaga, Utton, & Nair, 1996). Weight-bearing exercises help offset the normal processes of loss of muscle tone and bone density, improving balance and reducing the likelihood of falls. Experimental studies of the effects of exercise on cognitive functioning show that it also leads to improvements in various central nervous system functions. These benefits of exercise are attributed in part to higher levels of oxygen, which improve the metabolism of glucose and neurotransmitters in the brain, as well as to increased levels of arousal, which increase response speed (Newell, Vaillancourt, & Sosnoff, 2006).

Sleep and Rest

Older adults seem to need about the same amount of sleep, 7 to 9 hours a night, as younger adults. However, older adults tend to go to sleep earlier and wake up earlier than when they were younger, and spend less time in deep sleep, which may be why older adults often report being light sleepers (National Institute on Aging, 2009c). More significant sleep problems occur for older adults who have various medical conditions that involve pain, sleep apnea, movement disorders, and urinary problems (Ohayon, Carskadon, Guilleminault, & Vitiello, 2004).

The most common sleep problem in elderhood is **insomnia**, which involves difficulties falling asleep or staying asleep. Insomnia may be a temporary problem associated with particular worries, excitement over an upcoming event, or preoccupation with an unresolved challenge. On the other hand, insomnia may be a symptom of other medical conditions, such as unmanaged pain, or difficulty breathing. An interesting problem is that people who have had a bout of insomnia may exacerbate their problem by worrying about whether they will be able to fall asleep (National Institute on Aging, 2009c).

Many older adults take daytime naps; an estimated 15% of those ages 55–64 and 25% of those ages 75–84 nap. There may be benefits from the practice of napping. In a study that tracked over 23,000 Greek adults for 6 years, those who napped 3 times a week or more for about half an hour had a substantially lower risk of heart attacks than those who did not nap (Naska et al., 2007). Napping may help reduce stress and allow a person to engage the remainder of the day with more energy. In a study of napping among older adults, those who had a regular habit of sleeping at about the same time each day and waking themselves up after about half an hour had a greater sense of self-efficacy and less experience of sluggishness in the afternoon and evening (Kaida et al., 2006).

The relationship of napping to well-being is not fully understood. People who are able to nap during the day may also be in greater control of their lives and less exposed to stress. On the other hand, taking a nap may be a deliberate way to reduce stress, relax, and prepare to engage more fully in the remaining hours of the day. Not surprising, napping several times a day is associated with unusual feelings of sleepiness during the day, depression, and pain (Foley et al., 2007).

Behavioral Slowing

One of the most commonly noted markers of aging is a gradual slowing in response to stimuli. **Behavioral slowing** is observed in motor responses, reaction time, problem-solving abilities, memory skills, and information processing (Salthouse, 1996). **Reaction time** is a composite outcome of the time it takes to perceive a stimulus, retrieve related information from memory, integrate it with other relevant stored information, reason as necessary about the required action, and then take action—whether that means the time it takes to press a button after detecting a signal, or the time it takes to complete a crossword puzzle or solve a math problem. Age-related slowing is more readily observable in complex tasks requiring mental processing than in routine tasks (Lemaire, Arnaud, & Lecacheur, 2004). The more complex the task, the greater the **processing load**—that is, the more domains of information are called into play and the more time it takes to select response strategies.

The number of tasks presented in a sequence and the complexity or choice required to make a response are all factors that influence response time. Under conditions where a choice of response is required, older adults do not show evidence of slowing in the early phase of processing the stimuli but in the executive functions associated with enacting the appropriate response (Yordanova, Kolev, Hohnsbein, & Falkenstein, 2004). In many studies, older adults show improvements in response time when given opportunity for practice. However, when older and younger adults are both given opportunities for practice, the older adults do not improve as much as the younger, and the performance gap may actually increase (Hein & Schubert, 2004).

Biological, learned, and motivational factors have been identified to account for behavioral slowing. At the biological level, there is evidence of the slowing of neural firing in certain brain areas, which may result in a slower speed of information processing. The extent of this slowing depends on the kinds of tasks and specific cognitive processes involved. Speed of processing may be only one of many factors responsible for age-related changes in cognitive processing (Hartley, 2006).

The slowing of responses may also be a product of learned cautiousness. With experience, people learn to respond slowly in order to avoid making mistakes. When confronted with new, experimental problem-solving tasks, older adults may take longer because they are not confident in using a new strategy. They may revert to a more familiar, if more time-consuming, approach in order to solve the problem correctly. Thus, a conservative orientation to the selection of problem-solving strategies may result in slower responses but not be strictly due to neurological causes (Touron & Hertzog, 2004). Depending upon the task, cautiousness may be related to prior experiences of instability or falling. As older adults step down from the sidewalk to the street, or step off an elevator or onto an escalator, they move more slowly to ensure that they have good footing and will not slip or fall. Finally, response slowing may be a product of a low level of motivation to perform a task. In experiments in which reaction time is being tested, adult participants may be uninterested in the task and thus unwilling to try to respond quickly.

The implications of the consequences of behavioral slowing are currently being examined. Some researchers have argued that even the slightest reduction in the speed of neural firing may result in reduced sensory and information-processing capacities. Furthermore, response slowing may reduce a person's chances of survival if a situation arises in which a sudden evasive action or immediate response is required. Others have suggested that if a moment of thought is required before an action is taken, slowness may increase a person's chances of survival.

©2010 Noel Hendrickson/Jupiterimages Corporation

As a result of behavioral slowing, it takes longer for elders to perform daily tasks. Her trips to the market take May more time than they did 10 years ago, but she still enjoys her shopping and the satisfaction of preparing her meals with the best ingredients.

A common consequence of slowing is its impact on cognitive functioning. If the nervous system functions at a slower rate, it takes more time to scan and perceive information, search long-term memory, integrate information from various knowledge domains, and make a response (Madden, 2001). With increased input each year, it is possible that the time needed for processing information increases. In the face of complex cognitive tasks, information may be lost, or distractions may intervene if the process takes too long (Birren & Fisher, 1992). For example, Hertzog (1989) examined the relationship of age and speed of performance in a variety of mental abilities among people ranging in age from 43 to 89. He found that the speed of performance measure was a better predictor of mental abilities than was age. Other research looked at crystallized and fluid intelligence. Recall from Chapter 13 (Later Adulthood) that crystallized intelligence tends to increase with age, whereas fluid intelligence declines. When the factor of speed of responding was removed from the tests of fluid intelligence, the decline with age was significantly less. These studies support the claim that changes in the speed of responding account for much—though probably not all—of the documented evidence of decline in intellectual performance with age.

The debate continues, however, about whether this slowing is general—influencing all types of cognitive and motor activity—or specific to certain domains. There is considerable evidence that contemporary circumstances—especially physical fitness and health, as well as the kinds of medications one is taking and the presence of immediate stressors in one's life—influence the speed of responding. In each situation, motor performance results from the adaptive self-organization of responses that are a product of how the person assesses the situation; the person's physical strength, flexibility, and endurance; and the person's ability to control posture, movement, and dexterity. Speed of responding will vary depending on what type of response is required and which systems constrain behavior (Newell, Vaillancourt, & Sosnoff, 2006). One 80-year-old woman may be able to walk through an airport quickly to get to her gate, but may be slow in reading and evaluating the information that tells whether her flight is on time or delayed. Another 80-year-old woman may be able to read the information about the flight and quickly assess whether her flight is on time, but may take much longer to get to the departure gate.

Because slowing occurs gradually, most adults compensate for it by making their environments more convenient or by changing their lifestyles. However, slowing becomes more hazardous in situations that require the older adult to keep pace with a tempo that cannot be modified, such as highway driving or crossing the street with the light. For instance, some older people encounter problems because the amount of time the light stays green at a pedestrian crosswalk is insufficient to permit them to get to the other side of the street safely. As older people recognize some situations in which they have trouble responding quickly, they must review the tempo of their day. Very old people may become more selective in their choice of activities so that they can allocate enough time for the tasks most important to them and perform them satisfactorily. This means exercising greater control over their time and being less concerned about whether they are in harmony with the tempo of others.

Sensory Changes

Every sense modality—vision, hearing, taste, touch, and smell—is vulnerable to age-related changes. With age, greater intensity of stimulation is required to make the same impact on the sensory system that was once achieved with lower levels of stimulation. Some of the changes in vision, hearing, and taste and smell are given in Table 14.1. These changes begin in early adulthood, and their effects increase throughout the remainder of life (Erber, 2005).

Vision. Visual adaptation involves the ability to adjust to changes in the level of illumination. Pupil size decreases with age, so that less light reaches the retina. Thus, older adults need higher levels of illumination to see clearly, and

TABLE 14.1 Changes in Sensory Systems After Age 20

AGE GROUP	VISION	HEARING	TASTE AND SMELL
20–35	Constant decline in accommodation as lenses begin to harden at about age 20	Pitch discrimination for high-frequency tones begins to decline	No documented changes
35–65	Sharp decline in acuity after 40; delayed adjustment to shifts in light and dark	Continued gradual loss in pitch discrimination to age 50	Loss of taste buds begins
65+	Sensitivity to glare; increased problems with daily visual tasks; increases in diseases of the eye that produce partial or total blindness	Sharp loss in pitch discrimination after 70; sound must be more intense to be heard	Higher thresholds for detecting sour, salt, and bitter tastes; higher threshold for detecting smells, and errors in identifying odors

Source: Based on Newman and Newman, 1983.

it takes them longer to adjust from dark to light and from light to dark. Many older adults are increasingly sensitive to glare and may draw the shades in their rooms to prevent bright light from striking their eyes. Slower adaptation time and sensitivity to glare interfere with night driving. Some of the visual problems of people older than 75 are difficulties with tasks that require speed of visual performance, such as reading signs in a moving vehicle; a decline in near vision, which interferes with reading and daily tasks; and difficulties in searching for or tracking visual information (National Institute on Aging, 2009a). About 16.5% of those 75 and older report that they have trouble seeing (National Center for Health Statistics, 2010).

Several physiological conditions seriously impair vision and can result in partial or total blindness in old age. These conditions include cataracts, which are a clouding of the lenses, making them less penetrable by light; deterioration or detachment of the retina; corneal disease, which can result in redness, watery eyes, pain, and difficulties seeing; and glaucoma, which is an increase in pressure from the fluid in the eyeball. The incidence of visual impairments, especially cataracts, increases dramatically from later adulthood (65 to 74) to elderhood (beyond 75) (He, Sengupta, Velkoff, & Barros, 2005).

About 18% to 20% of elders experience problems with cataracts. According to vision experts, recent medical innovations have made cataract surgery much less complicated than it was in the past. Nine out of 10 people who have cataract surgery regain very good vision, somewhere between 20/40 and 20/20 (Lee, 2002). Problems with glaucoma can be treated with eyedrops, lasers, or surgery. Retinal disorders, especially age-related macular degeneration, can be prevented or treated with dietary supplements.

Loss of vision poses serious challenges to adaptation—it has the effect of separating people from contact with the world. Such impairment is especially linked with feelings of helplessness. Most older adults are not ready to cope with the challenge of learning to function in their daily world without being able to see. For them, the loss of vision reduces their activity level, autonomy, and willingness to leave a familiar setting. For many older adults, impaired vision results in the decision to give up driving altogether, or at least night driving, causing a significant loss of independence. However, this loss can be minimized by the availability of inexpensive, flexible public transportation.

Hearing. Hearing loss increases with age. About 45% of those ages 75 and older have some trouble with their hearing (National Center for Health Statistics, 2010). The most common effects of hearing loss are a reduced sensitivity to both high-frequency (high-pitched) and low-intensity (quiet) sounds and a somewhat decreased ability to understand spoken messages. Certain environmental factors—including exposure to loud, unpredictable noise, and injuries, such as damage to the bones in the middle ear—influence the extent of hearing loss.

Loss of hearing interferes with a basic mode of human connectedness—the ability to participate in conversation. Hearing impairment may be linked to feelings of isolation or suspiciousness. A person may hear things imperfectly, miss parts of conversations, or perceive conversations as occurring in whispers rather than in ordinary tones. There are a variety of devices that can help support individuals who have hearing loss. These include hearing aids, amplifying devices that can make it easier to hear on the phone, alert systems coordinated with doorbells or smoke detectors, and cochlear implants that are surgically implanted to help overcome certain specific types of hearing loss (National Institute on Aging, 2009b).

Being aware of one's hearing loss and its impact on social interactions is the first step in learning to compensate for diminished auditory sensitivity. Knowing the people one is with and believing that one is valued by them can help reassure a person about the nature of conversations and allay suspicions. Elders with hearing loss may ask for a quiet spot in a restaurant, or ask friends to speak one at a time in a group setting. Self-esteem plays an important part in this process. The older person with high self-esteem is likely to be able to make the intellectual adjustment needed to interpret interactions and to request clarification when necessary. Such requests may even serve to stimulate greater interaction and produce greater clarity in communication. Older people with a hearing loss and high self-esteem tend to insist that people who want to communicate with them should face them when they speak.

In contrast, older people who have low self-esteem are likely to be more vulnerable to suspicions about the behavior of others because they doubt their own worth. They are more likely to perceive inaudible comments as attempts to ridicule or exclude them. These experiences contribute to feelings of rejection and can produce irritability and social withdrawal.

About 20% of those ages 75 and older have multiple sensory impairments. Those who have both visual and hearing impairments are more likely to report reduced social interactions, difficulty getting together with friends, and are at greater risk for falls, possibly due to the lack of sensory cues that help support navigation in unfamiliar settings (He et al., 2005).

Taste and Smell. There are taste receptors throughout the mouth, including on your tongue, the roof of your mouth, and your throat. These taste receptors detect flavors of food based on five tastes: sweet, salty, bitter, sour, and tangy. In addition, the smell of food contributes to its flavor, and many would argue that the appearance of food contributes to its appeal. With age, the number of taste buds decreases. Older adults have a higher threshold than young adults for detecting sweet, sour, bitter, and salty tastes. Some of this reduced sensitivity may be related to the impact of certain medications, gum disease, dentures, some infections, cancer treatments, or alcohol consumption (National Institute on Aging, 2009d). In order to improve the taste of food, older adults may add salt or sugar, which may aggravate existing conditions such as high blood pressure or diabetes.

Lester takes great delight in the smell of freshly baked bread, one of the foods he selects every other day at the market near his home.

© Juice Images/Alamy

Older adults also require greater intensity to detect odors and are more likely to misidentify them (Receputo, Mazzoleni, Rapisarda, & Di Fazio, 1996). The sense of smell can keep a person safe. Smells related to smoke, gas leaks, spoiled food, or household chemicals are important indications of a possible environmental problem. Loss of smell in older adults can increase their vulnerability to illness or accidents if they ignore these cues. Changes in the senses of smell and taste may result in a loss of appetite or a disruption of normal eating habits. Loss of appetite (which may accompany illness and new medications), pain due to dental problems, and changes in the digestive system all contribute to malnutrition among the elderly.

Coping with Sensory Changes. As a result of the various patterns of aging among the very old, it is impossible to prescribe an ideal pattern of coping. The SOC model, which was introduced in Chapter 13 (Later Adulthood), becomes increasingly relevant as sensory and motor functions are impaired. According to this model, in order to cope effectively, older adults must select the areas where they are most invested in sustaining optimal functioning and direct their resources to enhancing those areas, while compensating for the areas in which functioning is more limited. What one hopes to achieve is a balance between self-sufficiency and willingness to accept help, preserving one's dignity as much as possible and optimizing day-to-day mobility. This is described in the following excerpt from Erikson's study of the very old:

> Appropriate dependence can be accommodated and accepted by elders when they realistically appraise their own physical capacities. One of our more practical elders simply states, "Of course, you're still interested in everything. But you don't

expect yourself to do everything, the way you used to. Some things you just have to let go." However, inappropriate restriction can be, in its way, insulting and belittling. In describing his current life, one widowed man expresses both his refusal to accept restriction and his willingness to rely on appropriate assistance: "I can stay up here in the woods because I know if I really need help, my son will be here inside of three hours. Now, this deal with fixing my own water pipes, I'd have never tried that without my son so nearby, and I didn't even need him." (Erikson et al., 1986, pp. 309–310)

Health, Illness, and Functional Independence

How can we characterize the level of health, illness, and **functional independence** in later life? A mild but persistent decline in the immune system is observed as a correlate of aging. As a result, older adults are more susceptible to infections and take a longer time to heal. Substantial numbers of older adults are afflicted with one or more chronic conditions, such as arthritis, osteoporosis, diabetes, or high blood pressure, which may require medication and interfere with daily functioning.

Osteoarthritis is the most common type of arthritis for older adults. This type of arthritis results when the cartilage that pads bones in a joint wears away. The joints may feel stiff when a person has not moved for a while. Other symptoms include temporary or chronic pain, and gradual loss of mobility in the affected joints. **Osteoporosis** is a disease that weakens bones so that they break easily. Bone tissue is continuously broken down and replaced. With age, more bone is lost than is replaced. Although women are at greater risk of osteoporosis than men, after age 70 men and women lose bone at about the same rate (National Institute on Aging, 2009e, 2009f).

Data from the National Health Interview Survey (National Center for Health Statistics, 2010) provide a look at the relationship of age to difficulties in physical functioning.

Participants were asked about whether they had certain upper-body and lower-body limitations. Upper-body limitations included such things as reaching up over one's head or using one's fingers to grasp a handle. Lower-body limitations included walking for a quarter mile or stooping, crouching, or kneeling. The percentage of respondents who reported difficulty in one or more areas increased from 28% of those ages 65 to 74, to 48% among those 75 and older. The area of most difficulty was standing for 2 hours, with 33% of those over age 75 reporting difficulties. This suggests that many elders would not go to an outdoor concert without bringing a chair.

One of the most difficult health challenges of elderhood is a group of disorders referred to as **organic brain syndromes**. These conditions, which result in confusion, disorientation, and loss of control over basic daily functions, present obstacles for adaptation to the person with the disease as well as the caregivers who are responsible for the older person's well-being (see the box on dementia).

Do people generally experience a rapid, general decline in health after age 65 or 70? Not according to self-ratings. In a national survey of older adults, people were asked to rate their health from poor to excellent. In the 75 to 84 age range, 71% of non-Hispanic Whites, 54% of non-Hispanic Blacks, and 50% of Hispanics rated their health as good, very good, or excellent. Among those 85 and older, the percentage who rated their health as good, very good, or excellent declined somewhat for the three groups, to 67%, 52%, and 53%, respectively (Federal Interagency Forum on Aging Related Statistics, 2004).

Among those in their eighties and early nineties, one health-related crisis may result in a marked decline in other areas. For example, the loss of a spouse may result in social withdrawal, loss of appetite, sleep disturbance, loss of energy, unwillingness to take medication, and decline in physical activity. All of these changes can produce a rapid deterioration of the respiratory, circulatory, and metabolic systems.

Studies of people in their later nineties and older find that these elders demonstrate unexpectedly good health. They appear to be more disease free than those who are 10 or 15 years younger. Perls (2004) suggested that a combination of genetic factors protect some people from the diseases of aging through two complementary processes. First, they are less vulnerable to some of the damaging effects of *oxygen radicals* that destroy DNA and cells. Thus, during their seventies and eighties, they do not suffer from the major diseases such as heart disease, cancer, stroke, or Alzheimer's disease. Second, they have a greater *functional reserve*, meaning that they require less of their organs to perform basic adaptive functions, so that they can tolerate a degree of damage without losing basic capacities. Studies of centenarians confirm this view of aging; they typically have a short period of poor health before death rather than suffering from prolonged disease-torn illness and disability.

In contrast to negative stereotypes about later life, the level of independent functioning among adults 80 years and older is high. Figure 14.1 shows the percentages of non-institutionalized people in three age groups who needed help in six **activities of daily living** (ADLs): bathing/showering,

dressing, eating, getting in and out of bed or a chair, walking, and using the toilet. The area of greatest limitation is walking, The percentage of adults needing assistance is small for those ages 65 to 74, increases slightly for those

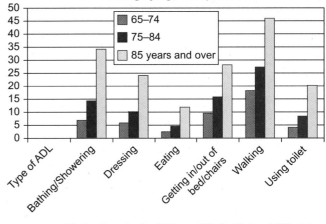

FIGURE 14.1 Limitations in Activities of Daily Living (ADLs) by Age, 2006

Source: © Cengage Learning.

Those who survive into their nineties demonstrate surprising good health. Solly has been bowling since he was 10; at age 96, he still enjoys the sport and carries a 123 average in the 80 and older league.

© Syracuse Newspapers/C.W. McKeen/The Image Works

Dementia

DEMENTIA IS THE loss of thinking, memory, and reasoning skills that significantly impairs a person's ability to carry out daily tasks. Symptoms include the inability to remember information, asking the same questions over and over again, becoming lost or confused in familiar places, being unable to follow directions, or neglecting personal safety, hygiene, or nutrition (National Institute on Aging, 2009g). Two of the most common causes of dementia in older people are vascular dementia or repeated small strokes and Alzheimer's disease. With vascular dementia, the supply of blood to the brain is disrupted, resulting in the death of brain cells. The loss of function may be gradual or relatively sudden. The symptoms vary depending upon which area of the brain has been damaged. Memory, language, reasoning, or motor coordination can be disrupted. Supportive counseling, attention to diet, and skilled physical therapy to reestablish control of daily functions may restore much of the person's previous level of adaptive behavior provided that additional strokes do not occur.

Alzheimer's disease produces a more gradual loss of memory, reduced intellectual functioning, and an increase of mood disturbances—especially hostility and depression. The incidence of this disease increases with age, with fewer than 2% of people below the age of 60 affected by it, whereas an estimated 30% to 50% of those ages 85

to 100 experience some symptoms. The severity of the disease also increases with age (He, Sengupta, Velkoff, & DeBarros, 2005).

A person with Alzheimer's disease experiences gradual brain failure over a period of 7 to 10 years. Symptoms include severe problems in cognitive functioning, especially increased memory impairment and a rapid decline in the complexity of written and spoken language; problems with self-care; and behavioral problems, such as wandering, asking the same questions repeatedly, and becoming suddenly angry or stubborn (O'Leary, Haley, & Paul, 1993; Kemper, Thompson, & Marquis, 2001). Currently, there is no treatment that will reverse Alzheimer's disease. Treatments address specific symptoms—especially mood and memory problems—and attempt to slow its progress.

As the number of older adults with Alzheimer's disease and related disorders has grown, the plight of their caregivers has aroused increasing concern (Roth et al., 2001; Kantrowitz & Springen, 2007). Most Alzheimer's patients are cared for at home, often by their adult children and their spouse. The caregiving process is ongoing, with an accumulation of stressors and periodic transitions as the patient's condition changes. As the symptoms of the disease progress, caregivers have to restructure their personal, work, and family life. Caregivers often experience high levels of stress and depression as they attempt to cope with their responsibilities and assess the

effectiveness or ineffectiveness of their efforts. Over time, they are likely to experience physical symptoms of their own, associated with the physical and emotional strains of this role.

When people with dementia are cared for at home by their spouse, children, or other relatives, three spheres of functioning intersect: home life, intimate or close relationships, and custodial care. The latter, custodial care, often involves routinization, surveillance, and indignities as a result of lost capacities, such as needing help with toileting, bathing, or dressing. Observations and interviews with caregivers and care recipients who live together suggest that these features of custodial care disrupt intimate relationships and home life, making daily experiences more monotonous, restrictive, and constraining. As their symptoms worsen, care recipients gradually lose many of the functions that support their identities as homemakers, parents, or intimate partners (Askham, Briggs, Norman, & Redfern, 2007).

The care of an older person with some form of dementia is fraught with problems and frustrations, but it also provides some opportunities for satisfaction and feelings of encouragement (Pinquart & Sörensen, 2003). The uplifts and hassles frequently reported by caregivers give some insight into the typical day-to-day experience of caring for a person who is suffering from Alzheimer's disease (Kinney & Stephens, 1989; Donovan & Corcoran, 2010).

75 to 84, and increases markedly for those 85 and older. However, even among this oldest group, fewer than half require help with walking, and fewer than 35% need help with other basic tasks of self-care (American Administration on Aging, 2010). Over the past decade, the proportion of elderly people reporting such needs has declined. Many factors may account for this improvement in daily functioning for recent cohorts of the very old, including improved design of interior space in senior housing, new devices that make it easier for older adults to compensate for physical limitations, and medications that help alleviate the symptoms of chronic illness (National Center for Health Statistics, 2004).

Developing a Psychohistorical Perspective

Objective 3. To develop the concept of an altered perspective on time and history that emerges among the long-lived.

Development in elderhood includes gains as well as losses. Through encounters with diverse experiences, decision making, parenting and other forms of tutoring or mentoring of younger generations, and efforts to formulate a personal

The uplifts include the following:

- Seeing care recipient calm
- Sharing a joke, laughing together with the care recipient
- Seeing care recipient responsive
- Care recipient showing affection
- Friends and family showing understanding about caregiving
- Care recipient recognizing familiar people, smiling or winking
- Care recipient being cooperative
- Leaving care recipients with others at home

Some of the hassles include:

- Care recipient being confused or not making sense
- Care recipient's forgetfulness, asking repetitive questions
- Care recipient's agitation, anger, or refusing help
- Care recipient's bowel or bladder accidents
- Seeing care recipient withdrawn or unresponsive
- Dressing and bathing care recipient, assisting with toileting
- Care recipient declining physically
- Care recipient not sleeping through the night

Two of the symptoms that are most difficult to manage are sleep disturbances and wandering. As cognitive functioning declines, the pattern of sleep deteriorates. A person with Alzheimer's disease sleeps for only short periods, napping on and off during the day and night. Often, the napping is accompanied by wakeful periods at night, during which the person is confused, upset, and likely to wander. Caregivers must therefore be continuously alert, night and day. Their own sleep is disturbed as they try to remain alert to the person's whereabouts. When the disease reaches this level, family caregivers are most likely to find it necessary to institutionalize the family member. Alzheimer's disease is a major cause of hospitalization and nursing home placement among the elderly; an estimated 50% of nursing home residents have Alzheimer's disease or a related form of dementia (He, Sengupta, Velkoff, & DeBarros, 2005).

A woman who remembers her mother as independent, with strong views and a deep commitment to social justice, describes some of the ups and downs as she witnesses her mother's condition:

> My mother also had strong views on quality of life issues for the elderly. We had often spoken about the importance of being able to die in a dignified way. She has a living will and opposes heroic measures to prolong life. I am convinced that Mom wouldn't want the quality of life she now has. She can't express herself, is unable to hold a knife or fork, has no control over her bodily functions and can't walk.

However, on a recent visit to her mother, who is living in a group home, she describes the following scene:

> I worried … that Mom wouldn't recognize me this time. But when I got there, she looked up at me and broke into a huge smile. She was truly excited to see me. She laughed and as I hugged her, we both cried. Then she began to speak nonstop gibberish. Although she can't tell us otherwise, my mother appears to be happy…. I honestly don't know if she has any thoughts about quality of life. (Simon, 2002, p. B7)

Critical Thinking Questions

1. Imagine that you are responsible for the care of a loved one who has Alzheimer's disease. What steps could you take to help support their optimal functioning?
2. Why do you think attention to diet is a recuperative component for people with vascular dementia?
3. Do you think that psychosocial development continues for people who have Alzheimer's disease? What about the caregivers? How might the responsibilities of care contribute to or impede their psychosocial development?
4. Why might sleep disturbances and wandering be the symptoms that are most likely to lead to institutionalization for those with Alzheimer's disease?
5. Why might an adult child want to care for a parent who has Alzheimer's disease rather than place him or her in a nursing home or extended care facility?
6. If you were to take on the responsibilities for someone with dementia, how would you prepare for this role? How would you plan for the long-term nature of this responsibility and the continuing deterioration of your loved one?

philosophy, adults reach new levels of conscious thought. Very old adults are more aware of alternatives; they can look deeply into both the past and the future, and can recognize that opposing forces can exist side by side (Riegel, 1973; Kunzmann & Baltes, 2005). The product of this integration of past, present, and future is the formation of a **psychohistorical perspective**. Through a process of creative coping, elders in each generation blend the salient events of their past histories with the demands of current reality. They are able to consider the contextual variations and uncertainties that are inherent in trying to make sense of life's challenges. Having lived a long time, and envisioning less time in the future, elders are more likely to be more forgiving, less interested in material accumulation, and more focused on the emotional satisfactions of life (Allemand, 2008; Brandtstädter, Rothermund, Kranz, & Kühn, 2010).

Think about what it means to have lived for 75 or more years. Those adults who were 80 years old in 2010 lived through the Great Depression; World War II; the Korean war; the Vietnam war; the Gulf war; the Afghan and Iraqi wars; the assassination of President Kennedy; Watergate; the Clinton impeachment trials; the AIDS epidemic; the terrorist attacks of September 11, 2001; the floods that destroyed much of New Orleans; and the election of the first African

American president. They have experienced the political leadership of 14 presidents. During their lives, they have adapted to dramatic technological innovations in communication, transportation, manufacturing, economics, food production, leisure activities, and health care. They have also experienced striking changes in cultural and political values.

One consequence of a long life is the accumulation of experiences. Another is the realization that change is a basic element of all life at the individual and social levels. Sometimes, these changes appear cyclical; at other times, they appear to bring real transformations. For example, people who are now age 80 lived during World War II, when women were involved in the labor market while men served in the military; the 1950s, when many women withdrew from the labor market and committed themselves to working at home; and the 1970s up to the present, when it has become normative for women to be employed outside the home, even when they have very young children. The patterns of behavior that younger adults might view as normative and necessary, elders may recognize as part of fluctuating social or historical conditions. Within the framework of an extended life, very old adults have opportunities to gain a special perspective on conditions of continuity and change within their culture. In the process of developing such a psychohistorical perspective, they develop a personal understanding of the effects of history on individual lives and of one's place in the chain of events. As society becomes more accustomed to having a significant group of very old adults functioning in the community, some scholars anticipate that a *culture of aging* will emerge in technological societies. This culture is likely to provide more opportunities for the expression of the pragmatic wisdom accumulated over a long lifetime through theater, music, the arts, and critical commentary. At the same time, new roles will evolve for successful agers as mentors and advisors to the young (Kunzmann & Baltes, 2005). In the United Kingdom, pensioners have created the Retirement Lounge, an online setting where retirees can interact and share their experiences:

> Social interaction is extremely important when we leave work for good. We are no longer in the working environment to share a joke or gossip with our colleagues. Sadly, many retirees get trapped in their home environment with no one to talk to apart from their family members, if they are fortunate to have them around. With that in mind, this portal is set up to serve the needs of senior citizens. This is a Pensioners Corner. With our pool of experience and knowledge base we should be able to help each other. (retirement-lounge.com, 2010)

Another online resource is sponsored by TIAA, myretirement.org. It has over 13,000 members who share ideas about weekly topics, access information about current trends, respond to surveys about topics of relevance to older adults and read about the results, share aspirations, thoughts, and photos with others. Other sites where older adults are sharing their expertise include: coolgrandma.com, senior.com, eldercareonline (econline.com), seniornet.org, and senioryears.com.

An international group of leaders, *The Elders*, is a different example of how people can bring their life experiences to bear to address critical issues (www.theelders.org). *The Elders* has formed to help address some of the serious and seemingly intractable problems that plague our world. A premise of this group is that in traditional societies, the oldest members of the group were looked to for their wisdom and guidance in efforts to resolve difficult conflicts. In today's world, where the conflicts are often of an international and intercultural nature, the global community is in need of a group of respected and trusted leaders who can offer guidance without a vested interest in a particular national, industrial, or religious advantage. The founding members of the *The Elders* are characterized as "trusted, respected worldly-wise individuals with a proven commitment and record of contributing to solving global problems." The current group of *Elders* includes: Martti Ahtisarri, Nelson Mandela, Graça Machel, Desmond Tutu, Kofi Annan, Ela Bhatt, Lakhdar Brahimi, Gro Brundtland, Jimmy Carter, Fernando H. Cardoso, Mary Robinson, and Aung San Suu Kyi. *The Elders* hope to share their wisdom, forged over a long lifetime and opportunities for international leadership.

A current effort by *The Elders* is to support worldwide immunization of children for polio and measles. They are working to support reunification of Cyprus, and to facilitate peaceful negotiations in the Middle East (The Elders, 2010).

As the example of *The Elders* suggests, a psychohistorical perspective contributes to the wisdom that the very old bring to their understanding of the meaning of life. As a result of living a long time, a person becomes aware of life's lessons as well as its uncertainties. The integration of a long-term past, present, and future combined with an appreciation for the relativistic nature of human experience allows these adults to bring an acceptance of alternative solutions and a commitment to essential positive values (Baltes & Staudinger, 2000).

We are all part of the process of psychosocial evolution. Each generation adds to the existing knowledge base and reinterprets the norms of society for succeeding generations. The very old are likely to be parents, grandparents, and great-grandparents. Many are seeing their lines of descent continue into the fourth generation, which will dominate the 21st century. The opportunity to see several generations of offspring brings a new degree of continuity to life, linking memories of one's own grandparents to observations of one's great-grandchildren (Wentowski, 1985). We can expect the value of the oral tradition of history and storytelling to take on new meaning as the very old help their great-grandchildren feel connected to the distant past. We can also expect a greater investment in the future, as the very old see in their great-grandchildren the concrete extension of their ancestry three generations into the future.

Erikson (Erikson et al., 1986) identified the emergence of these tendencies in the very old in the following excerpt:

> The elder has a reservoir of strength in the wellsprings of history and storytelling. As collectors of time and preservers

Wendell tells his young listeners what it was like to be a soldier in World War II. Through his stories, he makes this period of American history come alive for a new generation.

Copyright © Bill Aron/Photo Edit

of memory, those healthy elders who have survived into a reasonably fit old age have time on their side—time that is to be dispensed wisely and creatively, usually in the form of stories, to those younger ones who will one day follow in their footsteps. Telling these stories, and telling them well, marks a certain capacity for one generation to entrust itself to the next, by passing on a certain shared and collective identity to the survivors of the next generation: the future. (p. 331)

Traveling Uncharted Territory: Life Structures in Elderhood

Objective 4. To explore elements of the lifestyle structure in elderhood, especially living arrangements and gender roles.

How should elders behave? What norms exist to guide their social relationships or the structure of their daily lives? What does a healthy 85-year-old woman consider appropriate behavior, and what expectations do others have for her? When we talk about traveling uncharted territory, we are assuming that elderhood is a time of life for which there are few age-specific social norms. The very old are creating their own definitions of this life stage. You may have heard the expression "Life begins at 80." One interpretation of this adage is that because there are so few norms for behavior and so few responsibilities when one reaches elderhood, one can do whatever one wants.

Changes in role relationships—especially role loss in later adulthood—present significant challenges to the

preservation of a coherent self-concept. In early adulthood, there is an opportunity to engage in many new roles and to establish a lifestyle that expresses the priorities of one's personal identity. In middle adulthood, the pressure of life roles and their competing demands may be at their peak. During later adulthood, the challenge is to establish an integrated sense of self that helps to compensate for the loss of salient life roles and to protect the person from a sense of despair. In elderhood, those who cope most effectively have been able to focus on certain valued characteristics of the self and to optimize them despite difficult changes in their social and physical resources (Diehl, Hastings, & Stanton, 2001).

The MacArthur Foundation Research Network on Successful Aging (Rowe & Kahn, 1998) has offered a new, interdisciplinary perspective on the distinction between usual and successful aging. Those characterized by **usual aging** may be functioning well but are at high risk for disease, disability, and reduced capacity for functional independence. In contrast, the **successful agers** are characterized by three interdependent features (see Figure 14.2). They have a "low risk of disease and disease-related disabilities; high mental and physical function; and active engagement with life" (p. 38). This last feature, **active engagement**, is a frequently repeated theme in the field of gerontology.

In an effort to describe the norms that older adults use to guide their conduct, researchers asked older adults from New York City and Savannah, Georgia, to respond to six pictures similar to the two drawings in Figure 14.3 (Offenbacher & Poster, 1985). The responses to the following two questions were used to construct a code of conduct: "How do you think that people who know this person, such as family or friends, feel about him or her?" and "How do you

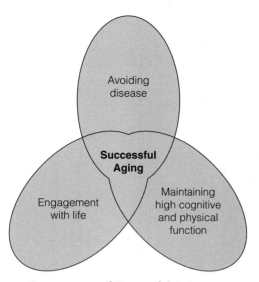

FIGURE 14.2 Components of Successful Aging

Source: Components of Successful Aging, Adapted from J.W. Rowe & R.L. Kahn, 1998, *Successful Aging.*

feel about this person?" Four normative principles were found in the responses:

1. Don't be sorry for yourself.
2. Try to be independent.
3. Don't just sit there; do something.
4. Above all, be sociable.

This code of conduct suggests that older people believe that being sociable, active, and independent constitute successful living in later life. Of course, older adults are not alone in valuing these qualities. However, these norms are important as sources of self-esteem for this age group. They promote a sense of vigor and a shield against depression or discouragement.

The themes "Don't be sorry for yourself" and "Don't just sit there" suggest that the very old continue to see their lives as precious resources that are not to be wasted in self-pity and passivity. The emphasis on activity as opposed to meditation reflects the Western cultural value of a *sense of agency*—thinking is not as highly valued as action. In contrast, doing things, having an impact, and receiving the feedback that action stimulates provide the keys to successful living. Subsequent studies have supported the idea that finding meaning in one's existence, continuing to experience a sense of social competence, and perceptions of self-efficacy help older adults maintain a sense of well-being (Onedera & Stickle, 2008). For example, by continuing to participate in intellectually complex and challenging leisure activities— such as reading stimulating books and magazines; going to museums, concerts, and plays; or participating in hobbies that require decision making and problem solving—older adults contribute to preserving their intellectual flexibility (Schooler & Mulatu, 2001).

The desire to preserve a sense of control and agency despite health problems, loss of loved ones, and poverty

is expressed across ethnic groups. However, the ways that women define empowerment and experience successful aging is related, in part, to their cultural values and worldview. In a study of women between the ages of 60 and 80, nine different ethnic groups were self-defined by the participants: English, British Muslim, African Caribbean, Dominican, British Irish, Pakistani, British Polish, Indian, and Bangladeshi (Wray, 2003). For some of these women, freedom from the burdens of care for their aging family members or children was a valued opportunity for empowerment in later life. A number of women engaged in forms of group religious services and the related opportunities for social interaction, volunteer work, and prayer, which created feelings of social inclusion and agency.

> I am baptized Sikh and value religion to guide me and have focus in life. My religion has influenced my life very positively; this has helped me to care for my husband and cope with stressful events. I have planned days when I visit friends and attend religious activities. These are also my means of socializing. We offer each other support and get involved in charity work. (Wray, 2003, p. 519)

For some women, paid employment or volunteer work keeps them connected to society and provides feelings of being in control of their daily lives. Finally, some women spoke of their time with their grandchildren and the responsibilities they had for their grandchildren's care as contributing to a sense of purpose and well-being. In some cultural groups, the opportunity to strengthen their connection with their religious and ethnic communities created a form of collective agency. In other cultural groups, the opportunity to continue to express self-reliance and control over daily life was especially significant. Among most of the women, some form of interdependence and participation in meaningful social relationships played a key role in sustaining feelings of agency and continued self-worth.

The fact that older adults must carve out new patterns of adapting to later life is illustrated in the following sections in two specific areas of functioning: living arrangements and gender role definitions.

Living Arrangements

Approximately 78% of U.S. adults ages 75 and older own their own homes. However, the pattern of **living arrangements** changes after age 75, especially for women (see Figure 14.4). Before that age, the majority of older adults live in family households, mostly as married couples. Among adults ages 75 and older, however, only 45% live with a spouse; the others either live alone or with family or nonrelatives. The pattern differs by gender. Among women ages 75 and older, 48% live alone; among men ages 75 and older, only 23% live alone (U.S. Census Bureau, 2008). Older women are less likely than men to remarry after the death of their spouse, and older women are less likely to live with other family members than they were in the past. For unmarried elders, functional status and cognitive functioning

FIGURE 14.3 Typical Drawings That Researchers Might Use to Establish the Social Norms of Very Old People

Source: Drawings based on Offenbacher and Poster, 1985.

are key factors that lead to living with one's children or other relatives (Liang et al., 2005).

Living arrangements among older adults are linked to cultural values associated with individualism and independence or collectivism and interdependence. In a comparison of living arrangements of older adults in 43 countries, older adults were the most likely age group to live alone. However, in Africa it was more common for older adults to head up a large household that included young children than in other countries. In Asia co-residence with adult children was more common than in Africa. When older adults lived with their children, co-residence with adult sons and their families was more common in Asia and Africa, but co-residence with adult daughters and their families was more common in Latin America. In countries with higher levels of education for the general population, families were more likely to have nuclear households with older adults living alone (Bongaarts & Zimmer, 2002).

Living Alone. One implication of these trends in living arrangements is that increasing numbers of women are establishing a new single lifestyle in which they function as heads of households at ages 75 and older. Though still in need of social interaction and support services, they are often relieved of the responsibilities of caring for spouses who were ill. Depending on their own health, these women may be freer to direct their time and interests toward their friends, grandchildren, hobbies, and activities than they have

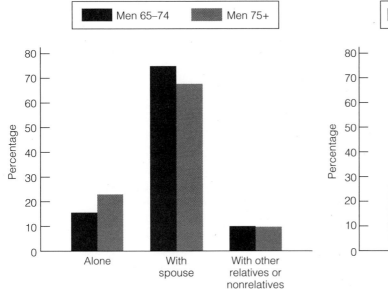
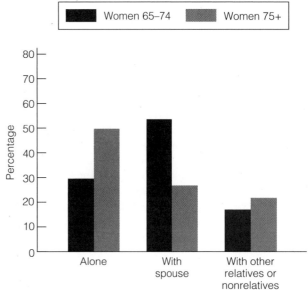

FIGURE 14.4 Living Arrangements for Older Adults by Age and Sex: 2003

Source: U.S. Census Bureau, 2004b.

been at any other time in their lives. In a qualitative study of older widows' experiences, four themes emerged: (1) making aloneness acceptable, (2) going my own way, (3) reducing my risks, and (4) sustaining myself (Porter, 1994). One aspect of this process of adaptation, often linked to "going my own way" and "reducing my risks," is a decision to move from one's residence. In a longitudinal study of residential mobility, individuals were interviewed over a 20-year period. Widowhood was found to be a significant event that triggered a decision to move, often within the first year after becoming widowed (Chevan, 1995).

The pattern of elderly women living alone is similar in Canada, the United Kingdom, and many other northern European countries, but it is not as common in southern Europe and developing countries, where both older men and women, whether married or widowed, live in multigenerational families. For example, data gathered in four Asian countries—Thailand, Singapore, Philippines, and Vietnam—in the mid-1990s found that from 60% to 90% of older adults lived with their children and grandchildren. The case of Japan illustrates the possible impact of modernization on the living arrangements of the elderly. In 1960, about 90% of older adults lived with their children (or one might say that the children lived with them in their households). By 1990, this type of living arrangement had declined to 50%. Both the increasing longevity and improved financial resources of older adults contribute to this trend toward independent housing, which is coupled with a continued desire for close kinship ties (Kinsella & Velkoff, 2001).

In the United States, living arrangements for older women differ by race and ethnic group. Older unmarried Asian American women, for example, are much more likely to live with other family members than to live alone in comparison to European American women of similar economic and educational backgrounds. Within the Asian American ethnic groups, acculturation appears to increase the likelihood of choosing to live alone. Those who immigrated to the United States before 1965 or who were born in the United States are more likely to live alone than the more recent immigrants. In a comparison among the Asian American cultures, older Japanese women were more likely to live alone than the Chinese, Filipino, and Korean women. Consistent with patterns for European American women, the more children these Asian American women had, the less likely they were to be institutionalized (Burr & Mutchler, 1993).

Older African Americans are more likely than other ethnic groups to live in large households where the membership is changing over time. In a sample of older Floridians, the African American elders were more likely than other groups to form co-resident relationships with their grandchildren and other nonrelatives. As marital status, aging, and disability or health needs of family and fictive kin dictated, African American households were more likely to add new members (Peek, Koropeckyj-Cox, Zsembik, & Coward, 2004).

The majority of very old men—about 70%—are married and live with their spouses; only 21% are widowed. In contrast, 33% of very old women are married, and 57% are

Most older women who live alone adapt well to this independent life style. Charlotte enjoys her needlepoint, has frequent visits from family and friends, and does not have to take care of anyone but herself.

widowed (U.S. Census Bureau, 2007). Widowed men are much more likely to remarry, which they tend to do quickly. However, remarriage among the very old is still a new frontier. Sexual and social stereotypes inhibit some older people from considering remarriage. Also, potential financial consequences may make remarriage undesirable. For instance, a widow may lose her husband's pension or her social security benefits if she remarries. However, some older couples cope with this problem by living together instead of marrying. In 2003, there were 280,000 men and women ages 65 and older living as unmarried heterosexual couples (Fields, 2003). Those who do remarry usually view the new relationship quite positively.

In contrast to those older women who live alone and those who live with a male partner, an emerging strategy is for several older women to live together. This alternative addresses the increasing costs of housing in many communities as well as the growing research evidence about the health and mental health risks of social isolation and loneliness in later life. Women of the baby boom generation are more likely to have experienced divorce and have smaller families than the previous generation of older adults. Many of these women have developed and nurtured friendships with other women from their high school and college years, in the workplace, and through community participation. As they begin planning for later adulthood, the idea of sharing the costs and responsibilities with good friends can be quite appealing. "We lived together in dorms and sororities. We shared apartments after graduation. We traveled together. We helped each other through divorce and the death of our parents. Why not take it to the next level?" (Gross, 2004, p. 1).

Interstate Migration. The great majority of older adults (more than 90%) remain in their home communities as

iStockphoto.com/Bob Thomas

they age, many preferring to stay in their own home, even after their children move out and their spouse dies. Yet the trend toward interstate migration has increased since the mid-1960s. Each year, roughly 1% to 2% of those 75 and older move to a new residence across state lines (U.S. Census Bureau, 2004b). Many of these older interstate migrants will live out their lives in communities in which they did not grow up, work, or raise their children. They are pioneers, establishing new friendships, community involvements, and lifestyles. Another significantly large group of older adults return to their birth state, especially after one's spouse dies or, in the case of serious disability, in order to be close to family caregivers (Stoller & Longino, 2001). In the face of some new physical limitations, older adults may want to be able to remain independent but require more help. By moving back to their home community, they are more confident about being able to draw on needed support from family and friends (Rowles & Ravdal, 2002). In addition to these permanent moves, many older adults participate in seasonal migration—residents from southern states go north for the summer, and residents of northern states go south for the winter. Over time, some of these seasonal migrants decide to establish a permanent residence in the state they visit. This is especially likely for northern residents who establish permanent residence in the South (Hogan & Steinnes, 1998).

Housing Options. Differences in lifestyle, health, interest, ability to perform daily activities, marital status, and income enter into the very old person's preference for housing arrangements. Housing for the elderly—sometimes referred to as *retirement housing*—has expanded dramatically, and developers have experimented with a great variety of housing configurations that are intended to meet the special needs of particular aging populations (Shapiro, 2001). These options range from inner-city hotels for those with minimal incomes to sprawling luxury villages with apartments, medical clinics, and sponsored activities. Retirement communities are typically age-restricted residences. They may be apartments in a high-rise, townhouses, or homes with shared recreational resources, like a fitness center, pool, or golf course, and social and cultural programming. Often, they provide the option for prepared meals or a communal dining center. Life satisfaction in a retirement community may depend on the fit between one's marital status and the demographics of the community. For example, one study assessed the life satisfaction of widows who were living alone in retirement communities. When widows outnumbered married couples in the community, the widows had a high frequency of seeing friends and participating in activities. However, when married couples outnumbered widows, the widows experienced less satisfaction and were more socially isolated (Hong & Duff, 1994).

The majority of older adults live in urban areas, and 31% live in inner-city neighborhoods. As a result, any economic factors that affect the **housing options** in urban communities have a significant impact on the living arrangements of older adults (see the box on the impact of gentrification on the very old). Because older adults tend to have a limited income and depend on the quality of community resources and social support for their well-being, moving can be an especially difficult life event, adversely affecting their overall well-being (Pynoos, Caraviello, & Cicero, 2010).

Institutional Care. About 1.5 million adults older than 65 live in **nursing homes**. This includes any arrangement with three or more beds that provides nursing and personal care services (U.S. Census Bureau, 2007). Nursing homes provide nursing care and rehabilitation for people who have severe functional limitations as a result of acute illness, surgery, or advanced dementia. The likelihood of institutionalization increases with age and limitations in family support. About 75% of people in nursing homes do not have spouses. The likelihood of a person living in a nursing home increases when there is no family member who can help to manage daily living needs. Among nursing home residents, about 13% are 65 to 74 years old, 35% are 75 to 84, and 51% are 85 and older (U.S. Census Bureau, 2004b). People tend to think that once older adults are admitted to a nursing home, they stay there until they die. In fact, there is a high annual turnover among nursing home residents. Often, a person enters a nursing home for a period of convalescence after hospitalization and then returns home or to a setting that provides less intensive care.

Many nursing homes are part of a **continuing care retirement community**— a residential setting offering housing and medical, preventive health, and social services to residents who are well at the time they enter the community. Once admitted, they are guaranteed nursing care if they become ill or disabled (Shapiro, 2001). In an analysis of nursing home use among residents in continuing care retirement communities, the risk of being transferred to the nursing home facility appeared to be greater than the rate for older adults in the local community, but the length of stay per admission was shorter (Cohen, Tell, Bishop, Wallack, & Branch, 1989). The nursing home may be used for recuperative purposes rather than having patients stay in the hospital for a longer period. This practice may reduce overall medical costs and provide a better recovery environment than being discharged to one's home before one can fully manage all the demands of self-care.

The advantages of a continuing care community are described by Glenn Smith:

> "We'd seen a lot of people our age struggle when one went into a skilled nursing facility 6 miles away," says 76-year-old Glenn Smith. "Then someone has to drive Momma over to see Daddy every day." So Smith and his wife, Kathleen, moved to a CCRC (continuing care retirement community) atop a hill overlooking Oregon's Rogue River Valley. A nursing home is just a short walk from their spacious three bedroom cottage. Smith, who is a retired college administrator, has one bit of advice: Move in while you are younger and healthy in order to take full advantage of the activities—and pay a lower entry fee. (Shapiro, 2001, p. 60)

The Impact of Gentrification on the Elderly

GENTRIFICATION IS A process of urban renewal or renovation in which new home owners and developers invest in the rehabilitation of neighborhoods that have been declining or deteriorating due to lack of maintenance and upkeep of the properties. Middle and upper income residents move into areas that have been deteriorating, often displacing poorer residents who have lived in that area for some time. To make investment in new construction and rehabilitation of older housing stock profitable, developers must be able to attract residents who can pay higher rents such as professionals and managers (the urban gentry). Once this process gets under way, landlords have an incentive to evict low-income residents who may have lived in the neighborhood for a long time in favor of more affluent tenants who can afford higher rent (Wetzel, 2004).

Several consequences of gentrification can have a negative impact on the housing options of older adults (Singelakis, 1990). First, rental apartments are converted to condominiums, which older adults cannot afford. Second, in areas where there is no rent control, the rent rises above the rate that the older person is able to pay. Where there is rent regulation, some landlords use harassment to force out the original residents. Third, properties that have been used as single-room-occupancy hotels are demolished and new structures are built. Single-room-occupancy hotels provide low-cost housing and social support to many older adults who live alone. From 1970

to 1982, more than half the single-room-occupancy units in the United States were lost to various urban gentrification projects (Hopper & Hamberg, 1986). A similar study of gentrification in London found a significant displacement of the elderly, with the hidden costs of overcrowding in family, friends', or relatives' homes; homelessness; and expanded unmet housing needs (Atkinson, 2000).

In addition to reducing access to affordable housing, the disruption in older adults' living arrangements can have health implications due to dispersion of the person's social support network, reduced access to public transportation, and less readily accessible sources of basic goods and services (CDC, 2010a).

Although gentrification poses threats to housing for the elderly, the alternative of ongoing neglect and decay in urban neighborhoods brings its own risks—especially increased crime, health and safety hazards, and lack of services. Over time, people with more resources leave these neighborhoods, making them vulnerable to continued deterioration. Writing about the process of gentrification in Los Angeles, David Zahniser describes it as follows:

> That, in a nutshell, is the most maddening thing about gentrification—its very duality, the way in which it simultaneously delivers pleasure and pain, miraculous benefits and terrible consequences. As middle-income residents move in, neighborhoods that once heard low-flying helicopters and automatic-weapons fire have found a greater measure of peace. Working-class families who scraped together the money to buy homes in the mid-1990s have happily cashed out, making hundreds of thousands of dollars en route to a five-bedroom home in Fontana, Las Vegas or Phoenix. Those who stay behind, however, frequently find themselves in a neighborhood they don't

recognize. And those who rent in a rapidly gentrifying neighborhood discover that they gained physical security while losing economic security, with rents rising steadily and the inventory of reasonably priced homes shrinking. (Zahniser, 2006, p. 2)

More positive approaches suggest a gradual rehabilitation or redevelopment of urban communities that preserves the identity of the neighborhood but encourages new building and new businesses at a slower rate of growth (West, 1999; CDC, 2010a). Some cities have placed a freeze on the conversions of rental units to condominiums. Others have created community land trusts where residents own the units or homes they live in, but the community owns the land, thus helping to control its use. This strategy is intended to help protect the neighborhood atmosphere and tone that have been created by its long-term residents.

Critical Thinking Questions

1. Why might older adults be especially likely to be impacted by gentrification? Why might the increased costs of rental or condominium purchase be especially difficult for them?
2. What are the particular stressors that an older adult might face if gentrification results in a loss of their rental housing unit?
3. What might be the psychological effects of moving to a new neighborhood for people who are in their eighties or nineties?
4. Why do you think the elderly might want to remain in their apartment or home, even if the neighborhood is deteriorating?
5. What obligations do you think local governments and developers should assume for the housing needs of the elderly in neighborhoods when older housing stock is renovated or replaced?

Aging in Place. The fastest growing component of the Medicare program is **community-based long-term health care**, which provides medical and social services to those who are chronically ill and eligible for institutionalization but who, nevertheless, live in the community. At their best, these programs are designed to complement and support

informal caregiving, supplementing and providing relief for family members and friends who are trying to care for the very old. They bring comfort to the very old clients who prefer to remain in their homes.

These programs also offer flexibility by providing needed services and modifying them as a person's condition changes.

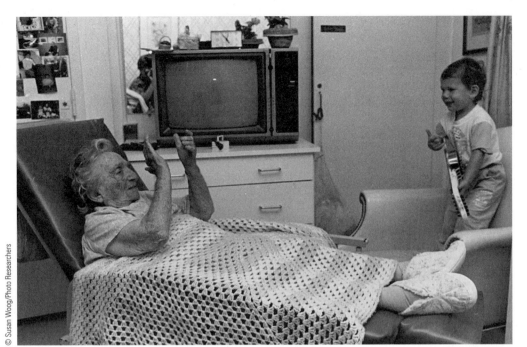

At 97 years of age, Stella has had to move into a nursing home because she can no longer walk. Periodic visits from her great-grandson keep her in good spirits. He plays, and she is a most appreciative audience.

© Susan Woog/Photo Researchers

For example, a home health service may provide a case manager who can identify the required services and coordinate a program of home care providers, services, and adult day care to meet the needs of the client and the client's support system. Long-term home health care programs evolve in response to the pattern of need that emerges in a community and the quality of the services available. As the programs develop, their emphasis tends to shift from providing services to those who would otherwise be institutionalized to preventing institutionalization among a high-risk population (Kaye, 1995; Kasper, 1997; U.S. Department of Health and Human Services, 2005).

The benefits of remaining in one's home, despite serious limitations in functional independence, are (1) preserving one's sense of autonomy and dignity, (2) reducing expenses, and (3) sustaining relationships with family and friends. In contrast, the move to a nursing home tends to be associated with higher levels of dependence and greater emphasis on "going along with the program" rather than on initiating one's own plans and projects. In a comparison of older women living in their homes and those living in a nursing care facility, researchers were interested in how the living arrangements might influence cognitive problem solving. The home-based group became more engaged in the hypothetical problems, their solutions suggested a greater sense of perceived control over the solutions, and they approached the problems in a more abstract, relativistic manner (Collins, Luszcz, Lawson, & Keeves, 1997). The results of this work suggest that the nursing home environment may operate to undermine cognitive functioning by reducing the need for independent problem-solving activity. However, as the case study about Mr. Z suggests, there are nursing home residents who retain their positive spirit and are able to help others while receiving the level of support they require given their serious physical disabilities.

CASE STUDY

MR. Z

The following case illustrates the importance of psychological attitudes in allowing a person with serious physical problems to play a meaningful role in a social setting for the frail elderly. Mr. Z's outlook helps him maintain his vitality and express his love of life.

Mr. M.L. Z is an 89-year-old White male of Eastern European origin. He lives in a midsized nursing home in the Midwest. Many of his daily activities revolve around circulating among the facility's residents, chatting, playing cards, reading to them, and "fetching things." Most important, Mr. Z carries his old battered violin with him and at the drop of a hat will play a tune or break into song in a surprisingly strong, clear, melodic voice. He claims to be able to sing songs in any one of seven languages, and with the least encouragement will try out several for anyone who will listen.

Mr. Z is small (5' 3"), frail looking, and completely bald. He has facial scars and wears extremely thick-lensed glasses. He seems to be known and well liked by practically all residents and staff of the facility in which he resides, and by many visitors there as well.

He recalls a colorful history. He "escaped" his homeland at the tender age of 16 to avoid compulsory military service and fled to Russia. There he was inducted into the army, and was subsequently sent off to duty in Siberia, where he lived for about 6 years. After another tour of duty in a border patrol he deserted, he made his way across Europe, and eventually came to the United States. Here he took odd jobs, educated himself, and in time "got into show business"; he became a vaudeville prompter. In time his contacts in entertainment took him around the world. Yet time took its toll.

He tells of marrying a woman with whom he lived for almost 40 years. They had no children and she died some 15 years ago. Following her death, he began to experience a series of physical difficulties. An operation for cataracts left him with the need for very thick glasses. At one time he had a toupee made, which he has not worn for some time. One leg was amputated because of a diabetic condition, and he now wears a prosthetic leg. In addition, he wears a hearing aid, false teeth, and, for the last year, a heart pacer. Several years ago he experienced what he calls a small stroke, which left him "mixed up" for a few days. But he "worked this out," he reports, by "walking a lot," an activity in which he engages frequently.

Mr. Z says he has never smoked and drinks only on occasions or holidays, and then only to a limited degree. He scorns food fads, and eats mostly fresh fruits and lots of vegetables; he loves fish and drinks lots of tea.

Despite all his troubles, Mr. Z maintains what is apparently a cheerful, optimistic view of life and circumstances, while he pursues his hobby of energetically helping his fellow residents keep their spirits up and their interests high. He is very highly regarded and seen as filling a very important role in his nursing home as a storyteller and entertainer.

Source: Excerpt from *Aging and Life: An Introduction to Gerontology* (2nd ed.). A.N. Schwartz, C.L. Snyder, & J.A. Peterson, pp. 33–34. Copyright © 1984. Austin, TX: Holt, Rinehart & Winston, Inc. Reprinted by permission of the publisher.

CRITICAL THINKING AND CASE ANALYSIS

1. Imagine that you were having lunch with Mr. Z. What questions would you want to ask him?
2. What are the physical challenges of aging with which Mr. Z must cope?
3. Why might Mr. Z be living in a nursing home?
4. How would you describe Mr. Z's psychohistorical perspective?
5. What are the unique, creative adaptations that characterize Mr. Z's story?
6. In what sense is the nursing home optimizing Mr. Z's functioning?

Gender Role Definitions

The way in which very old adults view masculinity and femininity is yet another aspect of traveling uncharted territory. How do the very old define gender roles? How does gender influence behavior? Do very old adults make the same distinctions as college-age individuals about the behaviors that are appropriate or desirable for men and women? These questions remain to be answered.

Evaluating the Concept of Gender Role Convergence. The idea of **gender role convergence** suggests a transformation of gender role orientation during midlife. According to this theoretical perspective, men become more nurturant and more concerned with social relationships. Women become more assertive and concerned with independence and achievement. As a result, men and women become more androgynous and, in that sense, more similar in gender orientation during later life (Gutmann, 1987).

The extent to which men and women become more similar in outlook and behavior in later adulthood and elderhood is a subject of controversy. Unfortunately, few data from longitudinal or cohort sequential studies are available to address this topic. Cross-sectional data collected from men and women across a wide age span from early adulthood to elderhood have focused on men's and women's endorsement of affiliative and instrumental values. Men and women appear to be similar in their **affiliative values**—that is, the values placed on helping or pleasing others, reflected in the amount of time they spend and the degree of satisfaction they achieve in such actions. At each age, men are more invested than women in **instrumental values**—that is, the values placed on doing things that are challenging, reflected in the amount of time they spend and the degree of satisfaction they achieve in such actions. However, the youngest age groups value instrumentality more highly and devote more time to it than the oldest age group. Thus, gender differences in instrumentality persist, but instrumentality becomes somewhat less important for older men and women. Affiliative behavior is equally important for men and women at both ages (Fultz & Herzog, 1991).

The stereotypes that are applied to aging men and women reflect similar patterns. College students and older adults (with a mean age of 70) were asked to generate characteristics in response to one of four target stimuli: a 35-year-old man, a 35-year-old woman, a 65-year-old man, and a 65-year-old woman (Kite, Deaux, & Miele, 1991). Age stereotypes were more prevalent than gender stereotypes. The attributes that were used to characterize older men and women were similar and distinct from the attributes used to characterize younger men and women.

In general, the older target people were evaluated more negatively by the younger participants, but not as negatively by the older participants. These negative judgments included unattractive physical qualities as well as irritable and depressed personality qualities. Moreover, younger participants were more likely to characterize both male and female older target people as lacking in instrumental traits, such as achievement orientation and self-confidence. However, they did not view older target people as lacking in affiliative traits, such as caring about others or being kind or generous. Thus, the gender role convergence that has been hypothesized as taking place with advanced age is reflected in the stereotypes that younger people apply to older adults.

Gender role convergence, where it is observed, may be due to changing circumstances rather than to a normative pattern of development in later life. For example, many older women experience a transition from living with their husbands to living alone after age 75. This change is linked to new demands for independence, self-reliance, and agency. Women who are able to meet these challenges by developing independent living skills, making effective use of social supports and community resources, and initiating new relationships are likely to experience a heightened sense of well-being.

After 60 years of marriage, Ann and Ted still get quite a kick out of being together. Their lives are sprinkled with many moments like this, when a glance or an expression brings out a loving smile.

For many older married couples, the physical effects of aging bring new needs for assistance in some of the tasks of daily living. Because men usually marry younger women, they are more likely to require the assistance of their wives in the later years of marriage, thus shifting the balance of power and increasing their sense of **dependency**. This may be especially true when husbands retire while their wives continue to work; when husbands can no longer drive and must depend on their wives for transportation; or when, due to health constraints, husbands are restricted from performing the types of household tasks that once were their domain, such as mowing the grass, shoveling snow, repairing the home, or other tasks requiring muscle strength and endurance. On the other hand, among adults of 75 years and older, more women than men have difficulties with mobility and require assistance in the tasks of independent living. Thus, health and fitness more than gender may guide the nature of dyadic interactions among older couples. As men and women become more equal with respect to power and resources in their marital relationship, there may be fewer clear-cut gender expectations. Still, to the extent that gender role distinctions help stabilize a relationship, older adults may be reluctant to make dramatic changes to the way their relationships have been structured (Silver, 2003).

Romance and Sexuality. Romance, intimacy, and sexuality remain important among older married couples. The majority of couples who have enjoyed a close, sexually active relationship report little change in satisfaction from age 60 to 85. Some couples explore different ways of experiencing sexual pleasure in later life, and others report a more relaxed, sexually satisfying quality in their lovemaking. Using Sternberg's (1988) model of the three dimensions of love relationships (see Chapter 11, Early Adulthood), long-lasting marriages tend to be more companionate in nature, emphasizing intimacy and commitment over passion. In this model, lovemaking may take on a different intensity and quality over time. Current research on sexuality in later life confirms that older adults have sexual needs, benefit from sexual expression, and are able to be sexually active. A national survey of adults ages 60 and older found that more than half were sexually active, meaning that they had intercourse, oral sex, anal intercourse, or masturbated at least once a month (Dunn & Cutler, 2000). This study found that sexual activity declined with age, but that 20% to 25% of those in their eighties were still sexually active. Older couples may find greater satisfaction in intimate physical contact, such as kissing and caressing, and experimentation with new ways of experiencing sexual stimulation as genital intercourse becomes less frequent. Following along with the idea of gender role convergence, men and women become more similar in their sexual behavior and more harmonious in their lovemaking (Crooks & Bauer, 2005).

Today's cohort of older men and women, born in the 1930s, tend to be tied to many of the traditional gender role standards of their historical era. For example, older women are likely to believe that the only kinds of relationships that are possible between men and women are romantic or courtship relationships. Few very old women have friendships with very old men, partly because few older men are available, but also because most older women have no models for independent friendship relationships with men. During their early and middle adult years, their friendships with men were either formed while they were part of a couple or mediated by some other situation, such as a work setting. Many men in the current elderhood cohort also behave in accordance with the gender role standards of their young adulthood. Although women far outnumber men at advanced ages, men still seem to prefer to remarry rather than play the field, although they have become a scarce and valuable commodity. The norm of serial monogamy guides these men's behavior. They are probably motivated to remarry by a desire to continue to be taken care of as well as to satisfy their sexual needs.

One of the greatest challenges to continued romantic and sexual intimacy in later life is widowhood. Despite the fact that older men are much more likely to remarry than older women, remarriage is relatively uncommon in later adulthood and elderhood. One estimate found that among 1,000 widowed men and women older than 65, 3 women and 17 men remarried (Clarke, 1995). These data do not address the question of whether older men and women would like to have a romantic relationship after widowhood. This question was addressed in a study of older couples that followed men and women 6 and 18 months after widowhood (Carr, 2004). Participants were asked two questions about their romantic interests: "At this point do you have any interest in dating?" which was answered *yes* or *no*, and "Some day I would like to remarry," answered on a scale from *not true at all* to *very true*. They were also asked if they were dating. At 6 months after widowhood, men were more likely to want to be dating than women (17% vs. 6%), more likely to want to remarry (30% vs. 16%), and more likely to be dating (15% vs. less than 1%). At 18 months after widowhood, men were still more likely to want to be dating (37% vs. 15%) and more likely to be dating (23% vs. 9%), but about equally likely to want to remarry (26% vs. 19%). The most important predictor of whether men or women wanted to date or remarry was the quality of their social support system. In general, women had more supportive relationships with friends than did men prior to widowhood. The more social support men had, the less likely they were to express interest in remarriage. Men and women who had comparable levels of social support from friends were equally disinterested in remarriage.

This research suggests that the picture we have about gender differences in motivations to find a new partner after widowhood needs to be revised. First, although more men than women are interested in new romantic relationships, the majority of men do not express this interest. Second, when social support systems are comparable, men and women are about equally likely to reject the idea of a new romantic relationship. One limitation of this research was the way in which interest in a new partner was defined, limiting the alternatives for romantic relationships to dating and marriage. Given the potential costs of remarriage in later life, older adults may be looking for a different kind of intimacy that does not require the responsibilities of co-residence and the legal commitments of marriage (Davidson, 2002; Ghazanfareeon, Karlsson, & Borrell, 2002).

Ageism and Sexuality. Older adults continue to face negative, ageist social attitudes about sexual activity that may inhibit their sexual behavior. These social attitudes include assumptions that very old adults do not have sexual desires, they cannot have intercourse because of sexual dysfunction, sex may be dangerous to their health, they are physically and sexually unattractive, and it is morally wrong or perverted for older adults to be sexually active (Crooks & Bauer, 2005). Current cohorts of very old adults have limited knowledge about sexuality and aging. A number of studies have demonstrated that increasing knowledge through various types of sex education programs can increase permissive attitudes about sexuality among older adults (Hillman & Stricker, 1994). These interventions have involved the elderly people themselves, nursing students, college students, nursing home staff, and adult children of aging parents. However, increased knowledge does not always result in more permissive attitudes. Especially among health care staff in institutional settings, the institutional regulations, personal moral values, and practical problems of permitting sexual activity among residents may combine to promote a more negative attitude even with advanced information about sexuality and aging.

Cohort factors may change the current societal attitudes toward sexuality among the very old. Because so many more adult women are in the workplace, they have more experience with male colleagues. Also, changing sexual norms have already led many more adults to experience nonmarital sexual relationships. A growing openness about homosexual relationships may reduce some of the stigma against forming same-sex bonds in later life. Acceptance of new sexual relationships in later life is more likely because many adults will have experienced a larger number of sexual relationships in their earlier years of adulthood. The high divorce rate since the mid-1970s means that in the future more women will have had the experience of developing a single lifestyle that includes a network of both male and female friends. As the value of intimacy for health and well-being is more fully recognized, we may expect future groups of older adults to be more comfortable about forming homosexual as well as heterosexual intimate relationships.

The Psychosocial Crisis: Immortality versus Extinction

Objective 5. To identify and describe the psychosocial crisis of immortality versus extinction, the central process of social support, the prime adaptive ego quality of confidence, and the core pathology of diffidence.

By the end of later adulthood, most people have developed a point of view about death. Although they may continue to experience anxiety about their impending death, they have found the courage to confront their fears and overcome them. If older adults have achieved integrity, they believe that their

© 2009 Jupiterimages

Participation in this ritual candle lighting and prayer connects Betty with all those who have prayed here before her over many generations, and all those who will come to this altar in the future.

life has made sense. This amplifies their confidence about the choices they have made and the goals they have achieved without despair over the failures, missed opportunities, or misfortunes that may have occurred. Thus armed, the very old can accept the end of life and view it as a natural part of the life span. They are capable of distilling wisdom from the events of their lives, including their successes and mistakes.

However, the very old are faced with a new challenge—a conflict between the acceptance of death and the intensifying hope for immortality. Having lived longer than their cohort of friends, family members, and even, in some cases, their children, the very old struggle to find meaning in their survival. All of us face a certain disbelief about our own mortality. Although we know that death is a certainty, an element of human thought prevents us from facing the full realization of death; we continue to hope for immortality. This quality may be adaptive, in that people who have a sense of hope cope with the reality of death better than those who do not.

Immortality

Elders have a unique appreciation of time. They recognize that there is a finite amount of future time until their death,

as well as an unlimited transcendental future time that begins with their death and extends onward into infinity (Boyd & Zimbardo, 1996; Zimbardo & Boyd, 2008). They begin to see themselves as links in a long, fluid chain of historical and biological growth and change. The positive pole of this crisis is a confidence in the continuity of life, a transcendence of death through the development of a symbolic sense of immortality. The achievement of this perspective, which may include the incorporation of transcendental goals such as reuniting with loved ones after death or being released from the limitations of an aging body, may be accompanied with sentiments of joy, which contribute to feelings of well-being, flexibility, and acceptance of the challenges of aging.

A psychosocial sense of **immortality** may be achieved and expressed in many ways (Lifton, 1973). Here, we explore five possible paths toward immortality. First, one may live on through one's children, sensing a connection and attachment to the future through one's life and the lives of one's offspring. This type of immortality can be extended to include devotion to one's country, social organizations or groups, or humankind.

Second, one may believe in an afterlife or a spiritual plane of existence that extends beyond one's biological life. Most religions espouse the concept of a state of harmony with natural forces, so that after death, one endures beyond this earthly life. Among many indigenous peoples, there is a sacred link between the living and the dead—a responsibility on the part of the living to protect and respect the sacred burial grounds, and a responsibility on the part of the dead ancestors to look after the spiritual well-being of the living. This belief is illustrated in the box on the responsibility of native Hawaiians for their ancestors' remains.

Third, one may achieve a sense of immortality through creative achievements and their impact on others. Many people find comfort in believing that they are part of a chain of positive influences on the lives of others. This sense of immortality is linked to the achievement of generativity in middle adulthood. Adults who have made a commitment to improving the quality of life for others during middle adulthood are likely to see evidence of this effort by the time they reach elderhood. The bond between an individual and community makes death less final. An African proverb advises that you live as long as someone knows your name. The more embedded you are in your community, and the more lives you have touched, the greater the sense of continuity or transcendence.

Fourth, one may develop the notion of participation in the chain of nature. In death, one's body returns to the earth, and one's energy is brought forth in a new form.

Fifth, one may achieve a sense of immortality through what Lifton (1973) described as **experiential transcendence**:

This state is characterized by extraordinary psychic unity and perceptual intensity. But there also occurs … a process of symbolic reordering…. Experiential transcendence includes a feeling of … "continuous present" that can be

HUMAN DEVELOPMENT AND DIVERSITY

HUMAN DEVELOPMENT AND DIVERSITY

The Responsibility of Native Hawaiians for Their Ancestors' Remains

THE FOLLOWING NARRATIVE describes the crisis of immortality versus extinction in the context of the desecration of a native Hawaiian burial site. In fighting to stop the destruction, those involved were reminded of the commitment that the living have for the care and protection of the burial grounds of their ancestors:

Hawai'i Nei was born December 1988 from the *kaumah a* (heaviness) and *aokanaka* (enlightenment) caused by the archaeological disinterment of over 1,100 ancestral Native Hawaiians from Honokahua, Maui. The ancestral remains were removed over the protests of the Native Hawaiian community in order to build the Ritz Carlton Hotel. The desecration was stopped following a 24-hour vigil at the State Capital. Governor John Waihe'e, a Native Hawaiian, approved of a settlement that returned the ancestral remains to their *one hanau* (birth sands), set aside the reburial site in perpetuity, and moved the hotel inland and away from the ancestral resting place.

In one sense Honokahua represents balance for from this tragedy came enlightenment: the realization by living Native Hawaiians that we were responsible for the care and protection of our ancestors and that cultural protocols needed to be relearned and laws effectively changed to create the empowerment necessary to carry out this important and time-honored responsibility to *malama* (take care) and *kupale* (protect) our ancestors.

Hui Malama I Na Kupuna O Hawai'i Nei members have trained under the direction of Edward and Pualani Kanahele of Hilo in traditional protocols relating to the care of *na iwi kupuna* (ancestral remains). These commitments were undertaken as a form of *aloha* and respect for our own families, ancestors, parents, and children.

Hui Malama I Na Kupuna O Hawai'i Nei has been taught by the Kanahele family about the importance of *pule* (prayer) necessary to *ho'olohe* (listen) to the calling of our ancestors. Through *pule* we request the assistance of *ke akua* and our ancestors to provide us with the tools necessary to conduct our work:

> *E homai ka ike, e homai ka ikaika, e homai ka akamai, e homai ka maopop o pono, e homai ka 'ike papalua, e homai ka man a.*

(Grant us knowledge, grant us strength, grant us intelligence, grant us righteous understanding, grant us visions and avenues of communication, grant us mana.)

Moreover, we have been taught that the relationship between our ancestors and ourselves is one of interdependence—as the living, we have a *kuleana* (responsibility) to care for our *kupuna* (ancestors). In turn, our ancestors respond by protecting us on the spiritual side. Hence, one side cannot completely exist without the other.

Source: Pell (2002)

Critical Thinking Questions

1. How would you characterize the belief system that connects native Hawaiians and their ancestors? In what ways is this belief system similar to or different from your own sense of connection to your ancestors?

2. How might the sense of interdependence between the living and the dead influence the day-to-day behavior of native Hawaiians?

3. What is the connection between a person's beliefs regarding their ancestors and their sense of immortality versus extinction?

4. Select a culture of interest to you. What is the relationship of the living to their ancestors in this culture? What beliefs, rituals, and actions reflect this relationship?

5. How might the trends of modernization help explain why Hawaiians may have lost touch with the traditional practices associated with the care of ancestral remains? What is gained by reviving these traditions?

equated with eternity or with "mythical time." This continuous present is perceived as not only "here and now" but as inseparable from past and future. (p. 10)

The notion of **cosmic transcendence** has been developed further in the writings of Lars Tornstam, a Swedish gerontologist, who writes about feelings of cosmic communion with the spirit of the universe, and a redefinition of time, space, life, and death (Tornstam, 2005). This expression of immortality is independent of religion, offspring, or creative achievement. It is an insight derived from moments of rapture or ecstasy in which all that one senses is the power of the moment. In these experiences, the duality of life and death dissolve, and what remains is continuous being.

Extinction

The negative pole of the psychosocial crisis of elderhood is a sense of being bound by the limits of one's own life history. In place of a belief in continuous existence and transformation, one views the end of life as an end to motion, attachment, and change. Instead of faith in the ideas of connection

APPLYING THEORY AND RESEARCH TO LIFE

Erikson on Coping with Aging

THE ERIKSONS' ADVICE (Erikson et al., 1986, pp. 332–333) suggests the achievement of experiential transcendence:

> With aging, there are inevitably constant losses—losses of those very close, and friends near and far. Those who have been rich in intimacy also have the most to lose. Recollection is one form of adaptation, but the effort skillfully to form new relationships is adaptive and more rewarding. Old age is necessarily a time of relinquishing—of giving up old friends, old roles, earlier work that was once meaningful, and even possessions that belong to a previous stage of life and are now an impediment to the resiliency and freedom that seem to be requisite for adapting to the unknown challenges that determine the final stage of life.
>
> Trust in interdependence. Give and accept help when it is needed. Old Oedipus well knew that the aged sometimes need three legs; pride can be an asset but not a cane. When frailty takes over, dependence is appropriate, and one has no choice but to trust in the compassion of others and be consistently surprised at how faithful some caretakers can be.
>
> Much living, however, can teach us only how little is known. Accept that essential "not-knowingness" of childhood and with it also that playful curiosity. Growing old can be an interesting adventure and is certainly full of surprises.
>
> One is reminded here of the image Hindu philosophy uses to describe the final letting go—that of merely being. The mother cat picks up in her mouth the kitten, which completely collapses every tension and hangs limp and infinitely trusting in the maternal benevolence. The kitten responds instinctively. We human beings require at least a whole lifetime of practice to do this.

Source: From *Vital Involvement in Old Age*, E.H. Erikson, J.M. Erikson, & H.Q. Kivnick (1986), pp. 332–333.

Critical Thinking Questions

1. How do you think the elderly cope with the reality that many of their friends and relatives die while they survive?
2. Given the full course of psychosocial development, why is it especially difficult for the elderly to accept help and depend upon others when they need it? What lessons from earlier stages of life might prepare a person to do this?
3. How might cultural beliefs, religious views, and a sense of meaning contribute to the ability of the elderly to see this last phase of their life as an adventure?
4. Read more about Erik Erikson. What can you find out about how well he was able to accept this advice in the last years of his life?
5. Critically evaluate the advice provided by Erikson. Do you think it would be good advice to give to older adults to help them find a sense of satisfaction? What advice would you offer in its place?

and continuity, one experiences a great fear of **extinction**—a fear that one's life and its end amount to nothing. Erikson's advice on coping with aging concerns responding to loss and dealing with diminished capacities (see the box).

The following quotations from a study of very old men suggest the range in sentiment about immortality and extinction (Rosenfeld, 1978, p. 10). About 28% of the adults in the study were described as having low morale and made statements such as "I feel I'm a forgotten man. I don't exist anymore.... I don't feel old.... I'm just living out my life." About 25% were stoic but not very positive about their condition: "You know you're getting old. You have to put your mind to it and take it as it comes. You can't get out of it. Take it gracefully." Almost half found their lives full and rewarding: "I go home with my cup overflowing. There are so many opportunities to do things for people. These are the happiest days of my life."

The possibility of ending one's life with a sense of extinction is reflected in the public health concern about suicide among the elderly. Data from the *World Health Statistical Annual* provide a basis for describing the incidence of suicide for men and women in the age groups from 65 to 74 and 75 years and older (Kennedy & Tanenbaum, 2000). Men commit suicide at higher rates than women at all ages, but the discrepancy increases with age. Suicide rates are much higher among those 75 years and older than in the younger group. Finally, national and geographic differences are substantial. For example, in Germany more than half the suicides are committed by people ages 65 and older.

In the analysis of factors associated with suicide in Germany, severe physical disease, loneliness and isolation, and feelings of meaninglessness were identified as forming a biopsychosocial context for late-life suicide (Schmitz-Scherzer, 1995). In Japan, suicide rates among older adults are greater in rural than in urban communities. The authors of this research suggested that changes in Japanese society have led to a reduced valuing of older family members and less extended family support. The rural elderly are less able to accept these changes, which undercut their sense of purpose and meaning (Watanabe, Hasegawa, & Yoshinaga, 1996). Without appropriate social support, and in the face of substantially reduced physical or psychological resources, a significant number of the very old end their own lives.

Happily, evidence on the outlook of the community-based population of the United States suggests that relatively few of the elderly experience a level of discouragement that is implied by the sense of extinction. Among those ages 75 and older, fewer than 6% report feelings of worthlessness or hopelessness all of the time, most of the time, or some of the time (National Center for Health Statistics, 2010).

The Central Process: Social Support

Social support has been defined as the social experiences that lead people to believe that they are cared for and loved, esteemed and valued, and belong to a network of communication and mutual obligation (Cobb, 1979). Social support is a broad term that includes the quantity and interconnectedness or web of social relationships in which a person is embedded, the strength of those ties, the frequency of contact, and the extent to which the support system is perceived as helpful and caring (Bergeman, Plomin, Pedersen, McClearn, & Nesselroade, 1990). It is commonly divided into two different but complementary categories: **socioemotional support**, which refers to expressions of affection, respect, and esteem, and **instrumental support**, which refers to direct assistance, including help with chores, medical care, or transportation. Both types of social support—but especially socioemotional support—contribute to maintaining well-being and fostering the possibility of transcending the physical limitations that accompany aging (Rowe & Kahn, 1998).

Social support can contribute to improved health. Jean and Carol exercise together three times a week, talking and laughing as they ride.

© 2010 Tim Hall/Jupiterimages Corporation

The Benefits of Social Support

Social support plays a direct role in promoting health, well-being, and life satisfaction even when a person is not facing a specific stressful situation (Gow et al., 2007). First, because social support involves meaningful social relationships, it reduces isolation. People who have intimate companions in later life have higher levels of life satisfaction. They feel valued and valuable. This kind of social support is likely to be most appreciated when it comes from friends and neighbors—members of the community who are not bound by familial obligation to care about the person, but who do so anyway.

Second, the presence of caring, familiar people provides a flow of affection, information, advice, transportation, and assistance with meals and daily activities, finances, and health care—all critical resources. The presence of a support system tends to reduce the impact of stressors and protect people from some of their negative consequences, especially serious illnesses and depression (Krause, 2006).

Third, social integration and membership in a meaningful social support network are associated with increased longevity. Five different longitudinal studies have demonstrated that a high level of social integration is associated with lower mortality rates (Rowe & Kahn, 1997). The support system often serves to encourage an older person to maintain health care practices and to seek medical attention when it is needed. Members of the immediate family, close relatives, and friends provide direct care during times of grave illness or loss, encouraging the older person to cope with difficulties and to remain hopeful. Very old people are likely to experience declines in physical stamina. They may also

have limited financial resources. In order for the very old to transcend the limitations of their daily living situations, they must be convinced that they are embedded in a network of social relationships in which they are valued. But their value cannot be based solely on a physical exchange of goods and services. Rather, it must be founded on an appreciation of the person's dignity and a history of reciprocal caring.

The Dynamics of Social Support

The benefits of receiving social support can be diminished if the recipients adhere to a strong cultural norm for reciprocity. The **norm of reciprocity** implies that you are obligated to return in full value what you receive: "One good turn deserves another." People want and expect to be able to give about the same as or more than they receive. What is given does not have to be identical to what is received, but it has to be perceived as having equal worth. Being in someone's debt may be considered stressful and shameful. In a study of Japanese American elderly people, receiving material support from their family was associated with higher levels of depression and less satisfaction in life, especially for those who had very traditional values about reciprocity. The general principle of trying to mobilize social support to enhance the functioning of the very old has to be modified to include sensitivity to the context and meaning of that support (Nemoto, 1998).

Most older adults continue to see themselves as involved in a reciprocal, supportive relationship with their friends. Feelings of usefulness and competence continue to be important correlates of well-being in later life. Older adults are especially likely to experience positive feelings of life satisfaction when they are able to provide assistance to others at times of significant life transition or need, such as unemployment or the divorce of a child (Davey & Eggebeen, 1998). Even though they are comforted by knowing that support would be available when needed, older adults are likely to experience negative feelings when the support received is more than was needed or when there is no opportunity for them to reciprocate (Liang, Krause, & Bennett, 2001).

Older adults may expect to receive more care from their children when they are ill than they can provide in exchange. By shifting to a life-span perspective, however, they can retain a sense of balance by seeing the help they receive now as comparable to the help they gave their children at earlier life stages (Ingersoll-Dayton & Antonucci, 1988). When very old people are highly valued, it is not as important that they reciprocate in the exchange of tangible resources. Wisdom, affection, joie de vivre, and a positive model of surviving into old age are intangible resources that are highly valued by members of the very old person's social support network. Being valued may also mean that the person's advice and conversation are adequate exchange for some of the services and assistance provided by family and friends.

Social relationships can include both positive and negative interactions. Within one's social network, positive interactions might include enjoying shared activities, confiding about one's worries, or asking for help when one is ill. Negative interactions might include being taken advantage of, having one's privacy invaded, or being insulted. Sometimes, the same people can be sources of both positive and negative interactions. Not surprisingly, the overall frequency of positive exchanges is related to lower levels of depression. When older adults experience the effects of negative social interactions in one relationship—for example, when they have an argument with their adult child—they can buffer these emotions by having positive interactions with another member of their social network—for example, a friend or spouse (Okun & Keith, 1998).

Many older adults are selective about the people in their social network, striving to interact primarily with people who engage in harmonious interactions. They also take steps to prevent conflict in the relationships they value. For example, they impose certain constraints on their interactions—not criticizing someone in public, respecting others' privacy, and keeping a confidence. These strategies help to avoid negative interactions and maximize the satisfaction and stability of their relationships. These strategies are not a sign of weakness or passivity, but a deliberate attempt to protect meaningful relationships and avoid the negative affect associated with interpersonal conflict (Sorkin & Rook, 2004).

The Social Support Network

Of course, being an integral part of a social system does not begin in later life. It has its origins in infancy, with the formation of a mutual relationship with a caregiver. Social support systems are extended in childhood and early adolescence through identification with a peer group, and in early and middle adulthood through marriage, childrearing, and relationships with coworkers and adult friends. In later life, family members are usually the primary sources of social support, especially one's spouse, children, and siblings. The quality of the relationship between an adult child and an aging parent has a long history. Clearly, the nature of the support that an aging parent is able to receive or that an adult child is willing to provide is influenced by the feelings of closeness and connection that were fashioned during the childrearing process and also by the child's relationship to the parents during early adulthood years.

In the United States, age is a predictor of the size of the social support network. Younger people have larger social support networks than do older people. This may be true for a variety of reasons. For very old people, especially women, the likelihood of living alone is high. After the death of a spouse, men and women must realign their social support systems from among relationships that include their adult children, friends, relatives, neighbors, and new acquaintances in order to satisfy their needs for interaction and companionship. In a study of social relationships following widowhood, women clearly benefited from the social network that existed prior to their husband's death. However, contrary to expectations, efforts to modify this network by renewing old acquaintances or forming new friendships did not help to reduce feelings of depression or loneliness, even 2 years after the loss (Zettel & Rook, 2004). Very old adults who are childless or have no surviving children or siblings are especially vulnerable to ending their lives in isolation. In contrast, those who are able to preserve a diverse social network are more likely to be the healthiest, make the most use of appropriate community services, and experience the highest levels of well-being (Bosworth & Schaie, 1997; Litwin, 1997; Antonucci et al., 2001).

For many older adults, religious participation provides an additional source of social support. Older adults are more likely than younger adults to describe themselves as religious in their beliefs and behavior. Mary, who at age 80 has experienced the deaths of three brothers, her husband, and her daughter-in-law, gives and receives emotional support through her faith:

> I always have a lot of faith. The good Lord has always given me the strength to go on. I was raised to believe and pray when I have problems. I go to Mass every Sunday, and we have other special days when we go to Mass. I'm a Eucharistic minister. God makes me do things to feel better—I serve people and God. I go to buildings to give communion to people who can't get out. (Rowe & Kahn, 1998, p. 164)

The place of religion in the lives of the very old is especially significant for African Americans, who are more likely than European Americans to attend religious services regularly, even at advanced ages. They are also more likely to describe themselves as very religious—a characterization that reflects the frequency of their private prayer, their strong emotional commitment, and their reading of religious material. Religious involvement among elderly African Americans is not predicted by income or education, however (Taylor, 1986). In one study of older African American residents in an urban area, church membership was significantly related to well-being, particularly as a result of the perceived support they received from other church members (Walls & Zarit, 1991).

Ethnic identity itself may also become an important vehicle for social support in later life (Cool, 1987). It can provide a variety of sources of nonfamilial support, from a loose network of associations to membership in formal clubs and organizations. Members of an ethnic group may feel a strong sense of community as a result of their shared exposure to past discrimination, a realization of common concerns, and a sense of responsibility to preserve some of the authenticity of their ethnic identity for future generations. Participation in such a support network may be another vehicle for contributing wisdom gained through life experiences to those who will follow. Insofar as members of ethnic groups have felt somewhat marginal in the larger society in the past, their mutual support in later life may protect them from some of the negative stereotypes that the society imposes on the very old.

Involvement in a social support system can be viewed as an essential ingredient in the achievement of a sense of immortality. The social support system confirms the value of elders, providing direct evidence of their positive impact on others and a sense of embeddedness in their social communities. The social support system of elders usually includes adult children. Positive interactions with them contribute to the sense of living on through one's offspring and their descendants. Interactions with members of the social support system—especially those marked by feelings of warmth, caring, and celebration—may be moments of experiential transcendence for elders. They feel the fullness and joy of existence that transcend physical and material barriers.

The Prime Adaptive Ego Quality and the Core Pathology

Confidence

In this discussion, **confidence** refers to a conscious trust in oneself and an assurance about the meaningfulness of life. In this definition, one finds the earliest psychosocial crisis of trust versus mistrust integrated with the crisis of integrity versus despair. In elderhood, after a lifetime of facing challenges and experiencing losses and gains, one has a new belief in the validity of one's intuition, a trust in one's worldview, and a continued belief in one's capacity to participate in the world on one's own terms. Confidence is sustained by a stable, supportive social network (Lang, Featherman, &

Nesselroade, 1997; Krause, 2007). Older adults who feel they are able to engage in the activities they enjoy and to interact with people they value are also more likely to believe that they can adapt to the challenges they face. As a result of their confidence, they are less disrupted by stressful events and more hopeful about being able to find successful solutions in the face of negative events (Pushkar, Arbuckle, Conway, Chaikelson, & Maag, 1997).

Physical health and age, per se, are not the best predictors of confidence. One's perceptions of physical health problems and how one sees oneself in comparison to others may be more important predictors of confidence than any objective measure of health status. Some people view themselves as more impaired and dependent than they actually are; others, who may be suffering from serious illnesses, continue to view their situation with optimism (Ryff, 1995). Similarly, one's perception of the adequacy of social support and its appropriateness in response to one's needs is more important to a sense of confidence than the financial value of the resources exchanged (Davey & Eggebeen, 1998).

Over the course of the life span, psychosocial theory predicts that each individual will confront issues related to the negative poles of the psychosocial crisis of each stage. We argue that finding ways to integrate the negative pole of each stage into an overall positive worldview strengthens and humanizes one's character. Encounters with each negative pole provide a deeper sense of empathy for the suffering of others and a more profound appreciation for the courage that it takes to live out one's life with an open, generous, hopeful outlook. Confidence emerges not because of a life of one success after the next, but out of a sequence of struggles in which creative energy is required to find a positive balance between positive and negative forces (J.M. Erikson, 1988).

Diffidence

Diffidence refers to an inability to act because of overwhelming self-doubt. It is considered one of the basic factors underlying personality disorders (Livesley, Jackson, & Schroeder, 1992). Diffidence is evidenced by an unusual amount of difficulty in making daily decisions without advice and reassurance from others, great reluctance in undertaking projects or becoming involved in activities because of lack of confidence, and fears of being unable to care for oneself, which result in the fear of being alone (American Psychiatric Association, 1994).

Diffidence is likely to be associated with hopelessness. Among the elderly, hopelessness is experienced as a negative expectancy about the future and a sense of futility about having an impact on impending events. The combination of hopelessness and depression are strongly associated with suicidal ideation among the elderly (Uncapher, Gallagher-Thompson, Osgood, & Bongar, 1998). Feelings of diffidence can result from increased dependency and loss of control due to physical illness, loss of social support, or marked reduction in the quality of life; or they can be a product of a continuous process of ego pathology, building on the negative resolutions of earlier psychosocial crises. It is clear that in later life, the courage and energy required to remain flexible and adaptive to change must be derived from the well of ego resources established over the life course. For some of the very old, this precious resource is missing, and they face the end of life in a state of passivity and doubt.

APPLIED TOPIC

Meeting the Needs of the Frail Elderly

Objective 6. To apply research and theory to concerns about meeting the needs of the frail elderly.

THE GOAL OF providing services or community resources to the frail elderly should be to enhance a realistic level of performance. On the one hand, one should not try to encourage 80-year-olds to live the lives of teenagers or people in their fifties. On the other hand, one should not hold such minimal expectations for the elderly that they are robbed of their autonomy and ability to meet challenges or to strive toward achievable goals. One of the current issues that has become a focus of research and policy debate is the extent to which physical frailty in elderhood is treatable or preventable, and how to reduce dependency, especially in long-term nursing care.

In 2004, the U.S. Administration on Aging announced a new initiative focused on supporting "Seniors Aging in Place" (ageinplace.org) in response to the strong preference among the very old to remain independent. Innovative projects were funded that provided new resources or access to services in the community, so that older adults with a wide range of needs and abilities could retain an optimal level of independent functioning. The National Aging in Place Council is a forum whose mission is to encourage professionals and corporations in specific communities to work together to provide the system of community resources that will permit older adults to remain in their homes as long as possible. The council provides suggestions to individuals about how to modify their homes to make them accessible and how to take advantage of community resources and services. It also sponsors innovative collaboration between health care, transportation, and corporate interests to create products and services that will facilitate optimal residential communities for the very old (National Aging in Place Council, 2007).

Defining Frailty

Frailty has typically been operationalized in terms of dependency. One common approach is to list any difficulties in the ADLs, including bathing, dressing, transferring from the bed to a chair, using the toilet, and eating. Sometimes, these assessments include walking a short distance because this degree of motor ability is usually required to function independently. Beyond these basic types of self-care, an expanded notion of dependency refers to difficulties in managing **instrumental activities of daily living** (IADLs), such as shopping, preparing meals, doing light housework, using transportation, or using the telephone. These tasks, though clearly more complex than the basic ADLs, are essential to maintaining one's daily life without

Because of his problems walking, Caleb was practically homebound. But once his children bought him this motorized chair he was able to enjoy going outdoors, interacting with neighbors, and taking Pebbles for a walk. What other technological inventions help support optimal functioning in elderhood?

Copyright © A. Ramey/Photo Edit

dependence on informal or formal community support services (Guralnik & Simonsick, 1993).

Dependency or difficulty in managing ADLs increases markedly after age 85. Many factors combine to produce this dependency. In most postindustrial societies, later adulthood is characterized by a sedentary lifestyle. Estimates suggest that only about 10% of older adults are active enough to sustain appropriate levels of muscle strength and cardiovascular capacity. Weakness resulting from disuse combines with certain biological changes, diseases, medications, and malnutrition to produce muscle atrophy, risk of falling, reduced arousal and cognitive capacity, and a gradual decline in confidence in being able to cope with even moderate types of physical exertion.

Measures of functional limitations often fail to differentiate between what people say they might be able to do in a hypothetical context (when completing a survey) and what they actually do in their day-to-day lives. For example, some people may respond to a questionnaire saying that they are able to walk half a mile without help, but they do not actually ever walk that much. Others may respond that they cannot walk half a mile without help, but in fact they walk several blocks on most days to go to the store near their home. When observed in their natural setting, many older adults use compensatory strategies to overcome some physical impairment or integrate the support of others so that they can enact certain functions even though they have serious disabilities. For example, in a sample of women who needed assistance in more than three areas of daily living, more than one fourth still managed to get to church services once a week or more. They did not allow their physical limitations to restrict their role involvement (Idler, 1987; Glass, 1998).

For many older adults, problems with remaining independent change from time to time. In the winter, when streets are icy and the weather is cold, a person may need more help because it is difficult to walk outside or to wait for the bus. In the event of an acute illness requiring a period of hospitalization, a person may temporarily need support during the posthospital recovery but does not require long-term institutionalization. Full recovery from a week or two of being bedridden may require additional physical therapy, rebuilding muscle tone and endurance, and rebuilding confidence in managing daily tasks. The outcome for the older person depends on the patient, caregiver, and health care system—all sharing expectations for recovery and rehabilitation rather than viewing the person as permanently weakened and destined for prolonged dependency (Schulz & Williamson, 1993).

Supporting Optimal Functioning

Optimal functioning is what a person is capable of doing when motivated and well prepared. To support optimal functioning of elderly people, one must accurately assess their limitations. One does not want to take away the supports that help very old adults sustain their independence or overreact to their physical or intellectual limitations. This tendency, however, is observed in the responses of some adult children to their aging parents. Once the children realize that their parents are not functioning at the same high level of competence that they enjoyed previously, the children move toward a **role reversal**. The children may infantilize or dominate their parents, insisting on taking over all financial matters or attempting to relocate their parents to a more protective housing arrangement. Gradually, some children take away all their parents' decision-making responsibilities.

Although children may view such actions as being in their parents' best interests, they may fail to take their parents' preferences into account. For example, adult children tend to overemphasize the importance of health and financial considerations for their parents and to overlook the significance of familiar housing in preserving the companionship and daily support that are critical to their parents' sense of well-being (Kahana, 1982). Adult children may also fail to realize how important decision-making tasks and responsibility for personal care are to the maintenance of their parents' personality structure. In mutually satisfying relationships between adult daughters and their aging mothers, the daughters made sure that their mothers were consistently involved in decisions that affected their lives, even when the mothers were heavily dependent on their daughters for daily care (Pratt, Jones, Shin, & Walker, 1989).

In many nursing homes, there is a similar tendency to reduce or eliminate expectations of autonomy by failing to give residents responsibilities for planning or performing the activities of daily life. Routine chores such as cooking, cleaning, shopping for groceries, doing laundry, planning meals, answering the phone, paying bills, and writing letters all give older adults the sense that life is going along as usual. Replacing these responsibilities with unstructured time may subject very old people to more stress than continuing to expect some forms of regular contribution to daily life. Thus, paid work assignments and structured daily responsibilities are activities that an institutional setting can provide to help maintain a high level of social and intellectual functioning among the residents. The Eden Alternative is an emerging concept in nursing home care that gives residents responsibilities for some aspect of their environment, depending on their level of functioning. These responsibilities—such as watering plants, volunteering in a nearby child care center, or reading to other residents—help overcome the negative impact of dependency and institutionalization (Hooyman & Kiyak, 2002).

Supporting the optimal functioning of frail elderly people requires an individualized approach. Each person has a unique profile of competencies and limitations. For some, the physical environment presents the greatest barriers to optimal functioning. For example, older adults who are in a wheelchair are likely to experience a fall every so often. However, those who have installed modifications in their home—including widened doorways and halls, railings, and easy-open doors—are less likely to fall than those whose homes have not been modified (Berg, Hines, & Allen, 2002). A person who cannot walk without fear of falling, see well, or grasp objects because of arthritis may need to have modifications in the home that will compensate for these limitations. Many creative strategies have been introduced that permit people with serious physical disabilities to retain an optimal level of autonomy in their homes.

The Role of the Community

Interventions at the community level may be necessary to meet the safety, health, and social needs of some older adults who want to remain in their communities. It is important for resources to be accessible. In promoting optimal functioning in urban settings, for example, it is important to provide health care settings that are more easily accessible for elderly people with limited mobility. Andrulis (2000) has taken this point of view one step further by arguing that as the number of elderly people in the urban centers of the United States increases, health care organizations and providers supported by local, state, and federal governments must be prepared to reach out to the growing population of elderly people. Many of these people are poor, have physical limitations, and experience psychological barriers such as perceived threat of violence, confusion, fear, and embarrassment over lack of financial resources. As a result, they may be unable or unwilling to leave their immediate environment. Community outreach would have to provide a wide variety of services to a culturally diverse population with special attention to poverty-related concerns.

In one community intervention service in New Haven, Connecticut, called LIFE (Learning Informally From the Elderly), community professionals charged with providing services to the frail elderly organized interviews and community meetings with them to learn what challenges they were facing in trying to remain as independent as possible in their neighborhood (Pallett-Hehn & Lucas, 1994). The professionals were surprised to find that the older adults brought safety concerns to the fore as a primary issue and that health and service concerns were secondary. In order to preserve and continue the dialogue, the professionals fostered the creation of Elder Forums—neighborhood groups where older adults discuss their mutual concerns and possible solutions. Each month, representatives from the Elder Forums come together in an assembly with professionals and policymakers to raise concerns that have been discussed in the Elder Forums and to identify community resources or changes in policy and procedures for addressing these concerns.

In a surprising essay, Clive Thompson (2007) wrote about the features of life in New York City that contribute to longevity. A major theme was the role of walking and climbing stairs as aspects of daily life in the city. "Driving in the city is maddening, pushing us onto the sidewalks and up and down the stairs to the subways. What's more, our social contract dictates that you should move your ass when you're on the sidewalk so as not to annoy your fellow walkers" (Thompson, 2007, p. 31). Living in areas that are densely populated means access to more markets, specialty shops, and interesting things to do in walking distance. People in New York City are more likely to walk a mile to get to something than people who live in suburban or rural areas. In a shift from earlier views of cities as crime-ridden, disease-promoting, alienating environments, some social scientists are starting to write about urban health advantages. Friendship groups are likely to form in neighborhoods; big cities may have bigger, more fully equipped hospitals; and population density can attract more parks, gyms, and recreational facilities. The causal relationship between urban life and health is probably bidirectional. As cities become safer, people with more resources (who generally have greater longevity) want to live there, attracting more of the lifestyle resources that support health.

For some elderly adults, the absence of meaningful interpersonal relationships is the greatest barrier to optimal functioning. The role of the informal social support system in meeting the needs of the frail elderly cannot be underestimated. Children, spouses, other relatives, and neighbors are all important sources of help. Within communities, the elderly are themselves likely to provide significant help to age-mates who may be ill, bereaved, or impaired in some way. Most older adults prefer not to have to ask for help. However, they are much better off if they have someone to turn to than if they have no one.

Beyond personal networks of social support, communities have been characterized by different levels of **collective efficacy**, which combines a strong sense of social cohesion with a high level of informal social control (Sampson, Raudenbush, & Earls, 1997). People who live in communities characterized by high collective efficacy are willing to take on important community concerns and to intervene on each other's behalf even if they do not know one another on a personal level. Examples of the impact of collective efficacy include reducing violent victimization, child or elder abuse, and illicit drug trafficking in a neighborhood. Communities that are high in collective efficacy will act to draw on the required resources to attract health care services, create new recreational settings, and improve transportation resources. In all these ways, communities characterized by collective efficacy can enhance the health and optimal functioning of the frail elderly (Browning & Cagney, 2003).

The Role of Creative Action

People can do a lot for themselves to promote a fulfilling later life. By identifying meaningful goals and coordinating action to achieve these goals, older adults can create lives that are both meaningful and manageable (Riediger, Freund, & Baltes, 2005). Very old adults can alter the structure of their environment to preserve optimal functioning and enhance their sense of well-being. They may move to a warmer climate, to a homogeneous-age community, or to a more

At age 85, George preserves his playful outlook by spending time with his great-granddaughter. They take turns surprising each other with new costumes, songs, and games.

Jose Luis Pelaez, Inc./CORBIS

modest home or apartment that entails fewer maintenance responsibilities. They may participate in exercise classes or other guided physical activity to improve their strength, endurance, and flexibility. Elders may select some family and friendship relationships that they sustain through frequent interaction, mutual help giving, and shared activities. They may participate in activities in community settings, including churches, senior centers, libraries, and volunteer organizations, through which they retain a sense of purpose and social connection. For example, 21% of people ages 75 and older participate in some form of charity work (U.S. Census Bureau, 2007). They may decide to focus their interest on a single remaining role that is most important to them. One study has found that older people may live longer if they are

able to maintain a sense of control over the role that is most important to them (Krause & Shaw, 2000). As at earlier ages, elders make certain choices that direct the course of their lives, provide a sense of meaning, and influence their overall level of adjustment.

In summary, the quality of life for the frail elderly depends on four factors: (1) the specific nature and timing of the health-related limitations that accompany aging; (2) the availability of appropriate resources within the home, family, and community to help compensate for or minimize these limitations; (3) the selective emphasis that the person gives to some life experiences over others as being central to well-being; and (4) the person's motivational orientation to continue to find creative strategies to adapt to change.

Chapter Summary

Objective 1. To identify elderhood as a unique developmental period for those of unusual longevity—a stage with its own developmental tasks and psychosocial crisis.

Elderhood is a period of new challenges and opportunities that will be faced by an increasing number of people in the years ahead. Those who are 80 years old and older are the fastest growing segment of the U.S. population. Having reached a sense of acceptance of one's death, the task is to find meaning and enjoyment in the bonus years of life. This requires ongoing adaptation to changing physical and cognitive capacities, a deepening sense of time and the place of one's life in the history of one's people, and a willingness to

find new and flexible solutions to the demands of daily life. This period of life requires ongoing adaptive self-organization.

In attempting to describe the psychosocial development of the very old, we are drawn to concepts that have a strong non-Western philosophical flavor. We have introduced such concepts as psychohistorical perspective, experiential transcendence, immortality, and social support—themes that reflect the need to assume a long-range perspective on life and its meaning.

Objective 2. To describe some of the physical changes associated with aging, including changes in fitness, behavioral slowing, sensory changes, and vulnerability to illness, and the challenges that these changes pose for continued psychosocial well-being.

The quality of daily life for the very old is influenced to a great extent by their physical health. For some, daily activities are restricted by one or more chronic diseases. Nevertheless, the majority of elders continue to live in their own households and perform tasks of daily living independently.

Objective 3. To develop the concept of an altered perspective on time and history that emerges among the long-lived.

The concept of time changes with advanced age, so that the continuity of past, present, and future becomes clearer.

Objective 4. To explore elements of the lifestyle structure in elderhood, especially living arrangements and gender roles.

An increasingly wide range of lifestyle alternatives are being invented in elderhood, including opportunities for travel, housing that provides varying levels of care, and patterns of close relationships in which traditional gender roles are modified to take into consideration new capacities and interests.

Objective 5. To identify and describe the psychosocial crisis of immortality versus extinction, the central process of social support, the prime adaptive ego quality of confidence, and the core pathology of diffidence.

Having lived well beyond their life expectancy, elders face the psychosocial crisis of immortality versus extinction. A key to their quality of life lies in whether they are integrated into effective social support networks. Social support provides help, resources, meaningful social interaction, and a psychological sense of being valued. Elders who survive within a support system can transcend the limitations of their mortality, finding comfort and continuity in their participation in a chain of loving relationships. Those who are isolated, however, are more likely to face the end of their lives bound to the tedium of struggling with their physical limitations and resenting their survival.

Objective 6. To apply research and theory to concerns about meeting the needs of the frail elderly.

The topic of the care of the frail elderly illustrates the relevance of a psychosocial framework. The resources and services available in the community can support optimal functioning. Children, grandchildren, and other family members need to be able to interpret the needs of their aging parents without underestimating their capacity or resilience. Finally, older adults can guide the direction of their care by the decisions they make, both in earlier periods of life and as they detect new signs of frailty.

Key Terms

active engagement, 577
activities of daily living (ADLs), 573
affiliative values, 584
behavioral slowing, 569
collective efficacy, 595
community-based long-term
    health care, 582
confidence, 592
continuing care retirement
    community, 581
cosmic transcendence, 588
dependency, 585
diffidence, 592
experiential transcendence, 587
extinction, 589

fitness, 567
frailty, 593
functional independence, 572
gender gap, 565
gender role convergence, 584
gentrification, 582
housing options, 581
immortality, 587
instrumental activities of
    daily living (IADLs), 593
instrumental support, 590
instrumental values, 584
life structure, 567
living arrangements, 578
norm of reciprocity, 590

nursing homes, 581
old-old, 566
optimal functioning, 594
organic brain syndromes, 573
physical changes of aging, 567
processing load, 569
psychohistorical perspective, 575
role reversal, 594
sexuality, 585
social support, 590
socioemotional support, 590
successful agers, 577
usual aging, 577
visual adaptation, 570
young-old, 566

Further Reflection

1. Imagine that you are now 85 years old. What kind of life do you hope to be living? What kinds of changes or modifications do you envision having to make from the period of your fifties and sixties in order to adapt in elderhood?
2. What is a psychohistorical perspective? What insights might come along with living a very long time?
3. The majority of the elderly are women. What are some implications of this for social policy and community development?
4. How would you describe the difference in the major challenges and areas for new growth between later adulthood and elderhood?
5. In what ways may the experiences of those who are elders today differ from those who will reach elderhood 50 years from now (those who are 25–30 today)?
6. Reflecting on your study of human development, what are the salient factors that promote optimal functioning at each stage of life?

Psychology CourseMate

To access additional course materials, including CourseMate, please visit www.cengagebrain.com. At the CengageBrain.com home page, search for the ISBN of your title (from the back cover of your book) using the search box at the top of the page. This will take you to the product page where these resources can be found.

Casebook

For additional cases related to this chapter, see "Still Going Strong," in *Life Span Development: A Case Book*, by Barbara and Philip Newman, Laura Landry-Meyer, and Brenda J. Lohman, pp. 215–218. This case highlights the importance of living arrangements for the health and well-being of an active 93-year-old woman.

Colombe avec Fleurs, 1957 (coloured pencil on paper)/Private Collection / The Bridgeman Art Library International/© 2011 Estate of Pablo Picasso/Artists Rights Society (ARS), New York

When the dove returned to the ark with an olive branch in its beak, Noah and his family perceived the sign that the period of turmoil was at an end and that life could begin anew. The dove has become a symbol of peace and hope—an image of comfort in a time of grief—providing the sense that rebirth accompanies death.

Understanding Death, Dying, and Bereavement

Chapter Objectives

1. To understand the role of mortality in shaping psychosocial development.

2. To define the biological state of death.

3. To describe factors associated with the process of dying and the modern ideal of a good death.

4. To describe death-related rituals and their functions.

5. To analyze factors that affect grief and bereavement.

LIKE BOOKENDS, BIRTH and death bracket the story of development. Birth is preceded by a long chain of biological transformations, in which the biochemical thread of DNA is passed from generation to generation. Pregnancy and birth occur in a psychosocial context of relationships, resources, and cultural beliefs and practices (see Chapter 4, The Period of Pregnancy and Prenatal Development). So, too, it is with death: The biological process of dying takes place in a psychosocial context of relationships, resources, and cultural beliefs and practices. As the psychosocial concept of immortality implies, death is accompanied by a series of transformations at the biological, psychological, and societal levels. It is the role of culture and religion to provide a narrative or explanation for the transformations of energy that occur in death. Because we cannot empirically test many of these explanations, it is the role of the ego to cope with the unknown aspects of death, to give it personal meaning.

Death is at once a certainty, in that all living things die, and a random event, in that the timing of death is unknown. We know for sure that we will die, but when and how are not known. Moreover, whereas through observation, systematic study, and the transmission of knowledge from generation to generation, we have a good idea about the trajectory of development beginning with the prenatal period until death, we have only speculations and belief systems to guide our understanding of what occurs at death and beyond. Thus, death is both inevitable and unknowable.

Thanatology is the field of science that addresses dying, death, and the psychological mechanisms of coping with them. This field includes an analysis of the attitudes toward dying, the meaning of death for individuals and societies, the rituals and practices associated with death, the bereavement process, and the expressions of bereavement across situations and cultures. ∎

Mortality and Psychosocial Development

Objective 1. To understand the role of mortality in shaping psychosocial development.

Psychosocial development focuses on the ongoing interactions between the person and the environment. The person's ability to understand the self and others matures and changes with each psychosocial crisis. At each stage of life, the ego is shaped by the perplexing nature of mortality. In infancy, as one achieves a balance between trust and mistrust, an outlook of hopefulness emerges. This outlook shapes one's orientation toward risk, transitions, and ultimately death. If one has lived a life of hopefulness about the future, this same orientation is likely to extend toward one's beliefs about death—a sense that whatever follows the death of the physical body is going to be good.

In the resolution of the crisis of identity versus role confusion, one confronts the need to impose a sense of meaning on one's life: Where am I going? What do I want out of life? What is my path? Even though one may believe that death is far off in the distant future, the creation of a personal identity reflects an understanding that one's life is finite; one's choices should count for something.

The crisis of generativity versus stagnation brings the issue of mortality even more to center stage. Here, one begins to consider the impact of one's life on future generations: What can I do to contribute to the quality of life for others, even after my death? How can I use my resources, talents, and creative abilities to ensure a good future for those who come after me? While still in the throes of caring for children, aging parents, colleagues, and communities, the generative action of middle adults suggests a concern for a time when the ego is not present to nurture and maintain.

Developing a point of view about death is a major developmental task during later adulthood. The resolution of the crisis of integrity versus despair requires recognition that

Courtesy of Philip Newman

In older communities it is common to find small family cemeteries where people are buried near their home or farmland. These cemeteries suggest a time when there was a greater intimacy between the living and their ancestors.

death is increasingly imminent. Integrity is achieved on the shoulders of earlier ego strengths that allow the person to celebrate personal achievements, cherish meaningful relationships, and look with satisfaction at the life thus far lived. The integrity expressed by those in later adulthood—an ability to celebrate life in the face of impending death—is a model for younger generations.

Finally, the crisis of immortality versus extinction brings the confidence of continuity. One is ready—though not necessarily eager—to close one door, confident that another will open. In this period, the possibility of death cannot dampen the joy of being and the certainty that one's life is intimately connected with all life.

Over time, direct personal experiences with dying and death have changed. One hundred years ago, most people died in their homes. Many women and infants died in childbirth. As a result, death was experienced by family members who cared for the dying and were present at the death. As you travel through New England, it is common to find small cemeteries near churches and homes, where you sense the intimate gathering of families who buried their dead nearby.

With the growth of modern medicine, people who were very ill were taken to hospitals. Those who were dying were removed from the home, and death occurred more in hospitals or nursing homes. Death was sanitized through embalming practices. A culture of death as medical failure emerged, leaving people increasingly alienated from the realities of dying. The discussion of topics related to death and dying became taboo. Children were shielded from experiences with death. Doctors often tried to protect people from the knowledge that they were dying. Once people became terminally ill, they were deprived of the right to have a voice in decisions related to their treatment and the conditions surrounding the end of life (Kastenbaum, 2009).

Beginning with the works of Elisabeth Kübler-Ross (1969, 1983), the needs of the dying person were given a voice again. Concern about allowing people to talk about their fears, to plan for their funeral, and to bring closure to their personal affairs led people to face death more openly and directly. This approach also led to new ways of thinking about the care of the dying. Currently, we have new technologies that allow for the prolongation of life, but are still caught in conflicts about how long and under what conditions we should sustain life.

Definitions of Death

Objective 2. To define the biological state of death.

The definition of death has changed. Historically, the criteria for death were lack of a heartbeat and lack of respiration, called **cardiopulmonary death**. This definition was used for hundreds of years. In 1981, the President's Commission for the Ethical Study of Problems in Medicine and Biomedical and Behavioral Research identified eight criteria for the determination of **whole-brain death**:

1. No spontaneous movement in response to any stimuli
2. No spontaneous respirations for at least 1 hour

3. Total lack of responsiveness to even the most painful stimuli
4. No eye movements, blinking, or pupil responses
5. No postural activity, swallowing, yawning, or vocalizing
6. No motor reflexes
7. A flat electroencephalogram (EEG) for at least 10 minutes
8. No change in any of these criteria when they are tested again 24 hours later

In addition to these eight criteria, certain other conditions, such as deep coma, have to be ruled out. Two areas in the brain control different types of life functions: the *brainstem* controls heartbeat and respiration, and the *cortex* controls sensory integration and cognitive function. It is possible for a person's brainstem functions to continue even when there is no cortical functioning. This condition is called **persistent vegetative state**. If you refer back to the list of eight criteria, you can see that the person in this state is not technically dead. When this state occurs, family members, doctors, and sometimes the courts are faced with the difficult decision about whether to let the person die.

In response to the report of the President's Commission, Congress passed the Uniform Determination of Death Act (UDDA). All 50 states and the District of Columbia recognize whole-brain death as the one legal standard. However, the UDDA allows physicians or hospitals to apply the cardiopulmonary definition or the whole-brain death definition, whichever applies first. On the one hand, because of the great need for transplantable organs, there is urgency in deciding whether or not a person has died. On the other hand, it is not legal to remove an organ when that removal would cause a person's death. Therefore, the decision whether to harvest organs from people who are experiencing whole-brain death poses a difficult ethical question (DeGrazia, 1998).

Advance Directives

Because there are a variety of technologies that can extend life when a person is no longer able to communicate, it is recommended that adults prepare some form of **advance directive**, such as a *living will* or *durable power of attorney* (Doukas & Reichel, 2007). These documents can inform a physician or hospital as to a person's wishes about life-sustaining procedures in the face of terminal illness or imminent death and designate someone to act on one's behalf. Through a **living will**, a person can direct physicians or a hospital to withhold life-sustaining procedures and prevent the use of unwanted medical measures when that person is unable to convey those wishes. Some older people wear bracelets that say, "living will—do not resuscitate (DNR)." The **durable power of attorney** authorizes someone to act on behalf of the person regarding financial and property matters and health care decisions. This directive can go into effect when either the agreement is signed or the disability occurs (Hooyman & Kiyak, 1993). One benefit of the living will is that it helps resolve potential conflicts between a dying person's wishes and family members' feelings of obligation to do

everything possible to keep the person alive. It is possible to register a living will online at www.uslivingwillregistry.com.

The following quotation describes the benefit that accompanied a woman's decision to register her advanced directive with the U.S. Living Will Registry:

> I am very glad I registered my advanced directive. As caregiver to my mother, my father, and my stepmother I cannot express the peace of mind that registering gives. My husband and daughter will never go through the stress of wondering if they are acting according to my wishes. It will be very clear for them. In a way, making my advanced directive is protecting my husband and daughter, even when I am seriously ill. When a loved one is seriously ill is the worst possible time to deal with the subtleties and ramifications of hospital and legal bureaucracies. This will free them from a lot of those worries. (U.S. Living Will Registry, 2010)

One of the more troubling health conditions is Alzheimer's disease, in which there is a gradual loss of mental competence, so that a decision must be made about when the person is no longer competent and the living will or durable power of attorney will go into effect. The preparation of advance directives requires that people think about the kind of care they want to receive and the conditions under which they want treatment to be withheld. Currently, most Americans do not complete advance directives, and many interventions that are designed to increase completion of advance directives are not effective (Kersting, 2004; Jezewski, Meeker, Sessana, & Finnell, 2007). Even though it is recommended that people consider these issues while they are flourishing, the fact remains that it seems to be difficult for people to face these issues and make decisions about their death.

The Process of Dying

Objective 3. To describe factors associated with the process of dying and the modern ideal of a good death.

People can experience death in many different ways. Their psychological coping strategies differ depending on the conditions of the experience. In Chapter 13 (Later Adulthood), we described Kübler-Ross' concept of stages in coming to terms with one's death: denial, anger and resentment, bargaining, depression and mourning one's death, and acceptance. Although these emotional reactions are all important aspects of understanding how people may cope with the reality of their death, the differences in the conditions of death mean that this stage process is not likely to be experienced universally.

Confronting One's Death

In contrast to the notion of stages, some people write about the **dying trajectory** (Lawton, 2001)—that is, the time during which the person's health goes from good to death. Certain illnesses such as some cancers or AIDS result in a gradual decline. Under these conditions, people have more time to acknowledge their death and to plan for it. They may be asked to make a number of decisions about their treatment, in each case weighing the risks or side effects of treatment against the chances of prolonging life. Some people experience unpredictable, sudden death in the midst of a healthy life, as in an automobile accident, by homicide, or by a heart attack. This trajectory does not allow the person to confront the reality of death. For some, death involves an ambiguous decline, in which periods of illness may alternate with periods of remission, as in the case of leukemia or muscular dystrophy. For these people, there is a complex process of learning to live with a terminal disease, in which there may be periods of health as well as periods of decline. In this scenario, the person may wrestle with the question of whether they are dying from the illness or living with the illness. The case study of Harriet McBryde Johnson illustrates the complex process of making meaning in the face of an ambiguous trajectory.

CASE STUDY

TOO LATE TO DIE YOUNG

Harriet McBryde Johnson was diagnosed with muscular dystrophy as a little girl. She has faced a life of surviving the expectation that she would die young.

I'm 3 or 4 years old. I'm sitting on the living room floor, playing with dolls. I look up at the TV and see a little boy. He's sitting on the floor, playing with toy soldiers. Then he's in Little League; he stumbles on his way to first base. He visits a doctor. His parents are sad. He's in a wheelchair. Then a bed. Then I see the toy soldiers. No boy. An unseen narrator says, "Little Billy's toy soldiers have lost their general." It's a commercial for the Muscular Dystrophy Association. As the narrator makes the pitch, a realization comes to me: I will die.

Is it really one of my earliest memories? Or was it manufactured by my imagination? I don't suppose it matters. Either way, it was my truth. I'm a little girl who knows she will die, but I don't say anything. Somehow my mother guesses. "That boy," she says, "has a different kind of muscular dystrophy. Girls don't get it." Maybe, I think, but he looks a lot like me. And pretty soon I see little girls on the telethon and hear that girls too have "killer diseases." I don't know the word, but I figure my mother is in denial.

By the time I am 5, I think of myself as a dying child. I've been sick a lot. There is some discussion before my parents decide to send me to kindergarten. I am glad they do. When I die, I think, I might as well die a kindergartner.

I've just turned 30. I've been lolling in bed for nearly 3 weeks; I say I've strained my neck, but really it's major depression. Just before my birthday my mother had brain surgery. She's come through it beautifully, but I'm terrified to think I could actually outlive my parents. I am further set adrift by the sudden death of the crazy German doctor who nursed me with pea soup and sausages when I refused to go to the hospital with pneumonia. My thoughts race by, but I manage to grab them and take a look. I find that I'm bonkers but rational. I know what's bothering me; my plan to die young hasn't worked out. What do I do now? My thoughts take on the structure of a song with a repeated chorus; it's too late to die young.

I decide to embrace the death sentence. No need to fear it; no need to hasten it. Mortality is something all people share, a unifying force. Every life, whether long or short, is a treasure of infinite value. These things are true, I figure, and it's my job to say so. When I die, I might as well die honest.

Source: Johnson, 2005, pp. 44–46.

CRITICAL THINKING AND CASE ANALYSIS

1. What are the challenges of facing an ambiguous dying trajectory? For the dying person? For close relatives?
2. What are some of the possible reasons for Harriet's depression at age 30?
3. According to psychosocial theory, what are some of the life themes that Harriet is facing at age 4? At age 30?
4. How might her psychosocial development be affected by her illness at age 4 and age 30? By her sense of herself as someone who is dying?
5. What are some of Harriet's coping strengths? Weaknesses?
6. If you were Harriet's parents, what would you do to try to prepare Harriet for her life? For her death?

The dying process may bring a high **degree of suffering**, including shortness of breath, inability to eat, limited mobility, and pain. In some instances, this suffering can be alleviated with medications, but in some cases it grows worse. Health care providers and family members often express great dissatisfaction with these end-of-life conditions for the dying person and the surviving loved ones.

Finally, the dying process may be conceptualized in different ways depending on the *age* of the dying person. The primary cause of death differs for people of various age groups, thus creating different contexts for dying. Children and adolescents are most likely to die of accidents including injuries due to fire and auto accidents, or abuse. In middle adulthood, cancer, heart disease, and AIDS are common causes of death, along with accidents and homicide. Older adults are most likely to die of the complications from chronic diseases, such as heart disease, diabetes, pneumonia, or cancer (U.S. Census Bureau, 2010).

People of different ages have differing cognitive abilities, psychological coping mechanisms, and views of the future that they bring to the tasks of preparing for death. Kübler-Ross reported the following poem that was written by Mike, a teenage boy, to his parents on the day of his death:

The time has come,
My job is done.
Now it's time for another one

The gates will open, open soon
I now will go.
See you soon.
Time, time will never stop
Everlasting time
Love is eternal
Forevermore love
I will always love you. (cited in Kübler-Ross, 1983, p. 189)

Because of the nature of his illness, Mike had time to prepare for his death. His mother reports that he taped messages to his family and friends, helped plan his funeral, and gave a few things away before he died. At this age, Mike appears to have a hopeful view about an everlasting life. He is able to conceptualize dying as a transition that allows some continuity between the life he had and the life he is going to have. He also sees a future in which he will be reunited with the other loved ones in his life before too long. Another teenager, John, who was terminally ill, stated that before he died he wanted two things: to own a van and to make love to a woman (Kübler-Ross, 1983, p. 184). Here we see a youthful approach to the dying process. John's goals are more fun loving and pragmatic, whereas Mike's approach is more spiritual and interpersonal.

Ray Bradbury provided a portrait of a great-grandmother's approach to her own death. At 90, Great-Grandma told her children and grandchildren:

I don't want any Halloween parties here tomorrow. Don't want anyone saying anything sweet about me; I said it all in my time and my pride. I've tasted every victual and danced every dance; now there's one last tart I haven't bit on, one tune I haven't whistled. But I'm not afraid. I'm truly curious. Death won't get a crumb by my mouth I won't keep and savor. So don't you worry over me. Now, all of you go, and let me find my sleep. (Bradbury, 1957/1964, pp. 140–141)

In this case, Great-Grandma reassures her children that she is ready—that she has experienced a full life and sees death as the next dance. In addition to the way death is perceived by the dying, the death will be perceived and conceptualized differently by caregivers. The death of a child or adolescent may be seen as quite tragic in the minds and hearts of parents and friends; the death of an older person may be seen as the natural close to a full life. In some cultures, the death of an elder is especially painful, as it results in the loss of wisdom and guidance for younger generations. In other cultures, the death of a child is especially tragic, because it results in the loss of promise and potential for the future.

The Good Death

Professionals who are responsible for the care of the dying have begun to define the characteristics of a good death or dying well (Webb, 1997; Emanuel & Emanuel, 1998; Kehl, 2006). The results of one British study group offered the following 12 principles of a good death (Smith, 2000):

- To know when death is coming, and to understand what can be expected
- To be able to retain control of what happens
- To be afforded dignity and privacy
- To have control over pain relief and other symptom control
- To have choice and control over where death occurs (at home or elsewhere)
- To have access to information and expertise of whatever kind is necessary
- To have access to any spiritual or emotional support required
- To have access to hospice care in any location, not only in the hospital
- To have control over who is present and who shares the end
- To be able to issue advanced directives, which ensure wishes are respected
- To have time to say good-bye, and control over other aspects of timing
- To be able to leave when it is time to go, and not to have life prolonged pointlessly

Research on perspectives about dying find that the definition of a **good death** is highly individual, shaped by the context of dying and changing over the course of the illness. In a research project (Carr, 2003), the ideals of a good death were studied by asking recent widows and widowers to rate their spouses' end-of-life experiences along the following dimensions:

- Spouse was at peace with the idea of dying
- Spouse was aware of the impending death
- Respondent and spouse discussed the death
- Respondent was with spouse at the moment of death
- Spouse led a full life
- Spouse was not in pain
- Spouse did not receive negligent care

These dimensions represent concrete evidence of what people perceive to be a good death. Of all these features, the greatest psychological distress for the survivor was associated with seeing the spouse in great pain at the end of life. Although roughly 70% of Americans say they would prefer to die at home, about 75% actually die in a hospital, many undergoing painful medical interventions in attempts to prolong life (Cloud, 2000).

In a study of what patients, family members, and their health care professionals were concerned about in preparing for the end of life, the following issues were highlighted: naming someone to make decisions, knowing what to expect about one's physical condition, having one's financial affairs in order, having one's treatment preferences in writing, and knowing that one's physician is comfortable talking about death. Dying patients were also concerned about planning their funeral (Steinhauser et al., 2001).

How well are people's needs being met at the end of their lives? Researchers attempted to address this question through a telephone interview with family members or close associates of more than 1,500 people who had died in the previous

9 to 15 months (Teno et al., 2004). The focus was on the location where people die and the quality of care received by the person in the last 48 hours of life. Two thirds of the deceased had been in a hospital or nursing home in the last 48 hours of life. Of the one third who died at home, 38% had no nursing services, 12% had some home nursing services, and 50% had home hospice services. Over 70% of those whose loved ones received hospice care rated that care as excellent. Fewer than 50% of those whose loved ones died in a hospital, nursing home, or at home with home nursing services rated their care as excellent. With the exception of those receiving hospice care, many of the bereaved felt that their loved ones did not receive the pain relief, respect, or emotional support they needed in the 2 days before their death.

There appear to be two different paths to achieving a good death among people who are in a slow, painful death trajectory. One is *hospice care*. The other is *euthanasia*.

Hospice Care

Hospice care is an integrated system of medicine, nursing, counseling, and spiritual care for the dying person and the family. Its goal is to achieve the highest possible quality of life for the dying person and the family, alleviating physical and emotional pain to the highest degree possible, while supporting family strengths to cope with the process of dying, loss of the loved one, and long-term bereavement (Smith, 1997; Knee, 2010). Hospice care can take place in a hospice setting or at home.

The Hospice Education Institute (2001) offers the following goals for high-quality end-of-life care:

- Promote relief from pain
- Integrate the psychological and spiritual aspects of patient care
- Offer a support system to help patients live as actively as possible until death
- Help the family cope during the patient's illness and their own bereavement

Hospice care differs from traditional hospital care in that the focus is on enhancing the quality of life for the dying person and the loved ones rather than on treating the disease or intervening to delay the end of life. The first role of hospice care is to relieve the person's pain and suffering through a variety of medical, physical, psychological, and spiritual means. Dying patients are encouraged to take an active role in as many aspects of their end-of-life care as their cognitive functioning and health permit. They are supported in talking about their death and interacting with their family. Hospice care has many advantages for those with a terminal illness. It prevents the experience of dying alone for those who do not have family and friends nearby. It allows the person to die in a more natural, familiar setting rather than in a hospital or nursing home. It offers emotional, spiritual, and physical comfort, helping more people experience a good death.

For example, Mary Wasacz is a spiritual care coordinator who works for the Hospice and Palliative Care of Westchester in New York. "Her job is to care for the spiritual lives of the dying and those who love them. She visits their homes . . . . She helps (patients) face their relationship with God, address their doubts, come to terms with their religious shortcomings, hold tighter to their faith (whether it's rich or flickering) and prepare for death. . . ." "This is sacred ground," says Wasacz. "It is such a sad time, but a privilege to be there, on this journey with them. It can be uplifting. What I do is facilitate peace" (Stern, 2007).

People come to the role of hospice work through many paths. Mary Wasacz is a devout Roman Catholic and

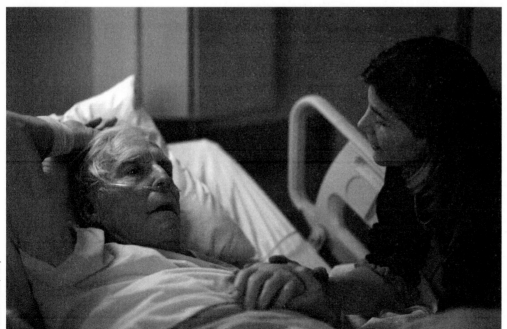

© Charles Mistral/Alamy

Regina and her dad both know that he is dying and the end is near. He is telling her about the time that he and her mother decided to have a child and about the feelings of wonder and awe they experienced when she was born. She is glad to be here with him and to be able to hold his hand. She is thankful that he is receiving wonderful care and comfort here in the hospice, but she is also very sorry that he will be leaving her soon.

Eucharistic minister (she has been specially trained by the clergy to administer the sacrament of the Eucharist or communion). She does not advocate her religion, or any particular religious orientation as a spiritual care coordinator, but her own faith helps her reassure people as they deal with their many fears and doubts. In contrast, Loretta Downs came to her role as a Hospice Partners volunteer patient companion after having experienced the death of many close friends who died of AIDS. She approaches her role in hospice through the lens of yoga training.

> Hospice is . . . a blanket of hope. It is a safe haven in which a team of specialists form a cocoon around the dying one and guide him or her through physical transformation while encouraging spiritual healing along the way. I am to be present in silence as well as in laughter and tears. I am to encourage all the appropriate activity and behavior my patients are able to perform while I create a space for them to engage in spiritual healing. . . . I am to be open to learn how to die myself. Now my patients and their families are my teachers. (Downs, 2004)

Angela Morrow described a third path, from intensive care nursing to hospice:

> I began my nursing career in an intensive care unit. The majority of deaths I witnessed there involved patients, most of whom were elderly, undergoing painful tests and treatments. . . . I'll never forget the 90-year-old male patient who had terminal cancer and was admitted to the intensive care unit with severe breathing problems. We had to place a tube down his throat to help him breathe and inserted several IV lines to give him medicine. His hands were tied to the bed and he was given medication to put him into a coma-like state. Then his heart stopped. We spent a long time trying to revive him and with every chest compression I gave him, I thought, "What are we doing? Why are we doing this?"

Now that I'm working in hospice, I have the pleasure of helping my patients achieve a "good death," one that is in accordance with their goals and priorities. (Morrow, 2008)

The story of the hospice movement illustrates how many factors converge to create a new set of policies and practices. The concept of the hospice as a setting for the care of terminally ill patients is attributed to Dr. Cicely Saunders, who founded St. Christopher's Hospice in London in 1967. In 1963, she gave a talk at Yale University about her work with terminally ill cancer patients and their families, illustrating the many ways in which patients benefited from an integrated approach to care. Following her talk, Florence Wald, the Dean of the Yale School of Nursing, invited Dr. Saunders to be a visiting faculty member for a semester. Subsequently, in 1968, Dr. Wald took a sabbatical and spent time with Dr. Saunders at St. Christopher's. These two health care leaders were supported in their efforts to create hospice settings in the United States by the publication of Dr. Kübler-Ross' book, *On Death and Dying*, in 1969. In 1972, the U.S. Senate Special Committee on Aging heard testimony from

Dr. Kübler-Ross about the negative impact of institutionalizing and isolating the dying. Between 1978 and 1982, several demonstration programs to explore the benefits of hospice care were funded by federal agencies and private foundations. As a result, the U.S. Congress included hospice care as a reimbursable Medicare benefit in 1982—a provision that became permanent in 1986.

Since that time, Congress has increased the level of reimbursement for hospice care, included hospice care as part of veterans' benefits, and included hospice care in the review of efforts to reduce waste and abuse in the Medicare and Medicaid systems. Clear guidelines have been established for the range and quality of services that hospices must offer in order to receive Medicare reimbursements, and an increasing range of educational and training programs have emerged to provide professional interdisciplinary training for those working in hospice and end-of-life care settings. In 1999, the U.S. Postal Service issued the Hospice Care Commemorative Stamp, marking the recognition of this successful model as part of the continuum of health care (National Hospice and Palliative Care Organization, 2005).

To take advantage of hospice through Medicare, one must make a decision to forgo any further life-saving or life-prolonging treatments. A physician must also submit certification that the person is terminally ill, with 6 months or less to live. This provision is one of the current limitations in the use of hospice care within the Medicare system. In advanced stages of Alzheimer's disease and other forms of dementia, the demands on caregivers can be intense, but survival can be prolonged beyond 6 months. As a result, only a small percentage of those with Medicare hospice coverage are patients with Alzheimer's disease (Kersting, 2004). To learn more about hospice care, you can visit the website of the National Hospice and Palliative Care Organization (www.hospiceinfo.org).

Euthanasia

Euthanasia is the practice of ending someone's life for reasons of mercy. In comparison to hospice care, euthanasia is considered when pain medication is ineffective in reducing suffering; when a person is in a persistent vegetative state, being kept alive by mechanical equipment; or when a person is in the final stages of a terminal illness. Euthanasia generally involves hastening the end of life by allowing people to have control over their death.

Passive Euthanasia. Imagine that a person in the late stages of Alzheimer's disease is diagnosed as having cancer. Should treatments including surgery, chemotherapy, and radiation be administered to prolong the life of someone who is already near death? Passive euthanasia refers to withholding treatment or removing life-sustaining nourishment and breathing aids. The result is that death occurs more quickly than if these procedures were continued. Through a living will, a person can make wishes known to others, including the hospital or care center, physicians, and family members or legal representatives. Through the durable power of attorney, a person assigns life-prolonging or life-ending decision making to a representative. Thus, by refusing treatment or by granting discretion to others to end heroic or extraordinary treatment, individuals may hasten their own death. In the preceding example, if the person had a living will or durable power of attorney, a decision could be made by someone else to withhold treatment for the cancer, even though the person is no longer capable of decision making.

Active Euthanasia. Activities designed to end a person's life are referred to as active euthanasia. There are several ways in which this may happen. **Mercy killing** involves actively taking a person's life. This is sometimes done in order to end a person's suffering. In our society, this is considered to be murder. States vary widely on whether the killer will be prosecuted for this act and whether juries will be willing to convict. In a Michigan case of a nurse who ended the lives of more than 20 patients at the Ann Arbor VA hospital, the jury found the nurse to be guilty of murder and sentenced her to life imprisonment. In a California case of a spouse who strangled her husband to end his suffering because she could not help him any longer, the state decided not to prosecute.

Physician-assisted suicide (PAS) involves either the administration of a lethal dose of some medication by a physician or arranging for a terminally ill patient to administer his or her own lethal dose of medication using a suicide machine. This is an extremely controversial procedure. In 1994, Oregon passed a Death with Dignity Act (ODDA) allowing individuals who are terminally ill to request a prescription from their physician for a lethal dose of medication. According to that act, doctors would be allowed to help patients commit suicide by prescribing a lethal dose of medication under the following conditions (Oregon Health Services, 2010a):

1. Patients must be 18 years old or over, and be residents of the state of Oregon.
2. Patients have been informed that they have a terminal disease and that they have less than 6 months to live; this must be confirmed by a second opinion.
3. The patient must make a written request for the lethal medication twice, at least 15 days apart, in the presence of two witnesses.
4. There must be an evaluation to determine that the person is capable of making an informed decision, that there is no psychological disorder that would impair the ability to make the decision and that the person is not suffering from depression.
5. The patient must be informed of the risks and possible results of taking the medication, and counseled as to feasible alternatives such as hospice, or palliative care.
6. The patient must be advised to have someone present at the time of taking the medication; and urged not to take the medication in public.
7. The patient is advised of the right to rescind the request at any time.

In 1997, the U.S. Supreme Court ruled that there is no constitutional right to physician-assisted suicide, leaving the issue up to the states. They did not overturn the Oregon law. In 1997, Oregon voters affirmed the decision to allow physician-assisted suicide by passing the measure again. In 2009, 95 people received prescriptions, and 53 took the medication. The most frequently mentioned end-of-life concerns were: loss of autonomy (96.6%), loss of dignity (91.5%), and

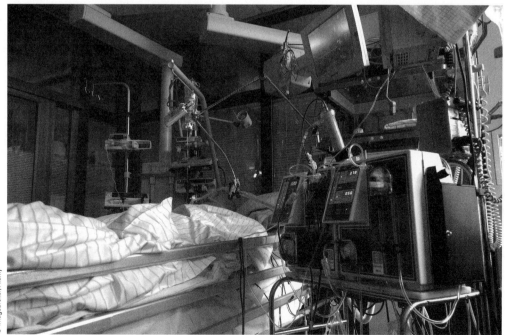

© imagebroker/Alamy

Technological innovations allow physicians to keep a person alive with the hope of saving them. These advances raise many ethical questions about conditions under which life should be sustained and treatment continued. Under what conditions do you think treatment should be terminated?

decreasing ability to participate in activities that made life enjoyable (86.4%) (Oregon Human Services, 2010b).

How common are these measures? In the United States, the Death with Dignity Act was passed in the State of Washington in 2008. In all other states beside Oregon and Washington, assisted suicide and active euthanasia are illegal, which makes it difficult to know how often these strategies are used. It is legal in several European countries including Belgium, Switzerland, Germany, and The Netherlands. In a study in The Netherlands, which has accurate records about requests for PAS, Wolf (1996) found that 38% of all deaths involved some kind of medical decision. Of these, 18% were the result of passive euthanasia where treatment was not provided, and 18% involved hastening death by providing pain medication or other care that led to death occurring more quickly than it might have by not using these treatments. Only about 2% of all cases involved the administration of a lethal drug or physician-assisted suicide. Thus, even in a country where assisted suicide is permitted, it is approached cautiously and used sparingly.

Ethical Issues at the End of Life

Ethical principles focus on standards of right and wrong, especially as they govern areas of moral and professional responsibility. Ethical issues surrounding end-of-life decisions bring to mind the applied topic of abortion that was discussed in Chapter 4. One might view abortion as a special case of decisions about ending life. End-of-life decisions are relevant not only for elderly people; they may be addressed when parents decide to limit treatment for a terminally ill child, when family members decide to remove life support for an adult who is in a vegetative state, or when a person seeks assisted suicide in order to avoid a decline into an immobile or helpless state. The matter is made even more complex because decisions about ending life conflict with the commitment of the medical profession to prolong life. As a result of many new technologies, medications, and genetic interventions, there are ongoing innovations that may be effective in slowing the progression of a disease or sustaining life even if the condition cannot be cured.

Public opinion about the acceptability of physicians helping patients end their lives depends on how the question is framed. In a 2007 Gallup Poll, 49% of respondents said that doctor-assisted suicide was morally acceptable, and 44% said that it was morally unacceptable. However, when framed slightly differently, the response rate shifted. The following question has been asked in polls from 1947 to 2007: "When a person has a disease that cannot be cured, do you think doctors should be allowed by law to end the patient's life by some painless means if the patient and his family request it?" In 1947, 37% of respondents said yes; in 2007, 71% said yes. Clearly, the public has a more accepting view of involving doctors in euthanasia today than in the past (Carroll, 2007). The range of techniques that are available to prolong life has expanded profoundly since 1947. One consequence of these improvements in medical technologies is the need for a new level of conscious decision-making among those who are dying and their families about the point at which medical treatment should be discontinued.

In contrast to PAS, some dying patients exercise a right to voluntarily refuse food and fluids as a way to hasten death. In interviews with 20 hospice workers, both nurses and social workers, 33 different cases were described where people wanted to hasten their death (Harvath et al., 2006). Two thirds sought PAS; one third chose refusal of food and fluids. The hospice workers who were interviewed perceived these two paths as substantially different, with different ethical considerations. Voluntary refusal of food and fluids was seen as "letting go of life" and most hospice workers viewed it as an expression of a dying person's autonomy.

> I don't have any dilemmas or ethical issues with a person not eating or drinking. It's a part of hospice that people have a right to determine what they will and will not do, how they want to die. There's a big difference between that and somebody taking (a lethal dose of) medicine. Nobody makes a decision to tell a person not to eat or drink. (Harvath et al., 2006, p. 209)

Despite public opinion supporting measures to actively end life, these measures are illegal in the United States—with the exception of the states of Oregon and Washington—and continue to be a topic of ethical controversy (Fraser & Walters, 2001; Walker, 2001). Those who support PAS argue that it respects the individual liberties and personal autonomy of those who are terminally ill but competent to make an informed decision about the end of life. It is also a compassionate response to help end suffering. Finally legalizing PAS would open the possibility for more reasoned, full discussion of alternatives between patients and their physicians. At present, these conversations are taking place covertly, without full access to information about alternatives.

Opponents of PAS argue that legalizing assisted suicide might put undue pressure on elderly people to end their lives rather than be a burden to their families or to use precious financial resources for end-of-life care. There is some sense that health care professionals in hospitals and nursing homes are less aggressive in using advanced technologies to prolong the life of elderly patients. Especially for those who have struggled to have access to quality health care during their adult lives, there is great mistrust about giving someone the right to withhold care or accelerate their death. Other opponents suggest that permitting those who are terminally ill to choose death would be one step toward a process of killing people who have mental disabilities or are born with serious defects that affect their quality of life. Some argue that the dying person who is in a great deal of pain may be depressed and lose sight of the possibilities for medical treatments that could improve the medical condition. With effective counseling, the person might be less desperate about the suffering and find ways to achieve a new sense of closeness with loved ones. Finally, there are those who feel that allowing someone to decide to end his or her own life is a violation of their religious or political views.

Death-Related Rituals

Objective 4. To describe death-related rituals and their functions.

Death is a powerful change of state that has mysterious qualities. Typically, it is accompanied by a range of symbolic rituals. These rituals address at least three critical aspects of the meaning of death. The first is how to treat the physical body—the corpse—in an appropriate way. The second is how to address the fate of the spiritual aspect of the person— the soul. The third is how to meet the emotional needs of the survivors and the needs of the society as a whole. Across cultures, people feel a strong need to carry out funeral rituals for the burial or cremation of the dead. Rituals have the advantage of offering a prescribed set of practices at a time when people may be too distressed to make complex decisions. Over one's life span, prior attendance and participation in funeral rituals provides some comfort and familiarity, which may help reduce the distress when a loved one dies.

Funeral rituals allow survivors to say good-bye to their loved one, honor the dead person, and, in the process, begin to detach themselves from the dead person. The concrete evidence of the body proves beyond a doubt to survivors that the person is dead. This helps break down natural tendencies to want to deny the loss. When there is no body, as sometimes happens in natural disasters, mass killings, and war, survivors may be overcome by distress and anxiety caused by uncertainty. Under these conditions, communities sometimes create memorial services or monuments to symbolically bury their dead (Boss, 2002a). The specific practices described in the following section are examples of traditional customs, which are often modified depending on the orthodoxy of the mourners, community practices, and the context of the death.

Care of the Body

Most funeral preparations include specific practices for caring for the corpse. Often, the corpse is washed and wrapped in a funeral shroud or cloth. Muslims wash the body in warm water and soap and, finally, with a scented water. Among American Indians, a powdery substance made of corn is used to cover the dead person's face. Among Protestants and Catholics in Europe and the United States, the body is usually washed, embalmed, and dressed in clothes selected by the family. Often, cosmetics are applied to make the person look as if he or she is sleeping. The corpse is placed in a casket and laid out for viewing. In some cultures, the body is cremated; in others, the body is buried. Cremation is typically associated with a belief in the liberation of the spirit. Burial is often tied to beliefs about the afterlife. For example, ancient Egyptians believed that in order for the person's soul to move on to the next life, the body needed to remain intact. As a result, they developed techniques for embalming and mummification to preserve the body as long as possible (Encarta, 2005).

Cultures have different practices concerning how quickly the body is to be disposed of after death. In most Protestant and Catholic families, there is a 1- to 3-day viewing period after death, when family and friends come to the funeral home to see the body and pay respects to family members. This precedes the actual funeral service and burial. In contrast, among Islamic families, the body is prepared by family members when possible, men caring for the body of men and women for the body of women. The burial is expected to take place as soon as possible after the death, preferably within 24 hours (IslamOnline, 2003). Viewing of the dead body after it has been prepared for burial is forbidden. In Japan, Buddhists allow 3 days to pass before the body is burned. On the first day, a priest comes to the home and recites a prayer called a *sutra*. On the second day, the family members burn incense sticks before the family altar. On the third day, the body is burned at a funeral hall, and the ashes are brought back to the house and then taken to the cemetery.

Care of the Spirit

Most cultures believe that there is a spiritual component of a person's being that is not destroyed as the body decomposes or burns. Certain ritual practices are designed to help the spirit make a transition to whatever existence the culture believes takes place after death. According to a Gallup Poll taken in 2007, over 80% of Americans believe in heaven (Newport, 2007). The concept of heaven, whether it is viewed as a beautiful garden or a perfect, golden city, is typically conceptualized as a paradise of safety and abundance where some form of pleasant existence continues after death (Miller, 2010).

The pathway to heaven depends on one's religious and cultural beliefs. For example, in the Roman Catholic religion, the Last Rites, or Viaticum (which in Latin refers to provision for the journey), is a ritual that is carried out at the end of life or in instances of serious illness. The ritual is a celebration of faith; a prayer for God to deliver the person from the illness of body, mind, and spirit; and a process of absolving the person of sins in preparation for life after death in a state of grace. As part of the ritual, the person confesses sins, takes communion, and prays with the priest or Eucharistic minister, reciting a set of familiar prayers and blessing (beliefnet, 2007).

Preparation of the spirit or soul may be achieved by reciting specific prayers or burying the person with possessions that may be useful in the afterlife. Singing, dancing, and

In India, the body of a dead woman is prepared for cremation as family members, friends, and members of the community look on.

© Yadid Levy/Alamy

playing musical instruments are sometimes used to speed the departed spirit on its way to the next life. Hindus believe that at death, the spirit leaves the body and enters a small flame that is lit next to the body. The spirit remains in the home because of attachments to family and possessions. The body is cremated, and there is a period of prayers in the person's home that lasts for 12 days. On the tenth day, the flame with the spirit is taken to the sea. Placing the flame in the sea is a signal to the spirit to leave the attachments of the earthly life and begin the transition to the afterlife.

In New Mexico, the Navajo believe that the dead person will need certain resources in the afterlife. The dead are often buried with an extra set of clothes, food, water, and other items that may be of value in the afterworld. The Navajo believe that everything a person creates has some part of the person's spirit in it. As a result, at death, many of the artifacts a person made, such as pottery or blankets, are cracked or torn in order to release the person's spirit (Santillanes, 1997).

Many societies also observe rituals in the years following the death to nurture and respect the spirit of the ancestor and establish a link between the living and the departed. In Estonia, it is thought that there is a day each year when the dead return to their home for a visit. Rooms are cleaned, and food is laid out for a banquet. This is to preserve and strengthen relationships between the living and the souls of the dead. Many Japanese families visit the cemetery four times each year. They also have small altars in their homes, where they pray to their ancestors. They believe that the ancestors are always with them, guiding their lives and providing protection. In America, many people of different cultures visit the cemetery for periods of reflection, solitude, and discussion with dead relatives. Practices of leaving flowers and wreaths at the gravesite are expressions of respect.

Care of the Surviving Family, Friends, and Community

In addition to addressing the treatment of the body and soul, death rituals are important for helping the people who remain to cope with their grief and reorient their lives in a world without the person who died. These rituals also allow the society to elaborate the meaning of death and decrease the ambiguity surrounding death. Most cultures have funerals for the dead. These funerals involve a gathering of family, friends, and spiritual leaders to carry out the rites for the dead person, provide a social context for expressions of grief, celebrate the life of the person who died, and begin the process of social support for those who remain. Depending on cultural custom, these social gatherings may occur before or after the burial or cremation. Funerals or memorial services provide a transition period surrounding death when people often have difficulty believing that the loved one has really died.

Among Africans who have migrated to the United States in recent years, a complex set of funeral rituals are observed that help mark the status of the deceased and to reaffirm traditional customs of the African community. The wake may last many days, as mourners gather from distant locations. The entire community contributes money to cover the costs of food, burial expenses, and the family's support during the period of mourning. The funeral begins with drumming, singing, and dancing, which continue when the funeral procession moves to the burial site or the airport if the person is returned to Africa to be buried with his or her ancestors. The more important the social position of the deceased, the more elaborate the funeral (Hazell, 1997).

In the Jewish tradition, the period of mourning is prescribed in some detail, taking the bereaved from the days immediately following the funeral through the first year, and annually thereafter. Special focus is given to the practices expected of children on the death of their parents. This may be related to the importance placed on the fifth commandment, to honor one's father and mother. Upon returning to the home after the burial, the family members light a *shiva* (shiva means 7) candle, which represents the everlasting soul of the deceased. They then begin 7 days of mourning. This is a time when family members stay at home and focus their attention on their grief and recollections of the deceased. Friends usually come by to visit, but no business is transacted. It is a solemn time, when luxuries and recreation are set aside. The Kaddish, a prayer that affirms life and faith in God, is recited daily. On the seventh day, the *shiva* candle is extinguished and the family members take a walk outside, symbolically escorting the loved one's soul out of the house and indicating that the family is strong enough to carry on their lives. The period of mourning typically lasts 12 months for those who have lost a parent and is marked by the unveiling of the tombstone or grave marker. After that time, children note the anniversary of their parents' death by lighting a *yahrzeit* (year's time) candle and attending services where the Kaddish is said (Louchheim, 1997).

Other rituals help to address the impact of the death on the larger social system. In the United States, people typically have a will, which is read to the heirs. This ritual provides for the distribution of resources and assets according to the deceased person's wishes. The reading of the will and distribution of the assets helps to realign the social system following a death. Obituaries, which are published in local newspapers, are another custom that notifies the larger community of a death. These statements often acknowledge the person's accomplishments and recognize their family members. This public statement can provide an opportunity for community members to offer support and condolences to the bereaved family members. A recent innovation is the practice of posting a **tribute** to a loved one on a website.

My grandma was the strongest and most beautiful person that I've ever known. She would light up a room when she walked in and had a wonderful warmth to her that made everyone love her. Although she has been gone from us for nearly 7 years—her spirit remains in each one of us. Life has not been the same without her here but we know that she is in a better place and that she looks over all of us. I've heard from many the famous quote of "it will get easier with time" but when you love someone that much it doesn't ever get easier. I think you just come to accept the outcome. Grandma—We miss you and Love you so much!! Not just today but Everyday!!! Love–your family. (Hospice of Michigan, 2007)

There are a variety of other ways that the lives of people are memorialized, including contributions to charities in the name of the dead person, the creation of monuments, naming of buildings or programs, listing of names on a wall or plaque, and the establishment of scholarships, grants, or other types of endowments. In the face of widespread catastrophes, such as the terrorist attacks of September 11, 2001, public memorial services are televised to permit international mourning.

The box on the Amish way of death illustrates how one culture openly incorporates death into every aspect of life. The service and ritual are expressions of the belief in a spiritual immortality and a simultaneous recognition of separation. Families customarily care for their aging parents in their own homes. Dying persons are surrounded by their families, who provide reassurance of generational continuity. The bereaved family members receive help and care from community members for at least the first year after a family death (Greksa & Korbin, 2004). In one study, Amish families found six conditions especially helpful for coping with death (Bryer, 1979, p. 260):

1. The continued presence of the family, both during the course of the illness and at the moment of death
2. Open communication about the process of dying and its impact on the family
3. Maintenance of a normal lifestyle by the family during the course of the illness
4. Commitment to as much independence of the dying person as possible
5. The opportunity to plan and organize one's own death
6. Continued support for the bereaved for at least a year following the funeral, with long-term support given to those who do not remarry

Religiosity leads to lower levels of anxiety and anger for the survivors and may provide them with an analysis of the meaning of the death of their loved one (Carr, 2003). The social support and dignity provided by religious rituals may also help survivors and decrease feelings of loneliness.

Bereavement and Grief

Objective 5. To analyze factors that affect grief and bereavement.

Three terms—bereavement, grief, and mourning—are often associated with the death or loss of a close relationship. Bereavement refers to the loss of a meaningful relationship; grief is the complex set of emotions and thoughts that accompany this loss; and mourning is the social and behavioral expressions of loss, often guided by cultural practices (Fontana & Keene, 2009).

Bereavement

Bereavement is a long-term process of adjustment to the death of a loved one and is more all-encompassing than grief. It commonly includes physical symptoms, role loss, cognitive manifestations, such as seeking meaning in the loss or trying

HUMAN DEVELOPMENT AND DIVERSITY

The Amish Way of Death

THE IMPORTANCE THAT the Amish place on their funeral ceremonies is reflected not only in familiarity with death but also in an intensified awareness of community. As an Amish man reported in a family interview, "The funeral is not for the one who dies, you know; it is for the family."

The Amish community takes care of all aspects of the funeral occasion, with the exception of the embalming procedure, coffin, and horse-drawn wagon. These matters are taken care of by a non-Amish funeral director who provides the type of service that the Amish desire.

The embalmed body is returned to the home within a day of the death. Family members dress the body in white garments in accordance with the biblical injunction found in Revelation 3:5. For a man, this consists of white trousers, a white shirt, and a white vest. For a woman, the usual clothing is a white cape and apron that she wore at both her baptism and marriage. At baptism, a black dress is worn with the white cape and apron; at marriage, a purple or blue dress is worn with the white cape and apron. It is only at her death that an Amish woman wears a white dress with the cape and apron that she put away for the occasion of her death. This is an example of the lifelong preparation for death as sanctioned by Amish society. The wearing of white clothes signifies the high ceremonial emphasis on the death event as the final rite of passage into a new and better life.

Several Amish women stated that making their parents', husbands', or children's funeral garments was a labor of love that represented the last thing they could do for their loved ones. One Amish woman related that each month, her aged grandmother carefully washed, starched, and ironed her own funeral clothing so that it would be in readiness for her death. This act appears to have reinforced for herself and her family her lifelong acceptance of death and

At the time of death, the whole Amish community comes together to support the mourners and say farewell to their friend.

AP Photo/Kentucky New Era, Peter Wright

to have contributed to laying the foundation for effective grief work for herself and her family. This can be seen as an example of the technique of preventive intervention called *anticipatory guidance* (Caplan, 1964), which focuses on helping individuals to cope with impending loss through open discussion and problem solving before the actual death.

After the body is dressed, it is placed in a plain wooden coffin that is made to specifications handed down through the centuries. The coffin is placed in a room that has been emptied of all furnishings, in order to accommodate the several hundred relatives, friends, and neighbors who will begin arriving as soon as the body is prepared for viewing. The coffin is placed in a central position in the house, both for practical considerations of seating and to underscore the importance of the death ceremony.

The funeral service is held in the barn in the warmer months and in the house during the colder seasons. The service is conducted in German and lasts 1½ hours, with the same order of service for every funeral. The guests

view the body when they arrive and again when they leave to take their places in the single-file procession of the carriages to the burial place.

Source: From "The Amish Way of Death: A Study of Family Support Systems," by K.B. Bryer, *American Psychologist, 34*, 255–261. Copyright © 1979 American Psychological Association. Reprinted by permission.

Critical Thinking Questions

1. How does the Amish way of death address the care of the body, spirit, and surviving loved ones?
2. What cultural worldview, values, and beliefs about life after death are reflected in this narrative about death-related rituals among the Amish?
3. What can you find out about the Amish beliefs regarding the afterlife?
4. What is the meaning of the various symbols in this narrative, including the white clothing, plain coffin, funeral taking place in the barn, and procession of horse-drawn carriages?
5. Compare the funeral rituals of the Amish with the rituals described for the Hindus and Navajo Indians. What might be some similarities and differences in beliefs that are reflected in these practices?

to solve problems that arise as a result of loss of the loved one, and a variety of intense emotions, including anger, sorrow, anxiety, and depression. Bereavement may be expressed in very individual ways and may also be guided by cultural practices that shape the behaviors and activities of those in mourning. The bereavement process can include both confronting the loss and seeking ways to move away from or beyond the loss. It can include the expression of pain, sorrow, and loneliness as well as the possibility of self-insight, redefinition, and psychosocial growth. The bereavement process can be viewed as a form of coping, as the person confronts the loss and its secondary stressors (Hansson & Stroebe, 2007).

Bereavement and Coping with Stress

Some authors conceptualize bereavement within a more general framework of coping with stress. In Reuben Hill's (1958) ABCX model of coping with stress, adaptation (X) is determined by the interaction among three factors: the initial stressor (A), the resources and social support a person has to deal with the stressor (B), and the perception or meaning the person makes of the situation (C). The model was expanded into the **double ABCX model** (McCubbin & Patterson, 1983) to reflect the changes in the family system over time as the initial stressor is met and subsequent events bring new stressors, alter the existing resources, and change perceptions of the event (Figure 15.1). As this model suggests, efforts to cope with the initial stressor result in changes in the situation that alter the family's adjustment. Initial coping strategies may reduce or improve the family's resources, perceptions of the original stressor may change with time, and new secondary stressors may arise that impact the family system.

The value of this model for understanding bereavement is its emphasis on individual contexts of the death, the dynamic and changing nature of the stressor and its impact over time, and the key role that meaning making plays in how a person will adapt to the loss of a loved one. For example, a death might be perceived as unfair, sudden, cruel, or too soon by some but perceived as a blessing, or timely, by others. Positive or negative appraisal of the loss may influence

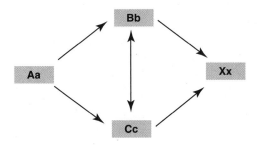

Aa: Build-up of stressor events
Bb: Resources build up to deal with situation
Cc: Family perceptions of this and previous stressor events
Xx: Outcome in terms of family adaptation

FIGURE 15.1 The Double ABCX Model of Coping with Stress

Source: © Cengage Learning.

the emotional state that emerges. If the person gains new insights into the loss and is able to construct positive meaning in the situation, some of the distressing negative emotions may subside and be replaced by positive emotions that could foster subsequent adjustment (Hansson & Stroebe, 2007).

With respect to resources, the loss of a life partner might be followed by the loss of social status, income, and companionship, but, over time, this same loss might result in new financial resources such as life insurance, fewer medical bills, and freedom from caregiving responsibilities. Over time, grief might have an impact on a survivor's health. The depression and confusion that accompany grieving may decrease the survivors' sensitivity to their own physical health and pose risks to their mental health as well. People in deep mourning may have feelings of uselessness or emptiness that prevent them from seeking help for their own physical or emotional health problems. Some people try to cope with their grief by increasing their use of medication, alcohol, or tranquilizers, which may threaten their physical health. Loss of appetite and lack of sleep are other symptoms of grief that contribute to the pattern of increased vulnerability during this time. In contrast, others may find a new sense of purpose and commitment to life as a consequence of bereavement. They may take new steps to improve their own health and to treasure their days, realizing that life is precious. In order to understand the adaptive nature of the bereavement process, one must appreciate that the meaning a surviving loved one gives to the death and the resources that are available to cope with the loss are changing over time.

Grief

Grief refers to the cognitive and emotional reactions that follow the death of a loved one. Grief reactions can vary in duration and intensity and can fade and reappear at unexpected moments. In a study of family members who were responsible for caring for a person suffering from later-life dementia, five aspects of grief were identified: (1) preoccupation with thoughts of the deceased person, (2) longing for the person, (3) painful emotions, (4) feelings of dissociation—feeling disconnected from reality, and (5) sensory illusions that led to the impression that the deceased person was still present. Of these five aspects of grief, preoccupation was the most common and lasted the longest after the person's death (Aneshensel et al., 1995).

Sometimes intense grief reactions are very similar to symptoms of mental illness (Hospice of Michigan, 2007). The following symptoms are not unusual:

Time distortion: Time seems to be frozen, the person is unsure what day it is, time moves unusually slowly or speeds by.
Obsessive rumination: Telling a story or incident over and over; thinking about a situation involving the dead person over and over.

Suicidal thoughts: Thoughts that the person cannot go on living without the deceased person in their lives.
Mystical experiences: Experiences of seeing or hearing the person who died, sensing them with you.
Identification symptoms: Experiences of symptoms that are similar to those of the person who died.
Increased use of drugs and alcohol: Used to buffer experiences of pain from the loss.
Confusion: Difficulty concentrating or making decisions.

There is no timetable for grief. One study followed the grief reactions of family members whose loved one died from cancer (Ringdal, Jordhov, Ringdal, & Kaasa, 2001). The intensity of grief response showed significant declines by the end of the first year after the death. In monitoring the grief response, however, one often finds conflicting evidence of devastation and impressive coping. A widow may be handling daily tasks at a high level of competence and still find herself in tears at seeing her husband's hat in the closet. Over time, one expects to see gradual improvement in the intense, disruptive feelings of grief, but it is hard to say if there is a time when mourning is completed. Perhaps the most important sign is that the person is able to reinvest in new activities and relationships, even while preserving affection for the deceased loved one.

Grief Work

In the face of bereavement, there is a need to work through the reality of the loss as well as the feelings that accompany it. The experience of the bereaved person is not that different from the experience of the person who is coping with his or her own death. Psychiatrist Erich Lindemann (1944) worked with many of the people whose relatives had died in the Coconut Grove fire in Boston. His writings continue to provide a basis for understanding the bereavement process.

Lindemann described the normal grief reaction as involving three phases. First, the person must achieve "emancipation from bondage to the deceased." This bondage may include feelings of guilt about ways in which he or she had criticized or even harmed the person who had died; feelings of regret for things left unsaid or undone. Second, the person must make an adjustment to all the aspects of the environment from which the deceased is missing. The more closely linked the lives of the living and the dead, the more difficult this may be. Third, the person must begin to form new relationships—what we have called redirecting energy to new roles. Lindemann found that one major obstacle to working through this loss is a desire to avoid the accompanying emotions and intense physical distress. According to his analysis, the strategy of avoiding grief only prolongs the survivor's physical, mental, and emotional preoccupation with the dead person.

Questions have been raised about how universally applicable Lindemann's idea of **grief work** really is. In some cultures, intense emotional expressions of grief are considered inappropriate. Under conditions of grave trauma, some counselors suggest that an early period of denial helps the person cope with immediate demands. For some, the loss of a loved one comes after a long period of painful illness. Death may be viewed as a relief from suffering and, as such, brings a form of comfort to those who are still living. Thus, the context of death and its meaning for those who mourn suggests a more individualized view of the adaptive process of bereavement (Hansson & Stroebe, 2007).

Bereavement and Grief Among Older Widows and Widowers

Among people who have lost a spouse, intense depression is more likely to be experienced by those who described their marriage as positive and vital. It is clear that this loss strikes at the core of an older adult's sense of attachment, social integration, and personal worth (Futterman, Gallagher, Thompson, Lovett, & Gilewski, 1990). In a comparison of older widows and widowers with adults who were not experiencing bereavement, the widowed adults showed greater signs of depression, psychopathology, and grief at 2 months after the loss (Thompson, Gallagher-Thompson, Futterman, Gilewski, & Peterson, 1991). At 12 and 30 months after the loss, the two groups were comparable in levels of depression and psychopathology, but the bereaved group continued to experience higher levels of grief than the nonbereaved group. This research, confirmed by other observations, suggests that among older adults, one may not expect a full resolution of the grief work associated with the death of a spouse. Rather, older adults come to accept a certain empty place in their hearts for their deceased partner and learn to find appropriate times to experience their profound sense of loss.

Five Patterns of Bereavement Among Widows

The complexity of bereavement as a coping process is illustrated in a study that followed older couples from before the death of a spouse until 18 months after the death. Five **patterns of bereavement**-related adjustment were identified (Bonanno, Wortman, & Nesse, 2004). These patterns, shown in Figure 15.2, were:

1. *Common grief pattern*. These people had low levels of depression before the spouse died. They experienced an increase in depression 6 months after the loss. After 18 months, they returned to the same low level of depression that characterized them before the loss.
2. *Resilient pattern*. People in this group had low levels of depression before the death of their spouse and continued to have low levels after the death of the spouse.
3. *Chronic grief pattern*. These people had low levels of depression before the loss but showed increased grief responses at both 6 months and 18 months after the loss.
4. *Chronic depression pattern*. These people had high levels of depression before the loss, and depression continued at high levels at both 6 and 18 months.

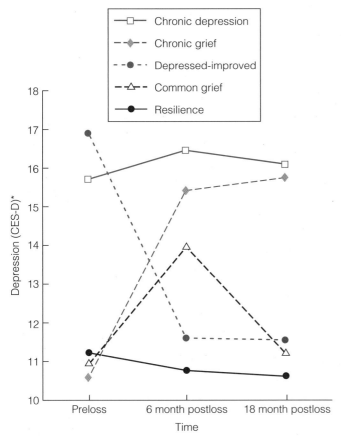

FIGURE 15.2 Five Patterns of Bereavement

*Note: Depression measured by the Center for Epidemiologic Studies of Depression (CES-D). Bonanno, Wortman, & Nesse, 2004, Fig. 1, p. 263. Copyright © 2004 by the American Psychological Association. Reprinted with permission.

5. *Depressed-improved pattern.* These people had elevated levels of depression before the loss, but lower depression scores at 6 and 18 months after the loss.

The results of this research help to clarify the importance of the context of loss as it affects the bereavement process. The context of the loss can include the nature of the relationship between the deceased person and the survivor, the sudden or gradual trajectory of death, the causes of death, the psychological health of the surviving spouse before the death of the partner, and the extent to which a spouse believes that the deceased had led a full life. The depressed-improved group, for example, was composed of people who were in unhappy or unsatisfying marriages; many had a substantial caregiving burden for an ailing spouse. Although people in this group did show evidence of grief responses at 6 months, they also reported benefits of widowhood and pride in the ability to cope with their new status.

In contrast, the chronic grievers comprised people whose lives were suddenly disrupted by the death of a healthy spouse. This group was especially preoccupied with a search for meaning as they tried to make sense of their spouse's death. They had sustained experiences of yearning for their spouse, thinking about their spouse, and talking with others about their spouse at 6 months, with some evidence of improvement in these aspects of grief by 18 months. The results of the study suggest that for some groups, especially the resilient and depressed-improved groups, the relative lack of expression of grief-related symptoms may not be due to denial of their loss, but to evidence of appropriate coping.

Bernice comes each month to visit with her husband at the cemetery. She never remarried and still thinks of herself as Bill's wife. She finds comfort knowing that her husband died bravely in the service of his country.

© Joseph Sohm/Visions of America/CORBIS

Factors That Affect the Distress of Survivors

As illustrated in the study of patterns of bereavement among widows, the bereavement path depends in part on the context of the loss. Grief may be more intense for those who lose a loved one in a sudden death. Under these conditions, there is no opportunity to discuss end-of-life decisions, for final expressions of caring and love, and for the bereaved to begin to anticipate life without the loved one (Howarth, 2007). Bereavement may be difficult if the dying person is unable to receive effective pain control in their last days of life. Survivors who feel that the death of their loved one was brought about by physicians' negligence feel greater distress and anger than survivors who feel that the loved one received high-quality medical care. An aspect of the dying process that is seen as negative for the dying person but is protective for the survivor is nursing home usage. It leads to reduced anxiety for the survivor and may prepare them for the separation that death finalizes, while sparing them from the burden and strain of direct caregiving.

Ambiguous loss is another especially difficult challenge for loved ones. Two types of ambiguous loss have been described (Boss, 1999). In the first instance, the person is missing and may be dead, as in soldiers who are missing in action or people who may have died in a disaster but there are no physical remains. In the second instance, the person is physically present but unable to participate in any meaningful way in family interactions, as when a person is in a coma or in the late stages of Alzheimer's disease. As a result of the destruction of the World Trade Center in New York, some children experienced both types of losses: One parent died in the destruction of the towers but no remains were recovered, and the other parent was so distraught by the spouse's death that he or she became unable to enact the parent role (Boss, 2004). The box on ambiguous loss describes some of the issues surrounding this unique context of bereavement.

Finally, bereavement may be difficult if the survivor has experienced many positive benefits of caregiving, including feelings of being needed, important, and effective, as they addressed the needs of an ailing spouse (Boerner, Schulz, & Horowitz, 2004). Although family caregiving is often viewed as a source of stress, some people find that they gain comfort and even a personal sense of worth through caregiving. In this context, the death of the ailing spouse or parent brings a double loss—loss of the loved one and loss of the meaningful caregiving role.

Unacknowledged and Stigmatized Loss

The bereavement process is influenced by a society's interpretation of who the legitimate mourners are and who has experienced a legitimate death. Some people who grieve may not be recognized as legitimate mourners. These might include former spouses, foster children, partners in a gay relationship, professional caregivers, extramarital lovers, families of addicts and criminals, and people who have had abortions. When communities do not sanction or support their grief, it may be difficult for these people to acknowledge that they have suffered a loss or to experience closure after the death. These **unacknowledged mourners** may be confused about their status and feel guilty or embarrassed by their attachment to the dead person (Murray, 2000).

There are also situations in which a person survives a loved one who had a stigmatized death. **Stigmatized deaths** are those in which people attribute the death to an immoral, illegal, or evil cause. Some survivors may feel conflict in their grief and anger toward the dead person because they believe that person was involved in immoral or unclean behavior. These feelings may lead the griever to secrecy and misrepresentations about the death. Social networks may shun people who are grieving for someone who died a stigmatized death. Negative stereotypes surround these deaths and are often extended to include survivors (Murray, 2000).

Death by suicide is an example of a stigmatized death, in which survivors may feel guilty about not having been able to prevent the death and angry at that person for the suicide. They may experience great conflict because of their love for the person who died and their belief that death by suicide is immoral. Communities look down on death by suicide and may not provide the customary rituals that help support the grieving persons. Many religions consider suicide to be a sin and will not provide religious services or burial rights for the deceased. In a qualitative study of adults who were mourning people who had committed suicide, two persistent themes are trying to make sense of the death and a struggle to manage the social uneasiness in interactions with others. Meaning making was a key factor in the coping process for these survivors, including the meaning of the suicide, the meaning of the relationship between the survivor and the person who committed suicide, and the meaning of the survivor's own life (Begley & Quayle, 2007).

AIDS is another example of a stigmatized loss. In the 1980s, as the AIDS epidemic was taking hold, many survivors found that there was little support for their grief. The devastating effects of AIDS and the associated end-of-life conditions, compounded by fear of contamination, left many survivors isolated and traumatized by their stigmatized loss. In 1985, gay rights activist Cleve Jones discovered that more than 1,000 people had died of AIDS in San Francisco alone. He and other activists conceived of the NAMES Project AIDS Memorial Quilt as a way of honoring and memorializing this loss. The first national display of the AIDS Quilt took place on the National Mall in Washington, D.C., at a lesbian and gay rights march in 1987. At the time, the quilt had 1,920 panels and was seen by more than half a million people. By 1988, the quilt was taken on a 20-city tour and had grown to 6,000 panels. Today, there are 18 NAMES chapters in the United States and 43 affiliates around the world. The quilt has 46,000 panels commemorating over 91,000 people who have died from AIDS (The Names Project Foundation, 2007). As a result of this and other initiatives, the focus shifted from shunning the ill to investing in new medical research for causes and cures. Resources were invested in research about AIDS,

Ambiguous Loss

IN 2005, THE CHIEF Medical Examiner's Office of the City of New York announced that it would stop efforts to identify body parts that were recovered from the destruction of the World Trade Center on September 11, 2001. Of the 2,749 people who were reported missing, 1,161 had not been identified from the remains. Despite the use of a variety of approaches to identification, more than 9,000 body fragments were not identified. These fragments were stored for future analysis, in case new technologies are developed that allow for their identification (Chen, 2005). At some point after the tragedy, the mayor of New York offered presumed-death certificates to families when there was no body that could be identified. Some families accepted those certificates, whereas others continued to wait for DNA testing results. Thousands of families suffered ambiguous loss—some for days not knowing if their loved one was in the buildings, many for months as they waited for the remains to be excavated from Ground Zero, and some are still suffering because there is no physical evidence of their loved one's body.

Pauline Boss (2002b, 2004, 2007) developed an understanding of ambiguous loss through clinical observation, theory, and research. She worked with many families who have experienced this type of loss, including merchant marine families, soldiers' families, families whose loved ones died in the terrorist attacks of September 11, 2001, and families in Kosovo. Much of this discussion is based on her observation and methods.

Ambiguous loss is a problem for the structural and functional characteristics of a family. Families may try to hold a place for the person in daily life. Confusion about whether a loved one is dead or alive may lead some families to ignore parental roles, put off decisions, neglect daily tasks, and isolate living family members. Many families stop carrying out rituals and celebrations, which leads to further disconnection among family members.

Psychologically, the chronic uncertainty and lack of new information produce feelings of hopelessness, passivity, and immobilization. Because they do not have proof of death, family members may become confused—they do not know what to think or how to act. They may become stagnant by denying the loss and continuing to hope. The result is that family members are not grieving, and they are not coping with their loss.

Questions arise such as, "Should you have a funeral if you do not have a body?" Families would get into protracted arguments about this. Some parents did not want to tell their children that their father or mother was dead. Many children got the impression that they were not supposed to talk about the missing parent. People in these families are trying to hold two opposing ideas in their minds: (1) the loved one is still alive, and (2) the loved one is dead. As a result, their grief process is blocked. It takes a very long time to create a family life that includes acceptance and integration of this ambiguity.

In working with the families whose loved ones died on September 11, 2001, Boss cited several techniques that helped people to cope with their loss. First, she created family storytelling meetings, where adults and children were encouraged to tell something they remembered about the missing person. Second, she arranged for groups of families who lived in the same community to meet together and tell stories about their missing family members. These meetings helped foster community connections. People were able to identify others who had the same needs, and they began to find ways to meet those needs. Third, she explained the idea of ambiguous loss and helped people see why it was causing them so much distress. This helped reduce self-blame and family discord. Fourth, she encouraged families to revise family rituals and celebrations but to continue having them, because they are so important to preserving the unity of a family. Fifth, she told them not to become agitated and distressed by pushing for closure. She believes that closure is a myth and that death always produces ambiguity and uncertainty. Being done with grief,

putting an end to mourning, and moving on are unrealistic expectations. People will always feel somewhat sad about the death of someone they love.

Some families were less distressed than others. The characteristics of these families included a belief that the loss of the loved one was predestined and perhaps a product of the will of God; some had a deep faith that God would care for their loved one and guide them; some had prior experience in coping with ambiguous loss; and some were cognitively or temperamentally better able to hold the two opposing ideas in their minds and still retain the ability to function. Boss (2004) reported some comments that were made to her by people who were less distressed: "My son has been missing so long now—he's probably dead, but I feel he's here with me, and always will be" (p. 559). "I must move on and organize life without my son, but at the same time I can hope and remember" (p. 559).

Critical Thinking Questions

1. What are some of the challenges of ambiguous loss that interfere with the bereavement process?

2. Critically evaluate each of the five techniques Boss has developed to help people cope with their loss. What might be helpful about these strategies? Why might these techniques be helpful? Are there aspects of these strategies that might not be helpful? Why not?

3. Which types of people might be most troubled by ambiguous loss? Why? Which types of people would be most likely to benefit from Boss's approach? Why?

4. Can you think of other kinds of interventions that might be helpful in supporting survivors of ambiguous loss?

5. What might be some differences in the challenges of coping with ambiguous loss and stigmatized loss?

6. Design research to investigate the long-term impact of ambiguous loss. What factors would you measure? What would be your indicators of effective bereavement and adjustment outcomes?

Four days after the earthquake hit Haiti, this woman in Port-au-Prince, the capital of Haiti, is completely traumatized by feelings of sudden loss of family, friends, property, and community.

AP Photo/Ariana Cubillos

AIDS education, and the discovery of treatments to slow the course of the illness and prolong life.

In the United States and throughout the world, the death of adult children as a result of AIDS is resulting in the increased involvement of grandparents who are parenting their orphaned grandchildren (Linsk & Mason, 2004; Winston, 2006). In a qualitative study of South Africans who had lost a loved one to AIDS, bereaved adults described their situation as so overwhelming that there was little time for the typical experiences of grief (Demmer, 2007). The struggle for daily survival was intensified as a result of the economic losses associated with the death of an adult member of the household. Older women were burdened with the tasks of caring for the sick and looking after the surviving children. In this context, customary practices associated with mourning and loss were set aside in order to continue to meet the pressing demands of daily life.

Psychosocial Growth Through Bereavement

Bereavement brings new possibilities for psychosocial growth. Just as happiness and joy are innate human emotions, so is sadness. Having these feelings is part of the human experience. Even though they are unpleasant, the emotions associated with grief connect people to their essential human nature. Expressions of grief have a social consequence. An infant's cries have the effect of bringing the caregiver into contact with the infant; the tears of grief communicate to others a person's needs for comfort and reassurance. Without experiences of grief, the moments of treasured happiness would mean less. These experiences help people understand the essence and limits of their existence. They provide a bridge for understanding the grief and unhappiness of others. Grief leads to greater levels of understanding of oneself and others.

The adaptive process of bereavement involves an oscillation between **loss-oriented coping**, which refers to confronting one's pain, sadness, and the loss of a loved one and finding a place for the deceased loved one in one's thoughts and memories in order to achieve emotional health and cognitive functioning, and **restoration-oriented coping**, which refers to finding ways to master the practical challenges of the loss in order to make meaning of the death and move along in one's life (Caserta & Lund, 2007; Hansson & Stroebe, 2007). When a person who is close dies, it stimulates reflection about that relationship. There may be a new appreciation of the qualities of the relationship and its importance. One may consider what the other person did to make the relationship especially valued. The bereaved person may begin to examine his or her own behavior, thinking of ways to bring some of the valued qualities of the relationship with the dead person to ongoing friendships and family ties. People may make resolutions to do a better job of supporting valued relationships by staying in touch, writing more often, or calling home. In the process of experiencing the death of a loved one, a person may become more appreciative of the value of these special, close relationships, realizing that they will not last forever. It is important to give valued relationships appropriate care and nurturance. This may lead to a growth in commitment to one's radius of significant relationships and to maintaining excellent quality in them.

The death of a loved one may stimulate a process of life review, leading one to reflect on the meaning of one's life. This process of taking stock may involve posing some of the

An aerial view of the AIDS Memorial Quilt displayed on the Mall in Washington, DC.

big questions of life: What is the purpose of your life? Are you spending time in ways that are meaningful? Is your work an expression of your real values? Are your relationships satisfying and meaningful? Are you making any contribution to your community and to the well-being of others? This kind of reflection may lead to a reformulation of one's lifestyle or a re-evaluation of certain life experiences.

The death of someone whose presence serves to help define your identity requires a redefinition of your identity. Social roles are typically reciprocal—children have parents, husbands have wives. The death of someone in a reciprocal role leads to the reorganization of that role and its enactment. When a parent dies, children may have to assume some elements of the parental role. These elements are often concerned with greater levels of responsibility and caregiving. When a spouse dies, the remaining spouse has a new identity as a widow or widower. This brings with it new social meaning and, sometimes, a change in social status.

When a person dies, the links to social identity and social network may no longer exist for the person who remains. As a result, the survivors have to redefine themselves and establish new personal identities. For example, when Carl died, his wife Lois was no longer invited to social events that were hosted by Carl's coworkers. Lois no longer maintained her membership at Carl's golf club. She found that it was awkward to introduce herself to new people without being able to say that she was Carl's wife. She recognized that her social status was based on Carl's work and leisure activities. Being Carl's widow did not carry the high level of social status and value that she was used to. Lois had to begin to create a new identity in her community. This work is not easy, but it is very important and necessary.

The death of a loved one may stimulate a revisitation of psychosocial crises. For example, upon the death of a parent, one may reflect on earlier issues of autonomy versus shame and doubt, realizing a new sense of responsibility for one's actions. When parents are alive, even as they get older, an adult child is somehow buffered from the full weight of autonomous self-determination. When parents die, one may reflect on the many ways in which their values and beliefs have guided one's attitudes and behavior.

When a spouse dies, in addition to the need to reconfigure one's identity, issues of intimacy versus isolation may be revisited. A person may reflect on the quality of his or her intimate relationship, thinking about the nature of trust, levels of disclosure, sense of mutual respect, and openness to change. One may reexamine some of the ways in which intimacy was expressed and some of the ways in which isolation was experienced in the relationship. If the opportunity arises for the formation of a new intimate relationship, this revisitation could lead the person to approach that new relationship with different strategies, assumptions, or expectations for self and other.

When a person you admire dies, it often promotes new levels of identification with the deceased. This process sometimes begins with the eulogy, where the community is reminded of the strengths and accomplishments of the person who died. In reflecting on the person's life, a survivor may take on a valued characteristic, such as integrity, fairness, sense of humor, or patience. Survivors may find themselves using expressions or participating in activities that were associated with the person who died. In this way, they expand their repertoire of behaviors, activities, and ego strengths. In addition to identification, the survivor may *introject* the lost person (i.e., take the person's essence inside themselves in thought and feelings). **Introjection** is different from identification, in that the person feels that the lost person is in them. They may carry on meaningful conversations with this person and sense their guiding presence. This is similar to having an imaginary companion. Introjection allows the bereaved person to keep the dead person alive and to preserve their relationship. While still carrying on a mature and sensible existence, the bereaved add a psychological dimension to their abilities by preserving the characteristics of the revered and adored loved one.

In bereavement, thoughts are likely to turn to one's own mortality. The manner of the loved one's demise and the way he or she faced death may help survivors prepare for the possibilities involved in their own death. The dead person's courage may lead the living person to work to develop courage. The creation of a living will by the deceased may be seen as beneficial by the surviving people, who proceed to establish their own living wills. The depth of emotion created by

the death of someone close helps individuals recognize the value of their own lives and the emotions that significant others will experience when they die. In bereavement, a person can find comfort in the faith, confidence, and hopefulness of the person who died, and be inspired to achieve that sense of integrity with regard to his or her own death.

Chapter Summary

The field of human development has come to a new openness about the topics of death and dying. There is an increasing sense that people can make decisions about the quality of their death and that these decisions can and should be discussed with family members as well as with health care professionals. In addition to experiences with death and the anticipation of one's own mortality, dialogues about death are taking place in families to a greater degree than they did in the past.

Objective 1. To understand the role of mortality in shaping psychosocial development.

The psychosocial perspective helps to direct attention to how people determine the meaning of the events of their lives as they interact with the environment over time. Death presents one of the greatest challenges to meaning making. At each stage of life, our understanding of death changes because of the different cognitive and emotional resources we have available and as a result of the salience and proximity to death. The way people conceptualize their own death and the death of others is influenced by the cultural context.

Objective 2. To define the biological state of death.

The definition of the biological state of death has changed as a result of the development of new technologies. In addition to the lack of a heartbeat and the lack of respiration, death is determined by a combination of eight criteria that confirm the end of brain functioning. New legal procedures or advance directives allow people to convey their preferences about end-of-life treatment and to appoint people to make decisions for them if they are incapacitated.

Objective 3. To describe factors associated with the process of dying and the modern ideal of a good death.

The process of dying can follow different trajectories, involve different degrees of suffering, and occur at different ages. Professionals have begun to define characteristics of a good death, and dying patients are having a greater voice in determining the nature of their death. Hospice care and euthanasia are two paths that people may choose when they are experiencing a slow, painful death trajectory. End-of-life decisions are a focus of ongoing ethical controversies and debate.

Objective 4. To describe death-related rituals and their functions.

Death-related rituals are found in all cultures. They tend to focus on three aspects of the meaning of death: (1) care of the body, (2) care of the spirit, and (3) care of the surviving family, friends, and community. These rituals provide a context for acknowledging the death, preparing the spirit for its transition, and legitimizing the grief of the bereaved survivors.

Objective 5. To analyze factors that affect grief and bereavement.

Bereavement is the long-term process of adjustment to the death of a loved one. Grief is the cognitive and emotional reaction to loss. The concept of grief work refers to the emotional expression, cognitive reorganization, and social adjustments that take place as a result of the death of a loved one. There are many patterns of bereavement, depending on the context of the death, relationship of the survivor to the dead person, religious orientation of the survivor, and finality or ambiguity surrounding the death. Communities play a role in supporting the bereavement process by the way they respect or stigmatize the death and the way they memorialize and honor the dead.

Key Terms

Further Reflection

1. How does the inevitability of death affect your own approach to life?
2. What is the meaning of a good death? How is this concept influenced by U.S. culture?
3. What are the functions of funerals?
4. What are the most important issues facing the survivors?
5. How does the community influence the process of bereavement?
6. What are likely outcomes for a person who denies a loved one's death and does not engage in grief work? As a professional, how would you help such a person?

Psychology CourseMate

To access additional course materials, including CourseMate, please visit www.cengagebrain.com. At the CengageBrain.com home page, search for the ISBN of your title (from the back cover of your book) using the search box at the top of the page. This will take you to the product page where these resources can be found.

Casebook

For additional case material related to this chapter, see the case "Till Death Do Us Part" in *Life Span Development: A Case Book*, by Barbara and Philip Newman, Laura Landry-Meyer, and Brenda J. Lohman, pp. 195–199. This case focuses on the role of a sudden illness in opening up communication about end-of-life issues for an older couple.

The Research Process

In this appendix, we highlight basic principles of the scientific process, including the positivist and qualitative approaches to inquiry, from which much of our knowledge about development is derived. Scholars depend on this process to guide inquiry, a process that imposes constraints of logic, methodology, and ethics in hopes of building a sound, unbiased understanding of patterns and processes of development. We review basic topics in research design including sampling, research methods, and designs for studying development. Finally we consider ethical guidelines for conducting research with human participants.

In approaching the challenges of conducting and interpreting research about development, remember that studies that summarize the responses or behaviors of groups of people will not necessarily account for the experiences of specific individuals. Similarly, the experiences of individuals will not necessarily be generalizable to larger groups. The study of life-span development is a quest for patterns of continuity and change over time and across historical eras. However, it is important to appreciate that some patterns that might characterize the experiences of one cohort may not apply across historical periods.

The Scientific Process

The **scientific process** allows us to create a body of knowledge that contains procedures for ensuring that the information will be correct. Two major positions have been taken on how to approach the discovery of knowledge: *positivism* and *qualitative inquiry*, which is sometimes referred to as *postpositivism* or phenomenology (Bordens & Abbott, 2011).

Positivism approaches the study of human behavior by seeking causal relationships among factors, with the goal of trying to predict outcomes. Often, this approach applies statistical analyses to data gathered from many participants in order to test specific hypotheses. In the positivist approach, the research hypotheses guide decisions about the nature and size of the sample, the site(s) where data are collected, the methods of data collection, and the statistical procedures used to analyze the data.

Qualitative inquiry approaches the study of human behavior by trying to understand the meanings, motives, and beliefs that underlie a person's experiences. This approach emphasizes the individual's point of view and the subjective understandings that help account for a person's actions. Often this approach begins with examination of a *personal experience*, such as a parent's experience of caring for a child who has a developmental disability; a *process*, such as staff-parent communication in a neonatal unit; or a *unique phenomenon*, such as a near-death experience. Approaches to data collection may change as the study evolves, depending on the nature of the participants, the ideas that emerge, and the researcher's reactions and **interpretation**s. Both positivism and qualitative inquiry strive to contribute to a new level of understanding of human behavior.

The Positivist Approach to Research

In this section, we describe the positivist research approach (see Figure A.1). The research process usually begins with a puzzling idea or observation. The fact that the observation is puzzling means there is something to be figured out. The research process assumes there is something to be explained or clarified that is currently not explained, or that certain observations lead to the possibility that current explanations are inadequate or incorrect. The observer tries to figure out how to explain the observation and thinks about what leads to what—which events or conditions cause other events or conditions. In this process of searching for explanations, one develops a set of interrelated ideas to account for the observation. These ideas—often referred to as assumptions, hypotheses, or predictions—constitute a **theory**. The theory is not an end in itself, but a way to begin.

Scientific Observation

The next step of the scientific process is to test the theory through **systematic observation**. A good theory contains specific predictions about cause and effect. After the predictions are stated, one must figure out how to test whether they are accurate. One must **operationalize** the concepts of a theory in order to test them. That is, one must translate an abstract concept into something that can be observed and measured.

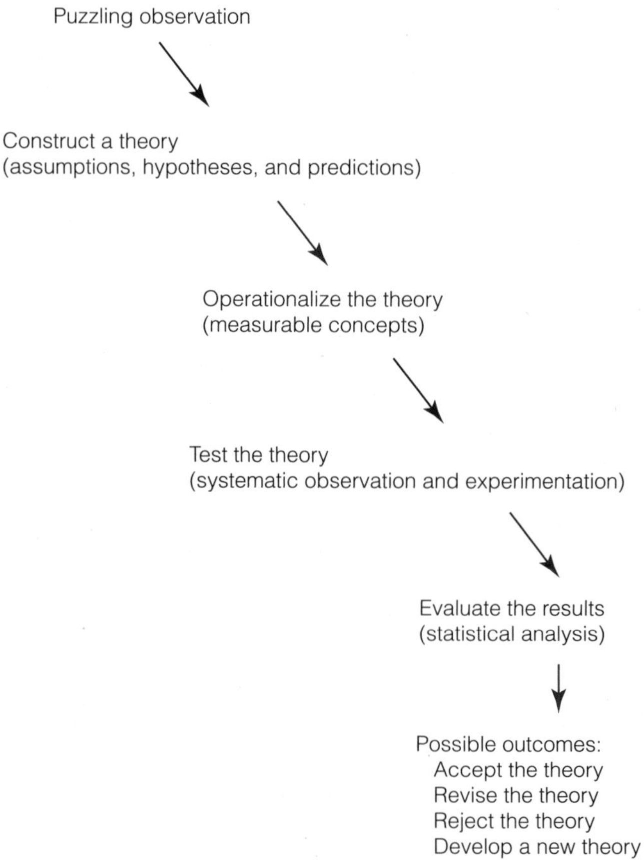

Puzzling observation

Construct a theory
(assumptions, hypotheses, and predictions)

Operationalize the theory
(measurable concepts)

Test the theory
(systematic observation and experimentation)

Evaluate the results
(statistical analysis)

Possible outcomes:
Accept the theory
Revise the theory
Reject the theory
Develop a new theory

FIGURE A.1 The Scientific Process

Scientific observation is characterized by three essential qualities: It must be *objective, repeatable, and systematic* (Creswell, 1994). **Objective observations** accurately reflect the events that are taking place. They are not unduly influenced by what the observer expects or hopes to see. Suppose, for example, that you want an objective assessment of your child's talent for playing the guitar. You are unlikely to get objective feedback from friends or relatives. Because they know you and presumably would not like to insult you, they may be inclined to slant their answers to please you.

A more objective approach might be to include an audiotape of your child's guitar playing with tapes of 10 other children. You would then ask another person to play the tapes for 10 people who do not know you or your child and ask each of them to rate the quality of musical ability demonstrated on each tape. You may or may not like the outcome, but at least your method would be more objective. It would reveal what other people think of your child's musical ability without being biased by any feelings about you or your child.

Social science research is always vulnerable to the theoretical biases and value orientations of the researchers. Certain practices of research design, sampling, and methodology are used to help overcome biases and build a higher level of objectivity into the process. However, many will argue that it is impossible to be entirely objective. One's orientation toward framing research questions and interpreting the results are always influenced by cultural and historical contexts that shape the values, beliefs, and assumptions that guide the research process. That is why it is so important that the research be carried out by more than one investigator and that the procedures are explained in enough detail to be repeatable.

If research is **repeatable**, then others could carry out a similar investigation and compare the results with those of the original investigator. In order for this to occur, the original investigator must carefully explain all the procedures used in the study, describe all the essential characteristics of the participants (e.g., age, sex, social class), and describe the setting or situation where the observations were made. Because there are many ways that one group of participants might differ from another and many different ways that observations can be made, repeatability is an important part of building a body of social science knowledge.

Usually, a problem or process is investigated by an individual or research team, taking great care to make sure that observations are unbiased, orderly, carefully collected and recorded, and comprehensive. In order to ensure that the results of a study are accurate, the original researchers encourage other investigators to repeat the study to see if the same results are observed.

A **systematic approach** ensures that research is done in a careful, orderly way. Researchers have a framework of essential questions that they strive to answer based on what is already known and what certain theories predict. They approach research by having clear objectives, carefully defining the purpose of the research, and the specific methods they will use to reach those objectives. Although some discoveries are made by accident, scientific research typically does not poke here and there at unrelated events.

Often the theory is not tested by the same person who develops it, because this person may have some personal investment in demonstrating that the theory is correct. The scientific process usually involves the ideas of more than one person. Sometimes, people with different points of view engage in debate, trying to refute positions they find flawed. At other times, two or more people work on different phases of theory building, experimentation, and **evaluation**.

If a theory is fruitful, many researchers working in independent groups will devise ways of testing and clarifying it. Working in this way, as a community of scholars, helps to ensure that a theory will not be confirmed simply because of the theorist's personal biases. For example, Erik Erikson was not the person who tested his own psychosocial theory. Many other researchers have devised strategies for operationalizing Erikson's concepts, thereby expanding our understanding of concepts such as hope, identity, intimacy, generativity, and wisdom—to name a few—and clarifying the relationship of development in childhood and adolescence to adulthood and later life.

The final phase of the scientific process involves an evaluation of the observations. **Statistical techniques** help determine the likelihood that observations could have happened by chance. Observations that appear to be a result of chance do not confirm the theory. If the observations have a low probability of having occurred by chance, one says that they are statistically significant. If statistically significant results support the theory's predictions, one is likely to accept them as providing evidence for the theory. Nevertheless, scientists may continue to examine the propositions of the theory, involving new participants or new methods.

What if the results do not fit the theory's predictions? One approach is to re-examine the methods and design of the study. Perhaps the key concepts were not measured appropriately or the sample was biased in some way. When results of research are inconclusive or contrary to the predictions, scholars may try another research approach before revising the theory. But when several different studies fail to support the hypotheses, we tend to lose confidence in the entire structure of the theory. We may revise or discard the theory and begin to develop an alternative explanation for the observations.

In summary, in the positivist approach, the scientific process consists of creating a theory, testing it through research, and modifying, rejecting, or accepting it. If confirmed through the research process, a theory helps us interpret many observations about reality.

The Qualitative Inquiry Approach to Research

Whereas the positivist perspective assumes that there is a truth that can be captured through the research process, the qualitative inquiry approach assumes that there are many versions of truth, depending on the informant and the context. Knowledge is not out there to be discovered; rather, it is invented, constructed, and continuously revised as one accumulates new information (Schwandt, 1998; Silverman, 2010). The approach begins with a beginner's mind. One looks at the world as if it were ripe for discovery. Theory typically emerges from the data, rather than guiding the methodology and data collection. When evidence is gathered that contradicts the theory, the theory is rejected or modified. Multiple methods are employed in order to learn as much as possible about the setting, the participants, and the contexts of behavior. In some instances, the observer's own experiences and beliefs are included as a guide to the meaningfulness of the observation. In other instances, the observer attempts to challenge a personal point of view by gathering as many different perspectives about the process as possible. Because qualitative inquiry assumes that there is not one truth, all perspectives and insights are considered equally valid. A major emphasis is on interpretation, made possible by the close acquaintance of the researcher with the details and voices of the participants.

In the study of human development, both positivist and qualitative inquiry are applied, often as complementary approaches to the same issue. The idea is that generalizations and categories used in the positivist approach can be reframed or refined using data from qualitative inquiry. Assumptions from the positivist perspective may be challenged by observations made through qualitative inquiry. For example, many children who live in households that may be characterized as female-headed, single-parent families actually have fathers, uncles, and grandfathers who participate actively in their daily lives, and many children who live in households that may be characterized as two-parent families actually have little daily contact with their fathers. Categories and definitions that are assumed to be meaningful from a positivist perspective are often shown to be more ambiguous or diversely defined when considered through the qualitative lens.

Research Design

Regardless of whether the positivist or qualitative approach is used, each empirical study needs to be designed. Research investigations are designed just as cars, bridges, and buildings are designed. **Research design** is often conducted in meetings where small groups of scholars try to think up the most appropriate approach for answering their questions. Scientists know that the information they gain from conducting research will be influenced by the characteristics of the participants who are involved in their study, the kind of data that are gathered, and the conditions under which the data are gathered. The principles of research design focus on the approach to selecting a sample, the methods used to gather information, the design for studying change, and the techniques used to analyze the data (Gliner & Morgan, 2000).

Sampling

Sampling is the method for choosing participants who will be included in the study. The nature of the questions that are being addressed usually has implications for the best way to identify the sample. If the study is about some universal principle of development, it should apply to individuals from a wide variety of family and social backgrounds. For example, studies of normal language development should include children from various ethnic, racial, social class, and cultural backgrounds. One cannot argue for universal principles if the research has shown the processes or patterns to be true only for a homogeneous group of children.

Every *sample* is taken from a population. The **population** is the large group to which the findings of the research are intended to apply. There is no single, predetermined population; the relevant population depends on the purpose and scope of the research. The sample is a smaller subgroup of the larger population that will participate in the study. For example, the population of interest might be adolescents in the United States who graduate from high school but do not go on to college. Roughly 975,000 adolescents who graduated from high school in the spring of 2007 were not enrolled in any postsecondary school in the fall of 2007 (U.S. Census Bureau, 2010). No research study is likely to include all of those adolescents. So a sample is drawn that is expected to be representative of the population. Under ideal conditions, the participants in any study of this population ought to have the same general characteristics (e.g., family income; race; gender; urban, suburban, or rural environment; and high school academic background) as the population from which the sample was selected. The sample and the population from which the sample is taken determine the **generalizability** of the research findings—the extent to which we can say with confidence that the observations made for this sample would apply to other groups. We must be careful not to assume that research findings based on one sample are generalizable for all ages, both sexes, all racial and ethnic groups, all social classes, or individuals from other cultures.

Five approaches to sampling, described in more detail in the following sections, are common in the research literature: *random samples, stratified samples, matched groups, volunteer samples, and qualitative sampling.* Each one has different implications for the generalizability of the findings (Henry, 1998).

Random Samples

In a **random sample**, each person in a given population has an equal chance of being included. The researcher may ensure equal opportunity by putting each person's name on a slip of paper and then choosing some of the slips blindly, or by selecting names from a list at random, using numbers produced by a random number generator. The Kaiser Family Foundation study of media use by infants, toddlers, and preschoolers discussed in Chapter 7 is an example of a study that used a random sampling of households (Rideout,

Vandewater, & Wartella, 2003). The study was a random, national telephone survey of families with children ages 6 months to 6 years old. The parent who spent the most time with the child was asked to complete the survey.

Stratified Samples

In a **stratified** sampling approach, participants are deliberately selected from a variety of levels (*strata*) or subgroups within the population. For example, one study used a stratified, random sample to examine the care received from family members by African American and European American adults ages 65 and older who lived in their own homes. The sample groups were selected in proportion to their numbers in the community. Within the African American and European American groups, participants were selected at random (Peek, Coward, & Peek, 2000).

Matched Groups

The researcher can also select two or more groups of participants who are similar on many dimensions. In most studies using **matched groups**, participants in one group receive some type of treatment or participate in some type of experimental intervention that the participants in the other group do not receive or participate in. In other studies, the impact of a naturally occurring difference is examined. For example, a matched group design was used to study the impact of low birth weight on later middle school performance. At age 11, children who had weighed less than 750 grams (1.65 pounds) at birth were compared to children who had weighed 750 to 1400 grams (1.65 to 3.08 pounds) and to children of normal birth weight. The groups were matched on age, sex, and other background variables. The design allowed researchers to evaluate the long-term risks for very small babies (Taylor, Klein, Minich, & Hack, 2000).

Volunteer Samples

Participants can be solicited by asking people directly, placing advertisements in newspapers or on bulletin boards, sending letters to teachers or parents asking for participants, or writing to professionals or groups of potential participants. Those who are included in the study are selected from among those who **volunteer**. Most studies that are conducted with students enrolled in introductory psychology courses involve volunteer samples. Although the students may be required to participate in research, they have a choice about which study they will volunteer for. In some sense, all research with human participants uses a volunteer sample. One cannot compel a person to participate in research.

The Qualitative Approach to Sampling

The primary objective of the qualitative approach to sampling is to learn as much as possible from each informant. Researchers enter a setting with some general idea of questions

they seek to understand. The strategy is to remain open to the information that is provided. Researchers may learn that they cannot get information about the question they started out with. For example, in a study of institutional wards for people with severe and profound retardation, Taylor (1987) wanted to know about residents' perspectives. However, many residents were nonverbal, and others were reticent to share their opinions. So Taylor shifted his attention to staff perspectives on the environment. Qualitative researchers emphasize that the **informants** should have the knowledge and experience that the researcher requires, be able to reflect and verbalize about the experiences, and be willing to participate in the study (Morse, 1998). The number of informants or settings in which research occurs is not decided in advance. Typically, the greater the depth and detail in each case, the fewer cases will be included. Additional cases are added as needed until the researcher believes that the variety of perspectives within a setting has been captured and the theoretical insights are well confirmed (Taylor & Bogdan, 1998).

Strengths and Weaknesses of Approaches to Sampling

What are some of the strengths and weaknesses of different approaches to sampling? Random sampling and stratified sampling are the most likely to ensure that a sample is *representative* of the population from which it is drawn. If each person in the population has an equal chance of being included in a study, then the outcome or results of the study ought to be equally likely to apply to those in the population who did not participate as to those who did. These sampling approaches are often used to provide statistical information about a population. They do not provide information about any specific person within the population. For example, the mean or arithmetic average income of a group of 100 people may not be the exact income of any single person in the group.

The use of matched samples allows one to examine the impact of naturally occurring events—such as unemployment, parental divorce, or low birth weight—that cannot be randomly assigned. By matching participants on a variety of background factors, such as IQ, family income, or birth order, one might be able to detect the impact of these events on emotional, social, or cognitive development. However, critics argue that one cannot match groups perfectly, and one might omit an important variable for which there is no match. For example, in the study described earlier about the impact of low birth weight on school achievement, sibling order was not included in the match. Because we know that firstborns typically do better on tests of academic achievement than siblings born later, this factor might explain more about the outcome than birth weight.

The method that places the greatest limits on generalization is volunteer sampling. One never knows what type of person will volunteer to participate in social science research. Can you think of how reliance on volunteers may produce special problems? For example, imagine a study that promises to pay $25 to those who participate. People who volunteer to participate in this research may be especially in need of money. Sometimes, volunteers have more free time, are hoping to find some kind of help as a result of participating in the research, or have greater faith in science than those who choose not to volunteer.

Regardless of these difficulties, volunteer samples are widely used. Most of the studies cited in this textbook are based on volunteer samples. All studies involving observation, interview, or experimentation with children require formal consent from parents and could be classified as volunteer samples. Frequently, the only way to study a certain question is to ask for volunteers.

Some of the research findings discussed in this text are based on **clinical samples**. This usually means that the participants have been involved in some type of treatment program or are on a waiting list to receive clinical treatment. These studies are especially important for understanding the causes of clinical conditions, the developmental paths or patterns that these conditions exhibit, or the impact of certain interventions on these conditions. Without voluntary participation, there would be no way to begin to document the effectiveness of treatment. At the same time, one must be cautious not to generalize findings from clinical studies to the population as a whole.

It will come as no surprise that the vast majority of studies reported in American journals are based on American samples. The U.S. population comprises only 5% of the world population. Thus, studies that presume to characterize normal development are limited to the extent that the results have not been repeated or confirmed across countries and cultures (Arnett, 2008). As international communication improves and the use of the Internet supports international collaboration, we are hopeful that cross-national research will increase.

Similarly, many studies of development during the period that we refer to as later adolescence are carried out with college students. Since roughly one third of later adolescents do not attend college, the results of these studies cannot be accurately generalized to the non-college population.

From a qualitative perspective, the best informants are those who willingly volunteer to share their experiences and reflect on them. If the informant is providing an authentic, open narrative, then insights can be drawn. Each informant's perspective is treated as one way of making meaning of the situation. The researcher's job is to try to build a complex picture of the topic by comparing the views of multiple informants.

Research Methods

A variety of methods have been used to study development. Each one has its strengths and weaknesses, allowing the investigator to focus on one set of behaviors at the expense of others. The choice of method must fit the problem under study. Six general categories of developmental research are described here: *observation, case study, interviews, surveys, tests,* and *experimentation*. These methods have all contributed to the discovery of knowledge, and as you read further,

you will find examples of each method. Some techniques—especially observation, case study, and interviews—are more commonly used in qualitative inquiry as investigators try to uncover basic themes or dimensions of a problem. Other methods—especially observation using a predetermined coding scheme, experimentation, structured interviews, surveys, and tests—tend to be used in the positivist approach to the research process.

Observation

One might argue that at the heart of all science is observation—taking note of events and trying to make sense of them (Adler & Adler, 1998). Direct **observation** of children in their home and school environments is one of the oldest methods for studying development (Kessen, 1965). Researchers have used mothers' diaries and observation logs to gather information about behavior in intimate settings that could not be known in any other way. Jean Piaget was guided by the observations of his own children in the formulation of his theory of cognition. Today, some researchers conduct observations in homes, schools, and day care centers where children typically spend their time. Others bring children and their families or friends into homelike laboratory settings, where they can watch children's behaviors under more constant and controlled physical conditions (Kochanska, Murray, & Harlan, 2000).

Naturalistic Observation. Naturalistic observation refers to research in which behavior in a setting is carefully observed without any other kinds of manipulation. This type of observation, sometimes referred to as **ethnography**, provides insight about how things occur in the real world (Fetterman, 2010). In some instances, researchers go into a setting to observe the full range of interactions and behavior patterns. Based on their field notes, they begin to develop hypotheses or tentative explanations about the meaning of the behaviors. Then, they may test these hypotheses through more focused observation or through controlled experimentation. In other instances, researchers use observation to examine a specific behavior or relationship. They may be looking for different forms of peer aggression, patterns of social cooperation, or conditions that promote cross-gender interactions. In these cases, the observers limit the scope of their observations to behaviors that are relevant to their concerns.

Participant Observation. A major methodological approach in qualitative inquiry is **participant observation**, in which the researcher actively engages in interactions with other members of a setting. This is done in order to gain a new understanding of how people in that setting experience the world or how the processes that take place in that setting might apply to broader issues such as socialization, control, or self-construction. To engage in this type of work, one must first obtain access to the setting and then gain the trust of the other people in the setting. Some participant observation takes place in public settings, such as parks, street corners, pool halls, or train stations, where the researcher can be accepted as a non-threatening participant. Even in these situations, it may take time for people to interact with the observer or be willing to confide in him or her. In Elliot Liebow's (1967, 2003) famous study of Black street-corner men, *Tally's Corner*, Liebow met his primary informant, Tally, while playing with a puppy outside a carryout restaurant. The friendship he formed with Tally led to introductions to other men on the street.

The participant observer usually gathers data through field notes, which are made after an observational session. Over time, the skilled observer learns to retain information about the details of a session and to record it in a systematic way. This is a very demanding process; it may take several hours to summarize what was observed in a single hour in the field. In addition to the observations, the researcher tries to capture his or her own reactions to the situation, using personal feelings and responses as a way of empathizing with the participants. In a study of a mental institution, Taylor made the following field notes:

> O.C. [observer's comments]: Although I don't show it, I tense up when the residents approach me when they're covered with food or excrement. Maybe this is what the attendants feel and why they often treat the residents as lepers. (Taylor & Bogdan, 1998, p. 73)

One of the challenges in participant observation is to check out and confirm one's insights from observation by comparing them with information drawn from other sources. This is especially important the more involved one becomes in the setting and the more attached one grows to the participants. This confirmatory approach is called *triangulation*, and it can be achieved by looking at written documents about the setting, interviewing other informants, and sharing observations with other members of a research team. This is often done toward the end of the study, as the researcher is preparing to leave the field (Taylor & Bogdan, 1998).

Correlation. Observational studies lend themselves to an examination of correlation rather than causation. **Correlation** refers to a statistical analysis of the strength and direction of the relationships among variables. It reflects the degree to which knowing the value of one variable, such as popularity, allows one to predict the level of another variable, such as aggressiveness.

The correlation coefficient is a numeric index of the strength of relationship between variables that can range from a value of +1.0 to −1.0. Let us take as an example the correlation between popularity with peers and aggressiveness. If, as popularity increases, so does aggressiveness, the correlation is *positive* (between 0 and +1.0). If, as popularity increases, aggressiveness decreases, the correlation is *negative* (between 0 and −1.0). If there is no systematic relationship between aggressiveness and popularity, the correlation is close to 0 (see Figure A.2). A correlation of .40 suggests that there is a positive relationship between aggressiveness and popularity, but that aggressiveness cannot be predicted entirely or even predominantly by knowing about a person's popularity.

A strong correlation between two variables shows only that there is an association between them. It does not provide information about causation. Knowing that aggression is negatively correlated with popularity does not necessarily mean that being aggressive causes children to be rejected by peers. It could be that some other factor, such as mistrust of others, accounts for both aggression and peer rejection.

Strengths and Limitations of the Observational Method. Many scholars agree that direct observation is an ideal way to study behavior (Bakeman, 2000). It avoids the interpretive issues that are raised when one asks people to report on their behavior, and it allows for the documentation of patterns of behavior that may not have been anticipated by the investigator. For example, in studying patterns of dominance among children, one might assume that hitting is a form of dominance. However, in observing play behavior, one may find that certain kinds of hitting are a type of affectionate interaction rather than a mechanism for achieving dominance. Another strength of observation is the ability to allow participants' behaviors to guide the researcher's conceptualization. Rather than setting up a specific task or group of questions and having people respond, the observer examines the full range of relevant behaviors and builds an interpretation of the meaning of the events from the patterns that have been observed.

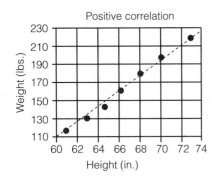
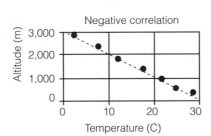
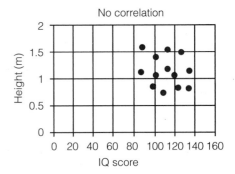

FIGURE A.2 Patterns Reflecting Positive, Negative, and Zero Correlations

Observational research also has weaknesses. It is often difficult to establish agreement among observers about exactly what occurred. Think about the times that you and a friend have been in the same situation but have entirely different reactions to what is happening or describe it very differently to a third party. Typically, two or more observers' codings of the same situation are compared to determine whether different observers interpreted the same event in the same way. This is called **interobserver reliability**. When interobserver reliability is high, one has confidence that all the observers are describing or coding the events in the same way. When interobserver reliability is low, the researchers must determine why and then correct the differences in observation techniques. This may result in changing the category scheme so that it is easier to link each behavior with a category, or it may result in more training, so that the observers know more precisely how to code each behavior.

Another difficulty with the observational method occurs when so much activity is taking place that it is difficult to select specific behaviors or to code fast enough to keep up with the pace of activity in the setting. The technology of video recording has helped address this problem. A video record can be reviewed over and over again. Several observers can watch a video, stop it, and discuss what they saw. The same events can be observed from several points of view. Video records allow one to track the sequences of interaction, turn taking, and the formation of cycles of interaction among family members, which often occur too subtly or quickly to be captured by direct observation (Johnson, Cowan, & Cowan, 1999; Heath, 2010).

Some research focuses on a particular kind of behavior or behavioral sequence, such as helping behavior, peer rejection, or conflict. In naturalistic observation, one cannot be assured that the behavior of interest will take place during the observational period. Finally, some researchers fear that the presence of the observer or the introduction of audio recording or videotaping equipment, or even note taking, may change the nature of the behaviors that take place in the setting. Although there are techniques to limit the impact of the observer on the setting, this is always a concern in direct observation.

Case Study

A **case study** is an in-depth description of a single person, family, social group, or social setting. The purpose of a case study may be to illuminate something very particular and interesting about the person or organization being studied, illustrate a general principle by providing specific details, examine a phenomenon that does not conform to theoretical predictions, or stimulate theory development in an area that has not been investigated (Yin, 2009).

Some case studies document the lives of great individuals. In *Gandhi's Truth*, Erikson (1969) provided a psychosocial analysis of the life of Mahatma Gandhi. Erikson considered Gandhi's childhood, adolescence, and young adulthood as they contributed to his personality, his moral philosophy, and to the contradictions between his personal relationships and his role as a powerful social leader.

Case studies can also focus on social groups, families, and organizations. One of Anna Freud's most famous cases described the attachments that developed among a group of orphans who had lived together in a concentration camp during World War II (Freud & Dann, 1951). The study focused on the strong feelings the children had for one another and their strategies for maintaining their sense of connectedness once they were placed in a more normal social environment. The case illustrated a unique phenomenon—the intense emotional attachment of young children to each other—that had not been documented before.

Case studies can be based on a variety of sources of information, including interviews, therapy sessions, prolonged observation, diaries or journals, letters, historical documents, and talks with people who know the subject of the study. The researcher usually spends a great deal of time with the subject of the case, in conversation, observation, and gathering information from documents and informants in order to fully understand what is happening. In addition to gathering information, the researcher engages in ongoing reflection in order to reach a new depth of insight about the case.

Strengths and Limitations of the Case Study Method. Case studies have the advantage of illustrating the complexity and uniqueness of the subject. They capture the interplay of complex, dynamic processes. Studies carried out with large samples often identify general principles, whereas case studies provide concrete examples of how these principles play out in the lives of specific individuals or groups. Some cases give the details of an experience that is rare and might not be captured in a large-scale study. Sometimes, the case study brings a problem to the attention of researchers, who then pursue it through other methods. Although case studies cannot provide the basis for broad generalizations, they can provide specific examples of instances where a broad generalization does not hold true. Throughout this book, you will find case study material that is intended to help you apply concepts from the text to specific examples and to serve as points of reflection about the relevance of human development content for understanding individuals' life stories.

Case studies have been criticized as unscientific. In the first place, they are obviously not representative of large groups of individuals. One must be cautious about generalizing the conclusions drawn from a case study to other individuals or groups. Moreover, if the information that provides the basis of the case study is gathered in a biased or subjective way, then the results or conclusions of the study will be of little worth. Of course, this criticism applies to any type of research. Finally, critics argue that there is no reliability in case studies. If different people were writing a case study on the same individual, they might come up with very different views of the events and their significance.

These limitations suggest that one must have a very clear idea of the study's purpose and a systematic approach to gathering information in order to conduct case studies that meet the standards of scientific observation. At the same time, vividly written, compelling case material has had a consistent impact in stimulating theory and research in the field of development. In some instances, the lucid recounting of case material is more convincing to policymakers than the results of studies based on large, national samples.

Interviews

Many case studies are based largely on face-to-face interviews. The **interview** method can also be used to gather data from large numbers of individuals and from people in clinical settings. Interviews can be highly structured, almost like a verbal survey, or very open ended, allowing the participant to respond freely to a series of general questions. There are at least three common uses of in-depth interviewing (Roulston, 2010). First, the life history or personal narrative allows the researcher to learn about a person's key life experiences and the meaning of those experiences. The researcher's role is to encourage the person being interviewed to cover all the important issues and to foster elaboration and reflection.

Second, through interviews, informants are asked to describe in detail events that occurred when the researcher was not present. This might be a historical event, a natural disaster, or the behaviors of a group to which the researcher does not have access. For example, a researcher may want to interview informants who have been members of a gang about the gang's initiation rites or practices. Third, interviews can be useful in gathering information from a number of people about a similar topic. For example, Harrington and Boardman (2000) interviewed 100 people they called pathmakers—people who achieved career success despite growing up in impoverished families and communities.

The success of the interview method depends heavily on the skill of the interviewer. Interviewers are trained to be nonjudgmental as they listen to a participant's responses. They try to create **rapport** with the participant by conveying a feeling of trustworthiness and acceptance. The goal, especially in qualitative interviewing, is to create a conversational atmosphere where the person feels at ease to talk. In unstructured interviews, the interviewer must make use of this rapport to encourage the participant to say more about a topic and to share thoughts that may be private or personal. Matching the race and gender of the interviewer and the participant being interviewed has been found to help foster rapport and improve the quality of the data that are produced.

The interview method has traditionally been associated with clinical research; however, it is becoming a common method in the study of cognition and language as well. Piaget's structured interview technique (Piaget, 1929) provides a model for the investigation of conceptual development. The researcher who uses this technique asks a child a question (e.g., "Are clouds living or dead?"), and then follows up on the child's answer with questions about how the child arrived at his or her conclusion. In other studies,

Piaget asked children to solve a problem, and then asked them to explain how they arrived at the solution. The child becomes an informant about his or her own conceptual capacities. This approach has been adapted in the study of moral development, interpersonal development, and positive, helping behavior.

Strengths and Limitations of the Interview Method. The interview method has the advantage of allowing individuals to contribute their own views on the topic being studied. They can tell the interviewer what is important to them, why they might choose one alternative over another, or what they think is wrong with the investigator's view of the situation. Interviews have the advantage of expediency when it might be difficult to gain access to a setting for observation or when one wants to gather information from a larger number of participants, rather than observing just a few.

There are also limitations to the interview method. Participants may present themselves in the way they want the interviewer to see them; when they do, they are said to be exhibiting a **self-presentation bias**. Research has suggested that young children's responses are especially vulnerable to influence by the interviewer. By smiling, nodding, frowning, or looking away, the interviewer can deliberately or inadvertently communicate approval or disapproval. There is a fine line between establishing rapport and influencing responses.

Another limitation of interviews is that people may not be aware of all the factors that influence their behaviors or decisions. Thus, in asking people about their lives and why they behave as they do, one is limited to the person's level of sensitivity and insight into their own situation. Whereas one might see certain forces at work through participant observation, relying solely on interviews limits the researchers' access to contextual factors that may influence a person's behavior (Taylor & Bogdan, 1998).

Surveys and Tests

Survey research is a means of collecting specific information from a large number of participants (Fowler, 2009). If people are to respond directly to surveys, they must be able to read and write, unless the survey questions are read to them. The survey method is, therefore, most commonly used with participants in middle childhood, adolescence, and adulthood. However, survey information about infants and toddlers is often collected from parents, child care workers, physicians, nurses, and others who are responsible for meeting the needs of young children. Thus, surveys have contributed a great deal to our knowledge about the way adults perceive the behaviors and needs of young children.

Survey methods can be used to collect information about attitudes ("Do you believe teachers should be permitted to use corporal punishment with their students?"), current behaviors and practices ("How many hours per day do you watch television?"), aspirations ("What do you hope to do when you graduate from high school?"), and perceptions

("How well does your mother/father or son/daughter understand your views?").

Survey questions are prepared in a standard form, and the responses are usually coded according to a prearranged set of categories. In well-designed surveys, the questions are stated clearly and offer response choices that are not ambiguous or overlapping. In the most powerful surveys, the sample of respondents is carefully selected to be representative of the population under study. Surveys may be conducted by telephone, through the mail, on the Internet, in classrooms, at work, or in the participants' homes (Fowler, 1993).

Tests are often similar in form to surveys. They consist of groups of questions or problems that the person is expected to answer. Usually, tests are designed to measure a specific ability or characteristic. You are no doubt familiar with the kinds of tests typically given in school. You are presented with a group of items and asked to produce the correct answer or select the correct answer from among several choices. Intelligence and achievement tests are of this nature. A researcher might give these tests along with some other measures in order to learn how intelligence relates to social life, emotions, or self-understanding.

Other tests are designed to measure specific psychological constructs such as creativity, conformity, depression, or extroversion. Some tests are administered to assess whether a person has some form of mental illness, learning disorder, or developmental or physical disability.

Psychological tests must be reliable and valid to be useful. Tests are **reliable** when the results are consistent. A person who takes a reliable test on 2 consecutive days should get approximately the same score on both days, unless some deliberate training or intervention has been introduced between test sessions. There ought to be a positive correlation (between 0 and +1.0) between the two scores.

Tests are **valid** when they measure what they claim to measure. The people who design the tests have to define what it is they are trying to measure. They also have to provide evidence that their test really measures this construct (Ray, 1993). For example, when designing a test to measure self-esteem, one should first consider, "What is meant by self-esteem?" and "What type of questions or tasks would provide evidence of self-esteem?" Consider the various tests that have been designed to measure intelligence in infants and very young children. The results of these tests are not very closely related to the results of tests of intelligence given in adolescence and adulthood (Slater, Carrick, Bell, & Roberts, 1999). In other words, correlations between intelligence tests given to infants and those given to the same individuals when they are older tend to be low (nearer to 0.0 than to +1.0 or −1.0). Why is this? One explanation is that the infant tests are not really tests of broad, adaptive intelligence, but measures of sensory processing and central nervous system coordination. As children get older, their symbolic capacities and acquired knowledge expand. As a result, they rely less on sensory processing and more on interpretation and experience to guide meaning making and problem solving.

Strengths and Limitations of Surveys and Tests.
Surveys and tests have certain advantages that make them widely used in developmental research. They allow the comparison of responses by large groups of respondents. Surveys and tests have been designed to address a wide variety of topics. With a prearranged coding or scoring system, many tests can be administered and evaluated without the extensive training that is usually necessary with participant observation or interview methods.

This method also has limitations. Some surveys create attitudes where none existed before. This is referred to as the **reactive** nature of surveys. For example, you might ask sixth-grade children questions about their satisfaction with their school curriculum. The students may answer a lot of questions on this topic, even though they had not given much thought to the issue before. Thus, reading the questions and response options on a survey may help participants formulate their opinions (Wilson, LaFleur, & Anderson, 1996).

Another problem is the gap between answers to survey questions or scores on tests and actual behavior. Parents may respond to a survey by indicating that they allow their children to participate in family decisions, but when it comes to real family decisions, they may not give their children much voice. Some survey questions are more difficult for some respondents to answer accurately than others. For example, consider the following question: How often did you go for medical treatment over the past 6 months? It would be easier for a person who went only once to respond accurately and with confidence than for a person who went six or eight times (Mathiowetz, 1999).

Experimentation

Experimentation is a method best suited for examining causal relationships. In an **experiment**, some variable or group of variables is systematically manipulated to examine the effect on an outcome. For example, in research on memory among older adults, the complexity of the material and the speed of presentation are varied in order to learn more about how these factors influence the ability of adults to recall information. The factor (or factors) manipulated by the experimenter is called the **independent variable**. The dimension of the participant's responses or reactions that is measured is the **dependent variable**. The research is carried out to determine whether the independent variable or some combination of independent variables can produce a change in the dependent variable.

In some experiments, one group of participants has a certain set of experiences or receives information (usually referred to as a **treatment**) that is not provided to another group. The group that experiences the experimenter's manipulation is called the **experimental group**. The group that does not experience the treatment or manipulation is called the **control group**. Differences in behavior between the two groups are then attributed to the treatment. For example, in a study of academic performance in human development courses, students enrolled in a course would be randomly assigned to the experimental group, in which they are linked as a study group through email, so they can contact one another, discuss questions from the course, and share their ideas. The other students, who are in the control group, do not receive this Internet support. Differences in course grades between the experimental and the control groups would be attributed to the Internet intervention.

In other experiments, the behavior of a single group of participants is compared before and after a treatment or across several treatments. Once again, systematic differences in behavior before and after the treatment are attributed to the experimental manipulation. In this case, each participant serves as his or her own control.

Control is the key to successful experimentation. The experimenter must exercise control in selecting the children or families who participate in a study. The participants must be able to bring equivalent competencies to the situation. If this condition is not met, one cannot assume that differences in behavior between groups are due to the treatment.

Experimenters control the way a task is presented to the participants so that such factors as the ability to understand the instructions, the order of events, and the degree of comfort and familiarity with the setting do not interfere with the participants' behavior. Control ensures that changes in behavior do, in fact, result from the experimental manipulation.

Many studies in human development are **quasi-experimental**. This means that the treatment was not controlled by the experimenter but was the result of some pattern of life events (Wilson, 1995). Suppose we are interested in the impact of unemployment on conflict between married couples. We cannot (nor do we want to) cause some adults to lose their jobs while others remain employed. We can, however, compare couples of about the same age and social class who have experienced unemployment with couples who have not. In these studies, assignment to a treatment occurs as a result of real-world events. One would select participants for the study who are as much alike as possible in other respects, except for their encounters with unemployment. It is the task of the researcher to compare some of the consequences of this treatment—the experience of unemployment—and to address the limitations that are imposed on the results because of how individuals come to be in one group or the other.

Strengths and Limitations of the Experimental Method. The experimental method has the advantage of providing conclusions about causal relationships. If the results suggest that the participants' behavior changes only when something about the experimental situation changes, we can conclude that the manipulation has caused the changes in behavior. This is a very powerful statement, particularly as we search for explanations for how conditions that occur early in development might influence later outcomes.

Experiments also have limitations. Despite careful control, one cannot entirely rule out factors that can interfere with the impact of the treatment or that influence the respondents

in ways that were not anticipated (Ray, 1993). For example, in a study of the impact of exposure to television violence, participants may have seen a televised documentary about the topic on the day before they came to participate in the research. In a study involving repeated observations, the participants might talk with each other about the study between testing sessions, thus influencing their responses. Any factor occurring outside the specific design of the study that influences the participants' responses is a threat to the **internal validity** or meaningfulness of the experiment.

Experiments may also be challenged on the basis of their **external validity**. We cannot be certain how applicable a controlled laboratory situation is to the real world. Would the behaviors that are observed in the laboratory also be observed at home, at school, or at work? For example, through studies of infant attachment (discussed in Chapter 5) we have learned that infants and young children do not behave the same way in the presence of their mothers as they do when their mothers are absent. Thus, experimental research conducted with children that does not allow their mothers to be present may produce behaviors that differ in quantity, quality, and sequence from the behavior that would be observed under conditions when the mothers are present.

Experimental studies suggest that event A causes response B. In many domains of development, however, a multifaceted, reciprocal process promotes change. Think a moment about the development of *friendship*. A friendship depends on so many domains and on the fit or lack of fit along each domain for the two people. Friendships may be influenced by physical appearance, abilities, temperaments, intelligence, family background, whether others support the friendship or ridicule it, and so on. Friendships are sustained and promoted by continuous feedback and interaction among the friends rather than by one or two factors that could be said to promote or inhibit friendship. Experiments tend to suggest a unidirectional, causal explanation for behaviors that may be more accurately described using an interactional model.

Advantages and disadvantages of the five research methods are summarized in Table A.1.

Designs for Studying Development

The primary concern of developmental research is to describe and account for patterns of continuity and change over time. We want to describe patterns of change and differences in these patterns across individuals, and to account for why groups of individuals who have been exposed to similar life situations differ from one another as they age. This is a very challenging task, which requires strategies for considering changing individuals in changing environments (Miller, 2007). Four major research approaches have been created for examining development: *retrospective studies, cross-sectional studies, longitudinal studies, and cohort sequential studies.*

TABLE A.1 Advantages and Disadvantages of the Methods of Developmental Research

METHOD	DEFINITION	ADVANTAGES	DISADVANTAGES
Observation	Systematic recording of behavior	Documents the variety of ongoing behavior, captures what happens naturally, without intervention	Time consuming: difficult to achieve inter-rater agreement; requires careful training; observer may interfere with what would normally occur; difficult to capture and code full range of ongoing activity
Case Study	In-depth description of a single person, family, or group	Focuses on complexity and unique experiences of individual; permits analysis of unusual cases	Lacks generalizability; conclusions may reflect bias of investigator; hard to replicate
Interviews	Face-to-face interaction in which each person can give a full account of his or her views	Provides complex, first-person account; flexible method; allows access to the other person's own meaning	Vulnerable to investigator bias; self-presentation bias; relies on participant's self-insight
Surveys and Tests	Standard questions administered to many participants	Permits data collection from large samples; permits group comparisons of responses in standard form; requires little training; flexible	Wording and way of presenting questions may influence responses; responses may not be closely related to behavior; tests may not be valid for certain groups
Experimentation	Analysis of cause-effects relations; manipulation of some conditions while others are held constant	Permits testing of causal hypotheses; permits isolation and control of specific variables; allows evaluation of treatment effects	Laboratory findings may lack ecological validity; unable to control for all threats to internal validity; focuses on a unidirectional model of causality

Retrospective Studies

A researcher engaged in a **retrospective** study asks the participants to report on experiences from an earlier time in their lives. Many early studies of childrearing used parents' recollections of their parenting techniques to evaluate their patterns of child care. Researchers who studied the effects of stress during pregnancy often asked women to recall their emotional state before, during, and after their child was born. Investigators of personality development use retrospective data by asking adolescent or adult subjects to recall important events of their childhood.

This approach produces a record of what a person has retained of past events. We cannot be certain that these events really occurred as they are remembered or, for that matter, whether they occurred at all. Piaget (1951) described a vivid memory from his second year of life:

> I was sitting in my pram, which my nurse was pushing in the Champs Elysées, when a man tried to kidnap me. I was held in by the strap fastened around me while my nurse bravely tried to stand between me and the thief. She received various scratches, and I can still see vaguely those on her face. (p. 188)

Thirteen years later, when Piaget was 15, the nurse joined a religious order. She wrote to his parents and returned a watch they had given her for protecting Jean from the kidnapper. She confessed that she had made up the story, even to the point of scratching her own face. Piaget believed he had created the visual memory from the story his parents had told him about the incident.

The passage of time may change the significance of certain past events in a person's memory. As we gain new levels of cognitive complexity or change our attitudes, we reorganize our memories of the past so as to bring them into line with our current level of understanding (Kotre, 1995b). Sometimes, people claim to have recovered memories of past events that have been long forgotten or repressed. It is difficult to determine the accuracy of these memories (Loftus, 1993). They may be entangled with current experiences or with ideas taken from books, movies, or conversations with others. They may be altered by the suggestion that something happened that actually did not, or by the suggestion that something did not happen that actually did. Because memory is so easily modified by suggestion, its usefulness in uncovering systematic data about the past is limited. However, retrospective data provide insight into how people make sense of their past and the role they give to past experiences in determining their present way of thinking. Studies that use the technique of life review provide insight into the way adults organize and structure key periods and events from their life history (McAdams et al., 1997).

Cross-Sectional Studies

Studies that compare people of different ages, social backgrounds, or from different school or community settings are called **cross-sectional studies**. Such studies are quite common in research on child development. Investigators may compare children at different levels of biological maturity or different chronological ages to learn how a particular developmental domain changes with age. Most studies of cognitive development discussed in Chapter 8, especially those that consider the shift from one type of reasoning to another, use the cross-sectional approach. They present children of different ages with the same kind of problem and then note differences in their approach to explaining and solving the problem. The main limitation of the cross-sectional method is that it measures group differences, not patterns of individual change over time. Often, however, these group differences are interpreted to suggest a pattern of development. With respect to studies on cognitive problem solving, the cross-sectional approach tells us that most 12-year-olds are more flexible in their reasoning than most 7-year-olds. It does not tell us how the same children actually change from the time they are 7 until they are 12, nor how the children who were most flexible at age 7 would perform at age 12 in comparison with those who were the least flexible.

Longitudinal Studies

A **longitudinal study** involves repeated observations of the same participants at different times. The time between observations may be brief, as from immediately after birth to 2 or 3 days after birth. Observations may be repeated over the entire life course, as in Leo Terman's longitudinal study of gifted children (Terman & Oden, 1947, 1959; Sears & Barbee, 1978; Holahan, Sears, & Cronbach, 1995).

Longitudinal studies have the advantage of tracking the course of development of a particular group of individuals. We can discover how certain characteristics of children in infancy or toddlerhood relate to those same characteristics when the individuals reach adolescence or adulthood. We can also learn whether certain qualities of childhood, such as intelligence or outgoingness, are related to overall social adjustment or life satisfaction in later years. Longitudinal studies permit us to trace intra-individual patterns over time—that is, how individuals change, for example, from the use of one-word expressions to two-word phrases. They also allow us to monitor changes in groups, for example, by comparing adults who have children in their early twenties to those who remain childfree and looking at their economic or occupational attainment by midlife (Schaie, 1994).

Longitudinal studies may be difficult to complete, especially if they are intended to cover a significant time period, such as the years from childhood to adulthood. Over this span of time, participants may drop out of the study, the investigators may lose funding or interest in the project, or the methods may become outdated. Questions that once seemed important may no longer be seen as vital. Another limitation is that repeated interactions with the participants may influence their behaviors. In other words, participation in the study could itself become a factor in their development. One of the greatest limitations of longitudinal studies is that they focus on only one generation or cohort of participants. Imagine studying the academic achievement and occupational attainment of a group of children born in 1980. Historical and social factors that may influence the course

of this group's development will be inextricably intertwined in the observations. One cannot tell if people growing up at other times in history would exhibit the pattern of changes that characterize this particular group.

Cohort Sequential Studies

A **cohort sequential design** combines the cross-sectional and longitudinal approaches into one method of study (Schaie, 1965, 1992). Groups of participants, called *cohorts*, are selected because they are a certain number of years apart in age. For example, we might begin with three groups of adolescents who are 11, 14, and 17, respectively. Every 3 years, these groups would be interviewed until the 11-year-olds have turned 17. Every 3 years, a new group of 11-year-olds would be added to the study. This combination of a longitudinal and cross-sectional design is a powerful developmental research method. It produces immediate cross-sectional data, longitudinal data after 3 and 6 years, and a comparison of children who were the same age (11, 14, or 17) at three different times. This third comparison permits us to identify social and historical factors that may influence age-related differences. This comparison also allows us to control for the possible impact of repeated measurement on the participants. Chapter 13 includes the results of a cohort sequential study of adult intellectual ability.

Comparisons of cohorts over long periods of time provide a way of controlling for the many historical factors—such as access to schooling, health, medical treatment, and nutrition—that might influence intellectual performance, separating these factors from age-related changes. The elements of a cohort sequential design are shown in Figure A.3. One drawback to the cohort sequential design is that data analysis requires more complex techniques in which time of response and frequency of response can both be included.

Evaluating Existing Research

In addition to collecting new data, social scientists devote considerable scholarly effort to reviewing and evaluating existing research. As a student, you may be asked to review research findings on a topic of interest to you. You will probably rely on online databases, such as InfoTrac College Edition, EBSCOHOST, PsychInfo, or the Social Science Citation Index, to find books, book chapters, and journal articles relevant to your topic. These sources provide information from published sources, most of which have undergone a **peer review** process. This means that other professionals have read and critically evaluated the materials before they were published. You may also find information using Internet search engines like Google or Bing. Internet resources are of a much more varied nature, including Web pages from professionals, reports of research institutes and centers, government documents, and ideas from teachers, students, and others who have opinions on the topic. The challenge

Age cohort comparisons

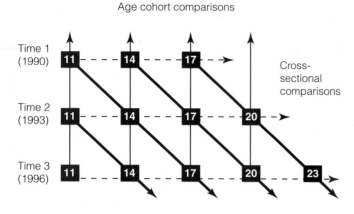

Cross-sectional comparisons

Longitudinal comparisons

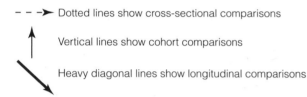

- - -▶ Dotted lines show cross-sectional comparisons

↑ Vertical lines show cohort comparisons

↘ Heavy diagonal lines show longitudinal comparisons

FIGURE A.3 The Cohort Sequential Design

in reviewing all this information is to apply a standard for judging its quality and validity as you formulate your own analysis of the topic.

Most researchers use this method of reading and reviewing the research of others to keep well informed about the research in their subject area. They analyze the work of others to generate new questions and to formulate well-founded conclusions about issues in their field of specialization. The study, analysis, and evaluation of current research literature constitute special skills in their own right (Fink, 2010).

Increasingly, websites provide information for researchers and report results of research. Because of the open access nature of the Web, there is no guarantee about the quality or validity of information. Using information from the Web requires a degree of care and caution over and above that used in the review of peer-reviewed journals. In reading about research from a website, one would ask many of the same questions about the research process that one would ask of a peer-reviewed journal article. In addition, the following issues need to be considered when evaluating Web-based information: the authority and **credibility** of the authors of the Web-based information; the scope, relevance, and timeliness of the information; and the potential **bias** of the author's point of view.

Authority and Credibility:

- Who publishes the website?
- Who is the author(s) of the website?
- What makes the author an authority on this subject?
- Does the author cite his/her experience/credentials?
- Does the website contain footnotes or references?

- If so, does material taken from other sources appear to be fully credited?

Scope, Relevance, and Timeliness:

- Who is the intended audience? (general, specialized, scholars)
- What is the level of the material? (basic, advanced)
- Is new research being reported or is the author reviewing/summarizing previously conducted research?
- What time period is covered?
- How recently has the website been updated?

Bias and Accuracy:

- How is the information presented? (fact, opinion, propaganda, etc.)
- If presented as fact, is it accurate?
- Is there a bias? (cultural, political, religious, etc.)
- If so, is the bias clearly stated or acknowledged by the authors?

One strategy in making use of Web-based information is to look for several sources on the same topic.

There are some wonderful resources of online information. All branches of the federal government have websites with information about policies, programs, and research reports. The U.S. Census publishes the Statistical Abstracts online as well as frequent reports on specific topics. Medical information is available from the National Institutes of Health as well as from ongoing medical research projects that provide results of their research online. Advocacy groups, such as the National Center for Children in Poverty, provide up-to-date information about the impact of policies or programs. With all this information available, the research process is at once more open, more accessible, and more vulnerable to viral mischief.

Ethics

In conducting research with living beings, and especially with children, social scientists continually confront ethical questions. **Ethics** refers to principles of conduct that are founded on a society's moral code. As part of their professional socialization, researchers are obligated to maintain humane, morally acceptable treatment of all living study participants (Sales & Folkman, 2000).

The ethical guidelines for research with humans encompass a variety of considerations. Because we are concerned about the right to **privacy**, the identities of individual participants and their responses must be kept **confidential**. Individuals must not be coerced into participating in a research project, and their refusal to participate should have no negative consequences. If children in a classroom, for example, decide that they do not want to participate in a research project, or if their parents do not give permission for them to participate, they should not be shamed, given an undesirable alternate assignment, or given a lower grade.

Researchers must protect participants from unnecessary painful physical and emotional experiences, including shame, failure, and social rejection. Researchers must weigh the benefits of the new information they may discover in a particular study against the potential risks or harm to the participants. Two questions must guide the researcher's decisions:

1. How would you feel if you or one of your family members were a participant in this study?
2. Can the problem be studied in ways that do not involve pain, deception, or emotional or physical stress?

The American Psychological Association has published a guide for researchers titled *Ethics in Research with Human Participants* (Sales & Folkman, 2000). This guide provides advice to researchers about how to manage all aspects of the research process in order to avoid any **conflict of interests** and to maintain the trust and safety of participants. Participants have a right to know how their privacy will be preserved and what steps will be taken to ensure that responses or behaviors observed in the research will remain confidential. The guidelines require that participants be told about all aspects of the research that may influence their decision to participate. They must be free to withdraw from the study at any time. They

are entitled to a full explanation of the study once it has been completed. When the participants are children, their parents must be given this information and must approve their children's participation.

Each university has an **institutional review** process that applies these or similar guidelines for the ethical conduct of research to proposals being prepared by faculty and students. Before a study can begin, the institutional review board considers the design of the study and its potential impact on participants. The investigators have to commit to a procedure of **informed consent**, so that participants are aware of the nature of the research, potential risks, conditions of confidentiality, and their freedom to withdraw from the study at any time if they choose. Approval for the research is typically given for 1 year. The institutional review process includes a mechanism for ongoing evaluation of research that takes place over longer periods of time. Most schools, day care centers, hospitals, nursing homes, and other treatment centers have their own review procedures for determining whether they will permit research to be carried out with the people in their programs. Ethical guidelines are important in order to prevent exploitation of participants and to prevent unintended negative consequences of participation in research.

Key Terms

Glossary

abortion   Termination of a pregnancy before the fetus is capable of surviving outside the uterus.

accommodation   (1) In Piaget's theory of cognitive development, the process of changing existing schemes in order to account for novel elements in the object or the event. (2) In vision, changes in the curvature of the lens in response to the distance of the stimulus.

active engagement   Continuing to be sociable and involved in doing things as you get older.

active euthanasia   Activities—such as mercy killing or physician-assisted suicide—that are designed to end a person's life, often to end a person's suffering.

activities of daily living (ADLs)   Basic types of self-care that are required to function independently.

adaptation   (1) In evolutionary theory, the total process of change in response to environmental conditions. (2) In Piaget's theory of cognitive development, a process of gradually modifying existing schemes and operations in order to take into account changes or discrepancies between what is known and what is being experienced.

adaptive self-organization   The process by which an open system retains its essential identity when confronted with new and constant environmental conditions. It creates new substructures, revises the relationships among components, and establishes new, higher levels of organization that coordinate existing substructures.

adaptive self-regulation   Adjustments made by an operating system in which feedback mechanisms identify and respond to environmental changes in order to

maintain and enhance the functioning of the system.

advance directive   A document that allows people to say what type of care they want to receive in case they cannot speak for themselves.

advocate   A person who pleads another's cause.

affect   Emotion, feeling, or mood.

affiliative values   The values placed on helping or pleasing others, reflected in the amount of time spent in and the degree of satisfaction achieved from such actions.

age-graded expectations   Views held within societies about what would be appropriate behavior at a given time in life.

ageism   A devaluation of older adults by the social community.

agency   Viewing the self as the originator of action.

aggressive-rejected   A path to peer rejection in which children are aggressive and attribute hostile intentions to others.

aggressive-withdrawn   A path to peer rejection in which children are both aggressive and self-conscious.

alienation   Withdrawal or separation of people or their affections from an object or position of former attachment.

allele   The alternate state of a gene at a given locus.

Alzheimer's disease   The most common form of chronic organic brain syndrome, involving gradual brain failure over a period of 7 to 10 years.

ambiguous loss   A condition in which death is uncertain because there is no verification of death, as when a soldier is missing in action and there is no body, or when a person is physically present but unable to participate in any meaningful way in interactions with others.

amniocentesis   The surgical insertion of a hollow needle through the abdominal wall and into the uterus of a pregnant woman to obtain fluid for the determination of sex or chromosomal abnormality of the fetus.

amniotic sac   A thin membrane forming a closed sac around the embryo and containing a fluid in which the embryo is immersed.

androgens   General term for male sex hormones, the most prevalent of which is testosterone.

androgyny   The capacity to express both masculine and feminine characteristics as the situation demands.

anomaly   Irregularity, something that is inconsistent with the normal condition; abnormality.

anorexia nervosa   An emotional disorder in which the person loses the ability to regulate eating behavior; the person is obsessed with a fear of being overweight and avoids food or becomes nauseated after eating.

anxious-avoidant attachment   Infants avoid contact with their mothers after separation or ignore their efforts to interact. They show less distress at being alone than other babies.

anxious-resistant attachment   Infants are very cautious in the presence of a stranger. Their exploratory behavior is noticeably disrupted by the caregiver's departure. When the caregiver returns, the infants appear to want to be close to the caregiver, but they are also angry, so they are very hard to soothe or comfort.

Apgar scoring method   Assessment method of the newborn based on heart rate, respiration, muscle tone, response to stimulation, and skin color.

applied behavioral analysis   An intervention that uses systematic operant-conditioning strategies to assist people who have severe behavior problems, including aggressive disorders and autism.

appraisal In coping, an estimate of the nature, quality, and importance of the stressors in a situation.

artificial insemination Injection of donor sperm into a woman's vagina to promote conception.

assimilation In Piaget's theory of cognitive development, the process of incorporating objects or events into existing schemes.

assisted living Housing or living arrangements for the elderly, infirm, or disabled, in which house-keeping, meals, medical care, and other assistance is available to residents as needed.

assisted reproductive technology (ART) Includes all fertility treatments in which both eggs and sperm are handled. In general, ART procedures involve surgically removing eggs from a woman's ovaries, combining them with sperm in the laboratory, and returning them to the woman's body or donating them to another woman.

assumption A fact, statement, or premise that is considered true and that guides the underlying logic of a theory.

attachment The tendency to remain close to a familiar individual who is ready and willing to give care, comfort, and aid in time of need.

attachment behavior system A complex set of reflexes and signaling behaviors that inspire caregiving and protective responses in adults; these responses shape a baby's expectations and help create an image of the parent in the child's mind.

attachment scheme A set of internal mental representations that an infant has of the anticipated responses of a caregiver.

auditory acuity The ability to recognize sounds of varying pitch and loudness.

authority relations All the hier-archical relationships that give one person decision-making authority and supervisory control over another.

autonomous morality A relatively mature moral perspective, in which rules are viewed as a product of cooperative agreements.

autonomy The ability to behave independently, to do things on one's own.

autosomal Being or pertaining to a chromosome other than a sex chromosome.

avoidance conditioning A kind of learning in which specific stimuli are identified as painful or unpleasant and are therefore avoided.

babbling The vocal sounds of infants after about the sixth week that are initially characterized by sounds used in many languages and then begin to reflect the sounds and intonation infants are most likely to hear in their caregivers' speech.

behavioral slowing Age-related delay in the speed of response to stimuli.

bereavement The long-term process of adjustment to the death of a loved one that is more all encompassing than grief and is commonly accompanied by physical symptoms, role loss, and a variety of intense emotions, including anger, sorrow, anxiety, and depression.

bilingualism The ability to speak two languages fluently.

binge drinking Quickly consuming five or more drinks in a row.

biological system Includes all those processes necessary for the physical functioning of the organism. Sensory capacities, motor responses, and the workings of the respiratory, endocrine, and circulatory systems are all biological processes.

birth culture A culture's beliefs, values, and guidelines for behavior regarding pregnancy and childbirth.

boundaries In family systems theory, what determines who is considered to be a family member and who is an outsider. They influence the way information, support, and validation of the family unit are sought and the way new members are admitted into the family.

bulimia A habitual disturbance in eating behavior, mostly affecting young women of normal weight, which is characterized by frequent episodes of grossly excessive food intake followed by self-induced vomiting to prevent weight gain.

cardiopulmonary death A set of criteria for death that includes lack of a heartbeat and lack of respiration.

care The commitment to be concerned.

career maturity The stage at which a person has developed decision-making strategies and the self-insight that permit a realistic career choice.

caregiving The nurturing responses of the caregiver that form a corresponding behavioral system we often refer to as parenting.

categorical identifications Self-understanding that relies on the categories one fits into, such as physical characteristics and religion.

categorization The process of arranging, classifying, or describing by labeling or naming.

causality The relation between a cause and an effect.

cell differentiation A process whereby cells take on specialized structures related to their function.

cell nucleus The part of the cell that contains the genetic material essential to reproduction and protein synthesis.

central process The dominant context or mechanism through which the psychosocial crisis is resolved.

cervix The narrow lower end of the uterus, which forms the beginning of the birth canal.

choice phase In Tiedeman's career decision model, the phase when the person decides which action alternative to follow. The decision is solidified in the person's mind as he or she elaborates the reasons why the decision is beneficial. There is a sense of relief and optimism as the person develops a commitment to executing the decision.

chromosome One of the rodlike bodies in a cell nucleus that contains genetic material and that divides when the cell divides. In humans, there are 23 pairs of chromosomes.

chronically depressed Experiencing depression over a long period of time.

chronosystem In Bronfenbrenner's theory, this is the temporal dimension: Individuals, the systems in which they are embedded, and resources all may change over time.

clarification phase In Tiedeman's career decision model, the phase when the person more fully understands the consequences of his or her commitment to the decision that has been made. He or she plans definite steps to take and may actually take them or may delay them until a more appropriate time. The self-image is prepared to be modified by the decision.

classical conditioning A form of learning in which a formerly neutral stimulus is repeatedly presented together with a stimulus that evokes a specific reflexive response. After repeated pairings, the neutral stimulus elicits a response similar to the reflexive response.

classification The action of grouping objects according to some specific characteristics they have in common, including all objects that show the characteristic and none that do not.

climacteric The period of menopause for women and a parallel period of reduced reproductive competence for men.

clinical samples Populations who are or have been treated for a problem, or who are waiting to be treated.

clique A small friendship group of 5 to 10 people.

codominance A condition in which both alleles of a specific gene contribute to the characteristic that is expressed, as in AB blood type.

coercive escalation A style of interaction in which the probability that a negative remark will be followed by another negative remark increases as the chain of communication gets longer and longer.

cognition The capacity for knowing, organizing perceptions, and problem solving.

cognitive competencies A person's knowledge, skills, and abilities.

cognitive functioning A very broad term that encompasses the range of cognitive abilities.

cognitive map An internal mental representation of the environment.

cognitive unconscious The range of mental structures and processes that operate outside awareness but play a significant role in conscious thought and action.

cohort In research design, a group of individuals who are studied during the same time period. In life course analysis, a group of people who are roughly the same age during a particular historical period.

cohort sequential study A research design that combines cross-sectional and longitudinal methods. Cohorts consist of participants in a certain age group. Different cohorts are studied at different times. New cohorts of younger groups are added in successive data collections to replace those who have grown older. This design allows the analysis of age differences, changes over time, and the effects of social and historical factors.

collective efficacy A strong sense of social cohesion with a high level of informal social control in a community.

collectivism Worldview in which social behavior is guided largely by the shared goals of a family, tribe, work group, or other collective.

combinatorial skills The ability to perform mathematical operations, including addition, subtraction, and multiplication. These skills are acquired during the stage of concrete operational thought.

commitment Consists of a demonstration of personal involvement in the areas of occupational choice, religion, and political ideology.

common bond Interpersonal ties that provide feelings of acceptance and emotional support.

common identity Shared roles involving pressure to comply with group expectations.

communication repairs Periods of recovery in normal mother-infant interactions that follow periods of mismatch, so that infants and mothers cycle again through points of coordination in their interactions.

communicative competence The ability to use all the aspects of language in one's culture, such as systems of meaning, rules of sentence formation, and adjustments for the social setting.

communion The commitment to and consideration for the well-being of others.

comparative assessments Self-understanding that relies on comparisons of oneself with social norms and standards or of oneself with≈specific other people.

competence The exercise of skill and intelligence in the completion of tasks; the sense that one is capable of exercising mastery over one's environment.

competence motivation The desire to exercise mastery by effectively manipulating objects or social interactions.

competition A contest between rivals.

compulsions Repetitive ritualized actions that serve as mechanisms for controlling anxiety.

compulsive sexual behavior A compulsive need to relieve anxiety through sex.

concrete operational thought In Piaget's theory, a stage of cognitive development in which rules of logic can be applied to observable or manipulable physical relations.

confidence A conscious trust in oneself and in the meaningfulness of life.

consensual union A relation between two people without civil or religious marriage ceremonies but regarded as a form of marital union.

conservation The concept that physical changes do not alter the mass, weight, number, or volume of matter. This concept is acquired during the concrete operational stage of cognitive development.

constructivist perspective The view that gender differences are a product of particular interactions that have a socially agreed-upon, gender-related meaning. In this view, the specific behaviors that are described as masculine or feminine depend largely on the situation, including expectations that people will behave in gender appropriate ways.

contactful interactions Interactions that are open to the other's point of view and clearly express the speaker's point of view.

contexts of development The interrelated conditions in which development occurs. Family, culture, and ethnic group are three of the major contexts that have an effect on development. Work organizations, community settings, child care programs, schools, religious groups, community clubs, athletic teams, cities, counties, states, and nations also may have influence. Economic and historical factors such as war, political revolution, famine, or economic collapse are additional factors that have been shown to affect development.

contextual dissonance The difference between the characteristics of the primary childrearing and home environment and other environments in which the child participates.

contextualization of learning Offering instruction in ways that first draw on a child's existing experiences, knowledge, and concepts and then expand them in new directions.

continuing care retirement community A residential setting offering housing and medical, preventive health, and social services to residents who are well at the time they enter the community.

continuity A condition that characterizes a culture when a child is given information and responsibilities that apply directly to his or her adult behavior.

continuous reinforcement In operant conditioning, the schedule in which reinforcement is given on every learning trial.

control group The participants in an experiment who do not experience the manipulation or treatment and whose responses or reactions are compared with those of participants who are treated actively to determine the effects of the manipulation.

controlling interactions Interactions in which one person expresses his or her point of view and does not take the other person's point of view into consideration.

conventional morality A stage of moral reasoning described by Kohlberg, in which right and wrong are closely associated with the rules created by legitimate authorities, including parents, teachers, or political leaders.

cooperation Working or acting together for a common purpose or benefit.

coordination Refers to two related characteristics of interaction—matching and synchrony.

coping behavior Active efforts to respond to stress. Coping includes gathering new information, maintaining control over one's emotions, and preserving freedom of movement.

core pathologies Destructive forces that result from severe, negative resolutions of the psychosocial crises.

correlation A measure of the strength and direction of the relationship among variables.

cosmic transcendence Feelings of cosmic communion with the spirit of the universe, and a redefinition of time, space, life, and death.

couvade A ritual in which an expectant father takes to his bed and observes specific taboos during the period shortly before birth.

creativity The ability to abandon old forms or patterns of doing things and to think in new ways.

crisis A dramatic emotional or circumstantial upheaval in a person's life. In psychosocial theory, this often refers to a normal set of stresses and strains rather than to an extraordinary set of events, and it consists of a period

of role experimentation and active decision making among alternative choices.

critical period A time of maximum sensitivity to or readiness for the development of a particular skill or behavior pattern.

cross-sectional study A research design in which the behavior of individuals of different ages, social backgrounds, or environmental settings is measured once to acquire information about the effects of these differences.

crowd A large group that is usually recognized by a few predominant characteristics, such as the "preppies," the "jocks," or the "druggies."

crystallization phase In Tiedeman's career decision model, the phase when the person becomes more aware of the alternatives for action and their consequences. Conflicts among alternatives are recognized, and some alternatives are discarded. The person develops a strategy for making the decision, in part by weighing the costs and benefits of each alternative.

crystallized intelligence (Gc) Skills and information that are acquired through education and socialization.

cultural determinism The theoretical concept that culture shapes individual experience.

cultural pathways Adults in each culture have values and goals for themselves and for their children that shape and organize the socialization process and activities of daily life.

cultural relativism Morality is viewed as a system of rules that are agreed upon in order to preserve human rights and social order. These rules are understood as having been created in cultural and historical contexts, and can be altered as the norms of the community change.

cultural tools Symbol systems such as language of one's society that permit individuals to alter their environments and guide, regulate, and redefine themselves.

culture Refers to the socially standardized ways of thinking, feeling, and acting that are shared by members of a society.

cumulative relation In heredity, when the allelic states of a gene in a single pair of chromosomes combine to influence a trait.

death anxiety Personal fear and worry about death.

decentering Gaining some objectivity over one's own point of view; reducing the dominance of one's subjective perspective in the interpretation of events.

defense mechanism A technique, usually unconscious, that attempts to alleviate the anxiety caused by the conflicting desires of the id and the superego in relation to impulses (e.g., repression, denial, projection).

degree of suffering Amount or intensity of pain and other symptoms, including shortness of breath, inability to eat, and limited mobility, that a person experiences at the end of life.

delay of gratification The exertion of willpower in order to resist the strong immediate pull or temptation of something desirable.

dementia Deterioration of intellectual faculties, such as memory, concentration, and judgment, sometimes accompanied by emotional disturbance and personality changes. Dementia is caused by organic damage to the brain (as in Alzheimer's disease), head trauma, metabolic disorders, or the presence of a tumor.

dependency In the study of aging, an assessment of difficulties in the activities of daily living usually required to function independently. Beyond very basic types of self-care, an expanded notion of dependency refers to difficulties in managing instrumental activities of daily living.

dependent variable A factor that is defined by a participant's responses or reactions and that may or may not be affected by the experimenter's manipulation of the independent variable.

depressed mood Refers to feelings of sadness, a loss of hope, a sense of

being overwhelmed by the demands of the world, and general unhappiness.

depression A state of feeling sad, often accompanied by feelings of low personal worth and withdrawal from relations with others.

depressive syndrome This term refers to a constellation of behaviors and emotions that occur together. The syndrome usually includes complaints about feeling depressed, anxious, fearful, worried, guilty, and worthless.

despair Feeling a loss of all hope and confidence.

developmental stage A period of life dominated by a particular quality of thinking or a particular mode of social relationships. The notion of stages suggests qualitative changes in competence at each phase of development.

developmental systems theory This perspective emphasizes the ongoing interaction and integration across many levels of the human organism from the genetic to the behavioral level, within the nested contexts of the person, family, community, and culture, to consider both continuity and change over individual and historical time.

developmental tasks Skills and competencies that are acquired at each stage of development.

differentiation The extent to which a social system encourages closeness while supporting the expression of differences.

diffidence The inability to act, due to overwhelming self-doubt.

dilation In childbirth, the gradual enlargement of the woman's cervix.

disclosure Sharing personal information with others.

discontinuity A condition that characterizes a culture when a child is either barred from activities that are open only to adults or forced to unlearn information or behaviors that are accepted in children but considered inappropriate for adults.

disdain A feeling of scorn for the weakness and frailty of oneself or others.

disengaged relationships Infrequent contact and a sense that the members of the family do not really seem to care about one another.

disequilibrium In Piaget's theory, a condition when changes in the organism or changes in the environment require a revision of schemes or mental structures.

dismissing avoidant attachment An attachment outcome in which people have a positive model of the self and a negative model of others.

disorganized attachment Babies' responses are particularly notable in the reunion sequence. In the other three attachment patterns, infants appear to use a coherent strategy for managing the stress of the situation. The disorganized babies have no consistent strategy: They behave in contradictory, unpredictable ways that seem to convey feelings of extreme fear or utter confusion.

dissociation A sense of separateness or withdrawal from others; an inability to experience the bond of mutual commitment.

division of labor Splitting the activities needed to accomplish a task between participants.

dizygotic twins Twins developed from two separate fertilized ova; also called fraternal twins.

DNA Deoxyribonucleic acid. DNA molecules are the chemical building blocks of the chromosomes found in the cell nucleus.

dominance If one allele is present, its characteristic is always observed, whether the other allele of the allelic pair is the same or not.

doubt A sense of uncertainty about one's abilities and one's worth.

Down syndrome A chromosomal irregularity in which the child has an extra chromosome 21. The condition results in mental retardation.

durable power of attorney A document that authorizes someone to act on behalf of a person in financial and property matters and health care decisions that can go into effect either when the agreement is signed or when a disability occurs.

dying trajectory   The time during which a person goes from good health to death.

early adolescence   The period of psychosocial development that begins with the onset of puberty and ends around 18 years of age, usually with graduation from high school.

ecological niche   The position or function of an organism in a community of plants and animals.

ecological validity   The applicability of a controlled laboratory situation in the real world.

effacement   The shortening of the cervical canal preceding childbirth.

efficacy   The capacity for producing a desired result, including planning intentional actions, guiding and directing one's own behaviors toward a goal, and reflecting on one's actions to assess their quality, impact, and purpose.

effortful control   A child's ability to suppress a dominant response and perform a subdominant response instead.

ego   In psychosexual theory, the mental structure that experiences and interprets reality. The ego includes most cognitive capacities, including perception, memory, reasoning, and problem solving.

egocentric empathy   When one recognizes distress in another person and responds to it in the same way one would respond if the distress were one's own.

egocentric speech   In Piaget's observation, toddlers use this to control and direct their behavior. The speech is considered egocentric because it is not intended to communicate with anyone else and often doesn't make sense to anyone else. Vygotsky suggested that egocentric speech is a component of the problem-solving function.

egocentrism   The perception of oneself at the center of the world; the view that others and events base their behavior on or occur as a result of one's own perceptions.

ego ideal   A set of positive standards, ideals, and ambitions that represent the way a person would like to be.

electronic fetal heart rate monitoring   The continuous monitoring of fetal heart rate using an electronic amplification device.

embryo   The developing human individual from the time of implantation to the end of the eighth week after conception.

emotional regulation   Strategies for coping with intense emotions, both positive and negative. Caregiver behavior and observation are important factors in the development of emotional regulation.

empathy   The capacity to recognize and experience the emotional state of another person.

empathy for another's feelings   When one shows empathy for a wide range of feelings and anticipates the kinds of reactions that might really comfort someone else.

empathy for another's life conditions   When one experiences empathy in understanding the life conditions or personal circumstances of a person or group.

enactive attainments   Personal experiences of mastery.

encodings   In cognitive behaviorism, the constructs that a person has about the self, the situation, and others in the situation.

enculturation   The process by which culture carriers teach, model, reward, punish, and use other symbolic strategies to transmit critical practices and values.

endogamy   Marriage within one's well-defined group, such as one's ethnic or religious group.

enmeshed relationships   Characterized by over-involvement in one another to the extent that any change in one family member is met by strong resistance by the others; individuality is viewed as a threat to the relationship.

enzymes   Complex proteins produced by living cells that act as catalysts for biochemical reactions.

epigenetic principle   A biological plan for growth such that each function emerges in a systematic sequence until the fully functioning organism has developed.

episodic memory   Recall of situations and data.

equilibration   Efforts to reconcile new perspectives and ideas about basic moral concepts, such as justice, intentionality, and social responsibility, with one's existing views about what is right and wrong when a stage change occurs.

equilibrium   In Piaget's theory, the balance that every organism strives to attain in which organized structures (sensory, motor, or cognitive) provide effective ways of interacting with the environment.

estrogen   The major female sex hormone.

ethics   Principles of conduct founded on a society's moral code.

ethnic group   A group of people who share a common cultural ancestry, language, or religion within a larger cultural context.

ethnic-group identity   Knowing that one is a member of a certain ethnic group; recognizing that aspects of one's thoughts, feelings, and actions are influenced by one's ethnic membership; and taking the ethnic group's values, outlook, and goals into account when making life choices.

ethology   The comparative investigation of the biological basis of behavior from an evolutionary perspective, to determine the proximal causes of behavioral acts, the relative contribution of inheritance and learning to these acts, and the adaptive significance and evolutionary history of different patterns of behavior within and across species.

euthanasia   The practice of ending someone's life for reasons of mercy.

evolutionary psychology   The study of the long-term, historical origins of behavior.

exclusivity   A shutting out of others for elitist reasons.

executive functioning Includes several cognitive capacities, including the ability to reject irrelevant information, formulate complex hypothetical arguments, organize an approach to a complex task, and follow a sequence of steps to task completion. Often associated with advances in the development of the prefrontal cortex.

exosystem One or more settings that do not involve the developing person as an active participant but in which events occur that affect or are affected by what happens in the setting containing the developing person.

expansion Elaborating on a child's expression by adding more words.

expectancies Expectations about one's ability to perform, the consequences of one's behavior, and the meaning of events in one's environment.

expectations Views held by oneself or by others about what would be appropriate behavior in a given situation or at a given stage of development.

experiential transcendence A way of experiencing immortality through achieving a sense of continuous presence.

experiment A research method best suited for examining causal relationships, in which some variable or group of variables is systematically manipulated to examine its effect on an outcome.

experimental group The participants who experience the manipulation or treatment in an experiment.

expertise A quality of individuals who focus their intelligence on intensive study, training, and repeated opportunities for problem solving within a domain in which they become specialists.

exploration phase In Tiedeman's career decision model, the phase when a person realizes that a career decision must be made and therefore begins to learn more about those aspects of the self and the occupational world that are relevant

to the impending decision. The person begins to generate alternatives for action. Uncertainty about the future and the many alternatives is accompanied by feelings of anxiety.

extended family The family group that includes family members other than the parents and children.

external frames of reference When a child evaluates his or her own performance in light of parent, teacher, or peer feedback and observations of the performance of other children in the class.

external validity The degree to which the results of an experiment are applicable to situations beyond the experiment itself.

extinction (1) In psychosocial theory, the negative pole of the psychosocial crisis of elderhood, in which it is feared that the end of one's life is the end of all continuity. (2) In evolutionary theory, the failure of a species to adapt to changing environmental conditions results in a gradual process in which the species no longer exists.

extroversion Personality dimension that includes such qualities as sociability, vigor, sensation seeking, and positive emotions.

fallopian tube The tube, extending from the uterus to the ovary, in which fertilization takes place.

family Two or more individuals living together who are related by birth, marriage, partnership agreement, or adoption.

family constellation The many variables that describe a family group, including the presence or absence of mother and father; the number, spacing, and sex of siblings; and the presence or absence of extended family members in the household.

family of origin The family into which one is born.

family of procreation The family one begins as an adult.

fast mapping Forming a rapid, initial, partial understanding of the meaning of a word by relating it to the known vocabulary and restructuring

the known-word storage space and its related conceptual categories.

fearful avoidant attachment An attachment outcome in which people have a negative model of both self and others.

feedback The process by which a system, often biological or ecological, is modulated, controlled, or changed by the product, output, or response it produces.

feedback loop The section of a control system that allows for feedback and self-correction and that adjusts its operation according to differences between the actual output and the desired output.

feedback mechanisms In systems theory, the operations in an open system that produce adaptive self-regulation by identifying and responding to changes in the environment.

femininity Gender traits associated with being expressive and communal (e.g., valuing interpersonal and spiritual development, and being tender, sympathetic, and concerned about the well-being of others).

fertilization The penetration of an egg by a sperm.

fetal alcohol syndrome A condition of the fetus involving central nervous system disorders, growth deficiency, low birth weight, and malformations of the skull and face; the condition is associated with use of alcohol by mothers during pregnancy.

fetal viability The maturational age at which the fetus can survive outside the uterus.

fetoscopy Examination of the fetus through the use of a fiber-optic lens.

fetus The unborn infant. Usually, the term fetus refers to infants between 8 weeks of gestational age and birth. See embryo.

fidelity The ability to freely pledge and sustain loyalties to others; the ability to freely pledge and sustain loyalties to values and ideologies.

filial obligation The responsibilities of adult children for their aging parents.

fitness (1) The genetic contribution of an individual to the next generation's gene pool relative to the average for the population, usually measured by the number of that individual's offspring or close kin that survive to reproductive age. (2) Patterns of activity or inactivity, endurance or frailty, and illness or health that influence the ability to manage tasks of independent daily living.

fluid intelligence (Gf) The ability to impose organization on information and to generate new hypotheses.

formal operational thought In Piaget's theory, the final stage of cognitive development, characterized by reasoning, hypothesis generation, and hypothesis testing.

formal operations Complex cognitive capacities, such as reasoning, hypothesis generation, and hypothesis testing.

foundational category In cognitive development, a fundamental mental classification, such as the distinction between human beings and inanimate objects.

fraternal twins Children born at the same time who developed from two different ova.

gamete A mature germ cell involved in reproduction; a sperm or an ovum.

gender Refers to the integrated cognitive, social, and emotional schemes associated with being male or female.

gender constancy When children learn the biological basis of gender and that one's gender does not change.

gender identification Incorporation into one's self-concept of the valued characteristics of male or female that become integrated into an early scheme for thinking of oneself as either male or female.

gender identity A set of beliefs, attitudes, and values about oneself as a man or woman in many areas of social life, including intimate relations, family, work, community, and religion.

gender label The word boy or girl. First component of gender identity, in which children learn to refer to themselves as a boy or girl and to

identify other children by applying the word correctly.

gender preference The development of a personal preference for the kinds of activities and attitudes associated with the masculine or feminine gender role.

gender role convergence A transformation in which men and women become more androgynous and more similar in gender orientation during later life.

gender role standards Attributes held by the culture for males and females. These attributes can include both precepts and sanctions.

gender scheme A personal theory about cultural expectations and stereotypes related to gender.

gene The fundamental physical unit of heredity. A gene is a linear sequence of nucleotides along a segment of DNA that carries the coded instructions for the synthesis of RNA, which, when translated into protein, leads to hereditary characteristics.

gene pool The genetic information contained in the genes of the population or culture that provides the ancestry for an individual.

generalizability The extent to which we can say with confidence that the observations made for a sample would apply to other groups.

generativity The capacity to contribute to the quality of life for future generations. A sense of generativity is attained toward the end of middle adulthood.

genetic anomalies Neurological or physical abnormalities that have a genetic cause.

genetic counseling Recent discoveries make it possible to identify the genes responsible for certain forms of disease and genetic anomalies. Couples who have reason to believe that they may carry genes for one of these disorders can be tested and advised about the probability of having children who may be afflicted.

genome The full set of chromosomes that carries all the inheritable traits of an organism.

genotype The hereditary information contained in the cells of an individual. Genotype may or may not be observable in the phenotype. See phenotype.

gentrification A pattern of real estate change in which a higher income group buys property and develops residential and commercial projects in an area that has previously been serving a lower income group.

gestation The period from conception to birth.

Glick effect Statistical evidence of a lack of persistence that relates dropping out of high school or college with a high probability of divorce.

global empathy Distress experienced and expressed as a result of witnessing someone else in distress.

goal The result or achievement toward which effort is directed.

goal-corrected partnership In Bowlby's attachment theory, the capacity that emerges in toddlerhood and early school age in which children begin to find more flexible and adaptive ways to maintain proximity with the object of attachment and to seek reassurance under stressful situations. As a result, children are able to manage negotiated separations more easily.

grammar Rules for the arrangement of words and phrases in a sentence and for the inflections that convey gender, tense, and number.

grief The cognitive and emotional reactions that follow the death of a loved one.

grief work A person's psychological efforts to work through the reality of loss of a loved one and the feelings in which the person must (1) achieve freedom from feelings of guilt about ways he or she had criticized or even harmed the person who died and feelings of regret for things left unsaid or undone; (2) make an adjustment to all the aspects of the environment from which the deceased is missing; and (3) begin to form new relationships.

group identity The positive pole of the psychosocial crisis of early adolescence, in which the person finds membership in and value convergence with a peer group.

guilt An emotion associated with doing something wrong or the anticipation of doing something wrong.

habituation A form of adaptation in which the child no longer responds to a stimulus that has been repeatedly presented.

heteronomous morality A child's moral perspective, in which rules are viewed as fixed and unchangeable.

heterozygous Characterized by the presence of different alleles of a particular gene at the same locus.

holophrase A single word functioning as a phrase or sentence.

homeostasis A relatively stable state of equilibrium.

homogamy When people are attracted to others who share important areas of similarity.

homozygous Characterized by the presence of two matched alleles of a particular gene at the same locus.

hope An enduring belief that one can attain one's essential wishes.

hormones A group of chemicals, each of which is released into the bloodstream by a particular gland or tissue and has a specific effect on tissues elsewhere in the body.

hospice care An integrated system of medicine, nursing, counseling, and spiritual care for the terminally ill and their family that emphasizes pain control and emotional support and typically refrains from extraordinary measures to prolong life.

household All persons who occupy a housing unit, including both related family members and all unrelated persons.

hyperarousal A response to exposure to violence and trauma, including low threshold for startle response, increases in heart rate, sleep disturbance, anxiety, and motor hyperactivity.

hypoactive sexual desire A decrease or absence of interest in sexual activity.

hypothesis A tentative proposition that can provide a basis for further inquiry.

hypothetico deductive reasoning A method of reasoning in which a hypothetical model based on observations is first proposed and then tested by deducing consequences from the model.

id In psychoanalytic theory, the mental structure that expresses impulses and wishes. Much of the content of the id is unconscious.

identical twins Children born at the same time who developed from the same ovum.

identification The process through which one person incorporates the values and beliefs of a valued other such as a parent.

identity In cognitive theory, the concept that an object is still the same object even though its shape or location has been changed.

identity achievement Individual identity status in which, after a crisis, a sense of commitment to family, work, political, and religious values is established.

identity confusion The negative pole of the psychosocial crisis of later adolescence, in which a person is unable to integrate various roles or make commitments.

identity foreclosure Individual identity status in which a commitment to family, work, politics, and religious values is established prematurely, without crisis.

illusion of incompetence Expressed by children who perform well in academic achievement tests yet perceive themselves as below average in academic ability and behave in accordance with this perception.

imaginary audience The preoccupation with what you believe other people are thinking about you.

imitation Repetition of another person's words, gestures, or behaviors.

immortality The positive pole of the psychosocial crisis of very old age, in which the person transcends death through a sense of symbolic continuity.

imprinting (1) The process of forming a strong social attachment at some point after birth. (2) A condition in which genes from either the mother or the father are silenced. At present, 83 imprinted genes have been identified, but many more are expected to be discovered. Under conditions of imprinting, the genes from both parents are present on the DNA strands and are copied by the RNA but only the genes from one parent are used in making proteins. As a result, even though there are two different alleles in the genotype, only the mother's or the father's allele is expressed in the phenotype.

impulse control The ability to delay gratification, and to suppress a dominant response in order to perform a subdominant response.

inclusive fitness The fitness of an individual organism as measured by the survival and reproductive success of its kin, each relative being valued according to the probability of shared genetic information, with an offspring or sibling having a value of 50% and a first cousin having a value of 25%.

independent variable The factor that is manipulated in an experiment, and the measured effects of the manipulation.

individual differences perspective The view that gender differences exist within the individual as persistent, internal attributes and that differences between boys and girls are stable characteristics that individuals bring to various situations.

individual identity The commitment to a personal integration of values, goals, and abilities that occurs as personal choices are made in response to anticipated or actual environmental demands at the end of adolescence.

individualism Worldview in which social behavior is guided largely by personal goals, ambitions, and pleasures.

induction (1) A form of discipline that points out the consequences of a child's actions for others. (2) In cognitive development, the realization that whatever holds true for one member of a category is likely to hold true for other members as well.

induction phase In Tiedeman's career decision model, the phase when a person encounters the new work environment for the first time. He or she wants to be accepted and looks to others for cues about how to behave. The person identifies with the new group and seeks recognition for his or her unique characteristics. Gradually, the self-image is modified as the person begins to believe in the values and goals of the work group.

industry A sense of pride and pleasure in acquiring culturally valued competences. The sense of industry is usually acquired by the end of the middle childhood years.

inertia A paralysis of thought and action that prevents productive work.

inferiority A sense of incompetence and failure that is built on negative evaluation and lack of skill.

infertility Inability to conceive or carry a fetus through the gestational period.

influence phase In Tiedeman's career decision model, the phase when the person is very much involved with the new group. He or she becomes more assertive in asking that the group perform better. The person also tries to influence the group to accommodate some of his or her values. The self is strongly committed to group goals. During this phase, the group's values and goals may be modified to include the orientation of the new member.

In-group A group of which one is a member; contrasted with outgroup.

inhibition A psychological restraint that prevents freedom of thought, expression, and activity.

initiative The ability to offer new solutions, to begin new projects, or to seek new social encounters; active investigation of the environment.

inner speech Language spoken softly or even silently to the self, which guides behavior. In Vygotsky's theory, the internalization of social language; a transition between spoken language and thought.

instrumental activities of daily living (IADLs) Basic tasks that are essential to maintaining one's daily life without dependence on informal or formal community support services.

instrumental reminiscence Reminiscence that emphasizes past accomplishments, past efforts to overcome difficulties, and the use of past experiences to approach current difficulties.

instrumental values The values placed on doing things that are challenging, reflected in the amount of time spent on and the degree of satisfaction achieved in such actions.

integration phase In Tiedeman's career decision model, the phase when group members react against the new member's attempts to influence them. The new member then compromises. In the process, he or she attains a more objective understanding of the self and the group. A true collaboration between the new member and the group is achieved. The new member feels satisfied and is evaluated as successful by the self and others.

integrative reminiscence Reminiscence that involves reviewing one's past in order to find meaning or to reconcile one's current and prior feelings about certain life events.

integrity The ability to accept the facts of one's life and to face death without great fear. The sense of integrity is usually acquired toward the end of later adulthood.

intellectual flexibility A person's ability to handle conflicting information, to take several perspectives on a problem, and to reflect on personal values in solving ethical problems.

intellectual vigor A person's ability to maintain and successfully utilize cognitive abilities.

interdependence A condition in which systems depend on each other, or in which all the elements in a system rely on one another for their continued growth.

intergenerational solidarity The closeness and commitment within parent-child and grandparent-grandchild relationships.

intermental In Vygotsky's theory, understanding or shared meaning between two or more people.

intermittent reinforcement A schedule of reinforcement that varies the amount of time or the number of trials between reinforcements.

internal frames of reference When a child compares how well he or she can perform in one domain versus another.

internalization A process in which the values, beliefs, and norms of the culture become the values, beliefs, and norms of the individual.

internal validity The sample and methods are appropriate in an experiment.

interobserver reliability Two or more observers' codings of the same situation are compared to determine whether different observers rated the same event in the same way.

intersubjectivity A shared repertoire of emotions that enables infants and their caregivers to understand each other and create shared meanings. They can engage in reciprocal, rhythmic interactions, appreciate state changes in one another, and modify their actions in response to emotional information about one another.

intimacy The ability to experience an open, supportive, tender relationship with another person without fear of losing one's own identity in the process of growing close. The sense of intimacy is usually acquired toward the end of early adulthood.

introjection An unconscious psychic process by which a person incorporates the characteristics of another person into his or her own personality.

introspection Deliberate self-evaluation and examination of private thoughts and feelings.

isolation A crisis resolution in which situational factors or a fragile sense of self lead a person to remain psychologically distant from others; the state of being alone.

justice orientation Moral decision making based on human rights, respect for others, and fairness.

labor In pregnancy, involuntary contractions of the uterine muscles that occur prior to giving birth.

language perception The ability to recognize sounds and differentiate among sound combinations before the meanings of these sounds are understood.

language production The generation of language material by an individual. One of the first significant events is the naming of objects.

latency stage In Freud's psychosexual theory, the fourth life stage, during which no significant conflicts or impulses are assumed to arise. Ego development proceeds during this period.

later adolescence The period of psychosocial development that begins around the time of graduation from high school and ends in the early twenties.

launching period The time in family life during which children leave home.

learned helplessness A belief that one's efforts have little to do with success or failure and that the outcome of task situations is largely outside one's control.

learning Any relatively permanent change in thought or behavior that is the consequence of experience.

life course Refers to the integration and sequencing of phases of work and family life.

life expectancy The average number of years from birth to death, as based on statistical analyses of the length of life for people born in a particular period.

life span Refers to the typical length of time that any particular organism can be expected to live.

lifestyle A relatively permanent structure of activity and experience, including the tempo of activity, the balance between work and leisure, and patterns of family and social relationships.

living will A document instructing physicians, relatives, or others to refrain from the use of extraordinary measures, such as life support equipment, to prolong one's life in the event of a terminal illness.

longevity The length or duration of life.

longitudinal study A research design in which repeated observations of the same participants are made at different times, in order to examine change over time.

long-term memory A complex network of information, concepts, and schemes related by associations, knowledge, and use. It is the storehouse of a lifetime of information.

loss-oriented coping Confronting one's pain, sadness, and the loss of a loved one and finding a place for the deceased in one's thoughts and memories in order to achieve emotional health and cognitive functioning.

love A profoundly tender, passionate affection for another person.

love withdrawal A form of discipline in which parents express disappointment or disapproval and become emotionally cold or distant.

low-birth-weight babies Infants who weigh less than 2,500 grams (about 5 pounds, 8 ounces) at birth. This may be a result of being born before the full period of gestation, or it may result from the mother's inadequate diet, smoking, or use of drugs.

macrosystem Refers to consistencies in the form and content of lower order systems (micro-, meso-, and exosystems) that exist or could exist at the level of the subculture or the culture as a whole, along with any belief systems of ideology underlying such consistencies.

major depressive disorder A disorder in which a person will have experienced five or more of the following symptoms for at least 2 weeks: depressed mood or irritable mood most of the day; decreased interest in pleasurable activities; changes in weight, or perhaps failure to make necessary weight gains in adolescence; sleep problems; psychomotor agitation or retardation; fatigue or loss of energy; feelings of worthlessness or abnormal amounts of guilt; reduced concentration and decision-making ability; and repeated suicidal ideation, attempts, or plans of suicide.

managerial resourcefulness Flexible, creative problem solving in the workplace, particularly when facing new problems and changing conditions.

masculinity Gender traits associated with being instrumental and agentic (e.g., having leadership abilities, being assertive, taking control).

matched groups sampling Two or more groups of participants who are similar on many dimensions are selected as the sample for an experiment. The effects of different treatments or manipulations are determined by comparing the behavior of these groups.

matching The infant and the caregiver are involved in similar behaviors or states at the same time.

menarche The beginning of regular menstrual periods.

mental image A form of representational thought that involves the ability to hold the picture of a person, object, or event in one's mind even in the absence of the stimulus itself.

mental operations A transformation—carried out in thought rather than action—that modifies an object, event, or idea.

mercy killing Taking a person's life in order to end their suffering. In our society, this is considered to be murder.

mesosystem The interrelations among two or more settings in which the developing person actively participates (e.g., for a child, the relations between home, school, and neighborhood peer groups; for an adult, between family, work, and social life).

metabolism A collective term for all the chemical processes that take place in the body: in some (catabolic), a complex substance is broken down into simpler ones, usually with the release of energy; in others (anabolic), a complex substance is built up from simpler ones, usually with the consumption of energy.

metacognition Thinking about one's own thinking, including what individuals understand about their reasoning capacities and about how information is organized, how knowledge develops, how reality is distinguished from belief or opinion, how to achieve a sense of certainty about what is known, and how to improve understanding.

microsystem A pattern of activities, roles, and interpersonal relations experienced by the developing person in a given setting with specific physical and material characteristics.

mirror neuron system A coordinated network of neural areas that underlies a person's ability to observe and then recreate the actions of others as well as to understand the emotions and intentions of others.

miscarriage Spontaneous termination of a pregnancy.

mismatch The infant and caregiver are not involved in the same behaviors or states at the same time.

mistrust A sense of unpredictability in the environment and suspicion about one's own worth. Experiences with mistrust are most critical during infancy.

monozygotic twins Twins who develop from a single fertilized egg. These twins have identical genetic characteristics.

moral development The acquisition of the principles or rules of right conduct and the distinction between right and wrong.

moral identity The sense in which a person defines himself or herself in moral terms and evaluates his or her behavior against moral standards that represent an integration of parental socialization about caring for others, an appreciation for the cultural and social contexts of moral actions, and experiences that have required moral action.

morality Conforming to rules of right or virtuous conduct that involves conceptions of the rights, dignity, and welfare of others.

mutuality The ability of two people to meet each other's needs and to share each other's concerns and feelings.

myelination The formation of a soft, white, fatty material called myelin around certain nerve axons to serve as an electrical insulator that speeds nerve impulses to muscles and other effectors.

narcissistic Extremely self-absorbed and self-loving.

natural selection A process whereby those individuals best suited to the characteristics of the immediate environment are most likely to survive and reproduce.

negative identity A clearly defined self-image that is contrary to the cultural values of the community.

neural tube The tube formed during the early embryonic period that later develops into the brain, spinal cord, nerves, and ganglia.

neuron A nerve cell with specialized processes; the fundamental functional unit of nervous tissue.

neuroticism A personality dimension consistently associated with discouragement, unhappiness, and hopelessness. Neuroticism includes such qualities as anxiety, hostility, and impulsiveness.

nonparental care Child care arrangements in which infants and toddlers are taken care of by persons who are not their parents. Center-based care includes day care centers, Head Start programs, preschool, pre-kindergarten, and other early child-hood programs.

norm of reciprocity The cultural norm that you are obligated to return in full value what you receive.

norms Collective expectations or rules for behavior held by members of a group or society.

nuclear family A household grouping that includes one or two parents and their children.

nuclear transplantation A procedure in which the nucleus of an egg cell, which contains its DNA, is removed and replaced with the DNA from an adult cell.

object permanence A scheme acquired during the sensorimotor stage of development, in which children become aware that an object continues to exist even when it is hidden or moved from place to place.

object relations The component of ego development that is concerned with the self, self-understanding, and self-other relationships.

object relations theory A modern adaptation of psychoanalytic theory that places less emphasis on the drives of aggression and sexuality as motivational forces and more emphasis on human relationships as the primary motivational force in life.

objective Based on facts and not influenced by personal feelings, interpretations, or prejudices.

observation A research method in which behavior is watched and recorded.

obsessions Persistent repetitive thoughts that serve as mechanisms for controlling anxiety.

obsessive-compulsive disorder An anxiety disorder that is characterized by recurrent, unwanted thoughts (obsessions) and/or repetitive behaviors (compulsions).

obsessive reminiscence Reminiscence that suggests an inability to resolve or accept certain past events and a persistent guilt or despair over these events.

old-old Among the very old, those who have suffered major physical or mental decrements.

open system A structure that maintains its organization even though its parts constantly change.

operant conditioning A form of learning in which new responses are strengthened by the presentation of reinforcements.

operation In Piaget's theory, an action that is performed on an object or a set of objects.

operational definition In research, the way an abstract concept is defined in terms of how it will be measured.

operationalize   To translate an abstract concept into something that can be observed and measured.

optimal functioning   What a person is capable of doing when motivated and well prepared.

optimism   A belief that one's decisions will lead to positive consequences and that situations will turn out well.

organic brain syndromes   Disorders involving memory loss, confusion, loss of ability to manage daily functions, and loss of ability to focus attention.

organ inferiority   In Adler's theory, a strong sense that some organ of one's body is weak and inferior. The person becomes preoccupied with thoughts of this weakness.

outgroup   A group that competes with one's own group; contrasted with ingroup.

overregularization   In language acquisition, the tendency to use a grammar rule for the formation of regular verbs or nouns when one cannot remember the irregular form. As a child's vocabulary grows, the need to apply the rule to unfamiliar words declines.

ovum   An egg; the female germ cell.

parenting   The rearing of children.

parenting alliance   The capacity of a spouse to acknowledge, respect, and value the parenting roles and tasks of the partner.

participant observation   Observation in which the researcher actively engages in interactions with other members of the setting.

passive euthanasia   Withholding treatment or removing life-sustaining nourishment and breathing aids for the dying person, with the result that death occurs more quickly than if these procedures were continued.

peer play   Play interactions with one's peers, which provide opportunities for physical, cognitive, social, and emotional development.

peer pressure   Expectations to conform and commit to the norms of one's peer group.

peer review   The process in which other professionals read and critically evaluate a researcher's materials before they are published.

persistent vegetative state   State in which a person's brainstem functions to continue to maintain heartbeat and respiration even when there is no cortical functioning.

personal choice   When children recognize a domain of personal freedom in decision making that is not guided by adult authority and regulations but by the child's own preferences.

personal fable   An intense investment in one's own thoughts and feelings and a belief that these thoughts are unique.

perspective taking   The ability to consider a situation from a point of view other than one's own.

phenotype   The observable characteristics that result from the interaction of a particular genotype and a particular environment.

physical culture   Encompasses the objects, technologies, structures, tools, and other artifacts of a culture.

physical state   In self-efficacy theory, the state of arousal or excitement that provides information as one makes a judgment whether one is likely to succeed or fail in a certain task.

physician-assisted suicide   The administration of a lethal dose of some medication by a physician or arranging for a terminally ill patient to administer his or her own lethal dose of medication using a suicide machine.

placenta   The vascular organ that connects the fetus to the maternal uterus and mediates metabolic exchanges.

plasticity   (1) The capability of being shaped and molded. (2) The capacity for continuous alteration of the neural circuits and synapses of the living brain and nervous system in response to experience or injury that involves the formation of new circuits and synapses and the elimination or modification of existing ones.

population   All units for potential observation.

positive reinforcer   In operant conditioning, a stimulus—such as food or a smile—that increases the rate of response when present.

positivism   An approach to the study of human behavior that seeks causal relationships among factors, with the goal of trying to predict outcomes.

postconventional morality   In Kohlberg's stages of moral reasoning, the most mature form of moral judgment. Moral decisions are based on an appreciation of the social contract that binds members of a social system and on personal values.

postformal thought   A qualitatively new form of thinking that emerges after formal operational thought, which involves a higher use of reflection and the integration of contextual, relativistic, and subjective knowledge.

postpartum depression   A period of sadness that may be experienced by the mother after giving birth, which appears to be related to hormonal activity.

post-traumatic stress disorder   A mental disorder that occurs after a traumatic event outside the range of usual human experience, characterized by symptoms such as reliving the event, reduced involvement with others, and manifestations of autonomic arousal such as hyperalertness and exaggerated startle response.

poverty   Commonly understood as the condition of having little money and few material possessions. Since poverty is defined at the family level and not the household level, the poverty status of the household is determined by the poverty status of the householder. Households are classified as poor when the total income of the householder's family is below the appropriate poverty threshold. (For nonfamily householders, their own income is compared with the appropriate threshold.) The income of people living in the household who are unrelated to the householder is not considered when determining the poverty status of a household, nor does their presence affect the family size in determining the appropriate threshold. The poverty thresholds vary depending on three criteria: size of family, number of related children, and, for one- and two-person families, age of householder.

power assertion A discipline technique involving physical force, harsh language, or control of resources.

preconventional morality In Kohlberg's stages of moral reasoning, the most immature form of moral judgment. Moral decisions are based on whether the act has positive or negative consequences, or whether it is rewarded or punished.

prediction Declaration in advance, usually with precision of calculation.

preoccupied attachment An outcome of attachment in which a person has a positive model of others and a negative model of the self.

preoperational thought In Piaget's theory of cognitive development, the stage in which representational skills are acquired.

prime adaptive ego qualities Mental states that form a basic orientation toward the interpretation of life experiences; new ego qualities emerge in the positive resolution of each psychosocial crisis.

private self Refers to a person's inner uniqueness and unity and the subjective experience of being the originator of one's thoughts and actions and of being self-reflective.

processing load In problem solving, the number of domains of information called into play and the amount of work necessary to select response strategies.

prohibitive moral judgment A judgment involving a conflict between violating a law and breaking a promise in order to achieve some other goal.

prompting Urging a child to say more about an incomplete expression.

prosocial moral judgment A judgment involving a conflict between doing something helpful for someone else and meeting one's own needs.

prospective memory Memory about events or actions taking place in the future.

proteome Constellation of all proteins in a cell. Unlike the relatively unchanging genome, the dynamic proteome changes from minute to minute in response to tens of thousands of intra- and extra-cellular environmental signals. A protein's chemistry and behavior are specified by the gene sequence and by the number and identities of other proteins made in the same cell at the same time and with which it associates and reacts. Thus, at the cellular level, genetic and environmental information are continuously interacting to influence the functions of the cells.

psychohistorical perspective An integration of past, present, and future time with respect to personal and societal continuity and change.

psychological system Includes those mental processes central to the person's ability to make meaning of experiences and take action. Emotion, memory and perception, problem solving, language, symbolic abilities, and orientation to the future all require the use of psychological processes. The psychological system provides the resources for processing information and navigating reality.

psychosocial Of or pertaining to the interaction between social and psychological factors.

psychosocial crisis A predictable life tension that arises as people experience some conflict between their own competencies and the expectations of their society.

psychosocial evolution The contribution of each generation to the knowledge and norms of society.

psychosocial moratorium A period of free experimentation before a final identity is achieved.

psychosocial theory A theory of psychological development that proposes that cognitive, emotional, and social growth are the result of the interaction between social expectations at each life stage and the competencies that people bring to each life challenge.

puberty The period of physical development at the onset of adolescence when the reproductive system matures.

public self The many roles that one plays and the expectations that social reference groups, including family members, neighbors, teachers, friends, religious groups, ethnic groups, and even national leaders, have for one's behavior.

punishment (1) A penalty or negative experience imposed on a person for improper behavior. (2) In operant conditioning, a negative stimulus applied in order to decrease the expression of an undesirable response. Compare negative reinforcer.

purpose The ability to imagine and pursue valued goals.

qualitative inquiry An approach to the study of human behavior that tries to understand the meanings, motives, and beliefs underlying a person's actions.

quasi-experimental study A study in which the assignment of participants to treatment was not controlled by the experimenter but was a result of some pattern of life events.

quickening Sensations of fetal movement, usually beginning during the second trimester of fetal growth.

radius of significant relationships The groups of important people in one's life. The breadth and complexity of these groups change over the life span.

random sampling A method for choosing the sample for a study in which each member of the population under investigation has an equal chance of being included.

range of applicability The nature of the concepts and principles that a theory is trying to explain.

rapport Conveying a feeling of trustworthiness and acceptance in an interview or in a counseling setting.

reaction range The range of possible responses to environmental conditions that is established through genetic influences.

reaction time The interval between the onset of a stimulus and a behavior in response.

reactive attachment disorder Clinical diagnosis that is linked to serious disturbances in infant attachment. Two expressions of this disorder have been described: inhibited type, in which the person is very withdrawn, hypervigilant in social contacts, and resistant to comfort; and uninhibited type, in which the person shows a lack of discrimination, being overly friendly and attaching to any new person.

reactive nature of surveys The ability of some surveys to create attitudes where none existed before.

reactivity A child's threshold for arousal, which indicates the likelihood of becoming distressed.

readiness A time when a child's physical, cognitive, social, and emotional maturation is at a level to undertake new learning or to engage in a more complex, demanding type of activity or relationship.

receptive language The ability to understand words.

reciprocity A scheme describing the interdependence of related dimensions, such as height and width or time and speed.

reference group A group with which an individual identifies and whose values the individual accepts as guiding principles.

reflex An involuntary motor response to a simple stimulus.

reinforcement In operant conditioning, the application of any stimulus that makes the repetition of a response more likely.

rejectivity The unwillingness to include certain others or groups of others in one's generative concerns.

relational paradigm In contemporary psychoanalytic theory, the view that humans have basic needs for connection, contact, and meaningful interpersonal relationships, and that the self is formed in an interpersonal context and emerges through interactions with others. Maturity requires the achievement of a sense of vitality, stability, and inner cohesiveness formulated through interpersonal transactions. Psychopathology or dysfunction arises when a person internalizes rigid, rejecting, or neglectful relational experiences and then uses these internalizations to anticipate or respond to real-life social encounters.

reliability The consistency of a test in measuring something.

reminiscence The process of thinking or telling about past experiences.

repeatable In research, it is important that others carry out a similar investigation and observe the same results as the original investigator. For this to occur, the original investigator must carefully define all the procedures and equipment used, describe all the essential characteristics of the participants (e.g., age, sex, and social class background), and describe the setting or situation where the observations were made.

representational skills Skills learned in the preoperational stage—including mental imagery, symbolic play, symbolic drawing, imitation, and language—that permit the child to represent experiences or feelings in a symbolic form.

repudiation Rejection of roles and values that are viewed as alien to oneself.

reputational identity Identity characteristics assigned to someone by those in their environment (such as a school) that is derived from their being associated with a crowd in the setting.

resilience The capacity to recover from stress, or the ability to withstand the effects of stressors that are typically associated with negative outcomes.

restoration-oriented coping Refers to finding ways to master the practical challenges of the loss of a loved one in order to make meaning of the death and move along in one's life.

retirement anxiety Apprehensions that adults have as they anticipate retirement.

retrospective study Research that asks the participants to report on experiences from an earlier time in their lives.

reversibility A scheme describing the ability to undo an action and return to the original state.

ritual A formal and customarily repeated act or series of acts.

role A set of behaviors with some socially agreed-upon functions and for which there exists an accepted code of norms, such as the role of teacher, child, or minister.

role compatibility When partners in a relationship approach situations in a manner that works well, their behaviors and responses complement one another.

role conflict The state of tension that occurs when the demands and expectations of various roles conflict with each other.

role enactment Patterned characteristics of social behavior that one performs as a result of being in a specific role.

role expectations Shared expectations for behavior that are linked to a social role.

role experimentation The central process for the resolution of the psychosocial crisis of later adolescence, which involves participation in a variety of roles before any final commitments are made.

role overload The state of tension that occurs when there are too many role demands and expectations to handle in the time allowed.

role reversal Assuming the behaviors of a person in a reciprocal role, as when a child acts toward his or her parent as a parent.

role sequencing The order of entry into new roles and age-related role transitions often based on normative expectations of members of one's ethnic group.

role spillover The state of tension that occurs when the demands or preoccupations about one role interfere with the ability to carry out another role.

role strain The conflict and competing demands made by

several roles that the person holds simultaneously.

rule   Principle or regulation governing conduct, action, procedure, or ritual.

sampling   A method of choosing participants in a study.

scaffolding   A process through which a child and an adult attempt to arrive at a shared understanding about a communication, at which point the adult interacts so as to expand or enrich the child's communicative competence.

schedules of reinforcement   The frequency and regularity with which reinforcements are given.

scheme   In Piaget's theory, the organization of actions into a unified whole, a mental construct.

secondary sex characteristics   The physical characteristics other than genitals that indicate sexual maturity, such as body hair, breasts, and deepened voice.

secular growth trend   A tendency, observed since approximately 1900, for more rapid physical maturation from one generation to the next, probably as a result of favorable nutrition, increased mobility, and greater protection from childhood diseases.

secure attachment   Infants actively explore their environment and interact with strangers while their mothers are present. After separation, the babies actively greet their mothers or seek interaction. If the babies were distressed during separation, the mothers' return reduces their distress, and the babies return to exploration of the environment. In adulthood, this is an attachment outcome in which a person has a positive model of the self and of others.

selection forces   Adolescents seek out friends who will support their involvement or their resistance to the use of alcohol and drugs as part of a more general pattern of behavior.

self-actualization   A motive that urges the person to make optimal use of his or her full potential, to become a more effective, creative participant in daily life.

self-efficacy   A sense of confidence that one can perform the behaviors that are demanded in a specific situation.

self-esteem   The evaluative dimension of the self that includes feelings of worthiness, pride, and discouragement.

self-fulfilling prophecy   False or inaccurate beliefs can produce a reality that corresponds with these beliefs.

self-labeling   Refers to applying a sexual label such as straight, gay, lesbian, or bisexual to oneself.

self-monitoring children   Some children appear to monitor their social environment more self-consciously than others. High self-monitoring children are more aware of the emotional and nonverbal behavior of others and make more use of social information to evaluate and regulate their own behavior than low self-monitoring children.

self-presentation bias   Research participants may present themselves in the way they want the interviewer to see them.

self-regulation   Behavior inhibition in response to stimuli.

self-regulatory plan   A strategy for achieving one's goals, including techniques for managing internal emotional states, creating a plan, and putting the plan into action.

self-theory   An organized set of ideas about the self, the world, and the meaning of interactions between the self and the environment.

semantic memory   Recall of basic knowledge, such as the meaning of words like "vegetable," "democracy," or "insect."

semiotic thinking   The understanding that one thing can stand for another.

sensitive period   A span of time during which a particular skill or behavior is most likely to develop.

sensitivity (of caregiver)   Attentiveness to an infant's state, accurate interpretation of the infant's signals, and well-timed responses that promote mutually rewarding interactions.

sensorimotor adaptation   Infants use their reflexes to explore their world, and they gradually alter their reflexive responses to take into account the unique properties of objects around them. This provides the basis for sensorimotor intelligence.

sensorimotor intelligence   In Piaget's theory of development, the first stage of cognitive growth, during which schemes are built on sensory and motor experiences.

sensorimotor play   Sensory exploration and motor manipulation that produce pleasure.

sensory register   The neurological processing activity that is required to take in visual, auditory, tactile, and olfactory information.

separation anxiety   Feelings of fear or sadness associated with the departure of the object of attachment.

sex   Refers to biological features or distinctions of men and women that are determined by chromosomal information.

sex-linked characteristics   Characteristics for which the allele is found on the sex chromosomes.

sexual orientation   Refers to one's preference for sexually intimate partners. The three common sexual orientations discussed in the literature are heterosexual, homosexual, and bisexual.

sexually transmitted diseases (STDs)   A wide range of bacterial, viral, and yeast infections that are transmitted through forms of sexual contact.

shame   An intense emotional reaction to being ridiculed or to a negative self-assessment.

short-term memory   The working capacity to encode and retrieve five to nine bits of information in the span of a minute or two. This is the scratch pad of memory that is used when someone tells you a telephone number or gives you his or her address.

sign   Something that represents something else, usually in an abstract, arbitrary way; for example, a word for an object.

small for gestational age (SGA) Fetus who does not weigh as much as a normal fetus of the same age. These fetuses are at greater risk for health problems than those who are born prematurely but are of average weight for their gestational age.

social clock Expectations for orderly and sequential changes that occur with the passage of time as individuals move through life.

social cognition Concepts related to understanding interpersonal behavior and the point of view of others.

social cognitive neuroscience The field of study that explores the neurological processes associated with the ways we perceive social information and reason about others. It is premised on the idea that articulating the biological, cognitive, and social levels of analysis contribute to more comprehensive explanations of human mind and behavior. While higher order metacognitive processes affect how we consciously operate in social interactions, automatic and unconscious mechanisms also account for much social interaction.

social construction In the study of gender, the view that gender differences are a product of cultural scripts and contextualized social expectations.

social conventions Socially accepted norms and regulations that guide behavior.

social culture Encompasses the norms, roles, beliefs, values, rites, and customs of a culture.

social evolutionary theory A theory that men and women differ in the features they emphasize in evaluating someone as a desirable partner.

social identity The aspect of the self-concept that is based on membership in a group or groups and the importance and emotional salience of that membership.

social integration Being comfortably involved in meaningful interpersonal associations and friendship relations.

socialization The process of teaching and enforcing group norms and values to the new group members.

social learning theory A theory of learning that emphasizes the ability to learn new responses through observation and imitation of others.

social play Children joining with other children in some activity.

social pretend play Children who coordinate their pretense. They establish a fantasy structure, take roles, agree on the make-believe meaning of props, and solve pretend problems.

social referencing The process by which infants use facial features and verbal expressions as clues to the emotional responses of another person, often the mother, and as information about how to approach an unfamiliar, ambiguous situation.

social role A set of behaviors with some socially agreed-upon functions and for which there exists an accepted code of norms, such as the role of teacher, child, or minister.

social role theory The theory that emphasizes participation in varied and more complex roles as a major factor in human development.

social support The social experiences leading people to believe that they are cared for and loved, that they are esteemed and valued, and that they belong to a network of communication and mutual obligation.

societal system Includes those processes through which a person becomes integrated into society. Societal influences include social roles, rituals, cultural myths, social expectations, leadership styles, communication patterns, family organization, ethnic and subcultural influences, political and religious ideologies, patterns of economic prosperity or poverty and war or peace, and exposure to racism, sexism, and other forms of discrimination, intolerance, or intergroup hostility. The impact of the societal system on psychosocial development results largely from interpersonal relationships, often relationships with close or significant others.

sociobiology The scientific study of the biological basis of social behavior that focuses on practices within populations that increase the likelihood of certain genes surviving in subsequent generations of offspring.

socioeconomic level One's ranking based on a number of social and financial indicators, including years of education, occupation, and income.

solicitude State of caring, attentiveness, and helpfulness.

solitary pretense Children are involved in their own fantasy activities, such as pretending that they are driving a car or giving a baby a bath.

sperm The male germ cell.

stagnation A lack of psychological movement or growth during middle adulthood that may result from self-aggrandizement or from the inability to cope with developmental tasks.

statistically significant Pertaining to observations that are unlikely to occur by chance and that therefore indicate a systematic cause.

status offense Behavior that is criminalized for minors, such as running away or truancy, which would not be against the law for adults.

stigmatized death People attributing someone's death to an immoral, illegal, or evil cause.

strange situation A standard laboratory procedure designed to study patterns of attachment behavior. A child is exposed during a 20-minute period to a series of events that are likely to stimulate the attachment system. Child and caregiver enter an unfamiliar laboratory setting; a stranger enters; the caregiver leaves briefly; and the caregiver and infant have opportunities for reunion while researchers observe child, caregiver, and their interactions.

stranger anxiety Feelings of fear or apprehension in the presence of unfamiliar people, especially during infancy.

stratified sampling A method for choosing the sample for a research study in which participants are selected from a variety of levels or types of people in the population.

substantive complexity The degree to which one's work requires thought, independent judgment, and frequent decision making.

superego In psychoanalytic theory, the mental function that embodies moral precepts and moral sanctions. The superego includes the ego ideal, or the goals toward which one strives, as well as the punishing conscience.

superordinate group identity The members of a team or other group who bring their own individual racial/ethnic, cultural, or socioeconomic group identities to a situation are willing to suppress their differences and work together for the success of the group.

swaddling The practice of wrapping a baby snugly in a soft blanket, which is a common technique for soothing a newborn in many cultures.

symbol An object or image that represents something. A symbol can be an image that represents an object, such as "chair," or an object that represents a concept, such as a dove.

symbolic play Imaginative or pretend activities that express emotions, problems, or roles.

synchrony Infant and caregiver move from one state to the next in a fluid manner. Interactions of the infant and caregiver are rhythmic, well timed, and mutually rewarding.

systematic In a careful, orderly way. Scientists have a framework of questions that they strive to answer based on what is already known and what theories predict. They approach research by having clear objectives, carefully defining the purpose of their work, and describing the specific methods they will use.

teachable moment A time when a person is most ready to acquire a new ability.

telegraphic speech Two-word sentences used by children that omit many parts of speech but convey meaning.

temperament Innate characteristics that determine the person's sensitivity to various sense experiences and his or her responsiveness to patterns of social interaction.

teratogens Agents that produce malformations during the formation of organs and tissues.

testis-determining factor (TDF) The gene or genes on the Y chromosome that are responsible for setting into motion the differentiation of the testes during embryonic development.

testosterone A hormone that fosters the development of male sex characteristics and growth.

thanatology The field of science that addresses dying and death as well as the psychological mechanisms of coping with them.

theory A logically interrelated system of concepts and statements that provides a framework for organizing, interpreting, and understanding observations, with the goal of explaining and predicting behavior.

theory of mind The natural way in which children understand each other's behavior. In day-to-day functioning, the theory of mind suggests that beliefs, desires, and actions are logically linked.

trajectory In the life course, the path of one's life experiences in a specific domain, particularly work and family life.

transgendered Refers to people who do not identify with or present themselves as reflecting the sex they were born with and who move across or combine gender boundaries.

transition In the life course, the beginning or close of an event or role relationship. For example, work transitions might be getting one's first job, being laid off, and going back to school for an advanced degree.

triangulation Confirming a researcher's insights by looking at written documents about the setting, interviewing other informants, and sharing observations with other members of the research team.

tribute A gift, testimonial, compliment, establishment of a public monument, or good works in the name of a deceased person given in acknowledgment of gratitude or esteem.

trust An emotional sense that both the environment and oneself are reliable and capable of satisfying basic needs.

ultrasound A technique for producing visual images of the fetus in utero through a pattern of deflected sound waves.

unconscious Psychological processes that occur outside of awareness, including problem solving.

usefulness/competence Personality dimension associated with well-being and high self-esteem through volunteer work, involvement with others, and a sense of purpose and structure in the use of time.

uterus In the female reproductive system, the hollow muscular organ in which the fertilized ovum normally becomes embedded and in which the developing embryo and fetus is nourished and grows.

vagal tone A process through which changes in heart rate vary during changes in environmental conditions. Typically, when you breathe in, heart rate increases, and when you breathe out, heart rate decreases. Under conditions when a task requires attention and concentration, heart rate increases, which allows for adaptive mobilization of resources. When the situation becomes more intense or threatening, heart rate slows, leading to conservation of resources and the ability to achieve a more calm state. The vagal system contributes to regulation of arousal and reactivity, and is considered to be a basic neural component of self-regulation, information processing, and emotion.

validity The extent to which a test measures what it is supposed to measure.

value A principle or quality that is intrinsically desirable.

verbal persuasion Encouragement from others.

very old age Or elderhood. A stage of development that emerges at the upper end of the life span, after one has exceeded the life expectancy for one's birth cohort.

viability Reaching the stage of development in which a fetus is capable of living outside the uterus.

vicarious experience An experience achieved through the imagined participation in events that happen to another person.

vicarious reinforcement Through observing others, a person can learn a behavior and also acquire the motivation to perform the behavior or resist performing that behavior depending on what is observed about the consequences of that behavior.

visual acuity The ability to detect visual stimuli under various levels of illumination.

visual adaptation The ability to adapt to changes in the level of illumination.

visual tracking Following an object's movement with one's eyes.

vocabulary A list of the words a person uses and understands.

volunteerism Involvement in some form of volunteer service.

volunteer sampling Sampling in which participants for a study are selected from volunteers.

whole-brain death A technical definition of death with eight criteria that was developed in 1981 by the President's Commission for the Ethical Study of Problems in Medicine and Biomedical and Behavioral Research.

will The determination to exercise free choice and self-control.

wisdom A type of expert knowledge that reflects sound judgment and good advice in the face of high levels of uncertainty.

withdrawal General orientation of wariness toward people and objects.

withdrawn A path to peer rejection in which children are shy and self-conscious.

word A unit of language, consisting of one or more spoken sounds or their written representation, that functions as a principal carrier of meaning.

work-family facilitation Individual coping strategies and family-friendly attitudes and resources of the workplace that make it easier for employees to address pressing family demands within the scope of their daily work.

working model of attachment An infant's expectations of the behavior of their caregiver that is based on the quality of attachment.

worldview A way of making meaning of the relationships, situations, and objects encountered in daily life in a culture.

young-old Among the very old, those who remain healthy, vigorous, and competent.

zone of proximal development The emergent developmental capacity that is just ahead of the level at which the person is currently functioning.

zygote The first phase of fetal development, when a single cell is formed from two gametes.

References

AARP. (2000). *Update on the older worker: 2000.* Retrieved January 30, 2002, from http://research.aarp.org/econ/dd62_worker.html

AARP. (2002). *AARP national survey on consumer preparedness and e-commerce: A survey of computer users age 45 and older.* Retrieved January 27, 2002, from http://research.aarp.org/consume/ecommerce_1.html

Abbey, A. (1995). Provision and receipt of social support and disregard: What is their impact on the marital life quality of infertile and fertile couples? *Journal of Personality and Social Psychology, 68,* 455–469.

Abel, E. L. (1984). *Fetal alcohol syndrome and fetal alcohol effects.* New York: Plenum.

Abel, K. (2010). Grandfamilies: Grandparents raising grandchildren. Retrieved on August 24, 2010, at http://life.familyeducation.com/grandparents/family/29678.html

Abele, A., & Wojciszke, B. (2007). Agency and communion from the perspective of self and others. *Journal of Personality and Social Psychology, 93,* 751–763.

Abell, S. C., & Richards, M. H. (1996). The relationship between body shape and satisfaction and self-esteem: An investigation of gender and class differences. *Journal of Youth and Adolescence, 25,* 691–703.

Aber, J. L. (1994). Poverty, violence, and child development: Untangling family and community level effects. In C. A. Nelson (Ed.), *Threats to optimal development: Integrating biological, psychological, and social risk factors* (pp. 229–272). Hillsdale, NJ: Erlbaum.

Aber, J. L., Belsky, J., Slade, A., & Crnic, K. (1999). Stability and change in mothers' representations of their relationship with their toddlers. *Developmental Psychology, 35,* 1038–1047.

Abma, J. C. & Martinez, G.M. (2006). Childlessness among older women in the United States: Trends and profiles. *Journal of Marriage and Family, 68,* 1045–1056.

About.com (2010). Discrimination stories. Retrieved on August 19, 2010, at http://jobsearch.about.com/u/sty/tipsforolderjobseekers/agediscrimination/I-Was-Called-an-Old-Lady.htm

Abrams, L. (2003). Contextual variations in young women's gender identity negotiations. *Psychology of Women Quarterly, 27,* 64–74.

Achenbach, T. M. (1991). *Manual for the youth self-report and 1991 profile.* Burlington, VT: University of Vermont, Department of Psychiatry.

Acitelli, L. K., Douvan, E., & Veroff, J. (1997). The changing influence of interpersonal perceptions on marital well-being among Black and White couples. *Journal of Social and Personal Relationships, 14,* 291–304.

Ackerman, G. L. (1993). A congressional view of youth suicide. *American Psychologist, 48,* 183–184.

Acredolo, L., Adams, A., & Schmid, J. (1984). On the understanding of the relationships between speed, duration, and distance. *Child Development, 55,* 2151–2159.

Acredolo, L., Goodwyn, S., & Abrams, D. (2002). *Baby signs: How to talk with your baby before your baby can talk.*

ADAM. (2004). *Hemophilia A.* Retrieved August 4, 2004, from http://www.nlm.nih.gov/medlineplus/ency/article/000538.htm

Adam, E. K., Snell, E. K., & Pendry, P. (2007). Sleep timing and quantity in ecological and family context: A nationally representative time-diary study. *Journal of Family Psychology, 21,* 4–19.

Adams, B. N. (1986). *The family: A sociological interpretation* (4th ed.). San Diego: Harcourt Brace Jovanovich.

Adams, G. R., & Archer, S. L. (1994). Identity: A precursor to intimacy. In S. L. Archer (Ed.), *Interventions for adolescent identity development* (pp. 193–213). Thousand Oaks, CA: Sage.

Adegoke, A. A. (1993). The experience of spermarche (the age of onset of sperm emission) among selected boys in Nigeria. *Journal of Youth and Adolescence, 22,* 201–209.

Adelman, C. (1999). *Answers in a Toolbox: Academic Intensity, Attendance Patterns, and Bachelor's Degree Attainment.* Washington, DC: U.S. Department of Education, Office of Educational Research and Improvement.

Adelson, J., & Doehrman, M. J. (1980). The psychodynamic approach to adolescence. In J. Adelson (Ed.), *Handbook of adolescent psychology* (pp. 99–116). New York: Wiley.

Ades, P. A., Ballor, D. L., Ashikaga, T., Utton, J. L., & Nair, K. S. (1996). Weight training improves walking endurance in healthy elderly persons. *Annals of Internal Medicine, 124,* 568–572.

Adler, A. (1935). The fundamental views of individual psychology. *International Journal of Individual Psychology, 1,* 5–8.

Adler, J. (1999, May 10). The truth about high school. *Newsweek,* pp. 56–58.

Adler, N. E., David, H. P., Major, B. N., Roth, S. H., Russo, N. F., & Wyatt, G. (1990). Psychological responses after abortion. *Science, 248,* 41–44.

Adler, P. A., & Adler, P. (1998). Observational techniques. In N. K. Denzin & Y. S. Lincoln (Eds.), *Collecting and interpreting qualitative materials* (pp. 79–109). Thousand Oaks, CA: Sage.

Adolph, K. E., & Berger, S. E. (2006). Motor development. In D. Kuhn, R. S. Siegler, W. Damon, & R. M. Lerner (Eds.), *Handbook of child psychology: Vol. 2, Cognition, perception, and language,* 6th edition. pp. 161–213. Hoboken, NJ: John Wiley & Sons.

Adolph, K. E., & Eppler, M. A. (2002). Flexibility and specificity in infant motor skill acquisition. In J. W. Fagen & H. Hayne (Eds.), *Progress in infancy research* (Vol. 2, pp. 121–167). Mahwah, NJ: Erlbaum.

AgriLife Extension (2010). Building positive relationships: Adult children and their Aging Parents. Retrieved on August 17, 2010, at http://fcs.tamu.edu/families/aging/elder_care/building_positive_relationships.php

Ainsworth, M. D. S. (1973). The development of infant–mother attachment. In B. M. Caldwell & H. N. Ricciuti (Eds.), *Review of child development research* (Vol. 3). Chicago: University of Chicago Press.

Ainsworth, M. D. S. (1979). Infant-mother attachment. *American Psychologist, 34,* 932–937.

Ainsworth, M. D. S. (1985). Patterns of infant–mother attachments: Antecedents and effects on development. *Bulletin of the New York Academy of Medicine, 61,* 771–791.

Ainsworth, M. D. S. (1989). Attachments beyond infancy. *American Psychologist, 44,* 709–716.

Ainsworth, M. D. S., Bell, S. M. V., & Stayton, D. J. (1971). Individual differences in strange situational behavior of one-year-olds. In H. A. Schaffer (Ed.), *The origins of human social relations.* London: Academic Press.

Ainsworth, M. D. S., Blehar, M. C., Waters, E., & Wall, S. (1978). *Patterns of attachment: A psychological study of the strange situation.* Hillsdale, NJ: Erlbaum.

Akhtar, N. & Gernsbacher, M. A. (2008). On privileging the role of gaze in infant social cognition. *Child Development Perspectives, 2,* 59–65.

Aksan, N., & Kochanska, G. (2005). Conscience in childhood: Old questions, new answers. *Developmental Psychology, 41,* 506–516.

Alan Guttmacher Institute. (1999). *Teen sex and pregnancy.* Retrieved November 3, 2001, from http://www.agi-usa.org/pubs/fb_teen_sex.html

Alan Guttmacher Institute. (2002). Sexuality education. *Facts in Brief.* Retrieved December 4, 2004, from http://www .agi-usa.org/pubs/fb_sex_ed02.pdf

Alan Guttmacher Institute. (2002). Teenagers' sexual and reproductive health. *Facts in Brief.* Retrieved December 4, 2004, from http:// www.agi-usa.org/pubs /fb_sex_ed02 .pdf

Alasker, F. D. (1995). Timing of puberty and reactions to pubertal changes. In M. Rutter (Ed.), *Psychosocial disturbances in young people: Challenges for prevention* (pp. 37–82). Cambridge, UK: Cambridge University Press.

Albert, M. S. (2002). Memory decline: The boundary between aging and age-related disease. *Annals of Neurology, 51,* 282–284.

Albom, M. (1997). *Tuesdays with Morrie: An old man, a young man, and life's greatest lesson.* New York: Doubleday.

Alessandri, S. M. (1992). Mother-child interactional correlates of maltreated and nonmaltreated children's play behavior. *Development and Psychopathology, 4,* 257–270.

Alexander, B. H., Checkoway, H., van Netten, C., Muller, C. H., Ewers, T. G., Kaufman, J. D., et al. (1996). Semen quality of men employed at a lead smelter. *Occupational and Environmental Medicine, 53,* 411–416.

Alexander, C. S., Somerfield, M. R., Ensminger, M. E., Johnson, K. E., & Kim, Y. J. (1993). Consistency of adolescents' self-report of sexual behavior in a longitudinal study. *Journal of Youth and Adolescence, 22,* 455–473.

Alexander, K. L., & Entwisle, D. R. (1988). Achievement in the first two years of school: Patterns of processes. *Monographs of the Society for Research in Child Development, 53* (2, Serial No. 218).

Alexander, K. L., Entwisle, D. R., & Kabbani, N. S. (2001). The dropout process in life course perspective: Early risk factors at home and school. *Teachers College Record, 103,* 760–822.

Alexander, K. L., Entwisle, D. R., & Olson, L. S. (2007). Lasting consequences of the summer learning gap. *American Sociological Review, 72,* 167–180.

Alexander, K. L., Entwisle, D. R., & Thompson, M. S. (1987). School performance, status relations, and the structure of sentiment: Bringing the teacher back in. *American Sociological Review, 52,* 655–682.

Allemand, M. (2008). Age differences in forgiveness: The role of future time perspective. *Journal of Research in Personality, 42,* 1137–1147.

Allen, J. P., & Land, D. (1999). Attachment in adolescence. In J. Cassidy & P. R. Shaver (Eds.), *Handbook of attachment: Theory, research, and clinical applications* (pp. 319–335). New York: Guilford Press.

Allen, K. R., Blieszner, R., & Roberto, K. (2001). Families in the middle and later years: A review and critique of the research in the 1990s. *Journal of Marriage and the Family, 62,* 911–926.

Allen, T. D. (2001). Family-supportive work environment. *Journal of Vocational Behavior, 38,* 414–435.

Allwood, M. A. (2007). The relations of violence exposure, trauma symptoms and aggressive cognitions to youth violent behavior. *Dissertation Abstracts International: Section B: The Sciences and Engineering, 67,* 5387.

Alter, R. C. (1984). Abortion outcome as a function of sex-role identification. *Psychology of Women Quarterly, 8,* 211–233.

Altschul, I., Oyserman, D., & Bybee, D. (2006). Racial-ethnic identity in mid-adolescence: Content and change as predictors of academic achievement. *Child Development, 77,* 1155–1169.

Amato, P. R. (1988). Parental divorce and attitudes toward marriage and family. *Journal of Marriage and the Family, 50,* 453–462.

Amato, P. R. (1996). Explaining the intergenerational transmission of divorce. *Journal of Marriage and the Family, 58,* 628–640.

Amato, P. R., & Booth, A. (1996). A prospective study of divorce and parent-child relationships. *Journal of Marriage and the Family, 58,* 356–365.

Amato, P. R., & De Boer, D. D. (2001). The transmission of marital instability across generations: Relationship skills or commitment to marriage? *Journal of Marriage and the Family, 63,* 1038–1051.

Ambady, N. & Bharucha, J. (2009). Culture and the brain. *Current Directions in Psychological Science, 18,* 342–345.

American Academy of Pediatrics. (1995). The inappropriate use of school "readiness" tests. *Pediatrics, 95,* 437–438.

American Academy of Pediatrics. (1996). Use and abuse of the Apgar score. *Pediatrics, 98,* 141–142.

American Academy of Pediatrics. (1999). *Caring for your baby and young child.* New York: Bantam.

American Academy of Pediatrics. (2001). Children, adolescents, and television. *Pediatrics, 107,* 423–426.

American Administration on Aging. (2010). *Profile of Older Americans, 2009.* U.S. Government Printing Office: U.S. Department of Health and Human Services.

American Association of Retired Persons (2010). Sex, romance and relationships. AARP survey of midlife and older adults. Retrieved on August 17, 2010, at http:// assets.aarp.org/rgcenter/general/srr_09.pdf

American Civil Liberties Union. (1996). *Violence chip.* Retrieved August 18, 2001, from http://www.aclu.org/library/aavchip.html

American Medical Association. (2004). *American Medical Association Family Medical Guide* (4th ed.). Hoboken, NJ: John Wiley & Sons.

American Psychiatric Association. (1994). *Diagnostic and statistical manual of mental disorders, DSM-IV* (4th ed.). Washington, DC: Author.

American Psychological Association. (1992). Ethical principles of psychologists and code of conduct. *American Psychologist, 47,* 1597–1611.

American Psychological Association. (1996). *Reducing violence: A research agenda.* Washington, DC. Author.

American Psychological Association Task Force in Gender Identity and Gender Variance. (2009). *Report of the task force on gender identity and gender variance.* Washington, DC: Author.

American Psychological Association. (2010). *Stress in America, 2009.* Washington, DC: Author.

Amundson, N. E. (2001). Three-dimensional living. *Journal of Employment Counseling, 38,* 114–127.

Anderson, D. R., Huston, A. C., Schmitt, K., Linebarger, D. L., & Wright, J. C. (2001). Early childhood television viewing and adolescent behavior: The recontact study. *Monographs of the Society for Research in Child Development, 66* (Serial No. 264).

Anderson, K. J., & Leaper, C. (1998). Meta-analyses of gender effects on conversational interruption: Who, what, when where, and how. *Sex roles, 39,* 225–252.

Anderson, S. M., Downey, G., & Tyler, T. R. (2005). Becoming engaged in the community: A relational perspective on social identity and community engagement. In G. Downey, J. S. Eccles, & C. M. Chatman (Eds.), *Navigating the future: Social identity, coping and life tasks.* New York: Russell Sage Foundation, pp. 210–251.

Anderssen, N., Amlie, C., & Ytteroy, E. A. (2002). Outcomes for children with lesbian or gay parents: A review of studies from 1978 to 2000. *Scandinavian Journal of Psychology, 43,* 335–351.

Andrulis, D. P. (2000). Community, service, and policy strategies to improve health care access in the changing urban environment. *American Journal of Public Health, 90,* 858–862.

Aneshensel, C. S., Pearlin, L. I., Mullan, J. T., Zarit, S. H., & Whitlatch, C. J. (1995). *Profiles in caregiving: The unexpected career.* San Diego: Academic Press.

Anglin, J. M. (1993). Vocabulary development: A morphological analysis. *Monographs of the Society for Research in Child Development, 58.*

Annan, J., Brier, M., & Aryemo, F. (2009). From "rebel" to "returnee": Daily life and reintegration for young soldiers in Northern Uganda. *Journal of Adolescent Research, 24,* 639–667.

Annie E. Casey Foundation. (1999). *Kids count data book.* Baltimore: Author.

Anthony, S. (1972). *The discovery of death in childhood and after.* New York: Basic Books.

Antonio, A. L., Chang, M. J., Hakuta, K., Kenny, D. A., Levin, S., & Milem, J. F. (2004). Effects of racial diversity on complex thinking in college students. *Psychological Science, 15,* 507–510.

Antonucci, T. C., Lansford, J. E., Schaberg, L., Smith, J., Baltes, M., Akiyama, H., et al. (2001). Widowhood and illness: A comparison of social network characteristics in France, Germany, Japan, and the United States. *Psychology and Aging, 16,* 655–665.

Aoki, C., & Siekevitz, P. (1988). Plasticity in brain development. *Scientific American, 259,* 56–64.

Apgar, V. (1953). Proposal for a new method of evaluating the newborn infant. *Anesthesia and Analgesia, 32,* 260–267.

Arbuckle, T. Y., Gold, D. P., Andres, D., Schwartzman, A., & Chaikelson, J. (1992). The role of psychosocial context, age, and intelligence in memory performance of older men. *Psychology and Aging, 7,* 25–36.

Arcus, D. & Chambers, P. (2008). Childhood risks associated with adoption: Family influences on childhood behavior and development. In T. P. Gulotta & G. M. Blau (Eds.), *Family influences on childhood behavior and development: Evidence-based prevention and treatment approaches* (pp. 117–142). New York: Routledge/Taylor & Francis.

Archer, J. (1991). Human sociobiology: Basic concepts and limitations. *Journal of Social Issues, 47*, 11–26.

Archer, S. L. (1992). A feminist's approach to identity research. In G. R. Adams, T. P. Gullotta, & R. Montemayor (Eds.), *Adolescent identity formation: Advances in adolescent development* (pp. 25–49). Newbury Park, CA: Sage.

Ardelt, M. (2004). Wisdom as expert knowledge system: A critical review of a contemporary operationalization of an ancient concept. *Human Development, 47*, 257–285.

Ardila-Rey, A., & Killen, M. (2001). Middle class Colombian children's evaluations of personal, moral, and social-conventional interactions in the classroom. *International Journal of Behavioral Development, 25*, 246–255.

Arias, E. (2007). United States life tables, 2004. *National Vital Statistics Reports, 56* (9).

Aries, E. (1998). Gender differences in interaction: A reexamination. In D. J. Canary & K. Dindia (Eds.), *Sex differences and similarities in communication: Critical essays and empirical investigations of sex and gender in interaction* (pp. 65–81). Mahwah, NJ: Erlbaum.

Armstrong, B., Cohall, A. T., Vaughan, R. D., Scott, M., Tiezzi, L., and McCarthy, J. F. (1999). Involving men in reproductive health: The young men's clinic. *American Journal of Public Health, 89*, 902–905.

Arnett, J. J. (2000). Emerging adulthood: A theory of development from the late teens through the twenties. *American Psychologist, 55*, 469–480.

Arnett, J. J. (2004a). *Adolescence and emerging adulthood: A cultural approach* (2nd ed.). Upper Saddle River, NJ: Prentice Hall.

Arnett, J. J. (2004b). *Emerging adulthood: The winding road from late teens through the twenties.* Oxford University Press.

Arnett, J. J. (2006). Emerging adulthood: Understanding the new way of coming of age. In J. J. Arnett & J. L. Tanner (Eds.), *Emerging adults in America: Coming of age in the 21st century* (pp. 3–19). Washington, DC: American Psychological Association.

Arnold, M. L. (2000). Stage, sequence, and sequels: Changing conceptions of morality, post-Kohlberg. *Educational Psychology Review, 12*, 365–383.

Aron, A., Fisher, H., Mashek, D., Strong, G., Li, H., & Brown, L. (2005). Reward, motivation and emotion systems associated with early-stage intense romantic love. *Journal of Neurophysiology, 93*, 327–337.

Aronfreed, J. (1969). The concept of internalization. In D. A. Goslin (Ed.), *Handbook of socialization theory and research.* Chicago: Rand McNally.

Arsenio, W. F., & Gold, J. (2006). The effects of social injustice and inequality on children's moral judgments and behavior: Towards a theoretical model. *Cognitive Development, 21*, 388–400.

Aseltine, R. H., Jr. (2003). Evaluation of a school based suicide prevention program. *Adolescent & Family Health, 3*, 81–88.

Asher, S. R., & Gazelle, H. (1999). Loneliness, peer relations, and language disorder in childhood. *Topics in Language Disorders, 19*, 16–33.

Asher, S. R., & Paquette, J. A. (2003). Loneliness and peer relations in childhood. *Current Directions in Psychological Science, 12*, 75–78.

Asher, S. R., Parkhurst J. T., Hymel, S., & Williams, G. A. (1999). Peer rejection and loneliness in childhood. In S. R. Asher & J. D. Coie (Eds.), *Peer rejection in childhood* (pp. 253–273). New York: Cambridge University Press.

Askham, J., Briggs, K., Norman, I., & Redfern, S. (2007). Care at home for people with dementia: As in a total institution? *Aging and Society, 27*, 3–24.

Aslin, R. N. (1987). Visual and auditory development in infancy. In J. D. Osofsky (Ed.), Handbook of infant development (2nd ed., pp. 5–97). New York: Wiley.

Associated Press. (2001). *Boys, like girls, may be hitting puberty earlier, study suggests.* Retrieved October 20, 2001, from http://stacks.msnbc.com/news/628473.asp

Astin, A., Korn, W., & Green, K. (1987). Retaining and Satisfying Students. *Educational Record, 68*(1) 36–42.

Astone, N. M. (1993). Are adolescent mothers just single mothers? *Journal of Research on Adolescence, 3*, 353–372.

Atchley, R. C. (1975). The life course, age grading, and age-linked demands for decision making. In N. Datan & L. H. Ginsberg (Eds.), *Life-span developmental psychology: Normative life crises.* New York: Academic Press.

Atchley, R. C. (2001). *Continuity and adaptation in aging.* Baltimore: Johns Hopkins University Press.

Atchley, R. C. (2003). Why most people cope well with retirement. In J. L. Ronch and J. A. Goldfield (Eds.), *Mental wellness in aging: Strengths-based approaches.* Baltimore, MD, US: Health Professions Press, pp. 123–138.

Atkinson, D. R., Morten, G., & Sue, D. W. (1983). *Counseling American minorities: A cross-cultural perspective* (2nd ed.). Dubuque, IA: William C. Brown.

Atkinson, J. W., & Birch, D. (1978). *Introduction to motivation* (2nd ed.). New York: Van Nostrand.

Atkinson, R. H. (2000). Measuring gentrification and displacement in Greater London. *Urban Studies, 37*, 149–166.

Atkinson, R. H. (2001). *Standardized tests and access to American universities.* Retrieved November 18, 2004, from http://www.ucop.edu/news/sat/speech.html

Au, T. K., Sidle, A. L., & Rollins, K. B. (1993). Developing an intuitive understanding of conservation: Invisible particles as a plausible mechanism. *Developmental Psychology, 29*, 286–299.

Aubé, C., & Rousseau, V. (2005). Team goal commitment and team effectiveness: The role of task interdependence and supportive behaviors. *Group Dynamics: Theory, Research, and Practice, 9*, 189–204.

Augustine, J. M., Nelson, T., & Edin, K. (2009). Why do poor men have children? Intentions among low-income unmarried U.S. fathers. *The Annals of the American Academy of Political and Social Science, 624*, 99–117.

Avert.org (2010). Global HIV/AIDS estimates, end of 2008. Retrieved on April 25, 2010, at www.avert.org/worldstats.htm.

Avery, C. S. (1989). How do you build intimacy in an age of divorce? *Psychology Today, 23*(5), 21–31.

Azar, B. (1997). It may cause anxiety, but day care can benefit kids. *APA Monitor, 28*, 13.

BabyCenter.com (2006). Gestational Carriers (Surrogacy). Retrieved May 26, 2007, from http://www.babycenter.com/refcap/4099.html#4

BabyCenter.com (2007). 17 surprising facts about birth in the U.S. Retrieved June 4, 2007, from http://www.babycenter.com/refcap/pregnancy/childbirth/

Back, M.D., Stopfer, J.M., Vazire, S., Gaddis, S., Schmukle, S.C., Egloff, B., & Gosling, S.D. (2010). Facebook profiles reflect actual personality, not self-idealization. *Psychological Science, 21*, 372–374.

Bagwell, C. L., & Coie, J. D. (2004). The best friendships of aggressive boys: Relationship quality, conflict management, and rule-breaking behavior. *Journal of Experimental Child Psychology, 88*, 5–24.

Bahrick, L. E., Lickliter, R., & Flom, R. (2006). Up versus down: The role of intersensory redundancy in the development of infants' sensitivity to the orientation of moving objects. *Infancy, 9*, 73–96.

Bailey, J. M., Bobrow, D., Wolfe, M., & Mikach, S. (1995). Sexual orientation of adult sons of gay fathers. *Developmental Psychology, 31*, 124–129.

Bailey, J. M., & Pillard, R. (1991). A genetic study of male sexual orientation. *Archives of General Psychiatry, 48*, 1089–1096.

Bailey, J. M., & Pillard, R. (1994). The innateness of homosexuality. *The Harvard Mental Health Letter, 10*, 4–6.

Bailey, J. M., & Zucker, K. J. (1995). Childhood sex-typed behavior and sexual orientation: A conceptual analysis and quantitative review. *Developmental Psychology, 31*, 43–55.

Baillargeon, R. (1987). Object permanence in 3½ and 4½ month-old infants. *Developmental Psychology, 23*, 655–664.

Baillargeon, R. (2004). Infants' physical world. *Current Directions in Psychological Science, 13*, 89–94.

Baillargeon, R. (2008). Innate ideas revisited: For a principles of persistence in infants' physical reasoning. *Perspectives on Psychological Science, 3*, 2–13.

Baillargeon, R., & DeVos, J. (1991). Object permanence in young infants: Further evidence. *Child Development, 62,* 1227–1246.

Baillargeon, R., & Graber, M. (1988). Evidence of location memory in 8-month-old infants in a nonsearch AB task. *Developmental Psychology, 24,* 502–511.

Baillargeon, R. H., Zoccolillo, M., Kenan, K., Côte, S., Perusse, D., Wu, H.-X., Boivin, M., & Tremblay, R. E. (2007). Gender differences in physical aggression: A prospective population-based survey of children before and after 2 years of age. *Developmental Psychology, 43,* 13–36.

Bakeman, R. (2000). Behavioral observation and coding. In H. T. Reiss & C. M. Judd (Eds.), *Handbook of research methods in social and personality psychology* (pp. 138–159). New York: Cambridge University Press.

Baker, H. A., Jr. (1991). An apple for my teacher: Twelve writers tell about teachers who made all the difference. In H. L. Gates Jr. (Ed.), *Bearing witness: selections from African-American autobiography in the twentieth century* (pp. 317–319). New York: Pantheon Books.

Baker, T. B., McFall, R. M., & Shoham, V. (2009). Current status and future prospects of clinical psychology. *Psychological Science in the Public Interest, 9,* 67–103.

Bakken, L., Thompson, J., Clark, F. L., Johnson, N., & Dwyer, K. (2001). Making conservationists and classifiers of preoperational fifth-grade children. *Journal of Educational Research, 95,* 56–61.

Baltes, P. B. (1997). On the incomplete architecture of human ontogeny: Selection, optimization, and compensation as foundation of developmental theory. *American Psychologist, 52,* 366–380.

Baltes, P. B., & Lindenberger, U. (1997). Emergence of a powerful connection between sensory and cognitive functions across the adult life span. A new window to the study of cognitive aging? *Psychology and Aging, 12,* 12–21.

Baltes, P. B., & Smith, J. (1990). The psychology of wisdom and its ontogenesis. In R. J. Sternberg (Ed.), *Wisdom: Its nature, origins and development* (pp. 87–120). New York: Cambridge University Press.

Baltes, P. B., Smith, J., & Staudinger, U. M. (1992). Wisdom and successful aging. In T. B. Sonderegger (Ed.), *Psychology and aging* (pp. 123–168). Lincoln: University of Nebraska Press.

Baltes, P. B., & Staudinger, U. M. (2000). Wisdom: A metaheuristic (pragmatic) to orchestrate mind and virtue toward excellence. *American Psychologist, 55,* 122–136.

Bambra, C. (2010). Yesterday once more? Unemployment and health in the 21st century. *Journal of Epidemiology and Community Health, 64,* 213–215.

Bandura, A. (Ed.). (1971). *Psychological modeling.* Chicago: Aldine-Atherton.

Bandura, A. (1973). *Aggression: A social learning analysis.* Englewood Cliffs, NJ: Prentice Hall.

Bandura, A. (1977). *Social learning theory.* Englewood Cliffs, NJ: Prentice Hall.

Bandura, A. (1982). Self-efficacy mechanism in human agency. *American Psychologist, 37,* 122–147.

Bandura, A. (1986). *Social foundations of thought and action: A social cognitive theory.* Englewood Cliffs, NJ: Prentice Hall.

Bandura, A. (1989). Regulation of cognitive processes through perceived self-efficacy. *Developmental Psychology, 25,* 729–735.

Bandura, A. (1989). Social cognitive theory. *Annals of Child Development, 6,* 1–60.

Bandura, A. (1991). Social cognitive theory of moral thought and action. In W. M. Kurtines & J. L. Gewirtz (Eds.), *Handbook of moral behavior and development: Vol. 1. Theory* (pp. 45–103). Hillsdale, NJ: Erlbaum.

Bandura, A. (2000). Self efficacy: The foundation of agency. In W. J. Perrig & A. Grob (Eds.), *Control of human behavior, mental processes, and consciousness: Essays in honor of the 60th birthday of August Flammer* (pp. 17–33). Mahwah, NJ: Erlbaum.

Bandura, A. (2001). Social cognitive theory: An agentic perspective. *Annual Review of Psychology, 52,* 1–26.

Bandura, A., Barbaranelli, C., Caprara, G. V., & Pastorelli, C. (1996). Multifaceted impact of self-efficacy beliefs on academic functioning. *Child Development, 67,* 1206–1222.

Bandura, A., & Schunck, D. H. (1981). Cultivating competence, self-efficacy, and intrinsic interest through proximal self-motivation. *Journal of Personality and Social Psychology, 41,* 586–598.

Bandura, A., & Walters, R. H. (1963). *Social learning and personality development.* New York: Holt, Rinehart & Winston.

Banerjee, R. (2002). Individual differences in children's understanding of social evaluation concerns. *Infant and Child Development, 11,* 237–252.

Bank, B. J., & Hansford, S. L. (2000). Gender and friendship: Why are men's best same sex friendships less intimate and supportive? *Personal Relationships, 7,* 63–78.

Bank, L., Forgatch, M. S., Patterson, G. R., & Fetrow, R. A. (1993). Parenting practices of single mothers: Mediators of negative contextual factors. *Journal of Marriage and the Family, 55,* 371–384.

Bankart, B. (1989). Japanese perceptions of motherhood. *Psychology of Women Quarterly, 13,* 59–76.

Barber, J. S. (2000). Intergenerational influences on the entry into parenthood: Mothers' preferences for family and nonfamily behavior. *Social Forces, 79,* 319–348.

Barbu, S., Le Maner-Idrissi, G., & Jouanjean, A. (2000). The emergence of gender segregation: Towards an integrative perspective. *Current Psychology Letters: Behavior, Brain, and Cognition, 3,* 7–18.

Barbu-Roth, M., Anderson, D. I., Després, A., Provasi, J., Cabrol, D., & Campos, J. J. (2009). Neonatal stepping in relation to terrestrial optic flow. *Child Development, 80,* 8–14.

Bard, K. A., Coles, C. D., Platzman, K. A., & Lynch, M. E. (2000). The effects of prenatal drug exposure, term status and caregiving on arousal and arousal modulation in 8-week-old infants. *Psychobiology, 36,* 194–212.

Barger, S.D., Donoho, C.J., & Wayment, H.A. (2009). The relative contributions of race/ethnicity, socioeconomic status, health, and social relationships to life satisfaction in the United States. *Quality of Life Research: An International Journal of Quality of Life Aspects of Treatment, Care and Rehabilitation, 18,* 179–189.

Bargh, J. A. & Morsella, E. (2008). The unconscious mind. *Perspectives on Psychological Science, 3,* 73–79.

Barinaga, M. (1991). How long is the human life-span? *Science, 254,* 936–938.

Barnard, K. E., & Morisset, C. E. (1995). Preventive health and developmental care for children: Relationships as a primary factor in service delivery with at risk populations. In H. E. Fitzgerald, B. M. Lester, et al. (Eds.), *Children of poverty: Research, health, and policy issues* (pp. 167–195). New York: Garland.

Barnett, R. C. (2004). Preface: Women and work: Where are we, where did we come from, and where are we going? *Journal of Social Issues, 60,* 667–674.

Barnett, R. C., Brennan, R. T., & Gareis, K. C. (1999). A closer look at the measurement of burnout. *Journal of Applied Biobehavioral Research, 4,* 65–78.

Barnett, R. C., & Hyde, J. S. (2001). Women, men, work, and family. *American Psychologist, 56,* 781–796.

Barnett, W. S. (1996). *Lives in the balance: Age-27 benefit-cost analysis of the High/Scope Perry Preschool Program* (Monographs of the High/Scope Educational Research Foundation, 11). Ypsilanti, MI: High/Scope Press.

Bartholomew, K. (1990). Avoidance of intimacy: An attachment perspective. *Journal of Social and Personal Relationships, 7,* 147–178.

Bartz, K. W., & Levine, E. S. (1978, November). Child rearing by black parents: A description and comparison to Anglo and Chicano parents. *Journal of Marriage and the Family, 40,* 709–719.

Bashore, T. R., Osman, A., & Heffley, E. F., III. (1989). Mental slowing in elderly persons: A cognitive psychophysiological analysis. *Psychology and Aging, 4,* 235–244.

Bass, D. M., & Bowman, K. (1990). The transition from caregiving to bereavement: The relationship of care-related strain and adjustment to death. *The Gerontologist, 30,* 35–42.

Bassett, M. T. (2001). Keeping the M in MTCT: Women, mothers, and HIV prevention. *American Journal of Public Health, 91,* 701–702.

Bates, E., & Goodman, J. C. (2001). On the inseparability of grammar and the lexicon: Evidence from acquisition. In M. Tomasello & E. Bates (Eds.), *Language development: The essential readings* (pp. 134–162). Malden, MA: Blackwell.

Bates, E., O'Connell, B., & Shore, C. (1987). Language and communication in infancy. In J. Osofsky (Ed.), *Handbook of infant development* (2nd ed., pp. 149–203). New York: Wiley.

Bates, E., Reilly, J., Wulgeck, B., Dronkers, N., Opei, M., Fenson, J., et al. (2001). Differential effects of unilateral lesions on language production in children and adults. *Brain & Language, 79*, 223–265.

Bates, E., & Roe, K. (2001). Language development in children with unilateral brain injury. In C.A. Nelson & M. Luciana (Eds.), *Handbook of developmental cognitive neuroscience* (pp. 281–308). Cambridge, MA: MIT Press.

Bates, J. E. (1987). Temperament in infancy. In J. D. Osofsky (Ed.), *Handbook of infant development* (2nd ed., pp. 1101–1149). New York: Wiley.

Batson, C. D., Polycarpou, M. P., Harmon-Jones, E., Imhoff, H. J., Mitchener, E. C., Bednar, L. L., et al. (1997). Empathy and attitudes: Can feeling for a member of a stigmatized group improve feelings toward the group? *Journal of Personality and Social Psychology, 72*, 105–118.

Bauer, J. (2010). Workers tell stories on how job retraining changed their lives. *Grand Rapids Press*. Retrieved on August 6, 2010, at http://www.mlive.com/news/index.ssf/2010/02/job_retraining_trade_readjustm.html

Bauer, P. J. (1993). Memory for gender-consistent and gender-inconsistent event sequences by twenty-five-month-old children. *Child Development, 64*, 285–297.

Baulieu, E. (1989). Contragestion and other clinical applications of RU486, an antiprogesterone at the receptor. *Science, 245*, 1351–1357.

Baum, S. K. (1999). Who has no regrets? *Psychological Reports, 85*, 257–260.

Baumeister, R. F., & Leary, M. R. (1995). The need to belong: Desire for interpersonal attachments as a fundamental human motivation. *Psychological Bulletin, 117*, 497–529.

Baumgardner, A. H. (1990). To know oneself is to like oneself: Self-certainty and self-affect. *Journal of Personality and Social Psychology, 58*, 1062–1072.

Baumrind, D. (1995). Commentary on sexual orientation: Research and social policy implications. *Developmental Psychology, 31*, 130–136.

Baxter, K. (2009). (Re)inventing adolescence. *The Hedgehog Review, 11*, 18–30.

Beah, I. (2007). *A long way gone: Memoirs of a boy soldier.* New York: Farrar, Straus, & Giroux.

Beall, A. E., & Sternberg, R. J. (1995). The social construction of love. *Journal of Social and Personal Relationships, 12*, 417–438.

Beardsley, T. (1996). Vital data. *Scientific American, 274*, 100–105.

Bearman, P. S., & Brueckner, H. (2001). Promising the future: Virginity pledges and first intercourse. *American Journal of Sociology, 106*, 859–912.

Beck, A. T. (1976/1979). *Cognitive therapy and the emotional disorders.* New York: Penguin Books.

Beck, J. C., & Schouten, R. (2000). Workplace violence and psychiatric practice. *Bulletin of the Menninger Clinic, 64*, 36–48.

Beck, M. (2008). Sorting through the choices for menopause hormones. *Wall Street Journal,* p. D1.

Becker, G., Beyene, Y., Newsom, E., & Mayen, N. (2003). Creating continuity through mutual assistance: Intergenerational reciprocity in four ethnic groups. *Journals of Gerontology: Series B: Psychological Sciences and Social Sciences, 58B,* S151–S159.

Beckman, L. J., & Harvey, S. M. (2005). Current reproductive technologies: Increased access and choice? *Journal of Social Issues, 61*, 1–20.

Beere, C. A. (1990). *Gender roles: A handbook of tests and measures.* New York: Greenwood.

Begley, M., & Quayle, E. (2007). The lived experience of adults bereaved by suicide: A phenomenological study. *Crisis: The Journal of Crisis Intervention and Suicide Prevention, 28*, 26–34.

Begley, S. (1995, September 2). The baby myth. *Newsweek,* pp. 38–41.

Behrman, R. E., & Butler, A. S. (2007). *Preterm birth: Causes, consequences and prevention.* Washington, DC: National Academies Press.

Beit-Hallahmi, B. (1987). Critical periods in psychoanalytic theories of personality development. In M. H. Bornstein (Ed.), *Sensitive periods in development: Interdisciplinary perspectives* (pp. 211–221). Hillsdale, NJ: Erlbaum.

Belanger, N. D., & Desrochers, S. (2001). Can 6-month-old infants process causality in different types of causal events? *British Journal of Developmental Psychology, 19*, 11–21.

Beliefnet (2007). What are the last rites? Retrieved October 30, 2007, from http://www.beliefnet.com/story/163/story_16366.html

Bell, L., Burtless, G., Gornich, J., & Smeeding, T.M. (2007). Failure to launch: Cross-national trends in the transition to economic independence. In S. Danzinger & C.E. Rouse (Eds.), *The price of independence* (pp. 27–55). New York: Russell Sage Foundation.

Bell, S. M., & Ainsworth, M. D. S. (1972). Infant crying and maternal responsiveness. *Child Development, 43*, 1171–1190.

Belsky, J. (1996). Parent, infant, and social-contextual antecedents of father–son attachment security. *Development Psychology, 32*, 905–913.

Belsky, J. (2006). Determinants and consequences of infant-parent attachment. In L. Balter & C. S. Tamis-LeMonda (Eds.), *Child psychology: A handbook of contemporary issues* (2nd ed., pp. 53–77). New York, NY: Psychology Press.

Belsky, J., Campbell, S. B., Cohn, J. F., & Moore, G. (1996). Instability of infant–parent attachment security. *Developmental Psychology, 32*, 921–924.

Belsky, J., Fish, M., & Isabella, R. (1991). Continuity and discontinuity in infant negative and positive emotionality: Family antecedents and attachment consequences. *Developmental Psychology, 27*, 421–431.

Belsky, J. & Pluess, M. (2009). The nature (and nurture?) of plasticity in early human development. *Perspectives on Psychological Science, 4*, 345–351.

Belsky, J., & Rovine, M. (1990). Patterns of marital change across the transition to parenthood. *Journal of Marriage and the Family, 52*, 5–20.

Belsky, J., Vandell, D. L., Burchinal, M., Clarke-Stewart, K. A., McCartney, K., & Owen, M. T. (2007). Are there long-term effects of early child care? *Child Development, 78*, 681–701.

Bem, S. L. (1981). Gender schema theory: A cognitive account of sex-typing. *Psychological Review, 88*, 354–364.

Bem, S. L. (1989). Genital knowledge and gender constancy in preschool children. *Child Development, 60*, 649–662.

Bem, S. L. (1993). *The lenses of gender.* New Haven, CT: Yale University Press.

Benasich, A. A., & Leevers, H. J. (2003). Processing of rapidly presented auditory cues in infancy: Implications for later language development. In H. Hayne & J. W. Fagen (Eds.), Progress in infancy research (Vol. 3, pp. 245–288). Mahwah, NJ: Lawrence Erlbaum.

Ben-Dat Fisher, D., Serbin, L. A., Stack, D. M., Ruttle, P. L., Ledingham, J. E., & Schwartzman, A. E. (2007). Intergenerational predictors of diurnal cortisol secretions in early adulthood. *Infant and Child Development, 16*, 151–170.

Benedict, R. (1934/1950). *Patterns of culture.* New York: New American Library.

Benenson, J. F. (1993). Greater preference among females than males for dyadic interaction in early childhood. *Child Development, 64*, 544–555.

Bengston, V. L. (2001). Beyond the nuclear family: The increasing importance of multigenerational bonds. *Journal of Marriage and the Family, 63*, 1–16.

Benjet, C., & Hernandez-Guzman, L. (2002). A short-term longitudinal study of pubertal change, gender, and psychological wellbeing of Mexican early adolescents. *Journal of Youth and Adolescence, 31*, 429–442.

Benson, J. B., & Uzgiris, I. C. (1985). Effect of self-initiated locomotion on infant search activity. *Developmental Psychology, 21*, 923–931.

Benson, M. J., Harris, P. B., & Rogers, C. S. (1992). Identity consequences of attachment to mothers and fathers among late adolescents. *Journal of Research on Adolescence, 2*, 187–204.

Benson, P. L. (1992). *The troubled journey: A profile of American youth.* Minneapolis: RespecTeen/Lutheran Brotherhood.

Berg, J. H., & Peplau, L. A. (1982). Loneliness: The relationship of self-disclosure and androgyny. *Personality and Social Psychology Bulletin, 8*, 624–630.

Berg, K., Hines, M., & Allen, S. (2002). Wheelchair users at home: Few home modifications and many injurious falls. *American Journal of Public Health, 92*, 48.

Bergeman, C. S., Plomin, R., Pedersen, N. L., McClearn, G. E., & Nesselroade, J. R. (1990). Genetic and environmental influences on social support: The Swedish adoption/twin study of aging. *Journal of Gerontology, 45,* P101–P106.

Berk, L. E. (2004). *Infants, children, and adolescents* (5th ed.). Needham Heights, MA: Allyn & Bacon.

Berkman, L. F., Glass, T., Brisette, I., & Seeman, T. E. (2000). From social integration to health: Durkheim in the new millennium. Social Science and Medicine, *51,* 843-857.

Berlin, L. J., & Cassidy, J. (1999). Relations among relationships: Contributions from attachment theory and research. In J. Cassidy & P. R. Shaver (Eds.), *Handbook of attachment: Theory, research, and clinical applications* (pp. 688–712). New York: Guilford Press.

Berlin, L. J., Ispa, J. M., Fine, M. A., Malone, P. S., Brooks-Gunn, J., Brady-Smith, C., Ayoub, C., & Bai, Y. (2009). Correlates and consequences of spanking and verbal punishment for low-income white, African American, and Mexican American toddlers. *Child Development, 80,* 1403–1420.

Berman, W. H., & Sperling, M. B. (1991). Parental attachment and emotional distress in the transition to college. *Journal of Youth and Adolescence, 20,* 427–440.

Bernard, J. (1972). *The future of marriage.* New York: World.

Berndt, T. J., & Keefe, K. (1995). Friends' influence on adolescents' adjustment to school. *Child Development, 66,* 1312–1329.

Berndt, T. J., & Murphy, L. M. (2002). Influences of friends and friendships: Myths, truths, and research recommendations. In R. V. Kail (Ed.), *Advances in child development and behavior* (Vol. 30, pp. 275–310). San Diego: Academic Press.

Bernichon, T., Cook, K. E., & Brown, J. D. (2003). Seeking self-evaluative feedback: The interactive role of global self-esteem and specific self-views. *Journal of Personality and Social Psychology, 84,* 194–204.

Bernier, A., Larose, S., Boivin, M., & Soucy, N. (2004). Attachment state of mind: Implications for adjustment to college. *Journal of Adolescent Research, 19,* 783–806.

Berrueta-Clement, J. R., Schweinhart, L. J., Barnett, W. S., Epstein, A. S., & Weikart, D. P. (1984). *Changed lives: The effects of the Perry Preschool Program on youths through age 19.* Ypsilanti, MI: High/Scope Press.

Bertalanffy, L. von (1950). The theory of open systems in physics and biology. *Science, 111,* 23–28.

Bertalanffy, L. von (1968). *General systems theory* (rev. ed.). New York: Braziller.

Berzonsky, M. D. (1989). Identity style: Conceptualization and measurement. *Journal of Adolescent Research, 4,* 267–281.

Berzonsky, M. D. (1993). Identity style, gender, and social-cognitive reasoning. *Journal of Adolescent Research, 8,* 289–296.

Berzonsky, M. D. (2003). The structure of identity: Commentary on Jane Kroger's view of identity status transition. *Identity, 3,* 231–245.

Berzonsky, M. D., & Kinney, A. (2008). Identity processing style and defense mechanisms. *Polish Psychological Bulletin, 39,* 111–117.

Berzonsky, M. D., & Kuk, L. S. (2000). Identity status, identity processing style, and the transition to university. *Journal of Adolescent Research, 15,* 81–98.

Berzonsky, M. D., & Sullivan, C. (1992). Social-cognitive aspects of identity style: Need for cognition, experiential openness, and introspection. *Journal of Adolescent Research, 7,* 140–155.

Bess, A. (2001, August 26). Chocolatiers face slavery minefield in Africa. *Reuters.* Retrieved September 8, 2001, from http://biz.yahoo.com/rf/010826/n26310591.html

Best, K. M., Hauser, S. T., & Allen, J. P. (1997). Predicting young adult competencies: Adolescent era parent and individual influences. *Journal of Adolescent Research, 12,* 90–112.

Betancourt, H., & Lopez, S. R. (1993). The study of culture, ethnicity, and race in American psychology. *American Psychologist, 48,* 629–637.

Bettencourt, B. A., & Hume, D. (1999). The cognitive contents of social-group identity: Values, emotions, and relationships. *European Journal of Social Psychology, 29,* 113–121.

Betz, N. E. (2001). Career self efficacy. *Contemporary models in vocational psychology* (pp. 55–78). Mahwah, NJ: Lawrence Erlbaum.

Betz, N. E. (2007). Career self efficacy: Exemplary recent research and emerging directions. *Journal of Career Assessment, 15,* 403–422.

Beyers, W. & Seiffge-Krenke, I. (2010). Does identity precede intimacy? Testing Erikson's theory on romantic development in emerging adults of the 21st century. *Journal of Adolescent Research, 25,* 387–415.

Bialystok, E. & Craik, F. I. M. (2010). Cognitive and linguistic processing in the bilingual mind. *Current Directions in Psychological Science, 19,* 19–23.

Bick, D. & Howard, L. (2010). When should women be screened for postnatal depression? *The Expert Review of Neurotherapeutics, 10,* 151–154.

Biddle, B. J. (1979). *Role theory: Expectations, identities, and behaviors.* New York: Academic Press.

Biddle, B. J. (1986). Recent developments in role theory. In R. H. Turner & S. F. Short, Jr. (Eds.), *Annual Review of Sociology, 12,* 67–92.

Biddle, B. J., & Thomas, E. J. (1966). *Role theory: Concepts and research.* New York: Wiley.

Bigler, R. S., & Liben, L. S. (1992). Cognitive mechanisms in children's gender stereotyping: Theoretical and educational implications of a cognitive based intervention. *Child Development, 63,* 1351–1363.

Bigler, R. S., Spears Brown, C., & Markell, M. (2001). When groups are not created equal: Effects of group status on the formation of intergroup attitudes in children. *Child Development, 72,* 1151–1162.

Bijstra, J., Van Geert, P., & Jackson, S. (1989). Conservation and the appearance–reality distinction: What do children really know and what do they answer? *British Journal of Developmental Psychology, 7,* 43–53.

Bilsker, D., Schiedel, D., & Marcia, J. (1988). Sex differences in identity status. *Sex Roles, 18,* 231–236.

Biringen, Z., Emde, R. N., Campos, J. J., & Appelbaum, M. I. (1995). Affective reorganization in the infant, the mother, and the dyad: The role of upright locomotion and its timing. *Child Development, 66,* 499–514.

Birsch, K. H., Munz, D., Bemmerer-Mayer, K., Terinde, R., Kreienberg, R., & Kachele, H. (2003). Coping styles of pregnant women after prenatal ultrasound screening for fetal malformation. *Journal of Psychosomatic Research, 55,* 91–97.

Blackwell, D. L, & Lichter, D. T. (2000). Mate selection among married and cohabiting couples. *Journal of Family Issues, 21,* 275– 302.

Blackwell, D. L., & Lichter, D. T. (2004). Homogamy among dating, cohabiting and married couples. *Sociological Quarterly, 45,* 719–737.

Blain, M. D., Thompson, J. M., & Whiffen, V. E. (1993). Attachment and perceived social support in late adolescence: The interaction between working models of self and others. *Journal of Adolescent Research, 8,* 226–241.

Blair, C. (2002). Integrating cognition and emotion in a neurobiological conceptualization of children's functioning at school entry. *American Psychologist, 57,* 111–127.

Blair-Loy, M. (2001). Cultural constructions of family schemas: The case of women finance executives. *Gender & Society, 15,* 687–709.

Blanchard, C., Perreault, S., & Vallerand, R. J. (1998). Participation in team sport: A self-expansion perspective. *International Journal of Sport Psychology, 29,* 289–302.

Blanck, R., & Blanck, G. (1986). *Beyond ego psychology.* New York: Columbia University Press.

Blasi, A. (1991). The self as subject in the study of personality. In D. Ozer, J. Healy, & A. Stewart (Eds.), *Perspectives in personality* (Vol. 3, Part A, pp. 19–37). London: Kingsley.

Blass, E. M., & Ciaramitaro, V. (1994). A new look at some old mechanisms in human newborns: Taste and tactile determinants of state, affect, and action. *Monographs of the Society for Research in Child Development, 59* (Serial No. 1).

Blass, E. M., & Hoffmeyer, L. B. (1991). Sucrose as an analgesic for newborn infants. *Pediatrics, 87,* 215–218.

Bleeker, M. M., & Jacobs, J. E. (2004). Achievement in math and science: Do mothers' beliefs matter 12 years later?

Journal of Educational Psychology, 96, 97–109.

Bloom, L. (1993, Winter). World learning. *Society for Research in Child Development Newsletter,* pp. 1, 9, 13.

Bloom, M. (2009). Social competency: A blueprint for promoting academic and social competence in after-school programs. In T. P. Gullotta, M. Bloom, C. P. Gullotta, & J. C. Messina (Eds.), *A blueprint for promoting academic and social competence in after-school programs: Issues in children's and families' lives* (pp. 1–19). New York: Springer.

Blos, P. (1962). *On adolescence: A psychoanalytic interpretation.* New York: The Free Press.

Blos, P. (1967). The second individuation process of adolescence. *Psychoanalytic Study of the Child, 23,* 162–186.

Blos, P. (1979). *The adolescent passage.* New York: International Universities Press.

Bluck, S., & Gluck, J. (2004). Making things better and learning a lesson: Experiencing wisdom across the lifespan. *Journal of Personality, 72,* 543–572.

Blum, R. W., Beuhring, T., Shew, M. L., Bearinger, L. H., Sieving, R. E., & Resnick, M. D. (2000). The effects of race/ethnicity, income, and family structure on adolescent risk behaviors. *American Journal of Public Health, 90,* 1879–1884.

Blustein, D.L. (2008). The role of work in psychological health and well-being: A conceptual, historical and public policy perspective. *American Psychologist, 63,* 228–240.

Blyth, D. A., Bulcroft, R., & Simmons, R. G. (1981). *The impact of puberty on adolescents: A longitudinal study.* Paper presented at the annual convention of the American Psychological Association, Los Angeles, CA.

Boerner, K., Schulz, R., & Horowitz, A. (2004). Positive aspects of caregiving and adaptation to bereavement. *Psychology and Aging, 19,* 668–675.

Bohan, J. S. (1993). Regarding gender. *Psychology of Women Quarterly, 17,* 5–21.

Bohlin, G., Bengtsgard, K., & Andersson, K. (2000). Social inhibition and overfriendliness as related to socioemotional functioning in 7- and 8-year-old children. *Journal of Clinical Child Psychology, 29,* 414–423.

Bohlmeijer, E., Smit, F., & Cuijpers, P. (2003). Effects of reminiscence and life review on late-life depression: A meta-analysis. *International Journal of Geriatric Psychiatry, 18,* 1088–1094.

Bolton, F. G., Jr., & MacEachron, A. E. (1988). Adolescent male sexuality: A developmental perspective. *Journal of Adolescent Research, 3,* 259–273.

Bomar, J. A., & Sabatelli, R. M. (1996). Family system dynamics, gender, and psychosocial maturity in late adolescence. *Journal of Adolescent Research, 11,* 421–439.

Bombar, M. L., & Littig, L. W. (1996). Babytalk as a communication of intimate attachment: An initial study in adult romances and friendships. *Personal Relationships, 3,* 137–158.

Bonanno, G. A., Wortman, C. B., & Nesse, R. M. (2004). Prospective patterns of resilience and maladjustment during widowhood. *Psychology and Aging, 19,* 260–271.

Boom, J., Brugman, D., & van der Heijden, P. G. M. (2001). Hierarchical structure of moral stages assessed by a sorting task. *Child Development, 72,* 535–548.

Booth, A. E. (2009). Causal supports for early word learning. *Child Development, 80,* 1243–1250.

Booth, A., Johnson, D. R., Granger, D. A., Crouter, A. C., & McHale, S. (2003). Testosterone and child and adolescent adjustment: The moderating role of parent–child relationships. *Developmental Psychology, 39,* 85–98.

Bongaarts, J., & Zimmer, Z. (2002). Living arrangements of older adults in the developing world. *The Journals of Gerontology Series B: Psychological Sciences and Social Sciences, 57,* S145–S157.

Boonstra, H.D. (2009). The challenge in helping young adults better manage their reproductive lives. *Guttmacher Policy Review,* 12.

Borden, W. (2000). The relational paradigm in contemporary psychoanalysis: Toward a psychodynamically informed social work perspective. *Social Service Review, 74,* 352–380.

Borkenau, P., Riemann, R., Angleitner, A., & Spinath, F. M. (2001). Genetic and environmental influences on observed personality: Evidence from the German Observational Study of Adult Twins. *Journal of Personality and Social Psychology, 80,* 655–668.

Borman, K. M., & Hopkins, M. (1987). Leaving school for work. *Research in the Sociology of Education and Socialization, 7,* 131–159.

Bornstein, M. H. (1985). How infant and mother jointly contribute to developing cognitive competence in the child. *Proceedings of the National Academy of Science, USA, 82,* 7470–7473.

Bornstein, M. H. (Ed.). (1987). *Sensitive periods in development: Interdisciplinary perspectives* (pp. 211–221). Hillsdale, NJ: Erlbaum.

Bornstein, M. H. (1995). Parenting infants. In M. H. Bornstein (Ed.), *Handbook of parenting: Vol. I. Children and parenting* (pp. 3–41). Mahwah, NJ: Erlbaum.

Bornstein, M. H. (2001). Mother–infant interaction. In G. Bremner & A. Fogel (Eds.), *Blackwell handbook of infant development* (pp. 269–295). Malden, MA: Blackwell.

Bornstein, M. H. (Ed.). (2002a). *Handbook of parenting* (5 volumes). Mahwah, NJ: Erlbaum.

Bornstein, M. H. (2002b). Parenting infants. In M. H. Bornstein (Ed.), *Handbook of Parenting: Vol. 1. Children and parenting* (2nd ed., pp. 3–43). Mahwah, NJ: Erlbaum.

Bornstein, M. H., Kessen, W., & Weiskopf, S. (1976). The categories of hue in infancy. *Science, 191,* 201–202.

Bornstein, M. H., & Suess, P. E. (2000). Child and mother cardiac vagal tone: Continuity, stability and concordance across the first 5 years. *Developmental Psychology, 36,* 54–65.

Boss, P. (1999). *Ambiguous loss.* Cambridge, MA: Harvard University Press.

Boss, P. (2002a). Ambiguous loss: Working with the families of the missing. *Family Process, 41,* 14–17.

Boss, P. (2002b). *Family stress management: A contextual approach* (2nd ed.). Thousand Oaks, CA: Sage.

Boss, P. (2004). Ambiguous loss research, theory, and practice: Reflections after 9/11. *Journal of Marriage and the Family, 66,* 551–566.

Boss, P. (2007). Ambiguous loss theory: Challenges for scholars and practitioners. *Family Relations, 56,* 105–111.

Bosworth, H. B., & Schaie, K. W. (1997). The relationship of social environment, social networks, and health outcomes in the Seattle longitudinal study: Two analytical approaches. *Journal of Gerontology, 52,* P197–P205.

Bouchard, T. J., Jr., & Pederson, N. (1999). Twins reared apart: Nature's double experiment. In M. C. LaBuda & E. L. Grigorenko (Eds.), *On the way to individuality: Current methodological issues in behavioral genetics* (pp. 71–93). Huntington, NY: Nova Science.

Bouldin, P. (2006). An investigation of the fantasy predisposition and fantasy style of children with imaginary companions. *Journal of Genetic Psychology, 167,* 17–29.

Bouldin, P., & Pratt, C. (1999). Characteristics of preschool and school-age children with imaginary companions. *Journal of Genetic Psychology, 160,* 397–410.

Bowen, M. (1978). *Family therapy and clinical practice.* New York: Aronson.

Bower, T. G. R. (1987). *Development in infancy* (2nd ed.). New York: W. H. Freeman.

Bowlby, J. (1960). Separation anxiety. *International Journal of Psychoanalysis, 41,* 69–113.

Bowlby, J. (1969/1982). *Attachment and loss: Vol. 1. Attachment.* New York: Basic Books.

Bowlby, J. (1980). *Attachment and loss: Vol. 3. Loss, sadness, and depression.* New York: Basic Books.

Bowlby, J. (1988). *A secure base: Parent-child attachment and healthy human development.* New York: Basic Books.

Bowman, B. T., Donovan, M. S., & Burns, M. S. (2000). *Eager to learn: Educating our preschoolers.* Washington, DC: National Academy Press.

Boyatzis, C. J., & Watson, M. W. (1993). Preschool children's symbolic representation of objects through gestures. *Child Development, 64,* 729–735.

Boyd, D.M. & Ellison, N.B. (2007). Social network sites: Definition, history and scholarship. *The Journal of Computer-Mediated Communication, 13,* 210–230.

Boyd, J. & Zimbardo, P.G. (1996). Constructing time after death: The transcendental-future time perspective. *Time and Society, 6,* 35–54.

Boykin, A. W. (1994). Harvesting talent and culture. In R. J. Rossi (Ed.), *Schools and students at risk: Context and framework for positive change* (pp. 116–138). New York: Teachers College Press.

Bozick, R. (2007). Making it through the first year of college: The role of students' economic resources, employment and living arrangements. *Sociology of Education, 80,* 261–285.

Bradbury, R. (1957/1964). *Dandelion Wine.* New York: Bantam Books.

Bradford, K., & Hawkins, A. J. (2006). Learning competent fathering: A longitudinal analysis of marital intimacy and fathering. *Fathering, 4,* 215–234.

Bradley, C. B., McMurray, R. G., Harrell, J. S., & Deng, S. (2000). Changes in common activities of 3rd through 10th graders: The CHIC study. *Medicine and Science in Sports and Exercise, 32,* 2071–2078.

Bradley, C. L. (1997). Generativity-stagnation: Development of a status model. *Developmental Review, 17,* 262–290.

Bradley, C. L., & Marcia, J. E. (1998). Generativity-stagnation: A five-category model. *Journal of Personality, 66,* 39–64.

Bradley, R. H., Caldwell, B. M., & Rock, S. L. (1988). Home environment and school performance. A ten-year followup and examination of three models of environmental action. *Child Development, 59,* 852–867.

Bradley, R. H., & Corwyn, R. F. (2002). Socioeconomic status and child development. *Annual Review of Psychology, 53,* 371–399.

Bradmetz, J. (1999). Precursors of formal thought: A longitudinal study. *British Journal of Developmental Psychology, 17,* 61–81.

Bradshaw, Z., & Slade, P. (2003). The effects of induced abortion on emotional experiences and relationships: A critical review of the literature. *Clinical Psychology Review, 23,* 929–948.

Braine, M. D. S. (1976). *Children's first word combinations. Monographs of the Society for Research in Child Development, 41*(1).

Brainerd, C. J. (1977). Cognitive development and concept learning: An interpretive review. *Psychological Bulletin, 84,* 919–939.

Braithwaite, V. (2004). The hope process and social inclusion. In V. Braithwaite (Ed.), *Hope, power, and governance. The Annals of the American Academy of Political and Social Science* (pp. 128–151). Thousand Oaks, CA: Sage.

Bramlett, M. D., & Mosher, W. D. (2002). Cohabitation, marriage, divorce, and remarriage in the United States, NCHS. *Vital Health Stat, 23* (22).

Brandon, P. E. (2000). An analysis of kinprovided child care in the context of intrafamily exchanges: Linking components of family support for parents raising young children. *The American Journal of Economics and Sociology, 59,* 191.

Brandtstädter, J. (2002). Searching for paths to successful development and aging: Integrating developmental and action theoretical perspectives. In L. Pulkkinen & A. Caspi (Eds.), *Paths to successful development: Personality in the life course* (pp. 380–408). New York: Cambridge University Press.

Brandtstädter, J., Rothermund, K., Kranz, D., & Kühn, W. (2010). Final decentrations, personal goals, rationality perspectives, and the awareness of life's finitude. *European Psychologist, 15,* 152–163.

Braungart, J. M., Plomin, R., Defries, J. C., & Fulker, D. W. (1992). Genetic influence on tester-rated infant temperament as assessed by Bayley's Infant Behavior Record: Nonadoptive and adoptive siblings and twins. *Developmental Psychology, 28*(1), 40–47.

Braungart-Rieker, J. M., Garwood, M. M., Powers, B. P., & Wang, X. (2001). Parental sensitivity, infant affect, and affect regulation: Predictors of later attachment. *Child Development, 72,* 252–270.

Brazelton, T. B. (1974). *Toddlers and parents: A declaration of independence.* Delacorte Press.

Brazelton, T. B. (1987a). Behavioral competence of the newborn infant. In G. B. Avery (Ed.), *Neonatology: Pathophysiology and management of the newborn* (pp. 379–399). Philadelphia: Lippincott.

Brazelton, T. B. (1987b). *What every baby knows* (pp. 11–13). Reading, MA: Addison-Wesley.

Brazelton, T. B., Koslowski, B., & Main, M. (1974). The origins of reciprocity: The early mother-infant interaction. In M. Lewis & L. A. Rosenblum (Eds.), *The effect of the infant on its caregiver* (pp. 49–76). New York: Wiley-Interscience.

Brazelton, T. B., Nugent, J. K., & Lester, B. M. (1987). Neonatal behavioral assessment scale. In J. D. Osofsky (Ed.), *Handbook of infant development* (2nd ed., pp. 780–817). New York: Wiley.

Breakwell, G. M. (1986). *Coping with threatened identities.* London: Methuen.

Breault, K. D., & Kposowa, A. J. (1987). Explaining divorce in the United States, 1980. *Journal of Marriage and the Family, 49,* 549–558.

Brendgen, M., Lamarche, V., Wanner, B., & Vitaro, F. (2010). Links between friendship relations and early adolescents' trajectories of depressed mood. *Developmental Psychology, 46,* 491–501.

Brennan, K. A., & Morris, K. A. (1997). Attachment styles, self-esteem, and patterns of seeking feedback from romantic partners. *Personality and Social Psychology Bulletin, 23,* 23–31.

Brennan, K. A., & Shaver, P. R. (1995). Dimensions of adult attachment, affect regulation, and romantic relationship functioning. *Personality and Social Psychology Bulletin, 21,* 267–283.

Brennan, R. T., Barnett, R. C., & Gareis, K. C. (2001). When she earns more than he does: A longitudinal study of dual-earner couples. *Journal of Marriage and the Family, 63,* 168–182.

Bretherton, I. (1985). Attachment theory: Retrospect and prospect. In I. Bretherton & E. Everett (Eds.), *Growing points of attachment theory and research* (pp. 3–35). *Monographs of the Society for Research in Child Development, 50* (1–2, Serial No. 209).

Bretherton, I. (1988). Open communication and internal working models: Their roles in the development of attachment relationships. In R. Dienstbier & R. A. Thompson (Eds.), *Nebraska Symposium on Motivation, 1988: Socioemotional Development, 36,* 60–61.

Bretherton, I. (1990). Open communication and internal working models: Their role in the development of attachment relationships. In R. Dienstbier & R. A. Thompson (Eds.), *Nebraska Symposium on Motivation 1988: Vol. 36. Socioemotional Development* (pp. 57–113). Lincoln: University of Nebraska Press.

Bretherton, I., & Munholland, K. A. (1999). Internal working models in attachment relationships. In J. Cassidy & P. R. Shaver (Eds.), *Handbook of attachment: Theory, research, and clinical applications* (pp. 89–111). New York: Guilford Press.

Bretschneider, J. G., & McCoy, N. L. (1988). Sexual interest and behavior in healthy 80- to 102-year-olds. *Archives of Sexual Behavior, 17,* 109–129.

Brewster, A. L., Nelson, J. P., McCanne, T. R., Lucas, D. R., & Milner, J. S. (1998). Gender differences in physiological reactivity to infant cries and smiles in military families. *Child Abuse and Neglect, 22,* 775–788.

Bridges, L. J., Connell, J. P., & Belsky, J. (1988). Similarities and differences in infant–mother and infant–father interaction in the strange situation: A component process analysis. *Developmental Psychology, 24,* 92–100.

Brierley, J. (1993). *Growth in children.* London: Cassell.

Brim, O. G. (1966). Socialization through the life cycle. In O.G. Brim and S. Wheeler (Eds.) *Socialization after childhood: Two essays.* New York: Wiley.

Brim, G. (1992). *Ambition: How we manage success and failure throughout our lives.* New York: Basic Books.

Bringle, J. R. (2007). Psychosocial processes at the end of life: The relationship between generativity and fear of death. *Dissertation Abstracts International: Section B: The Sciences and Engineering, 68,* 1296.

Brinkmeyer, M. Y., & Eyberg, S. M. (2003). Parent-child interaction therapy for oppositional children. In A.E. Kazdin & J.R. Weisz (Eds.), *Evidence-based psychotherapies for children and adolescents.* New York: Guildford Press, pp. 204–223.

Brisch, K. H., Bechinger, D., Betzler, S., Heinemann, H., Kächele, H., Pohlandt, F., Schmücker, G., & Buchheim, A. (2005). Attachment quality in very low-birthweight premature infants in relation to maternal attachment representations and neurological development. *Parenting: Science and Practice, 5,* 311–331.

Brisch, K. H., Munz, D., Bemmerer-Mayer, K., Terinde, R., Kreienberg, R., & Kächele, H., (2003). Coping styles of pregnant women after prenatal ultrasound screening for fetal malformation. *Journal of Psychosomatic Research, 55,* 91–97.

Brockner, J. (1984). Low self-esteem and behavioral plasticity. In L. Wheeler (Ed.), *Review of personality and social psychology* (Vol. 4, pp. 237–271). Beverly Hills, CA: Sage.

Broderick, C. B. (1993). *Understanding family process: Basics of family systems theory.* Newbury Park, CA: Sage.

Broen, A. N., Moum, T., Bodtker, A. S., & Ekeberg, O. (2005). Reasons for induced abortion and their relation to women's emotional distress: A prospective, two-year follow-up study. *General Hospital Psychiatry, 27,* 36–43.

Bronfenbrenner, U. (1979). *The ecology of human development.* Cambridge, MA: Harvard University Press.

Bronfenbrenner, U. (1995). Developmental ecology through space and time: A future perspective. In P. Moen, G. H. Elder, et al. (Eds.), *Examining lives in context: Perspectives on the ecology of human development* (pp. 619–647). Washington, DC: American Psychological Association.

Bronfenbrenner, U. (1999). Environments in developmental perspective: Theoretical and operational models. In S. L. Friedman, T. D., & Wachs, (Eds). Measuring environment across the life span: Emerging methods and concepts. (pp. 3–28). Washington, DC, US: American Psychological Association.

Bronfenbrenner, U. (2004). *Making human beings human: Bioecological perspectives on human development.* Thousand Oaks, CA: Sage.

Bronson, G. W. (1973). Infants' reactions to an unfamiliar person. In L. J. Stone, H. T. Smith, & L. B. Murphy (Eds.), *The competent infant.* New York: Basic Books.

Bronstein, P., Duncan, P., Clauson, J., Abrams, C., Yannett, N., Ginsburg, G., & Milne, M. (1998). Preventing middle school adjustment problems for children from lower income families: A program for aware parenting. *Journal of Applied Developmental Psychology, 19,* 129–152.

Brookes, H., Slater, A., Quinn, P. C., Lewkowizc, D. J., Hayes, R., & Brown, E. (2001). Three-month-old infants learn arbitrary auditory-visual pairings between voices and faces. *Infant and Child Development, 10,* 75–82.

Brooks-Gunn, J., & Reiter, E. O. (1990). The role of pubertal processes. In S. S. Feldman & G. R. Elliott (Eds.), *At the threshold: The developing adolescent* (pp. 16–53). Cambridge, MA: Harvard University Press.

Brooks-Gunn, J., & Warren, M. P. (1988). The psychological significance of secondary sexual characteristics in 9- to 11-year-old girls. *Child Development, 59,* 161–169.

Brown, B. B. (1990). Peer groups and peer cultures. In S. S. Feldman & G. R. Elliott (Eds.), *At the threshold: The developing adolescent* (pp. 171–196). Cambridge, MA: Harvard University Press.

Brown, B. B. (2004). Adolescents' relationships with peers. In R. M. Lerner & L. Steinberg (Eds.), *Handbook of adolescent psychology* (2nd ed., pp. 363–394). New York: Wiley.

Brown, B. B., Mounts, N., Lamborn, S. D., & Steinberg, L. (1993). Parenting practices and peer group affiliation in adolescence. *Child Development, 64,* 467–482.

Brown, D. W., Balluz, L. S., Heath, G. W., Moriarty, D. G., Ford, E. S., Giles, W. H., & Mokdad, A. H. (2003). Associations between recommended levels of physical activity and health-related quality of life: Findings from the 2001 Behavioral Risk Factor Surveillance System (BRFSS) survey. *Preventive Medicine: An International Journal Devoted to Practice & Theory, 37,* 520–528.

Brown, I., Jr., & Inouye, D. K. (1978). Learned helplessness through modeling: The role of perceived similarity in competence. *Journal of Personality and Social Psychology, 36,* 900–908.

Brown, J. D. (2003). The self-enhancement motive in collectivistic cultures: The rumors of my death have been greatly exaggerated. *Journal of Cross-Cultural Psychology, 34,* 603–605.

Brown, J. D., Cohen, P., Chen, H., Smailes, E., & Johnson, J. G. (2004). Sexual trajectories of abused and neglected youths. *Journal of Developmental and Behavioral Pediatrics, 25,* 77–82.

Brown, J. D., Dutton, K. A., & Cook, K. E. (2001). From the top down: Self-esteem and self-evaluation. *Cognition and Emotion, 15,* 615–631.

Brown, J. D., & Gallagher, F. M. (1992). Coming to terms with failure: Private self-enhancement and public self-effacement. *Journal of Experimental Social Psychology, 28,* 3–22.

Brown, J. D., & Mankowski, T. A. (1993). Self-esteem, mood, and self-evaluation: Changes in mood and the way you see you. *Journal of Personality and Social Psychology, 64,* 421–430.

Brown, J. D., & Smart, S. A. (1991). The self and social conduct: Linking self-representation to prosocial behavior. *Journal of Personality and Social Psychology, 60,* 368–375.

Brown, J. L., & Pollitt, E. (1996). Malnutrition, poverty, and intellectual development. *Scientific American, 274,* 38–43.

Brown, J. R., & Dunn, J. (1992). Talk with your mother or your sibling? Developmental changes in early family conversations about feelings. *Child Development, 63,* 336–349.

Brown, J. V., Bakeman, R., Coles, C. D., Platzman, K. A., & Lynch, M. E. (2004). Prenatal cocaine exposure: A comparison of 2-year-old children in parental and nonparental care. *Child Development, 75,* 1282–1295.

Brown, R. (1965). *Social psychology.* New York: Free Press.

Brown, S. K. (2003). *Staying ahead of the curve 2003: The AARP working in retirement study.* Washington, DC: AARP. Retrieved October 17, 2007, from http://www.aarp.org/research/reference/publicopinions/aresearch-import-417.html

Brown, S. L., & Booth, A. (1996). Cohabitation versus marriage: A comparison of relationship quality. *Journal of Marriage and the Family, 58,* 668–678.

Brown, W. H., Pfeiffer, K. A., McIver, K. L., Dowda, M., Addy, C. L., & Pate, R. R. (2009). Social and environmental factors associated with preschoolers' non-sedentary physical activity. *Child Development, 80,* 45–58.

Browning, C. R., & Cagney, K. A. (2003). Moving beyond poverty: Neighborhood structure, social processes, and health. *Journal of Health and Social Behavior, 44,* 552–571.

Brownlee, S. (1998, June 15). Baby talk. *U.S. News and World Report,* 48–55.

Brownlee, S. (1999). Inside the teen brain. *U.S. News and World Report, 127,* 44–54.

Brown University. (2004). The female athlete triad. *Health Education.* Retrieved November 28, 2004, from http://www.brown.edu/Student_Services/Health_Services/Health_Education/nutrition/ec_fatriad.htm

Brubaker, T. H. (1990). Families in later life: A burgeoning research area. *Journal of Marriage and the Family, 52,* 959–981.

Bruner, J. (2001). Human infancy and the beginnings of human competence. In J. A. Bargh & D. K Apsley (Eds.), *Unraveling the complexities of social life: A festschrift in honor of Robert B. Zajonc* (pp. 133–139). Washington, DC: American Psychological Association.

Brustad, R. J. (1988). Affective outcomes in competitive youth sport: The influence of intra-personal and socialization factors. *Journal of Sport and Exercise Psychology, 10,* 307–321.

Bryant, J., Carveth, R. A., & Brown, D. (1981). Television viewing and anxiety: An experimental examination. *Journal of Communication, 31,* 106–119.

Bryer, K. B. (1979). The Amish way of death: A study of family support systems. *American Psychologist, 34,* 255–261.

Buckwalter, J. G., Stanczyk, F. A., McCleary, C. A., Bluestein, B. W., Buckwalter, D. K., Rankin, K. P., et al. (1999). Pregnancy, the postpartum, and steroid hormones: Effects on cognition and mood. *Psychoneuroendocrinology, 24,* 69–84.

Buhl, H.M. (2007). Well-being and the child-parent relationship at the transition from university to work life. *Journal of Adolescent Research, 22,* 550–571.

Buhler, C., & Massarik, F. (1968). *The course of human life: A study of goals in the humanistic perspective.* New York: Springer Verlag.

Bui, K.-V. T., Peplau, L. A., & Hill, C. T. (1996). Testing the Rusbult model of relationship commitment and stability in a 15-year study of heterosexual couples. *Personality and Social Psychology Bulletin, 22,* 1244–1257.

Bukowski, W. M. (2001). Friendship and the worlds of childhood. In D. W. Nangle & C. A. Erdley (Eds.), *The role of friendship in psychological adjustment* (pp. 93–105). San Francisco: Jossey-Bass.

Bukowski, W. M., Gauze, C., Hoza, B., & Newcomb, A. F. (1993). Differences and consistency between same-sex and other-sex peer relationships during early adolescence. *Developmental Psychology, 29,* 255–263.

Bullock, H. E., & Morales Waugh, I. (2004). Caregiving around the clock: How women in nursing manage career and family demands. *Journal of Social Issues, 60,* 767–786.

Bullock, K. (2005). Grandfathers and the impact of raising grandchildren. *Journal of Sociology and Social Welfare, 32,* 43–59.

Bullock, M., & Lutkenhaus, P. (1988). The development of volitional behavior in the toddler years. *Child Development, 59,* 664–674.

Bunting, L., & McAuley, C. (2004). Teenage pregnancy and motherhood: The contribution of support. *Child & Family Social Work, 9,* 201–215.

Burchinal, M. R., Roberts, J. E., Riggins, R., Jr., Zeisel, S. A., Neebe, E., & Bryant, D. (2000). Relating quality of center-based child care to early cognitive and language development longitudinally. *Child Development, 71,* 338–357.

Bureau of Labor Statistics (2010). Table 2. Labor force status of persons 16 to 24 years old by school enrollment, educational attainment, sex, race, and Hispanic or Latino ethnicity, October 2009. Retrieved on July 8, 2010, at www.bls .gov/news.release/hsgec.t02.htm.

Burgess, E. W., & Bogue, D. J. (1967). The delinquency research of Clifford R. Shaw and Henry D. McKay and associates. In E. W. Burgess & D. J. Bogue (Eds.), *Urban Sociology* (pp. 293–317). Chicago: University of Chicago Press.

Burleson, B. R., Kunkel, A. W., Samter, W., & Werking, K. J. (1996). Men's and women's evaluations of communication skills in personal relationships: When sex differences make a difference—and when they don't. *Journal of Social and Personal Relationships, 13,* 201–224.

Burnett, D. (1999). Social relationships of Latino grandparent caregivers: A role theory perspective. *The Gerontologist, 39,* 49–58.

Burr, J. A., & Mutchler, J. E. (1993). Nativity, acculturation, and economic statues: Explanation of Asian American living arrangements in later life. *Journal of Gerontology, 48,* S55–S63.

Burr, W. R., & Christensen, C. (1992). Undesirable side effects of enhancing self esteem. *Family Relations, 41,* 480–484.

Burt, R. D., Vaughan, T. L., & Daling, J. R. (1988). Evaluating the risks of cesarean section: Low Apgar score in repeat C-section and vaginal deliveries. *American Journal of Public Health, 78,* 1312–1314.

Burton, S., & Mitchell, P. (2003). Judging who knows best about yourself: Developmental change in citing the self across middle childhood. *Child Development, 74,* 426–443.

Bus, A. G., van IJzendoorn, M. H., & Pellegrini, A. D. (1995). Joint book reading makes for success in learning to read: A meta-analysis on intergenerational transmission of literacy. *Review of Educational Research, 65,* 1–21.

Buschman, T. J., & Miller, E. K. (2007). Top-down versus bottom-up control of attention in the prefrontal and posterior parietal cortices. *Science, 315,* 1860–1862.

Bushman, B. & Anderson, C. (2002). Violent video games and hostile expectations: A test of the general aggression model. *Personality and Social Psychology Bulletin, 28,* 1679–1686.

Buss, A. H., & Plomin, R. (1984). *Temperament: Early developing personality traits.* Hillsdale, NJ: Erlbaum.

Buss, A. H., & Plomin, R. (1986). The EAS approach to temperament. In R. Plomin & J. Dunn (Eds.), *The study of temperament: Changes, continuities, and challenges.* Hillsdale, NJ: Erlbaum.

Buss, D. M. (1994). *The evolution of desire: Strategies of human mating.* New York: Basic Books.

Buss, D. M. (2006). Strategies of human mating. *Psychological Topics, 15,* 239–260.

Buss, D. M., Haselton, M. G., Shackelford, T. K., Bleske, A. L., & Wakefield, J. C. (1998). Adaptations, exaptations, and spandrels. *American Psychologist, 53,* 533–548.

Buss, F. L. (1985). *Dignity: Lower income women tell of their lives and struggles* (pp. 153–154). Ann Arbor: University of Michigan Press.

Butler, C., & Weatherall, A. (2006). "No, we're not playing families": Membership categorization in children's play. *Research on Language and Social Interaction, 39,* 441–470.

Butler, R. (1990). The effects of mastery and competitive conditions on self-assessment at different ages. *Child Development, 61,* 201–210.

Butler, R., & Ruzany, N. (1993). Age and socialization effects on the development of social comparison motives and normative ability assessment in kibbutz and urban children. *Child Development, 64,* 532–543.

Butterfield, E. C., Nelson, T. O., & Peck, V. (1988). Developmental aspects of the feeling of knowing. *Developmental Psychology, 24,* 654–663.

Butterfield, N. (1994). Play as an assessment and intervention strategy for children with language and intellectual disabilities. In K. Linfoot (Ed.), *Communication strategies for people with developmental disabilities: Issues from theory and practice* (pp. 12–44). Baltimore: Brookes.

Buunk, B. P., Kijkstra, P., Kenrick, D. T., & Warntjes, A. (2001). Age preferences for mates as related to gender, own age, and involvement level. *Evolution and Human Behavior, 22,* 241–250.

Buunk, B. P., Zurriaga, R., Peiro, J. M., Nauta, A., & Gosalvez, I. (2005). Social comparisons at work as related to cooperative social climate and to individual differences in social comparison orientation. *Applied Psychology: An International Review, 54,* 61–80.

Buysse, A. (1996). Adolescents, young adults, and AIDS: A study of actual knowledge vs. perceived need for additional information. *Journal of Youth and Adolescence, 25,* 259–271.

Byers-Heinlein, K., Burns, T. C., & Werker, J. F. (2010). The roots of bilingualism in newborns. *Psychological Science, 21,* 343–348.

Cacioppo, J. T., Ernst, J. M, Burleson, M. H., McClintock, M. K., Malarkey, W. B., Hawkley, L. C., Kowalewski, R. B., Paulsen, A., Hobson, J. A., Hugdahl, K., Spiegel, D., & Bernstson, G. G. (2000). Lonely traits and concomitant physiological processes: The MacArthur social neuroscience studies. *International Journal of Psychophysiology, 35,* 143–154.

Cacioppo, J. T., Hawkley, L. C., Ernst, J. M, Burleson, M., Bernstson, G. G., Bita, N., & Spiegel, D. (2006). Loneliness within a nomological net: An evolutionary perspective. *Journal of Research in Personaltiy, 40,* 1054–1085.

Cain, C. S. (2006). *Attachment disorders: Treatment strategies for traumatized children.* Lanham, MD: Jason Aronson.

Cain, K. M., & Dweck, C. S. (1995). The relation between motivational patterns and achievement cognitions through the elementary school years. *Merrill-Palmer Quarterly, 41,* 25–52.

Cain, P. S., & Treiman, D. J. (1981). The DOT as a source of occupational data. *American Sociological Review, 46,* 253–278.

Caldas, S. J. (1993). Current theoretical perspectives on adolescent pregnancy and childbearing in the United States. *Journal of Adolescent Research, 8,* 4–20.

Caldera, Y. M., Huston, A. C., & O'Brien, M. (1989). Social interactions and play patterns of parents and toddlers with feminine, masculine, and neutral toys. *Child Development, 60,* 70–76.

Calkins, S. D. (2004). Early attachment processes and the development of emotional self-regulation. In R. F. Baumeister & K. D. Vohs (Eds.), *Handbook of self-regulation: Research, theory, and application* (pp. 324–339). New York: Guilford Press.

Calkins, S. D., & Dedmon, S. E. (2000). Physiological and behavioral regulation in two-year-old children with aggressive/destructive behavior problems. *Journal of Abnormal Child Psychology, 28,* 103–118.

Calkins, S. D., & Fox, N. A. (1992). The relations among infant temperament, security of attachment, and behavioral inhibition at twenty-four months. *Child Development, 63,* 1456–1472.

Calkins, S. D., & Fox, N. A. (2002). Self-regulatory processes in early personality development: A multilevel approach to the study of childhood, social withdrawal, and aggression. *Development and Psychopathology, 14,* 477–498.

Calkins, S. D., & Howse, R. B. (2004). Individual differences in self-regulation: Implications for childhood adjustment. In P. Philippot & R. S. Feldman (Eds.), *The regulation of emotion* (pp. 307–332). Mahwah, NJ: Erlbaum.

Calvert, G., Spence, C., & Stein, B. E. (2004). *The handbook of multisensory processes.* Cambridge, MA: MIT Press.

Campbell, J. (1990). Self-esteem and clarity of the self-concept. *Journal of Personality and Social Psychology, 59,* 538–549.

Campbell, S. M., Ward, A. J., Sonnenfeld, J. A., & Agle, B.R. (2008). Relational ties that bind: Leader-follower relationship dimensions and charismatic attribution. *The Leadership Quarterly, 19,* 556–568.

Campos, B., Graesch, A. P., Repetti, R., Bradbury, T., & Ochs, E. (2009). Opportunity for interaction? A naturalistic observation study of dual-earner families after work and school. *Journal of Family Psychology, 23,* 798–807.

Canobi, K. H. (2004). Individual differences in children's addition and subtraction knowledge. *Cognitive Development, 19,* 81–93.

Canobi, K. H., Reeve, R. A., & Pattison, P. E. (2003). Patterns of knowledge in children's addition. *Developmental Psychology, 39,* 521–534.

Capaldi, D. M. (1996). The reliability of retrospective report for timing first intercourse for adolescent males. *Journal of Adolescent Research, 11,* 375–387.

Caplan, G. (1964). *Principles of preventive psychiatry.* New York: Basic Books.

Caplan, L.J., & Schooler, C. (2007). Socioeconomic status and financial coping strategies: The mediating role of perceived control. *Social Psychology Quarterly, 70,* 43–58.

Cappeliez, P., & O'Rourke, N. (2002). Profiles of reminiscence among older adults: Perceived stress, life attitudes, and personality variables. *International Journal of Aging and Human Development, 54,* 255–266.

Carlo, G., Knight, G. P., Eisenberg, N., & Rotenberg, K. J. (1991). Cognitive processes and prosocial behaviors among children: The role of affective attributions and reconciliations. *Developmental Psychology, 27,* 456–461.

Carlson, M., & Earls, F. (1997). Psychological and neuroendocrinological sequelae of early social deprivation in institutionalized children in Romania. *Annals of the New York Academy of Sciences, 807,* 419–426.

Carlson, V., Cicchetti, D., Barnett, D., & Braunwold, K. (1989). Finding order in disorganization. Lessons from research on maltreated infants' attachment to their caregivers. In D. Cicchetti & V. Carlson (Eds.), *Child maltreatment: Theory and research on the causes and consequences of maltreatment* (pp. 494–528). New York: Cambridge University Press.

Carnagey, N. L., & Anderson, C. A. (2004). Violent video game exposure and aggression: A literature review. *Minerva Psichiatrica, 45,* 1–18.

Caro, F. G., & Bass, S. A. (1997). Receptivity to volunteering in the immediate postretirement period. *Journal of Applied Gerontology, 16,* 427–441.

Carp, F. M. (1997). Retirement and women. In J. M. Coyle (Ed.), *Handbook of women and aging* (pp. 112–128). Westport, CT: Greenwood Press.

Carpendale, J. I. M., & Krebs, D. L. (1992). Situational variation in moral judgment: In a stage or on a stage? *Journal of Youth and Adolescence, 21,* 203–224.

Carper, J. (1995). *Stop aging now: the ultimate plan for staying young and reversing the aging process.* New York: HarperCollins.

Carr, D. (2003). A "good death" for whom? Quality of spouse's death and psychological distress among older widowed persons. *Journal of Health and Social Behavior, 44,* 215–232.

Carr, D. (2004). The desire to date and remarry among older widows and widowers. *Journal of Marriage and the Family, 66,* 1051–1068.

Carr, D., House, J. S., Wortman, C., Neese, R., & Kessler, R. C. (2001). Psychological adjustment to sudden and anticipated spousal loss among older widowed persons. *Journal of Gerontology, 56B,* S237–S248.

Carroll, J. (2007). Public divided over moral acceptability of doctor-assisted suicide. Retrieved on September 4, 2010, at http://www.gallup.com/poll/

Carroll, J. L. (2009) *Sexuality now: Embracing diversity* (3rd ed.). Belmont, CA: Wadsworth/Cengage Learning.

Carroll, J. L., & Rest, J. R. (1982). Moral development. In B. B. Wolman (Ed.), *Handbook of developmental psychology* (pp. 434–451). Englewood Cliffs, NJ: Prentice Hall.

Carter, C. S. (1998). Neuroendocrine perspectives on social attachment and love. *Psychoneuroendocrinology, 23,* 779–818.

Carter, C. S. (2003). Developmental consequences of oxytocin. *Physiology and Behavior, 79,* 383–97.

Carver, L. J., & Vaccaro, B. G. (2007) 12 month old infants allocate increased neural resources to stimuli associated with negative adult emotion. *Developmental Psychology, 43,* 54–69.

Caserta, M. S., & Lund, D. A. (2007). Toward the development of an inventory of daily widowed life (IDWL): Guided by the dual process model of coping with bereavement. *Death Studies, 31,* 505–534.

Casimir, G., & Waldman, D. A. (2007). A cross cultural comparison of the importance of leadership traits for effective low-level and high-level leaders: Australia and China. *International Journal of Cross Cultural Management, 7,* 47–60.

Casper, L. M., & Bianchi, S. M. (2002). *Continuity and change in the American family.* Thousand Oaks, CA: Sage.

Caspi, A., & Moffitt, T. E. (1991). Individual differences are accentuated during periods of social change: The sample case of girls at puberty. *Journal of Personality and Social Psychology, 61,* 157–168.

Cassia, V. M., Turati, C., & Simion, F. (2004). Can a nonspecific bias toward top-heavy patterns explain newborns' face preference? *Psychological Science, 15,* 379–383.

Cassia, V. M., Valenza, E., Simion, F., & Leon, I. (2008). Congruency as a nonspecific perceptual property contributing to newborns' face preference. *Child Development, 79,* 807–820.

Cassidy, J. (1999). The nature of the child's ties. In J. Cassidy & P. R. Shaver (Eds.), *Handbook of attachment: Theory, research, and clinical* applications (pp. 3–20). New York: Guilford Press.

Castleman, M. (2001). Depression. *SeniorNet's Healthy Aging Enrichment Center.* Retrieved January 29, 2002, from http://www.seniornet.org

Catherwood, D., Freiberg, K., Green, V., & Holt, C. (2001). Intra-hemispheric dynamics in infant encoding of coloured facial patterns. *Infant and Child Development, 10,* 47–57.

Caughy, M. O., Nettles, S. M., O'Campo, P. J., & Lohrfink, K. F. (2006). Neighborhood matters: Racial socialization of African American children. *Child Development, 77,* 1220-1236.

Ceballo, R., & McLoyd, V. C. (2002). Social support and parenting in poor, dangerous neighborhoods. *Child Development, 73,* 1320–1321.

Cedeno, L. A., Elias, M. J., Kelly, S., & Chu, B. C. (2010). School violence, adjustment, and the influence of hope on low-income, African American youth. *American Journal of Orthopsychiatry, 80,* 213–226.

Center for the Study and Prevention of Violence (2001). Bullying prevention: Recommendations for schools. *Safe Communities-Safe Schools Fact Sheet,* Retrieved August 14, 2007, from http://www.colorado.edu/cspv/publications/factsheets/safeschools/pdf/FS-SC08.pdf

Centers for Disease Control and Prevention (CDC). (2003). *2001 Assisted reproductive technology success rates: National summary and fertility clinic reports.* Washington, DC: U.S. Department of Health and Human Services.

Centers for Disease Control and Prevention (CDC). (2006). Youth risk behavior surveillance-United States, 2005. *Surveillance Summaries, 55,* Whole No. SS–5.

Centers for Disease Control and Prevention (CDC). (2007). Fetal Alcohol Spectrum Disorders. Retrieved June 3, 2007, from http://www.cdc.gov/ncbddd/fas/

Centers for Disease Control and Prevention (CDC). (2010a). Health effects of gentrification. Retrieved on August 28, 2010, at http://www.cdc.gov/healthyplaces/helathtopics/gentrificaiton.htm

Centers for Disease Control and Prevention (CDC). (2010b). HIV/AIDS Surveillance Report: 2007. Retrieved on July 9, 2010, at www.cdc.gov/hiv/topics/surveillance/basic.htm#aidsage

Centers for Disease Control and Prevention (CDC). (2010c). Youth Online: High School YRBS. Retrieved on July 4, 2010, at http://apps.nccd.cdc.gov/youthonline.

Central Intelligence Agency. (2007). Afghanistan, *The World Fact Book.* Retrieved August 17, 2007, from http://www.cia.gov/library/publications/the-world-factbook/geos/af.html#People

CEO Forum on Education and Technology. (2001). *The CEO Forum: School technology and readiness report. Key building blocks for student achievement in the 21st century.* Retrieved September 30, 2001, from http://www.ceoforum.org/downloads/report4.pdf

Cerella, J. (1990). Aging and information processing rate. In J. E. Birren & K. W. Schaie (Eds.), *Handbook of cognitive aging* (3rd ed., pp. 201–221). New York: Academic Press.

Cernoch, J. M., & Porter, R. H. (1985). Recognition of maternal axillary odors by infants. *Child Development, 56,* 1593–1598.

Cesarone, B. (1994). *Video games and children.* ERIC Digest EDO-PS-94-3. Retrieved August 18, 2001, from http://www.kidsource.com/kidsource/content2/video.games.html

Cha, Y. (2010). Reinforcing separate spheres: The effect of spousal overwork on men's and women's employment in dual earner households. *American Sociological Review, 75,* 303–329.

Chalmers, J. B., & Townsend, M. A. R. (1990). The effects of training in social perspective taking on socially maladjusted girls. *Child Development, 61,* 178–190.

Chandler, L. S., & S. J. Lane (Eds.). (1996). *Children with prenatal drug exposure* (pp. 111–128). New York: Haworth Press.

Chang, E. C., & Sanna, L. J. (2001). Optimism, pessimism, and positive and negative affectivity in middle-aged adults: A test of a cognitive-affective model of psychological adjustment. *Psychology and Aging, 16,* 524–531.

Chang, J. (1991). *Wild swans: Three daughters of China.* New York: Random House.

Chapman, M. (1988). *Constructive evolution: Origin and development of Piaget's thought.* New York: Cambridge University Press.

Chapman, M., & McBride, M. L. (1992). Beyond competence and performance: Children's class inclusion strategies, superordinate class cues, and verbal justifications. *Developmental Psychology, 28,* 319–327.

Charlesworth, W. R. (1992). Darwin and developmental psychology: Past and present. *Developmental Psychology, 28,* 5–16.

Chase-Lansdale, P. L. (1993). The impact of poverty on family process. *Child, Youth, and Family Services Quarterly, 16,* 5–8.

Chavez, A., Martinez, C., & Soberanes, B. (1995). Effects of early malnutrition on late mental and behavioral performance. *Developmental Brain Dysfunction, 8,* 90–102.

Chazan, S. E. (1981). Development of object permanence as a correlate of dimensions of maternal care. *Developmental Psychology, 17,* 79–81.

Chen, I. (2009, June). The social brain. *Smithsonian,* 38–43.

Chen, S., Boucher, H. C., & Tapias, M. P. (2006). The relational self revealed: Integrative conceptualization and implications for interpersonal life. *Psychological Bulletin, 132,* 151–179.

Cheng, S-T., & Chan, A. C. M. (2006). Relationship with others and life satisfaction in later life: Do gender and widowhood make a difference? *Journals of Gerontology: Series B: Psychological Sciences and Social Sciences, 61B,* P46–P53.

Cherlin, A. J. (2009). *The marriage-go-round: The state of marriage and the family in America today.* New York: Alfred A. Knopf/Random House.

Cherney, I. D., & London, K. (2006). Gender-linked differences in the toys, television shows, computer games and outdoor activities of 5- to 13-year-old children. *Sex Roles, 54,* 717–726.

Chevan, A. (1995). Holding on and letting go: Residential mobility during widowhood. *Research on Aging, 17,* 278–302.

Chickering, A. W., & Reisser, L. (1993). *Education and identity* (2nd ed.). San Francisco: Jossey-Bass.

Childbirthconnection.org (2007). Quotes from mothers. Labor induction. Retrieved June 4, 2007, from http://www.childbirthconnection.org

Child Health USA. (2005). Health Status: Infants. Rockville, MD: U.S. Department of Health and Human Services. Retrieved June 15, 2007, from http://mchb.hrsa.gov/mchirc/chusa_05/index.htm

Children's Defense Fund. (2003). *Key facts about America's children.* Retrieved September 15, 2004, from http://www.childrensdefense.org/data/default.aspx

ChildTrends. (2005). Mothers who smoke while pregnant. ChildTrends Data Bank. Retrieved June 2, 2007, from http://www.ChildTrendsdatabank.org/indicators/11 MothersWhoSmokeWhilePregnant.cfm

Chilman, C. S. (1993). Hispanic families in the United States: Research perspective. In H. P. McAdoo (Ed.), *Family ethnicity: Strength in diversity* (pp. 141–163). Newbury Park, CA: Sage.

Chouinard, M. M. (2007). Children's questions: A mechanism for cognitive development. *Monographs of the Society for Research in Child Development, Serial No. 286, Vol. 72, No. 1.* pp. 1–112.

Christiansen, S. L., & Palkovitz, R. (1998). Exploring Erikson's psychosocial theory of development: Generativity and its relationship to paternal identity, intimacy, and involvement in childcare. *Journal of Men's Studies, 7,* 133–156.

Chronicle of Higher Education. (2009). College dropout hall of fame (2010). Famous college dropouts. Retrieved on July 15, 2010, at www.collegedropoutshalloffame.com.

Church, J. (1966). *Three babies: Biographies of cognitive development.* New York: Random House.

Cicatelli Associates. (2004). *Best practices in adolescent pregnancy prevention.* Retrieved December 5, 2004, from http://www.cicatelli.org/BPAPP/default.htm

Cicirelli, V. G. (1999). Personality and demographic factors in older adults' fear of death. *The Gerontologist, 39,* 569–579.

Cicirelli, V. G. (2001). Personal meanings of death in older adults and young adults in relation to their fears of death. *Death Studies, 25,* 663–683.

Cincinnati Children's Hospital Medical Center. (1998). *Wellness: Infant safety tips.* Retrieved July 8, 2004, from http://www.cincinnatichildrens.org/health/info/newborn/well/infant-tips.htm

Cincinnati Children's Hospital Medical Center. (2004). *Installing and using child safety seats and booster seats.* Retrieved July 8, 2004, from http://www.cincinnatichildrens.org/health/info/safety/vehicle/harness.htm

Cinq-Mars, C., Wright, J., Cyr, M., & McDuff, P. (2003). Sexual at-risk behaviors of sexually abused adolescent girls. *Journal of Child Sexual Abuse, 12,* 2–18.

Cirino, P. T., Vaughn, S., Linan-Thompson, S., Cardena-Hagan, E., Fletcher, J. M., & Francis, D. J. (2009). One-year follow-up outcomes of Spanish and English interventions for English language learners at risk for reading problems. *American Educational Research Journal, 46,* 744–781.

CIRP (2006). American Freshman National Norms for Fall 2006. Retrieved on July 12, 2010, at www.gseis.ucla.edu/heri/PDFs/06CIRPFS_Norms_Narrative.pdf

Clancy, S. M., & Dollinger, S. J. (1993). Identity, self, and personality: 1. Identity status and the five-factor model of personality. *Journal of Research on Adolescence, 3,* 227–246.

Clark, A. L., & Howland, R. I. (1978). The American Samoan. In A. L. Clark (Ed.), *Culture, childbearing, and the health professionals* (pp. 154–172). Philadelphia: Davis.

Clark, J. E., Phillips, S. J., & Petersen, R. (1989). Developmental stability in jumping. *Developmental Psychology, 25,* 929–935.

Clark, M., & Arnold, J. (2008). The nature, prevalence, and correlates of generativity among men in middle career. *Journal of Vocational Behavior, 73,* 473–484.

Clark, M. L. (1991). Social identity, peer relations, and academic competence of African-American adolescents. *Education and Urban Society, 24,* 41–52.

Clark, M. L., & Ayers, M. (1988). The role of reciprocity and proximity in junior high school friendships. *Journal of Youth and Adolescence, 17,* 403–411.

Clark, M.S. & Lemay, E.P. Jr. (2010). Close relationships. In S.T. Fiske & D.Gilbert (Eds.), *Handbook of social psychology* (pp. 898–940). New York: Oxford University Press.

Clark, M. S., Lemay, E. P. Jr., Graham, S. M., Pataki, S. P., & Finkel, E. J. (2010). Ways of giving benefits in marriage: Norm use, relationship satisfaction, and attachment-related variability. *Psychological Science, 21,* 944–951.

Clark, S. D., Long, M. M., & Schiffman, L. G. (1999). The mind–body connection: The relationship among physical activity level, life satisfaction, and cognitive age among mature females. *Journal of Social Behavior and Personality, 14,* 221–240.

Clarke, S. C. (1995, July 14). *Advance report of final marriage statistics, 1989 and 1990.* (Monthly Vital Statistics Report, Vol. 43, No. 12, Supplement Table 6). Hyattsville, MD: National Center for Health Statistics.

Clarke-Stewart, K. A. (1989). Infant day care: Maligned or malignant? *American Psychologist, 44,* 266–273.

Clarke-Stewart, K. A., & Fein, G. G. (1983). Early childhood programs. In P. H. Mussen (Ed.), *Handbook of child psychology: Vol. 2. Infancy and developmental psychobiology* (pp. 917–1000). New York: Wiley.

Clark-Ibanez, M., & Felmlee, D. (2004). Interethnic relationship: The role of social network diversity. *Journal of Marriage and the Family, 66*, 293–305.

Clasen, D. R., & Brown, B. B. (1985). The multidimensionality of peer pressure in adolescence. *Journal of Youth and Adolescence, 14*, 451–468.

Clausen, J. A. (1975). The social meaning of differential physical and sexual maturation. In S. E. Dragastin & G. H. Elder (Eds.), *Adolescence in the life cycle: Psychological change and social context.* Washington, DC: Hemisphere.

Claxton, A. & Perry-Jenkins, M. (2008). No fun anymore: Leisure and marital quality across the transition to parenthood. *Journal of Marriage and the Family, 70*, 28–43.

Clifton, R., Perris, E., & Bullinger, A. (1991). Infants' perception of auditory space. *Developmental Psychology, 27*, 187–197.

Cloud, J. (2000, September 18). A kinder, gentler death. *Time*, pp. 60–67.

Cloud, J. (2001). Should SATs matter? *Time, 157*, 62–76.

Cloud, J. (2010). Why genes aren't destiny. *Time Magazine, 175*, 48–53.

CNN.com (2005, February 10). Centenarians reveal longevity secrets. *World.* Retrieved February 21, 2005, from http://www.cnn.com/2005/WORLD/americas/02/09/cuban.centenarians.ap/

Coalition to stop the use of child soldiers. (2008). *Child soldiers global report, 2008.* Retrieved on June 7, 2010, at www.childsoldiersglobalreport.org/

Coats, P. B., & Overman, S. J. (1992). Childhood play experiences of women in traditional and nontraditional professions. *Sex Roles, 26*, 261–271.

Coats, S., Smith, E. R., Claypool, H. M., & Banner, M. J. (2000). Overlapping mental representations of self and in-group: Reaction time evidence and its relationship with explicit measures of group identification. *Journal of Experimental Social Psychology, 36*, 304–315.

Cobb, S. (1979). Social support and health through the life course. In M. W. Riley (Ed.), *Aging from birth to death.* Boulder, CO: Westview.

Cody, H., & Kamphaus, R. W. (1999). Down syndrome. In S. Goldstein & C. R. Reynolds (Eds.), *Handbook of neurodevelopmental and genetic disorders in children* (pp. 385–405). New York: Guilford Press.

Cohane, G. H., & Pope, H. G., Jr. (2000). Body image in boys: A review of the literature. *International Journal of Eating Disorders, 29*, 373–379.

Cohen, B. (2004). Introduction. In N.B. Anderson, R.A. Bulatao, and B. Cohen (Eds.), *Critical Perspectives on Racial and Ethnic Differences in Health in Late Life*, National Research Council, Panel on Race, Ethnicity, and Health in Later Life, Committee on Population, Division of Behavioral and Social Sciences and Education, Washington: The National Academies Press, p. 16.

Cohen, J., & Sandy, S. V. (2007). The social, emotional and academic education of children: Theories, goals, methods and assessments. In R. Bar-On, J. G. Maree, & M. J. Elias (Eds.), *Educating people to be emotionally intelligent.* Westport, CT: Praeger, pp. 63–77.

Cohen, L. B., & Cashon, C. H. (2001). Do 7-month-old infants process independent features or facial configurations? *Infant and Child Development, 10*, 83–92.

Cohen, L. S., Wang, B., Nonacs, R., Viguera, A. C., Lemon, E. L., & Freeman, M. P. (2010). Treatment of mood disorders during pregnancy and postpartum. *Psychiatric Clinics of North America, 33*, 273–293.

Cohen, M. A., Tell, E. J., Bishop, C. E., Wallack, S. S., & Branch, L. G. (1989). Patterns of nursing home use in a prepaid managed care system: The continuing care retirement community. *The Gerontologist, 29*, 74–80.

Cohen, R. S., & Weissman, S. H. (1984). The parenting alliance. In R. S. Cohen, B. J. Cohler, & S. H. Weissman (Eds.), *Parenthood: A psychodynamic perspective* (pp. 33–49). New York: Guilford Press.

Cohn, B. (1998, March/April). What a wife's worth. *Stanford*, pp. 14–15.

Coie, J. D., & Krehbiel, G. (1984). Effects of academic tutoring on the social status of low achieving, socially rejected children. *Child Development, 55*, 1465–1478.

Colby, A., & Damon, W. (1994). Listening to a different voice: A review of Gilligan's "In a Different Voice." In B. Puka (Ed.), *Caring voices and women's moral frames: Gilligan's view. Moral development: A compendium*, Vol. 6 (pp. 275–283). New York: Garland.

Colby, A., & Damon, W. (1999). The development of extraordinary moral commitment. In M. Killen & D. Hart (Eds.), *Morality in everyday life: Developmental perspectives.* New York: Cambridge University Press, pp. 342–370.

Colby, A., & Kohlberg, L. (1987). The measurement of moral judgment: Vol. 1. Theoretical foundations and research validation. Cambridge, UK: Cambridge University Press.

Colby, A., Kohlberg, L., Gibbs, J., & Lieberman, M. (1983). A longitudinal study of moral judgment. *Monographs of the Society for Research in Child Development, 48* (1, Serial No. 200).

Cole, C. L., & Cole, A. L. (1985). Husbands and wives should have an equal share in making the marriage work. In H. Feldman & M. Feldman (Eds.), *Current controversies in marriage and family* (pp. 131–141). Newbury Park, CA: Sage.

Cole, D., & La Voie, J. C. (1985). Fantasy play and related cognitive development in 2 to 6 year olds. *Developmental Psychology, 21*, 233–240.

Coleman, E. (2003). Compulsive sexual behavior: What to call it, how to treat it? *SIECUS Report, 31*, 12–16.

Coleman, J. S. (1987). Families and schools. *Educational Researcher, 16*, 32–38.

Colin, V. (1996). *Human attachment.* New York: McGraw-Hill.

Coll, C. G. (2004). The interpenetration of culture and biology in human development. *Research in Human Development, 1*, 145–160.

Coll, C. T. G. (1990). Developmental outcome of minority infants: A process-oriented look into our beginnings. *Child Development, 61*, 270–289.

Collin, A., & Young, R. A. (2000). *The future of career.* New York: Cambridge University Press.

Collins, K., Luszcz, M., Lawson, M., & Keeves, J. (1997). Everyday problem solving in elderly women: Contributions of residence, perceived control and age. *The Gerontologist, 37*, 293–302.

Collins, W. (1995). Relationship and development: Family adaptation to individual change. In S. Shulman (Ed.), *Close relationships and socioemotional development* (pp. 128–154). Norwood, NJ: Ablex.

Collins, W. A., & Laursen, B. (2006). Parent-adolescent relationships. In P. Noller, & J. A. Feeney (Eds.), *Close relationships: Functions, forms and processes.* Hove, England: Taylor & Francis, pp. 111–125.

Colombo, J., Mitchell, D. W., Coldren, J. T., & Freeseman, L. J. (1991). Individual differences in infant visual attention: Are short lookers faster processors or feature processors? *Child Development, 62*, 1247–1257.

Commons, M. L., Galaz-Fontes, J. F., Morse, S. J. (2006). Leadership, cross-cultural contact, socio-economic status, and formal operational reasoning about moral dilemmas among Mexican non-literate adults and high school students. *Journal of Moral Education, 35*(2), 247–267.

Commons, M. L., & Richards, F. A. (2003). Four postformal stages. In J. Demick & C. Andreoletti (Eds.), *Handbook of adult development.* New York: Kluwer Academic/Plenum Publishers, pp. 199–219.

ComScore (2008). *Social networking explodes worldwide as sites increase their focus on cultural relevance.* Retrieved on August 12, 2008, from www.comscore.com/press/release.asp?press=2396.

Comstock, G. A. (with H. Paik). (1991). *Television and the American child.* San Diego: Academic Press.

Conger, J. A., & Kanungo, R. N. (1998). *Charismatic leadership in organizations.* Thousand Oaks, CA: Sage.

Conger, R. D., Conger, K. J., Elder, G. H., Lorenz, F. O., Simons, R. L., & Whitbeck, L. B. (1993). Family economic stress and adjustment of early adolescent girls. *Developmental Psychology, 29*, 206–219.

Conger, R. D., Wallace, L. E., Sun, Y., Simons, R. L., McLoyd, V. C., & Brody, G. H. (2002). Economic pressure in African American families: A replication and extension of the family stress model. *Developmental Psychology, 38*, 179–193.

Congress and RU-486. (2001, April 26). *Washington Post*, p. A26.

Connolly, C. (2004, December 1). Some abstinence programs mislead teens, report says. Washington Post, p. AO1. Retrieved December 4, 2004, from http://www.washingtonpost.com/wp-dyn/articles/A26623-2004Dec1.html

Connolly, J., Furman, W., & Konarski, R. (2000). The role of peers in the emergence of heterosexual romantic relationship in adolescence. *Child Development, 71,* 1395–1408.

Connolly, K., & Dalgleish, M. (1989). The emergence of a tool-using skill in infancy. *Developmental Psychology, 25,* 894–912.

Constantinople, A. (1969). An Eriksonian measure of personality development in college students. *Developmental Psychology, 1,* 357–372.

Consumer Product Safety Commission. (1999). *Safety hazards in child care settings.* Washington, DC: Author. Retrieved December 21, 2001, from http://www.cpsc.gov/library/ccstudy.html

Conte, H. R., Weiner, M. B., & Plutchik, R. (1982). Measuring death anxiety: Conceptual, psychometric, and factor-analytic aspects. *Journal of Personality and Social Psychology, 43,* 775–785.

Contreras, J. M., Lopez, I. R., Rivera-Mosquera, E. T., Raymond-Smith, L., & Rothstein, K. (1999). Social support and adjustment in Puerto Rican adolescent mothers: The moderating effect of acculturation. *Journal of Family Psychology, 13,* 228–243.

Conway, M. A., & Holmes, A. (2004). Psychosocial stages and the accessibility of autobiographical memories across the life cycle. *Journal of Personality, 73,* 461-480.

Cool, L. E. (1987). The effects of social class and ethnicity on the aging process. In P. Silverman (Ed.), *The elderly as modern pioneers* (pp. 263–282). Bloomington: Indiana University Press.

Cooney, T. M., & Mortimer, J. T. (1999). Family structure differences in the timing of leaving home: Exploring mediating factors. *Journal of Research in Adolescence, 9,* 367–393.

Cooney, T. M., Pedersen, F. A., Indelicato, S., & Palkovitz, R. (1993). Timing of fatherhood: Is "on-time" optimal? *Journal of Marriage and the Family, 55,* 205–215.

Copple, C. (2003). Fostering young children's representation, planning and reflection: A focus in three current early childhood models. *Journal of Applied Developmental Psychology, 24,* 763–771.

Corcoran, M. E., & Chaudry, A. (1997). The dynamics of childhood poverty. *Future of Children, 7.*

Coreter, C. M., & Fleming, A. S. (2002). Psychobiology of maternal behavior in human beings. In M. H. Bornstein (Ed.), *Handbook of parenting: Vol. 2. Biology and ecology of parenting* (pp. 141–181). Mahwah, NJ: Erlbaum.

Corijn, M., Liefbroer, A. C., & Gierveld, J. De J. (1996). It takes two to tango, doesn't it? The influence of couple characteristics on the timing of the birth of the first child. *Journal of Marriage and the Family, 58,* 117–126.

Corina, D. P., Vaid, J., & Bellugi, U. (1992). The linguistic basis of left hemisphere specialization, *Science, 255,* 1258–1260.

Cornelius, M. D. (1996). Adolescent pregnancy and the complications of prenatal substance use. In L. S. Chandler & S. J. Lane (Eds.), *Children with prenatal drug exposure* (pp. 111–128). New York: Haworth Press.

Cornelius, M. D., Goldshmidt, L., Taylor, P. M., & Day, N. L. (1999). Prenatal alcohol use among teenagers: Effects on neonatal outcomes. *Alcoholism: Clinical and Experimental Research, 23,* 1238–1244.

Correll, S. J. (2001). Gender and the career choice process: The role of biased self-assessments. *American Journal of Sociology, 106,* 1691–1730.

Corter, C. M., & Fleming, A. S. (2002). Psychobiology of maternal behavior in human beings. In M. H. Bornstein (Ed.), *Handbook of parenting: Vol. 2. Biology and ecology of parenting* (pp. 141–181). Mahwah, NJ: Erlbaum.

Cosden, M., Peerson, S., & Elliott, K. (1997). Effects of prenatal drug exposure on birth outcomes and early child development. *Journal of Drug Issues, 27,* 525–539.

Cosmides, L., & Tooby, J. (1997). *Evolutionary psychology: A primer.* Retrieved November 6, 2002, from http://www.psych.ucsb.edu/research/cep/primer.html

Costa, P. T., Metter, E. J., & McCrae, R. R. (1994). Personality stability and its contribution to successful aging. *Journal of Geriatric Psychiatry, 27,* 41–59.

Cota-Robles, S., Neiss, M., & Rowe, D. C. (2002). The role of puberty in violent and nonviolent delinquency among Anglo American, Mexican American, and African American boys. *Journal of Adolescent Research, 17,* 364–376.

Cotten, S. R. (1999). Marital status and mental health revisited: Examining the importance of risk factors and resources. *Family Relations, 48,* 225–233.

Cougle, J. R., Reardon, D. C., & Coleman, P. K. (2005). Generalized anxiety following unintended pregnancies resolved through childbirth and abortion: A cohort study of the 1995 National Survey of Family Growth. *Journal of Anxiety Disorders, 19,* 137–142.

Couzin, J. (2003, October). Is long life in the blood? *Science Now,* pp. 2–4.

Cowan, C. P., & Cowan, P. A. (1988). Who does what when partners become parents: Implications for men, women, and marriage. In R. Palkovitz & M. B. Sussman (Eds.), *Transitions to parenthood* (pp. 105–132). New York: Hawthorn Press.

Cowan, P. A., Cohn, D. A., Cowan, C. P., & Pearson, J. L. (1996). Parents' attachment histories and children's externalizing and internalizing behavior: Exploring family systems models of linkage. *Journal of Consulting and Clinical Psychology, 64,* 53–63.

Cowley, G. (1997, June 30). How to live to 100. *Newsweek,* pp. 56–67.

Cox, M. J., Owen, M. T., Henderson, V. K., & Margand, N. A. (1992). Prediction of infant–father and infant–mother attachment. *Developmental Psychology, 28,* 474–483.

Cox, M. J., Owen, M. T., Lewis, J. M., & Henderson, V. K. (1989). Marriage, adult adjustment, and early parenting. *Child Development, 60,* 1015–1024.

Crack-using woman admits guilt in the death of her fetus. (1997, December 3). *New York Times,* Sec. A., p. 33.

Craig-Bray, L., Adams, G. R., & Dobson, W. R. (1988). Identity formation and social relations during late adolescence. *Journal of Youth and Adolescence, 17,* 173–188.

Crain, W. C. (2000). *Theories of development: Concepts and applications* (4th ed.). Upper Saddle River, NJ: Prentice Hall.

Crain-Thoreson, C., & Dale, P. S. (1992). Do early talkers become early readers? Linguistic precocity, preschool language, and emergent literacy. *Developmental Psychology, 28,* 421–429.

Crawford, T. N., Cohen, P., Midlarsky, E., & Brook, J. (2001). Internalizing symptoms in adolescents: Gender differences in vulnerability to parental distress and discord. *Journal of Research on Adolescence, 11,* 95–118.

Creswell, J., & Thomas, L. Jr. (2009, January 24). The talented Mr. Madoff. *The New York Times.* Retrieved on August 19, 2010 at www.nytimes.com/2009/01/25/business/25bernie.html?pagewanted=1&_r=1

Creswell, J. W. (1994). *Research design: Qualitative and quantitative approaches.* Thousand Oaks, CA: Sage.

Crick, N. R., & Ladd, G. W. (1993). Children's perceptions of their peer experiences: Attributions, loneliness, social anxiety, and social avoidance. *Developmental Psychology, 29,* 244–254.

Crinion, J., Turner, R., Grogan, A., Hanakawa, T., Noppeney, U., Devlin, J. T., Aso, T., Urayama, S., Fukuyama, H., Stockton, K., Usuai, K., Green, D. W., & Price, C. J. (2006). Language control in the bilingual brain. *Science, 312,* 1537–1540.

Crocetti, E., Rubini, M., & Meeus, W. (2008). Capturing the dynamics of identity formation in various ethnic groups: Development and validation of a three-dimensional model. *Journal of Adolescence, 31,* 207–222.

Crockenberg, S. C., Leerkes, E. M., & Lekka, S. K. (2007). Pathways from marital aggression to infant emotion regulation: The development of withdrawal in infancy. *Infant Behavior and Development, 30,* 97–113.

Crockett, L. J., Bingham, C. R., Chopak, J. S., & Vicary, J. R. (1996). Timing of first sexual intercourse: The role of social control, social learning, and problem behavior. *Journal of Youth and Adolescence, 25,* 89–111.

Crohan, S. E. (1996). Marital quality and conflict across the transition to parenthood in African American and White couples. *Journal of Marriage and the Family, 58,* 933–944.

Crooks, R. L., & Baur, K. (2005). *Our sexuality* (9th ed.). Belmont, CA: Wadsworth.

Crooks, T. J. (1988). The impact of classroom evaluation practices on students. *Review of Educational Research, 58,* 438–481.

Crosby, R. A., DiClemente, R. J., Wingood, G. M., Rose, E., & Lang, D. (2003). Correlates of unplanned and unwanted pregnancy among African-American female teens. *American Journal of Preventive Medicine, 25*, 255–258.

Crosnoe, R. (2009). Low-income students and the socioeconomic composition of public high schools. *American Sociological Review, 74*, 709–730.

Crosnoe, R., & Elder, G. H., Jr. (2002a). Life course transitions, the generational stake, and grandparent-grandchild relationships. *Journal of Marriage and Family, 64*, 1089–1096.

Crosnoe, R., & Elder, G. H., Jr. (2002b). Successful adaptation in the later years: A life course approach to aging. *Social Psychology Quarterly, 65*, 309–328.

Crosnoe, R., & Elder, G. H., Jr. (2004). From childhood to the later years: Pathways of human development. *Research on aging, 26*, 623–654.

Crosnoe, R., & Huston, A. (2007). Socioeconomic status, schooling, and the developmental trajectories of adolescents. *Developmental Psychology, 43*, 1097–1110.

Cross, W. E., Jr. (1991). *Shades of black: Diversity in African-American identity.* Philadelphia: Temple University Press.

Cross, W. E., Jr., & Fhagen-Smith, P. (2001). Patterns of African American identity development: A life span perspective. In B. Jackson & C. Wijeyesinghe (Eds.), *New perspectives on racial identity development: A theoretical and practical anthology.* New York: New York University Press, pp. 243–270.

Crouter, A. C., & Bumpus, M. F. (2001). Linking parents' work stress to children's and adolescents' psychological adjustment. *Current Directions in Psychological Science, 10*, 156–159.

Crouter, A. C., & Manke, B. (1997). Development of a typology of dual-earner families: A window into differences between and within families in relationships, roles, and activities. *Journal of Family Psychology, 11*, 62–75.

Crowe, J., Elementary School Social Worker (2001). Retrieved December 18, 2001, from www.wetfeet.com

Crowell, J. A., Fraley, R. C., & Shaver, P. R. (1999). Measurement of individual differences in adolescent and adult attachment. In J. Cassidy & P. R. Shaver (Eds.), *Handbook of attachment: Theory, research, and clinical applications* (pp. 434–465). New York: Guilford Press.

Cuddy, A. J. C., Fiske, S. T., & Glick, P. (2004). When professionals become mothers, warmth doesn't cut the ice. *Journal of Social Issues, 60*, 701–718.

Cukan, A. (2001). FedEx sued for dreadlocks discrimination. *United Press International.* Retrieved January 7, 2002, from http://www.hirediversity.com/news/newsbyid.asp?id_4736

Cumsille, P., Darling, N., Flaherty, B., & Martinez, M.L. (2009). Heterogeneity and change in the patterning of adolescents' perceptions of the legitimacy of parental authority: A latent transition model. *Child Development, 80*, 418–432.

Cunningham, F. G., Gant, N., Gilstrap, L., Leveno, G., Hauth, J., & Wenstrom, K. (2001). *Williams' Obstetrics* (21st ed.). New York: McGraw-Hill.

Cunningham, P. B., Henggeler, S. Q., Limber, S. P., Melton, G. B., & Nation, M. A. (2000). Pattern and correlates of gun ownership among nonmetropolitan and rural middle school students. *Journal of Clinical Child Psychology, 29*, 432–442.

Currie, L. A. (1999). "Mr. Homunculus the Reading Detective": A cognitive approach to improving reading comprehension. *Educational and Child Psychology, 16*, 37–42.

Cutler, D. M., & Leiras-Muney, A. (2006). Education and health: Evaluating theories and evidence. NBER Working Paper No. 12352. Retrieved from http://www.nber.org/papers/w12352 on 2/12/2007.

Dahl, R. E., & Carskadon, M. A. (1995). Sleep and its disorders in adolescence. In R. Ferber & M. H. Kryger (Eds.), *Principles and practice of sleep medicine in the child* (pp. 19–27). Philadelphia: Saunders.

Dalgleish, T., Moradi, A. R., Taghavi, M. R., Neshat-Doost, H. T., & Yule, W. (2001). An experimental investigation of hypervigilance for threat in children and adolescents with post-traumatic stress disorder. *Psychological Medicine, 31*, 541–547.

Dalirazar, N. (2007). Reasons people do not work: 2004. *Current Population Reports*, Washington, DC: U.S. Census Bureau.

Damasio, A. (2005). Brain trust. *Nature, 435*, 571–572.

Damon, W. (1980). Patterns of change in children's social reasoning: A two-year longitudinal study. *Child Development, 51*, 1010–1017.

Damon, W. (1996). The lifelong transformation of moral goals through social influence. In P. B. Baltes & V. M. Staudinger (Eds.), *Interactive minds: Life-span perspectives on the social foundation of cognition* (pp. 198–220). New York: Cambridge University Press.

Damon, W. (2000). Setting the stage for the development of wisdom: Self-understanding and moral identity during adolescence. In W. S. Brown (Ed.), *Understanding wisdom: Sources, science, and society. Laws of science symposia series: Vol. 3.* West Conshohocken, PA: Templeton foundation Press, pp. 339–360.

Damon, W., & Hart, D. (1988). *Self-understanding in childhood and adolescence.* New York: Cambridge University Press.

Daniluk, J. C. (1999). When biology isn't destiny: Implications for the sexuality of women without children. *Canadian Journal of Counseling, 33*, 79–94.

Darling-Fisher, C. S., & Leidy, N. K. (1988). Measuring Eriksonian development in the adult: The Modified Erikson Psychosocial Stage Inventory. *Psychological Reports, 62*, 747–754.

Darwin, C. (1859/1979). *The illustrated "Origin of species."* (Abridged and introduced by Richard E. Leakey). New York: Hill & Wang.

Darwin, C. (1872/1965). *The expression of emotions in man and animals.* Chicago: University of Chicago Press.

Dasen, P. R. (1984). The cross cultural study of intelligence: Piaget and the Baoulé. *The International Journal of Psychology, 19*, 407–434.

Dating site reviews.com (2010). Match.com releases study on trends in online dating. Retrieved on July 28, 2010, at www.datingsitesreviews.com.

Davey, A., & Eggebeen, D. J. (1998). Patterns of intergenerational exchange and mental health. *Journal of Gerontology, 53*, P86–P95.

D'Augelli, A. R. (1991). Gay men in college: Identity processes and adaptation. *Journal of College Student Development, 32*, 140–146.

Davidson, K. (2002). Gender differences in new partnership choices and constraints for older widows and widowers. *Ageing International, 27*, 43–60.

Davies, P. L., & Rose, J. D. (1999). Assessment of cognitive development in adolescents by means of neuropsychological tasks. *Developmental Neuropsychology, 15*, 227–248.

Davies, P. T. & Woitach, M. J. (2008). Children's emotional security in the interparental relationship. *Current Directions in Psychological Science, 17*, 269–274.

Davis, A. (1995). The experimental method in psychology. In G. Breakwell, S. Hammond, & C. Fyfe-Schaw (Eds.), *Research methods in psychology* (pp. 42–58). Thousand Oaks, CA: Sage.

Davis, J. E. (2010). Painful numbers. *The Hedgehog Review, 12.3.*

Davis, K. E. (1985, February). Near and dear: Friendship and love compared. *Psychology Today, 19*, pp. 22–30.

Davis-Floyd, R. E. (1990). The role of obstetrical rituals in the resolution of cultural anomaly. *Social Science and Medicine, 31*, 175–189.

Davis-Kean, P. E., & Sandler, H. M. (2001). A meta-analysis of measures of self-esteem for young children: A framework for future measures. *Child Development, 72*, 887–906.

Davison, M. L., King, P. M., Kitchener, K. S., & Parker, C. A. (1980). The stage sequence concept in cognitive and social development. *Developmental Psychology, 16*, 121–131.

Davydov, V. V. (1995). The influence of L. S. Vygotsky on education theory, research, and practice (S. T. Kerr, Trans.). *Educational Researcher, 24*, 12–21.

Daw, J. (2001). Road rage, air rage and now "desk rage." *Monitor on Psychology, 32*, 52–54.

Dawson, T. L. (2002). New tools, new insights: Kohlberg's moral judgement stages revisited. *International Journal of Behavioral Development, 26*, 154–166.

Dawson, T. L. (2003). A stage is a stage is a stage: A direct comparison of two scoring systems. *Journal of Genetic Psychology, 164,* 335–364.

Dawson-Tunik, T. L., Commons, M., Wilson, M., & Fischer, K. W. (2005). The shape of development. *European Journal of Developmental Psychology, 2,* 163–195.

DeAngelis, T. (1997a). APA co-sponsors briefing on anorexia. *APA Monitor, 28,* 51.

DeAngelis, T. (1997b). When children don't bond with parents. *APA Monitor, 28,* 10–12.

DeAngelis, T. (2010). Social awareness and emotional skills equal successful kids. *Monitor on Psychology, 41,* 46–49.

Dearing, E., McCartney, K., & Taylor, B. A. (2009). Does higher quality early child care promote low-income children's math and reading achievement in middle childhood? *Child Development, 80,* 1329–1349.

Deater-Deckard, K., & O'Connor, T. G. (2000). Parent–child mutuality in early childhood: Two behavioral genetic studies. *Developmental Psychology, 36,* 561–570.

Deater-Deckard, K., Pickering, K., Dunn, J. F., & Golding, J. (1998). Family structure and depressive symptoms in men preceding and following the birth of a child. *American Journal of Psychiatry, 155,* 818–823.

Deaux, K., Reid, A., Mizrahi, K., & Ethier, K. A. (1995). Parameters of social identity. *Journal of Personality and Social Psychology, 68,* 280–291.

DeCasper, A. J., & Fifer, W. (1980). Of human bonding: Newborns prefer their mothers' voices. *Science, 208,* 1174–1176.

DeCasper, A. J., Lecanuet, J. P., Busnel, M. C., Granier-Deferre, C., et al. (1994). Fetal reactions to recurrent maternal speech. *Infant Behavior and Development, 17,* 159–164.

Decety, J., & Chaminade, T. (2003). When the self represents the other: A new cognitive neuroscience view on psychological identification. *Consciousness and Cognition, 12,* 577–596.

Declerq, E. R., Sakala, C., Corry, M. P., & Applebaum, S. (2006). Executive Summary. In *Listening to Mothers II: Report of the second national U.S. survey of women's childbearing experiences.* New York: Childbirth Connection, p. 1–9.

De Dreu, C. K. W., Greer, L. L., et al. (2010). The neuropeptide oxytocin regulates parochial altruism in intergroup conflict among humans. *Science, 328,* 1408–1411.

Deeg, D. J. H., Kardaun, J. W. P. F., & Fozard, J. L. (1996). Health, behavior, and aging. In J. E. Birren, K. W. Schaie, R. P. Abeles, M. Gatz, & T. A. Salthouse (Eds.), *Handbook of the psychology of aging* (pp. 129–149). San Diego: Academic Press.

Deenen, A. A., Gijs, L., & van Naerssen, A. X. (1994). Intimacy and sexuality in gay male couples. *Archives of Sexual Behavior, 23,* 421–431.

De Frias, C. M., & Schaie, K. W. (2001). Perceived work environment and cognitive style. *Experimental Aging Research, 27,* 67–81.

DeGenova, M. K. (1997). *Families in cultural context: Strengths and challenges in diversity.* Mountain View, CA: Mayfield.

DeGrazia, D. (1998). *Biology, consciousness, and the definitions of death.* Report from the Institute for Philosophy & Public Policy. Retrieved March 4, 2005, from http://www.puaf.umd.edu/IPPP/winter98/biology_consciousness.htm

Dekeyser, M., Verfaillie, K., & Vanrie, J. (2002). Creating stimuli for the study of biological motion perception. *Behavior Research Methods, Instruments, & Computers, 34,* 375–382.

Delsing, M. J.M. H., ter Bogt, T. F. M., Engles, R. C. M. E., & Meeus, W. H. J. (2007). Adolescents' peer crowd identification in the Netherlands: Structure and associations with problem behaviors. *Journal of Research on Adolescence, 17,* 467–480.

De Magalhaes, J. P. (2003). Winning the war against aging. *Futurist, 37,* 48–51.

DeMaris, A., & Rao, K. V. (1992). Premarital cohabitation and subsequent marital stability in the United States: A reassessment. *Journal of Marriage and the Family, 54,* 178–190.

Demetriou, A., & Efklides, A. (1985). Structure and sequence of formal and postformal thought: General patterns and individual differences. *Child Development, 56,* 1062–1091.

Demmer, C. (2007). Grief is a luxury: AIDS-related loss among the poor in South Africa. *Illness, Crisis & Loss, 15,* 39–51.

Demo, D. H., Fine, M. A., & Ganong, L. H. (2000). Divorce as a family stressor. In P. C. McKenry & S. J. Price (Eds.), *Families and change: Coping with stressful events and transitions* (pp. 279–302). Thousand Oaks, CA: Sage.

DenHartog, D. N., DeHoogh, A. H. B., & Keegan, A. E. (2007). The interactive effects of belongingness and charisma on helping and compliance. *Journal of Applied Psychology, 92,* 1131–1139.

Denissen, J. J. A., Zarrett, N. R., & Eccles, J. S. (2007). I like to do it, I'm able, and I know I am: Longitudinal couplings between domain-specific achievement, self-concept, and interest. *Child Development, 78,* 430–447.

Denmark, F. L., Griffin, A., & Blumenthal, S. J. (Eds.), (1996). *Women and mental health. Annals of the New York Academy of Sciences* (Vol. 789, pp. 101–117).

Denner, J., & Dunbar, N. (2004). Negotiating femininity: Power and strategies of Mexican American girls. *Sex Roles, 50,* 301–314.

Denton, W. H., Burleson, B. R., & Sprenkle, D. H. (1994). Motivation in marital communication: Comparison of distressed and nondistressed husbands and wives. *American Journal of Family Therapy, 22,* 17–26.

Denzin, N. K., & Lincoln, Y. S. (1998). *Strategies of qualitative inquiry.* Thousand Oaks, CA: Sage.

de Rosnay, M., Cooper, P. J., Tsigara, N., & Murray, L. (2006). Transmission of social anxiety from mother to infant: An

experimental study using a social referencing paradigm. *Behaviour Research and Therapy, 44,* 1165–1175.

de St. Aubin, E., McAdams, D. P., & Kim, T. (2004). *The generative society: Caring for future generations.* Washington, DC: American Psychological Association.

DeVoe, J., Peter, K., Noonan, M., Snyder, T., & Baum, K. (2005). *Indicators of school crime and safety: 2005* (NCES 2006-001/NCJ210697). Washington, DC: U.S. Government Printing Office.

DeVries, M. W., & DeVries, M. R. (1977). Cultural relativity of toilet training readiness: A perspective from East Africa. *Pediatrics, 60,* 170–177.

DeVries, R., Hildebrandt, C., & Zan, B. (2000). Constructivist early education for moral development. *Early Education and Development, 11,* 9–35.

Dewey, J. (1896). The reflex arc concept in psychology. *Psychological Review, 3,* 357–370.

De Wolff, M. S., & van IJzendoorn, M. H. (1997). Sensitivity and attachment: A meta-analysis on parental antecedents of infant attachment. *Child Development, 68,* 571–591.

Diamond, A. (2002). Normal development of the prefrontal cortex from birth to young adulthood: Cognitive functions, anatomy, and biochemistry. In D. T. Stuss & R. T. Knight (Eds.), *Principles of frontal lobe function* (pp. 466–503). London: Oxford University Press.

Diamond, L. M. (2000). Passionate friendships among adolescent sexual-minority women. *Journal of Research on Adolescence, 10,* 191–209.

Diaz, R. M. (1983). Thought and two languages: The impact of bilingualism on cognitive development. *Review of Research in Education, 10,* 23–54.

Dickinson, D. K., & Tabors, P. O. (2001). *Beginning literacy with language: Young children learning at home and school.* Baltimore: Brookes.

Dickstein, S., & Parke, R. D. (1988). Social referencing in infancy: A glance at fathers and marriage. *Child Development, 59,* 506–511.

Diehl, M., Hastings, C. T., & Stanton, J. M. (2001). Self-concept differentiation across the adult life span. *Psychology and Aging, 16,* 643–654.

Dielman, T. (1994). School-based research on the prevention of adolescent alcohol use and misuses: Methodological issues and advances. *Journal of Research on Adolescence, 4,* 271–293.

Diemer, M. A., & Blustein, D. L. (2006). Critical consciousness and career development among urban youth. *Journal of Vocational Behavior, 68,* 220–232.

Diener, C. I., & Dweck, C. S. (1980). An analysis of learned helplessness: 2. The processing of success. *Journal of Personality and Social Psychology, 39,* 940–952.

Dijkstra, J. K., Lindenberg, S., & Veenstra, R. (2007). Same-gender and cross-gender peer acceptance and peer rejection and their relation with bullying and helping among preadolescents: A goal-framing approach. *Developmental Psychology, 43,* 1377–1389.

Dill, K. E. (2009). *How fantasy becomes reality: Seeing through media influence.* New York: Oxford University Press.

DiMatteo, M. R., Morton, S. C., Lepper, H. S., Damush, T. M., et al. (1996). Cesarean childbirth and psychosocial outcomes: A meta-analysis. *Health Psychology, 15,* 303–314.

Dindia, K., & Allen, M. (1992). Sex differences in self-disclosure: A meta-analysis. *Psychological Bulletin, 112,* 106–124.

DiPietro, J. A. (2004). The role of prenatal maternal stress in child development. *Current Directions in Psychological Science, 13,* 71–74.

DiPietro, J. A., Caulfield, L. E., Costigan, K. A., Merialdi, M., Nguyen, R. H. N., Zavaleta, N., & Gurewisch, E. D. (2004). Fetal neurobehavioral development: A tale of two cities. *Developmental Psychology, 40,* 445–456.

DiPietro, J. A., Caulfield, L. E., Irizarry, R. A., Chen, P., Merialdi, M., & Zavaleta, N. (2006). Prenatal development of intrafetal and maternal-fetal synchrony. *Behavioral Neuroscience, 120,* 687–701.

DiPietro, J. A., Porges, S. W., & Uhly, B. (1992). Re-activity and developmental competence in preterm and full-term infants. *Developmental Psychology, 28,* 831–841.

DiPietro, L. (2001). Physical activity in aging: Changes in patterns and their relationship to health and function. *Journals of Gerontology: Series A: Biological Sciences and Medical Sciences, 56A,* 13–22.

Dirix, C. E. H., Nijhuis, J. G., Jongsma, H. W., & Hornstra, G. (2009). Aspects of fetal learning and memory. *Child Development, 80,* 1251–1258.

Dishion, T. J., Patterson, G. R., Stoolmiller, M., & Skinner, M. L. (1991). Family, school, and behavioral antecedents to early adolescent involvement with antisocial peers. *Developmental Psychology, 27,* 172–180.

Dishion, T. J., Poulin, F., & Medici-Skaggs, N. (2000). The ecology of premature autonomy in adolescence: Biological and social influences. In K. A. Kerns, A. M. Neal-Barnett, & J. M. Contreras (Eds.), *Family and peers: Linking two social worlds* (pp. 27–46). Westport, CT: Praeger.

Dixon, R. A. (1992). Contextual approaches to adult intellectual development. In R. J. Sternberg & C. A. Berg (Eds.), *Intellectual development* (pp. 350–380). New York: Cambridge University Press.

Dobek, J. C., White, K.N., & Gunter, K.B. (2007). The effect of a Nevel ADL-based training program on performance of activities of daily living and physical fitness. *Journal of Aging and Physical Activity, 15,* 13–25.

Dodge, K. A. (1989). Coordinating responses to aversive stimuli: Introduction to a special section on the development of emotion regulation. *Developmental Psychology, 25,* 339–342.

Dodge, K. A., Pettit, G. S., McClaskey, C. L., & Brown, M. M. (1986). Social competence in children. *Monographs of the Society for Research in Child Development, 51* (2, Serial No. 213).

Dolbin-MacNab, M. L., & Keiley, M. K. (2006). A systemic examination of grandparents' emotional closeness with their custodial grandchildren. *Research in Human Development, 3,* 59–71.

Dole, N., Savitz, D. A., Siega-Riz, A. M., Hertz-Picciotto, I., McMahon, M. J., & Buekens, P. (2004). Psychosocial factors and preterm birth among African American and White women in central North Carolina. *American Journal of Public Health, 94,* 1358–1365.

Domar, A. D., Clapp, D., Slawsby, E., Kessel, B., Orav, J., & Freizinger, M. (2000). The impact of group psychological interventions on distress in infertile women. *Health Psychology, 19,* 568–575.

Dominguez, T.P., Dunkel-Schetter, C., et al. (2008). Racial differences in birth outcomes: The role of general, pregnancy, and racism stress. *Health Psychology, 27,* 194-203.

Domino, G., & Affonso, D. D. (1990). Erikson's life stages: The Inventory of Psychosocial Balance. *Journal of Personality Assessment, 54,* 576–588.

Donald, M. (2001). *A mind so rare: The evolution of human consciousness.* New York: Norton.

Donald, M., Lucke, J., Dunne, M., & Raphael, B. (1995). Gender differences associated with young people's emotional reactions to sexual intercourse. *Journal of Youth and Adolescence, 24,* 453–464.

Donoghue, A.M. (2004). Occupational health hazards in mining: An overview. *Occupational Medicine, 54,* 283–289.

Donovan, M.L. & Corcoran, M.A. (2010). Description of dementia caregiver uplifts and implications for occupational therapists. *American Journal of Occupational Therapy, 64,* 590–595.

Dorfman, L., Woodruff, K., Chavez, V., & Wallack, L. (1997). Youth and violence on local television news in California. *American Journal of Public Health, 87,* 1311–1316.

Dorn, L. D., Dahl, R. E., Woodward, H. R., & Biro, F. (2006). Defining the boundaries of early adolescence: A user's guide to assessing pubertal status and pubertal timing in research with adolescents. *Applied Developmental Science, 10,* 30–56.

Dombeck, M., & Wells-Moran, J. (2010). Applying learning principles to thought: Cognitive restructuring. Retrieved on June 19, 2010, at www.centersite.net/poc/view_doc.php?type=doc&id=9746&cn=353

Doucet, A. (2009). Dad and baby in the first year: Gendered responsibilities and embodiment. *Annals of the Academy of Political and Social Science, 624,* 78–98.

Doukas, D. J., & Reichel, W. (2007). *Planning for uncertainty: Living wills and other advance directives for you and your family.* (2nd ed.) Baltimore, MD: Johns Hopkins University Press.

Doulas of North America. (1998). *The doula's contribution to modern maternity care.* Retrieved August 11, 2004, from http://www.dona.org

Downey, G., & Walker, E. (1989). Social cognition and adjustment in children at risk for psychopathology. *Developmental Psychology, 25,* 835–845.

Downs, L. S. (2004). Facing dying: A hospice worker tells how. *Yoga Chicago.* Retrieved October 31, 2007, from http://www.yogachicago.com/may04/dying.shtml

Dowrick, P. W. (1991). *Practical guide to using video in the behavioral sciences.* New York: Wiley.

Draganski, B.,Winkler, J., Flügel, D., May, A. (2004). Selective activation of ectopic grey matter during motor task. *Neuroreport: For Rapid Communication of Neuroscience Research., 15*(2), 251–253.

Dreman, S. (1997). *The family on the threshold of the 21st century: Trends and implications.* Mahwah, NJ: Erlbaum.

Drew, L. M., & Smith, P. K. (1999). The impact of parental separation/divorce on grandparent–grandchild relationships. *International Journal of Aging and Human Development, 48,* 191–215.

Driver, J., Tabares, A., Shapiro, A., Nahm, E.Y., & Gottman, J. (2003). Interactional patterns in marital success and failure: Gottman laboratory studies. In F. Walsh (Ed.), *Normal family processes: Growing diversity and complexity* (3rd ed.). New York: Guilford Press, pp. 493–513.

Dryfoos, J. G. (1999). The role of the school in children's out-of-school time. *The Future of Children, 9,* 117–134.

Dubler, N. N., & Sabatino, C. P. (1991). Age-based rationing and the law: An exploration. In R. H. Binstock & S. G. Post (Eds.), *Too old for health care? Controversies in medicine, law, economics, and ethics* (pp. 92–119). Baltimore: Johns Hopkins University.

Duckworth, A. L., Peterson, C., Matthews, M. D., & Kelly, D. R. (2007). Grit: Perseverance and passion for long-term goals. *Journal of Personality and Social Psychology, 92,* 1087–1101.

Duckworth, A. L., & Seligman, M. E. P. (2005). Self-discipline outdoes IQ in predicting academic performance of adolescents. *Psychological Science, 16,* 939–944.

Dudgeon, M. R., & Inhorn, M. C. (2004). Men's influence on women's reproductive health: Medical anthropological perspectives. *Social Science and Medicine, 59,* 1379–1395.

Dunbar, E. (1997). The Personal Dimensions of Difference Scale: Measuring multigroup identity with four ethnic groups. *International Journal of Intercultural Relations, 21,* 1–28.

Dunbar, K. (2000). How scientists think in the real world: Implications for science education. *Journal of Applied Developmental Psychology, 21*, 49–58.

Duncan, G. J., Huston, A. C., & Weisner, T. S. (2007). *Higher ground: New Hope for the working poor and their children.* New York: Russell Sage Foundation.

Duncan, G. J., Ziol-Guest, K. M., & Kalil, A. (2010). Early-childhood poverty and adult attainment, behavior, and health. *Child Development, 81*, 306–325.

Dundes, L. (2003). *The manner born: Birth rites in cross-cultural perspective.* Lanham, MD: Alta Mira Press.

Dunkel-Schetter, C., Sagrestano, L. F., Feldman, P., & Killingsworth, C. (1996). Social support and pregnancy: A comprehensive review focusing on ethnicity and culture. In G. R. Pierce & B. R. Sarason (Eds.), *Handbook of social support and the family* (pp. 375–412). New York: Plenum.

Dunkley, T. L., Wertheim, E. H., & Paxton, S. J. (2001). Examination of a model of multiple sociocultural influences on adolescent girls' body dissatisfaction and dietary restraint. *Adolescence, 36*, 265–279.

Dunn, J., Brown, J., & Beardsall, L. (1991). Family talk about feeling states and children's later understanding of others' emotions. *Developmental Psychology, 27*, 448–455.

Dunn, J., Cutting, A. L., & Demetriou, H. (2000). Moral sensibility, understanding others, and children's friendship interactions in the preschool period. *British Journal of Developmental Psychology, 18*, 159–177.

Dunn, M., & Cutler, N. (2000). Sexual issues in older adults. *AIDS Patient Care and STDs, 14*, 67–69.

Dunphy, D. C. (1963). The social structure of urban adolescent peer groups. *Sociometry, 26*, 230–246.

Duran-Aydintug, C. (1995). Former spouses exiting role-identities. *Journal of Divorce and Remarriage, 24*, 23–40.

Durbin, D. L., Darling, N., Steinberg, L., & Brown, B. B. (1993). Parenting style and peer group membership among European-American adolescents. *Journal of Research on Adolescence, 3*, 87–100.

Durik, A. M., Hyde, J. S., & Clark, R. (2000). Sequelae of cesarean and vaginal deliveries: Psychosocial outcomes for mothers and infants. *Developmental Psychology, 36*, 251–260.

Dush, C.M. K., Cohan, C.L., & Amato, P.R. (2003). The relationship between cohabitation and marital quality and stability: Change across cohorts? *Journal of Marriage and Family, 65*, 539–549.

Dutton, Y. C., & Zisook, S. (2005). Adaptation to bereavement. *Death Studies, 29*, 877–903.

Dweck, C. S. (1992). The study of goals in psychology. *Psychological Science, 3*, 165–167.

Dye, J.L. (2008). *Fertility of American Women: 2006.* Current Population Reports, P20–558. U.S. Census Bureau.

Dyk, P. H., & Adams, G. R. (1990). Identity and intimacy: An initial investigation of three theoretical models using cross-lag panel correlations. *Journal of Youth and Adolescence, 19*, 91–110.

Eagly, A. H. (2009). The his and hers of prosocial behavior: An examination of the social psychology of gender. *American Psychologist, 64*, 644–658.

Early, D. M., Pianta, R. C., Taylor, L. C., & Cox, M. J. (2001). Transition practices: Findings from a national survey of kindergarten teachers. *Early Childhood Education Journal, 28*, 199–206.

East, P. L., Hess, L. E., & Lerner, R. M. (1987). Peer social support and adjustment of early adolescent peer groups. *Journal of Early Adolescence, 7*, 153–163.

East, P. L., & Rook, K. S. (1992). Compensatory patterns of support among children's peer relationships: A test using school friends, nonschool friends, and siblings. *Developmental Psychology, 28*, 163–172.

Easterbrook, M. A., Kisilevsky, B. S., Muir, D. W., & Laplante, D. P. (1999). Newborns discriminate normal faces from scrambled faces. *Canadian Journal of Experimental Psychology, 53*, 231–241.

Ebersbach, M. (2009). Achieving a new dimension: Children integrate three stimulus dimensions in volume estimations. *Developmental Psychology, 45*, 877–883.

Eccles, J. S. (1993). School and family effects on the ontogeny of children's interests, self perceptions, and activity choices. In J. E. Jacobs (Ed.), *Developmental perspectives on Motivation: Nebraska Symposium on Motivation, 1992* (pp. 145–208). Lincoln, NE: University of Nebraska Press.

Eccles, J. S., Jacobs, J. E., & Harold, R. D. (1990). Gender-role stereotypes, expectancy effects, and parents' role in the socialization of gender differences in self perceptions and skill acquisition. *Journal of Social Issues, 46*, 182–201.

Eccles, J. S., Wigfield, A., Harold, R. D., & Blumenfeld, P. (1993). Age and gender differences in children's self- and task perceptions during elementary school. *Child Development, 64*, 830–847.

Eckerman, C. O., & Didow, S. M. (1989). Toddlers' social coordinations: Changing responses to another's invitation to play. *Developmental Psychology, 25*, 794–804.

Eckerman, C. O., & Didow, S. M. (1996). Nonverbal imitation and toddlers' mastery of verbal means of achieving coordinated action. *Developmental Psychology, 32*, 141–152.

Eckstein, S., & Shemesh, M. (1992). The rate of acquisition of formal operational schemata in adolescence: A secondary analysis. *Journal of Research in Science Teaching, 29*, 441–451.

Edelstein, R. S., Alexander, K. W., Shaver, P. R., Schaaf, J. M., Quas, J. A., Lovas, G. S., & Goodman, G. S. (2004). Adult attachment style and parental responsiveness during a stressful event. *Attachment and Human Development, 6*, 31–52.

Eder, R. A. (1989). The emergent personologist: The structure and content of 3½-, 5½-, and 7½-year-olds' concepts of themselves and other persons. *Child Development, 60*, 1218–1228.

Eder, R. A., Gerlach, S. G., & Perlmutter, M. (1987). In search of children's selves: Development of the specific and general components of the self-concept. *Child Development, 58*, 1044–1050.

Edhborg, M., Lundh, W., Seimyr, L., & Widstroem, A. (2001). The long-term impact of postnatal depressed mood on mother-child interaction: A preliminary study. *Journal of Reproductive and Infant Psychology, 19*, 61–71.

Edin, K. (2000). What do low-income single mothers say about marriage? *Social Problems, 47*, 112–133.

Edin, K., Kefalas, M. J., & Reed, J. M. (2004). A peek inside the black box: What marriage means for poor unmarried parents. *Journal of Marriage and the Family, 66*, 1007–1014.

Edin, K., & Lein, L. (1997). *Making ends meet: How single mothers survive welfare and low-wage work.* New York: Russell Sage Foundation.

Education Week. (2001). Harris interactive poll of students and technology. *Technology Counts, 2001*, pp. 7–8.

Edwards, C. P., & Liu, W. (2002). Parenting toddlers. In M. H. Bornstein (Ed.), *Handbook of parenting: Vol. 1. Children and parenting* (pp. 45–71). Mahwah, NJ: Erlbaum.

Edwards, C. P., & Whiting, B. B. (1988). *Children of different worlds.* Cambridge, MA: Harvard University Press.

Egan, S. K., & Perry, D. G. (2001). Gender identity: A multidimensional analysis with implications for psychosocial adjustment. *Developmental Psychology, 37*, 451–463.

Egeland, B., Jacobvitz, D., & Sroufe, L. A. (1988). Breaking the cycle of abuse. *Child Development, 59*, 1080–1088.

Egeland, B., & Sroufe, L. A. (1981). Attachment and early maltreatment. *Child Development, 52*, 44–52.

Egley, A., Howell, J.C., & Moore, J.P. (2010). Highlights of the 2008 National Youth Gang Survey. Washington, DC: Office of Juvenile Justice and Delinquency Prevention.

Egley, A., Jr., & Major, A. K. (2004). Highlights of the 2002 National Youth Gang Survey. *Office of Juvenile Justice and Delinquency Prevention Fact Sheet.* Retrieved December 5, 2004, from http://www.ncjrs.org/pdffiles1/ojjdp/fs200401.pdf_Eisenberg,_N.(2000)

Eiden, R. D., Veira, Y., & Granger, D. A. (2009). Prenatal cocaine exposure and infant cortisol reactivity. *Child Development, 80*, 528–543.

Ein-Dor, T., Mikulincer, M., Doron, G., & Shaver, P. R. (2010). The attachment paradox: How can so many of us (the insecure ones) have no adaptive advantages? *Perspectives on Psychological Science, 5,* 123–141.

Eisenberg, N. (2000). Emotion, regulation, and moral development. *Annual Review of Psychology, 51,* 665–697.

Eisenberg, N., & Fabes, R. A. (1998). Prosocial development. In W. Damon & N. Eisenberg (Eds.). *Handbook of child psychology: Vol. 3. Social, emotional, and personality development* (5th ed., pp. 701–778). New York: Wiley.

Eisenberg, N., Fabes, R. A., Guthrie, I. K., & Reiser, M. (2002). The role of emotionality and regulation in children's social competence and adjustment. In L. Pulkkinen & A. Caspi (Eds.). *Paths to successful development: Personality in the life course* (pp. 46–70). New York: Cambridge Univ. Press.

Eisenberg, N., Guthrie, I. K., Murphy, B. C., Shepard, S. A., Cumberland, A., & Carlo, G. (1999). Consistency and development of prosocial dispositions: A longitudinal study. *Child Development, 70,* 1360–1372.

Eisenberg, N., & Morris, A. S. (2004). Moral cognitions and prosocial responding in adolescence. In R. M. Lerner & L. Steinberg (Eds.), *Handbook of adolescent psychology* (2nd ed., pp. 155–188). New York: Wiley.

Eisenberg, N., & Strayer, J. (1987). Critical issues in the study of empathy. In N. Eisenberg & J. Strayer (Eds.), *Empathy and its development* (pp. 3–13). Cambridge, UK: Cambridge University Press.

Ekerdt, D. J., Bosse, R., & Levkoff, S. (1985). An empirical test for phases of retirement: Findings from the normative aging study. *Journal of Gerontology, 40,* 95–101.

Elder, G. H. (1985). *Life course dynamics: Trajectories and transitions, 1968–1980.* Ithaca, NY: Cornell University Press.

Elder, G. H. (1986). Military times and turning points in men's lives. *Developmental Psychology, 22,* 233–245.

Elder, G. H., Jr., Caspi, A., & van Nguyen, T. (1986). Resourceful and vulnerable children: Family influences in hard times. In R. K. Silbereisen et al. (Eds.), *Development as action in context* (pp. 167–186). Berlin: Springer Verlag.

Elder, G. H., Jr., George, L. K., & Shanahan, M. J. (1996). Psychosocial stress over the life course. In H. B. Kaplan (Ed.), *Psychosocial stress: Perspectives on structure, theory, life course, and methods* (pp. 247–291). Orlando, FL: Academic Press.

Elder, G. H., Jr., & Shanahan, M. J. (2006). The Life Course and Human Development. In R. M. Lerner & W. Damon (Eds.), *Handbook of child psychology (6th ed.): Vol. 1, Theoretical models of human development* (pp. 665–715). Hoboken, NJ: John Wiley & Sons.

Elder, G. H., Jr., Shanahan, M. J., & Clipp, E. C. (1997). Linking combat and physical health: The legacy of World War II in men's lives. *American Journal of Psychiatry, 154,* 330–336.

The Elders (2010). News. Retrieved on August 28, 2010, at http://www.theelders.org/media/news

Eldridge, K. A., & Christensen, A. (2002). Demand-withdraw communication during couple conflict: A review and analysis. In P. Noller & J. A. Feeney (Eds.), *Understanding marriage: Developments in the study of couple interaction.* Cambridge, England: Cambridge University Press, 289–322.

Eldridge, K. A., Sevier, M., Jones, J., Atkins, D. C., & Christensen, A. (2007). Demand-withdraw communication in severely distressed, moderately distressed, and nondistressed couples: Rigidity and polarity during relationship and personal problem discussions. *Journal of Family Psychology, 21,* 218–226.

Eldridge, N. S., & Gilbert, L. S. (1990). Correlates of relationship satisfaction in lesbian couples. *Psychology of Women Quarterly, 14,* 43–62.

Elias, M. (1998). Study: Most don't regret abortions. *USA Today: Health.* Retrieved November 18, 2001, from http//www.usatoday.com/life/health/women/abortion/1hwab009.htm

Elias, M. J., Beier, J. J., & Gara, M. A. (1989). Children's responses to interpersonal obstacles as a predictor of social competence. *Journal of Youth and Adolescence, 18,* 451–465.

Elkind, D. (1967). Egocentrism in adolescence. *Child Development, 38,* 1025–1034.

Elkind, D. (2007). *The power of play: Learning what comes naturally.* Philadelphia, PA: Da Capo Press.

Ellickson, P., Saner, H., & McGuigan, K. A. (1997). Profiles of violent youth: Substance use and other concurrent problems. *American Journal of Public Health, 87,* 985–991.

Elliott, G. C., Kao, S., & Grant, A. (2004). Mattering: Empirical validation of a social psychological concept. *Self and Identity, 3,* 339–354.

Ellsworth, C. P., Muir, C. P., & Hains, S. M. J. (1993). Social competence and person–object differentiation: An analysis of the still-face effect. *Developmental Psychology, 29,* 63–73.

Elwert, F., & Christakis, N. A. (2006). Widowhood and race. *American Sociological Review, 71,* 16–41.

Elwert, F., & Christakis, N. A. (2008). The effect of widowhood on mortality by the causes of death of both spouses. *American Journal of Public Health, 98,* 2092–2098.

Emanuel, E. J., & Emanuel, L. (1998). The promise of a good death. *The Lancet, 251,* 21–29.

Emde, R. N., & Buchsbaum, H. K. (1990). "Didn't you hear my mommy?" Autonomy with connectedness in moral self-emergence. In D. Cicchetti & M. Beeghly (Eds.), *The self in transition: Infancy to childhood* (pp. 35–60). Chicago: University of Chicago Press.

Enard, W., Przeworski, M., Fisher, S. E., Lai, C. S., Wiebe, V., Eitano, T., Monaco, A. P., & Paabo, S. (2002). Molecular evolution of FOXP2, a gene involved in speech and language. *Nature, 418,* 869–872.

Encarta. (2004). *Finland.* Retrieved November 18, 2004, from http://encarta.msn.com/encyclopedia_761578960_5/Finland.html

Encarta. (2005). *Funeral rites and customs.* Retrieved March 13, 2005, from http://au.encarta.msn.com/encyclopedia_761565630/Funeral_Rites_and_Customs.html

Ennett, S. T., & Bauman, K. E. (1996). Adolescent social networks: School, demographic and longitudinal considerations. *Journal of Adolescent Research, 11,* 194–215.

Ennett, S. T., et al. (2008). The social ecology of adolescent alcohol misuse. *Child Development, 79,* 1777–1791.

Entwisle, D. R., & Alexander, K. L. (1987). Long-term effects of cesarean delivery on parents' beliefs and children's schooling. *Developmental Psychology, 23,* 676–682.

Entwisle, D. R., Alexander, K. L., & Olson, L. S. (2005). Urban teenagers: Work and dropout. *Youth and Society, 37,* 3–32.

Entwisle, D. R., Alexander, K. L., Pallas, A. M., & Cadigan, D. (1987). The emergent academic self-image of first-graders: Its response to social structure. *Child Development, 58,* 1190–1206.

Epstein, S. (1973). The self-concept revisited; or, a theory of a theory. *American Psychologist, 28,* 404–416.

Epstein, S. (1991). Cognitive-experiential self theory: An integrative theory of personality. In R. Cutis (Ed.), *The self with others: Convergences in psychoanalytic, social, and personality psychology* (pp. 111–137). New York: Guilford Press.

Epstein, S. (1998). Cognitive-experiential self-theory. In D. F. Barone & M. Hersen (Eds.), *Advanced personality* (pp. 211–238). New York: Plenum Press.

Epstein, S. (2003). Cognitive-experiential self theory of personality. In T. Millon & M. J. Lerner (Eds.), *Handbook of psychology: Personality and social psychology* (Vol. 5, pp. 159–184). Hoboken, NJ: John Wiley & Sons.

Epstein, S. (2008). Intuition from the perspective of cognitive-experiential self theory. In H. Plessner, C. Betsch, & T. Betsch (Eds.), *Intuition in judgment and decision making* (pp. 23–37). Mahwah, NJ: Lawrence Erlbaum.

Epstein, S., Lipson, A., Holstein, C., & Huh, E. (1993). Irrational reactions to negative outcomes: Evidence for two conceptual systems. *Journal of Personality and Social Psychology, 62,* 328–339.

Equal Employment Opportunity Commission (EEOC). (2007). Types of discrimination. Retrieved October 3, 2007, from http://www.eeoc.gov/types/index.html

Equalrights.org (2010). Sex discrimination. Retrieved on August 19, 2010, at www.equalrights.org/publications/kyr/sexdiscrim.asp

Erber, J. T. (2005). *Aging and older adulthood.* Belmont, CA: Wadsworth.

Erez, A., Misangyi, V.F., Johnson, D.E., LePine, M.A., & Halverson, K.C. (2008). Stirring the hearts of followers: Charismatic leadership as the transferal of affect. *Journal of Applied Psychology, 93,* 601–616.

Erikson, E. H. (1959). The problem of ego identity. *Psychological Issues*, 1, 101–164.

Erikson, E. H. (1963). *Childhood and society* (2nd ed.). New York: Norton.

Erikson, E. H. (1968). *Identity: Youth and crisis.* New York: Norton.

Erikson, E. H. (1969). *Gandhi's truth: On the origins of militant nonviolence.* New York: Norton.

Erikson, E. H. (1972). Play and actuality. In M. W. Piers (Ed.), *Play and development* (pp. 127–167). New York: Norton.

Erikson, E. H. (1975). "Identity crisis" in autobiographic perspective. In E. H. Erikson (Ed.), *Life history and the historical moment* (pp. 17–47). New York: Norton.

Erikson, E. H. (1977). *Toys and reasons.* New York: Norton.

Erikson, E. H. (1978). Reflections on Dr. Borg's life cycle. In E. H. Erikson (Ed.), *Adulthood* (pp. 1–31). New York: Norton.

Erikson, E. H. (1980). Themes of adulthood in the Freud-Jung correspondence. In N.J. Smelser & E.H. Erikson (Eds.), *Themes of work and love in adulthood* (pp. 43–74). Cambridge, MA: Harvard University Press.

Erikson, E. H. (1982). *The life cycle completed: A review.* New York: Norton.

Erikson, E. H., Erikson, J. M., & Kivnick, H. Q. (1986). *Vital involvement in old age.* New York: Norton.

Erikson, J. M. (1988). *Wisdom and the senses: The way of creativity.* New York: Norton.

Erraji-Benchekroun, L., Underwood, M. D., Arango, V., Galfalvy, H., Pavlidis, P., Smyrniotopoulos, P., Mann, J. J., & Sibille, E. (2005). Molecular aging in human prefrontal cortex is selective and continuous throughout adult life. *Biological Psychiatry*, 57, 549–558.

Escalona, S. K. (1968). *The roots of individuality.* Chicago: Aldine.

Essau, C. A. (2004). Association between family factors and depressive disorders in adolescents. *Journal of Youth and Adolescence*, 33, 365–372.

Etzioni, A. (1976, November). The husband's rights in abortion. *Trial.*

Evans, C.D., & Diekman, A.B. (2009). On motivated role selection: Gender beliefs, distant goals, and career interest. *Psychology of Women Quarterly*, 33, 235–249.

Evans, D. W., Gray, F. L., & Leckman, J. F. (1999). The rituals, fears, and phobias of young children: Insights from development, psychopathology, and neurobiology. *Child Psychiatry and Human Development*, 29, 261–276.

Evans, G. W., Gonnella, C., Marcynyszyn, L. A., & Gentile, L., & Salpekar, N. (2005). The role of chaos in poverty and children's socioemotional adjustment. *Psychological Science*, 16, 560–565.

Evans, N., Gilpin, E., Farkas, A. J., Shenassa, E., & Pierce, J. P. (1995). Adolescents' perceptions of their peers' health norms. *American Journal of Public Health*, 85, 1064–1069.

Fabes, R. A., Eisenberg, N., McCormick, S. E., & Wilson, M. S. (1988). Preschoolers' attributions of the situational determinants of others' naturally occurring emotions. *Developmental Psychology*, 24, 376–385.

Fabes, R. A., Eisenberg, N., Nyman, M., & Michealieu, Q. (1991). Young children's appraisals of others' spontaneous emotional reactions. *Developmental Psychology*, 27, 858–866.

Fagot, B. I. (1995). Parenting boys and girls. In M. H. Bornstein (Ed.), *Handbook of Parenting: Vol. 1. Children and parenting* (pp. 163–183). Mahwah, NJ: Erlbaum.

Fagot, B. I., & Leinbach, M. D. (1989). The young child's gender schema: Environmental input, internal organization. *Child Development*, 60, 663–672.

Fan, J. X., & Zick, C. D. (2006). Expenditure flows near widowhood. *Journal of Family and Economic Issues*, 27, 335–353.

Farkas, G., Grobe, R. P., Sheehan, D., & Shuan, Y. (1990). Cultural resources and school success: Gender, ethnicity, and poverty groups. *American Sociological Review*, 55, 127–142.

Farmer, T. W., & Rodkin, P. C. (1996). Antisocial and prosocial correlates of classroom social positions: The social network centrality perspective. *Social Development*, 5, 174–188.

Farrar, M. J., Raney, G. E., & Boyer, M. E. (1992). Knowledge, concepts, and inferences in childhood. *Child Development*, 63, 673–691.

Farrell, A. D., Danish, S. J., & Howard, C. W. (1992). Risk factors for drug use in urban adolescents: Identification and crossvalidation. *American Journal of Community Psychology*, 20, 263–286.

Farrell, M. P., & Rosenberg, S. D. (1981). *Men at midlife.* Boston: Auburn House.

Fast, N.J. & Chen, S. (2009). When the boss feels inadequate: Power, incompetence and aggression. *Psychological Science, 20*, 1406–1413.

Feagin, J. R., & McKinney, K. D. (2003). *The many costs of racism.* Lanham, MD: Rowman & Littlefield.

Fearon, R. P., Bakermans-Kranenburg, M. J., van IJzendoorn, M. H., Lapsley, A., & Roisman, G. I. (2010). The significance of insecure attachment and disorganization in the development of children's externalizing behavior: A meta-analytic study. *Child Development, 81*, 435–456.

Federal Bureau of Investigation. (2005). Uniform Crime Reports, 1996 and 2005. Retrieved from http://www.fbi.gov/ucr/ucr.htm, on September 23, 2005.

Federal Interagency Forum on Aging Related Statistics. (2004). *Older Americans 2004: Key indicators of well being.* Retrieved February 20, 2005, from http://www.agingstats.gov/chartbook2004/default.htm

Federman, J. (1998). *National television violence study* (Vol. 3). Thousand Oaks, CA: Sage.

Feeney, J. A. (1999). Adult romantic attachment and couple relationships. In J. Cassidy & P. R. Shaver (Eds.), *Handbook of attachment: Theory, research, and clinical applications* (pp. 355–377). New York: Guilford Press.

Feinman, S., & Lewis, M. (1983). Social referencing at ten months: A second-order effect on infants' responses to strangers. *Child Development*, 54, 878–887.

Feinman, S., Roberts, D., Hsieh, K.-F., Sawyer, D., & Swanson, D. (1992). A critical review of social referencing in infancy. In S. Feinman (Ed.), *Social referencing and the social construction of reality in infancy* (pp. 15–54). New York: Plenum Press.

Feldman, R. (2003). Infant–mother and infant–father synchrony: The coregulation of positive arousal. *Infant Mental Health Journal*, 24, 1–23.

Feldman, R. (2004). Mother infant skin-to-skin contact and the development of emotion regulation. In S. P. Shohov (Ed.) *Advances in psychology research* (Vol. 27, pp. 113–131). Hauppauge, NY: Nova Science.

Feldman, R., & Eidelman, A. I. (2004). Mother-infant skin-to-skin contact (Kangaroo Care) accelerates autonomic and neurobehavioral maturation in premature infants. *Developmental Medicine and Child Neurology*, 45, 274–280.

Feldman, S., Byles, J. E., & Beaumont, R. (2000). "Is anybody listening?" The experiences of widowhood for older Australian women. *Journal of Women and Aging*, 12, 155–176.

Fenson, L., Dale, P. S., Reznick, J. S., Bates, E., Thal, D. J., & Pethick, S. J. (1994). Variability in early communicative development. *Monographs of the Society for Research in Child Development*, 59 (Serial No. 5).

Fenster, L., Eskenazi, B., Windham, G. C., & Swan, S. H. (1991). Caffeine consumption during pregnancy and fetal growth. *American Journal of Public Health*, 81, 458–461.

Fentress, J. C., & McLeod, P. J. (1986). Motor patterns in development. In E. M. Blass (Ed.), *Handbook of behavioral neurobiology: Vol. 8. Developmental psychobiology and developmental neurobiology.* New York: Plenum Press.

Fernald, A., Swingly, D., & Pinto, J. P. (2001). When half a word is enough: Infants can recognize spoken words using partial phonetic information. *Child Development*, 72, 1003–1015.

Fiedler, K. (2008). Language: A toolbox for sharing and influencing social reality. *Perspectives on Psychological Science*, 3, 38–47.

Fiel, C. M., Harris, D., & House, R. (1999). Charismatic leadership: Strategies for effecting social change. *Leadership Quarterly*, 10, 449–482.

Field, D. (1981). Can preschool children really learn to conserve? *Child Development*, 52, 326–334.

Field, T. M. (1991). Young children's adaptations to repeated separations from their mothers. *Child Development*, 62, 539–547.

Field, T. M. (2002). Prenatal effects of maternal depression. In S. H. Goodman & I. H. Gotlib (Eds.), *Children of depressed parents: Mechanisms of risk and implications for treatment* (pp. 59–88). Washington, DC: American Psychological Association.

Field, T. M., Cohen, D., Garcia, R., & Greenberg, R. (1984). Mother-stranger face discrimination by the newborn. *Infant Behavior and Development*, 7, 19–25.

Field, T. M., Diego, M., Hernandez-Reif, M., Schanberg, S., Kuhn, C., Yando, R., & Bendell, D. (2003). Pregnancy anxiety and comorbid depression and anger: Effects on the fetus and neonate. *Depression & Anxiety, 17,* 140–151.

Field, T. M., Healy, B., Goldstein, S., Perry, S., Bendell, D., Schanberg, S., et al. (1988). Infants of depressed mothers show "depressed" behavior even with nondepressed adults. *Child Development, 59,* 1569–1579.

Field, T. M., Woodson, R. W., Greenberg, R., & Cohen, C. (1982). Discrimination and imitation of facial expressions by neonates. *Science, 218,* 179–181.

Fife, B. L., & Wright, E. R. (2000). The dimensionality of stigma: A comparison of its impact on the self of persons with HIV/AIDS and Cancer. *Journal of Health and Social Behavior, 41,* 50–67.

Filion, K. (2009). Fact sheet for 2009 minimum wage increase. *Economic Policy Institute.* Retrieved from the Internet on November 11, 2009, at www.epi.org/publications/entry/mwig_fact_sheet/

Fincham, F., & Jaspars, J. (1979). Attribution of responsibility to the self and other in children and adults. *Journal of Personality and Social Psychology, 37,* 1589–1602.

Finer, L. B., & Henshaw, S. K. (2003). Abortion incidence and services in the United States in 2000. *Perspectives on Sexual and Reproductive Health, 35*(1), 1–15.

Finer, L. B., & Henshaw, S. K. (2006) *Estimates of U.S. abortion incidence, 2001–2003.* New York: Guttmacher Institute.

Fingerman, K., Miller, L., Birditt, K., & Zarit, S. (2009). Giving to the good and the needy: Parental support of grown children. *Journal of Marriage and the Family, 71,* 1220–1233.

Fingerman, K. L., Hay, E. L., & Birditt, K. S. (2004). The best of ties, the worst of ties: Close, problematic, and ambivalent social relationships. *Journal of Marriage and the Family, 66,* 792–808.

Finkenauer, C., Engels, R. C. M. E., Branje, S. J. T., & Meeus, W. (2004). Disclosure and relationship satisfaction in families. *Journal of Marriage and the Family, 66,* 195–209.

Finley, M. (1984). *Couvade and the cloud of unknowing.* Retrieved November 15, 2001, from http://www.mfinley.com/articles/couvade.htm

Finley, N. J. (1989). Gender differences in caregiving for elderly parents. *Journal of Marriage and the Family, 51,* 79–86.

Fiol, C. M., Harris, D., & House, R. (1999). Charismatic leadership: Strategies for effecting social change. *Leadership Quarterly, 10*(3) 449–482.

Firestone, R. W., Firestone, L. A., & Catlett, J. (2006). Couple relationships: Jealousy and sexual rivals. In F. W. Firestone, L. A. Firestone, & J. Catlett (Eds.), *Sex and love in intimate relationships.* Washington, DC: American Psychological Association, pp. 197–225.

Fischer, K. W. (1980). A theory of cognitive development: The control and construction of hierarchies of skills. *Psychological Review, 87,* 477–531.

Fischer, K. W., & Bidell, T. R. (1992, Winter). Ever younger ages: Constructive use of nativist findings about early development. *Newsletter of the Society for Research in Child Development,* pp. 1, 10, 11, 14.

Fischer, K. W., & Bidell, T. R. (2006). Dynamic development of action and thought. In W. Damon & R. M. Lerner (Eds.). *Theoretical Models of Human Development: Handbook of Child Psychology,* 6th Ed. (Vol. 1, pp. 313–399). New York: Wiley.

Fischer, K. W., Bullock, D., Rotenberg, E. J., & Raya, P. (1993). The dynamics of competence: How context contributes directly to skill. In R. Wozniak & K. Fischer (Eds.), *Development in context: Acting and thinking in specific environments* (JPS Series on Knowledge and Development, Vol. 1, pp. 93–117). Hillsdale, NJ: Erlbaum.

Fischer, K. W., & Rose, S. P. (1994). Dynamic development of coordination of components of brain and behavior: A framework for theory and research. In G. Dawson & K. W. Fischer (Eds.), *Human behavior and the developing brain* (pp. 3–66). New York: Guilford Press.

Fischer, K. W., & Silvern, L. (1985). Stages and individual differences in cognitive development. *Annual Review of Psychology, 36,* 613–648.

Fischer, K. W., & Wozniak, R. (Eds.) (2002). *Development in context: Acting and thinking in specific environments* (JPS Series on Knowledge and Development, Vol. 1, pp. 93–117). Hillsdale, NJ: Erlbaum.

Fischer, T. F. C., De Graaf, P. M., & Kalmijn, M. (2005). Friendly and antagonistic contact between former spouses after divorce: Patterns and determinants. *Journal of Family Issues, 26,* 1131–1163.

Fisher, L. & Trenkamp, B. (2010). *Income of the aged chartbook, 2008.* Social Security Administration. Retrieved on August 24, 2010, at http://www.socialsecurity.gov/policy/docs/chartbooks/income_aged/2008/iac08.pdf

Fitch, J. (1999). *White oleander.* Boston: Little, Brown.

Fitzgerald, B. (1999). Children of lesbian and gay parents: A review of the literature. *Marriage and Family Review, 29,* 57–75.

Fitzsimons, G. M., & Finkel, E. J. (2010). Interpersonal influences on self-regulation. *Current Directions in Psychological Science, 19,* 101–105.

Flavell, J. H. (1963). *The developmental psychology of Jean Piaget.* Princeton, NJ: Van Nostrand.

Flavell, J. H. (1974). The development of inferences about others. In W. Mischel (Ed.), *Understanding other persons.* Oxford: Blackwell, Basil & Mott.

Flavell, J. H. (1982). Structures, stages, and sequences in cognitive development. In W. A. Collins (Ed.), *The concept of development* (pp. 1–28). Hillsdale, NJ: Erlbaum.

Flavell, J. H., Flavell, E. R., & Green, F. L. (1987). Young children's knowledge about the apparent-real and pretend-real distinctions. *Developmental Psychology, 23,* 816–822.

Fleming, A. S., Ruble, D. N., Flett, G. L., & Shaul, D. L. (1988). Postpartum adjustment in first-time mothers: Relations between mood, maternal attitudes, and mother–infant interactions. *Developmental Psychology, 24,* 71–81.

Fletcher, W. L., & Hansson, R. O. (1991). Assessing the social components of retirement anxiety. *Psychology and Aging, 6,* 76–85.

Floet, A. M. W., & Maldonado-Duran, J. M. (2006). Motor skills disorders. *eMedicine.* Retrieved August 16, 2007, from http://www.emedicine.com/ped/topic2640.htm

Flom, R. & Bahrick, L. E. (2010). The effects of intersensory redundancy on attention and memory: Infants' long-term memory for orientation in audio-visual events. *Developmental Psychology, 46,* 428–436.

Florian, V., & Kravetz, S. (1983). Fear of personal death: Attribution structure and relation to religious belief. *Journal of Personality and Social Psychology, 44,* 600–607.

Floyd, F. J., Haynes, S. N., Doll, E. R., Winemiller, D., Lemsky, C., Burgy, T. M., et al. (1992). Assessing retirement satisfaction and perceptions of retirement experiences. *Psychology and Aging, 7,* 609–621.

Floyd, F. J., Stein, T. S., Harter, K. S. M., Allison, A., & Nye, C. L. (1999). Gay, lesbian, and bisexual youths: Separation-individuation, parental attitudes, identity consolidation, and well-being. *Journal of Youth and Adolescence, 28,* 719–739.

Flynn, K., & Fitzgibbon, M. (1996). Body image ideals of low-income African American mothers and their preadolescent daughters. *Journal of Youth and Adolescence, 25,* 615–630.

Fogel, A., Hsu, H-C., Shaprio, A. F., Nelson-Goens, G. C., & Secrist, C. (2006). Effects of normal and perturbed social play on the duration and amplitude of different types of infant smiles. *Developmental Psychology, 42,* 459–473.

Foley, D. J., Vitiello, M. V., Bilwise, D. L., Ancoli-Israel, S., Monjan, A. A., & Walsh, J. K. (2007). Frequent napping is associated with excessive daytime sleepiness, depression, pain, and nocturia in older adults. *American Journal of Geriatric Psychiatry, 15,* 344–350.

Folkman, S., & Moskowitz, J. T. (2000). Positive affect and the other side of coping. *American Psychologist, 55,* 647–654.

Fonagy, P. (1999). Psychoanalytic theory from the viewpoint of attachment theory and research. In J. Cassidy & P. R. Shaver (Eds.), *Handbook of attachment: Theory, research, and clinical applications* (pp. 595–624). New York: Guilford Press.

Fonagy, P. (2003). The development of psychopathology from infancy to adulthood: The mysterious unfolding of disturbance in time. *Infant Mental Health Journal, 24,* 212–239.

Fonagy, P., Steele, H., & Steele, M. (1991). Maternal representations of attachment during pregnancy predict the organization of infant-mother attachment at one year of age. *Child Development, 62,* 891–905.

Fontana, A., & Keene, J.R. (2009). *Death and dying in America.* Malden, MA: Polity Press.

Fontane, P. E. (1996). Exercise, fitness, feeling well. *American Behavioral Scientist, 39,* 288–305.

Ford, C. S. (1945). A comparative study of human reproduction. *Yale University Publications in Anthropology* (No. 32).

Fordham, K., & Stevenson-Hinde, J. (1999). Shyness, friendship quality, and adjustment during middle childhood. *Journal of Child Psychology and Psychiatry and Allied Disciplines, 40,* 757–768.

Forman, T. A. (2003). The social psychological costs of racial segmentation in the workplace: A study of African Americans' well-being. *Journal of Health and Social Behavior, 44,* 332–352.

Forret, M. L., Sullivan, S. E., & Miniero, L. A. (2010). Gender role differences in reactions to unemployment: Exploring psychological mobility and boundaryless careers. *Journal of Organizational Behavior, 31,* 647–666.

Fosburgh, L. (1977, August 7). The make-believe world of teen-age maturity. *New York Times Magazine,* pp. 29–34.

Fouad, N.A., & Bynner, J. (2008). Work transitions. *American Psychologist, 63,* 241–251.

Fowers, B. J., Montel, K. H., & Olson, D. H. (1996). Predicting marital success for premarital couple types based on PREPARE. *Journal of Marital and Family Therapy, 22,* 103–119.

Fowler, F. L., Jr. (1993). *Survey research methods* (2nd ed.). Thousand Oaks, CA: Sage.

Fox, N. A., Hane, A. A., & Pine, D. S. (2007). Plasticity for affective neurocircuitry. *Current Directions in Psychological Science, 16,* 1–5.

Fox, N. A., Kimmerly, N. L., & Schafer, W. D. (1991). Attachment to mother/attachment to father. *Child Development, 62,* 210–225.

Fraley, R. C., & Shaver, P. R. (2000). Adult romantic attachment: Theoretical developments, emerging controversies, and unanswered questions. *Review of General Psychology, 4,* 132–154.

Frankenberg, W. K., & Dodds, J. B. (1967). The Developmental Screening Test. *Journal of Pediatrics, 71,* 181–191.

Franklin, D. L. (1988). Race, class, and adolescent pregnancy: An ecological analysis. *American Journal of Orthopsychiatry, 58,* 339–355.

Franko, D. L., & Striegel-Moore, R. H. (2002). The role of body dissatisfaction as a risk factor for depression in adolescent girls: Are the differences Black and White? *Journal of Psychosomatic Research, 53,* 975–983.

Fraser, S. I., & Walters, J. W. (2000). Death—whose decision? Euthanasia and the terminally ill. *Journal of Medical Ethics, 26,* 121–125.

Frazier, P., Byer, A. L., Fischer, A. R., Wright, D. M., & DeBord, K. A. (1996). Adult attachment style and partner choice: Correlational and experimental findings. *Personal Relationships, 3,* 117–136.

Fredriksen, K., Rhodes, J., Reddy, R., & Way, N. (2004). Sleepless in Chicago: Tracking the effects of adolescent sleep loss during the middle school years. *Child Development, 75,* 84–95.

Freedman, D. J., Riesenhuber, M., Poggio, T., & Miller, E. K. (2001). Categorical representation of visual stimuli in the primate prefrontal cortex. *Science, 291,* 312–316.

Freeman, R. B., & Wise, D. A. (1982). *The youth labor market: Problems in the United States.* Chicago: University of Chicago Press.

Freiberg, K., Tually, K., & Crassini, B. (2001). Use of an auditory looming task to test infants' sensitivity to sound pressure level as an auditory distance cue. *British Journal of Developmental Psychology, 19,* 1–10.

French, D. C. (1984). Children's knowledge of the social functions of younger, older and same-age peers. *Child Development, 55,* 1429–1433.

French, D. C. (1988). Heterogeneity of peer-rejected boys: Aggressive and nonaggressive subtypes. *Child Development, 59,* 976–985.

French, D. C. (1990). Heterogeneity of peer-rejected girls. *Child Development, 61,* 2028–2031.

French, S. B., Seidman, E., Allen, L., & Aber, J. L. (2000). Racial/ethnic identity, congruence with the social context, and the transition to high school. *Journal of Adolescent Research, 15,* 587–603.

Frese, M. (2001). Personal initiative: The theoretical concept and empirical findings. In M. Erez & U. Kleinbeck (Eds.), *Work motivation in the context of a globalizing economy* (pp. 99–110). Mahwah, NJ: Erlbaum.

Freud, A. (1936/1946). *The ego and the mechanisms of defense.* New York: International Universities Press.

Freud, A. (1965). Normality and pathology in childhood. In *Writings of Anna Freud (Vol. 6)* (pp. 3–235). New York: International Universities Press.

Freud, A., & Dann, S. (1951). An experiment in group upbringing. In R. Eissler, A. Freud, H. Hartmann, & E. Kris (Eds.), *The psychoanalytic study of the child* (Vol. 6, pp. 127–168). New York: International Universities Press.

Freud, S. (1905/1953). Three essays on the theory of sexuality. In J. Strachey (Ed.), *The standard edition of the complete psychological works of Sigmund Freud* (Vol. 7, pp. 125–245). London: Hogarth Press.

Freud, S. (1909/1955). An analysis of a phobia in a 5-year-old boy. In J. Strachey (Ed.), *The standard edition of the complete psychological works of Sigmund Freud* (Vol. 10, 5–149). London: Hogarth Press.

Freud, S. (1925/1961). Some psychical consequences of the anatomical distinction between the sexes. In J. Strachey (Ed.), *The standard edition of the complete psychological works of Sigmund Freud* (Vol. 19, pp. 248–258). London: Hogarth Press.

Freud, S. (1933/1964). New introductory lectures on psychoanalysis. In J. Strachey (Ed.), *The standard edition of the complete psychological works of Sigmund Freud* (Vol. 22, pp. 3–182). London: Hogarth Press.

Freud, S. (1994). The social construction of gender. *Journal of Adult Development, 1,* 37–46.

Freund, A. M., & Baltes, P. B. (1998). Selection, optimization, and compensation as strategies of life management: Correlations with subjective indicators of successful aging. *Psychology and Aging, 13,* 531–543.

Frey, K. S., & Ruble, D. N. (1987). What children say about classroom performance: Sex and grade differences in perceived competence. *Child Development, 58,* 1066–1078.

Frey, P. S. (2003). Perceived self-efficacy domains as predictors of fear of the unknown and fear of dying among older adults. *Psychology and Aging, 18,* 474–486.

Friedman, C. K., Leaper, C., & Bigler, R. S. (2007). Do mothers' gender-related attitudes or comments predict young children's gender beliefs? *Parenting: Science and Practice, 7,* 357–366.

Friedman, W. J., Robinson, A. B., & Friedman, B. L. (1987). Sex differences in moral judgments? A test of Gilligan's theory. *Psychology of Women Quarterly, 11,* 37–46.

Froming, W. J., Allen, L., & Jensen, R. (1985). Altruism, role-taking, and self-awareness: The acquisition of norms governing altruistic behavior. *Child Development, 56,* 1123–1228.

Froming, W. J., Nasby, W., & McManus, J. (1998). Prosocial self-schemas, self-awareness, and children's prosocial behavior. *Journal of Personality and Social Psychology, 75,* 766–777.

Frone, M. R. (2003). Work–family balance. In J. C. Quick & L. E. Tetrick (Eds.), *Handbook of occupational health psychology* (pp. 143–162). Washington, DC: American Psychological Association.

Fruhauf, C. A., Jarrott, S. E., & Allen, K. R. (2006). Grandchildren's perceptions of caring for grandparents. *Journal of Family Issues, 27,* 887–911.

Fuller, B., Kagan, S. L., Caspary, G. L., & Gauthier, C. A. (2002). Welfare reform and childcare options for low-income families. *The Future of Children, 12,* 97–119.

Fultz, N. H., & Herzog, A. R. (1991). Gender differences in affiliation and instrumentality across adulthood. *Psychology and Aging, 6,* 579–586.

Funk, J. B., Baldacci, H. B., Pasold, T., & Baumgardner, J. (2004). Violence exposure in real-life, video games, television, movies, and the Internet: Is there desensitization? *Journal of Adolescence, 27,* 23–39.

Furman, W., & Wehner, E. A. (1997). Adolescent romantic relationships: A developmental perspective. In S. Shulman & W. A. Collins (Eds.), *Romantic relationships in adolescence: Developmental perspectives* (pp. 21–36). San Francisco: Jossey-Bass.

Furstenberg, F.F. (2010). Passage to adulthood. *The Prevention Researcher, 17,* 3–7.

Futterman, A., Gallagher, D., Thompson, L. W., Lovett, S., & Gilewski, M. (1990). Retrospective assessment of marital adjustment and depression during the first two years of spousal bereavement. *Psychology and Aging, 5*, 277–283.

Gabrieli, J. D. E. (2009). Dyslexia: A new synergy between education and cognitive neuroscience. *Science, 325*, 280–283.

Gaddis, A., & Brooks-Gunn, J. (1985). The male experience of pubertal change. *Journal of Youth and Adolescence, 14*, 61–69.

Gaina, A., Sekine, M., Chen, X., Hamanishi, S., & Kagamimori, S. (2004). Sleep parameters recorded by Actiwatch® in elementary school children and junior high school adolescents: Schooldays vs. weekends. *Sleep and Hypnosis, 6*, 66–77.

Galindo, C., & Fuller, B. (2010). The social competence of Latino kindergarteners and growth in mathematical understanding. *Developmental Psychology, 46*, 579–592.

Galinsky, E. (2007). Dual-centric: A new concept of work-life. Retrieved on September 26, 2007, from http://familiesandwork.org/site/research/reports/main.html

Gall, T. L., Evans, D. R., & Howard, J. (1997). The retirement adjustment process: Changes in the well-being of male retirees across time. *Journal of Gerontology, 52*, P110–P117.

Gallahue, D. L., & Ozmun, J. C. (2006). Motor development in young children. In B. Spodek & O. N. Saracho (Eds.), *Handbook of research on the education of young children* (2nd edition, pp. 105–120). Mahwah, NJ: Lawrence Erlbaum.

Galler, J. R., & Tonkiss, J. (1998). The effects of prenatal protein malnutrition and cocaine on the development of the rat. In J. A. Harvey & B. E. Kosofsky (Eds.), *Cocaine: Effects on the developing brain* (pp. 29–39). New York: New York.

Gallese, V. (2006). Intentional attunement: A neurophysiological perspective on social cognition and its disruption in autism. *Brain Research, 1079*, 15–24.

Galotti, K. M. (1989). Gender differences in self-reported moral reasoning: A review of new evidence. *Journal of Youth and Adolescence, 18*, 475–488.

Galotti, K. M., Kozberg, S. F., & Farmer, M. C. (1991). Gender and developmental differences in adolescents' conceptions of moral reasoning. *Journal of Youth and Adolescence, 20*, 13–30.

Galt, A. H. (1991). Magical misfortune in Locorotondo. *American Ethnologist, 18*, 735–750.

Galyer, K. T., & Evans, I. M. (2001). Pretend play and the development of emotion regulation in preschool children. *Early Child Development and Care, 166*, 93–108.

Ganea, P. A., Lillard, A. S., & Turkheimer, E. (2004). Preschoolers' understanding of the role of mental states and action in pretense. *Journal of Cognition and Development, 5*, 213–238.

Garbarino, J. (2001). An ecological perspective on the effects of violence on children. *Journal of Community Psychology, 29*, 361–378.

Gardiner, H. W., & Kosmitzki, C. (2005). *Lives across cultures: Cross-cultural human development* (3rd ed.). Boston: Pearson.

Gardner, H. (1983). *Frames of mind: The theory of multiple intelligences.* New York: Basic Books.

Gardner, H. (1993). *Creating minds.* New York: Basic Books.

Gardner, H., Kornhaber, M. L., & Wake, W. K. (1996). *Intelligence: Multiple perspectives.* Fort Worth, TX: Harcourt Brace.

Garguilo, J., Attie, I., Brooks-Gunn, J., & Warren, M. P. (1987). Dating in middle school girls: Effects of social context, maturation, and grade. *Developmental Psychology, 23*, 730–737.

Garland, A. F., & Zigler, E. (1993). Adolescent suicide prevention: Current research and social policy implications. *American Psychologist, 48*, 169–182.

Garmezy, N. (1991). Resilience in children's adaptation to negative life events and stressed environments. *Pediatric Annals, 20*, 459–466.

Garrett-Peters, R. (2009). "If I don't have to work anymore, who am I?": Job loss and collaborative self-concept repair. *Journal of Contemporary Ethnography, 38*, 547–583.

Garrison, C. Z., Schluchter, M. D., Schoenbach, V. J., & Kaplan, B. K. (1989). Epidemiology of depressive symptoms in young adolescents. *Journal of the American Academy of Child and Adolescent Psychiatry, 28*, 343–351.

Garrison, M. M., & Christakis, D. A. (2005). *A teacher in the living room.* The Kaiser Family Foundation. Retrieved on May 30, 2010, at www.kff.org/entmedia/upload/7427.pdf

Garton, A. F. (1992). *Social interaction and the development of language and cognition.* Hillsdale, NJ: Erlbaum.

Gartstein, M. A., Bridgett, D. J., Rothbart, M. K., Robertson, C., Iddins, E., Ramsay, K., & Schlect, S. (2010). A latent growth examination of fear development in infancy: Contributions of maternal depression and the risk for toddler anxiety. *Developmental Psychology, 46*, 651–668.

Gati, I., Osipow, S. H., & Givon, M. (1995). Gender differences in career decision making: The content and structure of preference. *Journal of Counseling Psychology, 42*, 204–215.

Gattai, F. B., & Musatti, T. (1999). Grandmothers' involvement in grandchildren's care: Attitudes, feelings, and emotions. *Family Relations: Interdisciplinary Journal of Applied Family Studies, 48*, 35–42.

Gavin, L. A., & Furman, W. (1989). Age differences in adolescents' perceptions of their peer groups. *Developmental Psychology, 25*, 827–834.

Gazelle, H. (2008). Behavioral profiles of anxious solitary children and heterogeneity in peer relations. *Developmental Psychology, 44*, 1604–1624.

Gazelle, H., & Druhen, M. J. (2009). Anxious solitude and peer exclusion predict social helplessness, upset affect, and vagal regulation in response to behavioral rejection from a friend. *Developmental Psychology, 45*, 1077–1096.

Ge, X., Conger, R. D., & Elder, G. H., Jr. (2001). The relation between puberty and psychological distress in adolescent boys. *Journal of Research on Adolescence, 11*, 49–70.

Ge, X., & Natsuaki, M.N. (2009). In search of explanations for early pubertal timing effects on developmental psychopathology. *Current Directions in Psychological Science, 18*, 327–331.

Geary, D. C., & Brown, S. C. (1991). Cognitive addition: Strategy choice and speed of processing differences in gifted, normal, and mathematically disabled children. *Developmental Psychology, 27*, 398–406.

Geary, D. C., Brown, S. C., & Samaranayake, V. A. (1991). Cognitive addition: A short longitudinal study of strategy choice and speed-of-processing differences in normal and mathematically disabled children. *Developmental Psychology, 27*, 787–797.

Geary, D. C., Hoard, M. K., Byrd-Craven, J., & DeSoto, M. C. (2004). Strategy choices in simple and complex addition: Contributions of working memory and counting knowledge for children with mathematical disability. *Journal of Experimental Child Psychology, 88*, 121–151.

Geary, D. C., Vigil, J., & Byrd-Craven, J. (2004). Evolution of human mate choice. *Journal of Sex Research, 41*, 27–42.

Geffken, G., Sajid, M., & MacNaughton, K. (2005). The course of childhood OCD, its antecedents, onset, comorbidities, remission, and reemergence: A 12-year case report. *Clinical Case Studies, 4*, 380–394.

Gelbach, H. (2006). How changes in students' goal orientations relate to outcomes in social studies. *Journal of Educational Research, 99*, 358–370.

Gelissen, J. P. T. M. 2003. Cross-national differences in public consent to divorce: Effects of cultural, structural and compositional factors. In W. Arts, L. C. J. M. Halman, & J. A. P. Hagenaars (Eds.), *The Cultural Diversity of European Unity: Findings, Explanations and Reflections from the European Values Study.* Brill Academic Publishers, Leiden, pp. 339–370.

Gelles, R. J. (1989). Child abuse and violence in single-parent families: Parent absence and economic deprivation. *American Journal of Orthopsychiatry, 59*, 492–501.

Gelman, D. (1992, February 24). Born or bred: The origins of homosexuality. *Newsweek*, pp. 46–53.

Gentile, D. A., & Walsh, D. A. (2002). A normative study of family media habits. *Applied Developmental Psychology, 23*, 157–178.

George, C., Kaplan, N., & Main, M. (1996). *Adult Attachment Interview Protocol* (3rd ed.) Unpublished manuscript, Department of Psychology, University of California at Berkeley.

George, C., & Solomon, J. (1999). Attachment and caregiving: The caregiving behavioral system. In J. Cassidy & P. R. Shaver (Eds.), *Handbook of attachment: Theory, research, and clinical applications* (pp. 649–670). New York: Guilford Press.

Gerbner, G., Gross, L., Morgan, M., & Signorelli, N. (1980). The "mainstreaming" of America: Violence profile no. 11. *Journal of Communication, 30,* 10–29.

Gerhold, M., Laucht, M., Texdorf, C., Schmidt, M. H., & Esser, G. (2002). Early mother–infant interaction as a precursor to childhood social withdrawal. *Child Psychiatry & Human Development, 32,* 277–293.

Gernsbacher, M. A., & Kaschak, M. P. (2003). Neuroimaging studies of language production and comprehension. *Annual Review of Psychology, 54,* 91–114.

Gershoff, E. T. (2003). Low-income and hardship among America's kindergartners (Living at the edge, No. 3). New York, NY: National Center for Children in Poverty, Columbia University Mailman School of Public Health.

Getchell, N., & Robertson, M. A. (1989). Whole body stiffness as a function of developmental level in children's hopping. *Developmental Psychology, 25,* 920–928.

Geyman, J. P., Oliver, L. M., & Sullivan, S. D. (1999). Expectant, medical, or surgical treatment of spontaneous abortion in first trimester of pregnancy? A pooled quantitative literature evaluation. *Journal of the American Board of Family Practice, 12,* 55–64.

Ghazanfareeon Karlsson, S., & Borrell, K. (2002). Intimacy and autonomy, gender and ageing: Living apart together. *Ageing International, 27,* 11–26.

Giambra, L. M., Arenberg, D., Zonderman, A. B., & Kawas, C. (1995). Adult life span changes in immediate visual memory and verbal intelligence. *Psychology and Aging, 10,* 123–139.

Giarrusso, R., Silverstein, M., & Bengston, V. L. (1996). Family complexity and the grandparenting role. *Generations: Quarterly Journal of the American Society on Aging, 20,* 17–23.

Gibbons, A. (2008). The birth of childhood. *Science, 322,* 1040–1043.

Gibbs, J. C. (1979). Kohlberg's moral stage theory: A Piagetian revision. *Human Development, 22,* 89–112.

Gibson, E. J., & Pick, A. D. (2000). *An ecological approach to perceptual learning and development.* London: Oxford University Press.

Gibson, E. J., & Walker, A. S. (1984). Development of knowledge of visual-tactual affordances of substance. *Child Development, 55,* 453–460.

Gibson, F. L., Ungerer, J. A., McMahon, C. A., Leslie, G. I., & Saunders, D. M. (2000). The mother-child relationship following in vitro fertilisation (IVF): Infant attachment, responsivity, and maternal sensitivity. *Journal of Child Psychology and Psychiatry and Allied Disciplines, 41,* 1015–1023.

Gielen, U. P., & Markoulis, D. C. (2001). Preference for principled moral reasoning: A developmental and cross-cultural perspective. In L. L Adler & U. P. Gielen (Eds.), *Cross-cultural topics in psychology* (2nd ed., pp. 81–101). Westport, CT: Praeger/Greenwood.

Gielen, U. P., & Miao, E. S. C. Y. (2000). Perceived parental behavior and the development of moral reasoning in students from Taiwan. In A. L. Comunian & U. P. Gielen (Eds.), *International perspectives on human development* (pp. 479–503). Lengerich, Germany: Pabst.

Gifford-Smith, M. E., & Brownell, C. A. (2003). Childhood peer relationships: Social acceptance, friendships, and peer networks. *Journal of School Psychology, 41,* 235–284.

Giles, D., Shaw, R.L., & Morgan, W. (2009). Representations of voluntary childlessness in the U.K. press, 1990–2008. *Journal of Health Psychology, 14,* 1218–1228.

Gilissen, R., Koolstra, C. M., van IJzendoorn, M. H., Bakermans-Kranenburg, M. J., & van der Veer, R. (2007). Physiological reactions of preschoolers to fear-inducing film clips: Effects of temperamental fearfulness and quality of the parent-child relationship. *Developmental Psychobiology, 49,* 187–195.

Gillath, O., & Shaver, P. R. (2007). Effects of attachment style and relationship context on selection among relational strategies. *Journal of Research in Personality, 41,* 968–976.

Gillen, M. & Kim, H. (2009). Older women and poverty transition: Consequences of income source changes from widowhood. *Journal of Applied Gerontology, 28,* 320–341.

Gillespie, C. (1989). *Hormones, hot flashes, and mood swings.* New York: Harper & Row.

Gilligan, C. (1977). In a different voice: Women's conceptions of self and morality. *Harvard Educational Review, 47,* 481–517.

Gilligan, C. (1988). *Mapping the moral domain: A contribution of women's thinking to psychological theory and education.* Cambridge, MA: Harvard University Press.

Ginsburg, H. P., Lee, J. S., & Boyd, J. S. (2008). Mathematics education for young children: What it is and how to promote it. *Social Policy Report, 22,* Whole.

Ginsburg, H. P., & Pappas, S. (2004). SES, ethnic, and gender differences in young children's informal addition and subtraction: A clinical interview investigation. *Journal of Applied Developmental Psychology, 25,* 171–192.

Ginsburg, S. D., & Orlofsky, J. L. (1981). Ego identity status, ego development, and focus of control in college women. *Journal of Youth and Adolescence, 10,* 297–307.

Gladwell, M. (2008). *Outliers: The story of success.* Boston: Little, Brown.

Glass, T. A. (1998). Conjugating the "tenses" of function: Discordance among hypothetical, experimental, and enacted function in older adults. *The Gerontologist, 38,* 101–112.

Gleason, T. R. (2002). Social provisions of real and imaginary relationships in early childhood. *Developmental Psychology, 38,* 979–992.

Gleason, T. R., Sebanc, A. M., & Hartup, W. W. (2003). Imaginary companions of preschool children. In M. E. Hertzig & E. A. Farber (Eds.), *Annual progress in child psychiatry and child development: 2000–2001* (pp. 101–121). New York: Brunner-Routledge.

Glenn, N. D., & Kramer, K. B. (1987). Marriages and divorces of children of divorce. *Journal of Marriage and the Family, 49,* 811–826.

Glick, P. C. (1957). *American families.* New York: Wiley.

Gliner, J. A., & Morgan, G. A. (2000). *Research methods in applied settings: An integrated approach to design and analysis.* Mahwah, NJ: Erlbaum.

Glodis, K. A., & Blasi, A. (1993). The sense of self and identity among adolescents and adults. *Journal of Adolescent Research, 8,* 356–380.

Glover, V. (1997). Maternal stress or anxiety in pregnancy and emotional development of the child. *British Journal of Psychiatry, 171,* 105–106.

Godina, E. Z. (2009). The secular trend: History and prospects. *Human Physiology, 35,* 770–776.

Goldbaum, S., Craig, W. M., Pepler, D., & Connolly, J. (2003). Developmental trajectories of victimization: Identifying risk and protective factors. *Journal of Applied School Psychology, 19,* 139–156.

Goldberg, E. (2001). Starboys. In A. Walker, M. Manoogan-O'Dell, L. McGraw, & D. L. White (Eds.), *Families in later life: Connections and transitions* (pp. 250–251). Thousand Oaks, CA: Pine Forge Press/ Sage Publications.

Goldberg, S. (1977). Infant development and mother–infant interaction in urban Zambia. In P. H. Leiderman, S. R. Tulkin, & A. Rosenfeld (Eds.), *Culture and infancy: Variations in the human experience* (pp. 211–244). New York: Academic Press.

Goldberg, S., & DiVitto, B. (1995). Parenting children born preterm. In M. H. Bornstein (Ed.), *Handbook of parenting, Vol. 1. Children and parenting* (pp. 209–232). Mahwah, NJ: Erlbaum.

Goldberg, W. A., Clarke-Stewart, K. A., Rice, J. A., & Dellis, E. (2002). Emotional energy as an explanatory construct for fathers' engagement with their infants. *Parenting: Science & Practice, 2,* 379–408.

Goldenberg, C. N. (1989). Parents' effects on academic grouping for reading: Three case studies. *American Educational Research Journal, 26,* 329–352.

Goldfield, E. C. (1989). Transition from rocking to crawling: Postural constraints on infant movement. *Developmental Psychology, 25,* 913–919.

Goldman, H. I. (2001). Parental reports of 'MAMA' sounds in infants: An exploratory study. *Journal of Child Language, 28,* 497–506.

Goldscheider, F. K., Thornton, A., & Yang, L. (2001). Helping out the kids: Expectations about parental support in young adulthood. *Journal of Marriage and the Family, 63,* 727–740.

Goldsmith, D. J., & Dun, S. A. (1997). Sex differences and similarities in the communication of social support. *Journal of Social and Personal Relationships, 14,* 317–337.

Goldsmith, H. H., Buss, A. H., Plomin, R., Rothbart, M. K., Thomas, A., Chess, S., et al.

(1987). Roundtable: What is temperament? Four approaches. *Child Development, 58,* 505–529.

Goldsmith, H. H., & Campos, J. J. (1986). Fundamental issues in the study of early development: The Denver twin temperament study. In M. E. Lamb & A. Brown (Eds.), *Advances in developmental psychology* (pp. 231–283). Hillsdale, NJ: Erlbaum.

Goldston, D. B., Molock, S. D., Whitbeck, L. B., Murakami, J. L., Zayas, L. H., & Hall, G. C. N. (2008). Cultural considerations in adolescent suicide prevention and psychosocial treatment. *American Psychologist, 63,* 14–31.

Goleman, D. (2006). *Social intelligence: The new science of human relationships.* New York: Bantam Books.

Golinkoff, R. M., Hirsh-Pasek, K., Bailey, L. M., & Wenger, N. R. (1992). Young children and adults use lexical principles to learn new nouns. *Developmental Psychology, 28,* 99–108.

Golombok, S., Cook, R., Bish, A., & Murray, C. (1995). Families created by the new reproductive technologies: Quality of parenting and social and emotional development of the children. *Child Development, 66,* 285–298.

Golombok, S., MacCallum, F., & Goodman, E. (2001). The "test-tube" generation: Parent–child relationships and the psychological well-being of in vitro fertilization children at adolescence. *Child Development, 72,* 599–608.

Golombok, S., Murray, C., Jadva, V., MacCallum, F., & Lycett, E. (2004). Families created through surrogacy arrangements: Parent-child relationships in the first year of life. *Developmental Psychology, 40,* 400–411.

Good, T. L., & Nichols, S. L. (2001). Expectancy effects in the classroom: A special focus on improving the reading performance of minority students in first-grade classrooms. *Educational Psychologist, 36,* 113–126.

Goodfellow, J., & Laverty, J. (2003). Grandparents supporting working families: Satisfaction and choice in the provision of child care. *Family Matters, 66,* 14–19.

Goodman, C. C. (2003). Intergenerational triads in grandparent-headed families. *Journal of Gerontology: Series B: Psychological Sciences and Social Sciences, 58B,* S281–S289.

Goodman, E., & Whitaker, R. C. (2002). A prospective study of the role of depression in the development and persistence of adolescent obesity. *Pediatrics, 110,* 497–504.

Goodwin, R. D., & Friedman, H. S. (2006). Health status and the five-factor personality traits in a nationally representative sample. *Journal of Health Psychology, 11,* 643–654.

Goodwyn, S., Acredolo, L., & Brown, C. (2000). Impact of symbolic gesturing on early language development. *Journal of Nonverbal Behavior, 24,* pp. 81–103.

Gopnik, A., & Meltzoff, A. N. (1987). The development of categorization in the sec-

ond year and its relation to other cognitive and linguistic developments. *Child Development, 58,* 1523–1531.

Gopnik, A., & Meltzoff, A. N. (1992). Categorization and naming: Basic-level sorting in eighteen-month-olds and its relation to language. *Child Development, 63,* 1091–1103.

Gopnik, A., & Meltzoff, A. N. (1997). *Words, thoughts, and theories.* Cambridge, MA: MIT Press.

Gore, S., Aseltine, R. H., & Colten, M. E. (1993). Gender, social-relational involvement, and depression. *Journal of Research on Adolescence, 3,* 101–126.

Gorer, G. (1938). *Himalayan village: An account of the Lepchas of Sikkim.* London: Michael Joseph.

Gornick, V. (1971, January 10). Consciousness. *New York Times Magazine.*

Gottesman, I. I. (1997). Twins: En route to QTLs for cognition. *Science, 276,* 1522–1523.

Gottman, J. M., Coan, J., Carrere, S., & Swanson, C. (1998). Predicting marital happiness and stability from newlywed interactions. *Journal of Marriage and the Family, 60,* 5–22.

Gottman, J. M., & Levenson, R. W. (1986). Assessing the role of emotion in marriage. *Behavioral Assessment, 8,* 31–48.

Gottman, J. M., & Silver, N. (2000). *The seven principles for making marriage work.* New York: Crown.

Gow, A. J., Pattie, A., Whiteman, M. C., Whalley, L. J., & Deary, I. J. (2007). Social support and successful aging: Investigating the relationships between lifetime cognitive change and life satisfaction. *Journal of Individual Differences, 28,* 103–115.

Graber, J. A. (2004). Internalizing problems during adolescence. In R. M. Lerner & L. Steinberg (Eds.), *Handbook of adolescent psychology* (2nd ed., pp. 587–626). New York: Wiley.

Graham, M. J., Larsen, U., & Xu, X. (1999). Secular trend in age at menarche in China: A case study of two rural counties in Anhui province. *Journal of Biosocial Science, 31,* 257–267.

Graham, S. (2004). Ethnicity and peer harassment during early adolescence. In T. Urdan & F. Pajares (Eds.), *Educating adolescents: Challenges and strategies.* Greenwich, CT: Information Age Publishing.

Graham, S., & Juvonen, J. (2002). Ethnicity, peer harassment, and adjustment in middle school: An exploratory study. *Journal of Early Adolescence, 22,* 173–199.

Graham, S., & Weiner, B. (1986). From an attributional theory of emotion to developmental psychology: A round-trip ticket? *Social Cognition, 4,* 152–179.

Graham, S., & Weiner, B. (1991). Testing judgments about attribution-emotion-action linkages: A lifespan approach. *Social Cognition, 9,* 254–276.

Grandquist, H. (1950). *Child problems among the Arabs.* Helsinki: Soderstrom.

Grantham-McGregor, S., Cheung, Y. B., Cueto, S., Glewwe, P., Richter, L., &

Strupp, B. (2007). Developmental potential in the first 5 years for children in developing countries. *The Lancet, 369,* 60–70.

Gratch, G., & Schatz, J. A. (1987). Cognitive development: The relevance of Piaget's infancy books. In J. D. Osofsky (Ed.), *Handbook of infant development* (2nd ed., pp. 204–237). New York: Wiley.

Gray, W. M. (1990). Formal operational thought. In W. F. Overton (Ed.), *Reasoning, necessity, and logic: Developmental perspectives* (pp. 227–253). Hillsdale, NJ: Erlbaum.

Green, C. D. (2009). Darwinian theory, functionalism, and the first American psychological revolution. *American Psychologist, 64,* 75–83.

Green, L., Fein, D., Joy, S., & Waterhouse, L. (1995). Cognitive functioning in autism: An overview (pp. 13–31). In E. Schopler & G. B. Mesibov (Eds.), *Learning and cognition in autism.* New York: Plenum Press.

Green, R. J., Bettinger, M., & Zacks, E. (1996). Are lesbian couples fused and gay male couples disengaged? Questioning gender straightjackets. In J. Laird & R. J. Green (Eds.), *Lesbians and gays in couples and families: A handbook for therapists* (pp. 185–230). San Francisco: Jossey-Bass.

Green, R. J., & Hill, J. H. (2003). Sex and higher education: Do men and women attend college for different reasons? *College Student Journal, 37,* 557–563.

Greenberg, E. F., & Nay, W. R. (1982). The intergenerational transmission of marital instability reconsidered. *Journal of Marriage and the Family, 44,* 335–347.

Greenberg, J. (2008). Understanding the vital human quest for self-esteem. *Perspectives on Psychological Science, 3,* 48–55.

Greenberg, M. T., Riggs, N. R., & Blair, C. (2007). The role of preventive interventions in enhancing neurocognitive functioning and promoting competence in adolescence. In D. Romer & E. F. Walker (Eds.), *Adolescent psychopathology and the developing brain: Integrating brain and prevention science* (pp. 441–462). New York: Oxford University Press.

Greene, R. R. (2008). Psychosocial theory. In B. A. Thyer, K. M. Sowers, & C. N. Dulmus (Eds.), *Comprehensive handbook of social work and social welfare, Vol. 2: Human behavior in the social environment* (pp. 229–255). Hoboken, NJ: John Wiley & Sons.

Greenfield, P. M. (2009). Linking social change and developmental change: Shifting pathways of human development. *Developmental Psychology, 45,* 401–418.

Greenfield, P. M., & Childs, C. P. (1991). Developmental continuity in biocultural context. In R. Cohen & A. W. Siegel (Eds.), *Context and development* (pp. 135–159). Hillsdale, NJ: Erlbaum.

Greenfield, P. M., Keller, H., Fuglini, A., & Maynard, A. (2003). Cultural pathways through universal development. *Annual Review of Psychology, 54,* 461–490.

Greenfield, P. M., & Suzuki, L. (1998). Culture and human development: Implications for parenting, education, pediatrics, and mental health. In I. Sigel & K. Renninger (Eds.), *Handbook of child psychology, Vol. 4: Child psychology in practice* (5th ed., pp. 1059–1109). New York: Wiley.

Gregg, T. R. (2004). *Use of functional magnetic resonance imaging to investigate brain functioning.* Retrieved August 24, 2004, from http://www.neuroguide.com/gregg.html

Gregor, T. (1977). *Mehinaku: The drama of daily life in a Brazilian Indian village.* Chicago: University of Chicago Press.

Gregory, K. M., Kim, A. S., & Whiren, A. (2003). The effect of verbal scaffolding on the complexity of preschool children's block constructions. In D. E. Lytle (Ed.), *Play and educational theory and practice* (pp. 117–133). Westport, CT: Praeger/Greenwood.

Gregory, L. W. (1995). The "turnaround" process: Factors influencing the school success of urban youth. *Journal of Adolescent Research, 10,* 136–154.

Greksa, L.P., & Korbin, J.E. (2004). Amish. In C.R. Ember & M. Ember (Eds.), *Encyclopedia of medical anthropology* (pp. 557–563). New York: Springer.

Grigsby, C., Baumann, D., Gregorich, S. E., & Roberts-Gray, C. (1990). Disaffiliation to entrenchment: A model for understanding homelessness. *Journal of Social Issues, 46,* 141–156.

Grolnick, W. S., Bridges, L. J., & Connell, J. P. (1996). Emotion regulation in two-year-olds: Strategies and emotional expression in four contexts. *Child Development, 67,* 928–941.

Groome, L. J., Mooney, D. M., Holland, S. B., Smith, Y. D., Atterbury, J. L., & Dykman, R. A. (2000). Temporal pattern and spectral complexity as stimulus parameters for eliciting a cardiac orienting reflex in human fetuses. *Perception and Psychophysics, 62,* 313–320.

Groome, L. J., Swiber, M. J., Bentz, L. S., Lynn, S., Holland, S. B., et al. (1995). Maternal anxiety during pregnancy: Effect on fetal behavior at 38 to 40 weeks of gestation. *Journal of Developmental and Behavioral Pediatrics, 16,* 391–396.

Gross, H., & Pattison, H. (2007). *Sanctioning pregnancy.* London: Routledge.

Gross, J. (2004). Older women team up to face future together. *New York Times.* Retrieved October 27, 2007, from http://query.nytimes.com/gst/fullpage.html?res=9F01E3DF113CF934A15751C0A9629C8B63&sec=&spon=&pagewanted=1

Grossman, F. K., Eichler, L. S., & Winickoff, S. A. (1980). *Pregnancy, birth, and parenthood.* San Francisco: Jossey-Bass.

Grotevant, H. D. (2009). Emotional distance regulation over the life course in adoptive kinship networks. In G.M. Wrobel & E. Neil (Eds.), *International advances in adoption research for practice* (pp. 295–316). New York: Wiley-Blackwell.

Grott, W., & van den Brink, H. M. (2005). The health effects of education: A survey and meta-analysis. Working paper, University of Amsterdam. http://wwwl.fee.uva.nl/scholar/wp/wp50-04.pdf

Grunfeld, F. V. (1975). *Games of the world: How to make them, how to play them, how they came to be.* New York: Holt, Rinehart & Winston.

Grusec, J. E. (1992). Social learning theory and developmental psychology: The legacies of Robert Sears and Albert Bandura. *Developmental Psychology, 28,* 776–786.

Grusec, J. E., & Abramovitch, R. (1982). Imitation of peers and adults in a natural setting: A functional analysis. *Child Development, 53,* 636–642.

Guay, R., Ratelle, C. F., Senécal, C., Larose, S., & Deschênes, A. (2006). Distinguishing developmental from chronic career indecision: Self-efficacy, autonomy, and social support. *Journal of Career Assessment, 14,* 235–251.

Gulko, J., Doyle, A., Serbin, L. A., & White, D. R. (1988). Conservation skills: A replicated study of order of acquisition across tasks. *Journal of Genetic Psychology, 149,* 425–439.

Gunnar, M.R. (2000). Early adversity and the development of stress reactivity and regulation. In C. Nelson (Ed.), *Minnesota Symposium on Child Psychology: Vol. 31. The effects of adversity on neurobehavioral development.* Mahwah, NJ: Erlbaum, pp. 163–200.

Gunnar, M. R., Larson, M. C., Hertsgaard, L., Harris, M. L., & Brodersen, L. (1992). The stressfulness of separation among 9-month-old infants: Effects of social context variables and infant temperament. *Child Development, 63,* 290–303.

Gur, R. C., Turetsky, B. I., Matsui, M., Yan, M., Bilker, W., Hughett, P., & Gur, R. E. (1999). Sex differences in brain gray and white matter in healthy young adults: Correlations with cognitive performance. *The Journal of Neuroscience, 19,* 4065–4072.

Guralnik, J. M., & Kaplan, G. A. (1989). Predictors of healthy aging: Prospective evidence from the Alameda County study. *American Journal of Public Health, 79,* 703–708.

Guralnik, J. M., & Simonsick, E. M. (1993). Physical disability in older Americans. *Journal of Gerontology, 48,* 3–10.

Gurin, P., & Markus, H. (1988). Group identity: The psychological mechanisms of durable salience. *Revue Internationale de Psychologie Sociale, 1,* 257–274.

Gurung, R.A.R., Dunkel-Schetter, C., et al. (2004). Psychosocial predictors of prenatal anxiety. *Journal of Social and Clinical Psychology, 24,* 497-519.

Gutman, L., & Midgley, C. (2000). The role of protective factors in supporting the academic achievement of poor African American students during the middle school transition. *Journal of Youth and Adolescence, 29,* 223–248.

Gutmann, D. (1987). *Reclaimed powers: Toward a new psychology of men and women in later life.* New York: Basic Books.

Guttmacher Institute. (2007). Get in the know: Medical abortions. Retrieved June 5, 2007, from http://www.guttmacher.org/in-the-know/medical.html

Guttmacher Institute. (2008). Facts on induced abortion in the United States. Retrieved on April 25, 2010, at www.guttmacher.org/pubs/fb_induced_abortion.html

Guttman, M. (1998, January 2–4). Who's healthier: Men or women? *USA Weekend,* pp. 4–13.

Guttmann, B. (1932). *Die Stammeslehvender des Chagga* (Vol. 1). Munich: Beck.

Ha, J.-H., Carr, D., Utz, R. L., & Nesse, R. (2006). Older adults' perceptions of intergenerational support after widowhood: How do men and women differ? *Journal of Family Issues, 27,* 3–30.

Habib, M. (2001). Online dating becoming common. *Canadian Press.* Retrieved December 23, 2001, from http://www.canoe.ca/CNEWSTech-News0102/07_dating-cp.html

Hack, M., & Fanaroff, A. A. (1999). Outcomes of children of extremely low birth weight and gestational age in the 1990s. *Early Human Development, 53,* 192–218.

Haffner, D. W. (1998). Facing facts: Sexual health for American adolescents. *Journal of Adolescent Health, 22,* 453–459.

Hahn, R. A., & Muecke, M. A. (1987). The anthropology of birth in five U.S. ethnic populations: Implications for obstetrical practice. *Current Problems in Obstetrics, Gynecology, and Fertility, 10,* 133–171.

Haidt, J. (2007). The new synthesis in moral psychology. *Science, 316,* 998–1002.

Haidt, J. (2008). Morality. *Perspective on Psychological Science, 3,* 65–72.

Hair, E.C., Moore, K.A., Ling, T.J., McPhee, G., Baker, C., & Brown, B.V. (2009). Youth who are disconnected and those who then reconnect: Assessing the influence of family, programs, peers and communities. *Child Trends, Inc. research brief #2009-37.* Washington, DC: Child Trends, Inc.

Hakuta, K., & Garcia, E. E. (1989). Bilingualism and education. *American Psychologist, 44,* 374–379.

Halfon, N., Inkelas, M., & Hochstein, M. (2000). The health development organization: An organizational approach to achieving child health development. *Milbank Quarterly, 78,* 447–497.

Halford, G. S., & Boyle, F. M. (1985). Do young children understand conservation of number? *Child Development, 56,* 165–176.

Halford, W. K., Hahlweg, K., & Dunne, M. (1990). Cross-cultural study of marital communication and marital distress. *Journal of Marriage and the Family, 52,* 487–500.

Halisch, F. & Geppert, U. (2001). Motives, personal goals and life satisfaction in old age: First results from the Munich twin study (GOLD). In A. Efklides, J. Kuhl, & R.M. Sorrentino (Eds.), *Trends and prospects in motivation research* (pp. 389–409). Dordrecht, Netherlands: Kluwer Academic Publishers.

Haller, E., & Waterman, M. (1985). The criteria of reading group assignments. *Reading Teacher, 38,* 772–782.

Hamachek, D. (1985). The self's development and ego growth: Conceptual analysis and implications for counselors. *Journal of Counseling and Development, 64,* 136–142.

Hamachek, D. (1994). Changes in the self from a developmental/psychosocial perspective. In T. M. Brinthaupt & R. P. Lipka (Eds.), *Changing the self: Philosophies, techniques, and experiences* (pp. 21–68). Albany: State University of New York Press.

Hamarat, E., Thompson, D., Zabrucky, K. M., Steele, D., Matheny, K. B., & Aysan, F. (2001). Perceived stress and coping resource availability as predictors of life satisfaction in young, middle-aged, and older adults. *Experimental Aging Research, 27,* 181–196.

Hamblen, J. (2003). PTSD in children and adolescents. *National Center for Post-Traumatic Stress Disorder.* Retrieved November 25, 2004, from http://www.ncptsd.org/facts/specific/fs_children.html

Hamilton, B. E. (2004). Reproduction rates for 1990–2002 and intrinsic rates for 2000–2001: United States. *National Vital Statistics Reports, 52* (Whole No. 17).

Hamilton, W. D. (1964). The genetical evolution of social behavior. *Journal of Theoretical Biology, 7,* 1–52.

Hammen, C. (2009). Adolescent depression: Stressful interpersonal contexts and risk for recurrence. *Current Direction in Psychological Science, 18,* 200–204.

Hammer, C. S. (2001). Come and sit down and let Mama read: Book reading interactions between African American mothers and their infants. In J. L. Harris & A. G. Kamhi (Eds.), *Literacy in African American communities* (pp. 21–43). Mahwah, NJ: Erlbaum.

Hammill, D. D. (2004). What we know about correlates of reading. *Exceptional Children, 70,* 453–468.

Hamon, R. R., & Blieszner, R. (1990). Filial responsibility expectations among adult child–older parent pairs. *Journal of Gerontology, 45,* P110–P112.

Han, W.-J. & Huang, C.-C. (2010). The forgotten treasure: Bilingualism and Asian children's emotional and behavioral health. *American Journal of Public Health, 100,* 831–838.

Handy, C. (2001). A world of fleas and elephants. In W. Bennis & G. M. Spreitzer (Eds.), *The future of leadership: Today's top leadership thinkers speak to tomorrow's leaders* (pp. 29–40). San Francisco: Jossey-Bass.

Handy, C. (2008). *Myself and other more important matters.* New York: AMACOM.

Haney, M., & Hill, J. (2004). Relationships between parent-teaching activities and emergent literacy in preschool children. *Early Child Development and Care, 174,* 215–228.

Hans, S. L. (1987). Maternal drug addiction and young children. *Division of Child, Youth, and Family Services Newsletter, 10,* 5, 15.

Hansell, S. (1985). Adolescent friendship networks and distress in school. *Social Forces, 63,* 698–715.

Hansson, R. D., & Stroebe, M. S. (2007). *Bereavement in late life: Coping, adaptation and developmental influences.* Washington, DC: American Psychological Association.

Hao, L., & Cherlin, A. J. (2004). Welfare reform and teenage pregnancy, childbirth, and school dropout. *Journal of Marriage and the Family, 66,* 179–194.

Harding, D. J. (2003). Counterfactual models of neighborhood effects: The effect of neighborhood poverty on dropping out and teenage pregnancy. *American Journal of Sociology, 109,* 676–719.

Hardy, J. B., & Duggan, A. K. (1988). Teenage fathers and the fathers of infants of urban teenage mothers. *American Journal of Public Health, 78,* 919–922.

Harel, J., & Scher, A. (2003). Insufficient responsiveness in ambivalent mother–infant relationships: Contextual and affective aspects. *Infant Behavior and Development, 26,* 371–383.

Harkness, S., & Super, C. H. (1995). Culture and parenting. In M. H. Bornstein (Ed.), *Handbook of parenting: Vol. 2. Biology and ecology of parenting* (pp. 211–234). Hillsdale, NJ: Erlbaum.

Harman, D., Holliday, R., & Meydani, M. (1998). *Towards the prolongation of the healthy life span: Practical approaches to intervention.* New York: New York Academy of Sciences.

Harrington, C. C., & Boardman, S. K. (2000). *Paths to success: Beating the odds in American society.* Cambridge, MA: Harvard University Press.

Harris, M. (1992). *Language experience and early language development: From input to uptake.* Hillsdale, NJ: Erlbaum.

Harris, P. L., & Kavanaugh, R. D. (1993). *Young children's understanding of pretense. Monographs of the Society for Research in Child Development, 58*(1).

Harris, P. L. (2007). Commentary: Time for questions. *Monographs of the Society for Research in Child Development, Serial No. 286, Vol. 72, No. 1.* pp. 113–120.

Harris, T., Kovar, M. G., Suzman, R., Kleinman, J. C., & Feldman, J. J. (1989). Longitudinal study of physical ability in the oldest old. *American Journal of Public Health, 79,* 698–702.

Hart, B., & Risley, T. R. (1992). American parenting of language-learning children: Persisting differences in family-child interactions observed in natural home environments. *Developmental Psychology, 28,* 1096–1105.

Hart, C. H., Ladd, G. W., & Burleson, B. R. (1990). Children's expectations of the outcomes of social strategies: Relations with sociometric status and maternal disciplinary styles. *Child Development, 61,* 127–137.

Hart, C. H., Newell, L. D., & Olsen, S. F. (2003). Parenting skills and social-communicative competence in childhood. In J. O. Greene & B. R. Burleson (Eds.), *Handbook of communication and social interaction skills* (pp. 753–797). Mahwah, NJ: Erlbaum.

Hart, D., & Fegley, S. (1995). Prosocial behavior and caring in adolescence: Relations to self-understanding and social judgment. *Child Development, 66,* 1346–1359.

Hart, H. M., McAdams, D. P., Hirsch, B. J., & Bauer, J. J. (2001). Generativity and social involvement among African Americans and White adults. *Journal of Research in Personaltiy, 35,* 209–230.

Harter, S. (1982). The perceived competence scale for children. *Child Development, 53,* 87–97.

Harter, S. (1985). *The self-perception profile for children* (Manual). Denver, CO: University of Denver Press.

Harter, S. (1993). Visions of self: Beyond the me in the mirror. In J. E. Jacobs (Ed.), *Nebraska Symposium on Motivation: 1992* (Vol. 40, pp. 99–144). Lincoln: University of Nebraska Press.

Harter, S. (1998). The development of self-representations. In W. Damon & N. Eisenberg (Eds.), *Handbook of child psychology* (pp. 553–617). New York: Wiley.

Harter, S., Whitesell, N. R., & Kowalski, P. (1992). Individual differences in the effects of educational transitions on young adolescents' perceptions of competence and motivational orientation. *American Educational Research Journal, 29,* 777–807.

Hartlage, S. A., Brandenburg, D. L., & Kravitz, H. M. (2004). Premenstrual exacerbation of depressive disorders in a community-based sample in the United States. *Psychosomatic Medicine, 66,* 698–706.

Hartley, A. (2006). Changing role of the speed of processing construct in the cognitive psychology of human aging. In J. E. Birren & K. W. Schaie (Eds.), *Handbook of the psychology of aging* (6th ed., pp. 183–207). Amsterdam, Netherlands: Elsevier.

Hartmann, H. (1939/1958). *Ego psychology and the problem of adaptation.* New York: International Universities Press.

Hartshorne, J. K., & Salem-Hartshorne, N. (2009). Birth order effects in the formation of long-term relationships. *Journal of Individual Psychology, 65,* 156–176.

Hartup, W. W. (1989). Social relationships and their developmental significance. *American Psychologist, 44,* 120–126.

Harvard Health Publications. (2007). Gender matters: Heart disease risk in women. Harvard Medical School. Retrieved October 8, 2007, from http://www.health.harvard.edu/newsweek/Gender_matters_Heart_disease_risk_in_women.htm#top

Harvath, T. S., Miller, L. L., Smith, K. A., Clark, L. D., Jackson, A., & Ganzini, L. (2006). Dilemmas encountered by hospice workers when patients wish to hasten death. *Journal of Hospice and Palliative Nursing, 8,* 200–209.

Harvey, J. H., Stein, S. K., & Scott, P. K. (1995). Fifty years of grief: Accounts and reported psychological reactions of Normandy invasion veterans. *Journal of Narrative and Life History, 5,* 315–332.

Harwood, R. L. (1992). The influence of culturally derived values on Anglo and Puerto Rican mothers' perceptions of attachment behavior. *Child Development, 63,* 822–839.

Haskett, M. E., & Kistner, J. A. (1991). Social interactions and peer perceptions of young physically abused children. *Child Development, 62,* 979–990.

Hatfield, E. (1988). Passionate and companionate love. In R. J. Sternberg & M. L. Barnes (Eds.), *The psychology of love* (pp. 191–217). New Haven, CT: Yale University Press.

Hatfield, E., & Sprecher, S. (1995). Men's and women's preferences in marital partners in the United States, Russia, and Japan. *Journal of Cross-Cultural Psychology, 26,* 728–750.

Hauser, M. (2006). *Moral minds: How nature designed our universal sense of right and wrong.* New York: HarperCollins.

Havighurst, R. J. (1972). *Developmental tasks and education* (3rd ed.). New York: David McKay.

Hawkins, A. J., & Dollahite, D. C. (1997). *Generative fathering: Beyond the deficit perspectives.* Thousand Oaks, CA: Sage.

Hawkins, J. L., Weisberg, C., & Ray, D. W. (1980). Spouse differences in communication style preference, perception, behavior. *Journal of Marriage and the Family, 42,* 585–593.

Hawley, G. A. (1988). *Measures of psychosocial development.* Odessa, FL: Psychological Assessment Resources.

Hayflick, L. (2000). The future of aging. *Nature, 408,* 267–269.

Haynes, J., & Miller, J. (2003). *Inconceivable conceptions: Psychological aspects of infertility and reproductive technology.* New York: Brunner-Routledge.

Hayward, M. D., Crimmins, E. M., Miles, T. P., & Yang, Y. (2000). The significance of socioeconomic status in explaining the racial gap in chronic health conditions. *American Sociological Review, 65,* 910–930.

Hazan, C., Campa, M., & Gur-Yaish, N. (2006). Attachment across the lifespan. In P. Noller & J. Feeney (Eds.), *Close relationships: Functions, forms and processes* (pp. 189–209). Hove, England: Psychology Press, Taylor/Francis.

Hazan, C., & Shaver, P. R. (1987). Attachment as an organizational framework for research on close relationships. *Journal of Personality and Social Psychology, 52,* 511–524.

Hazell, L. V. (1997) Cross-cultural funeral rites. *The Director, 69,* 53–55.

He, W., Sengupta, M., Velkoff, V., & DeBarros, K.A. (2005). *65+ in the United States: 2005. Current Population Reports, P23-209.* Washington, DC: U.S. Government Printing Office.

Healthy People 2000: National Health Promotion and Disease Prevention Objectives. (1990). Washington, DC: U.S. Department of Health and Human Services, Public Health Service, DHHS publication PHS 91-50212.

Healthy People 2010. (2001). Retrieved October 3, 2001, from http://www.health.gov/healthypeople/LHI/lhiwhat.htm

Healthy People 2020. (2010). Proposed *Healthy People 2020* objectives. Retrieved on August 7, 2010, at www.healthypeople.gov/hp2020/objectives/TopicAreas.aspx.

Hearold, S. (1986). A synthesis of 1043 effects of television on social behavior. In G. Comstock (Ed.), *Public communications and behavior* (Vol. 1, pp. 65–133). New York: Academic Press.

Heath, S. B. (1989). Oral and literate traditions among black Americans living in poverty. *American Psychologist, 44,* 367–372.

Heatherington, E. M., Cox, M., & Cox, R. (1985). Long-term effects of divorce and remarriage on the adjustment of children. *Journal of the American Academy of Psychiatry, 24,* 518–530.

Heatherington, E. M., Stanley-Hagan, M., & Anderson, E. R. (1989). Marital transitions: A child's perspective. *American Psychologist, 44,* 303–312.

Heatherton, T. F. (2000). Having and losing control: Understanding self-regulation failure. *Psychological Science Agenda, 13,* 8–9.

Heckhausen, J. (1987). Balancing for weaknesses and challenging developmental potential: A longitudinal study of mother-infant dyads in apprenticeship interactions. *Developmental Psychology, 23,* 762–770.

Heckhausen, J., Dixon, R. A., & Baltes, P. B. (1989). Gains and losses in development throughout adulthood as perceived by different adult age groups. *Developmental Psychology, 25,* 109–121.

Hegarty, P. (2009). Toward an LGBT-Informed paradigm for children who break gender norms: Comment on Drummond et al. (2008) and Rieger et al. (2008). *Developmental Psychology, 45,* 895–900.

Heifetz, R., Grashow, A., & Linsky, M. (2009). *The practice of adaptive leadership: Tools and tactics for changing your organization and the world.* Cambridge, MA: Harvard Business Press.

Heilman, M. E. (2001). Description and prescription: How gender stereotypes prevent women's ascent up the organizational ladder. *Journal of Social Issues, 57,* 657–674.

Heimpel, S. A., Wood, J. V., Marshall, M. A., & Brown, J. D. (2002). Do people with low self-esteem really want to feel better? Self-esteem differences in motivation to repair negative moods. *Journal of Personality and Social Psychology, 82,* 128–147.

Hein, G., & Schubert, T. (2004). Aging and input processing in dual-task situations. *Psychology and Aging, 19,* 416–432.

Heinicke, C. M. (1995). Determinants of the transition to parenting. In M. H. Bornstein (Ed.), *Handbook of parenting: Vol. 3. Status and social conditions of parenting* (pp. 277–303). Mahwah, NJ: Erlbaum.

Heinicke, C. M., & Guthrie, D. (1992). Stability and change in husband-wife adaptation and the development of positive parent-child relationships. *Infant and Behavior Development, 15,* 109–127.

Heinze, S. D., & Sleigh, M. J. (2003). Epidural or no epidural anaesthesia: Relationships between beliefs about childbirth and pain control. *Journal of Reproductive & Infant Psychology, 21,* 323–333.

Heitlinger, A. (1989). Current medical, legal, and demographic perspectives on artificial reproduction in Czechoslovakia. *American Journal of Public Health, 79,* 57–61.

Helman, C. G. (1990). *Culture, health, and illness* (2nd ed.). London: Wright.

Helwig, C. C., Zelazo, P. D., & Wilson, M. (2001). Children's judgments of psychological harm in normal and noncanonical situations. *Child Development, 72,* 66–81.

Henderson, A. J. Z., Bartholomew, K., Trinke, S. J., & Kwong, M. J. (2005). When loving means hurting: An exploration of attachment and intimate abuse in a community sample. *Journal of Family Violence, 20,* 219–230.

Henderson, H. A., Fox, N. A., & Rubin, K. H. (2001). Temperamental contributions to social behavior: The moderating roles of frontal EEG asymmetry and gender. *Journal of the American Academy of Child and Adolescent Psychiatry, 40,* 68–74.

Hendricks, L. E., & Fullilove, R. E. (1983). Locus of control and use of contraception among unmarried Black adolescent fathers and their controls: A preliminary report. *Journal of Youth and Adolescence, 12,* 225–233.

Henkens, K., & Tazelaar, F. (1997). Explaining retirement decisions of civil servants in the Netherlands: Intentions, behavior, and the discrepancy between the two. *Research on Aging, 19,* 139–173.

Henrich, C. C., Brown, J. L., & Aber, J. L. (1999). Evaluating the effectiveness of school-based violence prevention: Developmental approaches. *Social Policy Report, 13,* 1–17.

Henry, G. T. (1998). Practical sampling. In L. Bickman & D. J. Rog (Eds.), *Handbook of applied social research methods* (pp. 101–126). Thousand Oaks, CA: Sage.

Henry, J. D., MacLeod, M. S., Phillips, L. H., & Crawford, J. R. (2004). A meta-analytic review of prospective memory and aging. *Psychology and Aging, 19,* 27–39.

Henry J. Kaiser Family Foundation (2002). Abortion in the U.S. Retrieved June 5, 2007, from http://www.kff.org

Herbert, W. (1996). The moral child. *U.S. News and World Report, 120,* 52–59.

Herdt, G., & McClintock, M. (2000). The magical age of 10. *Archives of Sexual Behavior, 29,* 587–606.

Herek, G. M. (2006). Legal recognition of same-sex relationships in the United States: A social science perspective. *American Psychologist, 61,* 607–621.

Hergovich, A., Sirsch, U., & Felinger, M. (2002). Self-appraisals, actual appraisals, and reflected appraisals of preadolescent children. *Social Behavior and Personality, 30,* 603–612.

Herkovits, M. (1948). *Man and his works*. New York: Knopf.

Herman, M. R., Dornbusch, S. M., Herron, M. C., & Herting, J. R. (1997). The influence of family regulation, connection, and psychological autonomy on six measures of adolescent functioning. *Journal of Adolescent Research, 12*, 34–67.

Herman-Giddens, M. E., Slora, E. J., Wasserman, R. C., Bourdony, C. J., Bhapkar, M. V., Koch, G. G., & Hasemeier, C. M. (1997). Secondary sex characteristics and menses in young girls seen in office practice: A study from the pediatric research in office settings network. *Pediatrics, 99*, 505–512.

Hernandez, D. J. (1993). Childhood poverty: Trends, causes, and policies. *Child, Youth, and Family Services Quarterly, 16*, 3–4.

Herold, E. S., & Marshall, S. K. (1996). Adolescent sexual development. In G. R. Adams, R. Montemayor, & T. P. Gullotta (Eds.), *Psychosocial development during adolescence: Advances in adolescent development* (Vol. 8, pp. 62–94). Thousand Oaks, CA: Sage.

Herpertz-Dahlmann, B., Wewetzer, C., Hennighausen, K., & Remschmidt, H. (1996). Outcome, psychosocial functioning, and prognostic factors in adolescent anorexia nervosa as determined by prospective follow-up assessment. *Journal of Youth and Adolescence, 25*, 455–472.

Herring, C., & Wilson-Sadberry, K. R. (1993). Preference or necessity? Changing work roles of Black and White women, 1973–1990. *Journal of Marriage and the Family, 55*, 315–325.

Hertzog, C. (1989). Influences of cognitive slowing on age differences in intelligence. *Developmental Psychology, 25*, 636–651.

Hertzog, D., & Schaie, K. W. (1988). Stability and change in adult intelligence: 2. Simultaneous analysis of longitudinal means and covariance structures. *Psychology and Aging, 3*, 122–130.

Herzog, A. R., House, J. S., & Morgan, J. N. (1991). Relation of work and retirement to health and well-being in older age. *Psychology and Aging, 6*, 202–211.

Herzog, D. B., Dorer, D. J., Keel, P. K., Selwyn, S. E., Ekeblad, E. R., Flores, A. T., et al. (1999). Recovery and relapse in anorexia and bulimia nervosa: A 7.5-year follow-up study. *Journal of the American Academy of Child and Adolescent Psychiatry, 38*, 829–837.

Hespos, S. J., & Baillargeon, R. (2001). Reasoning about containment events in very young infants. *Cognition, 78*, 207–245.

Heuveline, P., & Timberlake, J. M. (2004). The role of cohabitation in family formation: The United States in comparative perspective. *Journal of Marriage and the Family, 66*, 1214–1230.

Heynen, J. (1990). *One hundred over 100: Moments with one hundred North American centenarians*. Golden, CO: Fulcrum.

Hickson, F. C., Davies, P. M., Hunt, A. J., & Weatherburn, P. (1992). Maintenance of open gay relationships: Some strategies for protection against HIV. *AIDS Care, 4*, 409–419.

Higher Education Research Institute. (2010). Financial concerns of first-year college students have wide impact. Retrieved on July 12, 2010, at www.heri.ucla.edu/pr-display.php?prQry=42

High/Scope. (2003). *Perry Preschool Project: Significant benefits*. Retrieved August 29, 2004, from http://www.highscope.org/Research/PerryProject/perrymain.htm

Hilgenkamp, T. I. M., van Wijck, R., & Evenhuis, H.M. (2010). Physical fitness in older people with ID—Concept and measuring instruments: *A review. Research in Developmental Disabilities, 31*, 1027–1038.

Hill, E. J., Yang, C., Hawkins, A. J., & Ferris, M. (2004). A cross-cultural test of the work-family interface in 48 countries. *Journal of Marriage and the Family, 66*, 1300–1316.

Hill, J. P. (1988). Adapting to menarche: Familial control and conflict. In M. R. Gunnar & W. A. Collins (Eds.), Development during the transition to adolescence. *Minnesota Symposium on Child Psychology* (Vol. 21, pp. 43–77). Hillsdale, NJ: Erlbaum.

Hill, N. E., & Taylor, L. C. (2004). Parental school involvement and children's academic achievement: Pragmatics and issues. *Current Directions in Psychological Science, 13*, 161–164.

Hill, R. (1958). Generic features of families under stress. *Social Casework, 39*, 139–150.

Hillman, J. L., & Stricker, G. (1994). A linkage of knowledge and attitudes toward elderly sexuality: Not necessarily a uniform relationship. *The Gerontologist, 34*, 256–260.

Hinchliff, S., Gott, M., & Ingleton, C. (2010). Sex, menopause and social context: A qualitative study with heterosexual women. *Journal of Health Psychology, 15*, 724–733.

Hing, E., & Bloom, B. (1990). Long-term care for the functionally dependent elderly. *Vital Health Statistics, 13*, No. 104.

Hinrichsen, G. A., & Clougherty, K. F. (2006). Depression and older adults. In G.A. Hinrichsen & K. F. Clougherty (Authors). *Interpersonal psychotherapy for depressed older adults*. Washington, DC: American Psychological Association, pp. 21–41.

Hipwell, A. E., Keenan, K., Loeber, R., & Battista, D. (2010). Early predictors of sexually intimate behaviors in an urban sample of young girls. *Developmental Psychology, 46*, 366–378.

Hirschfeld, L. A. (1994). The child's representation of human groups. In D. L. Medin et al. (Eds.), *The psychology of learning and motivation: Advances in research and theory* (Vol. 31, pp. 133–185). San Diego: Academic Press.

Hodges, J., & Tizard, B. (1989). Social and family relationships of ex-institutional adolescents. *Journal of Child Psychology and Psychiatry, 30*, 77–97.

Hodnett, E. D. (2003). Caregiver support for women during childbirth. *The Cochrane Library, 2*, 1–72. Retrieved August 12, 2004, from http://www.maternitywise.org/pdfs/continuous_support.pdf

Hodson, D. S., & Skeen, P. (1994). Sexuality and aging: The hammerlock of myths. *Journal of Applied Gerontology, 13*, 219–235.

Hodson, R., & Sullivan, T. A. (1995) *The social organization of work* (2nd ed.). Belmont, CA: Wadsworth.

Hoehl, S., Reid, V. M., Parise, E., Handle, A., Palumbo, L., & Striano, T. (2009). Looking at eye gaze processing and its neural correlates in infancy—Implications for social development and autism spectrum disorder. *Child Development, 80*, 968–985.

Hoeksma, J. B., Oosterlaan, J., & Schipper, E. M. (2004). Emotion regulation and the dynamics of feelings: A conceptual and methodological framework. *Child Development, 75*, 354–360.

Hof, L., & Miller, W. R. (1981). *Marriage enrichment: Philosophy, process, and program*. Bowie, MD: Brady.

Hoff, E. (2004). *Language Development* (3rd ed.). Pacific Grove, CA: Wadsworth.

Hoffman, M. L. (1970). Moral development. In P. H. Mussen (Ed.), *Carmichael's manual of child psychology* (3rd ed., Vol. 2). New York: Wiley.

Hoffman, M. L. (1977). Moral internalization: Current theory and research. In L. Berkowitz (Ed.), *Advances in experimental social psychology* (Vol. 10). New York: Academic Press.

Hoffman, M. L. (1982). Development of prosocial motivation: Empathy and guilt. In N. Eisenberg (Ed.), *The development of prosocial behavior* (pp. 281–313). New York: Academic Press.

Hoffman, M. L. (1987). The contribution of empathy to justice and moral development. In N. Eisenberg & J. Strayer (Eds.), *Empathy and its development* (pp. 47–80).

Hoffman, M. L., & Powlishta, K. K. (2001). Gender segregation in childhood: A test of the interaction style theory. *Journal of Genetic Psychology, 162*, 298–313.

Hoffman, S. J. (1985). Play and the acquisition of literacy. *Quarterly Newsletter of the Laboratory of Comparative Human Cognition, 7*, 89–95.

Hogan, D. P., Eggebeen, D. J., & Clogg, C. C. (1993). The structure of intergenerational exchanges in American families. *American Journal of Sociology, 98*, 1428–1458.

Hogan, T. D., & Steinnes, D. N. (1998). A logistic model of the seasonal migration decision for elderly households in Arizona and Minnesota. *The Gerontologist, 38*, 152–158.

Holahan, C. K., Sears, R. R., & Cronbach, L. J. (1995). *The gifted group in later maturity*. Stanford, CA: Stanford University Press.

Holland, J. L. (1997). *Making vocational choices: A theory of vocational personalities and work environments* (3rd ed.). Odessa, FL: Psychological Assessment Resources.

Hollingsworth, L. D. (2005). Ethical considerations in prenatal sex selection. *Health and Social Work, 30*, 126–134.

Holloway & Fuller, 1992: Holloway, S. D., & Fuller, B. (1992). The great childcare experiment: What are the lessons for school improvement? *Educational Researcher, 21*, 12–19.

Holmberg, L. I., & Wahlberg, V. (2000). The process of decision-making on abortion: A grounded theory study of young men in Sweden. *Journal of Adolescent Health, 26,* 230–234.

Holmboe, K., Nemoda, Z., Fearon, R. M. P., Csibra, G., Sasvari-Szekely, M., & Johnson, M. H. (2010). Polymorphisms in dopamine system genes are associated with individual differences in attention in infancy. *Developmental Psychology, 46,* 404–416.

Holmes, T. H., & Rahe, R. H. (1967). The social readjustment rating scale. *Journal of Psychosomatic Research, 11,* 213–218.

Holokawa, S., Brosseau-Laprè, F., & Pettito, L.A. (2002). Semantic and conceptual knowledge underlying bilingual babies' first signs and words. *Language Learning, 52,* 205–262.

Holstein, J. A., & Gubrium, J. F. (1995). *The active interview.* Thousand Oaks, CA: Sage.

Holzman, C., Eyster, J., Kleyn, M., Messer, L. C., Kaufman, J. S., Laraia, B. A., O'Campo, P., Burke, J. G., Culhane, J., & Elo, I. T. (2009). Maternal weathering and risk of preterm delivery. *American Journal of Public Health, 99,* 1864–1869.

Hong, L. K., & Duff, R. W. (1994). Widows in retirement communities: The social context of subjective well-being. *The Gerontologist, 34,* 347–352.

Honig, A. S. (1995). Choosing child care for young children. In M. H. Bornstein (Ed.), *Handbook of parenting: Applied and practical parenting* (Vol. 4, pp. 411–435). Mahwah, NJ: Erlbaum.

Honig, A. S. (2002). Choosing childcare for young children. In M. H. Bornstein (Ed.), *Handbook of parenting: Practical issues in parenting* (Vol. 5., pp. 375–405). Mahwah, NJ: Erlbaum.

Hooyman, N. R., & Kiyak, H. A. (2002). *Social gerontology: A multidisciplinary perspective* (6th ed.). Boston: Allyn & Bacon.

Hope, T. L., Wilder, E. I., & Watt, T. T. (2003). The relationship among adolescent pregnancy, pregnancy resolution, and juvenile delinquency. *Sociological Inquiry, 44,* 555–576.

Hopkins, B., & Westra, T. (1990). Motor development, maternal expectation, and the role of handling. *Infant Behavior and Development, 13,* 117–122.

Hopkins, D. R., Murrah, B., Hoeger, W. W. K., & Rhodes, R. C. (1990). Effect of low-impact aerobic dance on the functional fitness of elderly women. *The Gerontologist, 30,* 189–192.

Hopkins, J. R. (1995). Erik Homburger Erikson (1902–1994). *American Psychologist, 50,* 796–797.

Hopper, K. (1990). Public shelter as "a hybrid institution": Homeless men in historical perspective. *Journal of Social Issues, 46,* 13–29.

Hopper, K., & Hamberg, L. (1986). The making of America's homeless: From skid row to new poor, 1945–1984. In R. Bratt, C. Harman, & A. Meyerson (Eds.), *Critical perspectives on housing.* Philadelphia: Temple University Press.

Horn, J. L. (1979). The rise and fall of human abilities. *Journal of Research and Development in Education, 12,* 59–78.

Horn, J. L., & Masunaga, H. (2000). New directions for research into aging and intelligence: The development of expertise. In T. J. Perfect & E. A. Maylor (Eds.), *Models of cognitive aging* (pp. 125–159). London: Oxford University Press.

Hornblower, M. (1996). It takes a school. *Time, 147,* 36–38.

Hornik, R., & Gunnar, M. R. (1988). A descriptive analysis of infant social referencing. *Child Development, 59,* 626–634.

Hornik, R., Risenhoover, N., & Gunnar, M. (1987). The effects of maternal positive, neutral, and negative affective communications on infant responses to new toys. *Child Development, 58,* 937–944.

Horobin, K., & Acredolo, C. (1989). The impact of probability judgments on reasoning about multiple possibilities. *Child Development, 60*(1), 183–200.

Horst, E. A. (1995). Reexamining gender issues in Erikson's stages of identity and intimacy. *Journal of Counseling and Development, 73,* 271–278.

Horwitz, A. V., White, H. R., & Howell-White, S. (1996). Becoming married and mental health: A longitudinal study of a cohort of young adults. *Journal of Marriage and the Family, 58,* 895–907.

Hospice Education Institute. (2001). *A short history of hospice and palliative care.* Essex, CT: The Hospice Education Institute.

Hospice of Michigan. (2007). Grief support services. Retrieved November 2, 2007, from http://www.hom.org/griefami.asp

Hostile Aggressive Parenting. (2010). Observable effects on children resulting from exposure to hostile-aggressive parenting. Retrieved on July 5, 2010, at www.hostile-aggressive-parenting.com/effects_of_HAP.asp

Howarth, G. (2007). *Death and dying: A sociological introduction.* Malden, MA: Polity Press.

Howell, C. (1994, February 2). Coroner delivers primer to directors. *Arkansas-Democrat Gazette.*

Howell, E. M., Heiser, N., & Harrington, M. (1999). A review of recent findings on substance abuse treatment for pregnant women. *Journal of Substance Abuse Treatment, 16,* 195–219.

Howell, K. K. (2005) Ten most frequently asked questions about consuming caffeine during pregnancy. Emory Department of Psychiatry and Behavioral Sciences. Retrieved June 2, 2007, from http://www.psychiatry.emory.edu/PROGRAMS/GADrug/caffeine.htm

Howes, C. (1987). Peer interaction of young children. *Monographs of the Society for Research in Child Development, 53* (1, Serial No. 217).

Howes, C., & Phillipsen, L. (1992). Gender and friendship: Relationships within peer groups of young children. *Social Development, 1,* 230–242.

Howes, C., & Stewart, P. (1987). Child's play with adults, toys, and peers: An examination of family and child-care influences. *Developmental Psychology, 23,* 423–430.

Howes, C., Unger, O., & Seidner, L. B. (1989). Social pretend play in toddlers: Parallels with social play and with solitary pretend. *Child Development, 60,* 77–84.

How RU-486 works. (1997, March 3). *U.S. News and World Report,* pp. 66–69.

Hoyer, W. J., & Rybash, J. M. (1994). Characterizing adult cognitive development. *Journal of Adult Development, 1,* 7–12.

Hoyer, W. J., & Verhaeghen, P. (2006). Memory aging. In J. E. Birren and K. W. Schaie (Eds.), *Handbook of the psychology of aging* (pp. 209–232). Amsterdam, Netherlands: Elsevier.

Hruschka, D. J. (2010). *Friendship: Development, ecology and evolution of a relationship.* Berkeley: University of California Press.

Hsu, L. K. G. (1996). Outcome of early onset anorexia nervosa: What do we know? *Journal of Youth and Adolescence, 25,* 563–568.

Huber, J. (1990). Macro-micro links in gender stratification. *American Sociological Review, 55,* 1–10.

Hubert, N. C., Wachs, T. D., Peters-Martin, P., & Gandour, M. J. (1982). The study of early temperament: Measurement and conceptual issues. *Child Development, 53,* 571–600.

Huesmann, L. R., & Eron, L. D. (1986). *Television and the aggressive child: A crossnational comparison.* Hillsdale, NJ: Erlbaum.

Huesmann, L. R., & Malamuth, N. M. (1986). Media violence and antisocial behavior: An overview. *Journal of Social Issues, 42,* 1–6.

Huesmann, L. R., Moise-Titus, J., Podolski, C. L., & Eron, L. D. (2003). Longitudinal relations between children's exposure to TV violence and their aggressive behavior in young adulthood: 1977–1992. *Developmental Psychology, 39,* 210–221.

Huesmann, L. R., & Skoric, M. M. (2003). Regulating media violence: Why, how, and by whom? In E. L. Palmer & B. M. Young (Eds.), *The faces of televisual media: Teaching, violence, selling to children* (2nd ed., pp. 219–240). Mahwah, NJ: Erlbaum.

Hughes, F. M., Gordon, K. C., & Gaertner, L. (2004). Predicting spouses' perceptions of their parenting alliance. *Journal of Marriage and the Family, 66,* 506–514.

Human Rights Watch. (2004). *Child labor.* Retrieved November 10, 2004, from http://www.hrw.org/children/labor.htm

Human Rights Watch. (2006). *Children's rights: Child Labor.* Retrieved August 13, 2007, from http://hrw.org/children/labor.htm

Hunter, A. G. (1997). Counting on grandmothers: Black mothers' and fathers' reliance on grandmothers for parenting support. *Journal of Family Issues, 18,* 251–269.

Hupp, S. D. A., & Reitman, D. (1999). Improving sports skills and sportsmanship in children diagnosed with attention-deficit/hyperactivity disorder. *Child and Family Behavior Therapy, 21,* 35–51.

Huston, A. C., Donnerstein, E., Fairchild, H., Feshbach, N. D., Katz, P. A., Murray, J. P., et al. (1992). *Big world, small screen: The role of television in American society*. Lincoln: University of Nebraska Press.

Huston, T. L. (2000). The social ecology of marriage and other intimate unions. *Journal of Marriage and the Family, 62*, 298–320.

Huston, T. L., Caughlin, J. P., Houts, R. M., Smith, S. E., & George, L. J. (2001). The connubial crucible: Newlywed years as predictors of marital delight, distress, and divorce. *Journal of Personality and Social Psychology, 80*, 237–252.

Huston, T. L., & Melz, H. (2004). The case for (promoting) marriage: The devil is in the details. *Journal of Marriage and the Family, 66*, 943–958.

Huston, T. L., Niehuis, S., & Smith, S. E. (2001). The early marital roots of conjugal distress and divorce. *Current Directions in Psychological Science, 10*, 116–119.

Huston, T. L. & Vangelisti, A. L. (1995). How parenthood affects marriage: Explaining family interactions. In M. A. Fitzpatrick & A. L. Vagelisti (Eds.), *Exploring family interactions* (pp. 147–176). Thousand Oaks, CA: Sage.

Hutt, S. J., Tyler, S., Hutt, C., & Foy, H. (1988). *Play exploration and learning: A natural history of the preschool*. New York: Routledge.

Huttenlocher, P. R., & Dabholkar, A. S. (1997). Regional differences in synaptogenesis in human cerebral cortex. *The Journal of Comparative Neurology, 387*, 167–178.

Huxley, J. (1941). *The uniqueness of man*. London: Chatto & Windus.

Huxley, J. (1942). *Evolution: The magic synthesis*. New York: Harper.

Hyde, J. S. (2005). The gender similarities hypothesis. *American Psychologist, 60*, 581–592.

Hymel, S., Bowker, A., & Woody, E. (1993). Aggressive versus withdrawn unpopular children: Variations in peer and self-perceptions of multiple domains. *Child Development, 64*, 879–896.

Hymel, S., Wagner, E., & Butler, L. J. (1990). Reputational bias: View from the peer group. In S. Asher & J. D. Coie (Eds.). *Peer rejection in childhood* (pp. 156–186). New York: Cambridge University Press.

Iacoboni, M., & Dapretto, M. (2006). The mirror neuron system and the consequences of its dysfunction. *Nature Reviews/Neuroscience, 7*, 942–951, published online at http://www.nature.com/reviews/neuro

Iannotti, R. J. (1985). Naturalistic and structured assessments of prosocial behavior in preschool children: The influence of empathy and perspective taking. *Developmental Psychology, 21*, 46–55.

Iannotti, R. J., & Bush, P. J. (1992). Perceived versus actual friends' use of alcohol, cigarettes, marijuana, and cocaine: Which has the most influence? *Journal of Youth and Adolescence, 21*, 375–389.

Idler, E. L. (1987). Religious involvement and the health of the elderly: Some hypotheses and an initial test. *Social Forces, 66*, 226–238.

Ikels, C. (1998). Grandparenthood in cross-cultural perspective. In M. Szinovacz (Ed.), *Handbook on grandparenthood* (pp. 40–52). Westport, CT: Greenwood Press.

Impett, E. A., & Tolman, D. L. (2006). Late adolescent girls' sexual experiences and sexual satisfaction. *Journal of Adolescent Research, 21*, 628–646.

Ingersoll-Dayton, B., & Antonucci, T. C. (1988). Reciprocal and nonreciprocal social support: Contrasting sides of intimate relationships. *Journal of Gerontology, 43*, S65–S73.

Inhelder, B., & Piaget, J. (1958). *The growth of logical thinking from childhood to adolescence*. New York: Basic Books.

Insel, T. R. (2007). Shining light on depression. *Science, 317*, 757–758.

Institute of Medicine of the National Academies (2006). *Preterm birth: Causes, consequences, and prevention*. Washington, DC: National Academies Press.

InteliHealth.com (2002). *Words, not bullets, make the workplace hostile*. Retrieved January 7, 2002, from http://www.intelihealth.com/IH/ihtIH/WSIHW000/20813/23598/263562.html?d_dmt-Content

Irwin, C. E., Jr., Burg, S. J., & Cart, C. U. (2002). America's adolescents: Where have we been, where are we going? *Journal of Adolescent Health, 31*, 91–121.

Isaacowitz, D. M., Vaillant, G. E., & Seligman, M. E. P. (2003). Strengths and satisfaction across the lifespan. *International Journal of Aging & Human Development, 57*, 181–201.

Isabella, R. A., & Belsky, J. (1991). Interactional synchrony and the origins of infant-mother attachment: A replication study. *Child Development, 62*, 373–384.

Ishii-Kuntz, M. (1997). Japanese American families. In M. K. DeGenova (Ed.), *Families in cultural context: Strengths and challenges in diversity* (pp. 131–153). Mountain View, CA: Mayfield.

IslamOnline. (2003). *Fatwa: What is the sequence of rituals in an Islamic funeral service?* Retrieved March 13, 2005, from http://www.islamonline.net/fatwa/english/FatwaDisplay.asp?hFatwaID_94057

Ivarsson, T., & Valderhaug, R. (2006). Symptom patterns in children and adolescents with obsessive-compulsive disorder (OCD). *Behaviour Research and Therapy, 44*, 1105–1116.

Iverson, J. M., & Thelen, E. (1999). Hand, mouth, and brain: The dynamic emergence of speech and gesture. *Journal of Consciousness Studies, 6*, 11–12.

Izard, C. E. (1977). *Human emotion*. New York: Plenum Press.

Izard, C. E., Haynes, O. M., Chisholm, G., & Baak, K. (1991). Emotional determinants of infant-mother attachment. Child Development, 62, 906–917.

Jack, D. C., & Dill, D. (1992). The silencing the self scale: The schemas of intimacy associated with depression in women. *Psychology of Women Quarterly, 16*, 97–106.

Jacklin, C. N., & Maccoby, E. E. (1978). Social behavior at 33 months in same-sex and mixed-sex dyads. *Child Development, 49*, 557–569.

Jackson, J. S., Keioper, S. K., Brown, K. T., Brown, T. N., & Manuel, W. (2002). Athletic identity, racial attitudes and aggression in first-year Black and White intercollegiate athletes. In M. Gatz, M. A. Messner, & S. J. Ball-Rokeach (Eds.), *Paradoxes of youth and sport*. Albany: SUNY Press, pp. 159–172.

Jackson, P. B. (2004). Role sequencing: Does order matter for mental health? *Journal of Health and Social Behavior, 45*, 132–154.

Jacobs, J. N., & Kelley, M. L. (2006). Predictors of paternal involvement in childcare in dual-earner families with young children. *Fathering, 4*, 23–47.

Jacobson, E. (1964). *The self and the object world*. New York: International Universities Press.

Jacobson, S. W., Fein, G. G., Jacobson, J. L., Schwartz, P. M., & Dowler, J. K. (1985). The effect of intrauterine PCB exposure on visual recognition memory. *Child Development, 56*, 853–860.

Jacobson, S. W., Jacobson, J. L., O'Neill, J. M., Padgett, R. J., Frankowski, J. J., & Bihun, J. T. (1992). Visual expectation and dimensions of infant information processing. *Child Development, 63*, 711–724.

Jahoda, M. (1982). *Employment and unemployment*. Cambridge, UK: Cambridge University Press.

Jahromi, L. B., Putnam, S. P., & Stifter, C. A. (2004). Maternal regulation of infant reactivity from 2 to 6 months. *Developmental Psychology, 40*, 477–487.

James, W. (1890). *Principles of psychology (2 vols.)* New York: Henry Holt.

James, W. (1892/1961). *Psychology: The briefer course*. New York: Harper & Row.

Jamieson, A., Curry, A., & Martinez, G. (2001). School enrollment in the United States—Social and economic characteristics of students: 1999. *Current Population Reports*, P20-533.

Jarboe, P. J. (1986). *A comparison study of distress and marital adjustment in infertile and expectant couples*. Unpublished doctoral dissertation, Ohio State University.

Jayakody, R., Chatters, L. M., & Taylor, R. J. (1993). Family support to single and married African-American mothers: The provision of financial, emotional, and child care assistance. *Journal of Marriage and the Family, 55*, 261–276.

Jecker, N. S., & Schneiderman, L. J. (1994). Is dying young worse than dying old? *The Gerontologist, 34*, 66–72.

Jeffries, V. (1993). Virtue and attraction: Validation of measure of love. *Journal of Social and Personal Relationships, 10*, 99–118.

Jenkins, J. M., Turrell, S. L., Kogushi, Y., Lollis, S., & Ross, H. S. (2003). A longitudinal investigation of the dynamics of mental state talk in families. *Child Development, 74*, 905–920.

Jenkins, L. E. (1989). The Black family and academic achievement. In G. L. Berry & J. K. Asamen (Eds.), *Black students* (pp. 138–152). Newbury Park, CA: Sage.

Jetten, J., Spears, R., & Manstead, A. S. R. (1996). Intergroup norms and intergroup discrimination: Distinctive self-categorization and social identity effects. *Journal of Personality and Social Psychology, 71,* 1222–1233.

Jezewski, M. A., Meeker, M. S., Sessanna, L., & Finnell, D. S. (2007). The effectiveness of interventions to increase advance directive completion rates. *Journal of Aging and Health, 19,* 519–536.

Jirtle, R. L., & Weidman, J. R. (2007). Imprinted and more equal. *American Scientist, 95,* 143–149.

Jockin, V., McGue, M., & Lykken, D. T. (1996). Personality and divorce: A genetic analysis. *Journal of Personality and Social Psychology, 71,* 288–299.

Johnson, H. B. (2005, March–April). My word. Too late to die young. *AARP: The Magazine, 48,* 44–46, 99.

Johnson, K. P. (2004). Adolescent sleep patterns: Biological, social, and psychological influences. *Journal of the American Academy of Child and Adolescent Psychiatry, 43,* 374–375.

Johnson, M. (1999). Ontogenetic constraints on neural and behavioral plasticity: Evidence from imprinting and face processing. *Canadian Journal of Experimental Psychology, 53,* 77–90.

Johnson, M. H. (2000). State of the art: How babies' brains work. *The Psychologist, 13,* 298–301.

Johnson, M. H. (2001). Functional brain development in humans. *Nature Reviews Neuroscience, 2,* 475–483.

Johnson, M. P. (2002). An exploration of men's experience and role at childbirth. *Journal of Men's Studies, 10,* 165–182.

Johnson, R. E. (2003). Age and the remembering of text. *Developmental Review, 23,* 261–346.

Johnson, S. P. (2000). The development of visual surface perception: Insights into the ontogeny of knowledge. In C. Rovee-Collier, L. P. Lipsitt, & H. Hayne (Eds.), *Progress in infancy research* (Vol. 1, pp. 113–154). Mahwah, NJ: Erlbaum.

Johnson, V. K., Cowan, P. A., & Cowan, C. P. (1991). Children's classroom behavior: The unique contribution of family organization. *Journal of Family Psychology, 13,* 355–371.

Johnston, L. D., O'Malley, P. M., Bachman, J. G., & Schulenberg, J. E. (2010). *Monitoring the future: National results on adolescent drug use. Overview of key findings: 2009.* (NIH Publication yet to be assigned). Bethesda, MD: National Institute on Drug Abuse.

Johnston, L. D., O'Malley, P. M., Bachman, J. G., & Schulenberg, J. E. (2004). *Monitoring the Future: National results on adolescent drug use: Overview of key findings, 2003* (NIH Publication No. 04-5506). Bethesda, MD: National Institute on Drug Abuse.

Johnston, T. (2005). In one's own image: Ethics and the reproduction of deafness. *Journal of Deaf Studies and Deaf Education, 10,* 426–441.

Jokela, M. (2010). Characteristics of the first child predict the parents' probability of having another child. *Developmental Psychology, 46,* 915–926.

Jones, B.C., Main, J.C., DeBruine, L.M., Little, A.C., & Welling, L.L.M. (2010). Reading the look of love: Sexually dimorphic cues in opposite sex faces influence gaze categorization. *Psychological Science, 21,* 796–798.

Jones, J. (2008). Adoption experiences of women and men and demand for children to adopt by women 18–44 years of age in the United States, 2002. National Center for Health Statistics. *Vital Health Stat 23(27).* 2008.

Jones, J. T., & Cunningham, J. D. (1996). Attachment styles and other predictors of relationship satisfaction in dating couples. *Personal Relationships, 3,* 387–399.

Jones, R. M. (1992). Ego identity and adolescent problem behavior. In G. R. Adams, T. P. Gullota, & R. Montemayor (Eds.), *Adolescent identity formation* (pp. 216–233). Newbury Park, CA: Sage.

Jones, S. S., Smith, L. B., & Landau, B. (1991). Object properties and knowledge in early lexical learning. *Child Development, 62,* 499–516.

Jones-Webb, R. J., & Snowden, L. R. (1993). Symptoms of depression among Blacks and Whites. *American Journal of Public Health, 83,* 240–244.

Jonker, C., Launer, L. J., Hooijer, C., & Lindeboom, J. (1996). Memory complaints and memory impairment in older individuals. *Journal of the American Geriatrics Society, 44,* 44–49.

Jordan, B. (1983). *Birth in four cultures: A cross-cultural investigation of childbirth in Yucatan, Holland, Sweden and the United States* (3rd ed.). Montreal: Eden Press.

Jordan, C. H., Spencer, S. J., Zanna, M. P., Hoshino-Browne, E., & Correll, J. (2003). Secure and defensive high self-esteem. *Journal of Personality and Social Psychology, 85,* 969–978.

Jordan, J. V. (1997). Relational development through mutual empathy. In A. C. Bohart & L. S. Greenberg (Eds.), *Empathy reconsidered: New directions in psychotherapy* (pp. 343–351). Washington, DC: American Psychological Association.

Jordan, K. F., Lyons, T. S., & McDonough, J. T. (1992). *Funding and financing for programs to serve K–3 at-risk children: A research review.* Washington, DC: National Education Association.

Jordan, N. C., Kaplan, D., Ramineni, C., & Locuniak, M. N. (2009). Early math matters: Kindergarten number competence and later mathematics outcomes. *Developmental Psychology, 45,* 850–867.

Jordyn, M., & Byrd, M. (2003). The relationship between the living arrangements of university students and their identity development. *Adolescence, 38,* 267–278.

Jose, A., O'Leary, D.K., & Moyer, A. (2010). Does premarital cohabitation predict subsequent marital stability and marital quality? A meta-analysis. *Journal of Marriage and the Family, 72,* 105–116.

Josephson, W. L. (1987). Television violence and children's aggression: Testing the priming, social script, and disinhibition predictions. *Journal of Personality and Social Psychology, 53,* 882–890.

Josselson, R. (2003). Revisions: Processes of development in midlife women. In J. Demick & C. Andreoletti (Eds.), *Handbook of adult development* (pp. 431–441). New York: Kluwer Academic/Plenum Publishers.

Juvonen, J., Graham, S., & Schuster, M. A. (2003). Bullying among young adolescents: The strong, the weak, and the troubled. *Pediatrics, 112,* 1231–1237.

Jussim, L. (1990a). Expectancies and social issues: Introduction. *Journal of Social Issues, 46,* 1–8.

Jussim, L. (1990b). Social realities and social problems: The role of expectancies. *Journal of Social Issues, 46,* 9–34.

Justice, L. M., & Ezell, H. K. (2000). Enhancing children's print and word awareness through home-based parent intervention. *American Journal of Speech-Language Pathology, 9,* 257–269.

Kagan, J. (1958). The concept of identification. *Psychological Review, 65,* 296–305.

Kagan, J., Snidman, N., & Arcus, D. (1998). Childhood derivatives of high and low reactivity in infancy. *Child Development, 69,* 1483–1493.

Kagan, S. L. (1990). Readiness 2000: Rethinking rhetoric and responsibility. *Phi Delta Kappan, 1,* 21–23.

Kagitcibasi, C. (1990). Family and socialization in cross-cultural perspective: A model of change. In J. J. Berman (Ed.), *Nebraska Symposium on Motivation, 1989: Crosscultural perspectives* (pp. 135–200). Lincoln: University of Nebraska Press.

Kahana, B. (1982). Social behavior and aging. In B. B. Wolman (Ed.), *Handbook of developmental psychology* (pp. 871–889). Englewood Cliffs, NJ: Prentice Hall.

Kaida, K., Ogawa, K., Matsuura, N., Takkahashi, M., & Hori, T. (2006). Relationship between the habit of napping with self-awakening and generalized self-efficacy. *Japanese Journal of Health Psychology, 19,* 1–9.

Kaiser, S. & Sachser, N. (2009). Effects of prenatal social stress on offspring development. *Current Directions in Psychological Science, 18,* 118-121.

Kalb, C. (1997, May 5). How old is too old? *Newsweek,* p. 64.

Kalb, C. (2001, August 13). Should you have your baby now? *Newsweek,* pp. 40–48.

Kalil, K. M., Gruber, J. E., Conley, J., & Sytniac, M. (1993). Social and family pressures on anxiety and stress during pregnancy. *Pre- and Peri-natal Psychology Journal, 8,* 113–118.

Kalish, C. W., & Gelman, S. A. (1992). On wooden pillows: Multiple classification and children's category-based inductions. *Child Development, 63,* 1536–1557.

Kalleberg, A. L., & Rosenfeld, R. A. (1990). Work in the family and in the labor market. *Journal of Marriage and the Family, 52,* 331–346.

Kalman, M. B. (2003). Taking a different path: Menstrual preparation for adolescent girls living apart from their mothers. *Health Care for Women International, 24*, 868–879.

Kalmijn, M. (1998). Intermarriage and homogamy: Causes, patterns, trends. *Annual Review of Sociology, 24*, 395–421.

Kalmijn, M., & Bernasco, W. (2001). Joint and separated lifestyles in couple relationships. *Journal of Marriage and the Family, 63*, 639–654.

Kalmijn, M., De Graaf, P.M., & Poortman, A. R. (2004). Interactions between cultural and economic determinants of divorce in the Netherlands. *Journal of Marriage and Family. 66*, 75–89.

Kalmijn, M., & Flap, H. (2001). Assortative meeting and mating: Unintended consequences of organized settings for partner choices. *Social Forces, 79*, 1289–1312.

Kalmijn, M., & Monden, C. W. S. (2006). Are the negative effects of divorce on well-being dependent on marital quality? *Journal of Marriage and Family, 68*, 1197–1213.

Kamii, C., Lewis, B.A., & Kirkland, L. (2001). Manipulatives: When are they useful? *Journal of Mathematical Behavior, 20*, 21–31.

Kamii, C., Rummelsburg, J., & Kari, A. (2005). Teaching arithmetic to low-performing, low-SES first graders. *Journal of Mathematical Behavior, 24*, 39–50.

Kamii, C. K. (1985). *Young children reinvent arithmetic*. New York: Teachers College Press.

Kamii, C. K. (1994). *Young children continue to reinvent arithmetic: 3rd grade*. New York: Teachers College Press.

Kamo, Y. (1993). Determinants of marital satisfaction: A comparison of the United States and Japan. *Journal of Social and Personal Relationships, 10*, 551–568.

Kang, S. M., & Shaver, P. R. (2004). Individual differences in emotional complexity: Their psychological implications. *Journal of Personality, 72*, 687–726.

Kanter, R. M. (2004). *Confidence: How winning and losing streaks begin and end*. New York: Crown.

Kantrowitz, B., & Springen, K. (2007). Confronting Alzheimer's. *Newsweek*, June 18, 55–61.

Kanungo, R. N., & Misra, S. (1992). Managerial resourcefulness: A reconceptualization of management skills. *Human Relations, 45*, 1311–1332.

Kaplan, B. J. (1986). A psychobiological review of depression during pregnancy. *Psychology of Women Quarterly, 10*, 35–48.

Kaplevn, A., Smith, J.P., & van Soest, A. (2010). Life satisfaction. International differences in well-being. In E. Diener, J.F. Helliwell, & D. Kahneman (Eds.), *International differences in well-being* (pp. 70–104). New York: Oxford University Press.

Karmel, M. (1983). *Thank you, Dr. Lamaze*. Philadelphia: Lippincott.

Kasper, J. D. (1997). Long-term care moves into the mainstream. *The Gerontologist, 37*, 274–276.

Kastenbaum, R. (1981). *Death, society, and human experience* (2nd ed.). Palo Alto, CA: Mayfield.

Kastenbaum, R. (1985). Dying and death: A life-span approach. In J. Birren and K. W. Schaie (Eds.), *Handbook of the psychology of aging* (pp. 619–643). New York: Van Nostrand Reinhold.

Kastenbaum, R. J. (1992). *The psychology of death* (2nd ed.). New York: Springer Verlag.

Kastenbaum, R. J. (2009). *Death, society and the human experience* (10th ed.). Boston, MA: Allyn & Bacon.

Katchadourian, H. (1990). Sexuality. In S. S. Feldman & G. R. Elliott (Eds.), *At the threshold: The developing adolescent* (pp. 330–351). Cambridge, MA: Harvard University Press.

Kaufman, G. (1989). *The psychology of shame*. New York: Springer Verlag.

Kavanaugh, R. D., & Engel, S. (1998). The development of pretense and narrative in early childhood. In O. N. Saracho & B. Spodek (Eds.), *Multiple perspectives on play in early childhood education* (pp. 80–99). Albany: University of New York Press.

Kaye, L. W. (1995). *New developments in home care services for the elderly: Innovations in policy, program, and practice*. Binghamton, NY: Haworth Press.

Keating, D. P. (1990). Adolescent thinking. In S. S. Feldman & G. R. Elliott (Eds.), *At the threshold: The developing adolescent* (pp. 54–90). Cambridge, MA: Harvard University Press.

Keating, D. P. (2004). Cognitive and brain development. In R. M. Lerner & L. Steinberg (Eds.), *Handbook of adolescent psychology* (2nd ed., pp. 45–84). New York: Wiley.

Kegan, R. (1982). *The evolving self: Problems and process in human development*. Cambridge, MA: Harvard University Press.

Kehl, K. (2006). Moving toward peace: An analysis of the concept of a good death. *American Journal of Hospice and Palliative Medicine, 23*, 277–286.

Keith, V. M., & Finlay, B. (1988). Parental divorce and children's education, marriage, and divorce. *Journal of Marriage and the Family, 50*, 797–810.

Keller, H., Lohaus, A., Kuensemueller, M. A., Yovsi, R., Voelker, S., Jensen, H., et al. (2004). The bio-culture of parenting: Evidence from five cultural communities. *Parenting: Science and Practice, 4*, 25–50.

Kelly, M. L., Power, T. G., & Wimbush, D. D. (1992). Determinants of disciplinary practices in low-income Black mothers. *Child Development, 63*, 573–582.

Kelly, S. J., Ostrowski, N. L., & Wilson, M. A. (1999). Gender differences in brain and behavior: Hormonal and neural bases. *Pharmacology, Biochemistry and Behavior, 64*, 655–664.

Kelly, Y., Sacker, A., Schoon, I., & Nazroo, J. (2006). Ethnic differences in achievement of developmental milestones by 9 months of age: The Millenium Cohort Study. *Developmental Medicine & Child Neurology, 48*, 825–830.

Kemp, C. L. (2005). Dimensions of grandparent-adult grandchild relationships: From family ties to intergenerational friendships. *Canadian Journal on Aging, 24*, 161–178.

Kemper, S., Thompson, M., & Marquis, J. (2001). Longitudinal change in language production: Effects of aging and dementia on grammatical complexity and propositional content. *Psychology and Aging, 16*, 600–614.

Kennedy, A. C. (2006). Urban adolescent mothers exposed to community, family, and partner violence: Prevalence, outcomes and welfare policy implications. *American Journal of Orthopsychiatry, 76*, 44–54.

Kennedy, G. J., & Tanenbaum, S. (2000). Suicide and aging: International perspectives. *Psychiatric Quarterly, 71*, 345–362.

Kenny, D.A. & Acitelli, L.K. (2001). Accuracy and bias in the perception of the partner in a close relationship. *Journal of Personality and Social Psychology, 80*, 439–448.

Kenyan, D.B., & Koerner, S.S. (2009). Examining emerging adults' and parents' expectations about autonomy during the transition to college. *Journal of Adolescent Research, 24*, 293–320.

Kermoian, R., & Campos, J. J. (1988). Locomotor experience: A facilitator of spatial cognitive development. *Child Development, 59*, 908–917.

Kernan, C. L., & Greenfield, P. M. (2005). Becoming a team: Individualism, collectivism, ethnicity and group socialization in Los Angeles girls' basketball. *Ethos, 33*, 542–566.

Kernberg, O. F. (2005). Object relations theories and technique. In E. S. Person, A. M. Cooper, & G. O. Gabbard (Eds.), *The American psychiatric publishing textbook of psychoanalysis*. Washington, DC: American Psychiatric Publishing, Inc., pp. 57–75.

Kernis, M. H. (2003). Toward a conceptualization of optimal self-esteem. *Psychological Inquiry, 14*, 1–26.

Kersting, K. (2004). Improving the end of life for older adults. *Monitor on Psychology, 35*, 53–54.

Kessen, W. (1965). *The child*. New York: Wiley.

Kim, H.-J. K. (2002). *Taegyo (fetal education)*. Retrieved August 12, 2004, from http://fieldworking.com/historical/kim.html

Kimura, D. (1992). Sex differences in the brain. *Scientific American, 267*, 119–125.

Kimura, D. (2002). Sex differences in the brain. *Scientific American.com*. Retrieved May 29, 2007, from http://www.sciam.com

Kindermann, T. A. (1996). Strategies for the study of individual development within naturally-existing peer groups. *Social Development, 5*, 158–173.

King, L. A. (1993). Emotional expression, ambivalence over expression, and marital satisfaction. *Journal of Social and Personal Relationships, 10*, 601–607.

King, P. M., & Kitchener, K. S. (1994). *Developing reflective judgment: Understanding and promoting intellectual growth and critical thinking in adolescents and adults*. San Francisco: Jossey-Bass.

King, R. A., Schwab-Stone, M., Flisher, A. J., Greenwald, S., Kramer, R. A., Goodman, S. H., et al. (2001). Psychosocial and risk behavior correlates of youth suicide attempts and suicidal ideation. *Journal of the American Academy of Child and Adolescent Psychiatry, 40*, 837–846.

King, S. V., Burgess, E. O., Akinyela, M., Counts-Spriggs, M., & Parker, N. (2006). The religious dimension of the grandparent role in three-generation African American households. *Journal of Religion, Spirituality & Aging, 19*, 75–96.

Kinney, J. M., & Stephens, M. A. P. (1989). Hassles and uplifts of giving care to a family member with dementia. *Psychology and Aging, 4*, 402–408.

Kinnunen, U., Feldt, T., Mauno, S., & Rantanen, J. (2010). Interface between work and family: A longitudinal individual and cross-over perspective. *Journal of Occupational and Organizational Psychology, 83*, 119–137.

Kins, E., Beyers, W., Soenens, B., & Bansteenkiste, M. (2009). Patterns of home leaving and subjective well-being in emerging adulthood: The role of motivational processes and parental autonomy support. *Developmental Psychology, 45*, 1416–1429.

Kinsella, K., & Velkoff, V. A. (2001). An aging world: 2001. U.S. Census Bureau, Series P95/01-1, US Government Printing Office, Washington, DC.

Kirkman, M., Rosenthal, D., & Smtih, A. M. A. (1998). Adolescent sex and the romantic narrative: Why some young heterosexuals use condoms to prevent pregnancy but not disease. *Psychology, Health & Medicine, 3*, 355–370.

Kirkorian, H. L., Pempek, T. A., Murphy, L. A., Schmidt, M. E., & Anderson, D. R. (2009). The impact of background television on parent-child interactions. *Child Development, 80*, 1350–1359.

Kirkwood, T. B. L. (2001). Where will it all end? *The Lancet, 357*, 576–577.

Kirsch, P., Esslinger, C., Chen, Q., Mier, D., Lis, S., Siddhanti, S., Gruppe, H., Mattay, V. S., Gallhofer, B., & Meyer-Lindenberg, A. (2005). Oxytocin modulates neural circuitry for social cognition and fear in humans. *Neuroscience, 25*, 11489–11493.

Kiselica, M. S., Gorcynski, J., & Capps, S. (1998). Teen mothers and fathers: School counselor perceptions of service needs. *Professional School Counseling, 2*, 146–152.

Kiser, P. (2010). Who uses Face Book, Twitter, MySpace, and LinkedIn? Retrieved on August 7, 2010, at http://paulkiser.wordpress.com/2010/04/01/who-uses-facebook-twitter-myspace-linkedin/.

Kistner, J. A., Ziegert, D. I., Castro, R., & Robertson, B. (2001). Helplessness in early childhood: Prediction of symptoms associated with depression and negative self-worth. *Merrill-Palmer Quarterly, 47*, 336–354.

Kiston, J. M. (1994). Contemporary Eriksonian theory: A psychobiographical illustration. *Gerontology and Geriatrics Education, 14*, 81–91.

Kitayama, S., Karasawa, M., & Mesquita, B. (2004). Collective and personal processes in regulating emotions: Emotion and self in Japan and the United States. In P. Philippot & R. S. Feldman (Eds.), *The regulation of emotion* (pp. 251–276). Mahwah, NJ: Erlbaum.

Kite, M. E. (1996). Age, gender, and occupational label: A test of social role theory. *Psychology of Women Quarterly, 20*, 361–374.

Kite, M. E., Deaux, K., & Miele, M. (1991). Stereotypes of young and old: Does age outweigh gender? *Psychology and Aging, 6*, 19–27.

Kitson, G. C. (1982). Attachment to the spouse in divorce: A scale and its application. *Journal of Marriage and the Family, 44*, 379–393.

Kitzinger, C., & Coyle, A. (1995). Lesbian and gay couples: Speaking of difference. *Psychologist, 8*, 64–69.

Kitzinger, S. (1982). The social context of birth: Some comparisons between childbirth in Jamaica and Britain. In C. P. MacCormack (Ed.), *Ethnography of fertility and birth* (pp. 181–203). London: Academic Press.

Kitzmann, K. M., & Cohen, R. (2003). Parents' versus children's perceptions of interparental conflict as predictors of children's friendship quality. *Journal of Social and Personal Relationships, 20*, 689–700.

Kitzmann, K. M., Cohen, R., & Lockwood, R. L. (2002). Are only children missing out? Comparison of the peer-related social competence of only children and siblings. *Journal of Social and Personal Relationships, 19*, 295–316.

Kivnick, H. Q. (1988). Grandparenthood, life review, and psychosocial development. *Journal of Gerontological Social Work, 12*, 63–81.

Klein, H. (1991). Couvade syndrome: Male counterpart to pregnancy. *International Journal of Psychiatry in Medicine, 21*, 57–69.

Klein, L. & Knitzer, J. (2007). *Promoting effective early learning: What every policy maker and educator should know.* New York: National Center for Children in Poverty, Columbia University Mailman School of Public Health.

Klein, M. (1932/1975). *The psychoanalysis of children* (The International Psychoanalytic Library, No. 22). Oxford, UK: Hogarth Press.

Klein, M. (1948). *Contributions to psychoanalysis, 1921–1945.* London: Hogarth Press.

Klesges, L. M., Pahor, M., Shorr, R. I., Wan, J. Y., Williamson, J. D., & Guralnik, J. M. (2001). Financial difficulty in acquiring food among elderly disabled women: Results from the Women's Health and Aging Study. *American Journal of Public Health, 91*, 68–75.

Kliegman, R. M., Behrman, R. E., Jenson, H. B., & Stanton, B. F. (2007). *Nelson textbook of pediatrics* (18th ed.). Philadelphia: Saunders Elsevier.

Klimstra, T. A., et al. (2010). Short-term fluctuations in identity: Introducing a micro-level approach to identity formation. *Journal of Personality and Social Psychology, 99*, 191–202.

Kline, D. W., & Scialfa, C. T. (1997). Sensory and perceptual functioning: Basic research and human factors implications. In A. D. Fisk & W. A. Rogers (Eds.), *Handbook of human factors and the older adult* (pp. 27–54). San Diego: Academic Press.

Kluger, J. (1997, March 10). Will we follow the sheep? *Time*, pp. 67–72.

Klump, K. L., & Culbert, K. M. (2007). Molecular genetic studies of eating disorders: Current status and future directions. *Current Directions in Psychological Science, 16*, 37–41.

Kluwer, E. S., Heesink, J. A., & Van de Vliert, E. (2000). The division of labor in close relationships: An asymmetrical conflict issue. *Personal Relationships, 7*, 263–282.

Knee, D.O. (2010). Hospice care for the aging population in the United States. In J.C. Cavanaugh & C.K. Cavanaugh (Eds.), *Aging in America* (Vol. 3, pp. 203–221). Santa Barbara, CA: Praeger.

Knight, C. C., & Fischer, K. W. (1992). Learning to read words: Individual differences in developmental sequences. *Journal of Applied Developmental Psychology, 13*, 377–404.

Knitzer, J. (2007). Testimony of Jane Knitzer, Ed.D. to the House Ways and Means Committee, U.S. Congress Hearing on Economic and Societal Costs of Poverty. New York: National Center for Children in Poverty, Columbia University Mailman School of Public Health. http://nccp.org/media/wmt07_text.pdf

Knitzer, J. & Cooper, J. (2006). Beyond integration: Challenges for children's mental health. *Health Affairs, 25*, 670.

Knox, D., Zusman, M., & Nieves, W. (1997). College students' homogamous preferences for a date and mate. *College Student Journal, 31*, 445–448.

Kobak, R. (1999). The emotional dynamics of disruptions in attachment relationships. In J. Cassidy & P. Shaver (Eds.), *The handbook of attachment: Theory, research, and clinical applications* (pp. 21–43). New York: Guilford Press.

Koblinsky, S. A., & Anderson, E. A. (1993, Spring–Summer). Studying homeless children and their families: Issues and challenges. *Division 7 Newsletter*, pp. 1–3.

Kochanek, K. D., & Martin, J. A. (2004). *Supplemental analysis of recent trends in infant mortality.* National Center for Health Statistics, U.S. Department of Health and Human Services. Retrieved August 10, 2004, from http://www.cdc.gov/nchs/products/pubs/pubd/hestats/infantmort/infantmort.htm

Kochanska, G. (1997). Multiple pathways to conscience for children with different temperaments: From toddlerhood to age 5. *Developmental Psychology, 33*, 228–240.

Kochanska, G., Aksan, N., & Joy, M. E. (2007). Children's fearfulness as a moderator of parenting in early socialization: Two longitudinal studies. *Developmental Psychology, 43*, 222–237.

Kochanska, G., Aksan, N., & Koenig, A. L. (1995). A longitudinal study of the roots of preschoolers' conscience: Committed compliance and emerging internalization. *Child Development, 66,* 1752–1769.

Kochanska, G., Forman, D. R., Aksan, N., & Dunbar, S. B. (2005). Pathways to conscience: Early mother-child mutually responsive orientation and children's moral emotion, conduct, and cognition. *Journal of Child Psychology and Psychiatry, 46,* 19–34.

Kochanska, G., & Knaack, A. (2003). Effortful control as a personality characteristic of young children: Antecedents, correlates, and consequences. *Journal of Personality, 71,* 1087–1112.

Kochanska, G., Murray, K. T., & Harlan, E. T. (2000). Effortful control in early childhood: Continuity and change, antecedents, and implications for social development. *Developmental Psychology, 36,* 220–232.

Kochanska, G., & Radke-Yarrow, M. (1992). Inhibition in toddlerhood and the dynamics of the child's interactions with an unfamiliar peer at age 5. *Child Development, 63,* 325–335.

Kochenderfer-Ladd, B. J., & Wardrop, J. L. (2001). Chronicity and instability of children's peer victimization experiences as predictors of loneliness and social satisfaction trajectories. *Child Development, 72,* 134–151.

Kohlberg, L. (1964). Development of moral character and moral ideology. In M. L. Hoffman & L. W. Hoffman (Eds.), *Review of child development research* (Vol. 1). New York: Sage.

Kohlberg, L. (1966). A cognitive-developmental analysis of children's sex-role concepts and attitudes. In E. E. Maccoby (Ed.), *The development of sex differences.* Stanford, CA: Stanford University Press.

Kohlberg, L. (1969). Stage and sequence: The cognitive-developmental approach to socialization. In D. A. Goslin (Ed.), *Handbook of socialization theory and research.* Chicago: Rand McNally.

Kohlberg, L. (1976). Moral stages and moralization: The cognitive-developmental approach. In T. Lickona (Ed.), *Moral development and behavior.* New York: Holt, Rinehart & Winston.

Kohn, M. L. (1980). Job complexity and adult personality. In N. J. Smelser & E. H. Erikson (Eds.), *Themes of work and love in adulthood* (pp. 193–210). Cambridge, MA: Harvard University Press.

Kohn, M.L. (2006). *Change and stability: A cross national analysis of social structure and personality.* Greenbrae, CA: Paradigm Press.

Kohn, P. M., & Milrose, J. A. (1993). The inventory of high-school students' recent life experiences: A decontaminated measure of adolescents' life hassles. *Journal of Youth and Adolescence, 22,* 43–55.

Kohut, H. (1971). *The analysis of the self.* New York: International Universities Press.

Kolata, G. (2007). A surprising secret to long life, according to studies: Stay in school. *New York Times,* January 3, A1, A16.

Konopka, G. (1976). *Young girls: A portrait of adolescence.* Englewood Cliffs, NJ: Prentice Hall.

Konrad, P. (1990, August 6). Welcome to the woman-friendly company. *Business Week,* pp. 48–55.

Kopp, C. B. (1982). Antecedents of self-regulation: A developmental perspective. *Developmental Psychology, 18,* 199–214.

Kopp, C. B. (1989). Regulation of distress and negative emotions: A developmental view. *Developmental Psychology, 25,* 343–354.

Kornfield, S. (1990). *Impact of parental marital status, gender, and pubertal development on adolescent.* Unpublished manuscript, University of Georgia.

Kornhaber, A. (2004). *Grandparents' visitation rights.* Retrieved July 27, 2004, from http://www.grandparenting.org/Grandparent%20Visitation.htm

Kosfield, M., Heinrichs, M., Zak, P. J., Fischbacher, U., & Fehr, E. (2005). Oxytocin increases trust in humans. *Nature, 435,* 673–676.

Kotre, J. N. (1995a). Generative outcome. *Journal of Aging Studies, 9,* 33–41.

Kotre, J. N. (1995b). *White gloves: How we create ourselves through memory.* New York: Free Press.

Kotre, J. N., & Kotre, K. B. (1998). Intergenerational buffers: The damage stops here. In D. P. McAdams & E. de St. Aubin (Eds.), *Generativity and adult development: Psychosocial perspectives on caring for and contributing to the next generation* (pp. 367–389). Washington, DC: American Psychological Association.

Kovacs, A. M., & Mehler, J. (2009). Flexible learning of multiple speech structures in bilingual infants. *Science, 325,* 611–612.

Kowaz, A. M., & Marcia, J. E. (1991). Development and validation of a measure of Eriksonian industry. *Journal of Personality and Social Psychology, 60,* 390–397.

Kram, K. E. (1985). *Mentoring at work: Developmental relationships in organizational life.* Glenview, IL: Scott, Foresman.

Kramer, A. F., & Willis, S. L. (2002). Enhancing the cognitive vitality of older adults. *Current Directions in Psychological Science, 11,* 173–177.

Kramer, D.A. (2003). The ontogeny of wisdom in its variations. In J. Demick & C. Andreoletti (Eds.), *Handbook of adult development* (pp. 131–151). New York: Plenum Press.

Krampe, R. T., & Charness N. (2006). Aging and expertise. In K. A. Ericsson, N. Charness, P. Feltovich, & R. Hoffman (Eds.), *Cambridge handbook of expertise and expert performance* (pp. 725–744). New York: Cambridge University Press.

Krause, N. (2004). Stressors in highly valued roles, meaning in life, and the physical health status of older adults. *Journals of Gerontology, Series B: Psychological Sciences and Social Sciences, 59,* S287–S297.

Krause, N. (2006). Social relationships in late life. In R. H. Binstock & L. K. George (Eds.), *Handbook of aging and the social sciences* (pp. 181–200). San Diego, CA: Academic Press.

Krause, N. (2007). Longitudinal study of social support and meaning in life. *Psychology and Aging, 22,* 456–469.

Krause, N., & Shaw, B. A. (2000). Role-specific feelings of control and mortality. *Psychology and Aging, 15,* 617–626.

Kreider, R. M. (2005). Number, timing and duration of marriages and divorces: 2001. *Current Population Reports,* P70-97. Retrieved on August 18, 2010, at www.census.gov/prod/2005pubs/p70-97.pdf

Kreider, R. M., & Fields, J. M. (2002). Number, timing, and duration of marriages and divorces: Fall, 1996. *Current Population Reports,* P70–80. Washington, DC: U.S. Census Bureau.

Kremar, M., & Cooke, M. C. (2001). Children's moral reasoning and their perceptions of television violence. *Journal of Communication, 51,* 300–316.

Kroger, J. (1993). *Discussions on ego identity.* Hillsdale, NJ: Erlbaum.

Kroger, J. (1997). Gender and identity: The intersection of structure, content, and context. *Sex Roles, 36,* 747–770.

Kroger, J. (2000). *Identity development: Adolescence through adulthood.* Thousand Oaks, CA: Sage.

Kroger, J. (2002). Commentary on "Feminist perspectives on Erikson's theory: Their relevance for contemporary identity development research." *Identity: An International Journal of Theory and Research, 2,* Issue 3, 257–266.

Kroger, J. (2003). Identity development during adolescence. In G. R. Adams & M. D. Berzonsky (Eds.), *Blackwell handbook of adolescence* (pp. 205–226). Malden, MA: Blackwell.

Kroger, J. (2004). *Identity in adolescence: The balance between self and other.* New York: Routledge.

Krones, T., Schlüter, E., Neuwohner, E., Ansari, S. E., Wissner, T., & Richter, G. (2006). What is the preimplantation embryo? *Social Science and Medicine, 63,* 1–20.

Kropp, J. P., & Haynes, O. M. (1987). Abusive and nonabusive mothers' ability to identify general and specific emotion signals of infants. *Child Development, 58,* 187–190.

Kruger, J., & Dunning, D. (1999). Unskilled and unaware of it: How difficulties in recognizing one's own incompetence lead to inflated self-assessments. *Journal of Personality and Social Psychology, 77,* 1121–1134.

Kruk, E. (1995). Grandparent–grandchild contact loss: Findings from a study of "grandparents' rights" members. *Canadian Journal on Aging, 14,* 737–754.

Kubler-Ross, E. (1969). *On death and dying.* New York: Macmillan.

Kubler-Ross, E. (1972, February). On death and dying. *Journal of the American Medical Association, 219,* 10–15.

Kubler-Ross, E. (1981). *Living with dying.* New York: Macmillan.

Kubler-Ross, E. (1983). *On children and death.* New York: Macmillan.

Kuczaj, S. A., & Hill, H. M. (2003). The development of language. In A. Slater & G. Bremner (Eds.), *An introduction to developmental psychology* (pp. 211–236). Malden, MA: Blackwell.

Kuhl, P. K. (1987). Perception of speech and sound in early infancy. In P. Salapatek & L. Cohen (Eds.), *Handbook of infant perception* (Vol. 1). Orlando, FL: Academic Press.

Kuhn, D., Garcia-Mila, M., Zohar, A., & Andersen, C. (1995). Strategies of knowledge acquisition. *Monographs of the Society for Research in Child Development, 60* (4, Serial No. 245).

Kunjufu. (2004). *Fathers and childbirth.* Retrieved August 11, 2004, from http://www.blackchat.co.uk/theblackforum/forum2/2969.html

Kunz, J., & Kunz, P. R. (1995). Social support during the process of divorce: It does make a difference. *Journal of Divorce and Remarriage, 24,* 111–119.

Kunzmann, U., & Baltes, P. B. (2005). The psychology of wisdom: Theoretical and empirical challenges. In R. J. Sternberg & J. Jordan (Eds.). *A handbook of wisdom: Psychological perspectives* (pp. 110–135). New York: Cambridge University Press.

Kurdek, L. A. (1995). Lesbian and gay couples. In A. R. D'Augelli & C. J. Patterson (Eds.), *Lesbian, gay, and bisexual identities over the lifespan: Psychological perspectives* (pp. 243–261). New York: Oxford University Press.

Kurdek, L. A. (2003). Differences between gay and lesbian cohabiting couples. *Journal of Social and Personal Relationships, 20,* 411–436.

Kurdek, L. A. (2004). Are gay and lesbian cohabiting couples *really* different from heterosexual married couples? *Journal of Marriage and the Family, 66,* 880–900.

Kurdek, L. A. (2005). What do we know about gay and lesbian couples? *Current Directions in Psychological Science, 14,* 251–254.

Kurdek, L. A. (2006a). The nature and correlates of deterrents to leaving a relationship. *Personal Relationships, 13,* 521–535.

Kurdek, L. A. (2006b). Differences between partners from heterosexual, gay and lesbian cohabiting couples. *Journal of Marriage and Family, 68,* 509–528.

Kwon, Y.-J., & Lawson, A. E. (2000). Linking brain growth with the development of scientific reasoning ability and conceptual change during adolescence. *Journal of Research in Science Teaching, 37,* 44–62.

Laberge, L., Petit, D., Simard, C., Vitaro, F., Tremblay, R. E., & Montplaisir, J. (2001). Development of sleep patterns in early adolescence. *Journal of Sleep Research, 10,* 59–67.

Labouvie-Vief, G. (1992). A neo-Piagetian perspective on adult cognitive development. In R. J. Sternberg & C. A. Berg (Eds.), *Intellectual development* (pp. 197–228). New York: Cambridge University Press.

Labouvie-Vief, G., & Diehl, M. (2000). Cognitive complexity and cognitive-affective integration: Related or separate domains of adult development? *Psychology and Aging, 15,* 490–504.

Lacombe, A. C., & Gay, J. (1998). The role of gender in adolescent identity and intimacy decisions. *Journal of Youth and Adolescence, 27,* 795–802.

Lacroix, V., Pomerleau, A., Malcuit, G., Seguin, R., & Lamarre, G. (2001). Language and cognitive development of the child during the first three years in relation to the duration of maternal vocalizations and the toys present in the environment: Longitudinal study of populations at risk. *Canadian Journal of Behavioural Science, 33,* 65–76.

Ladd, G. W., Herald-Brown, S. L., & Reiser, M. (2008). Does chronic peer rejection predict the development of children's classroom participation during the grade school years? *Child Development, 79,* 1001–1015.

Laflamme, D., Pomerleau, A., & Malcuit, G. (2002). A comparison of fathers' and mothers' involvement in childcare and stimulation behaviors during free-play with their infants at 9 and 15 months. *Sex Roles, 47,* 507–518.

LaFreniere, P. J. (2000). *Emotional development: A biosocial perspective.* Belmont, CA: Wadsworth.

Lagattuta, K. H., & Wellman, H. M. (2001). Thinking about the past: Early knowledge about links between prior experience, thinking, and emotion. *Child Development, 72,* 82–102.

Laible, D. J., & Thompson, R. A. (2000). Mother–child discourse, attachment security, shared positive affect, and early conscience development. *Child Development, 71,* 1424–1440.

Lakin, J. L., Chartrand, T. L., & Arkin, R. M. (2008). I am too just like you. *Psychological Science, 19,* 816–822.

LaMastro, V. (2001). Childless by choice? Attributions and attitudes concerning family size. *Social Behavior and Personality, 29,* 231–243.

Lamb, M. E. (1976). Twelve-month-olds and their parents: Interaction in a laboratory playroom. *Developmental Psychology, 12,* 237–244.

Lambert, J. D., & Thomasson, G. C. (1997). Mormon American families. In M. K. DeGenova (Ed.), *Families in cultural context: Strengths and challenges in diversity* (pp. 85–108). Mountain View, CA: Mayfield.

Lambert, S. (2005). Gay and lesbian families: What we know and were to go from here. *The Family Journal, 13,* 43–51.

Lamborn, S. D., & Steinberg, L. D. (1993). Emotional autonomy redux: Revisiting Ryan and Lynch. *Child Development, 64,* 483–499.

Lamm, B., & Keller, H. (2007). Understanding cultural models of parenting. *Journal of Cross-Cultural Psychology, 38,* 50–57.

Landale, N. S., & Fennelly, K. S. (1992). Informal unions among mainland Puerto Ricans: Cohabitation or an alternative to legal marriage. *Journal of Marriage and the Family, 54,* 269–280.

Landry, S. H., Miller-Loncar, C. L., Smith, K. E., & Swank, P. R. (2002). The role of early parenting in children's development of executive processes. *Developmental Neuropsychology, 21,* 15–41.

Landry, S. H., Smith, K. E., Swank, P. R., Assel, M. A., & Vellet, S. (2001). Does early responsive parenting have a special importance for children's development or is consistency across early childhood necessary? *Developmental Psychology, 37,* 387–403.

Landry-Meyer, L. (1999). Research into action: Recommended intervention strategies for grandparent caregivers. *Family Relations: Interdisciplinary Journal of Applied Family Studies, 48,* 381–389.

Landry-Meyer, L., Gerard, J. M., & Guzell, J. R. (2005). Caregiver stress among grandparents raising grandchildren: The functional role of social support. *Marriage and Family Review, 37,* 171–190.

Lang, F. R., Featherman, D. L., & Nesselroade, J. R. (1997). Social self-efficacy and short-term variability in social relationships: The MacArthur successful aging study. *Psychology and Aging, 12,* 657–666.

Langlois, J. H., Ritter, J. M., Casey, R. J., & Sawin, D. B. (1995). Infant attractiveness predicts maternal behaviors and attitudes. *Developmental Psychology, 31,* 464–472.

Lankford, M. D., & Milone, K. (Illustrator). (1996). *Hopscotch around the world: Nineteen ways to play the game.* New York: Morrow.

Lansford, J. E., & Parker, J. G. (1999). Children's interactions in triads: Behavioral profiles and effects of gender and patterns of friendship among members. *Developmental Psychology, 35,* 80–93.

Lanz, M., & Tagliabue, S. (2007). Do I really need someone in order to become an adult? Romantic relationships during emerging adulthood in Italy. *Journal of Adolescent Research, 22,* 531–549.

Lapierre, S., Bouffard, L., & Bastin, E. (1997). Personal goals and subjective well-being in later life. *The International Journal of Aging and Human Development, 45,* 287–303.

Larson, E. A. (2006). Stress in the lives of college women: "Lots to do and not much time." *Journal of Adolescent Research, 21,* 579–606.

Larson, M. C., Gunnar, M. R., & Hertsgaard, L. (1991). The effects of morning naps, car trips, and maternal separation on adrenocortical activity in human infants. *Child Development, 62,* 362–372.

Larson, R., & Lampman-Petraitis, C. (1989). Daily emotional states as reported by children and adolescents. *Child Development, 60,* 1250–1260.

LaSala, M. C. (2000). Gay male couples: The importance of coming out and being out to parents. *Journal of Homosexuality, 39,* 47–71.

Laszlo, E. (1972). *Introduction to systems philosophy: Toward a new paradigm of contemporary thought.* New York: Harper & Row.

Laumann, E. Q., Ganon, J. H., Michael, R. T., & Michaels, S. (1994). *The social organization of sexuality.* Chicago: University of Chicago Press.

Laurenceau, J., Barrett, L. F., & Rovine, M. J. (2005). The interpersonal process model of intimacy in marriage: A daily-diary and multilevel modeling approach. *Journal of Family Psychology, 19,* 314–323.

Laursen, B., Coy, K., & Collins, W.A. (1998). Reconsidering changes in parent-child conflict across adolescence: A meta-analysis. *Child Development, 69,* 817–832.

Lawler, E. J., Thye, S. R., & Yoon, J. (2009). *Social commitments in a depersonalized world.* New York: Russell Sage Foundation.

Lawler, S. (2008). *Identity: Sociological perspectives.* Malden, MA: Polity Press.

Lawn, R. M., & Vehar, G. A. (1986). The molecular genetics of hemophilia. *Scientific American, 254,* 48–56.

Laws, G., Byrne, A., & Buckley, S. (2000). Language and memory development in children with Down syndrome at mainstream schools and special schools: A comparison. *Educational Psychology, 20,* 447–457.

Lawton, M. P. (2001). Quality of life and the end of life. In J. E. Birren & K. W. Schaie (Eds.), *Handbook of the psychology of aging* (5th ed., pp. 592–616) San Diego: Academic Press.

Lazarus, R. S. (2000). Toward better research on stress and coping. *American Psychologist, 55,* 655–673.

Lazarus, R. S., & Folkman, S. (1984). *Stress, appraisal, and coping.* New York: Springer Verlag.

Le, H.-N., Munoz, R. F., Ippen, C. G., & Stoddard, J. L. (2003). Treatment is not enough: We must prevent major depression in women. *Prevention & Treatment, 6.*

Leadbeater, B. J., Kuperminc, G. P., Blatt, S. J., & Hertzog, C. (1999). A multivariate model of gender differences in adolescents' internalizing and externalizing problems. *Developmental Psychology, 35,* 1268–1282.

Leahy, R. L. (2006). *Contemporary cognitive therapy: Theory, research, and practice.* New York: Guildford.

Leaper, C. (2000). Gender, affiliation, assertion, and the interactive context of parent-child play. *Developmental Psychology, 36,* 381–393.

Leaper, C., Anderson, K. J., & Sanders, P. (1998). Moderators of gender effects on parents' talk to their children: A metaanalysis. *Developmental Psychology, 34,* 3–27.

Leaper, C., Tenenbaum, H. R., & Shaffer, T. G. (1999). Communication patterns of African American girls and boys from low-income, urban background. *Child Development, 70,* 1489–1503.

Lecanuet, J. P., Graniere-Deferre, C., Jacquet, A. Y., & DeCasper, A. J. (2000). Fetal discrimination of low-pitched musical notes. *Developmental Psychobiology, 36,* 29–39.

Lee, C. (2002). *Cataracts.* Retrieved February 3, 2002, from http://www.allaboutvision.com/conditions/cataracts.htm

Lee, G. R., DeMaris, A., Bavin, S., & Sullivan, R. (2001). Gender differences in the depressive effect of widowhood in later life. *Journal of Gerontology, 56,* S56–S61.

Lee, K., & Allen, N. J. (2002). Organizational citizenship behavior and workplace deviance: The role of affect and cognitions. *Journal of Applied Psychology, 87,* 131–142.

Lee, K., Ashton, M. C., & Shin, K.-H. (2005). Correlates of workplace anti-social behavior. *Applied Psychology, 54,* 81–98.

Lee, K., & Freire, A. (2003). Cognitive development. In A. Slater & G. Bremner (Eds.), *An introduction to developmental psychology* (pp. 359–387). Malden, MA: Blackwell.

Lee, M. J., Whitehead, J., & Balchin, N. (2000). The measurement of values in youth sport: Development of the Youth Sport Values Questionnaire. *Journal of Sport and Exercise Psychology, 22,* 307–326.

Lee, M. J., Whitehead, J., & Ntoumanis, N. (2007). Development of the attitudes to moral decision-making in youth sport questionnaire. *Psychology of Sport and Exercise, 8,* 369–392.

Lee, V. E. & Burkham, D. T. (2002). *Inequality at the starting gate: Social background differences in achievement as children begin school.* New York: Economic Policy Institute.

Leerkes, E. M., Blankson, A. N., & O'Brien, M. (2009). Differential effects of maternal sensitivity to infant distress and non-distress on social-emotional functioning. *Child Development, 80,* 762–775.

Leffel, G.M., Fritz, M.E., & Stevens, M.R. (2008). Who cares? Generativity and the moral emotions, Part III. A social intuitionist "ecology of virtue." *Journal of Psychology and Theology, 36,* 202–221.

Lehr, U., Seiler, E., & Thomae, H. (2000). Aging in a cross-cultural perspective. In A. L. Comunian & U. P. Gielen (Eds.), *International perspectives on human development* (pp. 571–589). Lengerich, Germany: Pabst.

Leiderman, S., Tulkin, R., & Rosenfeld, A. (Eds.), *Culture and infancy: Variations in the human experience* (pp. 15–28). New York: Academic Press.

Leiras-Muney, A. (2005). The relationship between education and adult mortality in the United States. *The Review of Economic Studies, 72,* 189–221.

Lemaire, P., Arnaud, L., & Lecacheur, M. (2004). Adults' age-related differences in adaptivity of strategy choices: Evidence from computational estimation. *Psychology and Aging, 19,* 467–481.

Lemkau, J. R. (1988). Emotional sequelae of abortion: Implications for clinical practice. *Psychology of Women Quarterly, 12,* 461–472.

Lemonick, M. D. (2000). Teens before their time. *Time, 156,* 66–74.

Lenton, A.P. & Francesconi, M. (2010). How humans cognitive manage of abundance of mate options. *Psychological Sciences, 21,* 528–533.

Lenneberg, E.H. (1967), *Biological foundations of language.* Oxford, England: Wiley.

Lenroot, R. K., & Giedd, J. N. (2006). Brain development in children and adolescents: Insights from anatomical magnetic resonance imaging. *Neuroscience and Biobehavioral Reviews, 30,* 718–729.

Leong, F. T. L., Kao, E. M.-C., & Lee, S.-H. (2004). The relationship between family dynamics and career interests among Chinese Americans and European Americans. *Journal of Career Assessment, 12,* 65–84.

Lerman, R. (1993). A national profile of young unwed fathers. In R. Lerman, R. Ooms, & T. Ooms (Eds.), *Young unwed fathers: Changing roles and emerging policies* (pp. 27–51). Philadelphia: Temple University Press.

Lerner, J. V., & Lerner, R. M. (1983). Temperament and adaptation across life: Theoretical and empirical issues. In P. B. Baltes & O. G. Brim (Eds.), *Life span development and behavior, 5* (pp. 197–231). New York: Academic Press.

Lerner, R. M. (2002). *Concepts and theories of human development* (3rd ed.) Mahwah, NJ: Erlbaum.

Lerner, R. M., Dowling, E., & Roth, S. L. (2003). Contributions of lifespan psychology to the future elaboration of developmental systems theory. In U. M. Staudinger & U. Lindenberger (Eds.), *Understanding human development: Dialogues with lifespan psychology* (pp. 413–422). Dordrecht, Netherlands: Kluwer.

Lerner-Geva, L., Boyko, V., Blumstein, T., & Benyamini, Y. (2010). The impact of education, cultural background, and lifestyle on symptoms of the menopausal transition; The Woman's Health at Midlife study. *The Journal of Women's Health, 19,* 975–985.

Lervåg, A., & Hulme, C. (2009). Rapid automatized naming (RAN) taps a mechanism that places constraints on the development of early reading fluency. *Psychological Science, 20,* 1040–1048.

LeVay, S. (1991). A difference in hypothalamic structure between heterosexual and homosexual men. *Science, 253,* 1034–1037.

Levine, A., & Nidiffer, J. (1996). *Beating the odds: How the poor get to college.* San Francisco: Jossey-Bass.

Levine, R. A. (1977). Child rearing as cultural adaptation. In P. H. Leiderman, S. R. Tulkin, & A. Rosenfeld (Eds.), *Culture and infancy: Variations in the human experience* (pp. 15–28). New York: Academic Press.

Levine, R. A. (1980). Adulthood among the Gusii of Kenya. In N. J. Smelser & E. H. Erikson (Eds.), *Themes of work and love in adulthood* (pp. 77–119). Cambridge, MA: Harvard University Press.

Levine, R. A., Levine, S., Dixon, S., Richman, A., Liederman, P. H., Keefer, C. H., & Brazelton, T. B. (1996). *Child care and culture: Lessons from Africa.* New York: Cambridge University Press.

Levine, S. (2003). Erectile dysfunction: Why drug therapy isn't always enough. *Cleveland Clinic Journal of Medicine, 70,* 241–246.

Levinger, G. (1983). Development and change. In H. H. Kelley, et al. (Eds.), *Close relationships* (pp. 315–359). New York: Freeman.

Levitt, M. J., Weber, R. A., & Clark, M. C. (1986). Social network relationships as sources of maternal support and well-being. *Developmental Psychology, 22,* 310–316.

Levitt, M. J., Weber, R. A., & Guacci, N. (1993). Convoys of social support: An intergenerational analysis. *Psychology and Aging, 8,* 323–326.

Levy, G. D. (1998). Effects of gender constancy and figure's height and sex on young children's gender-typed attributions. *Journal of General Psychology, 125,* 65–68.

Levy, G. D., Barth, J. M., & Zimmerman, B. J. (1998). *Journal of Genetic Psychology, 159,* 121–126.

Levy, R. I. (1996). Essential contrasts: Differences in parental ideas about learners and teaching in Tahiti and Nepal. In S. Harkness & C. M. Super (Eds.), *Parents' cultural belief systems* (pp. 123–142). New York: Guilford Press.

Lewis, H. B. (1987). Shame and the narcissistic personality. In D. L. Nathanson (Ed.), *The many faces of shame* (pp. 93–132). New York: Guilford Press.

Lewis, M. (2005). The child and its family: The social network model. *Human Development, 48,* 8–27.

Lewis, M., & Carmody, D. P. (2008). Self representation and brain development. *Developmental Psychology, 44,* 1329–1334.

Lewit, E. M., & Baker, L. S. (1995). School readiness. *The Future of Children, 5,* 128–139.

Li, Q., Kirby, R.S., Sigler, R.T., Hwang, S-S., LaGory, M.E., & Goldenberg, R.L. (2010). A multilevel analysis of individual, household, and neighborhood correlates of intimate partner violence among low-income pregnant women in Jefferson County, Alabama. *American Journal of Public Health, 100,* 531–539.

Liang, J., Brown, J. W., Krause, N. M., Ofstedal, M. B., & Bennett, J. (2005). Health and living arrangements among older Americans. *Journal of Aging and Health, 17,* 305–335.

Liang, J., Krause, N. M., & Bennett, J. M. (2001). Social exchange and well-being: Is giving better than receiving? *Psychology and Aging, 16,* 511–523.

Liben, L. S., & Signorella, M. L. (1993). Gender-schematic processing in children: The role of initial interpretations of stimuli. *Developmental Psychology, 29,* 141–149.

Liburd, J. D. A. (2006). Eating disorder: Anorexia. *eMedicine.* Retrieved August 23, 2007, from http://www.emedicine.com/ped/topic115.htm

Lieberman, A. F., Weston, D. R., & Pawl, J. H. (1991). Preventive intervention and outcome with anxiously attached dyads. *Child Development, 62,* 199–209.

Liebert, R. M., & Sprafkin, J. (1988). *The early window: Effects of television on children and youth* (3rd ed.). New York: Pergamon Press.

Liebow, E. (1966). *Tally's corner.* Boston: Little, Brown.

Lifton, R. J. (1973). The sense of immortality: On death and the continuity of life. *American Journal of Psychoanalysis, 33,* 3–15.

Li-Grining, C. P. (2007). Effortful control among low-income preschoolers in three cities: Stability, change and individual differences. *Developmental Psychology, 43,* 208–221.

Lin, H.-L., Lawrence, F. R., & Gorrell, J. (2003). Kindergarten teachers' views of children's readiness for school. *Early Childhood Research Quarterly, 18,* 225–237.

Lin, R.-G., II. (2001, February 23). Nation's colleges anticipate end of SATs at UC schools. *Daily Californian,* University of California, Berkeley. Retrieved February 3, 2005, from http://www.studentadvantage.com_article_0,1075,c0-i0-t0-a1333686,00.html

Lindbohm, M., Hemminki, K., Bonhomme, M. G., Anttila, A., Rantala, K., Heikkila, P., & Rosenberg, M. J. (1991). Effects of paternal occupational exposure on spontaneous abortions. *American Journal of Public Health, 81,* 1029–1033.

Lindemann, E. (1944). Symptomology and management of acute grief. *American Journal of Psychiatry, 101,* 141–148.

Lindsey, E. W. (1994). Homelessness. In P. C. McKenry & S. J. Price (Eds.), *Families and change: Coping with stressful events* (pp. 281–302). Thousand Oaks, CA: Sage.

Lindsey, E. W., & Colwell, M. J. (2003). Preschoolers' emotional competence: Links to pretend and physical play. *Child Study Journal, 33,* 39–52.

Lindsey, E. W., Mize, J., & Pettit, G. S. (1997). Mutuality in parent–child play: Consequences for children's peer competence. *Journal of Social and Personal Relationships, 14,* 523–538.

Link, B., Phelan, J., Bresnahan, M., & Stueve, A. (1995). Life-time and five-year prevalence of homelessness in the United States: New evidence on an old debate. *American Journal of Orthopsychiatry, 65,* 347–354.

Linsk, N. L., & Mason, S. (2004). Stresses on grandparents and other relatives caring for children affected by HIV/AIDS. *Health & Social Work, 29,* 127–136.

Lippert, T., & Prager, K. J. (2001). Daily experiences of intimacy: A study of couples. *Personal Relationships, 8,* 283–298.

Littlefield, D., Robison, C. C., Engelbrecht, L., Gonzalez, B., & Hutcheson, H. (2002). Mobilizing women for minority health and social justice in California. *American Journal of Public Health, 92,* 576–579.

Litwin, H. (1997). Support network type and health service utilization. *Research on Aging, 19,* 274–299.

Litwin, H., Vogel, C., Künemund, H., & Kohli, M. (2008). The balance of intergenerational exchange: Correlates of net transfers in Germany and Israel. *European Journal of Ageing, 5,* 91–102.

Livesley, W. J., Jackson, D. N., & Schroeder, M. L. (1992). Factorial structure of traits delineating personality disorders in clinical and general population samples, *Journal of Abnormal Psychology, 101,* 432–440.

Lo, R., & Brown, R. (1999). Stress and adaptation: Preparation for successful retirement. *Australian and New Zealand Journal of Mental Health Nursing, 8,* 30–38.

Lobel, T. E., & Menashri, J. (1993). Relations of conceptions of gender-role transgressions and gender constancy to gender-typed toy preferences. *Developmental Psychology, 29,* 150–155.

Lobo, F., & Watkins, G. (1995). Late career unemployment in the 1990s: Its impact on the family. *Journal of Family Studies, 1,* 103–113.

Locker, J., & Cropley, M. (2004). Anxiety, depression, and self-esteem in secondary school children: An investigation into the impact of standard assessment tests (SATs) and other important school examinations. *School Psychology International, 25,* 333–345.

Lockery, S. (1991). Caregiving among racial and ethnic minority elders. *Generations, 15,* 58–62.

Loehlin, J. C. (1992). *Genes and environment in personality development.* Thousand Oaks, CA: Sage.

Loevinger, J. (1976). *Ego development.* San Francisco: Jossey-Bass. NACBT.org (2007). Cognitive behavior therapy. Retrieved from the Internet at http://nacbt.org/whatiscbt.htm

Loftus, E. F. (1993). The reality of repressed memories. *American Psychologist, 48,* 518–537.

Lohman, B. J. (2000). *School and family contexts: Relationship to coping with conflict during the individuation process.* Unpublished doctoral dissertation, Ohio State University.

Loizou, E. (2005). Infant humor: The theory of the absurd and the empowerment theory. *International Journal of Early Years Education, 13,* 43–53

Lombardi, D. N., Melchior, E. J., Murphy, J. G., & Brinkerhoff, A. L. (1996). The ubiquity of life-style. *Individual Psychology: Journal of Adlerian Theory, Research and Practice, 52,* 31–41.

Longoria, R.A. (2010). Grandparents raising grandchildren: The association of grandparents' self-reported use of alcohol and drugs and their emotional well-being. *American Journal of Orthopsychiatry, 80,* 401–411.

Lopata, H. Z. (1978). Widowhood: Social norms and social integration. In H. Z. Lopata (Ed.), *Family factbook.* Chicago: Marquis Academic Media.

López, A., Correa-Chávez, M., Rogoff, B., & Gutiérrez, K. (2010). Attention to instruction directed to another by U.S. Mexican-heritage children of varying cultural backgrounds. *Developmental Psychology, 46,* 593–601.

Lopez, A., Gelman, S. A., Gutheil, G., & Smith, E. (1992). The development of category-based inductions. *Child Development, 63,* 1070–1090.

Lopez, S. J., & Snyder, C. R. (2003). *Positive psychological assessment: A handbook of models and measures.* Washington, DC: American Psychological Association.

Lorenz, K. F. (1935). Der Kumpan in der Urwelt des Vogels. *Journal Ornithologie, 83*, 137.

Lorenz, K. F. (1937/1961). Imprinting. In R. C. Birney & R. C. Teevan (Eds.), *Instinct*. Princeton, NJ: Van Nostrand.

Lott, B., & Bullock, H. E. (2001). Who are the poor? *Journal of Social Issues, 57*, 189–206.

Louchheim, T. (1997). *Jewish customs of mourning*. Retrieved March 13, 2005, from http://scheinerman.net/judaism/life-cycle/mourning.html

Lowenstein, A., & Daatland, S. O. (2006). Filial norms and family support in a comparative cross-national context: Evidence from the OASIS study. *Ageing and Society, 26*, 203–223.

Lu, T., Pan, Y., Kao, S-Y., Li, C., Kohane, I., Chan, J., & Yankner, B. A. (2004). Gene regulation and DNA damage in the ageing human brain. *Nature, 429*, 883–891.

Luby, J. L. (2010). Preschool depression: The importance of identification of depression early in development. *Current Directions in Psychological Science, 19*, 91–95.

Lucariello, J. (1987). Spinning fantasy: Themes, structure, and the knowledge base. *Child Development, 58*, 434–442.

Ludemann, P. M., & Nelson, C. A. (1988). Categorical-representation of facial expressions by 7-month-old infants. *Developmental Psychology, 24*, 492–501.

Ludwig, J., & Phillips, D. (2007). The benefits and costs of Head Start. *SRCD Social Policy Report, 21*, 3–18.

Luedi, P. P., Dietrich, F. S., Weidman, J. R., Bosko, J. N., Jirtle, R. L., & Hartemink, A. J. (2007). Computational and experimental identification of novel human imprinted genes. *Genome Research, 17*, 1723–1730.

Luger, T., Cotter, K. A., & Sherman, A. M. (2009). It's all in how you view it: Pessimism, social relations, and life satisfaction in older adults with osteoarthritis. *Aging and Mental Health, 13*, 635–647.

Lugo-Gil, J. & Tamis-LeMonda, C. S. (2008). Family resources and parenting quality: Links to children's cognitive development across the first three years. *Child Development, 79*, 1065–1085.

Luhtanen, R., & Crocker, J. (1992). A collective self-esteem scale: Self-evaluation of one's social identity. *Personality and Social Psychology Bulletin, 18*, 302–318.

Lukas, W. D., & Campbell, B. C. (2000). Evolutionary and ecological aspects of early brain malnutrition in humans. *Human Nature, 11*, 1–26.

Luo, S. & Snider, A.G. (2009). Accuracy and biases in newlyweds' perceptions of each other. *Psychological Science, 11*, 1332–1339.

Lydon, J., Dunkel-Schetter, C., Cohan, C. L., & Pierce, T. (1996). Pregnancy decision making as a significant life event: A commitment approach. *Journal of Personality and Social Psychology, 71*, 141–151.

Lyerly, A. D., Little, M. O., & Faden, R. R. (2009). The National Children's Study: A golden opportunity to advance the health of pregnant women. *American Journal of Public Health, 99*, 1742–1745.

Lyles, L. (1991). What I learned from my mother. In H. L. Gates Jr. (Ed.), *Bearing witness: Selections from African-American autobiography in the twentieth century* (p.242). New York: Pantheon Books.

Lynam, D. R., & Henry, G. (2001). The role of neuropsychological deficits in conduct disorders. In J. Hill & B. Maughan (Eds.), *Conduct disorders in childhood and adolescence* (pp. 235–263). New York: Cambridge University Press.

Lyons, A. (2004). A profile of financially at-risk college students. *Journal of Consumer Affairs, 38*, 56–81.

Lyons, K. S., Zarit, S. H., Sayer, A. G., & Whitlatch, C. J. (2002). Caregiving as a dyadic process: Perspectives from caregiver and receiver. *Journal of Gerontology: Psychological Science 57B*, P195–P204.

Lyons-Ruth, K., Connell, D. B., Zoll, D., & Stahl, J. (1987). Infants at social risk: Relations among infant maltreatment, maternal behavior, and infant attachment behavior. *Developmental Psychology, 23*, 223–232.

Lyons-Ruth, K., Lyubchik, A., Wolfe, R., & Bronfman, E. (2002). Parental depression and child attachment: Hostile and helpless profiles of parent and child behavior among families at risk. In S. H. Goodman & I. H. Gotlib (Eds.), *Children of depressed parents: Mechanisms of risk and implications for treatment* (pp. 89–120). Washington, DC: American Psychological Association.

Maccoby, E. E. (1988). Gender as a social category. *Developmental Psychology, 24*, 755–765.

Maccoby, E. E. (1990). Gender and relationships: A developmental account. *American Psychologist, 45*, 513–520.

Maccoby, E. E. (1992). The role of parents in the socialization of children: An historical overview. *Developmental Psychology, 28*, 1006–1017.

Maccoby, E. E. (2002). Perspectives on gender development. In W. W. Hartup & R. K. Silbereisen (Eds.), *Growing points in developmental science* (pp. 202–222). New York: Psychology Press.

Maccoby, E. E., & Jacklin, C. N. (1987). Gender segregation in childhood. In E. H. Reese (Ed.), *Advances in child development and behavior* (Vol. 20, pp. 239–287). New York: Academic Press.

MacDermid, S. M., Huston, T. L., & McHale, S. M. (1990). Changes in marriage associated with transition to parenthood. *Journal of Marriage and the Family, 52*, 475–486.

MacDonald, M. G., Sheshia, M. M. K., & Mullett, M. D. (2005). *Avery's Neonatology: Pathophysiology and Management of the Newborn*. Philadelphia: Lippincott Williams & Wilkins.

Mace, D. R. (1982). *Close companions*. New York: Continuum.

MacFarlane, J. A. (1975). Olfaction in the development of social preferences in the human neonate. In Parent-infant interaction. *Ciba Foundation Symposium, 33*, 103–113.

MacKain, S. J. (1997). *"I know he's a boy because my tummy tells me": Social and cognitive contributions to children's understanding of gender*. Unpublished doctoral dissertation, University of North Carolina, Chapel Hill.

MacLean, A. & Elder, G.H. Jr. (2007). Military service in the life course. *Annual Review of Sociology 36*, 175–196.

MacLean, D. J., & Schuler, M. (1989). Conceptual development in infancy: The understanding of containment. *Child Development, 60*, 1126–1137.

MacLean, N. (2006). *Freedom is not enough: The opening of the American workplace*. Cambridge, MA: Harvard University Press.

MacMurray, B., & Aslin, R. N. (2004). Anticipatory eye movements reveal infants' auditory and visual categories. *Infancy, 6*, 203–229.

MacTurk, R. H., McCarthy, M. E., Vietze, P. M., & Yarrow, L. J. (1987). Sequential analysis of mastery behavior in 6- and 12-month-old infants. *Developmental Psychology, 23*, 199–203.

Madden, D. J. (2001). Speed and timing of behavioral processes. In J. E. Birren & K. W. Schaie (Eds.), *Handbook of the psychology of aging* (5th ed., pp. 288–312). San Diego: Academic Press.

Madden, N. A., Slavin, R. E., Karweit, N. L., Doaln, L. J., & Wasik, B. A. (1993). Success for All: Longitudinal effects of a restructuring program for inner-city elementary schools. *American Educational Research Journal, 30*, 123–148.

Madon, S., Jussim, L., & Eccles, J. (1997). In search of the powerful self-fulfilling prophecy. *Journal of Personality and Social Psychology, 72*, 791–809.

Mahanian, M. (2008). In their own words. *UCLA College Report, 10*, 27.

Mahay, J., & Lewin, A. C. (2007). Age and the desire to marry. *Journal of Family Issues, 28*, 706–723.

Mahler, M. S. (1963). Thoughts about development and individuation. *Psychoanalytic Study of the Child, 18*, 307–324.

Mahler, M. S. & Furer, M. (1968). *On human symbiosis and the vicissitudes of individuation*. New York: International Universities Press.

Mahler, M., Pine, F., & Bergman, A. (1975). *The psychological birth of the human infant*. New York: Basic Books.

Main, N., Kaplan, N., & Cassidy, J. (1985). Security in infancy, childhood, and adulthood: A move to the level of representation. In I. Bretherton & E. Everett (Eds.), *Growing points of attachment theory and research* (pp. 60–104). *Monographs of the Society for Research in Child Development, 50* (1–2, Serial No. 209).

Major, B., Appelbaum, M., et al. (2009). Abortion and mental health. *American Psychologist, 64*, 863-890.

Malanowski, J. (1997, November 3). Generation www. *Time digital*, pp. 42–49.

Malatesta, C. A., & Izard, C. E. (1984). The ontogenesis of human social signals: From biological imperative to symbol utilization. In N. A. Fox & R. J. Davidson (Eds.), *The psychobiology of affective development* (pp. 161–206). Hillsdale, NJ: Erlbaum.

Malle, B. F., & Horowitz, L. M. (1995). The puzzle of negative self-views: An explanation using the schema concept. *Journal of Personality and Social Psychology, 68,* 470–484.

Malone, L., West, J., Flanagan, K. D., & Park, J. (2006). The early reading and mathematics achievement of children who repeated kindergarten or who began school a year late. *Statistics in Brief.* Retrieved August 7, 2007 from http://nces .ed.gov/pubs2006/2006064.pdf

Maloy, K., & Patterson, M. J. (1992). *Birth or abortion? Private struggles in a political world.* New York: Plenum Press.

Mandel, D. R., Jusczyk, P. W., & Pisoni, D. B. (1995). Infants' recognition of the sound patterns of their own names. *Psychological Science, 6,* 314–317.

Mandel, J. L., Monaco, A. P., Nelson, D. L., Schlessinger, D., & Willard, H. (1992). Genome analysis and the human X chromosome. *Science, 258,* 103–109.

Mangelsdorf, S. C., Plunkett, J. W., Dedrick, C. F., Berlin, M., Meisels, S. J., McHale, J. L., & Dichtellmiller, M. (1996). Attachment security in very low birth weight infants. *Developmental Psychology, 32,* 914–920.

Mannix, M. (1999). The credit card binge. *U.S. News & World Report, 127*(9).

Marchand, A. (2010, January 21). Cost of college is a big worry of freshmen in national survey. *The Chronicle of Higher Education.*

Marcia, J. E. (1980). Identity in adolescence. In J. Adelson (Ed.), *Handbook of adolescent psychology* (pp. 159–187). New York: Wiley.

Marcia, J. E. (1993). The relational roots of identity. In J. Kroger (Ed.), *Discussions on ego identity* (pp. 101–120). Hillsdale, NJ: Erlbaum.

Marcia, J. E. (2002). Identity and psychosocial development in adulthood. *Identity, 2,* 7–28.

Marcus, G. F. (1996). Why do children say "breaked"? *Current Directions in Psychological Science, 5,* 81–85.

Marcus, G. F. (2000). *Pabiku* and *Ga Ti Ga*: Two mechanisms infants use to learn about the world. *Current Directions in Psychological Science, 9,* 145–147.

Margolin, G., Talovic, S., & Weinstein, C. D. (1983). Areas of change questionnaire: A practical approach to marital assessment. *Journal of Consulting and Clinical Psychology, 51,* 930–931.

Marini, Z. A., Dane, A. V., Bosacki, S. L., & YLC-CURA. (2006). Direct and indirect bully-victims: Different psychosocial risk factors associated with adolescents involved in bullying and victimization. *Aggressive Behavior, 32,* 551–569.

Marjoribanks, K. (1997–1998). Family background, social and academic capital, and adolescents' aspirations: A mediational analysis. *Social Psychology of Education, 2,* 177–197.

Markman, H. I., & Notarius, C. I. (1987). Coding marital and family interaction: Current status. In T. Jacob (Ed.), *Family interaction and psychopathology* (pp. 329–390). New York: Plenum Press.

Markovits, H., Benenson, J., & Dolenszky, E. (2001). Evidence that children and adolescents have internal models of peer interactions that are gender differentiated. *Child Development, 72,* 879–886.

Markovsky, B., & Chaffee, M. (1995). Social identification and solidarity: A reformulation. In B. Markovsky & K. Heimer (Eds.), *Advances in group processes* (Vol. 12, pp. 249–270). Greenwich, CT: Jai Press.

Marks, S. R. (1989). Toward a systems theory of marital quality. *Journal of Marriage and the Family, 51,* 15–26.

Marks, S. R., Huston, T. L., Johnston, E.M., & MacDermid, S. M. (2001). Role balance among white married couples. *Journal of Marriage and the Family, 63,* 1083–1098.

Markstrom, C. A., & Marshall, S. K. (2007). The psychosocial inventory of ego strengths: Examination of theory and psychometric properties. *Journal of Adolescence, 30,* 63-79.

Markstrom, C. A., Sabino, V. M., Turner, B. J., & Berman, R. C. (1997). The psychosocial inventory of ego strengths: Development and validation of a new Eriksonian measure. *Journal of Youth and Adolescence, 26,* 705–732.

Markus, H. R., & Kitayama, S. (1991). Culture and the self: Implications for cognition, emotion, and motivation. *Psychological Review, 98,* 224–253.

Markus, H. R., Mullally, P., & Kitayama, S. (1997). Selfways: Diversity in modes of cultural participation. In U. Neisser & D. A. Jopling (Eds.), *The conceptual self in context: Culture, experience, self-understanding* (pp. 13–61). Cambridge, UK: Cambridge University Press.

Marquardt, M., Seng, N.C., & Goodson, H. (2010). Team development via action learning. *Advances in developing human resources, 12,* 241–259.

Marsh, H. W., & Kleitman, S. (2005). Consequences of employment during high school: Character building, subversion of academic goals, or a threshold? *American Educational Research Journal, 42,* 331–370.

Marshall, S. K. (2004). Relative contributions of perceived mattering to parents and friends in predicting adolescents' psychological well-being. *Perceptual and Motor Skills, 99,* 591–601.

Marsiglio, W. (1988). Adolescent male sexuality and heterosexual masculinity: A conceptual model and review. *Journal of Adolescent Research, 3,* 285–303.

Marsiglio, W. (1989). Adolescent males' pregnancy resolution preferences and family formation intentions: Does family background make a difference for Blacks and Whites? *Journal of Adolescent Research, 4,* 214–237.

Marsiglio, W. (1993). Adolescent males' orientation toward paternity and contraception. *Family Planning Perspectives, 25,* 22–31.

Marsiglio, W. (2004). When stepfathers claim stepchildren: A conceptual analysis. *Journal of Marriage and the Family, 66,* 22–39.

Marsiglio, W., & Pleck, J. H. (2005). Fatherhood and masculinities. In R. W. Connell, J. Hearn, & M. Kimmel (Eds.), *The handbook of studies on men and masculinities* (pp. 249–269). Thousand Oaks CA: Sage.

Martin, C. L. (1989). Children's use of gender-related information in making social judgments. *Developmental Psychology, 25,* 80–88.

Martin, C. L., Eisenbud, L., & Rose, H. (1995). Children's gender-based reasoning about toys. *Child Development, 66,* 1453–1471.

Martin, C. L., & Halverson, C. F. (1987). The roles of cognition in sex roles acquisition. In D. B. Carter (Ed.), *Current conceptions of sex roles and sex typing: Theory and research* (pp. 123–137). New York: Praeger.

Martin, C. L., & Ruble, D. N. (1997). A developmental perspective of self-construals and sex differences: Comment on Cross and Madson (1997). *Psychological Bulletin, 122,* 45–50.

Martin, C. L., & Ruble, D. N. (2004). Children's search for gender cues: Cognitive perspectives on gender development. *Current Directions in Psychological Science, 13,* 67–70.

Martin, C. L., Ruble, D. N., & Szkrybalo, J. (2002). Cognitive theories of early gender development. *Psychological Bulletin, 128,* 903–933.

Martin, C. L., Wood, C. H., & Little, J. K. (1990). The development of gender stereotype components. *Child Development, 61,* 1891–1904.

Martin, G. B., & Clark, R. D., III. (1982). Distress crying in neonates: Species and peer specificity. *Developmental Psychology, 18,* 3–9.

Martin, J. A., Hamilton, B. E., Sutton, P. D., Ventura, S. J., Menacker, F., & Munson, M. L. (2003). Births: Final data for 2002. *National Vital Statistics Reports, 52,* No. 10.

Martin, P., Poon, L. W., Kim, E., & Johnson, M. A. (1996). Social and psychological resources in the oldest old. *Experimental Aging Research, 22,* 121–139.

Martin, S., Houseley, K., McCoy, H., Greenhouse, P., Stigger, F., Kenney, M. A., et al. (1988). Self-esteem of adolescent girls as related to weight. *Perceptual and Motor Skills, 67,* 879–884.

Marvin, R. S., & Brittner, P. A. (1999). Normative development: The ontogeny of attachment. In J. Cassidy & P. R. Shaver (Eds.), *Handbook of attachment: Theory, research, and clinical applications* (pp. 44–67). New York: Guilford Press.

Maslow, A. H. (1943). A theory of human motivation. *Psychological Review, 50,* 370–396.

Maslow, A. H. (1968). *Toward a psychology of being* (2nd ed.). Princeton, NJ: Van Nostrand.

Massey, Z., Rising, S. S., & Ickovics, J. (2005). Centering Pregnancy group prenatal care: Promoting relationship-centered care. *Journal of Obstetric Gynecologic and Neonatal Nursing, 35,* 286–294.

Masten, A. S. (2001). Ordinary magic: Resilience processes in development. *American Psychologist, 56,* 227–238.

Masten, A. S., Obradović, J., & Burt, K. B. (2006). Resilience in emerging adulthood: Developmental perspectives on continuity and transformation. In J. J. Arnett & J. S. Tanner (Eds.), *Emerging adults in America: Coming of age in the 21st century* (pp. 173–190). Washington, DC: American Psychological Association.

Masters, W., & Johnson, V. (1966). *Human sexual response.* Boston: Little, Brown.

Masuda, M. (1994). Exclusivity in heterosexual romantic relationships. *Japanese Journal of Experimental Social Psychology, 34,* 164–182.

Masunaga, H., & Horn, J. (2000). Characterizing mature human intelligence: Expertise development. *Learning and Individual Differences, 12,* 5–33.

Masunaga, H., & Horn, J. (2001). Expertise and age-related changes in components of intelligence. *Psychology and Aging, 16,* 293–311.

Masur, E. F., & Turner, M. (2001). Stability and consistency in mothers' and infants' interactive styles. *Merrill-Palmer Quarterly, 47,* 100–120.

Mathiowetz, N. A. (1999). Respondent uncertainty as indicator of response quality. *International Journal of Public Opinion Research, 11,* 289–296.

Mattessich, P., & Hill, R. (1987). Life cycle and family development. In M. B. Sussman & S. K. Steinmetz (Eds.), *Handbook of marriage and the family* (pp. 437–469). New York: Plenum Press.

Mattson, M. P., & Magnus, T. (2006). Ageing and neuronal vulnerability. *Nature Reviews Neuroscience, 7,* 278–294.

Mau, R. Y. (1992). The validity and devolution of a concept: Student alienation. *Adolescence, 27,* 731–741.

May, R. B., & Norton, J. M. (1981). Training task orders and transfer in conservation. *Child Development, 52,* 904–913.

Mayer, R. (1992). *Thinking, problem solving, and cognition* (2nd ed.). New York: Freeman.

Mayr, E. W. (1991) *One long argument: Charles Darwin and the genesis of modern evolutionary thought.* Cambridge: Harvard Univ. Press.

Mayser, S., Scheib, S., & Riediger, M. (2008). Un-reachable? An empirical differentiation of goals and life longings. *European Psychologist, 13,* 126–140.

McAdams, D.P. & Bowman, P.J. (2001). Narrating life's turning points: Redemption and contamination. In D.P. McAdams, R. Josselson, & A. Lieblich (Eds.), *Turns in the road: Narrative studies of lives in transition.* Washington, DC: American Psychological Association.

McAdams, D. P., & de St. Aubin, E. (1992). A theory of generativity and its assessment through self-report, behavioral acts, and narrative themes in autobiography. *Journal of Personality and Social Psychology, 62,* 1003–1015.

McAdams, D. P., & de St. Aubin, E. (1998). *Generativity and adult development: How and why we care for the next generation.* Washington, DC: American Psychological Association.

McAdams, D. P., de St. Aubin, E., & Logan, R. L. (1993). Generativity among young, midlife, and older adults. *Psychology and Aging, 8,* 221–230.

McAdams, D. P., Diamond, A., de St. Aubin, E., & Mansfield, E. D. (1997). Stories of commitment: The psychosocial construction of generative lives. *Journal of Personality and Social Psychology, 72,* 678–694.

McAdoo, H. P. (1985). Racial attitude and self-concept of young Black children over time. In H. P. McAdoo & J. L. McAdoo (Eds.), *Black children: Social, educational, and parental environments* (pp. 213–242). Newbury Park, CA: Sage.

McAllister, L. E., & Boyle, J. S. (1998). Without money, means, or men: African American women receiving prenatal care in a housing project. *Family and Community Health, 21,* 67–79.

McArdle, J. J., Ferrer-Caja, E., Hamagami, F., & Woodcock, R. W. (2002). Comparative longitudinal structural analyses of the growth and decline of multiple intellectual abilities over the lifespan. *Developmental Psychology, 38,* 115–142.

McAuley, E., Duncan, T. E., & McElroy, M. (1989). Self-efficacy cognitions and causal attributions for children's motor performance: An exploratory investigation. *Journal of Genetic Psychology, 150,* 65–73.

McAuliffe, G. (1997). A constructive developmental perspective on career counseling. In *The Hatherleigh guide to vocational and career counseling* (pp. 1–16). New York: Hatherleigh Press.

McCabe, A. E., Siegel, L. S., Spence, I., & Wilkinson, A. (1982). Class-inclusion reasoning: Patterns of performance from three to eight years. *Child Development, 53,* 780–785.

McCabe, M. P., & Ricciardelli, L. A. (2001). Parent, peer, and media influences on body image and strategies to both increase and decrease body size among adolescent boys and girls. *Adolescence, 36,* 225–240.

McCarthy, J., & Hardy, J. (1993). Age at first birth and birth outcomes. *Journal of Research on Adolescence, 3,* 373–392.

McClearn, G. E., Johansson, B., Berg, S., Pedersen, N. L., Ahern, F., Petrill, S. A., & Plomin, R. (1997). Substantial genetic influence on cognitive abilities in twins 80 or more years old. *Science, 276,* 1560–1563.

McClelland, J. L., & Rumelhart, D. E. (1986). *Parallel distributed processing* (Vol. 2). Cambridge, MA: MIT Press.

McCloskey, L. A., & Stuewig, J. (2001). The quality of peer relationship among children exposed to family violence. *Development and Psychopathology, 13,* 83–96.

McClure, E. B. (2000). A meta-analytic review of sex differences in facial expression processing and their development in infants, children and adolescents. *Psychological Bulletin, 126,* 424–453.

McConatha, J. T., McConatha, D., Jackson, J. A., & Bergen, A. (1998). The control factor: Life satisfaction in later adulthood. *Journal of Clinical Geropsychology, 4,* 159–168.

McCool, W. R., Dorn, L. D., & Susman, E. J. (1994). The relation to cortisol reactivity and anxiety to perinatal outcome in primiparous adolescents. *Research in Nursing and Health, 17,* 411–420.

McCord, J. (1990). Problem behaviors. In S. S. Feldman & G. R. Elliott (Eds.), *At the threshold: The developing adolescent* (pp. 414–430). Cambridge, MA: Harvard University Press.

McCreary, L. L., & Dancy, B. L. (2004). Dimensions of family functioning: Perspectives of low-income African American single-parent families. *Journal of Marriage and the Family, 66,* 690–701.

McCubbin, H. I., & Patterson, J. M. (1982). Family adaptation to crisis. In H. I. McCubbin, A. E. Cauble, & J. M. Patterson (Eds.), *Family stress, coping, and social support* (pp. 26–47). Springfield, IL: Thomas.

McCubbin, H. I., & Patterson, J. M. (1983). The family stress process: The double ABCX model of adjustment and adaptation. *Marriage and Family Review, 6,* 7–37.

McDonald, A. D., Armstrong, B. G., & Sloan, M. (1992). Cigarette, alcohol, and coffee consumption and prematurity. *American Journal of Public Health, 82,* 87–90.

McDonough, L. (2002). Basic-level nouns: First learned but misunderstood. *Journal of Child Language, 29,* 357–377.

McGonagle, K. A., Kessler, R. C., & Gotlib, I. H. (1993). The effects of marital disagreement style, frequency, and outcome on marital disruption. *Journal of Social and Personal Relationships, 10,* 385–404.

McGowen, K. R., & Hart, L. E. (1990). Still different after all these years: Gender differences in professional identity formation. *Professional Psychology: Research and Practice, 21,* 118–123.

McGuffin, P., Riley, B., & Plomin, R. (2001). Toward behavioral genomics. *Science, 291,* 1232–1249.

McHale, J.P., Kuersten-Hogan, R., & Rao, M. (2004). Growing points for coparenting theory and research. *Journal of Adult Development, II* (3), 221–234.

McHale, J. P., Vinden, P. G., Bush, L., Richer, D., Shaw, D., & Smith, B. (2005). Patterns of personal and social adjustment among sport-involved and non-involved urban middle-school children. *Sociology of Sport Journal, 22,* 119–136.

McIntosh, J. L. (1999). *U.S.A. Suicide: 1999 official final data.* Retrieved October 20, 2001, from http://www.suicidology.org/index.html

McLeod, J. D., & Shanahan, M. J. (1993). Poverty, parenting, and children's mental health. *American Sociological Review, 58,* 351–366.

McLoyd, V. C. (1990). The impact of economic hardship on Black families and children: Psychological distress, parenting, and socioemotional development. *Child Development, 61,* 311–346.

McLoyd, V. C. (1998). Socioeconomic disadvantage and child development. *American Psychologist, 53,* 185–204.

McLoyd, V. C., & Smith, J. (2002). Physical discipline and behavior problems in African American, European American, and Hispanic children: Emotional support as a moderator. *Journal of Marriage and the Family, 64,* 40–63.

McMunn, A., Bartley, M., Hardy, R., & Kuh, D. (2006). Life course social roles and women's health in mid-life: Causation or selection. *Journal of Epidemiology & Community Health, 60,* 484–489.

McRae, S. (1997). Cohabitation: A trial run for marriage? *Sexual and Marital Therapy, 12,* 259–273.

Meacham, J. A. (1995). Reminiscing as a process of social construction. In B. K. Haight & J. D. Webster (Eds.), *The art and science of reminiscing: Theory, research, methods, and applications* (pp. 37–48). Philadelphia: Taylor & Francis.

Mead, M. (1928/1950). *Coming of age in Samoa.* New York: New American Library.

Mead, M. (1935). *Sex and temperament in three primitive societies.* New York: Morrow.

Mead, M. (1949/1955). *Male and female: A study of the sexes in a changing world.* New York: Mentor.

Mead, M., & Newton, N. (1967). Cultural patterning of perinatal behavior. In S. A. Richardson & A. F. Guttmacher (Eds.), *Childbearing: Its social and psychological aspects.* Baltimore: Williams & Wilkins.

Means-Christensen, A., Snyder, D., & Negy, C. (2003). Assessing nontraditional couples: Validity of the Marital Satisfaction Inventory–Revised with gay, lesbian, and cohabiting heterosexual couples. *Journal of Marital and Family Therapy, 29,* 69–83.

Medline Plus (2010). Genetic counseling. Retrieved on April 24, 2010, at www.nlm.nih.gov/medlineplus/geneticcounseling.html#cat47

Meer, J. (1985, July). Loneliness. *Psychology Today, 19,* 28–33. Meeus, W. (1996). Studies on identity development in adolescence: An overview of research and some new data. *Journal of Youth and Adolescence, 25,* 569–598.

Meeus, W., Iedema, J., Helsen, M., & Vollenbergh, W. (1999). Patterns of adolescent identity development: Review of literature and longitudinal analysis. *Developmental Review, 19,* 419–461.

Meghdari, A., & Aryanpour, M. (2003). Dynamic modeling and analysis of the human jumping process. *Journal of Intelligent and Robotic Systems, 37,* 97–115.

Meins, E. (2003). Emotional development and early attachment relationships. In A. Slater & G. Bremner (Eds.), *An introduction to developmental psychology* (pp. 141–164). Malden, MA: Blackwell.

Melender, H. (2002). Experiences of fears associated with pregnancy and childbirth: A study of 329 pregnant women. *Birth: Issues in Perinatal Care, 29,* 101–111.

Mellor, S. (1989). Gender differences in identity formation as a function of self–other relationships. *Journal of Youth and Adolescence, 18,* 361–375.

Meltzoff, A. N. (1995). Understanding the intentions of others: Reenactment of intended acts by 18-month-old children. *Developmental Psychology, 31,* 838–850.

Meltzoff, A. N. (2002). Imitation as a mechanism of social cognition: Origins of empathy, theory of mind, and the representation of action. In U. Goswami (Ed.), *Blackwell handbook of childhood cognitive development* (pp. 6–25). Malden, MA: Blackwell.

Meltzoff, A. N., & Borton, R. W. (1979). Intermodal matching by human neonates. *Nature, 282,* 403–404.

Mendel, G. (1866). Experiments with plant hybrids. *Proceedings of the Brunn Natural History Society.*

Merkle, E. R., & Richardson, R. A. (2000). Digital dating and virtual relating: Conceptualizing computer mediated romantic relationships. *Family Relations, 49,* 187–192.

Merton, R. K. (1948). The self-fulfilling prophecy. *Antioch Review, 8,* 193–210.

Meschke, L. L., Bartholomae, S., & Zentall, S. R. (2002). Adolescent sexuality and parent–adolescent processes: Promoting healthy teen choices. *Journal of Adolescent Health, 31,* 264–279.

Meschke, L. L., Zweig, J. M., Barber, B. L., & Eccles, J. S. (2000). Demographic, biological, psychological, and social predictors of the timing of first intercourse. *Journal of Research on Adolescence, 10,* 315–338.

Messer, D. J. (2000). State of the art: Language acquisition. *Psychologist, 13,* 138–143.

Messer, D. J., Rachford, D., McCarthy, M. E., & Yarrow, L. J. (1987). Assessment of mastery behavior at 30 months: Analysis of task-directed activities. *Developmental Psychology, 23,* 771–781.

Messer, S., & Warren, S. (1995). *Models of brief psychodynamic therapy.* New York: Guilford Press.

Metz, M. E., Rosser, B. R. S., & Strapko, N. (1994). Differences in conflict-resolution styles among heterosexual, gay, and lesbian couples. *Journal of Sex Research, 31,* 293–308.

Meyer, V. (1991). A critique of adolescent pregnancy prevention research: The invisible White male. *Adolescence, 26,* 217–222.

Meyers, L. (2006). Office bullies: Still wearing the 'kick me' sign. *Monitor on Psychology, 37,* 68–70.

Mikulincer, M. (1998). Attachment working models and a sense of trust: An exploration of interaction goals and affect regulation. *Journal of Personality and Social Psychology, 74,* 1209–1224.

Mikulincer, M. & Shaver, P. R. (2007). *Attachment in adulthood: Structure, dynamics and change.* New York: Guilford Press.

Miles, L. K., Nind, L. K., & Macrae, C. N. (2010). Moving through time. *Psychological Science, 21,* 222–223.

Milkman, K. L., Rogers, T., & Bazerman, M. H. (2008). Harnessing our inner angels and demons: What we have learned about want/should conflicts and how that knowledge can help us reduce short-sighted decision making. *Perspectives on Psychological Science, 3,* 324–338.

Miller, E., & Almon, J. (2009). *Crisis in the kindergarten: Why children need to play in school.* College Park, MD: Alliance for Childhood.

Miller, E. K., Freedman, D. J., & Wallis, J. D. (2003). The prefrontal cortex: Categories, concepts, and cognition. In A. Parker, A. Derrington, & C. Blakemore (Eds.) *The physiology of cognitive processes.* (pp. 252–273). NY: Oxford University Press.

Miller, G. A., & Gildea, P. M. (1987). How children learn words. *Scientific American, 257,* 94–99.

Miller, J., Slomczynski, K. M., & Kohn, M. L. (1988). Continuity of learning-generalization: The effect of job on men's intellective process in the United States and Poland. In J. T. Mortimer & K. M. Borman (Eds.), *Work experience and psychological development through the lifespan* (pp. 79–107). Boulder, CO: Westview Press.

Miller, L. (2010). *Heaven: Our enduring fascination with the afterlife.* New York: Harper/Collins.

Miller, N. B., Smerglia, V. L., Gaudet, D. S., & Kitson, G. C. (1998). Stressful life events, social support, and the distress of widowed and divorced women: A counteractive model. *Journal of Family Issues, 19,* 181–203.

Miller, P. H. (1993). *Theories of developmental psychology* (3rd ed.). New York: Freeman.

Miller, P. H. (2002). *Theories of developmental psychology* (4th ed.). New York: Worth.

Miller, P. H. (2009). *Theories of developmental psychology* (5th ed.). New York: Worth.

Miller, P. J., & Sperry, L. L. (1987). The socialization of anger and aggression. *Merrill-Palmer Quarterly, 34,* 217–222.

Miller, W. B. (1992). An empirical study of the psychological antecedents and consequences of induced abortion. *Journal of Social Issues, 48,* 67–93.

Miller-Tiedeman, A. (1999). Development, decision making, and the new (quantum) careering. In A. Miller-Tiedeman (Ed.), *Learning, practicing, and living the new careering* (pp. 96–120). Philadelphia: Accelerated Development.

Mills, T. L., Gomez-Smith, Z., & DeLeon, J. M. (2005). Skipped generation families: Sources of psychological distress among grandmothers of grandchildren who live in homes where neither parent is present. *Marriage and Family Review, 37,* 191–212.

Min, Y. I., Correa-Villasenor, A., & Stewart, P. A. (1996). Parental occupational lead exposure and low birth weight. *American Journal of Industrial Medicine, 30,* 569–578.

Minami, T., & Inui, T. (2005). Roles of the prefrontal neurons in delayed matching-to-category task: A modeling study. *Neurocomputing: An International Journal. 65–66,* 609–616

Minkler, M., & Fuller-Thomson, E. (2005). African American grandparents raising grandchildren: A national study using the census 2000 American Community Survey. *Journals of Gerontology: Series B: Psychological Sciences and Social Sciences, 60B,* S82–S92.

Minuchin, S. (1978). Structural family therapy: Activating alternatives within a therapeutic system. In I. Zwerling (Ed.), *The American family*. Philadelphia: Smith, Kline & French.

Mischel, W. (1973). Toward a cognitive social learning reconceptualization of personality. *Psychological Review, 80*, 252–283.

Mischel, W. (1979). On the interface of cognition and personality: Beyond the person-situation debate. *American Psychologist, 34*, 740–754.

Mischel, W., & Ayduk, O. (2002). Self-regulation in a cognitive-affective personality system: Attentional control in the service of the self. *Self & Identity, 1*, 113–120.

Mischel, W., & Ayduk, O. (2004). Willpower in a cognitive-affective processing system: The dynamics of delay of gratification. In R. F. Baumeisster & K. D. Vohs (Eds.), *Handbook of self-regulation: Research, theory, and applications* (pp. 99–129). New York: Guilford Press.

Mischel, W., & Shoda Y. (1995). A cognitive-affective system theory of personality: Reconceptualizing situations, dispositions, dynamics, and invariance in personality structure. *Psychological Review, 102*, 246–268.

Mischel, W., Shoda, Y., & Rodriguez, M. L. (1989). Delay of gratification in children. *Science, 244*, 933–938.

Mistretta, C. M., & Bradley, R. M. (1977). Taste in utero: Theoretical considerations. In J. M. Weiffenbach (Ed.), *Taste and development* (pp. 279–291). DHEW Publication No. NIH 77-1068. Bethesda, MD: U.S. Department of Health, Education, and Welfare.

Mitchell, R. W. (2001). Americans' talk to dogs: Similarities and differences with talk to infants. *Research on Language and Social Interaction, 34*, 183–210.

Moen, P., Kim, J., & Hofmeister, H. (2001). Couples' work/retirement transitions, gender, and marital quality. *Social Psychology Quarterly, 64*, 55–71.

Moffitt, T. E., Caspi, A., Harrington, H., Milne, B. J., Melchior, M., Goldberg, D., & Poulton, R. (2007). Generalized anxiety disorder and depression: Childhood risk factors in a birth cohort followed to age 32. *Psychological Medicine, 37*, 441–452.

Mollborn, S., & Morningstar, E. (2009). Investigating the relationship between teenage childbearing and psychological distress using longitudinal evidence. *Journal of Health and Social Behavior, 50*, 310–326.

Monroe, S., Rohde, P., Seeley, J., & Lewisohn, P. (1999). Life events and depression in adolescence: Relationship loss as a prospective risk factor for first onset of major depressive disorder. *Journal of Abnormal Psychology, 108*, 606–614.

Montague, M. (2006). Self-regulation strategies for better math performance in middle school. In M. Montague & A.K. Jitendra (Eds.), *Teaching mathematics to middle school students with learning difficulties*. New York: Guildford, pp. 89–107.

Montemayor, R. (1983). Parents and adolescents in conflict: All families some of the time and some families most of the time. *Journal of Early Adolescence, 3*, 83–103.

Montgomery, D. E. (1993). Young children's understanding of interpretive diversity between different-age listeners. *Developmental Psychology, 29*, 337–345.

Moore, B. E. (1995). Narcissism. In B. R. Moore & B. D. Fine (Eds.), *Psychoanalysis: The major concepts* (pp. 229–251). New Haven: Yale University Press.

Moore, C. (2008). The development of gaze following. *Child Development Perspectives, 2*, 66–70.

Moore, C. (2009). Fairness in children's resource allocation depends on the recipient. *Psychological Science, 20*, 944–948.

Moore, K. A., Miller, B. C. et al. (1995). *Beginning too soon: Adolescent sexual behavior, pregnancy, and parenthood. Executive summary*. Washington, DC: Child Trends.

Moore, K. A., Myers, D. E., Morrison, D. R., Nord, C. W., Brown, B., & Edmonston, B. (1993). Age at first childbirth and later poverty. *Journal of Research on Adolescence, 3*, 393–422.

Moore, K. L., & Persaud, T. V. N. (1998). *The developing human: Clinically oriented embryology* (6th ed.). Philadelphia: Saunders.

Moore, K. L., & Persaud, T. V. N. (2003). *Before we were born: Essentials of embryology and birth defects*. Philadelphia, PA: W.B. Saunders & Company.

Moore, S., & Rosenthal, D. (2006). *Sexuality in adolescence: Current trends*. London: Routledge.

Monden, C. (2007). Partners in health? Exploring resemblance in health between partners in married and cohabiting couples. *Sociology of Health & Illness, 29*, 391–411.

Montgomery, M. (2005). Psychosocial intimacy and identity: From early adolescence to emerging adulthood. *Journal of Adolescent Research, 20*, 346–374.

Moreno, M. A., & Judd, R. (2006). Eating disorder: Bulimia. *eMedicine*. Retrieved August 23, 2007, from http://www.emedicine.com/ped/topic298.htm

Morf, C. C., & Mischel, W. (2002). Epilogue: Self-regulation, vulnerability, and implications for mental health. *Self & Identity, 1*, 191–199.

Morgan, C., Isaac, J. D., & Sansone, C. (2001). The role of interest in understanding the career choices of female and male college students. *Sex Roles, 44*, 295–320.

Morgan, D. M. (1989). Adjusting to widowhood: Do social networks really make it easier? *The Gerontologist, 29*, 101–107.

Morgan, S. (2005). Health benefits of gardening. University of Illinois Cooperative Extension. Retrieved October 14, 2007 from http://web.extension.uiuc.edu/champaign/homeowners/050103.html

Morgane, P. J., Austin-LaFrance, R., Bronzino, J. D., Tonkiss, J., et al. (1993). Prenatal malnutrition and development of the brain. *Neuroscience and Biobehavioral Reviews, 17*, 91–128.

Morrison, A. P. (1989). *Shame: The underside of narcissism*. Hillsdale, NJ: Analytic Press.

Morrissey, T. W. (2009). Multiple child care arrangements and young children's behavioral outcomes. *Child Development, 80*, 59–76.

Morrow, A. (2008). "A good death"? Palliative care blog. Retrieved on September 4, 2010, at http://dying.about.com/b/2008/02/25/a-good-death.htm

Morse, J. M. (1998). Designing funded qualitative research. In N. K. Denzin & Y. S. Lincoln (Eds.), *Strategies of qualitative inquiry* (pp. 56–85). Thousand Oaks, CA: Sage.

Mortenson, T. (2001). Trends in college participation by family income, 1970–1999, *Postsecondary Education Opportunity, 106*, 1–14. Retrieved August 8, 2007, from http://www.postsecondary.org/last12/106401TRENDS.pdf

Mortimer, J. T., Finch, M., Shanahan, M., & Ryu, S. (1992). Work experience, mental health, and behavioral adjustment in adolescence. *Journal of Research on Adolescence, 2*, 25–57.

Mortimer, J. T., & Johnson, M. K. (1999). Adolescent part-time work and postsecondary transition pathways in the United States. In W. R. Heinz (Ed.), *From education to work: Cross-national perspectives* (pp. 111–148). New York: Cambridge University Press.

Moshman, D. (2004). From inference to reasoning: The construction of rationality. *Thinking and Reasoning, 10*, 221–239.

Mosselson, J. R. (2009). Where am I? Refugee youth living in the United States. *Journal of the History of Childhood and Youth, 2.3*, 453–469.

Mounts, N. S. (2004). Adolescents' perceptions of parental management of adolescent peer relationships in an ethnically diverse sample. *Journal of Adolescent Research, 19*, 446–467.

Mounts, N. S. (2007). Adolescents' and their mothers' perceptions of parental management of peer relationships. *Journal of Research on Adolescence, 17*, 169–178.

Moussavi, S., Chatterji, S., Verdes, E., Tandon, A., Patel, V., & Ustan, B. (2007). Depression, chronic diseases, and decrements in health: Results for the World Health Surveys. *Lancet, 370*, 851–858.

Mowling, C. M., Brock, S. J., & Hastie, P. A. (2006). Fourth grade students' drawing interpretations of a sport education soccer unit. *Journal of Teaching in Physical Education, 25*, 9–35.

Mueller, M., Pearson, J., Muller, C., Frank, K., & Turner, A. (2010). Sizing up peers: Adolescent girls' weight control and social comparison in the school context. *Journal of Health and Social Behavior, 51*, 64–78.

Muir, D., & Lee, K. (2003). The still face effect: Methodological issues and new applications. *Infancy, 4*, 483–491.

Mulder, E. J. H., deMedina, P. G. R., Huizink, A. C., Van den Bergh, B. R. H., Buitelaar, J. K, & Visser, G. H. A. (2002). Prenatal maternal stress: Effects on pregnancy and the (unborn) child. *Early Human Development, 70*, 3–14.

Mullis, I. V. S., Martin, M. O., Kennedy, A. M., & Foy, P. (2007). *IEA's progress in international reading literacy study in primary school in 40 countries*. Chestnut Hill, MA: TIMSS & PIRLS International Study Center. Retrieved on June 26, 2010, at http://timss.bc.edu/PDF/P06_IR_Ch4.pdf

Mulrane, A. (2001). Are boys the weaker sex? *U.S. News and World Report, 131*, 40–47.

Munsey, C. (2010). The kids aren't all right. *Monitor on Psychology, 41*, 22–25.

Murakumi, J. (2002, Spring). Gender and depression: Explaining the different rates of depression between men and women. *Perspectives in Psychology*, 27–34.

Muraskin, L. & Lee, J. (2004). *Raising the graduation rates of low-income college students*. Washington, D.C.: The Pell Institute for the Study of Opportunity in Higher Education.

Murdock, G. P., & White, D. R. (1969). Standard cross-cultural sample: *Ethnology, 8*, 329–369.

Murphy, L. B. (1956). *Personality in young children: Vol. 2. Colin, a normal child*. New York: Basic Books.

Murphy, L. B. (1962). *The widening world of childhood: Paths toward mastery*. New York: Basic Books.

Murphy, L. B. (1972). *Infant's play and cognitive development* (pp. 99–126). New York: Norton.

Murphy, L. W., Vagins, D. J., & Parker, A. (2010). Statement before the House Education and Labor Subcommittee on Healthy Families and Communities Hearing on "Corporal Punishment in Schools and Its Effect on Academic Success." American Civil Liberties Union and Human Rights Watch. Retrieved on June 7, 2010, at www.hrw.org

Murray, B. (1997). Why aren't antidrug programs working? *APA Monitor, 28*, p. 30.

Murray, C. I. (2000). Coping with death, dying, and grief in families. In P. C. McKenry & S. J. Price (Eds.), *Families and change: Coping with stressful events and transitions* (2nd ed., pp. 120–153) Thousand Oaks, CA: Sage.

Murray, S. L., Homes, J. G., & Griffin, D. W. (1996). The self-fulfilling nature of positive illusions in romantic relationships: Love is not blind, but prescient. *Journal of Personality and Social Psychology, 71*, 1155–1180.

Murray-Close, D., & Ostrov, J. M. (2009). A longitudinal study of forms and functions of aggressive behavior in early childhood. *Child Development, 80*, 828–842.

Murtaugh, P. A., Burns, L. D., & Schuster, J. (1999). Predicting the Retention of University Students. *Research in Higher Education, 40*, 355–371.

Musch, J., & Grondin, S. (2001). Unequal competition as an impediment to personal development: A review of the relative age effect in sport. *Developmental Review, 21*, 147–167.

Mussen, P. H., & Jones, M. C. (1957). Self-conceptions, motivations, and interpersonal attitudes of late and early maturing boys. *Child Development, 28*, 243–256.

Musser, L. M., & Browne, B. A. (1991). Self-monitoring in middle childhood: Personality and social correlates. *Developmental Psychology, 27*, 994–999.

Myers, S., & Gramick, H. G. (1990). The social rights and responsibilities of pregnant women: An application of Parson's sick role model. *Journal of Applied Behavioral Science, 26*, 157–172.

Myers, S. M. (2006). Religious homogamy and marital quality: Historical and generational patterns, 1980-1997. *Journal of Marriage and Family, 68*, 292–304.

Myrseth, K. O. R., & Fishbach, A. (2009). Self control: A function of knowing when and how to exercise restraint. *Current Directions in Psychological Science, 18*, 247–252.

Namy, L. L., & Waxman, S. R. (2002). Patterns of spontaneous production of novel words and gestures within an experimental setting in children ages 1.6 and 2.2. *Journal of Child Language, 29*, 911–921.

Nanda, S. (1998). *Neither Man nor Woman: The Hijras of India*. Belmont, CA: Wadsworth Publishing.

Nanda, S. (1999). *Gender diversity: Cross-cultural variations*. Prospect Heights, IL: Waveland Press.

Nanda, S. (2004). The Xanith: An intermediate gender in Oman. Retrieved on July 10, 2010, at www.galva108.org/xanith.html.

Nangle, D. W., Erdley, C. A., Newman, J. E., Mason, C. A., & Carpenter, E. M. (2003). Popularity, friendship quantity, and friendship quality: Interactive influences on children's loneliness and depression. *Journal of Clinical Child and Adolescent Psychology, 32*, 546–555.

Nash, J. M. (1997, February 3). Fertile minds. *Time*, pp. 48–56.

Nasir, N. S., & Kirshner, B. (2003). The cultural construction of moral and civic identities. *Applied Developmental Science, 7*, 138–147.

Naska, A., Oikonomou, E., Trichopoulou, A., Psaltopoulou, T., & Trichopouolos, D. (2007). Siesta in healthy adults and coronary mortality in the general population. *Archives of Internal Medicine, 167*, 296–301.

Nathanielsz, P. W. (1996). The timing of birth. *American Scientist, 84*, 562–569.

National Academy on an Aging Society. (2000). Depression: A treatable disease. *Challenges for the 21st Century, 9* (Whole).

National Academy on an Aging Society. (2001). What are the attitudes of young retirees and older workers? *Data Profiles: Young Retirees and Older Workers, 5* (Whole).

National Aging in Place Council. (2007). Home page. Retrieved October 28, 2007, from http://www.naipc.org/NAIPCHome/tabid/36/Default.aspx#

National Association of School Psychologists. (2002). *Position paper on ability grouping*. Retrieved November 20, 2004, from http://www.nasponline.org/information/pospaper_ag.html

National Center for Children in Poverty (2009). Demographics of low-income children. Retrieved from the Internet on November 11, 2009, at www.nccp.org/profiles/US_profile_6.html

National Center for Education Statistics. (2003). *The condition of education*. Washington, DC: U.S. Government Printing Office.

National Center for Education Statistics. (2004). *Highlights from the TIMSS 1999 video study of eighth-grade mathematics teaching study*. Retrieved November 20, 2004, from http://nces.ed.gov/pubs2003/timssvideo/3E.asp?nav_3

National Center for Education Statistics. (2006). *Digest for Education Statistics*. Tables 187, 317. Retrieved September 7, 2007, from http://nces.ed.gov/programs/digest/d06/tables/dt06_187.asp

National Center for Education Statistics. (2010). Trends in international mathematics and science study, mathematics achievement in 4th and 8th graders, 2007. Retrieved on June 26, 2010, at http://nces.ed.gov/timss/results07_math07.asp

National Center for Health Statistics. (2004). *NCHS Data on Aging. Factsheet*. Retrieved February 20, 2005, from http://www.cdc.gov/nchs/data/factsheets/agingfactsheet.pdf

National Center for Health Statistics. (2007). *Healthy People 2010*. Retrieved May 29, 2007, from http://www.cdc.gov/nchs/hphome.htm

National Center for Health Statistics (2010). *Summary health statistics for U.S. adults: National Health Interview study, 2009*. U.S. Department of Health and Human Services.

National Center for Higher Education Management. (2004). *Graduation rates. Six-year graduation rates of Bachelor's students—2004*. Retrieved from the Internet at http://www.higheredinfo.org/dbrowser/index.php?year=2004&level=nation&mode=map&state=0&submeasure=27 on September 5, 2007.

National Center for Higher Education Management, (2007). *Difference in median earnings between a high school diploma and a bachelors degree by age group*. Retrieved from the Internet at http://www.higheredinfo.org/dbrowser/index.php?measure=83 on September 5, 2007.

National Center for Learning Disabilities. (2001). *Learning disabilities at a glance*. Retrieved August 16, 2007, from http://www.ncld.org/index.php?option=content&task=view&id=448

National Coalition for the Homeless. (2002). *Why are people homeless?* Retrieved February 12, 2005, from http://www.nationalhomeless.org/causes.html

National Coalition for the Homeless (2009). How many people experience homelessness? Why are people homeless? Who is homeless? Retrieved on August 18, 2010, at www.nationalhomeless.org

National Coalition for the Homeless and the National Law Center on Homelessness and Poverty. (2006). *A dream denied: The criminalization of homelessness in U.S. cities*. Retrieved October 4, 2007, from http://www.nationalhomeless.org/publications/crimreport/summary.html

National Coalition on Television Violence. (1990). Nintendo tainted by extreme violence. *NCTV News, 11*(1–2), 1, 3–4.

National Commission on Children. (1993). *Just the facts: A summary of recent information on America's children and their families*. Washington, DC: Author.

National Dissemination Center for Children with Disabilities. (2004). *Speech and Language Impairments*. Retrieved August 16,

2007, from http://www.nichcy.org/pubs/factshe/fs11txt.htm.

National Hospice and Palliative Care Organization. (2005). *History of hospice care.* Retrieved March 5, 2005, from http://www.nhpco.org/i4a/pages/index.cfm?pageid_3285

National Institute on Aging. (2009a). Aging and your eyes. Retrieved on August 26, 2010, at www.nia.nih.gov/HealthInformation/Publications/eyes.htm

National Institute on Aging. (2009b). Hearing loss. Retrieved on August 26, 2010, at http://www.nia.nih.gov/HealthInformation/Publications/hearing.htm

National Institute on Aging. (2009c). A good night's sleep. Retrieved on August 26, 2010, at http://www.nia.nih.gov/HealthInformation/Publications/sleep.htm

National Institute on Aging. (2009d). Smell and taste: Spice of life. Retrieved on August 26, 2010, at http://www.nia.nih.gov/HealthInformation/Publications/smell.htm

National Institute on Aging. (2009e). Arthritis advice. Retrieved on August 26, 2010, at http://www.nia.nih.gov/HealthInformation/Publications/arthritis.htm

National Institute on Aging. (2009f). Osteoporosis: The bone thief. Retrieved on August 26, 2010, at http://www.nia.nih.gov/HealthInformation/Publications/osteoporosis.htm

National Institute on Aging. (2009g). Forgetfulness: Knowing when to ask for help. Retrieved on August 26, 2010, at http://www.nia.nih.gov/HealthInformation/Publications/forgetfulness.htm

National Institutes of Health. (2000). The relation of child care to cognitive and language development. *Child Development, 71,* 960–980.

National Institutes of Health. (2007). *Specific genetic disorders.* Retrieved May 25, 2007, from http://www.genome.gov/10001204

National Institutes of Health. (2009). Stem cell information. Retrieved on April 24, 2010, at http://stemcells.nih.gov/info/basics/basics1.asp.

National Research Council. (1993). *Losing generations: Adolescents in high risk settings.* Washington, DC: National Academy Press.

National Research Council and Institute of Medicine. (2000). *From neurons to neighborhoods: The science of early childhood development.* Washington, DC: National Academy Press.

National Telecommunications and Information Administration. (2002). *Trendline study on electronic access by households: 1984–1998.* Retrieved January 27, 2002, from http://www.ntia.doc.gov/ntiahome/fttn99/appendix.html

National Urban League. (1987). *Adolescent male responsibility, pregnancy prevention, and parenting program: A program development guide.* New York: Author.

Naughton, K., & Thomas, E. (2000, March 13). Did Kayla have to die? *Newsweek,* pp. 24–29.

Naulty, J. S. (1987). Obstetric anesthesia. In G. B. Avery (Ed.), *Neonatology: Pathophysiology and management of the newborn.* Philadelphia: Lippincott.

Navaro, L., & Schwartzberg, S.L. (2007). *Envy, competition, and gender: Theory, clinical applications and group work.* New York: Routledge/Taylor & Francis Group.

Nazzi, T., & Gopnik, A. (2001). Linguistic cognitive abilities in infancy: When does language become a tool for categorization? *Cognition, 80,* B11–B20.

NCES (2010). Contexts of postsecondary education. Retrieved on July 15, 2010, at http://nces.ed.gov/programs/coe/2010/section5/table-cst-1.asp.

NCHEMS (2010). Information Center. Retrieved on July 15, 2010, at www.higheredinfo.org/.

Neckerman, H. J. (1996). The stability of social groups in childhood and adolescence: The role of the classroom social environment. *Social Development, 5,* 131–145.

Needham, A. (2001). Object recognition and object segregation in 4.5-month-old infants. *Journal of Experimental Child Psychology, 78,* 3–24.

Needham, B. L., Epel, E. S., Adler, N. E., & Kiefe, C. (2010). Trajectories of change in obesity and symptoms of depression: The CARDIA study. *American Journal of Public Health, 100,* 1040–1046.

Neeman, J., Hubbard, J., & Masten, A. (1995). The changing importance of romantic relationship involvement to competence from late childhood to late adolescence. *Development and Psychopathology, 7,* 727–750.

Neff, K. D., & Harter, S. (2003). Relationship styles of self-focused autonomy, other-focused connectedness, and mutuality across multiple relationship contexts. *Journal of Social and Personal Relationships, 20,* 81–99.

Neil, E. (2009). The corresponding experiences of adoptive parents and birth relatives in open adoptions. In G.M. Wrobel & E. Neil (Eds.), *International advances in adoption research for practice.* New York: Wiley-Blackwell, pp. 269–293.

Neimark, E. D. (1975). Longitudinal development of formal operations thought. *Genetic Psychology Monographs, 91,* 171–225.

Neimark, E. D. (1982). Adolescent thought: Transition to formal operations. In B. B. Wolman (Ed.), *Handbook of developmental psychology* (pp. 486–499). Englewood Cliffs, NJ: Prentice Hall.

Neisser, U., Boodoo, G., Bouchard, T. J., Jr., Bodkin, A. W., Brody, N., Ceci, S. J., et al. (1996). Intelligence: Knowns and unknowns. *American Psychologist, 51,* 77–101.

Neiworth, J. J. (2009). Thinking about me: How social awareness evolved. *Current Directions in Psychological Science, 18,* 143–147.

Nelson, C. A. (2001). The development and neural bases of face recognition. *Infant and Child Development, 10,* 3–18.

Nelson, E. (1987). Learned helplessness and children's achievement. In S. Moore & K. Kolb (Eds.), *Reviews of research for practitioners and parents* (No. 3, pp. 11–22). Minneapolis: Center for Early Education and Development.

Nelson, H.D. (2008). Menopause. *The Lancet, 372,* 760–770.

Nelson, K. (1973). Structure and strategy in learning to talk. *Monographs of the Society for Research in Child Development, 38,* 1–2.

Nelson, K. (1981). Individual differences in language development: Implications for development and language. *Developmental Psychology, 17,* 170–187.

Nelson, K. (2000). Narrative, time and the emergence of the encultured self. *Culture and Psychology, 6,* 183–196.

Nelson, K. (2005). Cognitive functions of language in early childhood. In B. D. Homer & C. S. Tomis-LeMonda (Eds.), *The development of social cognition* (pp. 7–28). Mahwah, NJ: Erlbaum.

Nelson, K. (2010). Developmental narratives of the experiencing child. *Child Development Perspectives, 4,* 43–47.

Nemoto, T. (1998). Subjective norms toward social support among Japanese American elderly in New York City: Why help does not always help. *Journal of Community Psychology, 26,* 293–316.

Nepomnyaschy, L. (2009). Socioeconomic gradients in infant health across race and ethnicity. *Maternal and child Health Journal, 13,* 720–731.

Nesdale, D., & Flesser, D. (2001). Social identity and the development of children's group attitudes. *Child Development, 72,* 506–517.

Neugarten, B. L. (1981). Growing old in 2020: How will it be different? *National Forum, 61*(3), 28–30.

Neugarten, B. L. (1990). The changing meanings of age. In M. Bergener & S. I. Finkel (Eds.), *Clinical and scientific psychogeriatrics: Vol. 1. The holistic approaches* (pp. 1–6). New York: Springer Verlag.

Neugarten, B. L., Moore, J. W., & Lowe, J. C. (1965). Age norms, age constraints, and adult socialization. *American Journal of Sociology, 70,* 710–717.

Neugarten, B. L., & Weinstein, R. (1964). The changing American grandparent. *Journal of Marriage and the Family, 26,* 199–204.

Neugebauer, R., Hoek, H. W., & Susser, E. (1999). Prenatal exposure to wartime famine and development of antisocial personality disorder in early adulthood. *Journal of the American Medical Association, 282,* 455–462.

Neville, H. J., Bavelier, D., Corina, D., Rauschecker, J., Karni, A., Lalwani, A., Braun, A, Clark, V., Jezzard, P., & Turner, R. (1998). Cerebral organization for language in deaf and hearing subjects: Biological constraints and effects of experience. *Proceedings of the National Academy of Sciences, 95,* 922–929.

Neville, H. J., & Mills, D. I. (1997). Epigenesis of language. *Mental Retardation and Developmental Disabilities Research Reviews, 3,* 1–11.

Newcombe, N. S., Ambady, N., et al. (2009). Psychology's role in mathematics and science education. *American Psychologist, 64,* 538–550.

Newell, K. M., Vaillancourt, D. E., & Sosnoff, J. J. (2006). Aging, complexity and motor performance. In J. E. Birren & K. W. Schaie (Eds.), *Handbook of the psychology of aging* (6th ed., pp. 163–182). Amsterdam, Netherlands: Elsevier.

Newman, B. M. (1989). The changing nature of the parent–adolescent relationship from early to late adolescence. *Adolescence, 24,* 916–924.

Newman, B. M. (2000). The challenges of parenting infants and children. In P. C. McKenry & S. J. Price (Eds.), *Families and change: Coping with stressful events and transitions* (pp. 45–70). Thousand Oaks, CA: Sage.

Newman, B. M. (2010). Teacher's corner. *Developments, 53*(1), 6–7.

Newman, B. M., & Newman, P. R. (2001). Group identity and alienation: Giving the We its due. *Journal of Youth and Adolescence, 30,* 515–538.

Newman, J. L., Roberts, L. R., & Syre, C. R. (1993). Concepts of family among children and adolescents: Effect of cognitive level, gender, and family structure. *Developmental Psychology, 29,* 951–962.

Newman, P. R. (1982). The peer group. In B. B. Wolman (Ed.), *Handbook of developmental psychology* (pp. 526–535). Englewood Cliffs, NJ: Prentice Hall.

Newman, P. R., & Newman, B. M. (1999). What does it take to have a positive impact on minority students' college retention? *Adolescence, 34,* 483–492.

Newman, R. (2001, October 1). The day the world changed, I did too. *Newsweek,* p. 9.

Newman, S., Karip, E., & Faux, R. B. (1995). Everyday memory function of older adults: The impact of intergenerational school volunteer programs. *Educational Gerontology, 21,* 569–580.

Newport, F. (2007). Americans more likely to believe in God than the devil; heaven more than hell. Gallup New Service. Retrieved on September 5, 2010 at http://www.gallup.com/poll/27877/americans-more-likely-believe-god-than-devil-heaven-more-than-hell.aspx

Newser.com (2010). Race discrimination. Retrieved on August 19, 2010, at www.newser.com/story/55858/white-fire-fighters-bias-claims-head-to-high-court.html#ixzz0x4OZM8dZ

NHSA.org (2007). *Head Start Basics.* Retrieved July 18, 2007, from http://www.nhsa.org/download/advocacy/fact/HSBasics.pdf

NIAAA. (2004). *Alcohol Alert.* No. 63. U.S. Department of Health and Human Services. Retrieved August 25, 2007 from http://pubs.niaaa.nih.gov/publications/aa63/aa63.pdf

NICHD. (2007). *Puberty.* Retrieved August 24, 2007, from http://www.nichd.nih.gov/health/topics/Puberty.cfm

NICHD Early Child Care Research Network. (2002). Early child care and children's development prior to school entry: Results from the NICHD Study of Early Child Care. *American Educational Research Journal, 39,* 51–62.

Nichols, M. R. (1993). Paternal perspectives of the childbirth experience. *Maternal-Child Nursing Journal, 21,* 99–108.

Nicoladis, E. (1998). First clues to the existence of two input languages: Pragmatic and lexical differentiation in a bilingual child. *Bilingualism: Language and Cognition, 1,* 105–116.

Nicoladis, E., & Secco, G. (2000). The role of a child's productive vocabulary in the language choice of a bilingual family. *First Language, 20,* 3–28.

NIH. (2007). Small infants have greater survival rate in high level intensive care facilities. *NIH NEWS.* Retrieved on May 2, 2010, at www.nichd.nih.gov/news/releases/infants_survival_rate_052307.cfm?from=sids

NIH/CEPH Collaborative Mapping Group. (1992). A comprehensive genetic linkage map of the human genome. *Science, 258,* 7–86.

Nijhuis, J.G. (2003). Fetal behavior. *Neurobiology of Aging, 24,* Supplement 1, pp. S41–S46.

Ninio, A., & Rinott, N. (1988). Fathers' involvement in the care of their infants and their attributions of cognitive competence to infants. *Child Development, 59,* 652–663.

Nisan, M., & Kohlberg, L. (1982). Universality and variation in moral judgment: A longitudinal and cross-sectional study in Turkey. *Child Development, 53,* 865–876.

Nolen-Hoeksema, S., & Girgus, J. S. (1994). The emergence of gender differences in depression during adolescence. *Psychology Bulletin, 115,* 424–443.

Noller, P., & Feeney, J. A. (2002). Communication, relationship concerns, and satisfaction in early marriage. In A. L.Vangelisti, H. T. Reis, & M. A. Fitzpatrick, (Eds). *Stability and change in relationships.* (pp. 129–155). Advances in personal relationships. New York, NY, US: Cambridge University Press

Noppe, I. C., & Noppe, L. D. (1997). Evolving meanings of death during early, middle, and later adolescence. *Death Studies, 21,* 253–275.

Norem, J. K., & Cantor, N. (1988). Capturing the "flavor" of behavior: Cognition, affect, and integration. In A. Isen & B. Moore (Eds.), *Affect and social behavior.* New York: Academic Press.

North American Menopause Society (2010). Menopause: A time of new beginnings. Retrieved on August 18, 2010, at www.menopause.org/newbeginnings.aspx

Northoff, G., & Bermpohl, F. (2004). Cortical midline structures and the self. *Trends in Cognitive Science, 8,* 102–127.

Norvilitis, J., & Santa Maria, P. (2002). Credit card debt on college campuses: Causes, consequences, and solutions. *College Student Journal, 36*(3), 356–364.

Novotney, A. (2009). A new American dream? *Monitor on Psychology, 40,* 46–49.

Nsamenang, A. B. (1992). *Human development in cultural context: A Third World perspective* (Cross-cultural research and methodology series, Vol. 16). Newbury Park, CA: Sage.

Ntoumanis, N., Vazou, S., & Duda, J. L. (2007). Peer-created motivational climate. In S. Jowette & D. Lavallee (Eds.). *Social psychology in sport,* Champaign, IL: Human Kinetics, pp. 145–156.

Nucci, L. P., & Turiel, E. (2002). The moral and the personal: Sources of social conflict. In L. P. Nucci & Saxe G. B. (Eds.), *Culture, thought, and development* (pp. 115–137). Mahwah, NJ: Erlbaum.

Nucci, L., & Turiel, E. (2009). Capturing the complexity of moral development and education. *Mind, Brain, and Education, 3,* 151–159.

Nunez, R. (2004). *Beyond the shelter wall: Homeless families speak out.* New York: White Tiger Press.

Nurmi, J.-E. (2004). Socialization and self-development: Channeling, selection, adjustment, and reflection. In R. M. Lerner & L. Steinberg (Eds.), *Handbook of adolescent psychology* (2nd ed., pp. 85–124). New York: Wiley.

O'Brien, S. F., & Bierman, K. L. (1988). Conceptions and perceived influence of peer groups: Interviews with preadolescents and adolescents. *Child Development, 59,* 1360–1365.

O'Bryant, S. L. (1988). Sibling support and older widows' well-being. *Journal of Marriage and the Family, 50,* 173–183.

O'Bryant, S. L., & Morgan, L. A. (1990). Recent widows' kin support and orientations to self-sufficiency. *The Gerontologist, 30,* 391–398.

O'Campo, P., Gielen, A. C., Faden, R. R., Xue, X., Kass, N., & Wang, M. (1995). Violence by male partners against women during the childbearing year: A contextual analysis. *American Journal of Public Health, 85,* 1092–1097.

O'Leary, P. A., Haley, W. E., & Paul, P. B. (1993). Behavioral assessment in Alzheimer's disease: Use of a 24-hr log. *Psychology and Aging, 8,* 139–143.

O'Leary, S. (1995). Parental discipline mistakes. *Current Directions in Psychological Science, 4,* 11–13.

O'Neil, J. M., Ohlde, C., Barke, C., Prosser-Gelwick, B., & Garfield, N. (1980). Research on a workshop to reduce the effects of sexism and sex-role socialization on women's career planning. *Journal of Counseling Psychology, 27,* 355–363.

O'Neil, J. M., Ohlde, C., Tollefson, N., Barke, C., Piggott, T., & Watts, D. (1980). Factors, correlates, and problem areas affecting career decision making of a cross-sectional sample of students. *Journal of Counseling Psychology, 27,* 571–580.

O'Neill, D. K., & Gopnik, A. (1991). Young children's ability to identify the sources of their beliefs. *Developmental Psychology, 27*, 390–397.

O'Rahilly, R., & Muller, F. (2001). *Human embryology and teratology* (3rd ed.) New York: Wiley.

O'Sullivan, L. F., Meyer-Bahlburg, H. F. L, & Watkins, B. X. (2000). Social cognitions associated with pubertal development in a sample of urban, low-income, African-American and Latina girls and mothers. *Journal of Adolescent Health, 27*, 227–235.

Oates, W. E. (1997). Reconciling with unful-filled dreams at the end of life. In T. D. Hargrave & S. M. Hanna (Eds.), *The aging family: New visions in theory, practice, and reality* (pp. 259–269). New York: Brunner/Mazel.

Obeidallah, D. A., Brennan, R. T., Brooks-Gunn, J., Kindlon, D., & Earls, F. (2000). Socioeconomic status, race, and girls' pubertal maturation: Results from the project on human development in Chicago neighborhoods. *Journal of Research on Adolescence, 10*, 443–464.

Ochberg, R. L. (1986). College dropouts: The developmental logic of psychosocial moratoria. *Journal of Youth and Adolescence, 15*, 287–302.

OECD (2010). Average annual hours actually worked per worker, 2009. Retrieved on August 14, 2010, at http://stats.oecd.org/Index.aspx?DatasetCode=ANHRS

Offenbacher, D. I., & Poster, C. H. (1985). Aging and the baseline code: An alterna-tive to the "normless elderly." *The Geron-tologist, 25*, 526–531.

Ofman, U. (2004). ". . . And how are things sexually?": Helping patients adjust to sex-ual changes before, during and after can-cer treatment. *Supportive Cancer Therapy, 1*, 243–247.

Ogbu, J. U. (1987). Variability in minority school performance: A problem in search of an explanation. *Anthropology and Educa-tion Quarterly, 18*, 312–334.

Ohannessian, C. M., & Crockett, L. J. (1993). A longitudinal investigation of the rela-tionship between educational investment and adolescent sexual activity. *Journal of Adolescent Research, 8*, 167–182.

Ohayon, M. M., Carskadon, M. A., Guil-leminault, C., & Vitiello, M. V. (2004). Meta-analysis of quantitative sleep param-eters from childhood to old age in healthy individuals: Development normative sleep values across the human lifespan. *Journal of Sleep and Sleep Disorder Research, 27*, 1255–1273.

Okimoto, J. T. (2001). The appeal cycle in three cultures: An exploratory compari-son of child development. *Journal of the American Psychoanalytic Association, 49*, 187–215.

Okun, M. A., & Keith, V. M. (1998). Effects of positive and negative social exchanges with various sources on depressive symp-toms in younger and older adults. *Journal of Gerontology: Psychological Sciences, 53B*, 4–20.

Okundaye, J. N. (2004). Drug trafficking and urban African American youth: Risk factors for PTSD. *Child & Adolescent Social Work Journal, 21*, 285–302.

Olds, D. L., Henderson, C. R., Jr., Tatelbaum, R., & Chamberlin, R. (1988). Improving the life-course development of socially dis-advantaged mothers: A randomized trial of nurse home visitation. *American Journal of Public Health, 78*, 1436–1445.

Ollech, D., & McCarthy, J. (1997). Impedi-ments to identity formation in female adolescents. *Psychoanalytic Psychology, 14*, 65–80.

Olshansky, S. J., Carnes, B. A., & Desesquelles, A. (2001). Prospects for human longevity. *Science, 291*, 1492–1492.

Olshansky, S. J., Carnes, B. A., & Grahn, D. (1998). Confronting the boundaries of human longevity. *American Scientist, 86*, 52–61.

Olweus, D. (1993). *Bullying at school: What we know and what we can do.* Cambridge, MA: Blackwell Press.

Olweus, D. (1995). Bullying or peer abuse at school: Facts and intervention. *Cur-rent Directions in Psychological Science, 4*, 196–200.

Olweus, D., Limber, S., & Mihalic, S. F. (1999). *Blueprints for violence prevention, Book 9: Bullying prevention program.* Boul-der, CO: Center for the Study and Preven-tion of Violence.

Oosterwegel, A., & Oppenheimer, L. (1993). *The self-system: Developmental changes between and within self-concepts.* Hillsdale, NJ: Erlbaum.

Operario, D., Tschann, J., Flores, E., Bridges, M. (2006). Brief report: Associations of parental warmth, peer support, and gender with adolescent emotional distress. *Journal of Adolescence. 29(2)*, 299–305.

Oppenheim, D., Sagi, A., & Lamb, M. E. (1988). Infant-adult attachments on the kibbutz and their relation to socio-emotional development four years later. *Development Psychology, 24*, 427–433.

Oregon Health Services (2010a). Death with Dignity Act. Retrieved on September 5, 2010, at http://www.oregon.gov/DHS/ph/pas/pasforms.shtml

Oregon Health Services (2010b). 2009 Sum-mary of Oregon's Death with Dignity Act. Retrieved on September 5, 2010, at http://www.oregon.gov/DHS/ph/pas/docs/year12.pdf

Orenstein, P. (1994). *Schoolgirls: Young women, self-esteem, and the confidence gap.* New York: Anchor Books.

Orenstein, P. (2000). *Schoolgirls: Young women, self-esteem, and the confidence gap.* (Second paperback edition) New York: Anchor Books.

Osipow, S. H. (1986). Career issues through the life span. In M. S. Pallak & R. Perloff (Eds.), *Psychology and work: Productivity, change, and employment* (pp. 137–168). Washington, DC: American Psychological Association.

Osofsky, J. D. (1995). The effect of exposure to violence on young children. *American Psychologist, 50*, 782–788.

Oster, H., Hegley, D., & Nagel, L. (1992). Adult judgments and fine-grained analysis of infant facial expressions: Testing the validity of a priori coding formulas. *Devel-opmental Psychology, 28*, 1115–1131.

Ostrov, E., Offer, D., & Howard, K. I. (1989). Gender differences in adolescent symp-tomatology: A normative study. *Journal of the American Academy of Child and Adoles-cent Psychiatry, 28*, 394–398.

Ott, M. A., Millstein, S. G., Ofner, S., & Halp-ern-Felsher, B. L. (2006). Greater expecta-tions: Adolescents' positive motivations for sex. *Perspectives on Sexual and Reproductive Health, 38*, 84–89.

Owen, M. T. (1997). *Mother-child interaction and cognitive outcomes associated with early child care: Results of the NICHD study.* Sym-posium presented at the Biennial Meeting of the Society for Research in Child Devel-opment, Symposium No. 2–210.

Pahl, K., & Way, N. (2006). Longitudinal tra-jectories of ethnic identity among urban, low-income Black and Latino adolescents. *Child Development, 77*, 1403–1415.

Pajares, F. (1996). Self-efficacy beliefs in academic settings. *Review of Educational Research, 66*, 543–578.

Palacios, J. & Brodzinsky, D. (2010). Adop-tion research: Trends, topics and out-comes. *International Journal of Behavioral Development, 34*, 270–284.

Palermo, G. B. (1995). Should physician-assisted suicide be legalized? A challenge for the 21st century. *International Journal of Offender Therapy and Comparative Crimi-nology, 39*, 367–376.

Palkovitz, R. (1985). Fathers' attendance, early contact, and extended care with their newborns: A critical review. *Child Develop-ment, 56*, 392–406.

Palkovitz, R. (2002). *Involved fathering and men's adult development: Provisional bal-ances.* Mahwah, NJ: Lawrence Erlbaum Associates.

Palladino-Schultheiss, D., & Blustein, D. (1994). Contributions of family relationship factors to the identity formation process. *Journal of Counseling Development, 73*, 159–166.

Pallett-Hehn, P., & Lucas, M. (1994). LIFE: Learning informally from elders. *The Ger-ontologist, 34*, 267–271.

Palm, G. F., & Palkovitz, R. (1988). The chal-lenge of working with new fathers: Implica-tions for support providers. In R. Palkovitz & M. B. Sussman (Eds.), *Transitions to par-enthood* (pp. 357–376). New York: Haworth.

Palmer, C. F. (1989). The discriminating nature of infants' exploratory actions. *Developmental Psychology, 25*, 885–893.

Palmore, E. B., Nowlin, J. B., & Wang, H. S. (1985). Predictors of function among the old-old: A 10-year follow-up. *Journal of Gerontology, 40*, 244–250.

Papp, L.M. (2010). Course and quality of inti-mate relationships among psychologically distressed mothers. *American Journal of Orthopsychiatry, 80*, 71–79.

Parents should talk to college students about alcohol. (1997, October 12). *Columbus Dispatch*, p. 7H.

Park, K. (2002). Stigma management among the voluntarily childless. *Sociological Perspectives, 45*, 21–45.

Park, K. A., Lay, K., & Ramsay, L. (1993). Individual differences and developmental changes in preschoolers' friendships. *Developmental Psychology, 29*, 264–270.

Park, K. A., & Waters, E. (1989). Security of attachment and preschool friendships. *Child Development, 60*, 1076–1081.

Park, S.-Y., Belsky, J., Putnam, S., & Crnic, K. (1997). Infant emotionality, parenting, and 3-year inhibition: Exploring stability and lawful discontinuity in a male sample. *Developmental Psychology, 33*, 218–227.

Parker, J. G., & Asher, S. R. (1993). Friendship and friendship quality in middle childhood: Links with peer group acceptance and feelings of loneliness and social dissatisfaction. *Developmental Psychology, 29*, 611–621.

Parkhurst, J. T., & Asher, S. R. (1992). Peer rejection in middle school: Subgroup differences in behavior, loneliness, and interpersonal concerns. *Developmental Psychology, 28*, 231–241.

Parsons, J. E., Adler, T. F., & Kaczala, C. M. (1982). Socialization of achievement attitudes and beliefs: Parental influences. *Child Development, 53*, 310–321.

Parsons, J. E., & Ruble, D. N. (1977). The development of achievement-related expectancies. *Child Development, 48*, 1075–1079.

Parsons, T., & Bales, R. F. (Eds.). (1955). *Family socialization and interaction process.* Glencoe, IL: Free Press.

Paschal, A. M. (2006). *Voices of African American teen fathers: I'm doing what I got to do.* New York: Haworth Press.

Passman, R. H., & Longeway, K. P. (1982). The role of vision in maternal attachment: Giving 2-year-olds a photograph of their mother during separation. *Developmental Psychology, 18*, 530–533.

Paterson, G., & Sanson, A. (1999). The association of behavioural adjustment to temperament, parenting and family characteristics among 5-year-old children. *Social Development, 8*, 293–309.

Patterson, C. J. (1995). Families of the lesbian baby boom: Parents' division of labor and children's adjustment. *Developmental Psychology, 31*, 115–123.

Patterson, C. J. (2006). Children of lesbian and gay parents. *Current Directions in Psychological Science, 15*, 241–244.

Patterson, C. J. (2009). Children of lesbian and gay parents: Psychology, law, and policy. *American Psychologist, 64*, 727–736.

Patterson, G. R. (1982). *Coercive family processes.* Eugene, OR: Castalia.

Patterson, G. R. (1992). Developmental changes in antisocial behavior. In R. D. Peters, R. J. McMahon, & V. L. Quignsey (Eds.), *Aggression and violence throughout the lifespan* (pp. 52–82). Newbury Park, CA: Sage.

Patterson, I. (1996). Participation in leisure activities by older adults after a stressful life event: The loss of a spouse. *International Journal of Aging and Human Development, 42*, 123–142.

Patterson, L. E. (1997). *Client resistance to career counseling.* In The Hatherleigh guide to vocational and career counseling (pp. 17–33). New York: Hatherleigh Press. Patterson, M. L., & Werker, J. F. (1999).

Patterson, M. L., & Werker, J. F. (1999). Matching phonetic information in lips and voice is robust in 4.5-month-old infants. *Infant Behavior and Development, 22*, 237–247.

Patton, W., & McMahon, M. (2006). *Career development and systems theory* (2nd ed.). Rotterdam, The Netherlands: Sense Publishers.

Pauli-Pott, U., Mertesacker, B., & Beckman, D. (2004). Predicting the development of infant emotionality from maternal characteristics. *Development and Psychopathology, 16*, 19–42.

Paulsen, A. M., & Betz, N. E. (2004). Basic confidence predictors of career decision-making self efficacy. *Career Development Quarterly, June.* Retrieved on July 13, 2010, at http://findarticles.com/p/articles/mi_m0JAX/is_4_52/ai_n6148413/

Paulussen-Hoogeboom, M. C., Stams, G. J. J. M., Hermanns, J. M. A., & Peetsma, T. T. D. (2007). Child negative emotionality and parenting from infancy to preschool: A meta-analytic review. *Developmental Psychology, 43*, 438–453.

Paus, T. (2005). Mapping brain maturation and cognitive development during adolescence. *Trends in Cognitive Science, 9*, 60–68.

Pavetti, L. A. (2000). Creating a new welfare reality: Early implementation of the Temporary Assistance for Needy Families program. *Journal of Social Issues, 56*, 601–615.

Pearce, L.D. (2002). The influence of early life course religious exposure on young adults' dispositions toward childbearing. *Journal for the Scientific Study of Religion, 41*, 325–340.

Pearn, J. (2003). Children and war. *Journal of Paediatrics & Child Health, 39*, 166–172.

Pearson, D., Rouse, H., Doswell, S., Ainsworth, C., Dawson, O., Simms, K., et al. (2001). Prevalence of imaginary companions in a normal child population. *Child Care, Health, & Development, 27*, 13–22.

Pearson, R.M., Cooper, R.M., Penton-Voak, I.S., Lightman, S.L., & Evans, J. (2010). Depressive symptoms in early pregnancy disrupt attentional processing of infant emotion. *Psychological Medicine: A Journal of Research in Psychiatry and the Allied Sciences, 40*, 621–631.

Peek, C.W., Koropeckyj-Cox, T., Zsembik, B.A., & Coward, R. T. (2004). Race comparisons of the household dynamics of older adults. *Research on Aging, 26*, 179-201.

Peek, M. K., Coward, R. T., & Peek, C. W. (2000). *Research on Aging, 22*, 117–142.

Pelham, B. W. (1991). On the benefits of misery: Self-serving biases in the depressive

self concept. *Journal of Personality and Social Psychology, 61*, 670–681.

Pell, R. W. (2002). *Hui Malama I Na Kupuna 'O Hawai'i Nei.* Retrieved February 6, 2000, from http://www.pixi.com/huimalam/#beliefs

Pellegrini, A. D. (2009). Research and policy on children's play. *Child Development Perspectives, 3*, 131–136.

Pellegrini, A. D., & Bjorklund, D. F. (2004). The ontogeny and phylogeny of children's object and fantasy play. *Human Nature, 15*, 23–43.

Pellegrini, D. S. (1985). Social cognition and competence in middle childhood. *Child Development, 56*, 253–264.

Peltonen, L., & McKusick, V. A. (2001). Dissecting human disease in the postgenomic era. *Science, 291*, 1224–1229.

Pembrey, M. E. (2008). Human inheritance, differences and diseases: Putting genes in their place. Part I & II. *Paediatric and Perinatal Epidemiology, 22*, 497–513.

Pembrey, M. E., Bygren, L. O., Kaati, G., Edvinsson, S., Northstone, K., Sjöström, M., & Golding, J. (2006). Sex-specific, male line transgenerational responses in humans. *European Journal of Human Genetics, 14*, 159–166.

Pennisi, E. (2009). On the origin of cooperation. *Science, 325*, 1196–1199.

Peplau, L. A., & Beals, K. P. (2004). The family lives of lesbians and gay men. In A. L. Vangelisti (Ed.), *Handbook of family communication* (pp. 233–248). Mahwah, NJ: Lawrence Erlbaum.

Perfect, T. J. (1994). What can Brinley Plots tell us about cognitive aging? *Journal of Gerontology, 49*, P60–P64.

Pergament, E. (1998). Smoking and pregnancy. *Risk Newsletter, 6*(4). Retrieved January 25, 2002, from http://www.fetal-exposure.org/smoke.html

Peris, A. (2000). *Therapies: Artificial insemination.* Retrieved October 14, 2001, from http://www.fertilitext.org/p2_doctor/ai.html

Perls, T. T. (2004). The oldest old. *Scientific American, 14*, 6–11.

Perls T. T., Kunkel L., & Puca, A. (2002). The genetics of exceptional human longevity. *Journal of the American Geriatric Society, 50*, 359–368.

Perls, T. T., & Terry, D. (2007) *The New England Centenarian Study. Overview.* Retrieved October 24, 2007, from http://www.bumc.bu.edu/Dept/Content.aspx?DepartmentID=361&PageID=5924

Perosa, L. M., Perosa, S. L., & Tam, H. P. (1996). The contribution of family structure and differentiation to identity development in females. *Journal of Youth and Adolescence, 25*, 817–837.

Perret-Clermont, A., Perret, J., & Bell, N. (1991). The social construction of meaning and cognitive activity in elementary school children. In L. B. Resnick, J. M. Levine, & S. D. Teasley (Eds.), *Perspectives on socially shared cognition* (pp. 41–62). Washington, DC: American Psychological Association.

Perrucci, C. C., Perrucci, R., & Targ, D. B. (1997). Gender differences in the economic, psychological, and social effects of plant closings in an expanding economy. *Social Science Journal, 34,* 217–233.

Perry, B. D. (1994). Neurobiological sequelae of childhood trauma: PTSD in children. In M. M. Murburg (Ed.), *Catecholamine function in posttraumatic stress disorder: Emerging concepts* (pp. 233–255). Washington, DC: American Psychiatric Press.

Perry, B. D., Pollard, R., Blakley, T., Baker, W., & Vigilante, D. (1995). Childhood trauma, the neurobiology of adaptation and "use-dependent" development of the brain: How states become traits. *Infant Mental Health Journal, 16,* 271–291.

Perry, M. A., & Fantuzzo, J. W. (2010). A multivariate investigation of maternal risks and their relationship to low-income, preschool children's competences. *Applied Developmental Science, 14,* 1–17.

Pertman, A. (2000). *Adoption nation: How the adoption revolution is transforming America.* New York: Basic Books.

Perusse, D. (1994). Mate choice in modern societies: Testing evolutionary hypotheses with behavioral data. *Human Nature, 5,* 255–278.

Pete, J. M., & DeSantis, L. (1990). Sexual decision making in young Black adolescent females. *Adolescence, 25,* 145–154.

Peter, J., Valkenburg, P.M., & Schouten, A. P. (2005). Developing a model of adolescent friendship formation on the Internet. *CyberPsychology & Behavior, 8,* 423–430.

Petersen, A. C., Compas, B. E., Brooks-Gunn, J., Stemmler, M., Ey, S., & Grant, K. E. (1993). Depression in adolescence. *American Psychologist, 48,* 155–168.

Petersen, A. C., Sarigiani, P. A., & Kennedy, R. E. (1991). Adolescent depression: Why more girls? *Journal of Youth and Adolescence, 20,* 247–272.

Peterson, B. D., Newton, C. R., & Rosen, K. H. (2003). Examining congruence between partners' perceived infertility-related stress and its relationship to marital adjustment and depression in infertile couples. *Family Process, 42,* 59–70.

Peterson, B. E., & Stewart, A. J. (1993). Generativity and social motives in young adults. *Journal of Personality and Social Psychology, 65,* 186–198.

Peterson, C., & Seligman, M. E. P. (2003). Character strengths before and after September 11. *Psychological Science, 14,* 381–384.

Peterson, G. (2001). *Infertility is taking its toll.* Retrieved August 9, 2004, from http://www.parentsplace.com/fertility/conception/qas/0,,238711_270929,00.html

Peterson, M. M. (2005). Assisted reproductive technologies and equity of access issues. *Journal of Medical Ethics, 31,* 280–285.

Pettit, G. S., Dodge, K. A., & Brown, M. M. (1988). Early family experience, social problem-solving patterns, and children's social competence. *Child Development, 59,* 107–120.

Pettis, R. (2004). Hijras. Retrieved on July 10, 2010, at www.glbtq.com/social-sciences/hijras.html.

Pfefferbaum, B., Seale, T. W., McDonald, N. B., Brandt, E. N., Jr., Rainwater, S. C., Maynard, B. T., et al. (2000). Posttraumatic stress two years after the Oklahoma City bombing in youth geographically distant from the explosion. *Psychiatry: Interpersonal and Biological Processes, 63,* 358–370.

Phillips, D. A. (1984). The illusion of incompetence among academically competent children. *Child Development, 55,* 2000–2016.

Phillips, D. A. (1987). Socialization of perceived academic competence among highly competent children. *Child Development, 58,* 1308–1320.

Phinney, J. S. (1989). Stages of ethnic identity development in minority group adolescents. *Journal of Early Adolescence, 9,* 34–49.

Phinney, J. S. (1992). The multigroup ethnic identity measure: A new scale for use with adolescents and young adults from diverse groups. *Journal of Adolescent Research, 7,* 156–176.

Phinney, J. S. (1996a). Understanding ethnic diversity: The role of ethnic identity. *American Behavioral Scientist, 40,* 143–152.

Phinney, J. S. (1996b). When we talk about American ethnic groups, what do we mean? *American Psychologist, 51,* 918–927.

Phinney, J. S. (1997). Variations in bicultural identification among African American and Mexican American adolescents. *Journal of Research on Adolescence, 7,* 3–32.

Piaget, J. (1926). *The language and thought of the child.* New York: Harcourt Brace.

Piaget, J. (1929). *The child's conception of physical causality.* New York: Harcourt Brace. (Originally published in French 1926)

Piaget, J. (1932/1948). *The moral judgment of the child.* Glencoe, IL: Free Press.

Piaget, J. (1936/1952). *The origins of intelligence in children.* New York: International Universities Press.

Piaget, J. (1941/1952). *The child's conception of number.* London: Kegan Paul, Trench & Trubner.

Piaget, J. (1951). *Play, dreams, and imitation in childhood.* New York: Norton.

Piaget, J. (1952). *The language and thought of the child.* London: Routledge & Kegan Paul.

Piaget, J. (1954). *The construction of reality in the child.* New York: Basic Books.

Piaget, J. (1962). *Play, dreams, and imitation in childhood.* New York: Norton.

Piaget, J. (1963). The attainment of invariant and reversible operations in the development of thinking. *Social Research, 30,* 283–299.

Piaget, J. (1970). Piaget's theory. In P. H. Mussen (Ed.), *Carmichael's manual of child psychology* (3rd ed., Vol. 1). New York: Wiley.

Piaget, J. (1972a). Intellectual evolution from adolescence to adulthood. *Human Development, 15,* 1–12.

Piaget, J. (1972b). *The psychology of intelligence.* Totowa, NJ: Littlefield Adams.

Piaget, J. (1978/1985). *The equilibration of cognitive structures.* Chicago: University of Chicago Press.

Piaget, J., & Inhelder, B. (1966/1969). *The psychology of the child.* New York: Basic Books.

Pick, H. L., Jr. (1989). Motor development: The control of action. *Developmental Psychology, 25,* 867–870.

Pick, H. L., Jr., & Rosengren, K. S. (1991). Perception and representation in the development of mobility. In R. R. Hoffman & D. S. Palermo (Eds.), *Cognition and the symbolic processes: Applied and ecological perspectives* (pp. 433–454). Hillsdale, NJ: Erlbaum.

Piek, J. P. (2006). *Infant motor development.* Champaign, IL: Human Kinetics Publishers.

Piers, M. W., & Landau, G. M. (1980). *The gift of play.* New York: Walker.

Pillow, B. H. (1991). Children's understanding of biased social cognition. *Developmental Psychology, 27,* 539–551.

Pine, D., Cohen, P., Gurley, D., Brook, J., & Ma, Y. (1998). The risk for early adulthood anxiety and depressive disorders in adolescents with anxiety and depressive disorders. *Archives of General Psychiatry, 55,* 56–64.

Pinquart, M., & Schindler, I. (2007). Changes in life satisfaction in the transition to retirement: A latent-class approach. *Psychology and Aging, 22,* 442–455.

Pinquart, M. & Sörensen, S. (2003). Associations of stressors and uplifts of caregiving with caregiver burden and depressive moods: A meta-analysis. *Journals of Gerontology B: Psychological Science and Social Science, 58,* P112–P128.

Pirog-Good, M. A. (1995). The family background and attitudes of teen fathers. *Youth and Society, 26,* 351–376.

Planned Parenthood. (2000). *Mifepristone: A brief history.* Retrieved October 23, 2001, from http://www.plannedparenthood.org/library/ABORTION/Mifepristone.html

Pleck, J. H., & Masciadrelli, B. P. (2004). Paternal involvement by U.S. residential fathers: Levels, sources, and consequences. In M. E. Lamb (Ed), *The role of the father in child development* (4th ed., pp. 222–271). Hoboken, NJ: John Wiley & Sons.

Plomin, R. (1994). *Genetics and experience.* Thousand Oaks, CA: Sage.

Plomin, R. (2004). Genetics and developmental psychology. *Merrill-Palmer Quarterly. 50*(3) 341–352.

Plomin, R., DeFries, J. C., Craig, I. W., & McGuffin, P. (Eds.). (2003). *Behavioral genetics in the postgenomic era.* Washington, DC: American Psychological Association.

Plomin, R., & Spinath, F. M. (2004). Intelligence, genetics, genes, and genomics. *Journal of Personality and Social Psychology. 86*(1) 112–129.

Plotnick, R. D. (1992). The effects of attitudes on teenage premarital pregnancy and its resolution. *American Sociological Review, 57*, 800–811.

Pluess, M., & Belsky, J. (2010). Differential susceptibility to parenting and quality child care. *Developmental Psychology, 46*, 379–390.

Plutchik, R. (2001). The nature of emotions. *American Scientist, 89*, 344–350.

Pöhlmann, K. (2001). Agency- and communion-orientation in life goals: Impacts on goal pursuit strategies and psychological well-being. In P. Schmuck & K.M. Sheldon (Eds.), *Life goals and well-being: Towards a positive psychology of human striving* (pp. 68–84). Ashland Ohio: Hogrefe and Huber.

Polednak, A. P. (1991). Black-White differences in infant mortality in 38 standard metropolitan statistical areas. *American Journal of Public Health, 81*, 1480–1482.

Pollack, D. (2001, August 17). Seeking secret of longevity in genes of centenarians. *Forward.* Retrieved February 20, 2005, from http://www.forward.com/issues/2001/01.08.17/genetic5.html

Pollack, H. (2000). When pregnant women use crack. *FAS Drug Policy Bulletin, 8.* Retrieved August 11, 2004, from http://www.fas.org/drugs/issue8.htm

Pollard, I. (2000). Substance abuse and parenthood: Biological mechanisms—bioethical challenges. *Women and Health, 30*, 1–24.

Pollitt, E. (1994). Poverty and child development: Relevance of research in developing countries to the United States. *Child Development, 65*, 283–295.

Pomerantz, E. M., & Easton, M. M. (2000). Developmental differences in children's conceptions of parental control: "They love me, but they make me feel incompetent." *Merrill-Palmer Quarterly, 46*, 140–167.

Ponitz, C. C., McClelland, M. M., Matthews, J. S., & Morrison, F. J. (2009). A structured observation of behavioral self-regulation and its contribution to kindergarten outcomes. *Developmental Psychology, 45*, 605–619.

Porcaro, C., Zappasodi, F., Barbati, G., Salustri, C., Pizzella, V., Rossini, P. M., & Tecchio, F. (2006). Fetal auditory responses to external sounds and mother's heart beat: Detection improved by Independent Component Analysis. *Brain Research, 1101*, 51–58.

Porter, E. J. (1994). Older widows' experiences of living alone at home. *Image: Journal of Nursing Scholarship, 26*, 19–24.

Porter, R. H., Balogh, R. D., & Makin, J. W. (1988). Olfactory influences on mother-infant interactions. In C. Rovee-Collier & L. Lipsitt (Eds.), *Advances in infancy research* (Vol. 5, pp. 39–68). Norwood, NJ: Ablex.

Portrie, T., & Hill, N.R. (2005). Blended families: A critical review of the current research. *The Family Journal, 13*, 445–451.

Posada, G., Gao, Y., Wu, F., Posada, R., Tascon, M., & Schoelmerich, A. (1995). The secure-base phenomenon across cultures: Children's behavior, mothers' preferences, and experts' concepts. *Monographs of the Society for Research in Child Development, 60*, 27–48.

Posada, G., Jacobs, A., Richmond, M. K., Carbonell, O. A., Alzate, G., Bustamante, M. R., & Quiceno, J. (2002). Maternal caregiving and infant security in two cultures. *Developmental Psychology, 38*, 67–78.

Posner, A. (2001). *Skills: Your key to success in the 21st century workplace.* Retrieved December 18, 2001, from http://www.wetfeet.com/asp/article.asp?aid_311&atype_general

Posttraumatic stress two years after the Oklahoma City bombing in youth geographically distant from the explosion. *Psychiatry: Interpersonal and Biological Processes, 63*, 358–370.

Poulin, F. W., & Boivin, M. (2000). The role of proactive and reactive aggression in the formation and development of boys' friendships. *Developmental Psychology, 36*, 233–240.

Poulin, R., Dishion, T. J., & Haas, E. (1999). The peer influence paradox: Friendship quality and deviancy training within male adolescent friendships. *Merrill-Palmer Quarterly, 45*, 42–61.

Power, T. G. (1985). Mother- and father-infant play: A developmental analysis. *Child Development, 56*, 1514–1524.

Powers, S. M. (2002). Merge as a basic mechanism of language: Evidence from language acquisition. In E. Witruk & A. D. Friederici (Eds.), *Basic functions of language, reading and reading disability* (pp. 105–117). Dordrecht, Netherlands: Kluwer.

Pratt, C. C., Jones, L. L., Shin, H., & Walker, A. J. (1989). Autonomy and decision making between single older women and their caregiving daughters. *The Gerontologist, 29*, 792–797.

Pratt, M.W., Arnold, M.L., & Lawford, H. (2009). Growing toward care: A psychosocial approach to moral identity and generativity of personality in emerging adulthood. In D. Narvaez & D.K. Lapsley (Eds.), *Personality, identity, and character: Explorations in moral psychology* (pp. 295–315). New York: Cambridge University Press.

Pratt, M.W., Norris, J.E., Hebblethwaite, S., & Arnold, M.L. (2008). Intergenerational transmission of values: Family generativity and adolescents' narratives of parent and grandparent value teaching. *Journal of Personality, 76*, 171–198.

Prawat, R. S., Byers, J. L., & Anderson, A. H. (1983). An attributional analysis of teachers' affective reactions to student success and failure. *American Educational Research Journal, 20*, 137–152.

Premack, D. (2010). Why humans are unique: Three theories. *Perspectives on Psychological Science, 5*, 22–32.

Preski, S., & Shelton, D. (2001). The role of contextual, child and parent factors in predicting criminal outcomes in adolescence. *Issues in Mental Health Nursing, 22*, 197–205.

Price, S., Price, C., & McKenry, P. (2010). Families and change. Thousand Oaks, CA: Sage.

Prinstein, M. J., & LaGreca, A. M. (2002). Peer crowd identification and internalizing distress in childhood and adolescence: A longitudinal follow-back study. *Journal of Research on Adolescence, 12*, 325–351.

Project Interaction (2010). Two spirited people. Retrieved on July 10, 2020 at www.mcgill.ca/interaction/mission/twospirit/

Pruchno, R.A., Cartwright, F.P., & Wilson-Genderson, M. (2009). Effects of marital closeness on the transition to caregiving to widowhood. *Aging and Mental Health, 13*, 808–817.

Puma, et al. (2005). Puma, M., Bell, S., Cook, R., Heid, C. & Lopez, M. (2005). *Head Start impact study: First year findings.* Washington, DC: U.S. Department of Health and Human Services.

Purhonen, M., Kilpelainen-Lees, R., Valkonen-Korhonen, M., Karhu, J., & Lehtonen, J. (2005). Four-month-old infants process own mother's voice faster than unfamiliar voices. *Cognitive Brain Research, 24*, 627–633.

Purhonen, M., Kilpeläinen-Lees, R., Valkonen-Korhonen, M., Karhu, J., Lehtonen, J. R. H. T. (2006). Implications of attachment theory for research on intimacy. In M. Mikulincer & G. S. Goodman (Eds.), *Dynamics of romantic love: Attachment, caregiving, and sex* (pp. 383–403). New York, NY: Guilford Press.

Pushkar, D., Arbuckle, T., Conway, M., Chaikelson, J., & Maag, U. (1997). Everyday activity parameters and competence in older adults. *Psychology and Aging, 12*, 600–609.

Putnam, S. P., Sanson, A. V., & Rothbart, M. K. (2002). Child temperament and parenting. In M. H. Bornstein (Ed.), *Handbook of parenting. Vol. 1. Children and parenting* (2nd ed., pp. 255–277). Mahwah, NJ: Erlbaum.

Pye, C. (1986). Quiché Mayan speech to children. *Journal of Child Language, 13*, 85–100.

Pyle, R. P. (2002). Best practices in assessing kindergarten readiness. *California School Psychologist, 7*, 63–73.

Pynoos, J., Caraviello, R., & Cicero, C. (2010). Housing in an aging America. In J.C. Cavanaugh & C.K. Cavanaugh (Eds.), *Aging in America, Vol. 3: Societal Issues* (pp. 128–159). Santa Barbara, CA: Praeger.

Qian, Z., & Preston, S. H. (1993). Changes in American marriage, 1972 to 1987: Availability and forces of attraction by age and education. *American Sociological Review, 58*, 482–495.

Quadrel, M. J., Fischhoff, B., & Davis, W. (1993). Adolescent (in)vulnerability. *American Psychologist, 48*, 102–116.

Quakenbush, S. W., & Barnett, M. A. (1995). Correlates of reminiscence activity among elderly individuals. *International Journal of Aging and Human Development, 41*, 169–181.

Quiggle, N. L., Garber, J., Panak, W. F., & Dodge, K. A. (1992). Social information processing in aggressive and depressed children. *Child Development, 63*, 1305–1320.

Quindlen, A. (2009, May 11–18). Stepping aside. *Newsweek*, pp. 69–70.

Quinn, P. C., Eimas, P. D., & Tarr, M. J. (2001). Perceptual categorization of cat and dog silhouettes by 3-to 4-month-old infants. *Journal of Experimental Child Psychology, 79*, 78–94.

Quintana, S. M., Aboud, F. E., Chao, R. K., Contreras-Grau, J., Cross, W. E. Jr., Hudley, C., Hughes, D., Liben, L. S., Nelson-LeGall, S., & Vietze, D. L. (2006). Race, ethnicity and culture in child development: Contemporary research and future directions. *Child Development, 77*, 1129–1141.

Radin, N. (1982) Primary caregiver and role sharing fathers. In M. E. Lamb (Ed.), *Nontraditional families* (pp. 173–204). Hillsdale, NJ: Erlbaum.

Radin, N. (1988). Primary caregiving fathers of long duration. In P. Bronstein & C. P. Cowan (Eds.), *Fatherhood today* (pp. 127–143). New York: Wiley.

Radin, N. (1993). Primary caregiving fathers in intact families. In A. Gottfried & A. Gottfried (Eds.), *Redefining families* (pp. 11–54). New York: Plenum Press.

Radke-Yarrow, M., Cummings, E. M., Kuczynski, L., & Chipman, M. (1985). Patterns of attachment in two- and three-year-olds in normal families and families with parental depression. *Child Development, 56*, 591–615.

Raeff, C. (2010). Independence and interdependence in children's developmental experiences. *Child Development Perspectives, 4*, 31–36.

Ragins, B. R. & Kram, K. E. (2007). *The handbook of mentoring at work: Theory, research and practice*. Thousand Oaks, CA: Sage.

Raina, G., Malhi, P., Malhotra, D., & Jerath, J. M. (2003). Does preference for sons have a differential impact on the intelligence of boys and girls? Evidence from India. *Psychologia: An International Journal of Psychology in the Orient, 46*, 182–189.

Raja, S. N., McGee, R., & Stanton, W. R. (1992). Perceived attachment to parents and peers and psychological well-being in adolescence. *Journal of Youth and Adolescence, 21*, 471–486.

Rakison, D. H., & Poulin-Dubois, D. (2001). Developmental origin of the animate–inanimate distinction. *Psychological Bulletin, 127*, 209–228.

Rakoczy, J., Tomasello, M., & Striano, T. (2004). Young children know that trying is not pretending: A test of the "behaving as if" construal of children's early concept of pretense. *Developmental Psychology, 40*, 388–399.

Raley, R. K. (1996). A shortage of marriageable men? A note on the role of cohabitation in Black–White differences in marriage rates. *American Sociological Review, 61*, 973–983.

Ramey, C. T., Campbell, F. A., & Ramey, S. L. (1999). Early intervention: Successful pathways to improving intellectual development. *Developmental Neuropsychology, 16*, 385–392.

Ramirez, A. Y. F. (2003). Dismay and disappointment: Parental involvement of Latino immigrant parents. *Urban Review, 35*(2) 93–110.

Ramsey, J. L., Langlois, J. H., Hoss, R. A., Rubenstein, A. J., & Griffin, A. M. (2004). Origins of a stereotype: Categorization of facial attractiveness by 6-month-old infants. *Developmental Science, 7*, 201–211.

Ranzijn, R., Keeves, J., Luszcz, M., & Feather, N. T. (1998). The role of self-perceived usefulness and competence in the self-esteem of elderly adults: Confirmatory factor analyses of the Bachman revision of Rosenberg's self-esteem scale. *Journal of Gerontology, 53*, P96–P104.

Raschick, M., & Ingersoll-Dayton, B. (2004). The costs and rewards of caregiving among aging spouses and adult children. *Family Relations, 53*, 317–325.

Rathbun, A., West, J., & Hausken, E. G. (2004). *From kindergarten through 3rd grade: Children's beginning school experiences*. Washington, DC: U.S. Department of Education.

Ray, W. J. (1993). *Methods toward a science of behavior and experience*. Pacific Grove, CA: Brooks/Cole.

Recchia, H. E., & Howe, N. (2009). Associations between social understanding, sibling relationship quality, and siblings' conflict strategies and outcomes. *Child Development, 80*, 1564–1578.

Receputo, G., Mazzoleni, G., DiFazio, I., & Alessandria, I. (1996). Study on the sense of taste in a group of Sicilian centenarians. *Archives of Gerontology and Geriatrics, Suppl. 5*, 411–414.

Receputo, G., Mazzoleni, G., Rapisarda, R., & Di Fazio, I. (1996). Sense of smell in centenarians from eastern Sicily. *Archives of Gerontology and Geriatrics, Suppl. 5*, 407–410.

Reddy, V. (2000). Coyness in infancy. *Developmental Science, 3*, 186–192.

Reed, R. K. (2005). *Birthing Fathers: The Transformation of Men in American Rites of Birth*. NJ: Rutgers University Press

Reese, E., & Cox, A. (1999). Quality of adult book reading affects children's emergent literacy. *Developmental Psychology, 35*, 20–28.

Reich, J. A., & Brindis, C. D. (2006). Conceiving risk and responsibility: A qualitative examination of men's experiences of unintended pregnancy and abortion. *Journal of Men's Health, 5*, 133–152.

Reicher, S., Levine, R. M., & Gordijn, E. (1998). More on deindividuation, power relations between groups, and the expression of social identity: Three studies on the effects of visibility to the in-group. *British Journal of Social Psychology, 37*, 15–40.

Reidiger, M., Freund, A. M., & Baltes, P. B. (2005). Managing life through personal goals: Intergoal facilitations and intensity of goal pursuit in younger and older adulthood. *Journals of Gerontology: Series B: Psychological Sciences and Social Sciences, 60B*, P84–P91.

Reimer, K. (2003). Committed to caring: Transformation in adolescent moral identity. *Applied Developmental Science, 7*, 129–137.

Reis, H. T. (2006). Implications of attachment theory for research on intimacy. In M. Mikulincer and G. S. Goodman (Eds.). *Dynamics of Romantic Love: Attachment, Caregiving, and Sex*. (pp. 383–403). New York: Guilford Press.

Reis, H. T. & Aron, A. (2008). Love: What is it, why does it matter, and how does it operate? *Perspectives on Psychological Science, 3*, 80–86.

Reischl, T. M., & Hirsch, B. J. (1989). Identity commitments and coping with a difficult developmental transition. *Journal of Youth and Adolescence, 18*, 55–70.

Reker, G. T. (1997). Personal meaning, optimism and choice: Existential predictors of depression in community and institutional elderly. *The Gerontologist, 37*, 709–716.

Remafedi, G. (1987). Adolescent sexuality: Psychosocial and medical implications. *Pediatrics, 79*, 326–330.

Remennick, L. (2000). Childless in the land of imperative motherhood: Stigma and coping among infertile Israeli women. *Sex Roles, 43*, 821–841.

Repacholi, B. M., & Meltzoff, A. N. (2007). Emotional eavesdropping: Infants selectively respond to indirect emotional signals. *Child Development, 78*, 503–521.

Repetti, R. L., Taylor, S. E., & Seeman, T. E. (2002). Risky families: Family social environments and the mental and physical health of offspring. *Psychological Bulletin, 128*, 330–366.

Repokari, L., Punamaki, R, Poikkeus, P., Tiitinen, A., Vilska, S., Unkila-Kallio, L., Sinkkonen, J., Amqvist, F., & Tulppala, M. (2006). Ante-and perinatal factors and child characteristics predicting parenting experience among formerly infertile couples during the child's first year: A controlled study. *Journal of Family Psychology, 20*, 670–679.

Republic of Kenya Ministry of Health (2004). *Status and trends of Millennium Development Goals (MDG) in Kenya*. Retrieved September 25, 2007, from http://www.health.go .ke/

Rest, J. R. (1983). Morality. In P. H. Mussen (Gen. Ed.), J. H. Flavell, & E. M. Markman (Vol. Eds.), *Handbook of child psychology: Vol. 3. Cognitive development*. New York: Wiley.

Rettew, D. C., Stanger, C., McKee, L., Doyle, A., & Hudziak, J. J., (2006). Interactions between child and parent temperament and child behavior problems. *Comprehensive Psychiatry, 47*, 412–420.

Reyna, V. F., & Farley, F. (2006). Risk and rationality in adolescent decision making: Implications for theory, practice, and public policy. *Psychological Science in the Public Interest, 7*, 2–44.

Rice, P. L. (2000). Baby, souls, name, and health: Traditional customs for a newborn infant among the Hmong in Melbourne. *Early Human Development, 57*, 189–203.

Richards, F., & Commons, M. L. (1990). Postformal cognitive-developmental theory and research: A review of its current status. In C. N. Alexander & E. J. Langer (Eds.), *Higher stages of human development: Perspectives on adult growth* (pp. 229–257). New York: Oxford University Press.

Richards, M. H., & Larson, R. (1993). Pubertal development and the daily subjective states of young adolescents. *Journal of Research on Adolescence, 3*, 145–169.

Richman, J. (2001). Humor and creative life styles. *American Journal of Psychotherapy, 55*, 420–428.

Richter, L. M. (2006). Studying adolescence, *Science, 312*, 1902–1905.

Ricks, M. H. (1985). The social transmission of parental behavior: Attachment across generations. In I. Bretherton & E. Waters (Eds.), *Growing points of attachment: Theory and research* (pp. 211–227). *Monographs of the Society for Research in Child Development, 50* (1–2, Serial No. 209).

Rideout, V. J., Vandewater, E. A., & Wartella, E. A. (2003). *Zero to six: Electronic media in the lives of infants, toddlers and preschoolers. A Kaiser Family Foundation Report.* Retrieved September 19, 2004, from http://www.kff.org/entmedia/loader.cfm?url_/commonspot/security/getfile.cfm&PageID_22754

Ridgeway, C. L., & Correll, S. J. (2004). Motherhood as a status characteristic. *Journal of Social Issues, 60*, 683–700.

Riebe, D., Burbank, P., & Garber, C. E. (2002). Setting the stage for active older adults. In P. M. Burbank & D. Riebe (Eds.), *Promoting exercise and behavior change in older adults: Interventions with the transtheoretical model* (pp. 1–28). New York: Springer Verlag.

Riediger, M., Freund, A.M., & Baltes, B. (2005). Managing life through personal goals: Intergoal facilitation and intensity of goal pursuit in younger and older adulthood. *The Journals of Gerontology: Series B: Psychological Sciences and Social Sciences, 60B*, 84–91.

Riegel, K. F. (1973). Dialectic operations: The final period of cognitive development. *Human Development, 16*, 346–370.

Riegel, K. F., & Riegel, R. M. (1972). Development, drop, and death. *Developmental Psychology, 6*, 306–319.

Rieser-Danner, L. A. (2003). Individual differences in infant fearfulness and cognitive performance: A testing, performance, or competence effect? *Genetic, Social,and General Psychology Monographs, 129*, 41-71.

Rindfuss, R. R., & VandenHeuvel, A. (1990). Cohabitation: Precursor to marriage or alternative to being single? *Population and Development Review, 16*, 703–726.

Ringdal, G. I., Jordhoy, M. S., Ringdal, K., & Kaasa, S. (2001). The first year of grief and bereavement in close family members to individuals who have died of cancer. *Palliative Medicine, 15*, 91–105.

Rispoli, M. (2003). Changes in the nature of sentence production during the period of grammatical development. *Journal of Speech, Language, & Hearing Research, 46*, 818–830.

Ritchie, S., & Howes, C. (2003). Program practices, caregiver stability, and child-caregiver relationships. *Journal of Applied Developmental Psychology, 24*, 497–516.

Ritter, C., Hobfoll, S. E., Lavin, J., Cameron, R. P., & Hulsizer, M. R. (2000). Stress, psychosocial resources, and depressive symptomatology during pregnancy in low-income, inner-city women. *Health Psychology, 19*, 576–585.

Ritvo, S., & Solnit, A J. (1995). Instinct theory. In B. R. Moore & B. D. Fine (Eds.), *Psychoanalysis: Themajor concepts* (pp. 327–333). NewHaven: Yale University Press.

Robbins, R. N., & Bryan, A. (2004). Relationships between future orientation, impulsive sensation seeking, and risk behavior among adjudicated adolescents. *Journal of Adolescent Research, 19*, 428–445.

Robert, P.M. & Harlan, S.L. (2006). Mechanisms of disability discrimination in large bureaucratic organizations: Ascriptive inequalities in the workplace. *Sociological Quarterly, 47*, 599–630.

Roberts, J. E., Burchinal, M., & Durham, M. (1999). Parents' reports of vocabulary and grammatical development of African American preschoolers: Child and environmental associations. *Child Development, 70*, 92–106.

Roberts, J. S., & Rosenwald, G. C. (2001). Ever upward and not turning back: Social mobility and identity formation among first-generation college students. In D. P. McAdams, R. Josselson, & A. Lieblich (Eds.), *Turns in the road: Narrative studies of lives in transition* (pp. 91–119). Washington, DC: American Psychological Association.

Roberts, L. J., & Krokoff, L. J. (1990). Withdrawal, hostility, and displeasure in marriage. *Journal of Marriage and the Family, 52*, 95–105.

Roberts, R. E., Phinney, J. S., Masse, L. C., Chen, Y. R., Roberts, C. R., & Romero. A. (1999). The structure of ethnic identity of young adolescents from diverse ethnocultural groups. *Journal of Early Adolescence, 19*, 301–322.

Roberts, R. E., & Sobhan, M. (1992). Symptoms of depression in adolescents: A comparison of Anglo, African, and Hispanic Americans. *Journal of Youth and Adolescence, 21*, 639–652.

Robertson, J., & Robertson, J. (1989). *Separation and the very young.* New York: Free Association Books.

Robertson, J. F., & Simons, R. L. (1989). Family factors, self-esteem, and adolescent depression. *Journal of Marriage and the Family, 51*, 125–138.

Robertson, S. M., Zarit, S. H., Duncan, L. G., Rovine, M. J., & Femia, E E (2007). Family caregivers' patterns of positive and negative affect. *Family Relations, 56*, 12–23.

Robin, D. J., Berthier, N. E., & Clifton, R. K. (1996). Infants' predictive reaching for moving objects in the dark. *Developmental Psychology, 32*, 824–835.

Robinson, B. E. (1988). Teenage pregnancy from the father's perspective. *American Journal of Orthopsychiatry, 58*, 46–51.

Robinson, J. L., & Acevedo, M. C. (2001). Infant reactivity and reliance on mother during emotion challenges: Prediction of cognition and language skills in a low-income sample. *Child Development, 72*, 402–415.

Robinson, J. L., & Emde, R. N. (2004). Mental health moderators of Early Head Start on parenting and child development: Maternal depression and relationship attitudes. *Parenting: Science and Practice, 4*, 73–97.

Rochat, P. (1989). Object manipulation and exploration in 2-to 5-month-old infants. *Developmental Psychology, 25*, 871–884.

Rochat, P., Querido, J. G., & Striano, T. (1999). Emerging sensitivity to the timing and structure of protoconversation in early infancy. *Developmental Psychology, 35*, 950–957.

Rodgers, A., & Rodgers, E. M. (2004.) *Scaffolding literacy instruction: Strategies for K-4 classrooms.* Portsmouth, NH: Heinemann.

Rodier, P. (2004). Environmental causes of central nervous system maldevelopment. *Pediatrics 2004, 113*, 1076–1083.

Rodriguez, R. (2006). Diversity finds its place. *HRMagazine, 51*, No. 8. Retrieved October 4, 2005, from http://www.shrm.org/hrmagazine/articles/0806/0806rodriguez.asp

Rodriguez-Fornells, A., Rotte, M., Heinze, H.-J., Nosselt, T., & Munte, T. F. (2002). Brain potential and functional MRI evidence for how to handle two languages with one brain. *Nature, 415*, 1026–1029.

Rogers, C. R. (1972). *Becoming partners: Marriage and its alternatives.* New York: Delacorte Press.

Rogers, C. R. A. (1959). A theory of therapy, personality, and interpersonal relationships as developed in the client-centered framework. In S. Koch (Ed.), *Psychology: A study of a science* (Vol. 3, pp. 184–156). New York: McGraw-Hill.

Rogers, C. R. A. (1961). *On becoming a person.* Boston: Houghton Mifflin.

Rogers, S. J. (2004). Dollars, dependency, and divorce: Four perspectives on the role of wives' income. *Journal of Marriage and the Family, 66*, 59–74.

Rogers, S. J., & Williams, J. H. G. (2006). *Imitation and the social mind: Autism and typical development.* New York: Guilford.

Rogoff, B., & Angelillo, C. (2002). Investigating the coordinated functioning of multifaceted cultural practices in human development. *Human Development, 45*, 211–216.

Rogoff, B., Mistry, J., Goncu, A., & Mosier, C. (1993). Guided participation in cultural activity by toddlers and caregivers. *Monograph of the Society for Research in Child Development, 58* (8 Serial No. 236).

Rogoff, B., & Morelli, G. (1989). Perspectives on children's development from cultural psychology. *American Psychologist, 44*, 343–348.

Rogoff, B., Paradise, R., Arauz, R. M., Correa-Chavez, M., & Angellilo, C. (2003). Firsthand learning through intent participation. *Annual Review of Psychology, 54*, 175–203.

Rohner, R. P. (1984). Toward a conception of culture for cross-cultural psychology. *Journal of Cross-Cultural Psychology, 15*, 111–138.

Rokach, A., Bacanli, H., & Ramberan, G., (2000). Coping with loneliness: A cross-cultural comparison. *European Psychologist, 5*, 302–311.

Rokach, A., & Neto, F. (2001). The experience of loneliness in adolescence: A crosscultural comparison. *International Journal of Adolescence and Youth, 9*, 159–173.

Ron, P. (2010). Elderly people's death and dying anxiety. A comparison between elderly living within the community and in nursing homes in Israel. *Illness, Crisis & Loss, 18*, 3–17.

Roney, J. R., Hanson, K. N., Durante, K. M., & Maestripieri, D. (2006). Reading men's faces: Women's mate attractiveness judgments track men's testosterone and interest in infants. *Proceedings of the Royal Society:B, 273*, 2169–2175.

Roosa, M. W. (1984). Maternal age, social class, and the obstetric performance of teenagers. *Journal of Youth and Adolescence, 13*, 365–374.

Roscigno, V., & Ainsworth-Darnell, J. (1999). Race, cultural capital and educational resources: Persistent inequalities and achievement returns. *Sociology of Education, 72*, 158–178.

Rose, S. A., Feldman, J. F., & Wallace, I. F. (1992). Infant information processing in relation to six-year cognitive outcomes. *Child Development, 63*, 1126–1141.

Rose, S. A., & Ruff, H. A. (1987). Cross-modal abilities in human infants. In J. D. Osofsky (Ed.), *Handbook of infant development* (2nd ed., pp. 318–362). New York: Wiley.

Rosellini, L. (1992, July 6). Sexual desire. *U.S. News and World Report, 113*(1), 60–66.

Rosen, A. B., & Rozin, P. (1993). Now you see it, now you don't: The preschool child's conception of invisible particles in the context of dissolving. *Developmental Psychology, 29*, 300–311.

Rosen, C. S., Schwebel, D. C., & Singer, J. L. (1997). Preschoolers' attributions of mental states in pretense. *Child Development, 68*, 1133–1142.

Rosen, K. S., & Rothbaum, F. (1993). Quality of parental caregiving and security of attachment. *Developmental Psychology, 29*, 358–367.

Rosen, W. D., Adamson, L. B., & Bakeman, R. (1992). An experimental investigation of infant social referencing: Mothers' messages and gender differences. *Developmental Psychology, 28*, 1172–1178.

Rosenbaum, J. E. (2009). Patient teenagers: A comparison of the sexual behavior of virgin pledgers and matched nonpledgers. *Pediatrics, 123*, 110–120.

Rosenberg, M. (1979). *Conceiving the self*. New York: Basic Books.

Rosenberg, M., & McCullough, B. C. (1981). Mattering: Inferred significance and mental health among adolescents. *Research in Community and Mental Health, 2*, 163–182.

Rosenblatt, R. A., Mattis, R., & Hart, L. G. (1995). Abortions in rural Idaho: Physicians' attitudes and practices. *American Journal of Public Health, 85*, 1423–1425.

Rosenfeld, M. J. (2007). *The age of independence: Interracial unions, same-sex unions, and the changing American family*. Cambridge, MA: Harvard University Press.

Rosenfeld, M. J., & Kim, B-S. (2005). The independence of young adults and the rise of interracial and same-sex unions. *American Sociological Review, 70*, 541–562.

Rosenfeld, S. (1992). The costs of sharing: Wives' employment and husbands' mental health. *Journal of Health and Social Behavior, 33*, 213–225.

Rosenfield, A., & Figdor, E. (2001). Where is the M in MTCT? The broader issues in mother-to-child transmission of HIV. *American Journal of Public Health, 91*, 703–704.

Rosenkoetter, L. I. (1999). The television situation comedy and children's prosocial behavior. *Journal of Applied Social Psychology, 29*, 979–993.

Rosenkoetter, M. M., & Garris, J. M. (2001). Retirement planning, use of time, and psychosocial adjustment. *Issues in Mental Health Nursing, 22*, 703–722.

Rosenthal, R. (1994). Interpersonal expectancy effects: A 30-year perspective. *Current Directions in Psychological Science, 3*, 176–179.

Rosenthal, R. (1995). Critiquing *Pygmalion*: A 25-year perspective. *Current Directions in Psychological Science, 4*, 171–172.

Rosenthal, R., & Jacobson, L. (1968). *Pygmalion in the classroom: Teacher expectations and student intellectual development*. New York: Holt, Rinehart & Winston.

Rosnick, C. B., Small, B. J., Graves, A. B., & Mortimer, J. A. (2004). The association between health and cognitive performance in a population-based study of older adults: The Charlotte county healthy aging study (CCHAS). *Aging, Neuropsychology, & Cognition, 11*, 89–99.

Ross, G., Kagan, J., Zelazo, P., & Kotelchuck, M. (1975). Separation protest in infants in home and laboratory. *Developmental Psychology, 11*, 256–257.

Ross, M. (1989). Relation of implicit theories to the construction of personal histories. *Psychological Review, 96*, 341–357.

Rostosky, S. S., & Travis, C. B. (1996). Menopause research and the dominance of the biomedical model 1984–1994. *Psychology of Women Quarterly, 20*, 285–312.

Rotenberg, K. J., McDougall, P., Boulton, M. J., Vaillancourt, T., Fox, C., & Hymel, S.

(2004). Cross-sectional and longitudinal relations among peer-reported trustworthiness, social relationships, and psychological adjustment in children and early adolescents from the United Kingdom and Canada. *Journal of Experimental Child Psychology, 88*, 46–67.

Roth, D. L., Haley, W. E., Owen, J. E., Clay, O. J., & Goode, K. T. (2001). Latent growth models of the longitudinal effects of dementia caregiving: A comparison of African American and White family caregivers. *Psychology and Aging, 16*, 427–436.

Roth, W. E. (1953). Precautions during pregnancy in New Guinea. In M. Mead & N. Calas (Eds.), *Primitive heritage*. New York: Random House.

Rothbart, M. K. (1991). Temperament: A developmental framework. In J. Strelau & A. Angleitner (Eds.), *Explorations in temperament: International perspectives on theory and measurement* (pp. 235–260). London: Plenum Press.

Rothbart, M. K., Ahadi, S. A., & Evans, D. E. (2000). Temperament and personality: Origins and outcomes. *Journal of Personality and Social Psychology, 78*, 122–135.

Rothbart, M. K., & Bates, J. E. (2006). Temperament. In W. Damon & R. M. Lerner (Series Eds.) & N. Eisenberg (Vol. Ed.), *Handbook of child psychology: Vol. 3, Social, emotional, and personality development* (6th ed., pp. 99–166). New York: Wiley.

Rothbart, M. K., & Derryberry, D. (1981). Development of individual differences in temperament. In M. E. Lamb & A. L. Brown (Eds.), *Advances in developmental psychology* (Vol. 1, pp. 37–86). Hillsdale, NJ: Erlbaum.

Rothbaum, F., Weisz, J., Pott, M., Miyake, J. 7 Morelli, G. (2000). Attachment and culture: Security in the United States and Japan. *American Psychologist, 55*, 1093–1104.

Rotheram-Borus, M. J., & Wyche, K. F. (1994). Ethnic differences in identity development in the United States. In S. L. Archer (Ed.), *Interventions for adolescent identity development* (pp. 62–83). Thousand Oaks, CA: Sage.

Rothrauff, T., & Cooney, T. M. (2008). The role of generativity in psychological well-being: Does it differ for childless adults and parents? *Journal of Adult Development, 15*, 148–159.

Rovee-Collier, C. (1987). Learning and memory in infancy. In J. D. Osofsky (Ed.), *Handbook of infant development* (2nd ed., pp. 98–148). New York: Wiley.

Rovee-Collier, C., Schechter, A., Shyi, G. C. W., & Shields, P. (1992). Perceptual identification of contextual attributes and infant memory retrieval. *Developmental Psychology, 28*, 307–318.

Rovet, J., Cole, S., Nulman, I., Scolnik, D., Altmann, D., & Koren, G. (1995). Effects of maternal epilepsy on children's neurodevelopment. *Child Neuropsychology, 1*, 150–157.

Rowe, J. W., & Kahn, R. L. (1997). Successful aging. *The Gerontologist, 37,* 433–440.

Rowe, J. W., & Kahn, R. L. (1998). *Successful aging.* New York: Pantheon Books.

Rowe, M. L., & Goldin-Meadow, S. (2009). Differences in early gesture explain SES disparities in child vocabulary size at school entry. *Science, 323,* 951–953.

Rowles, G. D., & Ravdal, H. (2002). Aging, place, and meaning in the face of changing circumstances. In R. S. Weiss & S. P. Bass (Eds.), *Challenges of the third age: Meaning and purpose in later life* (pp. 81–114). New York: Oxford University Press.

Rowold, J., & Laukamp, L. (2009). Charismatic leadership and objective performance indicators. *Applied Psychology: An International Review, 58,* 602–621.

Rubenstein, R. L. (2002). The third age. In R. S. Weiss & S. A. Bass (Eds.), *Challenges of the third age: Meaning and purpose in later life* (pp. 29–40). London: Oxford University Press.

Rubia, K., Smith, A. B., Woolley, J., Nosarti, C., Heyman, I., Taylor, E., & Brammer, M. (2006). Progressive increase of frontostriatal brain activation from childhood to adulthood during event-related tasks of cognitive control. *Human Brain Mapping, 27,* 973–993.

Rubin, K. H. (1980). Fantasy play: Its role in the development of social skills and social cognition. *New Directions in Child Development, 9,* 69–84.

Rubin, K. H., Coplan, R. J., & Bowker, J. C. (2009). Social withdrawal in childhood. *Annual Review of Psychology, 60,* 141–171.

Rubin, K. H., Hastings, P., Stewart, S. L., Henderson, H. A., & Chen, X. (1997). The consistency and concomitants of inhibition: Some of the children all of the time. *Child Development, 68,* 467–483.

Ruble, D. N., Alvarez, J., Bachman, M., Cameron, J., Fuligni, A., Coll, C. G., & Rhee, E. (2004). The development of a sense of "WE": The emergence and implications of children's collective identity. In M. Bennett & F. Sani (Eds.), *The development of the social self* (pp. 29–76). New York: Psychology Press.

Ruby, P., & Decety, J. (2001). Effect of subjective perspective taking during simulation of action: A PET investigation of agency. *Nature Neuroscience, 4,* 546–550.

Ruby, P., & Decety, J. (2004). How would you feel versus how do you think she would feel? A neuroimaging study of perspective-taking with social emotions. *Journal of Cognitive Neuroscience, 16,* 988–999.

Ruch, W., Proyer, R.T., & Weber, M. (2010). Humor as a character strength among the elderly: Empirical findings on age-related changes and its contribution to satisfaction with life. *Zeitschrift für Gerontologie und Geriatriei, 43,* 13–18.

Ruff, H. A., Saltarelli, L. M., Capozzoli, M., & Dubiner, K. (1992). The differentiation of activity in infants' exploration of objects. *Developmental Psychology, 28,* 851–861.

Rumelhart, D. E., & McClelland, J. L. (1986). *Parallel distributed processing* (Vol. 1). Cambridge, MA: MIT Press.

Rusbult, C. E., & Arriaga, X. B. (1997). Interdependence theory. In S. Duck (Ed.), *Handbook of personal relationships: Theory, research and interventions* (2nd ed., pp. 221–250). Chichester, UK: Wiley.

Rusbult, C. E., Finkel, E. J., & Kumashiro, M. (2009). The Michael Angelo phenomenon. *Current Directions in Psychological Science, 18,* 305–309.

Rusbult, C. E., Van Lange, P. A. M., Wildschut, T., Yovetich, N. A., & Verette, J. (2000). Perceived superiority in close relationships: Why it exists and persists. *Journal of Personality and Social Psychology, 79,* 521–545.

Russell, S. T., & Joyner, K. (2001). Adolescent sexual orientation and suicide risk: Evidence from a national study. *American Journal of Public Health, 91,* 1276–1281.

Rusting, R. L. (1992). Why do we age? *Scientific American, 267,* 130.

Rutkowska, J. C. (1994). Scaling up sensorimotor systems: Constraints from human infancy. *Adaptive Behavior, 2,* 349–373.

Rutter, M. (1990). Commentary: Some focus and process considerations regarding effects of parental depression on children. *Developmental Psychology, 26,* 60–67.

Rutter, M. (1995). Maternal deprivation. In M. H. Bornstein (Ed.), *Handbook of parenting: Vol. 4. Applied and practical parenting* (pp. 3–31). Hillsdale, NJ: Erlbaum.

Ryan, M. K., David, B., & Reynolds, K. J. (2004). Who cares? The effect of gender and context on the self and moral reasoning. *Psychology of Women Quarterly, 28,* 246–255.

Ryan, R. M., & Deci, E. L. (2000). Self-determination theory and the facilitation of intrinsic motivation, social development, and well-being. *American Psychologist, 55,* 68–78.

Ryan, R. M., & Lynch, J. H. (1989). Emotional autonomy versus detachment: Revisiting the vicissitudes of adolescence and young adulthood. *Child Development, 60,* 340–356.

Ryff, C. D., Keyes, C. L., & Hughes, D. L. (2003). Status inequalities, perceived discrimination, and eudaimonic well-being: Do the challenges of minority life hone purpose and growth? *Journal of Health and Social Behavior, 44,* 275–291.

Ryff, C. D., Kwan, C. M. L.,& Singer, B. H. (2001). Personality and aging: Flourishing agendas and future challenges. In J. E. Birren & K. W. Schaie (Eds.). *Handbook of the psychology of aging (5th ed.).* (pp. 477–499). San Diego, CA: Academic Press.

Sabatelli, R. M., Meth, R. L., & Gavazzi, S. M. (1988). Factors mediating the adjustment to involuntary childlessness. *Family Relations, 37,* 338–343.

Sabbagh, M. A., & Baldwin, D. A. (2001). Learning words from knowledgeable versus ignorant speakers: Links between preschoolers' theory of mind and semantic development. *Child Development, 72,* 1054–1070.

Sachs, S. (2001, October 7). The two worlds of Muslim American teenagers. *New York Times,* p. B1.

Saczynski, J. S., Willis, S. L., & Schaie, K. W. (2002). Strategy use in reasoning training with older adults. *Aging, Neuropsychology, & Cognition, 9,* 48–60.

Saffran, J., Aslin, R., & Newport, E. (1996). Statistical learning by 8-month-old infants. *Science, 274,* 1926–1928.

Sagi, A., & Hoffman, M. L. (1976). Empathetic distress in the newborn. *Developmental Psychology, 12,* 175–176.

Sagi, A., Koren-Karie, N., Gini, M., Ziv, Y., & Joels, T. (2002). Shedding further light on the effects of various types and quality of early child care on infant-mother attachment relationships: The Haifa study of early child care. *Child Development, 73,* 1166–1186.

Sagi, A., Lamb, M. E., Lewkowicz, K. S., Shoham, R., Dvir, R., & Estes, D. (1985). Security of infant-mother, -father, and -metapelet attachments among kibbutz-reared Israeli children. In I. Bretherton & E. Everett (Eds.), *Growing points of attachment theory and research* (pp. 257–275). *Monographs of the Society for Research in Child Development, 50* (1–2, Serial No. 209).

Sagi, A., & van IJzendoorn, M. H. (1996). Multiple caregiving environments: The kibbutz experience. In S. Harel & J. P. Shonkoff (Eds.), *Early childhood intervention and family support programs: Accomplishments and challenges* (pp. 143–162). Jerusalem: JDC-Brookdale Institute.

Sagrestano, L. M., Felman, P., Killingsworth Rini, C., Woo, G., & Dunkel-Schetter, C. (1999). Ethnicity and social support during pregnancy. *American Journal of Community Psychology, 27,* 869–898.

Sales, B. C., & Folkman, S. (Eds.). (2000). *Ethics in research with human participants.* Washington, DC: American Psychological Association.

Salisch, M. von (2001). Children's emotional development: Challenges in their relationships to parents, peers, and friends. *International Journal of Behavioral Development, 25,* 310–319.

Sallie Mae (2009). *How undergraduate students use credit cards.* Retrieved on July 8, 2010, at www.salliemae.com.

Salthouse, T. A. (1985). Speed of behavior and its implications for cognition. In J. W. Birren & K. W. Shaie (Eds.), *Handbook of the psychology of aging* (pp. 400–426). New York: Van Nostrand Reinhold.

Salthouse, T. A. (1996). The processing-speed theory of adult age differences in cognition. *Psychological Review, 103,* 403–428.

Saltz, R., & Saltz, E. (1986). Pretend play training and its outcomes. In G. Fein & M. Rivkin (Eds.), *The young child at play: Reviews of research* (Vol. 4, pp. 155–173). Washington, DC: National Association for the Education of Young Children.

Salvatore, N., & Sastre, M. T. M. (2001). Appraisal of life: "Area" versus "dimension" conceptualizations. *Social Indicators Research, 53,* 229–240.

Salzinger, S., Feldman, R. S., Hammer, M., & Rosario, M. (1993). The effects of physical abuse on children's social relationships. *Child Development, 64,* 168–187.

Sameroff, A. J. (1982). Development and the dialectic: The need for a systems approach. In W. A. Collins (Ed.), *The concept of development: The Minnesota Symposia on Child Psychology* (Vol. 15). Hillsdale, NJ: Erlbaum.

SAMHSA. (2001). *National Strategy for Suicide Prevention Goals and Objectives for Action.* Washington, DC: U.S. Department of Health and Human Services, Inventory Number SMA01-3517. Retrieved from http://mentalhealth.samhsa.gov/suicideprevention/strategy.asp on June 29, 2004

Sampson, R. J., Raudenbush, S. W., & Earls, F. (1997). Neighborhoods and violent crime: A multilevel study of collective efficacy. *Science, 227,* 918–923.

Sanders, R. E. (1997). Find your partner and do-si-do: The formation of personal relationships between social beings. *Journal of Social and Personal Relationships, 14,* 387–415.

Sandler, J., Holder, A., & Meers, P. M. (1963). The ego ideal and the ideal self. *Psychoanalytic Study of the Child, 18,* 139–158.

Sanoff, A. P. (2006). A perception gap over students' preparation. *The Chronicle of Higher Education, School & College special report.* March 10, pp. B9–B14.

Sansavini, A., Bertoncini, J., & Giovanelli, G. (1997). Newborns discriminate the rhythm of multisyllabic stressed words. *Developmental Psychology, 33,* 3–11.

Santelli, J. S., Abma, J., Ventura, S., Lindberg, L., Morrow, B., Anderson, J., et al. (2004). Can changes in sexual behaviors among high school students explain the decline in teen pregnancy rates in the 1990s? *Journal of Adolescent Health, 34,* 80–90.

Santillanes, G. F. (1997). Releasing the spirit: A lesson in Native American funeral rituals. *The Director, 69,* 32–34.

Saracho, O. N., & Shirakawa, Y. (2004). A comparison of the literacy development context of United States and Japanese families. *Early Childhood Education Journal, 31,* 261–266.

Sargrestano, L. M., Heavey, C. L., & Chistensen, A. (1999). Perceived power and physical violence in marital conflict. *Journal of Social Issues, 55,* 65–79.

Sarkisian, N., & Gerstel, N. (2004). Explaining the gender gap in help to parents: The importance of employment. *Journal of Marriage and the Family, 66,* 431–451.

Saudino, K. J. & Zapfe, J. A. (2008). Genetic influences on activity level in early childhood: do situations matter? *Child Development, 79,* 930–943.

Savani, K., Markus, H. R., Naidu, N. V. R., Kumar, S., & Berlia, N. (2010). What counts as a choice? U.S. Americans are more likely than Indians to construe actions as choices. *Psychological Science, 21,* 391–398.

Savaya, R., & Cohen, O. (2003). Perceptions of the societal image of Muslim Arab divorced men and women in Israel. *Journal of Social and Personal Relationships, 20,* 193–202.

Savin-Williams, R. C. (1996). Self-labeling and disclosure among gay, lesbian, and bisexual youths. In J. Laird & R.-J. Green (Eds.), *Lesbians and gays in couples and families: A Handbook for therapists* (pp. 153–182). San Francisco: Jossey-Bass.

Savin-Williams, R. C., & Diamond, L. M. (2004). Sex. In R. M. Lerner & L. Steinberg (Eds.), *Handbook of adolescent psychology* (2nd ed., pp. 189–231). New York: Wiley.

Savitz-Smith, J. (2003). Couples undergoing infertility treatment: Implications for counselors. *Family Journal—Counseling & Therapy for Couples and Families, 11,* 383–387.

Sax, L., & Astin, A. (1997). The benefits of service: Evidence from undergraduates. *Educational Record, 78,* 25–32.

Scarbrough, J. W. (2001). Welfare mothers' reflections on personal responsibility. *Journal of Social Issues, 57,* 261–276.

Scarr, S. (1992). Developmental theories for the 1990s: Development and individual differences. *Child Development, 63,* 1–19.

Schaffer, H. R., & Emerson, P. E. (1964). *The development of social attachments in infancy. Monographs of the Society for Research in Child Development, 29* (Whole No. 94).

Shaffer, K. & Kipp, D. R. *Developmental Psychology, Childhood & Adolescence,* Seventh Edition, Belmont: Thomson Wadsworth, 202

Schaie, K. W. (1965). A general model for the study of developmental problems. *Psychological Bulletin, 64,* 92–107.

Schaie, K. W. (1992). The impact of methodological changes in gerontology. *International Journal of Aging and Human Development, 35,* 19–29.

Schaie, K. W. (1994). The course of adult intellectual development. *American Psychologist, 49,* 304–313.

Schaie, K. W., & Elder, G. H. (Ed.). (2005). *Historical influences on lives and aging.* Societal impact on aging series. New York, NY: Springer Publishing Company.

Schaie, K. W., & Hertzog, C. (1983). Fourteen-year cohort-sequential analyses of adult intellectual development. *Developmental Psychology, 19,* 531–543.

Schaie, K. W., & Zuo, Y. (2001). Family environments and adult cognitive functioning. In R. Sternberg & E. L. Grigorenko (Eds.), *Environmental effects on cognitive abilities* (pp. 337–361). Mahwah, NJ: Erlbaum.

Schatz, M. (1983). Communication. In J. H. Flavell & E. M. Markman (Eds.), *Handbook of child psychology* (Vol. 3, pp. 841–889). New York: Wiley.

Scheff, T. J. (2003). Shame in self and society. *Symbolic Interaction, 26,* 239–262.

Schlein, S. (2007, Summer). Dimensions of relatedness, activation, and engagement: Erikson's interpersonal-relational method of psychoanalysis. *Psychologist-Psychoanalyst Newsletter, 59.*

Schickedanz, J. A. (1986). *More than the ABCs: The early stages of reading and writing.* Washington, DC: National Association for the Education of Young People.

Schiedel, D. G., & Marcia, J. E. (1985). Ego identity, intimacy, sex-role orientation, and gender. *Developmental Psychology, 21,* 149–160.

Schieffelin, B. B., & Cochran-Smith, M. (1984). Learning to read culturally: Literacy before schooling. In H. Goelman, A. A. Oberg, & F. Smith (Eds.), *Awakening to literacy* (pp. 3–23). Exeter, NH: Heinemann.

Schlein, S. (1987). *A way of looking at things: Selected papers from 1930 to 1980. Erik H. Erikson.* New York: Norton.

Schlein, S. (2007, Summer). Dimensions of relatedness, activation, and engagement: Erikson's interpersonal-relational method of psychoanalysis. *Psychologist-Psychoanalyst Newsletter, 59.*

Schmidt, L. A., Fox, N. A., Perez-Edar, K., & Hamer, D. H. (2009). Linking gene, brain, and behavior. *Psychological Science, 20,* 831–837.

Schmiege, S., & Russo, N. F. (2005). Depression and unwanted first pregnancy: Longitudinal cohort study. *British Medical Journal, 331.*

Schmitt-Rodermund, E., & Silbereisen, R. K. (1998). Career maturity determinants: Individual development, social context, and historical time. *Career Development Quarterly, 47,* 16–31.

Schmitz-Scherzer, R. (1995). Reflections on cultural influences on aging and old-age suicide in Germany. *International Psychogeriatrics, 7,* 231–238.

Schnall, S., Roper, J., & Fessler, D. M. T. (2010). Elevation leads to altruistic behavior. *Psychological Science, 21,* 315–320.

Schnarch, D. (2000). Desire problems: A systematic perspective. In S. Leiblum & R. Rosen (Eds.), *Principles and practice of sex therapy* (pp. 17–56). New York: Guilford Press.

Schneider, B. H., Atkinson, L., & Tardif, C. (2001). Child-parent attachment and children's peer relations: A quantitative review. *Developmental Psychology, 37,* 86–100.

Schneider, D. S., Sledge, P. A., Shuchter, S. R., & Zisook, S. (1996). Dating and remarriage over the first two years of widowhood. *Annals of Clinical Psychiatry, 8,* 51–57.

Schneider, W., & Bjorklund, D. F. (1992). Expertise, aptitude, and strategic remembering. *Child Development, 63,* 461–473.

Schoen, R. (1992). First unions and the stability of first marriages. *Journal of Marriage and the Family, 54,* 281–284.

Scholnick, E. K. (1995, Fall). Direction I: Knowing and constructing plans. *SRCD Newsletter,* 1–2.

Schöner, G., & Thelen, E. (2006). Using dynamic filed theory to rethink infant habituation. *Psychological Review, 113,* 273–299.

Schooler, C., & Mulatu, M. S. (2001). The reciprocal effects of leisure time activities and intellectual functioning in older people: A longitudinal analysis. *Psychology and Aging, 16,* 466–482.

Schootman, M., Fuortes, L. J., Zwerling, C., Albanese, M. A., & Watson, C. A. (1993). Safety behavior among Iowa junior high and high school students. *American Journal of Public Health, 83,* 1628–1629.

Schramm, D. G., Marshall, J. P., Harris, V. W., & Lee, T. R. (2005). After "I do": The newlywed transition. *Marriage & Family Review, 38,* 45–67.

Schrof, J. M. (1994). A lens on maternity. *U.S. News and World Report, 116*, 66–69.

Schulenberg, J., & Maggs, J. L. (2001). Moving targets: Modeling developmental trajectories of adolescent alcohol misuse, individual and peer risk factors, and intervention effects. *Applied Developmental Science, 5*, 237–253.

Schulenberg, J., Vondracek, F. W., & Kim, J. (1993). Career certainty and short-term changes in work values during adolescence. *Career Development Quarterly, 41*, 268–284.

Schultheiss, D. P., & Blustein, D. L. (1994). Contributions of family relationship factors to the identity formation process. *Journal of Counseling and Development, 73*, 159–166.

Schultz, A. (2001, March). 25 women making it big. *Fortune Small Business*, pp. 17–24.

Schultz, K. S., Morton, K. R., & Weckerle, J. R. (1998). The influence of push and pull factors on voluntary and involuntary early retirees' retirement decision and adjustment. *Journal of Vocational Behavior, 53*, 45–57.

Schultz, M. S., Cowan, P. A., Pape Cowan, C., & Brennan, R. T. (2004). Coming home upset: Gender, marital satisfaction and the daily spillover of workday experience into couple interactions. *Journal of Family Psychology, 18*, 250–253.

Schulz, M. S., Pruett, M. K., Kerig, P. K., & Parke, R. D. (2010). *Strengthening couple relationship for optimal child development: Lessons from research and intervention*. Washington, DC: American Psychological Association.

Schulz, R., & Willamson, G. M. (1993). Psychosocial and behavioral dimensions of physical frailty. *Journal of Gerontology, 48*, 39–43.

Schultz, R. I., Grelotti, D. J., & Pober, B. (2001). Genetics of childhood disorders: Vol. 26. Williams syndrome and brain–behavior relationships. *Journal of the American Academy of Child and Adolescent Psychiatry, 40*, 606–609.

Schuster, C. S. (1986). Intrauterine development. In C. S. Schuster & S. S. Ashburn (Eds.), *The process of human development* (pp. 67–94). Boston: Little, Brown.

Schwandt, T. A. (1998). Three epistemological stances for qualitative inquiry: Interpretivism, hermeneutics, and social constructionism. In N. K. Denzin & Y. S. Lincoln (Eds.), *The landscape of qualitative research: Theories and issues* (pp. 221–259). Thousand Oaks, CA: Sage.

Schwartz, A. N., Snyder, C. L., & Peterson, J. A. (1984). *Aging and life: An introduction to gerontology* (2nd ed.). New York: Holt, Rinehart & Winston.

Schwartz, S. J. (2001). The evolution of Eriksonian and neo-Eriksonian identity theory and research: A review and integration. *Identity, 1*, 7–58.

Schweinhart, L. J., Montie, J., Xiang, Z., Barnett, W.S., Belfield, C. R., & Norse, M. (2005). *Lifetime effects: The High/Scope Perry Preschool study through age 40*. Ypsilanti, MI: High/Scope Press.

Schweinhart, L. J., & Weikart, D. P. (1988). The High/Scope Perry Preschool Program.

In R. H. Price, E. L. Cowen, R. P. Lorion, & J. Ramos-McKay (Eds.), *Fourteen ounces of prevention* (pp. 53–66). Washington, DC: American Psychological Association.

Schwitzer, A. M., & Thomas, C. (1998). Implementation, utilization, and outcomes of a minority freshman peer mentor program at a predominantly white university. *Journal of the Freshman Year Experience & Students in Transition, 10*(1), 31–50.

Science Daily. (2005). *Fetal exposure to toxins could be behind rise in asthma*. Retrieved June 1, 2007, from http://www.sciencedaily.com/releases/2005/10/051011063818.htm

Science Daily. (2007). *Severe trauma affects kids' brain function, say researchers*. Retrieved August 16, 2007, from http://www.sciencedaily.com/releases/2007/07/070726184910.htm

Scogin, F., Storandt, M., & Lott, L. (1985). Memory-skills training, memory complaints, and depression in older adults. *Journal of Gerontology, 40*, 562–568.

Scopesi, A., Zanobini, M., & Carossino, P. (1997). Childbirth in different cultures: Psychophysical reactions of women delivering in U.S., German, French, and Italian hospitals. *Journal of Reproductive and Infant Psychology, 15*, 9–30.

Scott, J. P. (1987). Critical periods in processes of social organization. In M. H. Bornstein (Ed.), *Sensitive periods in development: Interdisciplinary perspectives* (pp. 247–268). Hillsdale, NJ: Erlbaum.

Scraton, S., & Holland, S. (2006). Grandfatherhood and leisure. *Leisure Studies, 25*, 233–250.

Seabrook, J. (2010). The last babylift: Adopting a child in Haiti. *The New Yorker, 86(12)*, May 10, 44–53.

Sears, D. O., Fu, M., Henry, P. J., & Bui, K. (2003). The origins and persistence of ethnic identity among the "new immigrant" groups. *Social Psychology Quarterly, 66*, 419–437.

Sears, P. S., & Barbee, A. H. (1978). Career and life satisfaction among Terman's gifted women. In J. Stanley, W. George, & C. Solano (Eds.), *The gifted and the creative: Fifty year perspective*. Baltimore: Johns Hopkins University Press.

Seaton, E. K., Yip, T., & Sellers, R. M. (2009). A longitudinal examination of racial identity and racial discrimination among African American adolescents. *Child Development, 80*, 406–417.

Seccombe, K. (1991). Assessing the costs and benefits of children: Gender comparisons among child-free husbands and wives. *Journal of Marriage and the Family, 53*, 191–202.

Seccombe, K. (2000). Families in poverty in the 1990s: Trends, causes, consequences, and lessons learned. *Journal of Marriage and the Family, 62*, 1094–1113.

Sedikides, C., Gaertner, L., & Toguchi, Y. (2003). Pancultural self-enhancement. *Journal of Personality and Social Psychology, 84*, 60–79.

Sedikides, C., Gaertner, L., & Vevea, J. L. (2005). Pancultural self-enhancement

reloaded: A meta-analytic reply to Heine (2005). *Journal of Personality and Social Psychology, 89*, 539–551.

Segal, L. B., Oster, H., Cohen, M., Caspi, B., Myers, M., & Brown, D. (1995). Smiling and fussing in seven-month-old preterm and full-term Black infants in the still-face situation. *Child Development, 66*, 1829–1843.

Sehdev, H. M. (2005). Cesarean Delivery. *eMedicine*. Retrieved May 29, 2007 from http://www.emedicine.com/med/topic3283.htm

Seider, S. (2007). Catalyzing a commitment to community service in emerging adults. *Journal of Adolescent Research, 22*, 612–639.

Seligman, M. E. P. (1975). *Helplessness*. San Francisco: Freeman.

Seligman, M. E. P., Parks, A. C., & Steen, T. (2006). A balanced psychology and a full life. In F. Huppert, B. Keverne, & N. Baylis (Eds.), *The science of well-being* (pp. 275–283), Oxford: Oxford University Press.

Sells, C. W., & Blum, R. W. (1996). Morbidity and mortality among U.S. adolescents: An overview of data and trends. *American Journal of Public Health, 86*, 513–519.

Selman, R. L. (1971). Taking another's perspective: Role-taking development in early childhood. *Child Development, 42*, 1721–1734.

Selman, R. L. (1980). *The growth of interpersonal understanding: Developmental and clinical analysis*. New York: Academic Press.

Selman, R. L. (1994). The relation of role taking to the development of moral judgment in children. In B. Puka (Ed.), *Fundamental research in moral development. Moral development: A compendium*, Vol. 2. (pp. 87–99). New York: Garland.

SeniorJournal.com (2004, September 13). *AoA awards $5.1 million to support seniors aging in place*. Retrieved February 22, 2005, from http://www.seniorjournal.com/NEWS/Eldercare/4-09-13AOA.htm

Sera, M. D., Troyer, D., & Smith, L. B. (1988). What do two-year-olds know about the sizes of things? *Child Development, 59*, 1489–1496.

Serbin, L. A., Powlishta, K. K., & Gulko, J. (1993). The development of sex typing in middle childhood. *Monographs of the Society for Research in Child Development, 58* (Whole No. 232).

Seriido, J., Almeida, D. M., & Wetherington, E. (2004). Chronic stressors and daily hassles: Unique and interactive relationship with psychological distress. *Journal of Health and Social Behavior, 45*, 17–33.

Setterlund, M. B., & Niedenthal, P. M. (1993). "Who am I? Why am I here?": Self-esteem, self-clarity, and prototype matching. *Journal of Personality and Social Psychology, 65*, 769–780.

Sexuality Information and Education Council of the United States. (2001). *Making the connection: Sexuality and reproductive health*. Retrieved November 18, 2001, from http://www.siecus.org/pubs/cnct/cnct0001.html

Shanahan, M. J., & Hofer, S. M. (2005). Social context in gene-environment interactions: Retrospect and prospect. *Journals of Gerontology: Series B: Psychological Sciences and Social Sciences, 60B*, 65–76.

Shapiro, J. P. (2001). Growing old in a good home. *U.S. News and World Report, 130*, 56–61.

Sharpley, C. F. (1997). Psychometric properties of the Self-Perceived Stress in Retirement Scale. *Psychological Reports, 81*, 319–322.

Sharpley, C. F., & Yardley, P. G. (1999). "What makes me happy now that I'm older": A retrospective report of attitudes and strategies used to adjust to retirement as reported by older persons. *Journal of Applied Health Behavior, 1*, 31–35.

Shaver, P. R., Collins, N., & Clark, C. L. (1996). Attachment styles and internal working models of self and relationship partners. In G. J. O. Fletcher & J. Fitness (Eds.), *Knowledge structures in close relationships: A social psychological approach* (pp. 25–61). Hillsdale, NJ: Erlbaum.

Sher, T. G., & Weiss, R. L. (1991). Negativity in marital communication? Where's the beef? Special Issue: Negative communication in marital interaction: A misnomer? *Behavioral Assessment, 13*, 1–5.

Sherkow, S. P. (2001). Reflections on the play state, play interruptions, and the capacity to play alone. *Journal of Clinical Psychoanalysis, 10*(3–4), 531–542.

Sherraden, M. S., & Barrera, R. E. (1996). Maternal support and cultural influences among Mexican immigrant mothers. *Families in Society, 77*, 298–313.

Shibley, P. K. (2000). *The concept of revisitation and the transition to parenthood.* Unpublished doctoral dissertation, Ohio State University.

Shirtcliff, E. A., Dahl, R. E., & Pollack, S. D. (2009). Pubertal development: Correspondence between hormonal and physical development. *Child Development, 80*, 327–337.

Shostak, A., & McLouth, G. (1985). *Men and abortion.* New York: Praeger.

Shrestha, L. B. (2006). Life expectancy in the United States. *CRS Report for Congress.* Congressional Research Service of the Library of Congress.

Siegel, B. (1996). Is the emperor wearing clothes? Social policy and the empirical support for full inclusion of children with disabilities in the preschool and early elementary grades. *Social Policy Report, 10*, 2–17.

Siegler, I. C., Poon, L. W., Madden, D. J., & Welsh, K. A. (1996). Psychological aspects of normal aging. In E. W. Busse & D. G. Blazer (Eds.), *The American Psychiatric Press textbook of geriatric psychiatry* (pp. 105–127). Washington, DC: American Psychiatric Press.

Siegler, R. S. (2000). Unconscious insights. *Current Directions in Psychological Science, 9*, 79–83.

Siegler, R. S., & Stern, E. (1998). A microgenetic analysis of conscious and unconscious strategy discoveries. *Journal of Experimental Psychology: General, 127*, 377–397.

Sigman, M. (1995). Nutrition and child development: More food for thought. *Current Directions in Psychological Science, 4*, 52–55.

Silver, C. B. (2003). Gendered identities in old age: Toward (de)gendering? *Journal of Aging Studies, 17*, 379–397.

Silver, M. (1995). Sex and violence on TV. *U.S. News and World Report, 119*, 62–68.

Silverman, J. G., Decker, M. R., McCauley, H. L., Gupta, J., Miller, E., Raj, A., & Goldberg, A. B. (2010). Male perpetration of intimate partner violence and involvement in abortions and abortion-related conflict. *American Journal of Public Health, 100*, 1415–1417.

Silverstein, A. B., Pearson, L. B., Aguinaldo, N. E., Friedman, S. L., Tokayama, D. L., & Weiss, Z. T. (1982). Identity conservation and equivalence conservation: A question of developmental priority. *Child Development, 53*, 819–821.

Simon, B., & Klandermans, B. (2001). Politicized collective identity. *American Psychologist, 56*, 319–331.

Simon, T. (2002, January 19). Dreaming of the mother who was. *Providence Journal*, p. B7.

Simons, F., Detenber, B. H., Cuthbert, B. N., Schwartz, D. D., & Reiss, J. E. (2003). Attention to Television: Alpha Power and Its Relationship to Image Motion and Emotional Content. *Media Psychology, 5*(3), 283–301.

Simons, R. L., Beaman, J., Conger, R. D., & Chao, W. (1993). Stress, support and antisocial behavior traits as determinants of emotional well-being and parenting practices among single mothers. *Journal of Marriage and the Family, 55*, 385–398.

Simonton, D. K. (1990). Creativity in the later years: Optimistic prospects for achievement. *The Gerontologist, 30*, 626–631.

Simonton, D. K. (1991). Creative productivity through the adult years. *Generations, 15*, 13–16.

Simonton, D. K. (1997). Creative productivity: A predictive and explanatory model of career trajectories and landmarks. *Psychological Review, 104*, 66–89.

Sinclair, W., & Pressinger, R. W. (2001). Environmental causes of infertility. *Infertility & Miscarriage Research Summaries.* Retrieved October 31, 2001, from http://www.chem-tox.com/infertility

Singer, D. G., & Singer, J. L. (1990). *The house of make-believe: Children's play and developing imagination.* Cambridge, MA: Harvard University Press.

Singer, D. G., & Singer, J. L. (2008). Make-believe play, imagination, and creativity: Links to children's media exposure. In S. L. Calvert & B. J. Wilson (Eds.), *The handbook of children, media and development. Handbooks in communication and media* (pp. 290–308). Malden: Blackwell.

Singer, J. L. (1975). *The inner world of daydreaming.* New York: Colophon Books.

Singer, L. T., Davillier, M., Bruening, P., Hawkins, S., & Yamashita, T. S. (1996). Social support, psychological distress, and parenting strains in mothers of very low birth weight infants. *Family Relations, 45*, 343–350.

Singer, W. (1995). Development and plasticity of cortical processing architectures. *Science, 270*, 758–764.

Singh, L., Morgan, J. L., & Best, C. T. (2002). Infants' listening preferences: Baby talk or happy talk? *Infancy, 3*, 365–394.

Sinnott, J. D., & Cavanaugh, J. C. (1991). *Bridging paradigms: Positive development in adulthood and cognitive aging.* New York: Praeger.

Sinoff, G., Iosipovici, A., Almog, R., & Barnett-Greens, O. (2008). Children of the elderly are inept in assessing death anxiety in their own parents. *International Journal of Geriatric Psychiatry, 23*, 1207–1208.

Sipsma, H., Biello, K. B., Cole-Lewis, H., & Kershaw, T. (2010). Like father like son: The intergenerational cycle of adolescent fatherhood. *American Journal of Public Health, 100*, 517–524.

Sirin, S. R. & Fine, M. (2008). *Muslim American youth: Understanding hyphenated identities through multiple methods.* New York: New York University Press.

Sirsch, U., Dreher, E., Mayr, E., & Willinger, U. (2009). What does it take to be an adult in Austria? Views of adulthood in Austrian adolescents, emerging adults and adults. *Journal of Adolescent Research, 24*, 275–292.

Skaalvik, S., & Skaalvik, E. M. (2004). Frames of reference for self-evaluation of ability in mathematics. *Psychological Reports, 94*, 619–632.

Skerrett, K. (1996). From isolation to mutuality: A feminist collaborative model of couples therapy. *Women and Therapy, 19*, 93–106.

Skinner, B. F. (1983). Intellectual self-management in old age. *American Psychologist, 38*, 239–244.

Slade, A. (1987). A longitudinal study of maternal involvement and symbolic play during the toddler period. *Child Development, 58*, 367–375.

Slater, A., Carrick, R., Bell, C., & Roberts, E. (1999). Can measures of infant information processing predict later intellectual ability? In A. Slater & D. Muir (Eds.), *The Blackwell reader in developmental psychology* (pp. 55–64). Malden, MA: Blackwell.

Slater, A., & Johnson, S. P. (1998). Visual sensory and perceptual abilities of the newborn: Beyond the blooming, buzzing confusion. In F. Simion & G. Butterworth (Eds.), *The development of sensory, motor, and cognitive capacities in early infancy: From perception to cognition* (pp. 121–141). Hove, UK: Psychology Press/Erlbaum.

Slavik, S. (1995). Presenting social interest to different life-styles. Special Issue: Counseling homosexuals and bisexuals. *Individual Psychology: Journal of Adlerian Theory, Research and Practice, 51*, 166–177.

Sliwinski, M. J., Hofer, S.M., Hall, C., Buschke, H., & Lipton, R. B. (2003). Modeling memory decline in older adults: The importance of preclinical dementia, attrition, and chronological age. *Psychology and Aging, 18,* 658– 671.

Sliwinski, M., Lipton, R. B., Buschke, H., & Stewart, W. (1996). The effects of pre-clinical dementia on estimates of normal cognitive functioning in aging. *Journal of Gerontology, 51,* P217–P225.

Slobin, D. I. (1985). *The cross-linguistic study of language acquisition* (Vols. 1, 2). Hillsdale, NJ: Erlbaum.

Sloutsky, V. M., & Fisher, A. V. (2004). Induction and categorization in young children: A similarity-based model. *Journal of Experimental Psychology: General, 133,* 166–188.

Slovak, K., & Singer, M. (2001). Gun violence exposure and trauma among rural youth. *Violence and Victims, 16,* 389–400.

Small, R., Rice, P. L., Yelland, J., & Lumley, J. (1999). Mothers in a new country: The role of culture and communication in Vietnamese, Turkish, and Filipino women's experiences of giving birth in Australia. *Women and Health, 28,* 77–101.

Small, S. A., & Kerns, D. (1993). Unwanted sexual activity among peers during early and middle adolescence: Incidence and risk factors. *Journal of Marriage and the Family, 55,* 941–952.

Small, S. A., Silverberg, S. B., & Kerns, D. (1993). Adolescents' perceptions of the costs and benefits of engaging in health-compromising behaviors. *Journal of Youth and Adolescence, 22,* 73–88.

Smedley, A., & Smedley, B. (2005). Race as biology is fiction, racism as a social problem is real: Anthropological and historical perspectives on the social construction of race. *American Psychologist, 60,* 16–26.

Smeeding, T. M. (2008). Poorer by comparison: Poverty, work and public policy in comparative perspective. *Pathways, Winter,* 3–5.

Smetana, J. G. (1985). Preschool children's conceptions of transgressions: Effects of varying moral and conventional domain-related attributes. *Developmental Psychology, 21,* 18–29.

Smetana, J. G. (1986). Preschool children's conceptions of sex-role transgressions. *Child Development, 57,* 862–871.

Smetana, J. G., Daddis, C., & Chuang, S. S. (2003). "Clean your room!" A longitudinal investigation of adolescent-parent conflict and conflict resolution in middle class African American families. *Journal of Adolescent Research, 18,* 631–650.

Smetana, J. G., Schlagman, N., & Adams, P. W. (1993). Preschool children's judgments about hypothetical and actual transgressions. *Child Development, 64,* 202–214.

Smetana, J. G., Yau, J., & Hanson, S. (1991). Conflict resolution in families with adolescents. *Journal of Research on Adolescence, 1,* 189–206.

Smith, A. C., & Smith, D. I. (2001). Emergency and transitional shelter population: 2000. *Census Special Reports,* Series CENSR /01-2. Washington, DC: U.S. Government Printing Office.

Smith, B. A., & Blass, E. M. (1996). Taste-mediated calming in premature, preterm, and full-term human infants. *Developmental Psychology, 32,* 1084–1089.

Smith, D. (2001). Children in the heat of war. *Monitor on Psychology, 32,* 29–31.

Smith, D. C. (1997). *Caregiving: Hospice-proven techniques for healing body and soul.* New York: Macmillan.

Smith, J., & Baltes, P. B. (1999). Life-span perspectives on development. In M. H. Bornstein & M. E. Lamb (Eds.), *Developmental psychology: An advanced textbook* (4th ed., pp. 47–72). Mahwah, NJ: Erlbaum.

Smith, L. B., Jones, S. S., & Landau, B. (1992). Count nouns, adjectives, and perceptual properties in children's novel word interpretations. *Developmental Psychology, 28,* 273–286.

Smith, P. K. (Ed.). (1991). *The psychology of grand-parenthood: An international perspective.* London: Routledge.

Smith, P. K., & Drew, L. M. (2002). Grand-parenthood. In M. H. Bornstein (Ed.), *Handbook of parenting: Vol. 3, Being and becoming a parent* (pp. 141–147). Mahwah, NJ: Erlbaum.

Smith, P. K., Hunter, T., Carvalho, A. M. A., & Costabile, A. (1992). Children's perceptions of play fighting, play chasing and real fighting: A cross-national interview study. *Social Development, 1,* 211–221.

Smith, R. (2000). A good death. *British Medical Journal, 320,* 129–130.

Smith, Y. L. S., van Goozen, S. H. M., & Cohen-Kettenis, P. T. (2001). Adolescents with gender identity disorder who were accepted or rejected for sex reassignment surgery: A prospective follow-up study. *Journal of the American Academy of Child and Adolescent Psychiatry, 40,* 472–481.

Smock, P. J., & Manning, W. D. (1997). Non-resident parents' characteristics and child support. *Journal of Marriage and the Family, 59,* 789–808.

Smolowe, J. (1997). A battle against biology; a victory in adoption. *Time, 150,* p. 46.

Snarey, J. R., Reimer, J., & Kohlberg, L. (1985). Development of social-moral reasoning among kibbutz adolescents: A longitudinal cross-sectional study. *Developmental Psychology, 21,* 3–17.

Snedeker, J., Geren, J., & Shafto, C. I. (2007). Starting over: International adoption as a natural experiment in language development. *Psychological Science, 18,* 79–87.

Snow, C. E. (1984). Parent-child interaction and the development of communicative ability. In R. L. Schiefelbusch & J. Pickar (Eds.), *Communicative competence: Acquisition and intervention* (pp. 69–108). Baltimore: University Park Press.

Snyder, C. R. (1994). *The psychology of hope: You can get there from here.* New York: Free Press.

Snyder, C. R. (2002). Hope theory: Rainbows in the mind. *Psychological Inquiry, 13,* 249–275.

Snyder, C. R., Cheavens, J., & Sympson, S. C. (1997). Hope: An individual motive for social commerce. *Group Dynamics: Theory, Research, and Practice, 1,* 107–118.

Snyder, C. R., Harris, C., Anderson, J. R., Holleran, S. A., Irving, L. M., Sigmon, S. T., et al. (1991). The will and the ways: Development and validation of an individual-differences measure of hope. *Journal of Personality and Social Psychology, 60,* 570–585.

Snyder, H. N., & Sickmund, M. (2006). *Juvenile Offenders and Victims: 2006 National Report.* National Center for Juvenile Justice. Retrieved August 24, 2007, from http://ojjdp.ncjrs.gov/ojstatbb/nr2006/downloads/NR2006.pdf

Sobel, D. M. (2004). Children's developing knowledge of the relationship between mental awareness and pretense. *Child Development, 75,* 704–729.

Soet, J. E., Brack, G. A., & Dilorio, C. (2003). Prevalence and predictors of women's experience of psychological trauma during childbirth. *Birth: Issues in Perinatal Care, 30,* 36–46.

Sokol, R. J., Delaney-Black, V., & Nordstrom, B. (2003). Fetal alcohol spectrum disorder. *Journal of the American Medical Association, 290,* 2996–2999.

Somerfield, M. R., & McCrae, R. R. (2000). Stress and coping research: Methodological challenges, theoretical advances, and clinical applications. *American Psychologist, 55,* 620–625.

Sonfield, A. (2002). Looking at men's sexual and reproductive health needs. *Guttmacher Report on Public Policy, 5.*

Sophian, C. (1998). A developmental perspective in children's counting. In C. Donlan (Ed.), *The development of mathematical skills* (pp. 27–46). Hove, England: Psychology Press/Taylor & Francis.

Sorkin, D. H., & Rook, K. S. (2004). Interpersonal control strivings and vulnerability to negative social exchanges in later life. *Psychology and Aging, 19,* 555–564.

Sorrell, G. T., & Montgomery, M. J. (2001). Feminist perspectives on Erikson's theory: Their relevance for contemporary identity development research. *Identity: An International Journal of Theory and Research, 1,* 97–128.

Sosa, R., Kennell, J., Klaus, M., Robertson, S., & Urrutia, J. (1980). The effect of a supportive companion on perinatal problems, length of labor, and mother-infant interaction. *The New England Journal of Medicine, 303,* 597–600.

Spear, L. P. (2000). The adolescent brain and age-related behavioral manifestations. *Neuroscience and Biobehavioral Reviews, 24,* 417–463.

Spearman, C. (1927). *The abilities of man.* New York: Macmillan.

Speckhard, A. C., & Rue, V. M. (1992). Postabortion syndrome: An emerging public health concern. *Journal of Social Issues, 48,* 95–119.

Spelke, E. S., von Hofsten, C., & Kestenbaum, R. (1989). Object perception in infancy: Interaction of spatial and kinetic information for object boundaries. *Developmental Psychology, 25,* 185–186.

Spencer, M. B. (1982). Personal and group identity of Black children: An alternative synthesis. *Genetic Psychology Monographs, 103,* 59–84.

Spencer, M. B. (2006). Revisiting the 1990 *Special Issue on Minority Children:* An editorial perspective 15 years later. *Child Development, 77,* 1149–1154.

Spencer, M. B., Cunningham, M., & Swanson, D. P. (1995). Identity as coping: Adolescent African-American males' adaptive responses to high-risk environments. In H. W. Harris, H. C. Blue, & E. E. H. Griffith (Eds.), *Racial and ethnic identity: Psychological development and creative expression* (pp. 31–52). New York: Routledge.

Spencer, M. B., & Markstrom-Adams, C. (1990). Identity processes among racial and ethnic minority children in America. *Child Development, 61,* 290–310.

Sperlich, M. & Seng, J. (2008). *Survivor moms: Women's stories of birthing, mothering and healing after sexual abuse.* Eugene, OR: Motherbaby Press.

Sperling, D. (1989, March 10). Success rate for in vitro is only 9%. *USA Today,* p. 1D.

Spitz, R. A. (1945). Hospitalism: An inquiry into the genesis of psychiatric conditions in early childhood. *Psychoanalytic Study of the Child, 1,* 113–117.

Spitz, R. A. (1946). Anaclitic depression. *Psychoanalytic Study of the Child, 2,* 313–342.

Spitze, G., & Logan, J. (1990). Sons, daughters, and intergenerational social support. *Journal of Marriage and the Family, 52,* 420–430.

SPLC Report. (2010, Spring). New SPLC film to address anti-gay bullying in schools, p. 5.

Sprecher, S., Sullivan, Q., & Hatfield, E. (1994). Mate selection preferences: Gender differences examined in a national sample. *Journal of Personality and Social Psychology, 66,* 1074–1080.

Spurlock, J. C., & Magistro, C. A. (1998). *New and improved: The transformation of American women's emotional culture.* New York: New York University Press.

Sroufe, L. A., & Fleeson, J. (1986). Attachment and the construction of relationships. In W. W. Hartup & Z. Rubin (Eds.), *Relationships and development* (pp. 51–72). Hillsdale, NJ: Erlbaum.

Stack, D. M., & Muir, D. W. (1992). Adult tactile stimulation during face-to-face interactions modulates five-month-olds' affect and attention. *Child Development, 63,* 1509–1525.

Stack, S. (1990). The impact of divorce on suicide, 1959–1980. *Journal of Marriage and the Family, 52,* 119–128.

Stake, R. E. (1998). Case studies. In N. K. Denzin & Y. S. Lincoln (Eds.), *Strategies of qualitative inquiry* (pp. 86–109). Thousand Oaks, CA: Sage.

Stallings, J. A. (1995). Ensuring teaching and learning in the 21st century. *Educational Researcher, 24,* 4–8.

Standley, K., Soule, B., & Copans, S. A. (1979). Dimensions of prenatal anxiety and their influence on pregnancy outcome. *American Journal of Obstetrics and Gynecology, 135,* 22–26.

Stapley, J. C., & Haviland, J. M. (1989). Beyond depression: Gender differences in normal adolescents' emotional experiences. *Sex Roles, 20,* 295–308.

Stattin, H., & Klackenberg-Larsson, I. (1991). The short-and long-term implications for parent-child relations of parents' prenatal preferences for their child's gender. *Developmental Psychology, 27,* 141–147.

Staudinger, U. M., Dorner, J., & Mickler, C. (2005). Wisdom and personality. In R. J. Sternberg & J. Jordan (Eds.), *A handbook of wisdom: Psychological perspectives* (pp. 191–219). New York: Cambridge University Press.

Stechler, G., & Halton, A. (1982). Prenatal influences on human development. In B. B. Wolman (Ed.), *Handbook of developmental psychology* (pp. 175–189). Englewood Cliffs, NJ: Prentice Hall.

Steele, K. (2010). *Biking and walking in the U.S. 2010: Benchmark report.* Washington, DC: Alliance for Biking and Walking.

Stein, C. H. (2009). "I owe it to them": Understanding felt obligation toward parents in adulthood. In K. Shifren (Ed.), *How caregiving affects development: Psychological implications for child, adolescent, and adult caregivers* (pp. 119–145). Washington, DC: American Psychological Association.

Steinberg, L. (2001). We know some things: Parent-adolescent relationships in retrospect and prospect. *Journal of Research on Adolescence, 11,* 1–19.

Steinberg, L. (2005). *Adolescence* (7th ed.). Boston: McGraw-Hill.

Steinhauser, K. E., Christakis, N. A., Clipp, E. C., McNeilly, M., Grambow, S., Parker, J., & Tulsky, J. A. (2001). Preparing for the end of life: Preferences of patients, families, physicians, and other care providers. *Journal of Pain and Symptom Management, 22,* 727–737.

Stephan, Y. (2009). Openness to experience and active older adults' life satisfaction: A trait and facet-level analysis. *Personality and Individual Differences, 47,* 637–641.

Stern, G. (2007, Ocober 28). Hospice worker attends to spiritual needs of the dying. *The Journal News,* Retrieved October 31, 2007 from http://www.thejournalnews.com/apps/pbcs.dll/article?AID=2007710280354

Sternberg, R. J. (1985). *Beyond IQ: A triarchic theory of human intelligence.* Cambridge, UK: Cambridge University Press.

Sternberg, R. J. (1988). *The triangle of love.* New York: Basic Books.

Sternberg, R. J. (1990). *Wisdom: Its nature, origins and development.* New York: Cambridge University Press.

Sternberg, R. J., Castejon, J. L., Prieto, M. D., Hautamaki, J., & Grigorenko, E. L. (2001). Confirmatory factor analysis of the Sternberg Triarchic Abilities Test in three international samples: An empirical test of the triarchic theory of intelligence. *European*

Journal of Psychological Assessment, 17, 1–16.

Sternberg, R. J., Grigorenko, E. L., & Singer, J. (2004). *Creativity: From potential to realization.* Washington, DC: American Psychological Association.

Sternberg, R. J., Torff, B., & Grigorenko, E. L. (1998). Teaching triarchically improves school achievement. *Journal of Educational Psychology, 90,* 374–384.

Stets, J. E., & Harrod, M. M. (2004). Verification across multiple identities: The role of status. *Social Psychology Quarterly, 67,* 155–171.

Stevens, J. H., Jr. (1988). Social support, locus of control, and parenting in three low-income groups of mothers: Black teenagers, Black adults, and White adults. *Child Development, 59,* 635–642.

Stevens, J. H., Jr., & Bakeman, R. (1985). A factor analytic study of the HOME scale for infants. *Developmental Psychology, 21,* 1196–1203.

Stevens-Long, J., & Commons, M. L. (1992). *Adult life: Developmental processes* (4th ed.). Mountain View, CA: Mayfield.

Stevens-Roseman, E. S. (2009). Older mentors for newer workers: Impact of a worker-driven intervention on later life satisfaction. *Journal of Workplace Behavioral Health, 24,* 419–426.

Stevenson, D. L., & Baker, D. P. (1987). The family-school relation and the child's school performance. *Child Development, 58,* 1348–1357.

Stevenson, H. W. (1992, December). Learning from Asian schools. *Scientific American, 267*(6), 70–77.

Stevenson, H. W., Chen, C., & Lee, S. (1993). Mathematics achievement of Chinese, Japanese, and American children: Ten years later. *Science, 259,* 53–58.

Stewart, A. J., & Vandewater, E. A. (1998). The course of generativity. In D. P. McAdams & E. de St. Aubin (Eds.), *Generativity and adult development* (pp. 75–100). Washington, DC: American Psychological Association.

Stice, E., & Shaw, H. (2002). Role of body dissatisfaction in the onset and maintenance of eating pathology: A synthesis of research findings. *Journal of Psychosomatic Research, 53,* 985–993.

Stice, E., & Shaw, H. (2004). Eating disorder prevention programs: A meta-analytic review. *Psychological Bulletin, 130,* 206–227.

Sticker, E. J. (1991). The importance of grandparenthood during the life cycle in Germany. In P. K. Smith (Ed.), *The psychology of grandparenthood: An international perspective* (pp. 32–49). London: Routledge.

Stinebrickner, T., & Stinebrickner, R. (2006). *The effect of credit constraints on the college drop out decision: A direct approach using a new panel study.* Unpublished manuscript. Retrieved September 11, 2007, from http://www.economics.uwo.ca/faculty/Stinebrickner/recentpapers/effectofcredit.pdf

Stipek, D., Recchia, S., & McClintic, S. (1992). Self-evaluation in young children. *Monographs of the Society for Research in Child Development, 57* (1, Serial No. 226).

Stoller, E. P., & Longino, C. F., Jr. (2001). "Going home" or "leaving home"? The impact of person and place ties on anticipated counterstream migration. *The Gerontologist, 41,* 96–102.

Strachan, S. M., Brawley, L. R., Spink, K., & Glazebrook, K. (2010). Older adults' physically-active identity: Relationships between social cognitions, physical activity, and satisfaction with life. *Psychology of Sport and Exercise, 11,* 114–121.

Strasburger, V. C., Wilson, B. J., & Jordan, A. B. (2009). *Children, adolescents and the media* (2nd ed.). Thousand Oaks, CA: Sage.

Strauss, K., Griffin, M. A., & Rafferty, A. E. (2009). Proactivity directed toward the team and organization: The role of leadership, commitment and role-breadth self-efficacy. *British Journal of Management, 20,* 279–291.

Streissguth, A. P., Barr, H. M., Sampson, P. D., Darby, B. L., & Martin, D. C. (1989). IQ at age 4 in relation to maternal alcohol use and smoking during pregnancy. *Developmental Psychology, 25,* 3–11.

Streri, A. (2005). Touching for knowing in infancy: The development of manual abilities in very young infants. *European Journal of Developmental Psychology, 2,* 325–343.

Stress and coping research: Methodological challenges, theoretical advances, and clinical applications. *American Psychologist, 55,* 620–625.

Stright, A. D., Neitzel, C., Sears, K. G., & Hoke-Sinex, L. (2001). Instruction begins in the home: Relations between parental instruction and children's self-regulation in the classroom. *Journal of Educational Psychology, 93,* 456–466.

Stringfellow, L. (1978). The Vietnamese. In A. L. Clark (Ed.), *Culture, childbearing, and the health professionals* (pp. 174–182). Philadelphia: Davis.

Strober, M. (1981). A comparative analysis of personality organization in juvenile anorexia nervosa. *Journal of Youth and Adolescence, 10,* 285–295.

Stromquist, N. P. (1991). *Daring to be different: The choice of nonconventional fields of study by international women.* New York: Institute of International Education.

Strouse, D. L. (1999). Adolescent crowd orientations: A social and temporal analysis. In J. A. McLellan & M. J. V. Pugh (Eds.), *The role of peer groups in adolescent social identity: Exploring the importance of stability and change* (pp. 37–54). San Francisco: Jossey-Bass.

Stuart-Hamilton, I. (1996). Intellectual changes in late life. In R. T. Woods (Ed.), *Handbook of the clinical psychology of ageing* (pp. 23–41). Oxford, England: John Wiley & Sons.

Subrahmanyam, K., Kraut, R., Greenfield, P., & Gross, E. (2001). New forms of electronic media. In D. Singer & J. Singer (Eds.), *Handbook of children and the family* (pp. 73–99). Thousand Oaks, CA: Sage.

Sui, J., Liu, C. H., & Han, S. (2009). Cultural difference in neural mechanisms of self-recognition. *Social Neuroscience, 4,* 402–411.

Sullivan, H. S. (1949). *The collected works of Harry Stack Sullivan* (Vols. 1, 2). New York: Norton.

Sullivan, H. S. (1953). *The interpersonal theory of psychiatry.* New York: Norton.

Sullivan, K., & Sullivan, A. (1980). Adolescent-parent separation. *Developmental Psychology, 16,* 93–104.

Sullivan, M. D. (2003). Hope and hopelessness at the end of life. *American Journal of Geriatric Psychiatry, 11,* 393–405.

Sullivan, M. W., Lewis, M., & Allesandri, S. M. (1992). Cross-age stability in emotional expressions during learning and extinction. *Developmental Psychology, 28,* 58–63.

Sun, S. S., Schubert, C. M., et al. (2005). Is sexual maturity occurring earlier among U.S. children? *Journal of Adolescent Health, 37,* 345–355.

Super, C. M., Kagan, J., Morrison, F. J., Haith, M. M., & Weiffenbach, J. (1972). Discrepancy and attention in the five-month infant. *Genetic Psychology Monographs, 85,* 305–331.

Susman, E. J., Dorn, L. D., & Chrousos, G. P. (1991). Negative hormones and affect levels in young adolescents: Concurrent and predictive perspectives. *Journal of Youth and Adolescence, 20,* 167–190.

Swann, W. B., Jr. (1990). To be known or be adored? The interplay of self-enhancement and self-verification. In E. T. Higgins & R. M. Sorrentino (Eds.), *Handbook of motivation and cognition: Foundations of social behavior* (pp. 404–448). New York: Guilford Press.

Swing, E. L., & Anderson, C. A. (2007). The unintended negative consequences of exposure to violent video games. *International Journal of Cognitive Technology, 12,* 3–13.

Swingley, D. (2007). Lexical exposure and word-form encoding in 1.5-year olds. *Developmental Psychology, 43,* 454–464.

Swisher, R., Sweet, S., & Moen, P. L. (2004). The family-friendly community and its life course fit for dual earner couples. *Journal of Marriage and the Family, 66,* 281–292.

Swyer, P. R. (1987). The organization of perinatal care with particular reference to the newborn. In G. B. Avery (Ed.), *Neonatology: Pathophysiology and management of the newborn* (pp. 13–44). Philadelphia: Lippincott.

Syed, M., & Azmitia, M. (2009). Longitudinal trajectories of ethnic identity during the college years. *Journal of Research on Adolescence, 19,* 587–600.

Tainaka, K., Takizawa, T., Katamoto, S., & Aoki, J. (2009). Six-year prospective study of physical fitness and incidents of disability among community-dwelling Japanese elderly women. *Geriatrics and Gerontology International, 9,* 21–28.

Tajfel, H. (1981). *Human groups and social categories.* Cambridge, UK: Cambridge University Press.

Takahashi, L. K., Baker, E. W., & Kalin, N. H. (1990). Ontogeny of behavioral and hormonal responses to stress in prenatally stressed male rat pups. *Physiology and Behavior, 47,* 357–364.

Takahashi, L. K., & Kalin, N. H. (1991). Early developmental and temporal characteristics of stress-induced secretion of pituitary-adrenal hormones in prenatally stressed rat pups. *Brain Research, 558,* 75–78.

Takata, Y., Ansai, T., et al. (2010). Quality of life and physical fitness in an 85-year-old population. *Archives of Gerontology and Geriatrics, 50,* 272–276.

Tallman, I., & Hsiao, Y.-L. (2004). Resources, cooperation, and problem solving in early marriages. *Social Psychology Quarterly, 67,* 172–188.

Tamis-LeMonda, C. S., Uzgiris, I. C., & Bornstein, M. H. (2002). Play in parent-child interactions. In M. H. Bornstein (Ed.), *Handbook of parenting. Vol. 5: Practical issues in parenting* (pp. 221–242). Mahwah, NJ: Erlbaum.

Tanfer, K. (1987). Premarital cohabitation among never-married women. *Journal of Marriage and the Family, 49,* 483–497.

Tang, C. S. K., Wong, C. S. Y., & Schwarzer, R. (1996). Psychosocial differences between occasional and regular adolescent users of marijuana and heroin. *Journal of Youth and Adolescence, 25,* 219–239.

Tang, C. S. K., Yeung, D. Y., & Lee, A. M. (2003). Psychosocial correlates of emotional responses to menarche among Chinese adolescent girls. *Journal of Adolescent Health, 33,* 193–201.

Tangney, J. P. (1991). Moral affect: The good, the bad, and the ugly. *Journal of Personality and Social Psychology, 61,* 598–607.

Tangney, J. P. (2001). Constructive and destructive aspects of shame and guilt. In A. C. Bohart & D. J. Stipek (Eds.), *Constructive and destructive behavior: Implications for family, school and society* (pp. 127–145). Washington, DC: American Psychological Association.

Tangney, J. P., Baumeister, R. F., & Boone, A. L. (2004). High self-control predicts good adjustment, less pathology, better grades, and interpersonal success. *Journal of Personality, 72,* 271–322.

Tangney, J. P., & Dearing, R. L. (2002). *Shame and guilt.* New York: Guilford Press.

Tangney, J. P., & Mashek, D. J. (2004). In search of the moral person: Do you have to feel really bad to be good? In J. Greenberg, S. L. Koole, & T. Pyszczynski, (Eds.) *Handbook of experimental existential psychology* (pp. 156–166). New York: Guilford Press.

Tangney, J. P., Wagner, P., Fletcher, C., & Gramzow, R. (1992). Shamed into anger? The relation of shame and guilt to anger and self-reported aggression. *Journal of Personality and Social Psychology, 62,* 669–675.

Tanner, E. M. & Finn-Stevenson, M. (2002). Nutrition and brain development: Social policy implications. *American Journal of Orthopsychiatry, 72,* 182–193.

Tanner, J. M. (1990). *Foetus into man: Physical growth from conception to maturity* (rev. ed.). Cambridge, MA: Harvard University Press.

Task Force on Community Preventive Services (2007). *The effectiveness of universal school-based programs for the prevention of violent and aggressive behavior.* Retrieved August 14, 2007, from http://www.cdc.gov/mmwr/preview/mmwrhtml/rr5607al.htm?s_cid=rr5607al_e

Tausig, M., & Fenwick, R. (2001). Unbinding time: Alternate work schedules and work-life balance. *Journal of Family and Economic Issues, 22,* 101–119.

Taylor, H. G., Klein, N., Minich, N. M., & Hack, M. (2000). Middle-school-age outcomes in children with very low birth weight. *Child Development, 71,* 1495–1511.

Taylor, J., & Turner, R. J. (2001). A longitudinal study of the role and significance of mattering to others for depressive symptoms. *Journal of Health and Social Behavior, 42,* 310–325.

Taylor, M., Cartwright, B. S., & Carlson, S. M. (1993). A developmental investigation of children's imaginary companions. *Developmental Psychology, 29,* 276–285.

Taylor, M., & Mannering, A. M. (2006). Of Hobbes and Harvey: The imaginary companions created by children and adults. In A. Göncü & S. Gaskins (Eds.), *Play and development: Evolutionary, sociocultural, and functional perspectives.* (pp. 227–245). The Jean Piaget symposium series. Mahwah, NJ: Lawrence Erlbaum.

Taylor, R. D., & Oskay, G. (1995). Identity formation in Turkish and American late adolescents. *Journal of Cross-Cultural Psychology, 26,* 8–22.

Taylor, R. J. (1986). Religious participation among elderly Blacks. *The Gerontologist, 26,* 630–636.

Taylor, R. J., Chatters, L. M., Tucker, M. B., & Lewis, E. (1990). Black families. *Journal of Marriage and the Family, 52,* 993–1014.

Taylor, S. E., Way, B.M., Welch, W.T., Hilmert, C.J., Lehman, B.J., & Eisenberger, N. I. (2006). Early family environment, cultural adversity, the serotonin transporter promoter polymorphism and depressive symptomatology. *Biological Psychiatry, 60,* 671–676.

Taylor, S. J. (1987) "They're not like you and me": Institutional attendants' perspectives on residents. *Children and Youth Services, 8,* 109–125.

Taylor, S. J., & Bogdan, R. (1998). *Introduction to qualitative research methods* (3rd ed.). New York: Wiley.

Taylor, W. C., Blair, S. N., Cummings, S. S., Wun, C. C., & Malina, R. M. (1999). Childhood and adolescent physical activity patterns and adult physical activity. *Medicine and Science in Sports and Exercise, 31,* 118–123.

Teachman, J. D., Polonko, K. A., & Scanzoni, J. (1987). Demography of the family. In M. B. Sussman & S. K. Steinmetz (Eds.), *Handbook of marriage and the family* (pp. 3–57). New York: Plenum Press.

Teller, D. Y., & Bornstein, J. H. (1987). Infant color vision and color perception. In P. Salapatek & L. Cohen (Eds.), *Handbook of infant perception* (Vol. 1). Orlando, FL: Academic Press.

Tennen, H., Affleck, G., Armeli, S., & Carney, M.A. (2000). A daily process approach to coping: Linking theory, research, and practice. *American Psychologist, 55,* 626–636.

Teno, J. M., Clarridge, B. R., Casey, V., Welch, L. C., Wetle, T., Shield, R., & More, V. (2004). Family perspectives on end-of-life care at the last place of care. *Journal of the American Medical Association, 291,* 88–93.

Teong, S. K. (2003). The effect of metacognitive training on mathematical word-problem solving. *Journal of Computer Assisted Learning, 19,* 46–55.

Terman, L. M., & Oden, M. H. (1947). *The gifted child grows up: Twenty-five years' follow-up of a superior group.* Stanford, CA: Stanford University Press.

Terman, L. M., & Oden, M. H. (1959). *The gifted group at mid-life: Thirty-five years' follow-up of a superior group.* Stanford, CA: Stanford University Press.

Terry-Humen, E., Manlove, J., & Cottingham, S. (2006). Trends and recent estimates: Sexual activity among U.S. teens. *Child Trends Research Brief, Publication #2006-08.*

Teti, D. M., & Lamb, M. E. (1989). Outcomes of adolescent marriage and adolescent childbirth. *Journal of Marriage and the Family, 51,* 203–212.

Thabes, V. (1997). Survey analysis of women's long-term postdivorce adjustment. *Journal of Divorce and Remarriage, 27,* 163–175.

Tharp, R. G. (1989). Psychocultural variables and constants: Effects on teaching and learning in schools. *American Psychologist, 44,* 349–359.

Tharp, R. G., & Gallimore, R. (1988). *Rousing minds to life: Teaching, learning, and schooling in social context.* Cambridge, UK: Cambridge University Press.

The Chronicle of Higher Education. (2005, August 26). *Almanac.*

The Names Project Foundation. (2005). *History of the quilt.* Retrieved March 10, 2005, from http://www.aidsquilt.org/history.htm

The Names Project Foundation. (2007). The AIDS Memorial Quilt. Retrieved on September 4, 2010, at www.aidsquilt.org/index.htm

The Retirement-Lounge.com (2010). Retirement—It's great to be out of the rat race. Retrieved on August 28, 2010, at http://www.retirement-lounge.com/index.html

Thelen, E. (1995). Motor development: A new synthesis. *American Psychologist, 50,* 79–95.

Thelen, E., & Fisher, D. M. (1982). Newborn stepping: An explanation for a "disappearing" reflex. *Developmental Psychology, 18,* 760–775.

Thelen, E., Fisher, D. M., & Ridley-Johnson, R. (1984). The relationship between physical growth and a newborn reflex. *Infant Behavior and Development, 7,* 479–493.

Thelen, E., & Smith, L. B. (1994). *A dynamic systems approach to the development of cognition and action.* Cambridge, MA: MIT Press.

Thoits, P. A. (1999). Self, identity, stress, and mental health. In C. S. Aneshensel & J. C. Phelan (Eds.), *Handbook of sociology of mental health* (pp. 345–368). New York: Kluwer Academic/Plenum.

Thomas, A., & Chess, S. (1977). *Temperament and development.* New York: Brunner/Mazel.

Thomas, A., & Chess, S. (1980). *The dynamics of psychological development.* New York: Brunner/Mazel.

Thomas, A., & Chess, S. (1986). The New York longitudinal study: From infancy to early adult life. In R. Plomin & J. Dunn (Eds.), *The study of temperament: Changes, continuities, and challenges.* Hillsdale, NJ: Erlbaum.

Thomas, A., Chess, S., & Birch, H. (1970). The origin of personality. *Scientific American, 223,* 102–109.

Thomas, M. H., & Drabman, R. S. (1977). *Effects of television violence on expectations of others' aggression.* Paper presented at the annual convention of the American Psychological Association, San Francisco, CA.

Thomas, V., & Striegel, P. (1994–1995). Stress and grief of a perinatal loss: Integrating qualitative and quantitative methods. *Omega: Journal of Death and Dying, 30,* 299–311.

Thompson, C. (2007, August 20). Why New Yorkers last longer. *New York,* pp. 28–33, 93.

Thompson, L. (1993). Conceptualizing gender in marriage: The case of marital care. *Journal of Marriage and the Family, 55,* 557–569.

Thompson, L. W., Gallagher-Thompson, D., Futterman, A., Gilewski, M. J., & Peterson, J. (1991). The effects of late-life spousal bereavement over a 30-month interval. *Psychology and Aging, 6,* 434–441.

Thompson, R. A. (1990). Emotion and self-regulation. In R. A. Thompson (Ed.), *Nebraska Symposium on Motivation, 1988* (Vol. 36, pp. 367–467). Lincoln: University of Nebraska Press.

Thompson, R. A., Connell, J. P., & Bridges, L. J. (1988). Temperament, emotion, and social interactive behavior in the strange situation: A component process analysis of attachment system functioning. *Child Development, 59,* 1102–1110.

Thomson, E., & Colella, U. (1992). Cohabitation and marital stability: Quality or commitment? *Journal of Marriage and the Family, 54,* 259–267.

Thornton, A., Axinn, W. G., & Teachman, J. D. (1995). The influence of school enrollment and accumulation on cohabitation and marriage in early adulthood. *American Sociological Review, 60,* 762–774.

Thornton, A., & Camburn, D. (1989). Religious participation and adolescent sexual behavior. *Journal of Marriage and the Family, 51,* 641–654.

Thornton, A., & Young-DeMarco, L. (2001). Four decades of trends in attitudes toward family issues in the United States: The 1960s through the 1990s. *Journal of Marriage and the Family, 63,* 1009–1037.

Thornton, A., Young-DeMarco, L., & Goldscheider, F. (1993). Leaving the parental nest: The experience of a young wife cohort in the 1980s. *Journal of Marriage and the Family, 55,* 216–229.

Thorpe, I. (2001). *Ian Thorpe's home page.* Retrieved October 21, 2001, from http://www.ianthorpe.telstra.com.au/

Thwaites, R., & Dagnan, D. (2004). Moderating variables in the relationship between social comparison and depression: An evolutionary perspective. *Psychology & Psychotherapy: Theory, Research & Practice, 77,* 309–323.

Tichauer, R. (1963). The Aymara children of Bolivia. *Journal of Pediatrics, 62,* 399–412.

Tiedeman, D. V., & Miller-Tiedeman, A. (1985). The trend of life in the human career. *Journal of Career Development, 11,* 221–250.

Tiedeman, D. V., & O'Hara, R. P. (1963). *Career development: Choice and adjustment.* New York: College Entrance Examination Board.

Tiedje, L. G. (2004). Processes of change in work/home incompatibilities: Employed mothers 1986–1999. *Journal of Social Issues, 60,* 787–800.

Timberlake, J. M., & Heuveline, P. (2005). Changes in nonmarital cohabitation and the family structure experiences of children across 17 countries. In L.E. Bass (Ed.), *Sociological studies of children and youth: Special international volume, Vol. 10:* Elsevier Science/JAI Press, pp. 257–278.

Tinsley, V. S., & Waters, H. S. (1982). The development of verbal control over motor behavior: A replication and extension of Luria's findings. *Child Development, 53,* 746–753.

Tither, J. M., & Ellis, B. J. (2008). Impact of fathers on daughters' age at menarche: A genetically and environmentally controlled sibling study. *Developmental Psychology, 44,* 1409–1420.

Tizaer, B., & Hughes, M. (1984). *Young children learning.* London: Fontana.

Tolman, E. C. (1932/1967). *Purposive behavior in rats and men.* New York: Appleton-Century-Crofts.

Tolman, E. C. (1948). Cognitive maps in rats and men. *Psychological Review, 55,* 189–208.

Tomarken, A. J., Dichter, G. S., Garber, J., & Simien, C. (2004). Resting frontal brain activity: Linkages to maternal depression and socio-economic status among adolescents. *Biological Psychology, 67,* 77–102.

Tomasello, M. (2006). Acquiring linguistic constructions. In D. Kuhn, R. S. Siegler, W. Damon, & R. M. Lerner (Eds.), *Handbook of child psychology: Vol. 2, Cognition, perception, and language* (6th ed., pp. 255–298). Hoboken, NJ: John Wiley & Sons.

Tomer, A., & Eliason, G. (2000). Attitudes about life and death: Toward a comprehensive model of death anxiety. In A. Tomer (Ed.), *Death attitudes and the older adult: Theories, concepts, and applications* (pp. 3–22). New York: Brunner-Routledge.

Toohey, S. B., Shinn, M., & Weitzman, B. C. (2004). Social networks and homelessness among women heads of household. *American Journal of Community Psychology, 33,* 7–20.

Torbert, W. R. (1994). Cultivating postformal adult development: Higher stages and contrasting interventions. In M. E. Miller & S. R. Cook-Greuter (Eds.), *Transcendence and mature thought in adulthood: The further reaches of adult development* (pp. 181–203). Lanham, MD: Rowman & Littlefield.

Tornstam, L. (2005). *Gerotranscendence: A developmental theory of positive aging.* New York: Springer.

Toth, S. L., Rogosch, F. A., Sturge-Apple, M., & Cicchetti, D. (2009). Maternal depression, children's attachment security, and representational development: An organizational perspective. *Child Development, 80,* 192–208.

Touron, D. R., & Hertzog, C. (2004). Distinguishing age differences in knowledge, strategy use, and confidence during strategic skill acquisition. *Psychology and Aging, 19,* 452–466.

Tracy, J. L., Shaver, P. R., Albino, A. W., & Cooper, M. L. (2003). Attachment styles and adolescent sexuality. In P. Florsheim (Ed.), *Adolescent romantic relationships and sexual behavior: Theory, research, and practical implications* (pp. 137–159). Mahwah, NJ: Erlbaum.

Tracy, R. L., & Ainsworth, M. D. S. (1981). Maternal affectionate behavior and infant-mother attachment patterns. *Child Development, 52,* 1341–1343.

Tracy, S. J., Lutgen-Sandvik, P., & Alberts, J. K. (2006). Nightmares, demons, and slaves: Exploring the painful metaphor of workplace bullying. *Management Communication Quarterly, 20,* 148–185.

Trawick-Smith, J. (1988). "Let's say you're the baby, OK?": Play leadership and following behavior of young children. *Young Children, 43,* 51–59.

Tremblay, R. E., Nagin, D. S., Séguin, J. R., Zoccolillo, M., Zelazo, P. D., Boivin, M., et al., (2004). Physical aggression during early childhood: Trajectories and predictors. *Pediatrics, 114,* 43–50.

Trethowan, W. (1972). The couvade syndrome. In J. Howells (Ed.), *Modern perspectives in psycho-obstetrics.* New York: Brunner/Mazel.

Trevarthen, C., & Aitken, K. J. (2001). Infant intersubjectivity: Research, theory, and clinical applications. *Journal of Child Psychology and Psychiatry and Allied Disciplines, 42,* 3–48.

Triandis, H. C. (1990). Cross-cultural studies of individualism and collectivism. In J. J. Berman (Ed.), *Nebraska Symposium on Motivation, 1989: Cross-cultural perspectives* (pp. 41–133). Lincoln: University of Nebraska Press.

Triandis, H. C. (1994). *Culture and social behavior.* New York: McGraw-Hill.

Triandis, H. C. (Ser. Ed.). (1995). *New directions in social psychology: Individualism and collectivism.* Boulder, CO: Westview Press.

Triandis, H. C. (1998). Vertical and horizontal individualism and collectivism: Theory and research implications for international comparative management. In J. L. C. Cheng & R. B. Peterson (Eds.), *Advances in international comparative management* (Vol. 12, pp. 7–35). Stamford, CT: JAI Press.

Triandis, H. C., Lambert, W., Berry, J., Lonner, W., Heron, A., Brislin, R., & Draguns, J. (Eds.). (1980). *Handbook of cross-cultural psychology: Vols. 1–6.* Boston: Allyn & Bacon.

Trionfi, G., & Reese, E. (2009). A good story: Children with imaginary companions create richer narratives. *Child Development, 80,* 1301–1313.

Troiden, R. R. (1993). The formation of homosexual identities. In L. D. Garnets & D. C. Kimmel (Eds.), *Psychological perspectives on lesbian and gay male experiences. Between men—between women* (pp. 191–217). New York: Columbia University Press.

Tronick, E. Z. (1989). Emotions and emotional communication in infants. *American Psychologist, 44,* 112–119.

Tronick, E. Z. (2003). Emotions and emotional communication with others. In J. Raphael-Leff (Ed.), *Parent-infant psychodynamics: Wild things, mirrors, and ghosts* (pp. 35–53). London: Whurr.

Tronick, E. Z., Als, H., & Brazelton, R. B. (1979). Early development of neonatal and infant behavior. In F. Falkner & J. M. Tanner (Eds.), *Human growth, Vol. 3, Neurobiology and nutrition* (pp. 305–328). New York: Plenum Press.

Tronick, E. Z., & Cohn, J. F. (1989). Infants-mother face-to-face interaction: Age and gender differences in coordination and the occurrence of miscoordination. *Child Development, 60,* 85–92.

Trumbull, E., Rothstein-Fisch, C., & Greenfield, P. M. (2000). *Bridging cultures in our schools: New approaches that work.* Retrieved June 18, 2004, from http://www.wested.org/online_pubs/bridging/ref.shtml

Trzesniewski, K. H., Donnellan, M. B., & Robins, R. W. (2003). Stability of self-esteem across the life span. *Journal of Personality and Social Psychology, 84,* 205–220.

Tsao, D. (2006). A dedicated system for processing faces. *Science, 314,* 72-73.

Tsao, F.-M., Liu, H.-M., & Kuhl, P. K. (2004). Speech perception in infancy predicts language development in the second year of life: A longitudinal study. *Child Development, 75,* 1067–1084.

Tschann, J. M., Johnston, J. R, & Wallerstein, J. S. (1989). Factors in adults' adjustment after divorce. *Journal of Marriage and the Family, 51,* 1033–1046.

Tucker, M. B., Taylor, R. J., & Mitchell-Kernan, C. (1993). Marriage and romantic involvement among aged African Americans. *Journal of Gerontology, 48,* S123– S132.

Tucker-Drob, E. M. (2009). Differentiation of cognitive abilities across the life span. *Developmental Psychology, 45,* 1097–1118.

Tudge, J., Putnam, S., & Valsiner, J. (1996). Culture and cognition in developmental perspective. In R. B. Cairns, G. H. Elder Jr., & E. J. Costello (Eds.), *Developmental science* (pp. 190–222). Cambridge, UK: Cambridge University Press.

Tudge, J. R. H. (1992). Processes and consequences of peer collaboration: A Vygotskian analysis. *Child Development, 63,* 1364–1379.

Tudge, J. R. H., & Winterhoff, P. A. (1993). Vygotsky, Piaget, and Bandura: Perspectives on the relations between the social world and cognitive development. *Human Development, 36,* 61–81.

Turiel, E. (1983). *The development of social knowledge: Morality and convention.* Cambridge, UK: Cambridge University Press.

Turiel, E. (2002). *The culture of morality: Social development, context, and conflict.* Cambridge, UK: Cambridge University Press.

Turiel, E. (2003). Resistance and subversion in everyday life. *Journal of Moral Education, 32,* 397–409.

Turiel, E. (2006). Social hierarchy, social conflicts and moral development. In C. Daiute, Z. Beykont, C. Higson-Smith, & L. Nucci (Eds.). *International perspectives on youth conflict and development.* New York: Oxford University Press, pp. 86–99.

Turner, J. S., & Rubinson, L. (1993). *Contemporary human sexuality.* Englewood Cliffs, NJ: Prentice Hall.

Turner, P. J., & Gervai, J. (1995). A multidimensional study of gender typing in preschool children and their parents: Personality, attitudes, preferences, behavior, and cultural differences. *Developmental Psychology, 31,* 759–772.

Twain, M. (1962). *The Adventures of Huckleberry Finn.* New York: Scholastic Book Services.

Tyler, R., Howard, J., Espinosa, M., & Doakes, S. S. (1997). Placement with substance-abusing mothers vs. placement with other relatives: Infant outcomes. *Child Abuse and Neglect, 21,* 337–349.

Tyson, P. (1996). Object relations, affect management, and psychic structure formation: The concept of object constancy. *Psychoanalytic Study of the Child, 51,* 172–189.

Tyson, P., & Tyson, R. L. (1995). Development. In B. R. Moore & B. D. Fine (Eds.), *Psychoanalysis: The major concepts* (pp. 395–420). NewHaven: Yale University Press.

Uchino, B. N., Cacciopo, J. T., & Kiecolt-Glaser, J. K. (1996). The relationship between social support and physiological processes: A review with emphasis on underlying mechanisms and implications for health. *Psychological Bulletin, 119,* 488–531.

Uddin, L. Q., Iacoboni, M., Lange, C., & Keenan, J. P. (2007). The self and social cognition: The role of cortical midline structures and mirror neurons. *Trends in Cognitive Science, 11,* 153–157.

Udry, J. R., & Billy, J. O. (1987). Initiation of coitus in early adolescence. *American Sociological Review, 52,* 841–855.

Udry, J. R., Billy, J. O., Morris, N. M., Groff, T. R, & Raj, M. S. (1985). Serum androgenic hormones motivate sexual behavior in adolescent boys. *Fertility and Sterility, 43,* 90–94.

Umaña-Taylor, A. J., Gonzales-Backen, M. A., & Guimond, A. B. (2009). Latino adolescents' ethnic identity: Is there a developmental progression and does growth in ethnic identity predict growth in self-esteem? *Child Development, 80,* 392–405.

Umbel, V. M., Pearson, B. Z., Fernandez, M. C., & Oller, D. K. (1992). Measuring bilingual children's receptive vocabularies. *Child Development, 63,* 1012–1020.

Umberson, D., Chen, M. D., House, J. S., Hopkins, K., & Slaten, E. (1996). The effect of social relationships on psychological well-being: Are men and women really so different? *American Sociological Review, 61,* 837–857.

Umberson, D., Wortman, C. B., & Kessler, R. C. (1992). Widowhood and depression: Explaining long-term gender differences in vulnerability. *Journal of Health and Social Behavior, 33,* 10–24.

UNAIDS. (2006). *Report on the global AIDS epidemic: Executive summary.* Geneva, Switzerland: Author.

Uncapher, H., Gallagher-Thompson, D., Osgood, N. J., & Bongar, B. (1998). Hopelessness and suicidal ideation in older adults. *The Gerontologist, 38,* 62–70.

Underhill, P.A., Shen, P. Lin, Li Jin, A.A., Passarino, G., Yang, W.H., Kauffman, E., Bonné-Tamir, B., Bertranpetit, J., Francalacci, P., Ibrahim, M., Jenkins, T., Kidd, J.R., Mehdi, S. Q., Seielstad, M.T., Wells, R.S., Piazza, A., Davis, R.W., Feldman, M.W., Cavalli-Sforza, L. L., & Oefner, P. J. (2000). Y chromosome sequence variation and the history of human populations. *Nature Genetics †26,* 358–361.

United Nations. (2000). *Child labor, conflict-induced trauma in children, among key topics in Third Committee Survey of children's rights.* Press Release GA /SHC/3590. Retrieved September 8, 2001, from http://srch1.un.org/plwebcgi/fastweb?state_id_999965071&view_unsearch&docrank_3&numhitsfound_12&query_child%20slavery&&docid_1804&docdb_pr2000&dbname_web&sorting _BYRELEVANCE&operator_adj&TemplateName_predoc.tmpl&set-Cookie_1

United Nations. (2006). *The Millennium Development Goals Report.* Retrieved May 30, 2007 from http://unstats.un.org/unsd/mdg/Resources/Static/Products/Progress2006/MDGReport2006.pdf

U.S. Bureau of Labor Statistics. (2009). Table 3.3. Civilian labor force participation rates by age, sex, race and ethnicity, 1988, 1998, 2008, and projected 2018. Retrieved on August 24, 2010, at http://www.bls.gov/emp/ep_table_303.htm

U.S. Bureau of Labor Statistics. (2009). Volunteers by selected characteristics, September 2009. Retrieved on August 24, 2010, at http://www.bls.gov/news.release/volun.t01.htm

U.S. Bureau of Labor Statistics. (2010). Table 7. Employment status of the civilian non-institutional population 25 years and over by educational attainment, sex, race, and Hispanic or Latino ethnicity. Retrieved on August 15, 2010, at www.bls.gov/cps/cpsaat7.pdf

U.S. Census Bureau. *Current Population Survey,* Table 429. U.S. Retrieved November 25, 2004, from http://nces.ed.gov/programs/digest/d03/tables/dt429.asp

U.S. Census Bureau. (1976). *Population profile of the United States, 1975.* Current Population Reports (Ser. P-20, No. 292). Washington, DC: U.S. Government Printing Office.

U.S. Census Bureau. (1983). *America in transition: An aging society.* Current Population Reports (Ser. P-23, No. 128). Washington, DC: U.S. Government Printing Office.

U.S. Census Bureau. (1984). *Demographic and socioeconomic aspects of aging in the United States.* Current Population Reports (Ser. P-23, No. 138), 59. Washington, DC: U.S. Government Printing Office.

U.S. Census Bureau. (1986). *Statistical abstract of the United States: 1986.* Washington, DC: U.S. Government Printing Office.

U.S. Census Bureau. (1987). *An aging world.* International Population Reports (Ser. P-95, No. 78). Washington, DC: U.S. Government Printing Office.

U.S. Census Bureau. (1989a). *Population profile of the United States, 1989.* Current Population Reports (Ser. P-23, No. 159). Washington, DC: U.S. Government Printing Office.

U.S. Census Bureau. (1989b). *The Black population in the United States, March, 1988.* Current Population Reports (Ser. P-20, No. 442). Washington, DC: U.S. Government Printing Office.

U.S. Census Bureau. (1991). *Statistical abstract of the United States: 1991.* Washington, DC: U.S. Government Printing Office.

U.S. Census Bureau. (1992). *Statistical abstract of the United States: 1992.* Washington, DC: U.S. Government Printing Office.

U.S. Census Bureau. (1995). *Statistical abstract of the United States: 1995.* Washington, DC: U.S. Government Printing Office.

U.S. Census Bureau. (1996). *Statistical abstract of the United States: 1996.* Washington, DC: U.S. Government Printing Office.

U.S. Census Bureau. (1997). *Statistical abstract of the United States: 1997.* Washington, DC: U.S. Government Printing Office.

U.S. Census Bureau. (1999). *Statistical abstract of the United States: 1999.* Washington, DC: U. S. Government Printing Office.

U.S. Census Bureau. (2000). *Statistical abstract of the United States: 2000.* Washington, DC: U.S. Government Printing Office.

U.S. Census Bureau. (2004). *Historical poverty tables.* Retrieved February 13, 2005, from http://www.census.gov/hhes/poverty/histpov/hstpov4.html

U.S. Census Bureau. (2006). *Statistical abstract of the United States: 2006.* Table 85, Washington, DC: U.S. Government Printing Office.

U.S. Census Bureau. (2006). *Statistical abstract of the United States: 2006.* Table 183, Retrieved October 26, 2007, from http://www.census.gov/compendia/statab/2006/2006edition.html

U.S. Census Bureau. (2006). *Statistical abstract of the United States: 2006.* Tables 50, 51, 624, 626. Retrieved September 15, 2007, from http://www.census.gov/compendia/statab/2006/population/pop.pdf

U.S. Census Bureau. (2006). *Statistical abstract of the United States: 2006.* Tables 51, 577, 685, 696. Retrieved October 14, 2007, from http://www.census.gov/compendia/statab/2006/2006edition.html

U.S. Census Bureau. (2006). *Statistical abstract of the United States: 2006.* Tables 52, 58, 604, 610, 615, 698. Retrieved September 29, 2007, from http://www.census.gov/compendia/statab/2006/2006edition.html

U.S. Census Bureau. (2006). *Statistical abstract of the United States: 2006.* Tables 577, 610. Retrieved September 7, 2007, from http://www.census.gov/compendia/statab/2006/labor_force_employment_earnings/labor.pdf

U.S. Census Bureau. (2007). *Statistical abstract of the United States: 2007.* Table 111. Deaths and death rates by leading causes of death and age: 2003. Retrieved August 24, 2007, from http://www.census.gov/prod/2006pubs/07statab/vitstat.pdf

U.S. Census Bureau. (2007). *Marital history by sex for selected birth cohorts, 1935–29 to 1980–84: 2004.* Retrieved September 23, 2007, from http://www.census.gov/population/socdemo/marital-hist/2004/Table1.2004.xls

U.S. Census Bureau. (2007). *Statistical abstract of the United States: 2006.* Washington, DC: U.S. Government Printing Office.

U.S. Census Bureau. (2007). *Statistical abstract of the United States: 2007.* Tables 55, 1222. Retrieved October 26, 2007, from http://www.census.gov/compendia/statab/population/

U.S. Census Bureau. (2007). *Statistical abstract of the United States: 2007.* Tables 78, 81, 584. Retrieved September 19, 2007, from http://www.census.gov/compendia/statab/tables/07s0584.xls

U.S. Census Bureau. (2008). *Statistical abstract of the United States, 2008.* Tables 56, 57, 72. Retrieved on August 28, 2010, at http://www.census.gov/prod/2007pubs/08abstract/pop.pdf

U.S. Census Bureau. (2009). *America's families and living arrangements: 2009.* Table A2. Retrieved on July 7, 2010, at www.census.gov/population/www/socdemo/hh-fam/cps2009.html

U.S. Census Bureau. (2009). *Statistical abstract of the United States: 2009.* Tables 100, 102. Retrieved from the Internet on November 22, 2009, at http://www.census.gov/compendia/statab/cats/births_deaths_marriages_divorces.html

U.S. Census Bureau. (2009). *Statistical abstract of the United States: 2009.* Tables 676, 697, 1199. Retrieved on August 24, 2010, at http://www.census.gov/prod/2008pubs/09statab/arts.pdf

U.S. Census Bureau. (2010). *America's families and living arrangements: 2008.* Table C4. Children with grandparents present, 2008. Retrieved on August 24, 2010, at http://www.census.gov/population/www/socdemo/hh-fam/cps2008.html

U.S. Census Bureau. (2010). *America's families and living arrangements: 2009.* Table A2, Family status and household relationships of people 15 years old and over by marital status, age and sex, 2009. Retrieved on August 17, 2010, at www.census.gov/population/www/socdemo/hh-fam/cps2009.html

U.S. Census Bureau. (2010). *America's families and living arrangements: Current Population Survey, 2009 Annual Social and Economic Supplement.* Table C8. Retrieved on August 18, 2010, at www.census.gov/population/www/socdemo/hh-fam/cps2009.html

U.S. Census Bureau. (2010). *Statistical abstract of the United States: 2010.* Tables 57, 85, 100, 224, 265, 267, 603, 609, 697. Retrieved on July 8, 2010, at www.census.gov/compendia/statab/cats/births_deaths_marriages_divorces.html

U.S. Census Bureau. (2010). *Statistical abstract of the United States: 2010.* Table 80. Retrieved on July 4, 2010, at www.census.gov/compendia/statab/2010/tables/10s0080.pdf

U.S. Census Bureau. (2010). *Statistical abstract of the United States: 2010.* Table 232. Preprimary school enrollment—Summary: 1970 to 2007. Retrieved on May 31, 2010, at www.census.gov/compendia/statab/2010/tables/10s0232.pdf

U.S. Census Bureau. (2010). *Statistical abstract of the United States: 2006.* Table 116. Retrieved on June 26, 2010, at www.census.gov/compendia/statab/2010/tables/10s0116.pdf

U.S. Census Bureau. (2010). *Statistical abstract of the United States: 2010.* Table 117. Retrieved on September 4, 2010, at http://www.census.gov/compendia/statab/2010/tables/10s0117.pdf

U.S. Census Bureau. (2010). *Statistical abstract of the United States: 2010.* Tables 7, 102, 207. Retrieved on August 26, 2010, at http://www.census.gov/compendia/statab/

U.S. Census Bureau. (2010). *Statistical abstract of the United States: 2010.* Table 57. Retrieved on August 24, 2010, at http://www.census.gov/compendia/statab/2010/tables/10s0057.pdf

U.S. Census Bureau. (2010). *Statistical abstract of the United States: 2010.* Tables 80, 85, 92, 584, 585, 597. Retrieved on July 31, 2010, at www.census.gov/compendia/

statab/cats/labor_force_employment_earnings.html

U.S. Census Bureau. (2010). *Statistical abstract of the United States: 2010.* Tables 7, 65. Retrieved on August 17, 2010, at www.census.gov/compendia/statab/cats/population.html

U.S. Census Bureau. (2010). *Statistical abstract of the United States: 2010.* Tables 100, 113. Retrieved on April 25, 2010 at http://www.census.gov/compendia/statab/

U.S. Code of Federal Regulations 45, CH. XIII (10-01-02 edition), §1304.21 *Program Performance Standards for Operation of Head Start-Education and Early Childhood Development.*

U.S. Conference of Mayors. (1998). *A status report on hunger and homelessness in America's cities.* Retrieved from http://usmayors.org

U.S. Conference of Mayors. (2008). *Status report on hunger and homelessness.* Retrieved on August 18, 2010, at http://usmayors.org/pressreleases/documents/hungerhomelessnessreport_121208.pdf

U.S. Department of Commerce. (2003). Student use of computers by level of enrollment and selected characteristics: 1993, 1997, and 2001.

U.S. Department of Education. (1995). *Digest of education statistics, 1995.* Washington, DC: U.S. Government Printing Office.

U.S. Department of Education. (2003). Table 2-1. Children ages 3 through 5 served under IDEA, Part B, by educational environment and state: Fall 2002. Retrieved on May 31, 2010, at www2.ed.gov/about/reports/annual/osep/2004/26th-vol-2-table-2.doc

U.S. Department of Education. (2005). *Early childhood program participation survey of the National Household Education Surveys Program (NHES),* National Center for Education Statistics. Retrieved July 18, 2007, from http://www.census.gov/compendia/statab/tables/07s0564.xls

U.S. Department of Energy. (2003). Human Genome Project: Genomics and Its Impact on Science and Society. *The Human Genome Project and Beyond.* Genomics 101: A Primer. Retrieved May 25, 2007, from http://www.ornl.gov/sci/techresources/Human_Genome/publicat/primer2001/1.shtml

U.S. Department of Energy (2007). *Human Genome Project Information.* Genetics privacy and legislation. Retrieved May 25, 2007, from http://www.ornl.gov/sci/techresources/Human_Genome/elsi/legislat.shtml

U.S. Department of Energy, Office of Science. (2004). *The science behind the Human Genome Project.* Retrieved August 3, 2004, from http://www.ornl.gov/sci/techresources/Human_Genome/project/info.shtml

U.S. Department of Health and Human Services (2009). *Assisted Reproductive Technologies (ART) report.* Retrieved on April 24, 2010, at http://apps.nccd.cdc.gov/ART/Marquee.aspx

U.S. Department of Health and Human Services. (1999). *Mental Health: A Report of* the Surgeon General—Executive Summary. Rockville, MD: U.S. Department of Health and Human Services, Substance Abuse and Mental Health Services Administration, Center for Mental Health Services, National Institutes of Health, National Institute of Mental Health. Chapter 5. Older Adults and Mental Health. Retrieved October 16, 2007, from http://www.mentalhealth.com

U.S. Department of Health and Human Services. (2001). *Healthy people 2010.* Washington, DC: U.S. Government Printing Office.

U.S. Department of Health and Human Services (2009). *Healthy People 2020:* Public Meetings. Retrieved on April 25, 2010, at www.healthypeople.gov/HP2020/

U.S. Department of Health and Human Services. (2005). *Home Health Care Fact Sheet.* Retrieved October 28, 2007, from http://www.eldercare.gov/eldercare/Public/resources/fact_sheets/home_care.asp

U.S. Department of Health and Human Services, Centers for Disease Control and Prevention. (2006). *2004 Assisted Reproductive Technology (ART) report.*

U.S. Department of Health and Human Services, Centers for Disease Control and Prevention. (2006). *2004 Assisted Reproductive Technology (ART) report.* Washington, DC: U.S. Government Printing Office.

U.S. Department of Labor. (1993). *Work and family: Turning thirty—job mobility and labor market attachment.* Report 862. Bureau of Labor Statistics.

U.S. Department of Labor. (2003). *O*NET.* Retrieved February 6, 2005, from http://www.doleta.gov/programs/onet/

U.S. Department of Labor. (2010). *Occupational outlook handbook: 2008–2018.* Retrieved on August 5, 2010, at www.bls.gov/oco/

U.S. Department of Labor, Employment and Training Administration. (1993). *Selected characteristics of occupations defined in the revised dictionary of occupational titles.* Washington, DC: U.S. Government Printing Office.

U.S. Living Will Registry. (2010). Testimonials from registrants. Retrieved on September 3, 2010, at "http://www.uslivingwillregistry.com/testimonials_registrants.shtm" www.uslivingwillregistry.com/testimonials_registrants.shtm

U.S. News & World Report. (2005). Mysteries of the Teen Years: An essential guide for parents (Special Edition).

U.S. Senate, Special Committee on Aging. (1986). *Aging America: Trends and projections.* Washington, DC: U.S. Government Printing Office.

University of California. (2004). *UC and the SAT.* Retrieved November 18, 2004, from http://www.ucop.edu/news/sat/welcome.html

Urban Institute. (2000). *A new look at homelessness in America.* Washington, DC: Author.

Urberg, K. A. (1992). Locus of peer influence: Social crowd and best friend. *Journal of Youth and Adolescence, 21,* 439–450.

Urberg, K. A., Shyu, S. J., & Liang, J. (1990). Peer influence in adolescent cigarette smoking. *Addictive Behavior, 115,* 247–255.

USA Today. (2004). Study: Abstinence pledges not reducing rates of STDs. *The Associated Press.* Retrieved December 4, 2004, from http://www.usatoday.com/news/health/2004-03-09-abstinence-study_x.htm

Utian, W. (2003). What are the key issues women face when ending hormone replacement therapy? *Cleveland Clinic Journal of Medicine, 70,* 93–94.

Valas, H. (2001). Learned helplessness and psychological adjustment II: Effects of learning disabilities and low achievement. *Scandinavian Journal of Educational Research, 45,* 101–114.

Valdez-Menchaca, M. S., & Whitehurst, G. J. (1992). Accelerating language development through picture book reading: A systematic extension to Mexican day care. *Developmental Psychology, 28,* 1106–1114.

Valk, A. (2000). Ethnic identity, ethnic attitudes, self-esteem, and esteem toward others among Estonian and Russian adolescents. *Journal of Adolescent Research, 15,* 637–651.

Valkenburg, P. M., & Peter, J. (2007). Preadolescents' and adolescents' online communication and their closeness to friends. *Developmental Psychology, 43,* 267–277.

Valsiner, J. (2000). *Culture and human development.* Thousand Oaks, CA: Sage.

Van Boxtel, M. P. J., Paas, F. G. W. C., Houx, P. J., & Adam, J. J. (1997). Aerobic capacity and cognitive performance in a cross-sectional aging study. *Medicine and Science in Sports and Exercise, 29,* 1357–1365.

Van der Mark, I. L., van IJzendoorn, M. H., & Bakermans-Kranenburg, M. J. (2002). Development of empathy in girls during the second year of life: Associations with parenting, attachment, and temperament. *Social Development, 11,* 451–468.

Van der Vegt, G., Emans, B. J. M., & Van De Vliert, E. (2001). Patterns of interdependence in work teams: A two-level investigation of the relations with job and team satisfaction. *Personnel Psychology, 54,* 51–69.

Van Geert, P. (1998). A dynamic systems model of basic developmental mechanisms: Piaget, Vygotsky and beyond. *Psychological Review, 105,* 634–677.

Van Hiel, A., Mervielde, I., & DeFruyt, F. (2006). Stagnation and generativity: Structure, validity and differential relationship with adaptive and maladaptive personality. *Journal of Personality, 74,* 543–574.

van IJzendoorn, M. H., Goldberg, S., Kroonenberg, P. M., & Frenkel, O. J. (1992). The relative effects of maternal and child problems on the quality of attachment: A meta-analysis of attachment in clinical samples. *Child Development, 63,* 840–858.

van IJzendoorn, M. H., & Kroonenberg, P. M. (1988). Cross-cultural patterns of attachment: A meta-analysis of the strange situation. *Child Development, 59,* 147–156.

van IJzendoorn, M. H., & Sagi, A. (1999). Cross-cultural patterns of attachment: Universal and contextual dimensions. In J. Cassidy & P. R. Shaver (Eds.), *Handbook of attachment: Theory, research, and clinical applications* (pp. 713–734). New York: Guilford Press.

Van Willigen, M. (2000). Differential benefits of volunteering across the life course. *Journal of Gerontology, 55,* S308–S318.

Vandell, D., Belsky, J., Burchinal, M., Steinberg, L., Vandergrift, N., & the NICHD Early Child Care Research Network. (2010). Do effects of early child care extend to age 15 years? Results from the NICHD Study of Early Child Care and Youth Development. *Child Development, 81*(3).

Vandell, D. L., Henderson, V. K., & Wilson, K. S. (1988). A longitudinal study of children with day-care experiences of varying quality. *Child Development, 59,* 1286–1292.

Vannoy, D. (1995). A paradigm of roles in the divorce process: Implications for divorce adjustment, future commitments, and personal growth. *Journal of Divorce and Remarriage, 24,* 71–87.

Vanzetti, N., & Duck, S. (1996). *A lifetime of relationships.* Pacific Grove, CA: Brooks/Cole.

Vaughn, B., Egeland, B., Sroufe, L. A., & Waters, E. (1979). Individual differences in infant-mother attachment at 12 and 18 months: Stability and change in families under stress. *Child Development, 50,* 971–975.

Vaughn, B. E., & Bost, K. K. (1999). Attachment and temperament. In J. Cassidy & P. R. Shaver (Eds.), *Handbook of attachment: Theory, research, and clinical applications* (pp. 198–225). New York: Guilford Press.

Vaughn, B. E., Colvin, T. N., Azria, M. R., Caya, L., & Krzysik, L. (2001). Dyadic analyses of friendship in a sample of preschool-age children attending Head Start: Correspondence between measures and implications for social competence. *Child Development, 72,* 862–878.

Vaughn, B. E., Lefever, G. B., Seifer, R., & Barglow, P. (1989). Attachment behavior, attachment security, and temperament during infancy. *Child Development, 60,* 728–737.

Veenhoven, R. (2000). Freedom and happiness: A comparative study in forty-four nations in the early 1990s. In E. Diener & E. M. Suh (Eds.), *Culture and subjective well-being* (pp. 257–288). Cambridge, MA: MIT Press.

Veenman, M. V. J., Wilhelm, P., & Beishuizen, J. J. (2004). The relation between intellectual and metacognitive skills from a developmental perspective. *Learning and Instruction, 14,* 89–109.

Veenstra, R., Lindenberg, S., Munniksma, A., & Dijkstra, J. K. (2010). The complex relation between bullying, victimization, acceptance, and rejection: Giving special attention to status, affection and sex differences. *Child Development, 81,* 480–486. http://timss.bc.edu/PDF/P06_IR_Ch4.pdf

Vega, W. A., Zimmerman, R. S., Warheit, G. J., Apospori, E., & Gil, A. G. (1993). Risk factors for adolescent drug use in four ethnic and racial groups. *American Journal of Public Health, 83,* 185–189.

Venter, J. C., et al. (2001). The sequence of the human genome. *Science, 291,* 1304–1351.

Verhaeghen, P., Geraerts, N., & Marcoen, A. (2000). Memory complaints, coping, and well-being in old age: A systemic approach. *The Gerontologist, 40,* 540–548.

Verhoef, H., & Michel, C. (1997). Studying morality within the African context: Model of moral analysis and construction. *Journal of Moral Education, 26,* 389–407.

Verhoeven, L. (2001). Prevention of reading difficulties. In L. Verhoeven & C. Snow (Eds.), *Literacy and motivation: Reading engagement in individuals and groups* (pp. 123–134). Mahwah, NJ: Erlbaum.

Verkuyten, M., & DeWolf, A. (2007). The development of in-group favoritism: Between social reality and group identity. *Developmental Psychology, 43,* 901–911.

Vinokur, A., Caplan, R. D., & Williams, C. C. (1987). Effects of recent and past stress on mental health: Coping with unemployment among Vietnam veterans and non-veterans. *Journal of Applied Social Psychology, 17,* 708–728.

Violato, C., & Holden, W. B. (1988). A confirmatory factor analysis of a four-factor model of adolescent concerns. *Journal of Youth and Adolescence, 17,* 101–113.

Vital Signs. (2010). Lack of sleep can lead to serious health problems. *47,* UCLA Health System, 6–7.

Vizziello, G. F., Antonioloi, M. E., Cocci, V., & Invernizzi, R. (1993). From pregnancy to motherhood: The structure of representative and narrative change. *Infant Mental Health Journal, 14,* 4–16.

Voelker-Rehage, C., Godde, B., & Staudinger, U.M. (2010). Physical and motor fitness are both related to cognition in old age. *European Journal of Neuroscience, 31,* 167–176.

Vogel, G. (2001). Human cloning plans spark talk of U.S. ban. *Science, 292,* 31.

Vogl-Bauer, S. (2003). Maintaining family relationships. In D. J. Canary & M. Dainton (Eds.), *Maintaining relationships through communication: Relational, contextual, and cultural variations* (pp. 31– 49). Mahwah, NJ: Erlbaum.

Volling, B. L., Youngblade, L. M., & Belsky, J. (1997). Young children's social relationships with siblings and friends. *American Journal of Orthopsychiatry, 67,* 102–111.

Vondracek, F. W., Schulenberg, J., Skorikov, V., & Gillespie, L. (1995). The relationship of identity status to career indecision during adolescence. *Journal of Adolescence, 18,* 17–29.

Vouloumanos, A., Hauser, M.D., Werker, J.F., & Martin, A. (2010). The tuning of human neonates' preference for speech. *Child Development, 81,* 517–527.

Voydanoff, P. (2004). The effects of work demands and resources on work-to-family conflict and facilitation. *Journal of Marriage and the Family, 66,* 398–412.

Voydanoff, P. (2005). Consequences of boundary-spanning demands and resources for work-to-family conflict and perceived stress. *Journal of Occupational Health Psychology, 10,* 491–503.

Vrijkotte, T. G. M., van der Wal, M. F., van Eijsden, M. & Bonsel, G. J. (2009). First-trimester working conditions and birthweight: A prospective cohort study. *American Journal of Public Health, 99,* 1409-1416.

Vuchinich, S. (1987). Starting and stopping spontaneous family conflicts. *Journal of Marriage and the Family, 49,* 591–601.

Vygotsky, L. S. (1962). *Thought and language.* Cambridge, MA: MIT Press.

Vygotsky, L.S. (1978a). Tool and symbol in child development. *Mind in society: The development of higher psychological processes.* (L.S. Cole, M., John-Steiner, V., Scribner, S. & Souberman, E. Editors) Cambridge, MA: Harvard University Press, pp. 19-30.

Vygotsky, L.S. (1978b). Interaction between learning and development. *Mind in society: The development of higher psychological processes.* (L.S. Cole, M., John-Steiner, V., Scribner, S. & Souberman, E. Editors) Cambridge, MA: Harvard University Press, pp. 79–92.

Vygotsky, L. S. (1978c). *Mind in society.* Cambridge, MA: Harvard University Press.

Vygotsky, L. S. (1987). Genetic roots of thinking and speech. In R. W. Rieber & A. S. Carton (Eds.), *The collected works of L. S. Vygotsky: Vol. 1: Problems of general psychology* (pp. 101–120). New York: Plenum.

Waas, G. A. (1988). Social attributional biases of peer-rejected and aggressive children. *Child Development, 59,* 969–975.

Wagner, B. M., & Phillips, D. A. (1992). Beyond beliefs: Parent and child behaviors and children's perceived academic competence. *Child Development, 63,* 1380–1391.

Wagner, M. (2005). Youth with disabilities leaving secondary school. In *Changes Over Time in the Early Post School Outcomes of Youth with Disabilities: A Report of Findings from the National Longitudinal Transition Study and the National Longitudinal Transition Study 2.* Menlo Park, CA: SRI International, 2.1-2.6.

Walasky, M., Whitbourne, S. K., & Nehrke, M. F. (1983–1984). Construction and validation of an ego-integrity status interview. *International Journal of Aging and Human Development, 18,* 61–72.

Waldman, I. R. (1996). Aggressive boys' hostile perceptual and response biases: The role of attention and impulsivity. *Child Development, 67,* 1015–1033.

Walker, A. (1991). Beauty: When the other dancer is the self. In H. L. Gates Jr. (Ed.), *Bearing witness: Selections from African-American autobiography in the twentieth century* (pp. 257–258). New York: Pantheon Books.

Walker, L. J. (1989). A longitudinal study of moral reasoning. *Child Development, 60,* 157–166.

Walker, L. J., de Vries, B., & Trevethan, S. D. (1987). Moral stages and moral orientations in real-life and hypothetical dilemmas. *Child Development, 58,* 842–858.

Walker, L. J., Gustafson, P., & Hennig, K. H. (2001). The consolidation/transition model in moral reasoning development. *Developmental Psychology, 37,* 187–197.

Walker, L. J., & Taylor, J. H. (1991). Family interactions and the development of moral reasoning. *Child Development, 62,* 262–283.

Walker, R. (2002). Case study, case records, and multimedia. *Cambridge Journal of Education, 32,* 109–127.

Walker, R. M. (2001). Physician-assisted suicide: The legal slippery slope. *Cancer Control, 8,* 25–31.

Walker-Andrews, A. S. (1986). Intermodal perception of expressive behaviors: Relation of eye and voice? *Developmental Psychology, 22,* 373–377.

Walker-Andrews, A. S., & Harris, P. L. (1993). Young children's comprehension of pretend causal sequences. *Developmental Psychology, 29,* 915–921.

Wallace, E., Hayes, D., & Jerger, J. (1994). Neurotology of aging: The auditory system. In M. L. Albert & J. E. Knoefel (Eds.), *Clinical neurology of aging* (2nd ed., pp. 448–464). New York: Oxford University Press.

Wallechinsky, D., & Wallace, A. (1993). *The book of lists.* New York: Little, Brown.

Wallechinsky, D., Wallace, I., & Wallace, A. (1977). *The book of lists.* New York: Morrow.

Wallerstein, I., & Smith, J. (1991). Households as an institution of the world economy. In R. L. Blumberg (Ed.), *Gender, family, and economy: The triple overlap* (pp. 225–242). Newbury Park, CA: Sage.

Wallerstein, J. S., & Blakeslee, S. (1995). *The good marriage.* New York: Houghton Mifflin.

Wallerstein, J. S., & Corbin, S. B. (1989). Daughters of divorce: Report from a 10-year follow-up. *American Journal of Orthopsychiatry, 59,* 593–604.

Wallien, M. S. C., van Goozen, S. H. M., & Cohen-Kettenis, P. T. (2007). Physiological correlates of anxiety in children with gender identity disorder. *European Child and Adolescent Psychiatry, 16,* 309–315.

Walls, C. T., & Zarit, S. H. (1991). Informal support from Black churches and the well-being of elderly Blacks. *The Gerontologist, 31,* 490–495.

Walther, F. J., den Ouden, A. L., & Verloove-Vanhorick, S. P. (2000). Looking back in time: Outcome of a national cohort of very preterm infants born in the Netherlands in 1983. *Early Human Development, 59,* 175–191.

Walther, J. B., & Parks, M. R. (2002). Cues filtered out, cues filtered in: Computer-mediated communication and relationships. In M. L. Knapp & Y. J. A.

Daly (Eds.), *Handbook of interpersonal communication*. Thousand Oaks, CA: Sage, pp. 529–563.

Wang, G.-Z., & Buffalo, M. D. (2004). Social and cultural determinants of attitudes toward abortion. *Social Science Journal, 41,* 93–105.

Wang, H., & Amato, P. R. (2000). Predictors of divorce adjustment: Stressors, resources, and definition. *Journal of Marriage and the Family, 62,* 655–668.

Wang, Q. (2001). Culture effects on adults' earliest childhood recollection and self-description: Implications for the relation between memory and the self. *Journal of Personality and Social Psychology, 81,* 220–233.

Wang, Q., Leichtman, M. D., & Davies, K. (2000). Sharing memories and telling stories: American and Chinese mothers and their 3-year-olds. *Memory, 8,* 159–177.

Wargo, E. (2008). Talk to the hand: New insights into the evolution of language and gesture. *Observer, 21,* 16–21.

Warren, E. (2003). *The two-income family trap: Why middle class mothers and fathers are going broke.* New York: Basic Books.

Warren, E. (2007). The vanishing middle class. In J. Edwards, M. Crain, & A.L. Kalleberg (Eds.), *Ending poverty in America: How to restore the American dream.* Chapel Hill, NC: The New Press.

Warren, P. N. (1998). Berdaches and assumptions about berdaches. Retrieved on July 10, 2010, at www.whosoever.org/v3i3/berdaches.html

Warshaw, G. (2006). Advances and challenges in care of older people with chronic illness. *Generations, 30,* 5–10.

Watanabe, N., Hasegawa, K., & Yoshinaga, Y. (1996). Suicide in later life in Japan: Urban and rural differences. In J. L. Pearson & Y. Conwell (Eds.), *Suicide and aging: International perspectives* (pp. 121–129). New York: Springer Verlag.

Waterman, A. S. (1982). Identity development from adolescence to adulthood: An extension of theory and a review of research. *Developmental Psychology, 18,* 341–358.

Waterman, A. S. (1992). Identity as an aspect of optimal psychological functioning. In G. Adams, T. P. Gullotta, & R. Montemayor (Eds.), *Adolescent identity formation: Advances in adolescent development* (Vol. 4., pp. 50–72). Newbury Park, CA: Sage.

Waterman, A. S., & Whitbourne, S. K. (1981). The inventory of psychosocial development. *Journal Supplement Abstract Service: Catalog of Selected Documents in Psychology, 11* (Ms. No. 2179).

Waters, E., Merick, S., Treboux, D., Crowell, J., & Albersheim, L. (2000). Attachment security in infancy and early adulthood: A twenty-year longitudinal study. *Child Development, 71,* 684–689.

Waxman, S. R., & Lidz, J. (2006). Early word learning. In D. Kuhn & R. Siegler (Eds.), *Handbook of child psychology: Cognition, perception, and language* (6th ed., pp. 299–335). New York: Wiley.

Weatherston, D. J. (2001). Infant mental health: A review of relevant literature. *Psychoanalytic Social Work, 8,* 39–69.

Webb, M. (1997). *The good death: The new American search to reshape the end of life.* New York: Bantam Books.

Weber, C., Hahne, A., Friedrich, M., & Friederici, A. D. (2004). Discrimination of word stress in early infant perception: Electrophysiological evidence. *Cognitive Brain Research, 18,* 149–161.

Weber, E. K. (1999). Children's personal prerogative in home and school contexts. *Early Education and Development, 10,* 499–515.

Webster, D. W., Gainer, P. S., & Champion, H. R. (1993). Weapon carrying among inner-city junior high school students: Defensive behavior vs. aggressive delinquency. *American Journal of Public Health, 83,* 1604–1608.

Weigel, D. J., Devereux, P., Leigh, G. K., & Ballard-Reisch, D. (1998). A longitudinal study of adolescents' perceptions of support and stress: Stability and change. *Journal of Adolescent Research, 13,* 158–177.

Weinfield, N. S., Sroufe, L. A., Egeland, B., & Carlson, E. A. (1999). The nature of individual differences in infant-caregiver attachment. In J. Cassidy & P. R. Shaver (Eds.), *Handbook of attachment: Theory, research, and clinical applications* (pp. 68–88). New York: Guilford Press.

Weinraub, M., Clemens, L. P., Sockloff, A., Ethridge, T., Gracely, E., & Meyers, B. (1984). The development of sex role stereotypes in the third year: Relationship to gender labeling, identity, sex-typed toy preference, and family characteristics. *Child Development, 55,* 1493–1503.

Weinreb, L., & Buckner, J. C. (1993). Homeless families: Program responses and public policies. *American Journal of Orthopsychiatry, 63,* 400–409.

Weinstein, R. S., Marshall, H. H., Sharp, L., & Botkin, M. (1987). Pygmalion and the student: Age and classroom differences in children's awareness of teacher expectations. *Child Development, 58,* 1079–1093.

Weinstock, H., Berman, S., & Cates, W., Jr. (2004). Sexually transmitted diseases among American youth: Incidence and prevalence estimates 2000. *Perspectives on Sexual and Reproductive Health, 36,* 6–10.

Weisgram, E. S., Bigler, R. S., & Liben, L. S. (2010). Gender, values, and occupational interests among children, adolescents and adults. *Child Development, 81,* 778–796.

Weismantle, M. (2001). Reasons people do not work, 1996. *Current Population Reports,* P70-76. Washington, DC: U.S. Department of Commerce.

Weisner, T. S. & Lowe, E. (2004). Globalization and the psychological anthropology of childhood and adolescence. In C. Casey & R. Edgerton (Eds.) *A companion to psychological anthropology: Modernity and psychocultural change.* Oxford, UK: Blackwell, pp. 1–48.

Weiss, B., Dodge, K. A., Bates, J. E., & Petit, G. S. (1992). Some consequences of early harsh discipline: Child aggression and a maladaptive social information processing style. *Child Development, 63,* 1321–1335.

Weiss, R. L., & Heyman, R. E. (1997). A clinical-research overview of couples interactions. In W. K. Halford & H. J. Markman (Eds.), *Clinical handbook of marriage and couples intervention* (pp. 13–41). Chichester, England: Wiley.

Weiss, R. S. (1997). Adaptation to retirement. In I. H. Gotlib & B. Wheaton (Eds.), *Stress and adversity over the life course: Trajectories and turning points* (pp. 232–245). New York: Cambridge University Press.

Weisner, T. S. (2005). Attachment as a cultural and ecological problem with pluralistic solutions. *Human Development, 48,* 89–94.

Weissberg, R. P., & O'Brien, M. U. (2004). What works in school-based social and emotional learning programs for positive youth development. *Annals of the American Academy of Political and Social Science, 591,* 86–97.

Weist, M. D., & Cooley-Quille, M. (2001). Advancing efforts to address youth violence involvement. *Journal of Clinical Child Psychology, 30,* 147–151.

Wellman, H. M. (1990). *The child's theory of mind.* Cambridge, MA: MIT Press.

Wellman, H. M., Cross, D., & Bartsch, K. (1986). Infant search and object permanence: A meta-analysis of the A-not-B error. *Monographs of the Society for Research in Child Development, 51* (3, Whole No. 214).

Wellman, H. M., Cross, D., & Watson, J. (2001). Meta-analysis of theory-of-mind development: The truth about false belief. *Child Development, 71,* 655–684.

Wenar, C. (1982). On negativism. *Human Development, 25,* 1–23.

Wentowski, G. J. (1985). Older women's perceptions of great-grandmotherhood: A research note. *The Gerontologist, 25,* 593–596.

Wentworth, N., & Haith, M. M. (1992). Event-specific expectations of 2-and 3-month-old infants. *Developmental Psychology, 28,* 842–850.

Wentzel, K. R., Barry, C. M., & Caldwell, K. A. (2004). Friendships in middle school: Influences on motivation and school adjustment. *Journal of Educational Psychology, 96,* 195–203.

Wenxin, Z., Meiping, W., & Fuligni, A. (2006). Expectations for autonomy, beliefs about parental authority, and parent-adolescent conflict. *Acta Psychologica Sinica, 38,* 868–876.

Werker, J. F., & Tees, R. C. (1999). Influences on infant speech processing: Toward a new synthesis. *Annual Review of Psychology, 50,* 509–535.

Wesley, P. W., & Buysse, V. (2003). Making meaning of school readiness in schools and communities. *Early Childhood Research Quarterly, 18,* 351–375.

West, J., Denton, K., & Germino-Hausken, E. (2000). *America's kindergartners: Findings from the early childhood longitudinal study, kindergarten class of 1998–99, Fall 1998.* Washington, DC: U.S. Department of Education, National Center for Education Statistics.

West, J. R. (1986). *Alcohol and brain development.* London: Oxford University Press.

West, K. (1999). Is there a solution to the "Charleston Problem"? Retrieved February 8, 2002, from http://www.crbj.com/articles/1999/04261999/Is there a solution to the Charleston problem.htm

West, M., & Newton, P. (1983). *The transition from school to work.* London: Croom Helm.

West, R. L., Crook, T. H., & Barron, K. L. (1992). Everyday memory performance across the life span: Effects of age and noncognitive individual differences. *Psychology and Aging, 7,* 72–82.

Wethington, E., Moen, P., Glasgow, N., & Pillemer, K. (2000). Multiple roles, social integration, and health. In K. Pillemer & P. Moen (Eds.), *Social integration in the second half of life* (pp. 48–71). Baltimore: Johns Hopkins University Press.

Wetzel, T. (2004). *What is gentrification?* Retrieved October 28, 2007, from http://www.uncanny.net/~wetzel/gentry.htm

Whisman, M. A., Uebelacker, L. A., Tolejko, N., Chatav, Y., & McKelvie, M. (2006). Marital discord and well-being in older adults: Is the association confounded by personality? *Psychology and Aging, 21,* 626–631.

Whitaker, M. (1993, November 15). White and black lies. *Newsweek,* pp. 52–54.

Whitall, J., & Getchell, N. (1995). From walking to running: Applying a dynamical systems approach to the development of locomotor skills. *Child Development, 66,* 1541–1553.

Whitbourne, J. (2002). The dropout dilemma: One in four college freshmen drop out. What is going on here? What does it take to stay in? *Findarticles.com.* Retrieved on July 15, 2010, at http://findarticles.com/p/articles/mi_m0BTR/is_4-22/ai_84599442/

Whitbourne, S. K. (1986). *The me I know: A study of adult identity.* New York: Springer Verlag.

Whitbourne, S. K., Sneed, J. R., & Sayer, A. (2009). Psychosocial development from college through midlife: A 34-year sequential study. *Developmental Psychology, 45,* 1328–1340.

Whitbourne, S. K., Zuschlag, M. K., Elliot, L. B., & Waterman, A. S. (1992). Psychosocial development in adulthood: A 22-year sequential study. *Journal of Personality and Social Psychology, 63,* 260–271.

White, B. L., Kaban, B. T., & Attanucci, J. S. (1979). *The origins of human competence.* Lexington, MA: Heath.

White, J. M., Wampler, R. S., & Winn, K. I. (1998). The identity style inventory: A revision with a sixth grade reading level (ISI-6G). *Journal of Adolescent Research, 13,* 223–245.

White, L., & Rogers, S. J. (2000). Economic circumstances and family outcomes: A review of the 1990s. *Journal of Marriage and the Family, 62,* 1035–1051.

White, N., & Cunningham, W. R. (1988). Is terminal drop pervasive or specific? *Journal of Gerontology, 43,* P141–P144.

White, N. R. (2002). "Not under my roof!" Young people's experience of home. *Youth and Society, 34,* 214–231.

White, R. W. (1959). Motivation reconsidered. The concept of competence. *Psychological Review, 66,* 297–333.

White, R. W. (1960). Competence and the psychosexual stages of development. In M. R. Jones (Ed.), *Nebraska Symposium on Motivation* (Vol. 8). Lincoln: University of Nebraska Press.

White, R. W. (1966). *Lives in progress* (2nd ed.). New York: Holt, Rinehart & Winston.

White, R. W. (1974). Strategies of adaptation: An attempt at systematic description. In G. V. Coelho, D. A. Hamburg, & J. E. Adams (Eds.), *Coping and adaptation* (pp. 47–68). New York: Basic Books.

Wholwend, K. E. (2009). Early adopters: Playing new literacies and pretending new technologies in print-centric classrooms. *Journal of Early Childhood Literacy, 9,* 117–140.

Wichstrom, L. (2001). The impact of pubertal timing on adolescents' alcohol use. *Journal of Research on Adolescence, 11,* 131–150.

Wierson, M., Long, P. J., & Forehand, R. L. (1993). Toward a new understanding of early menarche: The role of environmental stress in pubertal timing. *Adolescence, 28,* 912–924.

Wilcox, A. J., & Skjoerven, R. (1992). Birth weight and perinatal mortality. The effect of gestational age. *American Journal of Public Health, 82,* 378–382.

Wilcox, T., Schweinle, A., & Chapa, C. (2003). Object individuation in infancy. In H. Hayne & J. Fagen (Eds.), *Progress in infancy research* (Vol. 3, pp. 193–243). Mahwah, NJ: Erlbaum.

Wilcox, T., Woods, R., Tuggy, L., & Napoli, R. (2006). Shake, rattle, and … one or two objects? Young infants' use of auditory information to individuate objects. *Infancy, 9,* 97–123.

Wildsmith, E., Guzzo, K. B., & Hayford, S. R. (2010). Repeat unintended, unwanted and seriously mistimed childbearing in the United States. *Perspectives on Sexual and Reproductive Health, 42,* 14–22.

Wilhelm, M. O., & Bekkers, R. (2010). Helping behavior, dispositional empathic concern, and the principle of care. *Social Psychology Quarterly, 73,* 11–32.

Willetts, M. C. (2006). Union quality comparisons between long-term heterosexual cohabitation and legal marriage. *Journal of Family Issues, 27,* 110–127.

Williams, C., & Bybee, J. (1994). What do children feel guilty about? Development and gender differences. *Developmental Psychology, 30,* 617–623.

Williams, D. (2000). Ian Thorpe. *Time, 156,* 76–77.

Williams, J. C., & Cooper, H. C. (2004). The public policy of motherhood. *Journal of Social Issues, 60,* 849–865.

Williams, J. M., & Currie, C. (2000). Self-esteem and physical development in early adolescence: Pubertal timing and body image. *Journal of Early Adolescence, 20,* 129–149.

Williams, K. (2003). Has the future of marriage arrived? A contemporary examination of gender, marriage, and psychological well-being. *Journal of Health and Social Behavior, 44,* 470–487.

Williams, T. K., & Thornton, M. C. (1998). Social construction of ethnicity versus personal experience: The case of Afro-Amerasians. *Journal of Comparative Family Studies, 29,* 255–267.

Wilson, B. J., Smith, S. L., Potter, W. J., Kunkel, D., Linz, D., Colvin, C. M., & Donnerstein, E. (2002). Violence in children's television programming: Assessing the risks. *Journal of Communication, 52,* 5–35.

Wilson, E. (2007). Doctors fault designers' stance over thin models. *New York Times,* January 9, 2007. Retrieved August 23, 2007, from http://www.nytimes.com/2007/01/09/business/09thin.html?ex=1188014400&en=17872820f3627bc6&ei=5070

Wilson, R. S., & Matheny, A. P., Jr. (1986). Behavior genetics research in infant temperament: The Louisville twin study. In R. Plomin & J. Dunn (Eds.), *The study of temperament: Changes, continuities, and challenges.* Hillsdale, NJ: Erlbaum.

Wilson, S. (1995). Quasi-experimental designs. In G. Breakwell, S. Hammond, & C. Fyfe-Schaw (Eds.), *Research methods in psychology* (pp. 113–132). Thousand Oaks, CA: Sage.

Wilson, S. M., Peterson, G. W., & Wilson, P. (1993). The process of educational and occupational attainment of adolescent females from low-income, rural families. *Journal of Marriage and the Family, 55,* 158–175.

Wilson, T. A. (2006). Congenital adrenal hyperplasia. *eMedicine.* Retrieved August 6, 2007, from http://www.emedicine.com/ped/topic48.htm

Wilson, T. D. (2009). Know thyself. *Perspectives on Psychological Science, 4,* 384–389.

Wilson, T. D., LaFleur, S. J., & Anderson, D. E. (1996). The validity and consequences of verbal reports about attitudes. In N. Schwarz & S. Sudum (Eds.), *Answering questions: Methodology for determining cognitive processes in survey research* (pp. 91–114). San Francisco: Jossey Bass.

Wimmer, H. M., & Perner, J. (1983). Beliefs about beliefs: Representation and constraining function of wrong beliefs in young children's understanding of deception. *Cognition, 13,* 103–128.

Winerman, L. (2009). Playtime in peril. *Monitor on Psychology, 40,* 50–52.

Wingert, S., Harvey, C. D. H., Duncan, K. A., & Berry, R. E. (2005). Assessing the needs of assisted reproductive technology users on an online bulletin board. *International Journal of Consumer Studies, 29*, 468–478.

Winkleby, M. A., & Cubbin, C. (2004). Racial/ethnic disparities in health behaviors: A challenge to current assumptions. In N.B. Anderson, R.A. Bulatao, & B. Cohen (Eds.). *Critical Perspectives on Racial and Ethnic Differences in Health in Late Life*, National Research Council, Panel on Race, Ethnicity, and Health in Later Life, Committee on Population, Division of Behavioral and Social Sciences and Education, Washington: The National Academies Press, pp. 310–352.

Winnicut, D. W. (1948/1958). Paediatrics and psychiatry. In *Collected papers: Through paediatrics to psychoanalysis* (pp. 157–173). London: Tavistock.

Winston, C.A. (2006). African American grandmothers parenting AIDS orphans: Grieving and coping. *Qualitative Social Work: Research and Practice, 5*, 33–43.

Winston, R. M. L., & Handyside, A. H. (1993). New challenges in human in vitro fertilization. *Science, 260*, 932–936.

Witherspoon, D., Schotland, M., Way, N., & Hughes, D. (2009). Connecting the dots: How connectedness to multiple contexts influences the psychological and academic adjustment of urban youth. *Applied Developmental Science, 13*, 199–216.

Wittmann, M., Arce, E., & Santisteban, C. (2008). How impulsiveness, trait anger, and extracurricular activities might affect aggression in school children. *Personality and Individual Differences, 45*, 618–623.

Wolf, A. M., Gortmaker, S. L., Cheung, L., Gray, H. M., Herzog, D. B., & Colditz, G. A. (1993). Activity, inactivity, and obesity: Racial, ethnic, and age differences among schoolgirls. *American Journal of Public Health, 83*, 1625–1627.

Wolf, S. M. (1996). Gender, feminism, and death: Physician-assisted suicide and euthanasia. In S. M. Wolf (Ed.), *Feminism and bioethics: Beyond reproduction.* New York: Oxford University Press.

Wolff, P. H. (1963). Observations on the early development of smiling. In B. M. Foss (Ed.), *Determinants of infant behavior* (Vol. 2). New York: Wiley.

Wolff, P. H. (1966). Causes, controls, and organization of behavior in the neonate. *Psychological Issues, 5* (1, Whole No. 17).

Wolff, P. H. (1987). *The development of behavioral states and the expression of emotions in early infancy.* Chicago: University of Chicago Press.

Wolfinger, N. H. (2003). Family structure homogamy: The effects of parental divorce on partner selection and marital stability. *Social Science Research, 32*, 80–97.

Wong, C-K. & Lou, V.W.Q. (2010). "I wish to be self-reliant.": Aspiration for self-reliance, need and life satisfaction, and exit dilemma of welfare recipients in Hong Kong. *Social Indicators Research, 95*, 519–534.

Wong, P. T. P., & Watt, L. M. (1991). What types of reminiscence are associated with successful aging? *Psychology and Aging, 6*, 272–279.

Wood, J. J., & Repetti, R. L. (2004). What gets dad involved? A longitudinal study of change in parental child caregiving involvement. *Journal of Family Psychology, 18*, 237–249.

Wood, J. N. (2003). Social cognition and the prefrontal cortex. *Behavioral and Cognitive Neuroscience Reviews, 2*, 97–114.

Wood, W., & Eagly, A. H. (2002). A cross-cultural analysis of the behavior of women and men: Implications for the origins of sex differences. *Psychological Bulletin, 128*, 699–727.

Wood, W., Rhodes, N., & Biek, M. (1995). Working knowledge and attitude strength: An information-processing analysis. In K. E. Petty & J. A. Krosnick (Eds.), *Attitude strength: Antecedents and consequences* (pp. 283–313). Mahwah, NJ: Erlbaum.

Woodward, K. L. (1997, March 10). Today the sheep. *Newsweek*, p. 60.

Woollett, A., & Dosanjh-Matwala, N. (1990). Asian women's experience of childbirth in East London: The support of fathers and female relatives. *Journal of Reproductive and Infant Psychology, 8*, 11–22.

Woolley, J. D., & Wellman, H. M. (1993). Origin and truth: Young children's understanding of imaginary mental representations. *Child Development, 64*, 1–17.

Woolsey, B., & Schulz, M. (2010). Credit card statistics, industry facts and debt statistics. Retrieved on July 8, 2010, at www.creditcards.com/credit-card-news/credit-card-industry-facts-personal-debt-statistics-1276.php#Young-adults

Worchel, F. F., & Allen, M. (1997). Mothers' ability to discriminate cry types in low birth-weight premature and full-term infants. *Children's Health Care, 26*, 183–195.

Worchel, S. (1998). A developmental view of the search for group identity. In S. Worchel & J. F. Morales (Eds.), *Social identity: International perspectives* (pp. 53–74). Thousand Oaks, CA: Sage.

Wortman, C. B., & Boerner, K. (2007). Beyond the myths of coping with loss: Prevailing assumptions versus scientific evidence. In H. S. Friedman & R. C. Silver (Eds.). *Foundations of Health Psychology.* (pp. 285–324). New York: Oxford University Press.

Woyach, R. B. (1991). *Preparing for leadership: A young adult's guide to leadership skills in a global age.* Columbus: Mershon Center, Ohio State University.

WRAP, (2007). *Without housing.* Retrieved October 4, 2007, from http://www.nationalhomeless.org/publications/crimreport/summary.html

Wray, S. (2003). Women growing older: Agency, ethnicity and culture. *Sociology, 37*, 511–527.

Wright, J. D., & Devine, J. A. (1993). Family backgrounds and the substance-abusive homeless: The New Orleans experience. *The Community Psychologist, 26*, 35–37.

Wu, Y. (2010). Social skill in the workplace: What is social skill and how does it matter? *Dissertation Abstracts International Section A: Humanities and Social Sciences*, p. 3544.

Wulf, S. (1997). How to teach our children well. (It can be done.) *Time, 150*, 62–69.

Wylleman, P. (2000). Interpersonal relationships in sport: Uncharted territory in sport psychology research. *International Journal of Sport Psychology, 31*, 555–572.

www.IVF-infertility.com *Artificial insemination.* Retrieved May 25, 2007, from http://www.IVF-infertility.com

Xu, F. (2003). The development of object individuation in infancy. In H. Hayne & J. Fagen (Eds.), *Progress in infancy research* (Vol. 3, pp. 159–192). Mahwah, NJ: Erlbaum.

Yamauchi, L. A., Billig, S. H., Meyer, S., & Hofschire, L. (2006). Student outcomes associated with service-learning in a culturally relevant high school program. *Journal of Prevention & Intervention in the Community, 32*, 149–164.

Yang, L., Krampe, R. T., & Baltes, P. B. (2006). Basic forms of cognitive plasticitiy extended into the oldest-old: Retest learning, age and cognitive functioning. *Psychology and Aging, 21*, 372–378.

Yang, R. K., Zweig, A. R., Douthitt, T. C., & Federman, E. J. (1976). Successive relationships between maternal attitudes during pregnancy, analgesic medication during labor and delivery, and newborn behavior. *Developmental Psychology, 12*, 6–14.

Yarrow, L. J. (1963). Research in dimensions of early maternal care. *Merrill-Palmer Quarterly, 9*, 101–114.

Yarrow, L. J. (1964). Separation from parents in early childhood. In M. L. Hoffman & L. W. Hoffman (Eds.), *Review of child development research* (Vol. 1). New York: Sage.

Yarrow, L. J. (1970). The development of focused relationships during infancy. In J. Hellmuth (Ed.), *Exceptional infant* (Vol. 1). New York: Brunner/Mazel.

Yarrow, L. J., McQuiston, S., MacTurk, R. H., McCarthy, M. E., Klein, R. P., & Vietze, P. M. (1983). The assessment of mastery motivation during the first year of life. *Developmental Psychology, 19*, 159–171.

Yasui, M., Dorham, C. L., & Dishion, T. Y. (2004). Ethnic identity and psychological adjustment: A validity analysis for European American and African American adolescents. *Journal of Adolescent Research, 19*, 807–825.

Yates, A. (1989). Current perspectives on the eating disorders: 1. History, psychological, and biological aspects. *Journal of the American Academy of Child and Adolescent Psychiatry, 28*, 813–828.

Yates, M., & Youniss, J. (1996). Community service and political-moral identity in adolescents. *Journal of Research on Adolescence, 6*, 271–284.

Yau, J., & Smetana, J. G. (2003). Conceptions of moral, social-conventional, and personal events among Chinese preschoolers in Hong Kong. *Child Development, 74*, 647–658.

Yeung, W. J., Sandberg, J. F., Davis-Kean, P. E., & Hofferth, S. L. (2001). Children's time with fathers in intact families. *Journal of Marriage and the Family, 63,* 136–154.

Yin, R. K. (1994). *Case study research: Design and methods.* Thousand Oaks, CA: Sage.

Yip, T., Seaton, E. K., & Sellers, R. M. (2006). African American racial identity across the lifespan: Identity status, identity content, and depressive symptoms. *Child Development, 77,* 1504–1517.

Yoo, J. P., Slack, K. S., & Holl, J. I. (2009). Material hardship and the physical health of school-aged children in low-income households. *American Journal of Public Health, 99,* 829–836.

Yordanova, J., Kolev, V., Hohnsbein, J., & Falkenstein, M. (2004). Sensory slowing with ageing is mediated by a functional dysregulation of motor-generation processes: Evidence from high-resolution event-related potentials. *Brain, 127,* 351–362.

Yoshikawa, H. (2005). *Placing the first-year findings of the National Head Start Impact Study in context* (Brief prepared for the Society for Research in Child Development). Retrieved July 18, 2007, from http://srcd.org/documents/policy/Impactstudy.pdf

Youngblade, L. M., & Belsky, J. (1992). Parent-child antecedents of 5-year-olds' close friendships: A longitudinal analysis. *Developmental Psychology, 28,* 700–713.

Youngblade, L. M., & Dunn, J. (1995). Individual differences in young children's pretend play with mother and sibling: Links to relationships and understanding of other people's feelings and beliefs. *Child Development, 66,* 1472–1492.

Youniss, J. (1980). *Parents and peers in social development: A Sullivan-Piaget perspective.* Chicago: University of Chicago Press.

Youniss, J., McLellan, J. A., & Strouse, D. (1994). "We're popular, but we're not snobs": Adolescents describe their crowds. In R. Montemeyor, G. R. Adams, & T. P. Gwllotta (Eds.), *Personal relationships during adolescence. Advances in adolescent development* (Vol. 6, pp. 101–122). Thousand Oaks, CA: Sage.

Youth Risk Behavior Surveillance System. (2010). Trends in the prevalence of sexual behaviors: 1991–2009. Retrieved on July 4, 2010, at www.cdc.gov/healthyyouth/yrbs/pdf/us_sexual_trend_yrbs.pdf

Youth Risk Behavior Surveillance System. (2010). Trends in the prevalence of suicide related behaviors: 1991–2009. Retrieved on July 5, 2010, at www.cdc.gov/healthyyouth/yrbs/pdf/us_suicide_trend_yrbs.pdf

Yurdakok, K., Yavuz, T., & Taylor, C. E. (1990). Swaddling and acute respiratory infections. *American Journal of Public Health, 80,* 873–875.

Zahn-Waxler, C., & Kochanska, G. (1990). The origins of guilt. In R. A. Thompson (Ed.), *Nebraska Symposium on Motivation, 1988* (Vol. 36, pp. 183–258). Lincoln: University of Nebraska Press.

Zahn-Waxler, C., Kochanska, G., Krupnick, J., & McKnew, D. (1990). Patterns of guilt in children of depressed and well mothers. *Developmental Psychology, 26,* 51–59.

Zahn-Waxler, C., Radke-Yarrow, M., & King, R. A. (1977). *The impact of the affective environment on young children.* Paper presented at the biennial meeting of the Society for Research in Child Development, New Orleans, LA.

Zahn-Waxler, C., Radke-Yarrow, M., Wagner, E., & Chapman, M. (1992). Development of concern for others. *Developmental Psychology, 28,* 126–136.

Zahn-Waxler, C., Robinson, J. L., & Emde, R. N. (1992). The development of empathy in twins. *Developmental Psychology, 28,* 1038–1047.

Zahniser, D. (2006). Welcome to gentrification city. *LA Weekly News.* Retrieved October 28, 2007, from http://www.laweekly.com/news/features/welcome-to-gentrification-city/14285/

Zakriski, A. L., & Coie, J. D. (1996). A comparison of aggressive-rejected and nonaggressive-rejected children's interpretations of self-directed and other-directed rejection. *Child Development, 67,* 1048–1070.

Zarit, S.H., & Eggebeen, D.A. (2002). Parent-child relationships in adulthood and old age. In M.H. Bornstein (Ed.), *Handbook of parenting* (2nd ed., pp. 135–164). Mahwah, NJ: Erlbaum.

Zayas, L. H., & Solari, F. (1994). Early childhood socialization in Hispanic families: Context, culture, and practice implications. *Professional Psychology: Research and Practice, 25,* 200–206.

Zelinski, E. M., & Lewis, K. L. (2003). Adult age differences in multiple cognitive functions: Differentiation, dedifferentiation, or process-specific change. *Psychology and Aging, 18,* 727–745.

Zeskind, P. S. (1983). Cross-cultural differences in maternal perceptions of cries of low-and high-risk infants. *Child Development, 54,* 1119–1128.

Zeskind, P. S., Klein, L., & Marshall, T. R. (1992). Adult's perceptions of experimental modifications of durations of pauses and expiratory sounds in infant crying. *Developmental Psychology, 28,* 1153–1162.

Zettel, L. A., & Rook, K. S. (2004). Substitution and compensation in the social networks of older widowed women. *Psychology and Aging, 19,* 433–443.

Zhao, H., Brooks-Gunn, J., McLanahan, S., & Singer, B. (2000). Studying the real child rather than the ideal child: Bringing the person into developmental studies. In L. R. Bergman, R. B. Cairns, L. Nilsson, & L. Nystedt (Eds.), *Developmental science and the holistic approach* (pp. 393–419). Mahwah, NJ: Erlbaum.

Zhu, Y., Zhang, L., Fan, J., & Han, S. (2007). Neural basis of cultural influence on self-representation. *NeuroImage, 34,* 1320–1316.

Ziegert, D. I., Kistner, J. A., Castro, R., & Robertson, B. (2001). Longitudinal study of young children's responses to challenging achievement situations. *Child Development, 72,* 609–624.

Zigler, E. F., Kagan, S. L., & Hall, N. W. (1996). *Children, families, and government: Preparing for the twenty-first century.* Cambridge, UK: Cambridge University Press.

Zigler, E. F., & Styfco, S. (2004). Moving Head Start to the states: One experiment too many. *Applied Developmental Science, 8,* 51–55.

Zill, N., & West, J. (2000). *Entering kindergarten: A portrait of American children when they begin school.* Washington, DC: National Center for Educational Statistics. Retrieved August 21, 2001, from http://nces.ed.gov/pubs2000/coe2000/entering_kindergarten.html

Zimbardo, P. G. & Boyd, J. (2008). *The time paradox: The new psychology of time that will change your life.* New York: Free Press.

Zimmerman, B. J., Bandura, A., & Martinez-Pons, M. (1992). Self-motivation for academic attainment: The role of self-efficacy beliefs and personal goal setting. *American Educational Research Journal, 29,* 663–676.

Zimmerman, M. (2009, Spring). Why evolution is the organizing principle for biology. *Phi Kappa Phi Forum,* 4–7.

Zimmerman, M. A., Salem, D. A., & Maton, K. I. (1995). Family structure and psychosocial correlates among urban African-American adolescent males. *Child Development, 66,* 1598–1613.

Ziv, M., & Frye, D. (2003). The relation between desire and false belief in children's theory of mind: No satisfaction? *Developmental Psychology, 39,* 859–876.

Zosuls, K. M., Ruble, D. N., Tamis-LeMonda, C. S., Shrout, P. E., Bornstein, M. H., & Greulich, F. K. (2009). The acquisition of gender labels in infancy: Implications for gender-typed play. *Developmental Psychology, 45,* 688–701.

Zucker, A. N. (1999, May). The psychological impact of reproductive difficulties in women's lives. *Sex Roles: A Journal of Research,* 767–779.

Zucker, K. J. (1985). The infant's construction of his parents in the first six months of life. In T. M. Field & N. A. Fox (Eds.), *Social perception in infants.* Norwood, NJ: Ablex.

Zucker, K. J., Drummond, K. D., Bradley, S. J., & Peterson-Badali, M. (2009). Troubled meditations on psychosexual differentiation: Reply to Hegarty (2009). *Developmental Psychology, 45,* 904–908.

Zuckerman, B., Frank, D. A., & Hingson, R. (1989). Effects of maternal marijuana and cocaine use on fetal growth. *The New England Journal of Medicine, 320,* 762–768.

Zuckerman, C. (1997). Issues concerning end-of-life care. *Journal of Long Term Home Health Care, 16,* 26–34.

Zuo, J. (1992). The reciprocal relationship between marital interaction and marital happiness: A three-wave study. *Journal of Marriage and the Family, 54,* 870–878.

Zur, O., & Gelman, R. (2004). Young children can add and subtract by predicting and checking. *Early Childhood Research Quarterly, 19,* 121–137.

Zuravin, S. J. (1988). Child maltreatment and teenage first births: A relationship mediated by chronic sociodemographic stress? *American Journal of Orthopsychiatry, 58,* 91–103.

Name Index

Subject Index